DATE DUE

DEMCO 38-296

THE CHICANA STUDIES INDEX

Twenty Years of Gender Research
1971-1991

Compiled and Edited by
Lillian Castillo-Speed

Chicano Studies Library Publications Unit
University of California at Berkeley
1992

ISBN 0-918520-21-5
CHICANO STUDIES LIBRARY PUBLICATIONS SERIES, NO. 18
© **1992 by the Regents of the University of California. All rights reserved.**

Chicano Studies Library Publications Unit
3404 Dwinelle Hall
University of California at Berkeley
Berkeley, CA 94720
(510) 642-3859
FAX (510) 642-6456

Cover Art: Lorraine Nakata-García
Cover Design: René Bien
Typography: ATM Information Services

Library of Congress Cataloging-in-Publication Data

The Chicana studies index : twenty years of gender research, 1971-1991 /
compiled and edited by Lillian Castillo-Speed.

    p.   cm.
    Includes indexes
    ISBN 0-918520-21-5 : $90.00

    1. Mexican American women—Indexes. I. Castillo-Speed, Lillian.
Z1361.M4C457 1992

[E184.M5]
305.48'86872073—dc20   92-10870
                                    CIP

ACKNOWLEDGEMENTS

The present volume would not have been possible without the support and encouragement of several key people: my husband Richard B. Speed, my colleagues Richard Chabrán and Francisco García-Ayvens, and my
friend Carolyn Soto. Staff members who contributed
significantly were bibliographers Lisa Hernandez, Ermila
Carlin, and Julieta Carrillo. My thanks go out them and
to the rest of the Chicano Studies Library staff, volun-
teers, and loyal friends, whose commitment and hard
work are a constant inspiration.

DEDICATION

This book is dedicated to my mother Jennie Castillo, grandmother, great-grandmother, and day shift lead lady at Cal Mold, Inc., City of Industry, California.

TABLE OF CONTENTS

INTRODUCTION

The publication of the *Chicana Studies Index* by the Chicano Studies Library at UC Berkeley follows a well-established tradition of bibliography focused on women of Mexican heritage living in the United States. In 1976 the Library's Publications Unit produced *Bibliography of Writings: La Mujer* compiled by Cristina Portillo, Graciela Rios, and Martha Rodríguez. That same year two other classic bibliographies were published: *La Mujer Chicana: An Annotated Bibliography*, edited by Olivia Evey Chapa and Sally Andrade (Austin: Chicano Research and Learning Center) and *The Chicana: A Preliminary Bibliographic Study* by Roberto Cabello-Argandoña, Juan Gómez-Quiñones, and Patricia Herrera Durán (Los Angeles: Chicano Studies Research Center). In 1980, Catherine Loeb's "La Chicana: A Bibliographic Survey," published in *Frontiers*, updated these general and by then outdated works. In 1981 Sandra Balderrama concluded a project sponsored by the Chicano Studies Library and the Berkeley campus to compile a general bibliography which relied heavily on little known Chicana newspapers and journals, student papers and other ephemera. Her unpublished manuscript was entitled "A Comprehensive Bibliography on La Chicana."

In 1983 the Chicano Studies Library Publications Unit published *Unsettled Issues: Chicanas in the '80s* by Mujeres en Marcha. This document is a landmark in the history of Chicana feminist thought within the Chicano Movement. It reflected deep concerns with the role that gender played in Chicano Studies. As a result of the vigorous and diligent work of Chicana scholars to fight sexism in the academy, Chicana Studies has become a discipline in its own right. As it grows, more and more gender research is conducted by Chicanas themselves. This perspective is emphasized and celebrated in the *Chicana Studies Index*.

The *Chicana Studies Index* is a subject, author and title index to approximately 1150 journal articles, book articles, books, dissertations and reports on all aspects of the Chicana experience. This project began with the compilation of "Chicana Studies: A Selected List of Materials since 1980," a bibliography I published in *Frontiers* (1990). The *Chicana Studies Index* expands and updates that bibliography and provides subject access to the items listed. The source for journal articles was the Chicano Database, which contains over 38,000 journal article citations. The Chicano Database produces the *Chicano Index* and the *Chicano Database on CD-ROM* and is head-quartered at the Chicano Studies Library at the University of California at Berkeley. Book articles were derived from a separate file on the Chicano Database that contains citations used in producing the *Chicano Anthology Index*, compiled by Francisco García-Ayvens. Book citations were gathered by searching the resources of the Chicano Studies Library at the University of California, Berkeley, the Chicano Research Center Library at UCLA, and the Colección Tloque Nahuaque of the University of California, Santa Barbara. Most of the dissertation citations were gathered through an on-line search of *Dissertation Abstracts International.*

Materials included were chosen on the basis of usefulness for research. Biographical articles on Chicana engineers, businesspersons, or government officials were generally excluded. On the other hand, critical articles on the writings of Chicana authors are represented here. Individual poems and short stories were excluded for the most part. These and the biographical articles are readily found in the *Chicano Periodical Index* (continued by the *Chicano Index*) and are continually updated in the *Chicano Database on CD-ROM.* Creative works such as novels and collections of poetry by a single author were also omitted. Norma Alarcón's "Chicana Writers and Critics in a Social Context: Towards a Contemporary Bibliography" (*Third Woman*, 1989) is an excellent guide to creative works up to 1989.

The best general literature review for Chicana Studies is Cynthia Orozco's "Getting Started in Chicana Studies," published in *Women's Studies Quarterly* in 1990. A brief review of reference sources is included in my "Chicana Studies: An Updated List of Materials, 1980-1991," which will appear in 1992 in the premiere issue of the *Journal of Chicana Studies,* published jointly by the Chicana/Latina Research Project at the University of California at Davis, the MALCS (Mujeres Activas en Letras y Cambio Social) Editorial Board, and Third Woman Press of the University of California at Berkeley.

I would appreciate hearing about articles, books and other materials which should have been included. We will continue to add materials to the *Chicano Database on CD-ROM* and work towards publishing an update to the *Chicana Studies Index* at a later date.

HOW TO USE THE CHICANA STUDIES INDEX

The *Chicana Studies Index* consists of three sections: the SUBJECT INDEX, and the supplementary AUTHOR INDEX and TITLE INDEX. A brief description of each section follows.

SUBJECT INDEX

This is the main section of the *Chicana Studies Index*. Here are listed approximately 1150 citations arranged under appropriate descriptor (subject) terms. On average, each of the citations is indexed under three distinct terms, i.e., each of the citations is repeated in its entirety in three different locations. Each citation listing is numbered sequentially with the citation number serving as reference point for the supplementary author and title indexes. Each of the numbered citation entries provides the unique index number, full bibliographic description, and additional descriptor terms under which that particular citation is also indexed. The *Chicana Studies Index* uses subject headings from the fourth edition of the *Chicano Thesaurus*, which can be found in the fourth volume of the *Chicano Periodical Index* 1984-86 published in 1987 by the Chicano Studies Library Publications Unit. USE references from variant terms to the authorized form used in the Chicano Thesaurus are provided.

SAMPLE PERIODICAL CITATION

Chicana Studies ———— index term

citation number ——→ 280 Garcia, Alma M. The development of Chicana femi- ———— title
author ———— nist discourse, 1970-1980. GENDER & SOCIETY, ——— journal title
publication date ———— Vol. 3, no. 2 ,(June 1989), p. 217-238. English. ——— language
DESCR: Anglo Americans; *Chicano Movement;
index terms ———— *Feminism; Homosexuality; Machismo; National Association for Chicano Studies (NACS); Organiza-
tions: *Sexism; Women.

———— asterisk denotes major descriptor terms

SAMPLE BOOK CITATION

Canneries •———————— index term

citation number ——————→ 987 Ruiz, Vicki L. Cannery women/cannery lives: Mexi-
author ——————— can women, unionization, and the California food
processing industry, 1930-1950. Albuquerque, NM: •——— place of publication
Publisher, date ——————→ University of New Mexico Press, 1987. xviii, 194 p. ←——— pages
: ill. , English. DESCR: Agricultural labor unions; ←——— index terms
language ——————— California; Family; History; Industrial Workers; Labor
disputes; *Labor Unions; Trade Unions; United Can-
nery Agricultural Packing and Allied Workers of
America (UCAPAWA); Women.

book title ←——— (pointing to Cannery women/cannery lives)

SAMPLE BOOK ARTICLE CITATION

Employment •———————— index term

citation number ——————→ 1844 Curry Rodriguez, Julia E. Labor migration and famil-
author of article ————— ial responsibilities: experiences of Mexican women.
IN: Melville, Margarita, ed. MEXICANAS AT WORK ←——— title of book
editor of book ————— IN THE UNITED STATES. Houston, TX: Mexican
American Studies Program, University of Houston, ←——— publisher
date of publication ——————— 1988, p. 47-63. English. DESCR: Family; *Immi- ←——— index terms
language ——————— grants; Mexico; *Migrant Labor; Oral History; His-
tory; Sex Roles; Undocumented Workers; *Women;
*Working Women.

title of article ←——— (pointing to Labor migration and familial responsibilities)

SAMPLE DISSERTATION CITATION

Ramirez, Sara Estela •———————— index term

citation number ——————→ 4873 Hernandez, Ines. Sara Estela Ramirez: the early
author of thesis ————— twentieth century Texas-Mexican poet. Thesis
(Ph.D.)--University of Houston, 1984. 94 p. English ←——— language
index terms ——————→ DESCR: *Authors; *Biography; Feminism; Flores
Magon, Ricardo; Journalism; Literary Criticism;
Mexican Revolution-1910-1920; Mexico; *Poetry;
Texas; Women.

title of thesis ←——— (pointing to Sara Estela Ramirez: the early twentieth century Texas-Mexican poet)

AUTHOR INDEX

Garcia, Alma M. ⟵——— index term

title ———▸ The development of Chicana feminist discourse,
1980-1980, 280. ——— citation number

All of the citations in the Chicana Studies Index are listed according to the author's name, when provided. In the case of multiple authors, the citation is listed under each author up to a maximum of three. The author index groups entries alphabetically by author, lists the full titles, and provides the citation numbers in the subject index where full citations may be located. Name USE references are also provided here.

TITLE INDEX

title ———▸ The development of Chicana feminist discourse, 1970-
1980, 280. ⟵——— citation number

Specific titles may be located in the alphabetic listing that follows the author index. A title entry includes the full text of an individual title and the citation number in the subject index where a full citation may be located.

PERIODICALS INDEXED

ADOLESCENCE
Libra Publishers, Inc.
San Diego, CA

AFFILIA: JOURNAL OF WOMEN AND SOCIAL
WORK
Sage Publications
Newbury Park, CA

AGAINST THE CURRENT
Center for Changes
Detroit, MI

AGENDA
Office of Public Information
National Council of La Raza
Washington, DC

AGRICULTURAL HISTORY
Agricultural History Society
Washington, DC

AMERICAN BEHAVIORAL SCIENTIST
Sage Publications, Inc.
Newbury Park, CA

AMERICAN DEMOGRAPHICS
American Demographics, Inc.
Ithaca, NY

AMERICAN JOURNAL OF CLINICAL
NUTRITION
The American Society for Clinical Nutrition
Baltimore, MD

AMERICAN JOURNAL OF EPIDEMIOLOGY
The Johns Hopkins University School of
Hygiene and Public Health
Baltimore, MD

AMERICAN JOURNAL OF FAMILY THERAPY
Brunner/Mazel
New York, NY

AMERICAN JOURNAL OF PUBLIC HEALTH
American Public Health Association, Inc.
Washington, DC

AMERICAN JOURNAL OF SOCIOLOGY
The University of Chicago Press
Chicago, IL

AMERICAN PSYCHOLOGIST
American Psychological Association
Arlington, VA

THE AMERICAN SOCIOLOGIST
Transaction Periodicals Consortium
New Brunswick, NJ

AMERICAS 2001
Roberto Rodriguez
Los Angeles, CA

THE AMERICAS REVIEW
University of Houston
Houston, TX

ANS: ADVANCES IN NURSING SCIENCE
Aspen Systems Corp.
Germantown, MD

ANTHROPOLOGY AND EDUCATION
QUARTERLY
Council on Anthropology and Education
Washington, DC

ARCHIVES OF ENVIRONMENTAL HEALTH
Society for Occupational and
Environmental Health and International
Society for Environmental Epidemology
Washington, DC

ARCHIVES OF INTERNAL MEDICINE
American Medical Association
Chicago, IL

ARRIBA
Committee for Hispanic Arts
Austin, TX

ARTWEEK
Artweek, Inc.
Oakland, CA

ATISBOS: JOURNAL OF CHICANO RESEARCH
Stanford, CA

AZTLAN
Chicano Studies Research Center, UCLA
Los Angeles, CA

BERKELEY JOURNAL OF SOCIOLOGY: A
  CRITICAL REVIEW
  University of California Press
  Berkeley, CA

BERKELEY WOMEN OF COLOR
  Institute for the Study of Social Change
  Berkeley Women of Color Collective
  Berkeley, CA

BILINGUAL JOURNAL
  The Evaluation, Dissemination, and
  Assessment Center
  Cambridge, MA

BILINGUAL REVIEW
  Hispanic Research Center
  Arizona State University
  Tempe, AZ

BORDER HEALTH/SALUD FRONTERIZA
  Pan American Health Organization
  El Paso, TX

BORDERLANDS JOURNAL
  South Texas Institute of Latin and Mexican
  American Research
  Brownsville, TX

CALIFORNIA NURSE
  California Nurses Association
  San Francisco, CA

CALIFORNIA SOCIOLOGIST
  California State University
  Los Angeles, CA

CALIFORNIA WOMEN
  California Commission on the Status of
  Women
  Sacramento, CA

CALMECAC
  Calmécac de Aztlán en Los, Inc.
  Los Angeles, CA

CALYX: A JOURNAL OF ART AND
  LITERATURE BY WOMEN
  Calyx, Inc.
  Corvallis, OR

CAMINOS
  Caminos Corporation
  Los Angeles, CA

CANCER NURSING
  Raven Press
  New York, NY

CARACOL
  San Antonio, TX

CHICANO LAW REVIEW
  Chicano Law Student Association
  Los Angeles, CA

CHILD AND ADOLESCENT SOCIAL WORK
  JOURNAL
  Human Sciences Press, Inc.
  New York, NY

CHILD DEVELOPMENT
  The University of Chicago Press
  Society for Research in Child Development
  Chicago, IL

CHILD WELFARE
  Child Welfare League of America
  Washington, DC

CHISMEARTE
  Los Angeles Latino Writers Association
  Los Angeles, CA

CHRONICLE OF HIGHER EDUCATION
  Washington, DC

CHURCH AND SOCIETY
  The Program Agency, Presbyterian Church
  New York, NY

CLINICAL GERONTOLOGIST
  Haworth Press
  New York, NY

CLINICAL PEDIATRICS
  J.B. Lippincott Co.
  Hagerstown, MD

COMADRE
  San Jose, CA

COMMONGROUND MAGAZINE
  Women's Center
  Glendale, CA

LA COMUNIDAD [Sunday supplement]
  La Opinión
  Los Angeles, CA

CONFLUENCIA
  University of Northern Colorado
  Greenley, CO

CONTEMPORARY MARXISM
  Synthesis Publications
  San Francisco, CA

CONTEMPORARY POLICY ISSUES
  Western Economic Association International
  Huntington Beach, CA

CORAZÓN DE AZTLAN
  Los Angeles, CA

CORRESPONDENCIA
Mujer a Mujer
San Antonio, TX

CRIMINOLOGY: AN INTERDISCIPLINARY
JOURNAL
The American Society of Criminology
Seattle, WA

CRITICA
Chicano Studies
UCSD
La Jolla, CA

CRITICA HISPANICA
East Tennessee State University
Johnson City, TN

CRITICAL PERSPECTIVES OF THIRD WORLD
AMERICA
Ethnic Studies Student Union and Editorial
Board Council
Berkeley, CA

EL CUADERNO
La Academia de la Nueva Raza
Dixon, NM

CULTURAL CRITIQUE
Society for Cultural Critique
New York, NY

CULTURAL STUDIES
Routledge
London, England

CULTURAL SURVIVAL QUARTERLY
Cultural Survival, Inc.
Cambridge, MA

CURRENTS IN THEOLOGY AND MISSION
Christ Seminary-Seminex
Chicago, IL

DE COLORES
Pajarito Publications
Albuquerque, NM

DEMOGRAFIA Y ECONOMIA
El Colegio de México
México, DF

DEMOGRAPHY
Population Association of America
Alexandria, VA

DIFFERENCES: A JOURNAL OF FEMINIST
CULTURAL STUDIES
Pembroke Center for Teaching and
Research on Women
Brown University
Providence, RI

ECOLOGY OF FOOD AND NUTRITION
Gordon and Breach
New York, NY

EDUCATION
Project Innovation
Chula Vista, CA

EDUCATIONAL AND PSYCHOLOGICAL
MEASUREMENT
Durham, NC

ENCUENTRO FEMENIL
San Fernando, CA

ENVIRONMENT AND BEHAVIOR
Sage Publications
Newbury Park, CA

ETHNIC AND RACIAL STUDIES
Boston Routledge & Kegan Paul
London, England

FAMILY PLANNING PERSPECTIVES
Alan Guttmacher Institute
New York, NY

FAMILY RELATIONS
The National Council on Family Relations
Minneapolis, MN

FEM
Nueva Cultura Feminista
México, DF

FEMINIST ISSUES
Transaction Periodicals Consortium
New Brunswick, NJ

FEMINIST STUDIES
Feminist Studies, Inc.
University of Maryland
College Park, MD

FREE INQUIRY IN CREATIVE SOCIOLOGY
Sociology Consortium of Oklahoma
The University of Oklahoma
Norman, OK

FRONTIERS: A JOURNAL OF WOMEN
STUDIES
Women Studies Program
University of Colorado
Boulder, CO

GENDER & SOCIETY
   Sage Publications
   Beverly Hills, CA

GENETIC PSYCHOLOGY MONOGRAPHS
   The Journal Press
   Provincetown, MA

LA GENTE DE AZTLAN
   UCLA Communications Board of the
   Associated Students of UCLA
   Los Angeles, CA

GERONTOLOGIST
   The Gerontological Society of America
   Washington, DC

EL GRITO
   Quinto Sol Publications, Inc.
   Berkeley, CA

GUARDIAN
   New York, NY

HARVARD EDUCATIONAL REVIEW
   Cambridge, MA

HEALTH AND SOCIAL WORK
   National Association of Social Workers
   Silver Spring, MD

HEALTH PSYCHOLOGY
   Lawrence Erlbaum Associates, Inc.
   Hillsdale, NJ

HERESIES: A FEMINIST PUBLICATION ON
ART AND POLITICS
   Heresies Collective, Inc.
   New York, NY

HIGH PERFORMANCE
   Astro Artz
   Santa Monica, CA

HISPANIC JOURNAL OF BEHAVIORAL
SCIENCES
   Sage Publications
   Newbury Park, CA

HISTORIA MEXICANA
   Centro de Estudios Históricos de El Colegio
   de México
   México, D.F.

HOJAS
   Juarez-Lincoln Press
   Austin, TX

HOSPITAL AND COMMUNITY PSYCHIATRY
   American Psychiatric Association
   Washington, DC

HUMAN ORGANIZATION
   Society for Applied Anthropology
   Washington, DC

HUMAN RELATIONS
   Plenum Press
   New York, NY

IMAGES: ETHNIC STUDIES OCCASIONAL
PAPERS SERIES
   School of Ethnic Studies
   San Francisco State University
   San Francisco, CA

IMAGINE
   Imagine Publishers
   Boston, MA

IMPROVING COLLEGE AND UNIVERSITY
TEACHING
   Graduate School
   Oregon State College
   Corvallis, OR

INDUSTRIAL AND LABOR RELATIONS REVIEW
   New York School of Industrial Labor
   Relations
   Cornell University
   Ithaca, NY

INTERCAMBIOS FEMENILES
   National Network of Hispanic Women
   Los Angeles, CA

INTERNATIONAL JOURNAL OF AGING AND
HUMAN DEVELOPMENT
   Baywood Publishing Company, Inc.
   Amityville, NY

INTERNATIONAL JOURNAL OF GROUP
PSYCHOTHERAPY
   International Universities Press
   New York, NY

INTERNATIONAL JOURNAL OF HEALTH
SERVICES
   Baywood Publishing Company, Inc.
   Amityville, NY

INTERNATIONAL MIGRATION REVIEW
   International Migration Review
   Staten Island, NY

INTERNATIONAL QUARTERLY OF
COMMUNITY HEALTH AND EDUCATION
   Baywood Publishing Company, Inc.
   Farmingdale, NY

ISSUES IN RADICAL THERAPY
   The Saxifrage Publications Group
   Boulder, CO

JAMA: JOURNAL OF THE AMERICAN
MEDICAL ASSOCIATION
American Medical Association
Chicago, IL

JNCI: JOURNAL OF THE NATIONAL CANCER
INSTITUTE
U.S. Department of Health and Human
Services
Bethesda, MD

JOGN NURSING
Medical Department
Harper & Row
Hagerstown, MD

JOURNAL OF ADOLESCENT HEALTH CARE
Society for Adolescent Medicine
Elsevier Publishing Co., Inc.
New York, NY

JOURNAL OF ADOLESCENT RESEARCH
Sage Publications
Newbury Park, CA

JOURNAL OF ADULT EDUCATION
American Association for Adult Education
New York, NY

JOURNAL OF AMERICAN ETHNIC HISTORY
Transaction Periodicals Consortium
Rutgers University
New Brunswick, NJ

JOURNAL OF AMERICAN INDIAN EDUCATION
College of Education
Tempe, AZ

JOURNAL OF ANTHROPOLOGICAL RESEARCH
University of New Mexico
Albuquerque, NM

JOURNAL OF APPLIED BEHAVIORAL SCIENCE
NTL Institute For Applied Behavioral
Science
Arlington, VA

JOURNAL OF APPLIED PSYCHOLOGY
American Psychological Association
Bowling Green State University, OH

JOURNAL OF ARIZONA HISTORY
Arizona Pioneers' Historical Society
Tuscon, AZ

JOURNAL OF BORDERLAND STUDIES
New Mexico State University
Department of Economics
Las Cruces, NM

JOURNAL OF CLINICAL PSYCHOLOGY
Clinical Psychology Publishing Co.
Brandon, VT

JOURNAL OF COMMUNITY PSYCHOLOGY
Clinical Psychology Publishing Co., Inc.
Brandon, VT

JOURNAL OF CONSULTING AND CLINICAL
PSYCHOLOGY
American Psychological Association
Arlington, VA

JOURNAL OF COUNSELING PSYCHOLOGY
American Psychological Association
Arlington, VA

JOURNAL OF CROSS-CULTURAL
PSYCHOLOGY
Center for Cross-Cultural Research
International Association for Cross-Cultural
Psychology
Sage Publications
Newbury Park, CA

JOURNAL OF DIVORCE
Hawthorne Press
Binghamton, NY

JOURNAL OF DIVORCE AND REMARRIAGE
Hawthorne Press
New York, NY

JOURNAL OF DRUG ISSUES
Tallahasse, FL

JOURNAL OF EARLY ADOLESCENCE
H.E.L.P. Books
Tucson, AZ

JOURNAL OF EDUCATION
Boston, MA

JOURNAL OF ETHNIC STUDIES
College of Ethnic Studies
Western Washington University
Bellingham, WA

JOURNAL OF FAMILY HISTORY
JAI Press Inc.
Greenwich, CT

JOURNAL OF FAMILY PRACTICE
Appleton-Century-Crofts
New York, NY

JOURNAL OF FAMILY VIOLENCE
Plenum Publishing Corporation
New York, NY

JOURNAL OF GENETIC PSYCHOLOGY
Heldref Publications
New York, NY

JOURNAL OF GERONTOLOGY
Gerontological Society of America
Washington, DC

JOURNAL OF HEALTH AND SOCIAL
BEHAVIOR
American Sociological Association
Albany, NY

JOURNAL OF HISPANIC POLICY
Kennedy School Hispanic Student Caucus
Harvard University
Cambridge, MA

JOURNAL OF MARRIAGE AND THE FAMILY
National Council on Family Relations
Lincoln, NE

JOURNAL OF MEXICAN-AMERICAN HISTORY
Santa Barbara, CA

JOURNAL OF MULTICULTURAL COUNSELING
AND DEVELOPMENT
Association for Multicultural Counseling
and Development
Alexandria, VA

THE JOURNAL OF NARRATIVE TECHNIQUE
Eastern Michigan University
Ypsilanti, MI

JOURNAL OF NON-WHITE CONCERNS IN
PERSONNEL AND GUIDANCE
American Personnel and Guidance
Association
Washington, DC

JOURNAL OF POPULAR CULTURE
Bowling Green State University
Bowling Green, OH

JOURNAL OF QUANTITATIVE CRIMINOLOGY
Plenum Publishing Corporation
New York, NY

JOURNAL OF SOCIAL BEHAVIOR AND
PERSONALITY
Select Press
Corte Madera, CA

JOURNAL OF SOCIAL PSYCHOLOGY
Heldref Publications
Washington, DC

JOURNAL OF SOCIAL WORK AND HUMAN
SEXUALITY
Hawthorne Press
New York, NY

JOURNAL OF STUDIES ON ALCOHOL
Rutgers Center of Alcohol Studies
Alcohol Research Documentation
New Brunswick, NJ

JOURNAL OF THE AMERICAN ACADEMY OF
CHILD PSYCHOLOGY
The Academy
Baltimore, MD

JOURNAL OF THE NATIONAL CANCER
INSTITUTE
U.S. Government Print Office
Bethesda, MD

JOURNAL OF THE NATIONAL MEDICAL
ASSOCIATION
SLACK Inc.
Thorofare, NJ

JOURNAL OF TROPICAL PEDIATRICS
Oxford University Press
London, England

JOURNAL OF VOCATIONAL BEHAVIOR
Academic Press
New York, NY

LABOR HISTORY
Tamiment Institute
Washington, CT

LATIN AMERICAN PERSPECTIVES
Sage Publications, Inc.
Newbury Park, CA

LATIN AMERICAN THEATRE REVIEW
Center of Latin American Studies
University of Kansas
Lawrence, KS

LATIN QUARTER
Los Angeles, CA

LATINA
Charisma Enterprise
Santa Monica, CA

LATINO
League of United Latin American Citizens
Communications, Inc.
Denver, CO

LECTOR
Floricanto Press
Encino, CA

LEGACY: A JOURNAL OF
    NINETEENTH-CENTURY AMERICAN
    WOMEN WRITERS
    Gazette Printing Co.
    Easthampton, MA

LA LUZ
    La Luz Publications Co., Inc.
    Denver, CO

MAGAZIN
    Magazín, Inc.
    San Antonio, TX

MARRIAGE & FAMILY REVIEW
    Haworth Press
    New York, NY

MEDIA REPORT TO WOMEN
    Women's Institute for Freedom of the Press
    Washington, DC

MENTAL RETARDATION
    The American Association on Mental
    Retardation
    Washington, DC

MEXICAN STUDIES/ESTUDIOS MEXICANOS
    University of California Press
    Berkeley, CA

MIGRATION TODAY
    Center for Migration Studies of New York,
    Inc.
    Staten Island, NY

MIGRATION WORLD MAGAZINE
    Center for Migration Studies of New York,
    Inc.
    Staten Island, NY

MONOGRAPHIC REVIEW
    Genaro and Janet Perez
    Odessa, TX

MONTHLY LABOR REVIEW
    U.S. Department of Labor Statistics
    Washington, DC

MOVING ON
    New American Movement
    Chicago, IL

MULTICULTURAL INQUIRY AND RESEARCH
    ON AIDS (MIRA) NEWSLETTER
    Multicultural Inquiry and Research on AIDS
    San Francisco, CA

NABE JOURNAL
    National Association for Bilingual Education
    University of Southern California
    Los Angeles, CA

NACLA: REPORT ON THE AMERICAS
    North American Congress on Latin
    America, Inc.
    New York, NY

NATIONAL HISPANIC JOURNAL
    National Hispanic Institute
    Austin, TX

NEW ART EXAMINER
    Chicago New Art Examiner
    Chicago, IL

THE NEW ENGLAND JOURNAL OF MEDICINE
    Massachusetts Medical Society
    Waltham, MA

NEW MEXICO HISTORICAL REVIEW
    University of New Mexico
    Albuquerque, NM

NEW MEXICO MAGAZINE
    State of New Mexico
    Albuquerque, NM

NUESTRO
    Latin National Publishing Corporation
    New York, NY

NWSA JOURNAL
    National Women's Studies Association
    Ablex Publishing Corporation
    Norwood, NJ

OBSTETRICS GYNECOLOGY
    Year Book Publishers
    Chicago, IL

THE PACIFIC HISTORIAN
    Holt-Atherton Center for Western Studies
    University of the Pacific
    Stockton, CA

PACIFIC HISTORICAL REVIEW
    University of California Press
    Berkeley, CA

LA PALABRA
    Tempe, AZ

PALACIO
    Public Programs and Education
    Bureau of the Museum of New Mexico
    Santa Fe, NM

PEDIATRICS
American Academy of Pediatrics
Elk Grove Village, IL

PERSONNEL AND GUIDANCE JOURNAL
American Association for Counseling and
Development
Alexandria, VA

PERSPECTIVES IN MEXICAN AMERICAN
STUDIES
Mexican American Studies and Research
Center
Tucson, AZ

POPULATION BULLETIN
Population Reference Bureau
Washington, DC

POPULATION RESEARCH AND POLICY
REVIEW
Kluwer Academic Publishers
Hingham, MA

PREVENTIVE MEDICINE
Academic Press, Inc.
New York, NY

PROCEEDINGS OF THE PACIFIC COAST
COUNCIL ON LATIN AMERICAN STUDIES
San Diego State University Press
San Diego, CA

PSYCHOLOGICAL REPORTS
Missoula, MT

PSYCHOLOGY OF WOMEN QUARTERLY
American Psychological Association
Women's Studies Research Center
University of Wisconsin
Madison, WI

PUBLIC HEALTH BRIEFS
U.S. Government Printing Office
Washington, DC

PUBLIC HEALTH NURSING
Blackwell Scientific Publications, Inc.
Cambridge, MA

PUBLIC HEALTH REPORTS
Office of the Assistant Secretary for Health
Washington, DC

PUBLIC OPINION QUARTERLY
The American Association for Public
Opinion Research
The University of Chicago
Chicago, IL

QUALITATIVE SOCIOLOGY
Human Sciences Press
New York, NY

LA RAZA
Los Angeles, CA

LA RAZA HABLA
Chicano Affairs Office
New Mexico State University
Las Cruces, NM

READER'S DIGEST
The Reader's Digest Association
Pleasantville, NY

READING TEACHER
International Reading Association
Newark, DE

LA RED/THE NET
National Chicano Research Network
Institute for Social Research
University of Michigan
Ann Arbor, MI

REGENERACION [magazine]
Los Angeles, CA

RENATO ROSALDO LECTURE SERIES
MONOGRAPH
Mexican American Studies Research Center
University of Arizona
Tucson, AZ

RESEARCH BULLETIN (SPANISH SPEAKING
MENTAL HEALTH RESEARCH CENTER)
Spanish Speaking Mental Health Research
Center UCLA
Los Angeles, CA

RESEARCH IN NURSING AND HEALTH
John Wiley & Sons
New York, NY

RESEARCH ON AGING
Sage Publications
Newbury Park, CA

RESOURCES FOR FEMINIST RESEARCH
Ontario Institute for Studies in Education
Toronto, Ontario

RESPONSE TO THE VICTIMIZATION OF
WOMEN & CHILDREN
Guildford Press
New York, NY

REVIEW (FERNAND BRAUDEL CENTER)
Sage Publications
Beverly Hills, CA

REVIEW OF PUBLIC DATA USE
Clearinghouse and Laboratory for Census Data
Arlington, VA

REVIEW OF RADICAL POLITICAL ECONOMICS
Union for Radical Political Economics
New York, NY

REVISTA CANADIENSE DE ESTUDIOS HISPANICOS
La Asociación Canadiense de Hispanistas
Toronto, Ontario

REVISTA CHICANO-RIQUEÑA
Arte Público Press
Houston, TX

REVISTA IBEROAMERICA
Instituto Internacional de Literatura Iberamericana
Pittsburgh, PA

REVISTA MUJERES
Las Mujeres
University of California at Santa Cruz
Santa Cruz, CA

RURAL EDUCATOR
Department of Education
Colorado State University
Fort Collins, CO

SEX ROLES
Plenum Publishing Corporation
New York, NY

SIECUS REPORT
Sex Information and Education Council of the U.S.
New York, NY

SIGNS: JOURNAL OF WOMEN IN CULTURE AND SOCIETY
University of Chicago Press
Chicago, IL

SOCIAL CASEWORK: JOURNAL OF CONTEMPORARY SOCIAL WORK
Family Services Association of America
New York, NY

SOCIAL FORCES
The University of North Carolina Press
Chapel Hill, NC

SOCIAL PSYCHIATRY
Grune & Stratton
New York, NY

SOCIAL SCIENCE & MEDICINE
Pergamon Journals Limited
Elmsford, NY

SOCIAL SCIENCE JOURNAL
Western Social Science Association
JAI Press, Inc.
Greenwich, CT

SOCIAL SCIENCE QUARTERLY
The Southwestern Social Science Association
University of Texas Press
Austin, TX

SOCIAL STUDIES REVIEW
California Council for the Social Studies
Millbrae, CA

SOCIAL WORK
Journal of the National Association of Social Workers
Silver Springs, MD

SOCIOLOGICAL PERSPECTIVES
JAI Press, Inc.
Portland, OR

SOCIOLOGICAL QUARTERLY
Midwest Sociological Society
JAI Press, Inc.
Greenwich, CT

SOCIOLOGY AND SOCIAL RESEARCH
University of Southern California
Los Angeles, CA

SOUTHERN CALIFORNIA QUARTERLY
Historical Society of Southern California
Los Angeles, CA

SOUTHWEST ECONOMY AND SOCIETY
Albuquerque, NM

SOUTHWESTERN STUDIES
Texas Western Press
El Paso, TX

STUDIES IN FAMILY PLANNING
Population Council
New York, NY

SUICIDE AND LIFE-THREATENING BEHAVIOR
The American Association of Suicidology
New York, NY

TEXAS OBSERVER
Texas Observer Publishing Co.
Austin, TX

TEXAS TECH JOURNAL OF EDUCATION
School of Law Texas Tech University
Lubbock, TX

THEATRE JOURNAL
The University of College Theatre
Association
Johns Hopkins University
Baltimore, MD

THIRD WOMAN
Third Woman Press
Berkeley, CA

THIS WORLD [Sunday Supplement]
San Francisco Chronicle
San Francisco, CA

TRABAJOS MONOGRAFICOS
Mujeres Activas en Letras y Cambio Social
Davis, CA

TRIVIA: A JOURNAL OF IDEAS
N. Amherst, MA

TULSA STUDIES IN WOMEN'S LITERATURE
University of Tulsa
Tulsa, OK

URBAN ANTHROPOLOGY
The Institute for the Study of Man
Brockport, NY

VICTIMOLOGY
Visage Press
Washington, DC

VISTA
Vista Magazine
Coral Gables, FL

VOCATIONAL GUIDANCE QUARTERLY
National Vocational Guidance Association
Washington, DC

WOMANSPIRIT
Wolf Creek, OR

WESTERN FOLKLORE
California Folklore Society
Glendale, CA

WOMEN: A JOURNAL OF LIBERATION
Baltimore, MD

WOMEN & HEALTH
Haworth Press
Binghamton, NY

WOMEN AND PERFORMANCE
NYU/TSOA
New York, NY

WOMEN & POLITICS
Haworth Press
New York, NY

WOMEN AND THERAPY
Haworth Press
Binghamton, NY

WOMEN AND WORK
U.S. Dept. of Labor
Washington, DC

WOMEN'S STUDIES INTERNATIONAL FORUM
Fergamon Press
Elmsford, NY

WOMEN'S STUDIES QUARTERLY
The Feminist Press
The City University of New York
New York, NY

WORLD HEALTH
World Health Organization
Geneva

XALMAN
Santa Barbara, CA

YOUTH AND SOCIETY
Sage Publications
Newbury Park, CA

SUBJECT INDEX

1933 Cotton Strike

1 Weber, Devra Anne. Mexican women on strike:
memory, history and oral narratives. IN: Del
Castillo, Adelaida R., ed. BETWEEN BORDERS:
ESSAYS ON MEXICANA/CHICANA HISTORY. Encino,
CA: Floricanto Press, 1990, p. 175-200.
English. DESCR: Cotton Industry; History;
*Oral History; San Joaquin Valley, CA;
Strikes and Lockouts; *Valdez, Rosaura;
Working Women.

"A La Mujer" [essay]

2 Perez, Emma. "A la mujer": a critique of the
Partido Liberal Mexicano's gender ideology
on women. IN: Del Castillo, Adelaida R., ed.
BETWEEN BORDERS: ESSAYS ON MEXICANA/CHICANA
HISTORY. Encino, CA: Floricanto Press, 1990,
p. 459-482. English. DESCR: Essays;
*Feminism; Flores Magon, Ricardo; Guerrero,
Praxedis G.; Journalism; Mexican Revolution
- 1910-1920; Mexico; Newspapers; *Partido
Liberal Mexicano (PLM); Political Ideology;
Political Parties and Organizations;
*REGENERACION [newspaper]; Sex Roles; Women.

"A una madre de nuestros tiempos" [poem]

3 Lomas, Clara. Libertad de no procrear: la
voz de la mujer en "A una madre de nuestro
tiempo" de Margarita Cota-Cardenas. IN:
Cordova, Teresa, et al., eds. CHICANA
VOICES. Austin, TX: Center for Mexican
American Studies, 1986, p. 188-201.
Bilingual. DESCR: *Cota-Cardenas, Margarita;
Feminism; Literary Criticism; *Poetry; Sex
Stereotypes.

4 Lomas, Clara. Libertad de no procrear: la
voz de la mujer en "A una madre de nuestro
tiempo" de Margarita Cota-Cardenas. REVISTA
MUJERES, Vol. 2, no. 1 (January 1985), p.
30-35. Spanish. DESCR: *Cota-Cardenas,
Margarita; Feminism; Literary Criticism;
Poetry; Sex Stereotypes.

Abortion

5 Amaro, Hortensia. Abortion use and attitudes
among Chicanas: the need for research.
RESEARCH BULLETIN (SPANISH SPEAKING MENTAL
HEALTH RES. CENTER), Vol. 4, no. 3 (March
1980), p. 1-5. English. DESCR: *Attitudes;
Birth Control; Family Planning; Fertility;
Literature Reviews; Mental Health.

6 Amaro, Hortensia. Psychosocial determinants
of abortion attitudes among Mexican American
women. Thesis (Ph.D.)--University of
Calfor1ia, Los Angeles, 1982. 264 p.
English. DESCR: *Attitudes.

7 Amaro, Hortensia. Women in the
Mexican-American community: religion,
culture, and reproductive attitudes and
experiences. JOURNAL OF COMMUNITY
PSYCHOLOGY, Vol. 16, no. 1 (January 1988),
p. 6-20. English. DESCR: *Attitudes; Birth
Control; Family Planning; *Fertility;
Religion.

8 Aneshensel, Carol S., et al. Onset of
fertility-related events during adolescence:
a prospective comparison of Mexican American
and non-Hispanic white females. AMERICAN
JOURNAL OF PUBLIC HEALTH, Vol. 80, no. 8
(August 1990), p. 959-963. English. DESCR:
Anglo Americans; Birth Control; *Fertility;
*Sexual Behavior; Women; *Youth.

9 Del Zotto, Augusta. Latinas with AIDS: life
expectancy for Hispanic women is a startling

45 days after diagnosis. THIS WORLD, (April
9, 1989), p. 9. English. DESCR: AIDS
(Disease); Condom Use; Instituto Familiar de
la Raza, San Francisco, CA; Machismo; *Mano
a Mano; Quintero, Juanita; Sex Roles; Women
Men Relations.

10 Delgado, Sylvia. Chicana: the forgotten
woman. REGENERACION, Vol. 2, no. 1 (1971),
p. 2-4. English. DESCR: Free Clinics; *Women
Men Relations; Working Women.

11 Delgado, Sylvia. Young Chicana speaks up on
problems faced by young girls. REGENERACION,
Vol. 1, no. 10 (1971), p. 5-7. English.
DESCR: Feminism; Machismo; Marriage; Sex
Roles; *Women Men Relations.

12 Eisen, Marvin. Factors discriminating
pregnancy resolution decisions of unmarried
adolescents. GENETIC PSYCHOLOGY MONOGRAPHS,
Vol. 108, no. 1 (August 1983), p. 69-95.
English. DESCR: Attitudes; Decision Making;
*Fertility; *Single Parents; *Youth.

13 Eisen, Marvin and Zellman, Gail L. Factors
predicting pregnancy resolution decision
satisfaction of unmarried adolescents.
JOURNAL OF GENETIC PSYCHOLOGY, Vol. 145, no.
2 (December 1984), p. 231-239. English.
DESCR: Anglo Americans; Attitudes;
Counseling (Psychological); Family Planning;
*Fertility; Youth.

14 Fennelly, Katherine. Childbearing among
Hispanics in the United States: an annotated
bibliography. New York: Greenwood Press,
1987. xii, 167 p. English. DESCR:
*Bibliography; Birth Control; *Fertility;
Sterilization; *Women; Youth.

15 Flores, Francisca. Comision Femenil
Mexicana. REGENERACION, Vol. 2, no. 1
(1971), p. 6. English. DESCR: Children;
Comision Femenil Mexicana Nacional; *Family
Planning; Feminism; Organizations; Politics.

16 Flores, Francisca. Comision Femenil
Mexicana. REGENERACION, Vol. 2, no. 4
(1975), p. 24-25. English. DESCR: Child Care
Centers; Comision Femenil Mexicana Nacional;
Identity; Working Women.

17 Norris, Henry E. AIDS, women and
reproductive rights. MULTICULTURAL INQUIRY
AND RESEARCH ON AIDS (MIRA) NEWSLETTER, Vol.
1, no. 3 (Summer 1987), p. [2-3]. English.
DESCR: *AIDS (Disease); Center for
Constitutional Rights; Discrimination;
Preventative Medicine; Women.

18 Roraback, Rosanne Lisa. The effects of
occupational type, educational level,
marital status, and race/ethnicity on
women's attitudes towards feminist issues.
Thesis (M.A.)--Michigan State University,
1988. 62 p. English. DESCR: *Attitudes;
Equal Rights Amendment (ERA); *Feminism;
Identity; *Women.

19 Rosenhouse-Persson, Sandra and Sabagh,
Georges. Attitudes toward abortion among
Catholic Mexican-American women: the effects
of religiosity and education. DEMOGRAPHY,
Vol. 20, no. 1 (February 1983), p. 87-98.
English. DESCR: Attitudes; *Catholic Church;
Education; Religion.

20 Salazar, Sandra A. Reproductive choice for
Hispanas. AGENDA, Vol. 9, no. 4 (July,
August, 1979), p. 31-33, 36. English.
DESCR: Medical Care; *Public Health;
Sterilization.

Abortion (cont.)

21 Sex education, abortion views of Mexican Americans typical of U.S. beliefs. FAMILY PLANNING PERSPECTIVES, Vol. 15, (July, August, 1983), p. 197-201. English. **DESCR:** *Attitudes; Birth Control; Family Planning; *Sex Education.

22 Sosa Riddell, Adaljiza. The status of women in Mexico: the impact of the "International Year of the Woman". IN: Iglitzin, Lynn B. and Ross, Ruth A., eds. WOMEN IN THE WORLD, 1975-1985. Santa Barbara, CA: ABC-Clio, Inc., 1986, p. 305-324. English. **DESCR:** *Feminism; International Women's Year World Conference (1975: Mexico City); *Mexico; Political History and Conditions; Political Parties and Organizations; Rape; *Sexism; Social History and Conditions; *Women.

23 Urdaneta, Maria Luisa. Chicana use of abortion: the case of Alcala. IN: Melville, Margarita B., ed. TWICE A MINORITY. St. Louis, MO: Mosby, 1980, p. 33-51. English. **DESCR:** Alcala, TX; Fertility.

Academic Achievement

24 Achor, Shirley and Morales, Aida G. Chicanas holding doctoral degrees: social reproduction and cultural ecological approaches. ANTHROPOLOGY AND EDUCATION QUARTERLY, Vol. 21, no. 3 (September 1990), p. 269-287. English. **DESCR:** *Discrimination in Education; Graduate Schools; *Higher Education; Surveys.

25 Cardoza, Desdemona. College attendance and persistence among Hispanic women: an examination of some contributing factors. SEX ROLES, Vol. 24, no. 3-4 (January 1991), p. 133-147. English. **DESCR:** College Preparation; *Enrollment; High School and Beyond Project (HS&B); *Higher Education; *Sex Roles; Socialization; Socioeconomic Factors.

26 Chacon, Maria A., et al. Chicanas in California post secondary education: a comparative study of barriers to the program progress. Stanford, CA: Stanford Center for Chicano Research, 1985. viii, 217 p. English. **DESCR:** Colleges and Universities; Counseling (Educational); Educational Statistics; Enrollment; *Higher Education; Students; Surveys.

27 Daggett, Andrea Stuhlman. A comparison of occupational goal orientations of female Mexican-Americans and Anglo high-school seniors of the classes of 1972 and 1980. Thesis (Ph.D.)--University of Arizona, Tucson, 1983. xii, 134 p. English. **DESCR:** Anglo Americans; *Careers; *Secondary School Education; Sexism; Students; Women.

28 Del Castillo, Adelaida R., et al. An assessment of the status of the education of Hispanic American women. IN: McKenna, Teresa and Ortiz, Flora Ida, eds. THE BROKEN WEB: THE EDUCATIONAL EXPERIENCE OF HISPANIC WOMEN. Claremont, CA: Tomas Rivera Center; Berkeley, CA: Floricanto Press, 1988, p. 3-24. English. **DESCR:** Conferences and Meetings; Discrimination in Education; Dropouts; *Education; Higher Education; Public Policy; Research Methodology; The Educational Experience of Hispanic American Women [symposium] (1985: Claremont, CA); *Women.

29 Del Castillo, Adelaida R. and Torres, Maria. The interdependency of educational

institutions and cultural norms: the Hispana experience. IN: McKenna, Teresa and Ortiz, Flora Ida, eds. THE BROKEN WEB: THE EDUCATIONAL EXPERIENCE OF HISPANIC WOMEN. Claremont, CA: Tomas Rivera Center; Berkeley, CA: Floricanto Press, 1988, p. 39-60. English. **DESCR:** Acculturation; *Cultural Characteristics; *Education; *Literature Reviews; Research Methodology; *Values; Women.

30 Del Castillo, Adelaida R. Sobre la experiencia educativa chicana. FEM, Vol. 10, no. 48 (October, November, 1986), p. 7-10. Spanish. **DESCR:** *Education.

31 Flores, Laura Jane. A study of successful completion and attrition among Chicana Title VII Bilingual Education Doctoral Fellows at selected Southwestern universities. Thesis (Ed.D.)--New Mexico State University, 1984. 145 p. English. **DESCR:** Colleges and Universities; Graduate Schools; *Higher Education; Title VII Bilingual Education Doctoral Fellowship Program.

32 Gandara, Patricia. Passing through the eye of the needle: high-achieving Chicanas. HISPANIC JOURNAL OF BEHAVIORAL SCIENCES, Vol. 4, no. 2 (June 1982), p. 167-179. English. **DESCR:** Higher Education.

33 Gonzalez, Judith Teresa. Dilemmas of the high achieving Chicana: the double bind factor in male/female relationships. Tucson, AZ: Mexican American Studies & Research Center, University of Arizona, 1987. 31 leaves. English. **DESCR:** Higher Education; Identity; Males; Marriage; *Sex Roles; *Sex Stereotypes; Women Men Relations.

34 Gonzalez, Judith Teresa. Dilemmas of the high achieving Chicana: the double bind factor in male/female relationships. SEX ROLES, Vol. 18, no. 7-8 (April 1988), p. 367-380. English. **DESCR:** Higher Education; Identity; Males; Marriage; *Sex Roles; *Sex Stereotypes; Women Men Relations.

35 Guajardo, Maria Resendez. Educational attainment of Chicana adolescents. Thesis (Ph.D.)--University of Denver, 1988. 266 p. English. **DESCR:** *Dropouts; *Secondary School Education; *Youth.

36 Jaramillo, Mari-Luci. Institutional responsibility in the provision of educational experiences to the Hispanic American female student. IN: McKenna, Teresa and Ortiz, Flora Ida, eds. THE BROKEN WEB: THE EDUCATIONAL EXPERIENCE OF HISPANIC WOMEN. Claremont, CA: Tomaas Rivera Center; Berkeley, CA: Floricanto Press, 1988, p. 25-35. English. **DESCR:** *Discrimination in Education; Dropouts; *Education; Educational Administration; Enrollment; Higher Education; Students; *Women.

37 Lee, Valerie. Achievement and educational aspirations among Hispanic female high school students: comparison between public and Catholic schools. IN: McKenna, Teresa and Ortiz, Flora Ida, eds. THE BROKEN WEB: THE EDUCATIONAL EXPERIENCE OF HISPANIC WOMEN. Claremont, CA: Tomas Rivera Center; Berkeley, CA: Floricanto Press, 1988, p. 137-192. English. **DESCR:** Anglo Americans; Catholic Church; Education; Educational Statistics; Private Education; Religious Education; *Secondary School Education; *Women.

Academic Achievement
(cont.)

38 MacCorquodale, Patricia. Mexican-American women and mathematics: participation, aspirations, and achievement. IN: Cocking, Rodney R. and Mestre, Jose P., eds. LINGUISTIC AND CULTURAL DIFFERENCES ON LEARNING MATHEMATICS. Hillsdale, NJ: Erlbaum, 1988, p. 137-160. English. DESCR: Anglo Americans; Bilingualism; Family; *Mathematics.

39 McKenna, Teresa, ed. and Ortiz, Flora Ida, ed. The broken web: the educational experience of Hispanic American women. Claremont, CA: Tomas Rivera Center; Berkeley, CA: Floricanto Press, 1988. iii, 262 p. English. DESCR: *Education; Educational Statistics; The Educational Experience of Hispanic American Women [symposium] (1985: Claremont, CA); *Women.

40 Moore, Helen A. Hispanic women: schooling for conformity in public education. HISPANIC JOURNAL OF BEHAVIORAL SCIENCES, Vol. 5, no. 1 (March 1983), p. 45-63. English. DESCR: Education.

41 Morales, Aida G. Barriers, critical events, and support systems affecting Chicanas in their pursuit of an academic doctorate. Thesis (Ph.D.)--East Texas State University, 1988. 184 p. English. DESCR: *Higher Education; Natural Support Systems.

42 Munoz, Daniel G. Identifying areas of stress for Chicano undergraduates. IN: Olivas, Michael A., ed. LATINO COLLEGE STUDENTS. New York: Teachers College Press, 1986, p. 131-156. English. DESCR: *Attitudes; Colleges and Universities; Financial Aid; *Stress; Surveys.

43 Nieto Senour, Maria. Psychology of the Chicana. IN: Martinez, Joe L., Jr., ed. CHICANO PSYCHOLOGY. New York: Academic Press, 1977, p. 329-342. English. DESCR: Acculturation; Cultural Customs; Identity; *Psychology; Sex Roles.

44 Ortiz, Flora Ida. Hispanic American women in higher education: a consideration of the socialization process. AZTLAN, Vol. 17, no. 2 (Fall 1986), p. 125-152. English. DESCR: Counseling (Educational); Enrollment; *Higher Education; Sex Roles; *Sexism; Socialization; Students; University of California.

45 Palacios, Maria. Fear of success: Mexican-American women in two work environments. Thesis (Ph.D.)--New Mexico State University, 1988. 163 p. English. DESCR: *Assertiveness; *Careers; Income; Sex Roles; *Working Women.

46 Quezada, Rosa and Jones-Loheyde, Katherine. Hispanic women: academic advisees of high potential. IMPROVING COLLEGE & UNIVERSITY TEACHING, Vol. 32, no. 2-14 (1984), p. 95-98. English. DESCR: Counseling (Educational); *Higher Education.

47 Tienda, Marta. Sex, ethnicity and Chicano status attainment. INTERNATIONAL MIGRATION REVIEW, Vol. 16, no. 2 (Summer 1982), p. 435-473. English. DESCR: Discrimination in Education; Discrimination in Employment; Identity; Income; Language Proficiency; Sexism; *Social Classes; Social Mobility.

48 Vasquez, Melba J. T. Confronting barriers to the participation of Mexican American women in higher education. HISPANIC JOURNAL OF BEHAVIORAL SCIENCES, Vol. 4, no. 2 (June 1982), p. 147-165. English. DESCR: Higher Education; *Sex Roles; Socioeconomic Factors.

49 Vigil, James Diego. The nexus of class, culture and gender in the education of Mexican American females. IN: McKenna, Teresa and Ortiz, Flora Ida, eds. THE BROKEN WEB: THE EDUCATIONAL EXPERIENCE OF HISPANIC WOMEN. Claremont, CA: Tomas Rivera Center; Berkeley, CA: Floricanto Press, 1988, p. 79-103. English. DESCR: Acculturation; Discrimination in Education; *Education; Identity; Secondary School Education; Sex Roles; Social Classes; Students.

50 Zambrana, Ruth E. Toward understanding the educational trajectory and socialization of Latina women. IN: McKenna, Teresa and Ortiz, Flora Ida, eds. THE BROKEN WEB: THE EDUCATIONAL EXPERIENCE OF HISPANIC WOMEN. Claremont, CA: Tomas Rivera Center; Berkeley, CA: Floricanto Press, 1988, p. 61-77. English. DESCR: Anglo Americans; *Education; Feminism; Identity; Research Methodology; *Socialization; *Women.

Academic Performance
USE: Academic Achievement

Acapulco Fashion, Ciudad Juarez, Mexico

51 Preuss, Sabine. Die Frauen von Acapulco Fashion: Weiblicher Lebenszusammenhang und Industrialisierung in den Weltmarktfabriken Mexikos. Berlin: Express, c1985. 133 p.: ill. Other. DESCR: *Border Industries; *Employment; *Working Women.

Acculturation

52 Abney-Guardado, Armando J. Chicano intermarriage in the United States: a sociocultural analysis. Thesis (Ph.D.)--Notre Dame, 1983. viii, 142 p. English. DESCR: *Assimilation; *Intermarriage.

53 Alanis, Elsa. The relationship between state and trait anxiety and acculturation in Mexican-American women homemakers and Mexican-American community college female students. Thesis (Ph.D.)--United States International University, 1989. 161 p. English. DESCR: *Community Colleges; Family; Sex Roles; *Stress; Students.

54 Ashley, Laurel Maria. Self, family and community: the social process of aging among urban Mexican-American women. Thesis (Ph.D.)--University of California, Los Angeles, 1985. 306 p. English. DESCR: *Ancianos; *Family; Grandmothers; *Sex Roles; Southern California.

55 Baca Zinn, Maxine. Employment and education of Mexican-American women: the interplay of modernity and ethnicity in eight families. HARVARD EDUCATIONAL REVIEW, Vol. 50, no. 1 (February 1980), p. 47-62. English. DESCR: Decision Making; *Education; *Employment; *Family; Identity; Sex Roles; Social Classes; Values.

56 Baca Zinn, Maxine. Political familism: toward sex role equality in Chicano families. AZTLAN, Vol. 6, no. 1 (Spring 1975), p. 13-26. English. DESCR: Chicano Movement; Family; Machismo; *Sex Roles.

Acculturation (cont.)

57 Becerra, Rosina M. and de Anda, Diane. Pregnancy and motherhood among Mexican American adolescents. HEALTH AND SOCIAL WORK, Vol. 9, no. 2 (Spring 1984), p. 106-23. English. **DESCR:** Anglo Americans; Attitudes; Birth Control; *Fertility; Natural Support Systems; *Youth.

58 Chavez, John M. and Buriel, Raymond. Reinforcing children's effort: a comparison of immigrant, native-born Mexican American and Euro-American mothers. HISPANIC JOURNAL OF BEHAVIORAL SCIENCES, Vol. 8, no. 2 (June 1986), p. 127-142. English. **DESCR:** Immigrants; *Parenting.

59 Craver, Rebecca McDowell. The impact of intimacy: Mexican-Anglo intermarriage in New Mexico 1821-1846. SOUTHWESTERN STUDIES, no. 66 (1982), p. 1-79. English. **DESCR:** Anglo Americans; Assimilation; History; *Intermarriage; New Mexico; Rio Arriba Valley, NM.

60 Craver, Rebecca McDowell. The impact of intimacy: Mexican-Anglo intermarriage in New Mexico 1821-1846. El Paso, TX: Texas Western Press, University of Texas at El Paso, 1982. 79 p. English. **DESCR:** Anglo Americans; Assimilation; History; *Intermarriage; New Mexico; Rio Arriba Valley, NM.

61 Del Castillo, Adelaida R. and Torres, Maria. The interdependency of educational institutions and cultural norms: the Hispana experience. IN: McKenna, Teresa and Ortiz, Flora Ida, eds. THE BROKEN WEB: THE EDUCATIONAL EXPERIENCE OF HISPANIC WOMEN. Claremont, CA: Tomas Rivera Center; Berkeley, CA: Floricanto Press, 1988, p. 39-60. English. **DESCR:** Academic Achievement; *Cultural Characteristics; *Education; *Literature Reviews; Research Methodology; *Values; Women.

62 Enguidanos-Clark, Gloria M. Acculturative stress and its contribution to the development of depression in Hispanic women. Thesis (Ph.D.)--Wright Institute, Berkeley, 1986. 198 p. English. **DESCR:** *Depression (Psychological); Immigrants; Mental Health; *Stress.

63 Falicov, Celia Jaes. Mexican families. IN: McGoldrick, Monica, et al., eds. ETHNICITY AND FAMILY THERAPY. New York: The Guilford Press, 1982, p. 134-163. English. **DESCR:** Cultural Customs; *Family; Mental Health; Sex Roles.

64 Gilbert, M. Jean. Alcohol consumption patterns in immigrant and later generation Mexican American women. HISPANIC JOURNAL OF BEHAVIORAL SCIENCES, Vol. 9, no. 3 (September 1987), p. 299-313. English. **DESCR:** *Alcoholism; *Attitudes; Cultural Characteristics; *Immigrants; Mexico.

65 Gutierrez, Jeannie and Sameroff, Arnold. Determinants of complexity in Mexican-American and Anglo-American mothers' conceptions of child development. CHILD DEVELOPMENT, Vol. 61, no. 2 (April 1990), p. 384-394. English. **DESCR:** *Anglo Americans; Children; Cultural Characteristics; *Parenting; Values; *Women.

66 Hernandez, Leodoro. The socialization of a Chicano family. DE COLORES, Vol. 6, no. 1-2 (1982), p. 75-84. English. **DESCR:** Family; *Socialization.

67 Herrera-Sobek, Maria. The acculturation process of the Chicana in the corrido. DE COLORES, Vol. 6, no. 1-2 (1982), p. 7-16. English. **DESCR:** Corridos; Sex Roles.

68 Herrera-Sobek, Maria. The acculturation process of the Chicana in the corrido. PROCEEDINGS OF THE PACIFIC COAST COUNCIL ON LATIN AMER STUDIES, Vol. 9, (1982), p. 25-34. English. **DESCR:** *Corridos; Musical Lyrics; *Women Men Relations.

69 Jorgensen, Stephen R. and Adams, Russell P. Family planning needs and behavior of Mexican American women: a study of health care professionals and their clientele. HISPANIC JOURNAL OF BEHAVIORAL SCIENCES, Vol. 9, no. 3 (September 1987), p. 265-286. English. **DESCR:** *Attitudes; Birth Control; *Cultural Characteristics; *Family Planning; Fertility; Medical Personnel; Stereotypes; Sterilization.

70 Kranau, Edgar J.; Green, Vicki; and Valencia-Weber, Gloria. Acculturation and the Hispanic woman: attitudes toward women, sex-role attribution, sex-role behavior, and demographics. HISPANIC JOURNAL OF BEHAVIORAL SCIENCES, Vol. 4, no. 1 (March 1982), p. 21-40. English. **DESCR:** Population; *Sex Roles.

71 Lawrence, Alberto Augusto. Traditional attitudes toward marriage, marital adjustment, acculturation, and self-esteem of Mexican-American and Mexican wives. Thesis (Ph.D.)--United States International University, San Diego, CA, 1982. ix, 191 p. English. **DESCR:** *Attitudes; Machismo; *Marriage; Mental Health; Psychological Testing; San Ysidro, CA; Sex Roles; Sex Stereotypes; Tijuana, Baja California, Mexico; Women.

72 Lozano-Bull, Irma. Acculturative stress in Mexican-American women. Thesis (Ph.D.)--California School of Professional Psychology, Los Angeles, 1987. 201 p. English. **DESCR:** Natural Support Systems; *Stress.

73 Marin, Gerardo; Perez-Stable, Eliseo J.; and Marin, Barbara Van Oss. Cigarette smoking among San Francisco Hispanics: the role of acculturation and gender. PUBLIC HEALTH BRIEFS, Vol. 79, no. 2 (February 1989), p. 196-198. English. **DESCR:** Drug Use; Males; San Francisco, CA; *Smoking; Women.

74 Marshall, Maria Sandra Gonzalez. The childbearing beliefs and practices of pregnant Mexican-American adolescents living in Southwest border regions. Thesis (M.S.)--University of Arizona, 1987. 117 p. English. **DESCR:** Border Region; *Fertility; *Youth.

75 Martinez, Estella A. Child behavior in Mexican American/Chicano families: maternal teaching and child-rearing practices. FAMILY RELATIONS, Vol. 37, no. 3 (July 1988), p. 275-280. English. **DESCR:** Family; Maternal Teaching Observation Technique (MTOT); Parent and Child Relationships; *Parenting; *Psychological Testing; Socioeconomic Factors; Values.

76 McDuff, Mary Ann. Mexican-American women: a three-generational study of attitudes and behaviors. Thesis (M.A.)--Texas Women's University, 1989. 200 p. English. **DESCR:** *Age Groups; Family; San Antonio, TX; *Sex Roles.

Acculturation (cont.)

77 Melville, Margarita B. Cultural conflict. IN: Melville, Margarita B., ed. TWICE A MINORITY. St. Louis, MO: Mosby, 1980, p. 149-154. English.

78 Melville, Margarita B. Mexican women adapt to migration. IN: Rios-Bustamante, Antonio, ed. MEXICAN IMMIGRANT WORKERS IN THE U.S. Los Angeles, CA: Chicano Studies Research Center Publications, University of California, 1981, p. 119-124. English. DESCR: Attitudes; Immigrants; Sex Roles; Stress; *Undocumented Workers.

79 Melville, Margarita B. Selective acculturation of female Mexican migrants. IN: Melville, Margarita B., ed. TWICE A MINORITY. St. Louis, MO: Mosby, 1980, p. 155-163. English. DESCR: Identity; Migrant Labor; Working Women.

80 Miller, Michael V. Variations in Mexican American family life: a review synthesis of empirical research. AZTLAN, Vol. 9, no. 1 (1978), p. 209-231. Bibliography. English. DESCR: Compadrazgo; *Family; Intermarriage; Sex Roles; Stereotypes.

81 Murguia, Edward and Cazares, Ralph B. Intermarriage of Mexican Americans. MARRIAGE & FAMILY REVIEW, Vol. 5, no. 1 (Spring 1982), p. 91-100. English. DESCR: Anglo Americans; *Intermarriage; Social Mobility.

82 Nieto Senour, Maria. Psychology of the Chicana. IN: Martinez, Joe L., Jr., ed. CHICANO PSYCHOLOGY. New York: Academic Press, 1977, p. 329-342. English. DESCR: Academic Achievement; Cultural Customs; Identity; *Psychology; Sex Roles.

83 O'Guinn, Thomas C.; Imperia, Giovanna; and MacAdams, Elizabeth A. Acculturation and perceived family decision-making input among Mexican American wives. JOURNAL OF CROSS-CULTURAL PSYCHOLOGY, Vol. 18, no. 1 (March 1987), p. 78-92. English. DESCR: Attitudes; Consumers; Family; Sex Roles.

84 Ortiz, Sylvia. An analysis of the relationship between the values of sexual regulation, male dominance and motherhood, and Mexican-American women s attitudes, knowledge, and usage of birth control. Thesis (Ph.D.)--University of California, Santa Barbara, 1987. 128 p. English. DESCR: *Attitudes; *Birth Control; *Family Planning; Sexual Behavior.

85 Ortiz, Sylvia and Casas, Jesus Manuel. Birth control and low-income Mexican-American women: the impact of three values. HISPANIC JOURNAL OF BEHAVIORAL SCIENCES, Vol. 12, no. 1 (February 1990), p. 83-92. English. DESCR: Attitudes; *Birth Control; Fertility; *Low Income; *Sex Roles; Values.

86 Powell, Douglas R.; Zambrana, Ruth E.; and Silva-Palacios, Victor. Designing culturally responsive parent programs: a comparison of low-income Mexican and Mexican-American mothers' preferences. FAMILY RELATIONS, Vol. 39, no. 3 (July 1990), p. 298-304. English. DESCR: Children; Education; Immigrants; Los Angeles, CA; Low Income; *Parent and Child Relationships; *Parenting; Women.

87 Pumariega, Andres J. Acculturation and eating attitudes in adolescent girls: a comparative and correlational study. JOURNAL OF THE AMERICAN ACADEMY OF CHILD PSYCHIATRY, Vol. 25, no. 2 (March 1986), p. 276-279. English. DESCR: Anorexia Nervosa; Cultural Characteristics; Eating Attitudes Test (EAT); Nutrition; Socioeconomic Factors; Youth.

88 Rider, Kennon V. Relationship satisfaction of the Mexican American woman: effects of acculturation, socioeconomic status, and interaction structures. Thesis (Ph.D.)--Texas Tech University, 1988. 145 p. English. DESCR: *Interpersonal Relations; Sex Roles; *Socioeconomic Factors.

89 Sabogal, Fabio, et al. Hispanic familism and acculturation: what changes and what doesn't? HISPANIC JOURNAL OF BEHAVIORAL SCIENCES, Vol. 9, no. 4 (December 1987), p. 397-412. English. DESCR: Attitudes; Cultural Characteristics; Ethnic Groups; Extended Family; *Family; Natural Support Systems; Values.

90 Salgado de Snyder, Nelly and Padilla, Amado M. Cultural and ethnic maintenance of interethnically married Mexican-Americans. HUMAN ORGANIZATION, Vol. 41, no. 4 (Winter 1982), p. 359-362. English. DESCR: *Intermarriage.

91 Salgado de Snyder, Nelly; Lopez, Cynthia M.; and Padilla, Amado M. Ethnic identity and cultural awareness among the offspring of Mexican interethnic marriages. JOURNAL OF EARLY ADOLESCENCE, Vol. 2, no. 3 (Fall 1982), p. 277-282. English. DESCR: Children; *Identity; *Intermarriage; *Youth.

92 Salgado de Snyder, Nelly. Factors associated with acculturative stress and depressive symptomatology among married Mexican immigrant women. PSYCHOLOGY OF WOMEN QUARTERLY, Vol. 11, no. 4 (December 1987), p. 475-488. English. DESCR: Depression (Psychological); *Immigrants; Mental Health; Mexico; *Stress; Women.

93 Salgado de Snyder, Nelly. Mexican immigrant women: the relationship of ethnic loyalty and social support to acculturative stress and depressive symptomatology. Los Angeles, CA: Spanish Speaking Mental Health Research Center, 1987. 73 p. English. DESCR: Depression (Psychological); Identity; *Immigrants; Natural Support Systems; *Stress; Women.

94 Salgado de Snyder, Nelly. The role of ethnic loyalty among Mexican immigrant women. HISPANIC JOURNAL OF BEHAVIORAL SCIENCES, Vol. 9, no. 3 (September 1987), p. 287-298. English. DESCR: *Culture; *Identity; Immigrants; Mental Health; Mexico; *Women.

95 Sanchez, George J. "Go after the women": Americanization and the Mexican immigrant woman, 1915-1929. Stanford, CA: Stanford Center for Chicano Research [1984?]. [32] leaves. English. DESCR: *Assimilation; Biculturalism; *Immigrants; Social History and Conditions; Values; Women.

96 Sanchez, George J. "Go after the women": Americanization and the Mexican immigrant woman, 1915-1929. IN: DuBois, Ellen Carol and Ruiz, Vicki L., eds. UNEQUAL SISTERS: A MULTICULTURAL READER IN U.S. WOMEN'S HISTORY. New York: Routledge, 1990, p. 250-263. English. DESCR: *Assimilation; Biculturalism; *Immigrants; Social History and Conditions; Values; Women.

Acculturation (cont.)

97 Saracho, Olivia N. Women and education: sex role modifications of Mexican American women. EDUCATION, Vol. 109, no. 3 (Spring 1989), p. 295-301. English. **DESCR:** *Education; *Sex Roles.

98 Scrimshaw, Susan C.M., et al. Factors affecting breastfeeding among women of Mexican origin or descent in Los Angeles. AMERICAN JOURNAL OF PUBLIC HEALTH, Vol. 77, no. 4 (April 1987), p. 467-470. English. **DESCR:** *Breastfeeding; Immigrants; Los Angeles, CA; Working Women.

99 Sorenson, Ann Marie. Fertility, expectations and ethnic identity among Mexican-American adolescents: an expression of cultural ideals. SOCIOLOGICAL PERSPECTIVES, Vol. 28, no. 3 (July 1985), p. 339-360. English. **DESCR:** Anglo Americans; Cultural Characteristics; *Fertility; Identity; Values; Youth.

100 Stark, Miriam. La Chicana: changing roles in a changing society. Thesis (B.A)--University of Michigan, 1984. ii, 157 leaves. English. **DESCR:** Identity; Lansing, MI; *Sex Roles; *Social History and Conditions.

101 Vallez, Andrea. Acculturation, social support, stress and adjustment of the Mexican American college woman. Thesis (Ph.D.)--University of Colorado at Boulder, 1984. 121 p. English. **DESCR:** *Colleges and Universities; Depression (Psychological); Higher Education; Natural Support Systems; Southern California; Stress; *Students.

102 Valtierra, Mary. Acculturation, social support, and reported stress of Latina physicians. Thesis (Ph.D.)--California School of Professional Psychology, 1989. 136 p. English. **DESCR:** Careers; Cubanos; Immigration; Latin Americans; *Medical Personnel; Puerto Ricans; *Stress; *Women.

103 Vega, William A.; Kolody, Bohdan; and Valle, Juan Ramon. Migration and mental health: an empirical test of depression risk factors among immigrant Mexican women. INTERNATIONAL MIGRATION REVIEW, Vol. 21, no. 3 (Fall 1987), p. 512-530. English. **DESCR:** *Depression (Psychological); *Immigrants; Immigration; *Mental Health; Migration; Stress; Undocumented Workers; Women.

104 Vigil, James Diego. The nexus of class, culture and gender in the education of Mexican American females. IN: McKenna, Teresa and Ortiz, Flora Ida, eds. THE BROKEN WEB: THE EDUCATIONAL EXPERIENCE OF HISPANIC WOMEN. Claremont, CA: Tomas Rivera Center; Berkeley, CA: Floricanto Press, 1988, p. 79-103. English. **DESCR:** Academic Achievement; Discrimination in Education; *Education; Identity; Secondary School Education; Sex Roles; Social Classes; Students.

105 Walker, Todd. The relationship of nativity, social support and depression to the home environment among Mexican-American women. Thesis (Ph.D.)--University of Houston, 1989. 123 p. English. **DESCR:** Avance Parent-Child Education Program, San Antonio, TX; Children; Depression (Psychological); *Immigrants; Natural Support Systems; *Parenting; Women.

106 Yinger, Milton J. Assimilation in the United States: the Mexican-Americans. IN: Conner, Walker, ed. MEXICAN-AMERICANS IN COMPARATIVE PERSPECTIVE. Washington, DC: Urban Institute Press, 1985, p. 30-55. English. **DESCR:** *Assimilation; Culture of Poverty Model; Identity; Intermarriage.

107 Zayas, Luis H. Toward an understanding of suicide risks in young Hispanic females. JOURNAL OF ADOLESCENT RESEARCH, Vol. 2, no. 1 (Spring 1987), p. 1-11. English. **DESCR:** Cubanos; Cultural Characteristics; Depression (Psychological); Mental Health; Puerto Ricans; *Suicide; *Women; *Youth.

108 Zuniga, Maria E. Assessment issues with Chicanas: practice implications. PSYCHOTHERAPY, Vol. 25, no. 2 (Summer 1988), p. 288-293. English. **DESCR:** Colleges and Universities; Family; Identity; *Mental Health; Mexican-American Outreach Program, San Diego State University; *Psychotherapy; *Students.

Acculturation Rating Scale for Mexican Americans (ARSMA)

109 Cuellar, Israel, et al. Clinical psychiatric case presentation: culturally responsive diagnostic formulation and treatment in an Hispanic female. HISPANIC JOURNAL OF BEHAVIORAL SCIENCES, Vol. 5, no. 1 (March 1983), p. 93-103. English. **DESCR:** Case Studies; Medical Care; *Psychotherapy.

Acme Laundry, El Paso, TX

110 Garcia, Mario T. The Chicana in American history: the Mexican women of El Paso, 1880-1920 - a case study. PACIFIC HISTORICAL REVIEW, Vol. 49, no. 2 (May 1980), p. 315-337. English. **DESCR:** American Federation of Labor (AFL); Case Studies; Central Labor Union; Domestic Work; *El Paso, TX; Employment; *History; Immigrants; Income; Labor Unions; Sex Roles; Strikes and Lockouts; *Working Women.

Acquired Immunodeficiency Syndrome (AIDS)
    USE: AIDS (Disease)

Actors and Actresses

111 Broyles-Gonzalez, Yolanda and Rodriguez, Diane. The living legacy of Chicana performers: preserving history through oral testimony. FRONTIERS: A JOURNAL OF WOMEN STUDIES, Vol. 11, no. 1 (1990), p. [46]-52. English. **DESCR:** El Teatro Campesino; Latins Anonymous [comedy review]; Oral History; *Rodriguez, Diane; Sex Roles; Singers; Teatro.

112 Broyles-Gonzalez, Yolanda. Women in El Teatro Campesino: "A poco estaba molacha la Virgen de Guadalupe?". IN: Cordova, Teresa, et al., eds. CHICANA VOICES. Austin, TX: Center for Mexican American Studies, 1986, p. 162-187. English. **DESCR:** CORRIDOS [play]; *El Teatro Campesino; Stereotypes; Teatro; Valdez, Socorro.

113 Hadley-Freydberg, Elizabeth. Prostitutes, concubines, whores and bitches: Black and Hispanic women in contemporary American film. IN: McCluskey, Audrey T., ed. WOMEN OF COLOR: PERSPECTIVES ON FEMINISM AND IDENTITY. Bloomington, IN: Women's Studies Program, Indiana University, 1985, p. 46-65. English. **DESCR:** Blacks; *Films; Puerto Ricans; *Sex Stereotypes; Stereotypes; Women.

Actors and Actresses
(cont.)

114 Vega, Alicia. Three Latinas in Hollywood = Tres latinas en Hollywood. AMERICAS 2001, Vol. 1, no. 7 (July, August, 1988), p. 4-6. Bilingual. DESCR: Alonso, Maria Conchita; Martinez, Patrice; Ramos, Loyda.

115 Yarbro-Bejarano, Yvonne. Chicana's experience in collective theatre: ideology and form. WOMEN AND PERFORMANCE, Vol. 2, no. 2 (1985), p. 45-58. English. DESCR: Careers; El Teatro Campesino; El Teatro de la Esperanza; Political Ideology; *San Francisco Mime Troupe; Sex Roles; Teatro; Teatro Libertad; Valentina Productions; Women.

Actos

116 Bouknight, Jon. Language as a cure: an interview with Milcha Sanchez-Scott. LATIN AMERICAN THEATRE REVIEW, Vol. 23, no. 2 (Spring 1990), p. 63-74. English. DESCR: *Authors; ROOSTERS [play]; Sanchez-Scott, Milcha; *Teatro.

117 Mason, Terry. Symbolic strategies for change: a discussion of the Chicana women's movement. IN: Melville, Margarita B., ed. TWICE A MINORITY. St. Louis, MO: Mosby, 1980, p. 95-108. English. DESCR: Anglo Americans; *Feminism; Teatro; Women.

Acuna, Rodolfo

118 Orozco, Cynthia. Sexism in Chicano Studies and the community. IN: Cordova, Teresa, et al., eds. CHICANA VOICES. Austin, TX: Center for Mexican American Studies, 1986, p. 11-18. English. DESCR: Chicano Studies; Feminism; OCCUPIED AMERICA; *Sexism.

Adelante Mujer Hispana Conference--Education and Employment Conference (January 11-12, 1980: Denver, CO)

119 Adelante, mujer hispana. LATINO, Vol. 53, no. 2 (March, April, 1982), p. 26. English. DESCR: Conferences and Meetings; Leadership.

120 U.S. Department of Labor, Women's Bureau. Adelante mujer hispana: a conference model for Hispanic women. Washington, DC: The Bureau, 1980. 39 p.: ill. English. DESCR: *Conferences and Meetings; *Women.

La Adelita

121 Cantu, Norma. Women then and now: an analysis of the Adelita image versus the Chicana as political writer and philosopher. IN: Cordova, Teresa, et al., eds. CHICANA VOICES. Austin, TX: Center for Mexican American Studies, 1986, p. 3-10. English. DESCR: Chicano Studies; Discrimination; Higher Education; Stereotypes.

122 Leal, Luis. La soldadera en la narrativa de la Revolucion. IN: Leal, Luis. AZTLAN Y MEXICO: PERFILES LITERARIOS E HISTORICOS. Binghamton, NY: Bilingual Press/Editorial Bilingue, 1985, p. 185-193. Spanish. DESCR: LA VOZ DEL PUEBLO; *Literary Criticism; Mexican Literature; Mexican Revolution - 1910-1920; Women.

123 Longeaux y Vasquez, Enriqueta. The woman of La Raza. REGENERACION, Vol. 2, no. 4 (1975), p. 34-36. English. DESCR: Child Care Centers; Discrimination; Gallo, Juana; Housing; Machismo; Sex Roles; *Social History and Conditions; Working Women.

124 Longeaux y Vasquez, Enriqueta. The woman of La Raza. IN: Valdez, Luis and Steiner, Stan, eds. AZTLAN: AN ANTHOLOGY OF MEXICAN AMERICAN LITERATURE. New York: Vintage Books, 1972, p. 272-278. Also IN: Salinas, Luis Omar and Faderman, Lillian, compilers. FROM THE BARRIO: A CHICANO ANTHOLOGY. San Francisco, CA: Canfield Press, 1973, p. 20-24. English. DESCR: Child Care Centers; Discrimination; Gallo, Juana; Housing; Machismo; Sex Roles; *Social History and Conditions; Working Women.

125 Salas, Elizabeth. Soldaderas in the Mexican military: myth and history. Austin, TX: University of Texas Press, 1990. xiii, 163 p., [12] p. of plates: ill. English. DESCR: Aztecs; History; Mexican Revolution - 1910-1920; Mexico; *Military; Symbolism; War; *Women.

126 Salas, Elizabeth. Soldaderas in the Mexican military: myth and history. Thesis (Ph.D.)--University of California, Los Angeles, 1987. 313p. English. DESCR: Aztecs; History; Mexican Revolution - 1910-1920; Mexico; Military; Symbolism; War; *Women.

Adlerian "Life Style Inventory"

127 Zapata, Jesse T. and Jaramillo, Pat T. The Mexican American family: an Adlerian perspective. HISPANIC JOURNAL OF BEHAVIORAL SCIENCES, Vol. 3, no. 3 (September 1981), p. 275-290. English. DESCR: *Family; Parent and Child Relationships; Sex Roles; Stereotypes.

Administration of Justice

128 Martinez, Virginia. Chicanas and the law. IN: LA CHICANA: BUILDING FOR THE FUTURE, AN ACTION PLAN FOR THE 80s. Oakland, CA: National Hispanic University, 1981, p. 134-146. English. DESCR: Civil Rights; Feminism; Law.

129 Veyna, Angelina F. Women in early New Mexico: a preliminary view. IN: Cordova, Teresa, et al., eds. CHICANA VOICES. Austin, TX: Center for Mexican American Studies, 1986, p. 120-135. English. DESCR: History; New Mexico; *Women.

Adolescents
USE: Youth

Adult Education

130 Bova, Breda Murphy and Phillips, Rebecca R. Hispanic women at midlife: implications for higher and adult education. JOURNAL OF ADULT EDUCATION, Vol. 18, no. 1 (Fall 1989), p. 9-15. English. DESCR: Cultural Characteristics; *Higher Education; Identity; Sex Roles.

131 Esparza, Mariana Ochoa. The impact of adult education on Mexican-American women. Thesis (Ed.D.)--Texas A & I University, 1981. 168 p. English. DESCR: Careers; McAllen, TX; Sex Roles.

Affirmative Action

132 Dressel, Paula. Symposium. Civil rights, affirmative action, and the aged of the future: will life chances be different for Blacks, Hispanics, and women? An overview of the issues. GERONTOLOGIST, Vol. 26, no. 2 (April 1986), p. 128-131. English. DESCR: *Ancianos; Blacks; *Civil Rights; Women.

Affirmative Action
(cont.)

133 Romero, Mary. Twice protected?: assessing
the impact of affirmative action on
Mexican-American women. JOURNAL OF HISPANIC
POLICY, Vol. 3, (1988, 1989), p. 83-101.
English. DESCR: Careers; *Discrimination in
Employment; Statistics.

AFL-CIO

134 Vasquez, Mario F. Immigrant workers and the
apparel manufacturing industry in Southern
California. IN: Rios-Bustamante, Antonio,
ed. MEXICAN IMMIGRANT WORKERS IN THE U.S.
Los Angeles, CA: Chicano Studies Research
Center Publications, University of
California, 1981, p. 85-96. English. DESCR:
California; Garment Industry; Immigrants;
International Ladies Garment Workers Union
(ILGWU); *Labor Supply and Market; Labor
Unions; Undocumented Workers; Women.

AFL-CIO United Farmworkers Organizing Committee

135 Chavez, Henri. Unsung heroine of La Causa.
REGENERACION, Vol. 1, no. 10 (1971), p. 20.
English. DESCR: Agricultural Labor Unions;
Community Service Organization, Los Angeles,
(CSO); Family; Farm Workers; *Huerta,
Dolores; Poverty; Working Women.

Afro-Americans
USE: Blacks

Afro-Hispanics

136 Nieves-Squires, Sarah. Hispanic women:
making their presence on campus less
tenuous. Washington, DC: Association of
American Colleges, c1991. 14 p. English.
DESCR: Colleges and Universities; Cubanos;
*Discrimination in Education; *Higher
Education; Puerto Ricans; *Women.

Age Groups

137 Aneshensel, Carol S., et al. Participation
of Mexican American adolescents in a
longitudinal panel survey. PUBLIC OPINION
QUARTERLY, Vol. 53, no. 4 (Winter 1989), p.
548-562. English. DESCR: *Fertility; Los
Angeles County, CA; Social Science;
*Surveys; *Women Men Relations; *Youth.

138 Bean, Frank D. and Swicegood, Gray.
Generation, female education and Mexican
American fertility. SOCIAL SCIENCE
QUARTERLY, Vol. 63, (March 1982), p.
131-144. English. DESCR: Education; Family
Planning; *Fertility.

139 Bean, Frank D. and Swicegood, Gray. Mexican
American fertility patterns. Austin, TX:
University of Texas Press, 1985. x, 178 p.
English. DESCR: Census; Education;
*Fertility; Language Usage; *Population;
Research Methodology; *Socioeconomic
Factors; Statistics.

140 Bean, Frank D., et al. Generational
differences in fertility among Mexican
Americans: implications for assessing the
effects of immigration. SOCIAL SCIENCE
QUARTERLY, Vol. 65, no. 2 (June 1984), p.
573-582. English. DESCR: *Fertility;
Immigration; Vital Statistics.

141 Cazares, Ralph B.; Murguia, Edward; and
Frisbie, William Parker. Mexican American
intermarriage in a nonmetropolitan context.
SOCIAL SCIENCE QUARTERLY, Vol. 65, no. 2
(June 1984), p. 626-634. English. DESCR:
*Intermarriage; Pecos County, TX; Social
Classes; Texas.

142 Cazares, Ralph B.; Murguia, Edward; and
Frisbie, William Parker. Mexican American
intermarriage in a nonmetropolitan context.
IN: O. de la Garza, Rodolfo, et al., eds.
THE MEXICAN AMERICAN EXPERIENCE: AN
INTERDISCIPLINARY ANTHOLOGY. Austin, TX:
University of Texas Press, 1985, p. 393-401.
English. DESCR: *Intermarriage; Pecos
County, TX; Social Classes; Texas.

143 Facio, Elisa "Linda". The interaction of age
and gender in Chicana older lives: a case
study of Chicana elderly in a senior citizen
center. RENATO ROSALDO LECTURE SERIES
MONOGRAPH, Vol. 4, (1988), p. 21-38.
English. DESCR: *Ancianos; Poverty; Social
Classes.

144 Fennelly, Katherine, et al. The effect of
maternal age on the well-being of children.
JOURNAL OF MARRIAGE AND THE FAMILY, Vol. 46,
no. 4 (November 1984), p. 933-934. English.
DESCR: *Maternal and Child Welfare;
*Parenting; *Youth.

145 Frisbie, William Parker; Bean, Frank D.; and
Eberstein, Isaac W. Recent changes in
marital instability among Mexican Americans:
convergence with Black and Anglo trends.
SOCIAL FORCES, Vol. 58, no. 4 (June 1980),
p. 1205-1220. English. DESCR: Anglo
Americans; Blacks; *Divorce; *Marriage.

146 Griswold del Castillo, Richard. Chicano
family history--methodology and theory: a
survey of contemporary research directions.
IN: National Association for Chicano
Studies. HISTORY, CULTURE, AND SOCIETY:
CHICANO STUDIES IN THE 1980s. Ypsilanti, MI:
Bilingual Press/Editorial Bilingue, 1983, p.
95-106. English. DESCR: *Family;
Historiography.

147 Kearl, Michael C. and Murguia, Edward. Age
differences of spouses in Mexican American
intermarriage: exploring the cost of
minority assimilation. SOCIAL SCIENCE
QUARTERLY, Vol. 66, no. 2 (June 1985), p.
453-460. English. DESCR: *Assimilation;
*Intermarriage.

148 Markides, Kyriakos S. and Vernon, Sally W.
Aging, sex-role orientation and adjustment:
a three-generations study of Mexican
Americans. JOURNAL OF GERONTOLOGY, Vol. 39,
no. 5 (September 1984), p. 586-591. English.
DESCR: *Ancianos; Mental Health; *Sex Roles.

149 Markides, Kyriakos S. and Hoppe, Sue K.
Marital satisfaction in three generations of
Mexican Americans. SOCIAL SCIENCE QUARTERLY,
Vol. 66, no. 1 (March 1985), p. 147-154.
English. DESCR: *Marriage.

150 Markides, Kyriakos S., et al. Sample
representativeness in a three-generation
study of Mexican Americans. JOURNAL OF
MARRIAGE AND THE FAMILY, Vol. 45, no. 4
(November 1983), p. 911-916. English.
DESCR: *Marriage; Population; San Antonio,
TX; *Socioeconomic Factors.

151 Mason, Theresa Hope. Experience and meaning:
an interpretive study of family and gender
ideologies among a sample of
Mexican-American women of two generations.
Thesis (Ph.D.)--University of Texas, Austin,
1987. 406 p. English. DESCR: Culture;
Extended Family; *Family; *Sex Roles.

Age Groups (cont.)

152 Mayers, Raymond Sanchez. Use of folk medicine by elderly Mexican-American women. JOURNAL OF DRUG ISSUES, Vol. 19, no. 2 (1989), p. 283-295. English. DESCR: *Ancianos; Curanderas; Curanderismo; Folk Medicine.

153 McDuff, Mary Ann. Mexican-American women: a three-generational study of attitudes and behaviors. Thesis (M.A.)--Texas Women's University, 1989. 200 p. English. DESCR: *Acculturation; Family; San Antonio, TX; *Sex Roles.

154 Mink, Diane Leslie. Early grandmotherhood: an exploratory study. Thesis (Ph.D.)--California School of Professional Psychology, Los Angeles, 1987. 190 p. English. DESCR: *Ancianos; Assertiveness; Family; Fertility; Grandmothers; Natural Support Systems; *Sex Roles; Surveys; Youth.

155 Padilla, Eligio R. and O'Grady, Kevin E. Sexuality among Mexican Americans: a case of sexual stereotyping. JOURNAL OF PERSONALITY AND SOCIAL PSYCHOLOGY, Vol. 52, no. 1 (1987), p. 5-10. English. DESCR: Anglo Americans; Attitudes; California; Religion; *Sex Roles; *Sex Stereotypes; Sexual Behavior; Sexual Knowledge and Attitude Test; *Stereotypes; Students; Values.

156 Rogers, Linda Perkowski and Markides, Kyriakos S. Well-being in the postparental stage in Mexican-American women. RESEARCH ON AGING, Vol. 11, no. 4 (December 1989), p. 508-516. English. DESCR: Ancianos; Children; *"Empty Nest" Syndrome; *Parent and Child Relationships; San Antonio, TX.

157 Torres Raines, Rosario. The Mexican American woman and work: intergenerational perspectives of comparative ethnic groups. IN: Melville, Margarita, ed. MEXICANAS AT WORK IN THE UNITED STATES. Houston, TX: Mexican American Studies Program, University of Houston, 1988, p. 33-46. English. DESCR: Anglo Americans; Employment; Feminism; Marriage; Sex Roles; Social Classes; Socioeconomic Factors; *Working Women.

Aged

USE: Ancianos

Agricultural Extension Service

158 Jensen, Joan M. Crossing ethnic barriers in the Southwest: women's agricultural extension education, 1914-1940. AGRICULTURAL HISTORY, Vol. 60, no. 2 (Spring 1986), p. 169-181. English. DESCR: Agriculture; Cabeza de Baca, Fabiola; History; New Mexico; *Rural Education.

Agricultural Labor Unions

159 Calderon, Roberto R. and Zamora, Emilio, Jr. Manuela Solis Sager and Emma Tenayuca: a tribute. IN: Cordova, Teresa, et al., eds. CHICANA VOICES. Austin, TX: Center for Mexican American Studies, 1986, p. 30-41. English. DESCR: Biography; History; Labor; *Solis Sager, Manuela; South Texas Agricultural Worker's Union (STAWU); *Tenayuca, Emma; United Cannery Agricultural Packing and Allied Workers of America (UCAPAWA).

160 Calderon, Roberto R. and Zamora, Emilio, Jr. Manuela Solis Sager and Emma Tenayuca: a tribute. IN: Del Castillo, Adelaida R., ed. BETWEEN BORDERS: ESSAYS ON MEXICANA/CHICANA HISTORY. Encino, CA: Floricanto Press, 1990, p. 269-279. English. DESCR: Biography; History; Labor; *Solis Sager, Manuela; South Texas Agricultural Worker's Union (STAWU); *Tenayuca, Emma; United Cannery Agricultural Packing and Allied Workers of America (UCAPAWA).

161 Cantarow, Ellen and De la Cruz, Jessie Lopez. Jessie Lopez De la Cruz: the battle for farmworkers' rights. IN: Cantarow, Ellen. MOVING THE MOUNTAIN: WOMEN WORKING FOR SOCIAL CHANGE. Old Westbury, NY: Feminist Press, 1980, p. 94-151. English. DESCR: Chavez, Cesar E.; *De la Cruz, Jessie Lopez; *Farm Workers; Labor Disputes; Oral History; Parlier, CA; Sex Roles; Strikes and Lockouts; *United Farmworkers of America (UFW).

162 Chavez, Henri. Unsung heroine of La Causa. REGENERACION, Vol. 1, no. 10 (1971), p. 20. English. DESCR: AFL-CIO United Farmworkers Organizing Committee; Community Service Organization, Los Angeles, (CSO); Family; Farm Workers; *Huerta, Dolores; Poverty; Working Women.

163 Duran, Lucy. Lucy Duran--wife, mother, and organizer. IN: Mora, Magdalena and Del Castillo, Adelaida, eds. MEXICAN WOMEN IN THE UNITED STATES: STRUGGLES PAST AND PRESENT. Los Angeles, CA: Chicano Studies Research Center, UCLA, 1980, p. 183-184. English. DESCR: *Biography; Duran, Lucy; Farm Labor Organizing Committee (FLOC); Farm Workers; Working Women.

164 Echaveste, Beatrice and Huerta, Dolores. In the shadow of the eagle: Huerta = A la sombra del aguila: Huerta. AMERICAS 2001, Vol. 1, no. 3 (November, December, 1987), p. 26-30. Bilingual. DESCR: Boycotts; *Farm Workers; Huerta, Dolores; United Farmworkers of America (UFW).

165 Huerta, Dolores. Dolores Huerta talks about Republicans, Cesar, children and her home town. REGENERACION, Vol. 2, no. 4 (1975), p. 20-24. English. DESCR: *Biography; Chavez, Cesar E.; Community Service Organization, Los Angeles, (CSO); Democratic Party; Elected Officials; Flores, Art; Huerta, Dolores; McGovern, George; *Politics; Ramirez, Henry M.; Ross, Fred; Sanchez, Philip V.; United Farmworkers of America (UFW); Working Women.

166 Huerta, Dolores. Dolores Huerta talks about Republicans, Cesar, children and her home town. IN: Servin, Manuel P. ed. THE MEXICAN AMERICANS: AN AWAKENING MINORITY. 2nd ed. Beverly Hills, CA: Glencoe Press, 1974, p. 283-294. English. DESCR: *Biography; Chavez, Cesar E.; Community Service Organization, Los Angeles, (CSO); Democratic Party; Elected Officials; Flores, Art; Huerta, Dolores; McGovern, George; *Politics; Ramirez, Henry M.; Ross, Fred; Sanchez, Philip V.; United Farmworkers of America (UFW); Working Women.

167 Ruiz, Vicki L. Cannery women/cannery lives: Mexican women, unionization, and the California food processing industry, 1930-1950. Albuquerque, NM: University of New Mexico Press, 1987. xviii, 194 p.: ill. English. DESCR: California; *Canneries; Family; History; Industrial Workers; Labor Disputes; *Labor Unions; Trade Unions; United Cannery Agricultural Packing and Allied Workers of America (UCAPAWA); Women.

Agricultural Laborers
USE: Farm Workers

Agriculture

168 Jensen, Joan M. Crossing ethnic barriers in the Southwest: women's agricultural extension education, 1914-1940. AGRICULTURAL HISTORY, Vol. 60, no. 2 (Spring 1986), p. 169-181. English. **DESCR:** *Agricultural Extension Service; Cabeza de Baca, Fabiola; History; New Mexico; *Rural Education.

AGUEDA MARTINEZ [film]

169 Fregoso, Rosa Linda. La quinceanera of Chicana counter aesthetics. CENTRO BULLETIN, Vol. 3, no. 1 (Winter 1990, 1991), p. [87]-91. English. **DESCR:** ANIMA [film]; *CHICANA! [film]; *DESPUES DEL TERREMOTO [film]; Espana, Frances Salome; Feminism; *Films; Morales, Sylvia; Portillo, Lourdes; Vasquez, Esperanza.

Aid to Families with Dependent Children (AFDC)

170 Hancock, Paula F. The effect of welfare eligibility on the labor force participation of women of Mexican origin in California. POPULATION RESEARCH AND POLICY REVIEW, Vol. 5, no. 2 (1986), p. 163-185. English. **DESCR:** California; *Employment; Food Stamps; Immigrants; Medi-Cal; Single Parents; *Welfare; Women.

AIDS (Disease)

171 Alonso, Ana Maria and Koreck, Maria Teresa. Silences: "Hispanics", AIDS, and sexual practices. DIFFERENCES: A JOURNAL OF FEMINIST CULTURAL STUDIES, Vol. 1, no. 1 (Winter 1989), p. 101-124. English. **DESCR:** *Homosexuality; Human Immunodeficiency Virus (HIV); Machismo; Mexico; *Self-Referents; Sex Roles; *Sexual Behavior.

172 Amaro, Hortensia. Considerations for prevention of HIV infection among Hispanic women. PSYCHOLOGY OF WOMEN QUARTERLY, Vol. 12, no. 4 (December 1988), p. 429-443. English. **DESCR:** Attitudes; Population; *Women.

173 Arguelles, Lourdes and Rivero, Anne M. HIV infection/AIDS and Latinas in Los Angeles County: considerations for prevention, treatment, and research practice. CALIFORNIA SOCIOLOGIST, Vol. 11, no. 1-2 (1988), p. 69-89. English. **DESCR:** Cultural Characteristics; Health Education; Homosexuality; Human Immunodeficiency Virus (HIV); Los Angeles County, CA; Natural Support Systems; Parent and Child Relationships; Sexual Behavior; *Women.

174 Del Zotto, Augusta. Latinas with AIDS: life expectancy for Hispanic women is a startling 45 days after diagnosis. THIS WORLD, (April 9, 1989), p. 9. English. **DESCR:** Abortion; Condom Use; Instituto Familiar de la Raza, San Francisco, CA; Machismo; *Mano a Mano; Quintero, Juanita; Sex Roles; Women Men Relations.

175 Flaskerud, Jacquelyn H. and Nyamathi, Adeline M. Black and Latina womens' AIDS related knowledge, attitudes, and practices. RESEARCH IN NURSING AND HEALTH, Vol. 12, no. 6 (December 1989), p. 339-346. English. **DESCR:** Attitudes; *Blacks; Health Education; Los Angeles County, CA; Surveys; *Women.

176 Martinez, Ruben. AIDS in the Latino community. AMERICAS 2001, Vol. 1, no. 5

(March, April, 1988), p. [14-18]. Bilingual. **DESCR:** Sex Education.

177 Mays, Vicki M. and Cochran, Susan D. Issues in the perception of AIDS risk and risk reduction activities by Black and Hispanic/Latina women. AMERICAN PSYCHOLOGIST, Vol. 43, no. 11 (November 1988), p. 949-957. English. **DESCR:** Blacks; Condom Use; Fertility; Health Education; Preventative Medicine; *Sexual Behavior; Women.

178 Norris, Henry E. AIDS, women and reproductive rights. MULTICULTURAL INQUIRY AND RESEARCH ON AIDS (MIRA) NEWSLETTER, Vol. 1, no. 3 (Summer 1987), p. [2-3]. English. **DESCR:** Abortion; Center for Constitutional Rights; Discrimination; Preventative Medicine; Women.

179 Nyamathi, Adeline M. and Vasquez, Rose. Impact of poverty, homelessness, and drugs on Hispanic women at risk for HIV infection. HISPANIC JOURNAL OF BEHAVIORAL SCIENCES, Vol. 11, no. 4 (November 1989), p. 299-314. English. **DESCR:** Drug Use; Health Education; *Human Immunodeficiency Virus (HIV); Locus of Control; Mental Health; Needle-Sharing; *Poverty.

Aiken and Preger Revised Math Attitude Scale

180 Creswell, John L. Sex-related differences in the problem-solving abilities of rural Black, Anglo, and Chicano adolescents. TEXAS TECH JOURNAL OF EDUCATION, Vol. 10, no. 1 (Winter 1983), p. 29-33. English. **DESCR:** Anglo Americans; Blacks; California Achievement Test (CAT); *Mathematics; National Assessment of Educational Progress; National Council of Teachers of Mathematics (NCTM); Youth.

Alambristas
USE: Undocumented Workers

Alarcon, Norma

181 Quintana, Alvina E. O mama, with what's inside of me. REVISTA MUJERES, Vol. 3, no. 1 (January 1986), p. 38-40. English. **DESCR:** Feminism; *Literary Criticism; Poetry; "What Kind of Lover Have You Made Me, Mother?: Towards a Theory of Chicanas' Feminism and Cultural Identity Through Poetry" [article].

Albuquerque, NM

182 Zavella, Patricia. The impact of "sun belt industrialization" on Chicanas. FRONTIERS: A JOURNAL OF WOMEN STUDIES, Vol. 8, no. 1 (1984), p. 21-27. English. **DESCR:** Employment; *Industrial Workers; Industrialization; *Working Women.

183 Zavella, Patricia. The impact of "sun belt industrialization" on Chicanas. Stanford, CA: Stanford Center for Chicano Research, 1984. 25 leaves. English. **DESCR:** Employment; *Industrial Workers; Industrialization; *Working Women.

Alcala, TX

184 Urdaneta, Maria Luisa. Chicana use of abortion: the case of Alcala. IN: Melville, Margarita B., ed. TWICE A MINORITY. St. Louis, MO: Mosby, 1980, p. 33-51. English. **DESCR:** *Abortion; Fertility.

Alcoholism

185 Arevalo, Rodolfo, ed. and Minor, Marianne, ed. Chicanas and alcoholism: a sociocultural perspective of women. San Jose, CA: School of Social Work, San Jose State University, c1981. 55 p. English. DESCR: Drug Abuse Programs; Family; Feminism; Natural Support Systems; Preventative Medicine; Psychotherapy.

186 Cayer, Shirley. Chicago's new Hispanic health alliance. NUESTRO, Vol. 7, no. 5 (June, July, 1983), p. 44-48. English. DESCR: Chicago Hispanic Health Alliance; Family Planning; *Health Education; Latin Americans; *Medical Care.

187 Chase, Charlotte Fay. Alcohol-related problems of Mexican-American women in the San Francisco Bay Area. Thesis (M.S.)--University of California, San Francisco, 1988. ix, 121 leaves. English. DESCR: San Francisco Bay Area.

188 Corbett, Kitty; Mora, Juana; and Ames, Genevieve. Drinking patterns and drinking-related problems of Mexican-American husbands and wives. JOURNAL OF STUDIES ON ALCOHOL, Vol. 52, no. 3 (May 1991), p. 215-223. English. DESCR: *Marriage; *Sex Roles.

189 Gilbert, M. Jean. Alcohol consumption patterns in immigrant and later generation Mexican American women. HISPANIC JOURNAL OF BEHAVIORAL SCIENCES, Vol 9, no. 3 (September 1987), p. 299-313. English. DESCR: Acculturation; *Attitudes; Cultural Characteristics; *Immigrants; Mexico.

190 Holck, Susan E., et al. Alcohol consumption among Mexican American and Anglo women: results of a survey along the U.S.-Mexico border. JOURNAL OF STUDIES ON ALCOHOL, Vol. 45, no. 2 (March 1984), p. 149-154. English. DESCR: Anglo Americans; Border Region; Surveys.

191 Mata, Alberto Guardiola and Castillo, Valerie. Rural female adolescent dissatisfaction, support and helpseeking. FREE INQUIRY IN CREATIVE SOCIOLOGY, Vol. 14, no. 2 (November 1986), p. 135-138. English. DESCR: *Drug Use; Interpersonal Relations; *Natural Support Systems; Parent and Child Relationships; Rural Population; *Youth.

192 Panitz, Daniel R., et al. The role of machismo and the Hispanic family in the etiology and treatment of alcoholism in the Hispanic American males. AMERICAN JOURNAL OF FAMILY THERAPY, Vol. 11, no. 1 (Spring 1983), p. 31-44. English. DESCR: Children; Family; *Machismo; Puerto Rico; Socioeconomic Factors.

193 Stroup-Benham, Christine A.; Trevino, Fernando M.; and Trevino, Dorothy B. Alcohol consumption patterns among Mexican American mothers and among children from single- and dual-headed households: findings from HHANES 1982-84. AMERICAN JOURNAL OF PUBLIC HEALTH, Vol. 80, (December 1990), p. 36-41. English. DESCR: *Children; Hispanic Health and Nutrition Examination Survey (HHANES); Parent and Child Relationships; *Single Parents.

194 Trotter, Robert T. Ethnic and sexual patterns of alcohol use: Anglo and Mexican American college students. ADOLESCENCE, Vol. 17, no. 66 (Summer 1982), p. 305-325. English. DESCR: Anglo Americans; Colleges and Universities; Cultural Characteristics; Ethnic Groups; Sex Roles; Students; Youth.

195 Zambrana, Ruth E., et al. Ethnic differences in the substance use patterns of low-income pregnant women. FAMILY & COMMUNITY HEALTH, Vol. 13, no. 4 (January 1991), p. 1-11. English. DESCR: Blacks; *Drug Use; *Fertility; Immigrants; *Low Income; Smoking; Women.

Alonso, Luis Ricardo

196 Irizarry, Estelle. La abuelita in literature. NUESTRO, Vol. 7, no. 7 (September 1983), p. 50. English. DESCR: *Ancianos; Cotto-Thorner, Guillermo; Family; Grandmothers; Ulibarri, Sabine R.; Valero, Robert.

Alonso, Maria Conchita

197 Vega, Alicia. Three Latinas in Hollywood = Tres latinas en Hollywood. AMERICAS 2001, Vol. 1, no. 7 (July, August, 1988), p. 4-6. Bilingual. DESCR: *Actors and Actresses; Martinez, Patrice; Ramos, Loyda.

Altars

198 Altars as folk art. ARRIBA, Vol. 1, no. 1 (July 1980), p. 4. English. DESCR: Artists; De Leon, Josefina; Folk Art; Religious Art.

199 Lomas Garza, Carmen. Altares: arte espiritual del hogar. HOJAS, (1976), p. 105-111. English. DESCR: Artists; Folk Art; Lomas Garza, Carmen; Religious Art.

200 Navar, M. Margarita. La vela prendida: home altars. ARRIBA, Vol. 1, no. 5 (February 1980), p. 12. English. DESCR: Artists; Exhibits; Folk Art; Religious Art.

201 Texas Memorial Museum, University of Texas, Austin, TX. La vela prendida: Mexican-American women's home altars. Exhibition catalog, 1980. Bilingual. DESCR: Artists; Catalogues; Exhibits; Folk Art.

Alternative Education

202 Staudt, Kathleen. Programming women's empowerment: a case from northern Mexico. IN: Ruiz, Vicki L. and Tiano, Susan, eds. WOMEN ON THE U.S.-MEXICO BORDER: RESPONSES TO CHANGE. Boston, MA: Allen & Unwin, 1987, p. 155-173. English. DESCR: Border Region; Ciudad Juarez, Chihuahua, Mexico; Curriculum; Employment; *Feminism; Organizations; Women.

Alvarez, Linda

203 Olivera, Mercedes. The new Hispanic women. VISTA, Vol. 2, no. 11 (July 5, 1987), p. 6-8. English. DESCR: Esquiroz, Margarita; Garcia, Juliet; *Hernandez, Antonia A.; Mohr, Nicolasa; Molina, Gloria; Pabon, Maria; Working Women.

Alvarez, Robert R., Jr.

204 Garcia, Mario T. Family and gender in
    Chicano and border studies research. MEXICAN
    STUDIES/ESTUDIOS MEXICANOS, Vol. 6, no. 1
    (Winter 1990), p. 109-119. English. DESCR:
    *Border Region; CANNERY WOMEN, CANNERY
    LIVES; *Family; LA FAMILIA: MIGRATION AND
    ADAPTATION IN BAJA AND ALTA CALIFORNIA,
    1800-1975; *Literature Reviews; Ruiz, Vicki
    L.; Tiano, Susan B.; Women; WOMEN ON THE
    U.S.-MEXICO BORDER: RESPONSES TO CHANGE;
    WOMEN'S WORK AND CHICANO FAMILIES; Zavella,
    Pat.

American Federation of Labor (AFL)

205 Garcia, Mario T. The Chicana in American
    history: the Mexican women of El Paso,
    1880-1920 - a case study. PACIFIC HISTORICAL
    REVIEW, Vol. 49, no. 2 (May 1980), p.
    315-337. English. DESCR: Acme Laundry, El
    Paso, TX; Case Studies; Central Labor Union;
    Domestic Work; *El Paso, TX; Employment;
    *History; Immigrants; Income; Labor Unions;
    Sex Roles; Strikes and Lockouts; *Working
    Women.

American Indians
    USE: Native Americans

Americanization
    USE: Assimilation

Amnesty (Immigration)
    USE: Immigration Law and Legislation

Anaya, Rudolfo A.

206 Anderson, Robert K. Marez y Luna and the
    masculine-feminine dialectic. CRITICA
    HISPANICA, Vol. 6, no. 2 (1984), p. 97-105.
    English. DESCR: BLESS ME, ULTIMA; Literary
    Criticism; Novel; *Women Men Relations.

207 Herrera-Sobek, Maria. Women as metaphor in
    the patriarchal structure of HEART OF
    AZTLAN. IN: Gonzalez-T., Cesar A. RUDOLFO A.
    ANAYA: FOCUS ON CRITICISM. La Jolla, CA:
    Lalo Press, 1990, p. [165]-182. English.
    DESCR: *HEART OF AZTLAN; La Llorona;
    *Literary Characters; Literary Criticism;
    Sex Roles.

208 Mondin, Sandra. The depiction of the Chicana
    in BLESS ME ULTIMA and THE MILAGRO BEANFIELD
    WAR: a study in contrasts. IN: Luna Lawhn,
    Juanita, et al., eds. MEXICO AND THE UNITED
    STATES: INTERCULTURAL RELATIONS IN THE
    HUMANITIES. San Antonio, TX: San Antonio
    College, 1984, p. 137-150. English. DESCR:
    BLESS ME, ULTIMA; Literary Characters;
    Literary Criticism; Nichols, John;
    *Stereotypes; THE MILAGRO BEANFIELD WAR
    [novel].

209 Tatum, Charles M. Grappling with difference:
    gender, race, class, and ethnicity in
    contemporary Chicana/o literature. RENATO
    ROSALDO LECTURE SERIES MONOGRAPH, Vol. 6,
    (1988, 1989), p. 1-23. English. DESCR:
    Authors; BLESS ME, ULTIMA; *Feminism;
    Identity; Literary Characters; *Literary
    Criticism; Literature Reviews.

Ancianos

210 Ashley, Laurel Maria. Self, family and
    community: the social process of aging among
    urban Mexican-American women. Thesis
    (Ph.D.)--University of California, Los
    Angeles, 1985. 306 p. English. DESCR:
    Acculturation; *Family; Grandmothers; *Sex
    Roles; Southern California.

211 Balkwell, Carolyn Ann. An attitudinal
    correlate of the timing of a major life
    event: the case of morale in widowhood.
    FAMILY RELATIONS, Vol. 34, no. 4 (October
    1985), p. 577-581. English. DESCR:
    Counseling (Psychological); *Marriage;
    Mental Health; Natural Support Systems;
    Widowhood.

212 Balkwell, Carolyn Ann. Widowhood: its impact
    on morale and optimism among older persons
    of three ethnic groups. Thesis
    (Ph.D.)--University of Georgia, 1981. 170 p.
    English. DESCR: Anglo Americans; Blacks;
    Depression (Psychological); Ethnic Groups;
    Los Angeles County, CA; *Mental Health;
    Widowhood; *Women.

213 Bauer, Richard L., et al. Risk of
    postmenopausal hip fracture in
    Mexican-American women. AMERICAN JOURNAL OF
    PUBLIC HEALTH, Vol. 76, no. 8 (August 1986),
    p. 1020-1021. English. DESCR: *Public
    Health.

214 Bergdolt-Munzer, Sara L. Homemakers and
    retirement income benefits: the other home
    security issue. CHICANO LAW REVIEW, Vol. 8,
    (1985), p. 61-80. English. DESCR: Domestic
    Work; Feminism; Social Security; *Women.

215 Cuellar, Israel. Service delivery and mental
    health services for Chicano elders. IN:
    Miranda, Manuel and Ruiz, Rene A., eds.
    CHICANO AGING AND MENTAL HEALTH. Rockville,
    MD: U.S. Department of Health and Human
    Services, 1981, p. 185-211. English. DESCR:
    Attitudes; Cultural Customs; Cultural
    Pluralism; Language Usage; Mental Health;
    Mental Health Clinics; Religion; Sex Roles;
    Spanish Language.

216 Dressel, Paula. Symposium. Civil rights,
    affirmative action, and the aged of the
    future: will life chances be different for
    Blacks, Hispanics, and women? An overview of
    the issues. GERONTOLOGIST, Vol. 26, no. 2
    (April 1986), p. 128-131. English. DESCR:
    Affirmative Action; Blacks; *Civil Rights;
    Women.

217 Facio, Elisa "Linda". Constraints,
    resources, and self-definition: a case study
    of Chicano older women. Thesis
    (Ph.D.)--University of California, Berkeley,
    1988. 246 p. English. DESCR: *Family;
    Grandmothers; *Poverty; Sex Roles;
    Widowhood.

218 Facio, Elisa "Linda". Gender and aging: a
    case of Mexicana/Chicana elderly. TRABAJOS
    MONOGRAFICOS, Vol. 1, no. 1 (1985), p. 5-21.
    English.

219 Facio, Elisa "Linda". The interaction of age
    and gender in Chicana older lives: a case
    study of Chicana elderly in a senior citizen
    center. RENATO ROSALDO LECTURE SERIES
    MONOGRAPH, Vol. 4, (1988), p. 21-38.
    English. DESCR: Age Groups; Poverty; Social
    Classes.

220 Franklin, Gerald S. and Kaufman, Karen S.
    Group psychotherapy for elderly female
    Hispanic outpatients. HOSPITAL AND COMMUNITY
    PSYCHIATRY, Vol. 33, no. 5 (May 1982), p.
    385-387. English. DESCR: *Psychotherapy.

Ancianos (cont.)

221 Gonzalez del Valle, Amalia and Usher, Mary. Group therapy with aged Latino women: a pilot project and study. CLINICAL GERONTOLOGIST, Vol. 1, no. 1 (Fall 1982), p. 51-58. English. DESCR: Cultural Characteristics; Mental Illness; *Psychotherapy; San Mateo County, CA.

222 Irizarry, Estelle. La abuelita in literature. NUESTRO, Vol. 7, no. 7 (September 1983), p. 50. English. DESCR: Alonso, Luis Ricardo; Cotto-Thorner, Guillermo; Family; Grandmothers; Ulibarri, Sabine R.; Valero, Robert.

223 Markides, Kyriakos S. and Vernon, Sally W. Aging, sex-role orientation and adjustment: a three-generations study of Mexican Americans. JOURNAL OF GERONTOLOGY, Vol. 39, no. 5 (September 1984), p. 586-591. English. DESCR: *Age Groups; Mental Health; *Sex Roles.

224 Markides, Kyriakos S. Consequences of gender differentials in life expectancy for Black and Hispanic Americans. INTERNATIONAL JOURNAL OF AGING & HUMAN DEVELOPMENT, Vol. 29, no. 2 (1989), p. 95-102. English. DESCR: Blacks; Census; Cubanos; Latin Americans; Males; Population; Puerto Ricans; U.S. Bureau of the Census.

225 Mayers, Raymond Sanchez. Use of folk medicine by elderly Mexican-American women. JOURNAL OF DRUG ISSUES, Vol. 19, no. 2 (1989), p. 283-295. English. DESCR: Age Groups; Curanderas; Curanderismo; Folk Medicine.

226 Mink, Diane Leslie. Early grandmotherhood: an exploratory study. Thesis (Ph.D.)--California School of Professional Psychology, Los Angeles, 1987. 190 p. English. DESCR: Age Groups; Assertiveness; Family; Fertility; Grandmothers; Natural Support Systems; *Sex Roles; Surveys; Youth.

227 Padgett, Deborah. Aging minority women. WOMEN & HEALTH, Vol. 14, no. 3-4 (1988), p. 213-225. English. DESCR: Low Income; Public Health; *Women.

228 Richardson, Jean L., et al. Frequency and adequacy of breast cancer screening among elderly Hispanic women. PREVENTIVE MEDICINE, Vol. 16, no. 6 (November 1987), p. 761-774. English. DESCR: *Cancer; Diseases; *Health Education; Los Angeles, CA; *Medical Care; Preventative Medicine.

229 Rogers, Linda Perkowski and Markides, Kyriakos S. Well-being in the postparental stage in Mexican-American women. RESEARCH ON AGING, Vol. 11, no. 4 (December 1989), p. 508-516. English. DESCR: *Age Groups; Children; *"Empty Nest" Syndrome; *Parent and Child Relationships; San Antonio, TX.

230 Stephens, Richard C.; Oser, George T.; and Blau, Zena Smith. To be aged, Hispanic, and female: the triple risk. IN: Melville, Margarita B., ed. TWICE A MINORITY. St. Louis, MO: Mosby, 1980, p. 249-258. English.

231 Zepeda, Marlene. Las abuelitas. AGENDA, Vol. 9, no. 6 (November, December, 1979), p. 10-13. Bilingual. DESCR: Family.

"'And Miles to Go...': Mexican Women and Work, 1930-1985"

232 Dublin, Thomas. Commentary [on "And Miles to Go": Mexican Women and Work, 1930-1985]. IN: Schlissel, Lillian, et al., eds. WESTERN WOMEN: THEIR LAND, THEIR LIVES. Albuquerque, NM: University of New Mexico Press, 1988, p. 137-140. English. DESCR: Employment; Income; Labor Unions; Ruiz, Vicki L.; Undocumented Workers; Women; *Working Women.

233 Jensen, Joan M. Commentary [on "And Miles to Go": Mexican Women and Work, 1930-1985]. IN: Schlissel, Lillian, et al., eds. WESTERN WOMEN: THEIR LAND, THEIR LIVES. Albuquerque, NM: University of New Mexico Press, 1988, p. 141-144. English. DESCR: California; Employment; Income; Labor Unions; Public Policy; Ruiz, Vicki L.; Women; *Working Women.

234 Spence, Mary Lee. Commentary [on "And Miles to Go": Mexican Women and Work, 1930-1985]. IN: Schlissel, Lillian, et al., eds. WESTERN WOMEN: THEIR LAND, THEIR LIVES. Albuquerque, NM: University of New Mexico Press, 1988, p. 145-150. English. DESCR: Food Industry; Income; Labor Unions; Restaurants; Ruiz, Vicki L.; *Working Women.

AND THE EARTH DID NOT PART
USE: Y NO SE LO TRAGO LA TIERRA/AND THE EARTH DID NOT PART

Anglo Americans

235 Alarcon, Norma. The theoretical subject(s) of THIS BRIDGE CALLED MY BACK and Anglo-American feminism. IN: Calderon, Hector and Saldivar, Jose David, eds. CRITICISM IN THE BORDERLANDS: STUDIES IN CHICANO LITERATURE, CULTURE, AND IDEOLOGY. Durham, NC: Duke University Press, 1991, p. [28]-39. English. DESCR: Anzaldua, Gloria; *Feminism; Moraga, Cherrie; THIS BRIDGE CALLED MY BACK; *Women.

236 Alarcon, Norma. The theoretical subject(s) of THIS BRIDGE CALLED MY BACK and Anglo-American feminism. IN: Anzaldua, Gloria, ed. MAKING FACE, MAKING SOUL: HACIENDO CARAS: CREATIVE AND CRITICAL PERSPECTIVES BY WOMEN OF COLOR. San Francisco, CA: Aunt Lute Foundation Books, 1990, p. 356-369. English. DESCR: Anzaldua, Gloria; *Feminism; Literary Criticism; Moraga, Cherrie; THIS BRIDGE CALLED MY BACK; *Women.

237 Alba, Isabel Catherine. Achievement conflicts, sex-role orientation, and performance on sex-role appropriate and sex-role inappropriate tasks in women of three ethnic groups. Thesis (Ph.D.)--University of California, Riverside, 1987. 129 p. English. DESCR: *Assertiveness; Blacks; Ethnic Groups; Fear of Success Scale (FOSS); *Sex Roles; Women.

238 Aneshensel, Carol S.; Fielder, Eve P.; and Becerra, Rosina M. Fertility and fertility-related behavior among Mexican-American and non-Hispanic white female adolescents. JOURNAL OF HEALTH AND SOCIAL BEHAVIOR, Vol. 30, no. 1 (March 1989), p. 56-76. English. DESCR: *Fertility; Socioeconomic Factors; Youth.

239 Aneshensel, Carol S., et al. Onset of fertility-related events during adolescence: a prospective comparison of Mexican American and non-Hispanic white females. AMERICAN JOURNAL OF PUBLIC HEALTH, Vol. 80, no. 8 (August 1990), p. 959-963. English. DESCR: Abortion; Birth Control; *Fertility; *Sexual Behavior; Women; *Youth.

Anglo Americans (cont.)

240 Armas-Cardona, Regina. Anglo and Raza young women: a study of self-esteem, psychic distress and locus of control. Thesis (Ph.D.)--Wright Institute Graduate School of Psychology, 1985. 143 p. English. DESCR: Locus of Control; *Mental Health; Stress; *Women.

241 Atkinson, Donald R.; Winzelberg, Andrew; and Holland, Abby. Ethnicity, locus of control for family planning, and pregnancy counselor credibility. JOURNAL OF COUNSELING PSYCHOLOGY, Vol. 32, no. 3 (July 1985), p. 417-421. English. DESCR: Counseling (Psychological); *Family Planning; Fertility; Identity; *Locus of Control; Women.

242 Ayers-Nackamkin, Beverly, et al. Sex and ethnic differences in the use of power. JOURNAL OF APPLIED PSYCHOLOGY, Vol. 67, no. 4 (August 1982), p. 464-471. English. DESCR: Ethnic Groups; Management; *Personnel Management; Sex Roles; Social Psychology.

243 Balkwell, Carolyn Ann. Widowhood: its impact on morale and optimism among older persons of three ethnic groups. Thesis (Ph.D.)--University of Georgia, 1981. 170 p. English. DESCR: *Ancianos; Blacks; Depression (Psychological); Ethnic Groups; Los Angeles County, CA; *Mental Health; Widowhood; *Women.

244 Bauer, Richard L. Ethnic differences in hip fracture: a reduced incidence in Mexican-Americans. AMERICAN JOURNAL OF EPIDEMIOLOGY, Vol. 127, no. 1 (January 1988), p. 145-149. English. DESCR: Bexar County, TX; Blacks; Medical Care; Osteoporosis; *Public Health.

245 Bauer, Richard L. and Deyo, Richard A. Low risk of vertebral fracture in Mexican American women. ARCHIVES OF INTERNAL MEDICINE, Vol. 147, no. 8 (August 1987), p. 1437-1439. English. DESCR: *Osteoporosis; Preventative Medicine; Women.

246 Becerra, Rosina M. and de Anda, Diane. Pregnancy and motherhood among Mexican American adolescents. HEALTH AND SOCIAL WORK, Vol. 9, no. 2 (Spring 1984), p. 106-23. English. DESCR: Acculturation; Attitudes; Birth Control; *Fertility; Natural Support Systems; *Youth.

247 Belk, Sharyn S., et al. Impact of ethnicity, nationality, counseling orientation, and mental health standards on stereotypic beliefs about women. SEX ROLES, Vol. 21, no. 9-10 (November 1989), p. 671-695. English. DESCR: Beliefs About Women Scale (BAWS); *Comparative Psychology; *Counseling (Psychological); Cultural Characteristics; Identity; Mental Health; *Sex Stereotypes; Sexism; Women.

248 Bourque, Linda B.; Kraus, Jess F.; and Cosand, Beverly J. Attributes of suicide in females. SUICIDE AND LIFE-THREATENING BEHAVIOR, Vol. 13, no. 2 (Summer 1983), p. 123-138. English. DESCR: Sacramento County, CA; *Suicide; Women.

249 Braddom, Carolyn Lentz. The conceptualization of effective leadership as seen by women, Black and Hispanic superintendents. Thesis (Ed.D.)--University of Cincinnati, 1988. 232 p. English. DESCR: Blacks; *Educational Administration; *Leadership; Management; Women.

250 Calderon, Vivian. Maternal employment and career orientation of young Chicana, Black, and white women. Thesis (Ph.D.)--University of California, Santa Cruz, 1984. 150 p. English. DESCR: Blacks; *Careers; *Employment; Women; *Youth.

251 Castro, Felipe G.; Furth, Pauline; and Karlow, Herbert. The health beliefs of Mexican, Mexican American and Anglo American women. HISPANIC JOURNAL OF BEHAVIORAL SCIENCES, Vol. 6, no. 4 (December 1984), p. 365-383. English. DESCR: *Public Health.

252 Chavez, Ernest; Beauvais, Fred; and Oetting, E.R. Drug use by small town Mexican American youth: a pilot study. HISPANIC JOURNAL OF BEHAVIORAL SCIENCES, Vol. 8, no. 3 (September 1986), p. 243-258. English. DESCR: *Drug Use; Rural Population; Youth.

253 Codega, Susan A.; Pasley, B. Kay; and Kreutzer, Jill. Coping behaviors of adolescent mothers: an exploratory study and comparison of Mexican-Americans and Anglos. JOURNAL OF ADOLESCENT RESEARCH, Vol. 5, no. 1 (January 1990), p. 34-53. English. DESCR: Colorado; *Fertility; *Stress; Women; *Youth.

254 Cotera, Marta P. Feminism: the Chicana and Anglo versions: a historical analysis. IN: Melville, Margarita B., ed. TWICE A MINORITY. St. Louis, MO: Mosby, 1980, p. 217-234. English. DESCR: Chicano Movement; Conferences and Meetings; *Feminism; Organizations; Social History and Conditions; Voting Rights; *Women.

255 Craver, Rebecca McDowell. The impact of intimacy: Mexican-Anglo intermarriage in New Mexico 1821-1846. SOUTHWESTERN STUDIES, no. 66 (1982), p. 1-79. English. DESCR: Acculturation; Assimilation; History; *Intermarriage; New Mexico; Rio Arriba Valley, NM.

256 Craver, Rebecca McDowell. The impact of intimacy: Mexican-Anglo intermarriage in New Mexico 1821-1846. El Paso, TX: Texas Western Press, University of Texas at El Paso, 1982. 79 p. English. DESCR: Acculturation; Assimilation; History; *Intermarriage; New Mexico; Rio Arriba Valley, NM.

257 Creswell, John L. Sex-related differences in the problem-solving abilities of rural Black, Anglo, and Chicano adolescents. TEXAS TECH JOURNAL OF EDUCATION, Vol. 10, no. 1 (Winter 1983), p. 29-33. English. DESCR: Aiken and Preger Revised Math Attitude Scale; Blacks; California Achievement Test (CAT); *Mathematics; National Assessment of Educational Progress; National Council of Teachers of Mathematics (NCTM); Youth.

258 Cummings, Michele and Cummings, Scott. Family planning among the urban poor: sexual politics and social policy. FAMILY RELATIONS, Vol. 32, no. 1 (January 1983), p. 47-58. English. DESCR: Blacks; Discrimination; *Family Planning; Low Income; *Stereotypes.

259 Daggett, Andrea Stuhlman. A comparison of occupational goal orientations of female Mexican-Americans and Anglo high-school seniors of the classes of 1972 and 1980. Thesis (Ph.D.)--University of Arizona, Tucson, 1983. xii, 134 p. English. DESCR: Academic Achievement; *Careers; *Secondary School Education; Sexism; Students; Women.

Anglo Americans (cont.)

260 Daly, Mary B.; Clark, Gary M.; and McGuire, William L. Breast cancer prognosis in a mixed Caucasian-Hispanic population. JNCI: JOURNAL OF THE NATIONAL CANCER INSTITUTE, Vol. 74, no. 4 (April 1985), p. 753-757. English. DESCR: *Cancer; Women.

261 de Anda, Diane; Becerra, Rosina M.; and Fielder, Eve P. In their own words: the life experiences of Mexican-American and white pregnant adolescents and adolescent mothers. CHILD AND ADOLESCENT SOCIAL WORK, Vol. 7, no. 4 (August 1990), p. 301-318. English. DESCR: *Fertility; *Sexual Behavior; Women; *Youth.

262 de Anda, Diane; Becerra, Rosina M.; and Fielder, Eve P. Sexuality, pregnancy, and motherhood among Mexican-American adolescents. JOURNAL OF ADOLESCENT RESEARCH, Vol. 3, no. 3-4 (Fall, Winter, 1988), p. 403-411. English. DESCR: Attitudes; Birth Control; *Fertility; Sex Education; *Sexual Behavior; Women; *Youth.

263 De Llano, Carmen. Comparisons of the psychocultural characteristics of graduate school-bound and nongraduate school-bound Mexican American and Anglo American college women. Thesis (Ph.D.)--California School of Professional Psychology, 1986. 223 p. English. DESCR: Colleges and Universities; Comparative Psychology; Cultural Characteristics; *Graduate Schools; Higher Education; Students; *Women.

264 Del Castillo, Adelaida R. La vision chicana. REGENERACION, Vol. 2, no. 4 (1975), p. 46-48. English. DESCR: *Feminism; Women.

265 Deutsch, Sarah. Culture, class, and gender: Chicanas and Chicanos in Colorado and New Mexico, 1900-1940. Thesis (Ph.D.)--Yale University, 1985. xii, 510 p. English. DESCR: Colorado; Immigrants; New Mexico; *Sex Roles; *Social Classes; Social History and Conditions; Women; *Working Women.

266 Deutsch, Sarah. No separate refuge: culture, class, and gender on an Anglo-Hispanic frontier in the American Southwest, 1880-1940. New York: Oxford University Press, 1987. vi, 356 p. English. DESCR: Colorado; Immigrants; Immigration; Mining Industry; Missions; New Mexico; *Sex Roles; *Social Classes; *Social History and Conditions; Women; Working Women; World War I.

267 Dungy, Claibourne I. Breast feeding preference of Hispanic and Anglo women. CLINICAL PEDIATRICS, Vol. 28, no. 2 (February 1989), p. 92-94. English. DESCR: Attitudes; *Breastfeeding; Women.

268 Eisen, Marvin and Zellman, Gail L. Factors predicting pregnancy resolution decision satisfaction of unmarried adolescents. JOURNAL OF GENETIC PSYCHOLOGY, Vol. 145, no. 2 (December 1984), p. 231-239. English. DESCR: Abortion; Attitudes; Counseling (Psychological); Family Planning; *Fertility; Youth.

269 Enriquez-White, Celia. Attitudes of Hispanic and Anglo women managers toward women in management. Thesis (Ed.D.)--University of La Verne, 1982. 103 p. English. DESCR: *Attitudes; Leadership; *Management; Women.

270 Farkas, George; Barton, Margaret; and Kushner, Kathy. White, Black, and Hispanic female youths in central city labor markets. SOCIOLOGICAL QUARTERLY, Vol. 29, no. 4 (Winter 1988), p. 605-621. English. DESCR: Blacks; Employment; *Income; *Labor Supply and Market; Urban Communities; Women; *Youth.

271 Felice, Marianne E., et al. Clinical observations of Mexican-American, Caucasian, and Black pregnant teenagers. JOURNAL OF ADOLESCENT HEALTH CARE, Vol. 7, no. 5 (September 1986), p. 305-310. English. DESCR: Blacks; *Fertility; *Prenatal Care; San Diego, CA; Youth.

272 Finkelstein, Jordan W. and Von Eye, Alexander. Sanitary product use by white, Black, and Mexican American women. PUBLIC HEALTH REPORTS, Vol. 105, no. 5 (September, October, 1990), p. 491-496. English. DESCR: Blacks; *Menstruation; *Toxic Shock Syndrome (TSS); *Women.

273 Fleming, Marilyn B. Problems experienced by Anglo, Hispanic and Navajo Indian women college students. JOURNAL OF AMERICAN INDIAN EDUCATION, Vol. 22, no. 1 (October 1982), p. 7-17. English. DESCR: Community Colleges; Ethnic Groups; *Higher Education; Identity; Medical Education; Native Americans; Students; Women.

274 Flores, Francisca. Equality. REGENERACION, Vol. 2, no. 3 (1973), p. 4-5. English. DESCR: Chicano Movement; Discrimination; Elected Officials; Feminism; Income; *Machismo; *Working Women.

275 Forste, Renata T. and Heaton, Tim B. Initiation of sexual activity among female adolescents. YOUTH AND SOCIETY, Vol. 19, no. 3 (March 1988), p. 250-268. English. DESCR: Blacks; Family; Sex Education; *Sexual Behavior; Women; *Youth.

276 Frisbie, William Parker; Opitz, Wolfgang; and Kelly, William R. Marital instability trends among Mexican Americans as compared to Blacks and Anglos: new evidence. SOCIAL SCIENCE QUARTERLY, Vol. 66, no. 3 (September 1985), p. 587-601. English. DESCR: Blacks; Divorce; *Marriage.

277 Frisbie, William Parker; Bean, Frank D.; and Eberstein, Isaac W. Patterns of marital instability among Mexican Americans, Blacks, and Anglos. IN: Bean, Frank D. and Frisbie, W. Parker, eds. THE DEMOGRAPHY OF RACIAL AND ETHNIC GROUPS. New York: Academic Press, 1978, p. 143-163. English. DESCR: Blacks; Divorce; Family; *Marriage.

278 Frisbie, William Parker; Bean, Frank D.; and Eberstein, Isaac W. Recent changes in marital instability among Mexican Americans: convergence with Black and Anglo trends. SOCIAL FORCES, Vol. 58, no. 4 (June 1980), p. 1205-1220. English. DESCR: Age Groups; Blacks; *Divorce; *Marriage.

279 Gallegos, Placida I. Emerging leadership among Hispanic women: the role of expressive behavior and nonverbal skill. Thesis (Ph.D.)--University of California, Riverside, 1987. 101 p. English. DESCR: Comparative Psychology; Corporations; *Leadership; *Management; Women.

Anglo Americans (cont.)

280 Garcia, Alma M. The development of Chicana feminist discourse, 1970-1980. GENDER & SOCIETY, Vol. 3, no. 2 (June 1989), p. 217-238. English. **DESCR:** Chicana Studies; *Chicano Movement; *Feminism; Homosexuality; Machismo; National Association for Chicano Studies (NACS); Organizations; *Sexism; Women.

281 Garcia, Alma M. The development of Chicana feminist discourse, 1970-1980. IN: DuBois, Ellen Carol and Ruiz, Vicki L., eds. UNEQUAL SISTERS: A MULTICULTURAL READER IN U.S. WOMEN'S HISTORY. New York: Routledge, 1990, p. 418-431. English. **DESCR:** Chicana Studies; *Chicano Movement; *Feminism; Homosexuality; Machismo; National Association for Chicano Studies (NACS); Organizations; *Sexism; Women.

282 Gardea, Corina. A comparison of behavioral characteristics of Hispanic and Anglo female administrators in the resolution of critical incident situations. Thesis (Ph.D.)--University of Texas, Austin, 1984. 145 p. English. **DESCR:** *Community Colleges; *Educational Administration; Leadership; Women.

283 Golding, Jacqueline M. Division of household labor, strain, and depressive symptoms among Mexican Americans and non-Hispanic whites. PSYCHOLOGY OF WOMEN QUARTERLY, Vol. 14, no. 1 (March 1990), p. 103-117. English. **DESCR:** Comparative Psychology; *Depression (Psychological); Domestic Work; Employment; Identity; *Sex Roles; Women.

284 Gondolf, Edward W.; Fisher, Ellen; and McFerron, J. Richard. Racial differences among shelter residents: a comparison of Anglo, Black, and Hispanic battered. JOURNAL OF FAMILY VIOLENCE, Vol. 3, no. 1 (March 1988), p. 39-51. English. **DESCR:** Battered Women; Blacks; Comparative Psychology; Cultural Characteristics; Natural Support Systems; Socioeconomic Factors; *Violence; *Women.

285 Gonzalez, Alex. Sex roles of the traditional Mexican family: a comparison of Chicano and Anglo students' attitudes. JOURNAL OF CROSS-CULTURAL PSYCHOLOGY, Vol. 13, no. 3 (September 1982), p. 330-339. English. **DESCR:** Attitudes; Comparative Psychology; *Family; Hembrismo; Machismo; Sex Roles; Students.

286 Gould, Jeffrey B.; Davey, Becky; and Stafford, Randall S. Socioeconomic differences in rates of cesarean section. THE NEW ENGLAND JOURNAL OF MEDICINE, Vol. 321, no. 4 (July 27, 1989), p. 233-239. English. **DESCR:** Asian Americans; Blacks; *Cesarean Section; *Fertility; Los Angeles County, CA; *Socioeconomic Factors; Vital Statistics; Women.

287 Groessl, Patricia Ann. Depression and anxiety in postmenopausal women: a study of Black, white, and Hispanic women. Thesis (Ed.D.)--Western Michigan University, 1987. 87 p. English. **DESCR:** Blacks; *Depression (Psychological); Menopause; Michigan; Stress; Women.

288 Gutierrez, Jeannie and Sameroff, Arnold. Determinants of complexity in Mexican-American and Anglo-American mothers' conceptions of child development. CHILD DEVELOPMENT, Vol. 61, no. 2 (April 1990), p. 384-394. English. **DESCR:** Acculturation; Children; Cultural Characteristics; *Parenting; Values; *Women.

289 Hazuda, Helen P., et al. Employment status and women's protection against coronary heart disease. AMERICAN JOURNAL OF EPIDEMIOLOGY, Vol. 123, no. 4 (April 1986), p. 623-640. English. **DESCR:** Diseases; Employment; *Heart Disease; Nutrition; *Public Health; San Antonio, TX.

290 Holck, Susan E. Lung cancer mortality and smoking habits: Mexican-American women. AMERICAN JOURNAL OF PUBLIC HEALTH, Vol. 72, no. 1 (January 1982), p. 38-42. English. **DESCR:** Cancer; *Public Health; *Smoking.

291 Holck, Susan E., et al. Alcohol consumption among Mexican American and Anglo women: results of a survey along the U.S.-Mexico border. JOURNAL OF STUDIES ON ALCOHOL, Vol. 45, no. 2 (March 1984), p. 149-154. English. **DESCR:** *Alcoholism; Border Region; Surveys.

292 Holck, Susan E., et al. Need for family planning services among Anglo and Hispanic women in the United States counties bordering Mexico. FAMILY PLANNING PERSPECTIVES, Vol. 14, no. 3 (May, June, 1982), p. 155-159. English. **DESCR:** Border Region; *Family Planning; Women.

293 Hser, Yih-Ing; Chou, Chih-Ping; and Anglin, M. Douglas. The criminality of female narcotics addicts: a causal modeling approach. JOURNAL OF QUANTITATIVE CRIMINOLOGY, Vol. 6, no. 2 (June 1990), p. 207-228. English. **DESCR:** Criminal Acts; *Drug Addicts; Drug Traffic; Prostitution; Women.

294 Hurtado, Aida. Relating to privilege: seduction and rejection in the subordination of white women and women of color. SIGNS: JOURNAL OF WOMEN IN CULTURE AND SOCIETY, Vol. 14, no. 4 (Summer 1989), p. 833-855. English. **DESCR:** Asian Americans; Blacks; Ethnic Groups; *Feminism; Political Ideology; Political Socialization; *Women.

295 Isaacs, Barbara Gail. Anglo, Black, and Latin adolescents' participation in sports. Thesis (Ph.D.)--California School of Professional Psychology, Los Angeles, 1984. 283 p. English. **DESCR:** Blacks; Cultural Characteristics; *Secondary School Education; *Sports; *Women; Youth.

296 Jensen, Leif. Secondary earner strategies and family poverty: immigrant-native differentials, 1960-1980. INTERNATIONAL MIGRATION REVIEW, Vol. 25, no. 1 (Spring 1991), p. 113-140. English. **DESCR:** *Asian Americans; Blacks; Family; Immigrants; Immigration; Income; Poverty; Women; Working Women.

297 La Monica, Grace; Gulino, Claire; and Ortiz Soto, Irma. A comparative study of female Mexican and American working nurses in the border corridor. BORDER HEALTH/SALUD FRONTERIZA, Vol. 5, no. 2 (April, June, 1989), p. 2-6. Bilingual. **DESCR:** *Border Region; *Medical Personnel; Women; *Working Women.

Anglo Americans (cont.)

298 Laosa, Luis M. Maternal teaching strategies in Chicano and Anglo-American families: the influence of culture and education on maternal behavior. CHILD DEVELOPMENT, Vol. 51, no. 3 (September 1980), p. 759-765. English. DESCR: Comparative Psychology; *Cultural Characteristics; *Education; Family; Maternal Teaching Observation Technique (MTOT); *Parent and Child Relationships; Parenting; Women.

299 Lee, Valerie. Achievement and educational aspirations among Hispanic female high school students: comparison between public and Catholic schools. IN: McKenna, Teresa and Ortiz, Flora Ida, eds. THE BROKEN WEB: THE EDUCATIONAL EXPERIENCE OF HISPANIC WOMEN. Claremont, CA: Tomas Rivera Center; Berkeley, CA: Floricanto Press, 1988, p. 137-192. English. DESCR: *Academic Achievement; Catholic Church; Education; Educational Statistics; Private Education; Religious Education; *Secondary School Education; *Women.

300 MacCorquodale, Patricia. Mexican-American women and mathematics: participation, aspirations, and achievement. IN: Cocking, Rodney R. and Mestre, Jose P., eds. LINGUISTIC AND CULTURAL DIFFERENCES ON LEARNING MATHEMATICS. Hillsdale, NJ: Erlbaum, 1988, p. 137-160. English. DESCR: *Academic Achievement; Bilingualism; Family; *Mathematics.

301 Martinez, Marco Antonio. Conversational asymmetry between Mexican mothers and children. HISPANIC JOURNAL OF BEHAVIORAL SCIENCES, Vol. 3, no. 4 (December 1981), p. 329-346. English. DESCR: Language Usage; *Parent and Child Relationships.

302 Mary, Nancy L. Reactions of Black, Hispanic, and white mothers to having a child with handicaps. MENTAL RETARDATION, Vol. 28, no. 1 (February 1990), p. 1-5. English. DESCR: *Attitudes; Blacks; *Children; Comparative Psychology; *Mentally Handicapped; Parent and Child Relationships; *Women.

303 Mason, Terry. Symbolic strategies for change: a discussion of the Chicana women's movement. IN: Melville, Margarita B., ed. TWICE A MINORITY. St. Louis, MO: Mosby, 1980, p. 95-108. English. DESCR: Actos; *Feminism; Teatro; Women.

304 Michael, Robert T. and Tuma, Nancy Brandon. Entry into marriage and parenthood by young men and women: the influence of family background. DEMOGRAPHY, Vol. 22, no. 4 (November 1985), p. 515-544. Magazine. English. DESCR: Blacks; *Cultural Characteristics; *Fertility; *Marriage; Population; Youth.

305 Mullen, Julia Ann. Black, Anglo, and Chicana women's construction of mental illness. Thesis (Ph.D.)--University of California, Santa Barbara, 1985. 276 p. English. DESCR: Blacks; *Mental Illness; *Women.

306 Murguia, Edward and Cazares, Ralph B. Intermarriage of Mexican Americans. MARRIAGE & FAMILY REVIEW, Vol. 5, no. 1 (Spring 1982), p. 91-100. English. DESCR: Acculturation; *Intermarriage; Social Mobility.

307 Myres, Sandra Lynn. Mexican Americans and westering Anglos: a feminine perspective. NEW MEXICO HISTORICAL REVIEW, Vol. 57, no. 4 (October 1982), p. 317-333. English. DESCR: *Attitudes; *Ethnic Groups; Social History and Conditions; Southwestern United States; Stereotypes.

308 Neff, James Alan; Gilbert, Kathleen R.; and Hoppe, Sue K. Divorce likelihood among Anglos and Mexican Americans. JOURNAL OF DIVORCE AND REMARRIAGE, Vol. 15, no. 1-2 (1991), p. 75-98. English. DESCR: *Divorce; *Marriage; San Antonio, TX.

309 Nieto Gomez de Lazarin, Anna. La femenista [sic]. ENCUENTRO FEMENIL, Vol. 1, no. 2 (1974), p. 34-47. English. DESCR: Chicana Caucus, National Women's Political Caucus; Chicano Movement; Conferences and Meetings; Discrimination; *Feminism; National Women's Political Caucus (February 9-11, 1973: Houston, TX); *Sexism; Women.

310 Norinsky, Margaret Elaine. The relationship between sex-role identity and ethnicity to styles of assertiveness and aggression in women. Thesis (Ed.D.)--University of San Francisco, 1987. 164 p. English. DESCR: *Assertiveness; Blacks; Ethnic Groups; *Identity; *Sex Roles; *Women.

311 Notzon, Francis Claude. Factors associated with low birth weight in Mexican-Americans and Mexicans. Thesis (Ph.D.)--John Hopkins University, 1989. 190 p. English. DESCR: Fertility; *Maternal and Child Welfare; Mexico; *Prenatal Care; Public Health; *Women.

312 Ortiz, Vilma and Fennelly, Katherine. Early childbearing and employment among young Mexican origin, Black, and white women. SOCIAL SCIENCE QUARTERLY, Vol. 69, no. 4 (December 1988), p. 987-995. English. DESCR: Blacks; *Employment; *Fertility; *Women; *Youth.

313 Ortiz, Vilma and Cooney, Rosemary Santana. Sex-role attitudes and labor force participation among young Hispanic females and non-Hispanic white females. SOCIAL SCIENCE QUARTERLY, Vol. 65, no. 2 (June 1984), p. 392-400. English. DESCR: Attitudes; Employment; *Sex Roles; Working Women.

314 Ortiz, Vilma and Cooney, Rosemary Santana. Sex-role attitudes and labor force participation among young Hispanic females and non-Hispanic white females. IN: O. de la Garza, Rodolfo, et al., eds. THE MEXICAN AMERICAN EXPERIENCE: AN INTERDISCIPLINARY ANTHOLOGY. Austin, TX: University of Texas Press, 1985, p. 174-182. English. DESCR: Attitudes; Employment; *Sex Roles; Working Women.

315 Padilla, Eligio R. and O'Grady, Kevin E. Sexuality among Mexican Americans: a case of sexual stereotyping. JOURNAL OF PERSONALITY AND SOCIAL PSYCHOLOGY, Vol. 52, no. 1 (1987), p. 5-10. English. DESCR: Age Groups; Attitudes; California; Religion; *Sex Roles; *Sex Stereotypes; Sexual Behavior; Sexual Knowledge and Attitude Test; *Stereotypes; Students; Values.

316 Powers, Stephen and Jones, Patricia. Factorial invariance of the California achievement tests across race and sex. EDUCATIONAL AND PSYCHOLOGICAL MEASUREMENT, Vol. 44, no. 4 (Winter 1984), p. 967-970. English. DESCR: Blacks; *California Achievement Test (CAT); Educational Tests and Measurements; Males; Women.

Anglo Americans (cont.)

317 Quintana, Alvina E. Challenge and counter challenge: Chicana literary motifs. AGAINST THE CURRENT, Vol. 2, no. 2 (March, April, 1987), p. 25,28-32. English. **DESCR:** Authors; Cervantes, Lorna Dee; Cultural Studies; *Feminism; Identity; Literary Criticism; *Literature; Moraga, Cherrie; THERE ARE NO MADMEN HERE; Valdes, Gina; Women.

318 Quintana, Alvina E. Chicana literary motifs: challenge and counter-challenge. IMAGES: ETHNIC STUDIES OCCASIONAL PAPERS SERIES, (Fall 1986), p. 24-41. English. **DESCR:** Authors; Cervantes, Lorna Dee; Cultural Studies; *Feminism; *Identity; *Literary Criticism; Literature; Moraga, Cherrie; THERE ARE NO MADMEN HERE; Valdes, Gina; Women.

319 Ramirez, Alex, et al. The relationship between sociocultural variables and Chicano and Anglo high school student responses on the Potency Dimension of the Semantic Differential. HISPANIC JOURNAL OF BEHAVIORAL SCIENCES, Vol. 3, no. 2 (June 1981), p. 177-190. English. **DESCR:** Martinez, Joe L., Jr.; Martinez, Sergio R.; MULTIVARIATE ANALYSIS OF VARIANCE (MANOVA); Olmedo, Esteban L.; *Parent and Child Relationships; Sex Roles; Sex Stereotypes; Students.

320 Reimers, Cordelia W. A comparative analysis of the wages of Hispanics, Blacks, and non-Hispanic whites. IN: Borjas, George J. and Tienda, Marta, eds. HISPANICS IN THE U.S. ECONOMY. Orlando, FL: Academic Press, 1985, p. 27-75. English. **DESCR:** Blacks; *Income; Labor Supply and Market; Males; Survey of Income and Education (SIE).

321 Romero, Gloria J. and Garza, Raymond T. Attributions for the occupational success/failure of ethnic minority and nonminority women. SEX ROLES, Vol. 14, no. 7-8 (April 1986), p. 445-452. English. **DESCR:** *Attitudes; Careers; Identity; Sociology; Women.

322 Ross, Catherine E.; Mirowsky, John; and Ulbrich, Patricia. Distress and the traditional female role: a comparison of Mexicans and Anglos. AMERICAN JOURNAL OF SOCIOLOGY, Vol. 89, no. 3 (November 1983), p. 670-682. English. **DESCR:** Comparative Psychology; *Sex Roles; Stress; Women.

323 Ruiz, Vicki L., ed. and DuBois, Ellen Carol, ed. Unequal sisters: a multicultural reader in U.S. women's history. New York: Routledge, 1990. xvi, 473 p. English. **DESCR:** Asian Americans; Blacks; Feminism; *History; Native Americans; *Women.

324 Saldivar-Hull, Sonia. Feminism on the border: from gender politics to geopolitics. IN: Calderon, Hector and Saldivar, Jose David, eds. CRITICISM IN THE BORDERLANDS: STUDIES IN CHICANO LITERATURE, CULTURE, AND IDEOLOGY. Durham, NC: Duke University Press, 1991, p. [203]-220. English. **DESCR:** *Anzaldua, Gloria; *BORDERLANDS/LA FRONTERA: THE NEW MESTIZA; Feminism; Homosexuality; *Literary Criticism; Mestizaje; Moraga, Cherrie; Sexism; "The Cariboo Cafe" [short story]; Viramontes, Helena Maria; Women.

325 Salgado de Snyder, Nelly; Cervantes, Richard C.; and Padilla, Amado M. Gender and ethnic differences in psychosocial stress and generalized distress among Hispanics. SEX ROLES, Vol. 22, no. 7-8 (April, 1990), p. 441-453. English. **DESCR:** Central Americans; *Comparative Psychology; Depression (Psychological); Hispanic Stress Inventory (HSI); *Immigrants; Immigration; *Sex Roles; *Stress; Women.

326 Sanford, Judy, et al. Patterns of reported rape in a tri-ethnic population: Houston, Texas, 1974-1975. AMERICAN JOURNAL OF PUBLIC HEALTH, Vol. 69, no. 5 (May 1979), p. 480-484. English. **DESCR:** Blacks; Criminology; *Ethnic Groups; *Houston, TX; *Rape; Statistics; Women.

327 Schlissel, Lillian, ed.; Ruiz, Vicki L., ed.; and Monk, Janice, ed. Western women: their land, their lives. Albuquerque, NM: University of New Mexico Press, c1988. vi, 354 p. English. **DESCR:** History; Immigration; Intermarriage; Labor; Native Americans; *Social History and Conditions; Southwestern United States; *Women.

328 Smith, Bradford M. The measurement of narcissism in Asian, Caucasian, and Hispanic American women. PSYCHOLOGICAL REPORTS, Vol. 67, no. 3 (December 1990), p. 779-785. English. **DESCR:** Asian Americans; Comparative Psychology; Cultural Characteristics; *Narcissistic Personality Inventory; *Personality; *Psychological Testing; *Women.

329 Smith, Jack C. Trends in the incidence of breastfeeding for Hispanics of Mexican origin and Anglos on the US-Mexican border. AMERICAN JOURNAL OF PUBLIC HEALTH, Vol. 72, no. 1 (January 1982), p. 59-61. English. **DESCR:** Border Region; Breastfeeding; *Maternal and Child Welfare.

330 Sorenson, Ann Marie. The fertility and language characteristics of Mexican-American and non-Hispanic husbands and wives. SOCIOLOGICAL QUARTERLY, Vol. 29, no. 1 (March 1988), p. 111-130. English. **DESCR:** Fertility; Identity; *Language Usage; Marriage; Sex Roles.

331 Sorenson, Ann Marie. Fertility, expectations and ethnic identity among Mexican-American adolescents: an expression of cultural ideals. SOCIOLOGICAL PERSPECTIVES, Vol. 28, no. 3 (July 1985), p. 339-360. English. **DESCR:** Acculturation; Cultural Characteristics; *Fertility; Identity; Values; Youth.

332 Sorenson, Susan B. and Telles, Cynthia A. Self-reports of spousal violence in a Mexican-American and non-Hispanic white population. VIOLENCE AND VICTIMS, Vol. 6, no. 1 (1991), p. 3-15. English. **DESCR:** *Battered Women; Los Angeles, CA; Los Angeles Epidemiologic Catchment Area Research Program (LAECA); Rape; Violence; Women; *Women Men Relations.

333 Stewart, Kenneth L. and de Leon, Arnoldo. Fertility among Mexican Americans and Anglos in Texas, 1900. BORDERLANDS JOURNAL, Vol. 9, no. 1 (Spring 1986), p. 61-67. English. **DESCR:** *Fertility; Texas; Women.

334 Tienda, Marta and Angel, Ronald J. Headship and household composition among Blacks, Hispanics and other whites. SOCIAL FORCES, Vol. 61, no. 2 (December 1982), p. 508-531. English. **DESCR:** Blacks; Cultural Characteristics; Extended Family; *Family; Puerto Ricans; Single Parents.

Anglo Americans (cont.)

335 Tienda, Marta and Glass, Jennifer. Household structure and labor-force participation of Black, Hispanic, and white mothers. DEMOGRAPHY, Vol. 22, no. 3 (August 1985), p. 381-394. English. DESCR: Blacks; *Extended Family; *Family; *Sex Roles; *Working Women.

336 Torres Raines, Rosario. The Mexican American woman and work: intergenerational perspectives of comparative ethnic groups. IN: Melville, Margarita ed. MEXICANAS AT WORK IN THE UNITED STATES. Houston, TX: Mexican American Studies Program, University of Houston, 1988, p. 33-46. English. DESCR: Age Groups; Employment; Feminism; Marriage; Sex Roles; Social Classes; Socioeconomic Factors; *Working Women.

337 Torres, Sara. A comparative analysis of wife abuse among Anglo-American and Mexican-American battered women: attitudes, nature, severity, frequency and response to the abuse. Thesis (Ph.D.)--University of Texas, Austin, 1986. 265 p. English. DESCR: Attitudes; Battered Women; Family; *Violence; *Women.

338 Trotter, Robert T. Ethnic and sexual patterns of alcohol use: Anglo and Mexican American college students. ADOLESCENCE, Vol. 17, no. 66 (Summer 1982), p. 305-325. English. DESCR: *Alcoholism; Colleges and Universities; Cultural Characteristics; Ethnic Groups; Sex Roles; Students; Youth.

339 Vega, William A.; Warheit, George; and Meinhardt, Kenneth. Marital disruption and the prevalence of depressive symptomatology among Anglos and Mexican Americans. JOURNAL OF MARRIAGE AND THE FAMILY, Vol. 46, no. 4 (November 1984), p. 817-824. English. DESCR: Depression (Psychological); *Divorce; *Marriage; *Mental Health; Socioeconomic Factors.

340 Velasquez-Trevino, Gloria. Jovita Gonzalez, una voz de resistencia cultural en la temprana narrativa chicana. IN: Lopez-Gonzalez, Aralia, et al., eds. MUJER Y LITERATURA MEXICANA Y CHICANA: CULTURAS EN CONTACTO. Mexico: Colegio de la Frontera Norte, 1988, p. [77]-83. Spanish. DESCR: Authors; Feminism; Folklore; *Gonzalez, Jovita; Intergroup Relations; *League of United Latin American Citizens (LULAC).

341 Wagner, Roland M. Changes in extended family relationships for Mexican American and Anglo single mothers. JOURNAL OF DIVORCE, Vol. 11, no. 2 (Winter 1987), p. 69-87. English. DESCR: *Divorce; *Extended Family; Natural Support Systems; San Jose, CA; *Single Parents; Women.

342 Wagner, Roland M. Changes in the friend network during the first year of single parenthood for Mexican American and Anglo women. JOURNAL OF DIVORCE, Vol. 11, no. 2 (Winter 1987), p. 89-109. English. DESCR: Divorce; *Natural Support Systems; *Single Parents; Widowhood; Women.

343 Wagner, Roland M. and Schaffer, Diane M. Social networks and survival strategies: an exploratory study of Mexican American, Black, and Anglo female family heads in San Jose, California. IN: Melville, Margarita B., ed. TWICE A MINORITY. St. Louis, MO: Mosby, 1980, p. 173-190. English. DESCR: Blacks; Identity; *Natural Support Systems; San Jose, CA; *Single Parents; Stress.

344 Warren, Charles W.; Smith, Jack C.; and Rochat, Roger W. Differentials in the planning status of the most recent live birth to Mexican Americans and Anglos. PUBLIC HEALTH REPORTS, Vol. 98, no. 2 (March, April, 1983), p. 152-160. English. DESCR: *Family Planning; Fertility; Women.

345 Weiner, Raine. The needs of poverty women heading households: a return to postsecondary education. Thesis (Ph.D.)--California School of Professional Psychology, Los Angeles, 1986. 180 p. English. DESCR: Blacks; *Employment Training; Ethnic Groups; *Poverty; *Single Parents; Vocational Education; Welfare; Women.

346 Williams, Joyce E. Mexican American and Anglo attitudes about sex roles and rape. FREE INQUIRY IN CREATIVE SOCIOLOGY, Vol. 13, no. 1 (May 1985), p. 15-20. English. DESCR: Attitudes; *Feminism; *Rape; *Sex Roles; Women.

347 Zambrana, Ruth E. Toward understanding the educational trajectory and socialization of Latina women. IN: McKenna, Teresa and Ortiz, Flora Ida, eds. THE BROKEN WEB: THE EDUCATIONAL EXPERIENCE OF HISPANIC WOMEN. Claremont, CA: Tomas Rivera Center; Berkeley, CA: Floricanto Press, 1988, p. 61-77. English. DESCR: Academic Achievement; *Education; Feminism; Identity; Research Methodology; *Socialization; *Women.

348 Zeff, Shirley B. A cross-cultural study of Mexican American, Black American and white American women of a large urban university. HISPANIC JOURNAL OF BEHAVIORAL SCIENCES, Vol. 4, no. 2 (June 1982), p. 245-261. English. DESCR: Blacks; *Higher Education; Sex Roles; Students.

ANIMA [film]

349 Fregoso, Rosa Linda. La quinceanera of Chicana counter aesthetics. CENTRO BULLETIN, Vol. 3, no. 1 (Winter 1990, 1991), p. [87]-91. English. DESCR: *AGUEDA MARTINEZ [film]; *CHICANA! [film]; *DESPUES DEL TERREMOTO [film]; Espana, Frances Salome; Feminism; *Films; Morales, Sylvia; Portillo, Lourdes; Vasquez, Esperanza.

Anorexia Nervosa

350 Pumariega, Andres J. Acculturation and eating attitudes in adolescent girls: a comparative and correlational study. JOURNAL OF THE AMERICAN ACADEMY OF CHILD PSYCHIATRY, Vol. 25, no. 2 (March 1986), p. 276-279. English. DESCR: *Acculturation; Cultural Characteristics; Eating Attitudes Test (EAT); Nutrition; Socioeconomic Factors; Youth.

Anthropology

351 Newton, Frank; Olmedo, Esteban L.; and Padilla, Amado M. Hispanic mental health research: a reference guide. Berkeley, CA: University of California Press, c1982. 685 p. English. DESCR: *Bibliography; Education; Medical Care; *Mental Health; Psychology; Public Health; *Reference Works; Sociology.

Anthropology (cont.)

352 Quintana, Alvina E. Ana Castillo's THE MIXQUIAHUALA LETTERS: the novelist as ethnographer. IN: Calderon, Hector and Saldivar, Jose David, eds. CRITICISM IN THE BORDERLANDS: STUDIES IN CHICANO LITERATURE, CULTURE, AND IDEOLOGY. Durham, NC: Duke University Press, 1991, p. [72]-83. English. **DESCR:** Castillo, Ana; Cultural Studies; *Ethnology; Feminism; Geertz, Clifford; *Literary Criticism; Novel; THE MIXQUIAHUALA LETTERS.

Anzaldua, Gloria

353 Alarcon, Norma. The theoretical subject(s) of THIS BRIDGE CALLED MY BACK and Anglo-American feminism. IN: Calderon, Hector and Saldivar, Jose David, eds. CRITICISM IN THE BORDERLANDS: STUDIES IN CHICANO LITERATURE, CULTURE, AND IDEOLOGY. Durham, NC: Duke University Press, 1991, p. [28]-39. English. **DESCR:** *Anglo Americans; *Feminism; Moraga, Cherrie; THIS BRIDGE CALLED MY BACK; *Women.

354 Alarcon, Norma. The theoretical subject(s) of THIS BRIDGE CALLED MY BACK and Anglo-American feminism. IN: Anzaldua, Gloria, ed. MAKING FACE, MAKING SOUL: HACIENDO CARAS: CREATIVE AND CRITICAL PERSPECTIVES BY WOMEN OF COLOR. San Francisco, CA: Aunt Lute Foundation Books, 1990, p. 356-369. English. **DESCR:** *Anglo Americans; *Feminism; Literary Criticism; Moraga, Cherrie; THIS BRIDGE CALLED MY BACK; *Women.

355 de Lotbiniere-Harwood, Susanne and Anzaldua, Gloria. Conversations at the Book Fair: interview with Gloria Anzaldua. TRIVIA: A JOURNAL OF IDEAS, no. 14 (Spring 1989), p. 37-45. English. **DESCR:** *Authors; Biography; Feminism; Literary Criticism.

356 Harlow, Barbara. Sites of struggle: immigration, deportation, prison, and exile. IN: Calderon, Hector and Saldivar, Jose David, eds. CRITICISM IN THE BORDERLANDS: STUDIES IN CHICANO LITERATURE, CULTURE, AND IDEOLOGY. Durham, NC: Duke University Press, 1991, p. [149]-163. English. **DESCR:** BLACK GOLD; BORDERLANDS/LA FRONTERA: THE NEW MESTIZA; First, Ruth; Khalifeh, Sahar; *Literary Criticism; *Political Ideology; Sanchez, Rosaura; Social Classes; "The Cariboo Cafe" [short story]; "The Ditch" [short story]; Viramontes, Helena Maria; WILD THORNS; *Women; Working Women.

357 Quintana, Alvina E. Politics, representation and the emergence of a Chicana aesthetic. CULTURAL STUDIES, Vol. 4, no. 3 (October 1990), p. 257-263. English. **DESCR:** *Authors; Chavez, Denise; Chicana Studies; Cisneros, Sandra; Cultural Studies; Feminism; *Literary Criticism.

358 Saldivar-Hull, Sonia. Feminism on the border: from gender politics to geopolitics. IN: Calderon, Hector and Saldivar, Jose David, eds. CRITICISM IN THE BORDERLANDS: STUDIES IN CHICANO LITERATURE, CULTURE, AND IDEOLOGY. Durham, NC: Duke University Press, 1991, p. [203]-220. English. **DESCR:** Anglo Americans; *BORDERLANDS/LA FRONTERA: THE NEW MESTIZA; Feminism; Homosexuality; *Literary Criticism; Mestizaje; Moraga, Cherrie; Sexism; "The Cariboo Cafe" [short story]; Viramontes, Helena Maria; Women.

359 Spitta, Silvia D. Literary transculturation in Latin America. Thesis (Ph.D.)--University of Oregon, 1989. 184 p. English. **DESCR:** Arguedos, Jose Maria; Authors; Cultural Characteristics; Culture; *Intergroup Relations; *Latin American Literature; Spanish Influence.

360 Woodward, Carolyn. Dare to write: Virginia Woolf, Tillie Olsen, Gloria Anzaldua. IN: Cochran, Jo Whitehorse, et al., eds. CHANGING OUR POWER: AN INTRODUCTION TO WOMEN STUDIES. Dubuque, IA: Kendall/Hunt Publishing Co., 1988, p. 336-349. English. **DESCR:** *Authors; Feminism; Olsen, Tillie; Women; Woolf, Virginia.

Apodaca, Maria Linda

361 Sanchez, Rosaura. The history of Chicanas: a proposal for a materialist perspective. IN: Del Castillo, Adelaida R., ed. BETWEEN BORDERS: ESSAYS ON MEXICANA/CHICANA HISTORY. Encino, CA: Floricanto Press, 1990, p. 1-29. English. **DESCR:** *Chicana Studies; Del Castillo, Adelaida R.; Feminism; Historiography; History; Morales, Sylvia; Ruiz, Vicki L.

"The Apple Trees"

362 Castellano, Olivia. Of clarity and the moon: a study of two women in rebellion. DE COLORES, Vol. 3, no. 3 (1977), p. 25-30. English. **DESCR:** DAY OF THE SWALLOWS; *Literary Criticism; Portillo Trambley, Estela.

Aragon, Jesusita, 1908-

363 Buss, Fran Leeper. La partera: story of a midwife. Ann Arbor, MI: University of Michigan Press, 1980. 140 p.: ill. English. **DESCR:** Cultural Customs; *Curanderas; Folk Medicine; Herbal Medicine; *Midwives; New Mexico; San Miguel County, NM.

364 Perrone, Bobette; Stockel, H. Henrietta; and Krueger, Victoria. Medicine women, curanderas, and women doctors. Norman, OK: University of Oklahoma Press, c1989. xix, 252 p.:ill. English. **DESCR:** *Curanderas; *Curanderismo; *Folk Medicine; Herbal Medicine; Herrera, Sabinita; Medical Personnel; Native Americans; *Oral History; Rodriguez, Gregorita; Women.

Archives

365 Castaneda Garcia, Carmen. Fuentes para la historia de la mujer en los archivos de Guadalajara. IN: Del Castillo, Adelaida R., ed. BETWEEN BORDERS: ESSAYS ON MEXICANA/CHICANA HISTORY. Encino, CA: Floricanto Press, 1990, p. 102-112. Spanish. **DESCR:** *Guadalajara; History; *Mexico; *Women.

366 Driscoll, Barbara A. Chicana historiography: a research note regarding Mexican archival sources. IN: Cordova, Teresa, et al., eds. CHICANA VOICES. Austin, TX: Center for Mexican American Studies, 1986, p. 136-145. English. **DESCR:** *Historiography; Mexico.

367 Ruiz, Vicki L. Dead ends or gold mines?: using missionary records in Mexican-American women's history. FRONTIERS: A JOURNAL OF WOMEN STUDIES, Vol. 12, no. 1 (1991), p. 33-56. English. **DESCR:** Clergy; El Paso, TX; History; *Methodist Church; Protestant Church; *Research Methodology; *Rose Gregory Houchen Settlement House, El Paso, TX.

Archuleta, Eppie

368 Nelson, Kathryn J. Excerpts from los testamentos: Hispanic women folk artists of the San Luis Valley, Colorado. FRONTIERS: A JOURNAL OF WOMEN STUDIES, Vol. 5, no. 3 (Fall 1980), p. 34-43. English. DESCR: Artists; Biography; Folk Art; San Luis Valley, CO.

Arenal, Sandra

369 Lavrin, Asuncion. El segundo sexo en Mexico: experiencia, estudio e introspeccion, 1983-1987. MEXICAN STUDIES/ESTUDIOS MEXICANOS, Vol. 5, no. 2 (Summer 1989), p. 297-312. Spanish. DESCR: *Border Industries Carrillo, Jorge; Hernandez, Alberto; Iglesias, Norma; LA FLOR MAS BELLA DE LA MAQUILADORA; *Literature Reviews; Mexico; MUJERES FRONTERIZAS EN LA INDUSTRIA MAQUILADORA; SANGRE JOVEN: LAS MAQUILADORAS POR DENTRO; Women.

Arguedos, Jose Maria

370 Spitta, Silvia D. Literary transculturation in Latin America. Thesis (Ph.D.)--University of Oregon, 1989. 184 p. English. DESCR: Anzaldua, Gloria; Authors; Cultural Characteristics; Culture; *Intergroup Relations; *Latin American Literature; Spanish Influence.

Arguello, Concepcion

371 Mirande, Alfredo and Enriquez, Evangelina. Chicanas in the history of the Southwest. IN: Duran, Livie Isauro and Bernard, H. Russell, eds. INTRODUCTION TO CHICANO STUDIES. 2nd ed. New York: Macmillan, 1982, p. 156-179. English. DESCR: Barcelo, Gertrudes "La Tules"; Feges, Eulalia; *History; "Juanita of Downieville"; Robledo, Refugio; Urrea, Teresa.

ARISE CHICANO

372 Aguilar-Henson, Marcella. The multi-faceted poetic world of Angela de Hoyos. Austin, TX: Relampago Books Press, 1985, c1982. 81 p. English. DESCR: *Authors; CHICANO POEMS FOR THE BARRIO; de Hoyos, Angela; GATA POEMS; GOODBYE TO SILENCE; Language Usage; *Literary Criticism; *Poetry; SELECTED POEMS/SELECCIONES; YO, MUJER.

Arizona

373 Aulette, Judy and Mills, Trudy. Something old, something new: auxiliary work in the 1983-1986 copper strike. FEMINIST STUDIES, Vol. 14, no. 2 (Summer 1988), p. 251-268. English. DESCR: Clifton-Morenci Copper Strike, 1983-1986; Clifton-Morenci District, Arizona; Feminism; Labor Unions; Morenci Miners Women's Auxiliary (MMWA); Mutualistas; Phelps Dodge Corporation, Morenci, AZ; SALT OF THE EARTH [film]; Sex Roles; *Strikes and Lockouts.

374 Cabeza de Baca Gilbert, Fabiola. The pioneer women. IN: Valdez, Luis and Steiner, Stan, eds. AZTLAN: AN ANTHOLOGY OF MEXICAN AMERICAN LITERATURE. New York: Vintage Books, 1972, p. 260-263. English. DESCR: *History.

375 Fernandez, Celestino and Holscher, Louis M. Chicano-Anglo intermarriage in Arizona, 1960-1980: an exploratory study of eight counties. HISPANIC JOURNAL OF BEHAVIORAL SCIENCES, Vol. 5, no. 3 (September 1983), p. 291-304. English. DESCR: *Intermarriage.

376 Johnson, Susan L. Sharing bed and board: cohabitation and cultural difference in central Arizona mining towns. FRONTIERS: A JOURNAL OF WOMEN STUDIES, Vol. 7, no. 3 (1984), p. 36-42. English. DESCR: *Intermarriage; *Sex Roles.

377 MacCorquodale, Patricia. Social influences on the participation of Mexican-American women in science: final report. Unpublished report of study conducted at the Dept. of Sociology at the University of Arizona at Tucson and sponsored by the National Institute of Education. 1983, 81 p. (Eric Document: ED234944. English. DESCR: Careers; *Science as a Profession.

Arizona Farm Workers (AFW)

378 Arguelles, Lourdes. Undocumented female labor in the United States Southwest: an essay on migration, consciousness, oppression and struggle. IN: Del Castillo, Adelaida R., ed. BETWEEN BORDERS: ESSAYS ON MEXICANA/CHICANA HISTORY. Encino, CA: Floricanto Press, 1990, p. 299-312. English. DESCR: Immigrants; Immigration; *Undocumented Workers; Working Women.

Arredondo, Alicia

379 Goldman, Shifra M. Women artists of Texas: MAS = More + Artists + Women = MAS. CHISMEARTE, no. 7 (January 1981), p. 21-22. English. DESCR: Art Organizations and Groups; Barraza, Santa; Exhibits; Feminism; Flores, Maria; Folk Art; Gonzalez Dodson, Nora; *Mujeres Artistas del Suroeste (MAS), Austin, TX; Photography; Texas; Trevino, Modesta Barbina; WOMEN & THEIR WORK [festival] (Austin, TX: 1977).

Art

380 Alarcon, Norma. Hay que inventarnos/we must invent ourselves. THIRD WOMAN, Vol. 1, no. 1 (1981), p. 4-6. English. DESCR: Journals; Midwest Latina Writer's Workshop (1980: Chicago); Midwestern States; *THIRD WOMAN: OF LATINAS IN THE MIDWEST; Third World Literature (U.S.).

381 Brown, Betty Ann. Chicanas speak out. ARTWEEK, Vol. 15, no. 2 (January 14, 1984), p. 1+. English. DESCR: Carrasco, Barbara; Carrillo, Graciela; CHICANA VOICES & VISIONS [exhibit]; Exhibits; Goldman, Shifra M.; Hernandez, Ester; Lerma Bowerman, Liz; Rodriguez, Carmen; Rodriguez, Sandra Maria; Social and Public Art Resource Center, Venice, CA (SPARC).

382 CHISMEARTE: La mujer special issue. CHISMEARTE, Vol. 1, no. 4 (Fall, Winter, 1977), p. 1-39. Bilingual.

383 Cochran, Jo, et al., eds. Bearing witness/Sobreviviendo: an anthology of Native American/Latina art and literature. CALYX: A JOURNAL OF ART AND LITERATURE BY WOMEN, Vol. 8, no. 2 (Spring 1984), p. [1]-128. English. DESCR: Drawings; *Fiction; Native Americans; *Poems; Women.

384 Goldman, Shifra M. and Ybarra-Frausto, Tomas. Arte Chicano: a comprehensive annotated bibliography of Chicano art, 1965-1981. Berkeley, CA: Chicano Studies Library Publications Unit, 1985. viii, 778 p. English. DESCR: Art History; Artists; *Bibliography.

Art (cont.)

385 Goldman, Shifra M. Trabajadoras mexicanas y chicanas en las artes visuales. IN: Leal, Salvador, ed. A TRAVES DE LA FRONTERA. Mexico, D.F.: Centro de Estudios Economicos y Sociales del Tercer Mundo, A.C.; Instituto de Investigaciones Esteticas, U.N.A.M., 1983, p. 153-161. Spanish. **DESCR:** Gonzalez Parsons, Lucia; Huerta, Dolores; Moreno, Luisa [union organizer]; SALT OF THE EARTH [film]; Tenayuca, Emma; *Working Women.

386 Herrera-Sobek, Maria, ed. and Viramontes, Helena Maria, ed. Chicana creativity and criticism: charting new frontiers in American literature. Houston, TX: Arte Publico Press, 1988. 190 p. Bilingual. **DESCR:** Literary Criticism; *Literature; Poems; Prose.

387 Rios-C., Herminio; Romano-V., Octavio Ignacio; and Portillo Trambley, Estela. Chicanas en la literatura y el arte (El Grito Book Series: Book 1, September 1973). EL GRITO, Vol. 7, no. 1 (Fall 1973), p. 1-84. Bilingual. **DESCR:** Authors; *Poems; Teatro.

388 Vigil, Evangelina, ed. Woman of her word: Hispanic women write. REVISTA CHICANO-RIQUENA, Vol. 11, no. 3-4 (Fall, Winter, 1983), p. [1]-180. Bilingual. **DESCR:** Literary Criticism; *Literature; Poetry; Prose; *Women.

Art Criticism

389 Soberon, Mercedes. La revolucion se trata de amor: Mercedes Soberon. CHISMEARTE, Vol. 1, no. 1 (Fall 1976), p. 14-18. Spanish. **DESCR:** Concilio de Arte Popular, Los Angeles, CA; Cultural Organizations; La Mission Media Arts, San Francisco, CA; San Francisco, CA; *Sex Roles; Soberon, Mercedes.

390 Trujillo Gaitan, Marcella. The dilemma of the modern Chicana artist and critic. DE COLORES, Vol. 3, no. 3 (1977), p. 38-48. Bilingual. **DESCR:** Artists; *Chicano Movement; Gonzales, Sylvia Alicia; *Literary Criticism; Machismo; Malinche; *Poetry; Symbolism.

391 Trujillo Gaitan, Marcella. The dilemma of the modern Chicana artist and critic. HERESIES, Vol. 2, no. 4 (1979), p. 5-10. English. **DESCR:** Artists; Authors; *Chicano Movement; Gonzales, Sylvia Alicia; *Literary Criticism; Machismo; Malinche; *Poetry; Symbolism.

392 Venegas, Sybil. The artists and their work--the role of the Chicana artist. CHISMEARTE, Vol. 1, no. 4 (Fall, Winter, 1977), p. 3, 5. English. **DESCR:** *Artists; Carrasco, Barbara; Delgado, Etta; Hernandez, Ester; Las Mujeres Muralistas, San Francisco, CA; Mural Art.

Art History

393 Goldman, Shifra M. and Ybarra-Frausto, Tomas. Arte Chicano: a comprehensive annotated bibliography of Chicano art, 1965-1981. Berkeley, CA: Chicano Studies Library Publications Unit, 1985. viii, 778 p. English. **DESCR:** *Art; Artists; *Bibliography.

394 Stevens, Joanne Darsey. Santos by twentieth-century santeras: continuation of a traditional art form. Thesis (Ph.D.)--University of Texas at Dallas, 1986. 259 p. English. **DESCR:** *Artists; Dallas Museum of Art; New Mexico; *Santos.

Art Organizations and Groups

395 Goldman, Shifra M. Women artists of Texas: MAS = More + Artists + Women = MAS. CHISMEARTE, no. 7 (January 1981), p. 21-22. English. **DESCR:** Arredondo, Alicia; Barraza, Santa; Exhibits; Feminism; Flores, Maria; Folk Art; Gonzalez Dodson, Nora; *Mujeres Artistas del Suroeste (MAS), Austin, TX; Photography; Texas; Trevino, Modesta Barbina; WOMEN & THEIR WORK [festival] (Austin, TX: 1977).

396 Gonzales, Sylvia Alicia. Hispanic American voluntary organizations. Westport, CT: Greenwood Press, 1985. xx, 267 p. English. **DESCR:** *Community Organizations; Cultural Organizations; *Directories; Educational Organizations; *Organizations; Political Parties and Organizations; Professional Organizations.

397 Orozco, Sylvia. Las mujeres--Chicana artists come into their own. MOVING ON, Vol. 2, no. 3 (May 1978), p. 14-16. English. **DESCR:** Artists; Barraza, Santa; Flores, Maria; Gonzalez Dodson, Nora; *Mujeres Artistas del Suroeste (MAS), Austin, TX; Trevino, Modesta Barbina.

398 Pohl, Frances K. and Baca, Judith F. THE WORLD WALL: A VISION OF THE FUTURE WITHOUT FEAR: an interview with Judith F. Baca. FRONTIERS: A JOURNAL OF WOMEN STUDIES, Vol. 11, no. 1 (1990), p. [33]-43. English. **DESCR:** *Artists; *Baca, Judith F.; *Mural Art; Social and Public Art Resource Center, Venice, CA (SPARC); *THE WORLD WALL: A VISION OF THE FUTURE WITHOUT FEAR [mural].

Art Philosophy
USE: Art Criticism

Artists

399 Altars as folk art. ARRIBA, Vol. 1, no. 1 (July 1980), p. 4. English. **DESCR:** *Altars; De Leon, Josefina; Folk Art; Religious Art.

400 Burnham, Linda. Barbara Carrasco and public activist art. HIGH PERFORMANCE, Vol. 9, no. 3 (1986), p. 48. English. **DESCR:** Carrasco, Barbara; Mural Art; Politics.

401 Burnham, Linda. Patssi Valdez. HIGH PERFORMANCE, Vol. 9, no. 3 (1986), p. 54. English. **DESCR:** ASCO [art group], Los Angeles, CA; Los Angeles, CA; Performing Arts; Valdez, Patssi.

402 Campos Carr, Irene. Proyecto La Mujer: Latina women shaping consciousness. WOMEN'S STUDIES INTERNATIONAL FORUM, Vol. 12, no. 1 (1989), p. 45-49. English. **DESCR:** Aurora, IL; Authors; Barrios; Conferences and Meetings; Elgin, IL; *Feminism; Joliet, IL; Poetry; Proyecto La Mujer Conference (Spring, 1982: Northern Illinois); Women.

403 Goldman, Shifra M. and Ybarra-Frausto, Tomas. Arte Chicano: a comprehensive annotated bibliography of Chicano art, 1965-1981. Berkeley, CA: Chicano Studies Library Publications Unit, 1985. viii, 778 p. English. **DESCR:** *Art; Art History; *Bibliography.

Artists (cont.)

404 Goldman, Shifra M. Artistas chicanas texanas. FEM, Vol. 8, no. 34 (June, July, 1984), p. 29-31. Spanish. DESCR: Mujeres Artistas del Suroeste (MAS), Austin, TX; Texas.

405 Goldman, Shifra M. Artistas en accion: conferencia de las mujeres chicanas. LA COMUNIDAD, (August 10. 1980), p. 15. Spanish. DESCR: Chicano Studies; Conferences and Meetings; Flores, Gloriamalia; Lomas Garza, Carmen.

406 Goldman, Shifra M. Mujeres de California: Latin American women artists. IN: Moore, Sylvia, ed. YESTERDAY AND TOMORROW: CALIFORNIA WOMEN ARTISTS. New York, NY: Midmarch Arts Press, c1989, p. 202-229. English. DESCR: Baca, Judith F.; Biography; California; Carrasco, Barbara; Cervantez, Yreina; de Larios, Dora; Feminism; Hernandez, Judithe; Lomas Garza, Carmen; Lopez, Yolanda M.; Mesa-Bains, Amalia; Murillo, Patricia; Sanchez, Olivia; Valdez, Patssi; Vallejo Dillaway, Linda; Women; Zamora Lucero, Linda.

407 Johnston Hernandez, Beatriz. Life as art. VISTA, Vol. 3, no. 12 (August 7, 1988), p. 18,34. English. DESCR: *Lopez, Yolanda M.; Paintings.

408 La Duke, Betty. Trivial lives: artists Yolanda Lopez and Patricia Rodriguez. TRIVIA: A JOURNAL OF IDEAS, (Winter 1986), p. 74-85. English. DESCR: Biography; *Lopez, Yolanda M.; *Rodriguez, Patricia.

409 Lomas Garza, Carmen. Altares: arte espiritual del hogar. HOJAS, (1976), p. 105-111. English. DESCR: *Altars; Folk Art; Lomas Garza, Carmen; Religious Art.

410 Mesa-Bains, Amalia. Quest for identity: profile of two Chicana muralists: based on interviews with Judith F. Baca and Patricia Rodriguez. IN: Cockcroft, Eva Sperling and Barnet-Sanchez, Holly, eds. SIGNS FROM THE HEART: CALIFORNIA CHICANO MURALS. Venice, CA: Social and Public Art Resource Center, 1990, p. [68-83]. English. DESCR: Baca, Judith F.; Chicano Movement; GREAT WALL OF LOS ANGELES [mural]; *Mural Art; Rodriguez, Patricia.

411 Mesa-Bains, Amalia. A study of the influence of culture on the development of identity among a group of Chicana artists. Thesis (Ph.D.)--Wright Institute Graduate School of Psychology, 1983. 219 p. English. DESCR: *Culture; *Identity.

412 Moreno, Jose Adan and Lomas Garza, Carmen. Carmen Lomas Garza: traditional and non-traditional. CAMINOS, Vol. 5, no. 10 (November 1984), p. 44-45,53. English. DESCR: Lomas Garza, Carmen.

413 Navar, M. Margarita. La vela prendida: home altars. ARRIBA, Vol. 1, no. 5 (February 1980), p. 12. English. DESCR: *Altars; Exhibits; Folk Art; Religious Art.

414 Nelson, Kathryn J. Excerpts from los testamentos: Hispanic women folk artists of the San Luis Valley, Colorado. FRONTIERS: A JOURNAL OF WOMEN STUDIES, Vol. 5, no. 3 (Fall 1980), p. 34-43. English. DESCR: *Archuleta, Eppie; Biography; Folk Art; San Luis Valley, CO.

415 Orozco, Sylvia. Las mujeres--Chicana artists

come into their own. MOVING ON, Vol. 2, no. 3 (May 1978), p. 14-16. English. DESCR: Art Organizations and Groups; Barraza, Santa; Flores, Maria; Gonzalez Dodson, Nora; *Mujeres Artistas del Suroeste (MAS), Austin, TX; Trevino, Modesta Barbina.

416 Pohl, Frances K. and Baca, Judith F. THE WORLD WALL: A VISION OF THE FUTURE WITHOUT FEAR: an interview with Judith F. Baca. FRONTIERS: A JOURNAL OF WOMEN STUDIES, Vol. 11, no. 1 (1990), p. [33]-43. English. DESCR: Art Organizations and Groups; *Baca, Judith F.; *Mural Art; Social and Public Art Resource Center, Venice, CA (SPARC); *THE WORLD WALL: A VISION OF THE FUTURE WITHOUT FEAR [mural].

417 Rodriguez Aranda, Pilar E. and Cisneros, Sandra. On the solitary fate of being Mexican, female, wicked and thirty-three: an interview with writer Sandra Cisneros. THE AMERICAS REVIEW, Vol. 18, no. 1 (Spring 1990), p. 64-80. English. DESCR: *Cisneros, Sandra; Literature; MY WICKED WICKED WAYS; THE HOUSE ON MANGO STREET.

418 Stevens, Joanne Darsey. Santos by twentieth-century santeras: continuation of a traditional art form. Thesis (Ph.D.)--University of Texas at Dallas, 1986. 259 p. English. DESCR: Art History; Dallas Museum of Art; New Mexico; *Santos.

419 Stoller, Marianne L. The Hispanic women artists of New Mexico: present and past. PALACIO, Vol. 92, no. 1 (1986), p. 21-25. English. DESCR: *New Mexico; *Santeros.

420 Texas Memorial Museum, University of Texas, Austin, TX. La vela prendida: Mexican-American women's home altars. Exhibition catalog, 1980. Bilingual. DESCR: *Altars; Catalogues; Exhibits; Folk Art.

421 Three Latina artists = Tres artistas latinas. AMERICAS 2001, Vol. 1, no. 5 (March, April, 1988), p. 21. Bilingual. DESCR: *Baca, Judith F.; Biographical Notes; *Carrasco, Barbara; *Martinez, Esperanza.

422 Trujillo Gaitan, Marcella. The dilemma of the modern Chicana artist and critic. DE COLORES, Vol. 3, no. 3 (1977), p. 38-48. Bilingual. DESCR: Art Criticism; *Chicano Movement; Gonzales, Sylvia Alicia; *Literary Criticism; Machismo; Malinche; *Poetry; Symbolism.

423 Trujillo Gaitan, Marcella. The dilemma of the modern Chicana artist and critic. HERESIES, Vol. 2, no. 4 (1979), p. 5-10. English. DESCR: Art Criticism; Authors; *Chicano Movement; Gonzales, Sylvia Alicia; *Literary Criticism; Machismo; Malinche; *Poetry; Symbolism.

424 Venegas, Sybil. The artists and their work--the role of the Chicana artist. CHISMEARTE, Vol. 1, no. 4 (Fall, Winter, 1977), p. 3, 5. English. DESCR: Art Criticism; Carrasco, Barbara; Delgado, Etta; Hernandez, Ester; Las Mujeres Muralistas, San Francisco, CA; Mural Art.

ASCO [art group], Los Angeles, CA

425 Burnham, Linda. Patssi Valdez. HIGH PERFORMANCE, Vol. 9, no. 3 (1986), p. 54. English. DESCR: *Artists; Los Angeles, CA; Performing Arts; Valdez, Patssi.

Asian Americans

426 Dill, Bonnie Thornton. Our mothers' grief: racial ethnic women and the maintenance of families. JOURNAL OF FAMILY HISTORY, Vol. 13, no. 4 (October 1988), p. 415-431. English. DESCR: Blacks; Domestic Work; *Family; Fertility; *Sex Roles; *Women; *Working Women.

427 Galloway, Irma Nell. Trends in the employment of minority women as administrators in Texas public schools--1976-1981. Thesis (Ed.D.)--Texas Southern University, 1986. 129 p. English. DESCR: Blacks; Education; *Educational Administration; *Management; Native Americans; Texas; *Women.

428 Glenn, Evelyn Nakano. Racial ethnic women's labor: the intersection of race, gender and class oppression. REVIEW OF RADICAL POLITICAL ECONOMY, Vol. 17, no. 3 (Fall 1985), p. 86-108. English. DESCR: Blacks; *Discrimination; *Feminism; Laboring Classes; *Marxism; Sexism; Social Classes; Women; Working Women.

429 Gould, Jeffrey B.; Davey, Becky; and Stafford, Randall S. Socioeconomic differences in rates of cesarean section. THE NEW ENGLAND JOURNAL OF MEDICINE, Vol. 321, no. 4 (July 27, 1989), p. 233-239. English. DESCR: Anglo Americans; Blacks; *Cesarean Section; *Fertility; Los Angeles County, CA; *Socioeconomic Factors; Vital Statistics; Women.

430 Gurak, Douglas T. Assimilation and fertility: a comparison of Mexican American and Japanese American women. HISPANIC JOURNAL OF BEHAVIORAL SCIENCES, Vol. 2, no. 3 (September 1980), p. 219-239. English. DESCR: Assimilation; *Fertility; Japanese; Population; Women.

431 Hurtado, Aida. Relating to privilege: seduction and rejection in the subordination of white women and women of color. SIGNS: JOURNAL OF WOMEN IN CULTURE AND SOCIETY, Vol. 14, no. 4 (Summer 1989), p. 833-855. English. DESCR: *Anglo Americans; Blacks; Ethnic Groups; *Feminism; Political Ideology; Political Socialization; *Women.

432 Jensen, Leif. Secondary earner strategies and family poverty: immigrant-native differentials, 1960-1980. INTERNATIONAL MIGRATION REVIEW, Vol. 25, no. 1 (Spring 1991), p. 113-140. English. DESCR: Anglo Americans; Blacks; Family; Immigrants; Immigration; Income; Poverty; Women; Working Women.

433 Ruiz, Vicki L., ed. and DuBois, Ellen Carol, ed. Unequal sisters: a multicultural reader in U.S. women's history. New York: Routledge, 1990. xvi, 473 p. English. DESCR: Anglo Americans; Blacks; Feminism; *History; Native Americans; *Women.

434 Smith, Bradford M. The measurement of narcissism in Asian, Caucasian, and Hispanic American women. PSYCHOLOGICAL REPORTS, Vol. 67, no. 3 (December 1990), p. 779-785. English. DESCR: Anglo Americans; Comparative Psychology; Cultural Characteristics; *Narcissistic Personality Inventory; *Personality; *Psychological Testing; *Women.

La Asociacion Hispano-Americana de Madres y Esposas, Tucson, AZ

435 Marin, Christine. La Asociacion Hispano-Americana de Madres y Esposas: Tucson's Mexican American women in World War II. RENATO ROSALDO LECTURE SERIES MONOGRAPH, Vol. 1, (Summer 1985), p. [5]-18. English. DESCR: Cultural Organizations; History; Organizations; *Tucson, AZ; World War II.

Assertiveness

436 Alba, Isabel Catherine. Achievement conflicts, sex-role orientation, and performance on sex-role appropriate and sex-role inappropriate tasks in women of three ethnic groups. Thesis (Ph.D.)--University of California, Riverside, 1987. 129 p. English. DESCR: Anglo Americans; Blacks; Ethnic Groups; Fear of Success Scale (FOSS); *Sex Roles; Women.

437 Gutierrez, Lorraine M. Working with women of color: an empowerment perspective. SOCIAL WORK, Vol. 35, no. 2 (March 1990), p. 149-153. English. DESCR: Ethnic Groups; Feminism; Intergroup Relations; *Interpersonal Relations; *Social Work; *Women.

438 Jaramillo, Mari-Luci. How to suceed in business and remain Chicana. LA LUZ, Vol. 8, no. 7 (August, September, 1980), p. 33-35. English. DESCR: Cultural Characteristics; Family; Identity; *Natural Support Systems; *Working Women.

439 Kimbel, Charles E.; Marsh, Nancy B.; and Kiska, Andrew C. Sex, age, and cultural differences in self-reported assertiveness. PSYCHOLOGICAL REPORTS, Vol. 55, no. 2 (October 1984), p. 419-422. English. DESCR: Cultural Characteristics; Identity; Sex Roles.

440 McClelland, Judith Raymond. The relationship of independence to achievement: a comparative study of Hispanic women. Thesis (Ph.D.)--Fielding Institute, 1988. 164 p. English. DESCR: Attitudes; California Personality Inventory (CPI); Careers; Leadership; *Management; New Mexico; Personality; *Working Women.

441 Mink, Diane Leslie. Early grandmotherhood: an exploratory study. Thesis (Ph.D.)--California School of Professional Psychology, Los Angeles, 1987. 190 p. English. DESCR: Age Groups; *Ancianos; Family; Fertility; Grandmothers; Natural Support Systems; *Sex Roles; Surveys; Youth.

442 Moore, Helen A. and Porter, Natalie K. Leadership and nonverbal behaviors of Hispanic females across school equity environments. PSYCHOLOGY OF WOMEN QUARTERLY, Vol. 12, no. 2 (June 1988), p. 147-163. English. DESCR: Language Assessment; *Leadership; Primary School Education.

443 Norinsky, Margaret Elaine. The relationship between sex-role identity and ethnicity to styles of assertiveness and aggression in women. Thesis (Ed.D.)--University of San Francisco, 1987. 164 p. English. DESCR: Anglo Americans; Blacks; Ethnic Groups; *Identity; *Sex Roles; *Women.

Assertiveness (cont.)

444 Palacios, Maria. Fear of success: Mexican-American women in two work environments. Thesis (Ph.D.)--New Mexico State University, 1988. 163 p. English. DESCR: Academic Achievement; *Careers; Income; Sex Roles; *Working Women.

445 Ramirez Boulette, Teresa. Assertive training with low income Mexican American women. IN: Miranda, Manuel R., ed. PSYCHOTHERAPY WITH THE SPANISH-SPEAKING: ISSUES IN RESEARCH AND SERVICE DELIVERY. Los Angeles, CA: Spanish Speaking Mental Health Research Center, University of California, 1976, p. 67-71. English. DESCR: Low Income.

446 Young, Gay. Gender identification and working-class solidarity among maquila workers in Ciudad Juarez: stereotypes and realities. IN: Ruiz, Vicki L. and Tiano, Susan, eds. WOMEN ON THE U.S.-MEXICO BORDER RESPONSES TO CHANGE. Boston, MA: Allen & Unwin, 1987, p. 105-127. English. DESCR: Attitudes; Border Industrialization Program (BIP); *Border Industries; Border Region; Ciudad Juarez, Chihuahua, Mexico; Employment; Garment Industry; Sex Roles; Surveys; Working Women.

Assimilation

447 Abney-Guardado, Armando J. Chicano intermarriage in the United States: a sociocultural analysis. Thesis (Ph.D.)--Notre Dame, 1983. viii, 142 p. English. DESCR: *Acculturation; *Intermarriage.

448 Canino, Glorisa. The Hispanic woman: sociocultural influences on diagnoses and treatment. IN: Becerra, Rosina M., et al., eds. MENTAL HEALTH AND HISPANIC AMERICANS: CLINICAL PERSPECTIVES. New York: Grune & Stratton, 1982, p. 117-138. English. DESCR: Cultural Characteristics; Culture; *Depression (Psychological); Family; Feminism; Mental Health; Population; Sex Roles.

449 Craver, Rebecca McDowel. The impact of intimacy: Mexican-Anglo intermarriage in New Mexico 1821-1846. SOUTHWESTERN STUDIES, no. 66 (1982), p. 1-79. English. DESCR: Acculturation; Anglo Americans; History; *Intermarriage; New Mexico; Rio Arriba Valley, NM.

450 Craver, Rebecca McDowell. The impact of intimacy: Mexican-Anglo intermarriage in New Mexico 1821-1846. El Paso, TX: Texas Western Press, University of Texas at El Paso, 1982. 79 p. English. DESCR: Acculturation; Anglo Americans; History; *Intermarriage; New Mexico; Rio Arriba Valley, NM.

451 Fischer, Nancy A. and Marcum, John P. Ethnic integration, socioeconomic status, and fertility among Mexican Americans. SOCIAL SCIENCE QUARTERLY, Vol. 55, no. 2 (June 1984), p. 583-593. English. DESCR: *Fertility; Identity; Socioeconomic Factors.

452 Garcia, Mario T. La familia: the Mexican immigrant family, 1900-1930. IN: Barrera, Mario, et al., eds. WORK FAMILY, SEX ROLES, LANGUAGE: SELECTED PAPERS, 1979. Berkeley, CA: Tonatiuh-Quinto Sol, 1980, p. 117-139. English. DESCR: Cultural Customs; El Paso, TX; Family; *Historiography; History; Immigration; Labor; Sex Roles.

453 Gurak, Douglas T. Assimilation and fertility: a comparison of Mexican American and Japanese American women. HISPANIC JOURNAL OF BEHAVIORAL SCIENCES, Vol. 2, no. 3 (September 1980), p. 219-239. English. DESCR: Asian Americans; *Fertility; Japanese; Population; Women.

454 Kearl, Michael C. and Murguia, Edward. Age differences of spouses in Mexican American intermarriage: exploring the cost of minority assimilation. SOCIAL SCIENCE QUARTERLY, Vol. 66, no. 2 (June 1985), p. 453-460. English. DESCR: *Age Groups; *Intermarriage.

455 Lampe, Philip E. Female Mexican Americans: minority within a minority. BORDERLANDS JOURNAL, Vol. 6, no. 2 (Spring 1983), p. 99-109. English. DESCR: Identity.

456 Macklin, June and Teniente de Costilla, Alvina. Virgen de Guadalupe and the American dream: the melting pot bubbles on in Toledo, Ohio. IN: West, Stanley A. and Macklin, June, eds. THE CHICANO EXPERIENCE. Boulder, CO: Westview Press, 1979, p. 111-143. English. DESCR: Catholic Church; *Identity; Intermarriage; La Virgen de Guadalupe; Migration Patterns; Quinceaneras; Toledo, OH.

457 Miller, Darlis A. Cross-cultural marriages in the Southwest: the New Mexico experience, 1846-1900. NEW MEXICO HISTORICAL REVIEW, Vol. 57, no. 4 (October 1982), p. 335-359. English. DESCR: Attitudes; Ethnic Groups; *Intermarriage; New Mexico; Social History and Conditions.

458 Murguia, Edward. Chicano intermarriage: a theoretical and empirical study. San Antonio, TX: Trinity University Press, 1982. xiv, 134 p. English. DESCR: Attitudes; Ethnic Groups; *Intermarriage; Military; Social Classes; Weddings.

459 Salgado de Snyder, Nelly and Padilla, Amado M. Interethnic marriages of Mexican Americans after nearly two decades. [Los Angeles, CA]: Spanish Speaking Mental Health Research Center, 1985. 43 p. English. DESCR: Intergroup Relations; *Intermarriage; Los Angeles, CA.

460 Sanchez, George J. "Go after the women": Americanization and the Mexican immigrant woman, 1915-1929. Stanford, CA: Stanford Center for Chicano Research [1984?]. [32] leaves. English. DESCR: Acculturation; Biculturalism; *Immigrants; Social History and Conditions; Values; Women.

461 Sanchez, George J. "Go after the women": Americanization and the Mexican immigrant woman, 1915-1929. IN: DuBois, Ellen Carol and Ruiz, Vicki L., eds. UNEQUAL SISTERS: A MULTICULTURAL READER IN U.S. WOMEN'S HISTORY. New York: Routledge, 1990, p. 250-263. English. DESCR: Acculturation; Biculturalism; *Immigrants; Social History and Conditions; Values; Women.

462 Stephen, Elizabeth H. At the crossroads: fertility of Mexican-American women. New York: Garland Publishers, 1989. v, 184 p.: ill. English. DESCR: *Fertility; Immigration; *Population.

Assimilation (cont.)

463 Williams, Norma. Changes in funeral patterns and gender roles among Mexican Americans. IN: Ruiz, Vicki L. and Tiano, Susan, eds. WOMEN ON THE U.S.-MEXICO BORDER: RESPONSES TO CHANGE. Boston, MA: Allen & Unwin, 1987, p. 197-217. English. DESCR: Austin, TX; Cultural Customs; *Funerals; Sex Roles.

464 Yinger, Milton J. Assimilation in the United States: the Mexican-Americans. IN: Conner, Walker, ed. MEXICAN-AMERICANS IN COMPARATIVE PERSPECTIVE. Washington, DC: Urban Institute Press, 1985, p. 30-55. English. DESCR: Acculturation; Culture of Poverty Model; Identity; Intermarriage.

Attitudes

465 Amaro, Hortensia. Abortion use and attitudes among Chicanas: the need for research. RESEARCH BULLETIN (SPANISH SPEAKING MENTAL HEALTH RES. CENTER), Vol. 4, no. 3 (March 1980), p. 1-5. English. DESCR: *Abortion; Birth Control; Family Planning; Fertility; Literature Reviews; Mental Health.

466 Amaro, Hortensia. Considerations for prevention of HIV infection among Hispanic women. PSYCHOLOGY OF WOMEN QUARTERLY, Vol. 12, no. 4 (December 1988), p. 429-443. English. DESCR: *AIDS (Disease); Population; *Women.

467 Amaro, Hortensia. Psychosocial determinants of abortion attitudes among Mexican American women. Thesis (Ph.D.)--University of Calfornia, Los Angeles, 1982. 264 p. English. DESCR: *Abortion.

468 Amaro, Hortensia. Women in the Mexican-American community: religion, culture, and reproductive attitudes and experiences. JOURNAL OF COMMUNITY PSYCHOLOGY, Vol. 16, no. 1 (January 1988), p. 6-20. English. DESCR: Abortion; Birth Control; Family Planning; *Fertility; Religion.

469 Bean, Frank D. and Bradshaw, Benjamin S. Mexican American fertility. IN: Teller, Charles H., et al., eds. CUANTOS SOMOS: A DEMOGRAPHIC STUDY OF THE MEXICAN AMERICAN POPULATION. Austin, TX: Center for Mexican American Studies, University of Texas at Austin, 1977, p. 101-130. English. DESCR: Birth Control; *Fertility; Income; Population; Religion.

470 Becerra, Rosina M. and de Anda, Diane. Pregnancy and motherhood among Mexican American adolescents. HEALTH AND SOCIAL WORK, Vol. 9, no. 2 (Spring 1984), p. 106-23. English. DESCR: Acculturation; Anglo Americans; Birth Control; *Fertility; Natural Support Systems; *Youth.

471 Berger, Peggy S. Differences in importance of and satisfaction from job characteristics by sex and occupational type among Mexican-American employees. JOURNAL OF VOCATIONAL BEHAVIOR, Vol. 28, no. 3 (June 1986), p. 203-213. English. DESCR: *Employment; *Sex Roles.

472 Buriel, Raymond, et al. Mexican-American disciplinary practices and attitudes toward child maltreatment:a comparison of foreign and native-born mothers. HISPANIC JOURNAL OF BEHAVIORAL SCIENCES, Vol. 13, no. 1 (February 1991), p. 78-94. English. DESCR: *Child Abuse; Immigrants; *Parent and Child Relationships; *Parenting; Values; Violence.

473 Campoamor, Diana. Gender gap in politics: no laughing matter. VISTA, Vol. 4, no. 8 (October 24, 1988), p. 14. English. DESCR: Essays; Politics; *Women Men Relations.

474 Carrillo-Beron, Carmen. Raza mental health: perspectivas femeniles. IN: PERSPECTIVAS EN CHICANO STUDIES: PAPERS PRESENTED AT THE THIRD ANNUAL MEETING OF THE NATIONAL ASSOCIATION OF CHICANO SOCIAL SCIENCE, 1975. Los Angeles, CA: National Association of Chicano Social Science, 1977, p. 69-80. English. DESCR: Centro de Salud Mental, Oakland, CA; Conferences and Meetings; *Mental Health; Mujeres de Hoy Conference (Oakland, CA).

475 Cuellar, Israel. Service delivery and mental health services for Chicano elders. IN: Miranda, Manuel and Ruiz, Rene A., eds. CHICANO AGING AND MENTAL HEALTH. Rockville, MD: U.S. Department of Health and Human Services, 1981, p. 185-211. English. DESCR: *Ancianos; Cultural Customs; Cultural Pluralism; Language Usage; Mental Health; Mental Health Clinics; Religion; Sex Roles; Spanish Language.

476 de Anda, Diane; Becerra, Rosina M.; and Fielder, Eve P. Sexuality, pregnancy, and motherhood among Mexican-American adolescents. JOURNAL OF ADOLESCENT RESEARCH, Vol. 3, no. 3-4 (Fall, Winter, 1988), p. 403-411. English. DESCR: Anglo Americans; Birth Control; *Fertility; Sex Education; *Sexual Behavior; Women; *Youth.

477 Dungy, Claibourne I. Breast feeding preference of Hispanic and Anglo women. CLINICAL PEDIATRICS, Vol. 28, no. 2 (February 1989), p. 92-94. English. DESCR: Anglo Americans; *Breastfeeding; Women.

478 Eisen, Marvin. Factors discriminating pregnancy resolution decisions of unmarried adolescents. GENETIC PSYCHOLOGY MONOGRAPHS, Vol. 108, no. 1 (August 1983), p. 69-95. English. DESCR: Abortion; Decision Making; *Fertility; *Single Parents; *Youth.

479 Eisen, Marvin and Zellman, Gail L. Factors predicting pregnancy resolution decision satisfaction of unmarried adolescents. JOURNAL OF GENETIC PSYCHOLOGY, Vol. 145, no. 2 (December 1984), p. 231-239. English. DESCR: Abortion; Anglo Americans; Counseling (Psychological); Family Planning; *Fertility; Youth.

480 Enriquez-White, Celia. Attitudes of Hispanic and Anglo women managers toward women in management. Thesis (Ed.D.)--University of La Verne, 1982. 103 p. English. DESCR: Anglo Americans; Leadership; *Management; Women.

481 Estrada, Rosa Omega. A study of the attitudes of Texas Mexican American women toward higher education. Thesis (Ed.D.)--Baylor University, 1985. 280 p. English. DESCR: Education; *Higher Education; Texas.

482 Flaskerud, Jacquelyn H. and Nyamathi, Adeline M. Black and Latina womens' AIDS related knowledge, attitudes, and practices. RESEARCH IN NURSING AND HEALTH, Vol. 12, no. 6 (December 1989), p. 339-346. English. DESCR: *AIDS (Disease); *Blacks; Health Education; Los Angeles County, CA; Surveys; *Women.

Attitudes (cont.)

483 Garcia, Chris; Guerro, Connie Destito; and Mendez, Irene. La violacion sexual: the reality of rape. AGENDA, Vol. 8, no. 5 (September, October, 1978), p. 10-11. English. DESCR: Los Angeles, CA; *Rape.

484 Gilbert, M. Jean. Alcohol consumption patterns in immigrant and later generation Mexican American women. HISPANIC JOURNAL OF BEHAVIORAL SCIENCES, Vol. 9, no. 3 (September 1987), p. 299-313. English. DESCR: Acculturation; *Alcoholism; Cultural Characteristics; *Immigrants; Mexico.

485 Gonzalez, Alex. Sex roles of the traditional Mexican family: a comparison of Chicano and Anglo students' attitudes. JOURNAL OF CROSS-CULTURAL PSYCHOLOGY, Vol. 13, no. 3 (September 1982), p. 330-339. English. DESCR: Anglo Americans; Comparative Psychology; *Family; Hembrismo; Machismo; Sex Roles; Students.

486 Hawley, Peggy and Even, Brenda. Work and sex-role attitudes in relation to education and other characteristics. VOCATIONAL GUIDANCE QUARTERLY, Vol. 31, no. 2 (December 1982), p. 101-108. English. DESCR: Careers; Education; Ethnic Groups; Psychological Testing; *Sex Roles; Working Women.

487 Jorgensen, Stephen R. and Adams, Russell P. Family planning needs and behavior of Mexican American women: a study of health care professionals and their clientele. HISPANIC JOURNAL OF BEHAVIORAL SCIENCES, Vol. 9, no. 3 (September 1987), p. 265-286. English. DESCR: Acculturation; Birth Control; *Cultural Characteristics; *Family Planning; Fertility; Medical Personnel; Stereotypes; Sterilization.

488 Krause, Neal and Markides, Kyriakos S. Employment and psychological well-being in Mexican American women. JOURNAL OF HEALTH AND SOCIAL BEHAVIOR, Vol. 26, no. 1 (March 1985), p. 15-26. English. DESCR: *Employment; Identity; Mental Health; Sex Roles; Working Women.

489 Lawrence, Alberto Augusto. Traditional attitudes toward marriage, marital adjustment, acculturation, and self-esteem of Mexican-American and Mexican wives. Thesis (Ph.D.)--United States International University, San Diego, CA, 1982. ix, 191 p. English. DESCR: *Acculturation; Machismo; *Marriage; Mental Health; Psychological Testing; San Ysidro, CA; Sex Roles; Sex Stereotypes; Tijuana, Baja California, Mexico; Women.

490 Lucero, Aileen. Chicano sex role attitudes: a comparative study of sex differences in an urban barrio. Thesis (Ph.D.)--University of Colorado at Boulder, 1980. 160 p. English. DESCR: Colorado; Males; *Sex Roles.

491 Maez, Angelita. The effects of two parent training programs on parental attitudes and self-concepts of Mexican American mothers. Thesis (Ph.D.)--UCLA, 1987. xiv, 184 leaves. English. DESCR: Family; *Parenting.

492 Major, Linda Borsch. The psyche: changing role creates Latina's world of conflict. AGENDA, no. 4 (Spring 1974), p. 6-7. English. DESCR: *Identity

493 Mary, Nancy L. Reactions of Black, Hispanic, and white mothers to having a child with handicaps. MENTAL RETARDATION, Vol. 28, no. 1 (February 1990), p. 1-5. English. DESCR: Anglo Americans; Blacks; *Children; Comparative Psychology; *Mentally Handicapped; Parent and Child Relationships; *Women.

494 McClelland, Judith Raymond. The relationship of independence to achievement: a comparative study of Hispanic women. Thesis (Ph.D.)--Fielding Institute, 1988. 164 p. English. DESCR: *Assertiveness; California Personality Inventory (CPI); Careers; Leadership; *Management; New Mexico; Personality; *Working Women.

495 Medina Gonzales, Esther. Sisterhood. LA LUZ, Vol. 4, no. 5 (September, October, 1975), p. 7. English. DESCR: *Discrimination; *Sexism.

496 Melville, Margarita B. Mexican women adapt to migration. IN: Rios-Bustamante, Antonio, ed. MEXICAN IMMIGRANT WORKERS IN THE U.S. Los Angeles, CA: Chicano Studies Research Center Publications, University of California, 1981, p. 119-124. English. DESCR: Acculturation; Immigrants; Sex Roles; Stress; *Undocumented Workers.

497 Miller, Darlis A. Cross-cultural marriages in the Southwest: the New Mexico experience, 1846-1900. NEW MEXICO HISTORICAL REVIEW, Vol. 57, no. 4 (October 1982), p. 335-359. English. DESCR: Assimilation; Ethnic Groups; *Intermarriage; New Mexico; Social History and Conditions.

498 Munoz, Daniel G. Identifying areas of stress for Chicano undergraduates. IN: Olivas, Michael A., ed. LATINO COLLEGE STUDENTS. New York: Teachers College Press, 1986, p. 131-156. English. DESCR: Academic Achievement; Colleges and Universities; Financial Aid; *Stress; Surveys.

499 Murguia, Edward. Chicano intermarriage: a theoretical and empirical study. San Antonio, TX: Trinity University Press, 1982. xiv, 134 p. English. DESCR: Assimilation; Ethnic Groups; *Intermarriage; Military; Social Classes; Weddings.

500 Myres, Sandra Lynn. Mexican Americans and westering Anglos: a feminine perspective. NEW MEXICO HISTORICAL REVIEW, Vol. 57, no. 4 (October 1982), p. 317-333. English. DESCR: Anglo Americans; *Ethnic Groups; Social History and Conditions; Southwestern United States; Stereotypes.

501 O'Guinn, Thomas C.; Imperia, Giovanna; and MacAdams, Elizabeth A. Acculturation and perceived family decision-making input among Mexican American wives. JOURNAL OF CROSS-CULTURAL PSYCHOLOGY, Vol. 18, no. 1 (March 1987), p. 78-92. English. DESCR: *Acculturation; Consumers; Family; Sex Roles.

502 Ortiz, Sylvia. An analysis of the relationship between the values of sexual regulation, male dominance, and motherhood, and Mexican-American women's attitudes, knowledge, and usage of birth control. Thesis (Ph.D.)--University of California, Santa Barbara, 1987. 128 p. English. DESCR: Acculturation; *Birth Control; *Family Planning; Sexual Behavior.

Attitudes (cont.)

503 Ortiz, Sylvia and Casas, Jesus Manuel. Birth control and low-income Mexican-American women: the impact of three values. HISPANIC JOURNAL OF BEHAVIORAL SCIENCES, Vol. 12, no. 1 (February 1990), p. 83-92. English. **DESCR:** Acculturation; *Birth Control; Fertility; *Low Income; *Sex Roles; Values.

504 Ortiz, Vilma and Cooney, Rosemary Santana. Sex-role attitudes and labor force participation among young Hispanic females and non-Hispanic white females. SOCIAL SCIENCE QUARTERLY, Vol. 65, no. 2 (June 1984), p. 392-400. English. **DESCR:** Anglo Americans; Employment; *Sex Roles; Working Women.

505 Ortiz, Vilma and Cooney, Rosemary Santana. Sex-role attitudes and labor force participation among young Hispanic females and non-Hispanic white females. IN: O. de la Garza, Rodolfo, et al., eds. THE MEXICAN AMERICAN EXPERIENCE: AN INTERDISCIPLINARY ANTHOLOGY. Austin, TX: University of Texas Press, 1985, p. 174-182. English. **DESCR:** Anglo Americans; Employment; *Sex Roles; Working Women.

506 Padilla, Amado M. and Baird, Traci L. Mexican-American adolescent sexuality and sexual knowledge: an exploratory study. HISPANIC JOURNAL OF BEHAVIORAL SCIENCES, Vol. 13, no. 1 (February 1991), p. 95-104. English. **DESCR:** *Birth Control; Sex Roles; *Sexual Behavior; Surveys; *Youth.

507 Padilla, Eligio R. and O'Grady, Kevin E. Sexuality among Mexican Americans: a case of sexual stereotyping. JOURNAL OF PERSONALITY AND SOCIAL PSYCHOLOGY, Vol. 52, no. 1 (1987), p. 5-10. English. **DESCR:** Age Groups; Anglo Americans; California; Religion; *Sex Roles; *Sex Stereotypes; Sexual Behavior; Sexual Knowledge and Attitude Test; *Stereotypes; Students; Values.

508 Phillips, Melody. The Chicana: her attitudes towards the woman's liberation movement. COMADRE, no. 2 (Spring 1978), p. 42-50. English. **DESCR:** *Feminism; Sexism.

509 Romero, Gloria J. and Garza, Raymond T. Attributions for the occupational success/failure of ethnic minority and nonminority women. SEX ROLES, Vol. 14, no. 7-8 (April 1986), p. 445-452. English. **DESCR:** Anglo Americans; Careers; Identity; Sociology; Women.

510 Romero, Gloria J.; Cervantes, Richard C.; and Castro, Felipe G. Long-term stress among Latino women after a plant closure. SOCIOLOGY & SOCIAL RESEARCH, Vol. 71, no. 2 (January 1987), p. 85-88. English. **DESCR:** Employment; Family; *Stress; Wilmington, CA.

511 Roraback, Rosanne Lisa. The effects of occupational type, educational level, marital status, and race/ethnicity on women's attitudes towards feminist issues. Thesis (M.A.)--Michigan State University, 1988. 62 p. English. **DESCR:** Abortion; Equal Rights Amendment (ERA); *Feminism; Identity; *Women.

512 Rosenhouse-Persson, Sandra and Sabagh, Georges. Attitudes toward abortion among Catholic Mexican-American women: the effects of religiosity and education. DEMOGRAPHY, Vol. 20, no. 1 (February 1983), p. 87-98. English. **DESCR:** Abortion; *Catholic Church; Education; Religion.

513 Sabogal, Fabio, et al. Hispanic familism and acculturation: what changes and what doesn't? HISPANIC JOURNAL OF BEHAVIORAL SCIENCES, Vol. 9, no. 4 (December 1987), p. 397-412. English. **DESCR:** *Acculturation; Cultural Characteristics; Ethnic Groups; Extended Family; *Family; Natural Support Systems; Values.

514 Sex education, abortion views of Mexican Americans typical of U.S. beliefs. FAMILY PLANNING PERSPECTIVES, Vol. 15, (July, August, 1983), p. 197-201. English. **DESCR:** *Abortion; Birth Control; Family Planning; *Sex Education.

515 Shapiro, Johanna and Saltzer, Eleanor B. Attitudes toward breast-feeding among Mexican-American women. JOURNAL OF TROPICAL PEDIATRICS, Vol. 31, no. 1 (February 1985), p. 13-16. English. **DESCR:** *Breastfeeding.

516 Simoniello, Katina. On investigating the attitudes toward achievement and success in eight professional U.S. Mexican women. AZTLAN, Vol. 12, no. 1 (Spring 1981), p. 121-137. English. **DESCR:** *Sex Stereotypes.

517 Torres, Sara. A comparative analysis of wife abuse among Anglo-American and Mexican-American battered women: attitudes, nature, severity, frequency and response to the abuse. Thesis (Ph.D.)--University of Texas, Austin, 1986. 265 p. English. **DESCR:** Anglo Americans; Battered Women; Family; *Violence; *Women.

518 Vazquez-Nuttall, Ena; Romero-Garcia, Ivonne; and De Leon, Brunilda. Sex roles and perceptions of femininity and masculinity of Hispanic women: a review of the literature. PSYCHOLOGY OF WOMEN QUARTERLY, Vol. 11, no. 4 (December 1987), p. 409-425. English. **DESCR:** *Chicanismo; *Literature Reviews; Machismo; Puerto Ricans; *Sex Roles; *Women.

519 Weller, Susan C. and Dungy, Claibourne I. Personal preferences and ethnic variations among Anglo and Hispanic breast and bottle feeders. SOCIAL SCIENCE & MEDICINE, Vol. 23, no. 6 (1986), p. 539-548. English. **DESCR:** *Breastfeeding; *Maternal and Child Welfare; Orange, CA; Parenting; Socioeconomic Factors.

520 White, Marni, et al. Perceived crime in the neighborhood and mental health of women and children. ENVIRONMENT AND BEHAVIOR, Vol. 19, no. 5 (September 1987), p. 588-613. English. **DESCR:** Children; Criminology; Housing; *Mental Health; Women.

521 Williams, Joyce E. Mexican American and Anglo attitudes about sex roles and rape. FREE INQUIRY IN CREATIVE SOCIOLOGY, Vol. 13, no. 1 (May 1985), p. 15-20. English. **DESCR:** Anglo Americans; *Feminism; *Rape; *Sex Roles; Women.

522 Williams, Joyce E. Secondary victimization: confronting public attitudes about rape. VICTIMOLOGY, Vol. 9, no. 1 (1984), p. 66-81. English. **DESCR:** Natural Support Systems; *Rape; San Antonio, TX.

Attitudes (cont.)

523 Ybarra, Lea. Separating a myth from reality: socio-economic and cultural influences on Chicanas and the world of work. IN: Melville, Margarita, ec. MEXICANAS AT WORK IN THE UNITED STATES. Houston, TX: Mexican American Studies Program, University of Houston, 1988, p. 12-23. English. DESCR: *Cultural Characteristics; Income; Machismo; Sex Roles; *Socioeconomic Factors; Stereotypes; *Working Women.

524 Young, Gay. Gender identification and working-class solidarity among maquila workers in Ciudad Juarez: stereotypes and realities. IN: Ruiz, Vicki L. and Tiano, Susan, eds. WOMEN ON THE U.S.-MEXICO BORDER: RESPONSES TO CHANGE. Boston, MA: Allen & Unwin, 1987, p. 105-127. English. DESCR: Assertiveness; Border Industrialization Program (BIP); *Border Industries; Border Region; Ciudad Juarez, Chihuahua, Mexico; Employment; Garment Industry; Sex Roles; Surveys; Working Women.

Aurora, IL

525 Campos Carr, Irene. Proyecto La Mujer: Latina women shaping consciousness. WOMEN'S STUDIES INTERNATIONAL FORUM, Vol. 12, no. 1 (1989), p. 45-49. English. DESCR: Artists; Authors; Barrios; Conferences and Meetings; Elgin, IL; *Feminism; Joliet, IL; Poetry; Proyecto La Mujer Conference (Spring, 1982: Northern Illinois); Women.

Austin, TX

526 Williams, Norma. Changes in funeral patterns and gender roles among Mexican Americans. IN: Ruiz, Vicki L. and Tiano, Susan, eds. WOMEN ON THE U.S.-MEXICO BORDER: RESPONSES TO CHANGE. Boston, MA: Allen & Unwin, 1987, p. 197-217. English. DESCR: Assimilation; Cultural Customs; *Funerals; Sex Roles.

527 Williams, Norma. Role making among married Mexican American women: issues of class and ethnicity. JOURNAL OF APPLIED BEHAVIORAL SCIENCE, Vol. 24, no. 2 (1988), p. 203-217. English. DESCR: Corpus Christi, TX; Identity; Marriage; *Sex Roles; Social Classes.

Authors

528 Aguilar-Henson, Marcella. The multi-faceted poetic world of Angela de Hoyos. Austin, TX: Relampago Books Press, 1985, c1982. 81 p. English. DESCR: ARISE CHICANO; CHICANO POEMS FOR THE BARRIO; de Hoyos, Angela; GATA POEMS; GOODBYE TO SILENCE; Language Usage; *Literary Criticism; *Poetry; SELECTED POEMS/SELECCIONES; YO, MUJER.

529 Alarcon, Justo S. and Martinez, Julio A. [Bornstein-Somoza, Miriam]. IN: Martinez, Julio A. and Lomeli, Francisco A., eds. CHICANO LITERATURE: A REFERENCE GUIDE. Westport, CT: Greenwood Press, 1985, p. 74-77. English. DESCR: Biography; Bornstein-Somoza, Miriam; Literary Criticism.

530 Alarcon, Norma and Moraga, Cherrie. Interview with Cherrie Moraga. THIRD WOMAN, Vol. 3, no. 1-2 (1986), p. 127-134. English. DESCR: Biography; Homosexuality; *Moraga, Cherrie; Sex Roles.

531 Alarcon, Norma and Mora, Pat. Interview with Pat Mora. THIRD WOMAN, Vol. 3, no. 1-2 (1986), p. 121-126. English. DESCR: Biography; *Mora, Pat.

532 Alarcon, Norma. Latina writers in the United States. IN: Marting, Diane E., ed. SPANISH AMERICAN WOMEN WRITERS: A BIO-BIBLIOGRAPHICAL SOURCE BOOK. New York: Greenwood Press, 1990, p. [557]-567. English. DESCR: *Bibliography; BREAKING BOUNDARIES: LATINA WRITING AND CRITICAL READINGS; Cubanos; Intergroup Relations; Language Usage; *Literature Reviews; Puerto Ricans; THIRD WOMAN [journal]; *Women.

533 Binder, Wolfgang, ed. Partial autobiographies: interviews with twenty Chicano poets. Erlangen: Verlag Palm & Enke, 1985. xviii, 263 p. English. DESCR: *Autobiography; *Poetry.

534 Bornstein de Somoza, Miriam. La poetica chicana: vision panoramica. LA PALABRA, Vol. 2, no. 2 (Fall 1980), p. 43-66. Spanish. DESCR: *Literary Criticism; Literary Influence; *Poetry.

535 Bouknight, Jon. Language as a cure: an interview with Milcha Sanchez-Scott. LATIN AMERICAN THEATRE REVIEW, Vol. 23, no. 2 (Spring 1990), p. 63-74. English. DESCR: Actos; ROOSTERS [play]; Sanchez-Scott, Milcha; *Teatro.

536 Brinson-Pineda, Barbara and Binder, Wolfgang. [Interview with] Barbara Brinson-Pineda. IN: Binder, Wolfgang, ed. PARTIAL AUTOBIOGRAPHIES: INTERVIEWS WITH TWENTY CHICANO POETS. Erlangen, W. Germany: Verlag Palm & Enke, 1985, p. 16-27. English. DESCR: Autobiography; *Brinson-Pineda, Barbara; Poetry.

537 Bruce-Novoa, Juan. Bernice Zamora y Lorna Dee Cervantes: una estetica feminista. REVISTA IBEROAMERICANA, Vol. 51, (July, December, 1985), p. 565-573. English. DESCR: *Cervantes, Lorna Dee; EMPLUMADA; Literary Criticism; Poetry; RESTLESS SERPENTS; *Zamora, Bernice.

538 Campos Carr, Irene. Proyecto La Mujer: Latina women shaping consciousness. WOMEN'S STUDIES INTERNATIONAL FORUM, Vol. 12, no. 1 (1989), p. 45-49. English. DESCR: Artists; Aurora, IL; Barrios; Conferences and Meetings; Elgin, IL; *Feminism; Joliet, IL; Poetry; Proyecto La Mujer Conference (Spring, 1982: Northern Illinois); Women.

539 Castillo, Ana and Binder, Wolfgang. [Interview with] Ana Castillo. IN: Binder, Wolfgang, ed. PARTIAL AUTOBIOGRAPHIES: INTERVIEWS WITH TWENTY CHICANO POETS. Erlangen, W. Germany: Verlag Palm & Enke, 1985, p. 28-38. English. DESCR: Autobiography; *Castillo, Ana; Poetry.

540 Cervantes, Lorna Dee and Binder, Wolfgang. [Interview with] Lorna Dee Cervantes. IN: Binder, Wolfgang, ed. PARTIAL AUTOBIOGRAPHIES: INTERVIEWS WITH TWENTY CHICANO POETS. Erlangen, W. Germany: Verlag Palm & Enke, 1985, p. 39-53. English. DESCR: Autobiography; *Cervantes, Lorna Dee; Poetry.

541 Chavez, Denise. Heat and rain (testimonio). IN: Horno-Delgado, Asuncion, et al., eds. BREAKING BOUNDARIES: LATINA WRITING AND CRITICAL READINGS. Amherst, MA: University of Massachusetts Press, c1989, p. 27-32. English. DESCR: *Autobiography; Chavez, Denise; Essays.

Authors (cont.)

542 Cisneros, Sandra. Cactus flowers: in search of Tejana feminist poetry. THIRD WOMAN, Vol. 3, no. 1-2 (1986), p. 73-80. English. **DESCR:** *Feminism; Literary Criticism; *Poetry; Texas.

543 Cisneros, Sandra. Do you know me?: I wrote THE HOUSE ON MANGO STREET. THE AMERICAS REVIEW, Vol. 15, no. 1 (Spring 1987), p. 77-79. English. **DESCR:** Autobiography; Cisneros, Sandra; *Prose; THE HOUSE ON MANGO STREET.

544 Cisneros, Sandra. Ghosts and voices: writing from obsession. THE AMERICAS REVIEW, Vol. 15, no. 1 (Spring 1987), p. 69-73. English. **DESCR:** Autobiography; Cisneros, Sandra; *Prose.

545 Cisneros, Sandra and Binder, Wolfgang. [Interview with] Sandra Cisneros. IN: Binder, Wolfgang, ed. PARTIAL AUTOBIOGRAPHIES: INTERVIEWS WITH TWENTY CHICANO POETS. Erlangen, W. Germany: Verlag Palm & Enke, 1985, p. 54-74. English. **DESCR:** Autobiography; *Cisneros, Sandra; Poetry.

546 Cisneros, Sandra. Living as a writer: choice and circumstance. REVISTA MUJERES, Vol. 3, no. 2 (June 1986), p. 68-72. English. **DESCR:** Autobiography; Cisneros, Sandra.

547 Cisneros, Sandra. Notes to a young(er) writer. THE AMERICAS REVIEW, Vol. 15, no. 1 (Spring 1987), p. 74-76. English. **DESCR:** Autobiography; Cisneros, Sandra; *Prose.

548 Corpi, Lucha and Binder, Wolfgang. [Interview with] Lucha Corpi. IN: Binder, Wolfgang, ed. PARTIAL AUTOBIOGRAPHIES: INTERVIEWS WITH TWENTY CHICANO POETS. Erlangen, W. Germany: Verlag Palm & Enke, 1985, p. 75-85. English. **DESCR:** Autobiography; *Corpi, Lucha; Poetry.

549 Cunningham, Veronica and Binder, Wolfgang. [Interview with] Veronica Cunningham. IN: Binder, Wolfgang, ed. PARTIAL AUTOBIOGRAPHIES: INTERVIEWS WITH TWENTY CHICANO POETS. Erlangen, W. Germany: Verlag Palm & Enke, 1985, p. 86-92. English. **DESCR:** Autobiography; *Cunningham, Veronica; Poetry.

550 de Hoyos, Angela and Binder, Wolfgang. [Interview with] Angela de Hoyos. IN: Binder, Wolfgang, ed. PARTIAL AUTOBIOGRAPHIES: INTERVIEWS WITH TWENTY CHICANO POETS. Erlangen, W. Germany: Verlag Palm & Enke, 1985, p. 109-116. English. **DESCR:** Autobiography; *de Hoyos, Angela; Poetry.

551 de Lotbiniere-Harwood, Susanne and Anzaldua, Gloria. Conversations at the Book Fair: interview with Gloria Anzaldua. TRIVIA: A JOURNAL OF IDEAS, no. 14 (Spring 1989), p. 37-45. English. **DESCR:** *Anzaldua, Gloria; Biography; Feminism; Literary Criticism.

552 Del Rio, Carmen M. Chicana poets: re-visions from the margin. REVISTA CANADIENSE DE ESTUDIOS HISPANICOS, Vol. 14, no. 3 (Spring 1990), p. 431-445. English. **DESCR:** *Feminism; *Literary Criticism; *Poetry; Tafolla, Carmen; Villanueva, Alma.

553 Eger, Ernestina. A bibliography of criticism of contemporary Chicano literature. Berkeley, CA: Chicano Studies Library Publications Unit, 1982. xxi, 295 p.

English. **DESCR:** *Bibliography; *Literary Criticism; Literature.

554 Gonzales, Rebecca and Binder, Wolfgang. [Interview with] Rebecca Gonzales. IN: Binder, Wolfgang, ed. PARTIAL AUTOBIOGRAPHIES: INTERVIEWS WITH TWENTY CHICANO POETS. Erlangen, W. Germany: Verlag Palm & Enke, 1985, p. 93-94. English. **DESCR:** Autobiography; *Gonzales, Rebecca; Poetry.

555 Gonzalez, LaVerne. [Portillo Trambley, Estela]. IN: Martinez, Julio A. and Lomeli, Francisco A., eds. CHICANO LITERATURE: A REFERENCE GUIDE. Westport, CT: Greenwood Press, 1985, p. 316-322. English. **DESCR:** Biography; Literary Criticism; *Portillo Trambley, Estela.

556 Gonzalez, Maria R. El embrion nacionalista visto a traves de la obra de Sor Juana Ines de la Cruz. IN: Del Castillo, Adelaida R., ed. BETWEEN BORDERS: ESSAYS ON MEXICANA/CHICANA HISTORY. Encino, CA: Floricanto Press, 1990, p. 239-253. Spanish. **DESCR:** *Juana Ines de la Cruz, Sor; Mexico; *Nationalism; Women.

557 Hernandez, Ines. Sara Estela Ramirez: the early twentieth century Texas-Mexican poet. Thesis (Ph.D.)--University of Houston, 1984. 94 p. English. **DESCR:** *Biography; Feminism; Flores Magon, Ricardo; Journalism; Literary Criticism; Mexican Revolution - 1910-1920; Mexico; *Poetry; Ramirez, Sara Estela; Texas; Women.

558 Hernandez, Ines. Sara Estela Ramirez: sembradora. LEGACY: A JOURNAL OF NINETEENTH-CENTURY AMERICAN WOMEN WRITERS, Vol. 6, no. 1 (Spring 1989), p. 13-26. English. **DESCR:** *Biography; *Feminism; Flores Magon, Ricardo; *Journalism; LA CORREGIDORA [newspaper]; Mexican Revolution - 1910-1920; Mexico; Newspapers; Poetry; *Ramirez, Sara Estela; REGENERACION [newspaper].

559 Hispanic women writers: an interview with Rosaura Sanchez. LECTOR, Vol. 2, no. 3 (November, December, 1983), p. 5,7. English. **DESCR:** Sanchez, Rosaura.

560 Lizarraga, Sylvia S. Chicana women writers and their audience. LECTOR, Vol. 1, no. 1 (June 1982), p. 15-16,18. English. **DESCR:** Literature.

561 Lomas, Clara. Mexican precursors of Chicana feminist writing. IN: National Association for Chicano Studies. ESTUDIOS CHICANOS AND THE POLITICS OF COMMUNITY. [S.l.]: National Association for Chicano Studies, c1989, p. [149]-160. English. **DESCR:** de Cardenas, Isidra T.; *Feminism; Idar, Jovita; *Journalists; Literature; *Mexican Revolution - 1910-1920; Newspapers; Ramirez, Sara Estela; Villarreal, Andrea; Villegas de Magnon, Leonor.

562 Lomeli, Francisco A. Chicana novelists in the process of creating fictive voices. IN: Herrera-Sobek, Maria, ed. BEYOND STEREOTYPES: THE CRITICAL ANALYSIS OF CHICANA LITERATURE. Binghamton, NY: Bilingual Press/Editorial Bilingue, 1985, p. 29-46. English. **DESCR:** Literary Criticism; Literary History; *Novel.

Authors (cont.)

563 Lucero, Marcela Christine. The socio-historical implication of the valley as a metaphor in three Colorado Chicana poets. Thesis (Ph.D.)--University of Minnesota, 1981. 176 p. English. **DESCR:** Blea, Irene I.; Chicano Movement; Colorado; Feminism; Literary Criticism; Mondragon Valdez, Maria; Poetry; Zamora, Bernice.

564 Mora, Pat and Alarcon, Norma. A poet analyzes her craft. NUESTRO, Vol. 11, no. 2 (March 1987), p. 25-27. English. **DESCR:** BORDERS; CHANTS; *Mora, Pat; *Poetry.

565 Navarro, Marta A. and Castillo, Ana. Interview with Ana Castillo. IN: Trujillo, Carla, ed. CHICANA LESBIANS: THE GIRLS OUR MOTHERS WARNED US ABOUT. Berkeley, CA: Third Woman Press, 1991, p. 113-132. English. **DESCR:** Castillo, Ana; Homosexuality; Literature.

566 Ordonez, Elizabeth J. [Villanueva, Alma]. IN: Martinez, Julio A. and Lomeli, Francisco A., eds. CHICANO LITERATURE: A REFERENCE GUIDE. Westport, CT: Greenwood Press, 1985, p. 413-420. English. **DESCR:** Biography; *BLOODROOT; Literary Criticism; *Villanueva, Alma.

567 Padilla, Genaro. Imprisoned narrative? Or lies, secrets, and silence in New Mexico women's autobiography. IN: Calderon, Hector and Saldivar, Jose David, eds. CRITICISM IN THE BORDERLANDS: STUDIES IN CHICANO LITERATURE, CULTURE, AND IDEOLOGY. Durham, NC: Duke University Press, 1991, p. [43]-60. English. **DESCR:** *Autobiography; *Cabeza de Baca, Fabiola; *Jaramillo, Cleofas M.; Literary History; New Mexico; ROMANCE OF A LITTLE VILLAGE GIRL; WE FED THEM CACTUS.

568 Perez-Erdelyi, Mireya and Corpi, Lucha. Entrevista con Lucha Corpi: poeta chicana. THE AMERICAS REVIEW, Vol. 17, no. 1 (Spring 1989), p. 72-82. Spanish. **DESCR:** *Corpi, Lucha; Literature.

569 Quintana, Alvina E. Challenge and counter challenge: Chicana literary motifs. AGAINST THE CURRENT, Vol. 2, no. 2 (March, April, 1987), p. 25,28-32. English. **DESCR:** Anglo Americans; Cervantes, Lorna Dee; Cultural Studies; *Feminism; Identity; Literary Criticism; *Literature; Moraga, Cherrie; THERE ARE NO MADMEN HERE; Valdes, Gina; Women.

570 Quintana, Alvina E. Chicana discourse: negations and mediations. Thesis (Ph.D.)--University of California, Santa Cruz, 1989. 226 p. English. **DESCR:** Castillo, Ana; Chavez, Denise; Chicano Movement; Cisneros, Sandra; Ethnology; Feminism; Literary Criticism; *Literature; NOVENA NARRATIVES; Oral Tradition; Political Ideology; THE HOUSE ON MANGO STREET; THE LAST OF THE MENU GIRLS; THE MIXQUIAHUALA LETTERS.

571 Quintana, Alvina E. Chicana literary motifs: challenge and counter-challenge. IMAGES: ETHNIC STUDIES OCCASIONAL PAPERS SERIES, (Fall 1986), p. 24-41. English. **DESCR:** Anglo Americans; Cervantes, Lorna Dee; Cultural Studies; *Feminism; *Identity; *Literary Criticism; Literature; Moraga, Cherrie; THERE ARE NO MADMEN HERE; Valdes, Gina; Women.

572 Quintana, Alvina E. Politics, representation and the emergence of a Chicana aesthetic.

CULTURAL STUDIES, Vol. 4, no. 3 (October 1990), p. 257-263. English. **DESCR:** Anzaldua, Gloria; Chavez, Denise; Chicana Studies; Cisneros, Sandra; Cultural Studies; Feminism; *Literary Criticism.

573 Ramos, Luis Arturo. [Hoyos, Angela de]. IN: Martinez, Julio A. and Lomeli, Francisco A., eds. CHICANO LITERATURE: A REFERENCE GUIDE. Westport, CT: Greenwood Press, 1985, p. 260-265. English. **DESCR:** Biography; *de Hoyos, Angela; Literary Criticism.

574 Rebolledo, Tey Diana. Las escritoras: romances and realities. IN: Gonzales-Berry, Erlinda, ed. PASO POR AQUI: CRITICAL ESSAYS ON THE NEW MEXICAN LITERARY TRADITION. Albuquerque, NM: University of New Mexico Press, c1989, p. 199-214. English. **DESCR:** *Cabeza de Baca, Fabiola; *Jaramillo, Cleofas M.; Literary History; New Mexico; OLD SPAIN IN OUR SOUTHWEST; *Otero Warren, Nina; ROMANCE OF A LITTLE VILLAGE GIRL; WE FED THEM CACTUS; Women.

575 Rebolledo, Tey Diana. Hispanic women writers of the Southwest: tradition and innovation. IN: Lensink, Judy Nolte, ed. OLD SOUTHWEST/NEW SOUTHWEST: ESSAYS ON A REGION AND ITS LITERATURE. Tucson, AZ: The Tucson Public Library, 1987, p. 49-61. English. **DESCR:** Cabeza de Baca, Fabiola; Jaramillo, Cleofas M.; Literature; Mora, Pat; OLD SPAIN IN OUR SOUTHWEST; Otero Warren, Nina; Preciado Martin, Patricia; Sex Roles; Sex Stereotypes; Silva, Beverly; *Southwestern United States; Vigil-Pinon, Evangelina; WE FED THEM CACTUS; *Women.

576 Rebolledo, Tey Diana. Narrative strategies of resistance in Hispana writing. THE JOURNAL OF NARRATIVE TECHNIQUE, Vol. 20, no. 2 (Spring 1990), p. 134-146. English. **DESCR:** Cabeza de Baca, Fabiola; Fiction; Jaramillo, Cleofas M.; *Literary Criticism; Literature; New Mexico; OLD SPAIN IN OUR SOUTHWEST; *Oral Tradition; Otero Warren, Nina; ROMANCE OF A LITTLE VILLAGE GIRL; WE FED THEM CACTUS.

577 Rebolledo, Tey Diana. Tradition and mythology: signatures of landscape in Chicana literature. IN: Norwood, Vera and Mork, Janice, eds. THE DESERT IS NO LADY: SOUTHWESTERN LANDSCAPES IN WOMEN'S WRITING AND ART. New Haven, CT: Yale University Press, 1987, p. 96-124. English. **DESCR:** Cabeza de Baca, Fabiola; Chavez, Denise; Jaramillo, Cleofas M.; Literary Criticism; *Literary History; Literature; Mora, Pat; Mythology; Otero Warren, Nina; Portillo Trambley, Estela; Silva, Beverly; Southwestern United States; WE FED THEM CACTUS.

578 Rios-C., Herminio; Romano-V., Octavio Ignacio; and Portillo Trambley, Estela. Chicanas en la literatura y el arte (El Grito Book Series: Book 1, September 1973). EL GRITO, Vol. 7, no. 1 (Fall 1973), p. 1-84. Bilingual. **DESCR:** *Art; *Poems; Teatro.

Authors (cont.)

579 Saldivar, Ramon. The dialectics of subjectivity: gender and difference in Isabella Rios, Sandra Cisneros, and Cherrie Moraga. IN: Saldivar, Ramon. CHICANO NARRATIVE: THE DIALECTICS OF DIFFERENCE. Madison, WI: University of Wisconsin Press, 1990, p. 171-199. English. **DESCR:** Autobiography; *Cisneros, Sandra; Feminism; Fiction; *Literary Criticism; Literature; LOVING IN THE WAR YEARS; *Moraga, Cherrie; Political Ideology; *Rios, Isabella; THE HOUSE ON MANGO STREET; VICTUUM.

580 Sanchez, Rita. Chicana writer breaking out of the silence. DE COLORES, Vol. 3, no. 3 (1977), p. 31-37. English. **DESCR:** Castaneda Shular, Antonia; Correa, Viola; Cunningham, Veronica; Hernandez, Barbara; *Literary Criticism; Mendoza, Rita; *Poetry.

581 Sanchez, Rosaura. Chicana prose writers: the case of Gina Valdes and Sylvia Lizarraga. IN: Herrera-Sobek, Maria, ed. BEYOND STEREOTYPES: THE CRITICAL ANALYSIS OF CHICANA LITERATURE. Binghamton, NY: Bilingual Press/Editorial Bilingue, 1985, p. 61-70. English. **DESCR:** Literary Criticism; *Lizarraga, Sylvia; Prose; *Valdes, Gina.

582 Spitta, Silvia D. Literary transculturation in Latin America. Thesis (Ph.D.)--University of Oregon, 1989. 184 p. English. **DESCR:** Anzaldua, Gloria; Arguedos, Jose Maria; Cultural Characteristics; Culture; *Intergroup Relations; *Latin American Literature; Spanish Influence.

583 Tafolla, Carmen. Chicano literature: beyond beginnings. IN: Harris, Marie and Aguero, Kathleen, eds. A GIFT OF TONGUES: CRITICAL CHALLENGES IN CONTEMPORARY AMERICAN POETRY. Athens, GA: University of Georgia Press, 1987, p. 206-225. English. **DESCR:** Cota-Cardenas, Margarita; Language Usage; *Literary Criticism; *Literature; Portillo Trambley, Estela; Sex Stereotypes; Symbolism; Tafolla, Carmen; Vigil-Pinon, Evangelina.

584 Tatum, Charles M. Grappling with difference: gender, race, class, and ethnicity in contemporary Chicana/o literature. RENATO ROSALDO LECTURE SERIES MONOGRAPH, Vol. 6, (1988, 1989), p. 1-23. English. **DESCR:** Anaya, Rudolfo A.; BLESS ME, ULTIMA; *Feminism; Identity; Literary Characters; *Literary Criticism; Literature Reviews.

585 Trujillo Gaitan, Marcella. The dilemma of the modern Chicana artist and critic. HERESIES, Vol. 2, no. 4 (1979), p. 5-10. English. **DESCR:** Art Criticism; Artists; *Chicano Movement; Gonzales, Sylvia Alicia; *Literary Criticism; Machismo; Malinche; *Poetry; Symbolism.

586 Velasquez-Trevino, Gloria. Jovita Gonzalez, una voz de resistencia cultural en la temprana narrativa chicana. IN: Lopez-Gonzalez, Aralia, et al., eds. MUJER Y LITERATURA MEXICANA Y CHICANA: CULTURAS EN CONTACTO. Mexico: Colegio de la Frontera Norte, 1988, p. [77]-83. Spanish. **DESCR:** Anglo Americans; Feminism; Folklore; *Gonzalez, Jovita; Intergroup Relations; *League of United Latin American Citizens (LULAC).

587 Villanueva, Alma and Binder, Wolfgang. [Interview with] Alma Villanueva. IN: Binder, Wolfgang, ed. PARTIAL AUTOBIOGRAPHIES: INTERVIEWS WITH TWENTY CHICANO POETS. Erlangen, W. Germany: Verlag Palm & Enke, 1985, p. 201-202. English. **DESCR:** Autobiography; Poetry; *Villanueva, Alma.

588 Viramontes, Helena Maria. "Nopalitos": the making of fiction. IN: Horno-Delgado, Asuncion, et al., eds. BREAKING BOUNDARIES: LATINA WRITING AND CRITICAL READINGS. Amherst, MA: University of Massachusetts Press, c1989, p. 33-38. English. **DESCR:** *Autobiography; Essays; Viramontes, Helena Maria.

589 Woodward, Carolyn. Dare to write: Virginia Woolf, Tillie Olsen, Gloria Anzaldua. IN: Cochran, Jo Whitehorse, et al., eds. CHANGING OUR POWER: AN INTRODUCTION TO WOMEN STUDIES. Dubuque, IA: Kendall/Hunt Publishing Co., 1988, p. 336-349. English. **DESCR:** Anzaldua, Gloria; Feminism; Olsen, Tillie; Women; Woolf, Virginia.

590 Zamora, Bernice and Binder, Wolfgang. [Interview with] Bernice Zamora. IN: Binder, Wolfgang, ed. PARTIAL AUTOBIOGRAPHIES: INTERVIEWS WITH TWENTY CHICANO POETS. Erlangen, W. Germany: Verlag Palm & Enke, 1985, p. 221-229. English. **DESCR:** Autobiography; Poetry; *Zamora, Bernice.

Autobiography

591 Bello, Ruth T. Being Hispanic in Houston: a matter of identity. THE AMERICAS REVIEW, Vol. 16, no. 1 (Spring 1988), p. 31-43. English. **DESCR:** *Essays; *Houston, TX; *Identity; *Self-Referents.

592 Binder, Wolfgang, ed. Partial autobiographies: interviews with twenty Chicano poets. Erlangen: Verlag Palm & Enke, 1985. xviii, 263 p. English. **DESCR:** *Authors; *Poetry.

593 Brinson-Pineda, Barbara and Binder, Wolfgang. [Interview with] Barbara Brinson-Pineda. IN: Binder, Wolfgang, ed. PARTIAL AUTOBIOGRAPHIES: INTERVIEWS WITH TWENTY CHICANO POETS. Erlangen, W. Germany: Verlag Palm & Enke, 1985, p. 16-27. English. **DESCR:** Authors; *Brinson-Pineda, Barbara; Poetry.

594 Castillo, Ana and Binder, Wolfgang. [Interview with] Ana Castillo. IN: Binder, Wolfgang, ed. PARTIAL AUTOBIOGRAPHIES: INTERVIEWS WITH TWENTY CHICANO POETS. Erlangen, W. Germany: Verlag Palm & Enke, 1985, p. 28-38. English. **DESCR:** Authors; *Castillo, Ana; Poetry.

595 Cervantes, Lorna Dee and Binder, Wolfgang. [Interview with] Lorna Dee Cervantes. IN: Binder, Wolfgang, ed. PARTIAL AUTOBIOGRAPHIES: INTERVIEWS WITH TWENTY CHICANO POETS. Erlangen, W. Germany: Verlag Palm & Enke, 1985, p. 39-53. English. **DESCR:** Authors; *Cervantes, Lorna Dee; Poetry.

596 Chavez, Denise. Heat and rain (testimonio). IN: Horno-Delgado, Asuncion, et al., eds. BREAKING BOUNDARIES: LATINA WRITING AND CRITICAL READINGS. Amherst, MA: University of Massachusetts Press, c1989, p. 27-32. English. **DESCR:** *Authors; Chavez, Denise; Essays.

Autobiography (cont.)

597 Cisneros, Sandra. Do you know me?: I wrote
THE HOUSE ON MANGO STREET. THE AMERICAS
REVIEW, Vol. 15, no. 1 (Spring 1987), p.
77-79. English. DESCR: Authors; Cisneros,
Sandra; *Prose; THE HOUSE ON MANGO STREET.

598 Cisneros, Sandra. Ghosts and voices: writing
from obsession. THE AMERICAS REVIEW, Vol.
15, no. 1 (Spring 1987), p. 69-73. English.
DESCR: *Authors; Cisneros, Sandra; *Prose.

599 Cisneros, Sandra and Binder, Wolfgang.
[Interview with] Sandra Cisneros. IN:
Binder, Wolfgang, ed. PARTIAL
AUTOBIOGRAPHIES: INTERVIEWS WITH TWENTY
CHICANO POETS. Erlangen W. Germany: Verlag
Palm & Enke, 1985, p. 54-74. English.
DESCR: Authors; *Cisneros, Sandra; Poetry.

600 Cisneros, Sandra. Living as a writer: choice
and circumstance. REVISTA MUJERES, Vol. 3,
no. 2 (June 1986), p. 68-72. English.
DESCR: *Authors; Cisneros, Sandra.

601 Cisneros, Sandra. Notes to a young(er)
writer. THE AMERICAS REVIEW, Vol. 15, no. 1
(Spring 1987), p. 74-76. English. DESCR:
*Authors; Cisneros, Sandra; *Prose.

602 Corpi, Lucha and Binder, Wolfgang.
[Interview with] Lucha Corpi. IN: Binder,
Wolfgang, ed. PARTIAL AUTOBIOGRAPHIES:
INTERVIEWS WITH TWENTY CHICANO POETS.
Erlangen, W. Germany: Verlag Palm & Enke,
1985, p. 75-85. English. DESCR: Authors;
*Corpi, Lucha; Poetry.

603 Cunningham, Veronica and Binder, Wolfgang.
[Interview with] Veronica Cunningham. IN:
Binder, Wolfgang, ed. PARTIAL
AUTOBIOGRAPHIES: INTERVIEWS WITH TWENTY
CHICANO POETS. Erlangen, W. Germany: Verlag
Palm & Enke, 1985, p. 86-92. English.
DESCR: Authors; *Cunningham, Veronica;
Poetry.

604 de Hoyos, Angela and Binder, Wolfgang.
[Interview with] Angela de Hoyos. IN:
Binder, Wolfgang, ed. PARTIAL
AUTOBIOGRAPHIES: INTERVIEWS WITH TWENTY
CHICANO POETS. Erlangen, W. Germany: Verlag
Palm & Enke, 1985, p. 109-116. English.
DESCR: Authors; *de Hoyos, Angela; Poetry.

605 Gamio, Manuel. Senora Flores de Andrade. IN:
Mora, Magdalena and Del Castillo, Adelaida,
eds. MEXICAN WOMEN IN THE UNITED STATES:
STRUGGLES PAST AND PRESENT. Los Angeles, CA:
Chicano Studies Research Center, UCLA, 1980,
p. 189-192. English. DESCR: Flores de
Andrade, Senora; Immigrants; Mexican
Revolution - 1910-1920; *Oral History.

606 Gonzales, Rebecca and Binder, Wolfgang.
[Interview with] Rebecca Gonzales. IN:
Binder, Wolfgang, ed. PARTIAL
AUTOBIOGRAPHIES: INTERVIEWS WITH TWENTY
CHICANO POETS. Erlangen, W. Germany: Verlag
Palm & Enke, 1985, p. 93-94. English.
DESCR: Authors; *Gonzales, Rebecca; Poetry.

607 Gonzalez, Michelle. Reflexiones de una
estudiante chicana. FEM, Vol. 10, no. 48
(October, November, 1986), p. 40-41.
Spanish. DESCR: *Education.

608 Martinez, Elisa A. Sharing her tiny pieces
of the past. NUESTRO, Vol. 7, no. 7
(September 1983), p. 51-52. English. DESCR:
*Extended Family.

609 Mendoza, Lupe. Porque lo podemos hacer--a

poco no? REVISTA MUJERES, Vol. 1, no. 2
(June 1984), p. 33-37. Spanish. DESCR:
Higher Education; *Mendoza, Lupe.

610 Moraga, Cherrie. Loving in the war years: lo
que nunca paso por sus labios. Boston, MA:
South End Press, c1983. viii, 152 p.
English. DESCR: Homosexuality; Moraga,
Cherrie; *Poems.

611 Padilla, Genaro. Imprisoned narrative? Or
lies, secrets, and silence in New Mexico
women's autobiography. IN: Calderon, Hector
and Saldivar, Jose David, eds. CRITICISM IN
THE BORDERLANDS: STUDIES IN CHICANO
LITERATURE, CULTURE, AND IDEOLOGY. Durham,
NC: Duke University Press, 1991, p. [43]-60.
English. DESCR: Authors; *Cabeza de Baca,
Fabiola; *Jaramillo, Cleofas M.; Literary
History; New Mexico; ROMANCE OF A LITTLE
VILLAGE GIRL; WE FED THEM CACTUS.

612 Padilla, Genaro. "Yo sola aprendi":
contra-patriarchal containment in women's
nineteenth-century California personal
narratives. THE AMERICAS REVIEW, Vol. 16,
no. 3-4 (Fall, Winter, 1988), p. 91-109.
English. DESCR: California; *Literary
History; *Women.

613 Rips, Geoffrey and Tenayuca, Emma. Living
history: Emma Tenayuca tells her story.
TEXAS OBSERVER, (October 28, 1983), p.
7-15. English. DESCR: Communist Party; Food
Industry; Labor Unions; Leadership; Oral
History; Pecan Shelling Worker's Union, San
Antonio, TX; San Antonio, TX; Strikes and
Lockouts; Tenayuca, Emma; United Cannery
Agricultural Packing and Allied Workers of
America (UCAPAWA); Worker's Alliance (WA),
Los Angeles, CA; Working Women.

614 Ruelas, J. Oshi. Moments of change. REVISTA
MUJERES, Vol. 4, no. 1 (January 1987), p.
23-33. English. DESCR: Essays; *Ruelas, J.
Oshi; Sex Roles; Sexism.

615 Saldivar, Ramon. The dialectics of
subjectivity: gender and difference in
Isabella Rios, Sandra Cisneros, and Cherrie
Moraga. IN: Saldivar, Ramon. CHICANO
NARRATIVE: THE DIALECTICS OF DIFFERENCE.
Madison, WI: University of Wisconsin Press,
1990, p. 171-199. English. DESCR: Authors;
*Cisneros, Sandra; Feminism; Fiction;
*Literary Criticism; Literature; LOVING IN
THE WAR YEARS; *Moraga, Cherrie; Political
Ideology; *Rios, Isabella; THE HOUSE ON
MANGO STREET; VICTUUM.

616 San Miguel, Rachel. Being Hispanic in
Houston: my name is Carmen Quezada. THE
AMERICAS REVIEW, Vol. 16, no. 1 (Spring
1988), p. 44-52. English. DESCR: *Essays;
Houston, TX; Identity.

617 Villanueva, Alma and Binder, Wolfgang.
[Interview with] Alma Villanueva. IN:
Binder, Wolfgang, ed. PARTIAL
AUTOBIOGRAPHIES: INTERVIEWS WITH TWENTY
CHICANO POETS. Erlangen, W. Germany: Verlag
Palm & Enke, 1985, p. 201-202. English.
DESCR: Authors; Poetry; *Villanueva, Alma.

618 Viramontes, Helena Maria. "Nopalitos": the
making of fiction. IN: Horno-Delgado,
Asuncion, et al., eds. BREAKING BOUNDARIES:
LATINA WRITING AND CRITICAL READINGS.
Amherst, MA: University of Massachusetts
Press, c1989, p. 33-38. English. DESCR:
*Authors; Essays; Viramontes, Helena Maria.

Autobiography (cont.)

619 Williams, Norma. A Mexican American woman encounters sociology: an autobiographical perspective. AMERICAN SOCIOLOGIST, Vol. 19, no. 4 (Winter 1988), p. 340-346. English. **DESCR:** Sexism; Social Science; *Sociology; Williams, Norma.

620 Zamora, Bernice and Binder, Wolfgang. [Interview with] Bernice Zamora. IN: Binder, Wolfgang, ed. PARTIAL AUTOBIOGRAPHIES: INTERVIEWS WITH TWENTY CHICANO POETS. Erlangen, W. Germany: Verlag Palm & Enke, 1985, p. 221-229. English. **DESCR:** Authors; Poetry; *Zamora, Bernice.

621 Zavala, Iris M. Ideologias y autobiografias: perspectivas femeninas. THIRD WOMAN, Vol. 1, no. 2 (1982), p. 35-39. Spanish. **DESCR:** *Essays.

Avance Parent-Child Education Program, San Antonio, TX

622 Walker, Todd. The relationship of nativity, social support and depression to the home environment among Mexican-American women. Thesis (Ph.D.)--University of Houston, 1989. 123 p. English. **DESCR:** Acculturation; Children; Depression (Psychological); *Immigrants; Natural Support Systems; *Parenting; Women.

AWAKE IN THE RIVER

623 Crawford, John F. Notes toward a new multicultural criticism: three works by women of color. IN: Harris, Marie and Aguero, Kathleen, eds. A GIFT OF TONGUES: CRITICAL CHALLENGES IN CONTEMPORARY AMERICAN POETRY. Athens, GA: University of Georgia Press, 1987, p. 155-195. English. **DESCR:** Cervantes, Lorna Dee; EMPLUMADA; Harjo, Joy; *Literary Criticism; Mirikitani, Janice; SHE HAD SOME HORSES.

Aztecs

624 Anzaldua, Gloria. Borderlands/La frontera: the new mestiza. San Francisco, CA: Spinsters/Aunt Lute, 1987. 203 p. Bilingual. **DESCR:** Border Region; *Identity; Mythology; Poems; Prose; Sex Roles.

625 Blanco, Iris. La mujer en los albores de la conquista de Mexico. AZTLAN, Vol. 11, no. 2 (Fall 1980), p. 249-270. Spanish. **DESCR:** Mexico; Sex Roles; Women.

626 Blanco, Iris. Participacion de las mujeres en la sociedad prehispanica. IN: Sanchez, Rosaura and Martinez Cruz, Rosa, eds. ESSAYS ON LA MUJER. Los Angeles, CA: Chicano Studies Center Publications, UCLA, 1977, p. 48-81. Spanish. **DESCR:** Cultural Customs; *History; Indigenismo; Mexico; Precolumbian Society; Women.

627 Candelaria, Cordelia. La Malinche, feminist prototype. FRONTIERS: A JOURNAL OF WOMEN STUDIES, Vol. 5, no. 2 (Summer 1980), p. 1-6. English. **DESCR:** *Feminism; History; Malinche.

628 Del Castillo, Adelaida R. Malintzin Tenepal: a preliminary look into a new perspective. ENCUENTRO FEMENIL, Vol. 1, no. 2 (1974), p. 58-77. English. **DESCR:** Biography; Cortes, Hernan; *History; *Malinche; Precolumbian Society.

629 Del Castillo, Adelaida R. Malintzin Tenepal: a preliminary look into a new perspective.

IN: Sanchez, Rosaura and Martinez Cruz, Rosa, eds. ESSAYS ON LA MUJER. Los Angeles, CA: Chicano Studies Center Publications, UCLA, 1977, p. 124-149. English. **DESCR:** Biography; Cortes, Hernan; *History; *Malinche; Precolumbian Society.

630 Phillips, Rachel. Marina/Malinche: masks and shadows. IN: Miller, Beth, ed. WOMEN IN HISPANIC LITERATURE: ICONS AND FALLEN IDOLS. Berkeley, CA: University of California Press, 1983, p. 97-114. English. **DESCR:** History; Malinche; Psychohistory; *Symbolism.

631 Salas, Elizabeth. Soldaderas in the Mexican military: myth and history. Austin, TX: University of Texas Press, 1990. xiii, 163 p., [12] p. of plates: ill. English. **DESCR:** History; *La Adelita; Mexican Revolution - 1910-1920; Mexico; *Military; Symbolism; War; *Women.

632 Salas, Elizabeth. Soldaderas in the Mexican military: myth and history. Thesis (Ph.D.)--University of California, Los Angeles, 1987. 313p. English. **DESCR:** History; La Adelita; Mexican Revolution - 1910-1920; Mexico; Military; Symbolism; War; *Women.

Baca Barragan, Polly

633 Baca Barragan, Polly; Hamner, Richard; and Guerrero, Lena. [Untitled interview with State Senators (Colorado) Polly Baca-Barragan and Lena Guerrero]. NATIONAL HISPANIC JOURNAL, Vol. 1, no. 2 (Winter 1982), p. 8-11. English. **DESCR:** Carter, Jimmy (President); Democratic Party; Elected Officials; Guerrero, Lena; *Political Parties and Organizations.

634 Espinosa, Ann. Hispanas: our resourses [sic] for the eighties. LA LUZ, Vol. 8, no. 4 (October, November, 1979), p. 10-13. English. **DESCR:** *Civil Rights; Comision Femenil Mexicana Nacional; DIRECTORY OF HISPANIC WOMEN; Discrimination in Education; Elected Officials; Hernandez, Irene; Lacayo, Carmela; Lujan, Josie; Mexican American Women's National Association (MANA); Montanez Davis, Grace; Moreno, Olga; Mujeres Latinas en Accion (M.L.A.); National Conference of Puerto Rican Women, Inc. (NCOPRW); Organizations; Rangel, Irma.

Baca, Judith F.

635 Goldman, Shifra M. Mujeres de California: Latin American women artists. IN: Moore, Sylvia, ed. YESTERDAY AND TOMORROW: CALIFORNIA WOMEN ARTISTS. New York, NY: Midmarch Arts Press, c1989, p. 202-229. English. **DESCR:** *Artists; Biography; California; Carrasco, Barbara; Cervantez, Yreina; de Larios, Dora; Feminism; Hernandez, Judithe; Lomas Garza, Carmen; Lopez, Yolanda M.; Mesa-Bains, Amalia; Murillo, Patricia; Sanchez, Olivia; Valdez, Patssi; Vallejo Dillaway, Linda; Women; Zamora Lucero, Linda.

636 Mesa-Bains, Amalia. Quest for identity: profile of two Chicana muralists: based on interviews with Judith F. Baca and Patricia Rodriguez. IN: Cockcroft, Eva Sperling and Barnet-Sanchez, Holly, eds. SIGNS FROM THE HEART: CALIFORNIA CHICANO MURALS. Venice, CA: Social and Public Art Resource Center, 1990, p. [68-83]. English. **DESCR:** Artists; Chicano Movement; GREAT WALL OF LOS ANGELES [mural]; *Mural Art; Rodriguez, Patricia.

Baca, Judith F. (cont.)

637 Pohl, Frances K. and Baca, Judith F. THE
    WORLD WALL: A VISION OF THE FUTURE WITHOUT
    FEAR: an interview with Judith F. Baca.
    FRONTIERS: A JOURNAL OF WOMEN STUDIES, Vol.
    11, no. 1 (1990), p. [33]-43. English.
    DESCR: Art Organizations and Groups;
    *Artists; *Mural Art; Social and Public Art
    Resource Center, Venice, CA (SPARC); *THE
    WORLD WALL: A VISION OF THE FUTURE WITHOUT
    FEAR [mural].

638 Three Latina artists = Tres artistas
    latinas. AMERICAS 2001, Vol. 1, no. 5
    (March, April, 1988), p. 21. Bilingual.
    DESCR: *Artists; Biographical Notes;
    *Carrasco, Barbara; *Martinez, Esperanza.

Ballad
    USE: Corridos

BALLAD OF GREGORIO CORTEZ [film]

639 Morales, Sylvia. Chicano-produced celluloid
    mujeres. BILINGUAL REVIEW, Vol. 10, no. 2-3
    (May, December, 1983), p. 89-93. English.
    DESCR: Film Reviews; *Films; RAICES DE
    SANGRE [film]; SEGUIN [movie]; *Stereotypes;
    ZOOT SUIT [film].

Bancroft, Hubert Howe

640 Castaneda, Antonia I. Gender, race, and
    culture: Spanish-Mexican women in the
    historiography of frontier California.
    FRONTIERS: A JOURNAL OF WOMEN STUDIES, Vol.
    11, no. 1 (1990), p. [8]-20. English.
    DESCR: Bolton, Herbert Eugene; *California;
    Californios; *Historiography; History;
    Intermarriage; *Sex Stereotypes; Spanish
    Borderlands Theory; Spanish Influence;
    Stereotypes; Turner, Frederick Jackson;
    Women.

Banking Industry

641 Bustamante, Jorge A. Maquiladoras: a new
    face of international capitalism on Mexico's
    northern frontier. IN: Nash, June and
    Fernandez-Kelly, Patricia, eds. WOMEN, MEN,
    AND THE INTERNATIONAL DIVISION OF LABOR.
    Albany, NY: State University of New York
    Press, 1983, p. 224-256. English. DESCR:
    Border Industrialization Program (BIP);
    Border Industries; *Border Region; Foreign
    Trade; Industrial Workers International
    Economic Relations; Mexico; Population;
    Programa Nacional Fronterizo (PRONAF);
    United States-Mexico Relations; Women;
    Working Women.

Barcelo, Gertrudes "La Tules"

642 Mirande, Alfredo and Enriquez, Evangelina.
    Chicanas in the history of the Southwest.
    IN: Duran, Livie Isauro and Bernard, H.
    Russell, eds. INTRODUCTION TO CHICANO
    STUDIES. 2nd ed. New York: Macmillan, 1982,
    p. 156-179. English. DESCR: Arguello,
    Concepcion; Fages, Eulalia; *History;
    "Juanita of Downieville"; Robledo, Refugio;
    Urrea, Teresa.

Barraza, Santa

643 Goldman, Shifra M. Women artists of Texas:
    MAS = More + Artists + Women = MAS.
    CHISMEARTE, no. 7 (January 1981), p. 21-22.
    English. DESCR: Arredondo, Alicia; Art
    Organizations and Groups; Exhibits;
    Feminism; Flores, Maria; Folk Art; Gonzalez
    Dodson, Nora; *Mujeres Artistas del Suroeste
    (MAS), Austin, TX; Photography; Texas;

Trevino, Modesta Barbina; WOMEN & THEIR WORK
    [festival] (Austin, TX: 1977).

644 Orozco, Sylvia. Las mujeres--Chicana artists
    come into their own. MOVING ON, Vol. 2, no.
    3 (May 1978), p. 14-16. English. DESCR: Art
    Organizations and Groups; Artists; Flores,
    Maria; Gonzalez Dodson, Nora; *Mujeres
    Artistas del Suroeste (MAS), Austin, TX;
    Trevino, Modesta Barbina.

Barrios

645 Campos Carr, Irene. Proyecto La Mujer:
    Latina women shaping consciousness. WOMEN'S
    STUDIES INTERNATIONAL FORUM, Vol. 12, no. 1
    (1989), p. 45-49. English. DESCR: Artists;
    Aurora, IL; Authors; Conferences and
    Meetings; Elgin, IL; *Feminism; Joliet, IL;
    Poetry; Proyecto La Mujer Conference
    (Spring, 1982: Northern Illinois); Women.

646 Harris, Mary G. Cholas: Latino girls and
    gangs. New York: AMS Press, 1988. x, 220 p.
    English. DESCR: *Gangs; Juvenile
    Delinquency; Los Angeles, CA; San Fernando
    Valley, CA; *Youth.

647 Horowitz, Ruth. Passion, submission and
    motherhood: the negotiation of identity by
    unmarried innercity Chicanas. SOCIOLOGICAL
    QUARTERLY, Vol. 22, no. 2 (Spring 1981), p.
    241-252. English. DESCR: Birth Control;
    *Fertility; Identity; *Sex Roles; *Sexual
    Behavior; Single Parents; Youth.

648 Moore, Joan W. Mexican-American women
    addicts: the influence of family background.
    IN: Glick, Ronald and Moore, Joan, eds.
    DRUGS IN HISPANIC COMMUNITIES. New
    Brunswick, NJ: Rutgers University Press,
    c1990, p. 127-153. English. DESCR: *Drug
    Addicts; Drug Use; East Los Angeles, CA;
    *Family; *Gangs; Heroin; Hoyo-Mara Gang,
    East Los Angeles, CA; Pachucos; Sex Roles;
    Socialization; White Fence Gang; Youth.

Batos Locos
    USE: Pachucos

Battered Women

649 Gondolf, Edward W.; Fisher, Ellen; and
    McFerron, J. Richard. Racial differences
    among shelter residents: a comparison of
    Anglo, Black, and Hispanic battered. JOURNAL
    OF FAMILY VIOLENCE, Vol. 3, no. 1 (March
    1988), p. 39-51. English. DESCR: Anglo
    Americans; Blacks; Comparative Psychology;
    Cultural Characteristics; Natural Support
    Systems; Socioeconomic Factors; *Violence;
    *Women.

650 Hintz, Joy. Valiant migrant women = Las
    mujeres valerosas. Tiffin, OH: Sayger
    Printing, 1982. viii, 98 p. English. DESCR:
    *Farm Workers; Feminism; Florida; Marriage;
    Migrant Children; Migrant Health Services;
    Migrant Housing; *Migrant Labor; Migration
    Patterns; Ohio; Sex Roles; Texas.

651 Hogeland, Chris and Rosen, Karen. Dreams
    lost, dreams found: undocumented women in
    the land of opportunity. San Francisco, CA:
    Coalition for Immigrant and Refugee Rights
    and Services, c1991. 153 p. English. DESCR:
    *Coalition for Immigrant and Refugee Rights
    and Services, Immigrant Woman's Task Force;
    Discrimination; Immigrants; *San Francisco
    Bay Area; Sex Roles; Sexism; Social
    Services; Undocumented Workers; Violence;
    Women; Women Men Relations.

Battered Women (cont.)

652 Sorenson, Susan B. and Telles, Cynthia A. Self-reports of spousal violence in a Mexican-American and non-Hispanic white population. VIOLENCE AND VICTIMS, Vol. 6, no. 1 (1991), p. 3-15. English. DESCR: Anglo Americans; Los Angeles, CA; Los Angeles Epidemiologic Catchment Area Research Program (LAECA); Rape; Violence; Women; *Women Men Relations.

653 Torres, Sara. A comparative analysis of wife abuse among Anglo-American and Mexican-American battered women: attitudes, nature, severity, frequency and response to the abuse. Thesis (Ph.D.)--University of Texas, Austin, 1986. 265 p. English. DESCR: Anglo Americans; Attitudes; Family; *Violence; *Women.

654 Torres, Sara. Hispanic-American battered women: why consider cultural differences? RESPONSE TO THE VICTIMIZATION OF WOMEN & CHILDREN, Vol. 10, no. 3 (1987), p. 20-21. English. DESCR: Cultural Characteristics.

655 Zambrano, Myrna. Mejor sola que mal acompanada: para la mujer golpeada. Seattle, WA: Seal Press, 1985. 241 p. Bilingual. DESCR: Natural Support Systems; *Women.

Bay City Cannery Workers Committee

656 Zavella, Patricia. The politics of race and gender: organizing Chicana cannery workers in Northern California. IN: Bookman, Ann and Morgen, Sandra, eds. WOMEN AND THE POLITICS OF EMPOWERMENT. Philadelphia, PA: Temple University Press, 1988, p. 202-224. English. DESCR: *Canneries; Cannery Workers Committee (CWC); Discrimination; Garcia, Connie; Identity; *Labor Unions; Nationalism; Northern California; Santa Clara Valley, CA; Sex Roles; Sexism; *Working Women.

Beliefs About Women Scale (BAWS)

657 Belk, Sharyn S., et al. Impact of ethnicity, nationality, counseling orientation, and mental health standards on stereotypic beliefs about women. SEX ROLES, Vol. 21, no. 9-10 (November 1989), p. 671-695. English. DESCR: Anglo Americans; *Comparative Psychology; *Counseling (Psychological); Cultural Characteristics; Identity; Mental Health; *Sex Stereotypes; Sexism; Women.

Beltran, Beatriz

658 Lindstrom, Naomi. Four representative Hispanic women poets of Central Texas: a portrait of plurality. THIRD WOMAN, Vol. 2, no. 1 (1984), p. 64-70. English. DESCR: de Hoyos, Angela; Jimenez, Magali; *Literary Criticism; Poetry; Tafolla, Carmen; Texas.

Bem Sex Role Inventory (BSRI)

659 Lara-Cantu, M. Asuncion and Navarro-Arias, Roberto. Positive and negative factors in the measurement of sex roles: findings from a Mexican sample. HISPANIC JOURNAL OF BEHAVIORAL SCIENCES, Vol. 8, no. 2 (June 1986), p. 143-155. English. DESCR: Mexico; *Psychological Testing; *Sex Roles.

660 Reed-Sanders, Delores; Dodder, Richard A.; and Webster, Lucia. The Bem Sex-Role Inventory across three cultures. JOURNAL OF SOCIAL PSYCHOLOGY, Vol. 125, no. 4 (August 1985), p. 523-525. English. DESCR: Comparative Psychology; *Sex Roles.

BERNABE

661 Melville, Margarita B. Female and male in Chicano theatre. IN: Kanellos, Nicolas, ed. HISPANIC THEATRE IN THE UNITED STATES. Houston, TX: Arte Publico Press, 1984, p. 71-79. English. DESCR: BRUJERIAS [play]; Cultural Characteristics; DAY OF THE SWALLOWS; Duarte-Clark, Rodrigo; EL JARDIN [play]; Family; Feminism; Macias, Ysidro; Morton, Carlos; Portillo Trambley, Estela; RANCHO HOLLYWOOD [play]; *Sex Roles; *Teatro; THE ULTIMATE PENDEJADA [play]; Valdez, Luis; Women Men Relations.

Bexar County, TX

662 Bauer, Richard L. Ethnic differences in hip fracture: a reduced incidence in Mexican-Americans. AMERICAN JOURNAL OF EPIDEMIOLOGY, Vol. 127, no. 1 (January 1988), p. 145-149. English. DESCR: Anglo Americans; Blacks; Medical Care; Osteoporosis; *Public Health.

663 Valdez, Avelardo. Recent increases in intermarriage by Mexican American males: Bexar County, Texas from 1971 to 1980. SOCIAL SCIENCE QUARTERLY, Vol. 64, (March 1983), p. 136-144. English. DESCR: *Intermarriage; Males.

Bibliography

664 Alarcon, Norma. Chicana writers and critics in a social context : towards a contemporary bibliography. THIRD WOMAN, Vol. 4, (1989), p. 169-178. English. DESCR: *Literary Criticism; *Literature.

665 Alarcon, Norma. Latina writers in the United States. IN: Marting, Diane E., ed. SPANISH AMERICAN WOMEN WRITERS: A BIO-BIBLIOGRAPHICAL SOURCE BOOK. New York: Greenwood Press, 1990, p. [557]-567. English. DESCR: *Authors; BREAKING BOUNDARIES: LATINA WRITING AND CRITICAL READINGS; Cubanos; Intergroup Relations; Language Usage; *Literature Reviews; Puerto Ricans; THIRD WOMAN [journal]; *Women.

666 Amaro, Hortensia; Russo, Nancy Felipe; and Pares-Avila, Jose A. Contemporary research on Hispanic women: a selected bibliography of the social science literature. PSYCHOLOGY OF WOMEN QUARTERLY, Vol. 11, no. 4 (December 1987), p. 523-532. English. DESCR: *Psychology; Social Science; *Women.

667 Baezconde-Garbanati, Lourdes and Salgado de Snyder, Nelly. Mexican immigrant women: a selected bibliography. HISPANIC JOURNAL OF BEHAVIORAL SCIENCES, Vol. 9, no. 3 (September 1987), p. 331-358. English. DESCR: *Immigrants; *Women.

668 [Bibliography of Special Issue: Chicana Creativity and Criticism]. THE AMERICAS REVIEW, Vol. 15, no. 3-4 (Fall, Winter, 1987), p. 182-188. English. DESCR: *Literary Criticism; Literature.

669 Camarillo, Alberto M., ed. Latinos in the United States: a historical bibliography. Santa Barbara, CA: ABC-CLIO, 1986. x, 332 p.. English. DESCR: Political History and Conditions; Social History and Conditions.

Bibliography (cont.)

670 Carrillo V., Jorge and Hernandez H., Alberto. La industria maquiladora en Mexico: bibliografia, directorio e investigaciones recientes = Border assembly industry and recent research. La Jolla, CA: Program in United States-Mexican Studies, University of California, San Diego, 1981. 130 p. Spanish. DESCR: *Border Industries.

671 Castillo-Speed, Lillian. Chicana Studies: a selected list of materials since 1980. FRONTIERS: A JOURNAL OF WOMEN STUDIES, Vol. 11, no. 1 (1990), p. [66]-84. English. DESCR: Chicana Studies.

672 Chabran, Richard. Chicana reference sources. IN: Cordova, Teresa, et al., eds. CHICANA VOICES. Austin, TX: Center for Mexican American Studies, 1986, p. 146-156. English. DESCR: Literature Reviews; *Reference Works.

673 D'Andrea, Vaneeta-Marie. Ethnic women: a critique of the literature, 1971-1981. ETHNIC AND RACIAL STUDIES, Vol. 9, (April 1986), p. 235-246. English. DESCR: Ethnic Groups; *Literature Reviews; Periodical Indexes; *Women.

674 Eger, Ernestina. A bibliography of criticism of contemporary Chicano literature. Berkeley, CA: Chicano Studies Library Publications Unit, 1982. xxi, 295 p. English. DESCR: Authors; *Literary Criticism; Literature.

675 Fennelly, Katherine. Childbearing among Hispanics in the United States: an annotated bibliography. New York: Greenwood Press, 1987. xii, 167 p. English. DESCR: Abortion; Birth Control; *Fertility; Sterilization; *Women; Youth.

676 Flores, Estevan T. Chicanos and sociological research: 1970-1980. IN: CHICANOS AND THE SOCIAL SCIENCES: A DECADE OF RESEARCH AND DEVELOPMENT (1970-1980) SYMPOSIUM WORKING PAPER. Santa Barbara, CA: Center for Chicano Studies, University of California, 1983, p. 19-45. English. DESCR: Family; Internal Colony Model; Labor; Literature Reviews; Population; Research Methodology; *Sociology.

677 Garza-Livingston, M'Liss. Annotated bibliography of selected materials on la mujer y la Chicana. COMADRE, no. 1 (Summer 1977), p. 49-54. English.

678 Garza-Livingston, M'Liss. Annotated bibliography of selected materials on la mujer y la Chicana. COMADRE, no. 2 (Spring 1978), p. 51-56. English.

679 Goldman, Shifra M. and Ybarra-Frausto, Tomas. Arte Chicano: a comprehensive annotated bibliography of Chicano art, 1965-1981. Berkeley, CA: Chicano Studies Library Publications Unit, 1985. viii, 778 p. English. DESCR: *Art; Art History; Artists.

680 Loeb, Catherine. La Chicana: a bibliographic survey. FRONTIERS: A JOURNAL OF WOMEN STUDIES, Vol. 5, no. 2 (Summer 1980), p. 59-74. English.

681 McKenna, Teresa and Ortiz, Flora Ida. Select bibliography on Hispanic women and education. IN: McKenna, Teresa and Ortiz, Flora Ida, eds. THE BROKEN WEB: THE EDUCATIONAL EXPERIENCE OF HISPANIC WOMEN. Claremont, CA: Tomas Rivera Center; Berkeley, CA: Floricanto Press, 1988, p. 221-254. English. DESCR: *Education; *Women.

682 Miller, Elaine N. and Sternbach, Nancy Saporta. Selected bibliography. IN: Horno-Delgado, Asuncion, et al., eds. BREAKING BOUNDARIES: LATINA WRITING AND CRITICAL READINGS. Amherst, MA: University of Massachusetts Press, c1989, p. 251-263. English. DESCR: Cubanos; Literary Criticism; *Literature; Puerto Ricans; *Women.

683 Moraga, Cherrie. Third World women in the United States--by and about us: a selected bibliography. IN: Moraga, Cherrie and Anzaldua, Gloria, eds. THIS BRIDGE CALLED MY BACK: WRITINGS BY RADICAL WOMEN OF COLOR. Watertown, MA: Persephone Press, 1981, p. 251-261. English. DESCR: *Feminism; Women.

684 Newton, Frank; Olmedo, Esteban L.; and Padilla, Amado M. Hispanic mental health research: a reference guide. Berkeley, CA: University of California Press, c1982. 685 p. English. DESCR: Anthropology; Education; Medical Care; *Mental Health; Psychology; Public Health; *Reference Works; Sociology.

685 Ordonez, Elizabeth J. Chicana literature and related sources: a selected and annotated bibliography. BILINGUAL REVIEW, Vol. 7, no. 2 (May, August, 1980), p. 143-164. English. DESCR: *Literature.

686 Orozco, Cynthia. Getting started in Chicana Studies. WOMEN'S STUDIES QUARTERLY, no. 1-2 (1990), p. 46-69. English. DESCR: *Chicana Studies; *Literature Reviews.

687 Sable, Martin H. Las maquiladoras: assembly and manufacturing plants on the United States-Mexico border: an international guide. New York: Haworth Press, 1989. 150 p. English. DESCR: *Border Industries.

688 Sonntag, Iliana. Hacia una bibliografia de poesia femenina chicana. LA PALABRA, Vol. 2, no. 2 (Fall 1980), p. 91-109. Spanish. DESCR: *Poetry.

689 Sosa Riddell, Adaljiza. Bibliography on Chicanas and public policy. IN: Sosa Riddell, Adaljiza, ed. POLICY DEVELOPMENT: CHICANA/LATINA SUMMER RESEARCH INSTITUTE. Davis, CA: [Chicano Studies Program, University of California, Davis, 1989?], p. 27-29. English. DESCR: *Public Policy.

690 Timberlake, Andrea, et al. Women of color and southern women: a bibliography of social science research, 1975 to 1988. Memphis, TN: Center for Research on Women, Memphis State University, 1988. vii, 264 p. English. DESCR: Blacks; *Social Science; *Women.

691 Villalobos, Rolando M. Research guide to the literature on Northern Mexico's maquiladora assembly industry. [Stanford, CA?]: Zapata Underground Press, c1988. 59 leaves. English. DESCR: *Border Industries.

692 Zambrana, Ruth E. Bibliography on maternal and child health across class, race and ethnicity. Memphis, TN: Distributed by the Memphis State University Center for Research on Women, c1990. 58 leaves. English. DESCR: Ethnic Groups; *Maternal and Child Welfare; *Medical Care; Social Classes; *Women.

Bicultural Education
USE: Bilingual Bicultural Education

Biculturalism

693 Buriel, Raymond and Saenz, Evangelina. Psychocultural characteristics of college-bound and noncollege-bound Chicanas. JOURNAL OF SOCIAL PSYCHOLOGY, Vol. 110, (April 1980), p. 245-251. English. **DESCR:** *Biculturalism Inventory for Mexican American Students (BIMAS); Higher Education; Identity; Income; Psychological Testing; Sex Roles; Social Psychology.

694 Sanchez, George J. "Go after the women": Americanization and the Mexican immigrant woman, 1915-1929. Stanford, CA: Stanford Center for Chicano Research [1984?]. [32] leaves. English. **DESCR:** Acculturation; *Assimilation; *Immigrants; Social History and Conditions; Values; Women.

695 Sanchez, George J. "Go after the women": Americanization and the Mexican immigrant woman, 1915-1929. IN: DuBois, Ellen Carol and Ruiz, Vicki L., eds. UNEQUAL SISTERS: A MULTICULTURAL READER IN U.S. WOMEN'S HISTORY. New York: Routledge, 1990, p. 250-263. English. **DESCR:** Acculturation; *Assimilation; *Immigrants; Social History and Conditions; Values; Women.

696 Sanchez, Joaquin John. An investigation of the initial experience of a Chicana with higher education. Thesis (Ph.D.)--Saybrook Institute, 1983. 163 p. English. **DESCR:** Colleges and Universities; *Cultural Characteristics; *Higher Education.

697 Torres, Cynthia. Cultural and psychological attributes and their implications for career choice and aspirations among Mexican American females. Thesis (Ph.D.)--University of California, Los Angeles, 1986. 127 p. English. **DESCR:** *Careers; Counseling (Psychological); Cultural Characteristics.

698 Velasquez-Trevino, Gloria. Cultural ambivalence in early Chicana prose fiction. Thesis (Ph.D.)--Stanford University, 1985. 185 p. English. **DESCR:** *Fiction; Gonzalez, Jovita; Literary Criticism; Mena, Maria Cristina; Niggli, Josephina; Prose; Sex Roles.

Biculturalism Inventory for Mexican American Students (BIMAS)

699 Buriel, Raymond and Saenz, Evangelina. Psychocultural characteristics of college-bound and noncollege-bound Chicanas. JOURNAL OF SOCIAL PSYCHOLOGY, Vol. 110, (April 1980), p. 245-251. English. **DESCR:** Biculturalism; Higher Education; Identity; Income; Psychological Testing; Sex Roles; Social Psychology.

Bilingual Ballots
USE: Voting Rights

Bilingual Bicultural Education

700 Cotera, Marta P. Sexism in bilingual bicultural education. IN: Cotera, Martha and Hufford, Larry, eds. BRIDGING TWO CULTURES. Austin, TX: National Educational Laboratory Publishers, 1980, p. 181-190. English. **DESCR:** Sex Roles; Sexism; Stereotypes; Textbooks.

Bilingualism

701 Andrade, Sally J., ed. Latino families in the United States: a resource book for family life education = Las familias latinas en los Estados Unidos: recursos para la capacitacion familiar. [S.l.]: Planned Parenthood Federation of America, Inc., 1983. ix, 79, 70, xi p. Bilingual. **DESCR:** Community Organizations; Education; *Family; Mental Health; Public Health.

702 Carrasco, Frank F. Teaching strategies used by Chicano mothers with their Head Start children. Thesis (Ph.D.)--University of Colorado, Boulder, 1983. 177 p. English. **DESCR:** Children; *Education; Low Income; *Parent and Child Relationships; *Parenting.

703 MacCorquodale, Patricia. Mexican-American women and mathematics: participation, aspirations, and achievement. IN: Cocking, Rodney R. and Mestre, Jose P., eds. LINGUISTIC AND CULTURAL DIFFERENCES ON LEARNING MATHEMATICS. Hillsdale, NJ: Erlbaum, 1988, p. 137-160. English. **DESCR:** *Academic Achievement; Anglo Americans; Family; *Mathematics.

704 Ortega, Eliana and Sternbach, Nancy Saporta. At the threshold of the unnamed: Latina literary discourse in the eighties. IN: Horno-Delgado, Asuncion, et al., eds. BREAKING BOUNDARIES: LATINA WRITING AND CRITICAL READINGS. Amherst, MA: University of Massachusetts Press, c1989, p. [2]-23. English. **DESCR:** *Feminism; *Literary Criticism; Literary History; Political Ideology; Sex Roles; *Women.

705 Valdes, Guadalupe and Cardenas, Manuel. Positive speech accommodation in the language of Mexican American bilinguals: are women really more sensitive? HISPANIC JOURNAL OF BEHAVIORAL SCIENCES, Vol. 3, no. 4 (December 1981), p. 347-359. English. **DESCR:** *Language Usage; Spanish Language.

706 Valdes, Guadalupe; Garcia, Herman; and Storment, Diamantina. Sex-related speech accommodations among Mexican-American bilinguals: a pilot study of language choice in customer-server interactions. IN: Barkin, Florence, et al., eds. BILINGUALISM AND LANGUAGE CONTACT: SPANISH, ENGLISH, AND NATIVE AMERICAN LANGUAGES. New York: Teachers College, 1982, p. 187-200. English. **DESCR:** *Language Usage; Las Cruces, NM; Surveys.

Biographical Notes

707 Three Latina artists = Tres artistas latinas. AMERICAS 2001, Vol. 1, no. 5 (March, April, 1988), p. 21. Bilingual. **DESCR:** *Artists; *Baca, Judith F.; *Carrasco, Barbara; *Martinez, Esperanza.

708 Torano, Maria Elena and Alvarez, Lourdes. Hispanas: success in America. IN: THE STATE OF HISPANIC AMERICA II. Oakland, CA: National Hispanic Center for Advanced Studies and Policy Analysis, 1982, p. 151-167. English. **DESCR:** Social History and Conditions.

Biography

709 Alarcon, Justo S. and Martinez, Julio A. [Bornstein-Somoza, Miriam]. IN: Martinez, Julio A. and Lomeli, Francisco A., eds. CHICANO LITERATURE: A REFERENCE GUIDE. Westport, CT: Greenwood Press, 1985, p. 74-77. English. **DESCR:** *Authors; Bornstein-Somoza, Miriam; Literary Criticism.

--   --
Biography (cont.)

710 Alarcon, Norma and Moraga, Cherrie.
Interview with Cherrie Moraga. THIRD WOMAN,
Vol. 3, no. 1-2 (1986), p. 127-134. English.
DESCR: Authors; Homosexuality; *Moraga,
Cherrie; Sex Roles.

711 Alarcon, Norma and Mora, Pat. Interview with
Pat Mora. THIRD WOMAN, Vol. 3, no. 1-2
(1986), p. 121-126. English. **DESCR:** Authors;
*Mora, Pat.

712 Anzaldua, Gloria. La prieta. IN: Moraga,
Cherrie and Anzaldua, Gloria, eds. THIS
BRIDGE CALLED MY BACK: WRITINGS BY RADICAL
WOMEN OF COLOR. Watertown, MA: Persephone
Press, 1981, p. 198-209. English. **DESCR:**
Cultural Customs; Feminism.

713 Calderon, Roberto R. and Zamora, Emilio, Jr.
Manuela Solis Sager and Emma Tenayuca: a
tribute. IN: Cordova, Teresa, et al., eds.
CHICANA VOICES. Austin, TX: Center for
Mexican American Studies, 1986, p. 30-41.
English. **DESCR:** Agricultural Labor Unions;
History; Labor; *Solis Sager, Manuela; South
Texas Agricultural Worker's Union (STAWU);
*Tenayuca, Emma; United Cannery Agricultural
Packing and Allied Workers of America
(UCAPAWA).

714 Calderon, Roberto R. and Zamora, Emilio, Jr.
Manuela Solis Sager and Emma Tenayuca: a
tribute. IN: Del Castillo, Adelaida R., ed.
BETWEEN BORDERS: ESSAYS ON MEXICANA/CHICANA
HISTORY. Encino, CA: Floricanto Press, 1990,
p. 269-279. English. **DESCR:** Agricultural
Labor Unions; History; Labor; *Solis Sager,
Manuela; South Texas Agricultural Worker's
Union (STAWU); *Tenayuca, Emma; United
Cannery Agricultural Packing and Allied
Workers of America (UCAPAWA).

715 Carrillo, Teresa. The women's movement and
the left in Mexico: the presidential
candidacy of Dona Rosario Ibarra. IN:
Cordova, Teresa, et al., eds. CHICANA
VOICES. Austin, TX: Center for Mexican
American Studies, 1986, p. 96-113. English.
DESCR: Ibarra, Rosario; Mexico; Politics;
*Women.

716 de Lotbiniere-Harwood, Susanne and Anzaldua,
Gloria. Conversations at the Book Fair:
interview with Gloria Anzaldua. TRIVIA: A
JOURNAL OF IDEAS, no. 14 (Spring 1989), p.
37-45. English. **DESCR:** *Anzaldua, Gloria;
*Authors; Feminism; Literary Criticism.

717 Del Castillo, Adelaida R. Malintzin Tenepal:
a preliminary look into a new perspective.
ENCUENTRO FEMENIL, Vol. 1, no. 2 (1974), p.
58-77. English. **DESCR:** Aztecs; Cortes,
Hernan; *History; *Malinche; Precolumbian
Society.

718 Del Castillo, Adelaida R. Malintzin Tenepal:
a preliminary look into a new perspective.
IN: Sanchez, Rosaura and Martinez Cruz,
Rosa, eds. ESSAYS ON LA MUJER. Los Angeles,
CA: Chicano Studies Center Publications,
UCLA, 1977, p. 124-149. English. **DESCR:**
Aztecs; Cortes, Hernan; *History; *Malinche;
Precolumbian Society.

719 Duran Apodaca, Maria. North from Mexico. IN:
Jensen, Joan M. ed. WITH THESE HANDS: WOMEN
WORKING ON THE LAND. New York: McGraw-Hill,
1981, p. 120-122. English. **DESCR:** Duran
Apodaca, Maria; Oral History.

720 Duran, Lucy. Lucy Duran--wife, mother, and
organizer. IN: Mora, Magdalena and Del

Castillo, Adelaida, eds. MEXICAN WOMEN IN
THE UNITED STATES: STRUGGLES PAST AND
PRESENT. Los Angeles, CA: Chicano Studies
Research Center, UCLA, 1980, p. 183-184.
English. **DESCR:** Agricultural Labor Unions;
Duran, Lucy; Farm Labor Organizing
Committee (FLOC); Farm Workers; Working
Women.

721 Elsasser, Nan; MacKenzie, Kyle; and Tixier y
Vigil, Yvonne. Las mujeres: conversations
from a Hispanic community. Old Wesbury, NY:
Feminist Press; New York: McGraw-Hill, 1980.
xxv, 163 p.: ill. English. **DESCR:** *New
Mexico; Oral History.

722 Escalante, Virginia; Rivera, Nancy; and
Valle, Victor Manuel. Inside the world of
Latinas. IN: SOUTHERN CALIFORNIA'S LATINO
COMMUNITY: A SERIES OF ARTICLES REPRINTED
FROM THE LOS ANGELES TIMES. Los Angeles: Los
Angeles Times, 1983, p. 82-91. English.
DESCR: Castillo Fierro, Catalina (Katie);
Gaitan, Maria Elena; Gutierrez, Nancy; Luna
Mount, Julia; Ramirez, Cristina.

723 Goldman, Shifra M. Mujeres de California:
Latin American women artists. IN: Moore,
Sylvia, ed. YESTERDAY AND TOMORROW:
CALIFORNIA WOMEN ARTISTS. New York, NY:
Midmarch Arts Press, c1989, p. 202-229.
English. **DESCR:** *Artists; Baca, Judith F.;
California; Carrasco, Barbara; Cervantez,
Yreina; de Larios, Dora; Feminism;
Hernandez, Judithe; Lomas Garza, Carmen;
Lopez, Yolanda M.; Mesa-Bains, Amalia;
Murillo, Patricia; Sanchez, Olivia; Valdez,
Patssi; Vallejo Dillaway, Linda; Women;
Zamora Lucero, Linda.

724 Gonzalez, LaVerne. [Portillo Trambley,
Estela]. IN: Martinez, Julio A. and Lomeli,
Francisco A., eds. CHICANO LITERATURE: A
REFERENCE GUIDE. Westport, CT: Greenwood
Press, 1985, p. 316-322. English. **DESCR:**
Authors; Literary Criticism; *Portillo
Trambley, Estela.

725 Hernandez, Ines. Sara Estela Ramirez: the
early twentieth century Texas-Mexican poet.
Thesis (Ph.D.)--University of Houston, 1984.
94 p. English. **DESCR:** *Authors; Feminism;
Flores Magon, Ricardo; Journalism; Literary
Criticism; Mexican Revolution - 1910-1920;
Mexico; *Poetry; Ramirez, Sara Estela;
Texas; Women.

726 Hernandez, Ines. Sara Estela Ramirez:
sembradora. LEGACY: A JOURNAL OF
NINETEENTH-CENTURY AMERICAN WOMEN WRITERS,
Vol. 6, no. 1 (Spring 1989), p. 13-26.
English. **DESCR:** Authors; *Feminism; Flores
Magon, Ricardo; *Journalism; LA CORREGIDORA
[newspaper]; Mexican Revolution - 1910-1920;
Mexico; Newspapers; Poetry; *Ramirez, Sara
Estela; REGENERACION [newspaper].

727 Huerta, Dolores. Dolores Huerta talks about
Republicans, Cesar, children and her home
town. REGENERACION, Vol. 2, no. 4 (1975), p.
20-24. English. **DESCR:** *Agricultural Labor
Unions; Chavez, Cesar E.; Community Service
Organization, Los Angeles, (CSO); Democratic
Party; Elected Officials; Flores, Art;
Huerta, Dolores; McGovern, George;
*Politics; Ramirez, Henry M.; Ross, Fred;
Sanchez, Philip V.; United Farmworkers of
America (UFW); Working Women.

Biography (cont.)

728 Huerta, Dolores. Dolores Huerta talks about Republicans, Cesar, children and her home town. IN: Servin, Manuel P. ed. THE MEXICAN AMERICANS: AN AWAKENING MINORITY. 2nd ed. Beverly Hills, CA: Glencoe Press, 1974, p. 283-294. English. **DESCR**: *Agricultural Labor Unions; Chavez, Cesar E.; Community Service Organization, Los Angeles, (CSO); Democratic Party; Elected Officials; Flores, Art; Huerta, Dolores; McGovern, George; *Politics; Ramirez, Henry M.; Ross, Fred; Sanchez, Philip V.; United Farmworkers of America (UFW); Working Women.

729 La Duke, Betty. Trivial lives: artists Yolanda Lopez and Patricia Rodriguez. TRIVIA: A JOURNAL OF IDEAS, (Winter 1986), p. 74-85. English. **DESCR**: Artists; *Lopez, Yolanda M.; *Rodriguez, Patricia.

730 Meier, Matt S. Mexican American biographies: a historical dictionary, 1836-1987. Westport, CT: Greenwood Press, 1988. ix, 270 p. English. **DESCR**: *Dictionaries.

731 Mendoza, Hope Schecter and Chall, Malca. Activist in the labor movement, the Democratic Party, and the Mexican-American community: an interview. Berkeley, CA: Regional Oral History Office, Bancroft Library, University of California, Berkeley, 1980. xii, 170 p.: ill. English. **DESCR**: Chavez Ravine, Los Angeles, CA; Church, Frank; Community Organizations; Community Service Organization, Los Angeles, (CSO); Democratic Party; Elections; Garment Industry; Industrial Workers; *Labor Unions; Leadership; Mendoza, Hope Schecter; Snyder, Elizabeth; Warschaw, Carmen.

732 Moreno, Maria. I'm talking for justice. IN: Mora, Magdalena and Del Castillo, Adelaida, eds. MEXICAN WOMEN IN THE UNITED STATES: STRUGGLES PAST AND PRESENT. Los Angeles, CA: Chicano Studies Research Center, UCLA, 1980, p. 181-182. English. **DESCR**: Moreno, Maria.

733 Nelson, Kathryn J. Excerpts from los testamentos: Hispanic women folk artists of the San Luis Valley, Colorado. FRONTIERS: A JOURNAL OF WOMEN STUDIES, Vol. 5, no. 3 (Fall 1980), p. 34-43. English. **DESCR**: *Archuleta, Eppie; Artists; Folk Art; San Luis Valley, CO.

734 Oliveira, Annette. Remarkable Latinas. IN: HISPANICS AND GRANTMAKERS: A SPECIAL REPORT OF FOUNDATION NEWS. Washington, DC: Council on Foundations, 1981, p. 34. English. **DESCR**: Leadership; *Puerto Ricans; Women.

735 Ordonez, Elizabeth J. [Villanueva, Alma]. IN: Martinez, Julio A. and Lomeli, Francisco A., eds. CHICANO LITERATURE: A REFERENCE GUIDE. Westport, CT: Greenwood Press, 1985, p. 413-420. English. **DESCR**: Authors; *BLOODROOT; Literary Criticism; *Villanueva, Alma.

736 Ramos, Luis Arturo. [Hoyos, Angela de]. IN: Martinez, Julio A. and Lomeli, Francisco A., eds. CHICANO LITERATURE: A REFERENCE GUIDE. Westport, CT: Greenwood Press, 1985, p. 260-265. English. **DESCR**: Authors; *de Hoyos, Angela; Literary Criticism.

737 Sheridan, Thomas E. From Luisa Espinel to Lalo Guerrero: Tucson's Mexican musicians before World War II. JOURNAL OF ARIZONA HISTORY, Vol. 25, no. 3 (Fall 1984), p. 285-300. English. **DESCR**: Espinel, Luisa Ronstadt; Guerrero, Eduardo "Lalo"; History; Montijo, Manuel; *Musicians; Rebeil, Julia; Singers; *Tucson, AZ.

738 Zamora, Emilio, Jr. Sara Estela Ramirez: una rosa roja en el movimiento. IN: Mora, Magdalena and Del Castillo, Adelaida, eds. MEXICAN WOMEN IN THE UNITED STATES: STRUGGLES PAST AND PRESENT. Los Angeles, CA: Chicano Studies Research Center, UCLA, 1980, p. 163-169. English. **DESCR**: Literary Criticism; Poetry; *Ramirez, Sara Estela.

Birth Control

739 Amaro, Hortensia. Abortion use and attitudes among Chicanas: the need for research. RESEARCH BULLETIN (SPANISH SPEAKING MENTAL HEALTH RES. CENTER), Vol. 4, no. 3 (March 1980), p. 1-5. English. **DESCR**: *Abortion; *Attitudes; Family Planning; Fertility; Literature Reviews; Mental Health.

740 Amaro, Hortensia. Women in the Mexican-American community: religion, culture, and reproductive attitudes and experiences. JOURNAL OF COMMUNITY PSYCHOLOGY, Vol. 16, no. 1 (January 1988), p. 6-20. English. **DESCR**: Abortion; *Attitudes; Family Planning; *Fertility; Religion.

741 Andrade, Sally J. Chicana adolescents and contraception issues. LA RED/THE NET, no. 35 (October 1980), p. 2,14. English. **DESCR**: *Youth.

742 Andrade, Sally J. Family planning practices of Mexican Americans. IN: Melville, Margarita B., ed. TWICE A MINORITY. St. Louis, MO: Mosby, 1980, p. 17-32. English. **DESCR**: *Family Planning; *Fertility.

743 Aneshensel, Carol S., et al. Onset of fertility-related events during adolescence: a prospective comparison of Mexican American and non-Hispanic white females. AMERICAN JOURNAL OF PUBLIC HEALTH, Vol. 80, no. 8 (August 1990), p. 959-963. English. **DESCR**: Abortion; Anglo Americans; *Fertility; *Sexual Behavior; Women; *Youth.

744 Bean, Frank D. and Bradshaw, Benjamin S. Mexican American fertility. IN: Teller, Charles H., et al., eds. CUANTOS SOMOS: A DEMOGRAPHIC STUDY OF THE MEXICAN AMERICAN POPULATION. Austin, TX: Center for Mexican American Studies, University of Texas at Austin, 1977, p. 101-130. English. **DESCR**: Attitudes; *Fertility; Income; Population; Religion.

745 Becerra, Rosina M. and de Anda, Diane. Pregnancy and motherhood among Mexican American adolescents. HEALTH AND SOCIAL WORK, Vol. 9, no. 2 (Spring 1984), p. 106-23. English. **DESCR**: Acculturation; Anglo Americans; Attitudes; *Fertility; Natural Support Systems; *Youth.

746 Davis, Sally M. and Harris, Mary B. Sexual knowledge, sexual interests, and sources of sexual information of rural and urban adolescents from three cultures. ADOLESCENCE, Vol. 17, no. 66 (Summer 1982), p. 471-492. English. **DESCR**: Cultural Characteristics; Identity; Rural Population; *Sex Education; Sex Roles; Urban Communities; Youth.

Birth Control (cont.)

747 de Anda, Diane; Becerra, Rosina M.; and
    Fielder, Eve P. Sexuality, pregnancy, and
    motherhood among Mexican-American
    adolescents. JOURNAL OF ADOLESCENT RESEARCH.
    Vol. 3, no. 3-4 (Fall, Winter, 1988), p.
    403-411. English. DESCR: Anglo Americans;
    Attitudes; *Fertility; Sex Education;
    *Sexual Behavior; Women: *Youth.

748 Fennelly, Katherine. Childbearing among
    Hispanics in the United States: an annotated
    bibliography. New York: Greenwood Press,
    1987. xii, 167 p. English. DESCR: Abortion;
    *Bibliography; *Fertility; Sterilization;
    *Women; Youth.

749 Hernandez, Antonia A. Chicanas and the issue
    of involuntary sterilization: reforms needed
    to protect informed consent. CHICANO LAW
    REVIEW, Vol. 3, (1976), p. 3-37.
    Bibliography. English. DESCR:
    *Sterilization.

750 Horowitz, Ruth. Femininity and womanhood:
    virginity, unwed motherhood, and violence.
    IN: Horowitz, Ruth. HONOR AND THE AMERICAN
    DREAM: CULTURE AND IDENTITY IN A CHICANO
    COMMUNITY. New Brunswick, NJ: Rutgers
    University Press, 1983, p. 114-136. English.
    DESCR: *Fertility; Identity; Sex Roles;
    *Sexual Behavior; Single Parents; Violence;
    Women Men Relations; Youth.

751 Horowitz, Ruth. Passion, submission and
    motherhood: the negotiation of identity by
    unmarried innercity Chicanas. SOCIOLOGICAL
    QUARTERLY, Vol. 22, no. 2 (Spring 1981), p.
    241-252. English. DESCR: Barrios;
    *Fertility; Identity; *Sex Roles; *Sexual
    Behavior; Single Parents; Youth.

752 Hutchison, James. Teenagers and
    contraception in Cameron and Willacy
    Counties. BORDERLANDS JOURNAL, Vol. 7, no. 1
    (Fall 1983), p. 75-90. English. DESCR:
    Cameron County, TX; *Family Planning;
    Fertility; Sex Education; Willacy County,
    TX; Youth.

753 Jackson, Laurie Elizabeth. Self-care agency
    and limitations with respect to
    contraceptive behavior of Mexican-American
    women. Thesis (M.S.N.)--Medical College of
    Ohio at Toledo, 1988. 198 p. English.
    DESCR: *Fertility; Locus of Control.

754 Jorgensen, Stephen R. and Adams, Russell P.
    Family planning needs and behavior of
    Mexican American women: a study of health
    care professionals and their clientele.
    HISPANIC JOURNAL OF BEHAVIORAL SCIENCES,
    Vol. 9, no. 3 (September 1987), p. 265-286.
    English. DESCR: Acculturation; *Attitudes;
    *Cultural Characteristics; *Family Planning;
    Fertility; Medical Personnel; Stereotypes;
    Sterilization.

755 Ortiz, Sylvia. An analysis of the
    relationship between the values of sexual
    regulation, male dominance, and motherhood,
    and Mexican-American women's attitudes,
    knowledge, and usage of birth control.
    Thesis (Ph.D.)--University of California,
    Santa Barbara, 1987. 128 p. English. DESCR:
    Acculturation; *Attitudes; *Family Planning;
    Sexual Behavior.

756 Ortiz, Sylvia and Casas, Jesus Manuel. Birth
    control and low-income Mexican-American
    women: the impact of three values. HISPANIC
    JOURNAL OF BEHAVIORAL SCIENCES, Vol. 12, no.
    1 (February 1990), p. 83-92. English.

    DESCR: Acculturation; Attitudes; Fertility;
    *Low Income; *Sex Roles; Values.

757 Padilla, Amado M. and Baird, Traci L.
    Mexican-American sexuality and
    sexual knowledge: an exploratory study.
    HISPANIC JOURNAL OF BEHAVIORAL SCIENCES,
    Vol. 13, no. 1 (February 1991), p. 95-104.
    English. DESCR: *Attitudes; Sex Roles;
    *Sexual Behavior; Surveys; *Youth.

758 Sex education, abortion views of Mexican
    Americans typical of U.S. beliefs. FAMILY
    PLANNING PERSPECTIVES, Vol. 15, (July,
    August, 1983), p. 197-201. English. DESCR:
    *Abortion; *Attitudes; Family Planning; *Sex
    Education.

759 Stroup-Benham, Christine A. and Trevino,
    Fernando M. Reproductive characteristics of
    Mexican-American, mainland Puerto Rican, and
    Cuban-American women: data from the Hispanic
    Health and Nutrition Examination Survey.
    JAMA: JOURNAL OF THE AMERICAN MEDICAL
    ASSOCIATION, Vol. 265, no. 2 (January 9,
    1991), p. 222-226. English. DESCR:
    Breastfeeding; Cubanos; *Fertility; Hispanic
    Health and Nutrition Examination Survey
    (HHANES); Puerto Ricans; *Women.

760 Torres, Aida and Singh, Susheela.
    Contraceptive practice among Hispanic
    adolescents. FAMILY PLANNING PERSPECTIVES,
    Vol. 18, no. 4 (July, August, 1986), p.
    193-194. English. DESCR: *Family Planning;
    *Youth.

BLACK GOLD

761 Harlow, Barbara. Sites of struggle:
    immigration, deportation, prison, and exile.
    IN: Calderon, Hector and Saldivar, Jose
    David, eds. CRITICISM IN THE BORDERLANDS:
    STUDIES IN CHICANO LITERATURE, CULTURE, AND
    IDEOLOGY. Durham, NC: Duke University Press,
    1991, p. [149]-163. English. DESCR:
    Anzaldua, Gloria; BORDERLANDS/LA FRONTERA:
    THE NEW MESTIZA; First, Ruth; Khalifeh,
    Sahar; *Literary Criticism; *Political
    Ideology; Sanchez, Rosaura; Social Classes;
    "The Cariboo Cafe" [short story]; "The
    Ditch" [short story]; Viramontes, Helena
    Maria; WILD THORNS; *Women; Working Women.

Blacks

762 Abrahamse, Allan F.; Morrison, Peter A.; and
    Waite, Linda J. Teenagers willing to
    consider single parenthood: who is at
    greatest risk? FAMILY PLANNING PERSPECTIVES,
    Vol. 20, no. 1 (January, February, 1988), p.
    13-18. English. DESCR: Family Planning;
    *Fertility; High School and Beyond Project
    (HS&B); *Single Parents; Women; *Youth.

763 Alba, Isabel Catherine. Achievement
    conflicts, sex-role orientation, and
    performance on sex-role appropriate and
    sex-role inappropriate tasks in women of
    three ethnic groups. Thesis
    (Ph.D.)--University of California,
    Riverside, 1987. 129 p. English. DESCR:
    Anglo Americans; *Assertiveness; Ethnic
    Groups; Fear of Success Scale (FOSS); *Sex
    Roles; Women.

Blacks (cont.)

764 Balkwell, Carolyn Ann. Widowhood: its impact on morale and optimism among older persons of three ethnic groups. Thesis (Ph.D.)--University of Georgia, 1981. 170 p. English. **DESCR:** *Ancianos; Anglo Americans; Depression (Psychological); Ethnic Groups; Los Angeles County, CA; *Mental Health; Widowhood; *Women.

765 Bauer, Richard L. Ethnic differences in hip fracture: a reduced incidence in Mexican-Americans. AMERICAN JOURNAL OF EPIDEMIOLOGY, Vol. 127, no. 1 (January 1988), p. 145-149. English. **DESCR:** Anglo Americans; Bexar County, TX; Medical Care; Osteoporosis; *Public Health.

766 Braddom, Carolyn Lentz. The conceptualization of effective leadership as seen by women, Black and Hispanic superintendents. Thesis (Ed.D.)--University of Cincinnati, 1988. 232 p. English. **DESCR:** Anglo Americans; *Educational Administration; *Leadership; Management; Women.

767 Calderon, Vivian. Maternal employment and career orientation of young Chicana, Black, and white women. Thesis (Ph.D.)--University of California, Santa Cruz, 1984. 150 p. English. **DESCR:** Anglo Americans; *Careers; *Employment; Women; *Youth.

768 Creswell, John L. and Exezidis, Roxane H. Research brief: sex and ethnic differences in mathematics achievement of Black and Mexican-American adolescents. TEXAS TECH JOURNAL OF EDUCATION, Vol. 9, no. 3 (Fall 1982), p. 219-222. English. **DESCR:** *Mathematics; Youth.

769 Creswell, John L. Sex-related differences in the problem-solving abilities of rural Black, Anglo, and Chicano adolescents. TEXAS TECH JOURNAL OF EDUCATION, Vol. 10, no. 1 (Winter 1983), p. 29-33. English. **DESCR:** Aiken and Preger Revised Math Attitude Scale; Anglo Americans; California Achievement Test (CAT); *Mathematics; National Assessment of Educational Progress; National Council of Teachers of Mathematics (NCTM); Youth.

770 Cummings, Michele and Cummings, Scott. Family planning among the urban poor: sexual politics and social policy. FAMILY RELATIONS, Vol. 32, no. 1 (January 1983), p. 47-58. English. **DESCR:** Anglo Americans; Discrimination; *Family Planning; Low Income; *Stereotypes.

771 Dill, Bonnie Thornton. Our mothers' grief: racial ethnic women and the maintenance of families. JOURNAL OF FAMILY HISTORY, Vol. 13, no. 4 (October 1988), p. 415-431. English. **DESCR:** Asian Americans; Domestic Work; *Family; Fertility; *Sex Roles; *Women; *Working Women.

772 Dowling, Patrick T. and Fisher, Michael. Maternal factors and low birthweight infants: a comparison of Blacks with Mexican-Americans. JOURNAL OF FAMILY PRACTICE, Vol. 25, no. 2 (August 1987), p. 153-158. English. **DESCR:** Cook County, IL; *Infant Mortality; *Prenatal Care; *Public Health; *Socioeconomic Factors.

773 Dressel, Paula. Symposium. Civil rights, affirmative action, and the aged of the future: will life chances be different for Blacks, Hispanics, and women? An overview of the issues. GERONTOLOGIST, Vol. 26, no. 2 (April 1986), p. 128-131. English. **DESCR:** Affirmative Action; *Ancianos; *Civil Rights; Women.

774 Farkas, George; Barton, Margaret; and Kushner, Kathy. White, Black, and Hispanic female youths in central city labor markets. SOCIOLOGICAL QUARTERLY, Vol. 29, no. 4 (Winter 1988), p. 605-621. English. **DESCR:** Anglo Americans; Employment; *Income; *Labor Supply and Market; Urban Communities; Women; *Youth.

775 Felice, Marianne E., et al. Clinical observations of Mexican-American, Caucasian, and Black pregnant teenagers. JOURNAL OF ADOLESCENT HEALTH CARE, Vol. 7, no. 5 (September 1986), p. 305-310. English. **DESCR:** Anglo Americans; *Fertility; *Prenatal Care; San Diego, CA; Youth.

776 Finkelstein, Jordan W. and Von Eye, Alexander. Sanitary product use by white, Black, and Mexican American women. PUBLIC HEALTH REPORTS, Vol. 105, no. 5 (September, October, 1990), p. 491-496. English. **DESCR:** Anglo Americans; *Menstruation; *Toxic Shock Syndrome (TSS); *Women.

777 Flaskerud, Jacquelyn H. and Nyamathi, Adeline M. Black and Latina womens' AIDS related knowledge, attitudes, and practices. RESEARCH IN NURSING AND HEALTH, Vol. 12, no. 6 (December 1989), p. 339-346. English. **DESCR:** *AIDS (Disease); Attitudes; Health Education; Los Angeles County, CA; Surveys; *Women.

778 Forste, Renata T. and Heaton, Tim B. Initiation of sexual activity among female adolescents. YOUTH AND SOCIETY, Vol. 19, no. 3 (March 1988), p. 250-268. English. **DESCR:** Anglo Americans; Family; Sex Education; *Sexual Behavior; Women; *Youth.

779 Frisbie, William Parker; Opitz, Wolfgang; and Kelly, William R. Marital instability trends among Mexican Americans as compared to Blacks and Anglos: new evidence. SOCIAL SCIENCE QUARTERLY, Vol. 66, no. 3 (September 1985), p. 587-601. English. **DESCR:** Anglo Americans; Divorce; *Marriage.

780 Frisbie, William Parker; Bean, Frank D.; and Eberstein, Isaac W. Patterns of marital instability among Mexican Americans, Blacks, and Anglos. IN: Bean, Frank D. and Frisbie, W. Parker, eds. THE DEMOGRAPHY OF RACIAL AND ETHNIC GROUPS. New York: Academic Press, 1978, p. 143-163. English. **DESCR:** Anglo Americans; Divorce; Family; *Marriage.

781 Frisbie, William Parker; Bean, Frank D.; and Eberstein, Isaac W. Recent changes in marital instability among Mexican Americans: convergence with Black and Anglo trends. SOCIAL FORCES, Vol. 58, no. 4 (June 1980), p. 1205-1220. English. **DESCR:** Age Groups; Anglo Americans; *Divorce; *Marriage.

782 Galloway, Irma Nell. Trends in the employment of minority women as administrators in Texas public schools--1976-1981. Thesis (Ed.D.)--Texas Southern University, 1986. 129 p. English. **DESCR:** Asian Americans; Education; *Educational Administration; *Management; Native Americans; Texas; *Women.

Blacks (cont.)

783 Glenn, Evelyn Nakano. Racial ethnic women's labor: the intersection of race, gender and class oppression. REVIEW OF RADICAL POLITICAL ECONOMY, Vol. 17, no. 3 (Fall 1985), p. 86-108. English. DESCR: Asian Americans; *Discrimination; *Feminism; Laboring Classes; *Marxism; Sexism; Social Classes; Women; Working Women.

784 Gondolf, Edward W.; Fisher, Ellen; and McFerron, J. Richard. Racial differences among shelter residents: a comparison of Anglo, Black, and Hispanic battered. JOURNAL OF FAMILY VIOLENCE, Vol. 3, no. 1 (March 1988), p. 39-51. English. DESCR: Anglo Americans; Battered Women; Comparative Psychology; Cultural Characteristics; Natural Support Systems; Socioeconomic Factors; *Violence; *Women.

785 Gould, Jeffrey B.; Davey, Becky; and Stafford, Randall S. Socioeconomic differences in rates of cesarean section. THE NEW ENGLAND JOURNAL OF MEDICINE, Vol. 321, no. 4 (July 27, 1989), p. 233-239. English. DESCR: Anglo Americans; Asian Americans; *Cesarean Section; *Fertility; Los Angeles County, CA; *Socioeconomic Factors; Vital Statistics; Women.

786 Groessl, Patricia Ann. Depression and anxiety in postmenopausal women: a study of Black, white, and Hispanic women. Thesis (Ed.D.)--Western Michigan University, 1987. 87 p. English. DESCR: Anglo Americans; *Depression (Psychological); Menopause; Michigan; Stress; Women.

787 Hadley-Freydberg, Elizabeth. Prostitutes, concubines, whores and bitches: Black and Hispanic women in contemporary American film. IN: McCluskey, Audrey T., ed. WOMEN OF COLOR: PERSPECTIVES ON FEMINISM AND IDENTITY. Bloomington, IN: Women's Studies Program, Indiana University, 1985, p. 46-65. English. DESCR: *Actors and Actresses; *Films; Puerto Ricans; *Sex Stereotypes; Stereotypes; Women.

788 Hurtado, Aida. Relating to privilege: seduction and rejection in the subordination of white women and women of color. SIGNS: JOURNAL OF WOMEN IN CULTURE AND SOCIETY, Vol. 14, no. 4 (Summer 1989), p. 833-855. English. DESCR: *Anglo Americans; Asian Americans; Ethnic Groups; *Feminism; Political Ideology; Political Socialization; *Women.

789 Isaacs, Barbara Gail. Anglo, Black, and Latin adolescents' participation in sports. Thesis (Ph.D.)--California School of Professional Psychology, Los Angeles, 1984. 283 p. English. DESCR: Anglo Americans; Cultural Characteristics; *Secondary School Education; *Sports; *Women; Youth.

790 Jensen, Leif. Secondary earner strategies and family poverty: immigrant-native differentials, 1960-1980. INTERNATIONAL MIGRATION REVIEW, Vol. 25, no. 1 (Spring 1991), p. 113-140. English. DESCR: Anglo Americans; *Asian Americans; Family; Immigrants; Immigration; Income; Poverty; Women; Working Women.

791 Leonard, Jonathan S. The effect of unions on the employment of Blacks, Hispanics, and women. INDUSTRIAL AND LABOR RELATIONS REVIEW, Vol. 39, no. 1 (October 1985), p. 115-132. English. DESCR: Employment; *Labor Unions; Women.

792 Markides, Kyriakos S. Consequences of gender differentials in life expectancy for Black and Hispanic Americans. INTERNATIONAL JOURNAL OF AGING & HUMAN DEVELOPMENT, Vol. 29, no. 2 (1989), p. 95-102. English. DESCR: *Ancianos; Census; Cubanos; Latin Americans; Males; Population; Puerto Ricans; U.S. Bureau of the Census.

793 Mary, Nancy L. Reactions of Black, Hispanic, and white mothers to having a child with handicaps. MENTAL RETARDATION, Vol. 28, no. 1 (February 1990), p. 1-5. English. DESCR: Anglo Americans; *Attitudes; *Children; Comparative Psychology; *Mentally Handicapped; Parent and Child Relationships; *Women.

794 Mays, Vicki M. and Cochran, Susan D. Issues in the perception of AIDS risk and risk reduction activities by Black and Hispanic/Latina women. AMERICAN PSYCHOLOGIST, Vol. 43, no. 11 (November 1988), p. 949-957. English. DESCR: *AIDS (Disease); Condom Use; Fertility; Health Education; Preventative Medicine; *Sexual Behavior; Women.

795 Michael, Robert T. and Tuma, Nancy Brandon. Entry into marriage and parenthood by young men and women: the influence of family background. DEMOGRAPHY, Vol. 22, no. 4 (November 1985), p. 515-544. Magazine. English. DESCR: Anglo Americans; *Cultural Characteristics; *Fertility; *Marriage; Population; Youth.

796 Mullen, Julia Ann. Black, Anglo, and Chicana women's construction of mental illness. Thesis (Ph.D.)--University of California, Santa Barbara, 1985. 276 p. English. DESCR: Anglo Americans; *Mental Illness; *Women.

797 Norinsky, Margaret Elaine. The relationship between sex-role identity and ethnicity to styles of assertiveness and aggression in women. Thesis (Ed.D.)--University of San Francisco, 1987. 164 p. English. DESCR: Anglo Americans; *Assertiveness; Ethnic Groups; *Identity; *Sex Roles; *Women.

798 Ortiz, Vilma and Fennelly, Katherine. Early childbearing and employment among young Mexican origin, Black, and white women. SOCIAL SCIENCE QUARTERLY, Vol. 69, no. 4 (December 1988), p. 987-995. English. DESCR: Anglo Americans; *Employment; *Fertility; *Women; *Youth.

799 Powers, Stephen and Jones, Patricia. Factorial invariance of the California achievement tests across race and sex. EDUCATIONAL AND PSYCHOLOGICAL MEASUREMENT, Vol. 44, no. 4 (Winter 1984), p. 967-970. English. DESCR: Anglo Americans; *California Achievement Test (CAT); Educational Tests and Measurements; Males; Women.

800 Reimers, Cordelia W. A comparative analysis of the wages of Hispanics, Blacks, and non-Hispanic whites. IN: Borjas, George J. and Tienda, Marta, eds. HISPANICS IN THE U.S. ECONOMY. Orlando, FL: Academic Press, 1985, p. 27-75. English. DESCR: Anglo Americans; *Income; Labor Supply and Market; Males; Survey of Income and Education (SIE).

Blacks (cont.)

801 Ruiz, Vicki L., ed. and DuBois, Ellen Carol, ed. Unequal sisters: a multicultural reader in U.S. women's history. New York: Routledge, 1990. xvi, 473 p. English. **DESCR:** Anglo Americans; Asian Americans; Feminism; *History; Native Americans; *Women.

802 Sanford, Judy, et al. Patterns of reported rape in a tri-ethnic population: Houston, Texas, 1974-1975. AMERICAN JOURNAL OF PUBLIC HEALTH, Vol. 69, no. 5 (May 1979), p. 480-484. English. **DESCR:** Anglo Americans; Criminology; *Ethnic Groups; *Houston, TX; *Rape; Statistics; Women.

803 Tienda, Marta and Angel, Ronald J. Headship and household composition among Blacks, Hispanics and other whites. SOCIAL FORCES, Vol. 61, no. 2 (December 1982), p. 508-531. English. **DESCR:** Anglo Americans; Cultural Characteristics; Extended Family; *Family; Puerto Ricans; Single Parents.

804 Tienda, Marta and Glass, Jennifer. Household structure and labor-force participation of Black, Hispanic, and white mothers. DEMOGRAPHY, Vol. 22, no. 3 (August 1985), p. 381-394. English. **DESCR:** Anglo Americans; *Extended Family; *Family; *Sex Roles; *Working Women.

805 Timberlake, Andrea, et al. Women of color and southern women: a bibliography of social science research, 1975 to 1988. Memphis, TN: Center for Research on Women, Memphis State University, 1988. vii, 264 p. English. **DESCR:** *Bibliography; *Social Science; *Women.

806 Wagner, Roland M. and Schaffer, Diane M. Social networks and survival strategies: an exploratory study of Mexican American, Black, and Anglo female family heads in San Jose, California. IN: Melville, Margarita B., ed. TWICE A MINORITY. St. Louis, MO: Mosby, 1980, p. 173-190. English. **DESCR:** Anglo Americans; Identity; *Natural Support Systems; San Jose, CA; *Single Parents; Stress.

807 Weiner, Raine. The needs of poverty women heading households: a return to postsecondary education. Thesis (Ph.D.)--California School of Professional Psychology, Los Angeles, 1986. 180 p. English. **DESCR:** Anglo Americans; *Employment Training; Ethnic Groups; *Poverty; *Single Parents; Vocational Education; Welfare; Women.

808 Zambrana, Ruth E., et al. Ethnic differences in the substance use patterns of low-income pregnant women. FAMILY & COMMUNITY HEALTH, Vol. 13, no. 4 (January 1991), p. 1-11. English. **DESCR:** Alcoholism; *Drug Use; *Fertility; Immigrants; *Low Income; Smoking; Women.

809 Zeff, Shirley B. A cross-cultural study of Mexican American, Black American and white American women of a large urban university. HISPANIC JOURNAL OF BEHAVIORAL SCIENCES, Vol. 4, no. 2 (June 1982), p. 245-261. English. **DESCR:** Anglo Americans; *Higher Education; Sex Roles; Students.

Blea, Irene I.

810 Lucero, Marcela Christine. The socio-historical implication of the valley as a metaphor in three Colorado Chicana poets. Thesis (Ph.D.)--University of Minnesota, 1981. 176 p. English. **DESCR:** *Authors; Chicano Movement; Colorado; Feminism; Literary Criticism; Mondragon Valdez, Maria; Poetry; Zamora, Bernice.

BLESS ME, ULTIMA

811 Anderson, Robert K. Marez y Luna and the masculine-feminine dialectic. CRITICA HISPANICA, Vol. 6, no. 2 (1984), p. 97-105. English. **DESCR:** Anaya, Rudolfo A.; Literary Criticism; Novel; *Women Men Relations.

812 Mondin, Sandra. The depiction of the Chicana in BLESS ME ULTIMA and THE MILAGRO BEANFIELD WAR: a study in contrasts. IN: Luna Lawhn, Juanita, et al., eds. MEXICO AND THE UNITED STATES: INTERCULTURAL RELATIONS IN THE HUMANITIES. San Antonio, TX: San Antonio College, 1984, p. 137-150. English. **DESCR:** Anaya, Rudolfo A.; Literary Characters; Literary Criticism; Nichols, John; *Stereotypes; THE MILAGRO BEANFIELD WAR [novel].

813 Tatum, Charles M. Grappling with difference: gender, race, class, and ethnicity in contemporary Chicana/o literature. RENATO ROSALDO LECTURE SERIES MONOGRAPH, Vol. 6, (1988, 1989), p. 1-23. English. **DESCR:** Anaya, Rudolfo A.; Authors; *Feminism; Identity; Literary Characters; *Literary Criticism; Literature Reviews.

BLOODROOT

814 Ordonez, Elizabeth J. [Villanueva, Alma]. IN: Martinez, Julio A. and Lomeli, Francisco A., eds. CHICANO LITERATURE: A REFERENCE GUIDE. Westport, CT: Greenwood Press, 1985, p. 413-420. English. **DESCR:** Authors; Biography; Literary Criticism; *Villanueva, Alma.

Bojorquez, Frances

815 Matsuda, Gema. La Chicana organizes: the Comision Femenil Mexicana in perspective. REGENERACION, Vol. 2, no. 4 (1975), p. 25-27. English. **DESCR:** Chicano Movement; *Comision Femenil Mexicana Nacional; De la Cruz, Juana Ines; Flores, Francisca; History; Machismo; Malinche; Prisons; Sex Stereotypes; *Sexism.

Bolton, Herbert Eugene

816 Castaneda, Antonia I. Gender, race, and culture: Spanish-Mexican women in the historiography of frontier California. FRONTIERS: A JOURNAL OF WOMEN STUDIES, Vol. 11, no. 1 (1990), p. [8]-20. English. **DESCR:** Bancroft, Hubert Howe; *California; Californios; *Historiography; History; Intermarriage; *Sex Stereotypes; Spanish Borderlands Theory; Spanish Influence; Stereotypes; Turner, Frederick Jackson; Women.

Bonilla-Giannini, Roxanna

817 Ordonez, Elizabeth J. La imagen de la mujer en el nuevo cine chicano. CARACOL, Vol. 5, no. 2 (October 1978), p. 12-13. Spanish. **DESCR:** *Films; Lopez, Lexore; ONLY ONCE IN A LIFETIME [film]; *Photography; RAICES DE SANGRE [film]; Robelo, Miguel; Sex Stereotypes.

Book Industry
USE: Publishing Industry

Book Sellers and Distributors
    USE: Publishing Industry

Books

818 Introduction. ENCUENTRO FEMENIL, Vol. 1, no. 2 (1974), p. 3-7. English. DESCR: ENCUENTRO FEMENIL; Hijas de Cuauhtemoc; Organizations *Periodicals.

Border Industrialization Program (BIP)

819 Bustamante, Jorge A. Maquiladoras: a new face of international capitalism on Mexico's northern frontier. IN: Nash, June and Fernandez-Kelly, Patricia, eds. WOMEN, MEN, AND THE INTERNATIONAL DIVISION OF LABOR. Albany, NY: State University of New York Press, 1983, p. 224-256. English. DESCR: Banking Industry; Border Industries; *Border Region; Foreign Trade; Industrial Workers; International Economic Relations; Mexico; Population; Programa Nacional Fronterizo (PRONAF); United States-Mexico Relations; Women; Working Women.

820 Fernandez Kelly, Maria. Mexican border industrialization, female labor force participation and migration. IN: Nash, June and Fernandez-Kelly, Patricia, eds. WOMEN, MEN, AND THE INTERNATIONAL DIVISION OF LABOR. Albany, NY: State University of New York Press, 1983, p. 205-223. English. DESCR: *Border Industries; Ciudad Juarez, Chihuahua, Mexico; Immigration; Industrial Workers; Labor Supply and Market; Males; *Migration Patterns; Undocumented Workers; *Women; Working Women.

821 Iglesias, Norma. La flor mas bella de la maquiladora: historias de vida de la mujer obrera en Tijuana, B.C.N. Mexico, D.F.: Secretaria de Educacion Publica, CEFNOMEX, 1985. 166 p.: ill. Spanish. DESCR: *Border Industries; Cultural Customs; Labor Unions; Sindicato Independiente Solidev; Solidev Mexicana, S.A.; Tijuana, Baja California, Mexico; *Women; Working Women.

822 Seligson, Mitchell A. and Williams, Edward J. Maquiladoras and migration workers in the Mexico-United States Border Industrialization Program. Austin, TX: Mexico-United States Border Research Program, University of Texas at Austin, 1981. xviii, 202 p. English. DESCR: *Border Region; Employment; Immigration; Industrial Workers; Mexico; *Migration Patterns; Working Women.

823 Stoddard, Ellwyn R. Maquila: assembly plants in Northern Mexico. El Paso, TX: Texas Western Press, 1987. ix, 91 p., [4] p. of plates: ill. English. DESCR: *Border Industries; Immigration; Income; *Industrial Workers; Labor Supply and Market; Mexico; Sexism; Undocumented Workers.

824 Tiano, Susan B. Maquiladoras in Mexicali: integration or exploitation? IN: Ruiz, Vicki L. and Tiano, Susan, eds. WOMEN ON THE U.S.-MEXICO BORDER: RESPONSES TO CHANGE. Boston, MA: Allen & Unwin, 1987, p. 77-101. English. DESCR: *Border Industries; Border Region; Employment; Labor Supply and Market; Mexicali, Mexico; Women; Working Women.

825 Tiano, Susan B. Women's work and unemployment in northern Mexico. IN: Ruiz, Vicki L. and Tiano, Susan, eds. WOMEN ON THE U.S.-MEXICO BORDER: RESPONSES TO CHANGE. Boston, MA: Allen & Unwin, 1987, p. 17-39. English. DESCR: Border Industries; Border Region; Employment; Labor Supply and Market; Mexico; Multinational Corporations; *Women.

826 Young, Gay. Gender identification and working-class solidarity among maquila workers in Ciudad Juarez: stereotypes and realities. IN: Ruiz, Vicki L. and Tiano, Susan, eds. WOMEN ON THE U.S.-MEXICO BORDER: RESPONSES TO CHANGE. Boston, MA: Allen & Unwin, 1987, p. 105-127. English. DESCR: Assertiveness; Attitudes; *Border Industries; Border Region; Ciudad Juarez, Chihuahua, Mexico; Employment; Garment Industry; Sex Roles; Surveys; Working Women.

827 Young, Gay. Women, border industrialization program, and human rights. El Paso, TX: Center for InterAmerican and Border Studies, UTEP, 1984. 33 p. English. DESCR: *Border Industries; Economic Development; Employment; Industrial Workers; Mexico; Sex Roles; *Sexism; *Women; Working Women.

828 Young, Gay. Women, development and human rights: issues in integrated transnational production. JOURNAL OF APPLIED BEHAVIORAL SCIENCE, Vol. 20, no. 4 (November 1984), p. 383-401. English. DESCR: *Border Industries; Feminism; Mexico; Multinational Corporations; Women; Women Men Relations; *Working Women.

Border Industries

829 Arenal, Sandra. Sangre joven: las maquiladoras por dentro. Mexico, D.F.: Editorial Nuestro Tiempo, 1986. 130 p.: ill. Spanish. DESCR: *Border Region; Employment; *Oral History; Women; Working Women.

830 Blanco, Iris and Salorzano, Rosalia. O te aclimatas o te aclimueres. FEM, Vol. 8, no. 34 (June, July, 1984), p. 20-22. Spanish. DESCR: *Immigration; Mexico; Women; Working Women.

831 Bustamante, Jorge A. Maquiladoras: a new face of international capitalism on Mexico's northern frontier. IN: Nash, June and Fernandez-Kelly, Patricia, eds. WOMEN, MEN, AND THE INTERNATIONAL DIVISION OF LABOR. Albany, NY: State University of New York Press, 1983, p. 224-256. English. DESCR: Banking Industry; Border Industrialization Program (BIP); *Border Region; Foreign Trade; Industrial Workers; International Economic Relations; Mexico; Population; Programa Nacional Fronterizo (PRONAF); United States-Mexico Relations; Women; Working Women.

832 Carrillo V., Jorge and Hernandez H., Alberto. La industria maquiladora en Mexico: bibliografia, directorio e investigaciones recientes = Border assembly industry and recent research. La Jolla, CA: Program in United States-Mexican Studies, University of California, San Diego, 1981. 130 p. Spanish. DESCR: *Bibliography.

833 Carrillo V., Jorge and Hernandez H., Alberto. Mujeres fronterizas en la industria maquiladora. Mexico, D.F.: Secretaria de Educacion Publica; Tijuana, B.C.N.: Centro de Estudios Fronterizos del Norte de Mexico, 1985. 216 p. Spanish. DESCR: *Employment; *Women; Working Women.

Border Industries
(cont.)

834 Dixon, Marlene; Martinez, Elizabeth; and McCaughan, Ed. Theoretical perspectives on Chicanas, Mexicanas and the transnational working class. CONTEMPORARY MARXISM, no. 11 (Fall 1985), p. 46-76. English. DESCR: Capitalism; Economic History and Conditions; History; *Immigration; *Labor Supply and Market; *Laboring Classes; Mexico; Undocumented Workers; Women.

835 Fernandez Kelly, Maria. "Chavalas de maquiladora": a study of the female labor force in Ciudad Juarez' offshore production plants. Thesis (Ph.D.)--Rutgers University, 1980. xi, 391 leaves. English. DESCR: Ciudad Juarez, Chihuahua, Mexico; Electronics Industry; *Employment; Garment Industry; Industrial Workers; Mexico; Women; *Working Women.

836 Fernandez Kelly, Maria. For we are sold, I and my people: women and industry in Mexico's frontier. Albany, NY: State University of New York Press, 1983. vii, 217 p. English. DESCR: *Border Region; Ciudad Juarez, Chihuahua, Mexico; *Electronics Industry; *Garment Industry; Industrial Workers; Working Women.

837 Fernandez Kelly, Maria. The 'maquila' women. NACLA: REPORT ON THE AMERICAS, Vol. 14, no. 5 (September, October, 1980), p. 14-19. English. DESCR: Feminism; Industrial Workers; Stereotypes; Women; *Working Women.

838 Fernandez Kelly, Maria. Mexican border industrialization, female labor force participation and migration. IN: Nash, June and Fernandez-Kelly, Patricia, eds. WOMEN, MEN, AND THE INTERNATIONAL DIVISION OF LABOR. Albany, NY: State University of New York Press, 1983, p. 205-223. English. DESCR: Border Industrialization Program (BIP); Ciudad Juarez, Chihuahua, Mexico; Immigration; Industrial Workers; Labor Supply and Market; Males; *Migration Patterns; Undocumented Workers; *Women; Working Women.

839 Fuentes, Annette and Ehrenreich, Barbara. Women in the global factory. New York: Institute for New Communications; Boston: South End Press, 1983. 64 p.: ill. English. DESCR: Industrial Workers; *International Economic Relations; *Women; *Working Women.

840 Gettman, Dawn and Pena, Devon Gerardo. Women, mental health, and the workplace in a transnational setting. SOCIAL WORK, Vol. 31, no. 1 (January, February, 1986), p. 5-11. English. DESCR: Employment; *Mental Health; Mexico; United States-Mexico Relations; Women; *Working Women.

841 Hovell, Melbourne F., et al. Occupational health risks for Mexican women: the case of the maquiladora along the Mexican-United States border. INTERNATIONAL JOURNAL OF HEALTH SERVICES, Vol. 18, no. 4 (1988), p. 617-627. English. DESCR: Border Region; Mexico; *Occupational Hazards; Project Concern International (PCI), San Diego, CA; Public Health; Surveys; Tijuana, Baja California, Mexico; Women; Working Women.

842 Iglesias, Norma. La flor mas bella de la maquiladora: historias de vida de la mujer obrera en Tijuana, B.C.N. Mexico, D.F.: Secretaria de Educacion Publica, CEFNOMEX, 1985. 166 p.: ill. Spanish. DESCR: Border Industrialization Program (BIP); Cultural Customs; Labor Unions; Sindicato Independiente Solidev; Solidev Mexicana, S.A.; Tijuana, Baja California, Mexico; *Women; Working Women.

843 Iglesias, Norma. "Las mujeres somos mas responsables": la utilizacion de mano de obra femenina en las maquiladoras fronterizas. TRABAJOS MONOGRAFICOS, Vol. 2, no. 1 (1986), p. 19-30. Spanish. DESCR: Women; *Working Women.

844 Iglesias, Norma and Carrillo, Jorge. Que me dejo el trabajo? FEM, Vol. 10, no. 48 (October, November, 1986), p. 43-45. Spanish. DESCR: Women; *Working Women.

845 Iglesias, Norma and Carrillo, Jorge. Que me dejo el trabajo?: mi vida se pregunta. TRABAJOS MONOGRAFICOS, Vol. 2, no. 1 (1986), p. 10-18. Spanish. DESCR: *Oral History; *Working Women.

846 In the maquiladoras. CORRESPONDENCIA, no. 9 (December 1990), p. 3-9. English. DESCR: Labor Unions; Tijuana, Baja California, Mexico; Women; *Working Women.

847 Lavrin, Asuncion. El segundo sexo en Mexico: experiencia, estudio e introspeccion, 1983-1987. MEXICAN STUDIES/ESTUDIOS MEXICANOS, Vol. 5, no. 2 (Summer 1989), p. 297-312. Spanish. DESCR: Arenal, Sandra; Carrillo, Jorge; Hernandez, Alberto; Iglesias, Norma; LA FLOR MAS BELLA DE LA MAQUILADORA; *Literature Reviews; Mexico; MUJERES FRONTERIZAS EN LA INDUSTRIA MAQUILADORA; SANGRE JOVEN: LAS MAQUILADORAS POR DENTRO; Women.

848 Levy Oved, Albert and Alcocer Marban, Sonia. Las maquiladoras en Mexico. Mexico: Fondo de Cultura Economica, 1984. 125 p.: ill. Spanish. DESCR: *Border Region; International Economic Relations; United States-Mexico Relations; Women.

849 Pena, Devon Gerardo. Between the lines: a new perspective on the industrial sociology of women workers in transnational labor processes. IN: Cordova, Teresa, et al., eds. CHICANA VOICES. Austin, TX: Center for Mexican American Studies, 1986, p. 77-95. English. DESCR: *Labor; Marxism; *Women; Working Women.

850 Pena, Devon Gerardo. The class politics of abstract labor: organizational forms and industrial relations in the Mexican maquiladoras. Thesis (Ph.D.)--University of Texas, Austin, 1983. xix, 587 p. English. DESCR: Border Region; International Economic Relations; *Trade Unions; Women; Working Women.

851 Pena, Devon Gerardo. Las maquiladoras: Mexican women in class struggle in the border industries. AZTLAN, Vol. 11, no. 2 (Fall 1980), p. 159-229. English. DESCR: *Economic History and Conditions; Labor; Labor Unions; Mexico; Mexico-U.S. Border Development; Working Women.

852 Pena, Devon Gerardo. Tortuosidad: shop floor struggles of female maquiladora workers. IN: Ruiz, Vicki L. and Tiano, Susan, eds. WOMEN ON THE U.S.-MEXICO BORDER: RESPONSES TO CHANGE. Boston, MA: Allen & Unwin, 1987, p. 129-154. English. DESCR: Ciudad Juarez, Chihuahua, Mexico; Employment; Personnel Management; Population; Surveys; *Women; Working Women.

Border Industries
(cont.)

853 Preuss, Sabine. Die Frauen von Acapulco Fashion: Weiblicher Lebenszusammenhang und Industrialisierung in den Weltmarktfabriken Mexikos. Berlin: Express, c1985. 133 p.: ill. Other. **DESCR:** *Acapulco Fashion, Ciudad Juarez, Mexico; *Employment; *Working Women.

854 Ruiz, Vicki L., ed. and Tiano, Susan B., ed Women on the U.S.-Mexico border: responses to change. Boston, MA: Allen & Unwin, c1987. xi, 247 p. English. **DESCR:** *Border Region; Employment; Feminism; Immigrants; Mexico; Sex Roles; *Women.

855 Sable, Martin H. Las maquiladoras: assembly and manufacturing plants on the United States-Mexico border: an international guide. New York: Haworth Press, 1989. 150 p. English. **DESCR:** *Bibliography.

856 Stoddard, Ellwyn R. Maquila: assembly plants in Northern Mexico. El Paso, TX: Texas Western Press, 1987. ix, 91 p., [4] p. of plates: ill. English. **DESCR:** Border Industrialization Program (BIP); Immigration; Income; *Industrial Workers; Labor Supply and Market; Mexico; Sexism; Undocumented Workers.

857 Tiano, Susan B. Labor composition and gender stereotypes in the maquila. JOURNAL OF BORDERLAND STUDIES, Vol. 5, no. 1 (Spring 1990), p. 20-24. English. **DESCR:** Industrial Workers; Labor Supply and Market; *Sex Stereotypes; Women; *Working Women.

858 Tiano, Susan B. Maquiladoras in Mexicali: integration or exploitation? IN: Ruiz, Vicki L. and Tiano, Susan, eds. WOMEN ON THE U.S.-MEXICO BORDER: RESPONSES TO CHANGE. Boston, MA: Allen & Unwin, 1987, p. 77-101. English. **DESCR:** Border Industrialization Program (BIP); Border Region; Employment; Labor Supply and Market; Mexicali, Mexico; Women; Working Women.

859 Tiano, Susan B. Maquiladoras, women's work, and unemployment in northern Mexico. AZTLAN, Vol. 15, no. 2 (Fall 1984), p. 341-378. English. **DESCR:** Employment; Mexico; *Women; Working Women.

860 Tiano, Susan B. Women's work and unemployment in northern Mexico. IN: Ruiz, Vicki L. and Tiano, Susan, eds. WOMEN ON THE U.S.-MEXICO BORDER: RESPONSES TO CHANGE. Boston, MA: Allen & Unwin, 1987, p. 17-39. English. **DESCR:** Border Industrialization Program (BIP); Border Region; Employment; Labor Supply and Market; Mexico; Multinational Corporations; *Women.

861 Villalobos, Rolando M. Research guide to the literature on Northern Mexico's maquiladora assembly industry. [Stanford, CA?]: Zapata Underground Press, c1988. 59 leaves. English. **DESCR:** *Bibliography.

862 Williams, Edward J. and Passe-Smith, John T. Turnover and recruitment in the maquila industry: causes and solutions. Las Cruces, NM: Joint Border Research Institute, New Mexico State University, 1989. ii, 59 p. English. **DESCR:** *Employment; Income; *Labor Supply and Market; Personnel Management; Surveys; Women; *Working Women.

863 Young, Gay. Gender identification and working-class solidarity among maquila workers in Ciudad Juarez: stereotypes and realities. IN: Ruiz, Vicki L. and Tiano,

Susan, eds. WOMEN ON THE U.S.-MEXICO BORDER: RESPONSES TO CHANGE. Boston, MA: Allen & Unwin, 1987, p. 105-127. English. **DESCR:** Assertiveness; Attitudes; Border Industrialization Program (BIP); Border Region; Ciudad Juarez, Chihuahua, Mexico; Employment; Garment Industry; Sex Roles; Surveys; Working Women.

864 Young, Gay. Women, border industrialization program, and human rights. El Paso, TX: Center for InterAmerican and Border Studies, UTEP, 1984. 33 p. English. **DESCR:** Border Industrialization Program (BIP); Economic Development; Employment; Industrial Workers; Mexico; Sex Roles; *Sexism; *Women; Working Women.

865 Young, Gay. Women, development and human rights: issues in integrated transnational production. JOURNAL OF APPLIED BEHAVIORAL SCIENCE, Vol. 20, no. 4 (November 1984), p. 383-401. English. **DESCR:** Border Industrialization Program (BIP); Feminism; Mexico; Multinational Corporations; Women; Women Men Relations; *Working Women.

Border Patrol

866 Miller, George A. Latinas on border patrol. VISTA, Vol. 4, no. 18 (January 1, 1989), p. 8-10. English. **DESCR:** Border Region; Police; Statistics.

867 Solorzano-Torres, Rosalia. Women, labor, and the U.S.-Mexico border: Mexican maids in El Paso, Texas. IN: Melville, Margarita, ed. MEXICANAS AT WORK IN THE UNITED STATES. Houston, TX: Mexican American Studies Program, University of Houston, 1988, p. 75-83. English. **DESCR:** *Border Region; Domestic Work; El Paso, TX; Immigrants; Immigration and Naturalization Service (INS); Immigration Regulation and Control; *Labor Supply and Market; Undocumented Workers; *Women; *Working Women.

Border Region

868 Alvarez-Amaya, Maria. Determinants of breast and cervical cancer behavior among Mexican American women. BORDER HEALTH/SALUD FRONTERIZA, Vol. 5, no. 3 (July, September, 1989), p. 22-27. Bilingual. **DESCR:** *Breast Cancer; *Cancer; Diseases; Immigrants; Medical Care; *Preventative Medicine.

869 Anzaldua, Gloria. Borderlands/La frontera: the new mestiza. San Francisco, CA: Spinsters/Aunt Lute, 1987. 203 p. Bilingual. **DESCR:** Aztecs; *Identity; Mythology; Poems; Prose; Sex Roles.

870 Arenal, Sandra. Sangre joven: las maquiladoras por dentro. Mexico, D.F.: Editorial Nuestro Tiempo, 1986. 130 p.: ill. Spanish. **DESCR:** *Border Industries; Employment; *Oral History; Women; Working Women.

871 Bridges, Julian C. Family life. IN: Stoddard, Ellwyn R., et al., eds. BORDERLANDS SOURCEBOOK: A GUIDE TO THE LITERATURE ON NORTHERN MEXICO AND THE AMERICAN SOUTHWEST. Norman, OK: University of Oklahoma Press, 1983, p. 259-262. English. **DESCR:** *Family; Literature Reviews.

Border Region (cont.)

872 Bustamante, Jorge A. Maquiladoras: a new face of international capitalism on Mexico's northern frontier. IN: Nash, June and Fernandez-Kelly, Patricia, eds. WOMEN, MEN, AND THE INTERNATIONAL DIVISION OF LABOR. Albany, NY: State University of New York Press, 1983, p. 224-256. English. DESCR: Banking Industry; Border Industrialization Program (BIP); Border Industries; Foreign Trade; Industrial Workers; International Economic Relations; Mexico; Population; Programa Nacional Fronterizo (PRONAF); United States-Mexico Relations; Women; Working Women.

873 Castaneda, Antonia I. Comparative frontiers: the migration of women to Alta California and New Zealand. IN: Schlissel, Lillian, et al., eds. WESTERN WOMEN: THEIR LAND, THEIR LIVES. Albuquerque, NM: University of New Mexico Press, 1988, p. 283-300. English. DESCR: California; History; Immigrants; Immigration; Marriage; Mexico; Missions; Native Americans; New Zealand; Social History and Conditions; *Women.

874 Domenella, Ana Rosa. Al margen de un coloquio fronterizo mujer y literatura mexicana y chicana. FEM, Vol. 14, no. 89 (May 1990), p. 32-34. Spanish. DESCR: Coloquio Fronterizo Mujer y Literatura Mexicana y Chicana (1987: Tijuana, Baja California, Mexico); *Conferences and Meetings; *Literature; Mexican Literature; Mexico; Women.

875 Fernandez Kelly, Maria. For we are sold, I and my people: women and industry in Mexico's frontier. Albany, NY: State University of New York Press, 1983. vii, 217 p. English. DESCR: Border Industries; Ciudad Juarez, Chihuahua, Mexico; *Electronics Industry; *Garment Industry; Industrial Workers; Working Women.

876 Garcia, Mario T. Family and gender in Chicano and border studies research. MEXICAN STUDIES/ESTUDIOS MEXICANOS, Vol. 6, no. 1 (Winter 1990), p. 109-119. English. DESCR: Alvarez, Robert R., Jr.; CANNERY WOMEN, CANNERY LIVES; *Family; LA FAMILIA: MIGRATION AND ADAPTATION IN BAJA AND ALTA CALIFORNIA, 1800-1975; *Literature Reviews; Ruiz, Vicki L.; Tiano, Susan B.; Women; WOMEN ON THE U.S.-MEXICO BORDER: RESPONSES TO CHANGE; WOMEN'S WORK AND CHICANO FAMILIES; Zavella, Pat.

877 Gutierrez Castillo, Dina. La imagen de la mujer en la novela fronteriza. IN: Lopez-Gonzalez, Aralia, et al., eds. MUJER Y LITERATURA MEXICANA Y CHICANA: CULTURAS EN CONTACTO. Mexico: Colegio de la Frontera Norte, 1988, p. [55]-63. Spanish. DESCR: Islas, Arturo; Literary Characters; *Literary Criticism; Mendez M., Miguel; *Novel; PEREGRINOS DE AZTLAN; Sex Roles; Sex Stereotypes; THE RAIN GOD: A DESERT TALE; *Women.

878 Hedderson, John J. Fertility and mortality. IN: Stoddard, Ellwyn R., et al., eds. BORDERLANDS SOURCEBOOK: A GUIDE TO THE LITERATURE ON NORTHERN MEXICO AND THE AMERICAN SOUTHWEST. Norman, OK: University of Oklahoma Press, 1983, p. 232-236. English. DESCR: *Fertility; Population; *Vital Statistics.

879 Holck, Susan E., et al. Alcohol consumption among Mexican American and Anglo women: results of a survey along the U.S.-Mexico border. JOURNAL OF STUDIES ON ALCOHOL, Vol. 45, no. 2 (March 1984), p. 149-154. English. DESCR: *Alcoholism; Anglo Americans; Surveys.

880 Holck, Susan E., et al. Need for family planning services among Anglo and Hispanic women in the United States counties bordering Mexico. FAMILY PLANNING PERSPECTIVES, Vol. 14, no. 3 (May, June, 1982), p. 155-159. English. DESCR: Anglo Americans; *Family Planning; Women.

881 Hovell, Melbourne F., et al. Occupational health risks for Mexican women: the case of the maquiladora along the Mexican-United States border. INTERNATIONAL JOURNAL OF HEALTH SERVICES, Vol. 18, no. 4 (1988), p. 617-627. English. DESCR: *Border Industries; Mexico; *Occupational Hazards; Project Concern International (PCI), San Diego, CA; Public Health; Surveys; Tijuana, Baja California, Mexico; Women; Working Women.

882 La Monica, Grace; Gulino, Claire; and Ortiz Soto, Irma. A comparative study of female Mexican and American working nurses in the border corridor. BORDER HEALTH/SALUD FRONTERIZA, Vol. 5, no. 2 (April, June, 1989), p. 2-6. Bilingual. DESCR: Anglo Americans; *Medical Personnel; Women; *Working Women.

883 Levy Oved, Albert and Alcocer Marban, Sonia. Las maquiladoras en Mexico. Mexico: Fondo de Cultura Economica, 1984. 125 p.: ill. Spanish. DESCR: *Border Industries; International Economic Relations; United States-Mexico Relations; Women.

884 Marshall, Maria Sandra Gonzalez. The childbearing beliefs and practices of pregnant Mexican-American adolescents living in Southwest border regions. Thesis (M.S.)--University of Arizona, 1987. 117 p. English. DESCR: *Acculturation; *Fertility; *Youth.

885 Melville, Margarita B., ed. Mexicanas at work in the United States. Houston, TX: Mexican American Studies Program, University of Houston, 1988. 83 p. English. DESCR: *Employment; Family; *Labor; Migrant Labor; *Women; Working Women.

886 Miller, George A. Latinas on border patrol. VISTA, Vol. 4, no. 18 (January 1, 1989), p. 8-10. English. DESCR: *Border Patrol; Police; Statistics.

887 Pena, Devon Gerardo. The class politics of abstract labor: organizational forms and industrial relations in the Mexican maquiladoras. Thesis (Ph.D.)--University of Texas, Austin, 1983. xix, 587 p. English. DESCR: *Border Industries; International Economic Relations; *Trade Unions; Women; Working Women.

888 Pick, James B., et al. Socioeconomic influences on fertility in the Mexican borderlands region. MEXICAN STUDIES/ESTUDIOS MEXICANOS, Vol. 6, no. 1 (Winter 1990), p. 11-42. English. DESCR: *Employment; *Fertility; Labor Supply and Market; Literacy; Socioeconomic Factors; Working Women.

Border Region (cont.)

889 Ruiz, Vicki L., ed. and Tiano, Susan B., ed.
Women on the U.S.-Mexico border: responses
to change. Boston, MA: Allen & Unwin, c1987.
xi, 247 p. English. DESCR: *Border
Industries; Employment; Feminism;
Immigrants; Mexico; Sex Roles; *Women.

890 Seligson, Mitchell A. and Williams, Edward
J. Maquiladoras and migration workers in the
Mexico-United States Border
Industrialization Program. Austin, TX:
Mexico-United States Border Research
Program, University of Texas at Austin,
1981. xviii, 202 p. English. DESCR: Border
Industrialization Program (BIP); Employment;
Immigration; Industrial Workers; Mexico;
*Migration Patterns; Working Women.

891 Smith, Jack C. Trends in the incidence of
breastfeeding for Hispanics of Mexican
origin and Anglos on the US-Mexican border.
AMERICAN JOURNAL OF PUBLIC HEALTH, Vol. 72,
no. 1 (January 1982), p. 59-61. English.
DESCR: Anglo Americans; Breastfeeding;
*Maternal and Child Welfare.

892 Solorzano-Torres, Rosalia. Women, labor, and
the U.S.-Mexico border: Mexican maids in El
Paso, Texas. IN: Melville, Margarita, ed.
MEXICANAS AT WORK IN THE UNITED STATES.
Houston, TX: Mexican American Studies
Program, University of Houston, 1988, p.
75-83. English. DESCR: Border Patrol;
Domestic Work; El Paso, TX; Immigrants;
Immigration and Naturalization Service
(INS); Immigration Regulation and Control;
*Labor Supply and Market; Undocumented
Workers; *Women; *Working Women.

893 Staudt, Kathleen. Programming women's
empowerment: a case from northern Mexico.
IN: Ruiz, Vicki L. and Tiano, Susan, eds.
WOMEN ON THE U.S.-MEXICO BORDER: RESPONSES
TO CHANGE. Boston, MA: Allen & Unwin, 1987,
p. 155-173. English. DESCR: Alternative
Education; Ciudad Juarez, Chihuahua, Mexico;
Curriculum; Employment; *Feminism;
Organizations; Women.

894 Tiano, Susan B. Export processing, women's
work, and the employment problem in
developing countries: the case of the
maquiladora program in Northern Mexico. El
Paso, TX: Center for InterAmerican and
Border Studies, UTEP, 1985. 32 p. English.
DESCR: *Employment; Labor Supply and Market;
Mexico; *Sex Roles; Women; Working Women.

895 Tiano, Susan B. Maquiladoras in Mexicali:
integration or exploitation? IN: Ruiz, Vicki
L. and Tiano, Susan, eds. WOMEN ON THE
U.S.-MEXICO BORDER: RESPONSES TO CHANGE.
Boston, MA: Allen & Unwin, 1987, p. 77-101.
English. DESCR: Border Industrialization
Program (BIP); *Border Industries;
Employment; Labor Supply and Market;
Mexicali, Mexico; Women; Working Women.

896 Tiano, Susan B. Women's work and
unemployment in northern Mexico. IN: Ruiz,
Vicki L. and Tiano, Susan, eds. WOMEN ON THE
U.S.-MEXICO BORDER: RESPONSES TO CHANGE.
Boston, MA: Allen & Unwin, 1987, p. 17-39.
English. DESCR: Border Industrialization
Program (BIP); Border Industries;
Employment; Labor Supply and Market; Mexico;
Multinational Corporations; *Women.

897 Whiteford, Linda. Mexican American women as
innovators. IN: Melville, Margarita B., ed.
TWICE A MINORITY. St. Louis, MO: Mosby,
1980, p. 109-126. English. DESCR: Farm

Workers; Migrant Labor; *Working Women.

898 Young, Gay. Gender identification and
working-class solidarity among maquila
workers in Ciudad Juarez: stereotypes and
realities. IN: Ruiz, Vicki L. and Tiano,
Susan, eds. WOMEN ON THE U.S.-MEXICO BORDER:
RESPONSES TO CHANGE. Boston, MA: Allen &
Unwin, 1987, p. 105-127. English. DESCR:
Assertiveness; Attitudes; Border
Industrialization Program (BIP); *Border
Industries; Ciudad Juarez, Chihuahua,
Mexico; Employment; Garment Industry; Sex
Roles; Surveys; Working Women.

BORDERLANDS/LA FRONTERA: THE NEW MESTIZA

899 Harlow, Barbara. Sites of struggle:
immigration, deportation, prison, and exile.
IN: Calderon, Hector and Saldivar, Jose
David, eds. CRITICISM IN THE BORDERLANDS:
STUDIES IN CHICANO LITERATURE, CULTURE, AND
IDEOLOGY. Durham, NC: Duke University Press,
1991, p. [149]-163. English. DESCR:
Anzaldua, Gloria; BLACK GOLD; First, Ruth;
Khalifeh, Sahar; *Literary Criticism;
*Political Ideology; Sanchez, Rosaura;
Social Classes; "The Cariboo Cafe" [short
story]; "The Ditch" [short story];
Viramontes, Helena Maria; WILD THORNS;
*Women; Working Women.

900 Saldivar-Hull, Sonia. Feminism on the
border: from gender politics to geopolitics.
IN: Calderon, Hector and Saldivar, Jose
David, eds. CRITICISM IN THE BORDERLANDS:
STUDIES IN CHICANO LITERATURE, CULTURE, AND
IDEOLOGY. Durham, NC: Duke University Press,
1991, p. [203]-220. English. DESCR: Anglo
Americans; *Anzaldua, Gloria; Feminism;
Homosexuality; *Literary Criticism;
Mestizaje; Moraga, Cherrie; Sexism; "The
Cariboo Cafe" [short story]; Viramontes,
Helena Maria; Women.

BORDERS

901 Mora, Pat and Alarcon, Norma. A poet
analyzes her craft. NUESTRO, Vol. 11, no. 2
(March 1987), p. 25-27. English. DESCR:
*Authors; CHANTS; *Mora, Pat; *Poetry.

Bornstein-Somoza, Miriam

902 Alarcon, Justo S. and Martinez, Julio A.
[Bornstein-Somoza, Miriam]. IN: Martinez,
Julio A. and Lomeli, Francisco A., eds.
CHICANO LITERATURE: A REFERENCE GUIDE.
Westport, CT: Greenwood Press, 1985, p.
74-77. English. DESCR: *Authors; Biography;
Literary Criticism.

Boundaries
USE: Border Region

Bowerman, Liz Lerma
USE: Lerma Bowerman, Liz

Boycotts

903 Echaveste, Beatrice and Huerta, Dolores. In
the shadow of the eagle: Huerta = A la
sombra del aguila: Huerta. AMERICAS 2001,
Vol. 1, no. 3 (November, December, 1987), p.
26-30. Bilingual. DESCR: Agricultural Labor
Unions; *Farm Workers; Huerta, Dolores;
United Farmworkers of America (UFW).

Boycotts (cont.)

904 Rose, Margaret. From the fields to the
picket line: Huelga women and the boycott,
1965-1975. LABOR HISTORY, Vol. 31, no. 3
(1990), p. 271-293. English. **DESCR:** Family;
Farm Workers; Padilla, Esther; Padilla,
Gilbert; Rodriguez, Conrado; Rodriguez,
Herminia; *United Farmworkers of America
(UFW); Washington, D.C.

905 Rose, Margaret. Traditional and
nontraditional patterns of female activism
in the United Farm Workers of America,
1962-1980. FRONTIERS: A JOURNAL OF WOMEN
STUDIES, Vol. 11, no. 1 (1990), p. [26]-32.
English. **DESCR:** California; Chavez, Cesar
E.; *Chavez, Helen; *Huerta, Dolores; Labor
Disputes; Labor Unions; National Farm
Workers Association (NFWA); Sex Roles;
Strikes and Lockouts; *United Farmworkers of
America (UFW).

**BREAKING BOUNDARIES: LATINA WRITING AND CRITICAL
READINGS**

906 Alarcon, Norma. Latina writers in the United
States. IN: Marting, Diane E., ed. SPANISH
AMERICAN WOMEN WRITERS: A
BIO-BIBLIOGRAPHICAL SOURCE BOOK. New York:
Greenwood Press, 1990, p. [557]-567.
English. **DESCR:** *Authors; *Bibliography;
Cubanos; Intergroup Relations; Language
Usage; *Literature Reviews; Puerto Ricans;
THIRD WOMAN [journal]; *Women.

Breast Cancer

907 Alvarez-Amaya, Maria. Determinants of breast
and cervical cancer behavior among Mexican
American women. BORDER HEALTH/SALUD
FRONTERIZA, Vol. 5, no. 3 (July, September,
1989), p. 22-27. Bilingual. **DESCR:** Border
Region; *Cancer; Diseases; Immigrants;
Medical Care; *Preventative Medicine.

908 Gonzalez, Judith Teresa. Factors relating to
frequency of breast self-examination among
low-income Mexican American women:
implications for nursing practice. CANCER
NURSING, Vol. 13, no. 3 (June 1990), p.
134-142. English. **DESCR:** Cancer; Low Income;
Medical Care; Medical Personnel;
*Preventative Medicine.

Breastfeeding

909 Acosta Johnson, Carmen. Breast-feeding and
social class mobility: the case of Mexican
migrant mothers in Houston, Texas. IN:
Melville, Margarita B., ed. TWICE A
MINORITY. St. Louis, MO: Mosby, 1980, p.
66-82. English. **DESCR:** Herbal Medicine;
Maternal and Child Welfare; *Social Classes;
Social Mobility.

910 de la Torre, Adela and Rush, Lynda. The
determinants of breastfeeding for Mexican
migrant women. INTERNATIONAL MIGRATION
REVIEW, Vol. 21, no. 3 (Fall 1987), p.
728-742. English. **DESCR:** Farm Workers;
Maternal and Child Welfare; Migrant Health
Services; Migrant Labor; Migration; Public
Health; Working Women.

911 Dungy, Claibourne I. Breast feeding
preference of Hispanic and Anglo women.
CLINICAL PEDIATRICS, Vol. 28, no. 2
(February 1989), p. 92-94. English. **DESCR:**
Anglo Americans; Attitudes; Women.

912 Hendricks, Mary Lee. Factors relating to the
continuation of breast feeding by low income
Hispanic women. Thesis (M.S.)--California

State University, Long Beach, 1986. 94 p.
English. **DESCR:** *Low Income.

913 John, A. Meredith and Martorell, Reynaldo.
Incidence and duration of breast-feeding in
Mexican-American infants, 1970-1982.
AMERICAN JOURNAL OF CLINICAL NUTRITION, Vol.
50, no. 4 (October 1989), p. 868-874.
English. **DESCR:** Hispanic Health and
Nutrition Examination Survey (HHANES).

914 Kokinos, Mary and Dewey, Kathryn G. Infant
feeding practices of migrant
Mexican-American families in Northern
California. ECOLOGY OF FOOD AND NUTRITION,
Vol. 18, no. 3 (1986), p. 209-220. English.
DESCR: Farm Workers; Migrant Labor; Northern
California; Nutrition.

915 Magnus, Peter D. Breastfeeding among
Hispanics [letter]. AMERICAN JOURNAL OF
PUBLIC HEALTH, Vol. 73, no. 5 (May 1983), p.
597-598. English.

916 Romero-Gwynn, Eunice and Carias, Lucia.
Breast-feeding intentions and practice among
Hispanic mothers in Southern California.
PEDIATRICS, Vol. 84, no. 4 (October 1989),
p. 626-632. English. **DESCR:** Cubanos;
Expanded Food and Nutrition Education
Program; Immigrants; Puerto Ricans; Southern
California; Women.

917 Scrimshaw, Susan C.M., et al. Factors
affecting breastfeeding among women of
Mexican origin or descent in Los Angeles.
AMERICAN JOURNAL OF PUBLIC HEALTH, Vol. 77,
no. 4 (April 1987), p. 467-470. English.
DESCR: Acculturation; Immigrants; Los
Angeles, CA; Working Women.

918 Shapiro, Johanna and Saltzer, Eleanor B.
Attitudes toward breast-feeding among
Mexican-American women. JOURNAL OF TROPICAL
PEDIATRICS, Vol. 31, no. 1 (February 1985),
p. 13-16. English. **DESCR:** Attitudes.

919 Smith, Jack C. Trends in the incidence of
breastfeeding for Hispanics of Mexican
origin and Anglos on the US-Mexican border.
AMERICAN JOURNAL OF PUBLIC HEALTH, Vol. 72,
no. 1 (January 1982), p. 59-61. English.
DESCR: Anglo Americans; Border Region;
*Maternal and Child Welfare.

920 Stroup-Benham, Christine A. and Trevino,
Fernando M. Reproductive characteristics of
Mexican-American, mainland Puerto Rican, and
Cuban-American women: data from the Hispanic
Health and Nutrition Examination Survey.
JAMA: JOURNAL OF THE AMERICAN MEDICAL
ASSOCIATION, Vol. 265, no. 2 (January 9,
1991), p. 222-226. English. **DESCR:** *Birth
Control; Cubanos; *Fertility; Hispanic
Health and Nutrition Examination Survey
(HHANES); Puerto Ricans; *Women.

921 Sweeny, Mary Anne and Gulino, Claire. The
health belief model as an explanation for
breast-feeding practices in a Hispanic
population. ANS: ADVANCES IN NURSING
SCIENCE, Vol. 9, no. 4 (July 1987), p.
35-50. English. **DESCR:** *Cultural Customs;
*Public Health; San Diego, CA; Tijuana, Baja
California, Mexico; Women.

Breastfeeding (cont.)

922 Weller, Susan C. and Dungy, Claibourne I.
Personal preferences and ethnic variations
among Anglo and Hispanic breast and bottle
feeders. SOCIAL SCIENCE & MEDICINE, Vol. 23
no. 6 (1986), p. 539-548. English. DESCR:
Attitudes; *Maternal and Child Welfare;
Orange, CA; Parenting; Socioeconomic
Factors.

Brinson-Pineda, Barbara

923 Alarcon, Norma. What kind of lover have you
made me, Mother?: towards a theory of
Chicanas' feminism and cultural identity
through poetry. IN: McCluskey, Audrey T.,
ed. WOMEN OF COLOR: PERSPECTIVES ON FEMINISM
AND IDENTITY. Bloomington, IN: Women's
Studies Program, Indiana University, 1985,
p. 85-110. English. DESCR: Cervantes, Lorna
Dee; Cisneros, Sandra; Culture; *Feminism;
Identity; *Literary Criticism; Mora, Pat;
Moraga, Cherrie; *Poetry; Tafolla, Carmen;
Vigil-Pinon, Evangelina Villanueva, Alma.

924 Brinson-Pineda, Barbara and Binder,
Wolfgang. [Interview with] Barbara
Brinson-Pineda. IN: Binder, Wolfgang, ed.
PARTIAL AUTOBIOGRAPHIES: INTERVIEWS WITH
TWENTY CHICANO POETS. Erlangen, W. Germany:
Verlag Palm & Enke, 1985, p. 16-27. English.
DESCR: Authors; Autobiography; Poetry.

Brujas

925 Blea, Irene I. Brujeria: a sociological
analysis of Mexican American witches. IN:
Barrera, Mario, et al., eds. WORK, FAMILY,
SEX ROLES, LANGUAGE: SELECTED PAPERS, 1979.
Berkeley, CA: Tonatiuh-Quinto Sol, 1980, p.
177-193. English. DESCR: Colorado; Folklore;
Kiev, Ari; New Mexico.

BRUJERIAS [play]

926 Melville, Margarita B. Female and male in
Chicano theatre. IN: Kanellos, Nicolas, ed.
HISPANIC THEATRE IN THE UNITED STATES.
Houston, TX: Arte Publico Press, 1984, p.
71-79. English. DESCR: BERNABE; Cultural
Characteristics; DAY OF THE SWALLOWS;
Duarte-Clark, Rodrigo; EL JARDIN [play];
Family; Feminism; Macias, Ysidro; Morton,
Carlos; Portillo Trambley, Estela; RANCHO
HOLLYWOOD [play]; *Sex Roles; *Teatro; THE
ULTIMATE PENDEJADA [play]; Valdez, Luis;
Women Men Relations.

Business

927 Maymi, Carmen R. Fighting to open the doors
to opportunity. AGENDA, no. 4 (Spring 1974),
p. 8-10. English. DESCR: Business
Enterprises; Legislation; *Sexism.

928 Zambrana, Ruth E. Hispanic professional
women: work, family and health. Los Angeles,
CA: National Network of Hispanic Women,
1987. 75 leaves. English. DESCR: *Careers;
*Employment; Family; Management; Mental
Health; Social Classes; *Social Mobility;
*Women.

Business Enterprises

929 Fernandez Kelly, Maria and Garcia, Anna M.
Economic restructuring in the United States:
Hispanic women in the garment and
electronics industries. WOMEN AND WORK, Vol.
3, (1988), p. 49-65. English. DESCR:
Businesspeople; *Electronics Industry;
*Garment Industry; Industrial Workers;
*International Economic Relations; *Working
Women.

930 Maymi, Carmen R. Fighting to open the doors
to opportunity. AGENDA, no. 4 (Spring 1974),
p. 8-10. English. DESCR: Business;
Legislation; *Sexism.

931 Padilla, Steve. You've come a long way,
baby. Or have you? NUESTRO, Vol. 7, no. 6
(August 1983), p. 38-41. English. DESCR:
Minority Business Development Agency (MBDA);
National Alliance of Homebased
Businesswomen.

932 Valenzuela-Crocker, Elvira. Forging paths in
power and profit. AGENDA, no. 4 (Spring
1974), p. 15-21. English. DESCR:
Businesspeople.

Businesspeople

933 Fernandez Kelly, Maria and Garcia, Anna M.
Economic restructuring in the United States:
Hispanic women in the garment and
electronics industries. WOMEN AND WORK, Vol.
3, (1988), p. 49-65. English. DESCR:
Business Enterprises; *Electronics Industry;
*Garment Industry; Industrial Workers;
*International Economic Relations; *Working
Women.

934 Valenzuela-Crocker, Elvira. Forging paths in
power and profit. AGENDA, no. 4 (Spring
1974), p. 16-21. English. DESCR: *Business
Enterprises.

Cabeza de Baca, Fabiola

935 Jensen, Joan M. Crossing ethnic barriers in
the Southwest: women's agricultural
extension education, 1914-1940. AGRICULTURAL
HISTORY, Vol. 60, no. 2 (Spring 1986), p.
169-181. English. DESCR: *Agricultural
Extension Service; Agriculture; History; New
Mexico; *Rural Education.

936 Padilla, Genaro. Imprisoned narrative? Or
lies, secrets, and silence in New Mexico
women's autobiography. IN: Calderon, Hector
and Saldivar, Jose David, eds. CRITICISM IN
THE BORDERLANDS: STUDIES IN CHICANO
LITERATURE, CULTURE, AND IDEOLOGY. Durham,
NC: Duke University Press, 1991, p. [43]-60.
English. DESCR: Authors; *Autobiography;
*Jaramillo, Cleofas M.; Literary History;
New Mexico; ROMANCE OF A LITTLE VILLAGE
GIRL; WE FED THEM CACTUS.

937 Rebolledo, Tey Diana. Las escritoras:
romances and realities. IN: Gonzales-Berry,
Erlinda, ed. PASO POR AQUI: CRITICAL ESSAYS
ON THE NEW MEXICAN LITERARY TRADITION.
Albuquerque, NM: University of New Mexico
Press, c1989, p. 199-214. English. DESCR:
Authors; *Jaramillo, Cleofas M.; Literary
History; New Mexico; OLD SPAIN IN OUR
SOUTHWEST; *Otero Warren, Nina; ROMANCE OF A
LITTLE VILLAGE GIRL; WE FED THEM CACTUS;
Women.

938 Rebolledo, Tey Diana. Hispanic women writers
of the Southwest: tradition and innovation.
IN: Lensink, Judy Nolte, ed. OLD
SOUTHWEST/NEW SOUTHWEST: ESSAYS ON A REGION
AND ITS LITERATURE. Tucson, AZ: The Tucson
Public Library, 1987, p. 49-61. English.
DESCR: *Authors; Jaramillo, Cleofas M.;
Literature; Mora, Pat; OLD SPAIN IN OUR
SOUTHWEST; Otero Warren, Nina; Preciado
Martin, Patricia; Sex Roles; Sex
Stereotypes; Silva, Beverly; *Southwestern
United States; Vigil-Pinon, Evangelina; WE
FED THEM CACTUS; *Women.

Cabeza de Baca, Fabiola
(cont.)

939 Rebolledo, Tey Diana. Narrative strategies of resistance in Hispana writing. THE JOURNAL OF NARRATIVE TECHNIQUE, Vol. 20, no. 2 (Spring 1990), p. 134-146. English. **DESCR:** *Authors; Fiction; Jaramillo, Cleofas M.; *Literary Criticism; Literature; New Mexico; OLD SPAIN IN OUR SOUTHWEST; *Oral Tradition; Otero Warren, Nina; ROMANCE OF A LITTLE VILLAGE GIRL; WE FED THEM CACTUS.

940 Rebolledo, Tey Diana. Tradition and mythology: signatures of landscape in Chicana literature. IN: Norwood, Vera and Monk, Janice, eds. THE DESERT IS NO LADY: SOUTHWESTERN LANDSCAPES IN WOMEN'S WRITING AND ART. New Haven, CT: Yale University Press, 1987, p. 96-124. English. **DESCR:** *Authors; Chavez, Denise; Jaramillo, Cleofas M.; Literary Criticism; *Literary History; Literature; Mora, Pat; Mythology; Otero Warren, Nina; Portillo Trambley, Estela; Silva, Beverly; Southwestern United States; WE FED THEM CACTUS.

California

941 Allen, Jane and Guthrie, Derek. La mujer: a visual dialogue. NEW ART EXAMINER, Vol. 5, no. 10 (July 1978), p. 14. English. **DESCR:** Chicago, IL; *Feminism; Movimiento Artistico Chicano (MARCH), Chicago, IL; Stereotypes.

942 Arroyo, Laura E. Industrial and occupational distribution of Chicana workers. AZTLAN, Vol. 4, no. 2 (Fall 1973), p. 343-382. English. **DESCR:** *Employment; Farah Manufacturing Co., El Paso, TX; Farah Strike; Garment Industry; Industrial Workers; Strikes and Lockouts; Texas.

943 Arroyo, Laura E. Industrial and occupational distribution of Chicana workers. IN: Sanchez, Rosaura and Martinez Cruz, Rosa, eds. ESSAYS ON LA MUJER. Los Angeles, CA: Chicano Studies Center Publications, UCLA, 1977, p. 150-187. English. **DESCR:** *Employment; Farah Manufacturing Co., El Paso, TX; Farah Strike; Garment Industry; Industrial Workers; Strikes and Lockouts; Texas.

944 Barton, Amy E. and California Commission on the Status of Women. Campesinas: women farmworkers in the California agricultural labor force, report of a study project. Sacramento, CA: The Commission, [1978], vii, 23, 52 p. English. **DESCR:** *Farm Workers; Migrant Labor; Statistics; *Working Women.

945 Castaneda, Antonia I. Comparative frontiers: the migration of women to Alta California and New Zealand. IN: Schlissel, Lillian, et al., eds. WESTERN WOMEN: THEIR LAND, THEIR LIVES. Albuquerque, NM: University of New Mexico Press, 1988, p. 283-300. English. **DESCR:** Border Region; History; Immigrants; Immigration; Marriage; Mexico; Missions; Native Americans; New Zealand; Social History and Conditions; *Women.

946 Castaneda, Antonia I. Gender, race, and culture: Spanish-Mexican women in the historiography of frontier California. FRONTIERS: A JOURNAL OF WOMEN STUDIES, Vol. 11, no. 1 (1990), p. [8]-20. English. **DESCR:** Bancroft, Hubert Howe; Bolton, Herbert Eugene; Californios; *Historiography; History; Intermarriage; *Sex Stereotypes; Spanish Borderlands Theory; Spanish Influence; Stereotypes; Turner, Frederick Jackson; Women.

947 Castaneda, Antonia I. The political economy of nineteenth century stereotypes of Californianas. IN: Del Castillo, Adelaida R., ed. BETWEEN BORDERS: ESSAYS ON MEXICANA/CHICANA HISTORY. Encino, CA: Floricanto Press, 1990, p. 213-236. English. **DESCR:** *Californios; Dana, Richard Henry; Farnham, Thomas Jefferson; History; LIFE IN CALIFORNIA; *Political Economy; Robinson, Alfred; *Sex Stereotypes; TRAVELS IN CALIFORNIA AND SCENES IN THE PACIFIC OCEAN; TWO YEARS BEFORE THE MAST; Women.

948 de Anda, Diane and Becerra, Rosina M. Support networks for adolescent mothers. SOCIAL CASEWORK: JOURNAL OF CONTEMPORARY SOCIAL WORK, Vol. 65, no. 3 (March 1984), p. 172-181. English. **DESCR:** *Fertility; *Natural Support Systems; Spanish Language; *Youth.

949 Goldman, Shifra M. Mujeres de California: Latin American women artists. IN: Moore, Sylvia, ed. YESTERDAY AND TOMORROW: CALIFORNIA WOMEN ARTISTS. New York, NY: Midmarch Arts Press, c1989, p. 202-229. English. **DESCR:** *Artists; Baca, Judith F.; Biography; Carrasco, Barbara; Cervantez, Yreina; de Larios, Dora; Feminism; Hernandez, Judithe; Lomas Garza, Carmen; Lopez, Yolanda M.; Mesa-Bains, Amalia; Murillo, Patricia; Sanchez, Olivia; Valdez, Patssi; Vallejo Dillaway, Linda; Women; Zamora Lucero, Linda.

950 Hancock, Paula F. The effect of welfare eligibility on the labor force participation of women of Mexican origin in California. POPULATION RESEARCH AND POLICY REVIEW, Vol. 5, no. 2 (1986), p. 163-185. English. **DESCR:** Aid to Families with Dependent Children (AFDC); *Employment; Food Stamps; Immigrants; Medi-Cal; Single Parents; *Welfare; Women.

951 Jensen, Joan M. Commentary [on "And Miles to Go": Mexican Women and Work, 1930-1985]. IN: Schlissel, Lillian, et al., eds. WESTERN WOMEN: THEIR LAND, THEIR LIVES. Albuquerque, NM: University of New Mexico Press, 1988, p. 141-144. English. **DESCR:** "'And Miles to Go...': Mexican Women and Work, 1930-1985"; Employment; Income; Labor Unions; Public Policy; Ruiz, Vicki L.; Women; *Working Women.

952 Lara-Cea, Helen. Notes on the use of parish registers in the reconstruction of Chicana history in California prior to 1850. IN: Del Castillo, Adelaida R., ed. BETWEEN BORDERS: ESSAYS ON MEXICANA/CHICANA HISTORY. Encino, CA: Floricanto Press, 1990, p. 131-159. English. **DESCR:** Catholic Church; History; Indigenismo; Mission of Santa Clara; Population; *San Jose, CA; *Vital Statistics.

953 Monroy, Douglas. "They didn't call them 'padre' for nothing": patriarchy in Hispanic California. IN: Del Castillo, Adelaida R., ed. BETWEEN BORDERS: ESSAYS ON MEXICANA/CHICANA HISTORY. Encino, CA: Floricanto Press, 1990, p. 433-445. English. **DESCR:** Clergy; History; *Machismo; Rape; *Sex Roles; *Sexism; Spanish Influence; Women Men Relations.

California (cont.)

954 Padilla, Eligio R. and O'Grady, Kevin E.
Sexuality among Mexican Americans: a case of
sexual stereotyping. JOURNAL OF PERSONALITY
AND SOCIAL PSYCHOLOGY, Vol. 52, no. 1
(1987), p. 5-10. English. DESCR: Age Groups;
Anglo Americans; Attitudes; Religion; *Sex
Roles; *Sex Stereotypes; Sexual Behavior;
Sexual Knowledge and Attitude Test;
*Stereotypes; Students; Values.

955 Padilla, Genaro. "Yo sola aprendi":
contra-patriarchal containment in women's
nineteenth-century California personal
narratives. THE AMERICAS REVIEW, Vol. 16,
no. 3-4 (Fall, Winter, 1988), p. 91-109.
English. DESCR: Autobiography; *Literary
History; *Women.

956 Pavich, Emma Guerrero. A Chicana perspective
on Mexican culture and sexuality. JOURNAL OF
SOCIAL WORK AND HUMAN SEXUALITY, Vol. 4, no.
3 (Spring 1986), p. 47-65. English. DESCR:
Cultural Characteristics; Family; Feminism;
Homosexuality; Machismo; Sex Roles; Sex
Stereotypes; *Sexual Behavior; Women Men
Relations.

957 Rose, Margaret. Traditional and
nontraditional patterns of female activism
in the United Farm Workers of America,
1962-1980. FRONTIERS: A JOURNAL OF WOMEN
STUDIES, Vol. 11, no. 1 (1990), p. [26]-32.
English. DESCR: Boycotts; Chavez, Cesar E.;
*Chavez, Helen; *Huerta Dolores; Labor
Disputes; Labor Unions; National Farm
Workers Association (NFWA); Sex Roles;
Strikes and Lockouts; *United Farmworkers of
America (UFW).

958 Ruiz, Vicki L. California's early pioneers:
Spanish/Mexican women. SOCIAL STUDIES
REVIEW, Vol. 29, no. 1 (Fall 1989), p.
24-30. English. DESCR: *History; Ruiz
Burton, Maria Amparo; Sex Roles; *Women.

959 Ruiz, Vicki L. Cannery women/cannery lives:
Mexican women, unionization, and the
California food processing industry,
1930-1950. Albuquerque, NM: University of
New Mexico Press, 1987. xviii, 194 p.: ill.
English. DESCR: Agricultural Labor Unions;
*Canneries; Family; History; Industrial
Workers; Labor Disputes; *Labor Unions;
Trade Unions; United Cannery Agricultural
Packing and Allied Workers of America
(UCAPAWA); Women.

960 Vasquez, Mario F. Immigrant workers and the
apparel manufacturing industry in Southern
California. IN: Rios-Bustamante, Antonio,
ed. MEXICAN IMMIGRANT WORKERS IN THE U.S.
Los Angeles, CA: Chicano Studies Research
Center Publications, University of
California, 1981, p. 85-96. English. DESCR:
AFL-CIO; Garment Industry; Immigrants;
International Ladies Garment Workers Union
(ILGWU); *Labor Supply and Market; Labor
Unions; Undocumented Workers; Women.

California Achievement Test (CAT)

961 Creswell, John L. Sex-related differences in
the problem-solving abilities of rural
Black, Anglo, and Chicano adolescents. TEXAS
TECH JOURNAL OF EDUCATION, Vol. 10, no. 1
(Winter 1983), p. 29-33. English. DESCR:
Aiken and Preger Revised Math Attitude
Scale; Anglo Americans; Blacks;
*Mathematics; National Assessment of
Educational Progress; National Council of
Teachers of Mathematics (NCTM); Youth.

962 Powers, Stephen and Jones, Patricia.
Factorial invariance of the California
achievement tests across race and sex.
EDUCATIONAL AND PSYCHOLOGICAL MEASUREMENT,
Vol. 44, no. 4 (Winter 1984), p. 967-970.
English. DESCR: Anglo Americans; Blacks;
Educational Tests and Measurements; Males;
Women.

California Commission on the Status of Women

963 Nava, Yolanda. The Chicana and employment:
needs analysis and recommendations for
legislation. REGENERACION, Vol. 2, no. 3
(1973), p. 7-9. English. DESCR: Child Care
Centers; Comision Femenil Mexicana Nacional;
*Discrimination in Employment; Employment
Tests; Employment Training; Equal Rights
Amendment (ERA); Sexism; Statistics;
Stereotypes; Working Women.

California Personality Inventory (CPI)

964 McClelland, Judith Raymond. The relationship
of independence to achievement: a
comparative study of Hispanic women. Thesis
(Ph.D.)--Fielding Institute, 1988. 164 p.
English. DESCR: *Assertiveness; Attitudes;
Careers; Leadership; *Management; New
Mexico; Personality; *Working Women.

California Sanitary Canning Company, Los Angeles, CA

965 Ruiz, Vicki L. A promise fulfilled: Mexican
cannery workers in Southern California. THE
PACIFIC HISTORIAN, Vol. 30, no. 2 (Summer
1986), p. 51-61. English. DESCR: *Canneries;
Labor Unions; Moreno, Luisa [union
organizer]; Southern California; Strikes and
Lockouts; *United Cannery Agricultural
Packing and Allied Workers of America
(UCAPAWA); Working Women.

966 Ruiz, Vicki L. A promise fulfilled: Mexican
cannery workers in Southern California. IN:
DuBois, Ellen Carol and Ruiz, Vicki L., eds.
UNEQUAL SISTERS: A MULTICULTURAL READER IN
U.S. WOMEN'S HISTORY. New York: Routledge,
1990, p. 264-274. English. DESCR:
*Canneries; Labor Unions; Moreno, Luisa
[union organizer]; Southern California;
Strikes and Lockouts; *United Cannery
Agricultural Packing and Allied Workers of
America (UCAPAWA); Working Women.

967 Ruiz, Vicki L. A promise fulfilled: Mexican
cannery workers in Southern California. IN:
Del Castillo, Adelaida R., ed. BETWEEN
BORDERS: ESSAYS ON MEXICANA/CHICANA HISTORY.
Encino, CA: Floricanto Press, 1990, p.
281-298. English. DESCR: *Canneries; Labor
Unions; Moreno, Luisa [union organizer];
Southern California; Strikes and Lockouts;
United Cannery Agricultural Packing and
Allied Workers of America (UCAPAWA); Working
Women.

California State University, San Diego

968 Hernandez, Patricia. Lives of Chicana
activists: the Chicano student movement (a
case study). IN: Mora, Magdalena and Del
Castillo, Adelaida, eds. MEXICAN WOMEN IN
THE UNITED STATES: STRUGGLES PAST AND
PRESENT. Los Angeles, CA: Chicano Studies
Research Center, UCLA, 1980, p. 17-25.
English. DESCR: Case Studies; *Chicano
Movement; Colleges and Universities;
Movimiento Estudiantil Chicano de Aztlan
(MEChA); Student Movements; Student
Organizations.

Californios

969 Castaneda, Antonia I. Gender, race, and culture: Spanish-Mexican women in the historiography of frontier California. FRONTIERS: A JOURNAL OF WOMEN STUDIES, Vol. 11, no. 1 (1990), p. [8]-20. English. DESCR: Bancroft, Hubert Howe; Bolton, Herbert Eugene; *California; *Historiography; History; Intermarriage; *Sex Stereotypes; Spanish Borderlands Theory; Spanish Influence; Stereotypes; Turner, Frederick Jackson; Women.

970 Castaneda, Antonia I. The political economy of nineteenth century stereotypes of Californianas. IN: Del Castillo, Adelaida R., ed. BETWEEN BORDERS: ESSAYS ON MEXICANA/CHICANA HISTORY. Encino, CA: Floricanto Press, 1990, p. 213-236. English. DESCR: *California; Dana, Richard Henry; Farnham, Thomas Jefferson; History; LIFE IN CALIFORNIA; *Political Economy; Robinson, Alfred; *Sex Stereotypes; TRAVELS IN CALIFORNIA AND SCENES IN THE PACIFIC OCEAN; TWO YEARS BEFORE THE MAST; Women.

Calo

USE: Chicano Dialects

Cameron County, TX

971 Hutchison, James. Teenagers and contraception in Cameron and Willacy Counties. BORDERLANDS JOURNAL, Vol. 7, no. 1 (Fall 1983), p. 75-90. English. DESCR: *Birth Control; *Family Planning; Fertility; Sex Education; Willacy County, TX; Youth.

EL CAMINO [play]

972 Heard, Martha E. The theatre of Denise Chavez: interior landscapes with SABOR NUEVOMEXICANO. THE AMERICAS REVIEW, Vol. 16, no. 2 (Summer 1988), p. 83-91. English. DESCR: *Chavez, Denise; Literary Criticism; New Mexico; PLAZA [play]; *Teatro.

Canada

973 Romero-Cachinero, M. Carmen. Hispanic women in Canada: a framework for analysis. RESOURCES FOR FEMINIST RESEARCH, Vol. 16, no. 1 (March 1987), p. 19-20. English. DESCR: Population; Social History and Conditions; Women.

Canales, Alma

974 Chapa, Olivia Evey. Mujeres por la Raza unida. CARACOL, Vol. 1, no. 2 (October 1974), p. 3-5. English. DESCR: Cotera, Marta P.; Diaz, Elena; La Raza Unida Party; *Political Parties and Organizations; REPORT OF FIRST CONFERENCIA DE MUJERES POR LA RAZA UNIDA PARTY.

Cancer

975 Alvarez-Amaya, Maria. Determinants of breast and cervical cancer behavior among Mexican American women. BORDER HEALTH/SALUD FRONTERIZA, Vol. 5, no. 3 (July, September, 1989), p. 22-27. Bilingual. DESCR: Border Region; *Breast Cancer; Diseases; Immigrants; Medical Care; *Preventative Medicine.

976 Daly, Mary B.; Clark, Gary M.; and McGuire, William L. Breast cancer prognosis in a mixed Caucasian-Hispanic population. JNCI: JOURNAL OF THE NATIONAL CANCER INSTITUTE, Vol. 74, no. 4 (April 1985), p. 753-757. English. DESCR: Anglo Americans; Women.

977 Gonzalez, Judith Teresa. Factors relating to frequency of breast self-examination among low-income Mexican American women: implications for nursing practice. CANCER NURSING, Vol. 13, no. 3 (June 1990), p. 134-142. English. DESCR: *Breast Cancer; Low Income; Medical Care; Medical Personnel; *Preventative Medicine.

978 Gonzalez, Judith Teresa and Gonzalez, Virginia M. Initial validation of a scale measuring self-efficacy of breast self-examination among low-income Mexican American women. HISPANIC JOURNAL OF BEHAVIORAL SCIENCES, Vol. 12, no. 3 (August 1990), p. 277-291. English. DESCR: Low Income; Medical Care; Medical Education; Preventative Medicine.

979 Holck, Susan E. Lung cancer mortality and smoking habits: Mexican-American women. AMERICAN JOURNAL OF PUBLIC HEALTH, Vol. 72, no. 1 (January 1982), p. 38-42. English. DESCR: Anglo Americans; *Public Health; *Smoking.

980 Peters, Ruth K., et al. Risk factors for invasive cervical cancer among Latinas and non-Latinas in Los Angeles County. JOURNAL OF THE NATIONAL CANCER INSTITUTE, Vol. 77, no. 5 (November 1986), p. 1063-1077. English. DESCR: Diseases; Educational Levels; Los Angeles County, CA; *Public Health; Women.

981 Ponce-Adame, Merrihelen. Latinas and breast cancer. NUESTRO, Vol. 6, no. 8 (October 1982), p. 30-31. English. DESCR: *Public Health.

982 Ponce-Adame, Merrihelen. Women and cancer. CORAZON DE AZTLAN, Vol. 1, no. 2 (March, April, 1982), p. 32. English. DESCR: *Medical Care; Preventative Medicine.

983 Richardson, Jean L., et al. Frequency and adequacy of breast cancer screening among elderly Hispanic women. PREVENTIVE MEDICINE, Vol. 16, no. 6 (November 1987), p. 761-774. English. DESCR: Ancianos; Diseases; *Health Education; Los Angeles, CA; *Medical Care; Preventative Medicine.

Candelaria, Cordelia

984 Billings, Linda M. and Alurista. In verbal murals: a study of Chicana herstory and poetry. CONFLUENCIA, Vol. 2, no. 1 (Fall 1986), p. 60-68. English. DESCR: Cervantes, Lorna Dee; Cisneros, Sandra; EMPLUMADA; *Feminism; History; Literary Criticism; *Poetry; Xelina.

Canneries

985 Jensen, Joan M. Canning comes to New Mexico: women and the agricultural extension service, 1914-1919. NEW MEXICO HISTORICAL REVIEW, Vol. 57, no. 4 (October 1982), p. 361-386. English. DESCR: Food Industry; New Mexico; New Mexico Agricultural Extension Service.

986 Romero, Bertha. The exploitation of Mexican women in the canning industry and the effects of capital accumulation on striking workers. REVISTA MUJERES, Vol. 3, no. 2 (June 1986), p. 16-20. English. DESCR: Capitalism; Industrial Workers; Labor Unions; Strikes and Lockouts; *Watsonville Canning and Frozen Food Co.

Canneries (cont.)

987 Ruiz, Vicki L. Cannery women/cannery lives: Mexican women, unionization, and the California food processing industry, 1930-1950. Albuquerque, NM: University of New Mexico Press, 1987. xviii, 194 p.: ill. English. DESCR: Agricultural Labor Unions; California; Family; History; Industrial Workers; Labor Disputes; *Labor Unions; Trade Unions; United Cannery Agricultural Packing and Allied Workers of America (UCAPAWA); Women.

988 Ruiz, Vicki L. A promise fulfilled: Mexican cannery workers in Southern California. THE PACIFIC HISTORIAN, Vol. 30, no. 2 (Summer 1986), p. 51-61. English. DESCR: *California Sanitary Canning Company, Los Angeles, CA; Labor Unions; Moreno, Luisa [union organizer]; Southern California; Strikes and Lockouts; *United Cannery Agricultural Packing and Allied Workers of America (UCAPAWA); Working Women.

989 Ruiz, Vicki L. A promise fulfilled: Mexican cannery workers in Southern California. IN: DuBois, Ellen Carol and Ruiz, Vicki L., eds. UNEQUAL SISTERS: A MULTICULTURAL READER IN U.S. WOMEN'S HISTORY. New York: Routledge, 1990, p. 264-274. English. DESCR: *California Sanitary Canning Company, Los Angeles, CA; Labor Unions; Moreno, Luisa [union organizer]; Southern California; Strikes and Lockouts; *United Cannery Agricultural Packing and Allied Workers of America (UCAPAWA); Working Women.

990 Ruiz, Vicki L. A promise fulfilled: Mexican cannery workers in Southern California. IN: Del Castillo, Adelaida R., ed. BETWEEN BORDERS: ESSAYS ON MEXICANA/CHICANA HISTORY. Encino, CA: Floricanto Press, 1990, p. 281-298. English. DESCR: California Sanitary Canning Company, Los Angeles, CA; Labor Unions; Moreno, Luisa [union organizer]; Southern California; Strikes and Lockouts; United Cannery Agricultural Packing and Allied Workers of America (UCAPAWA); Working Women.

991 Ruiz, Vicki L. UCAPAWA, Chicanas, and the California food processing industry, 1937-1950. Thesis (Ph.D.)--Stanford University, 1982. x, 281 p. English. DESCR: Food Industry; *Labor Unions; Trade Unions; United Cannery Agricultural Packing and Allied Workers of America (UCAPAWA); Working Women.

992 Shapiro, Peter. Watsonville shows "it can be done". GUARDIAN, Vol. 39, no. 24 (March 25, 1987), p. 1,9. English. DESCR: Labor Unions; NorCal Frozen Foods; *Strikes and Lockouts; *Watsonville Canning and Frozen Food Co.; Working Women.

993 Zavella, Patricia. "Abnormal intimacy": the varying work networks of Chicana cannery workers. FEMINIST STUDIES, Vol. 11, no. 3 (Fall 1985), p. 541-557. English. DESCR: Discrimination in Employment; Labor Unions; *Natural Support Systems; *Working Women.

994 Zavella, Patricia. The politics of race and gender: organizing Chicana cannery workers in Northern California. IN: Bookman, Ann and Morgen, Sandra, eds. WOMEN AND THE POLITICS OF EMPOWERMENT. Philadelphia, PA: Temple University Press, 1988, p. 202-224. English. DESCR: Bay City Cannery Workers Committee; Cannery Workers Committee (CWC); Discrimination; Garcia, Connie; Identity; *Labor Unions; Nationalism; Northern

California; Santa Clara Valley, CA; Sex Roles; Sexism; *Working Women.

995 Zavella, Patricia. Women, work and family in the Chicano community: cannery workers of the Santa Clara Valley. Thesis (Ph.D.)--University of California, Berkeley, 1982. ix, 254 p. English. DESCR: Employment; *Family; Industrial Workers; Labor Unions; Santa Clara Valley, CA; *Sex Roles; *Working Women.

996 Zavella, Patricia. Women's work and Chicano families: cannery workers of the Santa Clara Valley. Ithaca, NY: Cornell University Press, 1987. xviii, 191 p. English. DESCR: Employment; Family; Industrial Workers; Labor Unions; Santa Clara Valley, CA; Sex Roles; *Working Women.

997 Zavella, Patricia. Work related networks and household organization among Chicana cannery workers. Stanford, CA: Stanford Center for Chicano Research, 1984. 12 leaves. English. DESCR: Industrial Workers; Natural Support Systems; *Working Women.

CANNERY WOMEN, CANNERY LIVES

998 Acuna, Rodolfo. The struggles of class and gender: current research in Chicano Studies [review essay]. JOURNAL OF AMERICAN ETHNIC HISTORY, Vol. 8, no. 2 (Spring 1989), p. 134-138. English. DESCR: *CHICANO ETHNICITY; Deutsch, Sarah; Keefe, Susan E.; Literature Reviews; *NO SEPARATE REFUGE; Padilla, Amado M.; Ruiz, Vicki L.; *WOMEN'S WORK AND CHICANO FAMILIES; Zavella, Pat.

999 Garcia, Mario T. Family and gender in Chicano and border studies research. MEXICAN STUDIES/ESTUDIOS MEXICANOS, Vol. 6, no. 1 (Winter 1990), p. 109-119. English. DESCR: Alvarez, Robert R., Jr.; *Border Region; *Family; LA FAMILIA: MIGRATION AND ADAPTATION IN BAJA AND ALTA CALIFORNIA, 1800-1975; *Literature Reviews; Ruiz, Vicki L.; Tiano, Susan B.; Women; WOMEN ON THE U.S.-MEXICO BORDER: RESPONSES TO CHANGE; WOMEN'S WORK AND CHICANO FAMILIES; Zavella, Pat.

Cannery Workers Committee (CWC)

1000 Zavella, Patricia. The politics of race and gender: organizing Chicana cannery workers in Northern California. IN: Bookman, Ann and Morgen, Sandra, eds. WOMEN AND THE POLITICS OF EMPOWERMENT. Philadelphia, PA: Temple University Press, 1988, p. 202-224. English. DESCR: Bay City Cannery Workers Committee; *Canneries; Discrimination; Garcia, Connie; Identity; *Labor Unions; Nationalism; Northern California; Santa Clara Valley, CA; Sex Roles; Sexism; *Working Women.

Capitalism

1001 Apodaca, Maria Linda. The Chicana woman: a historical materialist perspective. IN: Bollinger, William, et al., eds. WOMEN IN LATIN AMERICA: AN ANTHOLOGY FROM LATIN AMERICAN PERSPECTIVES. Riverside, CA: Latin American Perspectives, c1979, p. 81-100. English. DESCR: *Historiography; Immigrants; Imperialism; Marxism; Mexico; Oral History; Social Classes; Spanish Influence.

1002 Barton, Amy E. Women farmworkers: their workplace and capitalist patriarchy. REVISTA MUJERES, Vol. 3, no. 2 (June 1986), p. 11-13. English. DESCR: Discrimination; *Farm Workers; Sexism.

Capitalism (cont.)

1003 Dixon, Marlene; Martinez, Elizabeth; and McCaughan, Ed. Theoretical perspectives on Chicanas, Mexicanas and the transnational working class. CONTEMPORARY MARXISM, no. 11 (Fall 1985), p. 46-76. English. DESCR: Border Industries; Economic History and Conditions; History; *Immigration; *Labor Supply and Market; *Laboring Classes; Mexico; Undocumented Workers; Women.

1004 Fernandez Kelly, Maria and Garcia, Anna M. The making of an underground economy: Hispanic women, home work, and the advanced capitalist state. URBAN ANTHROPOLOGY, Vol. 14, no. 1-3 (Spring, Fall, 1985), p. 59-90. English. DESCR: Cubanos; Employment; Garment Industry; Industrial Workers; International Economic Relations; Labor Supply and Market; *Los Angeles County, CA; *Miami, FL; Women; Working Women.

1005 Romero, Bertha. The exploitation of Mexican women in the canning industry and the effects of capital accumulation on striking workers. REVISTA MUJERES, Vol. 3, no. 2 (June 1986), p. 16-20. English. DESCR: Canneries; Industrial Workers; Labor Unions; Strikes and Lockouts; *Watsonville Canning and Frozen Food Co.

CARACOL: LA REVISTA DE LA RAZA

1006 De la Torre, Susana and de Hoyos, Angela. Mujeres en el movimiento: platica de las mujeres de CARACOL. CARACOL, Vol. 4, no. 5 (January 1978), p. 16-18. Bilingual. DESCR: Feminism.

1007 Garcia-Camarillo, Mia. Mujeres en el movimiento: platica de las mujeres de CARACOL. CARACOL, Vol. 3, no. 1 (September 1976), p. 10-11. English. DESCR: *Chicano Movement; De la Torre, Susana.

Careers

1008 Alvarado, Anita L. The status of Hispanic women in nursing. IN: Melville, Margarita B., ed. TWICE A MINORITY. St. Louis, MO: Mosby, 1980, p. 208-216. English. DESCR: Medical Education; *Medical Personnel.

1009 Bauman, Raquel. A study of Mexican American women's perceptions of factors that influence academic and professional goal attainment. Thesis (Ed.D.)--University of Houston, 1984. 169 p. English. DESCR: *Educational Administration; *Higher Education; Management.

1010 Blair, Leita Mae. Characteristics of professional and traditional Mexican American women related to family of origin, role models, and conflicts: a case study. Thesis (Ed.D.)--East Texas State University, 1984. 348 p. English. DESCR: Case Studies; Education; *Family.

1011 Calderon, Vivian. Maternal employment and career orientation of young Chicana, Black, and white women. Thesis (Ph.D.)--University of California, Santa Cruz, 1984. 150 p. English. DESCR: Anglo Americans; Blacks; *Employment; Women; *Youth.

1012 Daggett, Andrea Stuhlman. A comparison of occupational goal orientations of female Mexican-Americans and Anglo high-school seniors of the classes of 1972 and 1980. Thesis (Ph.D.)--University of Arizona, Tucson, 1983. xii, 134 p. English. DESCR: Academic Achievement; Anglo Americans; *Secondary School Education; Sexism; Students; Women.

1013 Duran, Isabelle Sandoval. Grounded theory study: Chicana administrators in Colorado and New Mexico. Thesis (Ed.D.)--University of Wyoming, Laramie, 1982. ix, 114 p. English. DESCR: Colorado; *Educational Administration; Leadership; *Management; New Mexico.

1014 Esparza, Mariana Ochoa. The impact of adult education on Mexican-American women. Thesis (Ed.D.)--Texas A & I University, 1981. 168 p. English. DESCR: *Adult Education; McAllen, TX; Sex Roles.

1015 Hawley, Peggy and Even, Brenda. Work and sex-role attitudes in relation to education and other characteristics. VOCATIONAL GUIDANCE QUARTERLY, Vol. 31, no. 2 (December 1982), p. 101-108. English. DESCR: Attitudes; Education; Ethnic Groups; Psychological Testing; *Sex Roles; Working Women.

1016 Jaramillo, Mari-Luci. Profile of Chicanas and international relations. IN: LA CHICANA: BUILDING FOR THE FUTURE, AN ACTION PLAN FOR THE 80s. Oakland, CA: National Hispanic University, 1981, p. 37-58. English. DESCR: Feminism; *International Relations; Leadership.

1017 Lopez, Gloria Ann. Job satisfaction of the Mexican American woman administrator in higher education. Thesis (Ph.D.)--University of Texas, Austin, 1984. 193 p. English. DESCR: *Educational Administration; Higher Education; Leadership.

1018 MacCorquodale, Patricia. Social influences on the participation of Mexican-American women in science: final report. Unpublished report of study conducted at the Dept. of Sociology at the University of Arizona at Tucson and sponsored by the National Institute of Education. 1983, 81 p. (Eric Document: ED234944. English. DESCR: Arizona; *Science as a Profession.

1019 Madrid, Sandra Emilia. The effects of socialization on goal actualization of public school Chicana principals and superintendents. Thesis (Ph.D.)--University of Washington, 1985. 253 p. English. DESCR: *Educational Administration; Language Usage; *Socialization.

1020 Martinez, Diana. The double bind. AGENDA, (Summer 1976), p. 10-11. English. DESCR: Discrimination; *Sexism.

1021 McClelland, Judith Raymond. The relationship of independence to achievement: a comparative study of Hispanic women. Thesis (Ph.D.)--Fielding Institute, 1988. 164 p. English. DESCR: *Assertiveness; Attitudes; California Personality Inventory (CPI); Leadership; *Management; New Mexico; Personality; *Working Women.

1022 Nava, Yolanda. Chicanas in the television media. IN: LA CHICANA: BUILDING FOR THE FUTURE, AN ACTION PLAN FOR THE 80s. Oakland, CA: National Hispanic University, 1981, p. 120-133. English. DESCR: Employment; Stereotypes; *Television.

1023 Olivero, Magaly. Career Latinas: facing the challenges of a family and a career. NUESTRO, Vol. 5, no. 6 (August, September, 1981), p. 27-28. English. DESCR: Family.

Careers (cont.)

1024 Ortega, E. Astrid. Moving Hispanics into nursing. CALIFORNIA NURSE, Vol. 83, no. 3 (April 1987), p. 8. English. DESCR: *Medical Personnel.

1025 Palacios, Maria. Fear of success: Mexican-American women in two work environments. Thesis (Ph.D.)--New Mexico State University, 1988. 163 p. English. DESCR: Academic Achievement; *Assertiveness; Income; Sex Roles; *Working Women.

1026 Romero, Gloria J. and Garza, Raymond T. Attributions for the occupational success/failure of ethnic minority and nonminority women. SEX ROLES, Vol. 14, no. 7-8 (April 1986), p. 445-452. English. DESCR: Anglo Americans; *Attitudes; Identity; Sociology; Women.

1027 Romero, Mary. Twice protected?: assessing the impact of affirmative action on Mexican-American women. JOURNAL OF HISPANIC POLICY, Vol. 3, (1988, 1989), p. 83-101. English. DESCR: *Affirmative Action; *Discrimination in Employment; Statistics.

1028 Saavedra-Vela, Pilar. The dark side of Hispanic women's education. AGENDA, Vol. 8, no. 3 (May, June, 1978), p. 15-18. English. DESCR: *Education.

1029 Sullivan, Teresa A. The occupational prestige of women immigrants: a comparison of Cubans and Mexicans. INTERNATIONAL MIGRATION REVIEW, Vol. 18, no. 4 (Winter 1984), p. 1045-1062. English. DESCR: Cubanos; Employment; *Immigrants; Males; Mexico; Sex Roles; *Social Mobility; *Women; *Working Women.

1030 Torres, Cynthia. Cultural and psychological attributes and their implications for career choice and aspirations among Mexican American females. Thesis (Ph.D.)--University of California, Los Angeles, 1986. 127 p. English. DESCR: *Biculturalism; Counseling (Psychological); Cultural Characteristics.

1031 Valtierra, Mary. Acculturation, social support, and reported stress of Latina physicians. Thesis (Ph.D.)--California School of Professional Psychology, 1989. 136 p. English. DESCR: *Acculturation; Cubanos; Immigration; Latin Americans; *Medical Personnel; Puerto Ricans; *Stress; *Women.

1032 Yarbro-Bejarano, Yvonne. Chicana's experience in collective theatre: ideology and form. WOMEN AND PERFORMANCE, Vol. 2, no. 2 (1985), p. 45-58. English. DESCR: Actors and Actresses; El Teatro Campesino; El Teatro de la Esperanza; Political Ideology; *San Francisco Mime Troupe; Sex Roles; Teatro; Teatro Libertad; Valentina Productions; Women.

1033 Zambrana, Ruth E. Hispanic professional women: work, family and health. Los Angeles, CA: National Network of Hispanic Women, 1987. 75 leaves. English. DESCR: Business; *Employment; Family; Management; Mental Health; Social Classes; *Social Mobility; *Women.

1034 Zambrana, Ruth E. and Frith, Sandra. Mexican-American professional women: role satisfaction differences in single and multiple role lifestyles. JOURNAL OF SOCIAL BEHAVIOR AND PERSONALITY, Vol. 3, no. 4 (1988), p. 347-361. English. DESCR: Family; *Mental Health; *Sex Roles; Working Women.

Caribbean Region

1035 Yarbro-Bejarano, Yvonne. Primer encuentro de lesbianas feministas latinoamericanas y caribenas. THIRD WOMAN, Vol. 4, (1989), p. 143-146. English. DESCR: *Conferences and Meetings; First Meeting of Latin American and Caribbean Feminist Lesbians (October 14-17, 1987: Cuernavaca, Mexico); *Homosexuality; Latin Americans; Sexual Behavior; *Women.

"The Cariboo Cafe" [short story]

1036 Harlow, Barbara. Sites of struggle: immigration, deportation, prison, and exile. IN: Calderon, Hector and Saldivar, Jose David, eds. CRITICISM IN THE BORDERLANDS: STUDIES IN CHICANO LITERATURE, CULTURE, AND IDEOLOGY. Durham, NC: Duke University Press, 1991, p. [149]-163. English. DESCR: Anzaldua, Gloria; BLACK GOLD; BORDERLANDS/LA FRONTERA: THE NEW MESTIZA; First, Ruth; Khalifeh, Sahar; *Literary Criticism; *Political Ideology; Sanchez, Rosaura; Social Classes; "The Ditch" [short story]; Viramontes, Helena Maria; WILD THORNS; *Women; Working Women.

1037 Saldivar-Hull, Sonia. Feminism on the border: from gender politics to geopolitics. IN: Calderon, Hector and Saldivar, Jose David, eds. CRITICISM IN THE BORDERLANDS: STUDIES IN CHICANO LITERATURE, CULTURE, AND IDEOLOGY. Durham, NC: Duke University Press, 1991, p. [203]-220. English. DESCR: Anglo Americans; *Anzaldua, Gloria; *BORDERLANDS/LA FRONTERA: THE NEW MESTIZA; Feminism; Homosexuality; *Literary Criticism; Mestizaje; Moraga, Cherrie; Sexism; Viramontes, Helena Maria; Women.

Carrasco, Barbara

1038 Brown, Betty Ann. Chicanas speak out. ARTWEEK, Vol. 15, no. 2 (January 14, 1984), p. 1+. English. DESCR: *Art; Carrillo, Graciela; CHICANA VOICES & VISIONS [exhibit]; Exhibits; Goldman, Shifra M.; Hernandez, Ester; Lerma Bowerman, Liz; Rodriguez, Carmen; Rodriguez, Sandra Maria; Social and Public Art Resource Center, Venice, CA (SPARC).

1039 Burnham, Linda. Barbara Carrasco and public activist art. HIGH PERFORMANCE, Vol. 9, no. 3 (1986), p. 48. English. DESCR: *Artists; Mural Art; Politics.

1040 Goldman, Shifra M. Mujeres de California: Latin American women artists. IN: Moore, Sylvia, ed. YESTERDAY AND TOMORROW: CALIFORNIA WOMEN ARTISTS. New York, NY: Midmarch Arts Press, c1989, p. 202-229. English. DESCR: *Artists; Baca, Judith F.; Biography; California; Cervantez, Yreina; de Larios, Dora; Feminism; Hernandez, Judithe; Lomas Garza, Carmen; Lopez, Yolanda M.; Mesa-Bains, Amalia; Murillo, Patricia; Sanchez, Olivia; Valdez, Patssi; Vallejo Dillaway, Linda; Women; Zamora Lucero, Linda.

1041 Three Latina artists = Tres artistas latinas. AMERICAS 2001, Vol. 1, no. 5 (March, April, 1988), p. 21. Bilingual. DESCR: *Artists; Baca, Judith F.; Biographical Notes; *Martinez, Esperanza.

Carrasco, Barbara
     (cont.)

1042 Venegas, Sybil. The artists and their
     work--the role of the Chicana artist.
     CHISMEARTE, Vol. 1, no. 4 (Fall, Winter,
     1977), p. 3, 5. English. DESCR: Art
     Criticism; *Artists; Delgado, Etta;
     Hernandez, Ester; Las Mujeres Muralistas,
     San Francisco, CA; Mural Art.

Carrillo, Graciela

1043 Brown, Betty Ann. Chicanas speak out.
     ARTWEEK, Vol. 15, no. 2 (January 14, 1984),
     p. 1+. English. DESCR: *Art; Carrasco,
     Barbara; CHICANA VOICES & VISIONS [exhibit];
     Exhibits; Goldman, Shifra M.; Hernandez,
     Ester; Lerma Bowerman, Liz; Rodriguez,
     Carmen; Rodriguez, Sandra Maria; Social and
     Public Art Resource Center, Venice, CA
     (SPARC).

Carrillo, Jorge

1044 Lavrin, Asuncion. El segundo sexo en Mexico:
     experiencia, estudio e introspeccion,
     1983-1987. MEXICAN STUDIES/ESTUDIOS
     MEXICANOS, Vol. 5, no. 2 (Summer 1989), p.
     297-312. Spanish. DESCR: Arenal, Sandra;
     *Border Industries; Hernandez, Alberto;
     Iglesias, Norma; LA FLOR MAS BELLA DE LA
     MAQUILADORA; *Literature Reviews; Mexico;
     MUJERES FRONTERIZAS EN LA INDUSTRIA
     MAQUILADORA; SANGRE JOVEN: LAS MAQUILADORAS
     POR DENTRO; Women.

Carrillo Puerto, Felipe

1045 Macias, Anna. Against all odds: the feminist
     movement in Mexico to 1940. Westport, CT:
     Greenwood Press, 1982. xv, 195 p. English.
     DESCR: *Feminism; History; Mexican
     Revolution - 1910-1920; Mexico; *Women;
     Yucatan, Mexico.

Carter, Jimmy (President)

1046 Baca Barragan, Polly; Hamner, Richard; and
     Guerrero, Lena. [Untitled interview with
     State Senators (Colorado) Polly
     Baca-Barragan and Lena Guerrero]. NATIONAL
     HISPANIC JOURNAL, Vol. 1, no. 2 (Winter
     1982), p. 8-11. English. DESCR: Baca
     Barragan, Polly; Democratic Party; Elected
     Officials; Guerrero, Lena; *Political
     Parties and Organizations.

LA CASA DE BERNARDA ALBA

1047 Dewey, Janice. Dona Josefa: bloodpulse of
     transition and change. IN: Horno-Delgado,
     Asuncion, et al., eds. BREAKING BOUNDARIES:
     LATINA WRITING AND CRITICAL READINGS.
     Amherst, MA: University of Massachusetts
     Press, c1989, p. 39-47. English. DESCR: *DAY
     OF THE SWALLOWS; Garcia-Lorca, Federico;
     Literary Characters; Literary Criticism;
     *Portillo Trambley, Estela.

C.A.S.A.-H.G.T.
     USE: Centro de Accion Social Autonomo (CASA)

Case Studies

1048 Blair, Leita Mae. Characteristics of
     professional and traditional Mexican
     American women related to family of origin,
     role models, and conflicts: a case study.
     Thesis (Ed.D.)--East Texas State University,
     1984. 348 p. English. DESCR: *Careers;
     Education; *Family.

1049 Cuellar, Israel, et al. Clinical psychiatric
     case presentation; culturally responsive
     diagnostic formulation and treatment in an
     Hispanic female. HISPANIC JOURNAL OF
     BEHAVIORAL SCIENCES, Vol. 5, no. 1 (March
     1983), p. 93-103. English. DESCR:
     Acculturation Rating Scale for Mexican
     Americans (ARSMA); Medical Care;
     *Psychotherapy.

1050 Garcia, Mario T. The Chicana in American
     history: the Mexican women of El Paso,
     1880-1920 - a case study. PACIFIC HISTORICAL
     REVIEW, Vol. 49, no. 2 (May 1980), p.
     315-337. English. DESCR: Acme Laundry, El
     Paso, TX; American Federation of Labor
     (AFL); Central Labor Union; Domestic Work;
     *El Paso, TX; Employment; *History;
     Immigrants; Income; Labor Unions; Sex Roles;
     Strikes and Lockouts; *Working Women.

1051 Hernandez, Patricia. Lives of Chicana
     activists: the Chicano student movement (a
     case study). IN: Mora, Magdalena and Del
     Castillo, Adelaida, eds. MEXICAN WOMEN IN
     THE UNITED STATES: STRUGGLES PAST AND
     PRESENT. Los Angeles, CA: Chicano Studies
     Research Center, UCLA, 1980, p. 17-25.
     English. DESCR: California State University,
     San Diego; *Chicano Movement; Colleges and
     Universities; Movimiento Estudiantil Chicano
     de Aztlan (MEChA); Student Movements;
     Student Organizations.

Castaneda Shular, Antonia

1052 Sanchez, Rita. Chicana writer breaking out
     of the silence. DE COLORES, Vol. 3, no. 3
     (1977), p. 31-37. English. DESCR: Authors;
     Correa, Viola; Cunningham, Veronica;
     Hernandez, Barbara; *Literary Criticism;
     Mendoza, Rita; *Poetry.

Castillo, Ana

1053 Alarcon, Norma. The sardonic powers of the
     erotic in the work of Ana Castillo. IN:
     Horno-Delgado, Asuncion, et al., eds.
     BREAKING BOUNDARIES: LATINA WRITING AND
     CRITICAL READINGS. Amherst, MA: University
     of Massachusetts Press, c1989, p. 94-107.
     English. DESCR: Literary Criticism; OTRO
     CANTO; Poetry; Sex Roles; THE INVITATION;
     *THE MIXQUIAHUALA LETTERS; WOMEN ARE NOT
     ROSES.

1054 Castillo, Ana and Binder, Wolfgang.
     [Interview with] Ana Castillo. IN: Binder,
     Wolfgang, ed. PARTIAL AUTOBIOGRAPHIES:
     INTERVIEWS WITH TWENTY CHICANO POETS.
     Erlangen, W. Germany: Verlag Palm & Enke,
     1985, p. 28-38. English. DESCR: Authors;
     Autobiography; Poetry.

1055 Navarro, Marta A. and Castillo, Ana.
     Interview with Ana Castillo. IN: Trujillo,
     Carla, ed. CHICANA LESBIANS: THE GIRLS OUR
     MOTHERS WARNED US ABOUT. Berkeley, CA: Third
     Woman Press, 1991, p. 113-132. English.
     DESCR: *Authors; Homosexuality; Literature.

1056 Quintana, Alvina E. Ana Castillo's THE
     MIXQUIAHUALA LETTERS: the novelist as
     ethnographer. IN: Calderon, Hector and
     Saldivar, Jose David, eds. CRITICISM IN THE
     BORDERLANDS: STUDIES IN CHICANO LITERATURE,
     CULTURE, AND IDEOLOGY. Durham, NC: Duke
     University Press, 1991, p. [72]-83. English.
     DESCR: Anthropology; Cultural Studies;
     *Ethnology; Feminism; Geertz, Clifford;
     *Literary Criticism; Novel; THE MIXQUIAHUALA
     LETTERS.

Castillo, Ana (cont.)

1057 Quintana, Alvina E. Chicana discourse: negations and mediations. Thesis (Ph.D.)--University of California, Santa Cruz, 1989. 226 p. English. DESCR: Authors; Chavez, Denise; Chicano Movement; Cisneros, Sandra; Ethnology; Feminism; Literary Criticism; *Literature; NOVENA NARRATIVES; Oral Tradition; Political Ideology; THE HOUSE ON MANGO STREET; THE LAST OF THE MENU GIRLS; THE MIXQUIAHUALA LETTERS.

Castillo Fierro, Catalina (Katie)

1058 Escalante, Virginia; Rivera, Nancy; and Valle, Victor Manuel. Inside the world of Latinas. IN: SOUTHERN CALIFORNIA'S LATINO COMMUNITY: A SERIES OF ARTICLES REPRINTED FROM THE LOS ANGELES TIMES. Los Angeles: Los Angeles Times, 1983, p. 32-91. English. DESCR: *Biography; Gaitan, Maria Elena; Gutierrez, Nancy; Luna Mount, Julia; Ramirez, Cristina.

Catalogues

1059 Texas Memorial Museum, University of Texas, Austin, TX. La vela prencida: Mexican-American women's home altars. Exhibition catalog, 1980. Bilingual. DESCR: *Altars; Artists; Exhibits; Folk Art.

Catholic Church

1060 Bach-y-Rita, George. The Mexican-American: religious and cultural influences. IN: Becerra, Rosina M., et al., eds. MENTAL HEALTH AND HISPANIC AMERICANS: CLINICAL PERSPECTIVES. New York: Grune & Stratton, 1982, p. 29-40. English. DESCR: Cultural Characteristics; Culture; Language Usage; Machismo; *Mental Health; Psychotherapy; Religion.

1061 Erevia, Angela. Quinceanera. San Antonio, TX: Mexican American Cultural Center, 1980. xiii, 73 p. English. DESCR: *Cultural Customs; *Quinceaneras.

1062 Goldsmith, Raquel Rubio. Shipwrecked in the desert: a short history of the adventures and struggles for survival of the Mexican Sisters of the House of the Providence in Douglas, Arizona during their first twenty-two years of existence (1927-1949). RENATO ROSALDO LECTURE SERIES MONOGRAPH, Vol. 1, (Summer 1985), p. [39]-67. English. DESCR: Clergy; Douglas, AZ; History; *House of the Divine Providence [convent], Douglas, AZ; Women.

1063 Gutierrez, Ramon A. From honor to love: transformations of the meaning of sexuality in colonial New Mexico. IN: Smith, Raymond T., ed. KINSHIP IDEOLOGY AND PRACTICE IN LATIN AMERICA. Chapel Hill, NC: University of North Carolina Press, 1984, p. [237]-263. English. DESCR: *Marriage; New Mexico; *Sexual Behavior; Social Classes; Social History and Conditions; Spanish Influence; Values; Women.

1064 Iglesias, Maria and Hernandez, Maria Luz. Hermanas. IN: Stevens Arroyo, Antonio M., ed. PROPHETS DENIED HONOR: AN ANTHOLOGY ON THE HISPANO CHURCH OF THE UNITED STATES. Maryknoll, NY: Orbis Books, 1980, p. 141-142. English. DESCR: Clergy; Las Hermanas [organization]; Organizations.

1065 Isasi-Diaz, Ada Maria and Tarango, Yolanda. Hispanic women, prophetic voice in the Church: toward a Hispanic women's liberation theology. San Francisco, CA: Harper & Row, c1988. xx, 123 p. Bilingual. DESCR: *Feminism; Liberation Theology; Religion; *Women.

1066 Lara-Cea, Helen. Notes on the use of parish registers in the reconstruction of Chicana history in California prior to 1850. IN: Del Castillo, Adelaida R., ed. BETWEEN BORDERS: ESSAYS ON MEXICANA/CHICANA HISTORY. Encino, CA: Floricanto Press, 1990, p. 131-159. English. DESCR: *California; History; Indigenismo; Mission of Santa Clara; Population; *San Jose, CA; *Vital Statistics.

1067 Lee, Valerie. Achievement and educational aspirations among Hispanic female high school students: comparison between public and Catholic schools. IN: McKenna, Teresa and Ortiz, Flora Ida, eds. THE BROKEN WEB: THE EDUCATIONAL EXPERIENCE OF HISPANIC WOMEN. Claremont, CA: Tomas Rivera Center; Berkeley, CA: Floricanto Press, 1988, p. 137-192. English. DESCR: *Academic Achievement; Anglo Americans; Education; Educational Statistics; Private Education; Religious Education; *Secondary School Education; *Women.

1068 Macklin, June and Teniente de Costilla, Alvina. Virgen de Guadalupe and the American dream: the melting pot bubbles on in Toledo, Ohio. IN: West, Stanley A. and Macklin, June, eds. THE CHICANO EXPERIENCE. Boulder, CO: Westview Press, 1979, p. 111-143. English. DESCR: Assimilation; *Identity; Intermarriage; La Virgen de Guadalupe; Migration Patterns; Quinceaneras; Toledo, OH.

1069 Mosher, William D.; Johnson, David P.; and Horn, Marjorie C. Religion and fertility in the United States: the importance of marriage patterns and Hispanic origin. DEMOGRAPHY, Vol. 23, no. 3 (August 1986), p. 367-379. English. DESCR: *Fertility; Identity; Marriage; Population; *Religion.

1070 Ortiz, Carmen G. The influence of religious images on perceptions of femininity among women of Mexican origin. Thesis (Ph.D.)--California School of Professional Psychology, Berkeley, 1988. 210 p. English. DESCR: *Identity; *Religion; *Sexual Behavior; Symbolism.

1071 Rosenhouse-Persson, Sandra and Sabagh, Georges. Attitudes toward abortion among Catholic Mexican-American women: the effects of religiosity and education. DEMOGRAPHY, Vol. 20, no. 1 (February 1983), p. 87-98. English. DESCR: Abortion; Attitudes; Education; Religion.

1072 Sabagh, Georges and Lopez, David. Religiosity and fertility: the case of Chicanas. SOCIAL FORCES, Vol. 59, no. 2 (December 1980), p. 431-439. English. DESCR: *Family Planning; *Fertility; Immigrants; *Religion; Women.

1073 Urdaneta, Maria Luisa. Flesh pots, faith, or finances? Fertility rates among Mexican Americans. IN: West, Stanley A. and Macklin, June, eds. THE CHICANO EXPERIENCE. Boulder, CO: Westview Press, 1979, p. 191-206. English. DESCR: *Fertility; Machismo; Sex Roles.

Census

1074 Bean, Frank D. and Tienda, Marta. The Hispanic population of the United States. New York: Russell Sage Foundation, 1987. xxiv, 456 p. English. DESCR: Education; Employment; Fertility; Identity; Immigration; Income; *Population; Self-Referents; *Statistics.

1075 Bean, Frank D. and Swicegood, Gray. Mexican American fertility patterns. Austin, TX: University of Texas Press, 1985. x, 178 p. English. DESCR: Age Groups; Education; *Fertility; Language Usage; *Population; Research Methodology; *Socioeconomic Factors; Statistics.

1076 Estrada, Esther R. The importance of the 1980 census. IN: LA CHICANA: BUILDING FOR THE FUTURE, AN ACTION PLAN FOR THE '80s. Oakland, CA: National Hispanic University, 1981, p. 2-7. English. DESCR: Ethnic Groups; Self-Referents.

1077 Lorenzana, Noemi. La Chicana: transcending the old and carving out a new life and self-image. DE COLORES, Vol. 2, no. 3 (1975), p. 6-14. English. DESCR: Identity; Population; *Social History and Conditions.

1078 Markides, Kyriakos S. Consequences of gender differentials in life expectancy for Black and Hispanic Americans. INTERNATIONAL JOURNAL OF AGING & HUMAN DEVELOPMENT, Vol. 29, no. 2 (1989), p. 95-102. English. DESCR: *Ancianos; Blacks; Cubanos; Latin Americans; Males; Population; Puerto Ricans; U.S. Bureau of the Census.

Center for Autonomous Social Action (CASA)
USE: Centro de Accion Social Autonomo (CASA)

Center for Constitutional Rights

1079 Norris, Henry E. AIDS, women and reproductive rights. MULTICULTURAL INQUIRY AND RESEARCH ON AIDS (MIRA) NEWSLETTER, Vol. 1, no. 3 (Summer 1987), p. [2-3]. English. DESCR: Abortion; *AIDS (Disease); Discrimination; Preventative Medicine; Women.

Central Americans

1080 Salgado de Snyder, Nelly; Cervantes, Richard C.; and Padilla, Amado M. Gender and ethnic differences in psychosocial stress and generalized distress among Hispanics. SEX ROLES, Vol. 22, no. 7-8 (April, 1990), p. 441-453. English. DESCR: Anglo Americans; *Comparative Psychology; Depression (Psychological); Hispanic Stress Inventory (HSI); *Immigrants; Immigration; *Sex Roles; *Stress; Women.

Central Labor Union

1081 Garcia, Mario T. The Chicana in American history: the Mexican women of El Paso, 1880-1920 - a case study. PACIFIC HISTORICAL REVIEW, Vol. 49, no. 2 (May 1980), p. 315-337. English. DESCR: Acme Laundry, El Paso, TX; American Federation of Labor (AFL); Case Studies; Domestic Work; *El Paso, TX; Employment; *History; Immigrants; Income; Labor Unions; Sex Roles; Strikes and Lockouts; *Working Women.

Centro de Accion Social Autonomo (CASA)

1082 Marquez, Evelina and Ramirez, Margarita. Women's task is to gain liberation. IN:

Sanchez, Rosaura and Martinez Cruz, Rosa, eds. ESSAYS ON LA MUJER. Los Angeles, CA: Chicano Studies Center Publications, UCLA, 1977, p. 188-194. English. DESCR: *Feminism; Political Parties and Organizations.

1083 Mora, Magdalena. The Tolteca Strike: Mexican women and the struggle for union representation. IN: Rios-Bustamante, Antonio, ed. MEXICAN IMMIGRANT WORKERS IN THE U.S. Los Angeles, CA: Chicano Studies Research Center Publications, University of California, 1981, p. 111-117. English. DESCR: Food Industry; *Labor Unions; *Strikes and Lockouts; Toltec Foods, Richmond, CA.

Centro de Salud Mental, Oakland, CA

1084 Carrillo-Beron, Carmen. Raza mental health: perspectivas femeniles. IN: PERSPECTIVAS EN CHICANO STUDIES: PAPERS PRESENTED AT THE THIRD ANNUAL MEETING OF THE NATIONAL ASSOCIATION OF CHICANO SOCIAL SCIENCE, 1975. Los Angeles, CA: National Association of Chicano Social Science, 1977, p. 69-80. English. DESCR: Attitudes; Conferences and Meetings; *Mental Health; Mujeres de Hoy Conference (Oakland, CA).

Cervantes, Lorna Dee

1085 Alarcon, Norma. What kind of lover have you made me, Mother?: towards a theory of Chicanas' feminism and cultural identity through poetry. IN: McCluskey, Audrey T., ed. WOMEN OF COLOR: PERSPECTIVES ON FEMINISM AND IDENTITY. Bloomington, IN: Women's Studies Program, Indiana University, 1985, p. 85-110. English. DESCR: Brinson-Pineda, Barbara; Cisneros, Sandra; Culture; *Feminism; Identity; *Literary Criticism; Mora, Pat; Moraga, Cherrie; *Poetry; Tafolla, Carmen; Vigil-Pinon, Evangelina; Villanueva, Alma.

1086 Billings, Linda M. and Alurista. In verbal murals: a study of Chicana herstory and poetry. CONFLUENCIA, Vol. 2, no. 1 (Fall 1986), p. 60-68. English. DESCR: Candelaria, Cordelia; Cisneros, Sandra; EMPLUMADA; *Feminism; History; Literary Criticism; *Poetry; Xelina.

1087 Bruce-Novoa, Juan. Bernice Zamora y Lorna Dee Cervantes: una estetica feminista. REVISTA IBEROAMERICANA, Vol. 51, (July, December, 1985), p. 565-573. English. DESCR: *Authors; EMPLUMADA; Literary Criticism; Poetry; RESTLESS SERPENTS; *Zamora, Bernice.

1088 Cervantes, Lorna Dee and Binder, Wolfgang. [Interview with] Lorna Dee Cervantes. IN: Binder, Wolfgang, ed. PARTIAL AUTOBIOGRAPHIES: INTERVIEWS WITH TWENTY CHICANO POETS. Erlangen, W. Germany: Verlag Palm & Enke, 1985, p. 39-53. English. DESCR: Authors; Autobiography; Poetry.

1089 Crawford, John F. Notes toward a new multicultural criticism: three works by women of color. IN: Harris, Marie and Aguero, Kathleen, eds. A GIFT OF TONGUES: CRITICAL CHALLENGES IN CONTEMPORARY AMERICAN POETRY. Athens, GA: University of Georgia Press, 1987, p. 155-195. English. DESCR: AWAKE IN THE RIVER; EMPLUMADA; Harjo, Joy; *Literary Criticism; Mirikitani, Janice; SHE HAD SOME HORSES.

Cervantes, Lorna Dee
(cont.)

1090 Ordonez, Elizabeth J. The concept of cultural identity in Chicana poetry. THIRD WOMAN, Vol. 2, no. 1 (1984), p. 75-82. English. DESCR: Corpi, Lucha; *Literary Criticism; Poetry; Tafolla, Carmen; Villanueva, Alma.

1091 Quintana, Alvina E. Challenge and counter challenge: Chicana literary motifs. AGAINST THE CURRENT, Vol. 2, no. 2 (March, April, 1987), p. 25,28-32. English. DESCR: Anglo Americans; Authors; Cultural Studies; *Feminism; Identity; Literary Criticism; *Literature; Moraga, Cherrie; THERE ARE NO MADMEN HERE; Valdes, Gina; Women.

1092 Quintana, Alvina E. Chicana literary motifs: challenge and counter-challenge. IMAGES: ETHNIC STUDIES OCCASIONAL PAPERS SERIES, (Fall 1986), p. 24-41. English. DESCR: Anglo Americans; Authors; Cultural Studies; *Feminism; *Identity; *Literary Criticism; Literature; Moraga, Cherrie; THERE ARE NO MADMEN HERE; Valdes, Gina; Women.

1093 Zamora, Bernice. Archetypes in Chicana poetry. DE COLORES, Vol. 4, no. 3 (1978), p. 43-52. English. DESCR: Cunningham, Veronica; "Declaration on a Day of Little Inspiration" [poem]; Hernandez, Carlota; "I Speak in an Illusion" [poem]; *Literary Criticism; Lucero, Judy A.; Macias, Margarita; Mendoza, Rita; "Para Mi Hijita" [poem]; *Poetry; "Rape Report" [poem]; "The White Line" [poem]; "Working Mother's Song" [poem]; "You Can Only Blame the System for So Long" [poem]; Zamora, Katarina.

Cervantez, Yreina

1094 Goldman, Shifra M. Mujeres de California: Latin American women artists. IN: Moore, Sylvia, ed. YESTERDAY AND TOMORROW: CALIFORNIA WOMEN ARTISTS. New York, NY: Midmarch Arts Press, c1989, p. 202-229. English. DESCR: *Artists; Baca, Judith F.; Biography; California; Carrasco, Barbara; de Larios, Dora; Feminism; Hernandez, Judithe; Lomas Garza, Carmen; Lopez, Yolanda M.; Mesa-Bains, Amalia; Murillo, Patricia; Sanchez, Olivia; Valdez, Patssi; Vallejo Dillaway, Linda; Women; Zamora Lucero, Linda.

Cesarean Section

1095 Gould, Jeffrey B.; Davey, Becky; and Stafford, Randall S. Socioeconomic differences in rates of cesarean section. THE NEW ENGLAND JOURNAL OF MEDICINE, Vol. 321, no. 4 (July 27, 1989), p. 233-239. English. DESCR: Anglo Americans; Asian Americans; Blacks; *Fertility; Los Angeles County, CA; *Socioeconomic Factors; Vital Statistics; Women.

CHANTS

1096 Mora, Pat and Alarcon, Norma. A poet analyzes her craft. NUESTRO, Vol. 11, no. 2 (March 1987), p. 25-27. English. DESCR: *Authors; BORDERS; *Mora, Pat; *Poetry.

Chavez, Cesar E.

1097 Cantarow, Ellen and De la Cruz, Jessie Lopez. Jessie Lopez De la Cruz: the battle for farmworkers' rights. IN: Cantarow, Ellen. MOVING THE MOUNTAIN: WOMEN WORKING FOR SOCIAL CHANGE. Old Westbury, NY: Feminist Press, 1980, p. 94-151. English. DESCR: Agricultural Labor Unions; *De la Cruz, Jessie Lopez; *Farm Workers; Labor Disputes; Oral History; Parlier, CA; Sex Roles; Strikes and Lockouts; *United Farmworkers of America (UFW).

1098 Huerta, Dolores. Dolores Huerta talks about Republicans, Cesar, children and her home town. REGENERACION, Vol. 2, no. 4 (1975), p. 20-24. English. DESCR: *Agricultural Labor Unions; *Biography; Community Service Organization, Los Angeles, (CSO); Democratic Party; Elected Officials; Flores, Art; Huerta, Dolores; McGovern, George; *Politics; Ramirez, Henry M.; Ross, Fred; Sanchez, Philip V.; United Farmworkers of America (UFW); Working Women.

1099 Huerta, Dolores. Dolores Huerta talks about Republicans, Cesar, children and her home town. IN: Servin, Manuel P. ed. THE MEXICAN AMERICANS: AN AWAKENING MINORITY. 2nd ed. Beverly Hills, CA: Glencoe Press, 1974, p. 283-294. English. DESCR: *Agricultural Labor Unions; *Biography; Community Service Organization, Los Angeles, (CSO); Democratic Party; Elected Officials; Flores, Art; Huerta, Dolores; McGovern, George; *Politics; Ramirez, Henry M.; Ross, Fred; Sanchez, Philip V.; United Farmworkers of America (UFW); Working Women.

1100 Rose, Margaret. Traditional and nontraditional patterns of female activism in the United Farm Workers of America, 1962-1980. FRONTIERS: A JOURNAL OF WOMEN STUDIES, Vol. 11, no. 1 (1990), p. [26]-32. English. DESCR: Boycotts; California; *Chavez, Helen; *Huerta, Dolores; Labor Disputes; Labor Unions; National Farm Workers Association (NFWA); Sex Roles; Strikes and Lockouts; *United Farmworkers of America (UFW).

Chavez, Denise

1101 Chavez, Denise. Heat and rain (testimonio). IN: Horno-Delgado, Asuncion, et al., eds. BREAKING BOUNDARIES: LATINA WRITING AND CRITICAL READINGS. Amherst, MA: University of Massachusetts Press, c1989, p. 27-32. English. DESCR: *Authors; *Autobiography; Essays.

1102 Heard, Martha E. The theatre of Denise Chavez: interior landscapes with SABOR NUEVOMEXICANO. THE AMERICAS REVIEW, Vol. 16, no. 2 (Summer 1988), p. 83-91. English. DESCR: EL CAMINO [play]; Literary Criticism; New Mexico; PLAZA [play]; *Teatro.

1103 Quintana, Alvina E. Chicana discourse: negations and mediations. Thesis (Ph.D.)--University of California, Santa Cruz, 1989. 226 p. English. DESCR: Authors; Castillo, Ana; Chicano Movement; Cisneros, Sandra; Ethnology; Feminism; Literary Criticism; *Literature; NOVENA NARRATIVES; Oral Tradition; Political Ideology; THE HOUSE ON MANGO STREET; THE LAST OF THE MENU GIRLS; THE MIXQUIAHUALA LETTERS.

1104 Quintana, Alvina E. Politics, representation and the emergence of a Chicana aesthetic. CULTURAL STUDIES, Vol. 4, no. 3 (October 1990), p. 257-263. English. DESCR: Anzaldua, Gloria; *Authors; Chicana Studies; Cisneros, Sandra; Cultural Studies; Feminism; *Literary Criticism.

Chavez, Denise (cont.)

1105 Rebolledo, Tey Diana. Tradition and mythology: signatures of landscape in Chicana literature. IN: Norwood, Vera and Monk, Janice, eds. THE DESERT IS NO LADY: SOUTHWESTERN LANDSCAPES IN WOMEN'S WRITING AND ART. New Haven, CT: Yale University Press, 1987, p. 96-124. English. DESCR: *Authors; Cabeza de Baca, Fabiola; Jaramillo, Cleofas M.; Literary Criticism; *Literary History; Literature; Mora, Pat; Mythology; Otero Warren, Nina; Portillo Trambley, Estela; Silva, Beverly; Southwestern United States; WE FED THEM CACTUS.

1106 Rosaldo, Renato. Fables of the fallen guy. IN: Calderon, Hector and Saldivar, Jose David, eds. CRITICISM IN THE BORDERLANDS: STUDIES IN CHICANO LITERATURE, CULTURE AND IDEOLOGY. Durham, NC: Duke University Press, 1991, p. [84]-93. English. DESCR: Cisneros, Sandra; Fiction; Literary Characters; *Literary Criticism; Rios, Alberto; Sex Roles; THE HOUSE ON MANGO STREET; THE IGUANA KILLER: TWELVE STORIES OF THE HEART; THE LAST OF THE MENU GIRLS.

Chavez, Helen

1107 Rose, Margaret. Traditional and nontraditional patterns of female activism in the United Farm Workers of America, 1962-1980. FRONTIERS: A JOURNAL OF WOMEN STUDIES, Vol. 11, no. 1 (1990), p. [26]-32. English. DESCR: Boycotts; California; Chavez, Cesar E.; *Huerta, Dolores; Labor Disputes; Labor Unions; National Farm Workers Association (NFWA); Sex Roles; Strikes and Lockouts; *United Farmworkers of America (UFW).

Chavez Ravine, Los Angeles, CA

1108 Mendoza, Hope Schecter and Chall, Malca. Activist in the labor movement, the Democratic Party, and the Mexican-American community: an interview. Berkeley, CA: Regional Oral History Office, Bancroft Library, University of California, Berkeley, 1980. xii, 170 p.: ill. English. DESCR: *Biography; Church, Frank; Community Organizations; Community Service Organization, Los Angeles, (CSO); Democratic Party; Elections; Garment Industry; Industrial Workers; *Labor Unions; Leadership; Mendoza, Hope Schecter; Snyder, Elizabeth; Warschaw, Carmen.

Chicago Hispanic Health Alliance

1109 Cayer, Shirley. Chicago's new Hispanic health alliance. NUESTRO, Vol. 7, no. 5 (June, July, 1983), p. 44-48. English. DESCR: Alcoholism; Family Planning; *Health Education; Latin Americans; *Medical Care.

Chicago, IL

1110 Allen, Jane and Guthrie, Derek. La mujer: a visual dialogue. NEW ART EXAMINER, Vol. 5, no. 10 (July 1978), p. 14. English. DESCR: California; *Feminism; Movimiento Artistico Chicano (MARCH), Chicago, IL; Stereotypes.

1111 Ano Nuevo Kerr, Louise. Chicanas in the Great Depression. IN: Del Castillo, Adelaida R., ed. BETWEEN BORDERS: ESSAYS ON MEXICANA/CHICANA HISTORY. Encino, CA: Floricanto Press, 1990, p. 257-268. English. DESCR: *Great Depression, 1929-1933; Historiography; Mexican Mothers' Club, Chicago, IL; *Working Women.

1112 Stern, Gwen. Research, action, and social betterment. AMERICAN BEHAVIOR SCIENTISTS, Vol. 29, no. 2 (November, December, 1985), p. 229-248. English. DESCR: *Medical Care; Research Methodology; The Latina Mother-Infant Project, Chicago, IL.

THE CHICANA: A COMPREHENSIVE BIBLIOGRAPHIC STUDY

1113 Candelaria, Cordelia. Six reference works on Mexican-American women: a review essay. FRONTIERS: A JOURNAL OF WOMEN STUDIES, Vol. 5, no. 2 (Summer 1980), p. 75-80. English. DESCR: DIOSA Y HEMBRA: THE HISTORY AND HERITAGE OF CHICANAS IN THE U.S.; ESSAYS ON LA MUJER; LA CHICANA: THE MEXICAN AMERICAN WOMAN; *Literature Reviews; MEXICAN WOMEN IN THE UNITED STATES: STRUGGLES PAST AND PRESENT; TWICE A MINORITY: MEXICAN-AMERICAN WOMEN.

Chicana Caucus, National Women's Political Caucus

1114 Nieto Gomez de Lazarin, Anna. La femenista [sic]. ENCUENTRO FEMENIL, Vol. 1, no. 2 (1974), p. 34-47. English. DESCR: Anglo Americans; Chicano Movement; Conferences and Meetings; Discrimination; *Feminism; National Women's Political Caucus (February 9-11, 1973: Houston, TX); *Sexism; Women.

Chicana Conference (May 22, 1976: Austin TX)

1115 Mireles, Irma. La mujer en la comunidad: ayer, hoy, y siempre. CARACOL, Vol. 2, no. 11 (July 1976), p. 4, 11. Spanish. DESCR: Conferences and Meetings.

CHICANA! [film]

1116 Fregoso, Rosa Linda. La quinceanera of Chicana counter aesthetics. CENTRO BULLETIN, Vol. 3, no. 1 (Winter 1990, 1991), p. [87]-91. English. DESCR: *AGUEDA MARTINEZ [film]; ANIMA [film]; *DESPUES DEL TERREMOTO [film]; Espana, Frances Salome; Feminism; *Films; Morales, Sylvia; Portillo, Lourdes; Vasquez, Esperanza.

Chicana Regional Conference (May 8, 1971: Los Angeles, CA)

1117 Chicana regional conference. LA RAZA, Vol. 1, no. 6 (1971), p. 43-45. English. DESCR: *Chicano Movement; Conferences and Meetings; Feminism; Women Men Relations.

Chicana Rights Project

1118 Mexican American Legal Defense and Education Fund (MALDEF). Chicana rights: a major MALDEF issue (reprinted from MALDEF Newsletter, Fall 1977). COMADRE, no. 3 (Fall 1978), p. 31-35. English. DESCR: *Feminism; Mexican American Legal Defense and Educational Fund (MALDEF); Statistics; Vasquez, Patricia.

Chicana Studies

1119 Castillo-Speed, Lillian. Chicana Studies: a selected list of materials since 1980. FRONTIERS: A JOURNAL OF WOMEN STUDIES, Vol. 11, no. 1 (1990), p. [66]-84. English. DESCR: *Bibliography.

Chicana Studies (cont.)

1120 Cordova, Teresa, et al., eds. and National Association for Chicano Studies. Chicana voices: intersections of class, race, and gender. Austin, TX: Center for Mexican American Studies Publications, 1986. xi, 223 p. English. **DESCR**: Labor; Political History and Conditions; *Social History and Conditions.

1121 Garcia, Alma M. The development of Chicana feminist discourse, 1970-1980. GENDER & SOCIETY, Vol. 3, no. 2 (June 1989), p. 217-238. English. **DESCR**: Anglo Americans; *Chicano Movement; *Feminism; Homosexuality; Machismo; National Association for Chicano Studies (NACS); Organizations; *Sexism; Women.

1122 Garcia, Alma M. The development of Chicana feminist discourse, 1970-1980. IN: DuBois, Ellen Carol and Ruiz, Vicki L., eds. UNEQUAL SISTERS: A MULTICULTURAL READER IN U.S. WOMEN'S HISTORY. New York: Routledge, 1990, p. 418-431. English. **DESCR**: Anglo Americans; *Chicano Movement; *Feminism; Homosexuality; Machismo; National Association for Chicano Studies (NACS); Organizations; *Sexism; Women.

1123 Garcia, Alma M. Studying Chicanas: bringing women into the frame of Chicano Studies. IN: Cordova, Teresa, et al., eds. CHICANA VOICES. Austin, TX: Center for Mexican American Studies, 1986, p. 19-29. English. **DESCR**: *Chicano Studies; Discrimination; Labor Supply and Market; Literature Reviews.

1124 Klor de Alva, J. Jorge. Chicana history and historical significance: some theoretical considerations. IN: Del Castillo, Adelaida R., ed. BETWEEN BORDERS: ESSAYS ON MEXICANA/CHICANA HISTORY. Encino, CA: Floricanto Press, 1990, p. 61-86. English. **DESCR**: *Historiography; *History; Sexism.

1125 Lucero, Marcela Christine. Resources for the Chicana feminist scholar. IN: Treichler, Paula A., et al., eds. FOR ALMA MATER: THEORY AND PRACTICE IN FEMINIST SCHOLARSHIP. Urbana: University of Illinois Press, 1985, p. 393-401. English. **DESCR**: *Feminism; Literature Reviews; Publishing Industry; Research Methodology.

1126 Orozco, Cynthia. Getting started in Chicana Studies. WOMEN'S STUDIES QUARTERLY, no. 1-2 (1990), p. 46-69. English. **DESCR**: Bibliography; *Literature Reviews.

1127 Quintana, Alvina E. Politics, representation and the emergence of a Chicana aesthetic. CULTURAL STUDIES, Vol. 4, no. 3 (October 1990), p. 257-263. English. **DESCR**: Anzaldua, Gloria; *Authors; Chavez, Denise; Cisneros, Sandra; Cultural Studies; Feminism; *Literary Criticism.

1128 Sanchez, Rosaura. The history of Chicanas: a proposal for a materialist perspective. IN: Del Castillo, Adelaida R., ed. BETWEEN BORDERS: ESSAYS ON MEXICANA/CHICANA HISTORY. Encino, CA: Floricanto Press, 1990, p. 1-29. English. **DESCR**: Apodaca, Maria Linda; Del Castillo, Adelaida R.; Feminism; Historiography; History; Morales, Sylvia; Ruiz, Vicki L.

1129 Winkler, Karen J. Scholars say issues of diversity have "revolutionized" field of Chicano Studies. CHRONICLE OF HIGHER EDUCATION, Vol. 37, no. 4 (September 26, 1990), p. A4-A9. English. **DESCR**: Chicano Studies; Curriculum; *Feminism; Higher Education; Ruiz, Vicki L.; Saragoza, Alex M.

1130 Zavella, Patricia. The problematic relationship of feminism and Chicana Studies. WOMEN'S STUDIES QUARTERLY, Vol. 17, no. 1-2 (1989), p. 25-36. English. **DESCR**: *Feminism; *Women.

LA CHICANA: THE MEXICAN AMERICAN WOMAN

1131 Candelaria, Cordelia. Six reference works on Mexican-American women: a review essay. FRONTIERS: A JOURNAL OF WOMEN STUDIES, Vol. 5, no. 2 (Summer 1980), p. 75-80. English. **DESCR**: DIOSA Y HEMBRA: THE HISTORY AND HERITAGE OF CHICANAS IN THE U.S.; ESSAYS ON LA MUJER; *Literature Reviews; MEXICAN WOMEN IN THE UNITED STATES: STRUGGLES PAST AND PRESENT; THE CHICANA: A COMPREHENSIVE BIBLIOGRAPHIC STUDY; TWICE A MINORITY: MEXICAN-AMERICAN WOMEN.

1132 Pierce, Jennifer. The implications of functionalism for Chicano family research. BERKELEY JOURNAL OF SOCIOLOGY, Vol. 29, (1984), p. 93-117. English. **DESCR**: Enriquez, Evangelina; *Family; Machismo; Mirande, Alfredo; Research Methodology; Sex Roles.

CHICANA VOICES & VISIONS [exhibit]

1133 Brown, Betty Ann. Chicanas speak out. ARTWEEK, Vol. 15, no. 2 (January 14, 1984), p. 1+. English. **DESCR**: *Art; Carrasco, Barbara; Carrillo, Graciela; Exhibits; Goldman, Shifra M.; Hernandez, Ester; Lerma Bowerman, Liz; Rodriguez, Carmen; Rodriguez, Sandra Maria; Social and Public Art Resource Center, Venice, CA (SPARC).

Chicana Welfare Rights Organization

1134 Chicana Welfare Rights challenges Talmadge amendment. REGENERACION, Vol. 2, no. 3 (1973), p. 14. English. **DESCR**: *Feminism; Social Services; Talmadge Amendment to the Social Security Act, 1971; *Welfare.

1135 Escalante, Alicia. Chicana Welfare Rights vs. the Talmadge amendment. LA RAZA, Vol. 2, no. 1 (February 1974), p. 20-21. English. **DESCR**: Flores, Francisca; Talmadge Amendment to the Social Security Act, 1971; *Welfare.

1136 Escalante, Alicia. A letter from the Chicana Welfare Rights organization. ENCUENTRO FEMENIL, Vol. 1, no. 2 (1974), p. 15-19. English. **DESCR**: Child Care Centers; *Talmadge Amendment to the Social Security Act, 1971; Welfare; Working Women.

1137 Flores, Francisca. A reaction to discussions on the Talmadge Amendment to the Social Security Act. ENCUENTRO FEMENIL, Vol. 1, no. 2 (1974), p. 13-14. English. **DESCR**: Child Care Centers; Discrimination; Feminism; Income; *Social Security Act; Social Services; *Talmadge Amendment to the Social Security Act, 1971; Welfare; Working Women.

1138 Flores, Francisca. A reaction to discussions on the Talmadge Amendment to the Social Security Act. REGENERACION, Vol. 2, no. 3 (1973), p. 16. English. **DESCR**: Child Care Centers; Discrimination; Feminism; Income; *Social Security Act; Social Services; *Talmadge Amendment to the Social Security Act, 1971; Welfare; Working Women.

Chicana Welfare Rights Organization (cont.)

1139 Nieto Gomez de Lazarin, Anna. Madres por justicia! ENCUENTRO FEMENIL, Vol. 1, no. 1 (Spring 1973), p. 12-19. English. DESCR: Employment; Talmadge Amendment to the Social Security Act, 1971; *Welfare.

1140 Nieto Gomez de Lazarin, Anna. What is the Talmadge Amendment?: justicia para las madres. REGENERACION, Vol. 2, no. 3 (1973), p. 14-15. English. DESCR: *Child Care Centers; Community Work Experience Program (C.W.E.P.); Discrimination in Employment; Employment Tests; Escalante, Alicia; *Feminism; Nixon, Richard; Working Women.

Chicana/Latina Summer Research Institute (August 19, 1989: Santa Clara University)

1141 Sosa Riddell, Adaljiza, ed. Policy development: Chicana/Latina Summer Research Institute [handbook]. Davis, CA: [Chicano Studies Program, UC Davis, 1989?]. 29 p. English. DESCR: Conferences and Meetings; Public Policy.

CHICANAS SPEAK OUT

1142 Gonzales, Sylvia Alicia. The Chicana perspective: a design for self-awareness. IN: Trejo, Arnulfo D., ed. THE CHICANOS: AS WE SEE OURSELVES. Tucson, AZ: University of Arizona Press, 1979, p. 81-99. English. DESCR: Chicano Movement; Discrimination; Feminism; Identity; Machismo; Madsen, William; *Mexican Revolution - 1910-1920; Mexico; Sex Roles; THE MEXICAN-AMERICANS OF SOUTH TEXAS; Vidal, Mirta.

Chicanismo

1143 Lucero Trujillo, Marcela. The terminology of machismo. DE COLORES, Vol. 4, no. 3 (1978), p. 34-42. Bilingual. DESCR: *Machismo; *Sex Stereotypes; *Women Men Relations.

1144 Vazquez-Nuttall, Ena; Romero-Garcia, Ivonne; and De Leon, Brunilda. Sex roles and perceptions of femininity and masculinity of Hispanic women: a review of the literature. PSYCHOLOGY OF WOMEN QUARTERLY, Vol. 11, no. 4 (December 1987), p. 409-425. English. DESCR: Attitudes; *Literature Reviews; Machismo; Puerto Ricans; *Sex Roles; *Women.

Chicano Dialects

1145 Galindo, Letticia. Perceptions of pachuquismo and use of Calo/pachuco Spanish by various Chicana women. LA RED/THE NET, no. 48 (November 1981), p. 2,10. English. DESCR: Language Usage; *Texas.

CHICANO ETHNICITY

1146 Acuna, Rodolfo. The struggles of class and gender: current research in Chicano Studies [review essay]. JOURNAL OF AMERICAN ETHNIC HISTORY, Vol. 8, no. 2 (Spring 1989), p. 134-138. English. DESCR: *CANNERY WOMEN, CANNERY LIVES; Deutsch, Sarah; Keefe, Susan E.; Literature Reviews; *NO SEPARATE REFUGE; Padilla, Amado M.; Ruiz, Vicki L.; *WOMEN'S WORK AND CHICANO FAMILIES; Zavella, Pat.

Chicano Movement

1147 Abajo con los machos [letter to the editor]. LA RAZA, Vol. 1, no. 5 (1971), p. 3-4. English. DESCR: *Machismo; Women Men Relations.

1148 Arizmendi, Yareli. La mujer y el teatro chicano. IN: Lopez-Gonzalez, Aralia, et al., eds. MUJER Y LITERATURA MEXICANA Y CHICANA: CULTURAS EN CONTACTO. Mexico: Colegio de la Frontera Norte, 1988, p. [85]-91. Spanish. DESCR: *Teatro.

1149 Asuncion-Lande, Nobleza C. Problems and strategies for sexual identity and cultural integration: Mexican-American women on the move. IN: Newmark, Eileen, ed. WOMEN'S ROLES: A CROSS-CULTURAL PERSPECTIVE. New York, NY: Pergamon Press, 1980, p. 497-506. English. DESCR: *Feminism; *Identity; *Sexism.

1150 Baca Zinn, Maxine. Political familism: toward sex role equality in Chicano families. AZTLAN, Vol. 6, no. 1 (Spring 1975), p. 13-26. English. DESCR: Acculturation; Family; Machismo; *Sex Roles.

1151 Blea, Irene I. Mexican American female experience. IN: Blea, Irene I. TOWARD A CHICANO SOCIAL SCIENCE. New York: Praeger, 1988, p. [67]-89. English. DESCR: *Feminism; Sex Roles; Sexism.

1152 Chavez, Henri. Las Chicanas/The Chicanas. REGENERACION, Vol. 1, no. 10 (1971), p. 14. Bilingual. DESCR: Sexism; *Women Men Relations.

1153 Chicana regional conference. LA RAZA, Vol. 1, no. 6 (1971), p. 43-45. English. DESCR: Chicana Regional Conference (May 8, 1971: Los Angeles, CA); Conferences and Meetings; Feminism; Women Men Relations.

1154 Cotera, Marta P. Chicana caucus. MAGAZIN, Vol. 1, no. 6 (August 1972), p. 24-26. English. DESCR: La Raza Unida Party, Texas.

1155 Cotera, Marta P. Feminism: the Chicana and Anglo versions: a historical analysis. IN: Melville, Margarita B., ed. TWICE A MINORITY. St. Louis, MO: Mosby, 1980, p. 217-234. English. DESCR: *Anglo Americans; Conferences and Meetings; *Feminism; Organizations; Social History and Conditions; Voting Rights; *Women.

1156 Del Castillo, Adelaida R. Mexican women in organization. IN: Mora, Magdalena and Del Castillo, Adelaida, eds. MEXICAN WOMEN IN THE UNITED STATES: STRUGGLES PAST AND PRESENT. Los Angeles, CA: Chicano Studies Research Center, UCLA, 1980, p. 7-16. English. DESCR: Feminism; Leadership; Student Organizations; Students.

1157 Enriquez, Evangelina and Mirande, Alfredo. Liberation, Chicana style: colonial roots of feministas chicanas. DE COLORES, Vol. 4, no. 3 (1978), p. 7-21. Bilingual. DESCR: Feminism; Malinche; *Political History and Conditions; *Social History and Conditions.

1158 Flores, Francisca. Equality. REGENERACION, Vol. 2, no. 3 (1973), p. 4-5. English. DESCR: Anglo Americans; Discrimination; Elected Officials; Feminism; Income; *Machismo; *Working Women.

1159 Garcia, Alma M. The development of Chicana feminist discourse, 1970-1980. GENDER & SOCIETY, Vol. 3, no. 2 (June 1989), p. 217-238. English. DESCR: Anglo Americans; Chicana Studies; *Feminism; Homosexuality; Machismo; National Association for Chicano Studies (NACS); Organizations; *Sexism; Women.

Chicano Movement (cont.)

1160 Garcia, Alma M. The development of Chicana feminist discourse, 1970-1980. IN: DuBois, Ellen Carol and Ruiz, Vicki L., eds. UNEQUAL SISTERS: A MULTICULTURAL READER IN U.S. WOMEN'S HISTORY. New York: Routledge, 1990, p. 418-431. English. DESCR: Anglo Americans; Chicana Studies; *Feminism; Homosexuality; Machismo; National Association for Chicano Studies (NACS); Organizations; *Sexism; Women.

1161 Garcia-Camarillo, Mia. Mujeres en el movimiento: platica de las mujeres de CARACOL. CARACOL, Vol. 3, no. 1 (September 1976), p. 10-11. English. DESCR: CARACOL: LA REVISTA DE LA RAZA; De la Torre, Susana.

1162 Gonzales, Sylvia Alicia. The Chicana perspective: a design for self-awareness. IN: Trejo, Arnulfo D., ed. THE CHICANOS: AS WE SEE OURSELVES. Tucson, AZ: University of Arizona Press, 1979, p. 81-99. English. DESCR: CHICANAS SPEAK OUT; Discrimination; Feminism; Identity; Machismo; Madsen, William; *Mexican Revolution - 1910-1920; Mexico; Sex Roles; THE MEXICAN-AMERICANS OF SOUTH TEXAS; Vidal, Mirta.

1163 Gonzales, Sylvia Alicia. Toward a feminist pedagogy for Chicana self-actualization. FRONTIERS: A JOURNAL OF WOMEN STUDIES, Vol. 5, no. 2 (Summer 1980), p. 48-51. English. DESCR: Education; *Feminism; Identity; Malinche.

1164 Hernandez, Patricia. Lives of Chicana activists: the Chicano student movement (a case study). IN: Mora, Magdalena and Del Castillo, Adelaida, eds. MEXICAN WOMEN IN THE UNITED STATES: STRUGGLES PAST AND PRESENT. Los Angeles, CA: Chicano Studies Research Center, UCLA, 1980, p. 17-25. English. DESCR: California State University, San Diego; Case Studies; Colleges and Universities; Movimiento Estudiantil Chicano de Aztlan (MEChA); Student Movements; Student Organizations.

1165 Longeaux y Vasquez, Enriqueta. Soy Chicana primero. LA RAZA HABLA, Vol. 1, no. 1 (January 1976), p. 1-5. English. DESCR: *Feminism; Identity.

1166 Longeaux y Vasquez, Enriqueta. Soy Chicana primero. EL CUADERNO, Vol. 1, no. 1 (1971), p. 17-22. English. DESCR: *Feminism; Identity.

1167 Lopez, Sonia A. The role of the Chicana within the student movement. IN: Sanchez, Rosaura and Martinez Cruz, Rosa, eds. ESSAYS ON LA MUJER. Los Angeles, CA: Chicano Studies Center Publications, UCLA, 1977, p. 16-29. English. DESCR: Conferences and Meetings; Feminism; First National Chicana Conference (May 1971: Houston, TX); *Student Movements.

1168 Lucero, Marcela Christine. The socio-historical implication of the valley as a metaphor in three Colorado Chicana poets. Thesis (Ph.D.)--University of Minnesota, 1981. 176 p. English. DESCR: *Authors; Blea, Irene I.; Colorado; Feminism; Literary Criticism; Mondragon Valdez, Maria; Poetry; Zamora, Bernice.

1169 Matsuda, Gema. La Chicana organizes: the Comision Femenil Mexicana in perspective. REGENERACION, Vol. 2, no. 4 (1975), p. 25-27. English. DESCR: Bojorquez, Frances; *Comision Femenil Mexicana Nacional; De la

Cruz, Juana Ines; Flores, Francisca; History; Machismo; Malinche; Prisons; Sex Stereotypes; *Sexism.

1170 Mesa-Bains, Amalia. Quest for identity: profile of two Chicana muralists: based on interviews with Judith F. Baca and Patricia Rodriguez. IN: Cockcroft, Eva Sperling and Barnet-Sanchez, Holly, eds. SIGNS FROM THE HEART: CALIFORNIA CHICANO MURALS. Venice, CA: Social and Public Art Resource Center, 1990, p. [68-83]. English. DESCR: Artists; Baca, Judith F.; GREAT WALL OF LOS ANGELES [mural]; *Mural Art; Rodriguez, Patricia.

1171 El Movimiento and the Chicana. LA RAZA, Vol. 1, no. 6 (1971), p. 40-42. English. DESCR: Stereotypes.

1172 Nieto Gomez de Lazarin, Anna. Ana Nieto Gomez: sexism in the Movimiento. LA GENTE DE AZTLAN, Vol. 6, no. 4 (March 1976), p. 10. English. DESCR: Feminism; Sex Roles; *Sexism.

1173 Nieto Gomez de Lazarin, Anna. Chicanas identify. REGENERACION, Vol. 1, no. 10 (1971), p. 9. English.

1174 Nieto Gomez de Lazarin, Anna. La femenista [sic]. ENCUENTRO FEMENIL, Vol. 1, no. 2 (1974), p. 34-47. English. DESCR: Anglo Americans; Chicana Caucus, National Women's Political Caucus; Conferences and Meetings; Discrimination; *Feminism; National Women's Political Caucus (February 9-11, 1973: Houston, TX); *Sexism; Women.

1175 Ordonez, Elizabeth J. Sexual politics and the theme of sexuality in Chicana poetry. IN: Miller, Beth, ed. WOMEN IN HISPANIC LITERATURE: ICONS AND FALLEN IDOLS. Berkeley, CA: University of California Press, 1983, p. 316-339. English. DESCR: Feminism; *Literary Criticism; Poetry; Sexual Behavior.

1176 Quintana, Alvina E. Chicana discourse: negations and mediations. Thesis (Ph.D.)--University of California, Santa Cruz, 1989. 226 p. English. DESCR: Authors; Castillo, Ana; Chavez, Denise; Cisneros, Sandra; Ethnology; Feminism; Literary Criticism; *Literature; NOVENA NARRATIVES; Oral Tradition; Political Ideology; THE HOUSE ON MANGO STREET; THE LAST OF THE MENU GIRLS; THE MIXQUIAHUALA LETTERS.

1177 Rivero, Eliana S. La mujer y La Raza: Latinas y Chicanas [part I]. CARACOL, Vol. 4, no. 1 (September 1977), p. 8-9. Spanish. DESCR: Self-Referents.

1178 Santiago, Myrna I. La Chicana. FEM, Vol. 8, no. 34 (June, July, 1984), p. 5-9. Spanish. DESCR: *Feminism; History.

1179 Sosa Riddell, Adaljiza. Chicanas and el Movimiento. AZTLAN, Vol. 5, no. 1 (Spring 1974), p. 155-165. English. DESCR: Stereotypes.

1180 Trujillo Gaitan, Marcella. The dilemma of the modern Chicana artist and critic. DE COLORES, Vol. 3, no. 3 (1977), p. 38-48. Bilingual. DESCR: Art Criticism; Artists; Gonzales, Sylvia Alicia; *Literary Criticism; Machismo; Malinche; *Poetry; Symbolism.

Chicano Movement (cont.)

1181 Trujillo Gaitan, Marcella. The dilemma of the modern Chicana artist and critic. HERESIES, Vol. 2, no. 4 (1979), p. 5-10. English. **DESCR:** Art Criticism; Artists; Authors; Gonzales, Sylvia Alicia; *Literary Criticism; Machismo; Malinche; *Poetry; Symbolism.

1182 Vasquez, Carlos. Women in the Chicano Movement. IN: Mora, Magdalena and Del Castillo, Adelaida, eds. MEXICAN WOMEN IN THE UNITED STATES: STRUGGLES PAST AND PRESENT. Los Angeles, CA: Chicano Studies Research Center, UCLA, 1980, p. 27-28. English. **DESCR:** *Feminism.

1183 Vasquez, Enriqueta L. La Chicana. MAGAZIN, Vol. 1, no. 4 (April 1972), p. 66-68+. English. **DESCR:** Family; Working Women.

CHICANO POEMS FOR THE BARRIO

1184 Aguilar-Henson, Marcella. The multi-faceted poetic world of Angela de Hoyos. Austin, TX: Relampago Books Press, 1985, c1982. 81 p. English. **DESCR:** ARISE CHICANO; *Authors; de Hoyos, Angela; GATA POEMS; GOODBYE TO SILENCE; Language Usage; *Literary Criticism; *Poetry; SELECTED POEMS/SELECCIONES; YO, MUJER.

Chicano Studies

1185 Cantu, Norma. Women then and now: an analysis of the Adelita image versus the Chicana as political writer and philosopher. IN: Cordova, Teresa, et al., eds. CHICANA VOICES. Austin, TX: Center for Mexican American Studies, 1986, p. 8-10. English. **DESCR:** Discrimination; Higher Education; *La Adelita; Stereotypes.

1186 Garcia, Alma M. Studying Chicanas: bringing women into the frame of Chicano Studies. IN: Cordova, Teresa, et al., eds. CHICANA VOICES. Austin, TX: Center for Mexican American Studies, 1986, p. 19-29. English. **DESCR:** Chicana Studies; Discrimination; Labor Supply and Market; Literature Reviews.

1187 Goldman, Shifra M. Artistas en accion: conferencia de las mujeres chicanas. LA COMUNIDAD, (August 10, 1980), p. 15. Spanish. **DESCR:** *Artists; Conferences and Meetings; Flores, Gloriamalia; Lomas Garza, Carmen.

1188 Nieto Gomez de Lazarin, Anna. Un proposito para estudios femeniles de la chicana. REGENERACION, Vol. 2, no. 4 (1975), p. 30, 31-32. English. **DESCR:** Curriculum; *Education; History; Nava, Yolanda; Sexism.

1189 Orozco, Cynthia. Sexism in Chicano Studies and the community. IN: Cordova, Teresa, et al., eds. CHICANA VOICES. Austin, TX: Center for Mexican American Studies, 1986, p. 11-18. English. **DESCR:** Acuna, Rodolfo; Feminism; OCCUPIED AMERICA; *Sexism.

1190 Winkler, Karen J. Scholars say issues of diversity have "revolutionized" field of Chicano Studies. CHRONICLE OF HIGHER EDUCATION, Vol. 37, no. 4 (September 26, 1990), p. A4-A9. English. **DESCR:** Chicana Studies; Curriculum; *Feminism; Higher Education; Ruiz, Vicki L.; Saragoza, Alex M.

Chicanos in American Literature

1191 Dario Salaz, Ruben. The Chicana in American literature. LA LUZ, Vol. 4, no. 3 (June 1975), p. 28. English. **DESCR:** Literary Criticism; Sex Stereotypes.

1192 Dario Salaz, Ruben. The Chicana in American literature. LA LUZ, Vol. 6, no. 11 (November 1977), p. 15. English. **DESCR:** *Literary Criticism; Sex Stereotypes.

Child Abuse

1193 Buriel, Raymond, et al. Mexican-American disciplinary practices and attitudes toward child maltreatment:a comparison of foreign and native-born mothers. HISPANIC JOURNAL OF BEHAVIORAL SCIENCES, Vol. 13, no. 1 (February 1991), p. 78-94. English. **DESCR:** *Attitudes; Immigrants; *Parent and Child Relationships; *Parenting; Values; Violence.

Child Care Centers

1194 Escalante, Alicia. A letter from the Chicana Welfare Rights organization. ENCUENTRO FEMENIL, Vol. 1, no. 2 (1974), p. 15-19. English. **DESCR:** *Chicana Welfare Rights Organization; *Talmadge Amendment to the Social Security Act, 1971; Welfare; Working Women.

1195 Flores, Francisca. Comision Femenil Mexicana. REGENERACION, Vol. 2, no. 4 (1975), p. 24-25. English. **DESCR:** *Abortion; Comision Femenil Mexicana Nacional; Identity; Working Women.

1196 Flores, Francisca. A reaction to discussions on the Talmadge Amendment to the Social Security Act. ENCUENTRO FEMENIL, Vol. 1, no. 2 (1974), p. 13-14. English. **DESCR:** *Chicana Welfare Rights Organization; Discrimination; Feminism; Income; *Social Security Act; Social Services; *Talmadge Amendment to the Social Security Act, 1971; Welfare; Working Women.

1197 Flores, Francisca. A reaction to discussions on the Talmadge Amendment to the Social Security Act. REGENERACION, Vol. 2, no. 3 (1973), p. 16. English. **DESCR:** *Chicana Welfare Rights Organization; Discrimination; Feminism; Income; *Social Security Act; Social Services; *Talmadge Amendment to the Social Security Act, 1971; Welfare; Working Women.

1198 Longeaux y Vasquez, Enriqueta. The woman of La Raza. REGENERACION, Vol. 2, no. 4 (1975), p. 34-36. English. **DESCR:** Discrimination; Gallo, Juana; Housing; La Adelita; Machismo; Sex Roles; *Social History and Conditions; Working Women.

1199 Longeaux y Vasquez, Enriqueta. The woman of La Raza. IN: Valdez, Luis and Steiner, Stan, eds. AZTLAN: AN ANTHOLOGY OF MEXICAN AMERICAN LITERATURE. New York: Vintage Books, 1972, p. 272-278. Also IN: Salinas, Luis Omar and Faderman, Lillian, compilers. FROM THE BARRIO: A CHICANO ANTHOLOGY. San Francisco, CA: Canfield Press, 1973, p. 20-24. English. **DESCR:** Discrimination; Gallo, Juana; Housing; La Adelita; Machismo; Sex Roles; *Social History and Conditions; Working Women.

Child Care Centers
(cont.)

1200 Nava, Yolanda. The Chicana and employment: needs analysis and recommendations for legislation. REGENERACION, Vol. 2, no. 3 (1973), p. 7-9. English. DESCR: California Commission on the Status of Women; Comision Femenil Mexicana Nacional; *Discrimination in Employment; Employment Tests; Employment Training; Equal Rights Amendment (ERA); Sexism; Statistics; Stereotypes; Working Women.

1201 Nieto Gomez de Lazarin, Anna. What is the Talmadge Amendment?: justicia para las madres. REGENERACION, Vol. 2, no. 3 (1973), p. 14-15. English. DESCR: Chicana Welfare Rights Organization; Community Work Experience Program (C.W E.P.); Discrimination in Employment; Employment Tests; Escalante, Alicia; *Feminism; Nixon, Richard; Working Women.

1202 Ruiz, Vicki L. Obreras y madres: labor activism among Mexican women and its impact on the family. RENATO ROSALDO LECTURE SERIES MONOGRAPH, Vol. 1, (Summer 1985), p. [19]-38. English. DESCR: Children; History; *Labor Unions; *Mexico; Sex Roles; Women; *Working Women.

Child Rearing
USE: Parenting

Child Study

1203 de Leon Siantz, Mary Lou. Maternal acceptance/rejection of Mexican migrant mothers. PSYCHOLOGY OF WOMEN QUARTERLY, Vol. 14, no. 2 (June 1990), p 245-254. English. DESCR: Farm Workers; *Migrant Children; Migrant Labor; Natural Support Systems; *Parent and Child Relationships; Stress; Texas Migrant Council Headstart Program.

Children

1204 Carrasco, Frank F. Teaching strategies used by Chicano mothers with their Head Start children. Thesis (Ph.D.)—University of Colorado, Boulder, 1983. 177 p. English. DESCR: Bilingualism; *Education; Low Income; *Parent and Child Relationships; *Parenting.

1205 Flores, Francisca. Comision Femenil Mexicana. REGENERACION, Vol. 2, no. 1 (1971), p. 6. English. DESCR: Abortion; Comision Femenil Mexicana Nacional; *Family Planning; Feminism; Organizations; Politics.

1206 Gunther Enriquez, Martha. Studying maternal-infant attachment: a Mexican-American example. IN: Kay, Margarita Artschwager, ed. ANTHROPOLOGY OF HUMAN BIRTH. Philadelphia, PA: F.A. Davis, 1982, p. 61-79. English. DESCR: *Fertility; Immigrants; *Maternal and Child Welfare; *Parent and Child Relationships.

1207 Gutierrez, Jeannie and Sameroff, Arnold. Determinants of complexity in Mexican-American and Anglo-American mothers' conceptions of child development. CHILD DEVELOPMENT, Vol. 61, no. 2 (April 1990), p. 384-394. English. DESCR: Acculturation; *Anglo Americans; Cultural Characteristics; *Parenting; Values; *Women.

1208 Limon, Jose E. [anthropologist]. "La vieja Ines," a Mexican folkgame: a research note. IN: Melville, Margarita B., ed. TWICE A MINORITY. St. Louis, MO: Mosby, 1980, p. 88-94. English. DESCR: *Folklore; *Games; *Sex Roles.

1209 Mary, Nancy L. Reactions of Black, Hispanic, and white mothers to having a child with handicaps. MENTAL RETARDATION, Vol. 28, no. 1 (February 1990), p. 1-5. English. DESCR: Anglo Americans; *Attitudes; Blacks; Comparative Psychology; *Mentally Handicapped; Parent and Child Relationships; *Women.

1210 Miranda, Gloria E. Hispano-Mexican childrearing practices in pre-American Santa Barbara. SOUTHERN CALIFORNIA QUARTERLY, Vol. 65, no. 4 (Winter 1983), p. 307-320. English. DESCR: Cultural Characteristics; *Family; History; *Parenting; Santa Barbara, CA; Socialization.

1211 Moore, Joan W. and Devitt, Mary. The paradox of deviance in addicted Mexican American mothers. GENDER & SOCIETY, Vol. 3, no. 1 (March 1989), p. 53-70. English. DESCR: *Drug Addicts; *Drug Use; Family; *Fertility; Gangs; Parenting; Sex Roles.

1212 Olvera-Ezzell, Norma; Power, Thomas G.; and Cousins, Jennifer H. Maternal socialization of children's eating habits: strategies used by obese Mexican-American mothers. CHILD DEVELOPMENT, Vol. 61, no. 2 (April 1990), p. 395-400. English. DESCR: Food Practices; *Nutrition; *Obesity; *Parent and Child Relationships; *Socialization.

1213 Panitz, Daniel R., et al. The role of machismo and the Hispanic family in the etiology and treatment of alcoholism in the Hispanic American males. AMERICAN JOURNAL OF FAMILY THERAPY, Vol. 11, no. 1 (Spring 1983), p. 31-44. English. DESCR: *Alcoholism; Family; *Machismo; Puerto Rico; Socioeconomic Factors.

1214 Parra, Elena and Henderson, Ronald W. Mexican American perceptions of parent and teacher roles in child development. IN: Fishman, Joshua A. and Keller, Gary D., eds. BILINGUAL EDUCATION FOR HISPANIC STUDENTS IN THE UNITED STATES. New York: Teachers College Press, 1982, p. 289-299. English. DESCR: Family; *Parenting; Sex Roles; Teacher Attitudes.

1215 Powell, Douglas R.; Zambrana, Ruth E.; and Silva-Palacios, Victor. Designing culturally responsive parent programs: a comparison of low-income Mexican and Mexican-American mothers' preferences. FAMILY RELATIONS, Vol. 39, no. 3 (July 1990), p. 298-304. English. DESCR: Acculturation; Education; Immigrants; Los Angeles, CA; Low Income; *Parent and Child Relationships; *Parenting; Women.

1216 Rogers, Linda Perkowski and Markides, Kyriakos S. Well-being in the postparental stage in Mexican-American women. RESEARCH ON AGING, Vol. 11, no. 4 (December 1989), p. 508-516. English. DESCR: *Age Groups; Ancianos; *"Empty Nest" Syndrome; *Parent and Child Relationships; San Antonio, TX.

1217 Ruiz, Vicki L. Obreras y madres: labor activism among Mexican women and its impact on the family. RENATO ROSALDO LECTURE SERIES MONOGRAPH, Vol. 1, (Summer 1985), p. [19]-38. English. DESCR: Child Care Centers; History; *Labor Unions; *Mexico; Sex Roles; Women; *Working Women.

Children (cont.)

1218 Salgado de Snyder, Nelly; Lopez, Cynthia M.;
and Padilla, Amado M. Ethnic identity and
cultural awareness among the offspring of
Mexican interethnic marriages. JOURNAL OF
EARLY ADOLESCENCE, Vol. 2, no. 3 (Fall
1982), p. 277-282. English. **DESCR:**
*Acculturation; *Identity; *Intermarriage;
*Youth.

1219 Shapiro, Johanna and Tittle, Ken. Maternal
adaptation to child disability in a Hispanic
population. FAMILY RELATIONS, Vol. 39, no. 2
(April 1990), p. 179-185. English. **DESCR:**
*Handicapped; *Parent and Child
Relationships; Psychological Testing;
*Stress.

1220 Stroup-Benham, Christine A.; Trevino,
Fernando M.; and Trevino, Dorothy B. Alcohol
consumption patterns among Mexican American
mothers and among children from single- and
dual-headed households: findings from HHANES
1982-84. AMERICAN JOURNAL OF PUBLIC HEALTH,
Vol. 80, (December 1990), p. 36-41.
English. **DESCR:** *Alcoholism; Hispanic Health
and Nutrition Examination Survey (HHANES);
Parent and Child Relationships; *Single
Parents.

1221 Walker, Todd. The relationship of nativity,
social support and depression to the home
environment among Mexican-American women.
Thesis (Ph.D.)--University of Houston, 1989.
123 p. English. **DESCR:** Acculturation; Avance
Parent-Child Education Program, San Antonio,
TX; Depression (Psychological); *Immigrants;
Natural Support Systems; *Parenting; Women.

1222 White, Marni, et al. Perceived crime in the
neighborhood and mental health of women and
children. ENVIRONMENT AND BEHAVIOR, Vol. 19,
no. 5 (September 1987), p. 588-613. English.
DESCR: Attitudes; Criminology; Housing;
*Mental Health; Women.

1223 Zepeda, Marlene. Mother-infant behavior in
Mexican and Mexican-American women: a study
of the relationship of selected prenatal,
perinatal and postnatal events. Thesis
(Ph.D.)--University of California, Los
Angeles, 1984, 429 p. English. **DESCR:**
*Fertility; *Maternal and Child Welfare;
*Parent and Child Relationships; Prenatal
Care.

Chistes

1224 Castro, Rafaela. Mexican women's sexual
jokes. AZTLAN, Vol. 13, no. 1-2 (Spring,
Fall, 1982), p. 275-293. English. **DESCR:**
Humor; Sexual Behavior.

1225 Rebolledo, Tey Diana. Walking the thin line:
humor in Chicana literature. IN:
Herrera-Sobek, Maria, ed. BEYOND
STEREOTYPES: THE CRITICAL ANALYSIS OF
CHICANA LITERATURE. Binghamton, NY:
Bilingual Press/Editorial Bilingue, 1985, p.
91-107. English. **DESCR:** *Humor; Literary
Criticism; *Poetry.

Cholos
USE: Pachucos

Christianity
USE: Religion

Church, Frank

1226 Mendoza, Hope Schecter and Chall, Malca.
Activist in the labor movement, the
Democratic Party, and the Mexican-American
community: an interview. Berkeley, CA:
Regional Oral History Office, Bancroft
Library, University of California, Berkeley,
1980. xii, 170 p.: ill. English. **DESCR:**
*Biography; Chavez Ravine, Los Angeles, CA;
Community Organizations; Community Service
Organization, Los Angeles, (CSO); Democratic
Party; Elections; Garment Industry;
Industrial Workers; *Labor Unions;
Leadership; Mendoza, Hope Schecter; Snyder,
Elizabeth; Warschaw, Carmen.

Cinema
USE: Films

Cisneros, Sandra

1227 Alarcon, Norma. What kind of lover have you
made me, Mother?: towards a theory of
Chicanas' feminism and cultural identity
through poetry. IN: McCluskey, Audrey T.,
ed. WOMEN OF COLOR: PERSPECTIVES ON FEMINISM
AND IDENTITY. Bloomington, IN: Women's
Studies Program, Indiana University, 1985,
p. 85-110. English. **DESCR:** Brinson-Pineda,
Barbara; Cervantes, Lorna Dee; Culture;
*Feminism; Identity; *Literary Criticism;
Mora, Pat; Moraga, Cherrie; *Poetry;
Tafolla, Carmen; Vigil-Pinon, Evangelina;
Villanueva, Alma.

1228 Billings, Linda M. and Alurista. In verbal
murals: a study of Chicana herstory and
poetry. CONFLUENCIA, Vol. 2, no. 1 (Fall
1986), p. 60-68. English. **DESCR:** Candelaria,
Cordelia; Cervantes, Lorna Dee; EMPLUMADA;
*Feminism; History; Literary Criticism;
*Poetry; Xelina.

1229 Cisneros, Sandra. Do you know me?: I wrote
THE HOUSE ON MANGO STREET. THE AMERICAS
REVIEW, Vol. 15, no. 1 (Spring 1987), p.
77-79. English. **DESCR:** Authors;
Autobiography; *Prose; THE HOUSE ON MANGO
STREET.

1230 Cisneros, Sandra. Ghosts and voices: writing
from obsession. THE AMERICAS REVIEW, Vol.
15, no. 1 (Spring 1987), p. 69-73. English.
DESCR: *Authors; Autobiography; *Prose.

1231 Cisneros, Sandra and Binder, Wolfgang.
[Interview with] Sandra Cisneros. IN:
Binder, Wolfgang, ed. PARTIAL
AUTOBIOGRAPHIES: INTERVIEWS WITH TWENTY
CHICANO POETS. Erlangen, W. Germany: Verlag
Palm & Enke, 1985, p. 54-74. English.
DESCR: Authors; Autobiography; Poetry.

1232 Cisneros, Sandra. Living as a writer: choice
and circumstance. REVISTA MUJERES, Vol. 3,
no. 2 (June 1986), p. 68-72. English.
DESCR: *Authors; Autobiography.

1233 Cisneros, Sandra. Notes to a young(er)
writer. THE AMERICAS REVIEW, Vol. 15, no. 1
(Spring 1987), p. 74-76. English. **DESCR:**
*Authors; Autobiography; *Prose.

1234 Gonzalez-Berry, Erlinda and Rebolledo, Tey
Diana. Growing up Chicano: Tomas Rivera and
Sandra Cisneros. REVISTA CHICANO-RIQUENA,
Vol. 13, no. 3-4 (Fall, Winter, 1985), p.
109-119. English. **DESCR:** Cultural
Characteristics; *Literary Criticism;
Rivera, Tomas; Sex Roles; THE HOUSE ON MANGO
STREET; Y NO SE LO TRAGO LA TIERRA/AND THE
EARTH DID NOT PART.

Cisneros, Sandra (cont.)

1235 Herrera-Sobek, Maria. The politics of rape: sexual transgression in Chicana fiction. THE AMERICAS REVIEW, Vol. 15, no. 3-4 (Fall, Winter, 1987), p. 171-181. English. **DESCR:** *Feminism; Fiction; GIVING UP THE GHOST; *Literary Criticism; Lizarraga, Sylvia; Moraga, Cherrie; *Rape; "Red Clowns" [short story]; Sex Roles; "Silver Lake Road" [short story].

1236 McCracken, Ellen. Latina narrative and politics of signification: articulation, antagonism, and populist rupture. CRITICA, Vol. 2, no. 2 (Fall 1990), p. 202-207. English. **DESCR:** IN NUEVA YORK; *Literary Criticism; *Mohr, Nicolasa; Puerto Ricans; RITUALS OF SURVIVAL; Short Story; THE HOUSE ON MANGO STREET; Women.

1237 McCracken, Ellen. Sandra Cisneros' THE HOUSE ON MANGO STREET: community-oriented introspection and the demystification of patriarchal violence. IN: Horno-Delgado, Asuncion, et al., eds. BREAKING BOUNDARIES: LATINA WRITING AND CRITICAL READINGS. Amherst, MA: University of Massachusetts Press, c1989, p. 62-71. English. **DESCR:** Literary Criticism; *THE HOUSE ON MANGO STREET.

1238 Olivares, Julian. Sandra Cisneros' THE HOUSE ON MANGO STREET and the poetics of space. THE AMERICAS REVIEW, Vol. 15, no. 3-4 (Fall, Winter, 1987), p. 160-170. English. **DESCR:** *Literary Criticism; THE HOUSE ON MANGO STREET.

1239 Quintana, Alvina E. Chicana discourse: negations and mediations. Thesis (Ph.D.)--University of California, Santa Cruz, 1989. 226 p. English. **DESCR:** Authors; Castillo, Ana; Chavez, Denise; Chicano Movement; Ethnology; Feminism; Literary Criticism; *Literature; NOVENA NARRATIVES; Oral Tradition; Political Ideology; THE HOUSE ON MANGO STREET; THE LAST OF THE MENU GIRLS; THE MIXQUIAHUALA LETTERS.

1240 Quintana, Alvina E. Politics, representation and the emergence of a Chicana aesthetic. CULTURAL STUDIES, Vol. 4, no. 3 (October 1990), p. 257-263. English. **DESCR:** Anzaldua, Gloria; *Authors; Chavez, Denise; Chicana Studies; Cultural Studies; Feminism; *Literary Criticism.

1241 Rodriguez Aranda, Pilar E. and Cisneros, Sandra. On the solitary fate of being Mexican, female, wicked and thirty-three: an interview with writer Sandra Cisneros. THE AMERICAS REVIEW, Vol. 18, no. 1 (Spring 1990), p. 64-80. English. **DESCR:** *Artists; Literature; MY WICKED WICKED WAYS; THE HOUSE ON MANGO STREET.

1242 Rosaldo, Renato. Fables of the fallen guy. IN: Calderon, Hector and Saldivar, Jose David, eds. CRITICISM IN THE BORDERLANDS: STUDIES IN CHICANO LITERATURE, CULTURE AND IDEOLOGY. Durham, NC: Duke University Press, 1991, p. [84]-93. English. **DESCR:** Chavez, Denise; Fiction; Literary Characters; *Literary Criticism; Rios, Alberto; Sex Roles; THE HOUSE ON MANGO STREET; THE IGUANA KILLER: TWELVE STORIES OF THE HEART; THE LAST OF THE MENU GIRLS.

1243 Saldivar, Ramon. The dialectics of subjectivity: gender and difference in Isabella Rios, Sandra Cisneros, and Cherrie Moraga. IN: Saldivar, Ramon. CHICANO NARRATIVE: THE DIALECTICS OF DIFFERENCE.

Madison, WI: University of Wisconsin Press, 1990, p. 171-199. English. **DESCR:** Authors; Autobiography; Feminism; Fiction; *Literary Criticism; Literature; LOVING IN THE WAR YEARS; *Moraga, Cherrie; Political Ideology; *Rios, Isabella; THE HOUSE ON MANGO STREET; VICTUUM.

Cities
USE: Urban Communities

Citizenship
USE: Naturalization

City Terrace, CA

1244 Blanco, Gilbert M. Las Adelitas del Barrio. LATIN QUARTER, Vol. 1, no. 3 (January, February, 1975), p. 30-32. English. **DESCR:** Community Development; Gangs; *Latin Empresses; Youth.

Ciudad Juarez, Chihuahua, Mexico

1245 Fernandez Kelly, Maria. "Chavalas de maquiladora": a study of the female labor force in Ciudad Juarez' offshore production plants. Thesis (Ph.D.)--Rutgers University, 1980. xi, 391 leaves. English. **DESCR:** *Border Industries; Electronics Industry; *Employment; Garment Industry; Industrial Workers; Mexico; Women; *Working Women.

1246 Fernandez Kelly, Maria. For we are sold, I and my people: women and industry in Mexico's frontier. Albany, NY: State University of New York Press, 1983. vii, 217 p. English. **DESCR:** Border Industries; *Border Region; *Electronics Industry; *Garment Industry; Industrial Workers; Working Women.

1247 Fernandez Kelly, Maria. Mexican border industrialization, female labor force participation and migration. IN: Nash, June and Fernandez-Kelly, Patricia, eds. WOMEN, MEN, AND THE INTERNATIONAL DIVISION OF LABOR. Albany, NY: State University of New York Press, 1983, p. 205-223. English. **DESCR:** Border Industrialization Program (BIP); *Border Industries; Immigration; Industrial Workers; Labor Supply and Market; Males; *Migration Patterns; Undocumented Workers; *Women; Working Women.

1248 Pena, Devon Gerardo. Tortuosidad: shop floor struggles of female maquiladora workers. IN: Ruiz, Vicki L. and Tiano, Susan, eds. WOMEN ON THE U.S.-MEXICO BORDER: RESPONSES TO CHANGE. Boston, MA: Allen & Unwin, 1987, p. 129-154. English. **DESCR:** Border Industries; Employment; Personnel Management; Population; Surveys; *Women; Working Women.

1249 Staudt, Kathleen. Programming women's empowerment: a case from northern Mexico. IN: Ruiz, Vicki L. and Tiano, Susan, eds. WOMEN ON THE U.S.-MEXICO BORDER: RESPONSES TO CHANGE. Boston, MA: Allen & Unwin, 1987, p. 155-173. English. **DESCR:** Alternative Education; Border Region; Curriculum; Employment; *Feminism; Organizations; Women.

Ciudad Juarez, Chihuahua, Mexico
(cont.)

1250 Young, Gay. Gender identification and working-class solidarity among maquila workers in Ciudad Juarez: stereotypes and realities. IN: Ruiz, Vicki L. and Tiano, Susan, eds. WOMEN ON THE U.S.-MEXICO BORDER: RESPONSES TO CHANGE. Boston, MA: Allen & Unwin, 1987, p. 105-127. English. DESCR: Assertiveness; Attitudes; Border Industrialization Program (BIP); *Border Industries; Border Region; Employment; Garment Industry; Sex Roles; Surveys; Working Women.

Civil Rights

1251 Cota-Robles de Suarez, Cecilia, ed. and Anguiano, Lupe, ed. Every woman's right: the right to quality education and economic independence. Montebello, CA: National Chicana Foundation, [1981]. viii, 110 p. English. DESCR: Education; *Feminism.

1252 Cotera, Marta P. La nueva hispana y [sic] hispanidad. LA LUZ, Vol. 8, no. 4 (October, November, 1979), p. 8-10. English. DESCR: *Feminism; Women Men Relations.

1253 Dressel, Paula. Symposium. Civil rights, affirmative action, and the aged of the future: will life chances be different for Blacks, Hispanics, and women? An overview of the issues. GERONTOLOGIST, Vol. 26, no. 2 (April 1986), p. 128-131. English. DESCR: Affirmative Action; *Ancianos; Blacks; Women.

1254 Espinosa, Ann. Hispanas: our resourses [sic] for the eighties. LA LUZ, Vol. 8, no. 4 (October, November, 1979), p. 10-13. English. DESCR: Baca Barragan, Polly; Comision Femenil Mexicana Nacional; DIRECTORY OF HISPANIC WOMEN; Discrimination in Education; Elected Officials; Hernandez, Irene; Lacayo, Carmela; Lujan, Josie; Mexican American Women's National Association (MANA); Montanez Davis, Grace; Moreno, Olga; Mujeres Latinas en Accion (M.L.A.); National Conference of Puerto Rican Women, Inc. (NCOPRW); Organizations; Rangel, Irma.

1255 Martinez, Virginia. Chicanas and the law. IN: LA CHICANA: BUILDING FOR THE FUTURE, AN ACTION PLAN FOR THE 80s. Oakland, CA: National Hispanic University, 1981, p. 134-146. English. DESCR: *Administration of Justice; Feminism; Law.

Cixous, Helene

1256 Ordonez, Elizabeth J. Body, spirit, and the text: Alma Villanueva's LIFE SPAN. IN: Calderon, Hector and Saldivar, Jose David, eds. CRITICISM IN THE BORDERLANDS: STUDIES IN CHICANO LITERATURE, CULTURE, AND IDEOLOGY. Durham, NC: Duke University Press, 1991, p. [61]-71. English. DESCR: *Feminism; *LIFE SPAN; *Literary Criticism; Poetry; *Villanueva, Alma.

Class Distinction
USE: Social Classes

Clergy

1257 Goldsmith, Raquel Rubio. La Mexicana/Chicana. RENATO ROSALDO LECTURE SERIES MONOGRAPH, Vol. 1, (Summer 1985), p. 1-67. English. DESCR: House of the Divine Providence [convent], Douglas, AZ; Labor Unions; *Social History and Conditions;

Women; World War II.

1258 Goldsmith, Raquel Rubio. Shipwrecked in the desert: a short history of the adventures and struggles for survival of the Mexican Sisters of the House of the Providence in Douglas, Arizona during their first twenty-two years of existence (1927-1949). RENATO ROSALDO LECTURE SERIES MONOGRAPH, Vol. 1, (Summer 1985), p. [39]-67. English. DESCR: Catholic Church; Douglas, AZ; History; *House of the Divine Providence [convent], Douglas, AZ; Women.

1259 Iglesias, Maria and Hernandez, Maria Luz. Hermanas. IN: Stevens Arroyo, Antonio M., ed. PROPHETS DENIED HONOR: AN ANTHOLOGY ON THE HISPANO CHURCH OF THE UNITED STATES. Maryknoll, NY: Orbis Books, 1980, p. 141-142. English. DESCR: *Catholic Church; Las Hermanas [organization]; Organizations.

1260 Mercado, Olivia; Corrales, Ramona; and Segovia, Sara. Las hermanas. COMADRE, no. 2 (Spring 1978), p. 34-41. English. DESCR: Religion.

1261 Monroy, Douglas. "They didn't call them 'padre' for nothing": patriarchy in Hispanic California. IN: Del Castillo, Adelaida R., ed. BETWEEN BORDERS: ESSAYS ON MEXICANA/CHICANA HISTORY. Encino, CA: Floricanto Press, 1990, p. 433-445. English. DESCR: *California; History; *Machismo; Rape; *Sex Roles; *Sexism; Spanish Influence; Women Men Relations.

1262 Ruiz, Vicki L. Dead ends or gold mines?: using missionary records in Mexican-American women's history. FRONTIERS: A JOURNAL OF WOMEN STUDIES, Vol. 12, no. 1 (1991), p. 33-56. English. DESCR: Archives; El Paso, TX; History; *Methodist Church; Protestant Church; *Research Methodology; *Rose Gregory Houchen Settlement House, El Paso, TX.

Clifton-Morenci Copper Strike, 1983-1986

1263 Aulette, Judy and Mills, Trudy. Something old, something new: auxiliary work in the 1983-1986 copper strike. FEMINIST STUDIES, Vol. 14, no. 2 (Summer 1988), p. 251-268. English. DESCR: Arizona; Clifton-Morenci District, Arizona; Feminism; Labor Unions; Morenci Miners Women's Auxiliary (MMWA); Mutualistas; Phelps Dodge Corporation, Morenci, AZ; SALT OF THE EARTH [film]; Sex Roles; *Strikes and Lockouts.

Clifton-Morenci District, Arizona

1264 Aulette, Judy and Mills, Trudy. Something old, something new: auxiliary work in the 1983-1986 copper strike. FEMINIST STUDIES, Vol. 14, no. 2 (Summer 1988), p. 251-268. English. DESCR: Arizona; Clifton-Morenci Copper Strike, 1983-1986; Feminism; Labor Unions; Morenci Miners Women's Auxiliary (MMWA); Mutualistas; Phelps Dodge Corporation, Morenci, AZ; SALT OF THE EARTH [film]; Sex Roles; *Strikes and Lockouts.

La Clinica Familiar del Barrio, Los Angeles, CA

1265 Marin, Barbara Van Oss, et al. Health care utilization by low-income clients of a community clinic: an archival study. HISPANIC JOURNAL OF BEHAVIORAL SCIENCES, Vol. 3, no. 3 (September 1981), p. 257-273. English. DESCR: Family Planning; Low Income; *Medical Care; Medical Clinics.

Clinical Psychiatry
    USE: Psychiatry

Clothing Trade
    USE: Garment Industry

Coachella, CA

1266 Lopez-Trevino, Maria Elena. A radio model: a
    community strategy to address the problems
    and needs of Mexican-American women
    farmworkers. Thesis (M.S.)--California State
    University, Long Beach, 1989. 179 p.
    English. DESCR: *Farm Workers; Income; Low
    Income; Occupational Hazards; *Radio; *Sex
    Roles.

Coalition Against the Prison, East Los Angeles, CA

1267 Pardo, Mary. Mexican American women
    grassroots community activists: "Mothers of
    East Los Angeles". FRONTIERS: A JOURNAL OF
    WOMEN STUDIES, Vol. 11, no. 1 (1990), p.
    [1]-7. English. DESCR: *Community
    Organizations; East Los Angeles, CA; Family;
    *Feminism; *Mothers of East L.A. (MELA);
    Organizations; Political Parties and
    Organizations; Politics; Sex Roles.

**Coalition for Immigrant and Refugee Rights and
    Services, Immigrant Woman's Task Force**

1268 Hogeland, Chris and Rosen, Karen. Dreams
    lost, dreams found: undocumented women in
    the land of opportunity. San Francisco, CA:
    Coalition for Immigrant and Refugee Rights
    and Services, c1991. 153 p. English. DESCR:
    *Battered Women; Discrimination; Immigrants;
    *San Francisco Bay Area; Sex Roles; Sexism;
    Social Services; Undocumented Workers;
    Violence; Women; Women Men Relations.

Code-switching
    USE: Language Usage

Cognition

1269 Laosa, Luis M. Maternal teaching strategies
    and cognitive styles in Chicano families.
    IN: Duran, Richard P., ed. LATINO LANGUAGE
    AND COMMUNICATIVE BEHAVIOR. Norwood, NJ:
    ABLEX Publishing Corp., 1981, p. 295-310.
    English. DESCR: *Education; *Parent and
    Child Relationships; *Parenting.

Cohen, Lawrence E.

1270 Alba, Richard D. A comment on Schoen and
    Cohen. AMERICAN JOURNAL OF SOCIOLOGY, Vol.
    87, no. 4 (January 1982), p. 935-939.
    English. DESCR: ETHNIC ENDOGAMY AMONG
    MEXICAN AMERICAN GROOMS; Intermarriage;
    *Research Methodology; Schoen, Robert.

College Preparation

1271 Cardoza, Desdemona. College attendance and
    persistence among Hispanic women: an
    examination of some contributing factors.
    SEX ROLES, Vol. 24, no. 3-4 (January 1991),
    p. 133-147. English. DESCR: Academic
    Achievement; *Enrollment; High School and
    Beyond Project (HS&B); *Higher Education;
    *Sex Roles; Socialization; Socioeconomic
    Factors.

Colleges and Universities

1272 Chacon, Maria A. An overdue study of the
    Chicana undergraduate college experience. LA
    LUZ, Vol. 8, no. 8 (October, November,
    1980), p. 27. English. DESCR: *Educational
    Statistics; Higher Education; Stanford
    University, Stanford, CA; Students.

1273 Chacon, Maria A., et al. Chicanas in
    California post secondary education: a
    comparative study of barriers to the program
    progress. Stanford, CA: Stanford Center for
    Chicano Research, 1985. viii, 217 p.
    English. DESCR: *Academic Achievement;
    Counseling (Educational); Educational
    Statistics; Enrollment; *Higher Education;
    Students; Surveys.

1274 Chacon, Maria A., et al. Chicanas in
    postsecondary education. Stanford, CA:
    Center for Research on Women, Stanford
    University, 1982. iii, 106, [68] p. English.
    DESCR: *Higher Education; Public Policy;
    *Surveys.

1275 De Llano, Carmen. Comparisons of the
    psychocultural characteristics of graduate
    school-bound and nongraduate school-bound
    Mexican American and Anglo American college
    women. Thesis (Ph.D.)--California School of
    Professional Psychology, 1986. 223 p.
    English. DESCR: *Anglo Americans;
    Comparative Psychology; Cultural
    Characteristics; *Graduate Schools; Higher
    Education; Students; *Women.

1276 Espin, Oliva M. Perceptions of sexual
    discrimination among college women in Latin
    America and the United States. HISPANIC
    JOURNAL OF BEHAVIORAL SCIENCES, Vol. 2, no.
    1 (March 1980), p. 1-19. English. DESCR:
    CRITICAL INCIDENT TECHNIQUE; Feminism; Latin
    Americans; *Sexism; Students; Women Men
    Relations.

1277 Flores, Laura Jane. A study of successful
    completion and attrition among Chicana Title
    VII Bilingual Education Doctoral Fellows at
    selected Southwestern universities. Thesis
    (Ed.D.)--New Mexico State University, 1984.
    145 p. English. DESCR: Academic Achievement;
    Graduate Schools; *Higher Education; Title
    VII Bilingual Education Doctoral Fellowship
    Program.

1278 Hernandez, Patricia. Lives of Chicana
    activists: the Chicano student movement (a
    case study). IN: Mora, Magdalena and Del
    Castillo, Adelaida, eds. MEXICAN WOMEN IN
    THE UNITED STATES: STRUGGLES PAST AND
    PRESENT. Los Angeles, CA: Chicano Studies
    Research Center, UCLA, 1980, p. 17-25.
    English. DESCR: California State University,
    San Diego; Case Studies; *Chicano Movement;
    Movimiento Estudiantil Chicano de Aztlan
    (MEChA); Student Movements; Student
    Organizations.

1279 Kluessendorf, Avonelle Donneeta. Role
    conflict in Mexican-American college women.
    Thesis (Ph.D.)--California School of
    Professional Psychology, Fresno, 1985. 111
    p. English. DESCR: Locus of Control; *Sex
    Roles; *Stress; Students.

1280 Munoz, Daniel G. Identifying areas of stress
    for Chicano undergraduates. IN: Olivas,
    Michael A., ed. LATINO COLLEGE STUDENTS. New
    York: Teachers College Press, 1986, p.
    131-156. English. DESCR: Academic
    Achievement; *Attitudes; Financial Aid;
    *Stress; Surveys.

1281 Nieto Gomez de Lazarin, Anna. The Chicana:
    perspectives for education. ENCUENTRO
    FEMENIL, Vol. 1, no. 1 (Spring 1973), p.
    34-61. English. DESCR: Discrimination;
    Discrimination in Education; *Education;
    Family; Identity; Sexism.

Colleges and Universities
(cont.)

1282 Nieves-Squires, Sarah. Hispanic women: making their presence on campus less tenuous. Washington, DC: Association of American Colleges, c1991. 14 p. English. **DESCR:** Afro-Hispanics; Cubanos; *Discrimination in Education; *Higher Education; Puerto Ricans; *Women.

1283 Sanchez, Joaquin John. An investigation of the initial experience of a Chicana with higher education. Thesis (Ph.D.)--Saybrook Institute, 1983. 163 p. English. **DESCR:** Biculturalism; *Cultural Characteristics; *Higher Education.

1284 Trotter, Robert T. Ethnic and sexual patterns of alcohol use: Anglo and Mexican American college students. ADOLESCENCE, Vol. 17, no. 66 (Summer 1982), p. 305-325. English. **DESCR:** *Alcoholism; Anglo Americans; Cultural Characteristics; Ethnic Groups; Sex Roles; Students; Youth.

1285 Vallez, Andrea. Acculturation, social support, stress and adjustment of the Mexican American college woman. Thesis (Ph.D.)--University of Colorado at Boulder, 1984. 121 p. English. **DESCR:** *Acculturation; Depression (Psychological); Higher Education; Natural Support Systems; Southern California; Stress; *Students.

1286 Zuniga, Maria E. Assessment issues with Chicanas: practice implications. PSYCHOTHERAPY, Vol. 25, no. 2 (Summer 1988), p. 288-293. English. **DESCR:** Acculturation; Family; Identity; *Mental Health; Mexican-American Outreach Program, San Diego State University; *Psychotherapy; *Students.

Colonia
USE: Barrios

Coloquio Fronterizo Mujer y Literatura Mexicana y Chicana (1987: Tijuana, Baja California, Mexico)

1287 Domenella, Ana Rosa. Al margen de un coloquio fronterizo mujer y literatura mexicana y chicana. FEM, Vol. 14, no. 89 (May 1990), p. 32-34. Spanish. **DESCR:** *Border Region; *Conferences and Meetings; *Literature; Mexican Literature; Mexico; Women.

Colorado

1288 Blea, Irene I. Brujeria: a sociological analysis of Mexican American witches. IN: Barrera, Mario, et al., eds. WORK, FAMILY, SEX ROLES, LANGUAGE: SELECTED PAPERS, 1979. Berkeley, CA: Tonatiuh-Quinto Sol, 1980, p. 177-193. English. **DESCR:** *Brujas; Folklore; Kiev, Ari; New Mexico.

1289 Codega, Susan A.; Pasley, B. Kay; and Kreutzer, Jill. Coping behaviors of adolescent mothers: an exploratory study and comparison of Mexican-Americans and Anglos. JOURNAL OF ADOLESCENT RESEARCH, Vol. 5, no. 1 (January 1990), p. 34-53. English. **DESCR:** Anglo Americans; *Fertility; *Stress; Women; *Youth.

1290 Deutsch, Sarah. Culture, class, and gender: Chicanas and Chicanos in Colorado and New Mexico, 1900-1940. Thesis (Ph.D.)--Yale University, 1985. xii, 510 p. English. **DESCR:** Anglo Americans; Immigrants; New Mexico; *Sex Roles; *Social Classes; Social

History and Conditions; Women; *Working Women.

1291 Deutsch, Sarah. No separate refuge: culture, class, and gender on an Anglo-Hispanic frontier in the American Southwest, 1880-1940. New York: Oxford University Press, 1987. vi, 356 p. English. **DESCR:** Anglo Americans; Immigrants; Immigration; Mining Industry; Missions; New Mexico; *Sex Roles; *Social Classes; *Social History and Conditions; Women; Working Women; World War I.

1292 Deutsch, Sarah. Women and intercultural relations: the case of Hispanic New Mexico and Colorado. SIGNS: JOURNAL OF WOMEN IN CULTURE AND SOCIETY, Vol. 12, no. 4 (Summer 1987), p. 719-739. English. **DESCR:** Cultural Characteristics; Immigrants; Intercultural Communication; Mexico; New Mexico; Rural Population; Sex Roles; Social History and Conditions; *Women.

1293 Duran, Isabelle Sandoval. Grounded theory study: Chicana administrators in Colorado and New Mexico. Thesis (Ed.D.)--University of Wyoming, Laramie, 1982. ix, 114 p. English. **DESCR:** Careers; *Educational Administration; Leadership; *Management; New Mexico.

1294 Lucero, Aileen. Chicano sex role attitudes: a comparative study of sex differences in an urban barrio. Thesis (Ph.D.)--University of Colorado at Boulder, 1980. 160 p. English. **DESCR:** *Attitudes; Males; *Sex Roles.

1295 Lucero, Marcela Christine. The socio-historical implication of the valley as a metaphor in three Colorado Chicana poets. Thesis (Ph.D.)--University of Minnesota, 1981. 176 p. English. **DESCR:** *Authors; Blea, Irene I.; Chicano Movement; Feminism; Literary Criticism; Mondragon Valdez, Maria; Poetry; Zamora, Bernice.

Comision Femenil Mexicana Nacional

1296 Espinosa, Ann. Hispanas: our resourses [sic] for the eighties. LA LUZ, Vol. 8, no. 4 (October, November, 1979), p. 10-13. English. **DESCR:** Baca Barragan, Polly; *Civil Rights; DIRECTORY OF HISPANIC WOMEN; Discrimination in Education; Elected Officials; Hernandez, Irene; Lacayo, Carmela; Lujan, Josie; Mexican American Women's National Association (MANA); Montanez Davis, Grace; Moreno, Olga; Mujeres Latinas en Accion (M.L.A.); National Conference of Puerto Rican Women, Inc. (NCOPRW); Organizations; Rangel, Irma.

1297 Flores, Francisca. Comision Femenil Mexicana. REGENERACION, Vol. 2, no. 1 (1971), p. 6. English. **DESCR:** Abortion; Children; *Family Planning; Feminism; Organizations; Politics.

1298 Flores, Francisca. Comision Femenil Mexicana. REGENERACION, Vol. 2, no. 4 (1975), p. 24-25. English. **DESCR:** *Abortion; Child Care Centers; Identity; Working Women.

1299 Matsuda, Gema. La Chicana organizes: the Comision Femenil Mexicana in perspective. REGENERACION, Vol. 2, no. 4 (1975), p. 25-27. English. **DESCR:** Bojorquez, Frances; Chicano Movement; De la Cruz, Juana Ines; Flores, Francisca; History; Machismo; Malinche; Prisons; Sex Stereotypes; *Sexism.

Comision Femenil Mexicana Nacional
(cont.)

1300 Nava, Yolanda. The Chicana and employment: needs analysis and recommendations for legislation. REGENERACION, Vol. 2, no. 3 (1973), p. 7-9. English. DESCR: California Commission on the Status of Women; Child Care Centers; *Discrimination in Employment; Employment Tests; Employment Training; Equal Rights Amendment (ERA); Sexism; Statistics; Stereotypes; Working Women.

Comision Femenil Mexicana de California

1301 Prida, Dolores. Looking for room of one's own. NUESTRO, Vol. 3, no. 5 (June, July, 1979), p. 24-29. English. DESCR: *Feminism; Mexican American Women's National Association (MANA); National Association of Cuban American Women; National Conference of Puerto Rican Women, Inc. (NCOPRW); Organizations.

Commerce
USE: Business

Communist Party

1302 Rips, Geoffrey and Tenayuca, Emma. Living history: Emma Tenayuca tells her story. TEXAS OBSERVER, (October 28, 1983), p. 7-15. English. DESCR: *Autobiography; Food Industry; Labor Unions; Leadership; Oral History; Pecan Shelling Worker's Union, San Antonio, TX; San Antonio, TX; Strikes and Lockouts; Tenayuca, Emma; United Cannery Agricultural Packing and Allied Workers of America (UCAPAWA); Worker's Alliance (WA), Los Angeles, CA; Working Women.

Community Colleges

1303 Alanis, Elsa. The relationship between state and trait anxiety and acculturation in Mexican-American women homemakers and Mexican-American community college female students. Thesis (Ph.D.)--United States International University, 1989. 161 p. English. DESCR: *Acculturation; Family; Sex Roles; *Stress; Students.

1304 Chacon, Maria A.; Coher, Elizabeth G.; and Strover, Sharon. Chicanas and Chicanos: barriers to progress in higher education. IN: Olivas, Michael A., ed. LATINO COLLEGE STUDENTS. New York: Teachers College Press, 1986, p. 296-324. English. DESCR: Discrimination; Dropouts; *Higher Education; Stress; Surveys.

1305 Fleming, Marilyn B. Problems experienced by Anglo, Hispanic and Navajo Indian women college students. JOURNAL OF AMERICAN INDIAN EDUCATION, Vol. 22, no. 1 (October 1982), p. 7-17. English. DESCR: Anglo Americans; Ethnic Groups; *Higher Education; Identity; Medical Education; Native Americans; Students; Women.

1306 Gardea, Corina. A comparison of behavioral characteristics of Hispanic and Anglo female administrators in the resolution of critical incident situations. Thesis (Ph.D.)--University of Texas, Austin, 1984. 145 p. English. DESCR: Anglo Americans; *Educational Administration; Leadership; Women.

1307 Martinez-Metcalf, Rosario. Concerns of Hispanic community college women. Thesis (Ph.D.)--North Texas State University, 1985. 163 p. English. DESCR: *Students.

Community Development

1308 Blanco, Gilbert M. Las Adelitas del Barrio. LATIN QUARTER, Vol. 1, no. 3 (January, February, 1975), p. 30-32. English. DESCR: City Terrace, CA; Gangs; *Latin Empresses; Youth.

Community Organizations

1309 Andrade, Sally J., ed. Latino families in the United States: a resource book for family life education = Las familias latinas en los Estados Unidos: recursos para la capacitacion familiar. [S.l.]: Planned Parenthood Federation of America, Inc., 1983. ix, 79, 70, xi p. Bilingual. DESCR: Bilingualism; Education; *Family; Mental Health; Public Health.

1310 Gonzales, Sylvia Alicia. Hispanic American voluntary organizations. Westport, CT: Greenwood Press, 1985. xx, 267 p. English. DESCR: Art Organizations and Groups; Cultural Organizations; *Directories; Educational Organizations; *Organizations; Political Parties and Organizations; Professional Organizations.

1311 Mendoza, Hope Schecter and Chall, Malca. Activist in the labor movement, the Democratic Party, and the Mexican-American community: an interview. Berkeley, CA: Regional Oral History Office, Bancroft Library, University of California, Berkeley, 1980. xii, 170 p.: ill. English. DESCR: *Biography; Chavez Ravine, Los Angeles, CA; Church, Frank; Community Service Organization, Los Angeles, (CSO); Democratic Party; Elections; Garment Industry; Industrial Workers; *Labor Unions; Leadership; Mendoza, Hope Schecter; Snyder, Elizabeth; Warschaw, Carmen.

1312 Pardo, Mary. Mexican American women grassroots community activists: "Mothers of East Los Angeles". FRONTIERS: A JOURNAL OF WOMEN STUDIES, Vol. 11, no. 1 (1990), p. [1]-7. English. DESCR: Coalition Against the Prison, East Los Angeles, CA; East Los Angeles, CA; Family; *Feminism; *Mothers of East L.A. (MELA); Organizations; Political Parties and Organizations; Politics; Sex Roles.

Community School Relationships

1313 Ramirez, Carmen Cecilia. A study of the value orientation of Lane County, Oregon, Mexican American mothers with a special focus on family/school relationships. Thesis (Ph.D.)--University of Oregon, 1981. 183 p. English. DESCR: Family; Lane County, OR; *Values.

Community Service Organization, Los Angeles, (CSO)

1314 Chavez, Henri. Unsung heroine of La Causa. REGENERACION, Vol. 1, no. 10 (1971), p. 20. English. DESCR: AFL-CIO United Farmworkers Organizing Committee; Agricultural Labor Unions; Family; Farm Workers; *Huerta, Dolores; Poverty; Working Women.

Community Service Organization, Los Angeles, (CSO) (cont.)

1315 Huerta, Dolores. Dolores Huerta talks about Republicans, Cesar, children and her home town. REGENERACION, Vol. 2, no. 4 (1975), p. 20-24. English. **DESCR:** *Agricultural Labor Unions; *Biography; Chavez, Cesar E.; Democratic Party; Elected Officials; Flores, Art; Huerta, Dolores; McGovern, George; *Politics; Ramirez, Henry M.; Ross, Fred; Sanchez, Philip V.; United Farmworkers of America (UFW); Working Women.

1316 Huerta, Dolores. Dolores Huerta talks about Republicans, Cesar, children and her home town. IN: Servin, Manuel P. ed. THE MEXICAN AMERICANS: AN AWAKENING MINORITY. 2nd ed. Beverly Hills, CA: Glencoe Press, 1974, p. 283-294. English. **DESCR:** *Agricultural Labor Unions; *Biography; Chavez, Cesar E.; Democratic Party; Elected Officials; Flores, Art; Huerta, Dolores; McGovern, George; *Politics; Ramirez, Henry M.; Ross, Fred; Sanchez, Philip V.; United Farmworkers of America (UFW); Working Women.

1317 Mendoza, Hope Schecter and Chall, Malca. Activist in the labor movement, the Democratic Party, and the Mexican-American community: an interview. Berkeley, CA: Regional Oral History Office, Bancroft Library, University of California, Berkeley, 1980. xii, 170 p.: ill. English. **DESCR:** *Biography; Chavez Ravine, Los Angeles, CA; Church, Frank; Community Organizations; Democratic Party; Elections; Garment Industry; Industrial Workers; *Labor Unions; Leadership; Mendoza, Hope Schecter; Snyder, Elizabeth; Warschaw, Carmen.

Community Work Experience Program (C.W.E.P.)

1318 Nieto Gomez de Lazarin, Anna. What is the Talmadge Amendment?: justicia para las madres. REGENERACION, Vol. 2, no. 3 (1973), p. 14-15. English. **DESCR:** Chicana Welfare Rights Organization; *Child Care Centers; Discrimination in Employment; Employment Tests; Escalante, Alicia; *Feminism; Nixon, Richard; Working Women.

Compadrazgo

1319 Baca Zinn, Maxine. Urban kinship and Midwest Chicano families: evidence in support of revision. DE COLORES, Vol. 6, no. 1-2 (1982), p. 85-98. English. **DESCR:** *Extended Family; Family; Midwestern States; Urban Communities.

1320 Miller, Michael V. Variations in Mexican American family life: a review synthesis of empirical research. AZTLAN, Vol. 9, no. 1 (1978), p. 209-231. Bibliography. English. **DESCR:** Acculturation; *Family; Intermarriage; Sex Roles; Stereotypes.

Comparative Education

1321 Heathcote, Olivia D. Sex stereotyping in Mexican reading primers. READING TEACHER, Vol. 36, no. 2 (November 1982), p. 158-165. English. **DESCR:** Curriculum Materials; Mexico; Primary School Education; *Sex Stereotypes.

Comparative Psychology

1322 Belk, Sharyn S., et al. Impact of ethnicity, nationality, counseling orientation, and mental health standards on stereotypic beliefs about women. SEX ROLES, Vol. 21, no. 9-10 (November 1989), p. 671-695. English.

DESCR: Anglo Americans; Beliefs About Women Scale (BAWS); *Counseling (Psychological); Cultural Characteristics; Identity; Mental Health; *Sex Stereotypes; Sexism; Women.

1323 De Llano, Carmen. Comparisons of the psychocultural characteristics of graduate school-bound and nongraduate school-bound Mexican American and Anglo American college women. Thesis (Ph.D.)--California School of Professional Psychology, 1986. 223 p. English. **DESCR:** *Anglo Americans; Colleges and Universities; Cultural Characteristics; *Graduate Schools; Higher Education; Students; *Women.

1324 Fu, Victoria R.; Hinkle, Dennis E.; and Korslund, Mary K. A development study of ethnic self-concept among pre-adolescent girls. JOURNAL OF GENETIC PSYCHOLOGY, Vol. 14, (March 1983), p. 67-73. English. **DESCR:** *Identity; Junior High School; Self-Concept Self Report Scale; Students; Youth.

1325 Gallegos, Placida I. Emerging leadership among Hispanic women: the role of expressive behavior and nonverbal skill. Thesis (Ph.D.)--University of California, Riverside, 1987. 101 p. English. **DESCR:** Anglo Americans; Corporations; *Leadership; *Management; Women.

1326 Golding, Jacqueline M. Division of household labor, strain, and depressive symptoms among Mexican Americans and non-Hispanic whites. PSYCHOLOGY OF WOMEN QUARTERLY, Vol. 14, no. 1 (March 1990), p. 103-117. English. **DESCR:** Anglo Americans; *Depression (Psychological); Domestic Work; Employment; Identity; *Sex Roles; Women.

1327 Gondolf, Edward W.; Fisher, Ellen; and McFerron, J. Richard. Racial differences among shelter residents: a comparison of Anglo, Black, and Hispanic battered. JOURNAL OF FAMILY VIOLENCE, Vol. 3, no. 1 (March 1988), p. 39-51. English. **DESCR:** Anglo Americans; Battered Women; Blacks; Cultural Characteristics; Natural Support Systems; Socioeconomic Factors; *Violence; *Women.

1328 Gonzalez, Alex. Sex roles of the traditional Mexican family: a comparison of Chicano and Anglo students' attitudes. JOURNAL OF CROSS-CULTURAL PSYCHOLOGY, Vol. 13, no. 3 (September 1982), p. 330-339. English. **DESCR:** Anglo Americans; Attitudes; *Family; Hembrismo; Machismo; Sex Roles; Students.

1329 Laosa, Luis M. Maternal teaching strategies in Chicano and Anglo-American families: the influence of culture and education on maternal behavior. CHILD DEVELOPMENT, Vol. 51, no. 3 (September 1980), p. 759-765. English. **DESCR:** Anglo Americans; *Cultural Characteristics; *Education; Family; Maternal Teaching Observation Technique (MTOT); *Parent and Child Relationships; Parenting; Women.

1330 Martinez, Ruben and Dukes, Richard L. Race, gender and self-esteem among youth. HISPANIC JOURNAL OF BEHAVIORAL SCIENCES, Vol. 9, no. 4 (December 1987), p. 427-443. English. **DESCR:** *Identity; *Sex Roles; *Youth.

Comparative Psychology
(cont.)

1331 Mary, Nancy L. Reactions of Black, Hispanic
and white mothers to having a child with
handicaps. MENTAL RETARDATION, Vol. 28, no.
1 (February 1990), p. 1-5. English. DESCR:
Anglo Americans; *Attitudes; Blacks;
*Children; *Mentally Handicapped; Parent and
Child Relationships; *Women.

1332 Melgoza, Bertha; Roll, Samuel; and Baker,
Richard C. Conformity and cooperation in
Chicanos: the case of the missing
susceptibility to influence. JOURNAL OF
COMMUNITY PSYCHOLOGY, Vol. 11, no. 4
(October 1983), p. 323-333. English. DESCR:
*Cultural Characteristics; *Locus of
Control; Socialization; Stereotypes; Women.

1333 Reed-Sanders, Delores; Dodder, Richard A.;
and Webster, Lucia. The Bem Sex-Role
Inventory across three cultures. JOURNAL OF
SOCIAL PSYCHOLOGY, Vol. 125, no. 4 (August
1985), p. 523-525. English. DESCR: Bem Sex
Role Inventory (BSRI); *Sex Roles.

1334 Ross, Catherine E.; Mirowsky, John; and
Ulbrich, Patricia. Distress and the
traditional female role: a comparison of
Mexicans and Anglos. AMERICAN JOURNAL OF
SOCIOLOGY, Vol. 89, no. 3 (November 1983),
p. 670-682. English. DESCR: Anglo Americans;
*Sex Roles; Stress; Women.

1335 Salgado de Snyder, Nelly; Cervantes, Richard
C.; and Padilla, Amado M. Gender and ethnic
differences in psychosocial stress and
generalized distress among Hispanics. SEX
ROLES, Vol. 22, no. 7-8 (April, 1990), p.
441-453. English. DESCR: Anglo Americans;
Central Americans; Depression
(Psychological); Hispanic Stress Inventory
(HSI); *Immigrants; Immigration; *Sex Roles;
*Stress; Women.

1336 Smith, Bradford M. The measurement of
narcissism in Asian, Caucasian, and Hispanic
American women. PSYCHOLOGICAL REPORTS, Vol.
67, no. 3 (December 1990), p. 779-785.
English. DESCR: Anglo Americans; Asian
Americans; Cultural Characteristics;
*Narcissistic Personality Inventory;
*Personality; *Psychological Testing;
*Women.

1337 Velasquez, Roberto J.; Callahan, Wendell J.;
and Carrillo, Ricardo. MMPI differences
among Mexican-American male and female
psychiatric inpatients. PSYCHOLOGICAL
REPORTS, Vol. 68, no. 1 (February 1991), p
123-127. English. DESCR: Males; Minnesota
Multiphasic Personality Inventory (MMPI);
Personality; Psychiatry; *Psychological
Testing; Sex Roles.

Concilio de Arte Popular, Los Angeles, CA

1338 Soberon, Mercedes. La revolucion se trata de
amor: Mercedes Soberon. CHISMEARTE, Vol. 1,
no. 1 (Fall 1976), p. 14-18. Spanish.
DESCR: Art Criticism; Cultural
Organizations; La Mission Media Arts, San
Francisco, CA; San Francisco, CA; *Sex
Roles; Soberon, Mercedes.

Condom Use

1339 Del Zotto, Augusta. Latinas with AIDS: life
expectancy for Hispanic women is a startling
45 days after diagnosis. THIS WORLD, (April
9, 1989), p. 9. English. DESCR: Abortion;
AIDS (Disease); Instituto Familiar de la
Raza, San Francisco, CA; Machismo; *Mano a
Mano; Quintero, Juanita; Sex Roles; Women
Men Relations.

1340 Mays, Vicki M. and Cochran, Susan D. Issues
in the perception of AIDS risk and risk
reduction activities by Black and
Hispanic/Latina women. AMERICAN
PSYCHOLOGIST, Vol. 43, no. 11 (November
1988), p. 949-957. English. DESCR: *AIDS
(Disease); Blacks; Fertility; Health
Education; Preventative Medicine; *Sexual
Behavior; Women.

**Conference on the Educational and Occupational
Needs of Hispanic Women (1976: Denver, CO)**

1341 U.S. National Institute of Education.
Conference on the educational and
occupational needs of Hispanic women, June
29-30, 1976; December 10-12, 1976.
Washington, DC: U.S. Department of
Education, 1980. x, 301 p. English. DESCR:
Conferences and Meetings; *Education;
*Employment; Higher Education; Leadership;
Puerto Ricans; Sex Roles; *Women.

Conferences and Meetings

1342 Adelante, mujer hispana. LATINO, Vol. 53,
no. 2 (March, April, 1982), p. 26. English.
DESCR: *Adelante Mujer Hispana
Conference--Education and Employment
Conference (January 11-12, 1980: Denver,
CO); Leadership.

1343 Anonymous. Workshop resolutions - First
National Chicana Conference, May 1971. IN:
Garcia, Richard A., ed. CHICANOS IN AMERICA,
1540-1974: A CHRONOLOGY AND FACT BOOK. Dobbs
Ferry, NY: Oceana Publications, 1977, p.
142-144. English. DESCR: Feminism; *First
National Chicana Conference (May 1971:
Houston, TX).

1344 Avila, Consuelo. Ecos de una convencion.
MAGAZIN, Vol. 1, no. 9 (September 1973), p.
33-36. Spanish. DESCR: *Feminism; National
Women's Political Caucus (February 9-11,
1973: Houston, TX).

1345 Burciaga, Cecilia P. The 1977 National
Women's Conference in Houston: gains and
disappointments for Hispanics. LA LUZ, Vol.
7, no. 11 (November 1978), p. 8-9. English.
DESCR: *National Women's Conference
(November, 1977: Houston, TX).

1346 Campos Carr, Irene. Proyecto La Mujer:
Latina women shaping consciousness. WOMEN'S
STUDIES INTERNATIONAL FORUM, Vol. 12, no. 1
(1989), p. 45-49. English. DESCR: Artists;
Aurora, IL; Authors; Barrios; Elgin, IL;
*Feminism; Joliet, IL; Poetry; Proyecto La
Mujer Conference (Spring, 1982: Northern
Illinois); Women.

1347 Carrillo-Beron, Carmen. Raza mental health:
perspectivas femeniles. IN: PERSPECTIVAS EN
CHICANO STUDIES: PAPERS PRESENTED AT THE
THIRD ANNUAL MEETING OF THE NATIONAL
ASSOCIATION OF CHICANO SOCIAL SCIENCE, 1975.
Los Angeles, CA: National Association of
Chicano Social Science, 1977, p. 69-80.
English. DESCR: Attitudes; Centro de Salud
Mental, Oakland, CA; *Mental Health; Mujeres
de Hoy Conference (Oakland, CA).

1348 Chapa, Olivia Evey. Report from the National
Women's Political Caucus. MAGAZIN, Vol. 1,
no. 9 (September 1973), p. 37-39. English.
DESCR: *Feminism; National Women's Political
Caucus (February 9-11, 1973: Houston, TX).

Conferences and Meetings
(cont.)

1349 Chicana regional conference. LA RAZA, Vol. 1, no. 6 (1971), p. 43-45. English. **DESCR:** Chicana Regional Conference (May 8, 1971: Los Angeles, CA); *Chicano Movement; Feminism; Women Men Relations.

1350 Cotera, Marta P. Feminism: the Chicana and Anglo versions: a historical analysis. IN: Melville, Margarita B., ed. TWICE A MINORITY. St. Louis, MO: Mosby, 1980, p. 217-234. English. **DESCR:** *Anglo Americans; Chicano Movement; *Feminism; Organizations; Social History and Conditions; Voting Rights; *Women.

1351 Del Castillo, Adelaida R., et al. An assessment of the status of the education of Hispanic American women. IN: McKenna, Teresa and Ortiz, Flora Ida, eds. THE BROKEN WEB: THE EDUCATIONAL EXPERIENCE OF HISPANIC WOMEN. Claremont, CA: Tomas Rivera Center; Berkeley, CA: Floricanto Press, 1988, p. 3-24. English. **DESCR:** Academic Achievement; Discrimination in Education; Dropouts; *Education; Higher Education; Public Policy; Research Methodology; The Educational Experience of Hispanic American Women [symposium] (1985: Claremont, CA); *Women.

1352 Domenella, Ana Rosa. Al margen de un coloquio fronterizo mujer y literatura mexicana y chicana. FEM, Vol. 14, no. 89 (May 1990), p. 32-34. Spanish. **DESCR:** *Border Region; Coloquio Fronterizo Mujer y Literatura Mexicana y Chicana (1987: Tijuana, Baja California, Mexico); *Literature; Mexican Literature; Mexico; Women.

1353 Estrada, Iliad. Hispanic feminists meet--it's a trip. LA LUZ, Vol. 8, no. 7 (August, September, 1980), p. 35. English. **DESCR:** Feminism; National Hispanic Feminist Conference (March 28-31, 1980: San Jose, CA); *Puerto Ricans.

1354 Flores, Francisca. Conference of Mexican women un remolino. REGENERACION, Vol. 1, no. 10 (1971), p. 1-5. English. **DESCR:** Family; Feminism; First National Chicana Conference (May 1971: Houston, TX); Machismo; National Mexican American Issues Conference (October 11, 1970: Sacramento, CA); Sex Roles; Sex Stereotypes; Statistics; *Women Men Relations.

1355 Goldman, Shifra M. Artistas en accion: conferencia de las mujeres chicanas. LA COMUNIDAD, (August 10, 1980), p. 15. Spanish. **DESCR:** *Artists; Chicano Studies; Flores, Gloriamalia; Lomas Garza, Carmen.

1356 Gonzales, Sylvia Alicia. The Latina feminist: where we've been, where we're going. NUESTRO, Vol. 5, no. 6 (August, September, 1981), p. 45-47. English. **DESCR:** *Feminism; History; Leadership; National Hispanic Feminist Conference (March 28-31, 1980: San Jose, CA).

1357 Lopez, Sonia A. The role of the Chicana within the student movement. IN: Sanchez, Rosaura and Martinez Cruz, Rosa, eds. ESSAYS ON LA MUJER. Los Angeles, CA: Chicano Studies Center Publications, UCLA, 1977, p. 16-29. English. **DESCR:** Chicano Movement; Feminism; First National Chicana Conference (May 1971: Houston, TX); *Student Movements.

1358 Mireles, Irma. La mujer en la comunidad: ayer, hoy, y siempre. CARACOL, Vol. 2, no.

11 (July 1976), p. 4, 11. Spanish. **DESCR:** *Chicana Conference (May 22, 1976: Austin TX).

1359 Mujeres en Marcha, University of California, Berkeley. Chicanas in the 80s: unsettled issues. Berkeley, CA: Chicano Studies Library Publications Unit, 1983. 31 p. English. **DESCR:** Feminism; National Association for Chicano Studies (NACS); National Association for Chicano Studies Annual Conference (1982: Tempe, AZ); *Sexism.

1360 Nieto Gomez de Lazarin, Anna. La femenista [sic]. ENCUENTRO FEMENIL, Vol. 1, no. 2 (1974), p. 34-47. English. **DESCR:** Anglo Americans; Chicana Caucus, National Women's Political Caucus; Chicano Movement; Discrimination; *Feminism; National Women's Political Caucus (February 9-11, 1973: Houston, TX); *Sexism; Women.

1361 Robinson, Bea Vasquez. Are we racist? Are we sexist? AGENDA, (Winter 1976), p. 23-24. English. **DESCR:** Discrimination; Feminism; International Women's Year World Conference (1975: Mexico City); National Chicana Coalition; *Sexism.

1362 Saavedra-Vela, Pilar. Hispanic women in double jeopardy. AGENDA, Vol. 7, no. 6 (November, December, 1977), p. 4-7. English. **DESCR:** Discrimination; Houston, TX; National Women's Conference (November, 1977: Houston, TX); *Sexism.

1363 Saavedra-Vela, Pilar. Nosotras in Houston. AGENDA, Vol. 8, no. 2 (March, April, 1978), p. 26-31. English. **DESCR:** *Feminism; Houston, TX; National Women's Conference (November, 1977: Houston, TX).

1364 Santillanes, Maria. Women in prison--C.I.W.: an editorial. REGENERACION, Vol. 2, no. 4 (1975), p. 53. English. **DESCR:** Garcia, Dolly; La Mesa College Pinto and Pinta Program; Lopez, Tony; Mares, Rene; Martinez, Miguel; Pinto Conference (1973: UCLA); Player; *Prisons; Salazar, Peggy.

1365 Sosa Riddell, Adaljiza, ed. Policy development: Chicana/Latina Summer Research Institute [handbook]. Davis, CA: [Chicano Studies Program, UC Davis, 1989?]. 29 p. English. **DESCR:** *Chicana/Latina Summer Research Institute (August 19, 1989: Santa Clara University); Public Policy.

1366 Soto, Shirlene Ann. The women's movement in Mexico: the first and second feminist congresses in Yucatan, 1916. IN: Del Castillo, Adelaida R., ed. BETWEEN BORDERS: ESSAYS ON MEXICANA/CHICANA HISTORY. Encino, CA: Floricanto Press, 1990, p. 483-491. English. **DESCR:** *Feminism; *Feminist Congress (1916: Yucatan, Mexico); Mexico; Women.

1367 U.S. Department of Labor, Women's Bureau. Adelante mujer hispana: a conference model for Hispanic women. Washington, DC: The Bureau, 1980. 39 p.: ill. English. **DESCR:** *Adelante Mujer Hispana Conference--Education and Employment Conference (January 11-12, 1980: Denver, CO); *Women.

--   --

Conferences and Meetings
     (cont.)

1368 U.S. National Institute of Education.
     Conference on the educational and
     occupational needs of Hispanic women, June
     29-30, 1976; December 10-12, 1976.
     Washington, DC: U.S. Department of
     Education, 1980. x, 301 p. English. DESCR:
     Conference on the Educational and
     Occupational Needs of Hispanic Women (1976:
     Denver, CO); *Education; *Employment; Higher
     Education; Leadership; Puerto Ricans; Sex
     Roles; *Women.

1369 Vidal, Mirta. Women: new voice of La Raza.
     IN: Garcia, Richard A., ed. CHICANOS IN
     AMERICA, 1540-1974: A CHRONOLOGY AND FACT
     BOOK. Dobbs Ferry, NY: Oceana Publications,
     1977, p. 132-140. English. DESCR: Feminism;
     *First National Chicana Conference (May
     1971: Houston, TX).

1370 Yarbro-Bejarano, Yvonne. Primer encuentro de
     lesbianas feministas latinoamericanas y
     caribenas. THIRD WOMAN, Vol. 4, (1989), p.
     143-146. English. DESCR: Caribbean Region;
     First Meeting of Latin American and
     Caribbean Feminist Lesbians (October 14-17,
     1987: Cuernavaca, Mexico); *Homosexuality;
     Latin Americans; Sexual Behavior; *Women.

Conferencia de Mujeres Por La Raza (1971: Houston, TX)
     USE: First National Chicana Conference (May
     1971: Houston, TX)

Consumers

1371 O'Guinn, Thomas C.; Imperia, Giovanna; and
     MacAdams, Elizabeth A. Acculturation and
     perceived family decision-making input among
     Mexican American wives. JOURNAL OF
     CROSS-CULTURAL PSYCHOLOGY, Vol. 18, no. 1
     (March 1987), p. 78-92. English. DESCR:
     *Acculturation; Attitudes; Family; Sex
     Roles.

Contraception
     USE: Birth Control

Cook County, IL

1372 Dowling, Patrick T. and Fisher, Michael.
     Maternal factors and low birthweight
     infants: a comparison of Blacks with
     Mexican-Americans. JOURNAL OF FAMILY
     PRACTICE, Vol. 25, no. 2 (August 1987), p.
     153-158. English. DESCR: Blacks; *Infant
     Mortality; *Prenatal Care; *Public Health;
     *Socioeconomic Factors.

Coordinadora de Mujeres Trabajadoras

1373 Ruiz Funes, Concepcion and Tunon, Enriqueta.
     Panorama de las luchas de la mujer mexicana
     en el siglo XX. IN: Del Castillo, Adelaida
     R., ed. BETWEEN BORDERS: ESSAYS ON
     MEXICANA/CHICANA HISTORY. Encino, CA:
     Floricanto Press, 1990, p. 336-357. Spanish.
     DESCR: *Feminism; Frente Unido Pro Derechos
     de la Mujer; History; Labor Unions; *Mexico;
     Sex Roles; *Women.

Copyright
     USE: Publishing Industry

Corpi, Lucha

1374 Corpi, Lucha and Binder, Wolfgang.
     [Interview with] Lucha Corpi. IN: Binder,
     Wolfgang, ed. PARTIAL AUTOBIOGRAPHIES:
     INTERVIEWS WITH TWENTY CHICANO POETS.
     Erlangen, W. Germany: Verlag Palm & Enke,

1985, p. 75-85. English. DESCR: Authors;
     Autobiography; Poetry.

1375 Ordonez, Elizabeth J. The concept of
     cultural identity in Chicana poetry. THIRD
     WOMAN, Vol. 2, no. 1 (1984), p. 75-82.
     English. DESCR: Cervantes, Lorna Dee;
     *Literary Criticism; Poetry; Tafolla,
     Carmen; Villanueva, Alma.

1376 Perez-Erdelyi, Mireya and Corpi, Lucha.
     Entrevista con Lucha Corpi: poeta chicana.
     THE AMERICAS REVIEW, Vol. 17, no. 1 (Spring
     1989), p. 72-82. Spanish. DESCR: Authors;
     Literature.

Corporations

1377 Gallegos, Placida I. Emerging leadership
     among Hispanic women: the role of expressive
     behavior and nonverbal skill. Thesis
     (Ph.D.)--University of California,
     Riverside, 1987. 101 p. English. DESCR:
     Anglo Americans; Comparative Psychology;
     *Leadership; *Management; Women.

Corpus Christi, TX

1378 Williams, Norma. Role making among married
     Mexican American women: issues of class and
     ethnicity. JOURNAL OF APPLIED BEHAVIORAL
     SCIENCE, Vol. 24, no. 2 (1988), p. 203-217.
     English. DESCR: Austin, TX; Identity;
     Marriage; *Sex Roles; Social Classes.

Correa, Viola

1379 Sanchez, Rita. Chicana writer breaking out
     of the silence. DE COLORES, Vol. 3, no. 3
     (1977), p. 31-37. English. DESCR: Authors;
     Castaneda Shular, Antonia; Cunningham,
     Veronica; Fernandez, Barbara; *Literary
     Criticism; Mendoza, Rita; *Poetry.

LA CORREGIDORA [newspaper]

1380 Hernandez, Ines. Sara Estela Ramirez:
     sembradora. LEGACY: A JOURNAL OF
     NINETEENTH-CENTURY AMERICAN WOMEN WRITERS,
     Vol. 6, no. 1 (Spring 1989), p. 13-26.
     English. DESCR: Authors; *Biography;
     *Feminism; Flores Magon, Ricardo;
     *Journalism; Mexican Revolution - 1910-1920;
     Mexico; Newspapers; Poetry; *Ramirez, Sara
     Estela; REGENERACION [newspaper].

Corridos

1381 Fajardo, Ramon. Liberacion femenil: cancion
     corrido. XALMAN, Vol. 3, no. 2 (Fall 1980),
     p. 97-98. Spanish. DESCR: Feminism; Musical
     Lyrics.

1382 Fajardo, Ramon. Liberacion femenil: cancion
     corrido. IN: Bardeleben, Renate von, et al.,
     eds. MISSIONS IN CONFLICT: ESSAYS ON
     U.S.-MEXICAN RELATIONS AND CHICANO CULTURE.
     Tubingen, W. Germany: Gunter Narr Verlag,
     1986, p. 103-109. Spanish. DESCR: *Feminism;
     Musical Lyrics.

1383 Herrera-Sobek, Maria. The acculturation
     process of the Chicana in the corrido. DE
     COLORES, Vol. 6, no. 1-2 (1982), p. 7-16.
     English. DESCR: *Acculturation; Sex Roles.

1384 Herrera-Sobek, Maria. The acculturation
     process of the Chicana in the corrido.
     PROCEEDINGS OF THE PACIFIC COAST COUNCIL ON
     LATIN AMER STUDIES, Vol. 9, (1982), p.
     25-34. English. DESCR: *Acculturation;
     Musical Lyrics; *Women Men Relations.

Corridos (cont.)

1385 Herrera-Sobek, Maria. The Mexican corrido: a feminist analysis. Bloomington, IN: Indiana University Press, 1990. xix, 151 p.: ill. English. DESCR: Mexico; Military; *Sex Roles; Sex Stereotypes; Symbolism; *Women; Women Men Relations.

1386 Herrera-Sobek, Maria. The treacherous woman archetype: a structuring agent in the corrido. AZTLAN, Vol. 13, no. 1-2 (Spring, Fall, 1982), p. 135-148. English. DESCR: Folk Songs; Music.

1387 Saldivar, Jose David. Towards a Chicano poetics: the making of the Chicano subject. CONFLUENCIA, Vol. 1, no. 2 (Spring 1986), p. 10-17. English. DESCR: Feminism; *Literary Criticism; "Los Vatos" [poem]; Montoya, Jose E.; *Poetry; RESTLESS SERPENTS; Rios, Alberto; WHISPERING TO FOOL THE WIND; Zamora, Bernice.

CORRIDOS [play]

1388 Broyles-Gonzalez, Yolanda. Women in El Teatro Campesino: "A poco estaba molacha la Virgen de Guadalupe?". IN: Cordova, Teresa, et al., eds. CHICANA VOICES. Austin, TX: Center for Mexican American Studies, 1986, p. 162-187. English. DESCR: Actors and Actresses; *El Teatro Campesino; Stereotypes; Teatro; Valdez, Socorro.

Cortes, Hernan

1389 Del Castillo, Adelaida R. Malintzin Tenepal: a preliminary look into a new perspective. ENCUENTRO FEMENIL, Vol. 1, no. 2 (1974), p. 58-77. English. DESCR: Aztecs; Biography; *History; *Malinche; Precolumbian Society.

1390 Del Castillo, Adelaida R. Malintzin Tenepal: a preliminary look into a new perspective. IN: Sanchez, Rosaura and Martinez Cruz, Rosa, eds. ESSAYS ON LA MUJER. Los Angeles, CA: Chicano Studies Center Publications, UCLA, 1977, p. 124-149. English. DESCR: Aztecs; Biography; *History; *Malinche; Precolumbian Society.

Cota-Cardenas, Margarita

1391 Lomas, Clara. Libertad de no procrear: la voz de la mujer en "A una madre de nuestro tiempo" de Margarita Cota-Cardenas. IN: Cordova, Teresa, et al., eds. CHICANA VOICES. Austin, TX: Center for Mexican American Studies, 1986, p. 188-201. Bilingual. DESCR: "A una madre de nuestros tiempos" [poem]; Feminism; Literary Criticism; *Poetry; Sex Stereotypes.

1392 Lomas, Clara. Libertad de no procrear: la voz de la mujer en "A una madre de nuestro tiempo" de Margarita Cota-Cardenas. REVISTA MUJERES, Vol. 2, no. 1 (January 1985), p. 30-35. Spanish. DESCR: *"A una madre de nuestros tiempos" [poem]; Feminism; Literary Criticism; Poetry; Sex Stereotypes.

1393 Rebolledo, Tey Diana. The bittersweet nostalgia of childhood in the poetry of Margarita Cota-Cardenas. FRONTIERS: A JOURNAL OF WOMEN STUDIES, Vol. 5, no. 2 (Summer 1980), p. 31-35. English. DESCR: *Literary Criticism; Poetry.

1394 Tafolla, Carmen. Chicano literature: beyond beginnings. IN: Harris, Marie and Aguero, Kathleen, eds. A GIFT OF TONGUES: CRITICAL CHALLENGES IN CONTEMPORARY AMERICAN POETRY. Athens, GA: University of Georgia Press,

1987, p. 206-225. English. DESCR: *Authors; Language Usage; *Literary Criticism; *Literature; Portillo Trambley, Estela; Sex Stereotypes; Symbolism; Tafolla, Carmen; Vigil-Pinon, Evangelina.

Cotera, Marta P.

1395 Cardenas, Reyes. The machismo manifesto. CARACOL, Vol. 2, no. 8 (April 1976), p. 7. Bilingual. DESCR: *Machismo; Malinche; Women Men Relations.

1396 Chapa, Olivia Evey. Mujeres por la Raza unida. CARACOL, Vol. 1, no. 2 (October 1974), p. 3-5. English. DESCR: Canales, Alma; Diaz, Elena; La Raza Unida Party; *Political Parties and Organizations; REPORT OF FIRST CONFERENCIA DE MUJERES POR LA RAZA UNIDA PARTY.

Cotton Industry

1397 Weber, Devra Anne. Mexican women on strike: memory, history and oral narratives. IN: Del Castillo, Adelaida R., ed. BETWEEN BORDERS: ESSAYS ON MEXICANA/CHICANA HISTORY. Encino, CA: Floricanto Press, 1990, p. 175-200. English. DESCR: *1933 Cotton Strike; History; *Oral History; San Joaquin Valley, CA; Strikes and Lockouts; *Valdez, Rosaura; Working Women.

Cotto-Thorner, Guillermo

1398 Irizarry, Estelle. La abuelita in literature. NUESTRO, Vol. 7, no. 7 (September 1983), p. 50. English. DESCR: Alonso, Luis Ricardo; *Ancianos; Family; Grandmothers; Ulibarri, Sabine R.; Valero, Robert.

Counseling (Educational)

1399 Chacon, Maria A., et al. Chicanas in California post secondary education: a comparative study of barriers to the program progress. Stanford, CA: Stanford Center for Chicano Research, 1985. viii, 217 p. English. DESCR: *Academic Achievement; Colleges and Universities; Educational Statistics; Enrollment; *Higher Education; Students; Surveys.

1400 Ochoa, Mariaelena Lopez. Group counseling Chicana troubled youth: an exploratory group counseling project. Thesis (Ed.D.) --University of Massachusetts, 1981. 326 p. English. DESCR: *Youth.

1401 Ortiz, Flora Ida. Hispanic American women in higher education: a consideration of the socialization process. AZTLAN, Vol. 17, no. 2 (Fall 1986), p. 125-152. English. DESCR: *Academic Achievement; Enrollment; *Higher Education; Sex Roles; *Sexism; Socialization; Students; University of California.

1402 Quezada, Rosa and Jones-Loheyde, Katherine. Hispanic women: academic advisees of high potential. IMPROVING COLLEGE & UNIVERSITY TEACHING, Vol. 32, no. 2-14 (1984), p. 95-98. English. DESCR: Academic Achievement; *Higher Education.

Counseling (Psychological)

1403 Atkinson, Donald R.; Winzelberg, Andrew; and Holland, Abby. Ethnicity, locus of control for family planning, and pregnancy counselor credibility. JOURNAL OF COUNSELING PSYCHOLOGY, Vol. 32, no. 3 (July 1985), p. 417-421. English. DESCR: Anglo Americans; *Family Planning; Fertility; Identity; *Locus of Control; Women.

1404 Balkwell, Carolyn Ann. An attitudinal correlate of the timing of a major life event: the case of morale in widowhood. FAMILY RELATIONS, Vol. 34, no. 4 (October 1985), p. 577-581. English. DESCR: *Ancianos; *Marriage; Mental Health; Natural Support Systems; Widowhood.

1405 Belk, Sharyn S., et al. Impact of ethnicity, nationality, counseling orientation, and mental health standards on stereotypic beliefs about women. SEX ROLES, Vol. 21, no. 9-10 (November 1989), p. 671-695. English. DESCR: Anglo Americans; Beliefs About Women Scale (BAWS); *Comparative Psychology; Cultural Characteristics; Identity; Mental Health; *Sex Stereotypes; Sexism; Women.

1406 Eisen, Marvin and Zellman, Gail L. Factors predicting pregnancy resolution decision satisfaction of unmarried adolescents. JOURNAL OF GENETIC PSYCHOLOGY, Vol. 145, no. 2 (December 1984), p. 231-239. English. DESCR: Abortion; Anglo Americans; Attitudes; Family Planning; *Fertility; Youth.

1407 Palacios, Maria and Franco, Juan N. Counseling Mexican-American women. JOURNAL OF MULTICULTURAL COUNSELING AND DEVELOPMENT, Vol. 14, (July 1986), p. 124-131. English. DESCR: Cultural Characteristics; *Mental Health.

1408 Torres, Cynthia. Cultural and psychological attributes and their implications for career choice and aspirations among Mexican American females. Thesis (Ph.D.)--University of California, Los Angeles, 1986. 127 p. English. DESCR: *Biculturalism; *Careers; Cultural Characteristics.

Court Decisions
USE: Administration of Justice

Crime and Corrections
USE: Criminology

Criminal Acts

1409 Anglin, M. Douglas and Hser, Yih-Ing. Addicted women and crime. CRIMINOLOGY: AN INTERDISCIPLINARY JOURNAL, Vol. 25, no. 2 (1987), p. 359-397. English. DESCR: Drug Abuse Programs; *Drug Addicts; Statistics.

1410 Hser, Yih-Ing; Chou, Chih-Ping; and Anglin, M. Douglas. The criminality of female narcotics addicts: a causal modeling approach. JOURNAL OF QUANTITATIVE CRIMINOLOGY, Vol. 6, no. 2 (June 1990), p. 207-228. English. DESCR: Anglo Americans; *Drug Addicts; Drug Traffic; Prostitution; Women.

Criminal Justice System

1411 Blackwelder, Julia Kirk. Women of the depression: caste and culture in San Antonio, 1929-1939. College Station, TX: Texas A&M University Press, 1984. xviii, 279 p.: ill. English. DESCR: Cultural Characteristics; Employment; Family; Great Depression, 1929-1933; Labor Supply and Market; Labor Unions; Prostitution; San Antonio, TX; *Social Classes; *Women.

Criminology

1412 Sanford, Judy, et al. Patterns of reported rape in a tri-ethnic population: Houston, Texas, 1974-1975. AMERICAN JOURNAL OF PUBLIC HEALTH, Vol. 69, no. 5 (May 1979), p. 480-434. English. DESCR: Anglo Americans; Blacks; *Ethnic Groups; *Houston, TX; *Rape; Statistics; Women.

1413 White, Marni, et al. Perceived crime in the neighborhood and mental health of women and children. ENVIRONMENT AND BEHAVIOR, Vol. 19, no. 5 (September 1987), p. 588-613. English. DESCR: Attitudes; Children; Housing; *Mental Health; Women.

CRITICAL INCIDENT TECHNIQUE

1414 Espin, Oliva M. Perceptions of sexual discrimination among college women in Latin America and the United States. HISPANIC JOURNAL OF BEHAVIORAL SCIENCES, Vol. 2, no. 1 (March 1980), p. 1-19. English. DESCR: Colleges and Universities; Feminism; Latin Americans; *Sexism; Students; Women Men Relations.

Cuban Americans
USE: Cubanos

Cubanos

1415 Alarcon, Norma. Latina writers in the United States. IN: Marting, Diane E., ed. SPANISH AMERICAN WOMEN WRITERS: A BIO-BIBLIOGRAPHICAL SOURCE BOOK. New York: Greenwood Press, 1990, p. [557]-567. English. DESCR: *Authors; *Bibliography; BREAKING BOUNDARIES: LATINA WRITING AND CRITICAL READINGS; Intergroup Relations; Language Usage; *Literature Reviews; Puerto Ricans; THIRD WOMAN [journal]; *Women.

1416 Bean, Frank D.; Swicegood, Gray; and King, Allan G. Role incompatibility and the relationship between fertility and labor supply among Hispanic women. IN: Borjas, George J. and Tienda, Marta, eds. HISPANICS IN THE U.S. ECONOMY. Orlando, FL: Academic Press, 1985, p. 221-242. English. DESCR: *Employment; Fertility; Labor Supply and Market; Puerto Ricans.

1417 Fanelli-Kuczmarski, Marie T., et al. Folate status of Mexican American, Cuban, and Puerto Rican women. AMERICAN JOURNAL OF CLINICAL NUTRITION, Vol. 52, no. 2 (August 1990), p. 368-372. English. DESCR: *Folic Acid Deficiency; Hispanic Health and Nutrition Examination Survey (HHANES); *Nutrition; Puerto Ricans; *Women.

1418 Fernandez Kelly, Maria and Garcia, Anna M. The making of an underground economy: Hispanic women, home work, and the advanced capitalist state. URBAN ANTHROPOLOGY, Vol. 14, no. 1-3 (Spring, Fall, 1985), p. 59-90. English. DESCR: Capitalism; Employment; Garment Industry; Industrial Workers; International Economic Relations; Labor Supply and Market; *Los Angeles County, CA; *Miami, FL; Women; Working Women.

1419 Frisbie, William Parker. Variation in patterns of marital instability among Hispanics. JOURNAL OF MARRIAGE AND THE FAMILY, Vol. 48, no. 1 (February 1986), p. 99-106. English. DESCR: *Marriage; Puerto Ricans.

Cubanos (cont.)

1420 Markides, Kyriakos S. Consequences of gender differentials in life expectancy for Black and Hispanic Americans. INTERNATIONAL JOURNAL OF AGING & HUMAN DEVELOPMENT, Vol. 29, no. 2 (1989), p. 95-102. English. **DESCR:** *Ancianos; Blacks; Census; Latin Americans; Males; Population; Puerto Ricans; U.S. Bureau of the Census.

1421 Miller, Elaine N. and Sternbach, Nancy Saporta. Selected bibliography. IN: Horno-Delgado, Asuncion, et al., eds. BREAKING BOUNDARIES: LATINA WRITING AND CRITICAL READINGS. Amherst, MA: University of Massachusetts Press, c1989, p. 251-263. English. **DESCR:** *Bibliography; Literary Criticism; *Literature; Puerto Ricans; *Women.

1422 Nieves-Squires, Sarah. Hispanic women: making their presence on campus less tenuous. Washington, DC: Association of American Colleges, c1991. 14 p. English. **DESCR:** Afro-Hispanics; Colleges and Universities; *Discrimination in Education; *Higher Education; Puerto Ricans; *Women.

1423 Romero-Gwynn, Eunice and Carias, Lucia. Breast-feeding intentions and practice among Hispanic mothers in Southern California. PEDIATRICS, Vol. 84, no. 4 (October 1989), p. 626-632. English. **DESCR:** *Breastfeeding; Expanded Food and Nutrition Education Program; Immigrants; Puerto Ricans; Southern California; Women.

1424 Stroup-Benham, Christine A. and Trevino, Fernando M. Reproductive characteristics of Mexican-American, mainland Puerto Rican, and Cuban-American women: data from the Hispanic Health and Nutrition Examination Survey. JAMA: JOURNAL OF THE AMERICAN MEDICAL ASSOCIATION, Vol. 265, no. 2 (January 9, 1991), p. 222-226. English. **DESCR:** *Birth Control; Breastfeeding; *Fertility; Hispanic Health and Nutrition Examination Survey (HHANES); Puerto Ricans; *Women.

1425 Sullivan, Teresa A. The occupational prestige of women immigrants: a comparison of Cubans and Mexicans. INTERNATIONAL MIGRATION REVIEW, Vol. 18, no. 4 (Winter 1984), p. 1045-1062. English. **DESCR:** Careers; Employment; *Immigrants; Males; Mexico; Sex Roles; *Social Mobility; *Women; *Working Women.

1426 Valtierra, Mary. Acculturation, social support, and reported stress of Latina physicians. Thesis (Ph.D.)--California School of Professional Psychology, 1989. 136 p. English. **DESCR:** *Acculturation; Careers; Immigration; Latin Americans; *Medical Personnel; Puerto Ricans; *Stress; *Women.

1427 Zayas, Luis H. Toward an understanding of suicide risks in young Hispanic females. JOURNAL OF ADOLESCENT RESEARCH, Vol. 2, no. 1 (Spring 1987), p. 1-11. English. **DESCR:** Acculturation; Cultural Characteristics; Depression (Psychological); Mental Health; Puerto Ricans; *Suicide; *Women; *Youth.

Cuentos

1428 Jordan, Rosan Augusta. The vaginal serpent and other themes from Mexican-American women's lore. IN: Jordan, Rosan A. and Kalcik, Susan J., eds. WOMEN'S FOLKLORE, WOMEN'S CULTURE. Philadelphia: University of Pennsylvania Press, 1985, p. 26-44. English. **DESCR:** Fertility; *Folklore; La Llorona;

*Leyendas; *Sex Roles; Sexism; Sexual Behavior.

Cultural Characteristics

1429 Arce, Carlos H. and Abney-Guardado, Armando J. Demographic and cultural correlates of Chicano intermarriage. CALIFORNIA SOCIOLOGIST, Vol. 5, no. 2 (Summer 1982), p. 41-58. English. **DESCR:** Culture; *Intermarriage; Population; Social Psychology.

1430 Arguelles, Lourdes and Rivero, Anne M. HIV infection/AIDS and Latinas in Los Angeles County: considerations for prevention, treatment, and research practice. CALIFORNIA SOCIOLOGIST, Vol. 11, no. 1-2 (1988), p. 69-89. English. **DESCR:** *AIDS (Disease); Health Education; Homosexuality; Human Immunodeficiency Virus (HIV); Los Angeles County, CA; Natural Support Systems; Parent and Child Relationships; Sexual Behavior; *Women.

1431 Baca Zinn, Maxine. Chicano family research: conceptual distortions and alternative directions. JOURNAL OF ETHNIC STUDIES, Vol. 7, no. 3 (Fall 1979), p. 59-71. English. **DESCR:** Culture; *Family; Research Methodology; Stereotypes.

1432 Baca Zinn, Maxine. Chicano men and masculinity. JOURNAL OF ETHNIC STUDIES, Vol. 10, no. 2 (Summer 1982), p. 29-44. English. **DESCR:** Ethnic Stratification; *Machismo; Sex Roles; Sex Stereotypes; Socioeconomic Factors; Women Men Relations.

1433 Bach-y-Rita, George. The Mexican-American: religious and cultural influences. IN: Becerra, Rosina M., et al., eds. MENTAL HEALTH AND HISPANIC AMERICANS: CLINICAL PERSPECTIVES. New York: Grune & Stratton, 1982, p. 29-40. English. **DESCR:** Catholic Church; Culture; Language Usage; Machismo; *Mental Health; Psychotherapy; Religion.

1434 Belk, Sharyn S., et al. Impact of ethnicity, nationality, counseling orientation, and mental health standards on stereotypic beliefs about women. SEX ROLES, Vol. 21, no. 9-10 (November 1989), p. 671-695. English. **DESCR:** Anglo Americans; Beliefs About Women Scale (BAWS); *Comparative Psychology; *Counseling (Psychological); Identity; Mental Health; *Sex Stereotypes; Sexism; Women.

1435 Blackwelder, Julia Kirk. Women of the depression: caste and culture in San Antonio, 1929-1939. College Station, TX: Texas A&M University Press, 1984. xviii, 279 p.: ill. English. **DESCR:** Criminal Justice System; Employment; Family; Great Depression, 1929-1933; Labor Supply and Market; Labor Unions; Prostitution; San Antonio, TX; *Social Classes; *Women.

1436 Bova, Breda Murphy and Phillips, Rebecca R. Hispanic women at midlife: implications for higher and adult education. JOURNAL OF ADULT EDUCATION, Vol. 18, no. 1 (Fall 1989), p. 9-15. English. **DESCR:** *Adult Education; *Higher Education; Identity; Sex Roles.

Cultural Characteristics
(cont.)

1437 Canino, Glorisa. The Hispanic woman: sociocultural influences on diagnoses and treatment. IN: Becerra, Rosina M., et al., eds. MENTAL HEALTH AND HISPANIC AMERICANS: CLINICAL PERSPECTIVES. New York: Grune & Stratton, 1982, p. 117-138. English. DESCR: Assimilation; Culture; *Depression (Psychological); Family; Feminism; Mental Health; Population; Sex Roles.

1438 Cota-Robles de Suarez, Cecilia. Sexual stereotypes--psychological and cultural survival: a description of child-rearing practices attributed to the Chicana (the Mexican American woman) and its psychological and cultural implications. REGENERACION, Vol. 2, no. 3 (1973), p. 17, 20-21. English. DESCR: Family; Folklore; Language; Parenting; Sex Stereotypes; *Sexism; *Stereotypes.

1439 Cristo, Martha H. Stress and coping among Mexican women. Thesis (Ph.D.)--California School of Professional Psychology, Los Angeles, 1988. 336 p. English. DESCR: *Immigrants; Mental Health; Socioeconomic Factors; *Stress; *Women.

1440 Davis, Sally M. and Harris, Mary B. Sexual knowledge, sexual interests, and sources of sexual information of rural and urban adolescents from three cultures. ADOLESCENCE, Vol. 17, no. 66 (Summer 1982), p. 471-492. English. DESCR: Birth Control; Identity; Rural Population; *Sex Education; Sex Roles; Urban Communities; Youth.

1441 De Llano, Carmen. Comparisons of the psychocultural characteristics of graduate school-bound and nongraduate school-bound Mexican American and Anglo American college women. Thesis (Ph.D.)--California School of Professional Psychology, 1986. 223 p. English. DESCR: *Anglo Americans; Colleges and Universities; Comparative Psychology; *Graduate Schools; Higher Education; Students; *Women.

1442 Del Castillo, Adelaida R. and Torres, Maria. The interdependency of educational institutions and cultural norms: the Hispana experience. IN: McKenna, Teresa and Ortiz, Flora Ida, eds. THE BROKEN WEB: THE EDUCATIONAL EXPERIENCE OF HISPANIC WOMEN. Claremont, CA: Tomas Rivera Center; Berkeley, CA: Floricanto Press, 1988, p. 39-60. English. DESCR: Academic Achievement; Acculturation; *Education; *Literature Reviews; Research Methodology; *Values; Women.

1443 Deutsch, Sarah. Women and intercultural relations: the case of Hispanic New Mexico and Colorado. SIGNS: JOURNAL OF WOMEN IN CULTURE AND SOCIETY, Vol. 12, no. 4 (Summer 1987), p. 719-739. English. DESCR: Colorado; Immigrants; Intercultural Communication; Mexico; New Mexico; Rural Population; Sex Roles; Social History and Conditions; *Women.

1444 Fennelly, Katherine; Kandiah, Vasantha; and Ortiz, Vilma. The cross-cultural study of fertility among Hispanic adolescents in the Americas. STUDIES IN FAMILY PLANNING, Vol. 20, no. 2 (March, April, 1989), p. 96-101. English. DESCR: Ethnic Groups; *Fertility; Latin America; *Marriage; Youth.

1445 Gibson, Guadalupe. Hispanic women: stress and mental health issues. WOMEN AND THERAPY,

Vol. 2, no. 2-3 (Summer, Fall, 1983), p. 113-133. English. DESCR: *Mental Health; *Stress.

1446 Gilbert, M. Jean. Alcohol consumption patterns in immigrant and later generation Mexican American women. HISPANIC JOURNAL OF BEHAVIORAL SCIENCES, Vol. 9, no. 3 (September 1987), p. 299-313. English. DESCR: Acculturation; *Alcoholism; *Attitudes; *Immigrants; Mexico.

1447 Gondolf, Edward W.; Fisher, Ellen; and McFerron, J. Richard. Racial differences among shelter residents: a comparison of Anglo, Black, and Hispanic battered. JOURNAL OF FAMILY VIOLENCE, Vol. 3, no. 1 (March 1988), p. 39-51. English. DESCR: Anglo Americans; Battered Women; Blacks; Comparative Psychology; Natural Support Systems; Socioeconomic Factors; *Violence; *Women.

1448 Gonzalez del Valle, Amalia and Usher, Mary. Group therapy with aged Latino women: a pilot project and study. CLINICAL GERONTOLOGIST, Vol. 1, no. 1 (Fall 1982), p. 51-58. English. DESCR: *Ancianos; Mental Illness; *Psychotherapy; San Mateo County, CA.

1449 Gonzalez-Berry, Erlinda and Rebolledo, Tey Diana. Growing up Chicano: Tomas Rivera and Sandra Cisneros. REVISTA CHICANO-RIQUENA, Vol. 13, no. 3-4 (Fall, Winter, 1985), p. 109-119. English. DESCR: Cisneros, Sandra; *Literary Criticism; Rivera, Tomas; Sex Roles; THE HOUSE ON MANGO STREET; Y NO SE LO TRAGO LA TIERRA/AND THE EARTH DID NOT PART.

1450 Gutierrez, Jeannie and Sameroff, Arnold. Determinants of complexity in Mexican-American and Anglo-American mothers' conceptions of child development. CHILD DEVELOPMENT, Vol. 61, no. 2 (April 1990), p. 384-394. English. DESCR: Acculturation; *Anglo Americans; Children; *Parenting; Values; *Women.

1451 Isaacs, Barbara Gail. Anglo, Black, and Latin adolescents' participation in sports. Thesis (Ph.D.)--California School of Professional Psychology, Los Angeles, 1984. 283 p. English. DESCR: Anglo Americans; Blacks; *Secondary School Education; *Sports; *Women; Youth.

1452 Jaramillo, Mari-Luci. How to suceed in business and remain Chicana. LA LUZ, Vol. 8, no. 7 (August, September, 1980), p. 33-35. English. DESCR: Assertiveness; Family; Identity; *Natural Support Systems; *Working Women.

1453 Jorgensen, Stephen R. and Adams, Russell P. Family planning needs and behavior of Mexican American women: a study of health care professionals and their clientele. HISPANIC JOURNAL OF BEHAVIORAL SCIENCES, Vol. 9, no. 3 (September 1987), p. 265-286. English. DESCR: Acculturation; *Attitudes; Birth Control; *Family Planning; Fertility; Medical Personnel; Stereotypes; Sterilization.

1454 Kay, Margarita Artschwager. Mexican, Mexican American, and Chicana childbirth. IN: Melville, Margarita B., ed. TWICE A MINORITY. St. Louis, MO: Mosby, 1980, p. 52-65. English. DESCR: Herbal Medicine; *Maternal and Child Welfare; Midwives; Sex Roles.

Cultural Characteristics
(cont.)

1455 Kimbel, Charles E.; Marsh, Nancy B.; and Kiska, Andrew C. Sex, age, and cultural differences in self-reported assertiveness. PSYCHOLOGICAL REPORTS, Vol. 55, no. 2 (October 1984), p. 419-422. English. DESCR: *Assertiveness; Identity; Sex Roles.

1456 Laosa, Luis M. Maternal teaching strategies in Chicano and Anglo-American families: the influence of culture and education on maternal behavior. CHILD DEVELOPMENT, Vol. 51, no. 3 (September 1980), p. 759-765. English. DESCR: Anglo Americans; Comparative Psychology; *Education; Family; Maternal Teaching Observation Technique (MTOT); *Parent and Child Relationships; Parenting; Women.

1457 Manzanedo, Hector Garcia; Walters, Esperanza Garcia; and Lorig, Kate R. Health and illness perceptions of the Chicana. IN: Melville, Margarita B., ed. TWICE A MINORITY. St. Louis, MO: Mosby, 1980, p. 191-207. English. DESCR: Culture; *Medical Care; Public Health; Sex Roles; Values.

1458 Melgoza, Bertha; Roll, Samuel; and Baker, Richard C. Conformity and cooperation in Chicanos: the case of the missing susceptibility to influence. JOURNAL OF COMMUNITY PSYCHOLOGY, Vol. 11, no. 4 (October 1983), p. 323-333. English. DESCR: *Comparative Psychology; *Locus of Control; Socialization; Stereotypes; Women.

1459 Melville, Margarita B. Female and male in Chicano theatre. IN: Kanellos, Nicolas, ed. HISPANIC THEATRE IN THE UNITED STATES. Houston, TX: Arte Publico Press, 1984, p. 71-79. English. DESCR: BERNABE; BRUJERIAS [play]; DAY OF THE SWALLOWS; Duarte-Clark, Rodrigo; EL JARDIN [play]; Family; Feminism; Macias, Ysidro; Morton, Carlos; Portillo Trambley, Estela; RANCHO HOLLYWOOD [play]; *Sex Roles; *Teatro; THE ULTIMATE PENDEJADA [play]; Valdez, Luis; Women Men Relations.

1460 Michael, Robert T. and Tuma, Nancy Brandon. Entry into marriage and parenthood by young men and women: the influence of family background. DEMOGRAPHY, Vol. 22, no. 4 (November 1985), p. 515-544. Magazine. English. DESCR: Anglo Americans; Blacks; *Fertility; *Marriage; Population; Youth.

1461 Miranda, Gloria E. Hispano-Mexican childrearing practices in pre-American Santa Barbara. SOUTHERN CALIFORNIA QUARTERLY, Vol. 65, no. 4 (Winter 1983), p. 307-320. English. DESCR: *Children; *Family; History; *Parenting; Santa Barbara, CA; Socialization.

1462 Mirande, Alfredo. Que gacho es ser macho: it's a drag to be a macho man. AZTLAN, Vol. 17, no. 2 (Fall 1986), p. 63-89. English. DESCR: Identity; *Machismo; Personality; Sex Roles; *Sex Stereotypes; Values.

1463 Palacios, Maria and Franco, Juan N. Counseling Mexican-American women. JOURNAL OF MULTICULTURAL COUNSELING AND DEVELOPMENT, Vol. 14, (July 1986), p. 124-131. English. DESCR: *Counseling (Psychological); *Mental Health.

1464 Pavich, Emma Guerrero. A Chicana perspective on Mexican culture and sexuality. JOURNAL OF SOCIAL WORK AND HUMAN SEXUALITY, Vol. 4, no. 3 (Spring 1986), p. 47-65. English. DESCR: California; Family; Feminism; Homosexuality; Machismo; Sex Roles; Sex Stereotypes; *Sexual Behavior; Women Men Relations.

1465 Poma, Pedro A. Pregnancy in Hispanic women. JOURNAL OF THE NATIONAL MEDICAL ASSOCIATION, Vol. 79, no. 9 (September 1987), p. 929-935. English. DESCR: *Doctor Patient Relations; *Fertility; Machismo; Preventative Medicine; Women.

1466 Pumariega, Andres J. Acculturation and eating attitudes in adolescent girls: a comparative and correlational study. JOURNAL OF THE AMERICAN ACADEMY OF CHILD PSYCHIATRY, Vol. 25, no. 2 (March 1986), p. 276-279. English. DESCR: *Acculturation; Anorexia Nervosa; Eating Attitudes Test (EAT); Nutrition; Socioeconomic Factors; Youth.

1467 Sabogal, Fabio, et al. Hispanic familism and acculturation: what changes and what doesn't? HISPANIC JOURNAL OF BEHAVIORAL SCIENCES, Vol. 9, no. 4 (December 1987), p. 397-412. English. DESCR: *Acculturation; Attitudes; Ethnic Groups; Extended Family; *Family; Natural Support Systems; Values.

1468 Sanchez, Joaquin John. An investigation of the initial experience of a Chicana with higher education. Thesis (Ph.D.)--Saybrook Institute, 1983. 163 p. English. DESCR: Biculturalism; Colleges and Universities; *Higher Education.

1469 Smith, Bradford M. The measurement of narcissism in Asian, Caucasian, and Hispanic American women. PSYCHOLOGICAL REPORTS, Vol. 67, no. 3 (December 1990), p. 779-785. English. DESCR: Anglo Americans; Asian Americans; Comparative Psychology; *Narcissistic Personality Inventory; *Personality; *Psychological Testing; *Women.

1470 Sorenson, Ann Marie. Fertility, expectations and ethnic identity among Mexican-American adolescents: an expression of cultural ideals. SOCIOLOGICAL PERSPECTIVES, Vol. 28, no. 3 (July 1985), p. 339-360. English. DESCR: Acculturation; Anglo Americans; *Fertility; Identity; Values; Youth.

1471 Spitta, Silvia D. Literary transculturation in Latin America. Thesis (Ph.D.)--University of Oregon, 1989. 184 p. English. DESCR: Anzaldua, Gloria; Arguedos, Jose Maria; Authors; Culture; *Intergroup Relations; *Latin American Literature; Spanish Influence.

1472 Tienda, Marta and Angel, Ronald J. Headship and household composition among Blacks, Hispanics and other whites. SOCIAL FORCES, Vol. 61, no. 2 (December 1982), p. 508-531. English. DESCR: Anglo Americans; Blacks; Extended Family; *Family; Puerto Ricans; Single Parents.

1473 Torres, Cynthia. Cultural and psychological attributes and their implications for career choice and aspirations among Mexican American females. Thesis (Ph.D.)--University of California, Los Angeles, 1986. 127 p. English. DESCR: *Biculturalism; *Careers; Counseling (Psychological).

1474 Torres, Sara. Hispanic-American battered women: why consider cultural differences? RESPONSE TO THE VICTIMIZATION OF WOMEN & CHILDREN, Vol. 10, no. 3 (1987), p. 20-21. English. DESCR: *Battered Women.

Cultural Characteristics
(cont.)

1475 Trevathan, Wenda R. First conversations: verbal content of mother-newborn interaction. JOURNAL OF CROSS-CULTURAL PSYCHOLOGY, Vol. 19, no. 1 (March 1988), p. 65-77. English. DESCR: El Paso, TX; Language Arts; *Parent and Child Relationships.

1476 Triandis, Harry C. Role perceptions of Hispanic young adults. JOURNAL OF CROSS-CULTURAL PSYCHOLOGY, Vol. 15, no. 3 (September 1984), p. 297-320. English. DESCR: *Family; Parent and Child Relationships; *Sex Roles; Social Psychology; Values; Youth.

1477 Trotter, Robert T. Ethnic and sexual patterns of alcohol use: Anglo and Mexican American college students. ADOLESCENCE, Vol 17, no. 66 (Summer 1982), p. 305-325. English. DESCR: *Alcoholism; Anglo Americans; Colleges and Universities; Ethnic Groups; Sex Roles; Students; Youth.

1478 Williams, Norma. The Mexican American family: tradition and change. Dix Hills, NY General Hall, Inc., c1990. x, 170 p. English. DESCR: *Cultural Customs; *Family; Religion; *Sex Roles; Working Women.

1479 Worth, Dooley and Rodriguez, Ruth. Latina women and AIDS. SIECUS REPORT, (January, February, 1986), p. 5-7. English. DESCR: Drug Addicts; Drug Use; Health Education; Natural Support Systems; New York; Preventative Medicine; Puerto Ricans; Sex Roles; *Vital Statistics; Women.

1480 Ybarra, Lea. Separating a myth from reality: socio-economic and cultural influences on Chicanas and the world of work. IN: Melville, Margarita, ed. MEXICANAS AT WORK IN THE UNITED STATES. Houston, TX: Mexican American Studies Program, University of Houston, 1988, p. 12-23. English. DESCR: Attitudes; Income; Machismo; Sex Roles; *Socioeconomic Factors; Stereotypes; *Working Women.

1481 Zayas, Luis H. Toward an understanding of suicide risks in young Hispanic females. JOURNAL OF ADOLESCENT RESEARCH, Vol. 2, no. 1 (Spring 1987), p. 1-11. English. DESCR: Acculturation; Cubanos; Depression (Psychological); Mental Health; Puerto Ricans; *Suicide; *Women; *Youth.

Cultural Customs

1482 Anzaldua, Gloria. La prieta. IN: Moraga, Cherrie and Anzaldua, Gloria, eds. THIS BRIDGE CALLED MY BACK: WRITINGS BY RADICAL WOMEN OF COLOR. Watertown, MA: Persephone Press, 1981, p. 198-209. English. DESCR: *Biography; Feminism.

1483 Blanco, Iris. Participacion de las mujeres en la sociedad prehispanica. IN: Sanchez, Rosaura and Martinez Cruz, Rosa, eds. ESSAYS ON LA MUJER. Los Angeles, CA: Chicano Studies Center Publications, UCLA, 1977, p. 48-81. Spanish. DESCR: Aztecs; *History; Indigenismo; Mexico; Precolumbian Society; Women.

1484 Buss, Fran Leeper. La partera: story of a midwife. Ann Arbor, MI: University of Michigan Press, 1980. 140 p.: ill. English. DESCR: Aragon, Jesusita, 1908-; *Curanderas; Folk Medicine; Herbal Medicine; *Midwives; New Mexico; San Miguel County, NM.

1485 Cuellar, Israel. Service delivery and mental health services for Chicano elders. IN: Miranda, Manuel and Ruiz, Rene A., eds. CHICANO AGING AND MENTAL HEALTH. Rockville, MD: U.S. Department of Health and Human Services, 1981, p. 185-211. English. DESCR: *Ancianos; Attitudes; Cultural Pluralism; Language Usage; Mental Health; Mental Health Clinics; Religion; Sex Roles; Spanish Language.

1486 Erevia, Angela. Quinceanera. San Antonio, TX: Mexican American Cultural Center, 1980. xiii, 73 p. English. DESCR: Catholic Church; *Quinceaneras.

1487 Falicov, Celia Jaes. Mexican families. IN: McGoldrick, Monica, et al., eds. ETHNICITY AND FAMILY THERAPY. New York: The Guilford Press, 1982, p. 134-163. English. DESCR: Acculturation; *Family; Mental Health; Sex Roles.

1488 Garcia, Mario T. La familia: the Mexican immigrant family, 1900-1930. IN: Barrera, Mario, et al., eds. WORK, FAMILY, SEX ROLES, LANGUAGE: SELECTED PAPERS, 1979. Berkeley, CA: Tonatiuh-Quinto Sol, 1980, p. 117-139. English. DESCR: Assimilation; El Paso, TX; Family; *Historiography; History; Immigration; Labor; Sex Roles.

1489 Garcia-Bahne, Betty. La Chicana and the Chicano family. IN: Sanchez, Rosaura and Martinez Cruz, Rosa, eds. ESSAYS ON LA MUJER. Los Angeles, CA: Chicano Studies Center Publications, UCLA, 1977, p. 30-47. English. DESCR: *Family; Sex Roles; Social Classes; Socialization; Stereotypes.

1490 Iglesias, Norma. La flor mas bella de la maquiladora: historias de vida de la mujer obrera en Tijuana, B.C.N. Mexico, D.F.: Secretaria de Educacion Publica, CEFNOMEX, 1985. 166 p.: ill. Spanish. DESCR: Border Industrialization Program (BIP); *Border Industries; Labor Unions; Sindicato Independiente Solidev; Solidev Mexicana, S.A.; Tijuana, Baja California, Mexico; *Women; Working Women.

1491 Loustaunau, Martha Oehmke. Hispanic widows and their support systems in the Mesilla Valley of southern New Mexico, 1910-40. IN: Scadron, Arlene, ed. ON THEIR OWN: WIDOWS AND WIDOWHOOD IN THE AMERICAN SOUTHWEST 1843-1939. Urbana, IL: University of Illinois Press, c1988, p. [91]-116. English. DESCR: Extended Family; Mesilla Valley, NM; Natural Support Systems; Sex Roles; Single Parents; Widowhood; *Women.

1492 Nieto Senour, Maria. Psychology of the Chicana. IN: Martinez, Joe L., Jr., ed. CHICANO PSYCHOLOGY. New York: Academic Press, 1977, p. 329-342. English. DESCR: Academic Achievement; Acculturation; Identity; *Psychology; Sex Roles.

1493 Sweeny, Mary Anne and Gulino, Claire. The health belief model as an explanation for breast-feeding practices in a Hispanic population. ANS: ADVANCES IN NURSING SCIENCE, Vol. 9, no. 4 (July 1987), p. 35-50. English. DESCR: *Breastfeeding; *Public Health; San Diego, CA; Tijuana, Baja California, Mexico; Women.

Cultural Customs (cont.)

1494 Williams, Brett. Why migrant women feed their husbands tamales: foodways as a basis for a revisionist view of Tejano family life. IN: Brown, Linda Keller and Mussell, Kay, eds. ETHNIC AND REGIONAL FOODWAYS IN THE UNITED STATES: THE PERFORMANCE OF GROUP IDENTITY. Knoxville, TN: University of Tennessee Press, 1984, p. 113-126. English. DESCR: Extended Family; Family; *Food Practices; Illinois; *Migrant Labor; Sex Roles; Tamales; Texas.

1495 Williams, Norma. Changes in funeral patterns and gender roles among Mexican Americans. IN: Ruiz, Vicki L. and Tiano, Susan, eds. WOMEN ON THE U.S.-MEXICO BORDER: RESPONSES TO CHANGE. Boston, MA: Allen & Unwin, 1987, p. 197-217. English. DESCR: Assimilation; Austin, TX; *Funerals; Sex Roles.

1496 Williams, Norma. The Mexican American family: tradition and change. Dix Hills, NY: General Hall, Inc., c1990. x, 170 p. English. DESCR: Cultural Characteristics; *Family; Religion; *Sex Roles; Working Women.

Cultural Organizations

1497 Gonzales, Sylvia Alicia. Hispanic American voluntary organizations. Westport, CT: Greenwood Press, 1985. xx, 267 p. English. DESCR: Art Organizations and Groups; *Community Organizations; *Directories; Educational Organizations; *Organizations; Political Parties and Organizations; Professional Organizations.

1498 Marin, Christine. La Asociacion Hispano-Americana de Madres y Esposas: Tucson's Mexican American women in World War II. RENATO ROSALDO LECTURE SERIES MONOGRAPH, Vol. 1, (Summer 1985), p. [5]-18. English. DESCR: History; *La Asociacion Hispano-Americana de Madres y Esposas, Tucson, AZ; Organizations; *Tucson, AZ; World War II.

1499 Soberon, Mercedes. La revolucion se trata de amor: Mercedes Soberon. CHISMEARTE, Vol. 1, no. 1 (Fall 1976), p. 14-18. Spanish. DESCR: Art Criticism; Concilio de Arte Popular, Los Angeles, CA; La Mission Media Arts, San Francisco, CA; San Francisco, CA; *Sex Roles; Soberon, Mercedes.

Cultural Pluralism

1500 Cuellar, Israel. Service delivery and mental health services for Chicano elders. IN: Miranda, Manuel and Ruiz, Rene A., eds. CHICANO AGING AND MENTAL HEALTH. Rockville, MD: U.S. Department of Health and Human Services, 1981, p. 185-211. English. DESCR: *Ancianos; Attitudes; Cultural Customs; Language Usage; Mental Health; Mental Health Clinics; Religion; Sex Roles; Spanish Language.

1501 Valladolid-Cuaron, Alicia V.; Sutton, Arlene Vigil; and Renteria, Dorothy. La mujer en el ochenta. LA LUZ, Vol. 8, no. 3 (August, September, 1979), p. 16-17. English. DESCR: Discrimination in Employment.

1502 Zavella, Patricia. Reflections on diversity among Chicanas. FRONTIERS: A JOURNAL OF WOMEN STUDIES, Vol. 12, no. 2 (1991), p. 73-85. English. DESCR: Culture; *Feminism; Identity; Stereotypes.

Cultural Studies

1503 Alarcon, Norma. Chicana feminism: in the tracks of 'the' native woman. CULTURAL STUDIES, Vol. 4, no. 3 (October 1990), p. 248-256. English. DESCR: *Feminism; *Identity; *Indigenismo; Mestizaje; Women.

1504 Quintana, Alvina E. Ana Castillo's THE MIXQUIAHUALA LETTERS: the novelist as ethnographer. IN: Calderon, Hector and Saldivar, Jose David, eds. CRITICISM IN THE BORDERLANDS: STUDIES IN CHICANO LITERATURE, CULTURE, AND IDEOLOGY. Durham, NC: Duke University Press, 1991, p. [72]-83. English. DESCR: Anthropology; Castillo, Ana; *Ethnology; Feminism; Geertz, Clifford; *Literary Criticism; Novel; THE MIXQUIAHUALA LETTERS.

1505 Quintana, Alvina E. Challenge and counter challenge: Chicana literary motifs. AGAINST THE CURRENT, Vol. 2, no. 2 (March, April, 1987), p. 25,28-32. English. DESCR: Anglo Americans; Authors; Cervantes, Lorna Dee; *Feminism; Identity; Literary Criticism; *Literature; Moraga, Cherrie; THERE ARE NO MADMEN HERE; Valdes, Gina; Women.

1506 Quintana, Alvina E. Chicana literary motifs: challenge and counter-challenge. IMAGES: ETHNIC STUDIES OCCASIONAL PAPERS SERIES, (Fall 1986), p. 24-41. English. DESCR: Anglo Americans; Authors; Cervantes, Lorna Dee; *Feminism; *Identity; *Literary Criticism; Literature; Moraga, Cherrie; THERE ARE NO MADMEN HERE; Valdes, Gina; Women.

1507 Quintana, Alvina E. Politics, representation and the emergence of a Chicana aesthetic. CULTURAL STUDIES, Vol. 4, no. 3 (October 1990), p. 257-263. English. DESCR: Anzaldua, Gloria; *Authors; Chavez, Denise; Chicana Studies; Cisneros, Sandra; Feminism; *Literary Criticism.

Culture

1508 Alarcon, Norma. What kind of lover have you made me, Mother?: towards a theory of Chicanas' feminism and cultural identity through poetry. IN: McCluskey, Audrey T., ed. WOMEN OF COLOR: PERSPECTIVES ON FEMINISM AND IDENTITY. Bloomington, IN: Women's Studies Program, Indiana University, 1985, p. 85-110. English. DESCR: Brinson-Pineda, Barbara; Cervantes, Lorna Dee; Cisneros, Sandra; *Feminism; Identity; *Literary Criticism; Mora, Pat; Moraga, Cherrie; *Poetry; Tafolla, Carmen; Vigil-Pinon, Evangelina; Villanueva, Alma.

1509 Arce, Carlos H. and Abney-Guardado, Armando J. Demographic and cultural correlates of Chicano intermarriage. CALIFORNIA SOCIOLOGIST, Vol. 5, no. 2 (Summer 1982), p. 41-58. English. DESCR: Cultural Characteristics; *Intermarriage; Population; Social Psychology.

1510 Baca Zinn, Maxine. Chicano family research: conceptual distortions and alternative directions. JOURNAL OF ETHNIC STUDIES, Vol. 7, no. 3 (Fall 1979), p. 59-71. English. DESCR: Cultural Characteristics; *Family; Research Methodology; Stereotypes.

Culture (cont.)

1511 Bach-y-Rita, George. The Mexican-American: religious and cultural influences. IN: Becerra, Rosina M., et al., eds. MENTAL HEALTH AND HISPANIC AMERICANS: CLINICAL PERSPECTIVES. New York: Grune & Stratton, 1982, p. 29-40. English. DESCR: Catholic Church; Cultural Characteristics; Language Usage; Machismo; *Mental Health; Psychotherapy; Religion.

1512 Canino, Glorisa. The Hispanic woman: sociocultural influences on diagnoses and treatment. IN: Becerra, Rosina M., et al., eds. MENTAL HEALTH AND HISPANIC AMERICANS: CLINICAL PERSPECTIVES. New York: Grune & Stratton, 1982, p. 117-133. English. DESCR: Assimilation; Cultural Characteristics; *Depression (Psychological); Family; Feminism; Mental Health; Population; Sex Roles.

1513 Manzanedo, Hector Garcia; Walters, Esperanza Garcia; and Lorig, Kate R. Health and illness perceptions of the Chicana. IN: Melville, Margarita B., ed. TWICE A MINORITY. St. Louis, MO: Mosby, 1980, p. 191-207. English. DESCR: Cultural Characteristics; *Medical Care; Public Health; Sex Roles; Values.

1514 Mason, Theresa Hope. Experience and meaning: an interpretive study of family and gender ideologies among a sample of Mexican-American women of two generations. Thesis (Ph.D.)--University of Texas, Austin, 1987. 406 p. English. DESCR: *Age Groups; Extended Family; *Family; *Sex Roles.

1515 Mesa-Bains, Amalia. A study of the influence of culture on the development of identity among a group of Chicana artists. Thesis (Ph.D.)--Wright Institute Graduate School of Psychology, 1983. 219 p. English. DESCR: *Artists; *Identity.

1516 Rocard, Marcienne. The remembering voice in Chicana literature. THE AMERICAS REVIEW, Vol. 14, no. 3-4 (Fall Winter, 1986), p. 150-159. English. DESCR: *Literature.

1517 Salgado de Snyder, Nelly. The role of ethnic loyalty among Mexican immigrant women. HISPANIC JOURNAL OF BEHAVIORAL SCIENCES, Vol. 9, no. 3 (September 1987), p. 287-298. English. DESCR: Acculturation; *Identity; Immigrants; Mental Health; Mexico; *Women.

1518 Spitta, Silvia D. Literary transculturation in Latin America. Thesis (Ph.D.)--University of Oregon, 1989. 184 p. English. DESCR: Anzaldua, Gloria; Arguedos, Jose Maria; Authors; Cultural Characteristics; *Intergroup Relations; *Latin American Literature; Spanish Influence.

1519 Votaw, Carmen Delgado. Cultural influences on Hispanic feminism. AGENDA, Vol. 11, no. 4 (1981), p. 44-49. Bilingual. DESCR: *Feminism; Identity; Values.

1520 Zavella, Patricia. Reflections on diversity among Chicanas. FRONTIERS: A JOURNAL OF WOMEN STUDIES, Vol. 12, no. 2 (1991), p. 73-85. English. DESCR: *Cultural Pluralism; *Feminism; Identity; Stereotypes.

Culture of Poverty Model

1521 Yinger, Milton J. Assimilation in the United States: the Mexican-Americans. IN: Conner, Walker, ed. MEXICAN-AMERICANS IN COMPARATIVE PERSPECTIVE. Washington, DC: Urban Institute Press, 1985, p. 30-55. English. DESCR: Acculturation; *Assimilation; Identity; Intermarriage.

Cunningham, Veronica

1522 Cunningham, Veronica and Binder, Wolfgang. [Interview with] Veronica Cunningham. IN: Binder, Wolfgang, ed. PARTIAL AUTOBIOGRAPHIES: INTERVIEWS WITH TWENTY CHICANO POETS. Erlangen, W. Germany: Verlag Palm & Enke, 1985, p. 86-92. English. DESCR: Authors; Autobiography; Poetry.

1523 Sanchez, Rita. Chicana writer breaking out of the silence. DE COLORES, Vol. 3, no. 3 (1977), p. 31-37. English. DESCR: Authors; Castaneda Shular, Antonia; Correa, Viola; Hernandez, Barbara; *Literary Criticism; Mendoza, Rita; *Poetry.

1524 Zamora, Bernice. Archetypes in Chicana poetry. DE COLORES, Vol. 4, no. 3 (1978), p. 43-52. English. DESCR: Cervantes, Lorna Dee; "Declaration on a Day of Little Inspiration" [poem]; Hernandez, Carlota; "I Speak in an Illusion" [poem]; *Literary Criticism; Lucero, Judy A.; Macias, Margarita; Mendoza, Rita; "Para Mi Hijita" [poem]; *Poetry; "Rape Report" [poem]; "The White Line" [poem]; "Working Mother's Song" [poem]; "You Can Only Blame the System for So Long" [poem]; Zamora, Katarina.

Curanderas

1525 Buss, Fran Leeper. La partera: story of a midwife. Ann Arbor, MI: University of Michigan Press, 1980. 140 p.: ill. English. DESCR: Aragon, Jesusita, 1908-; Cultural Customs; Folk Medicine; Herbal Medicine; *Midwives; New Mexico; San Miguel County, NM.

1526 Espin, Oliva M. Spiritual power and the mundane world: Hispanic female healers in urban U.S. communities. WOMEN'S STUDIES QUARTERLY, Vol. 16, no. 3 (Fall 1988), p. 33-47. English. DESCR: Urban Communities.

1527 Mayers, Raymond Sanchez. Use of folk medicine by elderly Mexican-American women. JOURNAL OF DRUG ISSUES, Vol. 19, no. 2 (1989), p. 283-295. English. DESCR: Age Groups; *Ancianos; Curanderismo; Folk Medicine.

1528 Perrone, Bobette; Stockel, H. Henrietta; and Krueger, Victoria. Medicine women, curanderas, and women doctors. Norman, OK: University of Oklahoma Press, c1989. xix, 252 p.:ill. English. DESCR: Aragon, Jesusita, 1908-; *Curanderismo; *Folk Medicine; Herbal Medicine; Herrera, Sabinita; Medical Personnel; Native Americans; *Oral History; Rodriguez, Gregorita; Women.

1529 Rivera, George; Lucero, Aileen; and Regoli, Robert M. Contemporary curanderismo: a study of mental health agency and home clientele of a practicing curandera. ISSUES IN RADICAL THERAPY, Vol. 13, no. 1-2 (Winter, Spring, 1988), p. 52-57. English. DESCR: *Curanderismo; Mental Health; Socioeconomic Factors.

Curanderismo

1530 Macklin, June. "All the good and bad in this world": women, traditional medicine, and Mexican American culture. IN: Melville, Margarita B., ed. TWICE A MINORITY. St. Louis, MO: Mosby, 1980, p. 127-148. English. DESCR: Folk Medicine; Sex Roles.

1531 Mayers, Raymond Sanchez. Use of folk medicine by elderly Mexican-American women. JOURNAL OF DRUG ISSUES, Vol. 19, no. 2 (1989), p. 283-295. English. DESCR: Age Groups; *Ancianos; Curanderas; Folk Medicine.

1532 Perrone, Bobette; Stockel, H. Henrietta; and Krueger, Victoria. Medicine women, curanderas, and women doctors. Norman, OK: University of Oklahoma Press, c1989. xix, 252 p.:ill. English. DESCR: Aragon, Jesusita, 1908-; *Curanderas; *Folk Medicine; Herbal Medicine; Herrera, Sabinita; Medical Personnel; Native Americans; *Oral History; Rodriguez, Gregorita; Women.

1533 Rivera, George; Lucero, Aileen; and Regoli, Robert M. Contemporary curanderismo: a study of mental health agency and home clientele of a practicing curandera. ISSUES IN RADICAL THERAPY, Vol. 13, no. 1-2 (Winter, Spring, 1988), p. 52-57. English. DESCR: Curanderas; Mental Health; Socioeconomic Factors.

Current Population Survey

1534 Bachu, Amara and O'Connell, Martin. Developing current fertility indicators for foreign-born women from the Current Population Survey. REVIEW OF PUBLIC DATA USE, Vol. 12, no. 3 (October 1984), p. 185-195. English. DESCR: *Fertility; Latin America; Mexico; *Surveys; Vital Statistics; Women.

Curriculum

1535 Nieto Gomez de Lazarin, Anna. Un proposito para estudios femeniles de la chicana. REGENERACION, Vol. 2, no. 4 (1975), p. 30, 31-32. English. DESCR: Chicano Studies; *Education; History; Nava, Yolanda; Sexism.

1536 Staudt, Kathleen. Programming women's empowerment: a case from northern Mexico. IN: Ruiz, Vicki L. and Tiano, Susan, eds. WOMEN ON THE U.S.-MEXICO BORDER: RESPONSES TO CHANGE. Boston, MA: Allen & Unwin, 1987, p. 155-173. English. DESCR: Alternative Education; Border Region; Ciudad Juarez, Chihuahua, Mexico; Employment; *Feminism; Organizations; Women.

1537 Winkler, Karen J. Scholars say issues of diversity have "revolutionized" field of Chicano Studies. CHRONICLE OF HIGHER EDUCATION, Vol. 37, no. 4 (September 26, 1990), p. A4-A9. English. DESCR: Chicana Studies; Chicano Studies; *Feminism; Higher Education; Ruiz, Vicki L.; Saragoza, Alex M.

Curriculum Materials

1538 Heathcote, Olivia D. Sex stereotyping in Mexican reading primers. READING TEACHER, Vol. 36, no. 2 (November 1982), p. 158-165. English. DESCR: Comparative Education; Mexico; Primary School Education; *Sex Stereotypes.

Dallas Museum of Art

1539 Stevens, Joanne Darsey. Santos by twentieth-century santeras: continuation of a traditional art form. Thesis (Ph.D.)--University of Texas at Dallas, 1986. 259 p. English. DESCR: Art History; *Artists; New Mexico; *Santos.

Dana, Richard Henry

1540 Castaneda, Antonia I. The political economy of nineteenth century stereotypes of Californianas. IN: Del Castillo, Adelaida R., ed. BETWEEN BORDERS: ESSAYS ON MEXICANA/CHICANA HISTORY. Encino, CA: Floricanto Press, 1990, p. 213-236. English. DESCR: *California; *Californios; Farnham, Thomas Jefferson; History; LIFE IN CALIFORNIA; *Political Economy; Robinson, Alfred; *Sex Stereotypes; TRAVELS IN CALIFORNIA AND SCENES IN THE PACIFIC OCEAN; TWO YEARS BEFORE THE MAST; Women.

Day Care Centers
USE: Child Care Centers

DAY OF THE SWALLOWS

1541 Castellano, Olivia. Of clarity and the moon: a study of two women in rebellion. DE COLORES, Vol. 3, no. 3 (1977), p. 25-30. English. DESCR: *Literary Criticism; Portillo Trambley, Estela; "The Apple Trees".

1542 Dewey, Janice. Dona Josefa: bloodpulse of transition and change. IN: Horno-Delgado, Asuncion, et al., eds. BREAKING BOUNDARIES: LATINA WRITING AND CRITICAL READINGS. Amherst, MA: University of Massachusetts Press, c1989, p. 39-47. English. DESCR: Garcia-Lorca, Federico; LA CASA DE BERNARDA ALBA; Literary Characters; Literary Criticism; *Portillo Trambley, Estela.

1543 Melville, Margarita B. Female and male in Chicano theatre. IN: Kanellos, Nicolas, ed. HISPANIC THEATRE IN THE UNITED STATES. Houston, TX: Arte Publico Press, 1984, p. 71-79. English. DESCR: BERNABE; BRUJERIAS [play]; Cultural Characteristics; Duarte-Clark, Rodrigo; EL JARDIN [play]; Family; Feminism; Macias, Ysidro; Morton, Carlos; Portillo Trambley, Estela; RANCHO HOLLYWOOD [play]; *Sex Roles; *Teatro; THE ULTIMATE PENDEJADA [play]; Valdez, Luis; Women Men Relations.

1544 Salazar Parr, Carmen. La Chicana in literature. IN: Garcia, Eugene E., et al., eds. CHICANO STUDIES: A MULTIDISCIPLINARY APPROACH. New York: Teachers College Press, 1984, p. 120-134. English. DESCR: Literary Characters; Literary Criticism; *Literature; Portillo Trambley, Estela; Stereotypes; Teatro; "The Trees" [short story].

1545 Vallejos, Tomas. Estela Portillo Trambley's fictive search for paradise. FRONTIERS: A JOURNAL OF WOMEN STUDIES, Vol. 5, no. 2 (1980),p. 54-58. Also IN: Lattin, Vernon E., ed. CONTEMPORARY CHICANO FICTION. Binghamton, NY: Bilingual Press/Editorial Bilingue, 1986, p. 269-277. English. DESCR: *Literary Criticism; Novel; Portillo Trambley, Estela; RAIN OF SCORPIONS AND OTHER WRITINGS.

de Cardenas, Isidra T.

1546 Lomas, Clara. Mexican precursors of Chicana feminist writing. IN: National Association for Chicano Studies. ESTUDIOS CHICANOS AND THE POLITICS OF COMMUNITY. [S.l.]: National Association for Chicano Studies, c1989, p. [149]-160. English. DESCR: Authors; *Feminism; Idar, Jovita; *Journalists; Literature; *Mexican Revolution - 1910-1920; Newspapers; Ramirez, Sara Estela; Villarreal, Andrea; Villegas de Magnon, Leonor.

de Hoyos, Angela

1547 Aguilar-Henson, Marcella. The multi-faceted poetic world of Angela de Hoyos. Austin, TX: Relampago Books Press, 1985, c1982. 81 p. English. DESCR: ARISE CHICANO; *Authors; CHICANO POEMS FOR THE BARRIO; GATA POEMS; GOODBYE TO SILENCE; Language Usage; *Literary Criticism; *Poetry; SELECTED POEMS/SELECCIONES; YO, MUJER.

1548 de Hoyos, Angela and Binder, Wolfgang. [Interview with] Angela de Hoyos. IN: Binder, Wolfgang, ed. PARTIAL AUTOBIOGRAPHIES: INTERVIEWS WITH TWENTY CHICANO POETS. Erlangen, W. Germany: Verlag Palm & Enke, 1985, p. 109-116. English. DESCR: Authors; Autobiography; Poetry.

1549 Lindstrom, Naomi. Four representative Hispanic women poets of Central Texas: a portrait of plurality. THIRD WOMAN, Vol. 2, no. 1 (1984), p. 64-70. English. DESCR: Beltran, Beatriz; Jimenez, Magali; *Literary Criticism; Poetry; Tafolla, Carmen; Texas.

1550 Ramos, Luis Arturo. [Hoyos, Angela de]. IN: Martinez, Julio A. and Lomeli, Francisco A. eds. CHICANO LITERATURE: A REFERENCE GUIDE. Westwood, CT: Greenwood Press, 1985, p. 260-265. English. DESCR: Authors; Biography Literary Criticism.

De la Cruz, Jessie Lopez

1551 Cantarow, Ellen and De la Cruz, Jessie Lopez. Jessie Lopez De la Cruz: the battle for farmworkers' rights. IN: Cantarow, Ellen. MOVING THE MOUNTAIN: WOMEN WORKING FOR SOCIAL CHANGE. Old Westbury, NY: Feminist Press, 1980, p. 94-151. English. DESCR: Agricultural Labor Unions; Chavez, Cesar E.; *Farm Workers; Labor Disputes; Oral History; Parlier, CA; Sex Roles; Strikes and Lockouts; *United Farmworkers of America (UFW).

De la Cruz, Juana Ines

1552 De Ortego y Gasca, Felipe. The Hispanic woman: a humanistic perspective. LA LUZ, Vol. 6, no. 11 (November 1977), p. 7-10. English. DESCR: Dona Ximena; *Essays; History; Mistral, Gabriela; Ortiz de Dominguez, Josefa; *Women Men Relations; *Women's Suffrage.

1553 De Ortego y Gasca, Felipe. The Hispanic woman: a humanistic perspective. LA LUZ, Vol. 8, no. 8 (October, November, 1980), p. 6-9. English. DESCR: Dona Ximena; *Essays; History; Mistral, Gabriela; Ortiz de Dominguez, Josefa; *Women Men Relations; *Women's Suffrage.

1554 Matsuda, Gema. La Chicana organizes: the Comision Femenil Mexicana in perspective. REGENERACION, Vol. 2, no. 4 (1975), p. 25-27. English. DESCR: Bojorquez, Frances; Chicano Movement; *Comsion Femenil Mexicana

Nacional; Flores, Francisca; History; Machismo; Malinche; Prisons; Sex Stereotypes; *Sexism.

De la Torre, Susana

1555 Garcia-Camarillo, Mia. Mujeres en el movimiento: platica de las mujeres de CARACOL. CARACOL, Vol. 3, no. 1 (September 1976), p. 10-11. English. DESCR: CARACOL: LA REVISTA DE LA RAZA; *Chicano Movement.

de Larios, Dora

1556 Goldman, Shifra M. Mujeres de California: Latin American women artists. IN: Moore, Sylvia, ed. YESTERDAY AND TOMORROW: CALIFORNIA WOMEN ARTISTS. New York, NY: Midmarch Arts Press, c1989, p. 202-229. English. DESCR: *Artists; Baca, Judith F.; Biography; California; Carrasco, Barbara; Cervantez, Yreina; Feminism; Hernandez, Judithe; Lomas Garza, Carmen; Lopez, Yolanda M.; Mesa-Bains, Amalia; Murillo, Patricia; Sanchez, Olivia; Valdez, Patssi; Vallejo Dillaway, Linda; Women; Zamora Lucero, Linda.

De Leon, Josefina

1557 Altars as Folk art. ARRIBA, Vol. 1, no. 1 (July 1980), p. 4. English. DESCR: *Altars; Artists; Folk Art; Religious Art.

Decision Making

1558 Baca Zinn, Maxine. Employment and education of Mexican-American women: the interplay of modernity and ethnicity in eight families. HARVARD EDUCATIONAL REVIEW, Vol. 50, no. 1 (February 1980), p. 47-62. English. DESCR: Acculturation; *Education; *Employment; *Family; Identity; Sex Roles; Social Classes; Values.

1559 Eisen, Marvin. Factors discriminating pregnancy resolution decisions of unmarried adolescents. GENETIC PSYCHOLOGY MONOGRAPHS, Vol. 108, no. 1 (August 1983), p. 69-95. English. DESCR: Abortion; Attitudes; *Fertility; *Single Parents; *Youth.

"Declaration on a Day of Little Inspiration" [poem]

1560 Zamora, Bernice. Archetypes in Chicana poetry. DE COLORES, Vol. 4, no. 3 (1978), p. 43-52. English. DESCR: Cervantes, Lorna Dee; Cunningham, Veronica; Hernandez, Carlota; "I Speak in an Illusion" [poem]; *Literary Criticism; Lucero, Judy A.; Macias, Margarita; Mendoza, Rita; "Para Mi Hijita" [poem]; *Poetry; "Rape Report" [poem]; "The White Line" [poem]; "Working Mother's Song" [poem]; "You Can Only Blame the System for So Long" [poem]; Zamora, Katarina.

Del Castillo, Adelaida R.

1561 Sanchez, Rosaura. The history of Chicanas: a proposal for a materialist perspective. IN: Del Castillo, Adelaida R., ed. BETWEEN BORDERS: ESSAYS ON MEXICANA/CHICANA HISTORY. Encino, CA: Floricanto Press, 1990, p. 1-29. English. DESCR: Apodaca, Maria Linda; *Chicana Studies; Feminism; Historiography; History; Morales, Sylvia; Ruiz, Vicki L.

Del Rio, TX

1562 Canales, Genevieve and Roberts, Robert E. Gender and mental health in the Mexican origin population of South Texas. IN: Rodriguez, Reymund and Coleman, Marion Tolbert, eds. MENTAL HEALTH ISSUES OF THE MEXICAN ORIGIN POPULATION IN TEXAS. Austin, TX: Hogg Foundation for Mental Health, University of Texas, 1987, p. 89-99. English. DESCR: Depression (Psychological); Eagle Pass, TX; Health Education; *Males; *Mental Health; *Sex Roles; South Texas; Surveys.

Delgado, Etta

1563 Venegas, Sybil. The artists and their work--the role of the Chicana artist. CHISMEARTE, Vol. 1, no. 4 (Fall, Winter, 1977), p. 3, 5. English. DESCR: Art Criticism; *Artists; Carrasco, Barbara; Hernandez, Ester; Las Mujeres Muralistas, San Francisco, CA; Mural Art.

Democratic Party

1564 Baca Barragan, Polly; Hamner, Richard; and Guerrero, Lena. [Untitled interview with State Senators (Colorado) Polly Baca-Barragan and Lena Guerrero]. NATIONAL HISPANIC JOURNAL, Vol. 1, no. 2 (Winter 1982), p. 8-11. English. DESCR: Baca Barragan, Polly; Carter, Jimmy (President); Elected Officials; Guerrero, Lena; *Political Parties and Organizations.

1565 Huerta, Dolores. Dolores Huerta talks about Republicans, Cesar, children and her home town. REGENERACION, Vol. 2, no. 4 (1975), p. 20-24. English. DESCR: *Agricultural Labor Unions; *Biography; Chavez, Cesar E.; Community Service Organization, Los Angeles, (CSO); Elected Officials; Flores, Art; Huerta, Dolores; McGovern, George; *Politics; Ramirez, Henry M.; Ross, Fred; Sanchez, Philip V.; United Farmworkers of America (UFW); Working Women.

1566 Huerta, Dolores. Dolores Huerta talks about Republicans, Cesar, children and her home town. IN: Servin, Manuel P. ed. THE MEXICAN AMERICANS: AN AWAKENING MINORITY. 2nd ed. Beverly Hills, CA: Glencoe Press, 1974, p. 283-294. English. DESCR: *Agricultural Labor Unions; *Biography; Chavez, Cesar E.; Community Service Organization, Los Angeles, (CSO); Elected Officials; Flores, Art; Huerta, Dolores; McGovern, George; *Politics; Ramirez, Henry M.; Ross, Fred; Sanchez, Philip V.; United Farmworkers of America (UFW); Working Women.

1567 Mendoza, Hope Schecter and Chall, Malca. Activist in the labor movement, the Democratic Party, and the Mexican-American community: an interview. Berkeley, CA: Regional Oral History Office, Bancroft Library, University of California, Berkeley, 1980. xii, 170 p.: ill. English. DESCR: *Biography; Chavez Ravine, Los Angeles, CA; Church, Frank; Community Organizations; Community Service Organization, Los Angeles, (CSO); Elections; Garment Industry; Industrial Workers; *Labor Unions; Leadership; Mendoza, Hope Schecter; Snyder, Elizabeth; Warschaw, Carmen.

Demography
USE: Population

Depression (Psychological)

1568 Balkwell, Carolyn Ann. Widowhood: its impact on morale and optimism among older persons of three ethnic groups. Thesis (Ph.D.)--University of Georgia, 1981. 170 p. English. DESCR: *Ancianos; Anglo Americans; Blacks; Ethnic Groups; Los Angeles County, CA; *Mental Health; Widowhood; *Women.

1569 Canales, Genevieve and Roberts, Robert E. Gender and mental health in the Mexican origin population of South Texas. IN: Rodriguez, Reymund and Coleman, Marion Tolbert, eds. MENTAL HEALTH ISSUES OF THE MEXICAN ORIGIN POPULATION IN TEXAS. Austin, TX: Hogg Foundation for Mental Health, University of Texas, 1987, p. 89-99. English. DESCR: Del Rio, TX; Eagle Pass, TX; Health Education; *Males; *Mental Health; *Sex Roles; South Texas; Surveys.

1570 Canino, Glorisa. The Hispanic woman: sociocultural influences on diagnoses and treatment. IN: Becerra, Rosina M., et al., eds. MENTAL HEALTH AND HISPANIC AMERICANS: CLINICAL PERSPECTIVES. New York: Grune & Stratton, 1982, p. 117-138. English. DESCR: Assimilation; Cultural Characteristics; Culture; Family; Feminism; Mental Health; Population; Sex Roles.

1571 Dugan, Anna Baziak. Kin, social supports, and depression among women of Mexican heritage who are single parents. Thesis (Ph.D.)--Bryn Mawr College, 1982. vii, 188 p. English. DESCR: Detroit, MI; Family; *Natural Support Systems; *Single Parents.

1572 Enguidanos-Clark, Gloria M. Acculturative stress and its contribution to the development of depression in Hispanic women. Thesis (Ph.D.)--Wright Institute, Berkeley, 1986. 198 p. English. DESCR: *Acculturation; Immigrants; Mental Health; *Stress.

1573 Golding, Jacqueline M. Division of household labor, strain, and depressive symptoms among Mexican Americans and non-Hispanic whites. PSYCHOLOGY OF WOMEN QUARTERLY, Vol. 14, no. 1 (March 1990), p. 103-117. English. DESCR: Anglo Americans; Comparative Psychology; Domestic Work; Employment; Identity; *Sex Roles; Women.

1574 Groessl, Patricia Ann. Depression and anxiety in postmenopausal women: a study of Black, white, and Hispanic women. Thesis (Ed.D.)--Western Michigan University, 1987. 87 p. English. DESCR: Anglo Americans; Blacks; Menopause; Michigan; Stress; Women.

1575 Markides, Kyriakos S. and Farrell, Janice. Marital status and depression among Mexican Americans. SOCIAL PSYCHIATRY, Vol. 20, no. 2 (1985), p. 86-91. English. DESCR: Divorce; *Marriage; *Mental Health.

1576 Roberts, Robert E. and Roberts, Catharine Ramsay. Marriage, work and depressive symptoms among Mexican Americans. HISPANIC JOURNAL OF BEHAVIORAL SCIENCES, Vol. 4, no. 2 (June 1982), p. 199-221. English. DESCR: Employment; Marriage; *Mental Health.

1577 Rodriguez, Rogelio E. Psychological distress among Mexican-American women as a reaction to the new immigration law. Thesis (Ph.D.)--Loyola University of Chicago, 1989. 87 p. English. DESCR: Immigrants; *Immigration Law and Legislation; Immigration Reform and Control Act of 1986; *Mental Health; Mexico; Stress; Undocumented Workers; Women.

Depression (Psychological)
(cont.)

1578 Saenz, Rogelio; Goudy, Willis J.; and
Lorenz, Frederick O. The effects of
employment and marital relations on
depression among Mexican American women.
JOURNAL OF MARRIAGE AND THE FAMILY, Vol. 51,
no. 1 (February 1989), p. 239-251. English.
DESCR: Domestic Work; *Employment; Feminism;
*Marriage; Women Men Relations; Working
Women.

1579 Salgado de Snyder, Nelly. Factors associated
with acculturative stress and depressive
symptomatology among married Mexican
immigrant women. PSYCHOLOGY OF WOMEN
QUARTERLY, Vol. 11, no. 4 (December 1987),
p. 475-488. English. DESCR: *Acculturation;
*Immigrants; Mental Health; Mexico; *Stress;
Women.

1580 Salgado de Snyder, Nelly; Cervantes, Richard
C.; and Padilla, Amado M. Gender and ethnic
differences in psychosocial stress and
generalized distress among Hispanics. SEX
ROLES, Vol. 22, no. 7-8 (April, 1990), p.
441-453. English. DESCR: Anglo Americans;
Central Americans; *Comparative Psychology;
Hispanic Stress Inventory (HSI);
*Immigrants; Immigration; *Sex Roles;
*Stress; Women.

1581 Salgado de Snyder, Nelly. Mexican immigrant
women: the relationship of ethnic loyalty
and social support to acculturative stress
and depressive symptomatology. Los Angeles,
CA: Spanish Speaking Mental Health Research
Center, 1987. 73 p. English. DESCR:
*Acculturation; Identity; *Immigrants;
Natural Support Systems; *Stress; Women.

1582 Vallez, Andrea. Acculturation, social
support, stress and adjustment of the
Mexican American college woman. Thesis
(Ph.D.)--University of Colorado at Boulder,
1984. 121 p. English. DESCR: *Acculturation;
*Colleges and Universities; Higher
Education; Natural Support Systems; Southern
California; Stress; *Students.

1583 Vega, William A.; Warheit, George; and
Meinhardt, Kenneth. Marital disruption and
the prevalence of depressive symptomatology
among Anglos and Mexican Americans. JOURNAL
OF MARRIAGE AND THE FAMILY, Vol. 46, no. 4
(November 1984), p. 817-824. English.
DESCR: Anglo Americans; *Divorce; *Marriage;
*Mental Health; Socioeconomic Factors.

1584 Vega, William A.; Kolody, Bohdan; and Valle,
Juan Ramon. Migration and mental health: an
empirical test of depression risk factors
among immigrant Mexican women. INTERNATIONAL
MIGRATION REVIEW, Vol. 21, no. 3 (Fall
1987), p. 512-530. English. DESCR:
Acculturation; *Immigrants; Immigration;
*Mental Health; Migration; Stress;
Undocumented Workers; Women.

1585 Vega, William A.; Kolody, Bohdan; and Valle,
Juan Ramon. The relationship of marital
status, confidant support, and depression
among Mexican immigrant women. JOURNAL OF
MARRIAGE AND THE FAMILY, Vol. 48, no. 3
(August 1986), p. 597-605. English. DESCR:
*Immigrants; Low Income; *Marriage; San
Diego County, CA; Stress; Women.

1586 Vega, William A., et al. Depressive symptoms
and their correlates among immigrant Mexican
women in the United States. SOCIAL SCIENCE &
MEDICINE, Vol. 22, no. 6 (1986), p. 645-652.
English. DESCR: *Immigrants; *Mental Health;
Public Health; San Diego, CA.

1587 Walker, Todd. The relationship of nativity,
social support and depression to the home
environment among Mexican-American women.
Thesis (Ph.D.)--University of Houston, 1989.
123 p. English. DESCR: Acculturation; Avance
Parent-Child Education Program, San Antonio,
TX; Children; *Immigrants; Natural Support
Systems; *Parenting; Women.

1588 Zavala Martinez, Iris Zoraida. Depression
among women of Mexican descent. Thesis
(Ph.D.)--University of Massachusetts, 1984.
295 p. English. DESCR: Los Angeles, CA;
Mental Health.

1589 Zayas, Luis H. Toward an understanding of
suicide risks in young Hispanic females.
JOURNAL OF ADOLESCENT RESEARCH, Vol. 2, no.
1 (Spring 1987), p. 1-11. English. DESCR:
Acculturation; Cubanos; Cultural
Characteristics; Mental Health; Puerto
Ricans; *Suicide; *Women; *Youth.

DESPUES DEL TERREMOTO [film]

1590 Fregoso, Rosa Linda. La quinceanera of
Chicana counter aesthetics. CENTRO BULLETIN,
Vol. 3, no. 1 (Winter 1990, 1991), p.
[87]-91. English. DESCR: *AGUEDA MARTINEZ
[film]; ANIMA [film]; *CHICANA! [film];
Espana, Frances Salome; Feminism; *Films;
Morales, Sylvia; Portillo, Lourdes; Vasquez,
Esperanza.

Detroit, MI

1591 Dugan, Anna Baziak. Kin, social supports,
and depression among women of Mexican
heritage who are single parents. Thesis
(Ph.D.)--Bryn Mawr College, 1982. vii, 188
p. English. DESCR: *Depression
(Psychological); Family; *Natural Support
Systems; *Single Parents.

Deutsch, Sarah

1592 Acuna, Rodolfo. The struggles of class and
gender: current research in Chicano Studies
[review essay]. JOURNAL OF AMERICAN ETHNIC
HISTORY, Vol. 8, no. 2 (Spring 1989), p.
134-138. English. DESCR: *CANNERY WOMEN,
CANNERY LIVES; *CHICANO ETHNICITY; Keefe,
Susan E.; Literature Reviews; *NO SEPARATE
REFUGE; Padilla, Amado M.; Ruiz, Vicki L.;
*WOMEN'S WORK AND CHICANO FAMILIES; Zavella,
Pat.

Diabetes

1593 Henderson, Nancy. Perinatal service needs of
Hispanic women with diabetes. Thesis
(M.S.)--California State University, Long
Beach, 1987. 79 p. English. DESCR:
Fertility; Medical Care; *Social Services;
*Stress.

1594 Swinney, Gloria Luyas. The biocultural
context of low-income Mexican-American women
with type II non-insulin dependent diabetes
and its implications for health care
delivery. Thesis (Ph.D.)--University of
Texas, Austin, 1988. 277 p. English. DESCR:
Low Income; *Medical Care; Non-insulin
Dependent Diabetes Mellitus (NIDDM).

Diaz, Elena

1595 Chapa, Olivia Evey. Mujeres por la Raza
     unida. CARACOL, Vol. 1, no. 2 (October
     1974), p. 3-5. English. **DESCR:** Canales,
     Alma; Cotera, Marta P.; La Raza Unida Party;
     *Political Parties and Organizations; REPORT
     OF FIRST CONFERENCIA DE MUJERES POR LA RAZA
     UNIDA PARTY.

Dictionaries

1596 Meier, Matt S. Mexican American biographies:
     a historical dictionary, 1836-1987.
     Westport, CT: Greenwood Press, 1988. ix, 270
     p. English. **DESCR:** *Biography.

Dietetics
     USE: Nutrition

**DIOSA Y HEMBRA: THE HISTORY AND HERITAGE OF
CHICANAS IN THE U.S.**

1597 Candelaria, Cordelia. Six reference works on
     Mexican-American women: a review essay.
     FRONTIERS: A JOURNAL OF WOMEN STUDIES, Vol.
     5, no. 2 (Summer 1980), p. 75-80. English.
     DESCR: ESSAYS ON LA MUJER; LA CHICANA: THE
     MEXICAN AMERICAN WOMAN; *Literature Reviews;
     MEXICAN WOMEN IN THE UNITED STATES:
     STRUGGLES PAST AND PRESENT; THE CHICANA: A
     COMPREHENSIVE BIBLIOGRAPHIC STUDY; TWICE A
     MINORITY: MEXICAN-AMERICAN WOMEN.

Directories

1598 Amaro, Hortensia. Hispanic women in
     psychology: a resource directory.
     Washington, DC: American Psychological
     Association, 1984. ii, 41 p. English.
     DESCR: *Psychology; *Women.

1599 Castillo, Sylvia. A guide to Hispanic
     women's resources: a perspective on
     networking among Hispanic women. CALIFORNIA
     WOMEN, (December 1983), p. 2-6. English.
     DESCR: *Organizations; Professional
     Organizations; Women.

1600 Gonzales, Sylvia Alicia. Hispanic American
     voluntary organizations. Westport, CT:
     Greenwood Press, 1985. xx, 267 p. English.
     DESCR: Art Organizations and Groups;
     *Community Organizations; Cultural
     Organizations; Educational Organizations;
     *Organizations; Political Parties and
     Organizations; Professional Organizations.

1601 Soto, Shirlene Ann. The emerging Chicana: a
     review of the journals. SOUTHWEST ECONOMY
     AND SOCIETY, Vol. 2, no. 1 (October,
     November, 1976), p. 39-45. English. **DESCR:**
     Journals; *Literature Reviews.

1602 Varela, Vivian. Hispanic women's resource
     guide. COMMONGROUND MAGAZINE, Vol. 1, no. 3
     (May 1983), p. 14-15. English. **DESCR:**
     *Organizations.

DIRECTORY OF HISPANIC WOMEN

1603 Espinosa, Ann. Hispanas: our resourses [sic]
     for the eighties. LA LUZ, Vol. 8, no. 4
     (October, November, 1979), p. 10-13.
     English. **DESCR:** Baca Barragan, Polly; *Civil
     Rights; Comision Femenil Mexicana Nacional;
     Discrimination in Education; Elected
     Officials; Hernandez, Irene; Lacayo,
     Carmela; Lujan, Josie; Mexican American
     Women's National Association (MANA);
     Montanez Davis, Grace; Moreno, Olga; Mujeres
     Latinas en Accion (M.L.A.); National
     Conference of Puerto Rican Women, Inc.
     (NCOPRW); Organizations; Rangel, Irma.

Discrimination

1604 Aragon de Valdez, Theresa. Organizing as a
     political tool for the Chicana. FRONTIERS: A
     JOURNAL OF WOMEN STUDIES, Vol. 5, no. 2
     (Summer 1980), p. 7-13. English. **DESCR:**
     Feminism; *Leadership; Mexican American
     Legal Defense and Educational Fund (MALDEF);
     Social History and Conditions;
     Sterilization.

1605 Barton, Amy E. Women farmworkers: their
     workplace and capitalist patriarchy. REVISTA
     MUJERES, Vol. 3, no. 2 (June 1986), p.
     11-13. English. **DESCR:** Capitalism; *Farm
     Workers; Sexism.

1606 Cantu, Norma. Women then and now: an
     analysis of the Adelita image versus the
     Chicana as political writer and philosopher.
     IN: Cordova, Teresa, et al., eds. CHICANA
     VOICES. Austin, TX: Center for Mexican
     American Studies, 1986, p. 8-10. English.
     DESCR: Chicano Studies; Higher Education;
     *La Adelita; Stereotypes.

1607 Chacon, Maria A.; Cohen, Elizabeth G.; and
     Strover, Sharon. Chicanas and Chicanos:
     barriers to progress in higher education.
     IN: Olivas, Michael A., ed. LATINO COLLEGE
     STUDENTS. New York: Teachers College Press,
     1986, p. 296-324. English. **DESCR:** Community
     Colleges; Dropouts; *Higher Education;
     Stress; Surveys.

1608 Cummings, Michele and Cummings, Scott.
     Family planning among the urban poor: sexual
     politics and social policy. FAMILY
     RELATIONS, Vol. 32, no. 1 (January 1983), p.
     47-58. English. **DESCR:** Anglo Americans;
     Blacks; *Family Planning; Low Income;
     *Stereotypes.

1609 Diehl, Paula and Saavedra, Lupe. Hispanas in
     the year of the woman: many voices. AGENDA,
     (Winter 1976), p. 14-21. English. **DESCR:**
     *Feminism; International Women's Year World
     Conference (1975: Mexico City); Mexico City.

1610 Flores, Francisca. Equality. REGENERACION,
     Vol. 2, no. 3 (1973), p. 4-5. English.
     DESCR: Anglo Americans; Chicano Movement;
     Elected Officials; Feminism; Income;
     *Machismo; *Working Women.

1611 Flores, Francisca. A reaction to discussions
     on the Talmadge Amendment to the Social
     Security Act. ENCUENTRO FEMENIL, Vol. 1, no.
     2 (1974), p. 13-14. English. **DESCR:** *Chicana
     Welfare Rights Organization; Child Care
     Centers; Feminism; Income; *Social Security
     Act; Social Services; *Talmadge Amendment to
     the Social Security Act, 1971; Welfare;
     Working Women.

1612 Flores, Francisca. A reaction to discussions
     on the Talmadge Amendment to the Social
     Security Act. REGENERACION, Vol. 2, no. 3
     (1973), p. 16. English. **DESCR:** *Chicana
     Welfare Rights Organization; Child Care
     Centers; Feminism; Income; *Social Security
     Act; Social Services; *Talmadge Amendment to
     the Social Security Act, 1971; Welfare;
     Working Women.

1613 Garcia, Alma M. Studying Chicanas: bringing
     women into the frame of Chicano Studies. IN:
     Cordova, Teresa, et al., eds. CHICANA
     VOICES. Austin, TX: Center for Mexican
     American Studies, 1986, p. 19-29. English.
     DESCR: Chicana Studies; *Chicano Studies;
     Labor Supply and Market; Literature Reviews.

Discrimination (cont.)

1614 Glenn, Evelyn Nakano. Racial ethnic women's labor: the intersection of race, gender and class oppression. REVIEW OF RADICAL POLITICAL ECONOMY, Vol. 17, no. 3 (Fall 1985), p. 86-108. English. DESCR: Asian Americans; Blacks; *Feminism; Laboring Classes; *Marxism; Sexism; Social Classes; Women; Working Women.

1615 Gonzales, Sylvia Alicia. The Chicana perspective: a design for self-awareness. IN: Trejo, Arnulfo D., ed. THE CHICANOS: AS WE SEE OURSELVES. Tucson, AZ: University of Arizona Press, 1979, p. 81-99. English. DESCR: CHICANAS SPEAK OUT; Chicano Movement; Feminism; Identity; Machismo; Madsen, William; *Mexican Revolution - 1910-1920; Mexico; Sex Roles; THE MEXICAN-AMERICANS OF SOUTH TEXAS; Vidal, Mirta.

1616 Hogeland, Chris and Rosen, Karen. Dreams lost, dreams found: undocumented women in the land of opportunity. San Francisco, CA: Coalition for Immigrant and Refugee Rights and Services, c1991. 153 p. English. DESCR: *Battered Women; *Coalition for Immigrant and Refugee Rights and Services, Immigrant Woman's Task Force; Immigrants; *San Francisco Bay Area; Sex Roles; Sexism; Social Services; Undocumented Workers; Violence; Women; Women Men Relations.

1617 Longeaux y Vasquez, Enriqueta. The woman of La Raza. REGENERACION, Vol. 2, no. 4 (1975) p. 34-36. English. DESCR: Child Care Centers; Gallo, Juana; Housing; La Adelita; Machismo; Sex Roles; *Social History and Conditions; Working Women.

1618 Longeaux y Vasquez, Enriqueta. The woman of La Raza. IN: Valdez, Luis and Steiner, Stan. eds. AZTLAN: AN ANTHOLOGY OF MEXICAN AMERICAN LITERATURE. New York: Vintage Books, 1972, p. 272-273. Also IN: Salinas, Luis Omar and Faderman, Lillian, compilers. FROM THE BARRIO: A CHICANO ANTHOLOGY. San Francisco, CA: Canfield Press, 1973, p. 20-24. English. DESCR: Child Care Centers; Gallo, Juana; Housing; La Adelita; Machismo; Sex Roles; *Social History and Conditions; Working Women.

1619 Martinez, Diana. The double bind. AGENDA, (Summer 1976), p. 10-11. English. DESCR: Careers; *Sexism.

1620 Matute-Bianchi, Maria Eugenia. A Chicana in academe. WOMEN'S STUDIES QUARTERLY, Vol. 10, no. 1 (Spring 1982), p. 14-17. English. DESCR: *Higher Education; Matute-Bianchi, Maria Eugenia; Sex Roles; Sexism.

1621 Medina Gonzales, Esther. Sisterhood. LA LUZ, Vol. 4, no. 5 (September, October, 1975), p. 7. English. DESCR: *Attitudes; *Sexism.

1622 Mindiola, Tatcho, Jr. The cost of being a Mexican female worker in the 1970 Houston labor market. AZTLAN, Vol. 11, no. 2 (Fall 1980), p. 231-247. English. DESCR: *Discrimination in Employment; Houston, TX; Labor Supply and Market; Working Women.

1623 Nieto Gomez de Lazarin, Anna. The Chicana: perspectives for education. ENCUENTRO FEMENIL, Vol. 1, no. 1 (Spring 1973), p. 34-61. English. DESCR: Colleges and Universities; Discrimination in Education; *Education; Family; Identity; Sexism.

1624 Nieto Gomez de Lazarin, Anna. La femenista [sic]. ENCUENTRO FEMENIL, Vol. 1, no. 2 (1974), p. 34-47. English. DESCR: Anglo Americans; Chicana Caucus, National Women's Political Caucus; Chicano Movement; Conferences and Meetings; *Feminism; National Women's Political Caucus (February 9-11, 1973: Houston, TX); *Sexism; Women.

1625 Norris, Henry E. AIDS, women and reproductive rights. MULTICULTURAL INQUIRY AND RESEARCH ON AIDS (MIRA) NEWSLETTER, Vol. 1, no. 3 (Summer 1987), p. [2-3]. English. DESCR: Abortion; *AIDS (Disease); Center for Constitutional Rights; Preventative Medicine; Women.

1626 Peralta Aguilar, Linda. Unequal opportunity and the Chicana. LA LUZ, Vol. 1, no. 5 (September 1972), p. 52. English. DESCR: Discrimination in Employment; *Employment; *Feminism.

1627 Peralta Aguilar, Linda. Unequal opportunity and the Chicana. REGENERACION, Vol. 2, no. 4 (1975), p. 45-46. English. DESCR: *Discrimination in Employment; *Employment; Feminism.

1628 Peralta Aguilar, Linda. Unequal opportunity and the Chicana. LA LUZ, Vol. 6, no. 1 (January 1977), p. 29-30. English. DESCR: Discrimination in Employment; *Employment; *Feminism.

1629 Robinson, Bea Vasquez. Are we racist? Are we sexist? AGENDA, (Winter 1976), p. 23-24. English. DESCR: Conferences and Meetings; Feminism; International Women's Year World Conference (1975: Mexico City); National Chicana Coalition; *Sexism.

1630 Saavedra-Vela, Pilar. Hispanic women in double jeopardy. AGENDA, Vol. 7, no. 6 (November, December, 1977), p. 4-7. English. DESCR: Conferences and Meetings; Houston, TX; National Women's Conference (November, 1977: Houston, TX); *Sexism.

1631 Sanchez, Corina. Higher education y la Chicana? ENCUENTRO FEMENIL, Vol. 1, no. 1 (Spring 1973), p. 27-33. English. DESCR: Discrimination in Education; *Higher Education; Identity; Sexism.

1632 Sierra, Christine Marie. The university setting reinforces inequality. IN: Cordova, Teresa, et al., eds. CHICANA VOICES. Austin, TX: Center for Mexican American Studies, 1986, p. 5-7. English. DESCR: Discrimination in Education; Higher Education.

1633 Sosa Riddell, Adaljiza. Background: a critical overview on Chicanas/Latinas and public policies. IN: Sosa Riddell, Adaljiza, ed. POLICY DEVELOPMENT: CHICANA/LATINA SUMMER RESEARCH INSTITUTE. Davis, CA: [Chicano Studies Program, University of California, Davis, 1989?], p. 2-8. English. DESCR: Educational Administration; *Public Policy; Sexism.

1634 Sternbach, Nancy Saporta. "A deep racial memory of love": the Chicana feminism of Cherrie Moraga. IN: Horno-Delgado, Asuncion, et al., eds. BREAKING BOUNDARIES: LATINA WRITING AND CRITICAL READINGS. Amherst, MA: University of Massachusetts Press, c1989, p. 48-61. English. DESCR: Feminism; Homosexuality; Literary Criticism; *LOVING IN THE WAR YEARS; Machismo; Malinche; *Moraga, Cherrie; Sex Stereotypes; Sexism.

Discrimination (cont.)

1635 Tafolla, Carmen. To split a human: mitos, machos y la mujer chicana. San Antonio, TX: Mexican American Cultural Center, 1985. 115 p.: ill. English. **DESCR:** Education; *Feminism; Films; *Sex Roles; Sex Stereotypes; *Sexism.

1636 Talavera, Esther. Sterilization is not an alternative in family planning. AGENDA, Vol. 7, no. 6 (November, December, 1977), p. 8. English. **DESCR:** Family Planning; Feminism; *Fertility; Medical Care Laws and Legislation; Sterilization.

1637 Zavella, Patricia. The politics of race and gender: organizing Chicana cannery workers in Northern California. IN: Bookman, Ann and Morgen, Sandra, eds. WOMEN AND THE POLITICS OF EMPOWERMENT. Philadelphia, PA: Temple University Press, 1988, p. 202-224. English. **DESCR:** Bay City Cannery Workers Committee; *Canneries; Cannery Workers Committee (CWC); Garcia, Connie; Identity; *Labor Unions; Nationalism; Northern California; Santa Clara Valley, CA; Sex Roles; Sexism; *Working Women.

Discrimination in Education

1638 Achor, Shirley and Morales, Aida G. Chicanas holding doctoral degrees: social reproduction and cultural ecological approaches. ANTHROPOLOGY AND EDUCATION QUARTERLY, Vol. 21, no. 3 (September 1990), p. 269-287. English. **DESCR:** *Academic Achievement; Graduate Schools; *Higher Education; Surveys.

1639 Del Castillo, Adelaida R., et al. An assessment of the status of the education of Hispanic American women. IN: McKenna, Teresa and Ortiz, Flora Ida, eds. THE BROKEN WEB: THE EDUCATIONAL EXPERIENCE OF HISPANIC WOMEN. Claremont, CA: Tomas Rivera Center; Berkeley, CA: Floricanto Press, 1988, p. 3-24. English. **DESCR:** Academic Achievement; Conferences and Meetings; Dropouts; *Education; Higher Education; Public Policy; Research Methodology; The Educational Experience of Hispanic American Women [symposium] (1985: Claremont, CA); *Women.

1640 Espinosa, Ann. Hispanas: our resourses [sic] for the eighties. LA LUZ, Vol. 8, no. 4 (October, November, 1979), p. 10-13. English. **DESCR:** Baca Barragan, Polly; *Civil Rights; Comision Femenil Mexicana Nacional; DIRECTORY OF HISPANIC WOMEN; Elected Officials; Hernandez, Irene; Lacayo, Carmela; Lujan, Josie; Mexican American Women's National Association (MANA); Montanez Davis, Grace; Moreno, Olga; Mujeres Latinas en Accion (M.L.A.); National Conference of Puerto Rican Women, Inc. (NCOPRW); Organizations; Rangel, Irma.

1641 Garcia, Norma Varisto de. Education and the Spanish-speaking woman: a sad reality. NABE JOURNAL, Vol. 1, no. 1 (May 1976), p. 55-60. English. **DESCR:** *Education.

1642 Jaramillo, Mari-Luci. Institutional responsibility in the provision of educational experiences to the Hispanic American female student. IN: McKenna, Teresa and Ortiz, Flora Ida, eds. THE BROKEN WEB: THE EDUCATIONAL EXPERIENCE OF HISPANIC WOMEN. Claremont, CA: Tomaas Rivera Center; Berkeley, CA: Floricanto Press, 1988, p. 25-35. English. **DESCR:** Academic Achievement; Dropouts; *Education; Educational Administration; Enrollment; Higher

Education; Students; *Women.

1643 Mindiola, Tatcho, Jr. and Gutierrez, Armando. Education and discrimination against Mexican Americans in the Southwest. CALIFORNIA SOCIOLOGIST, Vol. 5, no. 2 (Summer 1982), p. 80-97. English. **DESCR:** Research Methodology; Social Classes.

1644 Nieto Gomez de Lazarin, Anna. The Chicana: perspectives for education. ENCUENTRO FEMENIL, Vol. 1, no. 1 (Spring 1973), p. 34-61. English. **DESCR:** Colleges and Universities; Discrimination; *Education; Family; Identity; Sexism.

1645 Nieves-Squires, Sarah. Hispanic women: making their presence on campus less tenuous. Washington, DC: Association of American Colleges, c1991. 14 p. English. **DESCR:** Afro-Hispanics; Colleges and Universities; Cubanos; *Higher Education; Puerto Ricans; *Women.

1646 Quezada, Rosa; Loheyde, Katherine Jones; and Kacmarczyk, Ronald. The Hispanic woman graduate student: barriers to mentoring in higher education. TEXAS TECH JOURNAL OF EDUCATION, Vol. 11, no. 3 (Fall 1984), p. 235-241. English. **DESCR:** *Graduate Schools; *Higher Education; *Mentoring; Students.

1647 Sanchez, Corina. Higher education y la Chicana? ENCUENTRO FEMENIL, Vol. 1, no. 1 (Spring 1973), p. 27-33. English. **DESCR:** Discrimination; *Higher Education; Identity; Sexism.

1648 Sierra, Christine Marie. The university setting reinforces inequality. IN: Cordova, Teresa, et al., eds. CHICANA VOICES. Austin, TX: Center for Mexican American Studies, 1986, p. 5-7. English. **DESCR:** *Discrimination; Higher Education.

1649 Tienda, Marta. Sex, ethnicity and Chicano status attainment. INTERNATIONAL MIGRATION REVIEW, Vol. 16, no. 2 (Summer 1982), p. 435-473. English. **DESCR:** Academic Achievement; Discrimination in Employment; Identity; Income; Language Proficiency; Sexism; *Social Classes; Social Mobility.

1650 Vigil, James Diego. The nexus of class, culture and gender in the education of Mexican American females. IN: McKenna, Teresa and Ortiz, Flora Ida, eds. THE BROKEN WEB: THE EDUCATIONAL EXPERIENCE OF HISPANIC WOMEN. Claremont, CA: Tomas Rivera Center; Berkeley, CA: Floricanto Press, 1988, p. 79-103. English. **DESCR:** Academic Achievement; Acculturation; *Education; Identity; Secondary School Education; Sex Roles; Social Classes; Students.

Discrimination in Employment

1651 Mindiola, Tatcho, Jr. The cost of being a Mexican female worker in the 1970 Houston labor market. AZTLAN, Vol. 11, no. 2 (Fall 1980), p. 231-247. English. **DESCR:** Discrimination; Houston, TX; Labor Supply and Market; Working Women.

Discrimination in Employment
(cont.)

1652 Nava, Yolanda. The Chicana and employment: needs analysis and recommendations for legislation. REGENERACION, Vol. 2, no. 3 (1973), p. 7-9. English. DESCR: California Commission on the Status of Women; Child Care Centers; Comision Femenil Mexicana Nacional; Employment Tests; Employment Training; Equal Rights Amendment (ERA); Sexism; Statistics; Stereotypes; Working Women.

1653 Nieto Gomez de Lazarin, Anna. Chicanas in the labor force. ENCUENTRO FEMENIL, Vol. 1, no. 2 (1974), p. 28-33. English. DESCR: Employment; *Working Women.

1654 Nieto Gomez de Lazarin, Anna. What is the Talmadge Amendment?: justicia para las madres. REGENERACION, Vol. 2, no. 3 (1973), p. 14-15. English. DESCR: Chicana Welfare Rights Organization; *Child Care Centers; Community Work Experience Program (C.W.E.P.); Employment Tests; Escalante, Alicia; *Feminism; Nixon, Richard; Working Women.

1655 Peralta Aguilar, Linda. Unequal opportunity and the Chicana. LA LUZ, Vol. 1, no. 5 (September 1972), p. 52. English. DESCR: *Discrimination; *Employment; *Feminism.

1656 Peralta Aguilar, Linda. Unequal opportunity and the Chicana. REGENERACION, Vol. 2, no. 4 (1975), p. 45-46. English. DESCR: *Discrimination; *Employment; Feminism.

1657 Peralta Aguilar, Linda. Unequal opportunity and the Chicana. LA LUZ, Vol. 6, no. 1 (January 1977), p. 29-30. English. DESCR: *Discrimination; *Employment; *Feminism.

1658 Romero, Mary. Twice protected?: assessing the impact of affirmative action on Mexican-American women. JOURNAL OF HISPANIC POLICY, Vol. 3, (1988, 1989), p. 83-101. English. DESCR: *Affirmative Action; Careers; Statistics.

1659 Segura, Denise. Conflict in social relations at work: a Chicana perspective. IN: National Association for Chicano Studies. ESTUDIOS CHICANOS AND THE POLITICS OF COMMUNITY. [S.l.]: National Association for Chicano Studies, c1989, p. [110]-131. English. DESCR: Employment Training; Immigrants; *Interpersonal Relations; Social Classes; Women; *Working Women.

1660 Segura, Denise. Labor market stratification: the Chicana experience. BERKELEY JOURNAL OF SOCIOLOGY, Vol. 29, (1984), p. 57-91. English. DESCR: Employment; *Labor Supply and Market; Socioeconomic Factors; *Working Women.

1661 Tienda, Marta. Sex, ethnicity and Chicano status attainment. INTERNATIONAL MIGRATION REVIEW, Vol. 16, no. 2 (Summer 1982), p. 435-473. English. DESCR: Academic Achievement; Discrimination in Education; Identity; Income; Language Proficiency; Sexism; *Social Classes; Social Mobility.

1662 Valladolid-Cuaron, Alicia V.; Sutton, Arlene Vigil; and Renteria, Dorothy. La mujer en el ochenta. LA LUZ, Vol. 8, no. 3 (August, September, 1979), p. 16-17. English. DESCR: *Cultural Pluralism.

1663 Vargas-Willis, Gloria and Cervantes, Richard C. Consideration of psychosocial stress in

the treatment of the Latina immigrant. HISPANIC JOURNAL OF BEHAVIORAL SCIENCES, Vol. 9, no. 3 (September 1987), p. 315-329. English. DESCR: *Immigrants; Mental Health; *Psychotherapy; *Stress.

1664 Zavella, Patricia. "Abnormal intimacy": the varying work networks of Chicana cannery workers. FEMINIST STUDIES, Vol. 11, no. 3 (Fall 1985), p. 541-557. English. DESCR: Canneries; Labor Unions; *Natural Support Systems; *Working Women.

Discriminatory Hiring Practices
USE: Discrimination in Employment

Disease Prevention and Control
USE: Preventative Medicine

Diseases

1665 Alvarez-Amaya, Maria. Determinants of breast and cervical cancer behavior among Mexican American women. BORDER HEALTH/SALUD FRONTERIZA, Vol. 5, no. 3 (July, September, 1989), p. 22-27. Bilingual. DESCR: Border Region; *Breast Cancer; *Cancer; Immigrants; Medical Care; *Preventative Medicine.

1666 Dinsmoor, Mara J. and Gibbs, Ronald S. Prevalence of asymptomatic hepatitis-B infection in pregnant Mexican-American women. OBSTETRICS AND GYNECOLOGY, Vol. 76, no. 2 (August 1990), p. 239-240. English. DESCR: *Fertility; *Hepatitis.

1667 Hazuda, Helen P., et al. Employment status and women's protection against coronary heart disease. AMERICAN JOURNAL OF EPIDEMIOLOGY, Vol. 123, no. 4 (April 1986), p. 623-640. English. DESCR: Anglo Americans; Employment; *Heart Disease; Nutrition; *Public Health; San Antonio, TX.

1668 Kay, Margarita Artschwager and Yoder, Marianne. Hot and cold in women's ethnotherapeutics: the American-Mexican West. SOCIAL SCIENCE & MEDICINE, Vol. 25, no. 4 (1987), p. 347-355. English. DESCR: *Folk Medicine; Herbal Medicine; Mexico; Southwestern United States.

1669 Peters, Ruth K., et al. Risk factors for invasive cervical cancer among Latinas and non-Latinas in Los Angeles County. JOURNAL OF THE NATIONAL CANCER INSTITUTE, Vol. 77, no. 5 (November 1986), p. 1063-1077. English. DESCR: *Cancer; Educational Levels; Los Angeles County, CA; *Public Health; Women.

1670 Richardson, Jean L., et al. Frequency and adequacy of breast cancer screening among elderly Hispanic women. PREVENTIVE MEDICINE, Vol. 16, no. 6 (November 1987), p. 761-774. English. DESCR: Ancianos; *Cancer; *Health Education; Los Angeles, CA; *Medical Care; Preventative Medicine.

"The Ditch" [short story]

1671 Harlow, Barbara. Sites of struggle: immigration, deportation, prison, and exile. IN: Calderon, Hector and Saldivar, Jose David, eds. CRITICISM IN THE BORDERLANDS: STUDIES IN CHICANO LITERATURE, CULTURE, AND IDEOLOGY. Durham, NC: Duke University Press, 1991, p. [149]-163. English. DESCR: Anzaldua, Gloria; BLACK GOLD; BORDERLANDS/LA FRONTERA: THE NEW MESTIZA; First, Ruth; Khalifeh, Sahar; *Literary Criticism; *Political Ideology; Sanchez, Rosaura; Social Classes; "The Cariboo Cafe" [short story]; Viramontes, Helena Maria; WILD THORNS; *Women; Working Women.

Divorce

1672 Duarte, Patricia. The post-lib tango: couples in chaos. NUESTRO, Vol. 3, no. 5 (June, July, 1979), p. 38-40. English. DESCR: Machismo; Marriage; *Sex Roles.

1673 Frisbie, William Parker; Opitz, Wolfgang; and Kelly, William R. Marital instability trends among Mexican Americans as compared to Blacks and Anglos: new evidence. SOCIAL SCIENCE QUARTERLY, Vol. 66, no. 3 (September 1985), p. 587-601. English. DESCR: Anglo Americans; Blacks; *Marriage.

1674 Frisbie, William Parker; Bean, Frank D.; and Eberstein, Isaac W. Patterns of marital instability among Mexican Americans, Blacks, and Anglos. IN: Bean, Frank D. and Frisbie, W. Parker, eds. THE DEMOGRAPHY OF RACIAL AND ETHNIC GROUPS. New York: Academic Press, 1978, p. 143-163. English. DESCR: Anglo Americans; Blacks; Family; *Marriage.

1675 Frisbie, William Parker; Bean, Frank D.; and Eberstein, Isaac W. Recent changes in marital instability among Mexican Americans: convergence with Black and Anglo trends. SOCIAL FORCES, Vol. 58, no. 4 (June 1980), p. 1205-1220. English. DESCR: Age Groups; Anglo Americans; Blacks; *Marriage.

1676 Markides, Kyriakos S. and Farrell, Janice. Marital status and depression among Mexican Americans. SOCIAL PSYCHIATRY, Vol. 20, no. 2 (1985), p. 86-91. English. DESCR: Depression (Psychological); *Marriage; *Mental Health.

1677 Neff, James Alan; Gilbert, Kathleen R.; and Hoppe, Sue K. Divorce likelihood among Anglos and Mexican Americans. JOURNAL OF DIVORCE AND REMARRIAGE, Vol. 15, no. 1-2 (1991), p. 75-98. English. DESCR: *Anglo Americans; *Marriage; San Antonio, TX.

1678 Vega, William A.; Warheit, George; and Meinhardt, Kenneth. Marital disruption and the prevalence of depressive symptomatology among Anglos and Mexican Americans. JOURNAL OF MARRIAGE AND THE FAMILY, Vol. 46, no. 4 (November 1984), p. 817-824. English. DESCR: Anglo Americans; Depression (Psychological); *Marriage; *Mental Health; Socioeconomic Factors.

1679 Wagner, Roland M. Changes in extended family relationships for Mexican American and Anglo single mothers. JOURNAL OF DIVORCE, Vol. 11, no. 2 (Winter 1987), p. 69-87. English. DESCR: Anglo Americans; *Extended Family; Natural Support Systems; San Jose, CA; *Single Parents; Women.

1680 Wagner, Roland M. Changes in the friend network during the first year of single parenthood for Mexican American and Anglo women. JOURNAL OF DIVORCE, Vol. 11, no. 2 (Winter 1987), p. 89-109. English. DESCR: Anglo Americans; *Natural Support Systems; *Single Parents; Widowhood; Women.

Doctor Patient Relations

1681 Poma, Pedro A. Pregnancy in Hispanic women. JOURNAL OF THE NATIONAL MEDICAL ASSOCIATION, Vol. 79, no. 9 (September 1987), p. 929-935. English. DESCR: *Cultural Characteristics; *Fertility; Machismo; Preventative Medicine; Women.

Dolores Madrigal, et al., Plaintiff, v. E.J. Quilligan, et al.

1682 Velez-I., Carlos G. The nonconsenting sterilization of Mexican women in Los Angeles: issues of psychocultural rupture and legal redress in paternalistic behavioral environments. IN: Melville, Margarita B., ed. TWICE A MINORITY. St. Louis, MO: Mosby, 1980, p. 235-248. English. DESCR: Legal Cases; Los Angeles, CA; *Sterilization.

Domestic Work

1683 Bergdolt-Munzer, Sara L. Homemakers and retirement income benefits: the other home security issue. CHICANO LAW REVIEW, Vol. 8, (1985), p. 61-80. English. DESCR: Ancianos; Feminism; Social Security; *Women.

1684 Dill, Bonnie Thornton. Our mothers' grief: racial ethnic women and the maintenance of families. JOURNAL OF FAMILY HISTORY, Vol. 13, no. 4 (October 1988), p. 415-431. English. DESCR: Asian Americans; Blacks; *Family; Fertility; *Sex Roles; *Women; *Working Women.

1685 Garcia, Mario T. The Chicana in American history: the Mexican women of El Paso, 1880-1920 - a case study. PACIFIC HISTORICAL REVIEW, Vol. 49, no. 2 (May 1980), p. 315-337. English. DESCR: Acme Laundry, El Paso, TX; American Federation of Labor (AFL); Case Studies; Central Labor Union; *El Paso, TX; Employment; *History; Immigrants; Income; Labor Unions; Sex Roles; Strikes and Lockouts; *Working Women.

1686 Golding, Jacqueline M. Division of household labor, strain, and depressive symptoms among Mexican Americans and non-Hispanic whites. PSYCHOLOGY OF WOMEN QUARTERLY, Vol. 14, no. 1 (March 1990), p. 103-117. English. DESCR: Anglo Americans; Comparative Psychology; *Depression (Psychological); Employment; Identity; *Sex Roles; Women.

1687 Kantorowski Davis, Sharon and Chavez, Virginia. Hispanic househusbands. HISPANIC JOURNAL OF BEHAVIORAL SCIENCES, Vol. 7, no. 4 (December 1985), p. 317-332. English. DESCR: Machismo; Marriage; *Sex Roles.

1688 Romero, Mary. Chicanas modernize domestic service. QUALITATIVE SOCIOLOGY, Vol. 11, no. 4 (Winter 1988), p. 319-334. English. DESCR: *Employment; Income; *Interpersonal Relations; Working Women.

Domestic Work (cont.)

1689 Romero, Mary. Day work in the suburbs: the work experience of Chicana private housekeepers. IN: Statham, Arne; Miller, Eleanor M; and Mauksch, Hans O., eds. THE WORTH OF WOMEN'S WORK: A QUALITATIVE SYNTHESIS. Albany, NY: State University of New York Press, 1988, p. 77-91. English. DESCR: Employment; Interpersonal Relations; *Natural Support Systems; Social Mobility; Working Women.

1690 Romero, Mary. Domestic service in the transition from rural to urban life: the case of la Chicana. WOMEN'S STUDIES QUARTERLY, Vol. 13, no. 3 (February 1987), p. 199-222. English. DESCR: Employment; Interpersonal Relations; Rural Population; Social Mobility; Sociology; Urban Communities; Working Women.

1691 Ruiz, Vicki L. By the day or week: Mexicana domestic workers in El Paso. TRABAJOS MONOGRAFICOS, Vol. 2, no. 1 (1986), p. 35-58. English. DESCR: El Paso, TX; Employment; Labor Supply and Market; *Working Women.

1692 Ruiz, Vicki L. By the day or week: Mexicana domestic workers in El Paso. IN: Ruiz, Vicki L. and Tiano, Susan, eds. WOMEN ON THE U.S.-MEXICO BORDER: RESPONSES TO CHANGE. Boston, MA: Allen & Urwin, 1987, p. 61-76. English. DESCR: El Paso, TX; Employment; Labor Supply and Market.

1693 Saenz, Rogelio; Goudy, Willis J.; and Lorenz, Frederick C. The effects of employment and marital relations on depression among Mexican American women. JOURNAL OF MARRIAGE AND THE FAMILY, Vol. 51, no. 1 (February 1989), p. 239-251. English. DESCR: *Depression (Psychological); *Employment; Feminism; *Marriage; Women Men Relations; Working Women.

1694 Solorzano-Torres, Rosalia. Women, labor, and the U.S.-Mexico border: Mexican maids in El Paso, Texas. IN: Melville, Margarita, ed. MEXICANAS AT WORK IN THE UNITED STATES. Houston, TX: Mexican American Studies Program, University of Houston, 1988, p. 75-83. English. DESCR: Border Patrol; *Border Region; El Paso, TX; Immigrants; Immigration and Naturalization Service (INS); Immigration Regulation and Control; *Labor Supply and Market; Undocumented Workers; *Women; *Working Women.

Dona Marina
USE: Malinche

Dona Ximena

1695 De Ortego y Gasca, Felipe. The Hispanic woman: a humanistic perspective. LA LUZ, Vol. 6, no. 11 (November 1977), p. 7-10. English. DESCR: De la Cruz, Juana Ines; *Essays; History; Mistral, Gabriela; Ortiz de Dominguez, Josefa; *Women Men Relations; *Women's Suffrage.

1696 De Ortego y Gasca, Felipe. The Hispanic woman: a humanistic perspective. LA LUZ, Vol. 8, no. 8 (October, November, 1980), p. 6-9. English. DESCR: De la Cruz, Juana Ines; *Essays; History; Mistral, Gabriela; Ortiz de Dominguez, Josefa; *Women Men Relations; *Women's Suffrage.

Douglas, AZ

1697 Goldsmith, Raquel Rubio. Shipwrecked in the desert: a short history of the adventures and struggles for survival of the Mexican Sisters of the House of the Providence in Douglas, Arizona during their first twenty-two years of existence (1927-1949). RENATO ROSALDO LECTURE SERIES MONOGRAPH, Vol. 1, (Summer 1985), p. [39]-67. English. DESCR: Catholic Church; Clergy; History; *House of the Divine Providence [convent], Douglas, AZ; Women.

Draft
USE: Military

Drawings

1698 Cochran, Jo, et al., eds. Bearing witness/Sobreviviendo: an anthology of Native American/Latina art and literature. CALYX: A JOURNAL OF ART AND LITERATURE BY WOMEN, Vol. 8, no. 2 (Spring 1984), p. [1]-128. English. DESCR: *Art; *Fiction; Native Americans; *Poems; Women.

Dropouts

1699 Chacon, Maria A.; Cohen, Elizabeth G.; and Strover, Sharon. Chicanas and Chicanos: barriers to progress in higher education. IN: Olivas, Michael A., ed. LATINO COLLEGE STUDENTS. New York: Teachers College Press, 1986, p. 296-324. English. DESCR: Community Colleges; Discrimination; *Higher Education; Stress; Surveys.

1700 de Anda, Diane. A study of the interaction of Hispanic junior high school students and their teachers. HISPANIC JOURNAL OF BEHAVIORAL SCIENCES, Vol. 4, no. 1 (March 1982), p. 57-74. English. DESCR: Junior High School; *Teacher-Pupil Interaction.

1701 Del Castillo, Adelaida R., et al. An assessment of the status of the education of Hispanic American women. IN: McKenna, Teresa and Ortiz, Flora Ida, eds. THE BROKEN WEB: THE EDUCATIONAL EXPERIENCE OF HISPANIC WOMEN. Claremont, CA: Tomas Rivera Center; Berkeley, CA: Floricanto Press, 1988, p. 3-24. English. DESCR: Academic Achievement; Conferences and Meetings; Discrimination in Education; *Education; Higher Education; Public Policy; Research Methodology; The Educational Experience of Hispanic American Women [symposium] (1985: Claremont, CA); *Women.

1702 Guajardo, Maria Resendez. Educational attainment of Chicana adolescents. Thesis (Ph.D.)--University of Denver, 1988. 266 p. English. DESCR: Academic Achievement; *Secondary School Education; *Youth.

1703 Jaramillo, Mari-Luci. Institutional responsibility in the provision of educational experiences to the Hispanic American female student. IN: McKenna, Teresa and Ortiz, Flora Ida, eds. THE BROKEN WEB: THE EDUCATIONAL EXPERIENCE OF HISPANIC WOMEN. Claremont, CA: Tomas Rivera Center; Berkeley, CA: Floricanto Press, 1988, p. 25-35. English. DESCR: Academic Achievement; *Discrimination in Education; *Education; Educational Administration; Enrollment; Higher Education; Students; *Women.

1704 Jaramillo, Mari-Luci. To serve Hispanic American female students: challenges and responsibilities for educational institutions. Claremont, CA: Tomas Rivera Center, c1987. 11 p. English. DESCR: *Education; Higher Education; Women.

Dropouts (cont.)

1705 Kaplan, Celia Patricia. Critical factors affecting school dropout among Mexican-American women. Thesis (Doctor of Public Health)--UCLA, 1990. xviii, 256 p. English. DESCR: Marriage; Secondary School Education.

Drug Abuse Programs

1706 Anglin, M. Douglas and Hser, Yih-Ing. Addicted women and crime. CRIMINOLOGY: AN INTERDISCIPLINARY JOURNAL, Vol. 25, no. 2 (1987), p. 359-397. English. DESCR: Criminal Acts; *Drug Addicts; Statistics.

1707 Arevalo, Rodolfo, ed. and Minor, Marianne, ed. Chicanas and alcoholism: a sociocultural perspective of women. San Jose, CA: School of Social Work, San Jose State University, c1981. 55 p. English. DESCR: *Alcoholism; Family; Feminism; Natural Support Systems; Preventative Medicine; Psychotherapy.

1708 Martinez, Thomas M. Alicia in Wonderland: Chicana drug addicts. ATISBOS, Vol. 3, (Summer, Fall, 1978), p. 194-200. English. DESCR: Drug Addicts; *Drug Use.

Drug Addicts

1709 Anglin, M. Douglas and Hser, Yih-Ing. Addicted women and crime. CRIMINOLOGY: AN INTERDISCIPLINARY JOURNAL, Vol. 25, no. 2 (1987), p. 359-397. English. DESCR: Criminal Acts; Drug Abuse Programs; Statistics.

1710 Hser, Yih-Ing; Chou, Chih-Ping; and Anglin, M. Douglas. The criminality of female narcotics addicts: a causal modeling approach. JOURNAL OF QUANTITATIVE CRIMINOLOGY, Vol. 6, no. 2 (June 1990), p. 207-228. English. DESCR: Anglo Americans; Criminal Acts; Drug Traffic; Prostitution; Women.

1711 Jurado, Marlo. Lack of communication. REGENERACION, Vol. 1, no. 10 (1971), p. 8. English. DESCR: *Prisons.

1712 Martinez, Thomas M. Alicia in Wonderland: Chicana drug addicts. ATISBOS, Vol. 3, (Summer, Fall, 1978), p. 194-200. English. DESCR: Drug Abuse Programs; *Drug Use.

1713 Moore, Joan W. Mexican-American women addicts: the influence of family background. IN: Glick, Ronald and Moore, Joan, eds. DRUGS IN HISPANIC COMMUNITIES. New Brunswick, NJ: Rutgers University Press, c1990, p. 127-153. English. DESCR: Barrios; Drug Use; East Los Angeles, CA; *Family; *Gangs; Heroin; Hoyo-Mara Gang, East Los Angeles, CA; Pachucos; Sex Roles; Socialization; White Fence Gang; Youth.

1714 Moore, Joan W. and Devitt, Mary. The paradox of deviance in addicted Mexican American mothers. GENDER & SOCIETY, Vol. 3, no. 1 (March 1989), p. 53-70. English. DESCR: Children; *Drug Use; Family; *Fertility; Gangs; Parenting; Sex Roles.

1715 Worth, Dooley and Rodriguez, Ruth. Latina women and AIDS. SIECUS REPORT, (January, February, 1986), p. 5-7. English. DESCR: Cultural Characteristics; Drug Use; Health Education; Natural Support Systems; New York; Preventative Medicine; Puerto Ricans; Sex Roles; *Vital Statistics; Women.

Drug Traffic

1716 Hser, Yih-Ing; Chou, Chih-Ping; and Anglin, M. Douglas. The criminality of female narcotics addicts: a causal modeling approach. JOURNAL OF QUANTITATIVE CRIMINOLOGY, Vol. 6, no. 2 (June 1990), p. 207-228. English. DESCR: Anglo Americans; Criminal Acts; *Drug Addicts; Prostitution; Women.

Drug Use

1717 Chavez, Ernest; Beauvais, Fred; and Oetting, E.R. Drug use by small town Mexican American youth: a pilot study. HISPANIC JOURNAL OF BEHAVIORAL SCIENCES, Vol. 8, no. 3 (September 1986), p. 243-258. English. DESCR: Anglo Americans; Rural Population; Youth.

1718 Marin, Gerardo; Perez-Stable, Eliseo J.; and Marin, Barbara Van Oss. Cigarette smoking among San Francisco Hispanics: the role of acculturation and gender. PUBLIC HEALTH BRIEFS, Vol. 79, no. 2 (February 1989), p. 196-198. English. DESCR: *Acculturation; Males; San Francisco, CA; *Smoking; Women.

1719 Martinez, Thomas M. Alicia in Wonderland: Chicana drug addicts. ATISBOS, Vol. 3, (Summer, Fall, 1978), p. 194-200. English. DESCR: Drug Abuse Programs; Drug Addicts.

1720 Mata, Alberto Guardiola and Castillo, Valerie. Rural female adolescent dissatisfaction, support and helpseeking. FREE INQUIRY IN CREATIVE SOCIOLOGY, Vol. 14, no. 2 (November 1986), p. 135-138. English. DESCR: Alcoholism; Interpersonal Relations; *Natural Support Systems; Parent and Child Relationships; Rural Population; *Youth.

1721 Moore, Joan W. Mexican-American women addicts: the influence of family background. IN: Glick, Ronald and Moore, Joan, eds. DRUGS IN HISPANIC COMMUNITIES. New Brunswick, NJ: Rutgers University Press, c1990, p. 127-153. English. DESCR: Barrios; *Drug Addicts; East Los Angeles, CA; *Family; *Gangs; Heroin; Hoyo-Mara Gang, East Los Angeles, CA; Pachucos; Sex Roles; Socialization; White Fence Gang; Youth.

1722 Moore, Joan W. and Devitt, Mary. The paradox of deviance in addicted Mexican American mothers. GENDER & SOCIETY, Vol. 3, no. 1 (March 1989), p. 53-70. English. DESCR: Children; *Drug Addicts; Family; *Fertility; Gangs; Parenting; Sex Roles.

1723 Nyamathi, Adeline M. and Vasquez, Rose. Impact of poverty, homelessness, and drugs on Hispanic women at risk for HIV infection. HISPANIC JOURNAL OF BEHAVIORAL SCIENCES, Vol. 11, no. 4 (November 1989), p. 299-314. English. DESCR: *AIDS (Disease); Health Education; *Human Immunodeficiency Virus (HIV); Locus of Control; Mental Health; Needle-Sharing; *Poverty.

1724 Worth, Dooley and Rodriguez, Ruth. Latina women and AIDS. SIECUS REPORT, (January, February, 1986), p. 5-7. English. DESCR: Cultural Characteristics; Drug Addicts; Health Education; Natural Support Systems; New York; Preventative Medicine; Puerto Ricans; Sex Roles; *Vital Statistics; Women.

--   --

Drug Use (cont.)

1725 Zambrana, Ruth E., et al. Ethnic differences in the substance use patterns of low-income pregnant women. FAMILY & COMMUNITY HEALTH, Vol. 13, no. 4 (January 1991), p. 1-11. English. DESCR: Alcoholism; Blacks; *Fertility; Immigrants *Low Income; Smoking; Women.

Duarte-Clark, Rodrigo

1726 Melville, Margarita B. Female and male in Chicano theatre. IN: Kanellos, Nicolas, ed. HISPANIC THEATRE IN THE UNITED STATES. Houston, TX: Arte Publico Press, 1984, p. 71-79. English. DESCR: BERNABE; BRUJERIAS [play]; Cultural Characteristics; DAY OF THE SWALLOWS; EL JARDIN [play]; Family; Feminism; Macias, Ysidro; Morton, Carlos; Portillo Trambley, Estela; RANCHO HOLLYWOOD [play]; *Sex Roles; *Teatro; THE ULTIMATE PENDEJADA [play]; Valdez, Luis; Women Men Relations.

Duran Apodaca, Maria

1727 Duran Apodaca, Maria. North from Mexico. IN: Jensen, Joan M. ed. WITH THESE HANDS: WOMEN WORKING ON THE LAND. New York: McGraw-Hill, 1981, p. 120-122. English. DESCR: *Biography; Oral History.

Duran, Flo

1728 Pesquera, Beatriz M. and Duran, Flo. Having a job gives you some sort of power: reflections of a Chicana working woman. FEMINIST ISSUES, Vol. 4, no. 2 (Fall 1984), p. 79-96. English. DESCR: Feminism; *Working Women.

Duran, Lucy

1729 Duran, Lucy. Lucy Duran--wife, mother, and organizer. IN: Mora, Magdalena and Del Castillo, Adelaida, eds. MEXICAN WOMEN IN THE UNITED STATES: STRUGGLES PAST AND PRESENT. Los Angeles, CA: Chicano Studies Research Center, UCLA 1980, p. 183-184. English. DESCR: Agricultural Labor Unions; *Biography; Farm Labor Organizing Committee (FLOC); Farm Workers; Working Women.

Dyadic Adjustment Scale (DAS)

1730 Casas, Jesus Manuel and Ortiz, Sylvia. Exploring the applicability of the Dyadic Adjustment Scale for assessing level of marital adjustment with Mexican Americans. JOURNAL OF MARRIAGE AND THE FAMILY, Vol. 47, no. 4 (November 1985), p. 1023-1027. English. DESCR: *Marriage.

Eagle Pass, TX

1731 Canales, Genevieve and Roberts, Robert E. Gender and mental health in the Mexican origin population of South Texas. IN: Rodriguez, Reymund and Coleman, Marion Tolbert, eds. MENTAL HEALTH ISSUES OF THE MEXICAN ORIGIN POPULATION IN TEXAS. Austin, TX: Hogg Foundation for Mental Health, University of Texas, 1987, p. 89-99. English. DESCR: Del Rio, TX; Depression (Psychological); Health Education; *Males; *Mental Health; *Sex Roles; South Texas; Surveys.

Earthquakes

1732 Arbelaez A., Marisol. Impacto social del sismo, Mexico 1985: las costureras. IN: Del Castillo, Adelaida R., ed. BETWEEN BORDERS: ESSAYS ON MEXICANA/CHICANA HISTORY. Encino, CA: Floricanto Press, 1990, p. 315-331. Spanish. DESCR: Frente de Costureras, Mexico; *Garment Industry; *Industrial Workers; Labor Unions; *Mexico; Mexico City Earthquake, September 19, 1985; *Women; Working Women.

East Los Angeles, CA

1733 Moore, Joan W. Mexican-American women addicts: the influence of family background. IN: Glick, Ronald and Moore, Joan, eds. DRUGS IN HISPANIC COMMUNITIES. New Brunswick, NJ: Rutgers University Press, c1990, p. 127-153. English. DESCR: Barrios; *Drug Addicts; Drug Use; *Family; *Gangs; Heroin; Hoyo-Mara Gang, East Los Angeles, CA; Pachucos; Sex Roles; Socialization; White Fence Gang; Youth.

1734 Pardo, Mary. Mexican American women grassroots community activists: "Mothers of East Los Angeles". FRONTIERS: A JOURNAL OF WOMEN STUDIES, Vol. 11, no. 1 (1990), p. [1]-7. English. DESCR: Coalition Against the Prison, East Los Angeles, CA; *Community Organizations; Family; *Feminism; *Mothers of East L.A. (MELA); Organizations; Political Parties and Politics; Sex Roles.

Eating Attitudes Test (EAT)

1735 Pumariega, Andres J. Acculturation and eating attitudes in adolescent girls: a comparative and correlational study. JOURNAL OF THE AMERICAN ACADEMY OF CHILD PSYCHIATRY, Vol. 25, no. 2 (March 1986), p. 276-279. English. DESCR: *Acculturation; Anorexia Nervosa; Cultural Characteristics; Nutrition; Socioeconomic Factors; Youth.

Economic Development

1736 Young, Gay. Women, border industrialization program, and human rights. El Paso, TX: Center for InterAmerican and Border Studies, UTEP, 1984. 33 p. English. DESCR: Border Industrialization Program (BIP); *Border Industries; Employment; Industrial Workers; Mexico; Sex Roles; *Sexism; *Women; Working Women.

Economic History and Conditions

1737 Dixon, Marlene; Martinez, Elizabeth; and McCaughan, Ed. Theoretical perspectives on Chicanas, Mexicanas and the transnational working class. CONTEMPORARY MARXISM, no. 11 (Fall 1985), p. 46-76. English. DESCR: Border Industries; Capitalism; History; *Immigration; *Labor Supply and Market; *Laboring Classes; Mexico; Undocumented Workers; Women.

1738 Falasco, Dee and Heer, David. Economic and fertility differences between legal and undocumented migrant Mexican families: possible effects of immigration policy changes. SOCIAL SCIENCE QUARTERLY, Vol. 65, no. 2 (June 1984), p. 495-504. English. DESCR: *Fertility; *Immigration Law and Legislation; Immigration Regulation and Control; Income; *Undocumented Workers.

1739 Pena, Devon Gerardo. Las maquiladoras: Mexican women in class struggle in the border industries. AZTLAN, Vol. 11, no. 2 (Fall 1980), p. 159-229. English. DESCR: Border Industries; Labor; Labor Unions; Mexico; Mexico-U.S. Border Development; Working Women.

Economically Disadvantaged
USE: Poverty

Edible Plants
USE: Herbal Medicine

Education

1740 Amodeo, Luiza B.; Edelson, Rosalyn; and Martin, Jeanette. The triple bias: rural, minority and female. RURAL EDUCATOR, Vol. 3, no. 3 (Spring 1982), p. 1-6. English. **DESCR:** Rural Population; Social History and Conditions; Women.

1741 Andrade, Sally J., ed. Latino families in the United States: a resource book for family life education = Las familias latinas en los Estados Unidos: recursos para la capacitacion familiar. [S.l.]: Planned Parenthood Federation of America, Inc., 1983. ix, 79, 70, xi p. Bilingual. **DESCR:** Bilingualism; Community Organizations; *Family; Mental Health; Public Health.

1742 Baca Zinn, Maxine. Employment and education of Mexican-American women: the interplay of modernity and ethnicity in eight families. HARVARD EDUCATIONAL REVIEW, Vol. 50, no. 1 (February 1980), p. 47-62. English. **DESCR:** Acculturation; Decision Making; *Employment; *Family; Identity; Sex Roles; Social Classes; Values.

1743 Bean, Frank D. and Swicegood, Gray. Generation, female education and Mexican American fertility. SOCIAL SCIENCE QUARTERLY, Vol. 63, (March 1982), p. 131-144. English. **DESCR:** Age Groups; Family Planning; *Fertility.

1744 Bean, Frank D. and Tienda, Marta. The Hispanic population of the United States. New York: Russell Sage Foundation, 1987. xxiv, 456 p. English. **DESCR:** *Census; Employment; Fertility; Identity; Immigration; Income; *Population; Self-Referents; *Statistics.

1745 Bean, Frank D. and Swicegood, Gray. Mexican American fertility patterns. Austin, TX: University of Texas Press, 1985. x, 178 p. English. **DESCR:** Age Groups; Census; *Fertility; Language Usage; *Population; Research Methodology; *Socioeconomic Factors; Statistics.

1746 Blair, Leita Mae. Characteristics of professional and traditional Mexican American women related to family of origin, role models, and conflicts: a case study. Thesis (Ed.D.)--East Texas State University, 1984. 348 p. English. **DESCR:** *Careers; Case Studies; *Family.

1747 Carrasco, Frank F. Teaching strategies used by Chicano mothers with their Head Start children. Thesis (Ph.D.)--University of Colorado, Boulder, 1983. 177 p. English. **DESCR:** Bilingualism; Children; Low Income; *Parent and Child Relationships; *Parenting.

1748 Cota-Robles de Suarez, Cecilia, ed. and Anguiano, Lupe, ed. Every woman's right: the right to quality education and economic independence. Montebello, CA: National Chicana Foundation, [1981]. viii, 110 p. English. **DESCR:** Civil Rights; *Feminism.

1749 Davis, Cary; Haub, Carl; and Willette, JoAnne. U.S. Hispanics: changing the face of America. POPULATION BULLETIN, Vol. 38, no. 3 (June 1983), p. 1-43. English. **DESCR:** Employment; Fertility; Immigration; Income; *Population; Statistics; Vital Statistics.

1750 Del Castillo, Adelaida R., et al. An assessment of the status of the education of Hispanic American women. IN: McKenna, Teresa and Ortiz, Flora Ida, eds. THE BROKEN WEB: THE EDUCATIONAL EXPERIENCE OF HISPANIC WOMEN. Claremont, CA: Tomas Rivera Center; Berkeley, CA: Floricanto Press, 1988, p. 3-24. English. **DESCR:** Academic Achievement; Conferences and Meetings; Discrimination in Education; Dropouts; Higher Education; Public Policy; Research Methodology; The Educational Experience of Hispanic American Women [symposium] (1985: Claremont, CA); *Women.

1751 Del Castillo, Adelaida R. and Torres, Maria. The interdependency of educational institutions and cultural norms: the Hispana experience. IN: McKenna, Teresa and Ortiz, Flora Ida, eds. THE BROKEN WEB: THE EDUCATIONAL EXPERIENCE OF HISPANIC WOMEN. Claremont, CA: Tomas Rivera Center; Berkeley, CA: Floricanto Press, 1988, p. 39-60. English. **DESCR:** Academic Achievement; Acculturation; *Cultural Characteristics; *Literature Reviews; Research Methodology; *Values; Women.

1752 Del Castillo, Adelaida R. Sobre la experiencia educativa chicana. FEM, Vol. 10, no. 48 (October, November, 1986), p. 7-10. Spanish. **DESCR:** *Academic Achievement.

1753 Escobedo, Theresa Herrera, ed. Thematic issue: Chicana issues. HISPANIC JOURNAL OF BEHAVIORAL SCIENCES, Vol. 4, no. 2 (June 1982), p. 145-286. English. **DESCR:** Higher Education; *Social History and Conditions.

1754 Estrada, Rosa Omega. A study of the attitudes of Texas Mexican American women toward higher education. Thesis (Ed.D.)--Baylor University, 1985. 280 p. English. **DESCR:** *Attitudes; *Higher Education; Texas.

1755 Galloway, Irma Nell. Trends in the employment of minority women as administrators in Texas public schools--1976-1981. Thesis (Ed.D.)--Texas Southern University, 1986. 129 p. English. **DESCR:** Asian Americans; Blacks; *Educational Administration; *Management; Native Americans; Texas; *Women.

1756 Garcia, Norma Varisto de. Education and the Spanish-speaking woman: a sad reality. NABE JOURNAL, Vol. 1, no. 1 (May 1976), p. 55-60. English. **DESCR:** Discrimination in Education.

1757 Gonzales, Sylvia Alicia. Toward a feminist pedagogy for Chicana self-actualization. FRONTIERS: A JOURNAL OF WOMEN STUDIES, Vol. 5, no. 2 (Summer 1980), p. 48-51. English. **DESCR:** Chicano Movement; *Feminism; Identity; Malinche.

1758 Gonzalez, Michelle. Reflexiones de una estudiante chicana. FEM, Vol. 10, no. 48 (October, November, 1986), p. 40-41. Spanish. **DESCR:** Autobiography.

1759 Hawley, Peggy and Even, Brenda. Work and sex-role attitudes in relation to education and other characteristics. VOCATIONAL GUIDANCE QUARTERLY, Vol. 31, no. 2 (December 1982), p. 101-108. English. **DESCR:** Attitudes; Careers; Ethnic Groups; Psychological Testing; *Sex Roles; Working Women.

Education (cont.)

1760 Jaramillo, Mari-Luci. Institutional responsibility in the provision of educational experiences to the Hispanic American female student. IN: McKenna, Teresa and Ortiz, Flora Ida, eds. THE BROKEN WEB: THE EDUCATIONAL EXPERIENCE OF HISPANIC WOMEN. Claremont, CA: Tomaas Rivera Center; Berkeley, CA: Floricarto Press, 1988, p. 25-35. English. DESCR: Academic Achievement; *Discrimination in Education; Dropouts; Educational Administration; Enrollment; Higher Education; Students; *Women.

1761 Jaramillo, Mari-Luci. To serve Hispanic American female students: challenges and responsibilities for educational institutions. Claremont, CA: Tomas Rivera Center, c1987. 11 p. English. DESCR: Dropouts; Higher Education; Women.

1762 Laosa, Luis M. Maternal teaching strategies and cognitive styles in Chicano families. IN: Duran, Richard P. ed. LATINO LANGUAGE AND COMMUNICATIVE BEHAVIOR. Norwood, NJ: ABLEX Publishing Corp., 1981, p. 295-310. English. DESCR: *Cognition; *Parent and Child Relationships; *Parenting.

1763 Laosa, Luis M. Maternal teaching strategies in Chicano and Anglo-American families: the influence of culture and education on maternal behavior. CHILD DEVELOPMENT, Vol. 51, no. 3 (September 1980), p. 759-765. English. DESCR: Anglo Americans; Comparative Psychology; *Cultural Characteristics; Family; Maternal Teaching Observation Technique (MTOT); *Parent and Child Relationships; Parenting; Women.

1764 Lee, Valerie. Achievement and educational aspirations among Hispanic female high school students: comparison between public and Catholic schools. IN: McKenna, Teresa and Ortiz, Flora Ida, eds. THE BROKEN WEB: THE EDUCATIONAL EXPERIENCE OF HISPANIC WOMEN. Claremont, CA: Tomas Rivera Center; Berkeley, CA: Floricanto Press, 1988, p. 137-192. English. DESCR: *Academic Achievement; Anglo Americans; Catholic Church; Educational Statistics; Private Education; Religious Education; *Secondary School Education; *Women.

1765 McKenna, Teresa and Ortiz, Flora Ida. Facts and figures on Hispanic Americans, women, and education. IN: McKenna, Teresa and Ortiz, Flora Ida, eds. THE BROKEN WEB: THE EDUCATIONAL EXPERIENCE OF HISPANIC WOMEN. Claremont, CA: Tomas Rivera Center; Berkeley, CA: Floricanto Press, 1988, p. 195-217. English. DESCR: *Educational Statistics; *Women.

1766 McKenna, Teresa and Ortiz, Flora Ida. Select bibliography on Hispanic women and education. IN: McKenna, Teresa and Ortiz, Flora Ida, eds. THE BROKEN WEB: THE EDUCATIONAL EXPERIENCE OF HISPANIC WOMEN. Claremont, CA: Tomas Rivera Center; Berkeley, CA: Floricanto Press, 1988, p. 221-254. English. DESCR: *Bibliography; *Women.

1767 McKenna, Teresa, ed. and Ortiz, Flora Ida, ed. The broken web: the educational experience of Hispanic American women. Claremont, CA: Tomas Rivera Center; Berkeley, CA: Floricanto Press, 1988. iii, 262 p. English. DESCR: *Academic Achievement; Educational Statistics; The Educational Experience of Hispanic American Women [symposium] (1985: Claremont, CA);

*Women.

1768 Moore, Helen A. Hispanic women: schooling for conformity in public education. HISPANIC JOURNAL OF BEHAVIORAL SCIENCES, Vol. 5, no. 1 (March 1983), p. 45-63. English. DESCR: *Academic Achievement.

1769 Newton, Frank; Olmedo, Esteban L.; and Padilla, Amado M. Hispanic mental health research: a reference guide. Berkeley, CA: University of California Press, c1982. 685 p. English. DESCR: Anthropology; *Bibliography; Medical Care; *Mental Health; Psychology; Public Health; *Reference Works; Sociology.

1770 Nieto Gomez de Lazarin, Anna. The Chicana: perspectives for education. ENCUENTRO FEMENIL, Vol. 1, no. 1 (Spring 1973), p. 34-61. English. DESCR: Colleges and Universities; Discrimination; Discrimination in Education; Family; Identity; Sexism.

1771 Nieto Gomez de Lazarin, Anna. Un proposito para estudios femeniles de la chicana. REGENERACION, Vol. 2, no. 4 (1975), p. 30, 31-32. English. DESCR: Chicano Studies; Curriculum; History; Nava, Yolanda; Sexism.

1772 Olivarez, Elizabeth. Women's rights and the Mexican American woman. REGENERACION, Vol. 2, no. 4 (1975), p. 40-42. English. DESCR: *Feminism; Identity; Politics; Psychology; Religion; Sex Roles.

1773 Powell, Douglas R.; Zambrana, Ruth E.; and Silva-Palacios, Victor. Designing culturally responsive parent programs: a comparison of low-income Mexican and Mexican-American mothers' preferences. FAMILY RELATIONS, Vol. 39, no. 3 (July 1990), p. 298-304. English. DESCR: Acculturation; Children; Immigrants; Los Angeles, CA; Low Income; *Parent and Child Relationships; *Parenting; Women.

1774 Rosenhouse-Persson, Sandra and Sabagh, Georges. Attitudes toward abortion among Catholic Mexican-American women: the effects of religiosity and education. DEMOGRAPHY, Vol. 20, no. 1 (February 1983), p. 87-98. English. DESCR: Abortion; Attitudes; *Catholic Church; Religion.

1775 Ruiz, Vicki L. "And miles to go...": Mexican women and work, 1930-1985. IN: Schlissel, Lillian, et al., eds. WESTERN WOMEN: THEIR LAND, THEIR LIVES. Albuquerque, NM: University of New Mexico Press, 1988, p. 117-136. English. DESCR: El Paso Women's Employment and Education Project (EPWEE); *Employment; Farah Manufacturing Co., El Paso, TX; Farah Strike; *Income; Industrial Workers; Labor Unions; Statistics; Undocumented Workers; United Cannery Agricultural Packing and Allied Workers of America (UCAPAWA); Women; *Working Women.

1776 Saavedra-Vela, Pilar. The dark side of Hispanic women's education. AGENDA, Vol. 8, no. 3 (May, June, 1978), p. 15-18. English. DESCR: Careers.

1777 Saracho, Olivia N. Women and education: sex role modifications of Mexican American women. EDUCATION, Vol. 109, no. 3 (Spring 1989), p. 295-301. English. DESCR: Acculturation; *Sex Roles.

Education (cont.)

1778 Schoen, Robert; Wooldredge, John; and Thomas, Barbara. Ethnic and educational effects on marriage choice. SOCIAL SCIENCE QUARTERLY, Vol. 70, no. 3 (September 1989), p. 617-630. English. DESCR: Identity; *Intermarriage; Marriage; Research Methodology; Social Classes.

1779 Tafolla, Carmen. To split a human: mitos, machos y la mujer chicana. San Antonio, TX: Mexican American Cultural Center, 1985. 115 p.: ill. English. DESCR: Discrimination; *Feminism; Films; *Sex Roles; Sex Stereotypes; *Sexism.

1780 U.S. National Institute of Education. Conference on the educational and occupational needs of Hispanic women, June 29-30, 1976; December 10-12, 1976. Washington, DC: U.S. Department of Education, 1980. x, 301 p. English. DESCR: Conference on the Educational and Occupational Needs of Hispanic Women (1976: Denver, CO); Conferences and Meetings; *Employment; Higher Education; Leadership; Puerto Ricans; Sex Roles; *Women.

1781 Vangie, Mary. Women at Frontera, CA. REGENERACION, Vol. 1, no. 10 (1971), p. 8. English. DESCR: *Mexican American Research Association (MARA), California Institution for Women; Prisons; Statistics.

1782 Vasquez, Josefina. Educacion y papel de la mujer en Mexico. IN: Del Castillo, Adelaida R., ed. BETWEEN BORDERS: ESSAYS ON MEXICANA/CHICANA HISTORY. Encino, CA: Floricanto Press, 1990, p. 377-398. Spanish. DESCR: History; *Mexico; *Sex Roles; *Women.

1783 Vigil, James Diego. The nexus of class, culture and gender in the education of Mexican American females. IN: McKenna, Teresa and Ortiz, Flora Ida, eds. THE BROKEN WEB: THE EDUCATIONAL EXPERIENCE OF HISPANIC WOMEN. Claremont, CA: Tomas Rivera Center; Berkeley, CA: Floricanto Press, 1988, p. 79-103. English. DESCR: Academic Achievement; Acculturation; Discrimination in Education; Identity; Secondary School Education; Sex Roles; Social Classes; Students.

1784 Zambrana, Ruth E. Toward understanding the educational trajectory and socialization of Latina women. IN: McKenna, Teresa and Ortiz, Flora Ida, eds. THE BROKEN WEB: THE EDUCATIONAL EXPERIENCE OF HISPANIC WOMEN. Claremont, CA: Tomas Rivera Center; Berkeley, CA: Floricanto Press, 1988, p. 61-77. English. DESCR: Academic Achievement; Anglo Americans; Feminism; Identity; Research Methodology; *Socialization; *Women.

Education Equalization
USE: Discrimination in Education

Educational Administration

1785 Bauman, Raquel. A study of Mexican American women's perceptions of factors that influence academic and professional goal attainment. Thesis (Ed.D.)--University of Houston, 1984. 169 p. English. DESCR: *Careers; *Higher Education; Management.

1786 Braddom, Carolyn Lentz. The conceptualization of effective leadership as seen by women, Black and Hispanic superintendents. Thesis (Ed.D.)--University of Cincinnati, 1988. 232 p. English. DESCR: Anglo Americans; Blacks; *Leadership; Management; Women.

1787 Duran, Isabelle Sandoval. Grounded theory study: Chicana administrators in Colorado and New Mexico. Thesis (Ed.D.)--University of Wyoming, Laramie, 1982. ix, 114 p. English. DESCR: Careers; Colorado; Leadership; *Management; New Mexico.

1788 Galloway, Irma Nell. Trends in the employment of minority women as administrators in Texas public schools--1976-1981. Thesis (Ed.D.)--Texas Southern University, 1986. 129 p. English. DESCR: Asian Americans; Blacks; Education; *Management; Native Americans; Texas; *Women.

1789 Gardea, Corina. A comparison of behavioral characteristics of Hispanic and Anglo female administrators in the resolution of critical incident situations. Thesis (Ph.D.)--University of Texas, Austin, 1984. 145 p. English. DESCR: Anglo Americans; *Community Colleges; Leadership; Women.

1790 Jaramillo, Mari-Luci. Institutional responsibility in the provision of educational experiences to the Hispanic American female student. IN: McKenna, Teresa and Ortiz, Flora Ida, eds. THE BROKEN WEB: THE EDUCATIONAL EXPERIENCE OF HISPANIC WOMEN. Claremont, CA: Tomaas Rivera Center; Berkeley, CA: Floricanto Press, 1988, p. 25-35. English. DESCR: Academic Achievement; *Discrimination in Education; Dropouts; *Education; Enrollment; Higher Education; Students; *Women.

1791 Lopez, Gloria Ann. Job satisfaction of the Mexican American woman administrator in higher education. Thesis (Ph.D.)--University of Texas, Austin, 1984. 193 p. English. DESCR: *Careers; Higher Education; Leadership.

1792 Madrid, Sandra Emilia. The effects of socialization on goal actualization of public school Chicana principals and superintendents. Thesis (Ph.D.)--University of Washington, 1985. 253 p. English. DESCR: *Careers; Language Usage; *Socialization.

1793 Ortiz, Flora Ida. The distribution of Mexican American women in school organizations. HISPANIC JOURNAL OF BEHAVIORAL SCIENCES, Vol. 4, no. 2 (June 1982), p. 181-198. English. DESCR: Educational Organizations; *Teaching Profession.

1794 Sosa Riddell, Adaljiza. Background: a critical overview on Chicanas/Latinas and public policies. IN: Sosa Riddell, Adaljiza, ed. POLICY DEVELOPMENT: CHICANA/LATINA SUMMER RESEARCH INSTITUTE. Davis, CA: [Chicano Studies Program, University of California, Davis, 1989?], p. 2-8. English. DESCR: Discrimination; *Public Policy; Sexism.

The Educational Experience of Hispanic American Women [symposium] (1985: Claremont, CA)

1795 Del Castillo, Adelaida R., et al. An assessment of the status of the education of Hispanic American women. IN: McKenna, Teresa and Ortiz, Flora Ida, eds. THE BROKEN WEB: THE EDUCATIONAL EXPERIENCE OF HISPANIC WOMEN. Claremont, CA: Tomas Rivera Center; Berkeley, CA: Floricanto Press, 1988, p. 3-24. English. DESCR: Academic Achievement; Conferences and Meetings; Discrimination in Education; Dropouts; *Education; Higher Education; Public Policy; Research Methodology; *Women.

1796 McKenna, Teresa, ed. and Ortiz, Flora Ida, ed. The broken web: the educational experience of Hispanic American women. Claremont, CA: Tomas Rivera Center; Berkeley, CA: Floricanto Press, 1988. iii, 262 p. English. DESCR: *Academic Achievement; *Education; Educational Statistics; *Women.

Educational Levels

1797 Peters, Ruth K., et al. Risk factors for invasive cervical cancer among Latinas and non-Latinas in Los Angeles County. JOURNAL OF THE NATIONAL CANCER INSTITUTE, Vol. 77, no. 5 (November 1986), p. 1063-1077. English. DESCR: *Cancer; Diseases; Los Angeles County, CA; *Public Health; Women.

Educational Materials
USE: Curriculum Materials

Educational Organizations

1798 Gonzales, Sylvia Alicia. Hispanic American voluntary organizations. Westport, CT: Greenwood Press, 1985. xx, 267 p. English. DESCR: Art Organizations and Groups; *Community Organizations; Cultural Organizations; *Directories; *Organizations; Political Parties and Organizations; Professional Organizations.

1799 Ortiz, Flora Ida. The distribution of Mexican American women in school organizations. HISPANIC JOURNAL OF BEHAVIORAL SCIENCES, Vol. 4, no. 2 (June 1982), p. 181-198. English. DESCR: Educational Administration; *Teaching Profession.

Educational Statistics

1800 Chacon, Maria A. An overdue study of the Chicana undergraduate college experience. LA LUZ, Vol. 8, no. 8 (October, November, 1980), p. 27. English. DESCR: Colleges and Universities; Higher Education; Stanford University, Stanford, CA; Students.

1801 Chacon, Maria A., et al. Chicanas in California post secondary education: a comparative study of barriers to the program progress. Stanford, CA: Stanford Center for Chicano Research, 1985. viii, 217 p. English. DESCR: *Academic Achievement; Colleges and Universities; Counseling (Educational); Enrollment; *Higher Education; Students; Surveys.

1802 Lee, Valerie. Achievement and educational aspirations among Hispanic female high school students: comparison between public and Catholic schools. IN: McKenna, Teresa and Ortiz, Flora Ida, eds. THE BROKEN WEB: THE EDUCATIONAL EXPERIENCE OF HISPANIC WOMEN. Claremont, CA: Tomas Rivera Center; Berkeley, CA: Floricanto Press, 1988, p. 137-192. English. DESCR: *Academic Achievement; Anglo Americans; Catholic Church; Education; Private Education; Religious Education; *Secondary School Education; *Women.

1803 Martinez, Douglas R. Hispanic origin women in the U.S. LA LUZ, Vol. 8, no. 8 (October, November, 1980), p. 11-12. English. DESCR: *Population; Statistics.

1804 McKenna, Teresa and Ortiz, Flora Ida. Facts and figures on Hispanic Americans, women, and education. IN: McKenna, Teresa and Ortiz, Flora Ida, eds. THE BROKEN WEB: THE EDUCATIONAL EXPERIENCE OF HISPANIC WOMEN. Claremont, CA: Tomas Rivera Center; Berkeley, CA: Floricanto Press, 1988, p. 195-217. English. DESCR: *Education; *Women.

1805 McKenna, Teresa, ed. and Ortiz, Flora Ida, ed. The broken web: the educational experience of Hispanic American women. Claremont, CA: Tomas Rivera Center; Berkeley, CA: Floricanto Press, 1988. iii, 262 p. English. DESCR: *Academic Achievement; *Education; The Educational Experience of Hispanic American Women [symposium] (1985: Claremont, CA); *Women.

Educational Tests and Measurements

1806 Powers, Stephen and Jones, Patricia. Factorial invariance of the California achievement tests across race and sex. EDUCATIONAL AND PSYCHOLOGICAL MEASUREMENT, Vol. 44, no. 4 (Winter 1984), p. 967-970. English. DESCR: Anglo Americans; Blacks; *California Achievement Test (CAT); Males; Women.

El Paso, TX

1807 Garcia, Mario T. The Chicana in American history: the Mexican women of El Paso, 1880-1920 - a case study. PACIFIC HISTORICAL REVIEW, Vol. 49, no. 2 (May 1980), p. 315-337. English. DESCR: Acme Laundry, El Paso, TX; American Federation of Labor (AFL); Case Studies; Central Labor Union; Domestic Work; Employment; *History; Immigrants; Income; Labor Unions; Sex Roles; Strikes and Lockouts; *Working Women.

1808 Garcia, Mario T. La familia: the Mexican immigrant family, 1900-1930. IN: Barrera, Mario, et al., eds. WORK, FAMILY, SEX ROLES, LANGUAGE: SELECTED PAPERS, 1979. Berkeley, CA: Tonatiuh-Quinto Sol, 1980, p. 117-139. English. DESCR: Assimilation; Cultural Customs; Family; *Historiography; History; Immigration; Labor; Sex Roles.

1809 Ruiz, Vicki L. By the day or week: Mexicana domestic workers in El Paso. TRABAJOS MONOGRAFICOS, Vol. 2, no. 1 (1986), p. 35-58. English. DESCR: *Domestic Work; Employment; Labor Supply and Market; *Working Women.

1810 Ruiz, Vicki L. By the day or week: Mexicana domestic workers in El Paso. IN: Ruiz, Vicki L. and Tiano, Susan, eds. WOMEN ON THE U.S.-MEXICO BORDER: RESPONSES TO CHANGE. Boston, MA: Allen & Unwin, 1987, p. 61-76. English. DESCR: *Domestic Work; Employment; Labor Supply and Market.

El Paso, TX (cont.)

1811 Ruiz, Vicki L. Dead ends or gold mines?:
using missionary records in Mexican-American
women's history. FRONTIERS: A JOURNAL OF
WOMEN STUDIES, Vol. 12, no. 1 (1991), p.
33-56. English. DESCR: Archives; Clergy;
History; *Methodist Church; Protestant
Church; *Research Methodology; *Rose Gregory
Houchen Settlement House, El Paso, TX.

1812 Solorzano-Torres, Rosalia. Women, labor, and
the U.S.-Mexico border: Mexican maids in El
Paso, Texas. IN: Melville, Margarita, ed.
MEXICANAS AT WORK IN THE UNITED STATES.
Houston, TX: Mexican American Studies
Program, University of Houston, 1988, p.
75-83. English. DESCR: Border Patrol;
*Border Region; Domestic Work; Immigrants;
Immigration and Naturalization Service
(INS); Immigration Regulation and Control;
*Labor Supply and Market; Undocumented
Workers; *Women; *Working Women.

1813 Trevathan, Wenda R. First conversations:
verbal content of mother-newborn
interaction. JOURNAL OF CROSS-CULTURAL
PSYCHOLOGY, Vol. 19, no. 1 (March 1988), p.
65-77. English. DESCR: Cultural
Characteristics; Language Arts; *Parent and
Child Relationships.

**El Paso Women's Employment and Education Project
(EPWEE)**

1814 Ruiz, Vicki L. "And miles to go...": Mexican
women and work, 1930-1985. IN: Schlissel,
Lillian, et al., eds. WESTERN WOMEN: THEIR
LAND, THEIR LIVES. Albuquerque, NM:
University of New Mexico Press, 1988, p.
117-136. English. DESCR: Education;
*Employment; Farah Manufacturing Co., El
Paso, TX; Farah Strike; *Income; Industrial
Workers; Labor Unions; Statistics;
Undocumented Workers; United Cannery
Agricultural Packing and Allied Workers of
America (UCAPAWA); Women; *Working Women.

Elected Officials

1815 Baca Barragan, Polly. La Chicana in
politics. IN: LA CHICANA: BUILDING FOR THE
FUTURE, AN ACTION PLAN FOR THE 80s. Oakland,
CA: National Hispanic University, 1981, p.
21-31. English. DESCR: Leadership; Political
Representation; *Politics.

1816 Baca Barragan, Polly; Hamner, Richard; and
Guerrero, Lena. [Untitled interview with
State Senators (Colorado) Polly
Baca-Barragan and Lena Guerrero]. NATIONAL
HISPANIC JOURNAL, Vol. 1, no. 2 (Winter
1982), p. 8-11. English. DESCR: Baca
Barragan, Polly; Carter, Jimmy (President);
Democratic Party; Guerrero, Lena; *Political
Parties and Organizations.

1817 Chacon, Peter. Chicanas and political
representation. IN: LA CHICANA: BUILDING FOR
THE FUTURE, AN ACTION PLAN FOR THE80s.
Oakland, CA: National Hispanic University,
1981, p. 32-36. English. DESCR: *Political
Representation; Politics; Voter Turnout.

1818 Espinosa, Ann. Hispanas: our resourses [sic]
for the eighties. LA LUZ, Vol. 8, no. 4
(October, November, 1979), p. 10-13.
English. DESCR: Baca Barragan, Polly; *Civil
Rights; Comision Femenil Mexicana Nacional;
DIRECTORY OF HISPANIC WOMEN; Discrimination
in Education; Hernandez, Irene; Lacayo,
Carmela; Lujan, Josie; Mexican American
Women's National Association (MANA);
Montanez Davis, Grace; Moreno, Olga; Mujeres

Latinas en Accion (M.L.A.); National
Conference of Puerto Rican Women, Inc.
(NCOPRW); Organizations; Rangel, Irma.

1819 Flores, Francisca. Equality. REGENERACION,
Vol. 2, no. 3 (1973), p. 4-5. English.
DESCR: Anglo Americans; Chicano Movement;
Discrimination; Feminism; Income; *Machismo;
*Working Women.

1820 Huerta, Dolores. Dolores Huerta talks about
Republicans, Cesar, children and her home
town. REGENERACION, Vol. 2, no. 4 (1975), p.
20-24. English. DESCR: *Agricultural Labor
Unions; *Biography; Chavez, Cesar E.;
Community Service Organization, Los Angeles,
(CSO); Democratic Party; Flores, Art;
Huerta, Dolores; McGovern, George;
*Politics; Ramirez, Henry M.; Ross, Fred;
Sanchez, Philip V.; United Farmworkers of
America (UFW); Working Women.

1821 Huerta, Dolores. Dolores Huerta talks about
Republicans, Cesar, children and her home
town. IN: Servin, Manuel P. ed. THE MEXICAN
AMERICANS: AN AWAKENING MINORITY. 2nd ed.
Beverly Hills, CA: Glencoe Press, 1974, p.
283-294. English. DESCR: *Agricultural Labor
Unions; *Biography; Chavez, Cesar E.;
Community Service Organization, Los Angeles,
(CSO); Democratic Party; Flores, Art;
Huerta, Dolores; McGovern, George;
*Politics; Ramirez, Henry M.; Ross, Fred;
Sanchez, Philip V.; United Farmworkers of
America (UFW); Working Women.

1822 Mora, Julio. Latina legislators: few and far
between. NUESTRO, Vol. 4, no. 2 (April
1980), p. 18-20. English.

Elections

1823 Mendoza, Hope Schecter and Chall, Malca.
Activist in the labor movement, the
Democratic Party, and the Mexican-American
community: an interview. Berkeley, CA:
Regional Oral History Office, Bancroft
Library, University of California, Berkeley,
1980. xii, 170 p.: ill. English. DESCR:
*Biography; Chavez Ravine, Los Angeles, CA;
Church, Frank; Community Organizations;
Community Service Organization, Los Angeles,
(CSO); Democratic Party; Garment Industry;
Industrial Workers; *Labor Unions;
Leadership; Mendoza, Hope Schecter; Snyder,
Elizabeth; Warschaw, Carmen.

Electronics Industry

1824 Fernandez Kelly, Maria. "Chavalas de
maquiladora": a study of the female labor
force in Ciudad Juarez' offshore production
plants. Thesis (Ph.D.)--Rutgers University,
1980. xi, 391 leaves. English. DESCR:
*Border Industries; Ciudad Juarez,
Chihuahua, Mexico; *Employment; Garment
Industry; Industrial Workers; Mexico; Women;
*Working Women.

1825 Fernandez Kelly, Maria and Garcia, Anna M.
Economic restructuring in the United States:
Hispanic women in the garment and
electronics industries. WOMEN AND WORK, Vol.
3, (1988), p. 49-65. English. DESCR:
Business Enterprises; Businesspeople;
*Garment Industry; Industrial Workers;
*International Economic Relations; *Working
Women.

Electronics Industry
(cont.)

1826 Fernandez Kelly, Maria. For we are sold, I and my people: women and industry in Mexico's frontier. Albany, NY: State University of New York Press, 1983. vii, 217 p. English. **DESCR:** Border Industries; *Border Region; Ciudad Juarez, Chihuahua, Mexico; *Garment Industry; Industrial Workers; Working Women.

1827 Fernandez Kelly, Maria and Garcia, Anna M. Invisible amidst the glitter: Hispanic women in the Southern California electronics industry. IN: Statham, Anne; Miller, Eleanor M.; and Mauksh, Hans O., eds. THE WORTH OF WOMEN'S WORK: A QUALITATIVE SYNTHESIS. Albany, NY: State University of New York Press, 1988, p. 265-290. English. **DESCR:** Employment; Immigrants; *Industrial Workers; Labor Supply and Market; Megatek, La Jolla, CA; Nova-Tech, San Diego, CA; Sex Roles; Southern California; *Working Women.

Elementary School Education
USE: Primary School Education

Elgin, IL

1828 Campos Carr, Irene. Proyecto La Mujer: Latina women shaping consciousness. WOMEN'S STUDIES INTERNATIONAL FORUM, Vol. 12, no. 1 (1989), p. 45-49. English. **DESCR:** Artists; Aurora, IL; Authors; Barrios; Conferences and Meetings; *Feminism; Joliet, IL; Poetry; Proyecto La Mujer Conference (Spring, 1982: Northern Illinois); Women.

Emigration
USE: Migration

Employment

1829 Arenal, Sandra. Sangre joven: las maquiladoras por dentro. Mexico, D.F.: Editorial Nuestro Tiempo, 1986. 130 p.: ill. Spanish. **DESCR:** *Border Industries; *Border Region; *Oral History; Women; Working Women.

1830 Arroyo, Laura E. Industrial and occupational distribution of Chicana workers. AZTLAN, Vol. 4, no. 2 (Fall 1973), p. 343-382. English. **DESCR:** California; Farah Manufacturing Co., El Paso, TX; Farah Strike; Garment Industry; Industrial Workers; Strikes and Lockouts; Texas.

1831 Arroyo, Laura E. Industrial and occupational distribution of Chicana workers. IN: Sanchez, Rosaura and Martinez Cruz, Rosa, eds. ESSAYS ON LA MUJER. Los Angeles, CA: Chicano Studies Center Publications, UCLA, 1977, p. 150-187. English. **DESCR:** California; Farah Manufacturing Co., El Paso, TX; Farah Strike; Garment Industry; Industrial Workers; Strikes and Lockouts; Texas.

1832 Baca Zinn, Maxine. Employment and education of Mexican-American women: the interplay of modernity and ethnicity in eight families. HARVARD EDUCATIONAL REVIEW, Vol. 50, no. 1 (February 1980), p. 47-62. English. **DESCR:** Acculturation; Decision Making; *Education; *Family; Identity; Sex Roles; Social Classes; Values.

1833 Bean, Frank D. and Tienda, Marta. The Hispanic population of the United States. New York: Russell Sage Foundation, 1987. xxiv, 456 p. English. **DESCR:** *Census; Education; Fertility; Identity; Immigration; Income; *Population; Self-Referents; *Statistics.

1834 Bean, Frank D.; Stephen, Elizabeth H.; and Opitz, Wolfgang. The Mexican origin population in the United States: a demographic overview. IN: O. de la Garza, Rodolfo, et al., eds. THE MEXICAN AMERICAN EXPERIENCE: AN INTERDISCIPLINARY ANTHOLOGY. Austin, TX: University of Texas Press, 1985, p. 57-75. English. **DESCR:** Fertility; Income; *Population; Vital Statistics.

1835 Bean, Frank D.; Swicegood, Gray; and King, Allan G. Role incompatibility and the relationship between fertility and labor supply among Hispanic women. IN: Borjas, George J. and Tienda, Marta, eds. HISPANICS IN THE U.S. ECONOMY. Orlando, FL: Academic Press, 1985, p. 221-242. English. **DESCR:** Cubanos; Fertility; Labor Supply and Market; Puerto Ricans.

1836 Becerra, Gloria V. and Lopez, Martha. Chicana employment--options for the future. IN: LA CHICANA: BUILDING FOR THE FUTURE, AN ACTION PLAN FOR THE 80s. Oakland, CA: National Hispanic University, 1981, p. 8-20. English. **DESCR:** Feminism.

1837 Berger, Peggy S. Differences in importance of and satisfaction from job characteristics by sex and occupational type among Mexican-American employees. JOURNAL OF VOCATIONAL BEHAVIOR, Vol. 28, no. 3 (June 1986), p. 203-213. English. **DESCR:** *Attitudes; *Sex Roles.

1838 Blackwelder, Julia Kirk. Women of the depression: caste and culture in San Antonio, 1929-1939. College Station, TX: Texas A&M University Press, 1984. xviii, 279 p.: ill. English. **DESCR:** Criminal Justice System; Cultural Characteristics; Family; Great Depression, 1929-1933; Labor Supply and Market; Labor Unions; Prostitution; San Antonio, TX; *Social Classes; *Women.

1839 Calderon, Vivian. Maternal employment and career orientation of young Chicana, Black, and white women. Thesis (Ph.D.)--University of California, Santa Cruz, 1984. 150 p. English. **DESCR:** Anglo Americans; Blacks; *Careers; Women; *Youth.

1840 Cardenas, Gilbert and Flores, Estevan T. The migration and settlement of undocumented women. Austin, TX: CMAS Publications, 1986. 69 p. English. **DESCR:** Houston, TX; *Immigration; Income; Labor Supply and Market; *Migration Patterns; Public Policy; Socioeconomic Factors; *Undocumented Workers.

1841 Cardenas, Gilbert; Shelton, Beth Anne; and Pena, Devon Gerardo. Undocumented immigrant women in the Houston labor force. CALIFORNIA SOCIOLOGIST, Vol. 5, no. 2 (Summer 1982), p. 98-118. English. **DESCR:** Houston, TX; *Immigrants; *Labor Supply and Market; *Undocumented Workers.

1842 Carrillo V., Jorge and Hernandez H., Alberto. Mujeres fronterizas en la industria maquiladora. Mexico, D.F.: Secretaria de Educacion Publica; Tijuana, B.C.N.: Centro de Estudios Fronterizos del Norte de Mexico, 1985. 216 p. Spanish. **DESCR:** *Border Industries; *Women; Working Women.

Employment (cont.)

1843 Cooney, Rosemary Santana. The Mexican
American female in the labor force. IN:
Teller, Charles H., et al., eds. CUANTOS
SOMOS: A DEMOGRAPHIC STUDY OF THE MEXICAN
AMERICAN POPULATION. Austin, TX: Center for
Mexican American Studies, University of
Texas at Austin, 1977, p. 183-196. English.
DESCR: Labor Supply and Market.

1844 Curry Rodriguez, Julia E. Labor migration
and familial responsibilities: experiences
of Mexican women. IN: Melville, Margarita,
ed. MEXICANAS AT WORK IN THE UNITED STATES.
Houston, TX: Mexican American Studies
Program, University of Houston, 1988, p.
47-63. English. **DESCR:** Family; *Immigrants;
Mexico; *Migrant Labor; Oral History; Sex
Roles; Undocumented Workers; *Women;
*Working Women.

1845 Curry Rodriguez, Julia E. Reconceptualizing
undocumented labor immigration: the causes,
impact and consequences in Mexican women's
lives. Thesis (Ph.D.)--University of Texas
at Austin, 1988. xiv, 329 p. English.
DESCR: *Immigrants; Mexico; Oral History;
*Undocumented Workers; *Women.

1846 Davis, Cary; Haub, Carl; and Willette,
JoAnne. U.S. Hispanics: changing the face of
America. POPULATION BULLETIN, Vol. 38, no. 3
(June 1983), p. 1-43. English. **DESCR:**
Education; Fertility; Immigration; Income;
*Population; Statistics; Vital Statistics.

1847 Dublin, Thomas. Commentary [on "And Miles to
Go": Mexican Women and Work, 1930-1985]. IN:
Schlissel, Lillian, et al., eds. WESTERN
WOMEN: THEIR LAND, THEIR LIVES. Albuquerque,
NM: University of New Mexico Press, 1988, p.
137-140. English. **DESCR:** "'And Miles to
Go...': Mexican Women and Work, 1930-1985";
Income; Labor Unions; Ruiz, Vicki L.;
Undocumented Workers; Women; *Working Women.

1848 Farkas, George; Barton, Margaret; and
Kushner, Kathy. White, Black, and Hispanic
female youths in central city labor markets.
SOCIOLOGICAL QUARTERLY, Vol. 29, no. 4
(Winter 1988), p. 605-621. English. **DESCR:**
Anglo Americans; Blacks; *Income; *Labor
Supply and Market; Urban Communities; Women;
*Youth.

1849 Fernandez Kelly, Maria. "Chavalas de
maquiladora": a study of the female labor
force in Ciudad Juarez' offshore production
plants. Thesis (Ph.D.)--Rutgers University,
1980. xi, 391 leaves. English. **DESCR:**
*Border Industries; Ciudad Juarez,
Chihuahua, Mexico; Electronics Industry;
Garment Industry; Industrial Workers;
Mexico; Women; *Working Women.

1850 Fernandez Kelly, Maria and Garcia, Anna M.
Invisible amidst the glitter: Hispanic women
in the Southern California electronics
industry. IN: Statham, Anne; Miller, Eleanor
M.; and Mauksh, Hans O., eds. THE WORTH OF
WOMEN'S WORK: A QUALITATIVE SYNTHESIS.
Albany, NY: State University of New York
Press, 1988, p. 265-290. English. **DESCR:**
*Electronics Industry; Immigrants;
*Industrial Workers; Labor Supply and
Market; Megatek, La Jolla, CA; Nova-Tech,
San Diego, CA; Sex Roles; Southern
California; *Working Women.

1851 Fernandez Kelly, Maria and Garcia, Anna M.
The making of an underground economy:
Hispanic women, home work, and the advanced
capitalist state. URBAN ANTHROPOLOGY, Vol.

14, no. 1-3 (Spring, Fall, 1985), p. 59-90.
English. **DESCR:** Capitalism; Cubanos; Garment
Industry; Industrial Workers; International
Economic Relations; Labor Supply and Market;
*Los Angeles County, CA; *Miami, FL; Women;
Working Women.

1852 Friaz, Guadalupe. Chicanas in the workforce
= Chicanas en la fuerza de trabajo: "Working
9 to 5". CAMINOS, Vol. 2, no. 3 (May 1981),
p. 37-39, 61+. Bilingual. **DESCR:** Labor
Unions; Laborers; *Working Women.

1853 Garcia, Mario T. The Chicana in American
history: the Mexican women of El Paso,
1880-1920 - a case study. PACIFIC HISTORICAL
REVIEW, Vol. 49, no. 2 (May 1980), p.
315-337. English. **DESCR:** Acme Laundry, El
Paso, TX; American Federation of Labor
(AFL); Case Studies; Central Labor Union;
Domestic Work; *El Paso, TX; *History;
Immigrants; Income; Labor Unions; Sex Roles;
Strikes and Lockouts; *Working Women.

1854 Gettman, Dawn and Pena, Devon Gerardo.
Women, mental health, and the workplace in a
transnational setting. SOCIAL WORK, Vol. 31,
no. 1 (January, February, 1986), p. 5-11.
English. **DESCR:** *Border Industries; *Mental
Health; Mexico; United States-Mexico
Relations; Women; *Working Women.

1855 Golding, Jacqueline M. Division of household
labor, strain, and depressive symptoms among
Mexican Americans and non-Hispanic whites.
PSYCHOLOGY OF WOMEN QUARTERLY, Vol. 14, no.
1 (March 1990), p. 103-117. English. **DESCR:**
Anglo Americans; Comparative Psychology;
*Depression (Psychological); Domestic Work;
Identity; *Sex Roles; Women.

1856 Hancock, Paula F. The effect of welfare
eligibility on the labor force participation
of women of Mexican origin in California.
POPULATION RESEARCH AND POLICY REVIEW, Vol.
5, no. 2 (1986), p. 163-185. English.
DESCR: Aid to Families with Dependent
Children (AFDC); California; Food Stamps;
Immigrants; Medi-Cal; Single Parents;
*Welfare; Women.

1857 Hancock, Paula F. The effects of nativity,
legal status and welfare eligibility on the
labor force participation of women of
Mexican origin in California. Thesis
(Ph.D.)--University of Southern California,
1985. English. **DESCR:** *Immigrants;
Undocumented Workers; *Welfare.

1858 Hart, John M. Working-class women in
nineteenth century Mexico. IN: Mora,
Magdalena and Del Castillo, Adelaida, eds.
MEXICAN WOMEN IN THE UNITED STATES:
STRUGGLES PAST AND PRESENT. Los Angeles, CA:
Chicano Studies Research Center, 1980, p.
151-157. English. **DESCR:** History; Mexico;
Women; Working Women.

1859 Hayghe, Howard. Married couples: work and
income patterns. MONTHLY LABOR REVIEW, Vol.
106, no. 12 (December 1983), p. 26-29.
English. **DESCR:** *Income; *Marriage; *Sex
Roles; Working Women.

1860 Hazuda, Helen P., et al. Employment status
and women's protection against coronary
heart disease. AMERICAN JOURNAL OF
EPIDEMIOLOGY, Vol. 123, no. 4 (April 1986),
p. 623-640. English. **DESCR:** Anglo Americans;
Diseases; *Heart Disease; Nutrition; *Public
Health; San Antonio, TX.

Employment (cont.)

1861 Jensen, Joan M. Commentary [on "And Miles to Go": Mexican Women and Work, 1930-1985]. IN Schlissel, Lillian, et al., eds. WESTERN WOMEN: THEIR LAND, THEIR LIVES. Albuquerque NM: University of New Mexico Press, 1988, p 141-144. English. DESCR: "'And Miles to Go...': Mexican Women and Work, 1930-1985"; California; Income; Labor Unions; Public Policy; Ruiz, Vicki L.; Women; *Working Women.

1862 Karnig, Albert K.; Welch, Susan; and Eribes Richard A. Employment of women by cities in the Southwest. SOCIAL SCIENCE JOURNAL, Vol. 21, no. 4 (October 1984), p. 41-48. English. DESCR: Local Government; Southwestern United States; Women.

1863 Kossoudji, Sherrie and Ranney, Susan. The labor market experience of female migrants: the case of temporary Mexican migration to the U.S. INTERNATIONAL MIGRATION REVIEW, Vol. 18, no. 4 (Winter 1984), p. 1120-1143. English. DESCR: Immigrants; Income; *Labor Supply and Market; *Migrant Labor; Sex Roles; *Women; Working Women.

1864 Krause, Neal and Markides, Kyriakos S. Employment and psychological well-being in Mexican American women. JOURNAL OF HEALTH AND SOCIAL BEHAVIOR, Vol. 26, no. 1 (March 1985), p. 15-26. English. DESCR: *Attitudes; Identity; Mental Health; Sex Roles; Working Women.

1865 Leonard, Jonathan S. The effect of unions or the employment of Blacks, Hispanics, and women. INDUSTRIAL AND LABOR RELATIONS REVIEW, Vol. 39, no. 1 (October 1985), p. 115-132. English. DESCR: Blacks; *Labor Unions; Women.

1866 Lopez-Garza, Maria C. Toward a reconceptualization of women's economic activities: the informal sector in urban Mexico. IN: Cordova, Teresa, et al., eds. CHICANA VOICES. Austin, TX: Center for Mexican American Studies, 1986, p. 66-76. English. DESCR: Mexico; *Women.

1867 Melville, Margarita B., ed. Mexicanas at work in the United States. Houston, TX: Mexican American Studies Program, University of Houston, 1988. 83 p. English. DESCR: Border Region; Family; *Labor; Migrant Labor; *Women; Working Women.

1868 Nava, Yolanda. Chicanas in the television media. IN: LA CHICANA: BUILDING FOR THE FUTURE, AN ACTION PLAN FOR THE 80s. Oakland, CA: National Hispanic University, 1981, p. 120-133. English. DESCR: Careers; Stereotypes; *Television.

1869 Nava, Yolanda. Employment counseling and the Chicana. ENCUENTRO FEMENIL, Vol. 1, no. 1 (Spring 1973), p. 20-26. English. DESCR: Employment Training; Sexism.

1870 Nieto Gomez de Lazarin, Anna. Chicanas in the labor force. ENCUENTRO FEMENIL, Vol. 1, no. 2 (1974), p. 28-33. English. DESCR: Discrimination in Employment; *Working Women.

1871 Nieto Gomez de Lazarin, Anna. Madres por justicia! ENCUENTRO FEMENIL, Vol. 1, no. 1 (Spring 1973), p. 12-19. English. DESCR: Chicana Welfare Rights Organization; Talmadge Amendment to the Social Security Act, 1971; *Welfare.

1872 O'Connor, Mary I. Women's networks and the social needs of Mexican immigrants. URBAN ANTHROPOLOGY, Vol. 19, no. 1-2 (Spring, Summer, 1990), p. 81-98. English. DESCR: *Immigrants; Labor Unions; *Natural Support Systems; *Sandyland Nursery, Carpinteria, CA; Undocumented Workers; United Farmworkers of America (UFW); Women.

1873 Ortiz, Vilma and Fennelly, Katherine. Early childbearing and employment among young Mexican origin, Black, and white women. SOCIAL SCIENCE QUARTERLY, Vol. 69, no. 4 (December 1988), p. 987-995. English. DESCR: Anglo Americans; Blacks; *Fertility; *Women; *Youth.

1874 Ortiz, Vilma and Cooney, Rosemary Santana. Sex-role attitudes and labor force participation among young Hispanic females and non-Hispanic white females. SOCIAL SCIENCE QUARTERLY, Vol. 65, no. 2 (June 1984), p. 392-400. English. DESCR: Anglo Americans; Attitudes; *Sex Roles; Working Women.

1875 Ortiz, Vilma and Cooney, Rosemary Santana. Sex-role attitudes and labor force participation among young Hispanic females and non-Hispanic white females. IN: O. de la Garza, Rodolfo, et al., eds. THE MEXICAN AMERICAN EXPERIENCE: AN INTERDISCIPLINARY ANTHOLOGY. Austin, TX: University of Texas Press, 1985, p. 174-182. English. DESCR: Anglo Americans; Attitudes; *Sex Roles; Working Women.

1876 Pena, Devon Gerardo. Tortuosidad: shop floor struggles of female maquiladora workers. IN: Ruiz, Vicki L. and Tiano, Susan, eds. WOMEN ON THE U.S.-MEXICO BORDER: RESPONSES TO CHANGE. Boston, MA: Allen & Unwin, 1987, p. 129-154. English. DESCR: Border Industries; Ciudad Juarez, Chihuahua, Mexico; Personnel Management; Population; Surveys; *Women; Working Women.

1877 Peralta Aguilar, Linda. Unequal opportunity and the Chicana. LA LUZ, Vol. 1, no. 5 (September 1972), p. 52. English. DESCR: *Discrimination; Discrimination in Employment; *Feminism.

1878 Peralta Aguilar, Linda. Unequal opportunity and the Chicana. REGENERACION, Vol. 2, no. 4 (1975), p. 45-46. English. DESCR: *Discrimination; *Discrimination in Employment; Feminism.

1879 Peralta Aguilar, Linda. Unequal opportunity and the Chicana. LA LUZ, Vol. 6, no. 1 (January 1977), p. 29-30. English. DESCR: *Discrimination; Discrimination in Employment; *Feminism.

1880 Pick, James B., et al. Socioeconomic influences on fertility in the Mexican borderlands region. MEXICAN STUDIES/ESTUDIOS MEXICANOS, Vol. 6, no. 1 (Winter 1990), p. 11-42. English. DESCR: *Border Region; *Fertility; Labor Supply and Market; Literacy; Socioeconomic Factors; Working Women.

1881 Popp, Gary E. and Muhs, William F. Fears of success and women employees. HUMAN RELATIONS, Vol. 35, no. 7 (July 1982), p. 511-519. English. DESCR: Women.

Employment (cont.)

1882 Preuss, Sabine. Die Frauen von Acapulco Fashion: Weiblicher Lebenszusammenhang und Industrialisierung in den Weltmarktfabriken Mexikos. Berlin: Express, c1985. 133 p.: ill. Other. **DESCR:** *Acapulco Fashion, Ciudad Juarez, Mexico; *Border Industries; *Working Women.

1883 Roberts, Robert E. and Roberts, Catharine Ramsay. Marriage, work and depressive symptoms among Mexican Americans. HISPANIC JOURNAL OF BEHAVIORAL SCIENCES, Vol. 4, no. 2 (June 1982), p. 199-221. English. **DESCR:** Depression (Psychological); Marriage; *Mental Health.

1884 Romero, Fred E. The labor market status of Chicanas. IN: Romero, Fred. CHICANO WORKERS: THEIR UTILIZATION AND DEVELOPMENT. Los Angeles: Chicano Studies Center Publications, UCLA, 1979, p. 82-95. English. **DESCR:** Income; Labor Supply and Market; *Statistics; *Working Women.

1885 Romero, Gloria J.; Castro, Felipe G.; and Cervantes, Richard C. Latinas without work: family, occupational, and economic stress following unemployment. PSYCHOLOGY OF WOMEN QUARTERLY, Vol. 12, no. 3 (September 1988), p. 281-297. English. **DESCR:** Family; Starkist Tuna Cannery, Wilmington, CA; *Stress.

1886 Romero, Gloria J.; Cervantes, Richard C.; and Castro, Felipe G. Long-term stress among Latino women after a plant closure. SOCIOLOGY & SOCIAL RESEARCH, Vol. 71, no. 2 (January 1987), p. 85-88. English. **DESCR:** Attitudes; Family; *Stress; Wilmington, CA.

1887 Romero, Mary. Chicanas modernize domestic service. QUALITATIVE SOCIOLOGY, Vol. 11, no. 4 (Winter 1988), p. 319-334. English. **DESCR:** *Domestic Work; Income; *Interpersonal Relations; Working Women.

1888 Romero, Mary. Day work in the suburbs: the work experience of Chicana private housekeepers. IN: Statham, Anne; Miller, Eleanor M; and Mauksch, Hans O., eds. THE WORTH OF WOMEN'S WORK: A QUALITATIVE SYNTHESIS. Albany, NY: State University of New York Press, 1988, p. 77-91. English. **DESCR:** Domestic Work; Interpersonal Relations; *Natural Support Systems; Social Mobility; Working Women.

1889 Romero, Mary. Domestic service in the transition from rural to urban life: the case of la Chicana. WOMEN'S STUDIES QUARTERLY, Vol. 13, no. 3 (February 1987), p. 199-222. English. **DESCR:** *Domestic Work; Interpersonal Relations; Rural Population; Social Mobility; Sociology; Urban Communities; Working Women.

1890 Ruiz, Vicki L. "And miles to go...": Mexican women and work, 1930-1985. IN: Schlissel, Lillian, et al., eds. WESTERN WOMEN: THEIR LAND, THEIR LIVES. Albuquerque, NM: University of New Mexico Press, 1988, p. 117-136. English. **DESCR:** Education; El Paso Women's Employment and Education Project (EPWEE); Farah Manufacturing Co., El Paso, TX; Farah Strike; *Income; Industrial Workers; Labor Unions; Statistics; Undocumented Workers; United Cannery Agricultural Packing and Allied Workers of America (UCAPAWA); Women; *Working Women.

1891 Ruiz, Vicki L. By the day or week: Mexicana domestic workers in El Paso. TRABAJOS MONOGRAFICOS, Vol. 2, no. 1 (1986), p.

35-58. English. **DESCR:** *Domestic Work; El Paso, TX; Labor Supply and Market; *Working Women.

1892 Ruiz, Vicki L. By the day or week: Mexicana domestic workers in El Paso. IN: Ruiz, Vicki L. and Tiano, Susan, eds. WOMEN ON THE U.S.-MEXICO BORDER: RESPONSES TO CHANGE. Boston, MA: Allen & Unwin, 1987, p. 61-76. English. **DESCR:** *Domestic Work; El Paso, TX; Labor Supply and Market.

1893 Ruiz, Vicki L. Working for wages: Mexican women in the Southwest, 1930-1980. Tucson, AZ: Southwest Institute for Research on Women, 1984. 24 p. English. **DESCR:** History; *Income; Labor Unions; *Women.

1894 Ruiz, Vicki L., ed. and Tiano, Susan B., ed. Women on the U.S.-Mexico border: responses to change. Boston, MA: Allen & Unwin, c1987. xi, 247 p. English. **DESCR:** *Border Industries; *Border Region; Feminism; Immigrants; Mexico; Sex Roles; *Women.

1895 Saenz, Rogelio; Goudy, Willis J.; and Lorenz, Frederick O. The effects of employment and marital relations on depression among Mexican American women. JOURNAL OF MARRIAGE AND THE FAMILY, Vol. 51, no. 1 (February 1989), p. 239-251. English. **DESCR:** *Depression (Psychological); Domestic Work; Feminism; *Marriage; Women Men Relations; Working Women.

1896 Sanchez, Rosaura. The Chicana labor force. IN: Sanchez, Rosaura and Martinez Cruz, Rosa, eds. ESSAYS ON LA MUJER. Los Angeles, CA: Chicano Studies Center Publications, UCLA, 1977, p. 3-15. English. **DESCR:** Income; Social Classes.

1897 Segura, Denise. Chicana and Mexican immigrant women at work: the impact of class, race, and gender on occupational mobility. GENDER & SOCIETY, Vol. 3, no. 1 (March 1989), p. 37-52. English. **DESCR:** *Immigrants; Labor Supply and Market; Laboring Classes; San Francisco Bay Area; *Social Mobility; Women; Working Women.

1898 Segura, Denise. Familism and employment among Chicanas and Mexican immigrant women. IN: Melville, Margarita, ed. MEXICANAS AT WORK IN THE UNITED STATES. Houston, TX: Mexican American Studies Program, University of Houston, 1988, p. 24-32. English. **DESCR:** *Extended Family; Family; Immigrants; Income; Machismo; Sex Roles; *Women; Working Women.

1899 Segura, Denise. The interplay of familism and patriarchy on employment among Chicana and Mexicana women. RENATO ROSALDO LECTURE SERIES MONOGRAPH, Vol. 5, (1989), p. 35-53. English. **DESCR:** *Family; Immigrants; Machismo; *Sex Roles; Women; Women Men Relations; *Working Women.

1900 Segura, Denise. Labor market stratification: the Chicana experience. BERKELEY JOURNAL OF SOCIOLOGY, Vol. 29, (1984), p. 57-91. English. **DESCR:** *Discrimination in Employment; *Labor Supply and Market; Socioeconomic Factors; *Working Women.

Employment (cont.)

1901 Seligson, Mitchell A. and Williams, Edward
J. Maquiladoras and migration workers in the
Mexico-United States Border
Industrialization Program. Austin, TX:
Mexico-United States Border Research
Program, University of Texas at Austin,
1981. xviii, 202 p. English. **DESCR:** Border
Industrialization Program (BIP); *Border
Region; Immigration; Industrial Workers;
Mexico; *Migration Patterns; Working Women.

1902 Solorzano-Torres, Rosalia. Female Mexican
immigrants in San Diego County. IN: Ruiz,
Vicki L. and Tiano, Susan, eds. WOMEN ON THE
U.S.-MEXICO BORDER: RESPONSES TO CHANGE.
Boston, MA: Allen & Unwin, 1987, p. 41-59.
English. **DESCR:** *Immigrants; Immigration;
Literature Reviews; San Diego County, CA;
Surveys; Undocumented Workers; Women.

1903 Staudt, Kathleen. Programming women's
empowerment: a case from northern Mexico.
IN: Ruiz, Vicki L. and Tiano, Susan, eds.
WOMEN ON THE U.S.-MEXICO BORDER: RESPONSES
TO CHANGE. Boston, MA: Allen & Unwin, 1987,
p. 155-173. English. **DESCR:** Alternative
Education; Border Region; Ciudad Juarez,
Chihuahua, Mexico; Curriculum; *Feminism;
Organizations; Women.

1904 Stewart, Kenneth L. and de Leon, Arnoldo.
Work force participation among Mexican
immigrant women in Texas, 1900. BORDERLANDS
JOURNAL, Vol. 9, no. 1 (Spring 1986), p.
69-74. English. **DESCR:** History; *Immigrants;
Texas; Women; *Working Women.

1905 Sullivan, Teresa A. The occupational
prestige of women immigrants: a comparison
of Cubans and Mexicans. INTERNATIONAL
MIGRATION REVIEW, Vol. 18, no. 4 (Winter
1984), p. 1045-1062. English. **DESCR:**
Careers; Cubanos; *Immigrants; Males;
Mexico; Sex Roles; *Social Mobility; *Women;
*Working Women.

1906 Taylor, Paul S. Mexican women in Los Angeles
industry in 1928. AZTLAN, Vol. 11, no. 1
(Spring 1980), p. 99-131. English. **DESCR:**
History; Industrial Workers; Los Angeles,
CA; *Working Women.

1907 Tiano, Susan B. Export processing, women's
work, and the employment problem in
developing countries: the case of the
maquiladora program in Northern Mexico. El
Paso, TX: Center for InterAmerican and
Border Studies, UTEP, 1985. 32 p. English.
DESCR: *Border Region; Labor Supply and
Market; Mexico; *Sex Roles; Women; Working
Women.

1908 Tiano, Susan B. Maquiladoras in Mexicali:
integration or exploitation? IN: Ruiz, Vicki
L. and Tiano, Susan, eds. WOMEN ON THE
U.S.-MEXICO BORDER: RESPONSES TO CHANGE.
Boston, MA: Allen & Unwin, 1987, p. 77-101.
English. **DESCR:** Border Industrialization
Program (BIP); *Border Industries; Border
Region; Labor Supply and Market; Mexicali,
Mexico; Women; Working Women.

1909 Tiano, Susan B. Maquiladoras, women's work,
and unemployment in northern Mexico. AZTLAN
Vol. 15, no. 2 (Fall 1984), p. 341-378.
English. **DESCR:** *Border Industries; Mexico;
*Women; Working Women.

1910 Tiano, Susan B. Women's work and
unemployment in northern Mexico. IN: Ruiz,
Vicki L. and Tiano, Susan, eds. WOMEN ON THE
U.S.-MEXICO BORDER: RESPONSES TO CHANGE.

Boston, MA: Allen & Unwin, 1987, p. 17-39.
English. **DESCR:** Border Industrialization
Program (BIP); Border Industries; Border
Region; Labor Supply and Market; Mexico;
Multinational Corporations; *Women.

1911 Tienda, Marta and Guhleman, Patricia. The
occupational position of employed Hispanic
women. IN: Borjas, George J. and Tienda,
Marta, eds. HISPANICS IN THE U.S. ECONOMY.
Orlando, FL: Academic Press, 1985, p.
243-273. English. **DESCR:** Identity; Puerto
Ricans.

1912 Torres Raines, Rosario. The Mexican American
woman and work: intergenerational
perspectives of comparative ethnic groups.
IN: Melville, Margarita, ed. MEXICANAS AT
WORK IN THE UNITED STATES. Houston, TX:
Mexican American Studies Program, University
of Houston, 1988, p. 33-46. English. **DESCR:**
Age Groups; Anglo Americans; Feminism;
Marriage; Sex Roles; Social Classes;
Socioeconomic Factors; *Working Women.

1913 U.S. National Institute of Education.
Conference on the educational and
occupational needs of Hispanic women, June
29-30, 1976; December 10-12, 1976.
Washington, DC: U.S. Department of
Education, 1980. x, 301 p. English. **DESCR:**
Conference on the Educational and
Occupational Needs of Hispanic Women (1976:
Denver, CO); Conferences and Meetings;
*Education; Higher Education; Leadership;
Puerto Ricans; Sex Roles; *Women.

1914 Waldman, Elizabeth. Profile of the Chicana:
a statistical fact sheet. IN: Mora,
Magdalena and Del Castillo, Adelaida, eds.
MEXICAN WOMEN IN THE UNITED STATES:
STRUGGLES PAST AND PRESENT. Los Angeles, CA:
Chicano Studies Research Center, UCLA, 1980,
p. 195-204. English. **DESCR:** Family;
Population; *Statistics.

1915 Williams, Edward J. and Passe-Smith, John T.
Turnover and recruitment in the maquila
industry: causes and solutions. Las Cruces,
NM: Joint Border Research Institute, New
Mexico State University, 1989. ii, 59 p.
English. **DESCR:** *Border Industries; Income;
*Labor Supply and Market; Personnel
Management; Surveys; Women; *Working Women.

1916 Young, Gay. Gender identification and
working-class solidarity among maquila
workers in Ciudad Juarez: stereotypes and
realities. IN: Ruiz, Vicki L. and Tiano,
Susan, eds. WOMEN ON THE U.S.-MEXICO BORDER:
RESPONSES TO CHANGE. Boston, MA: Allen &
Unwin, 1987, p. 105-127. English. **DESCR:**
Assertiveness; Attitudes; Border
Industrialization Program (BIP); *Border
Industries; Border Region; Ciudad Juarez,
Chihuahua, Mexico; Garment Industry; Sex
Roles; Surveys; Working Women.

1917 Young, Gay. Women, border industrialization
program, and human rights. El Paso, TX:
Center for InterAmerican and Border Studies,
UTEP, 1984. 33 p. English. **DESCR:** Border
Industrialization Program (BIP); *Border
Industries; Economic Development; Industrial
Workers; Mexico; Sex Roles; *Sexism; *Women;
Working Women.

1918 Zambrana, Ruth E. Hispanic professional
women: work, family and health. Los Angeles,
CA: National Network of Hispanic Women,
1987. 75 leaves. English. **DESCR:** Business;
*Careers; Family; Management; Mental Health;
Social Classes; *Social Mobility; *Women.

Employment (cont.)

1919 Zavella, Patricia. The impact of "sun belt industrialization" on Chicanas. FRONTIERS: A JOURNAL OF WOMEN STUDIES, Vol. 8, no. 1 (1984), p. 21-27. English. **DESCR:** Albuquerque, NM; *Industrial Workers; Industrialization; *Working Women.

1920 Zavella, Patricia. The impact of "sun belt industrialization" on Chicanas. Stanford, CA: Stanford Center for Chicano Research, 1984. 25 leaves. English. **DESCR:** Albuquerque, NM; *Industrial Workers; Industrialization; *Working Women.

1921 Zavella, Patricia. Women, work and family in the Chicano community: cannery workers of the Santa Clara Valley. Thesis (Ph.D.)--University of California, Berkeley, 1982. ix, 254 p. English. **DESCR:** *Canneries; *Family; Industrial Workers; Labor Unions; Santa Clara Valley, CA; *Sex Roles; *Working Women.

1922 Zavella, Patricia. Women's work and Chicano families: cannery workers of the Santa Clara Valley. Ithaca, NY: Cornell University Press, 1987. xviii, 191 p. English. **DESCR:** *Canneries; Family; Industrial Workers; Labor Unions; Santa Clara Valley, CA; Sex Roles; *Working Women.

Employment Tests

1923 Nava, Yolanda. The Chicana and employment: needs analysis and recommendations for legislation. REGENERACION, Vol. 2, no. 3 (1973), p. 7-9. English. **DESCR:** California Commission on the Status of Women; Child Care Centers; Comision Femenil Mexicana Nacional; *Discrimination in Employment; Employment Training; Equal Rights Amendment (ERA); Sexism; Statistics; Stereotypes; Working Women.

1924 Nieto Gomez de Lazarin, Anna. What is the Talmadge Amendment?: justicia para las madres. REGENERACION, Vol. 2, no. 3 (1973), p. 14-15. English. **DESCR:** Chicana Welfare Rights Organization; *Child Care Centers; Community Work Experience Program (C.W.E.P.); Discrimination in Employment; Escalante, Alicia; *Feminism; Nixon, Richard; Working Women.

Employment Training

1925 Nava, Yolanda. The Chicana and employment: needs analysis and recommendations for legislation. REGENERACION, Vol. 2, no. 3 (1973), p. 7-9. English. **DESCR:** California Commission on the Status of Women; Child Care Centers; Comision Femenil Mexicana Nacional; *Discrimination in Employment; Employment Tests; Equal Rights Amendment (ERA); Sexism; Statistics; Stereotypes; Working Women.

1926 Nava, Yolanda. Employment counseling and the Chicana. ENCUENTRO FEMENIL, Vol. 1, no. 1 (Spring 1973), p. 20-26. English. **DESCR:** *Employment; Sexism.

1927 Ridgely, Julia S. Health means jobs. WORLD HEALTH, (January, February, 1985), p. 18-20. English. **DESCR:** *Family Planning; Youth.

1928 Segura, Denise. Conflict in social relations at work: a Chicana perspective. IN: National Association for Chicano Studies. ESTUDIOS CHICANOS AND THE POLITICS OF COMMUNITY. [S.l.]: National Association for Chicano Studies, c1989, p. [110]-131. English. **DESCR:** *Discrimination in Employment; Immigrants; *Interpersonal Relations; Social Classes; Women; *Working Women.

1929 Weiner, Raine. The needs of poverty women heading households: a return to postsecondary education. Thesis (Ph.D.)--California School of Professional Psychology, Los Angeles, 1986. 180 p. English. **DESCR:** Anglo Americans; Blacks; Ethnic Groups; *Poverty; *Single Parents; Vocational Education; Welfare; Women.

EMPLUMADA

1930 Billings, Linda M. and Alurista. In verbal murals: a study of Chicana herstory and poetry. CONFLUENCIA, Vol. 2, no. 1 (Fall 1986), p. 60-68. English. **DESCR:** Candelaria, Cordelia; Cervantes, Lorna Dee; Cisneros, Sandra; *Feminism; History; Literary Criticism; *Poetry; Xelina.

1931 Bruce-Novoa, Juan. Bernice Zamora y Lorna Dee Cervantes: una estetica feminista. REVISTA IBEROAMERICANA, Vol. 51, (July, December, 1985), p. 565-573. English. **DESCR:** *Authors; *Cervantes, Lorna Dee; Literary Criticism; Poetry; RESTLESS SERPENTS; *Zamora, Bernice.

1932 Crawford, John F. Notes toward a new multicultural criticism: three works by women of color. IN: Harris, Marie and Aguero, Kathleen, eds. A GIFT OF TONGUES: CRITICAL CHALLENGES IN CONTEMPORARY AMERICAN POETRY. Athens, GA: University of Georgia Press, 1987, p. 155-195. English. **DESCR:** AWAKE IN THE RIVER; Cervantes, Lorna Dee; Harjo, Joy; *Literary Criticism; Mirikitani, Janice; SHE HAD SOME HORSES.

"Empty Nest" Syndrome

1933 Borland, Dolores C. A cohort analysis approach to the empty nest syndrome among three ethnic groups of women: a theoretical position. JOURNAL OF MARRIAGE AND THE FAMILY, Vol. 44, no. 1 (February 1982), p. 117-129. English. **DESCR:** Ethnic Groups; *Sex Roles; Social Psychology; Women.

1934 Rogers, Linda Perkowski and Markides, Kyriakos S. Well-being in the postparental stage in Mexican-American women. RESEARCH ON AGING, Vol. 11, no. 4 (December 1989), p. 508-516. English. **DESCR:** *Age Groups; Ancianos; Children; *Parent and Child Relationships; San Antonio, TX.

ENCUENTRO FEMENIL

1935 Introduction. ENCUENTRO FEMENIL, Vol. 1, no. 2 (1974), p. 3-7. English. **DESCR:** Books; Hijas de Cuauhtemoc; Organizations; *Periodicals.

Enriquez, Evangelina

1936 Pierce, Jennifer. The implications of functionalism for Chicano family research. BERKELEY JOURNAL OF SOCIOLOGY, Vol. 29, (1984), p. 93-117. English. **DESCR:** *Family; LA CHICANA: THE MEXICAN AMERICAN WOMAN; Machismo; Mirande, Alfredo; Research Methodology; Sex Roles.

Enrollment

1937 Cardoza, Desdemona. College attendance and persistence among Hispanic women: an examination of some contributing factors. SEX ROLES, Vol. 24, no. 3-4 (January 1991), p. 133-147. English. DESCR: Academic Achievement; College Preparation; High School and Beyond Project (HS&B); *Higher Education; *Sex Roles; Socialization; Socioeconomic Factors.

1938 Chacon, Maria A., et al. Chicanas in California post secondary education: a comparative study of barriers to the program progress. Stanford, CA: Stanford Center for Chicano Research, 1985. viii, 217 p. English. DESCR: *Academic Achievement; Colleges and Universities; Counseling (Educational); Educational Statistics; *Higher Education; Students; Surveys.

1939 Jaramillo, Mari-Luci. Institutional responsibility in the provision of educational experiences to the Hispanic American female student. IN: McKenna, Teresa and Ortiz, Flora Ida, eds. THE BROKEN WEB: THE EDUCATIONAL EXPERIENCE OF HISPANIC WOMEN. Claremont, CA: Tomaas Rivera Center; Berkeley, CA: Floricanto Press, 1988, p. 25-35. English. DESCR: Academic Achievement; *Discrimination in Education; Dropouts; *Education; Educational Administration; Higher Education; Students; *Women.

1940 Ortiz, Flora Ida. Hispanic American women in higher education: a consideration of the socialization process. AZTLAN, Vol. 17, no. 2 (Fall 1986), p. 125-152. English. DESCR: *Academic Achievement; Counseling (Educational); *Higher Education; Sex Roles; *Sexism; Socialization; Students; University of California.

Equal Opportunity
USE: Affirmative Action

Equal Rights Amendment (ERA)

1941 Cotera, Marta P. ERA: the Latina challenge. NUESTRO, Vol. 5, no. 8 (November 1981), p. 47-48. English. DESCR: Feminism; *Women Men Relations.

1942 Nava, Yolanda. The Chicana and employment: needs analysis and recommendations for legislation. REGENERACION, Vol. 2, no. 3 (1973), p. 7-9. English. DESCR: California Commission on the Status of Women; Child Care Centers; Comision Femenil Mexicana Nacional; *Discrimination in Employment; Employment Tests; Employment Training; Sexism; Statistics; Stereotypes; Working Women.

1943 Roraback, Rosanne Lisa. The effects of occupational type, educational level, marital status, and race/ethnicity on women's attitudes towards feminist issues. Thesis (M.A.)--Michigan State University, 1988. 62 p. English. DESCR: Abortion; *Attitudes; *Feminism; Identity; *Women.

Equality Before the Law
USE: Civil Rights

Equality in Education
USE: Discrimination in Education

Escalante, Alicia

1944 Nieto Gomez de Lazarin, Anna. What is the Talmadge Amendment?: justicia para las madres. REGENERACION, Vol. 2, no. 3 (1973), p. 14-15. English. DESCR: Chicana Welfare Rights Organization; *Child Care Centers; Community Work Experience Program (C.W.E.P.); Discrimination in Employment; Employment Tests; *Feminism; Nixon, Richard; Working Women.

Espana, Frances Salome

1945 Fregoso, Rosa Linda. La quinceanera of Chicana counter aesthetics. CENTRO BULLETIN, Vol. 3, no. 1 (Winter 1990, 1991), p. [87]-91. English. DESCR: *AGUEDA MARTINEZ [film]; ANIMA [film]; *CHICANA! [film]; *DESPUES DEL TERREMOTO [film]; Feminism; *Films; Morales, Sylvia; Portillo, Lourdes; Vasquez, Esperanza.

Espinel, Luisa Ronstadt

1946 Sheridan, Thomas E. From Luisa Espinel to Lalo Guerrero: Tucson's Mexican musicians before World War II. JOURNAL OF ARIZONA HISTORY, Vol. 25, no. 3 (Fall 1984), p. 285-300. English. DESCR: Biography; Guerrero, Eduardo "Lalo"; History; Montijo, Maruel; *Musicians; Rebeil, Julia; Singers; *Tucson, AZ.

Espiritismo
USE: Curanderismo

Esquiroz, Margarita

1947 Olivera, Mercedes. The new Hispanic women. VISTA, Vol. 2, no. 11 (July 5, 1987), p. 6-8. English. DESCR: Alvarez, Linda; Garcia, Juliet; *Hernandez, Antonia A.; Mohr, Nicolasa; Molina, Gloria; Pabon, Maria; Working Women.

Essays

1948 Agosin, Marjorie. Elucubraciones y antielucubraciones: critica feminista desde perspectivas poeticas. THIRD WOMAN, Vol. 1, no. 2 (1982), p. 65-69. Spanish. DESCR: Feminism; Literary Criticism; *Literature.

1949 Bello, Ruth T. Being Hispanic in Houston: a matter of identity. THE AMERICAS REVIEW, Vol. 16, no. 1 (Spring 1988), p. 31-43. English. DESCR: Autobiography; *Houston, TX; *Identity; *Self-Referents.

1950 Campoamor, Diana. Gender gap in politics: no laughing matter. VISTA, Vol. 4, no. 8 (October 24, 1988), p. 14. English. DESCR: Attitudes; Politics; *Women Men Relations.

1951 Chavez, Denise. Heat and rain (testimonio). IN: Horno-Delgado, Asuncion, et al., eds. BREAKING BOUNDARIES: LATINA WRITING AND CRITICAL READINGS. Amherst, MA: University of Massachusetts Press, c1989, p. 27-32. English. DESCR: *Authors; *Autobiography; Chavez, Denise.

1952 De Ortego y Gasca, Felipe. The Hispanic woman: a humanistic perspective. LA LUZ, Vol. 6, no. 11 (November 1977), p. 7-10. English. DESCR: De la Cruz, Juana Ines; Dona Ximena; History; Mistral, Gabriela; Ortiz de Dominguez, Josefa; *Women Men Relations; *Women's Suffrage.

1953 De Ortego y Gasca, Felipe. The Hispanic woman: a humanistic perspective. LA LUZ, Vol. 8, no. 8 (October, November, 1980), p. 6-9. English. DESCR: De la Cruz, Juana Ines; Dona Ximena; History; Mistral, Gabriela; Ortiz de Dominguez, Josefa; *Women Men Relations; *Women's Suffrage.

Essays (cont.)

1954 Delgado, Abelardo "Lalo". An open letter to Carolina... or relations between men and women. REVISTA CHICANO-RIQUENA, Vol. 10, no. 1-2 (Winter, Spring, 1982), p. 279-284. English. **DESCR:** Machismo; Sex Roles; Sex Stereotypes; Women Men Relations.

1955 Gonzales, Sylvia Alicia. The Chicana in literature. LA LUZ, Vol. 1, no. 9 (January 1973), p. 51-53. English. **DESCR:** Literature.

1956 Perez, Emma. "A la mujer": a critique of the Partido Liberal Mexicano's gender ideology on women. IN: Del Castillo, Adelaida R., ed. BETWEEN BORDERS: ESSAYS ON MEXICANA/CHICANA HISTORY. Encino, CA: Floricanto Press, 1990, p. 459-482. English. **DESCR:** *"A La Mujer" [essay]; *Feminism; Flores Magon, Ricardo; Guerrero, Praxedis G.; Journalism; Mexican Revolution - 1910-1920; Mexico; Newspapers; *Partido Liberal Mexicano (PLM); Political Ideology; Political Parties and Organizations; *REGENERACION [newspaper]; Sex Roles; Women.

1957 Ruelas, J. Oshi. Moments of change. REVISTA MUJERES, Vol. 4, no. 1 (January 1987), p. 23-33. English. **DESCR:** *Autobiography; *Ruelas, J. Oshi; Sex Roles; Sexism.

1958 San Miguel, Rachel. Being Hispanic in Houston: my name is Carmen Quezada. THE AMERICAS REVIEW, Vol. 16, no. 1 (Spring 1988), p. 44-52. English. **DESCR:** Autobiography; Houston, TX; Identity.

1959 Trujillo, Carla. Chicana lesbians: fear and loathing in the Chicano community. IN: Trujillo, Carla, ed. CHICANA LESBIANS: THE GIRLS OUR MOTHERS WARNED US ABOUT. Berkeley, CA: Third Woman Press, 1991, p. 186-194. English. **DESCR:** *Homosexuality; *Sex Roles; Sexual Behavior.

1960 Valdes-Fallis, Guadalupe. A liberated Chicana: a struggle against tradition. WOMEN: A JOURNAL OF LIBERATION, Vol. 3, no. 4 (1974), p. 20-21. English. **DESCR:** Feminism; Sex Roles; *Sexism.

1961 Viramontes, Helena Maria. "Nopalitos": the making of fiction. IN: Horno-Delgado, Asuncion, et al., eds. BREAKING BOUNDARIES: LATINA WRITING AND CRITICAL READINGS. Amherst, MA: University of Massachusetts Press, c1989, p. 33-38. English. **DESCR:** *Authors; *Autobiography; Viramontes, Helena Maria.

1962 Zavala, Iris M. Ideologias y autobiografias: perspectivas femeninas. THIRD WOMAN, Vol. 1, no. 2 (1982), p. 35-39. Spanish. **DESCR:** Autobiography.

ESSAYS ON LA MUJER

1963 Candelaria, Cordelia. Six reference works on Mexican-American women: a review essay. FRONTIERS: A JOURNAL OF WOMEN STUDIES, Vol. 5, no. 2 (Summer 1980), p. 75-80. English. **DESCR:** DIOSA Y HEMBRA: THE HISTORY AND HERITAGE OF CHICANAS IN THE U.S.; LA CHICANA: THE MEXICAN AMERICAN WOMAN; *Literature Reviews; MEXICAN WOMEN IN THE UNITED STATES: STRUGGLES PAST AND PRESENT; THE CHICANA: A COMPREHENSIVE BIBLIOGRAPHIC STUDY; TWICE A MINORITY: MEXICAN-AMERICAN WOMEN.

ESTAMPAS DEL VALLE Y OTRAS OBRAS

1964 de la Fuente, Patricia and Duke dos Santos, Maria I. The elliptic female presence as

Maria I. The elliptic female presence as unifying force in the novels of Rolando Hinojosa. REVISTA CHICANO-RIQUENA, Vol. 12, no. 3-4 (Fall, Winter, 1984), p. 64-75. English. **DESCR:** GENERACIONES Y SEMBLANZAS; Hinojosa-Smith, Rolando R.; *Literary Criticism; MI QUERIDO RAFA; RITES AND WITNESSES.

ETHNIC ENDOGAMY AMONG MEXICAN AMERICAN GROOMS

1965 Alba, Richard D. A comment on Schoen and Cohen. AMERICAN JOURNAL OF SOCIOLOGY, Vol. 87, no. 4 (January 1982), p. 935-939. English. **DESCR:** Cohen, Lawrence E.; Intermarriage; *Research Methodology; Schoen, Robert.

Ethnic Groups

1966 Alba, Isabel Catherine. Achievement conflicts, sex-role orientation, and performance on sex-role appropriate and sex-role inappropriate tasks in women of three ethnic groups. Thesis (Ph.D.)--University of California, Riverside, 1987. 129 p. English. **DESCR:** Anglo Americans; *Assertiveness; Blacks; Fear of Success Scale (FOSS); *Sex Roles; Women.

1967 Anzaldua, Gloria, ed. Making face, making soul = Haciendo caras: creative and critical perspectives by women of color. San Francisco, CA: Aunt Lute Foundation Books, 1990. English. **DESCR:** *Feminism; *Literature; Women.

1968 Ayers-Nackamkin, Beverly, et al. Sex and ethnic differences in the use of power. JOURNAL OF APPLIED PSYCHOLOGY, Vol. 67, no. 4 (August 1982), p. 464-471. English. **DESCR:** Anglo Americans; Management; *Personnel Management; Sex Roles; Social Psychology.

1969 Balkwell, Carolyn Ann. Widowhood: its impact on morale and optimism among older persons of three ethnic groups. Thesis (Ph.D.)--University of Georgia, 1981. 170 p. English. **DESCR:** *Ancianos; Anglo Americans; Blacks; Depression (Psychological); Los Angeles County, CA; *Mental Health; Widowhood; *Women.

1970 Borland, Dolores C. A cohort analysis approach to the empty nest syndrome among three ethnic groups of women: a theoretical position. JOURNAL OF MARRIAGE AND THE FAMILY, Vol. 44, no. 1 (February 1982), p. 117-129. English. **DESCR:** "Empty Nest" Syndrome; *Sex Roles; Social Psychology; Women.

1971 D'Andrea, Vaneeta-Marie. Ethnic women: a critique of the literature, 1971-1981. ETHNIC AND RACIAL STUDIES, Vol. 9, (April 1986), p. 235-246. English. **DESCR:** Bibliography; *Literature Reviews; Periodical Indexes; *Women.

1972 Estrada, Esther R. The importance of the 1980 census. IN: LA CHICANA: BUILDING FOR THE FUTURE, AN ACTION PLAN FOR THE '80s. Oakland, CA: National Hispanic University, 1981, p. 2-7. English. **DESCR:** *Census; Self-Referents.

Ethnic Groups (cont.)

1973 Fennelly, Katherine and Ortiz, Vilma. Childbearing among young Latino women in the United States. AMERICAN JOURNAL OF PUBLIC HEALTH, Vol. 77, no. 1 (January 1987), p. 25-28. English. DESCR: *Fertility; Puerto Ricans; Women; *Youth.

1974 Fennelly, Katherine; Kandiah, Vasantha; and Ortiz, Vilma. The cross-cultural study of fertility among Hispanic adolescents in the Americas. STUDIES IN FAMILY PLANNING, Vol. 20, no. 2 (March, April, 1989), p. 96-101. English. DESCR: Cultural Characteristics; *Fertility; Latin America; *Marriage; Youth.

1975 Fleming, Marilyn B. Problems experienced by Anglo, Hispanic and Navajo Indian women college students. JOURNAL OF AMERICAN INDIAN EDUCATION, Vol. 22, no. 1 (October 1982), p. 7-17. English. DESCR: Anglo Americans; Community Colleges; *Higher Education; Identity; Medical Education; Native Americans; Students; Women.

1976 Gibbs, Jewelle Taylor. Personality patterns of delinquent females: ethnic and sociocultural variations. JOURNAL OF CLINICAL PSYCHOLOGY, Vol. 38, no. 1 (January 1982), p. 198-206. English. DESCR: Identity; *Juvenile Delinquency; Personality; Psychological Testing; Socioeconomic Factors.

1977 Gutierrez, Lorraine M. Working with women of color: an empowerment perspective. SOCIAL WORK, Vol. 35, no. 2 (March 1990), p. 149-153. English. DESCR: *Assertiveness; Feminism; Intergroup Relations; *Interpersonal Relations; *Social Work; *Women.

1978 Hawley, Peggy and Even, Brenda. Work and sex-role attitudes in relation to education and other characteristics. VOCATIONAL GUIDANCE QUARTERLY, Vol. 31, no. 2 (December 1982), p. 101-108. English. DESCR: Attitudes; Careers; Education; Psychological Testing; *Sex Roles; Working Women.

1979 Hurtado, Aida. Relating to privilege: seduction and rejection in the subordination of white women and women of color. SIGNS: JOURNAL OF WOMEN IN CULTURE AND SOCIETY, Vol. 14, no. 4 (Summer 1989), p. 833-855. English. DESCR: *Anglo Americans; Asian Americans; Blacks; *Feminism; Political Ideology; Political Socialization; *Women.

1980 Miller, Darlis A. Cross-cultural marriages in the Southwest: the New Mexico experience, 1846-1900. NEW MEXICO HISTORICAL REVIEW, Vol. 57, no. 4 (October 1982), p. 335-359. English. DESCR: Assimilation; Attitudes; *Intermarriage; New Mexico; Social History and Conditions.

1981 Moraga, Cherrie, ed. and Castillo, Ana, ed. Esta [sic] puente, mi espalda: voces de mujeres tercermundistas en los Estados Unidos. San Francisco, CA: Ism Press, c1988. [19], 281 p.: ill. Spanish. DESCR: *Feminism; Literary Criticism; *Poems; *Prose; *Women.

1982 Moraga, Cherrie, ed. and Anzaldua, Gloria ed. This bridge called my back: writings by radical women of color. Watertown, MA: Persephone Press, c1981. xxvi, 261 p. English. DESCR: *Feminism; Literary Criticism; *Poems; *Prose; *Women.

1983 Murguia, Edward. Chicano intermarriage: a

theoretical and empirical study. San Antonio, TX: Trinity University Press, 1982. xiv, 134 p. English. DESCR: Assimilation; Attitudes; *Intermarriage; Military; Social Classes; Weddings.

1984 Myres, Sandra Lynn. Mexican Americans and westering Anglos: a feminine perspective. NEW MEXICO HISTORICAL REVIEW, Vol. 57, no. 4 (October 1982), p. 317-333. English. DESCR: Anglo Americans; *Attitudes; Social History and Conditions; Southwestern United States; Stereotypes.

1985 Norinsky, Margaret Elaine. The relationship between sex-role identity and ethnicity to styles of assertiveness and aggression in women. Thesis (Ed.D.)--University of San Francisco, 1987. 164 p. English. DESCR: Anglo Americans; *Assertiveness; Blacks; *Identity; *Sex Roles; *Women.

1986 Sabogal, Fabio, et al. Hispanic familism and acculturation: what changes and what doesn't? HISPANIC JOURNAL OF BEHAVIORAL SCIENCES, Vol. 9, no. 4 (December 1987), p. 397-412. English. DESCR: *Acculturation; Attitudes; Cultural Characteristics; Extended Family; *Family; Natural Support Systems; Values.

1987 Sanford, Judy, et al. Patterns of reported rape in a tri-ethnic population: Houston, Texas, 1974-1975. AMERICAN JOURNAL OF PUBLIC HEALTH, Vol. 69, no. 5 (May 1979), p. 480-484. English. DESCR: Anglo Americans; Blacks; Criminology; *Houston, TX; *Rape; Statistics; Women.

1988 Trotter, Robert T. Ethnic and sexual patterns of alcohol use: Anglo and Mexican American college students. ADOLESCENCE, Vol. 17, no. 66 (Summer 1982), p. 305-325. English. DESCR: *Alcoholism; Anglo Americans; Colleges and Universities; Cultural Characteristics; Sex Roles; Students; Youth.

1989 Weiner, Raine. The needs of poverty women heading households: a return to postsecondary education. Thesis (Ph.D.)--California School of Professional Psychology, Los Angeles, 1986. 180 p. English. DESCR: Anglo Americans; Blacks; *Employment Training; *Poverty; *Single Parents; Vocational Education; Welfare; Women.

1990 Zambrana, Ruth E. Bibliography on maternal and child health across class, race and ethnicity. Memphis, TN: Distributed by the Memphis State University Center for Research on Women, c1990. 58 leaves. English. DESCR: *Bibliography; *Maternal and Child Welfare; *Medical Care; Social Classes; *Women.

Ethnic Identity
USE: Identity

Ethnic Stratification

1991 Baca Zinn, Maxine. Chicano men and masculinity. JOURNAL OF ETHNIC STUDIES, Vol. 10, no. 2 (Summer 1982), p. 29-44. English. DESCR: Cultural Characteristics; *Machismo; Sex Roles; Sex Stereotypes; Socioeconomic Factors; Women Men Relations.

Ethnicity
USE: Identity

Ethnobotany
USE: Herbal Medicine

Ethnography
    USE: Ethnology

Ethnology

1992 Quintana, Alvina E. Ana Castillo's THE
     MIXQUIAHUALA LETTERS: the novelist as
     ethnographer. IN: Calderon, Hector and
     Saldivar, Jose David, eds. CRITICISM IN THE
     BORDERLANDS: STUDIES IN CHICANO LITERATURE,
     CULTURE, AND IDEOLOGY. Durham, NC: Duke
     University Press, 1991, p. [72]-83. English.
     DESCR: Anthropology; Castillo, Ana; Cultural
     Studies; Feminism; Geertz, Clifford;
     *Literary Criticism; Novel; THE MIXQUIAHUALA
     LETTERS.

1993 Quintana, Alvina E. Chicana discourse:
     negations and mediations. Thesis
     (Ph.D.)--University of California, Santa
     Cruz, 1989. 226 p. English. **DESCR:** Authors;
     Castillo, Ana; Chavez, Denise; Chicano
     Movement; Cisneros, Sandra; Feminism;
     Literary Criticism; *Literature; NOVENA
     NARRATIVES; Oral Tradition; Political
     Ideology; THE HOUSE ON MANGO STREET; THE
     LAST OF THE MENU GIRLS; THE MIXQUIAHUALA
     LETTERS.

1994 Ramos, Maria. A micro-ethnographic study of
     Chicana mother and daughter socialization
     practices. Thesis (Ph.D.)--University of
     Colorado at Boulder, 1982. 292 p. English.
     DESCR: *Interpersonal Relations; *Parent and
     Child Relationships; Parenting;
     *Socialization.

1995 Velez-I., Carlos G. Se me acabo la cancion:
     an ethnography of non-consenting
     sterilizations among Mexican women in Los
     Angeles. IN: Mora, Magdalena and Del
     Castillo, Adelaida, eds. MEXICAN WOMEN IN
     THE UNITED STATES: STRUGGLES PAST AND
     PRESENT. Los Angeles, CA: Chicano Studies
     Research Center, UCLA, 1980, p. 71-91.
     English. **DESCR:** Los Angeles, CA; Madrigal v.
     Quilligan; *Sterilization.

Ethnopsychology
    USE: Social Psychology

Excavations
    USE: Anthropology

Exhibits

1996 Brown, Betty Ann. Chicanas speak out.
     ARTWEEK, Vol. 15, no. 2 (January 14, 1984),
     p. 1+. English. **DESCR:** *Art; Carrasco,
     Barbara; Carrillo, Graciela; CHICANA VOICES
     & VISIONS [exhibit]; Goldman, Shifra M.;
     Hernandez, Ester; Lerma Bowerman, Liz;
     Rodriguez, Carmen; Rodriguez, Sandra Maria;
     Social and Public Art Resource Center,
     Venice, CA (SPARC).

1997 Goldman, Shifra M. Women artists of Texas:
     MAS = More + Artists + Women = MAS.
     CHISMEARTE, no. 7 (January 1981), p. 21-22.
     English. **DESCR:** Arredondo, Alicia; Art
     Organizations and Groups; Barraza, Santa;
     Feminism; Flores, Maria; Folk Art; Gonzalez
     Dodson, Nora; *Mujeres Artistas del Suroeste
     (MAS), Austin, TX; Photography; Texas;
     Trevino, Modesta Barbina; WOMEN & THEIR WORK
     [festival] (Austin, TX: 1977).

1998 Navar, M. Margarita. La vela prendida: home
     altars. ARRIBA, Vol. 1, no. 5 (February
     1980), p. 12. English. **DESCR:** *Altars;
     Artists; Folk Art; Religious Art.

1999 Texas Memorial Museum, University of Texas,
     Austin, TX. La vela prendida:

Mexican-American women's home altars.
Exhibition catalog, 1980. Bilingual. **DESCR:**
*Altars; Artists; Catalogues; Folk Art.

Expanded Food and Nutrition Education Program

2000 Romero-Gwynn, Eunice and Carias, Lucia.
     Breast-feeding intentions and practice among
     Hispanic mothers in Southern California.
     PEDIATRICS, Vol. 84, no. 4 (October 1989),
     p. 626-632. English. **DESCR:** *Breastfeeding;
     Cubanos; Immigrants; Puerto Ricans; Southern
     California; Women.

Expansionism
    USE: Imperialism

Export-Import Trade
    USE: Foreign Trade

Extended Family

2001 Alcalay, Rina. Hispanic women in the United
     States: family & work relations. MIGRATION
     TODAY, Vol. 12, no. 3 (1984), p. 13-20.
     English. **DESCR:** *Immigrants; Migration;
     *Women.

2002 Angel, Ronald J. and Tienda, Marta.
     Determinants of extended household
     structure: cultural pattern or economical
     need? AMERICAN JOURNAL OF SOCIOLOGY, Vol.
     87, no. 6 (May 1982), p. 1360-1383. English.
     DESCR: Income.

2003 Baca Zinn, Maxine. Urban kinship and Midwest
     Chicano families: evidence in support of
     revision. DE COLORES, Vol. 6, no. 1-2
     (1982), p. 85-98. English. **DESCR:**
     Compadrazgo; Family; Midwestern States;
     Urban Communities.

2004 Griswold del Castillo, Richard. "Only for my
     family...": historical dimensions of Chicano
     family solidarity--the case of San Antonio
     in 1860. AZTLAN, Vol. 16, no. 1-2 (1985), p.
     145-176. English. **DESCR:** *Family; History;
     Population; San Antonio, TX.

2005 Loustaunau, Martha Oehmke. Hispanic widows
     and their support systems in the Mesilla
     Valley of southern New Mexico, 1910-40. IN:
     Scadron, Arlene, ed. ON THEIR OWN: WIDOWS
     AND WIDOWHOOD IN THE AMERICAN SOUTHWEST
     1843-1939. Urbana, IL: University of
     Illinois Press, c1988, p. [91]-116. English.
     DESCR: Cultural Customs; Mesilla Valley, NM;
     Natural Support Systems; Sex Roles; Single
     Parents; Widowhood; *Women.

2006 Martinez, Elisa A. Sharing her tiny pieces
     of the past. NUESTRO, Vol. 7, no. 7
     (September 1983), p. 51-52. English. **DESCR:**
     Autobiography.

2007 Mason, Theresa Hope. Experience and meaning:
     an interpretive study of family and gender
     ideologies among a sample of
     Mexican-American women of two generations.
     Thesis (Ph.D.)--University of Texas, Austin,
     1987. 406 p. English. **DESCR:** *Age Groups;
     Culture; *Family; *Sex Roles.

2008 Sabogal, Fabio, et al. Hispanic familism and
     acculturation: what changes and what
     doesn't? HISPANIC JOURNAL OF BEHAVIORAL
     SCIENCES, Vol. 9, no. 4 (December 1987), p.
     397-412. English. **DESCR:** *Acculturation;
     Attitudes; Cultural Characteristics; Ethnic
     Groups; *Family; Natural Support Systems;
     Values.

Extended Family (cont.)

2009 Segura, Denise. Familism and employment among Chicanas and Mexican immigrant women. IN: Melville, Margarita, ed. MEXICANAS AT WORK IN THE UNITED STATES. Houston, TX: Mexican American Studies Program, University of Houston, 1988, p. 24-32. English. DESCR: *Employment; Family; Immigrants; Income; Machismo; Sex Roles; *Women; Working Women.

2010 Tienda, Marta and Angel, Ronald J. Headship and household composition among Blacks, Hispanics and other whites. SOCIAL FORCES, Vol. 61, no. 2 (December 1982), p. 508-531. English. DESCR: Anglo Americans; Blacks; Cultural Characteristics; *Family; Puerto Ricans; Single Parents.

2011 Tienda, Marta and Glass, Jennifer. Household structure and labor-force participation of Black, Hispanic, and white mothers. DEMOGRAPHY, Vol. 22, no. 3 (August 1985), p. 381-394. English. DESCR: Anglo Americans; Blacks; *Family; *Sex Roles; *Working Women.

2012 Wagner, Roland M. Changes in extended family relationships for Mexican American and Anglo single mothers. JOURNAL OF DIVORCE, Vol. 11, no. 2 (Winter 1987), p. 69-87. English. DESCR: Anglo Americans; *Divorce; Natural Support Systems; San Jose, CA; *Single Parents; Women.

2013 Williams, Brett. Why migrant women feed their husbands tamales: foodways as a basis for a revisionist view of Tejano family life. IN: Brown, Linda Keller and Mussell, Kay, eds. ETHNIC AND REGIONAL FOODWAYS IN THE UNITED STATES: THE PERFORMANCE OF GROUP IDENTITY. Knoxville, TN: University of Tennessee Press, 1984, p. 113-126. English. DESCR: Cultural Customs; Family; *Food Practices; Illinois; *Migrant Labor; Sex Roles; Tamales; Texas.

Fables
USE: Cuentos

FACE

2014 Bruce-Novoa, Juan. Deconstructing the dominant patriarchal text: Cecile Pineda's narratives. IN: Horno-Delgado, Asuncion, et al., eds. BREAKING BOUNDARIES: LATINA WRITING AND CRITICAL READINGS. Amherst, MA: University of Massachusetts Press, c1989, p. 72-81. English. DESCR: *FRIEZE; Identity; Literary Criticism; Novel; *Pineda, Cecile.

Fages, Eulalia

2015 Mirande, Alfredo and Enriquez, Evangelina. Chicanas in the history of the Southwest. IN: Duran, Livie Isauro and Bernard, H. Russell, eds. INTRODUCTION TO CHICANO STUDIES. 2nd ed. New York: Macmillan, 1982, p. 156-179. English. DESCR: Arguello, Concepcion; Barcelo, Gertrudes "La Tules"; *History; "Juanita of Downieville"; Robledo, Refugio; Urrea, Teresa.

Fairytales
USE: Cuentos

Familia
USE: Family

LA FAMILIA: MIGRATION AND ADAPTATION IN BAJA AND ALTA CALIFORNIA, 1800-1975

2016 Garcia, Mario T. Family and gender in Chicano and border studies research. MEXICAN STUDIES/ESTUDIOS MEXICANOS, Vol. 6, no. 1 (Winter 1990), p. 109-119. English. DESCR: Alvarez, Robert R., Jr.; *Border Region; CANNERY WOMEN, CANNERY LIVES; *Family; *Literature Reviews; Ruiz, Vicki L.; Tiano, Susan B.; Women; WOMEN ON THE U.S.-MEXICO BORDER: RESPONSES TO CHANGE; WOMEN'S WORK AND CHICANO FAMILIES; Zavella, Pat.

Family

2017 Alanis, Elsa. The relationship between state and trait anxiety and acculturation in Mexican-American women homemakers and Mexican-American community college female students. Thesis (Ph.D.)--United States International University, 1989. 161 p. English. DESCR: *Acculturation; *Community Colleges; Sex Roles; *Stress; Students.

2018 Andrade, Sally J. Family roles of Hispanic women: stereotypes, empirical findings, and implications for research. IN: Zambrana, Ruth E., ed. WORK, FAMILY, AND HEALTH: LATINA WOMEN IN TRANSITION. Bronx, NY: Hispanic Research Center, Fordham University, 1982, p. 95-106. English. DESCR: Puerto Ricans; *Research Methodology; *Sex Roles; Sex Stereotypes; Women.

2019 Andrade, Sally J., ed. Latino families in the United States: a resource book for family life education = Las familias latinas en los Estados Unidos: recursos para la capacitacion familiar. [S.l.]: Planned Parenthood Federation of America, Inc., 1983. ix, 79, 70, xi p. Bilingual. DESCR: Bilingualism; Community Organizations; Education; Mental Health; Public Health.

2020 Arevalo, Rodolfo, ed. and Minor, Marianne, ed. Chicanas and alcoholism: a sociocultural perspective of women. San Jose, CA: School of Social Work, San Jose State University, c1981. 55 p. English. DESCR: *Alcoholism; Drug Abuse Programs; Feminism; Natural Support Systems; Preventative Medicine; Psychotherapy.

2021 Ashley, Laurel Maria. Self, family and community: the social process of aging among urban Mexican-American women. Thesis (Ph.D.)--University of California, Los Angeles, 1985. 306 p. English. DESCR: Acculturation; *Ancianos; Grandmothers; *Sex Roles; Southern California.

2022 Baca Zinn, Maxine. Chicanas: power and control in the domestic sphere. DE COLORES, Vol. 2, no. 3 (1975), p. 19-31. English. DESCR: Immigration Regulation and Control; Machismo; *Sex Roles; Stereotypes; *Women Men Relations.

2023 Baca Zinn, Maxine. Chicanas: power and control in the domestic sphere. IN: Cotera, Martha and Hufford, Larry, eds. BRIDGING TWO CULTURES. Austin, TX: National Educational Laboratory Publishers, 1980, p. 270-281. English. DESCR: Immigration Regulation and Control; Machismo; Sex Roles; *Stereotypes; Women Men Relations.

2024 Baca Zinn, Maxine. Chicano family research: conceptual distortions and alternative directions. JOURNAL OF ETHNIC STUDIES, Vol. 7, no. 3 (Fall 1979), p. 59-71. English. DESCR: Cultural Characteristics; Culture; Research Methodology; Stereotypes.

Family (cont.)

2025 Baca Zinn, Maxine. Employment and education of Mexican-American women: the interplay of modernity and ethnicity in eight families. HARVARD EDUCATIONAL REVIEW, Vol. 50, no. 1 (February 1980), p. 47-62. English. DESCR: Acculturation; Decision Making; *Education; *Employment; Identity; Sex Roles; Social Classes; Values.

2026 Baca Zinn, Maxine. Ongoing questions in the study of Chicano families. IN: Valdez, Armando, et al., eds. THE STATE OF CHICANO RESEARCH ON FAMILY, LABOR, AND MIGRATION. Stanford, CA: Stanford Center for Chicano Research, 1983, p. 139-146. English. DESCR: *Research Methodology.

2027 Baca Zinn, Maxine. Political familism: toward sex role equality in Chicano families. AZTLAN, Vol. 6, no. 1 (Spring 1975), p. 13-26. English. DESCR: Acculturation; Chicano Movement; Machismo; *Sex Roles.

2028 Baca Zinn, Maxine. Qualitative methods in family research: a look inside Chicano families. CALIFORNIA SOCIOLOGIST, Vol. 5, no. 2 (Summer 1982), p. 58-79. English. DESCR: Marriage; *Research Methodology; *Sex Roles; Socioeconomic Factors.

2029 Baca Zinn, Maxine. Urban kinship and Midwest Chicano families: evidence in support of revision. DE COLORES, Vol. 6, no. 1-2 (1982), p. 85-98. English. DESCR: Compadrazgo; *Extended Family; Midwestern States; Urban Communities.

2030 Bays, Sharon Arlene. Women of the Valley of the Sun: women and family work culture in Woodlake, California. Thesis (M.A.)--UCLA, 1988. 89 leaves. English. DESCR: *Farm Workers; Woodlake, CA; Working Women.

2031 Blackwelder, Julia Kirk. Women of the depression: caste and culture in San Antonio, 1929-1939. College Station, TX: Texas A&M University Press, 1984. xviii, 279 p.: ill. English. DESCR: Criminal Justice System; Cultural Characteristics; Employment; Great Depression, 1929-1933; Labor Supply and Market; Labor Unions; Prostitution; San Antonio, TX; *Social Classes; *Women.

2032 Blair, Leita Mae. Characteristics of professional and traditional Mexican American women related to family of origin, role models, and conflicts: a case study. Thesis (Ed.D.)--East Texas State University, 1984. 348 p. English. DESCR: *Careers; Case Studies; Education.

2033 Bridges, Julian C. Family life. IN: Stoddard, Ellwyn R., et al., eds. BORDERLANDS SOURCEBOOK: A GUIDE TO THE LITERATURE ON NORTHERN MEXICO AND THE AMERICAN SOUTHWEST. Norman, OK: University of Oklahoma Press, 1983, p. 259-262. English. DESCR: Border Region; Literature Reviews.

2034 Briody, Elizabeth K. Patterns of household immigration into South Texas. INTERNATIONAL MIGRATION REVIEW, Vol. 21, no. 1 (Spring 1987), p. 27-47. English. DESCR: *Immigrants; Sex Roles; *Social Mobility; *South Texas.

2035 Canino, Glorisa. The Hispanic woman: sociocultural influences on diagnoses and treatment. IN: Becerra, Rosina M., et al.,

eds. MENTAL HEALTH AND HISPANIC AMERICANS: CLINICAL PERSPECTIVES. New York: Grune & Stratton, 1982, p. 117-138. English. DESCR: Assimilation; Cultural Characteristics; Culture; *Depression (Psychological); Feminism; Mental Health; Population; Sex Roles.

2036 Carr-Casanova, Rosario. Role-model history and demographic factors in the social composition of the family of forty Hispanic women leaders in four occupational groups. Thesis (Ph.D.)--Wright Institute, Berkeley, 1983. 136 p. English. DESCR: *Leadership; San Francisco Bay Area.

2037 Chavez, Henri. Unsung heroine of La Causa. REGENERACION, Vol. 1, no. 10 (1971), p. 20. English. DESCR: AFL-CIO United Farmworkers Organizing Committee; Agricultural Labor Unions; Community Service Organization, Los Angeles, (CSO); Farm Workers; *Huerta, Dolores; Poverty; Working Women.

2038 Cota-Robles de Suarez, Cecilia. Sexual stereotypes--psychological and cultural survival: a description of child-rearing practices attributed to the Chicana (the Mexican American woman) and its psychological and cultural implications. REGENERACION, Vol. 2, no. 3 (1973), p. 17, 20-21. English. DESCR: Cultural Characteristics; Folklore; Language; Parenting; Sex Stereotypes; *Sexism; *Stereotypes.

2039 Curry Rodriguez, Julia E. Labor migration and familial responsibilities: experiences of Mexican women. IN: Melville, Margarita, ed. MEXICANAS AT WORK IN THE UNITED STATES. Houston, TX: Mexican American Studies Program, University of Houston, 1988, p. 47-63. English. DESCR: Employment; *Immigrants; Mexico; *Migrant Labor; Oral History; Sex Roles; Undocumented Workers; *Women; *Working Women.

2040 Dill, Bonnie Thornton. Our mothers' grief: racial ethnic women and the maintenance of families. JOURNAL OF FAMILY HISTORY, Vol. 13, no. 4 (October 1988), p. 415-431. English. DESCR: Asian Americans; Blacks; Domestic Work; Fertility; *Sex Roles; *Women; *Working Women.

2041 Dugan, Anna Baziak. Kin, social supports, and depression among women of Mexican heritage who are single parents. Thesis (Ph.D.)--Bryn Mawr College, 1982. vii, 188 p. English. DESCR: *Depression (Psychological); Detroit, MI; *Natural Support Systems; *Single Parents.

2042 Facio, Elisa "Linda". Constraints, resources, and self-definition: a case study of Chicano older women. Thesis (Ph.D.)--University of California, Berkeley, 1988. 246 p. English. DESCR: *Ancianos; Grandmothers; *Poverty; Sex Roles; Widowhood.

2043 Falicov, Celia Jaes. Mexican families. IN: McGoldrick, Monica, et al., eds. ETHNICITY AND FAMILY THERAPY. New York: The Guilford Press, 1982, p. 134-163. English. DESCR: Acculturation; Cultural Customs; Mental Health; Sex Roles.

2044 La familia [special issue of DE COLORES]. DE COLORES, Vol. 6, no. 1-2 (1982), p. 1-149. Bilingual.

Family (cont.)

2045 Flores, Estevan T. Chicanos and sociological research: 1970-1980. IN: CHICANOS AND THE SOCIAL SCIENCES: A DECADE OF RESEARCH AND DEVELOPMENT (1970-1980) SYMPOSIUM WORKING PAPER. Santa Barbara, CA: Center for Chicano Studies, University of California, 1983, p. 19-45. English. DESCR: Bibliography; Internal Colony Model; Labor; Literature Reviews; Population; Research Methodology; *Sociology.

2046 Flores, Francisca. Conference of Mexican women un remolino. REGENERACION, Vol. 1, no. 10 (1971), p. 1-5. English. DESCR: Conferences and Meetings; Feminism; First National Chicana Conference (May 1971: Houston, TX); Machismo; National Mexican American Issues Conference (October 11, 1970: Sacramento, CA) Sex Roles; Sex Stereotypes; Statistics; *Women Men Relations.

2047 Forste, Renata T. and Heaton, Tim B. Initiation of sexual activity among female adolescents. YOUTH AND SOCIETY, Vol. 19, no. 3 (March 1988), p. 250-258. English. DESCR: Anglo Americans; Blacks; Sex Education; *Sexual Behavior; Women; *Youth.

2048 Frisbie, William Parker; Bean, Frank D.; and Eberstein, Isaac W. Patterns of marital instability among Mexican Americans, Blacks, and Anglos. IN: Bean, Frank D. and Frisbie, W. Parker, eds. THE DEMOGRAPHY OF RACIAL AND ETHNIC GROUPS. New York: Academic Press, 1978, p. 143-163. English. DESCR: Anglo Americans; Blacks; Divorce; *Marriage.

2049 Garcia, Mario T. La familia: the Mexican immigrant family, 1900-1930. IN: Barrera, Mario, et al., eds. WORK, FAMILY, SEX ROLES, LANGUAGE: SELECTED PAPERS, 1979. Berkeley, CA: Tonatiuh-Quinto Sol, 1980, p. 117-139 English. DESCR: Assimilation; Cultural Customs; El Paso, TX; *Historiography; History; Immigration; Labor; Sex Roles.

2050 Garcia, Mario T. Family and gender in Chicano and border studies research. MEXICAN STUDIES/ESTUDIOS MEXICANOS, Vol. 6, no. 1 (Winter 1990), p. 109-119. English. DESCR: Alvarez, Robert R., Jr.; *Border Region; CANNERY WOMEN, CANNERY LIVES; LA FAMILIA: MIGRATION AND ADAPTATION IN BAJA AND ALTA CALIFORNIA, 1800-1975; *Literature Reviews; Ruiz, Vicki L.; Tiano, Susan B.; Women; WOMEN ON THE U.S.-MEXICO BORDER: RESPONSES TO CHANGE; WOMEN'S WORK AND CHICANO FAMILIES; Zavella, Pat.

2051 Garcia-Bahne, Betty. La Chicana and the Chicano family. IN: Sanchez, Rosaura and Martinez Cruz, Rosa, eds. ESSAYS ON LA MUJER. Los Angeles, CA: Chicano Studies Center Publications, UCLA, 1977, p. 30-47. English. DESCR: Cultural Customs; Sex Roles; Social Classes; Socialization; Stereotypes.

2052 Gonzalez, Alex. Sex roles of the traditional Mexican family: a comparison of Chicano and Anglo students' attitudes. JOURNAL OF CROSS-CULTURAL PSYCHOLOGY, Vol. 13, no. 3 (September 1982), p. 330-339. English. DESCR: Anglo Americans; Attitudes; Comparative Psychology; Hembrismo; Machismo Sex Roles; Students.

2053 Gonzalez, Deena J. The widowed women of Santa Fe: assessments on the lives of an unmarried population, 1850-80. IN: Scadron, Arlene, ed. ON THEIR OWN: WIDOWS AND WIDOWHOOD IN THE AMERICAN SOUTHWEST 1843-1939. Urbana, IL: University of Illinois Press, c1988, p. [65]-90. English. DESCR: History; Income; Land Tenure; *Santa Fe, NM; Sex Roles; Single Parents; *Widowhood; *Women.

2054 Gonzalez, Deena J. The widowed women of Santa Fe: assessments on the lives of an unmarried population, 1850-80. IN: DuBois, Ellen Carol and Ruiz, Vicki L., eds. UNEQUAL SISTERS: A MULTICULTURAL READER IN U.S. WOMEN'S HISTORY. New York: Routledge, 1990, p. 34-50. English. DESCR: History; Income; Land Tenure; *Santa Fe, NM; Sex Roles; Single Parents; *Widowhood; *Women.

2055 Gonzalez, Rosalinda M. Chicanas and Mexican immigrant families 1920-1940: women's subordination and family exploitation. IN: Scharf, Lois and Jensen, Joan M., eds. DECADES OF DISCONTENT: THE WOMEN'S MOVEMENT, 1920-1940. Westport, CT: Greenwood Press, 1983, p. 59-84. English. DESCR: Farm Workers; History; Immigrants; Labor; Labor Unions; Mexico; Pecan Shelling Worker's Union, San Antonio, TX; Sex Roles; Strikes and Lockouts; United Cannery Agricultural Packing and Allied Workers of America (UCAPAWA); Working Women.

2056 Griswold del Castillo, Richard. Chicano family history--methodology and theory: a survey of contemporary research directions. IN: National Association for Chicano Studies. HISTORY, CULTURE, AND SOCIETY: CHICANO STUDIES IN THE 1980s. Ypsilanti, MI: Bilingual Press/Editorial Bilingue, 1983, p. 95-106. English. DESCR: Age Groups; Historiography.

2057 Griswold del Castillo, Richard. La familia: Chicano families in the urban Southwest, 1848 to the present. Notre Dame, IN: University of Notre Dame Press, c1984. xv, 173 p. English. DESCR: History; Intermarriage; Machismo; Parenting; *Sex Roles; Sexual Behavior; *Social History and Conditions.

2058 Griswold del Castillo, Richard. "Only for my family...": historical dimensions of Chicano family solidarity--the case of San Antonio in 1860. AZTLAN, Vol. 16, no. 1-2 (1985), p. 145-176. English. DESCR: Extended Family; History; Population; San Antonio, TX.

2059 Griswold del Castillo, Richard. Patriarchy and the status of women in the late nineteenth-century Southwest. IN: Rodriguez O., Jaime E., ed. THE MEXICAN AND MEXICAN AMERICAN EXPERIENCE IN THE 19TH CENTURY. Tempe, AZ: Bilingual Press/Editorial Bilingue, 1989, p. 85-99. English. DESCR: *Feminism; History; *Machismo; *Sex Roles.

2060 Hernandez, Leodoro. The socialization of a Chicano family. DE COLORES, Vol. 6, no. 1-2 (1982), p. 75-84. English. DESCR: Acculturation; *Socialization.

2061 Irizarry, Estelle. La abuelita in literature. NUESTRO, Vol. 7, no. 7 (September 1983), p. 50. English. DESCR: Alonso, Luis Ricardo; *Ancianos; Cotto-Thorner, Guillermo; Grandmothers; Ulibarri, Sabine R.; Valero, Robert.

2062 Jaramillo, Mari-Luci. How to suceed in business and remain Chicana. LA LUZ, Vol. 8, no. 7 (August, September 1980), p. 33-35. English. DESCR: Assertiveness; Cultural Characteristics; Identity; *Natural Support Systems; *Working Women.

Family (cont.)

2063 Jensen, Evelyn E. The Hispanic perspective of the ideal woman: a correlational study. Thesis (Ph.D.)--Fuller Theological Seminary, School of World Mission, 1987. 163 p. English. DESCR: *Hembrismo; *Machismo; *Sex Roles.

2064 Jensen, Leif. Secondary earner strategies and family poverty: immigrant-native differentials, 1960-1980. INTERNATIONAL MIGRATION REVIEW, Vol. 25, no. 1 (Spring 1991), p. 113-140. English. DESCR: Anglo Americans; *Asian Americans; Blacks; Immigrants; Immigration; Income; Poverty; Women; Working Women.

2065 Krause, Neal and Markides, Kyriakos S. Gender roles, illness, and illness behavior in a Mexican American population. SOCIAL SCIENCE QUARTERLY, Vol. 68, no. 1 (March 1987), p. 102-121. English. DESCR: Public Health; San Antonio, TX; *Sex Roles.

2066 Laosa, Luis M. Maternal teaching strategies in Chicano and Anglo-American families: the influence of culture and education on maternal behavior. CHILD DEVELOPMENT, Vol. 51, no. 3 (September 1980), p. 759-765. English. DESCR: Anglo Americans; Comparative Psychology; *Cultural Characteristics; *Education; Maternal Teaching Observation Technique (MTOT); *Parent and Child Relationships; Parenting; Women.

2067 Leon, Ana M., et al. Self-help support groups for Hispanic mothers. CHILD WELFARE, Vol. 63, no. 3 (May, June, 1984), p. 261-268. English. DESCR: Mental Health Clinics; *Natural Support Systems; *Parent and Child Relationships; Sex Roles.

2068 LeVine, Sarah Ethel; Correa, Clara Sunderland; and Uribe, F. Medardo Tapia. The marital morality of Mexican women--an urban study. JOURNAL OF ANTHROPOLOGICAL RESEARCH, Vol. 42, no. 2 (Summer 1986), p. 183-202. English. DESCR: Los Robles, Cuernavaca, Morelos, Mexico; *Machismo; Marriage; Parent and Child Relationships; *Sex Roles; Women; *Women Men Relations.

2069 MacCorquodale, Patricia. Mexican-American women and mathematics: participation, aspirations, and achievement. IN: Cocking, Rodney R. and Mestre, Jose P., eds. LINGUISTIC AND CULTURAL DIFFERENCES ON LEARNING MATHEMATICS. Hillsdale, NJ: Erlbaum, 1988, p. 137-160. English. DESCR: *Academic Achievement; Anglo Americans; Bilingualism; *Mathematics.

2070 Maez, Angelita. The effects of two parent training programs on parental attitudes and self-concepts of Mexican American mothers. Thesis (Ph.D.)--UCLA, 1987. xiv, 184 leaves. English. DESCR: *Attitudes; *Parenting.

2071 Martinez, Estella A. Child behavior in Mexican American/Chicano families: maternal teaching and child-rearing practices. FAMILY RELATIONS, Vol. 37, no. 3 (July 1988), p. 275-280. English. DESCR: *Acculturation; Maternal Teaching Observation Technique (MTOT); Parent and Child Relationships; *Parenting; *Psychological Testing; Socioeconomic Factors; Values.

2072 Mason, Theresa Hope. Experience and meaning: an interpretive study of family and gender ideologies among a sample of Mexican-American women of two generations. Thesis (Ph.D.)--University of Texas, Austin, 1987. 406 p. English. DESCR: *Age Groups; Culture; Extended Family; *Sex Roles.

2073 McDuff, Mary Ann. Mexican-American women: a three-generational study of attitudes and behaviors. Thesis (M.A.)--Texas Women's University, 1989. 200 p. English. DESCR: *Acculturation; *Age Groups; San Antonio, TX; *Sex Roles.

2074 Melville, Margarita B. Female and male in Chicano theatre. IN: Kanellos, Nicolas, ed. HISPANIC THEATRE IN THE UNITED STATES. Houston, TX: Arte Publico Press, 1984, p. 71-79. English. DESCR: BERNABE; BRUJERIAS [play]; Cultural Characteristics; DAY OF THE SWALLOWS; Duarte-Clark, Rodrigo; EL JARDIN [play]; Feminism; Macias, Ysidro; Morton, Carlos; Portillo Trambley, Estela; RANCHO HOLLYWOOD [play]; *Sex Roles; *Teatro; THE ULTIMATE PENDEJADA [play]; Valdez, Luis; Women Men Relations.

2075 Melville, Margarita B. Matrescence. IN: Melville, Margarita B., ed. TWICE A MINORITY. St. Louis, MO: Mosby, 1980, p. 11-16. English. DESCR: *Sex Roles.

2076 Melville, Margarita B., ed. Mexicanas at work in the United States. Houston, TX: Mexican American Studies Program, University of Houston, 1988. 83 p. English. DESCR: Border Region; *Employment; *Labor; Migrant Labor; *Women; Working Women.

2077 Miller, Michael V. Variations in Mexican American family life: a review synthesis of empirical research. AZTLAN, Vol. 9, no. 1 (1978), p. 209-231. Bibliography. English. DESCR: Acculturation; Compadrazgo; Intermarriage; Sex Roles; Stereotypes.

2078 Mink, Diane Leslie. Early grandmotherhood: an exploratory study. Thesis (Ph.D.)--California School of Professional Psychology, Los Angeles, 1987. 190 p. English. DESCR: Age Groups; *Ancianos; Assertiveness; Fertility; Grandmothers; Natural Support Systems; *Sex Roles; Surveys; Youth.

2079 Miranda, Gloria E. Hispano-Mexican childrearing practices in pre-American Santa Barbara. SOUTHERN CALIFORNIA QUARTERLY, Vol. 65, no. 4 (Winter 1983), p. 307-320. English. DESCR: *Children; Cultural Characteristics; History; *Parenting; Santa Barbara, CA; Socialization.

2080 Mirande, Alfredo and Enriquez, Evangelina. La Chicana: the Mexican-American woman. Chicago: University of Chicago Press, 1979. x, 283 p.: ill. English. DESCR: Feminism; *Social History and Conditions.

2081 Mirande, Alfredo. The Chicano family and sex roles: an overview and introduction. DE COLORES, Vol. 6, no. 1-2 (1982), p. 1-6. English. DESCR: Sex Roles.

2082 Moore, Joan W. Mexican-American women addicts: the influence of family background. IN: Glick, Ronald and Moore, Joan, eds. DRUGS IN HISPANIC COMMUNITIES. New Brunswick, NJ: Rutgers University Press, c1990, p. 127-153. English. DESCR: Barrios; *Drug Addicts; Drug Use; East Los Angeles, CA; *Gangs; Heroin; Hoyo-Mara Gang, East Los Angeles, CA; Pachucos; Sex Roles; Socialization; White Fence Gang; Youth.

Family (cont.)

2083 Moore, Joan W. and Devitt, Mary. The paradox of deviance in addicted Mexican American mothers. GENDER & SOCIETY, Vol. 3, no. 1 (March 1989), p. 53-70. English. DESCR: Children; *Drug Addicts; *Drug Use; *Fertility; Gangs; Parenting; Sex Roles.

2084 Navar, Isabelle. La Mexicana: an image of strength. AGENDA, no. 4 (Spring 1974), p. 3-5. English. DESCR: Feminism; *Identity; Psychology; Sexism; Working Women.

2085 Navar, Isabelle. La Mexicana: an image of strength. REGENERACION, Vol. 2, no. 4 (1974), p. 4-6. English. DESCR: Feminism; *Identity; Psychology; Sexism; Working Women.

2086 Nieto Gomez de Lazarin, Anna. The Chicana: perspectives for education. ENCUENTRO FEMENIL, Vol. 1, no. 1 (Spring 1973), p. 34-61. English. DESCR: Colleges and Universities; Discrimination; Discrimination in Education; *Education; Identity; Sexism.

2087 O'Guinn, Thomas C.; Imperia, Giovanna; and MacAdams, Elizabeth A. Acculturation and perceived family decision-making input among Mexican American wives. JOURNAL OF CROSS-CULTURAL PSYCHOLOGY, Vol. 18, no. 1 (March 1987), p. 78-92. English. DESCR: *Acculturation; Attitudes; Consumers; Sex Roles.

2088 Olivero, Magaly. Career Latinas: facing the challenges of a family and a career. NUESTRO, Vol. 5, no. 6 (August, September, 1981), p. 27-28. English. DESCR: *Careers.

2089 Panitz, Daniel R., et al. The role of machismo and the Hispanic family in the etiology and treatment of alcoholism in the Hispanic American males. AMERICAN JOURNAL OF FAMILY THERAPY, Vol. 11, no. 1 (Spring 1983), p. 31-44. English. DESCR: *Alcoholism; Children; *Machismo; Puerto Rico; Socioeconomic Factors.

2090 Pardo, Mary. Mexican American women grassroots community activists: "Mothers of East Los Angeles". FRONTIERS: A JOURNAL OF WOMEN STUDIES, Vol. 11, no. 1 (1990), p. [1]-7. English. DESCR: Coalition Against the Prison, East Los Angeles, CA; *Community Organizations; East Los Angeles, CA; *Feminism; *Mothers of East L.A. (MELA); Organizations; Political Parties and Organizations; Politics; Sex Roles.

2091 Parra, Elena and Henderson, Ronald W. Mexican American perceptions of parent and teacher roles in child development. IN: Fishman, Joshua A. and Keller, Gary D., eds. BILINGUAL EDUCATION FOR HISPANIC STUDENTS IN THE UNITED STATES. New York: Teachers College Press, 1982. p. 289-299. English DESCR: *Children; *Parenting; Sex Roles; Teacher Attitudes.

2092 Pavich, Emma Guerrero. A Chicana perspective on Mexican culture and sexuality. JOURNAL OF SOCIAL WORK AND HUMAN SEXUALITY, Vol. 4, no. 3 (Spring 1986), p. 47-65. English. DESCR: California; Cultural Characteristics; Feminism; Homosexuality; Machismo; Sex Roles; Sex Stereotypes; *Sexual Behavior; Women Men Relations.

2093 Pesquera, Beatriz M. Work and family: a comparative analysis of professional, clerical and blue-collar Chicana workers. Thesis (Ph.D.)--University of California, Berkeley, 1985. i, 212 p. English. DESCR: *Sex Roles; *Working Women.

2094 Pierce, Jennifer. The implications of functionalism for Chicano family research. BERKELEY JOURNAL OF SOCIOLOGY, Vol. 29, (1984), p. 93-117. English. DESCR: Enriquez, Evangelina; LA CHICANA: THE MEXICAN AMERICAN WOMAN; Machismo; Mirande, Alfredo; Research Methodology; Sex Roles.

2095 Ramirez, Carmen Cecilia. A study of the value orientation of Lane County, Oregon, Mexican American mothers with a special focus on family/school relationships. Thesis (Ph.D.)--University of Oregon, 1981. 183 p. English. DESCR: *Community School Relationships; Lane County, OR; *Values.

2096 Ramirez, Oscar and Arce, Carlos H. The contemporary Chicano family: an empirically based review. IN: Baron, Augustine, Jr., ed. EXPLORATIONS IN CHICANO PSYCHOLOGY. New York: Praeger, 1981, p. 3-28. English. DESCR: Fertility; Literature Reviews; Machismo; Population; Sex Roles.

2097 Ramos, Reyes. Discovering the production of Mexican American family structure. DE COLORES, Vol. 6, no. 1-2 (1982), p. 120-134. English. DESCR: Research Methodology.

2098 Romero, Gloria J.; Castro, Felipe G.; and Cervantes, Richard C. Latinas without work: family, occupational, and economic stress following unemployment. PSYCHOLOGY OF WOMEN QUARTERLY, Vol. 12, no. 3 (September 1988), p. 281-297. English. DESCR: *Employment; Starkist Tuna Cannery, Wilmington, CA; *Stress.

2099 Romero, Gloria J.; Cervantes, Richard C.; and Castro, Felipe G. Long-term stress among Latino women after a plant closure. SOCIOLOGY & SOCIAL RESEARCH, Vol. 71, no. 2 (January 1987), p. 85-88. English. DESCR: Attitudes; Employment; *Stress; Wilmington, CA.

2100 Rose, Margaret. From the fields to the picket line: Huelga women and the boycott, 1965-1975. LABOR HISTORY, Vol. 31, no. 3 (1990), p. 271-293. English. DESCR: *Boycotts; Farm Workers; Padilla, Esther; Padilla, Gilbert; Rodriguez, Conrado; Rodriguez, Herminia; *United Farmworkers of America (UFW); Washington, D.C.

2101 Ruiz, Vicki L. Cannery women/cannery lives: Mexican women, unionization, and the California food processing industry, 1930-1950. Albuquerque, NM: University of New Mexico Press, 1987. xviii, 194 p.: ill. English. DESCR: Agricultural Labor Unions; California; *Canneries; History; Industrial Workers; Labor Disputes; *Labor Unions; Trade Unions; United Cannery Agricultural Packing and Allied Workers of America (UCAPAWA); Women.

2102 Sabogal, Fabio, et al. Hispanic familism and acculturation: what changes and what doesn't? HISPANIC JOURNAL OF BEHAVIORAL SCIENCES, Vol. 9, no. 4 (December 1987), p. 397-412. English. DESCR: *Acculturation; Attitudes; Cultural Characteristics; Ethnic Groups; Extended Family; Natural Support Systems; Values.

Family (cont.)

2103 Saragoza, Alex M. The conceptualization of the history of the Chicano family. IN: Valdez, Armando, et al., eds. THE STATE OF CHICANO RESEARCH ON FAMILY, LABOR AND MIGRATION. Stanford, CA: Stanford Center for Chicano Research, 1983, p. 111-138. English. DESCR: *Social History and Conditions.

2104 Segura, Denise. Familism and employment among Chicanas and Mexican immigrant women. IN: Melville, Margarita, ed. MEXICANAS AT WORK IN THE UNITED STATES. Houston, TX: Mexican American Studies Program, University of Houston, 1988, p. 24-32. English. DESCR: *Employment; *Extended Family; Immigrants; Income; Machismo; Sex Roles; *Women; Working Women.

2105 Segura, Denise. The interplay of familism and patriarchy on employment among Chicana and Mexicana women. RENATO ROSALDO LECTURE SERIES MONOGRAPH, Vol. 5, (1989), p. 35-53. English. DESCR: Employment; Immigrants; Machismo; *Sex Roles; Women; Women Men Relations; *Working Women.

2106 Tienda, Marta and Angel, Ronald J. Headship and household composition among Blacks, Hispanics and other whites. SOCIAL FORCES, Vol. 61, no. 2 (December 1982), p. 508-531. English. DESCR: Anglo Americans; Blacks; Cultural Characteristics; Extended Family; Puerto Ricans; Single Parents.

2107 Tienda, Marta and Glass, Jennifer. Household structure and labor-force participation of Black, Hispanic, and white mothers. DEMOGRAPHY, Vol. 22, no. 3 (August 1985), p. 381-394. English. DESCR: Anglo Americans; Blacks; *Extended Family; *Sex Roles; *Working Women.

2108 Torres, Sara. A comparative analysis of wife abuse among Anglo-American and Mexican-American battered women: attitudes, nature, severity, frequency and response to the abuse. Thesis (Ph.D.)--University of Texas, Austin, 1986. 265 p. English. DESCR: Anglo Americans; Attitudes; Battered Women; *Violence; *Women.

2109 Triandis, Harry C. Role perceptions of Hispanic young adults. JOURNAL OF CROSS-CULTURAL PSYCHOLOGY, Vol. 15, no. 3 (September 1984), p. 297-320. English. DESCR: *Cultural Characteristics; Parent and Child Relationships; *Sex Roles; Social Psychology; Values; Youth.

2110 Valdez, Diana. Mexican American family research: a critical review and conceptual framework. DE COLORES, Vol. 6, no. 1-2 (1982), p. 48-63. English. DESCR: Research Methodology.

2111 Vasquez, Enriqueta L. La Chicana. MAGAZIN, Vol. 1, no. 4 (April 1972), p. 66-68+. English. DESCR: *Chicano Movement; Working Women.

2112 Waldman, Elizabeth. Profile of the Chicana: a statistical fact sheet. IN: Mora, Magdalena and Del Castillo, Adelaida, eds. MEXICAN WOMEN IN THE UNITED STATES: STRUGGLES PAST AND PRESENT. Los Angeles, CA: Chicano Studies Research Center, UCLA, 1980, p. 195-204. English. DESCR: Employment; Population; *Statistics.

2113 Whiteford, Linda. Migrants no longer: changing family structure of Mexican Americans in South Texas. DE COLORES, Vol. 6, no. 1-2 (1982), p. 99-108. English. DESCR: Sex Roles; South Texas.

2114 Williams, Brett. Why migrant women feed their husbands tamales: foodways as a basis for a revisionist view of Tejano family life. IN: Brown, Linda Keller and Mussell, Kay, eds. ETHNIC AND REGIONAL FOODWAYS IN THE UNITED STATES: THE PERFORMANCE OF GROUP IDENTITY. Knoxville, TN: University of Tennessee Press, 1984, p. 113-126. English. DESCR: Cultural Customs; Extended Family; *Food Practices; Illinois; *Migrant Labor; Sex Roles; Tamales; Texas.

2115 Williams, Norma. The Mexican American family: tradition and change. Dix Hills, NY: General Hall, Inc., c1990. x, 170 p. English. DESCR: Cultural Characteristics; *Cultural Customs; Religion; *Sex Roles; Working Women.

2116 Ybarra, Lea. Empirical and theoretical developments in the study of Chicano families. IN: Valdez, Armando, et al., eds. THE STATE OF CHICANO RESEARCH ON FAMILY, LABOR, AND MIGRATION. Stanford, CA: Stanford Center for Chicano Research, 1983, p. 91-110. English. DESCR: *Research Methodology; Sex Roles; Social Science; *Stereotypes.

2117 Ybarra, Lea. Marital decision-making and the role of machismo in the Chicano family. DE COLORES, Vol. 6, no. 1-2 (1982), p. 32-47. English. DESCR: *Machismo; Marriage; Sex Roles.

2118 Ybarra, Lea. When wives work: the impact on the Chicano family. JOURNAL OF MARRIAGE AND THE FAMILY, Vol. 44, (February 1982), p. 169-178. English. DESCR: *Working Women.

2119 Zambrana, Ruth E. Hispanic professional women: work, family and health. Los Angeles, CA: National Network of Hispanic Women, 1987. 75 leaves. English. DESCR: Business; *Careers; *Employment; Management; Mental Health; Social Classes; *Social Mobility; *Women.

2120 Zambrana, Ruth E. and Frith, Sandra. Mexican-American professional women: role satisfaction differences in single and multiple role lifestyles. JOURNAL OF SOCIAL BEHAVIOR AND PERSONALITY, Vol. 3, no. 4 (1988), p. 347-361. English. DESCR: *Careers; *Mental Health; *Sex Roles; Working Women.

2121 Zapata, Jesse T. and Jaramillo, Pat T. The Mexican American family: an Adlerian perspective. HISPANIC JOURNAL OF BEHAVIORAL SCIENCES, Vol. 3, no. 3 (September 1981), p. 275-290. English. DESCR: Adlerian "Life Style Inventory"; Parent and Child Relationships; Sex Roles; Stereotypes.

2122 Zavella, Patricia. Women, work and family in the Chicano community: cannery workers of the Santa Clara Valley. Thesis (Ph.D.)--University of California, Berkeley, 1982. ix, 254 p. English. DESCR: *Canneries; Employment; Industrial Workers; Labor Unions; Santa Clara Valley, CA; *Sex Roles; *Working Women.

Family (cont.)

2123 Zavella, Patricia. Women's work and Chicano families: cannery workers of the Santa Clara Valley. Ithaca, NY: Cornell University Press, 1987. xviii, 191 p. English. DESCR: *Canneries; Employment; Industrial Workers; Labor Unions; Santa Clara Valley, CA; Sex Roles; *Working Women.

2124 Zepeda, Marlene. Las abuelitas. AGENDA, Vol. 9, no. 6 (November, December, 1979), p. 10-13. Bilingual. DESCR: *Ancianos.

2125 Zuniga, Maria E. Assessment issues with Chicanas: practice implications. PSYCHOTHERAPY, Vol. 25, no. 2 (Summer 1988), p. 288-293. English. DESCR: Acculturation; Colleges and Universities; Identity; *Mental Health; Mexican-American Outreach Program, San Diego State University; *Psychotherapy; *Students.

Family Planning

2126 Abrahamse, Allan F.; Morrison, Peter A.; and Waite, Linda J. Teenagers willing to consider single parenthood: who is at greatest risk? FAMILY PLANNING PERSPECTIVES, Vol. 20, no. 1 (January, February, 1988), p. 13-18. English. DESCR: Blacks; *Fertility; High School and Beyond Project (HS&B); *Single Parents; Women; *Youth.

2127 Amaro, Hortensia. Abortion use and attitudes among Chicanas: the need for research. RESEARCH BULLETIN (SPANISH SPEAKING MENTAL HEALTH RES. CENTER), Vol. 4, no. 3 (March 1980), p. 1-5. English. DESCR: *Abortion; *Attitudes; Birth Control; Fertility; Literature Reviews; Mental Health.

2128 Amaro, Hortensia. Women in the Mexican-American community: religion, culture, and reproductive attitudes and experiences. JOURNAL OF COMMUNITY PSYCHOLOGY, Vol. 16, no. 1 (January 1988), p. 6-20. English. DESCR: Abortion; *Attitudes; Birth Control; *Fertility; Religion.

2129 Andrade, Sally J. Family planning practices of Mexican Americans. IN: Melville, Margarita B., ed. TWICE A MINORITY. St. Louis, MO: Mosby, 1980, p. 17-32. English. DESCR: Birth Control; *Fertility.

2130 Atkinson, Donald R.; Winzelberg, Andrew; and Holland, Abby. Ethnicity, locus of control for family planning, and pregnancy counselor credibility. JOURNAL OF COUNSELING PSYCHOLOGY, Vol. 32, no. 3 (July 1985), p. 417-421. English. DESCR: Anglo Americans; Counseling (Psychological); Fertility; Identity; *Locus of Control; Women.

2131 Bean, Frank D. and Swicegood, Gray. Generation, female education and Mexican American fertility. SOCIAL SCIENCE QUARTERLY, Vol. 63, (March 1982), p. 131-144. English. DESCR: Age Groups; Education; *Fertility.

2132 Cayer, Shirley. Chicago's new Hispanic health alliance. NUESTRO, Vol. 7, no. 5 (June, July, 1983), p 44-48. English. DESCR: Alcoholism; Chicago Hispanic Health Alliance; *Health Education; Latin Americans; *Medical Care.

2133 Cummings, Michele and Cummings, Scott. Family planning among the urban poor: sexual politics and social policy. FAMILY RELATIONS, Vol. 32, no. 1 (January 1983), p.

47-58. English. DESCR: Anglo Americans; Blacks; Discrimination; Low Income; *Stereotypes.

2134 Delgado, Jane L. Adolescent pregnancy: an overview. IN: National Hispanic Center for Advanced Studies and Policy Analysis and National Hispanic University. THE STATE OF HISPANIC AMERICA. VOL. VI. Oakland, CA: National Hispanic University, c1987, p. 37-49. English. DESCR: *Fertility; Public Policy; *Youth.

2135 Eisen, Marvin and Zellman, Gail L. Factors predicting pregnancy resolution decision satisfaction of unmarried adolescents. JOURNAL OF GENETIC PSYCHOLOGY, Vol. 145, no. 2 (December 1984), p. 231-239. English. DESCR: Abortion; Anglo Americans; Attitudes; Counseling (Psychological); *Fertility; Youth.

2136 Flores, Francisca. Comision Femenil Mexicana. REGENERACION, Vol. 2, no. 1 (1971), p. 6. English. DESCR: Abortion; Children; Comision Femenil Mexicana Nacional; Feminism; Organizations; Politics.

2137 Holck, Susan E., et al. Need for family planning services among Anglo and Hispanic women in the United States counties bordering Mexico. FAMILY PLANNING PERSPECTIVES, Vol. 14, no. 3 (May, June, 1982), p. 155-159. English. DESCR: Anglo Americans; Border Region; Women.

2138 Hutchison, James. Teenagers and contraception in Cameron and Willacy Counties. BORDERLANDS JOURNAL, Vol. 7, no. 1 (Fall 1983), p. 75-90. English. DESCR: *Birth Control; Cameron County, TX; Fertility; Sex Education; Willacy County, TX; Youth.

2139 Jorgensen, Stephen R. and Adams, Russell P. Family planning needs and behavior of Mexican American women: a study of health care professionals and their clientele. HISPANIC JOURNAL OF BEHAVIORAL SCIENCES, Vol. 9, no. 3 (September 1987), p. 265-286. English. DESCR: Acculturation; *Attitudes; Birth Control; *Cultural Characteristics; Fertility; Medical Personnel; Stereotypes; Sterilization.

2140 Marin, Barbara Van Oss, et al. Health care utilization by low-income clients of a community clinic: an archival study. HISPANIC JOURNAL OF BEHAVIORAL SCIENCES, Vol. 3, no. 3 (September 1981), p. 257-273. English. DESCR: La Clinica Familiar del Barrio, Los Angeles, CA; Low Income; *Medical Care; Medical Clinics.

2141 Ortiz, Sylvia. An analysis of the relationship between the values of sexual regulation, male dominance, and motherhood, and Mexican-American women's attitudes, knowledge, and usage of birth control. Thesis (Ph.D.)--University of California, Santa Barbara, 1987. 128 p. English. DESCR: Acculturation; *Attitudes; *Birth Control; Sexual Behavior.

2142 Radecki, Stephen E. and Bernstein, Gerald S. Use of clinic versus private family planning care by low-income women: access, cost and patient satisfaction. AMERICAN JOURNAL OF PUBLIC HEALTH, Vol. 79, no. 6 (June 1989), p. 692-697. English. DESCR: Los Angeles County, CA; *Low Income; Medical Care; *Medical Clinics; Medical Personnel.

Family Planning (cont.)

2143 Ridgely, Julia S. Health means jobs. WORLD HEALTH, (January, February, 1985), p. 18-20. English. DESCR: Employment Training; Youth.

2144 Sabagh, Georges and Lopez, David. Religiosity and fertility: the case of Chicanas. SOCIAL FORCES, Vol. 59, no. 2 (December 1980), p. 431-439. English. DESCR: Catholic Church; *Fertility; Immigrants; *Religion; Women.

2145 Sex education, abortion views of Mexican Americans typical of U.S. beliefs. FAMILY PLANNING PERSPECTIVES, Vol. 15, (July, August, 1983), p. 197-201. English. DESCR: *Abortion; *Attitudes; Birth Control; *Sex Education.

2146 Talavera, Esther. Sterilization is not an alternative in family planning. AGENDA, Vol. 7, no. 6 (November, December, 1977), p. 8. English. DESCR: Discrimination; Feminism; *Fertility; Medical Care Laws and Legislation; Sterilization.

2147 Torres, Aida and Singh, Susheela. Contraceptive practice among Hispanic adolescents. FAMILY PLANNING PERSPECTIVES, Vol. 18, no. 4 (July, August, 1986), p. 193-194. English. DESCR: Birth Control; *Youth.

2148 Warren, Charles W.; Smith, Jack C.; and Rochat, Roger W. Differentials in the planning status of the most recent live birth to Mexican Americans and Anglos. PUBLIC HEALTH REPORTS, Vol. 98, no. 2 (March, April, 1983), p. 152-160. English. DESCR: Anglo Americans; Fertility; Women.

Farah Manufacturing Co., El Paso, TX

2149 Arroyo, Laura E. Industrial and occupational distribution of Chicana workers. AZTLAN, Vol. 4, no. 2 (Fall 1973), p. 343-382. English. DESCR: California; *Employment; Farah Strike; Garment Industry; Industrial Workers; Strikes and Lockouts; Texas.

2150 Arroyo, Laura E. Industrial and occupational distribution of Chicana workers. IN: Sanchez, Rosaura and Martinez Cruz, Rosa, eds. ESSAYS ON LA MUJER. Los Angeles, CA: Chicano Studies Center Publications, UCLA, 1977, p. 150-187. English. DESCR: California; *Employment; Farah Strike; Garment Industry; Industrial Workers; Strikes and Lockouts; Texas.

2151 Coyle, Laurie; Hershatter, Gail; and Honig, Emily. Women at Farah: an unfinished story. IN: Mora, Magdalena and Del Castillo, Adelaida, eds. MEXICAN WOMEN IN THE UNITED STATES: STRUGGLES PAST AND PRESENT. Los Angeles, CA: Chicano Studies Research Center, UCLA, 1980, p. 117-143. English. DESCR: Farah Strike; Garment Industry; Labor Unions; *Strikes and Lockouts.

2152 Delgado Campbell, Dolores. Shattering the stereotype: Chicanas as labor union organizers. BERKELEY WOMEN OF COLOR, no. 11 (Summer 1983), p. 20-23. English. DESCR: Farah Strike; *Gonzalez Parsons, Lucia; Huerta, Dolores; *Labor Unions; Moreno, Luisa [union organizer]; Tenayuca, Emma; Working Women.

2153 Ruiz, Vicki L. "And miles to go...": Mexican women and work, 1930-1985. IN: Schlissel, Lillian, et al., eds. WESTERN WOMEN: THEIR LAND, THEIR LIVES. Albuquerque, NM: University of New Mexico Press, 1988, p. 117-136. English. DESCR: Education; El Paso Women's Employment and Education Project (EPWEE); *Employment; Farah Strike; *Income; Industrial Workers; Labor Unions; Statistics; Undocumented Workers; United Cannery Agricultural Packing and Allied Workers of America (UCAPAWA); Women; *Working Women.

Farah Strike

2154 Arroyo, Laura E. Industrial and occupational distribution of Chicana workers. AZTLAN, Vol. 4, no. 2 (Fall 1973), p. 343-382. English. DESCR: California; *Employment; Farah Manufacturing Co., El Paso, TX; Garment Industry; Industrial Workers; Strikes and Lockouts; Texas.

2155 Arroyo, Laura E. Industrial and occupational distribution of Chicana workers. IN: Sanchez, Rosaura and Martinez Cruz, Rosa, eds. ESSAYS ON LA MUJER. Los Angeles, CA: Chicano Studies Center Publications, UCLA, 1977, p. 150-187. English. DESCR: California; *Employment; Farah Manufacturing Co., El Paso, TX; Garment Industry; Industrial Workers; Strikes and Lockouts; Texas.

2156 Coyle, Laurie; Hershatter, Gail; and Honig, Emily. Women at Farah: an unfinished story. IN: Mora, Magdalena and Del Castillo, Adelaida, eds. MEXICAN WOMEN IN THE UNITED STATES: STRUGGLES PAST AND PRESENT. Los Angeles, CA: Chicano Studies Research Center, UCLA, 1980, p. 117-143. English. DESCR: Farah Manufacturing Co., El Paso, TX; Garment Industry; Labor Unions; *Strikes and Lockouts.

2157 Delgado Campbell, Dolores. Shattering the stereotype: Chicanas as labor union organizers. BERKELEY WOMEN OF COLOR, no. 11 (Summer 1983), p. 20-23. English. DESCR: Farah Manufacturing Co., El Paso, TX; *Gonzalez Parsons, Lucia; Huerta, Dolores; *Labor Unions; Moreno, Luisa [union organizer]; Tenayuca, Emma; Working Women.

2158 Ruiz, Vicki L. "And miles to go...": Mexican women and work, 1930-1985. IN: Schlissel, Lillian, et al., eds. WESTERN WOMEN: THEIR LAND, THEIR LIVES. Albuquerque, NM: University of New Mexico Press, 1988, p. 117-136. English. DESCR: Education; El Paso Women's Employment and Education Project (EPWEE); *Employment; Farah Manufacturing Co., El Paso, TX; *Income; Industrial Workers; Labor Unions; Statistics; Undocumented Workers; United Cannery Agricultural Packing and Allied Workers of America (UCAPAWA); Women; *Working Women.

Farm Labor Organizing Committee (FLOC)

2159 Duran, Lucy. Lucy Duran--wife, mother, and organizer. IN: Mora, Magdalena and Del Castillo, Adelaida, eds. MEXICAN WOMEN IN THE UNITED STATES: STRUGGLES PAST AND PRESENT. Los Angeles, CA: Chicano Studies Research Center, UCLA, 1980, p. 183-184. English. DESCR: Agricultural Labor Unions; *Biography; Duran, Lucy; Farm Workers; Working Women.

Farm Women
USE: Working Women

Farm Workers

2160 Barton, Amy E. and California Commission on the Status of Women. Campesinas: women farmworkers in the California agricultural labor force, report of a study project. Sacramento, CA: The Commission, [1978], vii, 23, 52 p. English. DESCR: California; Migrant Labor; Statistics; *Working Women.

2161 Barton, Amy E. Women Farmworkers: their workplace and capitalist patriarchy. REVISTA MUJERES, Vol. 3, no. 2 (June 1986), p. 11-13. English. DESCR: Capitalism; Discrimination; Sexism.

2162 Bays, Sharon Arlene. Women of the Valley of the Sun: women and family work culture in Woodlake, California. Thesis (M.A.)--UCLA, 1988. 89 leaves. English. DESCR: Family; Woodlake, CA; Working Women.

2163 Cantarow, Ellen and De la Cruz, Jessie Lopez. Jessie Lopez De la Cruz: the battle for farmworkers' rights. IN: Cantarow, Ellen. MOVING THE MOUNTAIN: WOMEN WORKING FOR SOCIAL CHANGE. Old Westbury, NY: Feminist Press, 1980, p. 94-151. English. DESCR: Agricultural Labor Unions; Chavez, Cesar E.; *De la Cruz, Jessie Lopez; Labor Disputes; Oral History; Parlier, CA; Sex Roles; Strikes and Lockouts; *United Farmworkers of America (UFW).

2164 Chavez, Henri. Unsung heroine of La Causa. REGENERACION, Vol. 1, no. 10 (1971), p. 20. English. DESCR: AFL-CIO United Farmworkers Organizing Committee; Agricultural Labor Unions; Community Service Organization, Los Angeles, (CSO); Family; *Huerta, Dolores; Poverty; Working Women.

2165 Chavira, Alicia. "Tienes que ser valiente": Mexicana migrants in a midwestern farm labor camp. IN: Melville, Margarita, ed. MEXICANAS AT WORK IN THE UNITED STATES. Houston, TX: Mexican American Studies Program, University of Houston, 1988, p. 64-74. English. DESCR: Immigrants; *Labor Camps; Midwestern States; Migrant Health Services; *Migrant Labor; Sex Roles; *Women.

2166 de la Torre, Adela and Rush, Lynda. The determinants of breastfeeding for Mexican migrant women. INTERNATIONAL MIGRATION REVIEW, Vol. 21, no. 3 (Fall 1987), p. 728-742. English. DESCR: *Breastfeeding; Maternal and Child Welfare; Migrant Health Services; Migrant Labor; Migration; Public Health; Working Women.

2167 de Leon Siantz, Mary Lou. Maternal acceptance/rejection of Mexican migrant mothers. PSYCHOLOGY OF WOMEN QUARTERLY, Vol. 14, no. 2 (June 1990), p. 245-254. English. DESCR: Child Study; *Migrant Children; Migrant Labor; Natural Support Systems; *Parent and Child Relationships; Stress; Texas Migrant Council Headstart Program.

2168 Duran, Lucy. Lucy Duran--wife, mother, and organizer. IN: Mora, Magdalena and Del Castillo, Adelaida, eds. MEXICAN WOMEN IN THE UNITED STATES: STRUGGLES PAST AND PRESENT. Los Angeles, CA: Chicano Studies Research Center, UCLA, 1980, p. 183-184. English. DESCR: Agricultural Labor Unions; *Biography; Duran, Lucy; Farm Labor Organizing Committee (FLOC); Working Women

2169 Echaveste, Beatrice and Huerta, Dolores. In the shadow of the eagle: Huerta = A la sombra del aguila: Huerta. AMERICAS 2001, Vol. 1, no. 3 (November, December, 1987), p.

26-30. Bilingual. DESCR: Agricultural Labor Unions; Boycotts; Huerta, Dolores; United Farmworkers of America (UFW).

2170 Fenster, Laura and Coye, Molly J. Birthweight of infants born to Hispanic women employed in agriculture. ARCHIVES OF ENVIRONMENTAL HEALTH, Vol. 45, no. 1 (January, February, 1990), p. 46-52. English. DESCR: *Prenatal Care; Women.

2171 Gonzalez, Rosalinda M. Chicanas and Mexican immigrant families 1920-1940: women's subordination and family exploitation. IN: Scharf, Lois and Jensen, Joan M., eds. DECADES OF DISCONTENT: THE WOMEN'S MOVEMENT, 1920-1940. Westport, CT: Greenwood Press, 1983, p. 59-84. English. DESCR: *Family; History; Immigrants; Labor; Labor Unions; Mexico; Pecan Shelling Worker's Union, San Antonio, TX; Sex Roles; Strikes and Lockouts; United Cannery Agricultural Packing and Allied Workers of America (UCAPAWA); Working Women.

2172 Hintz, Joy. Valiant migrant women = Las mujeres valerosas. Tiffin, OH: Sayger Printing, 1982. viii, 98 p. English. DESCR: Battered Women; Feminism; Florida; Marriage; Migrant Children; Migrant Health Services; Migrant Housing; *Migrant Labor; Migration Patterns; Ohio; Sex Roles; Texas.

2173 Jensen, Joan M. "I've worked, I'm not afraid of work": farm women in New Mexico, 1920-1940. NEW MEXICO HISTORICAL REVIEW, Vol. 61, no. 1 (January 1986), p. 27-52. English. DESCR: History; New Mexico; *Rural Economics; *Working Women.

2174 Kokinos, Mary and Dewey, Kathryn G. Infant feeding practices of migrant Mexican-American families in Northern California. ECOLOGY OF FOOD AND NUTRITION, Vol. 18, no. 3 (1986), p. 209-220. English. DESCR: *Breastfeeding; Migrant Labor; Northern California; Nutrition.

2175 Lopez-Trevino, Maria Elena. A radio model: a community strategy to address the problems and needs of Mexican-American women farmworkers. Thesis (M.S.)--California State University, Long Beach, 1989. 179 p. English. DESCR: Coachella, CA; Income; Low Income; Occupational Hazards; *Radio; *Sex Roles.

2176 Romero, Mary and Margolis, Eric. Tending the beets: campesinas and the Great Western Sugar Company. REVISTA MUJERES, Vol. 2, no. 2 (June 1985), p. 17-27. English. DESCR: Food Industry; Great Western Sugar Company, Hudson, CO; South Platte Valley, CO.

2177 Rose, Margaret. From the fields to the picket line: Huelga women and the boycott, 1965-1975. LABOR HISTORY, Vol. 31, no. 3 (1990), p. 271-293. English. DESCR: *Boycotts; Family; Padilla, Esther; Padilla, Gilbert; Rodriguez, Conrado; Rodriguez, Herminia; *United Farmworkers of America (UFW); Washington, D.C.

2178 Watkins, Elizabeth L.; Peoples, Mary D.; and Gates, Connie. Health and social needs of women farmworkers: receiving maternity care at a migrant health center. MIGRATION TODAY, Vol. 13, no. 2 (1985), p. 39-42. English. DESCR: *Maternal and Child Welfare; *Migrant Health Services; Women.

Farm Workers (cont.)

2179 Whiteford, Linda. Mexican American women as innovators. IN: Melville, Margarita B., ed. TWICE A MINORITY. St. Louis, MO: Mosby, 1980, p. 109-126. English. **DESCR:** Border Region; Migrant Labor; *Working Women.

Farnham, Thomas Jefferson

2180 Castaneda, Antonia I. The political economy of nineteenth century stereotypes of Californianas. IN: Del Castillo, Adelaida R., ed. BETWEEN BORDERS: ESSAYS ON MEXICANA/CHICANA HISTORY. Encino, CA: Floricanto Press, 1990, p. 213-236. English. **DESCR:** *California; *Californios; Dana, Richard Henry; History; LIFE IN CALIFORNIA; *Political Economy; Robinson, Alfred; *Sex Stereotypes; TRAVELS IN CALIFORNIA AND SCENES IN THE PACIFIC OCEAN; TWO YEARS BEFORE THE MAST; Women.

Fatalism
USE: Locus of Control

Fear of Success Scale (FOSS)

2181 Alba, Isabel Catherine. Achievement conflicts, sex-role orientation, and performance on sex-role appropriate and sex-role inappropriate tasks in women of three ethnic groups. Thesis (Ph.D.)--University of California, Riverside, 1987. 129 p. English. **DESCR:** Anglo Americans; *Assertiveness; Blacks; Ethnic Groups; *Sex Roles; Women.

Federal Aid

2182 Salazar, Sandra A. Chicanas as healers. IN: LA CHICANA: BUILDING FOR THE FUTURE, AN ACTION PLAN FOR THE 80s. Oakland, CA: National Hispanic University, 1981, p. 107-119. English. **DESCR:** *Medical Care; Public Health.

Fellowship
USE: Financial Aid

Feminism

2183 Agosin, Marjorie. Elucubraciones y antielucubraciones: critica feminista desde perspectivas poeticas. THIRD WOMAN, Vol. 1, no. 2 (1982), p. 65-69. Spanish. **DESCR:** Essays; Literary Criticism; *Literature.

2184 Alarcon, Norma. Chicana feminism: in the tracks of 'the' native woman. CULTURAL STUDIES, Vol. 4, no. 3 (October 1990), p. 248-256. English. **DESCR:** Cultural Studies; *Identity; *Indigenismo; Mestizaje; Women.

2185 Alarcon, Norma. Chicana's feminist literature: a re-vision through Malintzinl or Malintzin: putting flesh back on the object. IN: Moraga, Cherrie and Anzaldua, Gloria, eds. THIS BRIDGE CALLED MY BACK: WRITINGS BY RADICAL WOMEN OF COLOR. Watertown, MA: Persephone Press, 1981, p. 182-190. English. **DESCR:** Literature; Malinche; *Sex Roles; Stereotypes; Symbolism.

2186 Alarcon, Norma. The theoretical subject(s) of THIS BRIDGE CALLED MY BACK and Anglo-American feminism. IN: Calderon, Hector and Saldivar, Jose David, eds. CRITICISM IN THE BORDERLANDS: STUDIES IN CHICANO LITERATURE, CULTURE, AND IDEOLOGY. Durham, NC: Duke University Press, 1991, p. [28]-39. English. **DESCR:** *Anglo Americans; Anzaldua, Gloria; Moraga, Cherrie; THIS BRIDGE CALLED MY BACK; *Women.

2187 Alarcon, Norma. The theoretical subject(s) of THIS BRIDGE CALLED MY BACK and Anglo-American feminism. IN: Anzaldua, Gloria, ed. MAKING FACE, MAKING SOUL: HACIENDO CARAS: CREATIVE AND CRITICAL PERSPECTIVES BY WOMEN OF COLOR. San Francisco, CA: Aunt Lute Foundation Books, 1990, p. 356-369. English. **DESCR:** *Anglo Americans; Anzaldua, Gloria; Literary Criticism; Moraga, Cherrie; THIS BRIDGE CALLED MY BACK; *Women.

2188 Alarcon, Norma. Traddutora, traditora: a paradigmatic figure of Chicana feminism. CULTURAL CRITIQUE, Vol. 13, (Fall 1989), p. 57-87. English. **DESCR:** *Malinche; Paz, Octavio; Sex Roles; Symbolism.

2189 Alarcon, Norma. What kind of lover have you made me, Mother?: towards a theory of Chicanas' feminism and cultural identity through poetry. IN: McCluskey, Audrey T., ed. WOMEN OF COLOR: PERSPECTIVES ON FEMINISM AND IDENTITY. Bloomington, IN: Women's Studies Program, Indiana University, 1985, p. 85-110. English. **DESCR:** Brinson-Pineda, Barbara; Cervantes, Lorna Dee; Cisneros, Sandra; Culture; Identity; *Literary Criticism; Mora, Pat; Moraga, Cherrie; *Poetry; Tafolla, Carmen; Vigil-Pinon, Evangelina; Villanueva, Alma.

2190 Allen, Jane and Guthrie, Derek. La mujer: a visual dialogue. NEW ART EXAMINER, Vol. 5, no. 10 (July 1978), p. 14. English. **DESCR:** California; Chicago, IL; Movimiento Artistico Chicano (MARCH), Chicago, IL; Stereotypes.

2191 Anonymous. Workshop resolutions - First National Chicana Conference, May 1971. IN: Garcia, Richard A., ed. CHICANOS IN AMERICA, 1540-1974: A CHRONOLOGY AND FACT BOOK. Dobbs Ferry, NY: Oceana Publications, 1977, p. 142-144. English. **DESCR:** Conferences and Meetings; *First National Chicana Conference (May 1971: Houston, TX).

2192 Anzaldua, Gloria. Border crossings. TRIVIA: A JOURNAL OF IDEAS, no. 14 (Spring 1989), p. 46-51. English. **DESCR:** *Literary Criticism; Literature.

2193 Anzaldua, Gloria. La prieta. IN: Moraga, Cherrie and Anzaldua, Gloria, eds. THIS BRIDGE CALLED MY BACK: WRITINGS BY RADICAL WOMEN OF COLOR. Watertown, MA: Persephone Press, 1981, p. 198-209. English. **DESCR:** *Biography; Cultural Customs.

2194 Anzaldua, Gloria, ed. Making face, making soul = Haciendo caras: creative and critical perspectives by women of color. San Francisco, CA: Aunt Lute Foundation Books, 1990. English. **DESCR:** Ethnic Groups; *Literature; Women.

2195 Apodaca, Maria Linda. A double edge sword: Hispanas and liberal feminism. CRITICA, Vol. 1, no. 3 (Fall 1986), p. 96-114. English. **DESCR:** History; Women.

2196 Aragon de Valdez, Theresa. Organizing as a political tool for the Chicana. FRONTIERS: A JOURNAL OF WOMEN STUDIES, Vol. 5, no. 2 (Summer 1980), p. 7-13. English. **DESCR:** Discrimination; *Leadership; Mexican American Legal Defense and Educational Fund (MALDEF); Social History and Conditions; Sterilization.

---   ---

Feminism (cont.)

2197 Arevalo, Rodolfo, ed. and Minor, Marianne, ed. Chicanas and alcoholism: a sociocultural perspective of women. San Jose, CA: School of Social Work, San Jose State University, c1981. 55 p. English. DESCR: *Alcoholism; Drug Abuse Programs; Family; Natural Support Systems; Preventative Medicine; Psychotherapy.

2198 Asuncion-Lande, Nobleza C. Problems and strategies for sexual identity and cultural integration: Mexican-American women on the move. IN: Newmark, Eileen, ed. WOMEN'S ROLES: A CROSS-CULTURAL PERSPECTIVE. New York, NY: Pergamon Press, 1980, p. 497-506. English. DESCR: Chicano Movement; *Identity; *Sexism.

2199 Aulette, Judy and Mills, Trudy. Something old, something new: auxiliary work in the 1983-1986 copper strike. FEMINIST STUDIES, Vol. 14, no. 2 (Summer 1988), p. 251-268. English. DESCR: Arizona; Clifton-Morenci Copper Strike, 1983-1986; Clifton-Morenci District, Arizona; Labor Unions; Morenci Miners Women's Auxiliary (MMWA); Mutualistas; Phelps Dodge Corporation, Morenci, AZ; SALT OF THE EARTH [film]; Sex Roles; *Strikes and Lockouts.

2200 Avila, Consuelo. Ecos de una convencion. MAGAZIN, Vol. 1, no. 9 (September 1973), p. 33-36. Spanish. DESCR: Conferences and Meetings; National Women's Political Caucus (February 9-11, 1973: Houston, TX).

2201 Becerra, Gloria V. and Lopez, Martha. Chicana employment--options for the future. IN: LA CHICANA: BUILDING FOR THE FUTURE, AN ACTION PLAN FOR THE 80s. Oakland, CA: National Hispanic University, 1981, p. 8-20. English. DESCR: *Employment.

2202 Bergdolt-Munzer, Sara L. Homemakers and retirement income benefits: the other home security issue. CHICANO LAW REVIEW, Vol. 3, (1985), p. 61-80. English. DESCR: Ancianos; Domestic Work; Social Security; *Women.

2203 Billings, Linda M. and Alurista. In verbal murals: a study of Chicana herstory and poetry. CONFLUENCIA, Vol. 2, no. 1 (Fall 1986), p. 60-68. English. DESCR: Candelaria, Cordelia; Cervantes, Lorna Dee; Cisneros, Sandra; EMPLUMADA; History; Literary Criticism; *Poetry; Xelina.

2204 Blea, Irene I. Mexican American female experience. IN: Blea, Irene I. TOWARD A CHICANO SOCIAL SCIENCE. New York: Praeger, 1988, p. [67]-89. English. DESCR: Chicano Movement; Sex Roles; Sexism.

2205 Campos Carr, Irene. Proyecto La Mujer: Latina women shaping consciousness. WOMEN'S STUDIES INTERNATIONAL FORUM, Vol. 12, no. 1 (1989), p. 45-49. English. DESCR: Artists; Aurora, IL; Authors; Barrios; Conferences and Meetings; Elgin, IL; Joliet, IL; Poetry; Proyecto La Mujer Conference (Spring, 1982: Northern Illinois); Women.

2206 Candelaria, Cordelia. La Malinche, feminist prototype. FRONTIERS: A JOURNAL OF WOMEN STUDIES, Vol. 5, no. 2 (Summer 1980), p. 1-6. English. DESCR: Aztecs; History; Malinche.

2207 Canino, Glorisa. The Hispanic woman: sociocultural influences on diagnoses and treatment. IN: Becerra, Rosina M., et al., eds. MENTAL HEALTH AND HISPANIC AMERICANS:

CLINICAL PERSPECTIVES. New York: Grune & Stratton, 1982, p. 117-138. English. DESCR: Assimilation; Cultural Characteristics; Culture; *Depression (Psychological); Family; Mental Health; Population; Sex Roles.

2208 Chapa, Olivia Evey. Report from the National Women's Political Caucus. MAGAZIN, Vol. 1, no. 9 (September 1973), p. 37-39. English. DESCR: Conferences and Meetings; National Women's Political Caucus (February 9-11, 1973: Houston, TX).

2209 Chicana regional conference. LA RAZA, Vol. 1, no. 6 (1971), p. 43-45. English. DESCR: Chicana Regional Conference (May 8, 1971: Los Angeles, CA); *Chicano Movement; Conferences and Meetings; Women Men Relations.

2210 Chicana Welfare Rights challenges Talmadge amendment. REGENERACION, Vol. 2, no. 3 (1973), p. 14. English. DESCR: Chicana Welfare Rights Organization; Social Services; Talmadge Amendment to the Social Security Act, 1971; *Welfare.

2211 Cisneros, Sandra. Cactus flowers: in search of Tejana feminist poetry. THIRD WOMAN, Vol. 3, no. 1-2 (1986), p. 73-80. English. DESCR: Authors; Literary Criticism; *Poetry; Texas.

2212 Cordova, Marcella C. Women's rights: a Chicana's viewpoint. LA LUZ, Vol. 4, no. 2 (May 1975), p. 3. English. DESCR: *Machismo; *Women Men Relations.

2213 Cota-Robles de Suarez, Cecilia, ed. and Anguiano, Lupe, ed. Every woman's right: the right to quality education and economic independence. Montebello, CA: National Chicana Foundation, [1981]. viii, 110 p. English. DESCR: Civil Rights; Education.

2214 Cotera, Marta P. The Chicana feminist. Austin, TX: Information Systems Development, c1977. 68 p.: port. English. DESCR: Social History and Conditions.

2215 Cotera, Marta P. ERA: the Latina challenge. NUESTRO, Vol. 5, no. 8 (November 1981), p. 47-48. English. DESCR: Equal Rights Amendment (ERA); *Women Men Relations.

2216 Cotera, Marta P. Feminism: the Chicana and Anglo versions: a historical analysis. IN: Melville, Margarita B., ed. TWICE A MINORITY. St. Louis, MO: Mosby, 1980, p. 217-234. English. DESCR: *Anglo Americans; Chicano Movement; Conferences and Meetings; Organizations; Social History and Conditions; Voting Rights; *Women.

2217 Cotera, Marta P. Mexicano feminism. MAGAZIN, Vol. 1, no. 9 (September 1973), p. 30-32. English.

2218 Cotera, Marta P. La nueva hispana y [sic] hispanidad. LA LUZ, Vol. 8, no. 4 (October, November, 1979), p. 8-10. English. DESCR: *Civil Rights; Women Men Relations.

2219 De la Torre, Susana and de Hoyos, Angela. Mujeres en el movimiento: platica de las mujeres de CARACOL. CARACOL, Vol. 4, no. 5 (January 1978), p. 16-18. Bilingual. DESCR: *CARACOL: LA REVISTA DE LA RAZA.

Feminism (cont.)

2220 de Lotbiniere-Harwood, Susanne and Anzaldua, Gloria. Conversations at the Book Fair: interview with Gloria Anzaldua. TRIVIA: A JOURNAL OF IDEAS, no. 14 (Spring 1989), p. 37-45. English. **DESCR:** *Anzaldua, Gloria; *Authors; Biography; Literary Criticism.

2221 Del Castillo, Adelaida R., ed. Between borders: essays on Mexicana/Chicana history. Encino, CA: Floricanto Press, c1990. xv, 563 p. Bilingual. **DESCR:** Historiography; *History; Mexico; *Women; Working Women.

2222 Del Castillo, Adelaida R. Mexican women in organization. IN: Mora, Magdalena and Del Castillo, Adelaida, eds. MEXICAN WOMEN IN THE UNITED STATES: STRUGGLES PAST AND PRESENT. Los Angeles, CA: Chicano Studies Research Center, UCLA, 1980, p. 7-16. English. **DESCR:** *Chicano Movement; Leadership; Student Organizations; Students.

2223 Del Castillo, Adelaida R. La vision chicana. REGENERACION, Vol. 2, no. 4 (1975), p. 46-48. English. **DESCR:** Anglo Americans; Women.

2224 Del Rio, Carmen M. Chicana poets: re-visions from the margin. REVISTA CANADIENSE DE ESTUDIOS HISPANICOS, Vol. 14, no. 3 (Spring 1990), p. 431-445. English. **DESCR:** Authors; *Literary Criticism; *Poetry; Tafolla, Carmen; Villanueva, Alma.

2225 Delgado, Sylvia. Young Chicana speaks up on problems faced by young girls. REGENERACION, Vol. 1, no. 10 (1971), p. 5-7. English. **DESCR:** Abortion; Machismo; Marriage; Sex Roles; *Women Men Relations.

2226 Delgado Votaw, Carmen. Influencias culturales y feminismo en la mujer chicana. FEM, Vol. 10, no. 48 (October, November, 1986), p. 27-30. Spanish. **DESCR:** Identity.

2227 Diehl, Paula and Saavedra, Lupe. Hispanas in the year of the woman: many voices. AGENDA, (Winter 1976), p. 14-21. English. **DESCR:** Discrimination; International Women's Year World Conference (1975: Mexico City); Mexico City.

2228 Dixon, Marlene. The rise and demise of women's liberation: a class analysis. IN: Mora, Magdalena and Del Castillo, Adelaida, eds. MEXICAN WOMEN IN THE UNITED STATES: STRUGGLES PAST AND PRESENT. Los Angeles, CA: Chicano Studies Research Center, 1980, p. 37-43. English. **DESCR:** Sexism; Social Classes.

2229 Dunbar Ortiz, Roxanne. Toward a democratic women's movement in the United States. IN: Mora, Magdalena and Del Castillo, Adelaida, eds. MEXICAN WOMEN IN THE UNITED STATES: STRUGGLES PAST AND PRESENT. Los Angeles, CA: Chicano Studies Research Center, UCLA, 1980, p. 29-35. English. **DESCR:** *Sexism.

2230 Enriquez, Evangelina and Mirande, Alfredo. Liberation, Chicana style: colonial roots of feministas chicanas. DE COLORES, Vol. 4, no. 3 (1978), p. 7-21. Bilingual. **DESCR:** *Chicano Movement; Malinche; *Political History and Conditions; *Social History and Conditions.

2231 Enriquez, Evangelina. Towards a definition of, and critical approaches to, Chicano(a) literature. Thesis (Ph.D.)--University of California, Riverside, 1982. viii, 182 p. English. **DESCR:** *Literary Criticism;

Literary History; *Literature; Marxism.

2232 Espin, Oliva M. Perceptions of sexual discrimination among college women in Latin America and the United States. HISPANIC JOURNAL OF BEHAVIORAL SCIENCES, Vol. 2, no. 1 (March 1980), p. 1-19. English. **DESCR:** Colleges and Universities; CRITICAL INCIDENT TECHNIQUE; Latin Americans; *Sexism; Students; Women Men Relations.

2233 Estrada, Iliad. Hispanic feminists meet--it's a trip. LA LUZ, Vol. 8, no. 7 (August, September, 1980), p. 35. English. **DESCR:** Conferences and Meetings; National Hispanic Feminist Conference (March 28-31, 1980: San Jose, CA); *Puerto Ricans.

2234 Fajardo, Ramon. Liberacion femenil: cancion corrido. XALMAN, Vol. 3, no. 2 (Fall 1980), p. 97-98. Spanish. **DESCR:** *Corridos; Musical Lyrics.

2235 Fajardo, Ramon. Liberacion femenil: cancion corrido. IN: Bardeleben, Renate von, et al., eds. MISSIONS IN CONFLICT: ESSAYS ON U.S.-MEXICAN RELATIONS AND CHICANO CULTURE. Tubingen, W. Germany: Gunter Narr Verlag, 1986, p. 108-109. Spanish. **DESCR:** *Corridos; Musical Lyrics.

2236 Fernandez Kelly, Maria. The 'maquila' women. NACLA: REPORT ON THE AMERICAS, Vol. 14, no. 5 (September, October, 1980), p. 14-19. English. **DESCR:** *Border Industries; Industrial Workers; Stereotypes; Women; *Working Women.

2237 Flores, Francisca. Comision Femenil Mexicana. REGENERACION, Vol. 2, no. 1 (1971), p. 6. English. **DESCR:** Abortion; Children; Comision Femenil Mexicana Nacional; *Family Planning; Organizations; Politics.

2238 Flores, Francisca. Conference of Mexican women un remolino. REGENERACION, Vol. 1, no. 10 (1971), p. 1-5. English. **DESCR:** Conferences and Meetings; Family; First National Chicana Conference (May 1971: Houston, TX); Machismo; National Mexican American Issues Conference (October 11, 1970: Sacramento, CA); Sex Roles; Sex Stereotypes; Statistics; *Women Men Relations.

2239 Flores, Francisca. Equality. REGENERACION, Vol. 2, no. 3 (1973), p. 4-5. English. **DESCR:** Anglo Americans; Chicano Movement; Discrimination; Elected Officials; Income; *Machismo; *Working Women.

2240 Flores, Francisca. A reaction to discussions on the Talmadge Amendment to the Social Security Act. ENCUENTRO FEMENIL, Vol. 1, no. 2 (1974), p. 13-14. English. **DESCR:** *Chicana Welfare Rights Organization; Child Care Centers; Discrimination; Income; *Social Security Act; Social Services; *Talmadge Amendment to the Social Security Act, 1971; Welfare; Working Women.

2241 Flores, Francisca. A reaction to discussions on the Talmadge Amendment to the Social Security Act. REGENERACION, Vol. 2, no. 3 (1973), p. 16. English. **DESCR:** *Chicana Welfare Rights Organization; Child Care Centers; Discrimination; Income; *Social Security Act; Social Services; *Talmadge Amendment to the Social Security Act, 1971; Welfare; Working Women.

Feminism (cont.)

2242 Fox, Linda C. Obedience and rebellion: re-vision of Chicana myths of motherhood. WOMEN'S STUDIES QUARTERLY, Vol. 11, no. 4 (Winter 1983), p. 20-22. English. DESCR: La Llorona; Malinche; *Parent and Child Relationships.

2243 Fregoso, Rosa Linda. La quinceañera of Chicana counter aesthetics. CENTRO BULLETIN, Vol. 3, no. 1 (Winter 1990, 1991), p. [87]-91. English. DESCR: *AGUEDA MARTINEZ [film]; ANIMA [film]; *CHICANA! [film]; *DESPUES DEL TERREMOTO [film]; Espana, Frances Salome; *Films; Morales, Sylvia; Portillo, Lourdes; Vasquez, Esperanza.

2244 Garcia, Alma M. The development of Chicana feminist discourse, 1970-1980. GENDER & SOCIETY, Vol. 3, no. 2 (June 1989), p. 217-238. English. DESCR: Anglo Americans; Chicana Studies; *Chicano Movement; Homosexuality; Machismo; National Association for Chicano Studies (NACS); Organizations; *Sexism; Women.

2245 Garcia, Alma M. The development of Chicana feminist discourse, 1970-1980. IN: DuBois, Ellen Carol and Ruiz, Vicki L., eds. UNEQUAL SISTERS: A MULTICULTURAL READER IN U.S. WOMEN'S HISTORY. New York: Routledge, 1990, p. 418-431. English. DESCR: Anglo Americans; Chicana Studies; *Chicano Movement; Homosexuality; Machismo; National Association for Chicano Studies (NACS); Organizations; *Sexism; Women.

2246 Garcia, Alma M. El femenismo [sic] chicano un panorama historico. FEM, Vol. 10, no. 48 (October, November, 1986), p. 23-24. Spanish.

2247 Glenn, Evelyn Nakano. Racial ethnic women's labor: the intersection of race, gender and class oppression. REVIEW OF RADICAL POLITICAL ECONOMY, Vol. 17, no. 3 (Fall 1985), p. 86-108. English. DESCR: Asian Americans; Blacks; *Discrimination; Laboring Classes; *Marxism; Sexism; Social Classes; Women; Working Women.

2248 Goldman, Shifra M. Mujeres de California: Latin American women artists. IN: Moore, Sylvia, ed. YESTERDAY AND TOMORROW: CALIFORNIA WOMEN ARTISTS. New York, NY: Midmarch Arts Press, c1989, p. 202-229. English. DESCR: *Artists; Baca, Judith F.; Biography; California; Carrasco, Barbara; Cervantez, Yreina; de Larios, Dora; Hernandez, Judithe; Lomas Garza, Carmen; Lopez, Yolanda M.; Mesa-Bains, Amalia; Murillo, Patricia; Sanchez, Olivia; Valdez, Patssi; Vallejo Dillaway, Linda; Women; Zamora Lucero, Linda.

2249 Goldman, Shifra M. Women artists of Texas: MAS = More + Artists + Women = MAS. CHISMEARTE, no. 7 (January 1981), p. 21-22. English. DESCR: Arredondo, Alicia; Art Organizations and Groups; Barraza, Santa; Exhibits; Flores, Maria; Folk Art; Gonzalez Dodson, Nora; *Mujeres Artistas del Suroeste (MAS), Austin, TX; Photography; Texas; Trevino, Modesta Barbina; WOMEN & THEIR WORK [festival] (Austin, TX: 1977).

2250 Gonzales, Sylvia Alicia. The Chicana perspective: a design for self-awareness. IN: Trejo, Arnulfo D., ed. THE CHICANOS: AS WE SEE OURSELVES. Tucson, AZ: University of Arizona Press, 1979, p. 81-99. English. DESCR: CHICANAS SPEAK OUT; Chicano Movement; Discrimination; Identity; Machismo; Madsen,

William; *Mexican Revolution - 1910-1920; Mexico; Sex Roles; THE MEXICAN-AMERICANS OF SOUTH TEXAS; Vidal, Mirta.

2251 Gonzales, Sylvia Alicia. The Latina feminist: where we've been, where we're going. NUESTRO, Vol. 5, no. 6 (August, September, 1981), p. 45-47. English. DESCR: Conferences and Meetings; History; Leadership; National Hispanic Feminist Conference (March 28-31, 1980: San Jose, CA).

2252 Gonzales, Sylvia Alicia. Toward a feminist pedagogy for Chicana self-actualization. FRONTIERS: A JOURNAL OF WOMEN STUDIES, Vol. 5, no. 2 (Summer 1980), p. 48-51. English. DESCR: Chicano Movement; Education; Identity; Malinche.

2253 Griswold del Castillo, Richard. Patriarchy and the status of women in the late nineteenth-century Southwest. IN: Rodriguez O., Jaime E., ed. THE MEXICAN AND MEXICAN AMERICAN EXPERIENCE IN THE 19TH CENTURY. Tempe, AZ: Bilingual Press/Editorial Bilingue, 1989, p. 85-99. English. DESCR: Family; History; *Machismo; *Sex Roles.

2254 Gutierrez, Lorraine M. Working with women of color: an empowerment perspective. SOCIAL WORK, Vol. 35, no. 2 (March 1990), p. 149-153. English. DESCR: *Assertiveness; Ethnic Groups; Intergroup Relations; *Interpersonal Relations; *Social Work; *Women.

2255 Hernandez, Ines. Sara Estela Ramirez: the early twentieth century Texas-Mexican poet. Thesis (Ph.D.)--University of Houston, 1984. 94 p. English. DESCR: *Authors; *Biography; Flores Magon, Ricardo; Journalism; Literary Criticism; Mexican Revolution - 1910-1920; Mexico; *Poetry; Ramirez, Sara Estela; Texas; Women.

2256 Hernandez, Ines. Sara Estela Ramirez: sembradora. LEGACY: A JOURNAL OF NINETEENTH-CENTURY AMERICAN WOMEN WRITERS, Vol. 6, no. 1 (Spring 1989), p. 13-26. English. DESCR: Authors; *Biography; Flores Magon, Ricardo; *Journalism; LA CORREGIDORA [newspaper]; Mexican Revolution - 1910-1920; Mexico; Newspapers; Poetry; *Ramirez, Sara Estela; REGENERACION [newspaper].

2257 Herrera-Sobek, Maria. The politics of rape: sexual transgression in Chicana fiction. THE AMERICAS REVIEW, Vol. 15, no. 3-4 (Fall, Winter, 1987), p. 171-181. English. DESCR: Cisneros, Sandra; Fiction; GIVING UP THE GHOST; *Literary Criticism; Lizarraga, Sylvia; Moraga, Cherrie; *Rape; "Red Clowns" [short story]; Sex Roles; "Silver Lake Road" [short story].

2258 Hintz, Joy. Valiant migrant women = Las mujeres valerosas. Tiffin, OH: Sayger Printing, 1982. viii, 98 p. English. DESCR: Battered Women; *Farm Workers; Florida; Marriage; Migrant Children; Migrant Health Services; Migrant Housing; *Migrant Labor; Migration Patterns; Ohio; Sex Roles; Texas.

2259 Hurtado, Aida. Relating to privilege: seduction and rejection in the subordination of white women and women of color. SIGNS: JOURNAL OF WOMEN IN CULTURE AND SOCIETY, Vol. 14, no. 4 (Summer 1989), p. 833-855. English. DESCR: *Anglo Americans; Asian Americans; Blacks; Ethnic Groups; Political Ideology; Political Socialization; *Women.

Feminism (cont.)

2260 Isasi-Diaz, Ada Maria and Tarango, Yolanda. Hispanic women, prophetic voice in the Church: toward a Hispanic women's liberation theology. San Francisco, CA: Harper & Row, c1988. xx, 123 p. Bilingual. DESCR: Catholic Church; Liberation Theology; Religion; *Women.

2261 Jaramillo, Mari-Luci. Profile of Chicanas and international relations. IN: LA CHICANA: BUILDING FOR THE FUTURE, AN ACTION PLAN FOR THE 80s. Oakland, CA: National Hispanic University, 1981, p. 37-58. English. DESCR: Careers; *International Relations; Leadership.

2262 Larguia, Isabel and Dumoulin, John. Toward a science of women's liberation. IN: Mora, Magdalena and Del Castillo, Adelaida, eds. MEXICAN WOMEN IN THE UNITED STATES: STRUGGLES PAST AND PRESENT. Los Angeles, CA: Chicano Studies Research Center, 1980, p. 45-61. English. DESCR: Labor; Sex Roles; Social Classes.

2263 Limon, Jose E. [anthropologist]. La Llorona, the third legend of greater Mexico: cultural symbols, women, and the political unconscious. RENATO ROSALDO LECTURE SERIES MONOGRAPH, Vol. 2, (Spring 1986), p. [59]-93. English. DESCR: Folklore; *La Llorona; La Virgen de Guadalupe; *Leyendas; Malinche; Mexico; *Symbolism; Women.

2264 Limon, Jose E. [anthropologist]. La Llorona, the third legend of greater Mexico: cultural symbols, women, and the political unconscious. IN: Del Castillo, Adelaida R. BETWEEN BORDERS: ESSAYS ON MEXICANA/CHICANA HISTORY. Encino, CA: Floricanto Press, 1990, p. 399-432. English. DESCR: Folklore; *La Llorona; La Virgen de Guadalupe; *Leyendas; Malinche; Mexico; *Symbolism; Women.

2265 Lizarraga, Sylvia S. Hacia una teoria para la liberacion de la mujer. IN: Garcia, Juan R., ed. IN TIMES OF CHALLENGE: CHICANOS AND CHICANAS IN AMERICAN SOCIETY. Houston, TX: Mexican American Studies Program, University of Houston, 1988, p. 25-31. Spanish. DESCR: Laboring Classes; Social Classes; *Women; *Working Women.

2266 Lomas, Clara. Libertad de no procrear: la voz de la mujer en "A una madre de nuestro tiempo" de Margarita Cota-Cardenas. IN: Cordova, Teresa, et al., eds. CHICANA VOICES. Austin, TX: Center for Mexican American Studies, 1986, p. 188-201. Bilingual. DESCR: "A una madre de nuestros tiempos" [poem]; *Cota-Cardenas, Margarita; Literary Criticism; *Poetry; Sex Stereotypes.

2267 Lomas, Clara. Libertad de no procrear: la voz de la mujer en "A una madre de nuestro tiempo" de Margarita Cota-Cardenas. REVISTA MUJERES, Vol. 2, no. 1 (January 1985), p. 30-35. Spanish. DESCR: *"A una madre de nuestros tiempos" [poem]; *Cota-Cardenas, Margarita; Literary Criticism; Poetry; Sex Stereotypes.

2268 Lomas, Clara. Mexican precursors of Chicana feminist writing. IN: National Association for Chicano Studies. ESTUDIOS CHICANOS AND THE POLITICS OF COMMUNITY. [S.l.]: National Association for Chicano Studies, c1989, p. [149]-160. English. DESCR: Authors; de Cardenas, Isidra T.; Idar, Jovita; *Journalists; Literature; *Mexican Revolution - 1910-1920; Newspapers; Ramirez,

Sara Estela; Villarreal, Andrea; Villegas de Magnon, Leonor.

2269 Longeaux y Vasquez, Enriqueta. Soy Chicana primero. LA RAZA HABLA, Vol. 1, no. 1 (January 1976), p. 1-5. English. DESCR: Chicano Movement; Identity.

2270 Longeaux y Vasquez, Enriqueta. Soy Chicana primero. EL CUADERNO, Vol. 1, no. 1 (1971), p. 17-22. English. DESCR: *Chicano Movement; Identity.

2271 Lopez, Sonia A. The role of the Chicana within the student movement. IN: Sanchez, Rosaura and Martinez Cruz, Rosa, eds. ESSAYS ON LA MUJER. Los Angeles, CA: Chicano Studies Center Publications, UCLA, 1977, p. 16-29. English. DESCR: Chicano Movement; Conferences and Meetings; First National Chicana Conference (May 1971: Houston, TX); *Student Movements.

2272 Lucero, Marcela Christine. Resources for the Chicana feminist scholar. IN: Treichler, Paula A., et al., eds. FOR ALMA MATER: THEORY AND PRACTICE IN FEMINIST SCHOLARSHIP. Urbana: University of Illinois Press, 1985, p. 393-401. English. DESCR: *Chicana Studies; Literature Reviews; Publishing Industry; Research Methodology.

2273 Lucero, Marcela Christine. The socio-historical implication of the valley as a metaphor in three Colorado Chicana poets. Thesis (Ph.D.)--University of Minnesota, 1981. 176 p. English. DESCR: *Authors; Blea, Irene I.; Chicano Movement; Colorado; Literary Criticism; Mondragon Valdez, Maria; Poetry; Zamora, Bernice.

2274 Luna-Lawhn, Juanita. Victorian attitudes affecting the Mexican woman writing in LA PRENSA during the early 1900s and the Chicana of the 1980s. IN: Bardeleben, Renate von, et al., eds. MISSIONS IN CONFLICT: ESSAYS ON U.S.-MEXICAN RELATIONS AND CHICANO CULTURE. Tubingen, W. Germany: Gunter Narr Verlag, 1986, p. 65-71. English. DESCR: LA PRENSA, San Antonio, TX; Literary Criticism; *Newspapers; "Penitents" [poem]; Poetry; Zamora, Bernice.

2275 Macias, Anna. Against all odds: the feminist movement in Mexico to 1940. Westport, CT: Greenwood Press, 1982. xv, 195 p. English. DESCR: Carrillo Puerto, Felipe; History; Mexican Revolution - 1910-1920; Mexico; *Women; Yucatan, Mexico.

2276 Marquez, Evelina and Ramirez, Margarita. La tarea de la mujer es la liberacion. IN: Maciel, David R., compiler. LA OTRA CARA DE MEXICO: EL PUEBLO CHICANO. Mexico, D.F.: Ediciones "El Caballito," 1977, p. 173-181. Spanish. DESCR: Social Classes.

2277 Marquez, Evelina and Ramirez, Margarita. Women's task is to gain liberation. IN: Sanchez, Rosaura and Martinez Cruz, Rosa, eds. ESSAYS ON LA MUJER. Los Angeles, CA: Chicano Studies Center Publications, UCLA, 1977, p. 188-194. English. DESCR: Centro de Accion Social Autonomo (CASA); Political Parties and Organizations.

2278 Martinez, Virginia. Chicanas and the law. IN: LA CHICANA: BUILDING FOR THE FUTURE, AN ACTION PLAN FOR THE 80s. Oakland, CA: National Hispanic University, 1981, p. 134-146. English. DESCR: *Administration of Justice; Civil Rights; Law.

--   --
Feminism (cont.)

2279 Mason, Terry. Symbolic strategies for
     change: a discussion of the Chicana women's
     movement. IN: Melville, Margarita B., ed.
     TWICE A MINORITY. St. Louis, MO: Mosby,
     1980, p. 95-108. English. **DESCR**: Actos;
     Anglo Americans; Teatro; Women.

2280 Medina, Cecilia. Chicanas live in Aztlan
     also. IN: Poblano, Ralph (Rafa), ed. GHOSTS
     IN THE BARRIO: ISSUES IN
     BILINGUAL-BICULTURAL EDUCATION. San Rafael,
     CA: Leswing Press, 1973, p. 151-152.
     English.

2281 Melville, Margarita B. Female and male in
     Chicano theatre. IN: Kanellos, Nicolas, ed.
     HISPANIC THEATRE IN THE UNITED STATES.
     Houston, TX: Arte Publico Press, 1984, p.
     71-79. English. **DESCR**: BERNABE; BRUJERIAS
     [play]; Cultural Characteristics; DAY OF THE
     SWALLOWS; Duarte-Clark, Rodrigo; EL JARDIN
     [play]; Family; Macias, Ysidro; Morton,
     Carlos; Portillo Trambley, Estela; RANCHO
     HOLLYWOOD [play]; *Sex Roles; *Teatro; THE
     ULTIMATE PENDEJADA [play]; Valdez, Luis;
     Women Men Relations.

2282 Melville, Margarita B. Mexican women in the
     U.S. wage labor force. IN: Melville,
     Margarita, ed. MEXICANAS AT WORK IN THE
     UNITED STATES. Houston, TX: Mexican American
     Studies Program, University of Houston,
     1988, p. 1-11. English. **DESCR**: Sex
     Stereotypes; *Women; *Working Women.

2283 Mercado, Olivia. Chicanas: myths and roles.
     COMADRE, no. 1 (Summer 1977), p. 26-32.
     English. **DESCR**: Gallo, Juara; Huerta,
     Dolores; *Identity; Leadership; Sex Roles.

2284 Mexican American Legal Defense and Education
     Fund (MALDEF). Chicana rights: a major
     MALDEF issue (reprinted from MALDEF
     Newsletter, Fall 1977). COMADRE, no. 3 (Fall
     1978), p. 31-35. English. **DESCR**: Chicana
     Rights Project; Mexican American Legal
     Defense and Educational Fund (MALDEF);
     Statistics; Vasquez, Patricia.

2285 Mirande, Alfredo and Enriquez, Evangelina.
     La Chicana: the Mexican-American woman.
     Chicago: University of Chicago Press, 1979.
     x, 283 p.: ill. English. **DESCR**: Family;
     *Social History and Conditions.

2286 Molina de Pick, Gracia. Reflexiones sobre el
     feminismo y la Raza. LA LUZ, Vol. 1, no. 4
     (August 1972), p. 58. Spanish. **DESCR**:
     Sexism; *Stereotypes.

2287 Molina de Pick, Gracia. Reflexiones sobre el
     feminismo y la Raza. REGENERACION, Vol. 2,
     no. 4 (1975), p. 33-34. Spanish. **DESCR**:
     *Sexism; Stereotypes.

2288 Mora, Magdalena and Del Castillo, Adelaida
     R. Mexican women in the United States:
     struggles past and present. Los Angeles, CA:
     Chicano Studies Research Center
     Publications, c1980. 204 p. English. **DESCR**:
     *Social History and Conditions; *Working
     Women.

2289 Moraga, Cherrie. [Letter to Coordinadora
     Nacional de Lesbianas Feministas].
     CORRESPONDENCIA, no. 9 (December 1990), p.
     19-20. Bilingual. **DESCR**: *Homosexuality;
     Identity; Mexico-U.S. Lesbian Exchange.

2290 Moraga, Cherrie. Third World women in the
     United States--by and about us: a selected
     bibliography. IN: Moraga, Cherrie and

Anzaldua, Gloria, eds. THIS BRIDGE CALLED MY
BACK: WRITINGS BY RADICAL WOMEN OF COLOR.
Watertown, MA: Persephone Press, 1981, p.
251-261. English. **DESCR**: Bibliography;
Women.

2291 Moraga, Cherrie, ed. and Castillo, Ana, ed.
     Esta [sic] puente, mi espalda: voces de
     mujeres tercermundistas en los Estados
     Unidos. San Francisco, CA: Ism Press, c1988.
     [19], 281 p.: ill. Spanish. **DESCR**: Ethnic
     Groups; Literary Criticism; *Poems; *Prose;
     *Women.

2292 Moraga, Cherrie, ed. and Anzaldua, Gloria,
     ed. This bridge called my back: writings by
     radical women of color. Watertown, MA:
     Persephone Press, c1981. xxvi, 261 p.
     English. **DESCR**: Ethnic Groups; Literary
     Criticism; *Poems; *Prose; *Women.

2293 Morales, Patricia. Femenismo [sic] chicano.
     FEM, Vol. 8, no. 39 (April, May, 1985), p.
     41-44. Spanish.

2294 Mujeres en Marcha, University of California,
     Berkeley. Chicanas in the 80s: unsettled
     issues. Berkeley, CA: Chicano Studies
     Library Publications Unit, 1983. 31 p.
     English. **DESCR**: Conferences and Meetings;
     National Association for Chicano Studies
     (NACS); National Association for Chicano
     Studies Annual Conference (1982: Tempe, AZ);
     *Sexism.

2295 Navar, Isabelle. La Mexicana: an image of
     strength. AGENDA, no. 4 (Spring 1974), p.
     3-5. English. **DESCR**: Family; *Identity;
     Psychology; Sexism; Working Women.

2296 Navar, Isabelle. La Mexicana: an image of
     strength. REGENERACION, Vol. 2, no. 4
     (1974), p. 4-6. English. **DESCR**: Family;
     *Identity; Psychology; Sexism; Working
     Women.

2297 Nieto, Consuelo. The Chicana and the women's
     rights movement. LA LUZ, Vol. 3, no. 6
     (September 1974), p. 10-11. English.

2298 Nieto Gomez de Lazarin, Anna. Ana Nieto
     Gomez: sexism in the Movimiento. LA GENTE DE
     AZTLAN, Vol. 6, no. 4 (March 1976), p. 10.
     English. **DESCR**: *Chicano Movement; Sex
     Roles; *Sexism.

2299 Nieto Gomez de Lazarin, Anna. Chicana
     feminism. CARACOL, Vol. 2, no. 5 (January
     1976), p. 3-5. English.

2300 Nieto Gomez de Lazarin, Anna. La femenista
     [sic]. ENCUENTRO FEMENIL, Vol. 1, no. 2
     (1974), p. 34-47. English. **DESCR**: Anglo
     Americans; Chicana Caucus, National Women's
     Political Caucus; Chicano Movement;
     Conferences and Meetings; Discrimination;
     National Women's Political Caucus (February
     9-11, 1973: Houston, TX); *Sexism; Women.

2301 Nieto Gomez de Lazarin, Anna. What is the
     Talmadge Amendment?: justicia para las
     madres. REGENERACION, Vol. 2, no. 3 (1973),
     p. 14-15. English. **DESCR**: Chicana Welfare
     Rights Organization; *Child Care Centers;
     Community Work Experience Program
     (C.W.E.P.); Discrimination in Employment;
     Employment Tests; Escalante, Alicia; Nixon,
     Richard; Working Women.

2302 Oeste, Marcia. Mujeres arriba y adelante. LA
     LUZ, Vol. 1, no. 2 (May 1972), p. 39-40.
     English. **DESCR**: Ortega y Gasset, Jose;
     *Women Men Relations; Working Women.

2303 Olivarez, Elizabeth. Women's rights and the Mexican American woman. REGENERACION, Vol. 2, no. 4 (1975), p. 40-42. English. DESCR: Education; Identity; Politics; Psychology; Religion; Sex Roles.

2304 Ordonez, Elizabeth J. Body, spirit, and the text: Alma Villanueva's LIFE SPAN. IN: Calderon, Hector and Saldivar, Jose David, eds. CRITICISM IN THE BORDERLANDS: STUDIES IN CHICANO LITERATURE, CULTURE, AND IDEOLOGY. Durham, NC: Duke University Press, 1991, p. [61]-71. English. DESCR: Cixous, Helene; *LIFE SPAN; *Literary Criticism; Poetry; *Villanueva, Alma.

2305 Ordonez, Elizabeth J. Sexual politics and the theme of sexuality in Chicana poetry. IN: Miller, Beth, ed. WOMEN IN HISPANIC LITERATURE: ICONS AND FALLEN IDOLS. Berkeley, CA: University of California Press, 1983, p. 316-339. English. DESCR: Chicano Movement; *Literary Criticism; Poetry; Sexual Behavior.

2306 Orozco, Cynthia. Sexism in Chicano Studies and the community. IN: Cordova, Teresa, et al., eds. CHICANA VOICES. Austin, TX: Center for Mexican American Studies, 1986, p. 11-18. English. DESCR: Acuna, Rodolfo; Chicano Studies; OCCUPIED AMERICA; *Sexism.

2307 Orozco, Yolanda. La Chicana and "women's liberation". LA RAZA HABLA, Vol. 1, no. 5 (August 1976), p. 3-4. English. DESCR: University of California, San Diego.

2308 Ortega, Eliana and Sternbach, Nancy Saporta. At the threshold of the unnamed: Latina literary discourse in the eighties. IN: Horno-Delgado, Asuncion, et al., eds. BREAKING BOUNDARIES: LATINA WRITING AND CRITICAL READINGS. Amherst, MA: University of Massachusetts Press, c1989, p. [2]-23. English. DESCR: Bilingualism; *Literary Criticism; Literary History; Political Ideology; Sex Roles; *Women.

2309 Pardo, Mary. Mexican American women grassroots community activists: "Mothers of East Los Angeles". FRONTIERS: A JOURNAL OF WOMEN STUDIES, Vol. 11, no. 1 (1990), p. [1]-7. English. DESCR: Coalition Against the Prison, East Los Angeles, CA; *Community Organizations; East Los Angeles, CA; Family; *Mothers of East L.A. (MELA); Organizations; Political Parties and Organizations; Politics; Sex Roles.

2310 Pavich, Emma Guerrero. A Chicana perspective on Mexican culture and sexuality. JOURNAL OF SOCIAL WORK AND HUMAN SEXUALITY, Vol. 4, no. 3 (Spring 1986), p. 47-65. English. DESCR: California; Cultural Characteristics; Family; Homosexuality; Machismo; Sex Roles; Sex Stereotypes; *Sexual Behavior; Women Men Relations.

2311 Peralta Aguilar, Linda. Unequal opportunity and the Chicana. LA LUZ, Vol. 1, no. 5 (September 1972), p. 52. English. DESCR: *Discrimination; Discrimination in Employment; *Employment.

2312 Peralta Aguilar, Linda. Unequal opportunity and the Chicana. REGENERACION, Vol. 2, no. 4 (1975), p. 45-46. English. DESCR: *Discrimination; *Discrimination in Employment; *Employment.

2313 Peralta Aguilar, Linda. Unequal opportunity and the Chicana. LA LUZ, Vol. 6, no. 1 (January 1977), p. 29-30. English. DESCR: *Discrimination; Discrimination in Employment; *Employment.

2314 Perez, Emma. "A la mujer": a critique of the Partido Liberal Mexicano's gender ideology on women. IN: Del Castillo, Adelaida R., ed. BETWEEN BORDERS: ESSAYS ON MEXICANA/CHICANA HISTORY. Encino, CA: Floricanto Press, 1990, p. 459-482. English. DESCR: *"A La Mujer" [essay]; Essays; Flores Magon, Ricardo; Guerrero, Praxedis G.; Journalism; Mexican Revolution - 1910-1920; Mexico; Newspapers; *Partido Liberal Mexicano (PLM); Political Ideology; Political Parties and Organizations; *REGENERACION [newspaper]; Sex Roles; Women.

2315 Perez, Emma. Sexuality and discourse: notes from a Chicana survivor. IN: Trujillo, Carla, ed. CHICANA LESBIANS: THE GIRLS OUR MOTHERS WARNED US ABOUT. Berkeley, CA: Third Woman Press, 1991, p. 159-184. English. DESCR: Homosexuality; Intergroup Relations; Paz, Octavio; *Sex Roles; *Sexism; Skin Color.

2316 Pesquera, Beatriz M. and Duran, Flo. Having a job gives you some sort of power: reflections of a Chicana working woman. FEMINIST ISSUES, Vol. 4, no. 2 (Fall 1984), p. 79-96. English. DESCR: Duran, Flo; *Working Women.

2317 Phillips, Melody. The Chicana: her attitudes towards the woman's liberation movement. COMADRE, no. 2 (Spring 1978), p. 42-50. English. DESCR: Attitudes; Sexism.

2318 Prida, Dolores. Looking for room of one's own. NUESTRO, Vol. 3, no. 5 (June, July, 1979), p. 24-29. English. DESCR: Comision Femenil Mexicana de California; Mexican American Women's National Association (MANA); National Association of Cuban American Women; National Conference of Puerto Rican Women, Inc. (NCOPRW); Organizations.

2319 Quintana, Alvina E. Ana Castillo's THE MIXQUIAHUALA LETTERS: the novelist as ethnographer. IN: Calderon, Hector and Saldivar, Jose David, eds. CRITICISM IN THE BORDERLANDS: STUDIES IN CHICANO LITERATURE, CULTURE, AND IDEOLOGY. Durham, NC: Duke University Press, 1991, p. [72]-83. English. DESCR: Anthropology; Castillo, Ana; Cultural Studies; *Ethnology; Geertz, Clifford; *Literary Criticism; Novel; THE MIXQUIAHUALA LETTERS.

2320 Quintana, Alvina E. Challenge and counter challenge: Chicana literary motifs. AGAINST THE CURRENT, Vol. 2, no. 2 (March, April, 1987), p. 25,28-32. English. DESCR: Anglo Americans; Authors; Cervantes, Lorna Dee; Cultural Studies; Identity; Literary Criticism; *Literature; Moraga, Cherrie; THERE ARE NO MADMEN HERE; Valdes, Gina; Women.

2321 Quintana, Alvina E. Chicana discourse: negations and mediations. Thesis (Ph.D.)--University of California, Santa Cruz, 1989. 226 p. English. DESCR: Authors; Castillo, Ana; Chavez, Denise; Chicano Movement; Cisneros, Sandra; Ethnology; Literary Criticism; *Literature; NOVENA NARRATIVES; Oral Tradition; Political Ideology; THE HOUSE ON MANGO STREET; THE LAST OF THE MENU GIRLS; THE MIXQUIAHUALA LETTERS.

Feminism (cont.)

2322 Quintana, Alvina E. Chicana literary motifs: challenge and counter-challenge. IMAGES: ETHNIC STUDIES OCCASIONAL PAPERS SERIES, (Fall 1986), p. 24-41. English. DESCR: Anglo Americans; Authors; Cervantes, Lorna Dee; Cultural Studies; *Identity; *Literary Criticism; Literature; Moraga, Cherrie; THERE ARE NO MADMEN HERE; Valdes, Gina; Women.

2323 Quintana, Alvina E. Expanding a feminist view: challenge and counter-challenge in the relationship between women. REVISTA MUJERES, Vol. 2, no. 1 (January 1985), p. 11-18. English.

2324 Quintana, Alvina E. Language, power, and women: a hermeneutic interpretation. CRITICAL PERSPECTIVES, Vol. 2, no. 1 (Fall 1984), p. 10-19. English. DESCR: Literary Criticism; Malinche.

2325 Quintana, Alvina E. O mama, with what's inside of me. REVISTA MUJERES, Vol. 3, no. 1 (January 1986), p. 38-40. English. DESCR: Alarcon, Norma; *Literary Criticism; Poetry; "What Kind of Lover Have You Made Me, Mother?: Towards a Theory of Chicanas' Feminism and Cultural Identity Through Poetry" [article].

2326 Quintana, Alvina E. Politics, representation and the emergence of a Chicana aesthetic. CULTURAL STUDIES, Vol. 4, no. 3 (October 1990), p. 257-263. English. DESCR: Anzaldua, Gloria; *Authors; Chavez, Denise; Chicana Studies; Cisneros, Sandra; Cultural Studies; *Literary Criticism.

2327 Rincon, Bernice. La Chicana: her role in the past and her search for a new role in the future. REGENERACION, Vol. 1, no. 10 (1971), p. 15-18. English. DESCR: *Women Men Relations.

2328 Rincon, Bernice. La Chicana: her role in the past and her search for a new role in the future. REGENERACION, Vol. 2, no. 4 (1975), p. 36-39. English. DESCR: *Women Men Relations.

2329 Robinson, Bea Vasquez. Are we racist? Are we sexist? AGENDA, (Winter 1976), p. 23-24. English. DESCR: Conferences and Meetings; Discrimination; International Women's Year World Conference (1975: Mexico City); National Chicana Coalition; *Sexism.

2330 Roraback, Rosanne Lisa. The effects of occupational type, educational level, marital status, and race/ethnicity on women's attitudes towards feminist issues. Thesis (M.A.)--Michigan State University 1988. 62 p. English. DESCR: Abortion; *Attitudes; Equal Rights Amendment (ERA) Identity; *Women.

2331 Ruiz Funes, Concepcion and Tunon, Enriqueta Panorama de las luchas de la mujer mexicana en el siglo XX. IN: Del Castillo, Adelaida R., ed. BETWEEN BORDERS: ESSAYS ON MEXICANA/CHICANA HISTORY. Encino, CA: Floricanto Press, 1990, p. 336-357. Spanish. DESCR: Coordinadora de Mujeres Trabajadoras; Frente Unido Pro Derechos de la Mujer; History; Labor Unions; *Mexico; Sex Roles; *Women.

2332 Ruiz, Vicki L., ed. and DuBois, Ellen Carol, ed. Unequal sisters: a multicultural reader in U.S. women's history. New York: Routledge, 1990. xvi, 473 p. English.

DESCR: Anglo Americans; Asian Americans; Blacks; *History; Native Americans; *Women.

2333 Ruiz, Vicki L., ed. and Tiano, Susan B., ed. Women on the U.S.-Mexico border: responses to change. Boston, MA: Allen & Unwin, c1987. xi, 247 p. English. DESCR: *Border Industries; *Border Region; Employment; Immigrants; Mexico; Sex Roles; *Women.

2334 Saavedra-Vela, Pilar. Nosotras in Houston. AGENDA, Vol. 8, no. 2 (March, April, 1978), p. 26-31. English. DESCR: Conferences and Meetings; Houston, TX; National Women's Conference (November, 1977: Houston, TX).

2335 Saenz, Rogelio; Goudy, Willis J.; and Lorenz, Frederick O. The effects of employment and marital relations on depression among Mexican American women. JOURNAL OF MARRIAGE AND THE FAMILY, Vol. 51, no. 1 (February 1989), p. 239-251. English. DESCR: *Depression (Psychological); Domestic Work; *Employment; *Marriage; Women Men Relations; Working Women.

2336 Saldivar, Jose David. Towards a Chicano poetics: the making of the Chicano subject. CONFLUENCIA, Vol. 1, no. 2 (Spring 1986), p. 10-17. English. DESCR: Corridos; *Literary Criticism; "Los Vatos" [poem]; Montoya, Jose E.; *Poetry; RESTLESS SERPENTS; Rios, Alberto; WHISPERING TO FOOL THE WIND; Zamora, Bernice.

2337 Saldivar, Ramon. The dialectics of subjectivity: gender and difference in Isabella Rios, Sandra Cisneros, and Cherrie Moraga. IN: Saldivar, Ramon. CHICANO NARRATIVE: THE DIALECTICS OF DIFFERENCE. Madison, WI: University of Wisconsin Press, 1990, p. 171-199. English. DESCR: Authors; Autobiography; *Cisneros, Sandra; Fiction; *Literary Criticism; Literature; LOVING IN THE WAR YEARS; *Moraga, Cherrie; Political Ideology; *Rios, Isabella; THE HOUSE ON MANGO STREET; VICTUUM.

2338 Saldivar-Hull, Sonia. Feminism on the border: from gender politics to geopolitics. IN: Calderon, Hector and Saldivar, Jose David, eds. CRITICISM IN THE BORDERLANDS: STUDIES IN CHICANO LITERATURE, CULTURE, AND IDEOLOGY. Durham, NC: Duke University Press, 1991, p. [203]-220. English. DESCR: Anglo Americans; *Anzaldua, Gloria; *BORDERLANDS/LA FRONTERA: THE NEW MESTIZA; Homosexuality; *Literary Criticism; Mestizaje; Moraga, Cherrie; Sexism; "The Cariboo Cafe" [short story]; Viramontes, Helena Maria; Women.

2339 Sanchez, Rosaura. El discurso femenino en la literatura chicana. IN: Lopez-Gonzalez, Aralia, et al., eds. MUJER Y LITERATURA MEXICANA Y CHICANA: CULTURAS EN CONTACTO. Mexico: Colegio de la Frontera Norte, 1988, p. 37-43. Spanish. DESCR: *Literary Criticism; Ruiz Burton, Maria Amparo.

2340 Sanchez, Rosaura. The history of Chicanas: a proposal for a materialist perspective. IN: Del Castillo, Adelaida R., ed. BETWEEN BORDERS: ESSAYS ON MEXICANA/CHICANA HISTORY. Encino, CA: Floricanto Press, 1990, p. 1-29. English. DESCR: Apodaca, Maria Linda; *Chicana Studies; Del Castillo, Adelaida R.; Historiography; History; Morales, Sylvia; Ruiz, Vicki L.

2341 Santiago, Myrna I. La Chicana. FEM, Vol. 8, no. 34 (June, July, 1984), p. 5-9. Spanish. DESCR: *Chicano Movement; History.

Feminism (cont.)

2342 Sepulveda, Betty R. The Hispanic woman responding to the challenges that affect us all. LA LUZ, Vol. 1, no. 7 (November 1972), p. 56-59. English. **DESCR**: Identity.

2343 Sosa Riddell, Adaljiza. The status of women in Mexico: the impact of the "International Year of the Woman". IN: Iglitzin, Lynn B. and Ross, Ruth A., eds. WOMEN IN THE WORLD, 1975-1985. Santa Barbara, CA: ABC-Clio, Inc., 1986, p. 305-324. English. **DESCR**: Abortion; International Women's Year World Conference (1975: Mexico City); *Mexico; Political History and Conditions; Political Parties and Organizations; Rape; *Sexism; Social History and Conditions; *Women.

2344 Soto, Shirlene Ann. Emergence of the modern Mexican woman: her participation in revolution and struggle for equality, 1910-1940. Denver, CO: Arden Press, 1990. xvi, 199 p.: ill. English. **DESCR**: *Mexican Revolution - 1910-1920; *Mexico; Political History and Conditions; *Women.

2345 Soto, Shirlene Ann. The women's movement in Mexico: the first and second feminist congresses in Yucatan, 1916. IN: Del Castillo, Adelaida R., ed. BETWEEN BORDERS: ESSAYS ON MEXICANA/CHICANA HISTORY. Encino, CA: Floricanto Press, 1990, p. 483-491. English. **DESCR**: *Conferences and Meetings; *Feminist Congress (1916: Yucatan, Mexico); Mexico; Women.

2346 Staudt, Kathleen. Programming women's empowerment: a case from northern Mexico. IN: Ruiz, Vicki L. and Tiano, Susan, eds. WOMEN ON THE U.S.-MEXICO BORDER: RESPONSES TO CHANGE. Boston, MA: Allen & Unwin, 1987, p. 155-173. English. **DESCR**: Alternative Education; Border Region; Ciudad Juarez, Chihuahua, Mexico; Curriculum; Employment; Organizations; Women.

2347 Sternbach, Nancy Saporta. "A deep racial memory of love": the Chicana feminism of Cherrie Moraga. IN: Horno-Delgado, Asuncion, et al., eds. BREAKING BOUNDARIES: LATINA WRITING AND CRITICAL READINGS. Amherst, MA: University of Massachusetts Press, c1989, p. 48-61. English. **DESCR**: Discrimination; Homosexuality; Literary Criticism; *LOVING IN THE WAR YEARS; Machismo; Malinche; *Moraga, Cherrie; Sex Stereotypes; Sexism.

2348 Tafolla, Carmen. To split a human: mitos, machos y la mujer chicana. San Antonio, TX: Mexican American Cultural Center, 1985. 115 p.: ill. English. **DESCR**: Discrimination; Education; Films; *Sex Roles; Sex Stereotypes; *Sexism.

2349 Talavera, Esther. Sterilization is not an alternative in family planning. AGENDA, Vol. 7, no. 6 (November, December, 1977), p. 8. English. **DESCR**: Discrimination; Family Planning; *Fertility; Medical Care Laws and Legislation; Sterilization.

2350 Tatum, Charles M. Grappling with difference: gender, race, class, and ethnicity in contemporary Chicana/o literature. RENATO ROSALDO LECTURE SERIES MONOGRAPH, Vol. 6, (1988, 1989), p. 1-23. English. **DESCR**: Anaya, Rudolfo A.; Authors; BLESS ME, ULTIMA; Identity; Literary Characters; *Literary Criticism; Literature Reviews.

2351 Tavera Rivera, Margarita. Autoridad in absentia: la censura patriarcal en la narrativa chicana. IN: Lopez-Gonzalez,

Aralia, et al., eds. MUJER Y LITERATURA MEXICANA Y CHICANA: CULTURAS EN CONTACTO. Mexico: Colegio de la Frontera Norte, 1988, p. [65]-69. Spanish. **DESCR**: Fiction; *Literary Criticism; Sex Roles; *THE MOTHS AND OTHER STORIES; *Viramontes, Helena Maria.

2352 Torres Raines, Rosario. The Mexican American woman and work: intergenerational perspectives of comparative ethnic groups. IN: Melville, Margarita, ed. MEXICANAS AT WORK IN THE UNITED STATES. Houston, TX: Mexican American Studies Program, University of Houston, 1988, p. 33-46. English. **DESCR**: Age Groups; Anglo Americans; Employment; Marriage; Sex Roles; Social Classes; Socioeconomic Factors; *Working Women.

2353 Valdes-Fallis, Guadalupe. A liberated Chicana: a struggle against tradition. WOMEN: A JOURNAL OF LIBERATION, Vol. 3, no. 4 (1974), p. 20-21. English. **DESCR**: Essays; Sex Roles; *Sexism.

2354 Vasquez, Carlos. Women in the Chicano Movement. IN: Mora, Magdalena and Del Castillo, Adelaida, eds. MEXICAN WOMEN IN THE UNITED STATES: STRUGGLES PAST AND PRESENT. Los Angeles, CA: Chicano Studies Research Center, UCLA, 1980, p. 27-28. English. **DESCR**: Chicano Movement.

2355 Velasquez-Trevino, Gloria. Jovita Gonzalez, una voz de resistencia cultural en la temprana narrativa chicana. IN: Lopez-Gonzalez, Aralia, et al., eds. MUJER Y LITERATURA MEXICANA Y CHICANA: CULTURAS EN CONTACTO. Mexico: Colegio de la Frontera Norte, 1988, p. [77]-83. Spanish. **DESCR**: Anglo Americans; Authors; Folklore; *Gonzalez, Jovita; Intergroup Relations; *League of United Latin American Citizens (LULAC).

2356 Vidal, Mirta. Women: new voice of La Raza. IN: Garcia, Richard A., ed. CHICANOS IN AMERICA, 1540-1974: A CHRONOLOGY AND FACT BOOK. Dobbs Ferry, NY: Oceana Publications, 1977, p. 132-140. English. **DESCR**: Conferences and Meetings; *First National Chicana Conference (May 1971: Houston, TX).

2357 Votaw, Carmen Delgado. Cultural influences on Hispanic feminism. AGENDA, Vol. 11, no. 4 (1981), p. 44-49. Bilingual. **DESCR**: Culture; Identity; Values.

2358 Williams, Joyce E. Mexican American and Anglo attitudes about sex roles and rape. FREE INQUIRY IN CREATIVE SOCIOLOGY, Vol. 13, no. 1 (May 1985), p. 15-20. English. **DESCR**: Anglo Americans; Attitudes; *Rape; *Sex Roles; Women.

2359 Winkler, Karen J. Scholars say issues of diversity have "revolutionized" field of Chicano Studies. CHRONICLE OF HIGHER EDUCATION, Vol. 37, no. 4 (September 26, 1990), p. A4-A9. English. **DESCR**: Chicana Studies; Chicano Studies; Curriculum; Higher Education; Ruiz, Vicki L.; Saragoza, Alex M.

2360 Woodward, Carolyn. Dare to write: Virginia Woolf, Tillie Olsen, Gloria Anzaldua. IN: Cochran, Jo Whitehorse, et al., eds. CHANGING OUR POWER: AN INTRODUCTION TO WOMEN STUDIES. Dubuque, IA: Kendall/Hunt Publishing Co., 1988, p. 336-349. English. **DESCR**: Anzaldua, Gloria; *Authors; Olsen, Tillie; Women; Woolf, Virginia.

Feminism (cont.)

2361 Yarbro-Bejarano, Yvonne. Chicana literature from a Chicana feminist perspective. THE AMERICAS REVIEW, Vol. 15, no. 3-4 (Fall, Winter, 1987), p. 139-145. English. **DESCR:** *Literary Criticism; Literature.

2362 Yarbro-Bejarano, Yvonne. The female subject in Chicano theater: sexuality, race, and class. THEATRE JOURNAL, Vol. 38, no. 4 (December 1986), p. 389-407. English. **DESCR:** El Teatro Campesino; El Teatro de la Esperanza; El Teatro Nacional de Aztlan (TENAZ); *Malinche; *Sex Roles; *Teatro; Women in Teatro (WIT).

2363 Young, Gay. Women, development and human rights: issues in integrated transnational production. JOURNAL OF APPLIED BEHAVIORAL SCIENCE, Vol. 20, no. 4 (November 1984), p. 383-401. English. **DESCR:** Border Industrialization Program (BIP); *Border Industries; Mexico; Multinational Corporations; Women; Women Men Relations; *Working Women.

2364 Zambrana, Ruth E. Toward understanding the educational trajectory and socialization of Latina women. IN: McKenna, Teresa and Ortiz, Flora Ida, eds. THE BROKEN WEB: THE EDUCATIONAL EXPERIENCE OF HISPANIC WOMEN. Claremont, CA: Tomas Rivera Center; Berkeley, CA: Floricanto Press, 1988, p. 61-77. English. **DESCR:** Academic Achievement; Anglo Americans; *Education; Identity; Research Methodology *Socialization; *Women.

2365 Zavella, Patricia. The problematic relationship of feminism and Chicana Studies. WOMEN'S STUDIES QUARTERLY, Vol. 17, no. 1-2 (1989), p. 25-36. English. **DESCR:** Chicana Studies; *Women.

2366 Zavella, Patricia. Reflections on diversity among Chicanas. FRONTIERS: A JOURNAL OF WOMEN STUDIES, Vol. 12, no. 2 (1991), p. 73-85. English. **DESCR:** *Cultural Pluralism; Culture; Identity; Stereotypes.

Feminist Congress (1916: Yucatan, Mexico)

2367 Soto, Shirlene Ann. The women's movement in Mexico: the first and second feminist congresses in Yucatan, 1916. IN: Del Castillo, Adelaida R., ed. BETWEEN BORDERS: ESSAYS ON MEXICANA/CHICANA HISTORY. Encino, CA: Floricanto Press, 1990, p. 483-491. English. **DESCR:** *Conferences and Meetings; *Feminism; Mexico; Women.

Fertility

2368 Abrahamse, Allan F.; Morrison, Peter A.; and Waite, Linda J. Beyond stereotypes: who becomes a single teenage mother? Santa Monica, CA: RAND Corp., 1988. xv, 88 p. English. **DESCR:** Religion; Secondary School Education; *Single Parents; Statistics; *Women; *Youth.

2369 Abrahamse, Allan F.; Morrison, Peter A.; and Waite, Linda J. Teenagers willing to consider single parenthood: who is at greatest risk? FAMILY PLANNING PERSPECTIVES, Vol. 20, no. 1 (January, February, 1988), p. 13-18. English. **DESCR:** Blacks; Family Planning; High School and Beyond Project (HS&B); *Single Parents; Women; *Youth.

2370 Alba, Francisco. La fecundidad entre los Mexicano-Norteamericanos en relacion a los cambiantes patrones reproductivos en Mexico

y los Estados Unidos. DEMOGRAFIA Y ECONOMIA, Vol. 16, no. 2 (1982), p. 236-249. Spanish. **DESCR:** Mexico; Population.

2371 Amaro, Hortensia. Abortion use and attitudes among Chicanas: the need for research. RESEARCH BULLETIN (SPANISH SPEAKING MENTAL HEALTH RES. CENTER), Vol. 4, no. 3 (March 1980), p. 1-5. English. **DESCR:** *Abortion; *Attitudes; Birth Control; Family Planning; Literature Reviews; Mental Health.

2372 Amaro, Hortensia. Women in the Mexican-American community: religion, culture, and reproductive attitudes and experiences. JOURNAL OF COMMUNITY PSYCHOLOGY, Vol. 16, no. 1 (January 1988), p. 6-20. English. **DESCR:** Abortion; *Attitudes; Birth Control; Family Planning; Religion.

2373 Andrade, Sally J. Family planning practices of Mexican Americans. IN: Melville, Margarita B., ed. TWICE A MINORITY. St. Louis, MO: Mosby, 1980, p. 17-32. English. **DESCR:** Birth Control; *Family Planning.

2374 Aneshensel, Carol S.; Fielder, Eve P.; and Becerra, Rosina M. Fertility and fertility-related behavior among Mexican-American and non-Hispanic white female adolescents. JOURNAL OF HEALTH AND SOCIAL BEHAVIOR, Vol. 30, no. 1 (March 1989), p. 56-76. English. **DESCR:** Anglo Americans; Socioeconomic Factors; Youth.

2375 Aneshensel, Carol S., et al. Onset of fertility-related events during adolescence: a prospective comparison of Mexican American and non-Hispanic white females. AMERICAN JOURNAL OF PUBLIC HEALTH, Vol. 80, no. 8 (August 1990), p. 959-963. English. **DESCR:** Abortion; Anglo Americans; Birth Control; *Sexual Behavior; Women; *Youth.

2376 Aneshensel, Carol S., et al. Participation of Mexican American adolescents in a longitudinal panel survey. PUBLIC OPINION QUARTERLY, Vol. 53, no. 4 (Winter 1989), p. 548-562. English. **DESCR:** Age Groups; Los Angeles County, CA; Social Science; *Surveys; *Women Men Relations; *Youth.

2377 Atkinson, Donald R.; Winzelberg, Andrew; and Holland, Abby. Ethnicity, locus of control for family planning, and pregnancy counselor credibility. JOURNAL OF COUNSELING PSYCHOLOGY, Vol. 32, no. 3 (July 1985), p. 417-421. English. **DESCR:** Anglo Americans; Counseling (Psychological); *Family Planning; Identity; *Locus of Control; Women.

2378 Bachu, Amara and O'Connell, Martin. Developing current fertility indicators for foreign-born women from the Current Population Survey. REVIEW OF PUBLIC DATA USE, Vol. 12, no. 3 (October 1984), p. 185-195. English. **DESCR:** Current Population Survey; Latin America; Mexico; *Surveys; Vital Statistics; Women.

2379 Bean, Frank D. and Swicegood, Gray. Generation, female education and Mexican American fertility. SOCIAL SCIENCE QUARTERLY, Vol. 63, (March 1982), p. 131-144. English. **DESCR:** Age Groups; Education; Family Planning.

Fertility (cont.)

2380 Bean, Frank D. and Tienda, Marta. The Hispanic population of the United States. New York: Russell Sage Foundation, 1987. xxiv, 456 p. English. DESCR: *Census; Education; Employment; Identity; Immigration; Income; *Population; Self-Referents; *Statistics.

2381 Bean, Frank D. and Bradshaw, Benjamin S. Mexican American fertility. IN: Teller, Charles H., et al., eds. CUANTOS SOMOS: A DEMOGRAPHIC STUDY OF THE MEXICAN AMERICAN POPULATION. Austin, TX: Center for Mexican American Studies, University of Texas at Austin, 1977, p. 101-130. English. DESCR: Attitudes; Birth Control; Income; Population; Religion.

2382 Bean, Frank D. and Swicegood, Gray. Mexican American fertility patterns. Austin, TX: University of Texas Press, 1985. x, 178 p. English. DESCR: Age Groups; Census; Education; Language Usage; *Population; Research Methodology; *Socioeconomic Factors; Statistics.

2383 Bean, Frank D.; Stephen, Elizabeth H.; and Opitz, Wolfgang. The Mexican origin population in the United States: a demographic overview. IN: O. de la Garza, Rodolfo, et al., eds. THE MEXICAN AMERICAN EXPERIENCE: AN INTERDISCIPLINARY ANTHOLOGY. Austin, TX: University of Texas Press, 1985, p. 57-75. English. DESCR: Employment; Income; *Population; Vital Statistics.

2384 Bean, Frank D.; Swicegood, Gray; and King, Allan G. Role incompatibility and the relationship between fertility and labor supply among Hispanic women. IN: Borjas, George J. and Tienda, Marta, eds. HISPANICS IN THE U.S. ECONOMY. Orlando, FL: Academic Press, 1985, p. 221-242. English. DESCR: Cubanos; *Employment; Labor Supply and Market; Puerto Ricans.

2385 Bean, Frank D., et al. Generational differences in fertility among Mexican Americans: implications for assessing the effects of immigration. SOCIAL SCIENCE QUARTERLY, Vol. 65, no. 2 (June 1984), p. 573-582. English. DESCR: Age Groups; Immigration; Vital Statistics.

2386 Becerra, Rosina M. and de Anda, Diane. Pregnancy and motherhood among Mexican American adolescents. HEALTH AND SOCIAL WORK, Vol. 9, no. 2 (Spring 1984), p. 106-23. English. DESCR: Acculturation; Anglo Americans; Attitudes; Birth Control; Natural Support Systems; *Youth.

2387 Codega, Susan A.; Pasley, B. Kay; and Kreutzer, Jill. Coping behaviors of adolescent mothers: an exploratory study and comparison of Mexican-Americans and Anglos. JOURNAL OF ADOLESCENT RESEARCH, Vol. 5, no. 1 (January 1990), p. 34-53. English. DESCR: Anglo Americans; Colorado; *Stress; Women; *Youth.

2388 Davis, Cary; Haub, Carl; and Willette, JoAnne. U.S. Hispanics: changing the face of America. POPULATION BULLETIN, Vol. 38, no. 3 (June 1983), p. 1-43. English. DESCR: Education; Employment; Immigration; Income; *Population; Statistics; Vital Statistics.

2389 de Anda, Diane; Becerra, Rosina M.; and Fielder, Eve P. In their own words: the life experiences of Mexican-American and white pregnant adolescents and adolescent mothers.

CHILD AND ADOLESCENT SOCIAL WORK, Vol. 7, no. 4 (August 1990), p. 301-318. English. DESCR: Anglo Americans; *Sexual Behavior; Women; *Youth.

2390 de Anda, Diane; Becerra, Rosina M.; and Fielder, Eve P. Sexuality, pregnancy, and motherhood among Mexican-American adolescents. JOURNAL OF ADOLESCENT RESEARCH, Vol. 3, no. 3-4 (Fall, Winter, 1988), p. 403-411. English. DESCR: Anglo Americans; Attitudes; Birth Control; Sex Education; *Sexual Behavior; Women; *Youth.

2391 de Anda, Diane and Becerra, Rosina M. Support networks for adolescent mothers. SOCIAL CASEWORK: JOURNAL OF CONTEMPORARY SOCIAL WORK, Vol. 65, no. 3 (March 1984), p. 172-181. English. DESCR: California; *Natural Support Systems; Spanish Language; *Youth.

2392 Delgado, Jane L. Adolescent pregnancy: an overview. IN: National Hispanic Center for Advanced Studies and Policy Analysis and National Hispanic University. THE STATE OF HISPANIC AMERICA. VOL. VI. Oakland, CA: National Hispanic University, c1987, p. 37-49. English. DESCR: Family Planning; Public Policy; *Youth.

2393 Dill, Bonnie Thornton. Our mothers' grief: racial ethnic women and the maintenance of families. JOURNAL OF FAMILY HISTORY, Vol. 13, no. 4 (October 1988), p. 415-431. English. DESCR: Asian Americans; Blacks; Domestic Work; *Family; *Sex Roles; *Women; *Working Women.

2394 Dinsmoor, Mara J. and Gibbs, Ronald S. Prevalence of asymptomatic hepatitis-B infection in pregnant Mexican-American women. OBSTETRICS AND GYNECOLOGY, Vol. 76, no. 2 (August 1990), p. 239-240. English. DESCR: Diseases; *Hepatitis.

2395 Eisen, Marvin. Factors discriminating pregnancy resolution decisions of unmarried adolescents. GENETIC PSYCHOLOGY MONOGRAPHS, Vol. 108, no. 1 (August 1983), p. 69-95. English. DESCR: Abortion; Attitudes; Decision Making; *Single Parents; *Youth.

2396 Eisen, Marvin and Zellman, Gail L. Factors predicting pregnancy resolution decision satisfaction of unmarried adolescents. JOURNAL OF GENETIC PSYCHOLOGY, Vol. 145, no. 2 (December 1984), p. 231-239. English. DESCR: Abortion; Anglo Americans; Attitudes; Counseling (Psychological); Family Planning; Youth.

2397 Engle, Patricia L. Prenatal and postnatal anxiety in women giving birth in Los Angeles. HEALTH PSYCHOLOGY, Vol. 9, no. 3 (1990), p. 285-299. English. DESCR: Immigrants; Los Angeles, CA; *Maternal and Child Welfare; Medical Care; *Prenatal Care; *Stress; Women.

2398 Erickson, Pamela Irene. Pregnancy and childbirth among Mexican origin teenagers in Los Angeles. Thesis (Ph.D.)--UCLA, 1988. xiii, 277 leaves. English. DESCR: Los Angeles, CA; Medical Care; *Youth.

Fertility (cont.)

2399 Falasco, Dee and Heer, David. Economic and fertility differences between legal and undocumented migrant Mexican families: possible effects of immigration policy changes. SOCIAL SCIENCE QUARTERLY, Vol. 65, no. 2 (June 1984), p. 495-504. English. DESCR: *Economic History and Conditions; *Immigration Law and Legislation; Immigration Regulation and Control; Income; *Undocumented Workers.

2400 Felice, Marianne E., et al. Clinical observations of Mexican-American, Caucasian, and Black pregnant teenagers. JOURNAL OF ADOLESCENT HEALTH CARE, Vol. 7, no. 5 (September 1986), p. 305-310. English. DESCR: Anglo Americans; Blacks; *Prenatal Care; San Diego, CA; Youth.

2401 Fennelly, Katherine. Childbearing among Hispanics in the United States: an annotated bibliography. New York: Greenwood Press, 1987. xii, 167 p. English. DESCR: Abortion; *Bibliography; Birth Control; Sterilization; *Women; Youth.

2402 Fennelly, Katherine and Ortiz, Vilma. Childbearing among young Latino women in the United States. AMERICAN JOURNAL OF PUBLIC HEALTH, Vol. 77, no. 1 (January 1987), p. 25-28. English. DESCR: *Ethnic Groups; Puerto Ricans; Women; *Youth.

2403 Fennelly, Katherine; Kandiah, Vasantha; and Ortiz, Vilma. The cross-cultural study of fertility among Hispanic adolescents in the Americas. STUDIES IN FAMILY PLANNING, Vol. 20, no. 2 (March, April, 1989), p. 96-101. English. DESCR: Cultural Characteristics; Ethnic Groups; Latin America; *Marriage; Youth.

2404 Fennelly, Katherine. El embarazo precoz: childbearing among Hispanic teenagers in the United States. New York, NY: School of Public Health, Columbia University, c1988. 36 p.: ill. Bilingual. DESCR: Women; Youth.

2405 Fennelly, Katherine; Dryfoos, Joy; and Schwartz, Dana. Hispanic adolescent fertility. HISPANIC JOURNAL OF BEHAVIORAL SCIENCES, Vol. 8, no. 2 (June 1986), p. 157-171. English. DESCR: Youth.

2406 Fischer, Nancy A. and Marcum, John P. Ethnic integration, socioeconomic status, and fertility among Mexican Americans. SOCIAL SCIENCE QUARTERLY, Vol. 65, no. 2 (June 1984), p. 583-593. English. DESCR: Assimilation; Identity; Socioeconomic Factors.

2407 Franks, Adele L.; Binkin, Nancy J.; and Snider, Dixie E. Isoniazid hepatitis among pregnant and postpartum Hispanic patients. PUBLIC HEALTH REPORTS, Vol. 104, no. 2 (March, April, 1989), p. 151-155. English. DESCR: *Hepatitis; Public Health; Vital Statistics.

2408 Freier, Michelle Cyd. Psychosocial and physiological influences on birth outcomes among women of Mexican origin or descent. Thesis (Ph.D.)--UCLA, 1987. xiv, 197 leaves. English. DESCR: *Mental Health.

2409 Garn, Stanley M. and LaVelle, Marquisa. Reproductive histories of low weight girls and women. AMERICAN JOURNAL OF CLINICAL NUTRITION, Vol. 37, no. 5 (May 1983), p 862-866. English. DESCR: Nutrition; Youth.

2410 Gould, Jeffrey B.; Davey, Becky; and Stafford, Randall S. Socioeconomic differences in rates of cesarean section. THE NEW ENGLAND JOURNAL OF MEDICINE, Vol. 321, no. 4 (July 27, 1989), p. 233-239. English. DESCR: Anglo Americans; Asian Americans; Blacks; *Cesarean Section; Los Angeles County, CA; *Socioeconomic Factors; Vital Statistics; Women.

2411 Gunther Enriquez, Martha. Studying maternal-infant attachment: a Mexican-American example. IN: Kay, Margarita Artschwager, ed. ANTHROPOLOGY OF HUMAN BIRTH. Philadelphia, PA: F.A. Davis, 1982, p. 61-79. English. DESCR: Children; Immigrants; *Maternal and Child Welfare; *Parent and Child Relationships.

2412 Gurak, Douglas T. Assimilation and fertility: a comparison of Mexican American and Japanese American women. HISPANIC JOURNAL OF BEHAVIORAL SCIENCES, Vol. 2, no. 3 (September 1980), p. 219-239. English. DESCR: Asian Americans; Assimilation; Japanese; Population; Women.

2413 Hedderson, John J. Fertility and mortality. IN: Stoddard, Ellwyn R., et al., eds. BORDERLANDS SOURCEBOOK: A GUIDE TO THE LITERATURE ON NORTHERN MEXICO AND THE AMERICAN SOUTHWEST. Norman, OK: University of Oklahoma Press, 1983, p. 232-236. English. DESCR: Border Region; Population; *Vital Statistics.

2414 Henderson, Nancy. Perinatal service needs of Hispanic women with diabetes. Thesis (M.S.)--California State University, Long Beach, 1987. 79 p. English. DESCR: *Diabetes; Medical Care; *Social Services; *Stress.

2415 Horowitz, Ruth. Femininity and womanhood: virginity, unwed motherhood, and violence. IN: Horowitz, Ruth. HONOR AND THE AMERICAN DREAM: CULTURE AND IDENTITY IN A CHICANO COMMUNITY. New Brunswick, NJ: Rutgers University Press, 1983, p. 114-136. English. DESCR: *Birth Control; Identity; Sex Roles; *Sexual Behavior; Single Parents; Violence; Women Men Relations; Youth.

2416 Horowitz, Ruth. Passion, submission and motherhood: the negotiation of identity by unmarried innercity Chicanas. SOCIOLOGICAL QUARTERLY, Vol. 22, no. 2 (Spring 1981), p. 241-252. English. DESCR: Barrios; Birth Control; Identity; *Sex Roles; *Sexual Behavior; Single Parents; Youth.

2417 Hunt, Isabelle F., et al. Zinc supplementation during pregnancy in low-income teenagers of Mexican descent: effects on selected blood constituents and on progress and outcome of pregnancy. AMERICAN JOURNAL OF CLINICAL NUTRITION, Vol. 42, no. 5 (November 1985), p. 815-828. English. DESCR: *Nutrition; *Youth.

2418 Hurtado, Aida. A view from within: midwife practices in South Texas. INTERNATIONAL QUARTERLY OF COMMUNITY HEALTH AND EDUCATION, Vol. 8, no. 4 (1987, 1988), p. 317-339. English. DESCR: Medical Education; *Midwives; South Texas.

Fertility (cont.)

2419 Hutchison, James. Teenagers and
     contraception in Cameron and Willacy
     Counties. BORDERLANDS JOURNAL, Vol. 7, no. 1
     (Fall 1983), p. 75-90. English. **DESCR:**
     *Birth Control; Cameron County, TX; *Family
     Planning; Sex Education; Willacy County, TX;
     Youth.

2420 Jackson, Laurie Elizabeth. Self-care agency
     and limitations with respect to
     contraceptive behavior of Mexican-American
     women. Thesis (M.S.N.)--Medical College of
     Ohio at Toledo, 1988. 198 p. English.
     DESCR: *Birth Control; Locus of Control.

2421 Jordan, Rosan Augusta. The vaginal serpent
     and other themes from Mexican-American
     women's lore. IN: Jordan, Rosan A. and
     Kalcik, Susan J., eds. WOMEN'S FOLKLORE,
     WOMEN'S CULTURE. Philadelphia: University of
     Pennsylvania Press, 1985, p. 26-44. English.
     DESCR: Cuentos; *Folklore; La Llorona;
     *Leyendas; *Sex Roles; Sexism; Sexual
     Behavior.

2422 Jorgensen, Stephen R. and Adams, Russell P.
     Family planning needs and behavior of
     Mexican American women: a study of health
     care professionals and their clientele.
     HISPANIC JOURNAL OF BEHAVIORAL SCIENCES,
     Vol. 9, no. 3 (September 1987), p. 265-286.
     English. **DESCR:** Acculturation; *Attitudes;
     Birth Control; *Cultural Characteristics;
     *Family Planning; Medical Personnel;
     Stereotypes; Sterilization.

2423 Leblanc, Donna Marie. Quality of maternity
     care in rural Texas. Thesis (Dr. P.H.)
     --University of Texas H.S.C. at Houston
     School of Public Health, 1983. 266 p.
     English. **DESCR:** Low Income; *Maternal and
     Child Welfare; *Medical Care; Prenatal Care;
     *Rural Poor; Texas.

2424 Lee, Bun Song and Pol, Louis G. A comparison
     of fertility adaptation between Mexican
     immigrants to the U.S. and internal migrants
     in Mexico. CONTEMPORARY POLICY ISSUES, Vol.
     3, no. 3 (Spring, 1985), p. 91-101. English.
     DESCR: *Immigrants; Mexico; Migration
     Patterns; *Rural Urban Migration; Women.

2425 Lindemann, Constance and Scott, Wilbur. The
     fertility related behavior of Mexican
     American adolescents. JOURNAL OF EARLY
     ADOLESCENCE, Vol. 2, no. 1 (Spring 1982), p.
     31-38. English. **DESCR:** Migration Patterns;
     Youth.

2426 Lopez, Norma Y. Hispanic teenage pregnancy:
     overview and implications. Washington, DC:
     National Council of La Raza, 1987. 17
     leaves. English. **DESCR:** Statistics; Women;
     *Youth.

2427 Marshall, Maria Sandra Gonzalez. The
     childbearing beliefs and practices of
     pregnant Mexican-American adolescents living
     in Southwest border regions. Thesis
     (M.S.)--University of Arizona, 1987. 117 p.
     English. **DESCR:** *Acculturation; Border
     Region; *Youth.

2428 Mays, Vicki M. and Cochran, Susan D. Issues
     in the perception of AIDS risk and risk
     reduction activities by Black and
     Hispanic/Latina women. AMERICAN
     PSYCHOLOGIST, Vol. 43, no. 11 (November
     1988), p. 949-957. English. **DESCR:** *AIDS
     (Disease); Blacks; Condom Use; Health
     Education; Preventative Medicine; *Sexual
     Behavior; Women.

2429 Michael, Robert T. and Tuma, Nancy Brandon.
     Entry into marriage and parenthood by young
     men and women: the influence of family
     background. DEMOGRAPHY, Vol. 22, no. 4
     (November 1985), p. 515-544. Magazine.
     English. **DESCR:** Anglo Americans; Blacks;
     *Cultural Characteristics; *Marriage;
     Population; Youth.

2430 Mink, Diane Leslie. Early grandmotherhood:
     an exploratory study. Thesis
     (Ph.D.)--California School of Professional
     Psychology, Los Angeles, 1987. 190 p.
     English. **DESCR:** Age Groups; *Ancianos;
     Assertiveness; Family; Grandmothers; Natural
     Support Systems; *Sex Roles; Surveys; Youth.

2431 Moore, Joan W. and Devitt, Mary. The paradox
     of deviance in addicted Mexican American
     mothers. GENDER & SOCIETY, Vol. 3, no. 1
     (March 1989), p. 53-70. English. **DESCR:**
     Children; *Drug Addicts; *Drug Use; Family;
     Gangs; Parenting; Sex Roles.

2432 Mosher, William D.; Johnson, David P.; and
     Horn, Marjorie C. Religion and fertility in
     the United States: the importance of
     marriage patterns and Hispanic origin.
     DEMOGRAPHY, Vol. 23, no. 3 (August 1986), p.
     367-379. English. **DESCR:** *Catholic Church;
     Identity; Marriage; Population; *Religion.

2433 Notzon, Francis Claude. Factors associated
     with low birth weight in Mexican-Americans
     and Mexicans. Thesis (Ph.D.)--John Hopkins
     University, 1989. 190 p. English. **DESCR:**
     Anglo Americans; *Maternal and Child
     Welfare; Mexico; *Prenatal Care; Public
     Health; *Women.

2434 One birth in four. AMERICAN DEMOGRAPHICS,
     Vol. 6, no. 1 (January 1984), p. 15.
     English. **DESCR:** Population; *Vital
     Statistics.

2435 Ortiz, Sylvia and Casas, Jesus Manuel. Birth
     control and low-income Mexican-American
     women: the impact of three values. HISPANIC
     JOURNAL OF BEHAVIORAL SCIENCES, Vol. 12, no.
     1 (February 1990), p. 83-92. English.
     DESCR: Acculturation; Attitudes; *Birth
     Control; *Low Income; *Sex Roles; Values.

2436 Ortiz, Vilma and Fennelly, Katherine. Early
     childbearing and employment among young
     Mexican origin, Black, and white women.
     SOCIAL SCIENCE QUARTERLY, Vol. 69, no. 4
     (December 1988), p. 987-995. English.
     DESCR: Anglo Americans; Blacks; *Employment;
     *Women; *Youth.

2437 Perez, Robert. Effects of stress, social
     support and coping style on adjustment to
     pregnancy among Hispanic women. HISPANIC
     JOURNAL OF BEHAVIORAL SCIENCES, Vol. 5, no.
     2 (June 1983), p. 141-161. English. **DESCR:**
     Natural Support Systems; *Stress.

2438 Perez, Robert. Stress and coping as
     determinants of adaptation to pregnancy in
     Hispanic women. Thesis (Ph.D.)--University
     of California, Los Angeles, 1982. 343 p.
     English. **DESCR:** Medical Personnel; Natural
     Support Systems; *Stress.

Fertility (cont.)

2439 Pick, James B., et al. Socioeconomic influences on fertility in the Mexican borderlands region. MEXICAN STUDIES/ESTUDIOS MEXICANOS, Vol. 6, no. 1 (Winter 1990), p. 11-42. English. DESCR: *Border Region; *Employment; Labor Supply and Market; Literacy; Socioeconomic Factors; Working Women.

2440 Pletsch, Pamela K. Hispanics: at risk for adolescent pregnancy? PUBLIC HEALTH NURSING, Vol. 7, no. 2 (June 1990), p. 105-110. English. DESCR: *Maternal and Child Welfare; *Youth.

2441 Poma, Pedro A. Pregnancy in Hispanic women. JOURNAL OF THE NATIONAL MEDICAL ASSOCIATION, Vol. 79, no. 9 (September 1987), p. 929-935. English. DESCR: *Cultural Characteristics; *Doctor Patient Relations; Machismo; Preventative Medicine; Women.

2442 Ramirez, Oscar and Arce, Carlos H. The contemporary Chicano family: an empirically based review. IN: Baron, Augustine, Jr., ed. EXPLORATIONS IN CHICANO PSYCHOLOGY. New York: Praeger, 1981, p. 3-28. English. DESCR: *Family; Literature Reviews; Machismo; Population; Sex Roles.

2443 Remez, Lisa. Rates of adolescent pregnancy and childbearing are high among Mexican-born Mexican Americans. FAMILY PLANNING PERSPECTIVES, Vol. 23, no. 2 (March, April, 1991), p. 88-89. English. DESCR: *Immigrants; Los Angeles County, CA; *Sexual Behavior; *Youth.

2444 Sabagh, Georges. Fertility expectations and behavior among Mexican Americans in Los Angeles, 1973-82. SOCIAL SCIENCE QUARTERLY, Vol. 65, no. 2 (June 1984), p. 594-608. English. DESCR: Immigrants; Los Angeles, CA.

2445 Sabagh, Georges and Lopez, David. Religiosity and fertility: the case of Chicanas. SOCIAL FORCES, Vol. 59, no. 2 (December 1980), p. 431-439. English. DESCR: Catholic Church; *Family Planning; Immigrants; *Religion; Women.

2446 Sorenson, Ann Marie. The fertility and language characteristics of Mexican-American and non-Hispanic husbands and wives. SOCIOLOGICAL QUARTERLY, Vol. 29, no. 1 (March 1988), p. 111-130. English. DESCR: Anglo Americans; Identity; *Language Usage; Marriage; Sex Roles.

2447 Sorenson, Ann Marie. Fertility, expectations and ethnic identity among Mexican-American adolescents: an expression of cultural ideals. SOCIOLOGICAL PERSPECTIVES, Vol. 28, no. 3 (July 1985), p. 339-360. English. DESCR: Acculturation; Anglo Americans; Cultural Characteristics; Identity; Values; Youth.

2448 Stephen, Elizabeth H. At the crossroads: fertility of Mexican-American women. New York: Garland Publishers, 1989. v, 184 p.: ill. English. DESCR: Assimilation; Immigration; *Population.

2449 Stewart, Kenneth L. and de Leon, Arnoldo. Fertility among Mexican Americans and Anglos in Texas, 1900. BORDERLANDS JOURNAL, Vol. 9, no. 1 (Spring 1986), p. 61-67. English. DESCR: Anglo Americans; Texas; Women.

2450 Stroup-Benham, Christine A. and Trevino, Fernando M. Reproductive characteristics of Mexican-American, mainland Puerto Rican, and Cuban-American women: data from the Hispanic Health and Nutrition Examination Survey. JAMA: JOURNAL OF THE AMERICAN MEDICAL ASSOCIATION, Vol. 265, no. 2 (January 9, 1991), p. 222-226. English. DESCR: *Birth Control; Breastfeeding; Cubanos; Hispanic Health and Nutrition Examination Survey (HHANES); Puerto Ricans; *Women.

2451 Swicegood, Gray. Language opportunity costs and Mexican American fertility. Thesis (Ph.D.)--University of Texas, Austin, 1982. ix, 188 p. English. DESCR: *Language Usage.

2452 Swicegood, Gray, et al. Language usage and fertility in the Mexican-origin population of the United States. DEMOGRAPHY, Vol. 25, no. 1 (February 1988), p. 17-33. English. DESCR: Immigrants; *Language Usage; Population; Women.

2453 Tajalli, Irene Queiro. Selected cultural, organizational, and economic factors related to prenatal care utilization by middle-income Hispanic women. Thesis (Ph.D.)--University of Illinois at Urbana-Champaign, 1984. 139 p. English. DESCR: Indiana; Maternal and Child Welfare; *Medical Care; Prenatal Care; Preventative Medicine.

2454 Talavera, Esther. Sterilization is not an alternative in family planning. AGENDA, Vol. 7, no. 6 (November, December, 1977), p. 8. English. DESCR: Discrimination; Family Planning; Feminism; Medical Care Laws and Legislation; Sterilization.

2455 Urdaneta, Maria Luisa. Chicana use of abortion: the case of Alcala. IN: Melville, Margarita B., ed. TWICE A MINORITY. St. Louis, MO: Mosby, 1980, p. 33-51. English. DESCR: *Abortion; Alcala, TX.

2456 Urdaneta, Maria Luisa. Flesh pots, faith, or finances? Fertility rates among Mexican Americans. IN: West, Stanley A. and Macklin, June, eds. THE CHICANO EXPERIENCE. Boulder, CO: Westview Press, 1979, p. 191-206. English. DESCR: Catholic Church; Machismo; Sex Roles.

2457 Ventura, Stephanie J. and Taffel, Selma M. Childbearing characteristics of U.S.- and foreign-born Hispanic mothers. PUBLIC HEALTH REPORTS, Vol. 100, no. 6 (November, December, 1985), p. 647-652. English. DESCR: Identity; Immigrants; *Maternal and Child Welfare; *Statistics.

2458 Warren, Charles W.; Smith, Jack C.; and Rochat, Roger W. Differentials in the planning status of the most recent live birth to Mexican Americans and Anglos. PUBLIC HEALTH REPORTS, Vol. 98, no. 2 (March, April, 1983), p. 152-160. English. DESCR: Anglo Americans; *Family Planning; Women.

2459 Williams, Ronald L., et al. Pregnancy outcomes among Spanish-surname women in California. AMERICAN JOURNAL OF PUBLIC HEALTH, Vol. 76, no. 4 (April 1986), p. 387-391. English. DESCR: *Infant Mortality.

2460 Wolff, Cindy Brattan. Diet and pregnancy outcome in Mexican-American women. Thesis (Ph.D.)--Colorado State University, 1988. 257 p. English. DESCR: Food Practices; *Maternal and Child Welfare; *Nutrition.

Fertility (cont.)

2461 Zambrana, Ruth E., et al. Ethnic differences in the substance use patterns of low-income pregnant women. FAMILY & COMMUNITY HEALTH, Vol. 13, no. 4 (January 1991), p. 1-11. English. DESCR: Alcoholism; Blacks; *Drug Use; Immigrants; *Low Income; Smoking; Women.

2462 Zepeda, Marlene. Mother-infant behavior in Mexican and Mexican-American women: a study of the relationship of selected prenatal, perinatal and postnatal events. Thesis (Ph.D.)--University of California, Los Angeles, 1984, 429 p. English. DESCR: Children; *Maternal and Child Welfare; *Parent and Child Relationships; Prenatal Care.

Fiction

2463 Cochran, Jo, et al., eds. Bearing witness/Sobreviviendo: an anthology of Native American/Latina art and literature. CALYX: A JOURNAL OF ART AND LITERATURE BY WOMEN, Vol. 8, no. 2 (Spring 1984), p. [1]-128. English. DESCR: *Art; Drawings; Native Americans; *Poems; Women.

2464 Herrera-Sobek, Maria. The politics of rape: sexual transgression in Chicana fiction. THE AMERICAS REVIEW, Vol. 15, no. 3-4 (Fall, Winter, 1987), p. 171-181. English. DESCR: Cisneros, Sandra; *Feminism; GIVING UP THE GHOST; *Literary Criticism; Lizarraga, Sylvia; Moraga, Cherrie; *Rape; "Red Clowns" [short story]; Sex Roles; "Silver Lake Road" [short story].

2465 Rebolledo, Tey Diana. Narrative strategies of resistance in Hispana writing. THE JOURNAL OF NARRATIVE TECHNIQUE, Vol. 20, no. 2 (Spring 1990), p. 134-146. English. DESCR: *Authors; Cabeza de Baca, Fabiola; Jaramillo, Cleofas M.; *Literary Criticism; Literature; New Mexico; OLD SPAIN IN OUR SOUTHWEST; *Oral Tradition; Otero Warren, Nina; ROMANCE OF A LITTLE VILLAGE GIRL; WE FED THEM CACTUS.

2466 Rosaldo, Renato. Fables of the fallen guy. IN: Calderon, Hector and Saldivar, Jose David, eds. CRITICISM IN THE BORDERLANDS: STUDIES IN CHICANO LITERATURE, CULTURE AND IDEOLOGY. Durham, NC: Duke University Press, 1991, p. [84]-93. English. DESCR: Chavez, Denise; Cisneros, Sandra; Literary Characters; *Literary Criticism; Rios, Alberto; Sex Roles; THE HOUSE ON MANGO STREET; THE IGUANA KILLER: TWELVE STORIES OF THE HEART; THE LAST OF THE MENU GIRLS.

2467 Saldivar, Ramon. The dialectics of subjectivity: gender and difference in Isabella Rios, Sandra Cisneros, and Cherrie Moraga. IN: Saldivar, Ramon. CHICANO NARRATIVE: THE DIALECTICS OF DIFFERENCE. Madison, WI: University of Wisconsin Press, 1990, p. 171-199. English. DESCR: Authors; Autobiography; *Cisneros, Sandra; Feminism; *Literary Criticism; Literature; LOVING IN THE WAR YEARS; *Moraga, Cherrie; Political Ideology; *Rios, Isabella; THE HOUSE ON MANGO STREET; VICTUUM.

2468 Tavera Rivera, Margarita. Autoridad in absentia: la censura patriarcal en la narrativa chicana. IN: Lopez-Gonzalez, Aralia, et al., eds. MUJER Y LITERATURA MEXICANA Y CHICANA: CULTURAS EN CONTACTO. Mexico: Colegio de la Frontera Norte, 1988, p. [65]-69. Spanish. DESCR: Feminism; *Literary Criticism; Sex Roles; *THE MOTHS

AND OTHER STORIES; *Viramontes, Helena Maria.

2469 Velasquez-Trevino, Gloria. Cultural ambivalence in early Chicana prose fiction. Thesis (Ph.D.)--Stanford University, 1985. 185 p. English. DESCR: Biculturalism; Gonzalez, Jovita; Literary Criticism; Mena, Maria Cristina; Niggli, Josephina; Prose; Sex Roles.

Film Reviews

2470 Candelaria, Cordelia. Social equity in film criticism. BILINGUAL REVIEW, Vol. 10, no. 2-3 (May, December, 1983), p. 64-70. English. DESCR: Stereotypes.

2471 Cortes, Carlos E. Chicanas in film: history of an image. BILINGUAL REVIEW, Vol. 10, no. 2-3 (May, December, 1983), p. 94-108. English. DESCR: *Films; *Stereotypes.

2472 Morales, Sylvia. Chicano-produced celluloid mujeres. BILINGUAL REVIEW, Vol. 10, no. 2-3 (May, December, 1983), p. 89-93. English. DESCR: BALLAD OF GREGORIO CORTEZ [film]; *Films; RAICES DE SANGRE [film]; SEGUIN [movie]; *Stereotypes; ZOOT SUIT [film].

Films

2473 Candelaria, Cordelia. Film portrayals of La Mujer Hispana. AGENDA, Vol. 11, no. 3 (May, June, 1981), p. 32-36. English. DESCR: Stereotypes.

2474 Cortes, Carlos E. Chicanas in film: history of an image. BILINGUAL REVIEW, Vol. 10, no. 2-3 (May, December, 1983), p. 94-108. English. DESCR: Film Reviews; *Stereotypes.

2475 Fregoso, Rosa Linda. La quinceanera of Chicana counter aesthetics. CENTRO BULLETIN, Vol. 3, no. 1 (Winter 1990, 1991), p. [87]-91. English. DESCR: *AGUEDA MARTINEZ [film]; ANIMA [film]; *CHICANA! [film]; *DESPUES DEL TERREMOTO [film]; Espana, Frances Salome; Feminism; Morales, Sylvia; Portillo, Lourdes; Vasquez, Esperanza.

2476 Hadley-Freydberg, Elizabeth. Prostitutes, concubines, whores and bitches: Black and Hispanic women in contemporary American film. IN: McCluskey, Audrey T., ed. WOMEN OF COLOR: PERSPECTIVES ON FEMINISM AND IDENTITY. Bloomington, IN: Women's Studies Program, Indiana University, 1985, p. 46-65. English. DESCR: *Actors and Actresses; Blacks; Puerto Ricans; *Sex Stereotypes; Stereotypes; Women.

2477 Kernan, Lisa. Keep marching sisters: the second generation looks at SALT OF THE EARTH. NUESTRO, Vol. 9, no. 4 (May 1985), p. 23-25. English. DESCR: *SALT OF THE EARTH [film]; Strikes and Lockouts.

2478 Morales, Sylvia. Chicano-produced celluloid mujeres. BILINGUAL REVIEW, Vol. 10, no. 2-3 (May, December, 1983), p. 89-93. English. DESCR: BALLAD OF GREGORIO CORTEZ [film]; Film Reviews; RAICES DE SANGRE [film]; SEGUIN [movie]; *Stereotypes; ZOOT SUIT [film].

2479 Ordonez, Elizabeth J. La imagen de la mujer en el nuevo cine chicano. CARACOL, Vol. 5, no. 2 (October 1978), p. 12-13. Spanish. DESCR: Bonilla-Giannini, Roxanna; Lopez, Lexore; ONLY ONCE IN A LIFETIME [film]; *Photography; RAICES DE SANGRE [film]; Robelo, Miguel; Sex Stereotypes.

Films (cont.)

2480 Tafolla, Carmen. To split a human: mitos, machos y la mujer chicana. San Antonio, TX: Mexican American Cultural Center, 1985. 115 p.: ill. English. DESCR: Discrimination; Education; *Feminism; *Sex Roles; Sex Stereotypes; *Sexism.

Financial Aid

2481 Munoz, Daniel G. Identifying areas of stress for Chicano undergraduates. IN: Olivas, Michael A., ed. LATINO COLLEGE STUDENTS. New York: Teachers College Press, 1986, p. 131-156. English. DESCR: Academic Achievement; *Attitudes; Colleges and Universities; *Stress; Surveys.

First Meeting of Latin American and Caribbean Feminist Lesbians (October 14-17, 1987: Cuernavaca, Mexico)

2482 Yarbro-Bejarano, Yvonne. Primer encuentro de lesbianas feministas latinoamericanas y caribenas. THIRD WOMAN, Vol. 4, (1989), p. 143-146. English. DESCR: Caribbean Region; *Conferences and Meetings; *Homosexuality; Latin Americans; Sexual Behavior; *Women.

First National Chicana Conference (May 1971: Houston, TX)

2483 Anonymous. Workshop resolutions - First National Chicana Conference, May 1971. IN: Garcia, Richard A., ed. CHICANOS IN AMERICA, 1540-1974: A CHRONOLOGY AND FACT BOOK. Dobbs Ferry, NY: Oceana Publications, 1977, p. 142-144. English. DESCR: Conferences and Meetings; Feminism.

2484 Flores, Francisca. Conference of Mexican women un remolino. REGENERACION, Vol. 1, no. 10 (1971), p. 1-5. English. DESCR: Conferences and Meetings; Family; Feminism; Machismo; National Mexican American Issues Conference (October 11, 1970: Sacramento, CA); Sex Roles; Sex Stereotypes; Statistics; *Women Men Relations.

2485 Lopez, Sonia A. The role of the Chicana within the student movement. IN: Sanchez, Rosaura and Martinez Cruz, Rosa, eds. ESSAYS ON LA MUJER. Los Angeles, CA: Chicano Studies Center Publications, UCLA, 1977, p. 16-29. English. DESCR: Chicano Movement; Conferences and Meetings; Feminism; *Student Movements.

2486 Vidal, Mirta. Women new voice of La Raza. IN: Garcia, Richard A., ed. CHICANOS IN AMERICA, 1540-1974: A CHRONOLOGY AND FACT BOOK. Dobbs Ferry, NY: Oceana Publications, 1977, p. 132-140. English. DESCR: Conferences and Meetings; Feminism.

First, Ruth

2487 Harlow, Barbara. Sites of struggle: immigration, deportation, prison, and exile. IN: Calderon, Hector and Saldivar, Jose David, eds. CRITICISM IN THE BORDERLANDS: STUDIES IN CHICANO LITERATURE, CULTURE, AND IDEOLOGY. Durham, NC: Duke University Press, 1991, p. [149]-163 English. DESCR: Anzaldua, Gloria; BLACK GOLD; BORDERLANDS/LA FRONTERA: THE NEW MESTIZA; Khalifeh, Sahar; *Literary Criticism; *Political Ideology; Sanchez, Rosaura; Social Classes; "The Cariboo Cafe" [short story]; "The Ditch" [short story]; Viramontes, Helena Maria; WILD THORNS; *Women; Working Women.

LA FLOR MAS BELLA DE LA MAQUILADORA

2488 Lavrin, Asuncion. El segundo sexo en Mexico: experiencia, estudio e introspeccion, 1983-1987. MEXICAN STUDIES/ESTUDIOS MEXICANOS, Vol. 5, no. 2 (Summer 1989), p. 297-312. Spanish. DESCR: Arenal, Sandra; *Border Industries; Carrillo, Jorge; Hernandez, Alberto; Iglesias, Norma; *Literature Reviews; Mexico; MUJERES FRONTERIZAS EN LA INDUSTRIA MAQUILADORA; SANGRE JOVEN: LAS MAQUILADORAS POR DENTRO; Women.

Flores, Art

2489 Huerta, Dolores. Dolores Huerta talks about Republicans, Cesar, children and her home town. REGENERACION, Vol. 2, no. 4 (1975), p. 20-24. English. DESCR: *Agricultural Labor Unions; *Biography; Chavez, Cesar E.; Community Service Organization, Los Angeles, (CSO); Democratic Party; Elected Officials; Huerta, Dolores; McGovern, George; *Politics; Ramirez, Henry M.; Ross, Fred; Sanchez, Philip V.; United Farmworkers of America (UFW); Working Women.

2490 Huerta, Dolores. Dolores Huerta talks about Republicans, Cesar, children and her home town. IN: Servin, Manuel P. ed. THE MEXICAN AMERICANS: AN AWAKENING MINORITY. 2nd ed. Beverly Hills, CA: Glencoe Press, 1974, p. 283-294. English. DESCR: *Agricultural Labor Unions; *Biography; Chavez, Cesar E.; Community Service Organization, Los Angeles, (CSO); Democratic Party; Elected Officials; Huerta, Dolores; McGovern, George; *Politics; Ramirez, Henry M.; Ross, Fred; Sanchez, Philip V.; United Farmworkers of America (UFW); Working Women.

Flores de Andrade, Senora

2491 Gamio, Manuel. Senora Flores de Andrade. IN: Mora, Magdalena and Del Castillo, Adelaida, eds. MEXICAN WOMEN IN THE UNITED STATES: STRUGGLES PAST AND PRESENT. Los Angeles, CA: Chicano Studies Research Center, UCLA, 1980, p. 189-192. English. DESCR: Autobiography; Immigrants; Mexican Revolution - 1910-1920; *Oral History.

Flores, Francisca

2492 Escalante, Alicia. Chicana Welfare Rights vs. the Talmadge amendment. LA RAZA, Vol. 2, no. 1 (February 1974), p. 20-21. English. DESCR: Chicana Welfare Rights Organization; Talmadge Amendment to the Social Security Act, 1971; *Welfare.

2493 Matsuda, Gema. La Chicana organizes: the Comision Femenil Mexicana in perspective. REGENERACION, Vol. 2, no. 4 (1975), p. 25-27. English. DESCR: Bojorquez, Frances; Chicano Movement; *Comision Femenil Mexicana Nacional; De la Cruz, Juana Ines; History; Machismo; Malinche; Prisons; Sex Stereotypes; *Sexism.

2494 Rincon, Bernice. Chicanas on the move. REGENERACION, Vol. 2, no. 4 (1975), p. 52. English. DESCR: Population; *Sexism.

Flores, Gloriamalia

2495 Goldman, Shifra M. Artistas en accion: conferencia de las mujeres chicanas. LA COMUNIDAD, (August 10, 1980), p. 15. Spanish. DESCR: *Artists; Chicano Studies; Conferences and Meetings; Lomas Garza, Carmen.

Flores Magon, Ricardo

2496 Hernandez, Ines. Sara Estela Ramirez: the early twentieth century Texas-Mexican poet. Thesis (Ph.D.)--University of Houston, 1984. 94 p. English. DESCR: *Authors; *Biography; Feminism; Journalism; Literary Criticism; Mexican Revolution - 1910-1920; Mexico; *Poetry; Ramirez, Sara Estela; Texas; Women.

2497 Hernandez, Ines. Sara Estela Ramirez: sembradora. LEGACY: A JOURNAL OF NINETEENTH-CENTURY AMERICAN WOMEN WRITERS, Vol. 6, no. 1 (Spring 1989), p. 13-26. English. DESCR: Authors; *Biography; *Feminism; *Journalism; LA CORREGIDORA [newspaper]; Mexican Revolution - 1910-1920; Mexico; Newspapers; Poetry; *Ramirez, Sara Estela; REGENERACION [newspaper].

2498 Perez, Emma. "A la mujer": a critique of the Partido Liberal Mexicano's gender ideology on women. IN: Del Castillo, Adelaida R., ed. BETWEEN BORDERS: ESSAYS ON MEXICANA/CHICANA HISTORY. Encino, CA: Floricanto Press, 1990, p. 459-482. English. DESCR: *"A La Mujer" [essay]; Essays; *Feminism; Guerrero, Praxedis G.; Journalism; Mexican Revolution - 1910-1920; Mexico; Newspapers; *Partido Liberal Mexicano (PLM); Political Ideology; Political Parties and Organizations; *REGENERACION [newspaper]; Sex Roles; Women.

Flores, Maria

2499 Goldman, Shifra M. Women artists of Texas: MAS = More + Artists + Women = MAS. CHISMEARTE, no. 7 (January 1981), p. 21-22. English. DESCR: Arredondo, Alicia; Art Organizations and Groups; Barraza, Santa; Exhibits; Feminism; Folk Art; Gonzalez Dodson, Nora; *Mujeres Artistas del Suroeste (MAS), Austin, TX; Photography; Texas; Trevino, Modesta Barbina; WOMEN & THEIR WORK [festival] (Austin, TX: 1977).

2500 Orozco, Sylvia. Las mujeres--Chicana artists come into their own. MOVING ON, Vol. 2, no. 3 (May 1978), p. 14-16. English. DESCR: Art Organizations and Groups; Artists; Barraza, Santa; Gonzalez Dodson, Nora; *Mujeres Artistas del Suroeste (MAS), Austin, TX; Trevino, Modesta Barbina.

Florida

2501 Hintz, Joy. Valiant migrant women = Las mujeres valerosas. Tiffin, OH: Sayger Printing, 1982. viii, 98 p. English. DESCR: Battered Women; *Farm Workers; Feminism; Marriage; Migrant Children; Migrant Health Services; Migrant Housing; *Migrant Labor; Migration Patterns; Ohio; Sex Roles; Texas.

Folic Acid Deficiency

2502 Fanelli-Kuczmarski, Marie T., et al. Folate status of Mexican American, Cuban, and Puerto Rican women. AMERICAN JOURNAL OF CLINICAL NUTRITION, Vol. 52, no. 2 (August 1990), p. 368-372. English. DESCR: Cubanos; Hispanic Health and Nutrition Examination Survey (HHANES); *Nutrition; Puerto Ricans; *Women.

Folk Art

2503 Altars as folk art. ARRIBA, Vol. 1, no. 1 (July 1980), p. 4. English. DESCR: *Altars; Artists; De Leon, Josefina; Religious Art.

2504 Goldman, Shifra M. Women artists of Texas: MAS = More + Artists + Women = MAS. CHISMEARTE, no. 7 (January 1981), p. 21-22. English. DESCR: Arredondo, Alicia; Art Organizations and Groups; Barraza, Santa; Exhibits; Feminism; Flores, Maria; Gonzalez Dodson, Nora; *Mujeres Artistas del Suroeste (MAS), Austin, TX; Photography; Texas; Trevino, Modesta Barbina; WOMEN & THEIR WORK [festival] (Austin, TX: 1977).

2505 Lomas Garza, Carmen. Altares: arte espiritual del hogar. HOJAS, (1976), p. 105-111. English. DESCR: *Altars; Artists; Lomas Garza, Carmen; Religious Art.

2506 Navar, M. Margarita. La vela prendida: home altars. ARRIBA, Vol. 1, no. 5 (February 1980), p. 12. English. DESCR: *Altars; Artists; Exhibits; Religious Art.

2507 Nelson, Kathryn J. Excerpts from los testamentos: Hispanic women folk artists of the San Luis Valley, Colorado. FRONTIERS: A JOURNAL OF WOMEN STUDIES, Vol. 5, no. 3 (Fall 1980), p. 34-43. English. DESCR: *Archuleta, Eppie; Artists; Biography; San Luis Valley, CO.

2508 Texas Memorial Museum, University of Texas, Austin, TX. La vela prendida: Mexican-American women's home altars. Exhibition catalog, 1980. Bilingual. DESCR: *Altars; Artists; Catalogues; Exhibits.

Folk Medicine

2509 Buss, Fran Leeper. La partera: story of a midwife. Ann Arbor, MI: University of Michigan Press, 1980. 140 p.: ill. English. DESCR: Aragon, Jesusita, 1908-; Cultural Customs; *Curanderas; Herbal Medicine; *Midwives; New Mexico; San Miguel County, NM.

2510 Kay, Margarita Artschwager and Yoder, Marianne. Hot and cold in women's ethnotherapeutics: the American-Mexican West. SOCIAL SCIENCE & MEDICINE, Vol. 25, no. 4 (1987), p. 347-355. English. DESCR: *Diseases; Herbal Medicine; Mexico; Southwestern United States.

2511 Macklin, June. "All the good and bad in this world": women, traditional medicine, and Mexican American culture. IN: Melville, Margarita B., ed. TWICE A MINORITY. St. Louis, MO: Mosby, 1980, p. 127-148. English. DESCR: *Curanderismo; Sex Roles.

2512 Mayers, Raymond Sanchez. Use of folk medicine by elderly Mexican-American women. JOURNAL OF DRUG ISSUES, Vol. 19, no. 2 (1989), p. 283-295. English. DESCR: Age Groups; *Ancianos; Curanderas; Curanderismo.

2513 Perrone, Bobette; Stockel, H. Henrietta; and Krueger, Victoria. Medicine women, curanderas, and women doctors. Norman, OK: University of Oklahoma Press, c1989. xix, 252 p.:ill. English. DESCR: Aragon, Jesusita, 1908-; *Curanderas; *Curanderismo; Herbal Medicine; Herrera, Sabinita; Medical Personnel; Native Americans; *Oral History; Rodriguez, Gregorita; Women.

Folk Songs

2514 Herrera-Sobek, Maria. The treacherous woman archetype: a structuring agent in the corrido. AZTLAN, Vol. 13, no. 1-2 (Spring, Fall, 1982), p. 135-143. English. DESCR: *Corridos; Music.

Folklife
USE: Cultural Customs

Folklore

2515 Blea, Irene I. Brujeria: a sociological analysis of Mexican American witches. IN: Barrera, Mario, et al., eds. WORK, FAMILY, SEX ROLES, LANGUAGE: SELECTED PAPERS, 1979. Berkeley, CA: Tonatiuh-Quinto Sol, 1980, p. 177-193. English. DESCR: *Brujas; Colorado; Kiev, Ari; New Mexico.

2516 Cota-Robles de Suarez, Cecilia. Sexual stereotypes--psychological and cultural survival: a description of child-rearing practices attributed to the Chicana (the Mexican American woman) and its psychological and cultural implications. REGENERACION, Vol. 2, no. 3 (1973), p. 17, 20-21. English. DESCR: Cultural Characteristics; Family; Language; Parenting; Sex Stereotypes; *Sexism; *Stereotypes.

2517 Jones, Pamela. "There was a woman": La Llorona in Oregon. WESTERN FOLKLORE, Vol. 47, no. 3 (July 1988), p. 195-211. English. DESCR: *La Llorona; *Leyendas; Oregon; Research Methodology.

2518 Jordan, Rosan Augusta. The vaginal serpent and other themes from Mexican-American women's lore. IN: Jordan, Rosan A. and Kalcik, Susan J., eds. WOMEN'S FOLKLORE, WOMEN'S CULTURE. Philadelphia: University of Pennsylvania Press, 1985, p. 26-44. English. DESCR: Cuentos; Fertility; La Llorona; *Leyendas; *Sex Roles; Sexism; Sexual Behavior.

2519 Limon, Jose E. [anthropologist]. La Llorona, the third legend of greater Mexico: cultural symbols, women, and the political unconscious. RENATO ROSALDO LECTURE SERIES MONOGRAPH, Vol. 2, (Spring 1986), p. [59]-93. English. DESCR: *Feminism; *La Llorona; La Virgen de Guadalupe; *Leyendas; Malinche; Mexico; *Symbolism; Women.

2520 Limon, Jose E. [anthropologist]. La Llorona, the third legend of greater Mexico: cultural symbols, women, and the political unconscious. IN: Del Castillo, Adelaida R. BETWEEN BORDERS: ESSAYS ON MEXICANA/CHICANA HISTORY. Encino, CA: Floricanto Press, 1990, p. 399-432. English. DESCR: *Feminism; *La Llorona; La Virgen de Guadalupe; *Leyendas; Malinche; Mexico; *Symbolism; Women.

2521 Limon, Jose E. [anthropologist]. "La vieja Ines," a Mexican folkgame: a research note. IN: Melville, Margarita B., ed. TWICE A MINORITY. St. Louis, MO: Mosby, 1980, p. 88-94. English. DESCR: Children; *Games; *Sex Roles.

2522 Pena, Manuel. Class, gender, and machismo: the "treacherous-woman" folklore of Mexican male workers. GENDER & SOCIETY, Vol. 5, no. 1 (March 1991), p. 30-46. English. DESCR: Laborers; *Machismo; Males; *Sex Roles; Sex Stereotypes; Social Classes; *Undocumented Workers; Women Men Relations.

2523 Velasquez-Treviro, Gloria. Jovita Gonzalez,

una voz de resistencia cultural en la temprana narrativa chicana. IN: Lopez-Gonzalez, Aralia, et al., eds. MUJER Y LITERATURA MEXICANA Y CHICANA: CULTURAS EN CONTACTO. Mexico: Colegio de la Frontera Norte, 1988, p. [77]-83. Spanish. DESCR: Anglo Americans; Authors; Feminism; *Gonzalez, Jovita; Intergroup Relations; *League of United Latin American Citizens (LULAC).

Folktales
USE: Cuentos

Food Industry

2524 Jensen, Joan M. Canning comes to New Mexico: women and the agricultural extension service, 1914-1919. NEW MEXICO HISTORICAL REVIEW, Vol. 57, no. 4 (October 1982), p. 361-386. English. DESCR: *Canneries; New Mexico; New Mexico Agricultural Extension Service.

2525 Keremitsis, Dawn. Del metate al molino: la mujer mexicana de 1910 a 1940. HISTORIA MEXICANA, Vol. 33, no. 2 (1983), p. 285-302. Spanish. DESCR: History; Labor Unions; Mexico; Sex Roles; Strikes and Lockouts; Women; *Working Women.

2526 Mora, Magdalena. The Tolteca Strike: Mexican women and the struggle for union representation. IN: Rios-Bustamante, Antonio, ed. MEXICAN IMMIGRANT WORKERS IN THE U.S. Los Angeles, CA: Chicano Studies Research Center Publications, University of California, 1981, p. 111-117. English. DESCR: Centro de Accion Social Autonomo (CASA); *Labor Unions; *Strikes and Lockouts; Toltec Foods, Richmond, CA.

2527 Rips, Geoffrey and Tenayuca, Emma. Living history: Emma Tenayuca tells her story. TEXAS OBSERVER, (October 28, 1983), p. 7-15. English. DESCR: *Autobiography; Communist Party; Labor Unions; Leadership; Oral History; Pecan Shelling Worker's Union, San Antonio, TX; San Antonio, TX; Strikes and Lockouts; Tenayuca, Emma; United Cannery Agricultural Packing and Allied Workers of America (UCAPAWA); Worker's Alliance (WA), Los Angeles, CA; Working Women.

2528 Romero, Mary and Margolis, Eric. Tending the beets: campesinas and the Great Western Sugar Company. REVISTA MUJERES, Vol. 2, no. 2 (June 1985), p. 17-27. English. DESCR: *Farm Workers; Great Western Sugar Company, Hudson, CO; South Platte Valley, CO.

2529 Ruiz, Vicki L. UCAPAWA, Chicanas, and the California food processing industry, 1937-1950. Thesis (Ph.D.)--Stanford University, 1982. x, 281 p. English. DESCR: *Canneries; *Labor Unions; Trade Unions; United Cannery Agricultural Packing and Allied Workers of America (UCAPAWA); Working Women.

2530 Spence, Mary Lee. Commentary [on "And Miles to Go": Mexican Women and Work, 1930-1985]. IN: Schlissel, Lillian, et al., eds. WESTERN WOMEN: THEIR LAND, THEIR LIVES. Albuquerque, NM: University of New Mexico Press, 1988, p. 145-150. English. DESCR: "'And Miles to Go...': Mexican Women and Work, 1930-1985"; Income; Labor Unions; Restaurants; Ruiz, Vicki L.; *Working Women.

Food Practices

2531 Olvera-Ezzell, Norma; Power, Thomas G.; and Cousins, Jennifer H. Maternal socialization of children's eating habits: strategies used by obese Mexican-American mothers. CHILD DEVELOPMENT, Vol. 61, no. 2 (April 1990), p. 395-400. English. DESCR: Children; *Nutrition; *Obesity; *Parent and Child Relationships; *Socialization.

2532 Williams, Brett. Why migrant women feed their husbands tamales: foodways as a basis for a revisionist view of Tejano family life. IN: Brown, Linda Keller and Mussell, Kay, eds. ETHNIC AND REGIONAL FOODWAYS IN THE UNITED STATES: THE PERFORMANCE OF GROUP IDENTITY. Knoxville, TN: University of Tennessee Press, 1984, p. 113-126. English. DESCR: Cultural Customs; Extended Family; Family; Illinois; *Migrant Labor; Sex Roles; Tamales; Texas.

2533 Wolff, Cindy Brattan. Diet and pregnancy outcome in Mexican-American women. Thesis (Ph.D.)--Colorado State University, 1988. 257 p. English. DESCR: *Fertility; *Maternal and Child Welfare; *Nutrition.

Food Stamps

2534 Hancock, Paula F. The effect of welfare eligibility on the labor force participation of women of Mexican origin in California. POPULATION RESEARCH AND POLICY REVIEW, Vol. 5, no. 2 (1986), p. 163-185. English. DESCR: Aid to Families with Dependent Children (AFDC); California; *Employment; Immigrants; Medi-Cal; Single Parents; *Welfare; Women.

Foreign Policy
USE: International Relations

Foreign Trade

2535 Bustamante, Jorge A. Maquiladoras: a new face of international capitalism on Mexico's northern frontier. IN: Nash, June and Fernandez-Kelly, Patricia, eds. WOMEN, MEN, AND THE INTERNATIONAL DIVISION OF LABOR. Albany, NY: State University of New York Press, 1983, p. 224-256. English. DESCR: Banking Industry; Border Industrialization Program (BIP); Border Industries; *Border Region; Industrial Workers; International Economic Relations; Mexico; Population; Programa Nacional Fronterizo (PRONAF); United States-Mexico Relations; Women; Working Women.

Fotonovelas

2536 Carrillo, Loretta and Lyson, Thomas A. The fotonovela as a cultural bridge of Hispanic women in the United States. JOURNAL OF POPULAR CULTURE, Vol. 17, no. 3 (Winter 1983), p. 59-64. English.

Free Clinics

2537 Delgado, Sylvia. Chicana: the forgotten woman. REGENERACION, Vol. 2, no. 1 (1971), p. 2-4. English. DESCR: *Abortion; *Women Men Relations; Working Women.

Frente de Costureras, Mexico

2538 Arbelaez A., Marisol. Impacto social del sismo, Mexico 1985: las costureras. IN: Del Castillo, Adelaida R., ed. BETWEEN BORDERS: ESSAYS ON MEXICANA/CHICANA HISTORY. Encino, CA: Floricanto Press, 1990, p. 315-331. Spanish. DESCR: Earthquakes; *Garment Industry; *Industrial Workers; Labor Unions; *Mexico; Mexico City Earthquake, September 19, 1985; *Women; Working Women.

Frente Unido Pro Derechos de la Mujer

2539 Ruiz Funes, Concepcion and Tunon, Enriqueta. Panorama de las luchas de la mujer mexicana en el siglo XX. IN: Del Castillo, Adelaida R., ed. BETWEEN BORDERS: ESSAYS ON MEXICANA/CHICANA HISTORY. Encino, CA: Floricanto Press, 1990, p. 336-357. Spanish. DESCR: Coordinadora de Mujeres Trabajadoras; *Feminism; History; Labor Unions; *Mexico; Sex Roles; *Women.

FRIEZE

2540 Bruce-Novoa, Juan. Deconstructing the dominant patriarchal text: Cecile Pineda's narratives. IN: Horno-Delgado, Asuncion, et al., eds. BREAKING BOUNDARIES: LATINA WRITING AND CRITICAL READINGS. Amherst, MA: University of Massachusetts Press, c1989, p. 72-81. English. DESCR: *FACE; Identity; Literary Criticism; Novel; *Pineda, Cecile.

Funerals

2541 Williams, Norma. Changes in funeral patterns and gender roles among Mexican Americans. IN: Ruiz, Vicki L. and Tiano, Susan, eds. WOMEN ON THE U.S.-MEXICO BORDER: RESPONSES TO CHANGE. Boston, MA: Allen & Unwin, 1987, p. 197-217. English. DESCR: Assimilation; Austin, TX; Cultural Customs; Sex Roles.

Gaitan, Maria Elena

2542 Escalante, Virginia; Rivera, Nancy; and Valle, Victor Manuel. Inside the world of Latinas. IN: SOUTHERN CALIFORNIA'S LATINO COMMUNITY: A SERIES OF ARTICLES REPRINTED FROM THE LOS ANGELES TIMES. Los Angeles: Los Angeles Times, 1983, p. 82-91. English. DESCR: *Biography; Castillo Fierro, Catalina (Katie); Gutierrez, Nancy; Luna Mount, Julia; Ramirez, Cristina.

Galindo, P. (Pseud. for Rolando Hinojosa-Smith)
USE: Hinojosa-Smith, Rolando R.

Gallo, Juana

2543 Longeaux y Vasquez, Enriqueta. The woman of La Raza. REGENERACION, Vol. 2, no. 4 (1975), p. 34-36. English. DESCR: Child Care Centers; Discrimination; Housing; La Adelita; Machismo; Sex Roles; *Social History and Conditions; Working Women.

2544 Longeaux y Vasquez, Enriqueta. The woman of La Raza. IN: Valdez, Luis and Steiner, Stan, eds. AZTLAN: AN ANTHOLOGY OF MEXICAN AMERICAN LITERATURE. New York: Vintage Books, 1972, p. 272-278. Also IN: Salinas, Luis Omar and Faderman, Lillian, compilers. FROM THE BARRIO: A CHICANO ANTHOLOGY. San Francisco, CA: Canfield Press, 1973, p. 20-24. English. DESCR: Child Care Centers; Discrimination; Housing; La Adelita; Machismo; Sex Roles; *Social History and Conditions; Working Women.

2545 Mercado, Olivia. Chicanas: myths and roles. COMADRE, no. 1 (Summer 1977), p. 26-32. English. DESCR: Feminism; Huerta, Dolores; *Identity; Leadership; Sex Roles.

Games

2546 Limon, Jose E. [anthropologist]. "La vieja Ines," a Mexican folkgame: a research note. IN: Melville, Margarita B., ed. TWICE A MINORITY. St. Louis, MO: Mosby, 1980, p. 88-94. English. DESCR: Children; *Folklore; *Sex Roles.

Gangs

2547 Blanco, Gilbert M. Las Adelitas del Barrio. LATIN QUARTER, Vol. 1, no. 3 (January, February, 1975), p. 30-32. English. DESCR: City Terrace, CA; Community Development; *Latin Empresses; Youth.

2548 Harris, Mary G. Cholas: Latino girls and gangs. New York: AMS Press, 1988. x, 220 p. English. DESCR: Barrios; Juvenile Delinquency; Los Angeles, CA; San Fernando Valley, CA; *Youth.

2549 Moore, Joan W. Mexican-American women addicts: the influence of family background. IN: Glick, Ronald and Moore, Joan, eds. DRUGS IN HISPANIC COMMUNITIES. New Brunswick, NJ: Rutgers University Press, c1990, p. 127-153. English. DESCR: Barrios; *Drug Addicts; Drug Use; East Los Angeles, CA; *Family; Heroin; Hoyo-Mara Gang, East Los Angeles, CA; Pachucos; Sex Roles; Socialization; White Fence Gang; Youth.

2550 Moore, Joan W. and Levitt, Mary. The paradox of deviance in addicted Mexican American mothers. GENDER & SOCIETY, Vol. 3, no. 1 (March 1989), p. 53-70. English. DESCR: Children; *Drug Addicts; *Drug Use; Family; *Fertility; Parenting; Sex Roles.

Garcia, Connie

2551 Zavella, Patricia. The politics of race and gender: organizing Chicana cannery workers in Northern California. IN: Bookman, Ann and Morgen, Sandra, eds. WOMEN AND THE POLITICS OF EMPOWERMENT. Philadelphia, PA: Temple University Press, 1988, p. 202-224. English. DESCR: Bay City Cannery Workers Committee; *Canneries; Cannery Workers Committee (CWC); Discrimination; Identity; *Labor Unions; Nationalism; Northern California; Santa Clara Valley, CA; Sex Roles; Sexism; *Working Women.

Garcia, Dolly

2552 Santillanes, Maria. Women in prison--C.I.W.: an editorial. REGENERACION, Vol. 2, no. 4 (1975), p. 53. English. DESCR: Conferences and Meetings; La Mesa College Pinto and Pinta Program; Lopez, Tony; Mares, Rene; Martinez, Miguel; Pinto Conference (1973: UCLA); Player; *Prisons; Salazar, Peggy.

Garcia, Juliet

2553 Olivera, Mercedes. The new Hispanic women. VISTA, Vol. 2, no. 11 (July 5, 1987), p. 6-8. English. DESCR: Alvarez, Linda; Esquiroz, Margarita; *Hernandez, Antonia A.; Mohr, Nicolasa; Molina, Gloria; Fabon, Maria; Working Women.

Garcia-Lorca, Federico

2554 Dewey, Janice. Dona Josefa: bloodpulse of transition and change. IN: Horno-Delgado, Asuncion, et al. eds. BREAKING BOUNDARIES: LATINA WRITING AND CRITICAL READINGS. Amherst, MA: University of Massachusetts Press, c1989, p. 39-47. English. DESCR: *DAY OF THE SWALLOWS; LA CASA DE BERNARDA ALBA; Literary Characters; Literary Criticism; *Portillo Trambley, Estela.

Garment Industry

2555 Arbelaez A., Marisol. Impacto social del sismo, Mexico 1985: las costureras. IN: Del Castillo, Adelaida R., ed. BETWEEN BORDERS: ESSAYS ON MEXICANA/CHICANA HISTORY. Encino, CA: Floricanto Press, 1990, p. 315-331. Spanish. DESCR: Earthquakes; Frente de Costureras, Mexico; *Industrial Workers; Labor Unions; *Mexico; Mexico City Earthquake, September 19, 1985; *Women; Working Women.

2556 Arroyo, Laura E. Industrial and occupational distribution of Chicana workers. AZTLAN, Vol. 4, no. 2 (Fall 1973), p. 343-382. English. DESCR: California; *Employment; Farah Manufacturing Co., El Paso, TX; Farah Strike; Industrial Workers; Strikes and Lockouts; Texas.

2557 Arroyo, Laura E. Industrial and occupational distribution of Chicana workers. IN: Sanchez, Rosaura and Martinez Cruz, Rosa, eds. ESSAYS ON LA MUJER. Los Angeles, CA: Chicano Studies Center Publications, UCLA, 1977, p. 150-187. English. DESCR: California; *Employment; Farah Manufacturing Co., El Paso, TX; Farah Strike; Industrial Workers; Strikes and Lockouts; Texas.

2558 Coyle, Laurie; Hershatter, Gail; and Honig, Emily. Women at Farah: an unfinished story. IN: Mora, Magdalena and Del Castillo, Adelaida, eds. MEXICAN WOMEN IN THE UNITED STATES: STRUGGLES PAST AND PRESENT. Los Angeles, CA: Chicano Studies Research Center, UCLA, 1980, p. 117-143. English. DESCR: Farah Manufacturing Co., El Paso, TX; Farah Strike; Labor Unions; *Strikes and Lockouts.

2559 Duron, Clementina. Mexican women and labor conflict in Los Angeles: the ILGWU dressmakers' strike of 1933. AZTLAN, Vol. 15, no. 1 (Spring 1984), p. 145-161. English. DESCR: International Ladies Garment Workers Union (ILGWU); Labor Unions; *Strikes and Lockouts.

2560 Fernandez Kelly, Maria. "Chavalas de maquiladora": a study of the female labor force in Ciudad Juarez' offshore production plants. Thesis (Ph.D.)--Rutgers University, 1980. xi, 391 leaves. English. DESCR: *Border Industries; Ciudad Juarez, Chihuahua, Mexico; Electronics Industry; *Employment; Industrial Workers; Mexico; Women; *Working Women.

2561 Fernandez Kelly, Maria and Garcia, Anna M. Economic restructuring in the United States: Hispanic women in the garment and electronics industries. WOMEN AND WORK, Vol. 3, (1988), p. 49-65. English. DESCR: Business Enterprises; Businesspeople; *Electronics Industry; Industrial Workers; *International Economic Relations; *Working Women.

2562 Fernandez Kelly, Maria. For we are sold, I and my people: women and industry in Mexico's frontier. Albany, NY: State University of New York Press, 1983. vii, 217 p. English. DESCR: Border Industries; *Border Region; Ciudad Juarez, Chihuahua, Mexico; *Electronics Industry; Industrial Workers; Working Women.

Garment Industry (cont.)

2563 Fernandez Kelly, Maria and Garcia, Anna M. The making of an underground economy: Hispanic women, home work, and the advanced capitalist state. URBAN ANTHROPOLOGY, Vol. 14, no. 1-3 (Spring, Fall, 1985), p. 59-90. English. DESCR: Capitalism; Cubanos; Employment; Industrial Workers; International Economic Relations; Labor Supply and Market; *Los Angeles County, CA; *Miami, FL; Women; Working Women.

2564 Jaech, Richard E. Latin American undocumented women in the United States. CURRENTS IN THEOLOGY AND MISSION, Vol. 9, no. 4 (August 1982), p. 196-211. English. DESCR: Latin Americans; Protestant Church; Socioeconomic Factors; *Undocumented Workers; *Women.

2565 Mendoza, Hope Schecter and Chall, Malca. Activist in the labor movement, the Democratic Party, and the Mexican-American community: an interview. Berkeley, CA: Regional Oral History Office, Bancroft Library, University of California, Berkeley, 1980. xii, 170 p.: ill. English. DESCR: *Biography; Chavez Ravine, Los Angeles, CA; Church, Frank; Community Organizations; Community Service Organization, Los Angeles, (CSO); Democratic Party; Elections; Industrial Workers; *Labor Unions; Leadership; Mendoza, Hope Schecter; Snyder, Elizabeth; Warschaw, Carmen.

2566 Monroy, Douglas. La costura en Los Angeles, 1933-1939: the ILGWU and the politics of domination. IN: Mora, Magdalena and Del Castillo, Adelaida, eds. MEXICAN WOMEN IN THE UNITED STATES: STRUGGLES PAST AND PRESENT. Los Angeles, CA: Chicano Studies Research Center, UCLA, 1980, p. 171-178. English. DESCR: History; International Ladies Garment Workers Union (ILGWU); Labor Unions; Los Angeles, CA.

2567 Olivares, Yvette. The sweatshop: the garment industry's reborn child. REVISTA MUJERES, Vol. 3, no. 2 (June 1986), p. 55-62. English. DESCR: Labor; Public Health; Third World; *Undocumented Workers; *Women; Working Women.

2568 Vasquez, Mario F. The election day immigration raid at Lilli Diamond Originals and the response of the ILGWU. IN: Mora, Magdalena and Del Castillo, Adelaida, eds. MEXICAN WOMEN IN THE UNITED STATES: STRUGGLES PAST AND PRESENT. Los Angeles, CA: Chicano Studies Research Center, UCLA, 1980, p. 145-148. English. DESCR: Immigration Regulation and Control; International Ladies Garment Workers Union (ILGWU); Labor Unions; *Lilli Diamond Originals; Undocumented Workers; Women; Working Women.

2569 Vasquez, Mario F. Immigrant workers and the apparel manufacturing industry in Southern California. IN: Rios-Bustamante, Antonio, ed. MEXICAN IMMIGRANT WORKERS IN THE U.S. Los Angeles, CA: Chicano Studies Research Center Publications, University of California, 1981, p. 85-96. English. DESCR: AFL-CIO; California; Immigrants; International Ladies Garment Workers Union (ILGWU); *Labor Supply and Market; Labor Unions; Undocumented Workers; Women.

2570 Young, Gay. Gender identification and working-class solidarity among maquila workers in Ciudad Juarez: stereotypes and realities. IN: Ruiz, Vicki L. and Tiano, Susan, eds. WOMEN ON THE U.S.-MEXICO BORDER:

RESPONSES TO CHANGE. Boston, MA: Allen & Unwin, 1987, p. 105-127. English. DESCR: Assertiveness; Attitudes; Border Industrialization Program (BIP); *Border Industries; Border Region; Ciudad Juarez, Chihuahua, Mexico; Employment; Sex Roles; Surveys; Working Women.

Garment Workers
USE: Industrial Workers

Garzon, Luz

2571 Sanchez, Elba R. La realidad a traves de la inocencia en el cuento: "Un Paseo". IN: Cordova, Teresa, et al., eds. CHICANA VOICES. Austin, TX: Center for Mexican American Studies, 1986, p. 202-207. Spanish. DESCR: Literary Criticism; Short Story; *"Un Paseo" [short story].

GATA POEMS

2572 Aguilar-Henson, Marcella. The multi-faceted poetic world of Angela de Hoyos. Austin, TX: Relampago Books Press, 1985, c1982. 81 p. English. DESCR: ARISE CHICANO; *Authors; CHICANO POEMS FOR THE BARRIO; de Hoyos, Angela; GOODBYE TO SILENCE; Language Usage; *Literary Criticism; *Poetry; SELECTED POEMS/SELECCIONES; YO, MUJER.

Gays
USE: Homosexuality

Geertz, Clifford

2573 Quintana, Alvina E. Ana Castillo's THE MIXQUIAHUALA LETTERS: the novelist as ethnographer. IN: Calderon, Hector and Saldivar, Jose David, eds. CRITICISM IN THE BORDERLANDS: STUDIES IN CHICANO LITERATURE, CULTURE, AND IDEOLOGY. Durham, NC: Duke University Press, 1991, p. [72]-83. English. DESCR: Anthropology; Castillo, Ana; Cultural Studies; *Ethnology; Feminism; *Literary Criticism; Novel; THE MIXQUIAHUALA LETTERS.

GENERACIONES Y SEMBLANZAS

2574 de la Fuente, Patricia and Duke dos Santos, Maria I. The elliptic female presence as unifying force in the novels of Rolando Hinojosa. REVISTA CHICANO-RIQUENA, Vol. 12, no. 3-4 (Fall, Winter, 1984), p. 64-75. English. DESCR: ESTAMPAS DEL VALLE Y OTRAS OBRAS; Hinojosa-Smith, Rolando R.; *Literary Criticism; MI QUERIDO RAFA; RITES AND WITNESSES.

Generations
USE: Age Groups

Ghetto
USE: Barrios

GIVING UP THE GHOST

2575 Alarcon, Norma. Making "familia" from scratch: split subjectivities in the work of Helena Maria Viramontes and Cherrie Moraga. THE AMERICAS REVIEW, Vol. 15, no. 3-4 (Fall, Winter, 1987), p. 147-159. English. DESCR: *Literary Criticism; Moraga, Cherrie; *Sex Roles; "Snapshots" [short story]; THE MOTHS AND OTHER STORIES; Viramontes, Helena Maria.

GIVING UP THE GHOST
(cont.)

2576 Herrera-Sobek, Maria. The politics of rape: sexual transgression in Chicana fiction. THE AMERICAS REVIEW, Vol. 15, no. 3-4 (Fall, Winter, 1987), p. 171-181. English. DESCR: Cisneros, Sandra; *Feminism; Fiction; *Literary Criticism; Lizarraga, Sylvia; Moraga, Cherrie; *Rape; "Red Clowns" [short story]; Sex Roles; "Silver Lake Road" [short story].

2577 Yarbro-Bejarano, Yvonne. Cherrie Moraga's GIVING UP THE GHOST: the representation of female desire. THIRD WOMAN, Vol. 3, no. 1-2 (1986), p. 113-120. English. DESCR: Homosexuality; Moraga, Cherrie; Teatro.

Glue Sniffing
USE: Drug Use

Godparents
USE: Compadrazgo

Goldman, Shifra M.

2578 Brown, Betty Ann. Chicanas speak out. ARTWEEK, Vol. 15, no. 2 (January 14, 1984), p. 1+. English. DESCR: *Art; Carrasco, Barbara; Carrillo, Graciela; CHICANA VOICES & VISIONS [exhibit]; Exhibits; Hernandez, Ester; Lerma Bowerman, Liz; Rodriguez, Carmen; Rodriguez, Sandra Maria; Social and Public Art Resource Center, Venice, CA (SPARC).

Gomez-Quinones, Juan

2579 Sanchez, Marta E. Judy Lucero and Bernice Zamora: two dialectical statements in Chicana poetry. DE COLORES, Vol. 4, no. 3 (1978), p. 22-33. Bilingual. DESCR: *Literary Criticism; Lucero, Judy A.; *Poetry; Zamora, Bernice.

2580 Sanchez, Marta E. Judy Lucero and Bernice Zamora: two dialectical statements in Chicana poetry. IN: Sommers, Joseph and Ybarra-Frausto, Tomas, eds. MODERN CHICANO WRITERS: A COLLECTION OF CRITICAL ESSAYS. Englewood Cliffs, NJ: Prentice-Hall, 1979, p. 141-149. English. DESCR: *Literary Criticism; Lucero, Judy A.; *Poetry; Zamora, Bernice.

Gonzales, Rebecca

2581 Gonzales, Rebecca and Binder, Wolfgang. [Interview with] Rebecca Gonzales. IN: Binder, Wolfgang, ed. PARTIAL AUTOBIOGRAPHIES: INTERVIEWS WITH TWENTY CHICANO POETS. Erlangen. W. Germany: Verlag Palm & Enke, 1985, p. 93-94. English. DESCR: Authors; Autobiography; Poetry.

Gonzales, Sylvia Alicia

2582 Trujillo Gaitan, Marcella. The dilemma of the modern Chicana artist and critic. DE COLORES, Vol. 3, no. 3 (1977), p. 38-43. Bilingual. DESCR: Art Criticism; Artists; *Chicano Movement; *Literary Criticism; Machismo; Malinche; *Poetry; Symbolism.

2583 Trujillo Gaitan, Marcella. The dilemma of the modern Chicana artist and critic. HERESIES, Vol. 2, no. 4 (1979), p. 5-10. English. DESCR: Art Criticism; Artists; Authors; *Chicano Movement; *Literary Criticism; Machismo; Malinche; *Poetry; Symbolism.

Gonzalez Dodson, Nora

2584 Goldman, Shifra M. Women artists of Texas: MAS = More + Artists + Women = MAS. CHISMEARTE, no. 7 (January 1981), p. 21-22. English. DESCR: Arredondo, Alicia; Art Organizations and Groups; Barraza, Santa; Exhibits; Feminism; Flores, Maria; Folk Art; *Mujeres Artistas del Suroeste (MAS), Austin, TX; Photography; Texas; Trevino, Modesta Barbina; WOMEN & THEIR WORK [festival] (Austin, TX: 1977).

2585 Orozco, Sylvia. Las mujeres--Chicana artists come into their own. MOVING ON, Vol. 2, no. 3 (May 1978), p. 14-16. English. DESCR: Art Organizations and Groups; Artists; Barraza, Santa; Flores, Maria; *Mujeres Artistas del Suroeste (MAS), Austin, TX; Trevino, Modesta Barbina.

Gonzalez, Jovita

2586 Velasquez-Trevino, Gloria. Cultural ambivalence in early Chicana prose fiction. Thesis (Ph.D.)--Stanford University, 1985. 185 p. English. DESCR: Biculturalism; *Fiction; Literary Criticism; Mena, Maria Cristina; Niggli, Josephina; Prose; Sex Roles.

2587 Velasquez-Trevino, Gloria. Jovita Gonzalez, una voz de resistencia cultural en la temprana narrativa chicana. IN: Lopez-Gonzalez, Aralia, et al., eds. MUJER Y LITERATURA MEXICANA Y CHICANA: CULTURAS EN CONTACTO. Mexico: Colegio de la Frontera Norte, 1988, p. [77]-83. Spanish. DESCR: Anglo Americans; Authors; Feminism; Folklore; Intergroup Relations; *League of United Latin American Citizens (LULAC).

Gonzalez Parsons, Lucia

2588 Delgado Campbell, Dolores. Shattering the stereotype: Chicanas as labor union organizers. BERKELEY WOMEN OF COLOR, no. 11 (Summer 1983), p. 20-23. English. DESCR: Farah Manufacturing Co., El Paso, TX; Farah Strike; Huerta, Dolores; *Labor Unions; Moreno, Luisa [union organizer]; Tenayuca, Emma; Working Women.

2589 Goldman, Shifra M. Trabajadoras mexicanas y chicanas en las artes visuales. IN: Leal, Salvador, ed. A TRAVES DE LA FRONTERA. Mexico, D.F.: Centro de Estudios Economicos y Sociales del Tercer Mundo, A.C.; Instituto de Investigaciones Esteticas, U.N.A.M., 1983, p. 153-161. Spanish. DESCR: Art; Huerta, Dolores; Moreno, Luisa [union organizer]; SALT OF THE EARTH [film]; Tenayuca, Emma; *Working Women.

2590 Mirande, Alfredo and Enriquez, Evangelina. Chicanas in the struggle for unions. IN: Duran, Livie Isauro and Bernard, H. Russell, eds. INTRODUCTION TO CHICANO STUDIES. 2nd. ed. New York: Macmillan, 1973, p. 325-337. English. DESCR: *Labor Unions; Moreno, Luisa [union organizer]; Parsons, Albert; Tenayuca, Emma; United Cannery Agricultural Packing and Allied Workers of America (UCAPAWA).

GOODBYE TO SILENCE

2591 Aguilar-Henson, Marcella. The multi-faceted poetic world of Angela de Hoyos. Austin, TX: Relampago Books Press, 1985, c1982. 81 p. English. **DESCR:** ARISE CHICANO; *Authors; CHICANO POEMS FOR THE BARRIO; de Hoyos, Angela; GATA POEMS; Language Usage; *Literary Criticism; *Poetry; SELECTED POEMS/SELECCIONES; YO, MUJER.

Graduate Schools

2592 Achor, Shirley and Morales, Aida G. Chicanas holding doctoral degrees: social reproduction and cultural ecological approaches. ANTHROPOLOGY AND EDUCATION QUARTERLY, Vol. 21, no. 3 (September 1990), p. 269-287. English. **DESCR:** *Academic Achievement; *Discrimination in Education; *Higher Education; Surveys.

2593 De Llano, Carmen. Comparisons of the psychocultural characteristics of graduate school-bound and nongraduate school-bound Mexican American and Anglo American college women. Thesis (Ph.D.)--California School of Professional Psychology, 1986. 223 p. English. **DESCR:** *Anglo Americans; Colleges and Universities; Comparative Psychology; Cultural Characteristics; Higher Education; Students; *Women.

2594 Flores, Laura Jane. A study of successful completion and attrition among Chicana Title VII Bilingual Education Doctoral Fellows at selected Southwestern universities. Thesis (Ed.D.)--New Mexico State University, 1984. 145 p. English. **DESCR:** Academic Achievement; Colleges and Universities; *Higher Education; Title VII Bilingual Education Doctoral Fellowship Program.

2595 Quezada, Rosa; Loheyde, Katherine Jones; and Kacmarczyk, Ronald. The Hispanic woman graduate student: barriers to mentoring in higher education. TEXAS TECH JOURNAL OF EDUCATION, Vol. 11, no. 3 (Fall 1984), p. 235-241. English. **DESCR:** Discrimination in Education; *Higher Education; *Mentoring; Students.

Grandmothers

2596 Ashley, Laurel Maria. Self, family and community: the social process of aging among urban Mexican-American women. Thesis (Ph.D.)--University of California, Los Angeles, 1985. 306 p. English. **DESCR:** Acculturation; *Ancianos; *Family; *Sex Roles; Southern California.

2597 Binder, Wolfgang. Mothers and grandmothers: acts of mythification and remembrance in Chicano poetry. IN: Bardeleben, Renate von, et al., eds. MISSIONS IN CONFLICT: ESSAYS ON U.S.-MEXICAN RELATIONS AND CHICANO CULTURE. Tubingen, W. Germany: Gunter Narr Verlag, 1986, p. 133-143. English. **DESCR:** *Literary Criticism; Poetry.

2598 Facio, Elisa "Linda". Constraints, resources, and self-definition: a case study of Chicano older women. Thesis (Ph.D.)--University of California, Berkeley, 1988. 246 p. English. **DESCR:** *Ancianos; *Family; *Poverty; Sex Roles; Widowhood.

2599 Irizarry, Estelle. La abuelita in literature. NUESTRO, Vol. 7, no. 7 (September 1983), p. 50. English. **DESCR:** Alonso, Luis Ricardo; *Ancianos; Cotto-Thorner, Guillermo; Family; Ulibarri, Sabine R.; Valero, Robert.

2600 Mink, Diane Leslie. Early grandmotherhood: an exploratory study. Thesis (Ph.D.)--California School of Professional Psychology, Los Angeles, 1987. 190 p. English. **DESCR:** Age Groups; *Ancianos; Assertiveness; Family; Fertility; Natural Support Systems; *Sex Roles; Surveys; Youth.

2601 Rebolledo, Tey Diana. Abuelitas: mythology and integration in Chicana literature. REVISTA CHICANO-RIQUENA, Vol. 11, no. 3-4 (Fall 1983), p. 148-158. English. **DESCR:** *Literary Criticism; Poetry.

Grape Boycott
USE: Boycotts

Great Depression, 1929-1933

2602 Ano Nuevo Kerr, Louise. Chicanas in the Great Depression. IN: Del Castillo, Adelaida R., ed. BETWEEN BORDERS: ESSAYS ON MEXICANA/CHICANA HISTORY. Encino, CA: Floricanto Press, 1990, p. 257-268. English. **DESCR:** *Chicago, IL; Historiography; Mexican Mothers' Club, Chicago, IL; *Working Women.

2603 Blackwelder, Julia Kirk. Women of the depression: caste and culture in San Antonio, 1929-1939. College Station, TX: Texas A&M University Press, 1984. xviii, 279 p.: ill. English. **DESCR:** Criminal Justice System; Cultural Characteristics; Employment; Family; Labor Supply and Market; Labor Unions; Prostitution; San Antonio, TX; *Social Classes; *Women.

GREAT WALL OF LOS ANGELES [mural]

2604 Mesa-Bains, Amalia. Quest for identity: profile of two Chicana muralists: based on interviews with Judith F. Baca and Patricia Rodriguez. IN: Cockcroft, Eva Sperling and Barnet-Sanchez, Holly, eds. SIGNS FROM THE HEART: CALIFORNIA CHICANO MURALS. Venice, CA: Social and Public Art Resource Center, 1990, p. [68-83]. English. **DESCR:** Artists; Baca, Judith F.; Chicano Movement; *Mural Art; Rodriguez, Patricia.

Great Western Sugar Company, Hudson, CO

2605 Romero, Mary and Margolis, Eric. Tending the beets: campesinas and the Great Western Sugar Company. REVISTA MUJERES, Vol. 2, no. 2 (June 1985), p. 17-27. English. **DESCR:** *Farm Workers; Food Industry; South Platte Valley, CO.

Gringo
USE: Anglo Americans

Guadalajara

2606 Castaneda Garcia, Carmen. Fuentes para la historia de la mujer en los archivos de Guadalajara. IN: Del Castillo, Adelaida R., ed. BETWEEN BORDERS: ESSAYS ON MEXICANA/CHICANA HISTORY. Encino, CA: Floricanto Press, 1990, p. 102-112. Spanish. **DESCR:** *Archives; History; *Mexico; *Women.

Guadalupanismo

2607 Soto, Shirlene Ann. Tres modelos culturales: la Virgen de Guadalupe, la Malinche y la Llorona. FEM, Vol. 10, no. 48 (October, November, 1986), p. 13-16. Spanish. **DESCR:** *La Llorona; *La Virgen de Guadalupe; *Malinche; Symbolism; Women.

GUADALUPE [play]

2608 Yarbro-Bejarano, Yvonne. The image of the Chicana in teatro. IN: Cochran, Jo; Stewart, J.T.; and Tsutakawa, Mayumi, eds. GATHERING GROUND: NEW WRITING AND ART BY NORTHWEST WOMEN OF COLOR. Seattle, WA: Seal Press, 1984, p. 90-96. English. DESCR: El Teatro de la Esperanza; HIJOS: ONCE A FAMILY [play]; LA VICTIMA [play]; *Literary Characters; Sex Roles; Sex Stereotypes; Stereotypes; *Teatro; THE OCTOPUS [play]; Women Men Relations.

Guerrero, Eduardo "Lalo"

2609 Sheridan, Thomas E. From Luisa Espinel to Lalo Guerrero: Tucson's Mexican musicians before World War II. JOURNAL OF ARIZONA HISTORY, Vol. 25, no. 3 (Fall 1984), p. 285-300. English. DESCR: Biography; Espinel, Luisa Ronstadt; History; Montijo, Manuel; *Musicians; Rebeil, Julia; Singers; *Tucson, AZ.

Guerrero, Lena

2610 Baca Barragan, Polly; Hamner, Richard; and Guerrero, Lena. [Untitled interview with State Senators (Colorado) Polly Baca-Barragan and Lena Guerrero]. NATIONAL HISPANIC JOURNAL, Vol. 1, no. 2 (Winter 1982), p. 8-11. English. DESCR: Baca Barragan, Polly; Carter, Jimmy (President); Democratic Party; Elected Officials; *Political Parties and Organizations.

Guerrero, Praxedis G.

2611 Perez, Emma. "A la mujer": a critique of the Partido Liberal Mexicano's gender ideology on women. IN: Del Castillo, Adelaida R., ed. BETWEEN BORDERS: ESSAYS ON MEXICANA/CHICANA HISTORY. Encino, CA: Floricanto Press, 1990, p. 459-482. English. DESCR: *"A La Mujer" [essay]; Essays; *Feminism; Flores Magon, Ricardo; Journalism; Mexican Revolution - 1910-1920; Mexico; Newspapers; *Partido Liberal Mexicano (PLM); Political Ideology; Political Parties and Organizations; *REGENERACION [newspaper]; Sex Roles; Women.

Gutierrez, Nancy

2612 Escalante, Virginia; Rivera, Nancy; and Valle, Victor Manuel. Inside the world of Latinas. IN: SOUTHERN CALIFORNIA'S LATINO COMMUNITY: A SERIES OF ARTICLES REPRINTED FROM THE LOS ANGELES TIMES. Los Angeles: Los Angeles Times, 1983, p. 82-91. English. DESCR: *Biography; Castillo Fierro, Catalina (Katie); Gaitan, Maria Elena; Luna Mount, Julia; Ramirez, Cristina.

Handicapped

2613 Shapiro, Johanna and Tittle, Ken. Maternal adaptation to child disability in a Hispanic population. FAMILY RELATIONS, Vol. 39, no. 2 (April 1990), p. 179-185. English. DESCR: Children; *Parent and Child Relationships; Psychological Testing; *Stress.

Harjo, Joy

2614 Crawford, John F. Notes toward a new multicultural criticism: three works by women of color. IN: Harris, Marie and Aguero, Kathleen, eds. A GIFT OF TONGUES: CRITICAL CHALLENGES IN CONTEMPORARY AMERICAN POETRY. Athens, GA: University of Georgia Press, 1987, p. 155-195. English. DESCR: AWAKE IN THE RIVER; Cervantes, Lorna Dee; EMPLUMADA; *Literary Criticism; Mirikitani, Janice; SHE HAD SOME HORSES.

Health

USE: Public Health

Health Care

USE: Medical Care

Health Education

2615 Arguelles, Lourdes and Rivero, Anne M. HIV infection/AIDS and Latinas in Los Angeles County: considerations for prevention, treatment, and research practice. CALIFORNIA SOCIOLOGIST, Vol. 11, no. 1-2 (1988), p. 69-89. English. DESCR: *AIDS (Disease); Cultural Characteristics; Homosexuality; Human Immunodeficiency Virus (HIV); Los Angeles County, CA; Natural Support Systems; Parent and Child Relationships; Sexual Behavior; *Women.

2616 Canales, Genevieve and Roberts, Robert E. Gender and mental health in the Mexican origin population of South Texas. IN: Rodriguez, Reymund and Coleman, Marion Tolbert, eds. MENTAL HEALTH ISSUES OF THE MEXICAN ORIGIN POPULATION IN TEXAS. Austin, TX: Hogg Foundation for Mental Health, University of Texas, 1987, p. 89-99. English. DESCR: Del Rio, TX; Depression (Psychological); Eagle Pass, TX; *Males; *Mental Health; *Sex Roles; South Texas; Surveys.

2617 Cayer, Shirley. Chicago's new Hispanic health alliance. NUESTRO, Vol. 7, no. 5 (June, July, 1983), p. 44-48. English. DESCR: Alcoholism; Chicago Hispanic Health Alliance; Family Planning; Latin Americans; *Medical Care.

2618 Flaskerud, Jacquelyn H. and Nyamathi, Adeline M. Black and Latina womens' AIDS related knowledge, attitudes, and practices. RESEARCH IN NURSING AND HEALTH, Vol. 12, no. 6 (December 1989), p. 339-346. English. DESCR: *AIDS (Disease); Attitudes; *Blacks; Los Angeles County, CA; Surveys; *Women.

2619 Mays, Vicki M. and Cochran, Susan D. Issues in the perception of AIDS risk and risk reduction activities by Black and Hispanic/Latina women. AMERICAN PSYCHOLOGIST, Vol. 43, no. 11 (November 1988), p. 949-957. English. DESCR: *AIDS (Disease); Blacks; Condom Use; Fertility; Preventative Medicine; *Sexual Behavior; Women.

2620 Nyamathi, Adeline M. and Vasquez, Rose. Impact of poverty, homelessness, and drugs on Hispanic women at risk for HIV infection. HISPANIC JOURNAL OF BEHAVIORAL SCIENCES, Vol. 11, no. 4 (November 1989), p. 299-314. English. DESCR: *AIDS (Disease); Drug Use; *Human Immunodeficiency Virus (HIV); Locus of Control; Mental Health; Needle-Sharing; *Poverty.

2621 Richardson, Jean L., et al. Frequency and adequacy of breast cancer screening among elderly Hispanic women. PREVENTIVE MEDICINE, Vol. 16, no. 6 (November 1987), p. 761-774. English. DESCR: Ancianos; *Cancer; Diseases; Los Angeles, CA; *Medical Care; Preventative Medicine.

Health Education (cont.)

2622 Worth, Dooley and Rodriguez, Ruth. Latina women and AIDS. SIECUS REPORT, (January, February, 1986), p. 5-7. English. DESCR: Cultural Characteristics; Drug Addicts; Drug Use; Natural Support Systems; New York; Preventative Medicine; Puerto Ricans; Sex Roles; *Vital Statistics; Women.

Health Status
USE: Public Health

Heart Disease

2623 Hazuda, Helen P., et al. Employment status and women's protection against coronary heart disease. AMERICAN JOURNAL OF EPIDEMIOLOGY, Vol. 123, no. 4 (April 1986), p. 623-640. English. DESCR: Anglo Americans; Diseases; Employment; Nutrition; *Public Health; San Antonio, TX.

HEART OF AZTLAN

2624 Herrera-Sobek, Maria. Women as metaphor in the patriarchal structure of HEART OF AZTLAN. IN: Gonzalez-T., Cesar A. RUDOLFO A. ANAYA: FOCUS ON CRITICISM. La Jolla, CA: Lalo Press, 1990, p. [165]-182. English. DESCR: Anaya, Rudolfo A.; La Llorona; *Literary Characters; Literary Criticism; Sex Roles.

Hembrismo

2625 Gonzalez, Alex. Sex roles of the traditional Mexican family: a comparison of Chicano and Anglo students' attitudes. JOURNAL OF CROSS-CULTURAL PSYCHOLOGY, Vol. 13, no. 3 (September 1982), p. 330-339. English. DESCR: Anglo Americans; Attitudes; Comparative Psychology; *Family; Machismo; Sex Roles; Students.

2626 Jensen, Evelyn E. The Hispanic perspective of the ideal woman: a correlational study. Thesis (Ph.D.)--Fuller Theological Seminary, School of World Mission, 1987. 163 p. English. DESCR: Family; *Machismo; *Sex Roles.

2627 Vasquez, Melba J. T. and Gonzalez, Anna M. Sex roles among Chicanos: stereotypes, challenges and changes. IN: Baron, Augustine, Jr., ed. EXPLORATIONS IN CHICANO PSYCHOLOGY. New York: Praeger, 1981, p. 50-70. English. DESCR: Machismo; *Sex Roles; Social Science; Stereotypes.

Hepatitis

2628 Dinsmoor, Mara J. and Gibbs, Ronald S. Prevalence of asymptomatic hepatitis-B infection in pregnant Mexican-American women. OBSTETRICS AND GYNECOLOGY, Vol. 76, no. 2 (August 1990), p. 239-240. English. DESCR: Diseases; *Fertility.

2629 Franks, Adele L.; Binkin, Nancy J.; and Snider, Dixie E. Isoniazid hepatitis among pregnant and postpartum Hispanic patients. PUBLIC HEALTH REPORTS, Vol. 104, no. 2 (March, April, 1989), p. 151-155. English. DESCR: Fertility; Public Health; Vital Statistics.

Herbal Medicine

2630 Acosta Johnson, Carmen. Breast-feeding and social class mobility: the case of Mexican migrant mothers in Houston, Texas. IN: Melville, Margarita B., ed. TWICE A MINORITY. St. Louis, MO: Mosby, 1980, p.

66-82. English. DESCR: *Breastfeeding; Maternal and Child Welfare; *Social Classes; Social Mobility.

2631 Buss, Fran Leeper. La partera: story of a midwife. Ann Arbor, MI: University of Michigan Press, 1980. 140 p.: ill. English. DESCR: Aragon, Jesusita, 1908-; Cultural Customs; *Curanderas; Folk Medicine; *Midwives; New Mexico; San Miguel County, NM.

2632 Kay, Margarita Artschwager and Yoder, Marianne. Hot and cold in women's ethnotherapeutics: the American-Mexican West. SOCIAL SCIENCE & MEDICINE, Vol. 25, no. 4 (1987), p. 347-355. English. DESCR: *Diseases; *Folk Medicine; Mexico; Southwestern United States.

2633 Kay, Margarita Artschwager. Mexican, Mexican American, and Chicana childbirth. IN: Melville, Margarita B., ed. TWICE A MINORITY. St. Louis, MO: Mosby, 1980, p. 52-65. English. DESCR: *Cultural Characteristics; *Maternal and Child Welfare; Midwives; Sex Roles.

2634 Perrone, Bobette; Stockel, H. Henrietta; and Krueger, Victoria. Medicine women, curanderas, and women doctors. Norman, OK: University of Oklahoma Press, c1989. xix, 252 p.:ill. English. DESCR: Aragon, Jesusita, 1908-; *Curanderas; *Curanderismo; *Folk Medicine; Herrera, Sabinita; Medical Personnel; Native Americans; *Oral History; Rodriguez, Gregorita; Women.

Las Hermanas [organization]

2635 Iglesias, Maria and Hernandez, Maria Luz. Hermanas. IN: Stevens Arroyo, Antonio M., ed. PROPHETS DENIED HONOR: AN ANTHOLOGY ON THE HISPANO CHURCH OF THE UNITED STATES. Maryknoll, NY: Orbis Books, 1980, p. 141-142. English. DESCR: *Catholic Church; Clergy; Organizations.

Hernandez, Alberto

2636 Lavrin, Asuncion. El segundo sexo en Mexico: experiencia, estudio e introspeccion, 1983-1987. MEXICAN STUDIES/ESTUDIOS MEXICANOS, Vol. 5, no. 2 (Summer 1989), p. 297-312. Spanish. DESCR: Arenal, Sandra; *Border Industries; Carrillo, Jorge; Iglesias, Norma; LA FLOR MAS BELLA DE LA MAQUILADORA; *Literature Reviews; Mexico; MUJERES FRONTERIZAS EN LA INDUSTRIA MAQUILADORA; SANGRE JOVEN: LAS MAQUILADORAS POR DENTRO; Women.

Hernandez, Antonia A.

2637 Olivera, Mercedes. The new Hispanic women. VISTA, Vol. 2, no. 11 (July 5, 1987), p. 6-8. English. DESCR: Alvarez, Linda; Esquiroz, Margarita; Garcia, Juliet; Mohr, Nicolasa; Molina, Gloria; Pabon, Maria; Working Women.

Hernandez, Barbara

2638 Sanchez, Rita. Chicana writer breaking out of the silence. DE COLORES, Vol. 3, no. 3 (1977), p. 31-37. English. DESCR: Authors; Castaneda Shular, Antonia; Correa, Viola; Cunningham, Veronica; *Literary Criticism; Mendoza, Rita; *Poetry.

--   --

Hernandez, Carlota

2639 Zamora, Bernice. Archetypes in Chicana
    poetry. DE COLORES, Vol. 4, no. 3 (1978), p.
    43-52. English. DESCR: Cervantes, Lorna Dee;
    Cunningham, Veronica; 'Declaration on a Day
    of Little Inspiration" [poem]; "I Speak in
    an Illusion" [poem]; *Literary Criticism;
    Lucero, Judy A.; Macias, Margarita; Mendoza
    Rita; "Para Mi Hijita" [poem]; *Poetry;
    "Rape Report" [poem]; "The White Line"
    [poem]; "Working Mother's Song" [poem]; "You
    Can Only Blame the System for So Long"
    [poem]; Zamora, Katarina.

Hernandez, Ester

2640 Brown, Betty Ann. Chicanas speak out.
    ARTWEEK, Vol. 15, no. 2 (January 14, 1984),
    p. 1+. English. DESCR: *Art; Carrasco,
    Barbara; Carrillo, Graciela; CHICANA VOICES
    & VISIONS [exhibit]; Exhibits; Goldman,
    Shifra M.; Lerma Bowerman, Liz; Rodriguez,
    Carmen; Rodriguez, Sandra Maria; Social and
    Public Art Resource Center, Venice, CA
    (SPARC).

2641 Venegas, Sybil. The artists and their
    work--the role of the Chicana artist.
    CHISMEARTE, Vol. 1, no. 4 (Fall, Winter,
    1977), p. 3, 5. English. DESCR: Art
    Criticism; *Artists; Carrasco, Barbara;
    Delgado, Etta; Las Mujeres Muralistas, San
    Francisco, CA; Mural Art.

Hernandez, Irene

2642 Espinosa, Ann. Hispanas: our resourses [sic]
    for the eighties. LA LUZ, Vol. 8, no. 4
    (October, November, 1979), p. 10-13.
    English. DESCR: Baca Barragan, Polly; *Civil
    Rights; Comision Femenil Mexicana Naciona ;
    DIRECTORY OF HISPANIC WOMEN; Discrimination
    in Education; Elected Officials; Lacayo,
    Carmela; Lujan, Josie; Mexican American
    Women's National Association (MANA);
    Montanez Davis, Grace; Moreno, Olga; Mujeres
    Latinas en Accion (M.L.A.); National
    Conference of Puerto Rican Women, Inc.
    (NCOPRW); Organizations; Rangel, Irma.

Hernandez, Judithe

2643 Goldman, Shifra M. Mujeres de California:
    Latin American women artists. IN: Moore,
    Sylvia, ed. YESTERDAY AND TOMORROW:
    CALIFORNIA WOMEN ARTISTS. New York, NY:
    Midmarch Arts Press, c1989, p. 202-229.
    English. DESCR: *Artists; Baca, Judith F.;
    Biography; California; Carrasco, Barbara;
    Cervantez, Yreina; de Larios, Dora;
    Feminism; Lomas Garza, Carmen; Lopez,
    Yolanda M.; Mesa-Bains, Amalia; Murillo,
    Patricia; Sanchez, Olivia; Valdez, Patssi;
    Vallejo Dillaway, Linda; Women; Zamora
    Lucero, Linda.

Heroin

2644 Moore, Joan W. Mexican-American women
    addicts: the influence of family background.
    IN: Glick, Ronald and Moore, Joan, eds.
    DRUGS IN HISPANIC COMMUNITIES. New
    Brunswick, NJ: Rutgers University Press
    c1990, p. 127-153. English. DESCR: Barrios;
    *Drug Addicts; Drug Use; East Los Angeles,
    CA; *Family; *Gangs; Hoyo-Mara Gang, East
    Los Angeles, CA; Pachucos; Sex Roles;
    Socialization; White Fence Gang; Youth.

Herrera, Sabinita

2645 Perrone, Bobette; Stockel, H. Henrietta; and
    Krueger, Victoria. Medicine women,
    curanderas, and women doctors. Norman, OK:
    University of Oklahoma Press, c1989. xix,
    252 p.:ill. English. DESCR: Aragon,
    Jesusita, 1908-; *Curanderas; *Curanderismo;
    *Folk Medicine; Herbal Medicine; Medical
    Personnel; Native Americans; *Oral History;
    Rodriguez, Gregorita; Women.

Hidalgo County, TX

2646 Hurtado, Aida. Midwife practices in Hidalgo
    County, Texas. TRABAJOS MONOGRAFICOS, Vol.
    3, no. 1 (1987), p. 1-30. English. DESCR:
    *Maternal and Child Welfare; Midwives.

High Blood Pressure

2647 Sorel, Janet Elaine. The relationship
    between gender role incongruity on measures
    of coping and material resources and blood
    pressure among Mexican-American women.
    Thesis (Ph.D.)--University of North Carolina
    at Chapel Hill, 1988. 268 p. English.
    DESCR: Hispanic Health and Nutrition
    Examination Survey (HHANES); Hypertension;
    Public Health; *Sex Roles; *Stress.

High School and Beyond Project (HS&B)

2648 Abrahamse, Allan F.; Morrison, Peter A.; and
    Waite, Linda J. Teenagers willing to
    consider single parenthood: who is at
    greatest risk? FAMILY PLANNING PERSPECTIVES,
    Vol. 20, no. 1 (January, February, 1988), p.
    13-18. English. DESCR: Blacks; Family
    Planning; *Fertility; *Single Parents;
    Women; *Youth.

2649 Cardoza, Desdemona. College attendance and
    persistence among Hispanic women: an
    examination of some contributing factors.
    SEX ROLES, Vol. 24, no. 3-4 (January 1991),
    p. 133-147. English. DESCR: Academic
    Achievement; College Preparation;
    *Enrollment; *Higher Education; *Sex Roles;
    Socialization; Socioeconomic Factors.

High School Education
    USE: Secondary School Education

Higher Education

2650 Achor, Shirley and Morales, Aida G. Chicanas
    holding doctoral degrees: social
    reproduction and cultural ecological
    approaches. ANTHROPOLOGY AND EDUCATION
    QUARTERLY, Vol. 21, no. 3 (September 1990),
    p. 269-287. English. DESCR: *Academic
    Achievement; *Discrimination in Education;
    Graduate Schools; Surveys.

2651 Bauman, Raquel. A study of Mexican American
    women's perceptions of factors that
    influence academic and professional goal
    attainment. Thesis (Ed.D.)--University of
    Houston, 1984. 169 p. English. DESCR:
    *Careers; *Educational Administration;
    Management.

2652 Bova, Breda Murphy and Phillips, Rebecca R.
    Hispanic women at midlife: implications for
    higher and adult education. JOURNAL OF ADULT
    EDUCATION, Vol. 18, no. 1 (Fall 1989), p.
    9-15. English. DESCR: *Adult Education;
    Cultural Characteristics; Identity; Sex
    Roles.

Higher Education (cont.)

2653 Buriel, Raymond and Saenz, Evangelina. Psychocultural characteristics of college-bound and noncollege-bound Chicanas. JOURNAL OF SOCIAL PSYCHOLOGY, Vol. 110, (April 1980), p. 245-251. English. **DESCR:** Biculturalism; *Biculturalism Inventory for Mexican American Students (BIMAS); Identity; Income; Psychological Testing; Sex Roles; Social Psychology.

2654 Cantu, Norma. Women then and now: an analysis of the Adelita image versus the Chicana as political writer and philosopher. IN: Cordova, Teresa, et al., eds. CHICANA VOICES. Austin, TX: Center for Mexican American Studies, 1986, p. 8-10. English. **DESCR:** Chicano Studies; Discrimination; *La Adelita; Stereotypes.

2655 Cardoza, Desdemona. College attendance and persistence among Hispanic women: an examination of some contributing factors. SEX ROLES, Vol. 24, no. 3-4 (January 1991), p. 133-147. English. **DESCR:** Academic Achievement; College Preparation; *Enrollment; High School and Beyond Project (HS&B); *Sex Roles; Socialization; Socioeconomic Factors.

2656 Casas, Jesus Manuel and Ponterotto, Joseph G. Profiling an invisible minority in higher education: the Chicana. PERSONNEL AND GUIDANCE JOURNAL, Vol. 62, no. 6 (February 1984), p. 349-353. English.

2657 Chacon, Maria A.; Cohen, Elizabeth G.; and Strover, Sharon. Chicanas and Chicanos: barriers to progress in higher education. IN: Olivas, Michael A., ed. LATINO COLLEGE STUDENTS. New York: Teachers College Press, 1986, p. 296-324. English. **DESCR:** Community Colleges; Discrimination; Dropouts; Stress; Surveys.

2658 Chacon, Maria A. An overdue study of the Chicana undergraduate college experience. LA LUZ, Vol. 8, no. 8 (October, November, 1980), p. 27. English. **DESCR:** Colleges and Universities; *Educational Statistics; Stanford University, Stanford, CA; Students.

2659 Chacon, Maria A., et al. Chicanas in California post secondary education: a comparative study of barriers to the program progress. Stanford, CA: Stanford Center for Chicano Research, 1985. viii, 217 p. English. **DESCR:** *Academic Achievement; Colleges and Universities; Counseling (Educational); Educational Statistics; Enrollment; Students; Surveys.

2660 Chacon, Maria A., et al. Chicanas in postsecondary education. Stanford, CA: Center for Research on Women, Stanford University, 1982. iii, 106, [68] p. English. **DESCR:** Colleges and Universities; Public Policy; *Surveys.

2661 De Blassie, Richard R. and Franco, Juan N. The differences between personality inventory scores and self-rating in a sample of Hispanic subjects. JOURNAL OF NON-WHITE CONCERNS IN PERSONNEL AND GUIDANCE, Vol. 11, no. 2 (January 1983), p. 43-46. English. **DESCR:** Hispanic Education [program]; New Mexico State University; *Personality; Sixteen Personality Factor Questionnaire; Students.

2662 De Llano, Carmen. Comparisons of the psychocultural characteristics of graduate school-bound and nongraduate school-bound Mexican American and Anglo American college women. Thesis (Ph.D.)--California School of Professional Psychology, 1986. 223 p. English. **DESCR:** *Anglo Americans; Colleges and Universities; Comparative Psychology; Cultural Characteristics; *Graduate Schools; Students; *Women.

2663 Del Castillo, Adelaida R., et al. An assessment of the status of the education of Hispanic American women. IN: McKenna, Teresa and Ortiz, Flora Ida, eds. THE BROKEN WEB: THE EDUCATIONAL EXPERIENCE OF HISPANIC WOMEN. Claremont, CA: Tomas Rivera Center; Berkeley, CA: Floricanto Press, 1988, p. 3-24. English. **DESCR:** Academic Achievement; Conferences and Meetings; Discrimination in Education; Dropouts; *Education; Public Policy; Research Methodology; The Educational Experience of Hispanic American Women [symposium] (1985: Claremont, CA); *Women.

2664 Escobedo, Theresa Herrera, ed. Thematic issue: Chicana issues. HISPANIC JOURNAL OF BEHAVIORAL SCIENCES, Vol. 4, no. 2 (June 1982), p. 145-286. English. **DESCR:** Education; *Social History and Conditions.

2665 Estrada, Rosa Omega. A study of the attitudes of Texas Mexican American women toward higher education. Thesis (Ed.D.)--Baylor University, 1985. 280 p. English. **DESCR:** *Attitudes; Education; Texas.

2666 Fleming, Marilyn B. Problems experienced by Anglo, Hispanic and Navajo Indian women college students. JOURNAL OF AMERICAN INDIAN EDUCATION, Vol. 22, no. 1 (October 1982), p. 7-17. English. **DESCR:** Anglo Americans; Community Colleges; Ethnic Groups; Identity; Medical Education; Native Americans; Students; Women.

2667 Flores, Laura Jane. A study of successful completion and attrition among Chicana Title VII Bilingual Education Doctoral Fellows at selected Southwestern universities. Thesis (Ed.D.)--New Mexico State University, 1984. 145 p. English. **DESCR:** Academic Achievement; Colleges and Universities; Graduate Schools; Title VII Bilingual Education Doctoral Fellowship Program.

2668 Gandara, Patricia. Passing through the eye of the needle: high-achieving Chicanas. HISPANIC JOURNAL OF BEHAVIORAL SCIENCES, Vol. 4, no. 2 (June 1982), p. 167-179. English. **DESCR:** *Academic Achievement.

2669 Gonzales, Erlinda. La muerte de un refran. DE COLORES, Vol. 2, no. 3 (1975), p. 15-18. Spanish. **DESCR:** *Identity; *Social History and Conditions; Socialization.

2670 Gonzalez, Judith Teresa. Dilemmas of the high achieving Chicana: the double bind factor in male/female relationships. Tucson, AZ: Mexican American Studies & Research Center, University of Arizona, 1987. 31 leaves. English. **DESCR:** *Academic Achievement; Identity; Males; Marriage; *Sex Roles; *Sex Stereotypes; Women Men Relations.

Higher Education (cont.)

2671 Gonzalez, Judith Teresa. Dilemmas of the high achieving Chicana: the double bind factor in male/female relationships. SEX ROLES, Vol. 18, no. 7-8 (April 1988), p. 367-380. English. DESCR: *Academic Achievement; Identity; Males; Marriage; *Sex Roles; *Sex Stereotypes; Women Men Relations.

2672 Gonzalez-Huss, Mary Jane. Characteristics of college bound Mexican American females. Thesis (Ph.D.)--University of Nevada, Reno, 1984. xi, 136 leaves. English.

2673 Jaramillo, Mari-Luci. Institutional responsibility in the provision of educational experiences to the Hispanic American female student. IN: McKenna, Teresa and Ortiz, Flora Ida, eds. THE BROKEN WEB: THE EDUCATIONAL EXPERIENCE OF HISPANIC WOMEN. Claremont, CA: Tomaas Rivera Center; Berkeley, CA: Floricanto Press, 1988, p. 25-35. English. DESCR: Academic Achievement; *Discrimination in Education; Dropouts; *Education; Educational Administration; Enrollment; Students; *Women.

2674 Jaramillo, Mari-Luci. To serve Hispanic American female students: challenges and responsibilities for educational institutions. Claremont, CA: Tomas Rivera Center, c1987. 11 p. English. DESCR: Dropouts; *Education; Women.

2675 Lopez, Gloria Ann. Job satisfaction of the Mexican American woman administrator in higher education. Thesis (Ph.D.)--University of Texas, Austin, 1984. 193 p. English. DESCR: *Careers; *Educational Administration; Leadership.

2676 Matute-Bianchi, Maria Eugenia. A Chicana in academe. WOMEN'S STUDIES QUARTERLY, Vol. 10, no. 1 (Spring 1982), p. 14-17. English. DESCR: Discrimination; Matute-Bianchi, Maria Eugenia; Sex Roles; Sexism.

2677 Mendoza, Lupe. Porque lo podemos hacer--a poco no? REVISTA MUJERES, Vol. 1, no. 2 (June 1984), p. 33-37. Spanish. DESCR: Autobiography; *Mendoza, Lupe.

2678 Morales, Aida G. Barriers, critical events, and support systems affecting Chicanas in their pursuit of an academic doctorate. Thesis (Ph.D.)--East Texas State University, 1988. 184 p. English. DESCR: *Academic Achievement; Natural Support Systems.

2679 Nieves-Squires, Sarah. Hispanic women: making their presence on campus less tenuous. Washington, DC: Association of American Colleges, c1991. 14 p. English. DESCR: Afro-Hispanics; Colleges and Universities; Cubans; *Discrimination in Education; Puerto Ricans; *Women.

2680 Ortiz, Flora Ida. Hispanic American women in higher education: a consideration of the socialization process. AZTLAN, Vol. 17, no. 2 (Fall 1986), p. 125-152. English. DESCR: *Academic Achievement; Counseling (Educational); Enrollment; Sex Roles; *Sexism; Socialization; Students; University of California.

2681 Quezada, Rosa; Loheyde, Katherine Jones; and Kacmarczyk, Ronald. The Hispanic woman graduate student: barriers to mentoring in higher education. TEXAS TECH JOURNAL OF EDUCATION, Vol. 11, no. 3 (Fall 1984), p. 235-241. English. DESCR: Discrimination in Education; *Graduate Schools; *Mentoring; Students.

2682 Quezada, Rosa and Jones-Loheyde, Katherine. Hispanic women: academic advisees of high potential. IMPROVING COLLEGE & UNIVERSITY TEACHING, Vol. 32, no. 2-14 (1984), p. 95-98. English. DESCR: Academic Achievement; Counseling (Educational).

2683 Sanchez, Corina. Higher education y la Chicana? ENCUENTRO FEMENIL, Vol. 1, no. 1 (Spring 1973), p. 27-33. English. DESCR: Discrimination; Discrimination in Education; Identity; Sexism.

2684 Sanchez, Joaquin John. An investigation of the initial experience of a Chicana with higher education. Thesis (Ph.D.)--Saybrook Institute, 1983. 163 p. English. DESCR: Biculturalism; Colleges and Universities; *Cultural Characteristics.

2685 Sierra, Christine Marie. The university setting reinforces inequality. IN: Cordova, Teresa, et al., eds. CHICANA VOICES. Austin, TX: Center for Mexican American Studies, 1986, p. 5-7. English. DESCR: *Discrimination; Discrimination in Education.

2686 U.S. National Institute of Education. Conference on the educational and occupational needs of Hispanic women, June 29-30, 1976; December 10-12, 1976. Washington, DC: U.S. Department of Education, 1980. x, 301 p. English. DESCR: Conference on the Educational and Occupational Needs of Hispanic Women (1976: Denver, CO); Conferences and Meetings; *Education; *Employment; Leadership; Puerto Ricans; Sex Roles; *Women.

2687 Vallez, Andrea. Acculturation, social support, stress and adjustment of the Mexican American college woman. Thesis (Ph.D.)--University of Colorado at Boulder, 1984. 121 p. English. DESCR: *Acculturation; *Colleges and Universities; Depression (Psychological); Natural Support Systems; Southern California; Stress; *Students.

2688 Vasquez, Melba J. T. Confronting barriers to the participation of Mexican American women in higher education. HISPANIC JOURNAL OF BEHAVIORAL SCIENCES, Vol. 4, no. 2 (June 1982), p. 147-165. English. DESCR: Academic Achievement; *Sex Roles; Socioeconomic Factors.

2689 Winkler, Karen J. Scholars say issues of diversity have "revolutionized" field of Chicano Studies. CHRONICLE OF HIGHER EDUCATION, Vol. 37, no. 4 (September 26, 1990), p. A4-A9. English. DESCR: Chicana Studies; Chicano Studies; Curriculum; *Feminism; Ruiz, Vicki L.; Saragoza, Alex M.

2690 Zeff, Shirley B. A cross-cultural study of Mexican American, Black American and white American women of a large urban university. HISPANIC JOURNAL OF BEHAVIORAL SCIENCES, Vol. 4, no. 2 (June 1982), p. 245-261. English. DESCR: Anglo Americans; Blacks; Sex Roles; Students.

Hijas de Cuauhtemoc

2691 Introduction. ENCUENTRO FEMENIL, Vol. 1, no. 2 (1974), p. 3-7. English. DESCR: Books; ENCUENTRO FEMENIL; Organizations; *Periodicals.

HIJOS: ONCE A FAMILY [play]

2692 Yarbro-Bejarano, Yvonne. The image of the Chicana in teatro. IN: Cochran, Jo; Stewart, J.T.; and Tsutakawa, Mayumi, eds. GATHERING GROUND: NEW WRITING AND ART BY NORTHWEST WOMEN OF COLOR. Seattle, WA: Seal Press, 1984, p. 90-96. English. DESCR: El Teatro de la Esperanza; GUADALUPE [play]; LA VICTIMA [play]; *Literary Characters; Sex Roles; Sex Stereotypes; Stereotypes; *Teatro; THE OCTOPUS [play]; Women Men Relations.

Hinojosa-Smith, Rolando R.

2693 de la Fuente, Patricia and Duke dos Santos, Maria I. The elliptic female presence as unifying force in the novels of Rolando Hinojosa. REVISTA CHICANO-RIQUENA, Vol. 12, no. 3-4 (Fall, Winter, 1984), p. 64-75. English. DESCR: ESTAMPAS DEL VALLE Y OTRAS OBRAS; GENERACIONES Y SEMBLANZAS; *Literary Criticism; MI QUERIDO RAFA; RITES AND WITNESSES.

Hispanic Education [program]

2694 De Blassie, Richard R. and Franco, Juan N. The differences between personality inventory scores and self-rating in a sample of Hispanic subjects. JOURNAL OF NON-WHITE CONCERNS IN PERSONNEL AND GUIDANCE, Vol. 11, no. 2 (January 1983), p. 43-46. English. DESCR: Higher Education; New Mexico State University; *Personality; Sixteen Personality Factor Questionnaire; Students.

Hispanic Health and Nutrition Examination Survey (HHANES)

2695 Fanelli-Kuczmarski, Marie T., et al. Folate status of Mexican American, Cuban, and Puerto Rican women. AMERICAN JOURNAL OF CLINICAL NUTRITION, Vol. 52, no. 2 (August 1990), p. 368-372. English. DESCR: Cubanos; *Folic Acid Deficiency; *Nutrition; Puerto Ricans; *Women.

2696 John, A. Meredith and Martorell, Reynaldo. Incidence and duration of breast-feeding in Mexican-American infants, 1970-1982. AMERICAN JOURNAL OF CLINICAL NUTRITION, Vol. 50, no. 4 (October 1989), p. 868-874. English. DESCR: *Breastfeeding.

2697 Sorel, Janet Elaine. The relationship between gender role incongruity on measures of coping and material resources and blood pressure among Mexican-American women. Thesis (Ph.D.)--University of North Carolina at Chapel Hill, 1988. 268 p. English. DESCR: High Blood Pressure; Hypertension; Public Health; *Sex Roles; *Stress.

2698 Stroup-Benham, Christine A.; Trevino, Fernando M.; and Trevino, Dorothy B. Alcohol consumption patterns among Mexican American mothers and among children from single- and dual-headed households: findings from HHANES 1982-84. AMERICAN JOURNAL OF PUBLIC HEALTH, Vol. 80, (December 1990), p. 36-41. English. DESCR: *Alcoholism; *Children; Parent and Child Relationships; *Single Parents.

2699 Stroup-Benham, Christine A. and Trevino, Fernando M. Reproductive characteristics of Mexican-American, mainland Puerto Rican, and Cuban-American women: data from the Hispanic Health and Nutrition Examination Survey. JAMA: JOURNAL OF THE AMERICAN MEDICAL ASSOCIATION, Vol. 265, no. 2 (January 9, 1991), p. 222-226. English. DESCR: *Birth Control; Breastfeeding; Cubanos; *Fertility; Puerto Ricans; *Women.

Hispanic Stress Inventory (HSI)

2700 Salgado de Snyder, Nelly; Cervantes, Richard C.; and Padilla, Amado M. Gender and ethnic differences in psychosocial stress and generalized distress among Hispanics. SEX ROLES, Vol. 22, no. 7-8 (April, 1990), p. 441-453. English. DESCR: Anglo Americans; Central Americans; *Comparative Psychology; Depression (Psychological); *Immigrants; Immigration; *Sex Roles; *Stress; Women.

Historiography

2701 Ano Nuevo Kerr, Louise. Chicanas in the Great Depression. IN: Del Castillo, Adelaida R., ed. BETWEEN BORDERS: ESSAYS ON MEXICANA/CHICANA HISTORY. Encino, CA: Floricanto Press, 1990, p. 257-268. English. DESCR: *Chicago, IL; *Great Depression, 1929-1933; Mexican Mothers' Club, Chicago, IL; *Working Women.

2702 Apodaca, Maria Linda. The Chicana woman: a historical materialist perspective. IN: Bollinger, William, et al., eds. WOMEN IN LATIN AMERICA: AN ANTHOLOGY FROM LATIN AMERICAN PERSPECTIVES. Riverside, CA: Latin American Perspectives, c1979, p. 81-100. English. DESCR: Capitalism; Immigrants; Imperialism; Marxism; Mexico; Oral History; Social Classes; Spanish Influence.

2703 Camarillo, Alberto M. The "new" Chicano history: historiography of Chicanos of the 1970s. IN: CHICANOS AND THE SOCIAL SCIENCES: A DECADE OF RESEARCH AND DEVELOPMENT (1970-1980) SYMPOSIUM WORKING PAPER. Santa Barbara, CA: Center for Chicano Studies, University of California, 1983, p. 9-17. English. DESCR: History; Literature Reviews; Urban Communities.

2704 Cardenas de Dwyer, Carlota. Mexican American women: images and realities. IN: Cotera, Martha and Hufford, Larry, eds. BRIDGING TWO CULTURES. Austin, TX: National Educational Laboratory Publishers, 1980, p. 294-296. English. DESCR: *Stereotypes.

2705 Castaneda, Antonia I. Gender, race, and culture: Spanish-Mexican women in the historiography of frontier California. FRONTIERS: A JOURNAL OF WOMEN STUDIES, Vol. 11, no. 1 (1990), p. [8]-20. English. DESCR: Bancroft, Hubert Howe; Bolton, Herbert Eugene; *California; Californios; History; Intermarriage; *Sex Stereotypes; Spanish Borderlands Theory; Spanish Influence; Stereotypes; Turner, Frederick Jackson; Women.

2706 Del Castillo, Adelaida R., ed. Between borders: essays on Mexicana/Chicana history. Encino, CA: Floricanto Press, c1990. xv, 563 p. Bilingual. DESCR: Feminism; *History; Mexico; *Women; Working Women.

2707 Driscoll, Barbara A. Chicana historiography: a research note regarding Mexican archival sources. IN: Cordova, Teresa, et al., eds. CHICANA VOICES. Austin, TX: Center for Mexican American Studies, 1986, p. 136-145. English. DESCR: Archives; Mexico.

Historiography (cont.)

2708 Garcia, Mario T. La familia: the Mexican immigrant family, 1900-1930. IN: Barrera, Mario, et al., eds. WORK, FAMILY, SEX ROLES, LANGUAGE: SELECTED PAPERS, 1979. Berkeley, CA: Tonatiuh-Quinto Sol, 1980, p. 117-139. English. DESCR: Assimilation; Cultural Customs; El Paso, TX; Family; History; Immigration; Labor; Sex Roles.

2709 Gomez-Quinones, Juan. Questions within women's historiography. IN: Del Castillo, Adelaida R., ed. BETWEEN BORDERS: ESSAYS ON MEXICANA/CHICANA HISTORY. Encino, CA: Floricanto Press, 1990, p. 87-97. English. DESCR: *Mexico; *Women.

2710 Griswold del Castillo, Richard. Chicano family history--methodology and theory: a survey of contemporary research directions. IN: National Association for Chicano Studies. HISTORY, CULTURE, AND SOCIETY: CHICANO STUDIES IN THE 1980s. Ypsilanti, MI: Bilingual Press/Editorial Bilingue, 1983, p. 95-106. English. DESCR: Age Groups; *Family.

2711 Klor de Alva, J. Jorge. Chicana history and historical significance: some theoretical considerations. IN: Del Castillo, Adelaida R., ed. BETWEEN BORDERS: ESSAYS ON MEXICANA/CHICANA HISTORY. Encino, CA: Floricanto Press, 1990, p. 61-86. English. DESCR: Chicana Studies; *History; Sexism.

2712 Orozco, Cynthia. Chicana labor history: a critique of male consciousness in historical writing. LA RED/THE NET, no. 77 (January 1984), p. 2-5. English. DESCR: Labor; *Sexism; Working Women.

2713 Sanchez, Rosaura. The history of Chicanas: a proposal for a materialist perspective. IN: Del Castillo, Adelaida R., ed. BETWEEN BORDERS: ESSAYS ON MEXICANA/CHICANA HISTORY. Encino, CA: Floricanto Press, 1990, p. 1-29. English. DESCR: Apodaca, Maria Linda; *Chicana Studies; Del Castillo, Adelaida R.; Feminism; History; Morales, Sylvia; Ruiz Vicki L.

History

2714 Apodaca, Maria Linda. A double edge sword: Hispanas and liberal feminism. CRITICA, Vol. 1, no. 3 (Fall 1986), p. 96-114. English. DESCR: *Feminism; Women.

2715 Billings, Linda M. and Alurista. In verbal murals: a study of Chicana herstory and poetry. CONFLUENCIA, Vol. 2, no. 1 (Fall 1986), p. 60-68. English. DESCR: Candelaria, Cordelia; Cervantes, Lorna Dee; Cisneros, Sandra; EMPLUMADA; *Feminism; Literary Criticism; *Poetry; Xelina.

2716 Blanco, Iris. Participacion de las mujeres en la sociedad prehispanica. IN: Sanchez, Rosaura and Martinez Cruz, Rosa, eds. ESSAYS ON LA MUJER. Los Angeles, CA: Chicano Studies Center Publications, UCLA, 1977, p. 48-81. Spanish. DESCR: Aztecs; Cultural Customs; Indigenismo; Mexico; Precolumbian Society; Women.

2717 Cabeza de Baca Gilbert, Fabiola. The pioneer women. IN: Valdez Luis and Steiner, Stan, eds. AZTLAN: AN ANTHOLOGY OF MEXICAN AMERICAN LITERATURE. New York: Vintage Books, 1972, p. 260-263. English. DESCR: Arizona.

2718 Calderon, Roberto R. and Zamora, Emilio, Jr. Manuela Solis Sager and Emma Tenayuca: a tribute. IN: Cordova, Teresa, et al., eds. CHICANA VOICES. Austin, TX: Center for Mexican American Studies, 1986, p. 30-41. English. DESCR: Agricultural Labor Unions; Biography; Labor; *Solis Sager, Manuela; South Texas Agricultural Worker's Union (STAWU); *Tenayuca, Emma; United Cannery Agricultural Packing and Allied Workers of America (UCAPAWA).

2719 Calderon, Roberto R. and Zamora, Emilio, Jr. Manuela Solis Sager and Emma Tenayuca: a tribute. IN: Del Castillo, Adelaida R., ed. BETWEEN BORDERS: ESSAYS ON MEXICANA/CHICANA HISTORY. Encino, CA: Floricanto Press, 1990, p. 269-279. English. DESCR: Agricultural Labor Unions; Biography; Labor; *Solis Sager, Manuela; South Texas Agricultural Worker's Union (STAWU); *Tenayuca, Emma; United Cannery Agricultural Packing and Allied Workers of America (UCAPAWA).

2720 Camarillo, Alberto M. The "new" Chicano history: historiography of Chicanos of the 1970s. IN: CHICANOS AND THE SOCIAL SCIENCES: A DECADE OF RESEARCH AND DEVELOPMENT (1970-1980) SYMPOSIUM WORKING PAPER. Santa Barbara, CA: Center for Chicano Studies, University of California, 1983, p. 9-17. English. DESCR: *Historiography; Literature Reviews; Urban Communities.

2721 Campbell, Julie A. Madres y esposas: Tucson's Spanish-American Mothers and Wives Association. JOURNAL OF ARIZONA HISTORY, Vol. 31, no. 2 (Summer 1990), p. 161-182. English. DESCR: Military; Organizations; *Spanish-American Mothers and Wives Association, Tucson, AZ; Tucson, AZ; World War II.

2722 Candelaria, Cordelia. La Malinche, feminist prototype. FRONTIERS: A JOURNAL OF WOMEN STUDIES, Vol. 5, no. 2 (Summer 1980), p. 1-6. English. DESCR: Aztecs; *Feminism; Malinche.

2723 Castaneda, Antonia I. Comparative frontiers: the migration of women to Alta California and New Zealand. IN: Schlissel, Lillian, et al., eds. WESTERN WOMEN: THEIR LAND, THEIR LIVES. Albuquerque, NM: University of New Mexico Press, 1988, p. 283-300. English. DESCR: Border Region; California; Immigrants; Immigration; Marriage; Mexico; Missions; Native Americans; New Zealand; Social History and Conditions; *Women.

2724 Castaneda, Antonia I. Gender, race, and culture: Spanish-Mexican women in the historiography of frontier California. FRONTIERS: A JOURNAL OF WOMEN STUDIES, Vol. 11, no. 1 (1990), p. [8]-20. English. DESCR: Bancroft, Hubert Howe; Bolton, Herbert Eugene; *California; Californios; *Historiography; Intermarriage; *Sex Stereotypes; Spanish Borderlands Theory; Spanish Influence; Stereotypes; Turner, Frederick Jackson; Women.

2725 Castaneda, Antonia I. The political economy of nineteenth century stereotypes of Californianas. IN: Del Castillo, Adelaida R., ed. BETWEEN BORDERS: ESSAYS ON MEXICANA/CHICANA HISTORY. Encino, CA: Floricanto Press, 1990, p. 213-236. English. DESCR: *California; *Californios; Dana, Richard Henry; Farnham, Thomas Jefferson; LIFE IN CALIFORNIA; *Political Economy; Robinson, Alfred; *Sex Stereotypes; TRAVELS IN CALIFORNIA AND SCENES IN THE PACIFIC OCEAN; TWO YEARS BEFORE THE MAST; Women.

History (cont.)

2726 Castaneda Garcia, Carmen. Fuentes para la historia de la mujer en los archivos de Guadalajara. IN: Del Castillo, Adelaida R., ed. BETWEEN BORDERS: ESSAYS ON MEXICANA/CHICANA HISTORY. Encino, CA: Floricanto Press, 1990, p. 102-112. Spanish. **DESCR:** *Archives; *Guadalajara; *Mexico; *Women.

2727 Cotera, Marta P. Diosa y hembra, the history and heritage of Chicanas in the United States. Austin, TX: Information Systems Development, 1976. 202 p. English. **DESCR:** *Social History and Conditions.

2728 Cotera, Marta P. Profile on the Mexican American woman. Austin, TX: National Educational Laboratory Publishers, 1976. v, 264 p. English. **DESCR:** *Social History and Conditions.

2729 Craver, Rebecca McDowell. The impact of intimacy: Mexican-Anglo intermarriage in New Mexico 1821-1846. SOUTHWESTERN STUDIES, no. 66 (1982), p. 1-79. English. **DESCR:** Acculturation; Anglo Americans; Assimilation; *Intermarriage; New Mexico; Rio Arriba Valley, NM.

2730 Craver, Rebecca McDowell. The impact of intimacy: Mexican-Anglo intermarriage in New Mexico 1821-1846. El Paso, TX: Texas Western Press, University of Texas at El Paso, 1982. 79 p. English. **DESCR:** Acculturation; Anglo Americans; Assimilation; *Intermarriage; New Mexico; Rio Arriba Valley, NM.

2731 De Ortego y Gasca, Felipe. The Hispanic woman: a humanistic perspective. LA LUZ, Vol. 6, no. 11 (November 1977), p. 7-10. English. **DESCR:** De la Cruz, Juana Ines; Dona Ximena; *Essays; Mistral, Gabriela; Ortiz de Dominguez, Josefa; *Women Men Relations; *Women's Suffrage.

2732 De Ortego y Gasca, Felipe. The Hispanic woman: a humanistic perspective. LA LUZ, Vol. 8, no. 8 (October, November, 1980), p. 6-9. English. **DESCR:** De la Cruz, Juana Ines; Dona Ximena; *Essays; Mistral, Gabriela; Ortiz de Dominguez, Josefa; *Women Men Relations; *Women's Suffrage.

2733 Del Castillo, Adelaida R., ed. Between borders: essays on Mexicana/Chicana history. Encino, CA: Floricanto Press, c1990. xv, 563 p. Bilingual. **DESCR:** Feminism; Historiography; Mexico; *Women; Working Women.

2734 Del Castillo, Adelaida R. Malintzin Tenepal: a preliminary look into a new perspective. ENCUENTRO FEMENIL, Vol. 1, no. 2 (1974), p. 58-77. English. **DESCR:** Aztecs; Biography; Cortes, Hernan; *Malinche; Precolumbian Society.

2735 Del Castillo, Adelaida R. Malintzin Tenepal: a preliminary look into a new perspective. IN: Sanchez, Rosaura and Martinez Cruz, Rosa, eds. ESSAYS ON LA MUJER. Los Angeles, CA: Chicano Studies Center Publications, UCLA, 1977, p. 124-149. English. **DESCR:** Aztecs; Biography; Cortes, Hernan; *Malinche; Precolumbian Society.

2736 Dixon, Marlene; Martinez, Elizabeth; and McCaughan, Ed. Theoretical perspectives on Chicanas, Mexicanas and the transnational working class. CONTEMPORARY MARXISM, no. 11 (Fall 1985), p. 46-76. English. **DESCR:** Border Industries; Capitalism; Economic History and Conditions; *Immigration; *Labor Supply and Market; *Laboring Classes; Mexico; Undocumented Workers; Women.

2737 Garcia, Mario T. The Chicana in American history: the Mexican women of El Paso, 1880-1920 - a case study. PACIFIC HISTORICAL REVIEW, Vol. 49, no. 2 (May 1980), p. 315-337. English. **DESCR:** Acme Laundry, El Paso, TX; American Federation of Labor (AFL); Case Studies; Central Labor Union; Domestic Work; *El Paso, TX; Employment; Immigrants; Income; Labor Unions; Sex Roles; Strikes and Lockouts; *Working Women.

2738 Garcia, Mario T. La familia: the Mexican immigrant family, 1900-1930. IN: Barrera, Mario, et al., eds. WORK, FAMILY, SEX ROLES, LANGUAGE: SELECTED PAPERS, 1979. Berkeley, CA: Tonatiuh-Quinto Sol, 1980, p. 117-139. English. **DESCR:** Assimilation; Cultural Customs; El Paso, TX; Family; *Historiography; Immigration; Labor; Sex Roles.

2739 Goldsmith, Raquel Rubio. Shipwrecked in the desert: a short history of the adventures and struggles for survival of the Mexican Sisters of the House of the Providence in Douglas, Arizona during their first twenty-two years of existence (1927-1949). RENATO ROSALDO LECTURE SERIES MONOGRAPH, Vol. 1, (Summer 1985), p. [39]-67. English. **DESCR:** Catholic Church; Clergy; Douglas, AZ; *House of the Divine Providence [convent], Douglas, AZ; Women.

2740 Gonzales, Sylvia Alicia. The Latina feminist: where we've been, where we're going. NUESTRO, Vol. 5, no. 6 (August, September, 1981), p. 45-47. English. **DESCR:** Conferences and Meetings; *Feminism; Leadership; National Hispanic Feminist Conference (March 28-31, 1980: San Jose, CA).

2741 Gonzalez, Deena J. The widowed women of Santa Fe: assessments on the lives of an unmarried population, 1850-80. IN: Scadron, Arlene, ed. ON THEIR OWN: WIDOWS AND WIDOWHOOD IN THE AMERICAN SOUTHWEST 1843-1939. Urbana, IL: University of Illinois Press, c1988, p. [65]-90. English. **DESCR:** Family; Income; Land Tenure; *Santa Fe, NM; Sex Roles; Single Parents; *Widowhood; *Women.

2742 Gonzalez, Deena J. The widowed women of Santa Fe: assessments on the lives of an unmarried population, 1850-80. IN: DuBois, Ellen Carol and Ruiz, Vicki L., eds. UNEQUAL SISTERS: A MULTICULTURAL READER IN U.S. WOMEN'S HISTORY. New York: Routledge, 1990, p. 34-50. English. **DESCR:** Family; Income; Land Tenure; *Santa Fe, NM; Sex Roles; Single Parents; *Widowhood; *Women.

2743 Gonzalez, Rosalinda M. Chicanas and Mexican immigrant families 1920-1940: women's subordination and family exploitation. IN: Scharf, Lois and Jensen, Joan M., eds. DECADES OF DISCONTENT: THE WOMEN'S MOVEMENT, 1920-1940. Westport, CT: Greenwood Press, 1983, p. 59-84. English. **DESCR:** *Family; Farm Workers; Immigrants; Labor; Labor Unions; Mexico; Pecan Shelling Worker's Union, San Antonio, TX; Sex Roles; Strikes and Lockouts; United Cannery Agricultural Packing and Allied Workers of America (UCAPAWA); Working Women.

History (cont.)

2744 Green, George N. ILGWJ in Texas, 1930-1970. JOURNAL OF MEXICAN-AMERICAN HISTORY, Vol. 1, no. 2 (Spring 1971), p. 144-169. English. DESCR: International Ladies Garment Workers Union (ILGWU); *Labor Unions; Texas.

2745 Griswold del Castillo, Richard. La familia: Chicano families in the urban Southwest, 1848 to the present. Notre Dame, IN: University of Notre Dame Press, c1984. xv, 173 p. English. DESCR: *Family; Intermarriage; Machismo; Parenting; *Sex Roles; Sexual Behavior; *Social History and Conditions.

2746 Griswold del Castillo, Richard. "Only for my family...": historical dimensions of Chicano family solidarity--the case of San Antonio in 1860. AZTLAN, Vol 16, no. 1-2 (1985), p. 145-176. English. DESCR: Extended Family; *Family; Population; San Antonio, TX.

2747 Griswold del Castillo, Richard. Patriarchy and the status of women in the late nineteenth-century Southwest. IN: Rodriguez O., Jaime E., ed. THE MEXICAN AND MEXICAN AMERICAN EXPERIENCE IN THE 19TH CENTURY. Tempe, AZ: Bilingual Press/Editorial Bilingue, 1989, p. 85-99. English. DESCR: Family; *Feminism; *Machismo; *Sex Roles.

2748 Gutierrez, Ramon A. Marriage and seduction in Colonial New Mexico. IN: Del Castillo, Adelaida R., ed. BETWEEN BORDERS: ESSAYS ON MEXICANA/CHICANA HISTORY. Encino, CA: Floricanto Press, 1990, p. 447-457. English. DESCR: *Marriage; *New Mexico; Rape; *Sexual Behavior; Women.

2749 Hart, John M. Working-class women in nineteenth century Mexico. IN: Mora, Magdalena and Del Castillo, Adelaida, eds. MEXICAN WOMEN IN THE UNITED STATES: STRUGGLES PAST AND PRESENT. Los Angeles, CA Chicano Studies Research Center, 1980, p. 151-157. English. DESCR: *Employment; Mexico; Women; Working Women.

2750 Jensen, Joan M. Crossing ethnic barriers in the Southwest: women's agricultural extension education, 1914-1940. AGRICULTURAL HISTORY, Vol. 60, no. 2 (Spring 1986), p. 169-181. English. DESCR: *Agricultural Extension Service; Agriculture; Cabeza de Baca, Fabiola; New Mexico; *Rural Education.

2751 Jensen, Joan M. "I've worked, I'm not afraid of work": farm women in New Mexico, 1920-1940. NEW MEXICO HISTORICAL REVIEW, Vol. 61, no. 1 (January 1986), p. 27-52. English. DESCR: *Farm Workers; New Mexico; *Rural Economics; *Working Women.

2752 Keremitsis, Dawn. Del metate al molino: la mujer mexicana de 1910 a 1940. HISTORIA MEXICANA, Vol. 33, no. 2 (1983), p. 285-302. Spanish. DESCR: Food Industry; Labor Unions; Mexico; Sex Roles; Strikes and Lockouts; Women; *Working Women.

2753 Klor de Alva, J. Jorge. Chicana history and historical significance: some theoretical considerations. IN: Del Castillo, Adelaida R., ed. BETWEEN BORDERS: ESSAYS ON MEXICANA/CHICANA HISTORY. Encino, CA: Floricanto Press, 1990, p. 61-86. English. DESCR: Chicana Studies; *Historiography; Sexism.

2754 Lara-Cea, Helen. Notes on the use of parish registers in the reconstruction of Chicana history in California prior to 1850. IN: Del

Castillo, Adelaida R., ed. BETWEEN BORDERS: ESSAYS ON MEXICANA/CHICANA HISTORY. Encino, CA: Floricanto Press, 1990, p. 131-159. English. DESCR: *California; Catholic Church; Indigenismo; Mission of Santa Clara; Population; *San Jose, CA; *Vital Statistics.

2755 Macias, Anna. Against all odds: the feminist movement in Mexico to 1940. Westport, CT: Greenwood Press, 1982. xv, 195 p. English. DESCR: Carrillo Puerto, Felipe; *Feminism; Mexican Revolution - 1910-1920; Mexico; *Women; Yucatan, Mexico.

2756 Marin, Christine. La Asociacion Hispano-Americana de Madres y Esposas: Tucson's Mexican American women in World War II. RENATO ROSALDO LECTURE SERIES MONOGRAPH, Vol. 1, (Summer 1985), p. [5]-18. English. DESCR: Cultural Organizations; *La Asociacion Hispano-Americana de Madres y Esposas, Tucson, AZ; Organizations; *Tucson, AZ; World War II.

2757 Matsuda, Gema. La Chicana organizes: the Comision Femenil Mexicana in perspective. REGENERACION, Vol. 2, no. 4 (1975), p. 25-27. English. DESCR: Bojorquez, Frances; Chicano Movement; *Comision Femenil Mexicana Nacional; De la Cruz, Juana Ines; Flores, Francisca; Machismo; Malinche; Prisons; Sex Stereotypes; *Sexism.

2758 Miranda, Gloria E. Hispano-Mexican childrearing practices in pre-American Santa Barbara. SOUTHERN CALIFORNIA QUARTERLY, Vol. 65, no. 4 (Winter 1983), p. 307-320. English. DESCR: *Children; Cultural Characteristics; *Family; *Parenting; Santa Barbara, CA; Socialization.

2759 Mirande, Alfredo and Enriquez, Evangelina. Chicanas in the history of the Southwest. IN: Duran, Livie Isauro and Bernard, H. Russell, eds. INTRODUCTION TO CHICANO STUDIES. 2nd ed. New York: Macmillan, 1982, p. 156-179. English. DESCR: Arguello, Concepcion; Barcelo, Gertrudes "La Tules"; Fages, Eulalia; "Juanita of Downieville"; Robledo, Refugio; Urrea, Teresa.

2760 Monroy, Douglas. La costura en Los Angeles, 1933-1939: the ILGWU and the politics of domination. IN: Mora, Magdalena and Del Castillo, Adelaida, eds. MEXICAN WOMEN IN THE UNITED STATES: STRUGGLES PAST AND PRESENT. Los Angeles, CA: Chicano Studies Research Center, UCLA, 1980, p. 171-178. English. DESCR: *Garment Industry; International Ladies Garment Workers Union (ILGWU); Labor Unions; Los Angeles, CA.

2761 Monroy, Douglas. "They didn't call them 'padre' for nothing": patriarchy in Hispanic California. IN: Del Castillo, Adelaida R., ed. BETWEEN BORDERS: ESSAYS ON MEXICANA/CHICANA HISTORY. Encino, CA: Floricanto Press, 1990, p. 433-445. English. DESCR: *California; Clergy; *Machismo; Rape; *Sex Roles; *Sexism; Spanish Influence; Women Men Relations.

2762 Moreno, Dorinda. The image of the Chicana and the La Raza woman. CARACOL, Vol. 2, no. 12 (August 1976), p. 14-15. English.

2763 Nieto Gomez de Lazarin, Anna. Un proposito para estudios femeniles de la chicana. REGENERACION, Vol. 2, no. 4 (1975), p. 30, 31-32. English. DESCR: Chicano Studies; Curriculum; *Education; Nava, Yolanda; Sexism.

History (cont.)

Blacks; Feminism; Native Americans; *Women.

2764 Phillips, Rachel. Marina/Malinche: masks and shadows. IN: Miller, Beth, ed. WOMEN IN HISPANIC LITERATURE: ICONS AND FALLEN IDOLS. Berkeley, CA: University of California Press, 1983, p. 97-114. English. DESCR: Aztecs; Malinche; Psychohistory; *Symbolism.

2765 Rose, Margaret. Women in the United Farm Workers: a study of Chicana Mexicana participation in a labor union, 1950-1980. Thesis (Ph.D.)--University of California, Los Angeles, 1988. 403p. English. DESCR: Huerta, Dolores; *Labor Unions; *Sex Roles; United Farmworkers of America (UFW); Working Women.

2766 Rubio Goldsmith, Raquel. Oral history: considerations and problems for its use in the history of Mexicanas in the United States. IN: Del Castillo, Adelaida R., ed. BETWEEN BORDERS: ESSAYS ON MEXICANA/CHICANA HISTORY. Encino, CA: Floricanto Press, 1990, p. 161-173. English. DESCR: *Oral History; *Research Methodology.

2767 Ruiz Funes, Concepcion and Tunon, Enriqueta. Panorama de las luchas de la mujer mexicana en el siglo XX. IN: Del Castillo, Adelaida R., ed. BETWEEN BORDERS: ESSAYS ON MEXICANA/CHICANA HISTORY. Encino, CA: Floricanto Press, 1990, p. 336-357. Spanish. DESCR: Coordinadora de Mujeres Trabajadoras; *Feminism; Frente Unido Pro Derechos de la Mujer; Labor Unions; *Mexico; Sex Roles; *Women.

2768 Ruiz, Vicki L. California's early pioneers: Spanish/Mexican women. SOCIAL STUDIES REVIEW, Vol. 29, no. 1 (Fall 1989), p. 24-30. English. DESCR: *California; Ruiz Burton, Maria Amparo; Sex Roles; *Women.

2769 Ruiz, Vicki L. Cannery women/cannery lives: Mexican women, unionization, and the California food processing industry, 1930-1950. Albuquerque, NM: University of New Mexico Press, 1987. xviii, 194 p.: ill. English. DESCR: Agricultural Labor Unions; California; *Canneries; Family; Industrial Workers; Labor Disputes; *Labor Unions; Trade Unions; United Cannery Agricultural Packing and Allied Workers of America (UCAPAWA); Women.

2770 Ruiz, Vicki L. Dead ends or gold mines?: using missionary records in Mexican-American women's history. FRONTIERS: A JOURNAL OF WOMEN STUDIES, Vol. 12, no. 1 (1991), p. 33-56. English. DESCR: Archives; Clergy; El Paso, TX; *Methodist Church; Protestant Church; *Research Methodology; *Rose Gregory Houchen Settlement House, El Paso, TX.

2771 Ruiz, Vicki L. Obreras y madres: labor activism among Mexican women and its impact on the family. RENATO ROSALDO LECTURE SERIES MONOGRAPH, Vol. 1, (Summer 1985), p. [19]-38. English. DESCR: Child Care Centers; Children; *Labor Unions; *Mexico; Sex Roles; Women; *Working Women.

2772 Ruiz, Vicki L. Working for wages: Mexican women in the Southwest, 1930-1980. Tucson, AZ: Southwest Institute for Research on Women, 1984. 24 p. English. DESCR: *Employment; *Income; Labor Unions; *Women.

2773 Ruiz, Vicki L., ed. and DuBois, Ellen Carol, ed. Unequal sisters: a multicultural reader in U.S. women's history. New York: Routledge, 1990. xvi, 473 p. English. DESCR: Anglo Americans; Asian Americans;

2774 Salas, Elizabeth. Soldaderas in the Mexican military: myth and history. Austin, TX: University of Texas Press, 1990. xiii, 163 p., [12] p. of plates: ill. English. DESCR: Aztecs; *La Adelita; Mexican Revolution - 1910-1920; Mexico; *Military; Symbolism; War; *Women.

2775 Salas, Elizabeth. Soldaderas in the Mexican military: myth and history. Thesis (Ph.D.)--University of California, Los Angeles, 1987. 313p. English. DESCR: Aztecs; La Adelita; Mexican Revolution - 1910-1920; Mexico; Military; Symbolism; War; *Women.

2776 Sanchez, Rosaura. The history of Chicanas: a proposal for a materialist perspective. IN: Del Castillo, Adelaida R., ed. BETWEEN BORDERS: ESSAYS ON MEXICANA/CHICANA HISTORY. Encino, CA: Floricanto Press, 1990, p. 1-29. English. DESCR: Apodaca, Maria Linda; *Chicana Studies; Del Castillo, Adelaida R.; Feminism; Historiography; Morales, Sylvia; Ruiz, Vicki L.

2777 Santiago, Myrna I. La Chicana. FEM, Vol. 8, no. 34 (June, July, 1984), p. 5-9. Spanish. DESCR: *Chicano Movement; *Feminism.

2778 Santillan, Richard. Rosita the riveter: Midwest Mexican American women during World War II, 1941-1945. PERSPECTIVES IN MEXICAN AMERICAN STUDIES, Vol. 2, (1989), p. 115-147. English. DESCR: Industrial Workers; Intergroup Relations; Language Usage; *Midwestern States; Military; Mutualistas; Sexism; War; *Working Women; *World War II.

2779 Schlissel, Lillian, ed.; Ruiz, Vicki L., ed.; and Monk, Janice, ed. Western women: their land, their lives. Albuquerque, NM: University of New Mexico Press, c1988. vi, 354 p. English. DESCR: Anglo Americans; Immigration; Intermarriage; Labor; Native Americans; *Social History and Conditions; Southwestern United States; *Women.

2780 Sheridan, Thomas E. From Luisa Espinel to Lalo Guerrero: Tucson's Mexican musicians before World War II. JOURNAL OF ARIZONA HISTORY, Vol. 25, no. 3 (Fall 1984), p. 285-300. English. DESCR: Biography; Espinel, Luisa Ronstadt; Guerrero, Eduardo "Lalo"; Montijo, Manuel; *Musicians; Rebeil, Julia; Singers; *Tucson, AZ.

2781 Stewart, Kenneth L. and de Leon, Arnoldo. Work force participation among Mexican immigrant women in Texas, 1900. BORDERLANDS JOURNAL, Vol. 9, no. 1 (Spring 1986), p. 69-74. English. DESCR: Employment; *Immigrants; Texas; Women; *Working Women.

2782 Sweeney, Judith. Chicana history: a review of the literature. IN: Sanchez, Rosaura and Martinez Cruz, Rosa, eds. ESSAYS ON LA MUJER. Los Angeles, CA: Chicano Studies Center Publications, UCLA, 1977, p. 99-123. English. DESCR: Literature Reviews.

2783 Taylor, Paul S. Mexican women in Los Angeles industry in 1928. AZTLAN, Vol. 11, no. 1 (Spring 1980), p. 99-131. English. DESCR: Employment; Industrial Workers; Los Angeles, CA; *Working Women.

History (cont.)

2784 Vasquez, Josefina. Educacion y papel de la mujer en Mexico. IN: Del Castillo, Adelaida R., ed. BETWEEN BORDERS: ESSAYS ON MEXICANA/CHICANA HISTORY. Encino, CA: Floricanto Press, 1990, p. 377-398. Spanish. **DESCR:** *Education; *Mexico; *Sex Roles; *Women.

2785 Veyna, Angelina F. Una vista al pasado: la mujer en Nuevo Mexico, 1744-1767. TRABAJOS MONOGRAFICOS, Vol. 1, no. 1 (1985), p. 28-42. English. **DESCR:** *New Mexico; Sex Roles.

2786 Veyna, Angelina F. Women in early New Mexico: a preliminary view. IN: Cordova, Teresa, et al., eds. CHICANA VOICES. Austin, TX: Center for Mexican American Studies, 1986, p. 120-135. English. **DESCR:** Administration of Justice; New Mexico; *Women.

2787 Weber, Devra Anne. Mexican women on strike: memory, history and oral narratives. IN: Del Castillo, Adelaida R., ed. BETWEEN BORDERS: ESSAYS ON MEXICANA/CHICANA HISTORY. Encino, CA: Floricanto Press, 1990, p. 175-200. English. **DESCR:** *1933 Cotton Strike; Cotton Industry; *Oral History; San Joaquin Valley, CA; Strikes and Lockouts; *Valdez, Rosaura; Working Women.

Home Altars
USE: Altars

Homosexuality

2788 Alarcon, Norma and Moraga, Cherrie. Interview with Cherrie Moraga. THIRD WOMAN, Vol. 3, no. 1-2 (1986), p. 127-134. English. **DESCR:** Authors; Biography; *Moraga, Cherrie; Sex Roles.

2789 Alonso, Ana Maria and Koreck, Maria Teresa. Silences: "Hispanics", AIDS, and sexual practices. DIFFERENCES: A JOURNAL OF FEMINIST CULTURAL STUDIES, Vol. 1, no. 1 (Winter 1989), p. 101-124. English. **DESCR:** *AIDS (Disease); Human Immunodeficiency Virus (HIV); Machismo; Mexico; *Self-Referents; Sex Roles; *Sexual Behavior.

2790 Arguelles, Lourdes and Rivero, Anne M. HIV infection/AIDS and Latinas in Los Angeles County: considerations for prevention, treatment, and research practice. CALIFORNIA SOCIOLOGIST, Vol. 11, no. 1-2 (1988), p. 69-89. English. **DESCR:** *AIDS (Disease); Cultural Characteristics; Health Education; Human Immunodeficiency Virus (HIV); Los Angeles County, CA; Natural Support Systems; Parent and Child Relationships; Sexual Behavior; *Women.

2791 Castillo, Ana. La macha: toward a beautiful whole self. IN: Trujillo, Carla, ed. CHICANA LESBIANS: THE GIRLS OUR MOTHERS WARNED US ABOUT. Berkeley, CA: Third Woman Press, 1991, p. 24-48. English. **DESCR:** *Sexual Behavior.

2792 Garcia, Alma M. The development of Chicana feminist discourse, 1970-1980. GENDER & SOCIETY, Vol. 3, no. 2 (June 1989), p. 217-238. English. **DESCR:** Anglo Americans; Chicana Studies; *Chicano Movement; *Feminism; Machismo; National Association for Chicano Studies (NACS); Organizations; *Sexism; Women.

2793 Garcia, Alma M. The development of Chicana feminist discourse, 1970-1980. IN: DuBois, Ellen Carol and Ruiz, Vicki L., eds. UNEQUAL SISTERS: A MULTICULTURAL READER IN U.S. WOMEN'S HISTORY. New York: Routledge, 1990, p. 418-431. English. **DESCR:** Anglo Americans; Chicana Studies; *Chicano Movement; *Feminism; Machismo; National Association for Chicano Studies (NACS); Organizations; *Sexism; Women.

2794 Moraga, Cherrie. [Letter to Coordinadora Nacional de Lesbianas Feministas]. CORRESPONDENCIA, no. 9 (December 1990), p. 19-20. Bilingual. **DESCR:** Feminism; Identity; Mexico-U.S. Lesbian Exchange.

2795 Moraga, Cherrie. Loving in the war years: lo que nunca paso por sus labios. Boston, MA: South End Press, c1983. viii, 152 p. English. **DESCR:** *Autobiography; Moraga, Cherrie; *Poems.

2796 Navarro, Marta A. and Castillo, Ana. Interview with Ana Castillo. IN: Trujillo, Carla, ed. CHICANA LESBIANS: THE GIRLS OUR MOTHERS WARNED US ABOUT. Berkeley, CA: Third Woman Press, 1991, p. 113-132. English. **DESCR:** *Authors; Castillo, Ana; Literature.

2797 Pavich, Emma Guerrero. A Chicana perspective on Mexican culture and sexuality. JOURNAL OF SOCIAL WORK AND HUMAN SEXUALITY, Vol. 4, no. 3 (Spring 1986), p. 47-65. English. **DESCR:** California; Cultural Characteristics; Family; Feminism; Machismo; Sex Roles; Sex Stereotypes; *Sexual Behavior; Women Men Relations.

2798 Perez, Emma. Sexuality and discourse: notes from a Chicana survivor. IN: Trujillo, Carla, ed. CHICANA LESBIANS: THE GIRLS OUR MOTHERS WARNED US ABOUT. Berkeley, CA: Third Woman Press, 1991, p. 159-184. English. **DESCR:** *Feminism; Intergroup Relations; Paz, Octavio; *Sex Roles; *Sexism; Skin Color.

2799 Ramos, Juanita, ed. Companeras: Latina lesbians (an anthology). New York: Latina Lesbian History Project, 1987. xxix, 265 p. Bilingual. **DESCR:** *Literature; Poetry; Prose; *Women.

2800 Saldivar-Hull, Sonia. Feminism on the border: from gender politics to geopolitics. IN: Calderon, Hector and Saldivar, Jose David, eds. CRITICISM IN THE BORDERLANDS: STUDIES IN CHICANO LITERATURE, CULTURE, AND IDEOLOGY. Durham, NC: Duke University Press, 1991, p. [203]-220. English. **DESCR:** Anglo Americans; *Anzaldua, Gloria; *BORDERLANDS/LA FRONTERA: THE NEW MESTIZA; Feminism; *Literary Criticism; Mestizaje; Moraga, Cherrie; Sexism; "The Cariboo Cafe" [short story]; Viramontes, Helena Maria; Women.

2801 Sternbach, Nancy Saporta. "A deep racial memory of love": the Chicana feminism of Cherrie Moraga. IN: Horno-Delgado, Asuncion, et al., eds. BREAKING BOUNDARIES: LATINA WRITING AND CRITICAL READINGS. Amherst, MA: University of Massachusetts Press, c1989, p. 48-61. English. **DESCR:** Discrimination; Feminism; Literary Criticism; *LOVING IN THE WAR YEARS; Machismo; Malinche; *Moraga, Cherrie; Sex Stereotypes; Sexism.

Homosexuality (cont.)

2802 Trujillo, Carla. Chicana lesbians: fear and loathing in the Chicano community. IN: Trujillo, Carla, ed. CHICANA LESBIANS: THE GIRLS OUR MOTHERS WARNED US ABOUT. Berkeley, CA: Third Woman Press, 1991, p. 186-194. English. **DESCR:** Essays; *Sex Roles; Sexual Behavior.

2803 Trujillo, Carla, ed. Chicana lesbians: the girls our mothers warned us about. Berkeley, CA: Third Woman Press, 1991. xii, 202 p.: ill. English. **DESCR:** Literary Criticism; Poems; Prose.

2804 Yarbro-Bejarano, Yvonne. Cherrie Moraga's GIVING UP THE GHOST: the representation of female desire. THIRD WOMAN, Vol. 3, no. 1-2 (1986), p. 113-120. English. **DESCR:** *GIVING UP THE GHOST; Moraga, Cherrie; Teatro.

2805 Yarbro-Bejarano, Yvonne. De-constructing the lesbian body: Cherrie Moraga's LOVING IN THE WAR YEARS. IN: Trujillo, Carla, ed. CHICANA LESBIANS: THE GIRLS OUR MOTHERS WARNED US ABOUT. Berkeley, CA: Third Woman Press, 1991, p. 143-155. English. **DESCR:** Literary Criticism; *LOVING IN THE WAR YEARS; *Moraga, Cherrie; Skin Color.

2806 Yarbro-Bejarano, Yvonne. Primer encuentro de lesbianas feministas latinoamericanas y caribenas. THIRD WOMAN, Vol. 4, (1989), p. 143-146. English. **DESCR:** Caribbean Region; *Conferences and Meetings; First Meeting of Latin American and Caribbean Feminist Lesbians (October 14-17, 1987: Cuernavaca, Mexico); Latin Americans; Sexual Behavior; *Women.

House of the Divine Providence [convent], Douglas, AZ

2807 Goldsmith, Raquel Rubio. La Mexicana/Chicana. RENATO ROSALDO LECTURE SERIES MONOGRAPH, Vol. 1, (Summer 1985), p. 1-67. English. **DESCR:** Clergy; Labor Unions; *Social History and Conditions; Women; World War II.

2808 Goldsmith, Raquel Rubio. Shipwrecked in the desert: a short history of the adventures and struggles for survival of the Mexican Sisters of the House of the Providence in Douglas, Arizona during their first twenty-two years of existence (1927-1949). RENATO ROSALDO LECTURE SERIES MONOGRAPH, Vol. 1, (Summer 1985), p. [39]-67. English. **DESCR:** Catholic Church; Clergy; Douglas, AZ; History; Women.

THE HOUSE ON MANGO STREET

2809 Cisneros, Sandra. Do you know me?: I wrote THE HOUSE ON MANGO STREET. THE AMERICAS REVIEW, Vol. 15, no. 1 (Spring 1987), p. 77-79. English. **DESCR:** Authors; Autobiography; Cisneros, Sandra; *Prose.

2810 Gonzalez-Berry, Erlinda and Rebolledo, Tey Diana. Growing up Chicano: Tomas Rivera and Sandra Cisneros. REVISTA CHICANO-RIQUENA, Vol. 13, no. 3-4 (Fall, Winter, 1985), p. 109-119. English. **DESCR:** Cisneros, Sandra; Cultural Characteristics; *Literary Criticism; Rivera, Tomas; Sex Roles; Y NO SE LO TRAGO LA TIERRA/AND THE EARTH DID NOT PART.

2811 McCracken, Ellen. Latina narrative and politics of signification: articulation, antagonism, and populist rupture. CRITICA, Vol. 2, no. 2 (Fall 1990), p. 202-207.

English. **DESCR:** *Cisneros, Sandra; IN NUEVA YORK; *Literary Criticism; *Mohr, Nicolasa; Puerto Ricans; RITUALS OF SURVIVAL; Short Story; Women.

2812 McCracken, Ellen. Sandra Cisneros' THE HOUSE ON MANGO STREET: community-oriented introspection and the demystification of patriarchal violence. IN: Horno-Delgado, Asuncion, et al., eds. BREAKING BOUNDARIES: LATINA WRITING AND CRITICAL READINGS. Amherst, MA: University of Massachusetts Press, c1989, p. 62-71. English. **DESCR:** *Cisneros, Sandra; Literary Criticism.

2813 Olivares, Julian. Sandra Cisneros' THE HOUSE ON MANGO STREET and the poetics of space. THE AMERICAS REVIEW, Vol. 15, no. 3-4 (Fall, Winter, 1987), p. 160-170. English. **DESCR:** Cisneros, Sandra; *Literary Criticism.

2814 Quintana, Alvina E. Chicana discourse: negations and mediations. Thesis (Ph.D.)--University of California, Santa Cruz, 1989. 226 p. English. **DESCR:** Authors; Castillo, Ana; Chavez, Denise; Chicano Movement; Cisneros, Sandra; Ethnology; Feminism; Literary Criticism; *Literature; NOVENA NARRATIVES; Oral Tradition; Political Ideology; THE LAST OF THE MENU GIRLS; THE MIXQUIAHUALA LETTERS.

2815 Rodriguez Aranda, Pilar E. and Cisneros, Sandra. On the solitary fate of being Mexican, female, wicked and thirty-three: an interview with writer Sandra Cisneros. THE AMERICAS REVIEW, Vol. 18, no. 1 (Spring 1990), p. 64-80. English. **DESCR:** *Artists; *Cisneros, Sandra; Literature; MY WICKED WICKED WAYS.

2816 Rosaldo, Renato. Fables of the fallen guy. IN: Calderon, Hector and Saldivar, Jose David, eds. CRITICISM IN THE BORDERLANDS: STUDIES IN CHICANO LITERATURE, CULTURE AND IDEOLOGY. Durham, NC: Duke University Press, 1991, p. [84]-93. English. **DESCR:** Chavez, Denise; Cisneros, Sandra; Fiction; Literary Characters; *Literary Criticism; Rios, Alberto; Sex Roles; THE IGUANA KILLER: TWELVE STORIES OF THE HEART; THE LAST OF THE MENU GIRLS.

2817 Saldivar, Ramon. The dialectics of subjectivity: gender and difference in Isabella Rios, Sandra Cisneros, and Cherrie Moraga. IN: Saldivar, Ramon. CHICANO NARRATIVE: THE DIALECTICS OF DIFFERENCE. Madison, WI: University of Wisconsin Press, 1990, p. 171-199. English. **DESCR:** Authors; Autobiography; *Cisneros, Sandra; Feminism; Fiction; *Literary Criticism; Literature; LOVING IN THE WAR YEARS; *Moraga, Cherrie; Political Ideology; *Rios, Isabella; VICTUUM.

Housing

2818 Longeaux y Vasquez, Enriqueta. The woman of La Raza. REGENERACION, Vol. 2, no. 4 (1975), p. 34-36. English. **DESCR:** Child Care Centers; Discrimination; Gallo, Juana; La Adelita; Machismo; Sex Roles; *Social History and Conditions; Working Women.

Housing (cont.)

2819 Longeaux y Vasquez, Enriqueta. The woman of
La Raza. IN: Valdez, Luis and Steiner, Stan,
eds. AZTLAN: AN ANTHOLOGY OF MEXICAN
AMERICAN LITERATURE. New York: Vintage
Books, 1972, p. 272-273. Also IN: Salinas,
Luis Omar and Faderman, Lillian, compilers.
FROM THE BARRIO: A CHICANO ANTHOLOGY. San
Francisco, CA: Canfield Press, 1973, p.
20-24. English. DESCR: Child Care Centers;
Discrimination; Gallo, Juana; La Adelita;
Machismo; Sex Roles; *Social History and
Conditions; Working Women.

2820 White, Marni, et al. Perceived crime in the
neighborhood and mental health of women and
children. ENVIRONMENT AND BEHAVIOR, Vol. 19,
no. 5 (September 1987), p. 588-613. English.
DESCR: Attitudes; Children; Criminology;
*Mental Health; Women.

Houston, TX

2821 Bello, Ruth T. Being Hispanic in Houston: a
matter of identity. THE AMERICAS REVIEW,
Vol. 16, no. 1 (Spring 1988), p. 31-43.
English. DESCR: Autobiography; *Essays;
*Identity; *Self-Referents.

2822 Cardenas, Gilbert and Flores, Estevan T. The
migration and settlement of undocumented
women. Austin, TX: CMAS Publications, 1986.
69 p. English. DESCR: Employment;
*Immigration; Income; Labor Supply and
Market; *Migration Patterns; Public Policy;
Socioeconomic Factors; *Undocumented
Workers.

2823 Cardenas, Gilbert; Shelton, Beth Anne; and
Pena, Devon Gerardo. Undocumented immigrant
women in the Houston labor force. CALIFORNIA
SOCIOLOGIST, Vol. 5, no. 2 (Summer 1982), p.
98-118. English. DESCR: Employment;
*Immigrants; *Labor Supply and Market;
*Undocumented Workers.

2824 Mindiola, Tatcho, Jr. The cost of being a
Mexican female worker in the 1970 Houston
labor market. AZTLAN, Vol. 11, no. 2 (Fall
1980), p. 231-247. English. DESCR:
Discrimination; *Discrimination in
Employment; Labor Supply and Market; Working
Women.

2825 Saavedra-Vela, Pilar. Hispanic women in
double jeopardy. AGENDA, Vol. 7, no. 6
(November, December, 1977), p. 4-7. English.
DESCR: Conferences and Meetings;
Discrimination; National Women's Conference
(November, 1977: Houston, TX); *Sexism.

2826 Saavedra-Vela, Pilar. Nosotras in Houston.
AGENDA, Vol. 8, no. 2 (March, April, 1978),
p. 26-31. English. DESCR: Conferences and
Meetings; *Feminism; National Women's
Conference (November, 1977: Houston, TX)

2827 San Miguel, Rachel. Being Hispanic in
Houston: my name is Carmen Quezada. THE
AMERICAS REVIEW, Vol. 16, no. 1 (Spring
1988), p. 44-52. English. DESCR:
Autobiography; *Essays; Identity.

2828 Sanford, Judy, et al. Patterns of reported
rape in a tri-ethnic population: Houston,
Texas, 1974-1975. AMERICAN JOURNAL OF PUBLIC
HEALTH, Vol. 69, no. 5 (May 1979), p.
480-484. English. DESCR: Anglo Americans;
Blacks; Criminology; *Ethnic Groups; *Rape;
Statistics; Women.

Hoyo-Mara Gang, East Los Angeles, CA

2829 Moore, Joan W. Mexican-American women
addicts: the influence of family background.
IN: Glick, Ronald and Moore, Joan, eds.
DRUGS IN HISPANIC COMMUNITIES. New
Brunswick, NJ: Rutgers University Press,
c1990, p. 127-153. English. DESCR: Barrios;
*Drug Addicts; Drug Use; East Los Angeles,
CA; *Family; *Gangs; Heroin; Pachucos; Sex
Roles; Socialization; White Fence Gang;
Youth.

La Huelga
     USE: Boycotts

Huerta, Dolores

2830 Chavez, Henri. Unsung heroine of La Causa.
REGENERACION, Vol. 1, no. 10 (1971), p. 20.
English. DESCR: AFL-CIO United Farmworkers
Organizing Committee; Agricultural Labor
Unions; Community Service Organization, Los
Angeles, (CSO); Family; Farm Workers;
Poverty; Working Women.

2831 Delgado Campbell, Dolores. Shattering the
stereotype: Chicanas as labor union
organizers. BERKELEY WOMEN OF COLOR, no. 11
(Summer 1983), p. 20-23. English. DESCR:
Farah Manufacturing Co., El Paso, TX; Farah
Strike; *Gonzalez Parsons, Lucia; *Labor
Unions; Moreno, Luisa [union organizer];
Tenayuca, Emma; Working Women.

2832 Echaveste, Beatrice and Huerta, Dolores. In
the shadow of the eagle: Huerta = A la
sombra del aguila: Huerta. AMERICAS 2001,
Vol. 1, no. 3 (November, December, 1987), p.
26-30. Bilingual. DESCR: Agricultural Labor
Unions; Boycotts; *Farm Workers; United
Farmworkers of America (UFW).

2833 Goldman, Shifra M. Trabajadoras mexicanas y
chicanas en las artes visuales. IN: Leal,
Salvador, ed. A TRAVES DE LA FRONTERA.
Mexico, D.F.: Centro de Estudios Economicos
y Sociales del Tercer Mundo, A.C.; Instituto
de Investigaciones Esteticas, U.N.A.M.,
1983, p. 153-161. Spanish. DESCR: Art;
Gonzalez Parsons, Lucia; Moreno, Luisa
[union organizer]; SALT OF THE EARTH [film];
Tenayuca, Emma; *Working Women.

2834 Huerta, Dolores. Dolores Huerta talks about
Republicans, Cesar, children and her home
town. REGENERACION, Vol. 2, no. 4 (1975), p.
20-24. English. DESCR: *Agricultural Labor
Unions; *Biography; Chavez, Cesar E.;
Community Service Organization, Los Angeles,
(CSO); Democratic Party; Elected Officials;
Flores, Art; McGovern, George; *Politics;
Ramirez, Henry M.; Ross, Fred; Sanchez,
Philip V.; United Farmworkers of America
(UFW); Working Women.

2835 Huerta, Dolores. Dolores Huerta talks about
Republicans, Cesar, children and her home
town. IN: Servin, Manuel P. ed. THE MEXICAN
AMERICANS: AN AWAKENING MINORITY. 2nd ed.
Beverly Hills, CA: Glencoe Press, 1974, p.
283-294. English. DESCR: *Agricultural Labor
Unions; *Biography; Chavez, Cesar E.;
Community Service Organization, Los Angeles,
(CSO); Democratic Party; Elected Officials;
Flores, Art; McGovern, George; *Politics;
Ramirez, Henry M.; Ross, Fred; Sanchez,
Philip V.; United Farmworkers of America
(UFW); Working Women.

Huerta, Dolores (cont.)

2836 Mercado, Olivia. Chicanas: myths and roles. COMADRE, no. 1 (Summer 1977), p. 26-32. English. **DESCR:** Feminism; Gallo, Juana; *Identity; Leadership; Sex Roles.

2837 Rose, Margaret. Traditional and nontraditional patterns of female activism in the United Farm Workers of America, 1962-1980. FRONTIERS: A JOURNAL OF WOMEN STUDIES, Vol. 11, no. 1 (1990), p. [26]-32. English. **DESCR:** Boycotts; California; Chavez, Cesar E.; *Chavez, Helen; Labor Disputes; Labor Unions; National Farm Workers Association (NFWA); Sex Roles; Strikes and Lockouts; *United Farmworkers of America (UFW).

2838 Rose, Margaret. Women in the United Farm Workers: a study of Chicana Mexicana participation in a labor union, 1950-1980. Thesis (Ph.D.)--University of California, Los Angeles, 1988. 403p. English. **DESCR:** History; *Labor Unions; *Sex Roles; United Farmworkers of America (UFW); Working Women.

Human Immunodeficiency Virus (HIV)

2839 Alonso, Ana Maria and Koreck, Maria Teresa. Silences: "Hispanics", AIDS, and sexual practices. DIFFERENCES: A JOURNAL OF FEMINIST CULTURAL STUDIES, Vol. 1, no. 1 (Winter 1989), p. 101-124. English. **DESCR:** *AIDS (Disease); *Homosexuality; Machismo; Mexico; *Self-Referents; Sex Roles; *Sexual Behavior.

2840 Arguelles, Lourdes and Rivero, Anne M. HIV infection/AIDS and Latinas in Los Angeles County: considerations for prevention, treatment, and research practice. CALIFORNIA SOCIOLOGIST, Vol. 11, no. 1-2 (1988), p. 69-89. English. **DESCR:** *AIDS (Disease); Cultural Characteristics; Health Education; Homosexuality; Los Angeles County, CA; Natural Support Systems; Parent and Child Relationships; Sexual Behavior; *Women.

2841 Nyamathi, Adeline M. and Vasquez, Rose. Impact of poverty, homelessness, and drugs on Hispanic women at risk for HIV infection. HISPANIC JOURNAL OF BEHAVIORAL SCIENCES, Vol. 11, no. 4 (November 1989), p. 299-314. English. **DESCR:** *AIDS (Disease); Drug Use; Health Education; Locus of Control; Mental Health; Needle-Sharing; *Poverty.

Humor

2842 Castro, Rafaela. Mexican women's sexual jokes. AZTLAN, Vol. 13, no. 1-2 (Spring, Fall, 1982), p. 275-293. English. **DESCR:** *Chistes; Sexual Behavior.

2843 Rebolledo, Tey Diana. Walking the thin line: humor in Chicana literature. IN: Herrera-Sobek, Maria, ed. BEYOND STEREOTYPES: THE CRITICAL ANALYSIS OF CHICANA LITERATURE. Binghamton, NY: Bilingual Press/Editorial Bilingue, 1985, p. 91-107. English. **DESCR:** Chistes; Literary Criticism; *Poetry.

Hypertension

2844 Sorel, Janet Elaine. The relationship between gender role incongruity on measures of coping and material resources and blood pressure among Mexican-American women. Thesis (Ph.D.)--University of North Carolina at Chapel Hill, 1988. 268 p. English. **DESCR:** High Blood Pressure; Hispanic Health and Nutrition Examination Survey (HHANES); Public Health; *Sex Roles; *Stress.

"I Speak in an Illusion" [poem]

2845 Zamora, Bernice. Archetypes in Chicana poetry. DE COLORES, Vol. 4, no. 3 (1978), p. 43-52. English. **DESCR:** Cervantes, Lorna Dee; Cunningham, Veronica; "Declaration on a Day of Little Inspiration" [poem]; Hernandez, Carlota; *Literary Criticism; Lucero, Judy A.; Macias, Margarita; Mendoza, Rita; "Para Mi Hijita" [poem]; *Poetry; "Rape Report" [poem]; "The White Line" [poem]; "Working Mother's Song" [poem]; "You Can Only Blame the System for So Long" [poem]; Zamora, Katarina.

Ibarra, Rosario

2846 Carrillo, Teresa. The women's movement and the left in Mexico: the presidential candidacy of Dona Rosario Ibarra. IN: Cordova, Teresa, et al., eds. CHICANA VOICES. Austin, TX: Center for Mexican American Studies, 1986, p. 96-113. English. **DESCR:** Biography; Mexico; Politics; *Women.

Iconography
USE: Symbolism

Idar, Jovita

2847 Lomas, Clara. Mexican precursors of Chicana feminist writing. IN: National Association for Chicano Studies. ESTUDIOS CHICANOS AND THE POLITICS OF COMMUNITY. [S.l.]: National Association for Chicano Studies, c1989, p. [149]-160. English. **DESCR:** Authors; de Cardenas, Isidra T.; *Feminism; *Journalists; Literature; *Mexican Revolution - 1910-1920; Newspapers; Ramirez, Sara Estela; Villarreal, Andrea; Villegas de Magnon, Leonor.

Identity

2848 Adams, Russell P. Predictors of self-esteem and locus-of-control in Mexican-American women. Thesis (Ph.D.)--Texas Tech University, 1989. 138 p. English. **DESCR:** *Locus of Control; Mental Health; Research Methodology.

2849 Ainsworth, Diane. Cultural cross fires. IN: Duran, Livie Isauro and Bernard, H. Russell, eds. INTRODUCTION TO CHICANO STUDIES. 2nd ed. New York: Macmillan, c1982, p. 505-512. English. **DESCR:** Medical Care; *Sterilization; Velez Ibanez, Carlos.

2850 Alarcon, Norma. Chicana feminism: in the tracks of 'the' native woman. CULTURAL STUDIES, Vol. 4, no. 3 (October 1990), p. 248-256. English. **DESCR:** Cultural Studies; *Feminism; *Indigenismo; Mestizaje; Women.

2851 Alarcon, Norma. What kind of lover have you made me, Mother?: towards a theory of Chicanas' feminism and cultural identity through poetry. IN: McCluskey, Audrey T., ed. WOMEN OF COLOR: PERSPECTIVES ON FEMINISM AND IDENTITY. Bloomington, IN: Women's Studies Program, Indiana University, 1985, p. 85-110. English. **DESCR:** Brinson-Pineda, Barbara; Cervantes, Lorna Dee; Cisneros, Sandra; Culture; *Feminism; *Literary Criticism; Mora, Pat; Moraga, Cherrie; *Poetry; Tafolla, Carmen; Vigil-Pinon, Evangelina; Villanueva, Alma.

Identity (cont.)

2852 Alvarez, Robert R. A profile of the citizenship process among Hispanics in the United States. INTERNATIONAL MIGRATION REVIEW, Vol. 21, no. 2 (Summer 1987), p. 327-351. English. DESCR: Immigration and Naturalization Service (INS); *Naturalization.

2853 Anzaldua, Gloria. Borderlands/La frontera: the new mestiza. San Francisco, CA: Spinsters/Aunt Lute, 1987. 203 p. Bilingual. DESCR: Aztecs; Border Region; Mythology; Poems; Prose; Sex Roles.

2854 Asuncion-Lande, Nobleza C. Problems and strategies for sexual identity and cultural integration: Mexican-American women on the move. IN: Newmark, Eileen, ed. WOMEN'S ROLES: A CROSS-CULTURAL PERSPECTIVE. New York, NY: Pergamon Press, 1980, p. 497-506. English. DESCR: Chicano Movement; *Feminism; *Sexism.

2855 Atkinson, Donald R.; Winzelberg, Andrew; and Holland, Abby. Ethnicity, locus of control for family planning, and pregnancy counselor credibility. JOURNAL OF COUNSELING PSYCHOLOGY, Vol. 32, no. 3 (July 1985), p. 417-421. English. DESCR: Anglo Americans; Counseling (Psychological); *Family Planning; Fertility; *Locus of Control; Women.

2856 Baca Zinn, Maxine. Employment and education of Mexican-American women: the interplay of modernity and ethnicity in eight families. HARVARD EDUCATIONAL REVIEW, Vol. 50, no. 1 (February 1980), p. 47-62. English. DESCR: Acculturation; Decision Making; *Education; *Employment; *Family; Sex Roles; Social Classes; Values.

2857 Baca Zinn, Maxine. Gender and ethnic identity among Chicanos. FRONTIERS: A JOURNAL OF WOMEN STUDIES, Vol. 5, no. 2 (Summer 1980), p. 18-24. English. DESCR: Sex Roles.

2858 Bean, Frank D. and Tienda, Marta. The Hispanic population of the United States. New York: Russell Sage Foundation, 1987. xxiv, 456 p. English. DESCR: *Census; Education; Employment; Fertility; Immigration; Income; *Population; Self-Referents; *Statistics.

2859 Belk, Sharyn S., et al. Impact of ethnicity, nationality, counseling orientation, and mental health standards on stereotypic beliefs about women. SEX ROLES, Vol. 21, no. 9-10 (November 1989), p. 671-695. English. DESCR: Anglo Americans; Beliefs About Women Scale (BAWS); *Comparative Psychology; *Counseling (Psychological); Cultural Characteristics; Mental Health; *Sex Stereotypes; Sexism; Women.

2860 Bello, Ruth T. Being Hispanic in Houston: a matter of identity. THE AMERICAS REVIEW, Vol. 16, no. 1 (Spring 1988), p. 31-43. English. DESCR: Autobiography; *Essays; *Houston, TX; *Self-Referents.

2861 Bova, Breda Murphy and Phillips, Rebecca R. Hispanic women at midlife: implications for higher and adult education. JOURNAL OF ADULT EDUCATION, Vol. 18, no. 1 (Fall 1989), p. 9-15. English. DESCR: *Adult Education; Cultural Characteristics; *Higher Education; Sex Roles.

2862 Bruce-Novoa, Juan. Deconstructing the dominant patriarchal text: Cecile Pineda's narratives. IN: Horno-Delgado, Asuncion, et al., eds. BREAKING BOUNDARIES: LATINA WRITING AND CRITICAL READINGS. Amherst, MA: University of Massachusetts Press, c1989, p. 72-81. English. DESCR: *FACE; *FRIEZE; Literary Criticism; Novel; *Pineda, Cecile.

2863 Buriel, Raymond and Saenz, Evangelina. Psychocultural characteristics of college-bound and noncollege-bound Chicanas. JOURNAL OF SOCIAL PSYCHOLOGY, Vol. 110, (April 1980), p. 245-251. English. DESCR: Biculturalism; *Biculturalism Inventory for Mexican American Students (BIMAS); Higher Education; Income; Psychological Testing; Sex Roles; Social Psychology.

2864 Cabeza de Vaca, Darlene. Knowing the value God places on me... REVISTA MUJERES, Vol. 2, no. 1 (January 1985), p. 26-29. English.

2865 Davis, Sally M. and Harris, Mary B. Sexual knowledge, sexual interests, and sources of sexual information of rural and urban adolescents from three cultures. ADOLESCENCE, Vol. 17, no. 66 (Summer 1982), p. 471-492. English. DESCR: Birth Control; Cultural Characteristics; Rural Population; *Sex Education; Sex Roles; Urban Communities; Youth.

2866 Delgado Votaw, Carmen. Influencias culturales y feminismo en la mujer chicana. FEM, Vol. 10, no. 48 (October, November, 1986), p. 27-30. Spanish. DESCR: *Feminism.

2867 Fischer, Nancy A. and Marcum, John P. Ethnic integration, socioeconomic status, and fertility among Mexican Americans. SOCIAL SCIENCE QUARTERLY, Vol. 65, no. 2 (June 1984), p. 583-593. English. DESCR: Assimilation; *Fertility; Socioeconomic Factors.

2868 Fleming, Marilyn B. Problems experienced by Anglo, Hispanic and Navajo Indian women college students. JOURNAL OF AMERICAN INDIAN EDUCATION, Vol. 22, no. 1 (October 1982), p. 7-17. English. DESCR: Anglo Americans; Community Colleges; Ethnic Groups; *Higher Education; Medical Education; Native Americans; Students; Women.

2869 Flores, Francisca. Comision Femenil Mexicana. REGENERACION, Vol. 2, no. 4 (1975), p. 24-25. English. DESCR: *Abortion; Child Care Centers; Comision Femenil Mexicana Nacional; Working Women.

2870 Flores, Rosalie. The new Chicana and machismo. REGENERACION, Vol. 2, no. 4 (1975), p. 55-56. English. DESCR: *Machismo.

2871 Fu, Victoria R.; Hinkle, Dennis E.; and Korslund, Mary K. A development study of ethnic self-concept among pre-adolescent girls. JOURNAL OF GENETIC PSYCHOLOGY, Vol. 14, (March 1983), p. 67-73. English. DESCR: Comparative Psychology; Junior High School; Self-Concept Self Report Scale; Students; Youth.

2872 Gallegos y Chavez, Ester. The northern New Mexican woman: a changing silhouette. IN: Trejo, Arnulfo D., ed. THE CHICANOS: AS WE SEE OURSELVES. Tucson, AZ: University of Arizona Press, 1979, p. 67-79. English. DESCR: Machismo; New Mexico; Social History and Conditions.

Identity (cont.)

2873 Gibbs, Jewelle Taylor. Personality patterns of delinquent females: ethnic and sociocultural variations. JOURNAL OF CLINICAL PSYCHOLOGY, Vol. 38, no. 1 (January 1982), p. 198-206. English. **DESCR:** Ethnic Groups; *Juvenile Delinquency; Personality; Psychological Testing; Socioeconomic Factors.

2874 Golding, Jacqueline M. Division of household labor, strain, and depressive symptoms among Mexican Americans and non-Hispanic whites. PSYCHOLOGY OF WOMEN QUARTERLY, Vol. 14, no. 1 (March 1990), p. 103-117. English. **DESCR:** Anglo Americans; Comparative Psychology; *Depression (Psychological); Domestic Work; Employment; *Sex Roles; Women.

2875 Gonzales, Erlinda. La muerte de un refran. DE COLORES, Vol. 2, no. 3 (1975), p. 15-18. Spanish. **DESCR:** *Higher Education; *Social History and Conditions; Socialization.

2876 Gonzales, Sylvia Alicia. The Chicana perspective: a design for self-awareness. IN: Trejo, Arnulfo D., ed. THE CHICANOS: AS WE SEE OURSELVES. Tucson, AZ: University of Arizona Press, 1979, p. 81-99. English. **DESCR:** CHICANAS SPEAK OUT; Chicano Movement; Discrimination; Feminism; Machismo; Madsen, William; *Mexican Revolution - 1910-1920; Mexico; Sex Roles; THE MEXICAN-AMERICANS OF SOUTH TEXAS; Vidal, Mirta.

2877 Gonzales, Sylvia Alicia. Toward a feminist pedagogy for Chicana self-actualization. FRONTIERS: A JOURNAL OF WOMEN STUDIES, Vol. 5, no. 2 (Summer 1980), p. 48-51. English. **DESCR:** Chicano Movement; Education; *Feminism; Malinche.

2878 Gonzalez, Judith Teresa. Dilemmas of the high achieving Chicana: the double bind factor in male/female relationships. Tucson, AZ: Mexican American Studies & Research Center, University of Arizona, 1987. 31 leaves. English. **DESCR:** *Academic Achievement; Higher Education; Males; Marriage; *Sex Roles; *Sex Stereotypes; Women Men Relations.

2879 Gonzalez, Judith Teresa. Dilemmas of the high achieving Chicana: the double bind factor in male/female relationships. SEX ROLES, Vol. 18, no. 7-8 (April 1988), p. 367-380. English. **DESCR:** *Academic Achievement; Higher Education; Males; Marriage; *Sex Roles; *Sex Stereotypes; Women Men Relations.

2880 Horowitz, Ruth. Femininity and womanhood: virginity, unwed motherhood, and violence. IN: Horowitz, Ruth. HONOR AND THE AMERICAN DREAM: CULTURE AND IDENTITY IN A CHICANO COMMUNITY. New Brunswick, NJ: Rutgers University Press, 1983, p. 114-136. English. **DESCR:** *Birth Control; *Fertility; Sex Roles; *Sexual Behavior; Single Parents; Violence; Women Men Relations; Youth.

2881 Horowitz, Ruth. Passion, submission and motherhood: the negotiation of identity by unmarried innercity Chicanas. SOCIOLOGICAL QUARTERLY, Vol. 22, no. 2 (Spring 1981), p. 241-252. English. **DESCR:** Barrios; Birth Control; *Fertility; *Sex Roles; *Sexual Behavior; Single Parents; Youth.

2882 Jaramillo, Mari-Luci. How to suceed in business and remain Chicana. LA LUZ, Vol. 8, no. 7 (August, September, 1980), p. 33-35. English. **DESCR:** Assertiveness; Cultural Characteristics; Family; *Natural Support Systems; *Working Women.

2883 Jenoveva. La Chicana: principle of life, survival and endurance. CALMECAC, Vol. 1, (Summer 1980), p. 7-10. English. **DESCR:** *Sex Roles.

2884 Kimbel, Charles E.; Marsh, Nancy B.; and Kiska, Andrew C. Sex, age, and cultural differences in self-reported assertiveness. PSYCHOLOGICAL REPORTS, Vol. 55, no. 2 (October 1984), p. 419-422. English. **DESCR:** *Assertiveness; Cultural Characteristics; Sex Roles.

2885 Krause, Neal and Markides, Kyriakos S. Employment and psychological well-being in Mexican American women. JOURNAL OF HEALTH AND SOCIAL BEHAVIOR, Vol. 26, no. 1 (March 1985), p. 15-26. English. **DESCR:** *Attitudes; *Employment; Mental Health; Sex Roles; Working Women.

2886 Lampe, Philip E. Female Mexican Americans: minority within a minority. BORDERLANDS JOURNAL, Vol. 6, no. 2 (Spring 1983), p. 99-109. English. **DESCR:** *Assimilation.

2887 Longeaux y Vasquez, Enriqueta. Soy Chicana primero. LA RAZA HABLA, Vol. 1, no. 1 (January 1976), p. 1-5. English. **DESCR:** Chicano Movement; *Feminism.

2888 Longeaux y Vasquez, Enriqueta. Soy Chicana primero. EL CUADERNO, Vol. 1, no. 1 (1971), p. 17-22. English. **DESCR:** *Chicano Movement; *Feminism.

2889 Lorenzana, Noemi. La Chicana: transcending the old and carving out a new life and self-image. DE COLORES, Vol. 2, no. 3 (1975), p. 6-14. English. **DESCR:** *Census; Population; *Social History and Conditions.

2890 Lorenzana, Noemi. Hijas de Aztlan. DE COLORES, Vol. 1, no. 3 (Summer 1974), p. 39-44. Bilingual.

2891 Macklin, June and Teniente de Costilla, Alvina. Virgen de Guadalupe and the American dream: the melting pot bubbles on in Toledo, Ohio. IN: West, Stanley A. and Macklin, June, eds. THE CHICANO EXPERIENCE. Boulder, CO: Westview Press, 1979, p. 111-143. English. **DESCR:** Assimilation; Catholic Church; Intermarriage; La Virgen de Guadalupe; Migration Patterns; Quinceaneras; Toledo, OH.

2892 Major, Linda Borsch. The psyche: changing role creates Latina's world of conflict. AGENDA, no. 4 (Spring 1974), p. 6-7. English. **DESCR:** Attitudes.

2893 Martinez, Ruben and Dukes, Richard L. Race, gender and self-esteem among youth. HISPANIC JOURNAL OF BEHAVIORAL SCIENCES, Vol. 9, no. 4 (December 1987), p. 427-443. English. **DESCR:** *Comparative Psychology; *Sex Roles; *Youth.

2894 Melville, Margarita B. Introduction. IN: Melville, Margarita B., ed. TWICE A MINORITY. St. Louis, MO: Mosby, 1980, p. 1-9. English.

2895 Melville, Margarita B. Selective acculturation of female Mexican migrants. IN: Melville, Margarita B., ed. TWICE A MINORITY. St. Louis, MO: Mosby, 1980, p. 155-163. English. **DESCR:** *Acculturation; Migrant Labor; Working Women.

Identity (cont.)

2896 Mercado, Olivia. Chicanas: myths and roles. COMADRE, no. 1 (Summer 1977), p. 26-32. English. DESCR: Feminism; Gallo, Juana; Huerta, Dolores; Leadership; Sex Roles.

2897 Mesa-Bains, Amalia. A study of the influence of culture on the development of identity among a group of Chicana artists. Thesis (Ph.D.)--Wright Institute Graduate School of Psychology, 1983. 219 p. English. DESCR: *Artists; *Culture.

2898 Mirande, Alfredo. Que gacho es ser macho: it's a drag to be a macho man. AZTLAN, Vol. 17, no. 2 (Fall 1986), p. 63-89. English. DESCR: *Cultural Characteristics; *Machismo; Personality; Sex Roles; *Sex Stereotypes; Values.

2899 Moraga, Cherrie. [Letter to Coordinadora Nacional de Lesbianas Feministas]. CORRESPONDENCIA, no. 9 (December 1990), p. 19-20. Bilingual. DESCR: Feminism; *Homosexuality; Mexico-U.S. Lesbian Exchange.

2900 Mosher, William D.; Johnson, David P.; and Horn, Marjorie C. Religion and fertility in the United States: the importance of marriage patterns and Hispanic origin. DEMOGRAPHY, Vol. 23, no. 3 (August 1986), p. 367-379. English. DESCR: *Catholic Church; *Fertility; Marriage; Population; *Religion.

2901 Navar, Isabelle. Como Chicana mi madre. ENCUENTRO FEMENIL, Vol. 1, no. 2 (1974), p. 8-12. English.

2902 Navar, Isabelle. La Mexicana: an image of strength. AGENDA, no. 4 (Spring 1974), p. 3-5. English. DESCR: Family; Feminism; Psychology; Sexism; Working Women.

2903 Navar, Isabelle. La Mexicana: an image of strength. REGENERACION, Vol. 2, no. 4 (1974), p. 4-6. English. DESCR: Family; Feminism; Psychology; Sexism; Working Women.

2904 Nieto Gomez de Lazarin, Anna. The Chicana: perspectives for education. ENCUENTRO FEMENIL, Vol. 1, no. 1 (Spring 1973), p. 34-61. English. DESCR: Colleges and Universities; Discrimination; Discrimination in Education; *Education; Family; Sexism.

2905 Nieto Senour, Maria. Psychology of the Chicana. IN: Martinez, Joe L., Jr., ed. CHICANO PSYCHOLOGY. New York: Academic Press, 1977, p. 329-342. English. DESCR: Academic Achievement; Acculturation; Cultural Customs; *Psychology; Sex Roles.

2906 Norinsky, Margaret Elaine. The relationship between sex-role identity and ethnicity to styles of assertiveness and aggression in women. Thesis (Ed.D.)--University of San Francisco, 1987. 164 p. English. DESCR: Anglo Americans; *Assertiveness; Blacks; Ethnic Groups; *Sex Roles; *Women.

2907 Olivarez, Elizabeth. Women's rights and the Mexican American woman. REGENERACION, Vol. 2, no. 4 (1975), p. 40-42. English. DESCR: Education; *Feminism; Politics; Psychology; Religion; Sex Roles.

2908 Ortiz, Carmen G. The influence of religious images on perceptions of femininity among women of Mexican origin. Thesis (Ph.D.)--California School of Professional Psychology, Berkeley, 1988. 210 p. English. DESCR: Catholic Church; *Religion; *Sexual Behavior; Symbolism.

2909 Quintana, Alvina E. Challenge and counter challenge: Chicana literary motifs. AGAINST THE CURRENT, Vol. 2, no. 2 (March, April, 1987), p. 25,28-32. English. DESCR: Anglo Americans; Authors; Cervantes, Lorna Dee; Cultural Studies; *Feminism; Literary Criticism; *Literature; Moraga, Cherrie; THERE ARE NO MADMEN HERE; Valdes, Gina; Women.

2910 Quintana, Alvina E. Chicana literary motifs: challenge and counter-challenge. IMAGES: ETHNIC STUDIES OCCASIONAL PAPERS SERIES, (Fall 1986), p. 24-41. English. DESCR: Anglo Americans; Authors; Cervantes, Lorna Dee; Cultural Studies; *Feminism; *Literary Criticism; Literature; Moraga, Cherrie; THERE ARE NO MADMEN HERE; Valdes, Gina; Women.

2911 Rebolledo, Tey Diana. The maturing of Chicana poetry: the quiet revolution of the 1980s. IN: Treichler, Paula A., et al., eds. FOR ALMA MATER: THEORY AND PRACTICE IN FEMINIST SCHOLARSHIP. Urbana: University of Illinois Press, 1985, p. 143-158. English. DESCR: *Literary Criticism; *Poetry; Sexual Behavior.

2912 Romero, Gloria J. and Garza, Raymond T. Attributions for the occupational success/failure of ethnic minority and nonminority women. SEX ROLES, Vol. 14, no. 7-8 (April 1986), p. 445-452. English. DESCR: Anglo Americans; *Attitudes; Careers; Sociology; Women.

2913 Roraback, Rosanne Lisa. The effects of occupational type, educational level, marital status, and race/ethnicity on women's attitudes towards feminist issues. Thesis (M.A.)--Michigan State University, 1988. 62 p. English. DESCR: Abortion; *Attitudes; Equal Rights Amendment (ERA); *Feminism; *Women.

2914 Salgado de Snyder, Nelly; Lopez, Cynthia M.; and Padilla, Amado M. Ethnic identity and cultural awareness among the offspring of Mexican interethnic marriages. JOURNAL OF EARLY ADOLESCENCE, Vol. 2, no. 3 (Fall 1982), p. 277-282. English. DESCR: *Acculturation; Children; *Intermarriage; *Youth.

2915 Salgado de Snyder, Nelly. Mexican immigrant women: the relationship of ethnic loyalty and social support to acculturative stress and depressive symptomatology. Los Angeles, CA: Spanish Speaking Mental Health Research Center, 1987. 73 p. English. DESCR: *Acculturation; Depression (Psychological); *Immigrants; Natural Support Systems; *Stress; Women.

2916 Salgado de Snyder, Nelly. The role of ethnic loyalty among Mexican immigrant women. HISPANIC JOURNAL OF BEHAVIORAL SCIENCES, Vol. 9, no. 3 (September 1987), p. 287-298. English. DESCR: Acculturation; *Culture; Immigrants; Mental Health; Mexico; *Women.

2917 San Miguel, Rachel. Being Hispanic in Houston: my name is Carmen Quezada. THE AMERICAS REVIEW, Vol. 16, no. 1 (Spring 1988), p. 44-52. English. DESCR: Autobiography; *Essays; Houston, TX.

Identity (cont.)

2918 Sanchez, Corina. Higher education y la Chicana? ENCUENTRO FEMENIL, Vol. 1, no. 1 (Spring 1973), p. 27-33. English. DESCR: Discrimination; Discrimination in Education; *Higher Education; Sexism.

2919 Sanchez, Marta E. The birthing of the poetic "I" in Alma Villanueva's MOTHER MAY I?: the search for a feminine identity. IN: Herrera-Sobek, Maria, ed. BEYOND STEREOTYPES: THE CRITICAL ANALYSIS OF CHICANA LITERATURE. Binghamton, NY: Bilingual Press/Editorial Bilingue, 1985, p. 108-152. Also IN: Sanchez, Marta. CONTEMPORARY CHICANA POETRY. Berkeley, CA: University of California Press, 1985, p. 24-84. English. DESCR: Literary Criticism; MOTHER MAY I?; Poetry; Villanueva, Alma.

2920 Schoen, Robert; Wooldredge, John; and Thomas, Barbara. Ethnic and educational effects on marriage choice. SOCIAL SCIENCE QUARTERLY, Vol. 70, no. 3 (September 1989), p. 617-630. English. DESCR: Education; *Intermarriage; Marriage; Research Methodology; Social Classes.

2921 Sepulveda, Betty R. The Hispanic woman responding to the challenges that affect us all. LA LUZ, Vol. 1, no. 7 (November 1972), p. 56-59. English. DESCR: *Feminism.

2922 Sorenson, Ann Marie. The fertility and language characteristics of Mexican-American and non-Hispanic husbands and wives. SOCIOLOGICAL QUARTERLY, Vol. 29, no. 1 (March 1988), p. 111-130. English. DESCR: Anglo Americans; Fertility; *Language Usage; Marriage; Sex Roles.

2923 Sorenson, Ann Marie. Fertility, expectations and ethnic identity among Mexican-American adolescents: an expression of cultural ideals. SOCIOLOGICAL PERSPECTIVES, Vol. 28, no. 3 (July 1985), p. 339-360. English. DESCR: Acculturation; Anglo Americans; Cultural Characteristics; *Fertility; Values; Youth.

2924 Stark, Miriam. La Chicana: changing roles in a changing society. Thesis (B.A)--University of Michigan, 1984. ii, 157 leaves. English. DESCR: Acculturation; Lansing, MI; *Sex Roles; *Social History and Conditions.

2925 Tatum, Charles M. Grappling with difference: gender, race, class, and ethnicity in contemporary Chicana/o literature. RENATO ROSALDO LECTURE SERIES MONOGRAPH, Vol. 6, (1988, 1989), p. 1-23. English. DESCR: Anaya, Rudolfo A.; Authors; BLESS ME, ULTIMA; *Feminism; Literary Characters; *Literary Criticism; Literature Reviews.

2926 Terrazas, Olga Esperanza. The self-concept of Mexican-American adolescent females. Thesis (Ph.D.)--Wright Institute, 1980. 262 p. English. DESCR: Psychological Testing; *Youth.

2927 Tienda, Marta and Guhleman, Patricia. The occupational position of employed Hispanic women. IN: Borjas, George J. and Tienda, Marta, eds. HISPANICS IN THE U.S. ECONOMY. Orlando, FL: Academic Press, 1985, p. 243-273. English. DESCR: *Employment; Puerto Ricans.

2928 Tienda, Marta. Sex, ethnicity and Chicano status attainment. INTERNATIONAL MIGRATION REVIEW, Vol. 16, no. 2 (Summer 1982), p. 435-473. English. DESCR: Academic Achievement; Discrimination in Education; Discrimination in Employment; Income; Language Proficiency; Sexism; *Social Classes; Social Mobility.

2929 Treacy, Mary Jane. The ties that bind: women and community in Evangelina Vigil's THIRTY AN' SEEN A LOT. IN: Horno-Delgado, Asuncion, et al., eds. BREAKING BOUNDARIES: LATINA WRITING AND CRITICAL READINGS. Amherst, MA: University of Massachusetts Press, c1989, p. 82-93. English. DESCR: Literary Criticism; Poetry; Sexism; *THIRTY AN' SEEN A LOT; *Vigil-Pinon, Evangelina.

2930 Vasquez, Melba J. T. Power and status of the Chicana: a social-psychological perspective. IN: Martinez, Joe L., Jr., ed. CHICANO PSYCHOLOGY. 2nd. ed. Orlando, FL: Academic Press, 1984, p. 269-287. English. DESCR: Income; *Mental Health; Psychology; *Sex Roles; Socialization; Working Women.

2931 Veloz, Josefina Estrada. Chicana identity: gender and ethnicity. Thesis (Ph.D.)--New Mexico State University, 1981. 239 p. English. DESCR: Sex Roles.

2932 Ventura, Stephanie J. and Taffel, Selma M. Childbearing characteristics of U.S.- and foreign-born Hispanic mothers. PUBLIC HEALTH REPORTS, Vol. 100, no. 6 (November, December, 1985), p. 647-652. English. DESCR: *Fertility; Immigrants; *Maternal and Child Welfare; *Statistics.

2933 Vigil, James Diego. The nexus of class, culture and gender in the education of Mexican American females. IN: McKenna, Teresa and Ortiz, Flora Ida, eds. THE BROKEN WEB: THE EDUCATIONAL EXPERIENCE OF HISPANIC WOMEN. Claremont, CA: Tomas Rivera Center; Berkeley, CA: Floricanto Press, 1988, p. 79-103. English. DESCR: Academic Achievement; Acculturation; Discrimination in Education; *Education; Secondary School Education; Sex Roles; Social Classes; Students.

2934 Votaw, Carmen Delgado. Cultural influences on Hispanic feminism. AGENDA, Vol. 11, no. 4 (1981), p. 44-49. Bilingual. DESCR: Culture; *Feminism; Values.

2935 Wagner, Roland M. and Schaffer, Diane M. Social networks and survival strategies: an exploratory study of Mexican American, Black, and Anglo female family heads in San Jose, California. IN: Melville, Margarita B., ed. TWICE A MINORITY. St. Louis, MO: Mosby, 1980, p. 173-190. English. DESCR: Anglo Americans; Blacks; *Natural Support Systems; San Jose, CA; *Single Parents; Stress.

2936 Williams, Norma. Role making among married Mexican American women: issues of class and ethnicity. JOURNAL OF APPLIED BEHAVIORAL SCIENCE, Vol. 24, no. 2 (1988), p. 203-217. English. DESCR: Austin, TX; Corpus Christi, TX; Marriage; *Sex Roles; Social Classes.

2937 Yinger, Milton J. Assimilation in the United States: the Mexican-Americans. IN: Conner, Walker, ed. MEXICAN-AMERICANS IN COMPARATIVE PERSPECTIVE. Washington, DC: Urban Institute Press, 1985, p. 30-55. English. DESCR: Acculturation; *Assimilation; Culture of Poverty Model; Intermarriage.

Identity (cont.)

2938 Zambrana, Ruth E. Toward understanding the educational trajectory and socialization of Latina women. IN: McKenna, Teresa and Ortiz, Flora Ida, eds. THE BROKEN WEB: THE EDUCATIONAL EXPERIENCE OF HISPANIC WOMEN. Claremont, CA: Tomas Rivera Center; Berkeley, CA: Floricanto Press, 1988, p. 61-77. English. DESCR: Academic Achievement; Anglo Americans; *Education; Feminism; Research Methodology; *Socialization; *Women.

2939 Zavella, Patricia. The politics of race and gender: organizing Chicana cannery workers in Northern California. IN: Bookman, Ann and Morgen, Sandra, eds. WOMEN AND THE POLITICS OF EMPOWERMENT. Philadelphia, PA: Temple University Press, 1988, p. 202-224. English. DESCR: Bay City Cannery Workers Committee; *Canneries; Cannery Workers Committee (CWC); Discrimination; Garcia, Connie; *Labor Unions; Nationalism; Northern California; Santa Clara Valley, CA; Sex Roles; Sexism; *Working Women.

2940 Zavella, Patricia. Reflections on diversity among Chicanas. FRONTIERS: A JOURNAL OF WOMEN STUDIES, Vol. 12, no. 2 (1991), p. 73-85. English. DESCR: *Cultural Pluralism; Culture; *Feminism; Stereotypes.

2941 Zuniga, Maria E. Assessment issues with Chicanas: practice implications. PSYCHOTHERAPY, Vol. 25, no. 2 (Summer 1988), p. 288-293. English. DESCR: Acculturation; Colleges and Universities; Family; *Mental Health; Mexican-American Outreach Program, San Diego State University; *Psychotherapy; *Students.

Ideology
USE: Political Ideology

Idioms
USE: Chicano Dialects

Iglesias, Norma

2942 Lavrin, Asuncion. El segundo sexo en Mexico: experiencia, estudio e introspeccion, 1983-1987. MEXICAN STUDIES/ESTUDIOS MEXICANOS, Vol. 5, no. 2 (Summer 1989), p. 297-312. Spanish. DESCR: Arenal, Sandra; *Border Industries; Carrillo, Jorge; Hernandez, Alberto; LA FLOR MAS BELLA DE LA MAQUILADORA; *Literature Reviews; Mexico; MUJERES FRONTERIZAS EN LA INDUSTRIA MAQUILADORA; SANGRE JOVEN: LAS MAQUILADORAS POR DENTRO; Women.

THE IGUANA KILLER: TWELVE STORIES OF THE HEART

2943 Rosaldo, Renato. Fables of the fallen guy. IN: Calderon, Hector and Saldivar, Jose David, eds. CRITICISM IN THE BORDERLANDS: STUDIES IN CHICANO LITERATURE, CULTURE AND IDEOLOGY. Durham, NC: Duke University Press, 1991, p. [84]-93. English. DESCR: Chavez, Denise; Cisneros, Sandra; Fiction; Literary Characters; *Literary Criticism; Rios, Alberto; Sex Roles; THE HOUSE ON MANGO STREET; THE LAST OF THE MENU GIRLS.

Illegal Aliens
USE: Undocumented Workers

Illinois

2944 Williams, Brett. Why migrant women feed their husbands tamales: foodways as a basis for a revisionist view of Tejano family life. IN: Brown, Linda Keller and Mussell,

Kay, eds. ETHNIC AND REGIONAL FOODWAYS IN THE UNITED STATES: THE PERFORMANCE OF GROUP IDENTITY. Knoxville, TN: University of Tennessee Press, 1984, p. 113-126. English. DESCR: Cultural Customs; Extended Family; Family; *Food Practices; *Migrant Labor; Sex Roles; Tamales; Texas.

Illiteracy
USE: Literacy

Immigrants

2945 Alcalay, Rina. Hispanic women in the United States: family & work relations. MIGRATION TODAY, Vol. 12, no. 3 (1984), p. 13-20. English. DESCR: Extended Family; Migration; *Women.

2946 Alvarez-Amaya, Maria. Determinants of breast and cervical cancer behavior among Mexican American women. BORDER HEALTH/SALUD FRONTERIZA, Vol. 5, no. 3 (July, September, 1989), p. 22-27. Bilingual. DESCR: Border Region; *Breast Cancer; *Cancer; Diseases; Medical Care; *Preventative Medicine.

2947 Apodaca, Maria Linda. The Chicana woman: a historical materialist perspective. IN: Bollinger, William, et al., eds. WOMEN IN LATIN AMERICA: AN ANTHOLOGY FROM LATIN AMERICAN PERSPECTIVES. Riverside, CA: Latin American Perspectives, c1979, p. 81-100. English. DESCR: Capitalism; *Historiography; Imperialism; Marxism; Mexico; Oral History; Social Classes; Spanish Influence.

2948 Arguelles, Lourdes. Undocumented female labor in the United States Southwest: an essay on migration, consciousness, oppression and struggle. IN: Del Castillo, Adelaida R., ed. BETWEEN BORDERS: ESSAYS ON MEXICANA/CHICANA HISTORY. Encino, CA: Floricanto Press, 1990, p. 299-312. English. DESCR: Arizona Farm Workers (AFW); Immigration; *Undocumented Workers; Working Women.

2949 Baezconde-Garbanati, Lourdes and Salgado de Snyder, Nelly. Mexican immigrant women: a selected bibliography. HISPANIC JOURNAL OF BEHAVIORAL SCIENCES, Vol. 9, no. 3 (September 1987), p. 331-358. English. DESCR: *Bibliography; *Women.

2950 Baker, Susan Gonzalez. Many rivers to cross: Mexican immigrants, women workers, and the structure of labor markets in the urban Southwest. Thesis (Ph.D.)--University of Texas, Austin, 1989. 163 p. English. DESCR: Immigration Reform and Control Act of 1986; *Labor Supply and Market; Undocumented Workers; Women; *Working Women.

2951 Briody, Elizabeth K. Patterns of household immigration into South Texas. INTERNATIONAL MIGRATION REVIEW, Vol. 21, no. 1 (Spring 1987), p. 27-47. English. DESCR: *Family; Sex Roles; *Social Mobility; *South Texas.

2952 Buriel, Raymond, et al. Mexican-American disciplinary practices and attitudes toward child maltreatment:a comparison of foreign and native-born mothers. HISPANIC JOURNAL OF BEHAVIORAL SCIENCES, Vol. 13, no. 1 (February 1991), p. 78-94. English. DESCR: *Attitudes; *Child Abuse; *Parent and Child Relationships; *Parenting; Values; Violence.

Immigrants (cont.)

2953 Cardenas, Gilbert; Shelton, Beth Anne; and Pena, Devon Gerardo. Undocumented immigrant women in the Houston labor force. CALIFORNIA SOCIOLOGIST, Vol. 5, no. 2 (Summer 1982), p. 98-118. English. **DESCR:** Employment; Houston, TX; *Labor Supply and Market; *Undocumented Workers.

2954 Castaneda, Antonia I. Comparative frontiers: the migration of women to Alta California and New Zealand. IN: Schlissel, Lillian, et al., eds. WESTERN WOMEN: THEIR LAND, THEIR LIVES. Albuquerque, NM: University of New Mexico Press, 1988, p. 283-300. English. **DESCR:** Border Region; California; History; Immigration; Marriage; Mexico; Missions; Native Americans; New Zealand; Social History and Conditions; *Women.

2955 Chavez, John M. and Buriel, Raymond. Reinforcing children's effort: a comparison of immigrant, native-born Mexican American and Euro-American mothers. HISPANIC JOURNAL OF BEHAVIORAL SCIENCES, Vol. 8, no. 2 (June 1986), p. 127-142. English. **DESCR:** Acculturation; *Parenting.

2956 Chavira, Alicia. "Tienes que ser valiente": Mexicana migrants in a midwestern farm labor camp. IN: Melville, Margarita, ed. MEXICANAS AT WORK IN THE UNITED STATES. Houston, TX: Mexican American Studies Program, University of Houston, 1988, p. 64-74. English. **DESCR:** *Farm Workers; *Labor Camps; Midwestern States; Migrant Health Services; *Migrant Labor; Sex Roles; *Women.

2957 Cooney, Rosemary Santana and Ortiz, Vilma. Nativity, national origin, and Hispanic female participation in the labor force. SOCIAL SCIENCE QUARTERLY, Vol. 64, (September 1983), p. 510-523. English. **DESCR:** Women; *Working Women.

2958 Cristo, Martha H. Stress and coping among Mexican women. Thesis (Ph.D.)--California School of Professional Psychology, Los Angeles, 1988. 336 p. English. **DESCR:** Cultural Characteristics; Mental Health; Socioeconomic Factors; *Stress; *Women.

2959 Curry Rodriguez, Julia E. Labor migration and familial responsibilities: experiences of Mexican women. IN: Melville, Margarita, ed. MEXICANAS AT WORK IN THE UNITED STATES. Houston, TX: Mexican American Studies Program, University of Houston, 1988, p. 47-63. English. **DESCR:** Employment; Family; Mexico; *Migrant Labor; Oral History; Sex Roles; Undocumented Workers; *Women; *Working Women.

2960 Curry Rodriguez, Julia E. Reconceptualizing undocumented labor immigration: the causes, impact and consequences in Mexican women's lives. Thesis (Ph.D.)--University of Texas at Austin, 1988. xiv, 329 p. English. **DESCR:** Employment; Mexico; Oral History; *Undocumented Workers; *Women.

2961 Deutsch, Sarah. Culture, class, and gender: Chicanas and Chicanos in Colorado and New Mexico, 1900-1940. Thesis (Ph.D.)--Yale University, 1985. xii, 510 p. English. **DESCR:** Anglo Americans; Colorado; New Mexico; *Sex Roles; *Social Classes; Social History and Conditions; Women; *Working Women.

2962 Deutsch, Sarah. No separate refuge: culture, class, and gender on an Anglo-Hispanic frontier in the American Southwest, 1880-1940. New York: Oxford University Press, 1987. vi, 356 p. English. **DESCR:** Anglo Americans; Colorado; Immigration; Mining Industry; Missions; New Mexico; *Sex Roles; *Social Classes; *Social History and Conditions; Women; Working Women; World War I.

2963 Deutsch, Sarah. Women and intercultural relations: the case of Hispanic New Mexico and Colorado. SIGNS: JOURNAL OF WOMEN IN CULTURE AND SOCIETY, Vol. 12, no. 4 (Summer 1987), p. 719-739. English. **DESCR:** Colorado; Cultural Characteristics; Intercultural Communication; Mexico; New Mexico; Rural Population; Sex Roles; Social History and Conditions; *Women.

2964 Engle, Patricia L. Prenatal and postnatal anxiety in women giving birth in Los Angeles. HEALTH PSYCHOLOGY, Vol. 9, no. 3 (1990), p. 285-299. English. **DESCR:** *Fertility; Los Angeles, CA; *Maternal and Child Welfare; Medical Care; *Prenatal Care; *Stress; Women.

2965 Enguidanos-Clark, Gloria M. Acculturative stress and its contribution to the development of depression in Hispanic women. Thesis (Ph.D.)--Wright Institute, Berkeley, 1986. 198 p. English. **DESCR:** *Acculturation; *Depression (Psychological); Mental Health; *Stress.

2966 Fernandez Kelly, Maria and Garcia, Anna M. Invisible amidst the glitter: Hispanic women in the Southern California electronics industry. IN: Statham, Anne; Miller, Eleanor M.; and Mauksh, Hans O., eds. THE WORTH OF WOMEN'S WORK: A QUALITATIVE SYNTHESIS. Albany, NY: State University of New York Press, 1988, p. 265-290. English. **DESCR:** *Electronics Industry; Employment; *Industrial Workers; Labor Supply and Market; Megatek, La Jolla, CA; Nova-Tech, San Diego, CA; Sex Roles; Southern California; *Working Women.

2967 Gamio, Manuel. Senora Flores de Andrade. IN: Mora, Magdalena and Del Castillo, Adelaida, eds. MEXICAN WOMEN IN THE UNITED STATES: STRUGGLES PAST AND PRESENT. Los Angeles, CA: Chicano Studies Research Center, UCLA, 1980, p. 189-192. English. **DESCR:** Autobiography; Flores de Andrade, Senora; Mexican Revolution - 1910-1920; *Oral History.

2968 Garcia, Mario T. The Chicana in American history: the Mexican women of El Paso, 1880-1920 - a case study. PACIFIC HISTORICAL REVIEW, Vol. 49, no. 2 (May 1980), p. 315-337. English. **DESCR:** Acme Laundry, El Paso, TX; American Federation of Labor (AFL); Case Studies; Central Labor Union; Domestic Work; *El Paso, TX; Employment; *History; Income; Labor Unions; Sex Roles; Strikes and Lockouts; *Working Women.

2969 Gilbert, M. Jean. Alcohol consumption patterns in immigrant and later generation Mexican American women. HISPANIC JOURNAL OF BEHAVIORAL SCIENCES, Vol. 9, no. 3 (September 1987), p. 299-313. English. **DESCR:** Acculturation; *Alcoholism; *Attitudes; Cultural Characteristics; Mexico.

Immigrants (cont.)

2970 Gonzalez, Rosalinda M. Chicanas and Mexican immigrant families 1920-1940: women's subordination and family exploitation. IN: Scharf, Lois and Jensen, Joan M., eds. DECADES OF DISCONTENT: THE WOMEN'S MOVEMENT, 1920-1940. Westport, CT: Greenwood Press, 1983, p. 59-84. English. DESCR: *Family; Farm Workers; History; Labor; Labor Unions; Mexico; Pecan Shelling Worker's Union, San Antonio, TX; Sex Roles; Strikes and Lockouts; United Cannery Agricultural Packing and Allied Workers of America (UCAPAWA); Working Women.

2971 Guendelman, Sylvia. The incorporation of Mexican women in seasonal migration: a study of gender differences. HISPANIC JOURNAL OF BEHAVIORAL SCIENCES, Vol. 9, no. 3 (September 1987), p. 245-264. English. DESCR: Marriage; Mexico; *Migration Patterns; *Sex Roles; *Women; *Women Men Relations; Working Women.

2972 Gunther Enriquez, Martha. Studying maternal-infant attachment: a Mexican-American example. IN: Kay, Margarita Artschwager, ed. ANTHROPOLOGY OF HUMAN BIRTH. Philadelphia, PA: F.A. Davis, 1982, p. 61-79. English. DESCR: Children; *Fertility; *Maternal and Child Welfare; *Parent and Child Relationships.

2973 Hancock, Paula F. The effect of welfare eligibility on the labor force participation of women of Mexican origin in California. POPULATION RESEARCH AND POLICY REVIEW, Vol. 5, no. 2 (1986), p. 163-185. English. DESCR: Aid to Families with Dependent Children (AFDC); California; *Employment; Food Stamps; Medi-Cal; Single Parents; *Welfare; Women.

2974 Hancock, Paula F. The effects of nativity, legal status and welfare eligibility on the labor force participation of women of Mexican origin in California. Thesis (Ph.D.)--University of Southern California 1985. English. DESCR: *Employment; Undocumented Workers; *Welfare.

2975 Hogeland, Chris and Rosen, Karen. Dreams lost, dreams found: undocumented women in the land of opportunity. San Francisco, CA: Coalition for Immigrant and Refugee Rights and Services, c1991. 153 p. English. DESCR: *Battered Women; *Coalition for Immigrant and Refugee Rights and Services, Immigrant Woman's Task Force; Discrimination; *San Francisco Bay Area; Sex Roles; Sexism; Social Services; Undocumented Workers; Violence; Women; Women Men Relations.

2976 Jensen, Leif. Secondary earner strategies and family poverty: immigrant-native differentials, 1960-1980. INTERNATIONAL MIGRATION REVIEW, Vol. 25, no. 1 (Spring 1991), p. 113-140. English. DESCR: Anglo Americans; *Asian Americans; Blacks; Family; Immigration; Income; Poverty; Women; Working Women.

2977 Kossoudji, Sherrie and Ranney, Susan. The labor market experience of female migrants: the case of temporary Mexican migration to the U.S. INTERNATIONAL MIGRATION REVIEW, Vol. 18, no. 4 (Winter 1984), p. 1120-1143. English. DESCR: Employment; Income; *Labor Supply and Market; *Migrant Labor; Sex Roles; *Women; Working Women.

2978 Lee, Bun Song and Pol, Louis G. A comparison of fertility adaptation between Mexican immigrants to the U.S. and internal migrants in Mexico. CONTEMPORARY POLICY ISSUES, Vol. 3, no. 3 (Spring, 1985), p. 91-101. English. DESCR: *Fertility; Mexico; Migration Patterns; *Rural Urban Migration; Women.

2979 Melville, Margarita B. Mexican women adapt to migration. IN: Rios-Bustamante, Antonio, ed. MEXICAN IMMIGRANT WORKERS IN THE U.S. Los Angeles, CA: Chicano Studies Research Center Publications, University of California, 1981, p. 119-124. English. DESCR: Acculturation; Attitudes; Sex Roles; Stress; *Undocumented Workers.

2980 O'Connor, Mary I. Women's networks and the social needs of Mexican immigrants. URBAN ANTHROPOLOGY, Vol. 19, no. 1-2 (Spring, Summer, 1990), p. 81-98. English. DESCR: Employment; Labor Unions; *Natural Support Systems; *Sandyland Nursery, Carpinteria, CA; Undocumented Workers; United Farmworkers of America (UFW); Women.

2981 Powell, Douglas R.; Zambrana, Ruth E.; and Silva-Palacios, Victor. Designing culturally responsive parent programs: a comparison of low-income Mexican and Mexican-American mothers' preferences. FAMILY RELATIONS, Vol. 39, no. 3 (July 1990), p. 298-304. English. DESCR: Acculturation; Children; Education; Los Angeles, CA; Low Income; *Parent and Child Relationships; *Parenting; Women.

2982 Remez, Lisa. Rates of adolescent pregnancy and childbearing are high among Mexican-born Mexican Americans. FAMILY PLANNING PERSPECTIVES, Vol. 23, no. 2 (March, April, 1991), p. 88-89. English. DESCR: *Fertility; Los Angeles County, CA; *Sexual Behavior; *Youth.

2983 Rodriguez, Rogelio E. Psychological distress among Mexican-American women as a reaction to the new immigration law. Thesis (Ph.D.)--Loyola University of Chicago, 1989. 87 p. English. DESCR: Depression (Psychological); *Immigration Law and Legislation; Immigration Reform and Control Act of 1986; *Mental Health; Mexico; Stress; Undocumented Workers; Women.

2984 Rodriguez, Rogelio E. and DeWolfe, Alan. Psychological distress among Mexican-American and Mexican women as related to status on the new immigration law. JOURNAL OF CONSULTING AND CLINICAL PSYCHOLOGY, Vol. 58, no. 5 (October 1990), p. 548-553. English. DESCR: Immigration Law and Legislation; Immigration Reform and Control Act of 1986; Natural Support Systems; *Stress; Undocumented Workers; Women.

2985 Romero-Gwynn, Eunice and Carias, Lucia. Breast-feeding intentions and practice among Hispanic mothers in Southern California. PEDIATRICS, Vol. 84, no. 4 (October 1989), p. 626-632. English. DESCR: *Breastfeeding; Cubanos; Expanded Food and Nutrition Education Program; Puerto Ricans; Southern California; Women.

2986 Ruiz, Vicki L., ed. and Tiano, Susan B., ed. Women on the U.S.-Mexico border: responses to change. Boston, MA: Allen & Unwin, c1987. xi, 247 p. English. DESCR: *Border Industries; *Border Region; Employment; Feminism; Mexico; Sex Roles; *Women.

Immigrants (cont.)

2987 Sabagh, Georges. Fertility expectations and behavior among Mexican Americans in Los Angeles, 1973-82. SOCIAL SCIENCE QUARTERLY, Vol. 65, no. 2 (June 1984), p. 594-608. English. DESCR: *Fertility; Los Angeles, CA.

2988 Sabagh, Georges and Lopez, David. Religiosity and fertility: the case of Chicanas. SOCIAL FORCES, Vol. 59, no. 2 (December 1980), p. 431-439. English. DESCR: Catholic Church; *Family Planning; *Fertility; *Religion; Women.

2989 Saboonchi, Nasrin. The working women's reactions to the traditional marriage role: a crosscultural study within the symbolic interactionism framework. Thesis (Ph.D.)--United States International University, 1983. 173 p. English. DESCR: Iranians; *Marriage; *Sex Roles; Women; Working Women.

2990 Salgado de Snyder, Nelly. Factors associated with acculturative stress and depressive symptomatology among married Mexican immigrant women. PSYCHOLOGY OF WOMEN QUARTERLY, Vol. 11, no. 4 (December 1987), p. 475-488. English. DESCR: *Acculturation; Depression (Psychological); Mental Health; Mexico; *Stress; Women.

2991 Salgado de Snyder, Nelly; Cervantes, Richard C.; and Padilla, Amado M. Gender and ethnic differences in psychosocial stress and generalized distress among Hispanics. SEX ROLES, Vol. 22, no. 7-8 (April, 1990), p. 441-453. English. DESCR: Anglo Americans; Central Americans; *Comparative Psychology; Depression (Psychological); Hispanic Stress Inventory (HSI); Immigration; *Sex Roles; *Stress; Women.

2992 Salgado de Snyder, Nelly. Mexican immigrant women: the relationship of ethnic loyalty and social support to acculturative stress and depressive symptomatology. Los Angeles, CA: Spanish Speaking Mental Health Research Center, 1987. 73 p. English. DESCR: *Acculturation; Depression (Psychological); Identity; Natural Support Systems; *Stress; Women.

2993 Salgado de Snyder, Nelly. The role of ethnic loyalty among Mexican immigrant women. HISPANIC JOURNAL OF BEHAVIORAL SCIENCES, Vol. 9, no. 3 (September 1987), p. 287-298. English. DESCR: Acculturation; *Culture; *Identity; Mental Health; Mexico; *Women.

2994 Sanchez, George J. "Go after the women": Americanization and the Mexican immigrant woman, 1915-1929. Stanford, CA: Stanford Center for Chicano Research [1984?]. [32] leaves. English. DESCR: Acculturation; *Assimilation; Biculturalism; Social History and Conditions; Values; Women.

2995 Sanchez, George J. "Go after the women": Americanization and the Mexican immigrant woman, 1915-1929. IN: DuBois, Ellen Carol and Ruiz, Vicki L., eds. UNEQUAL SISTERS: A MULTICULTURAL READER IN U.S. WOMEN'S HISTORY. New York: Routledge, 1990, p. 250-263. English. DESCR: Acculturation; *Assimilation; Biculturalism; Social History and Conditions; Values; Women.

2996 Scrimshaw, Susan C.M., et al. Factors affecting breastfeeding among women of Mexican origin or descent in Los Angeles. AMERICAN JOURNAL OF PUBLIC HEALTH, Vol. 77, no. 4 (April 1987), p. 467-470. English. DESCR: Acculturation; *Breastfeeding; Los Angeles, CA; Working Women.

2997 Segura, Denise. Chicana and Mexican immigrant women at work: the impact of class, race, and gender on occupational mobility. GENDER & SOCIETY, Vol. 3, no. 1 (March 1989), p. 37-52. English. DESCR: *Employment; Labor Supply and Market; Laboring Classes; San Francisco Bay Area; *Social Mobility; Women; Working Women.

2998 Segura, Denise. Chicanas and Mexican immigrant women in the labor market: a study of occupational mobility and stratification. Thesis (Ph.D.)--University of California, Berkeley, 1986. iii, 282 p. English. DESCR: *Labor Supply and Market; Mexico; Women; *Working Women.

2999 Segura, Denise. Conflict in social relations at work: a Chicana perspective. IN: National Association for Chicano Studies. ESTUDIOS CHICANOS AND THE POLITICS OF COMMUNITY. [S.l.]: National Association for Chicano Studies, c1989, p. [110]-131. English. DESCR: *Discrimination in Employment; Employment Training; *Interpersonal Relations; Social Classes; Women; *Working Women.

3000 Segura, Denise. Familism and employment among Chicanas and Mexican immigrant women. IN: Melville, Margarita, ed. MEXICANAS AT WORK IN THE UNITED STATES. Houston, TX: Mexican American Studies Program, University of Houston, 1988, p. 24-32. English. DESCR: *Employment; *Extended Family; Family; Income; Machismo; Sex Roles; *Women; Working Women.

3001 Segura, Denise. The interplay of familism and patriarchy on employment among Chicana and Mexicana women. RENATO ROSALDO LECTURE SERIES MONOGRAPH, Vol. 5, (1989), p. 35-53. English. DESCR: Employment; *Family; Machismo; *Sex Roles; Women; Women Men Relations; *Working Women.

3002 Simon, Rita J. and DeLey, Margo. The work experience of undocumented Mexican women migrants in Los Angeles. INTERNATIONAL MIGRATION REVIEW, Vol. 18, no. 4 (Winter 1984), p. 1212-1229. English. DESCR: Income; *Los Angeles, CA; Population; Socioeconomic Factors; *Undocumented Workers; *Working Women.

3003 Solorzano-Torres, Rosalia. Female Mexican immigrants in San Diego County. IN: Ruiz, Vicki L. and Tiano, Susan, eds. WOMEN ON THE U.S.-MEXICO BORDER: RESPONSES TO CHANGE. Boston, MA: Allen & Unwin, 1987, p. 41-59. English. DESCR: Employment; Immigration; Literature Reviews; San Diego County, CA; Surveys; Undocumented Workers; Women.

3004 Solorzano-Torres, Rosalia. Women, labor, and the U.S.-Mexico border: Mexican maids in El Paso, Texas. IN: Melville, Margarita, ed. MEXICANAS AT WORK IN THE UNITED STATES. Houston, TX: Mexican American Studies Program, University of Houston, 1988, p. 75-83. English. DESCR: Border Patrol; *Border Region; Domestic Work; El Paso, TX; Immigration and Naturalization Service (INS); Immigration Regulation and Control; *Labor Supply and Market; Undocumented Workers; *Women; *Working Women.

Immigrants (cont.)

3005 Stewart, Kenneth L. and de Leon, Arnoldo. Work force participation among Mexican immigrant women in Texas, 1900. BORDERLANDS JOURNAL, Vol. 9, no. 1 (Spring 1986), p. 69-74. English. DESCR: Employment; History; Texas; Women; *Working Women.

3006 Sullivan, Teresa A. The occupational prestige of women immigrants: a comparison of Cubans and Mexicans. INTERNATIONAL MIGRATION REVIEW, Vol. 18, no. 4 (Winter 1984), p. 1045-1062. English. DESCR: Careers; Cubanos; Employment; Males; Mexico; Sex Roles; *Social Mobility; *Women; *Working Women.

3007 Swicegood, Gray, et al. Language usage and fertility in the Mexican-origin population of the United States. DEMOGRAPHY, Vol. 25, no. 1 (February 1988), p. 17-33. English. DESCR: *Fertility; *Language Usage; Population; Women.

3008 Vargas-Willis, Gloria and Cervantes, Richard C. Consideration of psychosocial stress in the treatment of the Latina immigrant. HISPANIC JOURNAL OF BEHAVIORAL SCIENCES, Vol. 9, no. 3 (September 1987), p. 315-329. English. DESCR: Discrimination in Employment; Mental Health; *Psychotherapy; *Stress.

3009 Vasquez, Mario F. Immigrant workers and the apparel manufacturing industry in Southern California. IN: Rios-Bustamante, Antonio, ed. MEXICAN IMMIGRANT WORKERS IN THE U.S. Los Angeles, CA: Chicano Studies Research Center Publications, University of California, 1981, p. 85-96. English. DESCR: AFL-CIO; California; Garment Industry; International Ladies Garment Workers Union (ILGWU); *Labor Supply and Market; Labor Unions; Undocumented Workers; Women.

3010 Vega, William A.; Kolody, Bohdan; and Valle Juan Ramon. Migration and mental health: an empirical test of depression risk factors among immigrant Mexican women. INTERNATIONAL MIGRATION REVIEW, Vol. 21, no. 3 (Fall 1987), p. 512-530. English. DESCR: Acculturation; *Depression (Psychological); Immigration; *Mental Health; Migration; Stress; Undocumented Workers; Women.

3011 Vega, William A.; Kolody, Bohdan; and Valle, Juan Ramon. The relationship of marital status, confidant support, and depression among Mexican immigrant women. JOURNAL OF MARRIAGE AND THE FAMILY, Vol. 48, no. 3 (August 1986), p. 597-605. English. DESCR: *Depression (Psychological); Low Income; *Marriage; San Diego County, CA; Stress; Women.

3012 Vega, William A., et al. Depressive symptoms and their correlates among immigrant Mexican women in the United States. SOCIAL SCIENCE & MEDICINE, Vol. 22, no. 6 (1986), p. 645-652. English. DESCR: Depression (Psychological); *Mental Health; Public Health; San Diego, CA.

3013 Ventura, Stephanie J. and Taffel, Selma M. Childbearing characteristics of U.S.- and foreign-born Hispanic mothers. PUBLIC HEALTH REPORTS, Vol. 100, no. 6 (November, December, 1985), p. 647-652. English. DESCR: *Fertility; Identity; *Maternal and Child Welfare; *Statistics.

3014 Walker, Todd. The relationship of nativity, social support and depression to the home environment among Mexican-American women. Thesis (Ph.D.)--University of Houston, 1989. 123 p. English. DESCR: Acculturation; Avance Parent-Child Education Program, San Antonio, TX; Children; Depression (Psychological); Natural Support Systems; *Parenting; Women.

3015 Zambrana, Ruth E., et al. Ethnic differences in the substance use patterns of low-income pregnant women. FAMILY & COMMUNITY HEALTH, Vol. 13, no. 4 (January 1991), p. 1-11. English. DESCR: Alcoholism; Blacks; *Drug Use; *Fertility; *Low Income; Smoking; Women.

Immigration

3016 Arguelles, Lourdes. Undocumented female labor in the United States Southwest: an essay on migration, consciousness, oppression and struggle. IN: Del Castillo, Adelaida R., ed. BETWEEN BORDERS: ESSAYS ON MEXICANA/CHICANA HISTORY. Encino, CA: Floricanto Press, 1990, p. 299-312. English. DESCR: Arizona Farm Workers (AFW); Immigrants; *Undocumented Workers; Working Women.

3017 Bean, Frank D. and Tienda, Marta. The Hispanic population of the United States. New York: Russell Sage Foundation, 1987. xxiv, 456 p. English. DESCR: *Census; Education; Employment; Fertility; Identity; Income; *Population; Self-Referents; *Statistics.

3018 Bean, Frank D., et al. Generational differences in fertility among Mexican Americans: implications for assessing the effects of immigration. SOCIAL SCIENCE QUARTERLY, Vol. 65, no. 2 (June 1984), p. 573-582. English. DESCR: Age Groups; *Fertility; Vital Statistics.

3019 Blanco, Iris and Salorzano, Rosalia. O te aclimatas o te aclimueres. FEM, Vol. 8, no. 34 (June, July, 1984), p. 20-22. Spanish. DESCR: *Border Industries; Mexico; Women; Working Women.

3020 Cardenas, Gilbert and Flores, Estevan T. The migration and settlement of undocumented women. Austin, TX: CMAS Publications, 1986. 69 p. English. DESCR: Employment; Houston, TX; Income; Labor Supply and Market; *Migration Patterns; Public Policy; Socioeconomic Factors; *Undocumented Workers.

3021 Castaneda, Antonia I. Comparative frontiers: the migration of women to Alta California and New Zealand. IN: Schlissel, Lillian, et al., eds. WESTERN WOMEN: THEIR LAND, THEIR LIVES. Albuquerque, NM: University of New Mexico Press, 1988, p. 283-300. English. DESCR: Border Region; California; History; Immigrants; Marriage; Mexico; Missions; Native Americans; New Zealand; Social History and Conditions; *Women.

3022 Corrales, Ramona. Undocumented Hispanas in America. IN: LA CHICANA: BUILDING FOR THE FUTURE, AN ACTION PLAN FOR THE 80s. Oakland, CA: National Hispanic University, 1981, p. 59-73. Also IN: THE STATE OF HISPANIC AMERICA II. Oakland, CA: National Hispanic Center Advanced Studies and Policy Analysis, 1982, p. 100-107. English. DESCR: Immigration Law and Legislation; Sex Roles; *Undocumented Workers.

Immigration (cont.)

3023 Davis, Cary; Haub, Carl; and Willette, JoAnne. U.S. Hispanics: changing the face of America. POPULATION BULLETIN, Vol. 38, no. 3 (June 1983), p. 1-43. English. **DESCR:** Education; Employment; Fertility; Income; *Population; Statistics; Vital Statistics.

3024 Deutsch, Sarah. No separate refuge: culture, class, and gender on an Anglo-Hispanic frontier in the American Southwest, 1880-1940. New York: Oxford University Press, 1987. vi, 356 p. English. **DESCR:** Anglo Americans; Colorado; Immigrants; Mining Industry; Missions; New Mexico; *Sex Roles; *Social Classes; *Social History and Conditions; Women; Working Women; World War I.

3025 Dixon, Marlene; Martinez, Elizabeth; and McCaughan, Ed. Theoretical perspectives on Chicanas, Mexicanas and the transnational working class. CONTEMPORARY MARXISM, no. 11 (Fall 1985), p. 46-76. English. **DESCR:** Border Industries; Capitalism; Economic History and Conditions; History; *Labor Supply and Market; *Laboring Classes; Mexico; Undocumented Workers; Women.

3026 Espin, Oliva M. Cultural and historical influences on sexuality in Hispanic/Latin women: implications for psychotherapy. IN: Vance, Carole S., ed. PLEASURE AND DANGER: EXPLORING FEMALE SEXUALITY. Boston, MA: Routledge & Kegan Paul, 1984, p. 149-164. English. **DESCR:** Language Usage; Machismo; *Psychotherapy; Sex Roles; *Sexual Behavior; Social History and Conditions; Spanish Influence; *Women.

3027 Fernandez Kelly, Maria. Mexican border industrialization, female labor force participation and migration. IN: Nash, June and Fernandez-Kelly, Patricia, eds. WOMEN, MEN, AND THE INTERNATIONAL DIVISION OF LABOR. Albany, NY: State University of New York Press, 1983, p. 205-223. English. **DESCR:** Border Industrialization Program (BIP); *Border Industries; Ciudad Juarez, Chihuahua, Mexico; Industrial Workers; Labor Supply and Market; Males; *Migration Patterns; Undocumented Workers; *Women; Working Women.

3028 Garcia, Mario T. La familia: the Mexican immigrant family, 1900-1930. IN: Barrera, Mario, et al., eds. WORK, FAMILY, SEX ROLES, LANGUAGE: SELECTED PAPERS, 1979. Berkeley, CA: Tonatiuh-Quinto Sol, 1980, p. 117-139. English. **DESCR:** Assimilation; Cultural Customs; El Paso, TX; Family; *Historiography; History; Labor; Sex Roles.

3029 Jensen, Leif. Secondary earner strategies and family poverty: immigrant-native differentials, 1960-1980. INTERNATIONAL MIGRATION REVIEW, Vol. 25, no. 1 (Spring 1991), p. 113-140. English. **DESCR:** Anglo Americans; *Asian Americans; Blacks; Family; Immigrants; Income; Poverty; Women; Working Women.

3030 Salgado de Snyder, Nelly; Cervantes, Richard C.; and Padilla, Amado M. Gender and ethnic differences in psychosocial stress and generalized distress among Hispanics. SEX ROLES, Vol. 22, no. 7-8 (April, 1990), p. 441-453. English. **DESCR:** Anglo Americans; Central Americans; *Comparative Psychology; Depression (Psychological); Hispanic Stress Inventory (HSI); *Immigrants; *Sex Roles; *Stress; Women.

3031 Schlissel, Lillian, ed.; Ruiz, Vicki L., ed.; and Monk, Janice, ed. Western women: their land, their lives. Albuquerque, NM: University of New Mexico Press, c1988. vi, 354 p. English. **DESCR:** Anglo Americans; History; Intermarriage; Labor; Native Americans; *Social History and Conditions; Southwestern United States; *Women.

3032 Seligson, Mitchell A. and Williams, Edward J. Maquiladoras and migration workers in the Mexico-United States Border Industrialization Program. Austin, TX: Mexico-United States Border Research Program, University of Texas at Austin, 1981. xviii, 202 p. English. **DESCR:** Border Industrialization Program (BIP); *Border Region; Employment; Industrial Workers; Mexico; *Migration Patterns; Working Women.

3033 Solorzano-Torres, Rosalia. Female Mexican immigrants in San Diego County. IN: Ruiz, Vicki L. and Tiano, Susan, eds. WOMEN ON THE U.S.-MEXICO BORDER: RESPONSES TO CHANGE. Boston, MA: Allen & Unwin, 1987. p. 41-59. English. **DESCR:** Employment; *Immigrants; Literature Reviews; San Diego County, CA; Surveys; Undocumented Workers; Women.

3034 Stephen, Elizabeth H. At the crossroads: fertility of Mexican-American women. New York: Garland Publishers, 1989. v, 184 p.: ill. English. **DESCR:** Assimilation; *Fertility; *Population.

3035 Stoddard, Ellwyn R. Maquila: assembly plants in Northern Mexico. El Paso, TX: Texas Western Press, 1987. ix, 91 p., [4] p. of plates: ill. English. **DESCR:** Border Industrialization Program (BIP); *Border Industries; Income; *Industrial Workers; Labor Supply and Market; Mexico; Sexism; Undocumented Workers.

3036 Valtierra, Mary. Acculturation, social support, and reported stress of Latina physicians. Thesis (Ph.D.)--California School of Professional Psychology, 1989. 136 p. English. **DESCR:** *Acculturation; Careers; Cubanos; Latin Americans; *Medical Personnel; Puerto Ricans; *Stress; *Women.

3037 Vega, William A.; Kolody, Bohdan; and Valle, Juan Ramon. Migration and mental health: an empirical test of depression risk factors among immigrant Mexican women. INTERNATIONAL MIGRATION REVIEW, Vol. 21, no. 3 (Fall 1987), p. 512-530. English. **DESCR:** Acculturation; *Depression (Psychological); *Immigrants; *Mental Health; Migration; Stress; Undocumented Workers; Women.

Immigration and Naturalization Service (INS)

3038 Alvarez, Robert R. A profile of the citizenship process among Hispanics in the United States. INTERNATIONAL MIGRATION REVIEW, Vol. 21, no. 2 (Summer 1987), p. 327-351. English. **DESCR:** Identity; *Naturalization.

3039 Solorzano-Torres, Rosalia. Women, labor, and the U.S.-Mexico border: Mexican maids in El Paso, Texas. IN: Melville, Margarita, ed. MEXICANAS AT WORK IN THE UNITED STATES. Houston, TX: Mexican American Studies Program, University of Houston, 1988, p. 75-83. English. **DESCR:** Border Patrol; *Border Region; Domestic Work; El Paso, TX; Immigrants; Immigration Regulation and Control; *Labor Supply and Market; Undocumented Workers; *Women; *Working Women.

Immigration Law and Legislation

3040 Corrales, Ramona. Undocumented Hispanas in America. IN: LA CHICANA: BUILDING FOR THE FUTURE, AN ACTION PLAN FOR THE 80s. Oakland, CA: National Hispanic University, 1981, p. 59-73. Also IN: THE STATE OF HISPANIC AMERICA II. Oakland, CA: National Hispanic Center Advanced Studies and Policy Analysis, 1982, p. 100-107. English. DESCR: Immigration; Sex Roles; *Undocumented Workers.

3041 Falasco, Dee and Heer, David. Economic and fertility differences between legal and undocumented migrant Mexican families: possible effects of immigration policy changes. SOCIAL SCIENCE QUARTERLY, Vol. 65, no. 2 (June 1984), p. 495-504. English. DESCR: *Economic History and Conditions; *Fertility; Immigration Regulation and Control; Income; *Undocumented Workers.

3042 Rodriguez, Rogelio E. Psychological distress among Mexican-American women as a reaction to the new immigration law. Thesis (Ph.D.)--Loyola University of Chicago, 1989. 87 p. English. DESCR: Depression (Psychological); Immigrants; Immigration Reform and Control Act of 1986; *Mental Health; Mexico; Stress; Undocumented Workers; Women.

3043 Rodriguez, Rogelio E. and DeWolfe, Alan. Psychological distress among Mexican-American and Mexican women as related to status on the new immigration law. JOURNAL OF CONSULTING AND CLINICAL PSYCHOLOGY, Vol. 58, no. 5 (October 1990), p. 548-553. English. DESCR: *Immigrants; Immigration Reform and Control Act of 1986; Natural Support Systems; *Stress; Undocumented Workers; Women.

Immigration Raids
USE: Immigration Regulation and Control

Immigration Reform and Control Act of 1986

3044 Baker, Susan Gonzalez. Many rivers to cross: Mexican immigrants, women workers, and the structure of labor markets in the urban Southwest. Thesis (Ph.D.)--University of Texas, Austin, 1989. 153 p. English. DESCR: *Immigrants; *Labor Supply and Market; Undocumented Workers; Women; *Working Women.

3045 Rodriguez, Rogelio E. Psychological distress among Mexican-American women as a reaction to the new immigration law. Thesis (Ph.D.)--Loyola University of Chicago, 1989. 87 p. English. DESCR: Depression (Psychological); Immigrants; *Immigration Law and Legislation; *Mental Health; Mexico; Stress; Undocumented Workers; Women.

3046 Rodriguez, Rogelio E. and DeWolfe, Alan. Psychological distress among Mexican-American and Mexican women as related to status on the new immigration law. JOURNAL OF CONSULTING AND CLINICAL PSYCHOLOGY, Vol. 58, no. 5 (October 1990), p. 548-553. English. DESCR: *Immigrants; Immigration Law and Legislation; Natural Support Systems; *Stress; Undocumented Workers; Women.

Immigration Regulation and Control

3047 Baca Zinn, Maxine. Chicanas: power and control in the domestic sphere. DE COLORES, Vol. 2, no. 3 (1975), p. 19-31. English. DESCR: *Family; Machismo; *Sex Roles; Stereotypes; *Women Men Relations.

3048 Baca Zinn, Maxine. Chicanas: power and control in the domestic sphere. IN: Cotera, Martha and Hufford, Larry, eds. BRIDGING TWO CULTURES. Austin, TX: National Educational Laboratory Publishers, 1980, p. 270-281. English. DESCR: Family; Machismo; Sex Roles; *Stereotypes; Women Men Relations.

3049 Falasco, Dee and Heer, David. Economic and fertility differences between legal and undocumented migrant Mexican families: possible effects of immigration policy changes. SOCIAL SCIENCE QUARTERLY, Vol. 65, no. 2 (June 1984), p. 495-504. English. DESCR: *Economic History and Conditions; *Fertility; *Immigration Law and Legislation; Income; *Undocumented Workers.

3050 Solorzano-Torres, Rosalia. Women, labor, and the U.S.-Mexico border: Mexican maids in El Paso, Texas. IN: Melville, Margarita, ed. MEXICANAS AT WORK IN THE UNITED STATES. Houston, TX: Mexican American Studies Program, University of Houston, 1988, p. 75-83. English. DESCR: Border Patrol; *Border Region; Domestic Work; El Paso, TX; Immigrants; Immigration and Naturalization Service (INS); *Labor Supply and Market; Undocumented Workers; *Women; *Working Women.

3051 Vasquez, Mario F. The election day immigration raid at Lilli Diamond Originals and the response of the ILGWU. IN: Mora, Magdalena and Del Castillo, Adelaida, eds. MEXICAN WOMEN IN THE UNITED STATES: STRUGGLES PAST AND PRESENT. Los Angeles, CA: Chicano Studies Research Center, UCLA, 1980, p. 145-148. English. DESCR: Garment Industry; International Ladies Garment Workers Union (ILGWU); Labor Unions; *Lilli Diamond Originals; Undocumented Workers; Women; Working Women.

Immunization
USE: Preventative Medicine

Imperialism

3052 Apodaca, Maria Linda. The Chicana woman: a historical materialist perspective. IN: Bollinger, William, et al., eds. WOMEN IN LATIN AMERICA: AN ANTHOLOGY FROM LATIN AMERICAN PERSPECTIVES. Riverside, CA: Latin American Perspectives, c1979, p. 81-100. English. DESCR: Capitalism; *Historiography; Immigrants; Marxism; Mexico; Oral History; Social Classes; Spanish Influence.

IN NUEVA YORK

3053 McCracken, Ellen. Latina narrative and politics of signification: articulation, antagonism, and populist rupture. CRITICA, Vol. 2, no. 2 (Fall 1990), p. 202-207. English. DESCR: *Cisneros, Sandra; *Literary Criticism; *Mohr, Nicolasa; Puerto Ricans; RITUALS OF SURVIVAL; Short Story; THE HOUSE ON MANGO STREET; Women.

Income

3054 Aguilar, Marian Angela. Patterns of health care utilization of Mexican American women. Thesis (Ph.D.)--University of Illinois at Urbana-Champaign, 1983. v, 147 p. English. DESCR: Insurance; *Medical Care; *Public Health; Public Policy.

Income (cont.)

3055 Angel, Ronald J. and Tienda, Marta. Determinants of extended household structure: cultural pattern or economical need? AMERICAN JOURNAL OF SOCIOLOGY, Vol. 87, no. 6 (May 1982), p. 1360-1383. English. **DESCR:** *Extended Family.

3056 Bean, Frank D. and Tienda, Marta. The Hispanic population of the United States. New York: Russell Sage Foundation, 1987. xxiv, 456 p. English. **DESCR:** *Census; Education; Employment; Fertility; Identity; Immigration; *Population; Self-Referents; *Statistics.

3057 Bean, Frank D. and Bradshaw, Benjamin S. Mexican American fertility. IN: Teller, Charles H., et al., eds. CUANTOS SOMOS: A DEMOGRAPHIC STUDY OF THE MEXICAN AMERICAN POPULATION. Austin, TX: Center for Mexican American Studies, University of Texas at Austin, 1977, p. 101-130. English. **DESCR:** Attitudes; Birth Control; *Fertility; Population; Religion.

3058 Bean, Frank D.; Stephen, Elizabeth H.; and Opitz, Wolfgang. The Mexican origin population in the United States: a demographic overview. IN: O. de la Garza, Rodolfo, et al., eds. THE MEXICAN AMERICAN EXPERIENCE: AN INTERDISCIPLINARY ANTHOLOGY. Austin, TX: University of Texas Press, 1985, p. 57-75. English. **DESCR:** Employment; Fertility; *Population; Vital Statistics.

3059 Buriel, Raymond and Saenz, Evangelina. Psychocultural characteristics of college-bound and noncollege-bound Chicanas. JOURNAL OF SOCIAL PSYCHOLOGY, Vol. 110, (April 1980), p. 245-251. English. **DESCR:** Biculturalism; *Biculturalism Inventory for Mexican American Students (BIMAS); Higher Education; Identity; Psychological Testing; Sex Roles; Social Psychology.

3060 Cardenas, Gilbert and Flores, Estevan T. The migration and settlement of undocumented women. Austin, TX: CMAS Publications, 1986. 69 p. English. **DESCR:** Employment; Houston, TX; *Immigration; Labor Supply and Market; *Migration Patterns; Public Policy; Socioeconomic Factors; *Undocumented Workers.

3061 Davis, Cary; Haub, Carl; and Willette, JoAnne. U.S. Hispanics: changing the face of America. POPULATION BULLETIN, Vol. 38, no. 3 (June 1983), p. 1-43. English. **DESCR:** Education; Employment; Fertility; Immigration; *Population; Statistics; Vital Statistics.

3062 Dublin, Thomas. Commentary [on "And Miles to Go": Mexican Women and Work, 1930-1985]. IN: Schlissel, Lillian, et al., eds. WESTERN WOMEN: THEIR LAND, THEIR LIVES. Albuquerque, NM: University of New Mexico Press, 1988, p. 137-140. English. **DESCR:** "'And Miles to Go...': Mexican Women and Work, 1930-1985"; Employment; Labor Unions; Ruiz, Vicki L.; Undocumented Workers; Women; *Working Women.

3063 Falasco, Dee and Heer, David. Economic and fertility differences between legal and undocumented migrant Mexican families: possible effects of immigration policy changes. SOCIAL SCIENCE QUARTERLY, Vol. 65, no. 2 (June 1984), p. 495-504. English. **DESCR:** *Economic History and Conditions; *Fertility; *Immigration Law and Legislation; Immigration Regulation and Control; *Undocumented Workers.

3064 Farkas, George; Barton, Margaret; and Kushner, Kathy. White, Black, and Hispanic female youths in central city labor markets. SOCIOLOGICAL QUARTERLY, Vol. 29, no. 4 (Winter 1988), p. 605-621. English. **DESCR:** Anglo Americans; Blacks; Employment; *Labor Supply and Market; Urban Communities; Women; *Youth.

3065 Flores, Francisca. Equality. REGENERACION, Vol. 2, no. 3 (1973), p. 4-5. English. **DESCR:** Anglo Americans; Chicano Movement; Discrimination; Elected Officials; Feminism; *Machismo; *Working Women.

3066 Flores, Francisca. A reaction to discussions on the Talmadge Amendment to the Social Security Act. ENCUENTRO FEMENIL, Vol. 1, no. 2 (1974), p. 13-14. English. **DESCR:** *Chicana Welfare Rights Organization; Child Care Centers; Discrimination; Feminism; *Social Security Act; Social Services; *Talmadge Amendment to the Social Security Act, 1971; Welfare; Working Women.

3067 Flores, Francisca. A reaction to discussions on the Talmadge Amendment to the Social Security Act. REGENERACION, Vol. 2, no. 3 (1973), p. 16. English. **DESCR:** *Chicana Welfare Rights Organization; Child Care Centers; Discrimination; Feminism; *Social Security Act; Social Services; *Talmadge Amendment to the Social Security Act, 1971; Welfare; Working Women.

3068 Garcia, Mario T. The Chicana in American history: the Mexican women of El Paso, 1880-1920 - a case study. PACIFIC HISTORICAL REVIEW, Vol. 49, no. 2 (May 1980), p. 315-337. English. **DESCR:** Acme Laundry, El Paso, TX; American Federation of Labor (AFL); Case Studies; Central Labor Union; Domestic Work; *El Paso, TX; Employment; *History; Immigrants; Labor Unions; Sex Roles; Strikes and Lockouts; *Working Women.

3069 Gonzalez, Deena J. The widowed women of Santa Fe: assessments on the lives of an unmarried population, 1850-80. IN: Scadron, Arlene, ed. ON THEIR OWN: WIDOWS AND WIDOWHOOD IN THE AMERICAN SOUTHWEST 1843-1939. Urbana, IL: University of Illinois Press, c1988. p. [65]-90. English. **DESCR:** Family; History; Land Tenure; *Santa Fe, NM; Sex Roles; Single Parents; *Widowhood; *Women.

3070 Gonzalez, Deena J. The widowed women of Santa Fe: assessments on the lives of an unmarried population, 1850-80. IN: DuBois, Ellen Carol and Ruiz, Vicki L., eds. UNEQUAL SISTERS: A MULTICULTURAL READER IN U.S. WOMEN'S HISTORY. New York: Routledge, 1990, p. 34-50. English. **DESCR:** Family; History; Land Tenure; *Santa Fe, NM; Sex Roles; Single Parents; *Widowhood; *Women.

3071 Hayghe, Howard. Married couples: work and income patterns. MONTHLY LABOR REVIEW, Vol. 106, no. 12 (December 1983), p. 26-29. English. **DESCR:** *Employment; *Marriage; *Sex Roles; Working Women.

Income (cont.)

3072 Jensen, Joan M. Commentary [on "And Miles to Go": Mexican Women and Work, 1930-1985]. IN Schlissel, Lillian, et al., eds. WESTERN WOMEN: THEIR LAND, THEIR LIVES. Albuquerque NM: University of New Mexico Press, 1988, p. 141-144. English. DESCR: "'And Miles to Go...': Mexican Women and Work, 1930-1985"; California; Employment; Labor Unions; Public Policy; Ruiz, Vicki L.; Women; *Working Women.

3073 Jensen, Leif. Secondary earner strategies and family poverty: immigrant-native differentials, 1960-1980. INTERNATIONAL MIGRATION REVIEW, Vol. 25, no. 1 (Spring 1991), p. 113-140. English. DESCR: Anglo Americans; *Asian Americans; Blacks; Family; Immigrants; Immigration; Poverty; Women; Working Women.

3074 Kossoudji, Sherrie and Ranney, Susan. The labor market experience of female migrants: the case of temporary Mexican migration to the U.S. INTERNATIONAL MIGRATION REVIEW, Vol. 18, no. 4 (Winter 1984), p. 1120-1143. English. DESCR: Employment; Immigrants; *Labor Supply and Market; *Migrant Labor; Sex Roles; *Women; Working Women.

3075 Lopez-Trevino, Maria Elena. A radio model: a community strategy to address the problems and needs of Mexican-American women farmworkers. Thesis (M.S.)--California State University, Long Beach, 1989. 179 p. English. DESCR: Coachella, CA; *Farm Workers; Low Income; Occupational Hazards; *Radio; *Sex Roles.

3076 Palacios, Maria. Fear of success: Mexican-American women in two work environments. Thesis (Ph.D.)--New Mexico State University, 1988. 163 p. English. DESCR: Academic Achievement; *Assertiveness; *Careers; Sex Roles; *Working Women.

3077 Reimers, Cordelia W. A comparative analysis of the wages of Hispanics, Blacks, and non-Hispanic whites. IN: Borjas, George J. and Tienda, Marta, eds. HISPANICS IN THE U.S. ECONOMY. Orlando, FL: Academic Press, 1985, p. 27-75. English. DESCR: Anglo Americans; Blacks; Labor Supply and Market; Males; Survey of Income and Education (SIE).

3078 Rivero, Eliana S. La mujer y La Raza: Latinas y Chicanas [part III]. CARACOL, Vol. 4, no. 4 (December 1977), p. 6, 17. Spanish.

3079 Romero, Fred E. The labor market status of Chicanas. IN: Romero, Fred. CHICANO WORKERS: THEIR UTILIZATION AND DEVELOPMENT. Los Angeles: Chicano Studies Center Publications, UCLA, 1979, p. 82-95. English. DESCR: *Employment; Labor Supply and Market; *Statistics; *Working Women.

3080 Romero, Mary. Chicanas modernize domestic service. QUALITATIVE SOCIOLOGY, Vol. 11, no. 4 (Winter 1988), p. 319-334. English. DESCR: *Domestic Work; *Employment; *Interpersonal Relations; Working Women.

3081 Ruiz, Vicki L. "And miles to go...": Mexican women and work, 1930-1985. IN: Schlissel, Lillian, et al., eds. WESTERN WOMEN: THEIR LAND, THEIR LIVES. Albuquerque, NM: University of New Mexico Press, 1988, p. 117-136. English. DESCR: Education; El Paso Women's Employment and Education Project (EPWEE); *Employment; Farah Manufacturing Co., El Paso, TX; Farah Strike; Industrial Workers; Labor Unions; Statistics; Undocumented Workers; United Cannery Agricultural Packing and Allied Workers of America (UCAPAWA); Women; *Working Women.

3082 Ruiz, Vicki L. Working for wages: Mexican women in the Southwest, 1930-1980. Tucson, AZ: Southwest Institute for Research on Women, 1984. 24 p. English. DESCR: *Employment; History; Labor Unions; *Women.

3083 Sanchez, Rosaura. The Chicana labor force. IN: Sanchez, Rosaura and Martinez Cruz, Rosa, eds. ESSAYS ON LA MUJER. Los Angeles, CA: Chicano Studies Center Publications, UCLA, 1977, p. 3-15. English. DESCR: *Employment; Social Classes.

3084 Segura, Denise. Familism and employment among Chicanas and Mexican immigrant women. IN: Melville, Margarita, ed. MEXICANAS AT WORK IN THE UNITED STATES. Houston, TX: Mexican American Studies Program, University of Houston, 1988, p. 24-32. English. DESCR: *Employment; *Extended Family; Family; Immigrants; Machismo; Sex Roles; *Women; Working Women.

3085 Simon, Rita J. and DeLey, Margo. The work experience of undocumented Mexican women migrants in Los Angeles. INTERNATIONAL MIGRATION REVIEW, Vol. 18, no. 4 (Winter 1984), p. 1212-1229. English. DESCR: Immigrants; *Los Angeles, CA; Population; Socioeconomic Factors; *Undocumented Workers; *Working Women.

3086 Spence, Mary Lee. Commentary [on "And Miles to Go": Mexican Women and Work, 1930-1985]. IN: Schlissel, Lillian, et al., eds. WESTERN WOMEN: THEIR LAND, THEIR LIVES. Albuquerque, NM: University of New Mexico Press, 1988, p. 145-150. English. DESCR: "'And Miles to Go...': Mexican Women and Work, 1930-1985"; Food Industry; Labor Unions; Restaurants; Ruiz, Vicki L.; *Working Women.

3087 Stoddard, Ellwyn R. Maquila: assembly plants in Northern Mexico. El Paso, TX: Texas Western Press, 1987. ix, 91 p., [4] p. of plates: ill. English. DESCR: Border Industrialization Program (BIP); *Border Industries; Immigration; *Industrial Workers; Labor Supply and Market; Mexico; Sexism; Undocumented Workers.

3088 Tienda, Marta. Sex, ethnicity and Chicano status attainment. INTERNATIONAL MIGRATION REVIEW, Vol. 16, no. 2 (Summer 1982), p. 435-473. English. DESCR: Academic Achievement; Discrimination in Education; Discrimination in Employment; Identity; Language Proficiency; Sexism; *Social Classes; Social Mobility.

3089 Vasquez, Melba J. T. Power and status of the Chicana: a social-psychological perspective. IN: Martinez, Joe L., Jr., ed. CHICANO PSYCHOLOGY. 2nd. ed. Orlando, FL: Academic Press, 1984, p. 269-287. English. DESCR: *Identity; *Mental Health; Psychology; *Sex Roles; Socialization; Working Women.

3090 Williams, Edward J. and Passe-Smith, John T. Turnover and recruitment in the maquila industry: causes and solutions. Las Cruces, NM: Joint Border Research Institute, New Mexico State University, 1989. ii, 59 p. English. DESCR: *Border Industries; *Employment; *Labor Supply and Market; Personnel Management; Surveys; Women; *Working Women.

Income (cont.)

3091 Ybarra, Lea. Separating a myth from reality: socio-economic and cultural influences on Chicanas and the world of work. IN: Melville, Margarita, ed. MEXICANAS AT WORK IN THE UNITED STATES. Houston, TX: Mexican American Studies Program, University of Houston, 1988, p. 12-23. English. DESCR: Attitudes; *Cultural Characteristics; Machismo; Sex Roles; *Socioeconomic Factors; Stereotypes; *Working Women.

Indexes

3092 Castillo-Speed, Lillian, ed.; Chabran, Richard, ed.; and Garcia-Ayvens, Francisco, ed. The Chicano index: a comprehensive subject, author, and title index to Chicano materials. Berkeley, CA: Chicano Studies Library Publications Unit, 1989-. English. DESCR: *Periodical Indexes.

Indiana

3093 Tajalli, Irene Queiro. Selected cultural, organizational, and economic factors related to prenatal care utilization by middle-income Hispanic women. Thesis (Ph.D.)--University of Illinois at Urbana-Champaign, 1984. 139 p. English. DESCR: *Fertility; Maternal and Child Welfare; *Medical Care; Prenatal Care; Preventative Medicine.

Indianapolis, IN

3094 Queiro-Tajalli, Irene. Hispanic women's perceptions and use of prenatal health care services. AFFILIA: JOURNAL OF WOMEN AND SOCIAL WORK, Vol. 4, no. 2 (Summer 1989), p. 60-72. English. DESCR: *Medical Care; *Prenatal Care; Surveys; Women.

Indianismo
USE: Indigenismo

Indigenismo

3095 Alarcon, Norma. Chicana feminism: in the tracks of 'the' native woman. CULTURAL STUDIES, Vol. 4, no. 3 (October 1990), p. 248-256. English. DESCR: Cultural Studies; *Feminism; *Identity; Mestizaje; Women.

3096 Blanco, Iris. Participacion de las mujeres en la sociedad prehispanica. IN: Sanchez, Rosaura and Martinez Cruz, Rosa, eds. ESSAYS ON LA MUJER. Los Angeles, CA: Chicano Studies Center Publications, UCLA, 1977, p. 48-81. Spanish. DESCR: Aztecs; Cultural Customs; *History; Mexico; Precolumbian Society; Women.

3097 Lara-Cea, Helen. Notes on the use of parish registers in the reconstruction of Chicana history in California prior to 1850. IN: Del Castillo, Adelaida R., ed. BETWEEN BORDERS: ESSAYS ON MEXICANA/CHICANA HISTORY. Encino, CA: Floricanto Press, 1990, p. 131-159. English. DESCR: *California; Catholic Church; History; Mission of Santa Clara; Population; *San Jose, CA; *Vital Statistics.

Industrial Workers

3098 Arbelaez A., Marisol. Impacto social del sismo, Mexico 1985: las costureras. IN: Del Castillo, Adelaida R., ed. BETWEEN BORDERS: ESSAYS ON MEXICANA/CHICANA HISTORY. Encino, CA: Floricanto Press, 1990, p. 315-331. Spanish. DESCR: Earthquakes; Frente de Costureras, Mexico; *Garment Industry; Labor

Unions; *Mexico; Mexico City Earthquake, September 19, 1985; *Women; Working Women.

3099 Arroyo, Laura E. Industrial and occupational distribution of Chicana workers. AZTLAN, Vol. 4, no. 2 (Fall 1973), p. 343-382. English. DESCR: California; *Employment; Farah Manufacturing Co., El Paso, TX; Farah Strike; Garment Industry; Strikes and Lockouts; Texas.

3100 Arroyo, Laura E. Industrial and occupational distribution of Chicana workers. IN: Sanchez, Rosaura and Martinez Cruz, Rosa, eds. ESSAYS ON LA MUJER. Los Angeles, CA: Chicano Studies Center Publications, UCLA, 1977, p. 150-187. English. DESCR: California; *Employment; Farah Manufacturing Co., El Paso, TX; Farah Strike; Garment Industry; Strikes and Lockouts; Texas.

3101 Bustamante, Jorge A. Maquiladoras: a new face of international capitalism on Mexico's northern frontier. IN: Nash, June and Fernandez-Kelly, Patricia, eds. WOMEN, MEN, AND THE INTERNATIONAL DIVISION OF LABOR. Albany, NY: State University of New York Press, 1983, p. 224-256. English. DESCR: Banking Industry; Border Industrialization Program (BIP); Border Industries; *Border Region; Foreign Trade; International Economic Relations; Mexico; Population; Programa Nacional Fronterizo (PRONAF); United States-Mexico Relations; Women; Working Women.

3102 Fernandez Kelly, Maria. "Chavalas de maquiladora": a study of the female labor force in Ciudad Juarez' offshore production plants. Thesis (Ph.D.)--Rutgers University, 1980. xi, 391 leaves. English. DESCR: *Border Industries; Ciudad Juarez, Chihuahua, Mexico; Electronics Industry; *Employment; Garment Industry; Mexico; Women; *Working Women.

3103 Fernandez Kelly, Maria and Garcia, Anna M. Economic restructuring in the United States: Hispanic women in the garment and electronics industries. WOMEN AND WORK, Vol. 3, (1988), p. 49-65. English. DESCR: Business Enterprises; Businesspeople; *Electronics Industry; *Garment Industry; *International Economic Relations; *Working Women.

3104 Fernandez Kelly, Maria. For we are sold, I and my people: women and industry in Mexico's frontier. Albany, NY: State University of New York Press, 1983. vii, 217 p. English. DESCR: Border Industries; *Border Region; Ciudad Juarez, Chihuahua, Mexico; *Electronics Industry; *Garment Industry; Working Women.

3105 Fernandez Kelly, Maria and Garcia, Anna M. Invisible amidst the glitter: Hispanic women in the Southern California electronics industry. IN: Statham, Anne; Miller, Eleanor M.; and Mauksh, Hans O., eds. THE WORTH OF WOMEN'S WORK: A QUALITATIVE SYNTHESIS. Albany, NY: State University of New York Press, 1988, p. 265-290. English. DESCR: *Electronics Industry; Employment; Immigrants; Labor Supply and Market; Megatek, La Jolla, CA; Nova-Tech, San Diego, CA; Sex Roles; Southern California; *Working Women.

Industrial Workers
(cont.)

3106 Fernandez Kelly, Maria and Garcia, Anna M. The making of an underground economy: Hispanic women, home work, and the advanced capitalist state. URBAN ANTHROPOLOGY, Vol. 14, no. 1-3 (Spring, Fall, 1985), p. 59-90. English. **DESCR:** Capitalism; Cubanos; Employment; Garment Industry; International Economic Relations; Labor Supply and Market; *Los Angeles County, CA; *Miami, FL; Women; Working Women.

3107 Fernandez Kelly, Maria. The 'maquila' women. NACLA: REPORT ON THE AMERICAS, Vol. 14, no. 5 (September, October, 1980), p. 14-19. English. **DESCR:** *Border Industries; Feminism; Stereotypes; Women; *Working Women.

3108 Fernandez Kelly, Maria. Mexican border industrialization, female labor force participation and migration. IN: Nash, June and Fernandez-Kelly, Patricia, eds. WOMEN, MEN, AND THE INTERNATIONAL DIVISION OF LABOR. Albany, NY: State University of New York Press, 1983, p. 205-223. English. **DESCR:** Border Industrialization Program (BIP); *Border Industries; Ciudad Juarez, Chihuahua, Mexico; Immigration; Labor Supply and Market; Males; *Migration Patterns; Undocumented Workers; *Women; Working Women.

3109 Fuentes, Annette and Ehrenreich, Barbara. Women in the global factory. New York: Institute for New Communications; Boston: South End Press, 1983. 64 p.: ill. English. **DESCR:** *Border Industries; *International Economic Relations; *Women; *Working Women.

3110 Mendoza, Hope Schecter and Chall, Malca. Activist in the labor movement, the Democratic Party, and the Mexican-American community: an interview. Berkeley, CA: Regional Oral History Office, Bancroft Library, University of California, Berkeley, 1980. xii, 170 p.: ill. English. **DESCR:** *Biography; Chavez Ravine, Los Angeles, CA; Church, Frank; Community Organizations; Community Service Organization, Los Angeles, (CSO); Democratic Party; Elections; Garment Industry; *Labor Unions; Leadership; Mendoza, Hope Schecter; Snyder, Elizabeth; Warschaw, Carmen.

3111 Romero, Bertha. The exploitation of Mexican women in the canning industry and the effects of capital accumulation on striking workers. REVISTA MUJERES, Vol. 3, no. 2 (June 1986), p. 16-20. English. **DESCR:** Canneries; Capitalism; Labor Unions; Strikes and Lockouts; *Watsonville Canning and Frozen Food Co.

3112 Ruiz, Vicki L. "And miles to go...": Mexican women and work, 1930-1985. IN: Schlissel, Lillian, et al., eds. WESTERN WOMEN: THEIR LAND, THEIR LIVES. Albuquerque, NM: University of New Mexico Press, 1988, p. 117-136. English. **DESCR:** Education; El Paso Women's Employment and Education Project (EPWEE); *Employment; Farah Manufacturing Co., El Paso, TX; Farah Strike; *Income; Labor Unions; Statistics; Undocumented Workers; United Cannery Agricultural Packing and Allied Workers of America (UCAPAWA); Women; *Working Women.

3113 Ruiz, Vicki L. Cannery women/cannery lives: Mexican women, unionization, and the California food processing industry, 1930-1950. Albuquerque, NM: University of New Mexico Press, 1987. xviii, 194 p.: ill.

English. **DESCR:** Agricultural Labor Unions; California; *Canneries; Family; History; Labor Disputes; *Labor Unions; Trade Unions; United Cannery Agricultural Packing and Allied Workers of America (UCAPAWA); Women.

3114 Santillan, Richard. Rosita the riveter: Midwest Mexican American women during World War II, 1941-1945. PERSPECTIVES IN MEXICAN AMERICAN STUDIES, Vol. 2, (1989), p. 115-147. English. **DESCR:** History; Intergroup Relations; Language Usage; *Midwestern States; Military; Mutualistas; Sexism; War; *Working Women; *World War II.

3115 Seligson, Mitchell A. and Williams, Edward J. Maquiladoras and migration workers in the Mexico-United States Border Industrialization Program. Austin, TX: Mexico-United States Border Research Program, University of Texas at Austin, 1981. xviii, 202 p. English. **DESCR:** Border Industrialization Program (BIP); *Border Region; Employment; Immigration; Mexico; *Migration Patterns; Working Women.

3116 Stoddard, Ellwyn R. Maquila: assembly plants in Northern Mexico. El Paso, TX: Texas Western Press, 1987. ix, 91 p., [4] p. of plates: ill. English. **DESCR:** Border Industrialization Program (BIP); *Border Industries; Immigration; Income; Labor Supply and Market; Mexico; Sexism; Undocumented Workers.

3117 Taylor, Paul S. Mexican women in Los Angeles industry in 1928. AZTLAN, Vol. 11, no. 1 (Spring 1980), p. 99-131. English. **DESCR:** Employment; History; Los Angeles, CA; *Working Women.

3118 Tiano, Susan B. Labor composition and gender stereotypes in the maquila. JOURNAL OF BORDERLAND STUDIES, Vol. 5, no. 1 (Spring 1990), p. 20-24. English. **DESCR:** *Border Industries; Labor Supply and Market; *Sex Stereotypes; Women; *Working Women.

3119 Young, Gay. Women, border industrialization program, and human rights. El Paso, TX: Center for InterAmerican and Border Studies, UTEP, 1984. 33 p. English. **DESCR:** Border Industrialization Program (BIP); *Border Industries; Economic Development; Employment; Mexico; Sex Roles; *Sexism; *Women; Working Women.

3120 Zavella, Patricia. The impact of "sun belt industrialization" on Chicanas. FRONTIERS: A JOURNAL OF WOMEN STUDIES, Vol. 8, no. 1 (1984), p. 21-27. English. **DESCR:** Albuquerque, NM; Employment; Industrialization; *Working Women.

3121 Zavella, Patricia. The impact of "sun belt industrialization" on Chicanas. Stanford, CA: Stanford Center for Chicano Research, 1984. 25 leaves. English. **DESCR:** Albuquerque, NM; Employment; Industrialization; *Working Women.

3122 Zavella, Patricia. Women, work and family in the Chicano community: cannery workers of the Santa Clara Valley. Thesis (Ph.D.)--University of California, Berkeley, 1982. ix, 254 p. English. **DESCR:** *Canneries; Employment; *Family; Labor Unions; Santa Clara Valley, CA; *Sex Roles; *Working Women.

Industrial Workers
(cont.)

3123 Zavella, Patricia. Women's work and Chicano families: cannery workers of the Santa Clara Valley. Ithaca, NY: Cornell University Press, 1987. xviii, 191 p. English. **DESCR:** *Canneries; Employment; Family; Labor Unions; Santa Clara Valley, CA; Sex Roles; *Working Women.

3124 Zavella, Patricia. Work related networks and household organization among Chicana cannery workers. Stanford, CA: Stanford Center for Chicano Research, 1984. 12 leaves. English. **DESCR:** *Canneries; Natural Support Systems; *Working Women.

Industrialization

3125 Zavella, Patricia. The impact of "sun belt industrialization" on Chicanas. FRONTIERS: A JOURNAL OF WOMEN STUDIES, Vol. 8, no. 1 (1984), p. 21-27. English. **DESCR:** Albuquerque, NM; Employment; *Industrial Workers; *Working Women.

3126 Zavella, Patricia. The impact of "sun belt industrialization" on Chicanas. Stanford, CA: Stanford Center for Chicano Research, 1984. 25 leaves. English. **DESCR:** Albuquerque, NM; Employment; *Industrial Workers; *Working Women.

Infant Mortality

3127 Dowling, Patrick T. and Fisher, Michael. Maternal factors and low birthweight infants: a comparison of Blacks with Mexican-Americans. JOURNAL OF FAMILY PRACTICE, Vol. 25, no. 2 (August 1987), p. 153-158. English. **DESCR:** Blacks; Cook County, IL; *Prenatal Care; *Public Health; *Socioeconomic Factors.

3128 Williams, Ronald L., et al. Pregnancy outcomes among Spanish-surname women in California. AMERICAN JOURNAL OF PUBLIC HEALTH, Vol. 76, no. 4 (April 1986), p. 387-391. English. **DESCR:** *Fertility.

Inner City
USE: Urban Communities

Instituto Familiar de la Raza, San Francisco, CA

3129 Del Zotto, Augusta. Latinas with AIDS: life expectancy for Hispanic women is a startling 45 days after diagnosis. THIS WORLD, (April 9, 1989), p. 9. English. **DESCR:** Abortion; AIDS (Disease); Condom Use; Machismo; *Mano a Mano; Quintero, Juanita; Sex Roles; Women Men Relations.

Instructional Materials
USE: Curriculum Materials

Insurance

3130 Aguilar, Marian Angela. Patterns of health care utilization of Mexican American women. Thesis (Ph.D.)--University of Illinois at Urbana-Champaign, 1983. v, 147 p. English. **DESCR:** Income; *Medical Care; *Public Health; Public Policy.

Intercultural Communication

3131 Deutsch, Sarah. Women and intercultural relations: the case of Hispanic New Mexico and Colorado. SIGNS: JOURNAL OF WOMEN IN CULTURE AND SOCIETY, Vol. 12, no. 4 (Summer 1987), p. 719-739. English. **DESCR:** Colorado; Cultural Characteristics; Immigrants; Mexico; New Mexico; Rural Population; Sex Roles; Social History and Conditions; *Women.

Intercultural Education
USE: Cultural Pluralism

Interethnic Relationships
USE: Intergroup Relations

Intergroup Relations

3132 Alarcon, Norma. Latina writers in the United States. IN: Marting, Diane E., ed. SPANISH AMERICAN WOMEN WRITERS: A BIO-BIBLIOGRAPHICAL SOURCE BOOK. New York: Greenwood Press, 1990, p. [557]-567. English. **DESCR:** *Authors; *Bibliography; BREAKING BOUNDARIES: LATINA WRITING AND CRITICAL READINGS; Cubanos; Language Usage; *Literature Reviews; Puerto Ricans; THIRD WOMAN [journal]; *Women.

3133 Gutierrez, Lorraine M. Working with women of color: an empowerment perspective. SOCIAL WORK, Vol. 35, no. 2 (March 1990), p. 149-153. English. **DESCR:** *Assertiveness; Ethnic Groups; Feminism; *Interpersonal Relations; *Social Work; *Women.

3134 Perez, Emma. Sexuality and discourse: notes from a Chicana survivor. IN: Trujillo, Carla, ed. CHICANA LESBIANS: THE GIRLS OUR MOTHERS WARNED US ABOUT. Berkeley, CA: Third Woman Press, 1991, p. 159-184. English. **DESCR:** *Feminism; Homosexuality; Paz, Octavio; *Sex Roles; *Sexism; Skin Color.

3135 Salgado de Snyder, Nelly and Padilla, Amado M. Interethnic marriages of Mexican Americans after nearly two decades. [Los Angeles, CA]: Spanish Speaking Mental Health Research Center, 1985. 43 p. English. **DESCR:** *Assimilation; *Intermarriage; Los Angeles, CA.

3136 Santillan, Richard. Rosita the riveter: Midwest Mexican American women during World War II, 1941-1945. PERSPECTIVES IN MEXICAN AMERICAN STUDIES, Vol. 2, (1989), p. 115-147. English. **DESCR:** History; Industrial Workers; Language Usage; *Midwestern States; Military; Mutualistas; Sexism; War; *Working Women; *World War II.

3137 Spitta, Silvia D. Literary transculturation in Latin America. Thesis (Ph.D.)--University of Oregon, 1989. 184 p. English. **DESCR:** Anzaldua, Gloria; Arguedos, Jose Maria; Authors; Cultural Characteristics; Culture; *Latin American Literature; Spanish Influence.

3138 Velasquez-Trevino, Gloria. Jovita Gonzalez, una voz de resistencia cultural en la temprana narrativa chicana. IN: Lopez-Gonzalez, Aralia, et al., eds. MUJER Y LITERATURA MEXICANA Y CHICANA: CULTURAS EN CONTACTO. Mexico: Colegio de la Frontera Norte, 1988, p. [77]-83. Spanish. **DESCR:** Anglo Americans; Authors; Feminism; Folklore; *Gonzalez, Jovita; *League of United Latin American Citizens (LULAC).

Intermarriage

3139 Abney-Guardado, Armando J. Chicano intermarriage in the United States: a sociocultural analysis. Thesis (Ph.D.)--Notre Dame, 1983. viii, 142 p. English. **DESCR:** *Acculturation; *Assimilation.

Intermarriage (cont.)

3140 Alba, Richard D. A comment on Schoen and Cohen. AMERICAN JOURNAL OF SOCIOLOGY, Vol. 87, no. 4 (January 1982), p. 935-939. English. DESCR: Cohen, Lawrence E.; ETHNIC ENDOGAMY AMONG MEXICAN AMERICAN GROOMS; *Research Methodology; Schoen, Robert.

3141 Arce, Carlos H. and Abney-Guardado, Armando J. Demographic and cultural correlates of Chicano intermarriage. CALIFORNIA SOCIOLOGIST, Vol. 5, no. 2 (Summer 1982), p. 41-58. English. DESCR: Cultural Characteristics; Culture; Population; Social Psychology.

3142 Castaneda, Antonia I. Gender, race, and culture: Spanish-Mexican women in the historiography of frontier California. FRONTIERS: A JOURNAL OF WOMEN STUDIES, Vol. 11, no. 1 (1990), p. [8]-20. English. DESCR: Bancroft, Hubert Howe; Bolton, Herbert Eugene; *California; Californios; *Historiography; History; *Sex Stereotypes; Spanish Borderlands Theory; Spanish Influence; Stereotypes; Turner, Frederick Jackson; Women.

3143 Cazares, Ralph B.; Murguia, Edward; and Frisbie, William Parker. Mexican American intermarriage in a nonmetropolitan context. SOCIAL SCIENCE QUARTERLY, Vol. 65, no. 2 (June 1984), p. 626-634. English. DESCR: Age Groups; Pecos County, TX; Social Classes; Texas.

3144 Cazares, Ralph B.; Murguia, Edward; and Frisbie, William Parker. Mexican American intermarriage in a nonmetropolitan context. IN: O. de la Garza, Rodolfo, et al., eds. THE MEXICAN AMERICAN EXPERIENCE: AN INTERDISCIPLINARY ANTHOLOGY. Austin, TX: University of Texas Press, 1985, p. 393-401. English. DESCR: Age Groups; Pecos County, TX; Social Classes; Texas.

3145 Craver, Rebecca McDowell. The impact of intimacy: Mexican-Anglo intermarriage in New Mexico 1821-1846. SOUTHWESTERN STUDIES, no. 66 (1982), p. 1-79. English. DESCR: Acculturation; Anglo Americans; Assimilation; History; New Mexico; Rio Arriba Valley, NM.

3146 Craver, Rebecca McDowell. The impact of intimacy: Mexican-Anglo intermarriage in New Mexico 1821-1846. El Paso, TX: Texas Western Press, University of Texas at El Paso, 1982. 79 p. English. DESCR: Acculturation; Anglo Americans; Assimilation; History; New Mexico; Rio Arriba Valley, NM.

3147 Fernandez, Celestino and Holscher, Louis M Chicano-Anglo intermarriage in Arizona, 1960-1980: an exploratory study of eight counties. HISPANIC JOURNAL OF BEHAVIORAL SCIENCES, Vol. 5, no. 3 (September 1983), p. 291-304. English. DESCR: Arizona.

3148 Griswold del Castillo, Richard. La familia Chicano families in the urban Southwest, 1848 to the present. Notre Dame, IN: University of Notre Dame Press, c1984. xv, 173 p. English. DESCR: *Family; History; Machismo; Parenting; *Sex Roles; Sexual Behavior; *Social History and Conditions.

3149 Holscher, Louis M. Hispanic intermarriage: changing trends in New Mexico. AGENDA, Vol. 10, no. 6 (November, December, 1980), p. 8-10. English. DESCR: *Marriage; New Mexico.

3150 Johnson, Susan L. Sharing bed and board: cohabitation and cultural difference in central Arizona mining towns. FRONTIERS: A JOURNAL OF WOMEN STUDIES, Vol. 7, no. 3 (1984), p. 36-42. English. DESCR: Arizona; *Sex Roles.

3151 Kearl, Michael C. and Murguia, Edward. Age differences of spouses in Mexican American intermarriage: exploring the cost of minority assimilation. SOCIAL SCIENCE QUARTERLY, Vol. 66, no. 2 (June 1985), p. 453-460. English. DESCR: *Age Groups; *Assimilation.

3152 Macklin, June and Teniente de Costilla, Alvina. Virgen de Guadalupe and the American dream: the melting pot bubbles on in Toledo, Ohio. IN: West, Stanley A. and Macklin, June, eds. THE CHICANO EXPERIENCE. Boulder, CO: Westview Press, 1979, p. 111-143. English. DESCR: Assimilation; Catholic Church; *Identity; La Virgen de Guadalupe; Migration Patterns; Quinceaneras; Toledo, OH.

3153 Miller, Darlis A. Cross-cultural marriages in the Southwest: the New Mexico experience, 1846-1900. NEW MEXICO HISTORICAL REVIEW, Vol. 57, no. 4 (October 1982), p. 335-359. English. DESCR: Assimilation; Attitudes; Ethnic Groups; New Mexico; Social History and Conditions.

3154 Miller, Michael V. Variations in Mexican American family life: a review synthesis of empirical research. AZTLAN, Vol. 9, no. 1 (1978), p. 209-231. Bibliography. English. DESCR: Acculturation; Compadrazgo; *Family; Sex Roles; Stereotypes.

3155 Murguia, Edward. Chicano intermarriage: a theoretical and empirical study. San Antonio, TX: Trinity University Press, 1982. xiv, 134 p. English. DESCR: Assimilation; Attitudes; Ethnic Groups; Military; Social Classes; Weddings.

3156 Murguia, Edward and Cazares, Ralph B. Intermarriage of Mexican Americans. MARRIAGE & FAMILY REVIEW, Vol. 5, no. 1 (Spring 1982), p. 91-100. English. DESCR: Acculturation; Anglo Americans; Social Mobility.

3157 Salgado de Snyder, Nelly and Padilla, Amado M. Cultural and ethnic maintenance of interethnically married Mexican-Americans. HUMAN ORGANIZATION, Vol. 41, no. 4 (Winter 1982), p. 359-362. English. DESCR: Acculturation.

3158 Salgado de Snyder, Nelly; Lopez, Cynthia M.; and Padilla, Amado M. Ethnic identity and cultural awareness among the offspring of Mexican interethnic marriages. JOURNAL OF EARLY ADOLESCENCE, Vol. 2, no. 3 (Fall 1982), p. 277-282. English. DESCR: *Acculturation; Children; *Identity; *Youth.

3159 Salgado de Snyder, Nelly and Padilla, Amado M. Interethnic marriages of Mexican Americans after nearly two decades. [Los Angeles, CA]: Spanish Speaking Mental Health Research Center, 1985. 43 p. English. DESCR: *Assimilation; Intergroup Relations; Los Angeles, CA.

Intermarriage (cont.)

3160 Schlissel, Lillian, ed.; Ruiz, Vicki L., ed.; and Monk, Janice, ed. Western women: their land, their lives. Albuquerque, NM: University of New Mexico Press, c1988. vi, 354 p. English. DESCR: Anglo Americans; History; Immigration; Labor; Native Americans; *Social History and Conditions; Southwestern United States; *Women.

3161 Schoen, Robert; Wooldredge, John; and Thomas, Barbara. Ethnic and educational effects on marriage choice. SOCIAL SCIENCE QUARTERLY, Vol. 70, no. 3 (September 1989), p. 617-630. English. DESCR: Education; Identity; Marriage; Research Methodology; Social Classes.

3162 Valdez, Avelardo. Recent increases in intermarriage by Mexican American males: Bexar County, Texas from 1971 to 1980. SOCIAL SCIENCE QUARTERLY, Vol. 64, (March 1983), p. 136-144. English. DESCR: Bexar County, TX; Males.

3163 Yinger, Milton J. Assimilation in the United States: the Mexican-Americans. IN: Conner, Walker, ed. MEXICAN-AMERICANS IN COMPARATIVE PERSPECTIVE. Washington, DC: Urban Institute Press, 1985, p. 30-55. English. DESCR: Acculturation; *Assimilation; Culture of Poverty Model; Identity.

Internal Colony Model

3164 Flores, Estevan T. Chicanos and sociological research: 1970-1980. IN: CHICANOS AND THE SOCIAL SCIENCES: A DECADE OF RESEARCH AND DEVELOPMENT (1970-1980) SYMPOSIUM WORKING PAPER. Santa Barbara, CA: Center for Chicano Studies, University of California, 1983, p. 19-45. English. DESCR: Bibliography; Family; Labor; Literature Reviews; Population; Research Methodology; *Sociology.

International Economic Relations

3165 Bustamante, Jorge A. Maquiladoras: a new face of international capitalism on Mexico's northern frontier. IN: Nash, June and Fernandez-Kelly, Patricia, eds. WOMEN, MEN, AND THE INTERNATIONAL DIVISION OF LABOR. Albany, NY: State University of New York Press, 1983, p. 224-256. English. DESCR: Banking Industry; Border Industrialization Program (BIP); Border Industries; *Border Region; Foreign Trade; Industrial Workers; Mexico; Population; Programa Nacional Fronterizo (PRONAF); United States-Mexico Relations; Women; Working Women.

3166 Fernandez Kelly, Maria and Garcia, Anna M. Economic restructuring in the United States: Hispanic women in the garment and electronics industries. WOMEN AND WORK, Vol. 3, (1988), p. 49-65. English. DESCR: Business Enterprises; Businesspeople; *Electronics Industry; *Garment Industry; Industrial Workers; *Working Women.

3167 Fernandez Kelly, Maria and Garcia, Anna M. The making of an underground economy: Hispanic women, home work, and the advanced capitalist state. URBAN ANTHROPOLOGY, Vol. 14, no. 1-3 (Spring, Fall, 1985), p. 59-90. English. DESCR: Capitalism; Cubanos; Employment; Garment Industry; Industrial Workers; Labor Supply and Market; *Los Angeles County, CA; *Miami, FL; Women; Working Women.

3168 Fuentes, Annette and Ehrenreich, Barbara. Women in the global factory. New York:

Institute for New Communications; Boston: South End Press, 1983. 64 p.: ill. English. DESCR: *Border Industries; Industrial Workers; *Women; *Working Women.

3169 Levy Oved, Albert and Alcocer Marban, Sonia. Las maquiladoras en Mexico. Mexico: Fondo de Cultura Economica, 1984. 125 p.: ill. Spanish. DESCR: *Border Industries; *Border Region; United States-Mexico Relations; Women.

3170 Pena, Devon Gerardo. The class politics of abstract labor: organizational forms and industrial relations in the Mexican maquiladoras. Thesis (Ph.D.)--University of Texas, Austin, 1983. xix, 587 p. English. DESCR: *Border Industries; Border Region; *Trade Unions; Women; Working Women.

International Ladies Garment Workers Union (ILGWU)

3171 Duron, Clementina. Mexican women and labor conflict in Los Angeles: the ILGWU dressmakers' strike of 1933. AZTLAN, Vol. 15, no. 1 (Spring 1984), p. 145-161. English. DESCR: Garment Industry; Labor Unions; *Strikes and Lockouts.

3172 Green, George N. ILGWU in Texas, 1930-1970. JOURNAL OF MEXICAN-AMERICAN HISTORY, Vol. 1, no. 2 (Spring 1971), p. 144-169. English. DESCR: History; *Labor Unions; Texas.

3173 Monroy, Douglas. La costura en Los Angeles, 1933-1939: the ILGWU and the politics of domination. IN: Mora, Magdalena and Del Castillo, Adelaida, eds. MEXICAN WOMEN IN THE UNITED STATES: STRUGGLES PAST AND PRESENT. Los Angeles, CA: Chicano Studies Research Center, UCLA, 1980, p. 171-178. English. DESCR: *Garment Industry; History; Labor Unions; Los Angeles, CA.

3174 Vasquez, Mario F. The election day immigration raid at Lilli Diamond Originals and the response of the ILGWU. IN: Mora, Magdalena and Del Castillo, Adelaida, eds. MEXICAN WOMEN IN THE UNITED STATES: STRUGGLES PAST AND PRESENT. Los Angeles, CA: Chicano Studies Research Center, UCLA, 1980, p. 145-148. English. DESCR: Garment Industry; Immigration Regulation and Control; Labor Unions; *Lilli Diamond Originals; Undocumented Workers; Women; Working Women.

3175 Vasquez, Mario F. Immigrant workers and the apparel manufacturing industry in Southern California. IN: Rios-Bustamante, Antonio, ed. MEXICAN IMMIGRANT WORKERS IN THE U.S. Los Angeles, CA: Chicano Studies Research Center Publications, University of California, 1981, p. 85-96. English. DESCR: AFL-CIO; California; Garment Industry; Immigrants; *Labor Supply and Market; Labor Unions; Undocumented Workers; Women.

International Relations

3176 Jaramillo, Mari-Luci. Profile of Chicanas and international relations. IN: LA CHICANA: BUILDING FOR THE FUTURE, AN ACTION PLAN FOR THE 80s. Oakland, CA: National Hispanic University, 1981, p. 37-58. English. DESCR: Careers; Feminism; Leadership.

International Women's Year World Conference (1975: Mexico City)

3177 Diehl, Paula and Saavedra, Lupe. Hispanas in the year of the woman: many voices. AGENDA, (Winter 1976), p. 14-21. English. DESCR: Discrimination; *Feminism; Mexico City.

3178 Robinson, Bea Vasquez. Are we racist? Are we sexist? AGENDA, (Winter 1976), p. 23-24. English. DESCR: Conferences and Meetings; Discrimination; Feminism; National Chicana Coalition; *Sexism.

3179 Sosa Riddell, Adaljiza. The status of women in Mexico: the impact of the "International Year of the Woman". IN: Iglitzin, Lynn B. and Ross, Ruth A., eds. WOMEN IN THE WORLD, 1975-1985. Santa Barbara, CA: ABC-Clio, Inc., 1986, p. 305-324. English. DESCR: Abortion; *Feminism; *Mexico; Political History and Conditions; Political Parties and Organizations; Rape; *Sexism; Social History and Conditions; *Women.

Interpersonal Relations

3180 Gutierrez, Lorraine M. Working with women of color: an empowerment perspective. SOCIAL WORK, Vol. 35, no. 2 (March 1990), p. 149-153. English. DESCR: *Assertiveness; Ethnic Groups; Feminism; Intergroup Relations; *Social Work; *Women.

3181 Mata, Alberto Guardiola and Castillo, Valerie. Rural female adolescent dissatisfaction, support and helpseeking. FREE INQUIRY IN CREATIVE SOCIOLOGY, Vol. 14, no. 2 (November 1986) p. 135-138. English DESCR: Alcoholism; *Drug Use; *Natural Support Systems; Parent and Child Relationships; Rural Population; *Youth.

3182 Ramos, Maria. A micro-ethnographic study of Chicana mother and daughter socialization practices. Thesis (Ph.D.)--University of Colorado at Boulder, 1982. 292 p. English. DESCR: Ethnology; *Parent and Child Relationships; Parenting; *Socialization.

3183 Rider, Kennon V. Relationship satisfaction of the Mexican American woman: effects of acculturation, socioeconomic status, and interaction structures. Thesis (Ph.D.)--Texas Tech University, 1988. 145 p. English. DESCR: *Acculturation; Sex Roles; *Socioeconomic Factors.

3184 Romero, Mary. Chicanas modernize domestic service. QUALITATIVE SOCIOLOGY, Vol. 11, no. 4 (Winter 1988), p. 319-334. English. DESCR: *Domestic Work; *Employment; Income; Working Women.

3185 Romero, Mary. Day work in the suburbs: the work experience of Chicana private housekeepers. IN: Statham, Anne; Miller, Eleanor M; and Mauksch, Hans O., eds. THE WORTH OF WOMEN'S WORK: A QUALITATIVE SYNTHESIS. Albany, NY: State University of New York Press, 1988, p. 77-91. English. DESCR: Domestic Work; Employment; *Natural Support Systems; Social Mobility; Working Women.

3186 Romero, Mary. Domestic service in the transition from rural to urban life: the case of la Chicana. WOMEN'S STUDIES QUARTERLY, Vol. 13, no. 3 (February 1987), p. 199-222. English. DESCR: *Domestic Work; Employment; Rural Population; Social Mobility; Sociology; Urban Communities; Working Women.

3187 Segura, Denise. Conflict in social relations at work: a Chicana perspective. IN: National Association for Chicano Studies. ESTUDIOS CHICANOS AND THE POLITICS OF COMMUNITY. [S.l.]: National Association for Chicano Studies, c1989, p. [110]-131. English. DESCR: *Discrimination in Employment; Employment Training; Immigrants; Social Classes; Women; *Working Women.

3188 Yanez, Rosa H. The complimenting speech act among Chicano women. IN: Bergen, John J., ed. SPANISH IN THE UNITED STATES: SOCIOLINGUISTIC ISSUES. Washington, DC: Georgetown University Press, 1990, p. 79-85. English. DESCR: *Sociolinguistics.

THE INVITATION

3189 Alarcon, Norma. The sardonic powers of the erotic in the work of Ana Castillo. IN: Horno-Delgado, Asuncion, et al., eds. BREAKING BOUNDARIES: LATINA WRITING AND CRITICAL READINGS. Amherst, MA: University of Massachusetts Press, c1989, p. 94-107. English. DESCR: *Castillo, Ana; Literary Criticism; OTRO CANTO; Poetry; Sex Roles; *THE MIXQUIAHUALA LETTERS; WOMEN ARE NOT ROSES.

Iranians

3190 Saboonchi, Nasrin. The working women's reactions to the traditional marriage role: a crosscultural study within the symbolic interactionism framework. Thesis (Ph.D.)--United States International University, 1983. 173 p. English. DESCR: Immigrants; *Marriage; *Sex Roles; Women; Working Women.

Islas, Arturo

3191 Gutierrez Castillo, Dina. La imagen de la mujer en la novela fronteriza. IN: Lopez-Gonzalez, Aralia, et al., eds. MUJER Y LITERATURA MEXICANA Y CHICANA: CULTURAS EN CONTACTO. Mexico: Colegio de la Frontera Norte, 1988, p. [55]-63. Spanish. DESCR: *Border Region; Literary Characters; *Literary Criticism; Mendez M., Miguel; *Novel; PEREGRINOS DE AZTLAN; Sex Roles; Sex Stereotypes; THE RAIN GOD: A DESERT TALE; *Women.

Jails

LSE: Prisons

Japanese

3192 Gurak, Douglas T. Assimilation and fertility: a comparison of Mexican American and Japanese American women. HISPANIC JOURNAL OF BEHAVIORAL SCIENCES, Vol. 2, no. 3 (September 1980), p. 219-239. English. DESCR: Asian Americans; Assimilation; *Fertility; Population; Women.

Jaramillo, Cleofas M.

3193 Jensen, Carol. Cleofas M. Jaramillo on marriage in territorial Northern New Mexico. NEW MEXICO HISTORICAL REVIEW, Vol. 58, no. 2 (April 1983), p. 153-171. English. DESCR: *Marriage; New Mexico.

Jaramillo, Cleofas M.
(cont.)

3194 Padilla, Genaro. Imprisoned narrative? Or
lies, secrets, and silence in New Mexico
women's autobiography. IN: Calderon, Hector
and Saldivar, Jose David, eds. CRITICISM IN
THE BORDERLANDS: STUDIES IN CHICANO
LITERATURE, CULTURE, AND IDEOLOGY. Durham,
NC: Duke University Press, 1991, p. [43]-60.
English. **DESCR:** Authors; *Autobiography;
*Cabeza de Baca, Fabiola; Literary History;
New Mexico; ROMANCE OF A LITTLE VILLAGE
GIRL; WE FED THEM CACTUS.

3195 Rebolledo, Tey Diana. Las escritoras:
romances and realities. IN: Gonzales-Berry,
Erlinda, ed. PASO POR AQUI: CRITICAL ESSAYS
ON THE NEW MEXICAN LITERARY TRADITION.
Albuquerque, NM: University of New Mexico
Press, c1989, p. 199-214. English. **DESCR:**
Authors; *Cabeza de Baca, Fabiola; Literary
History; New Mexico; OLD SPAIN IN OUR
SOUTHWEST; *Otero Warren, Nina; ROMANCE OF A
LITTLE VILLAGE GIRL; WE FED THEM CACTUS;
Women.

3196 Rebolledo, Tey Diana. Hispanic women writers
of the Southwest: tradition and innovation.
IN: Lensink, Judy Nolte, ed. OLD
SOUTHWEST/NEW SOUTHWEST: ESSAYS ON A REGION
AND ITS LITERATURE. Tucson, AZ: The Tucson
Public Library, 1987, p. 49-61. English.
DESCR: *Authors; Cabeza de Baca, Fabiola;
Literature; Mora, Pat; OLD SPAIN IN OUR
SOUTHWEST; Otero Warren, Nina; Preciado
Martin, Patricia; Sex Roles; Sex
Stereotypes; Silva, Beverly; *Southwestern
United States; Vigil-Pinon, Evangelina; WE
FED THEM CACTUS; *Women.

3197 Rebolledo, Tey Diana. Narrative strategies
of resistance in Hispana writing. THE
JOURNAL OF NARRATIVE TECHNIQUE, Vol. 20, no.
2 (Spring 1990), p. 134-146. English.
DESCR: *Authors; Cabeza de Baca, Fabiola;
Fiction; *Literary Criticism; Literature;
New Mexico; OLD SPAIN IN OUR SOUTHWEST;
*Oral Tradition; Otero Warren, Nina; ROMANCE
OF A LITTLE VILLAGE GIRL; WE FED THEM
CACTUS.

3198 Rebolledo, Tey Diana. Tradition and
mythology: signatures of landscape in
Chicana literature. IN: Norwood, Vera and
Monk, Janice, eds. THE DESERT IS NO LADY:
SOUTHWESTERN LANDSCAPES IN WOMEN'S WRITING
AND ART. New Haven, CT: Yale University
Press, 1987, p. 96-124. English. **DESCR:**
*Authors; Cabeza de Baca, Fabiola; Chavez,
Denise; Literary Criticism; *Literary
History; Literature; Mora, Pat; Mythology;
Otero Warren, Nina; Portillo Trambley,
Estela; Silva, Beverly; Southwestern United
States; WE FED THEM CACTUS.

EL JARDIN [play]

3199 Melville, Margarita B. Female and male in
Chicano theatre. IN: Kanellos, Nicolas, ed.
HISPANIC THEATRE IN THE UNITED STATES.
Houston, TX: Arte Publico Press, 1984, p.
71-79. English. **DESCR:** BERNABE; BRUJERIAS
[play]; Cultural Characteristics; DAY OF THE
SWALLOWS; Duarte-Clark, Rodrigo; Family;
Feminism; Macias, Ysidro; Morton, Carlos;
Portillo Trambley, Estela; RANCHO HOLLYWOOD
[play]; *Sex Roles; *Teatro; THE ULTIMATE
PENDEJADA [play]; Valdez, Luis; Women Men
Relations.

Jimenez, Magali

3200 Lindstrom, Naomi. Four representative

Hispanic women poets of Central Texas: a
portrait of plurality. THIRD WOMAN, Vol. 2,
no. 1 (1984), p. 64-70. English. **DESCR:**
Beltran, Beatriz; de Hoyos, Angela;
*Literary Criticism; Poetry; Tafolla,
Carmen; Texas.

Job Discrimination
USE: Discrimination in Employment

Jokes
USE: Chistes

Joliet, IL

3201 Campos Carr, Irene. Proyecto La Mujer:
Latina women shaping consciousness. WOMEN'S
STUDIES INTERNATIONAL FORUM, Vol. 12, no. 1
(1989), p. 45-49. English. **DESCR:** Artists;
Aurora, IL; Authors; Barrios; Conferences
and Meetings; Elgin, IL; *Feminism; Poetry;
Proyecto La Mujer Conference (Spring, 1982:
Northern Illinois); Women.

Journalism

3202 Hernandez, Ines. Sara Estela Ramirez: the
early twentieth century Texas-Mexican poet.
Thesis (Ph.D.)--University of Houston, 1984.
94 p. English. **DESCR:** *Authors; *Biography;
Feminism; Flores Magon, Ricardo; Literary
Criticism; Mexican Revolution - 1910-1920;
Mexico; *Poetry; Ramirez, Sara Estela;
Texas; Women.

3203 Hernandez, Ines. Sara Estela Ramirez:
sembradora. LEGACY: A JOURNAL OF
NINETEENTH-CENTURY AMERICAN WOMEN WRITERS,
Vol. 6, no. 1 (Spring 1989), p. 13-26.
English. **DESCR:** Authors; *Biography;
*Feminism; Flores Magon, Ricardo; LA
CORREGIDORA [newspaper]; Mexican Revolution
- 1910-1920; Mexico; Newspapers; Poetry;
*Ramirez, Sara Estela; REGENERACION
[newspaper].

3204 Perez, Emma. "A la mujer": a critique of the
Partido Liberal Mexicano's gender ideology
on women. IN: Del Castillo, Adelaida R., ed.
BETWEEN BORDERS: ESSAYS ON MEXICANA/CHICANA
HISTORY. Encino, CA: Floricanto Press, 1990,
p. 459-482. English. **DESCR:** *"A La Mujer"
[essay]; Essays; *Feminism; Flores Magon,
Ricardo; Guerrero, Praxedis G.; Mexican
Revolution - 1910-1920; Mexico; Newspapers;
*Partido Liberal Mexicano (PLM); Political
Ideology; Political Parties and
Organizations; *REGENERACION [newspaper];
Sex Roles; Women.

Journalists

3205 Lomas, Clara. Mexican precursors of Chicana
feminist writing. IN: National Association
for Chicano Studies. ESTUDIOS CHICANOS AND
THE POLITICS OF COMMUNITY. [S.l.]: National
Association for Chicano Studies, c1989, p.
[149]-160. English. **DESCR:** Authors; de
Cardenas, Isidra T.; *Feminism; Idar,
Jovita; Literature; *Mexican Revolution -
1910-1920; Newspapers; Ramirez, Sara Estela;
Villarreal, Andrea; Villegas de Magnon,
Leonor.

Journals

3206 Alarcon, Norma. Hay que inventarnos/we must
invent ourselves. THIRD WOMAN, Vol. 1, no. 1
(1981), p. 4-6. English. **DESCR:** Art; Midwest
Latina Writer's Workshop (1980: Chicago);
Midwestern States; *THIRD WOMAN: OF LATINAS
IN THE MIDWEST; Third World Literature
(U.S.).

Journals (cont.)

3207 Garza-Livingston, M'Liss, ed. and Mercado, Olivia, ed. Chicana journals. COMADRE, no. 3 (Fall 1978), p. 38. Bilingual.

3208 Soto, Shirlene Ann. The emerging Chicana: a review of the journals. SOUTHWEST ECONOMY AND SOCIETY, Vol. 2, no. 1 (October, November, 1976), p. 39-45. English. DESCR: Directories; *Literature Reviews.

Juana Ines de la Cruz, Sor

3209 Gonzalez, Maria R. El embrion nacionalista visto a traves de la obra de Sor Juana Ines de la Cruz. IN: Del Castillo, Adelaida R., ed. BETWEEN BORDERS: ESSAYS ON MEXICANA/CHICANA HISTORY. Encino, CA: Floricanto Press, 1990, p. 239-253. Spanish. DESCR: Authors; Mexico; *Nationalism; Women.

"Juanita of Downieville"

3210 Mirande, Alfredo and Enriquez, Evangelina. Chicanas in the history of the Southwest. IN: Duran, Livie Isauro and Bernard, H. Russell, eds. INTRODUCTION TO CHICANO STUDIES. 2nd ed. New York: Macmillan, 1982, p. 156-179. English. DESCR: Arguello, Concepcion; Barcelo, Gertrudes "La Tules"; Fages, Eulalia; *History; Robledo, Refugio; Urrea, Teresa.

Junior Colleges
USE: Community Colleges

Junior High School

3211 de Anda, Diane. A study of the interaction of Hispanic junior high school students and their teachers. HISPANIC JOURNAL OF BEHAVIORAL SCIENCES, Vol. 4, no. 1 (March 1982), p. 57-74. English. DESCR: Dropouts; *Teacher-Pupil Interaction.

3212 Fu, Victoria R.; Hinkle, Dennis E.; and Korslund, Mary K. A development study of ethnic self-concept among pre-adolescent girls. JOURNAL OF GENETIC PSYCHOLOGY, Vol. 14, (March 1983), p. 67-73. English. DESCR: Comparative Psychology; *Identity; Self-Concept Self Report Scale; Students; Youth.

Juvenile Delinquency

3213 Gibbs, Jewelle Taylor. Personality patterns of delinquent females: ethnic and sociocultural variations. JOURNAL OF CLINICAL PSYCHOLOGY, Vol. 38, no. 1 (January 1982), p. 198-206. English. DESCR: Ethnic Groups; Identity; Personality; Psychological Testing; Socioeconomic Factors.

3214 Harris, Mary G. Cholas: Latino girls and gangs. New York: AMS Press, 1988. x, 220 p. English. DESCR: Barrios; *Gangs; Los Angeles, CA; San Fernando Valley, CA; *Youth.

Keefe, Susan E.

3215 Acuna, Rodolfo. The struggles of class and gender: current research in Chicano Studies [review essay]. JOURNAL OF AMERICAN ETHNIC HISTORY, Vol. 8, no. 2 (Spring 1989), p. 134-138. English. DESCR: *CANNERY WOMEN, CANNERY LIVES; *CHICANO ETHNICITY; Deutsch, Sarah; Literature Reviews; *NO SEPARATE REFUGE; Padilla, Amado M.; Ruiz, Vicki L.; *WOMEN'S WORK AND CHICANO FAMILIES; Zavella, Pat.

Khalifeh, Sahar

3216 Harlow, Barbara. Sites of struggle: immigration, deportation, prison, and exile. IN: Calderon, Hector and Saldivar, Jose David, eds. CRITICISM IN THE BORDERLANDS: STUDIES IN CHICANO LITERATURE, CULTURE, AND IDEOLOGY. Durham, NC: Duke University Press, 1991, p. [149]-163. English. DESCR: Anzaldua, Gloria; BLACK GOLD; BORDERLANDS/LA FRONTERA: THE NEW MESTIZA; First, Ruth; *Literary Criticism; *Political Ideology; Sanchez, Rosaura; Social Classes; "The Cariboo Cafe" [short story]; "The Ditch" [short story]; Viramontes, Helena Maria; WILD THORNS; *Women; Working Women.

Kiev, Ari

3217 Blea, Irene I. Brujeria: a sociological analysis of Mexican American witches. IN: Barrera, Mario, et al., eds. WORK, FAMILY, SEX ROLES, LANGUAGE: SELECTED PAPERS, 1979. Berkeley, CA: Tonatiuh-Quinto Sol, 1980, p. 177-193. English. DESCR: *Brujas; Colorado; Folklore; New Mexico.

La Mesa College Pinto and Pinta Program

3218 Santillanes, Maria. Women in prison--C.I.W.: an editorial. REGENERACION, Vol. 2, no. 4 (1975), p. 53. English. DESCR: Conferences and Meetings; Garcia, Dolly; Lopez, Tony; Mares, Rene; Martinez, Miguel; Pinto Conference (1973: UCLA); Player; *Prisons; Salazar, Peggy.

Labels
USE: Self-Referents

Labor

3219 Almaguer, Tomas. Urban Chicano workers in historical perspective: a review of recent literature. LA RED/THE NET, no. 68 (May 1983), p. 2-6. English. DESCR: *Literature Reviews; Working Women.

3220 Calderon, Roberto R. and Zamora, Emilio, Jr. Manuela Solis Sager and Emma Tenayuca: a tribute. IN: Cordova, Teresa, et al., eds. CHICANA VOICES. Austin, TX: Center for Mexican American Studies, 1986, p. 30-41. English. DESCR: Agricultural Labor Unions; Biography; History; *Solis Sager, Manuela; South Texas Agricultural Worker's Union (STAWU); *Tenayuca, Emma; United Cannery Agricultural Packing and Allied Workers of America (UCAPAWA).

3221 Calderon, Roberto R. and Zamora, Emilio, Jr. Manuela Solis Sager and Emma Tenayuca: a tribute. IN: Del Castillo, Adelaida R., ed. BETWEEN BORDERS: ESSAYS ON MEXICANA/CHICANA HISTORY. Encino, CA: Floricanto Press, 1990, p. 269-279. English. DESCR: Agricultural Labor Unions; Biography; History; *Solis Sager, Manuela; South Texas Agricultural Worker's Union (STAWU); *Tenayuca, Emma; United Cannery Agricultural Packing and Allied Workers of America (UCAPAWA).

3222 Cordova, Teresa, et al., eds. and National Association for Chicano Studies. Chicana voices: intersections of class, race, and gender. Austin, TX: Center for Mexican American Studies Publications, 1986. xi, 223 p. English. DESCR: Chicana Studies; Political History and Conditions; *Social History and Conditions.

Labor (cont.)

3223 Flores, Estevan T. Chicanos and sociological research: 1970-1980. IN: CHICANOS AND THE SOCIAL SCIENCES: A DECADE OF RESEARCH AND DEVELOPMENT (1970-1980) SYMPOSIUM WORKING PAPER. Santa Barbara, CA: Center for Chicano Studies, University of California, 1983, p. 19-45. English. **DESCR:** Bibliography; Family; Internal Colony Model; Literature Reviews; Population; Research Methodology; *Sociology.

3224 Garcia, Mario T. La familia: the Mexican immigrant family, 1900-1930. IN: Barrera, Mario, et al., eds. WORK, FAMILY, SEX ROLES, LANGUAGE: SELECTED PAPERS, 1979. Berkeley, CA: Tonatiuh-Quinto Sol, 1980, p. 117-139. English. **DESCR:** Assimilation; Cultural Customs; El Paso, TX; Family; *Historiography; History; Immigration; Sex Roles.

3225 Gonzalez, Rosalinda M. Chicanas and Mexican immigrant families 1920-1940: women's subordination and family exploitation. IN: Scharf, Lois and Jensen, Joan M., eds. DECADES OF DISCONTENT: THE WOMEN'S MOVEMENT, 1920-1940. Westport, CT: Greenwood Press, 1983, p. 59-84. English. **DESCR:** *Family; Farm Workers; History; Immigrants; Labor Unions; Mexico; Pecan Shelling Worker's Union, San Antonio, TX; Sex Roles; Strikes and Lockouts; United Cannery Agricultural Packing and Allied Workers of America (UCAPAWA); Working Women.

3226 Larguia, Isabel and Dumoulin, John. Toward a science of women's liberation. IN: Mora, Magdalena and Del Castillo, Adelaida, eds. MEXICAN WOMEN IN THE UNITED STATES: STRUGGLES PAST AND PRESENT. Los Angeles, CA: Chicano Studies Research Center, 1980, p. 45-61. English. **DESCR:** *Feminism; Sex Roles; Social Classes.

3227 Melville, Margarita B., ed. Mexicanas at work in the United States. Houston, TX: Mexican American Studies Program, University of Houston, 1988. 83 p. English. **DESCR:** Border Region; *Employment; Family; Migrant Labor; *Women; Working Women.

3228 Olivares, Yvette. The sweatshop: the garment industry's reborn child. REVISTA MUJERES, Vol. 3, no. 2 (June 1986), p. 55-62. English. **DESCR:** Garment Industry; Public Health; Third World; *Undocumented Workers; *Women; Working Women.

3229 Orozco, Cynthia. Chicana labor history: a critique of male consciousness in historical writing. LA RED/THE NET, no. 77 (January 1984), p. 2-5. English. **DESCR:** *Historiography; *Sexism; Working Women.

3230 Pena, Devon Gerardo. Between the lines: a new perspective on the industrial sociology of women workers in transnational labor processes. IN: Cordova, Teresa, et al., eds. CHICANA VOICES. Austin, TX: Center for Mexican American Studies, 1986, p. 77-95. English. **DESCR:** Border Industries; Marxism; *Women; Working Women.

3231 Pena, Devon Gerardo. Las maquiladoras: Mexican women in class struggle in the border industries. AZTLAN, Vol. 11, no. 2 (Fall 1980), p. 159-229. English. **DESCR:** Border Industries; *Economic History and Conditions; Labor Unions; Mexico; Mexico-U.S. Border Development; Working Women.

3232 Schlissel, Lillian, ed.; Ruiz, Vicki L., ed.; and Monk, Janice, ed. Western women: their land, their lives. Albuquerque, NM: University of New Mexico Press, c1988. vi, 354 p. English. **DESCR:** Anglo Americans; History; Immigration; Intermarriage; Native Americans; *Social History and Conditions; Southwestern United States; *Women.

Labor Camps

3233 Chavira, Alicia. "Tienes que ser valiente": Mexicana migrants in a midwestern farm labor camp. IN: Melville, Margarita, ed. MEXICANAS AT WORK IN THE UNITED STATES. Houston, TX: Mexican American Studies Program, University of Houston, 1988, p. 64-74. English. **DESCR:** *Farm Workers; Immigrants; Midwestern States; Migrant Health Services; *Migrant Labor; Sex Roles; *Women.

Labor Classes
USE: Laboring Classes

Labor Disputes

3234 Cantarow, Ellen and De la Cruz, Jessie Lopez. Jessie Lopez De la Cruz: the battle for farmworkers' rights. IN: Cantarow, Ellen. MOVING THE MOUNTAIN: WOMEN WORKING FOR SOCIAL CHANGE. Old Westbury, NY: Feminist Press, 1980, p. 94-151. English. **DESCR:** Agricultural Labor Unions; Chavez, Cesar E.; *De la Cruz, Jessie Lopez; *Farm Workers; Oral History; Parlier, CA; Sex Roles; Strikes and Lockouts; *United Farmworkers of America (UFW).

3235 Rose, Margaret. Traditional and nontraditional patterns of female activism in the United Farm Workers of America, 1962-1980. FRONTIERS: A JOURNAL OF WOMEN STUDIES, Vol. 11, no. 1 (1990), p. [26]-32. English. **DESCR:** Boycotts; California; Chavez, Cesar E.; *Chavez, Helen; *Huerta, Dolores; Labor Unions; National Farm Workers Association (NFWA); Sex Roles; Strikes and Lockouts; *United Farmworkers of America (UFW).

3236 Ruiz, Vicki L. Cannery women/cannery lives: Mexican women, unionization, and the California food processing industry, 1930-1950. Albuquerque, NM: University of New Mexico Press, 1987. xviii, 194 p.: ill. English. **DESCR:** Agricultural Labor Unions; California; *Canneries; Family; History; Industrial Workers; *Labor Unions; Trade Unions; United Cannery Agricultural Packing and Allied Workers of America (UCAPAWA); Women.

3237 Saavedra, Lupe. It is only fair that women be allowed to... AGENDA, (Winter 1976), p. 12-13. English. **DESCR:** Labor Unions; SALT OF THE EARTH [film]; *Strikes and Lockouts.

Labor Supply and Market

3238 Baker, Susan Gonzalez. Many rivers to cross: Mexican immigrants, women workers, and the structure of labor markets in the urban Southwest. Thesis (Ph.D.)--University of Texas, Austin, 1989. 163 p. English. **DESCR:** *Immigrants; Immigration Reform and Control Act of 1986; Undocumented Workers; Women; *Working Women.

Labor Supply and Market
(cont.)

3239 Bean, Frank D.; Swicegood, Gray; and King, Allan G. Role incompatibility and the relationship between fertility and labor supply among Hispanic women. IN: Borjas, George J. and Tienda, Marta, eds. HISPANICS IN THE U.S. ECONOMY. Orlando, FL: Academic Press, 1985, p. 221-242. English. DESCR: Cubanos; *Employment; Fertility; Puerto Ricans.

3240 Blackwelder, Julia Kirk. Women of the depression: caste and culture in San Antonio, 1929-1939. College Station, TX: Texas A&M University Press, 1984. xviii, 279 p.: ill. English. DESCR: Criminal Justice System; Cultural Characteristics; Employment; Family; Great Depression, 1929-1933; Labor Unions; Prostitution; San Antonio, TX; *Social Classes; *Women.

3241 Cardenas, Gilbert and Flores, Estevan T. The migration and settlement of undocumented women. Austin, TX: CMAS Publications, 1986. 69 p. English. DESCR: Employment; Houston, TX; *Immigration; Income; *Migration Patterns; Public Policy; Socioeconomic Factors; *Undocumented Workers.

3242 Cardenas, Gilbert; Shelton, Beth Anne; and Pena, Devon Gerardo. Undocumented immigrant women in the Houston labor force. CALIFORNIA SOCIOLOGIST, Vol. 5, no. 2 (Summer 1982), p. 98-118. English. DESCR: Employment; Houston, TX; *Immigrants; *Undocumented Workers.

3243 Cooney, Rosemary Santana. The Mexican American female in the labor force. IN: Teller, Charles H., et al., eds. CUANTOS SOMOS: A DEMOGRAPHIC STUDY OF THE MEXICAN AMERICAN POPULATION. Austin, TX: Center for Mexican American Studies, University of Texas at Austin, 1977, p. 183-196. English. DESCR: *Employment.

3244 Dixon, Marlene; Martinez, Elizabeth; and McCaughan, Ed. Theoretical perspectives on Chicanas, Mexicanas and the transnational working class. CONTEMPORARY MARXISM, no. 11 (Fall 1985), p. 46-76. English. DESCR: Border Industries; Capitalism; Economic History and Conditions; History; *Immigration; *Laboring Classes; Mexico; Undocumented Workers; Women.

3245 Farkas, George; Barton, Margaret; and Kushner, Kathy. White, Black, and Hispanic female youths in central city labor markets. SOCIOLOGICAL QUARTERLY, Vol. 29, no. 4 (Winter 1988), p. 605-621. English. DESCR: Anglo Americans; Blacks; Employment; *Income; Urban Communities; Women; *Youth.

3246 Fernandez Kelly, Maria and Garcia, Anna M. Invisible amidst the glitter: Hispanic women in the Southern California electronics industry. IN: Statham, Anne; Miller, Eleanor M.; and Mauksh, Hans O., eds. THE WORTH OF WOMEN'S WORK: A QUALITATIVE SYNTHESIS. Albany, NY: State University of New York Press, 1988, p. 265-290. English. DESCR: *Electronics Industry; Employment; Immigrants; *Industrial Workers; Megatek, La Jolla, CA; Nova-Tech, San Diego, CA; Sex Roles; Southern California; *Working Women.

3247 Fernandez Kelly, Maria and Garcia, Anna M. The making of an underground economy: Hispanic women, home work, and the advanced capitalist state. URBAN ANTHROPOLOGY, Vol. 14, no. 1-3 (Spring, Fall, 1985), p. 59-90. English. DESCR: Capitalism; Cubanos; Employment; Garment Industry; Industrial Workers; International Economic Relations; *Los Angeles County, CA; *Miami, FL; Women; Working Women.

3248 Fernandez Kelly, Maria. Mexican border industrialization, female labor force participation and migration. IN: Nash, June and Fernandez-Kelly, Patricia, eds. WOMEN, MEN, AND THE INTERNATIONAL DIVISION OF LABOR. Albany, NY: State University of New York Press, 1983, p. 205-223. English. DESCR: Border Industrialization Program (BIP); *Border Industries; Ciudad Juarez, Chihuahua, Mexico; Immigration; Industrial Workers; Males; *Migration Patterns; Undocumented Workers; *Women; Working Women.

3249 Garcia, Alma M. Studying Chicanas: bringing women into the frame of Chicano Studies. IN: Cordova, Teresa, et al., eds. CHICANA VOICES. Austin, TX: Center for Mexican American Studies, 1986, p. 19-29. English. DESCR: Chicana Studies; *Chicano Studies; Discrimination; Literature Reviews.

3250 Garcia Castro, Mary. Migrant women: issues in organization and solidarity. MIGRATION WORLD MAGAZINE, Vol. 14, no. 1-2 (1986), p. 15-19. English. DESCR: *Migrant Labor; Organizations; Political Economy; Undocumented Workers; Women.

3251 Kossoudji, Sherrie and Ranney, Susan. The labor market experience of female migrants: the case of temporary Mexican migration to the U.S. INTERNATIONAL MIGRATION REVIEW, Vol. 18, no. 4 (Winter 1984), p. 1120-1143. English. DESCR: Employment; Immigrants; Income; *Migrant Labor; Sex Roles; *Women; Working Women.

3252 Mindiola, Tatcho, Jr. The cost of being a Mexican female worker in the 1970 Houston labor market. AZTLAN, Vol. 11, no. 2 (Fall 1980), p. 231-247. English. DESCR: Discrimination; *Discrimination in Employment; Houston, TX; Working Women.

3253 Pick, James B., et al. Socioeconomic influences on fertility in the Mexican borderlands region. MEXICAN STUDIES/ESTUDIOS MEXICANOS, Vol. 6, no. 1 (Winter 1990), p. 11-42. English. DESCR: *Border Region; *Employment; *Fertility; Literacy; Socioeconomic Factors; Working Women.

3254 Reimers, Cordelia W. A comparative analysis of the wages of Hispanics, Blacks, and non-Hispanic whites. IN: Borjas, George J. and Tienda, Marta, eds. HISPANICS IN THE U.S. ECONOMY. Orlando, FL: Academic Press, 1985, p. 27-75. English. DESCR: Anglo Americans; Blacks; *Income; Males; Survey of Income and Education (SIE).

3255 Romero, Fred E. The labor market status of Chicanas. IN: Romero, Fred. CHICANO WORKERS: THEIR UTILIZATION AND DEVELOPMENT. Los Angeles: Chicano Studies Center Publications, UCLA, 1979, p. 82-95. English. DESCR: *Employment; Income; *Statistics; *Working Women.

3256 Ruiz, Vicki L. By the day or week: Mexicana domestic workers in El Paso. TRABAJOS MONOGRAFICOS, Vol. 2, no. 1 (1986), p. 35-58. English. DESCR: *Domestic Work; El Paso, TX; Employment; *Working Women.

Labor Supply and Market
(cont.)

3257 Ruiz, Vicki L. By the day or week: Mexicana domestic workers in El Paso. IN: Ruiz, Vicki L. and Tiano, Susan, eds. WOMEN ON THE U.S.-MEXICO BORDER: RESPONSES TO CHANGE. Boston, MA: Allen & Unwin, 1987, p. 61-76. English. **DESCR**: *Domestic Work; El Paso, TX; Employment.

3258 Segura, Denise. Chicana and Mexican immigrant women at work: the impact of class, race, and gender on occupational mobility. GENDER & SOCIETY, Vol. 3, no. 1 (March 1989), p. 37-52. English. **DESCR**: *Employment; *Immigrants; Laboring Classes; San Francisco Bay Area; *Social Mobility; Women; Working Women.

3259 Segura, Denise. Chicanas and Mexican immigrant women in the labor market: a study of occupational mobility and stratification. Thesis (Ph.D.)--University of California, Berkeley, 1986. iii, 282 p. English. **DESCR**: *Immigrants; Mexico; Women; *Working Women.

3260 Segura, Denise. Labor market stratification: the Chicana experience. BERKELEY JOURNAL OF SOCIOLOGY, Vol. 29, (1984), p. 57-91. English. **DESCR**: *Discrimination in Employment; Employment; Socioeconomic Factors; *Working Women.

3261 Solorzano-Torres, Rosalia. Women, labor, and the U.S.-Mexico border: Mexican maids in El Paso, Texas. IN: Melville, Margarita, ed. MEXICANAS AT WORK IN THE UNITED STATES. Houston, TX: Mexican American Studies Program, University of Houston, 1988, p. 75-83. English. **DESCR**: Border Patrol; *Border Region; Domestic Work; El Paso, TX; Immigrants; Immigration and Naturalization Service (INS); Immigration Regulation and Control; Undocumented Workers; *Women; *Working Women.

3262 Stoddard, Ellwyn R. Maquila: assembly plants in Northern Mexico. El Paso, TX: Texas Western Press, 1987. ix, 91 p., [4] p. of plates: ill. English. **DESCR**: Border Industrialization Program (BIP); *Border Industries; Immigration; Income; *Industrial Workers; Mexico; Sexism; Undocumented Workers.

3263 Tiano, Susan B. Export processing, women's work, and the employment problem in developing countries: the case of the maquiladora program in Northern Mexico. El Paso, TX: Center for InterAmerican and Border Studies, UTEP, 1985. 32 p. English. **DESCR**: *Border Region; *Employment; Mexico; *Sex Roles; Women; Working Women.

3264 Tiano, Susan B. Labor composition and gender stereotypes in the maquila. JOURNAL OF BORDERLAND STUDIES, Vol. 5, no. 1 (Spring 1990), p. 20-24. English. **DESCR**: *Border Industries; Industrial Workers; *Sex Stereotypes; Women; *Working Women.

3265 Tiano, Susan B. Maquiladoras in Mexicali: integration or exploitation? IN: Ruiz, Vicki L. and Tiano, Susan, eds. WOMEN ON THE U.S.-MEXICO BORDER: RESPONSES TO CHANGE. Boston, MA: Allen & Unwin, 1987, p. 77-101. English. **DESCR**: Border Industrialization Program (BIP); *Border Industries; Border Region; Employment; Mexicali, Mexico; Women; Working Women.

3266 Tiano, Susan B. Women's work and unemployment in northern Mexico. IN: Ruiz,

Vicki L. and Tiano, Susan, eds. WOMEN ON THE U.S.-MEXICO BORDER: RESPONSES TO CHANGE. Boston, MA: Allen & Unwin, 1987, p. 17-39. English. **DESCR**: Border Industrialization Program (BIP); Border Industries; Border Region; Employment; Mexico; Multinational Corporations; *Women.

3267 Tienda, Marta. Hispanics in the U.S. labor market: an overview of recent evidence. LA RED/THE NET, no. 50 (January 1982), p. 4-7. English. **DESCR**: Laborers; Working Women.

3268 Vasquez, Mario F. Immigrant workers and the apparel manufacturing industry in Southern California. IN: Rios-Bustamante, Antonio, ed. MEXICAN IMMIGRANT WORKERS IN THE U.S. Los Angeles, CA: Chicano Studies Research Center Publications, University of California, 1981, p. 85-96. English. **DESCR**: AFL-CIO; California; Garment Industry; Immigrants; International Ladies Garment Workers Union (ILGWU); Labor Unions; Undocumented Workers; Women.

3269 Williams, Edward J. and Passe-Smith, John T. Turnover and recruitment in the maquila industry: causes and solutions. Las Cruces, NM: Joint Border Research Institute, New Mexico State University, 1989. ii, 59 p. English. **DESCR**: *Border Industries; *Employment; Income; Personnel Management; Surveys; Women; *Working Women.

Labor Unions

3270 Arbelaez A., Marisol. Impacto social del sismo, Mexico 1985: las costureras. IN: Del Castillo, Adelaida R., ed. BETWEEN BORDERS: ESSAYS ON MEXICANA/CHICANA HISTORY. Encino, CA: Floricanto Press, 1990, p. 315-331. Spanish. **DESCR**: Earthquakes; Frente de Costureras, Mexico; *Garment Industry; *Industrial Workers; *Mexico; Mexico City Earthquake, September 19, 1985; *Women; Working Women.

3271 Aulette, Judy and Mills, Trudy. Something old, something new: auxiliary work in the 1983-1986 copper strike. FEMINIST STUDIES, Vol. 14, no. 2 (Summer 1988), p. 251-268. English. **DESCR**: Arizona; Clifton-Morenci Copper Strike, 1983-1986; Clifton-Morenci District, Arizona; Feminism; Morenci Miners Women's Auxiliary (MMWA); Mutualistas; Phelps Dodge Corporation, Morenci, AZ; SALT OF THE EARTH [film]; Sex Roles; *Strikes and Lockouts.

3272 Blackwelder, Julia Kirk. Women of the depression: caste and culture in San Antonio, 1929-1939. College Station, TX: Texas A&M University Press, 1984. xviii, 279 p.: ill. English. **DESCR**: Criminal Justice System; Cultural Characteristics; Employment; Family; Great Depression, 1929-1933; Labor Supply and Market; Prostitution; San Antonio, TX; *Social Classes; *Women.

3273 Coyle, Laurie; Hershatter, Gail; and Honig, Emily. Women at Farah: an unfinished story. IN: Mora, Magdalena and Del Castillo, Adelaida, eds. MEXICAN WOMEN IN THE UNITED STATES: STRUGGLES PAST AND PRESENT. Los Angeles, CA: Chicano Studies Research Center, UCLA, 1980, p. 117-143. English. **DESCR**: Farah Manufacturing Co., El Paso, TX; Farah Strike; Garment Industry; *Strikes and Lockouts.

Labor Unions (cont.)

3274 Delgado Campbell, Dolores. Shattering the
stereotype: Chicanas as labor union
organizers. BERKELEY WOMEN OF COLOR, no. 11
(Summer 1983), p. 20-23. English. DESCR:
Farah Manufacturing Co., El Paso, TX; Farah
Strike; *Gonzalez Parsons, Lucia; Huerta,
Dolores; Moreno, Luisa [union organizer];
Tenayuca, Emma; Working Women.

3275 Dublin, Thomas. Commentary [on "And Miles to
Go": Mexican Women and Work, 1930-1985]. IN:
Schlissel, Lillian, et al., eds. WESTERN
WOMEN: THEIR LAND, THEIR LIVES. Albuquerque,
NM: University of New Mexico Press, 1988, p.
137-140. English. DESCR: "And Miles to
Go...': Mexican Women and Work, 1930-1985";
Employment; Income; Ruiz, Vicki L.;
Undocumented Workers; Women; *Working Women.

3276 Duron, Clementina. Mexican women and labor
conflict in Los Angeles: the ILGWU
dressmakers' strike of 1933. AZTLAN, Vol.
15, no. 1 (Spring 1984), p. 145-161.
English. DESCR: Garment Industry;
International Ladies Garment Workers Union
(ILGWU); *Strikes and Lockouts.

3277 Friaz, Guadalupe. Chicanas in the workforce
= Chicanas en la fuerza de trabajo: "Working
9 to 5". CAMINOS, Vol. 2, no. 3 (May 1981),
p. 37-39, 61+. Bilingual. DESCR: Employment;
Laborers; *Working Women.

3278 Garcia, Mario T. The Chicana in American
history: the Mexican women of El Paso,
1880-1920 - a case study. PACIFIC HISTORICAL
REVIEW, Vol. 49, no. 2 (May 1980), p.
315-337. English. DESCR: Acme Laundry, El
Paso, TX; American Federation of Labor
(AFL); Case Studies; Central Labor Union;
Domestic Work; *El Paso, TX; Employment;
*History; Immigrants; Income; Sex Roles;
Strikes and Lockouts *Working Women.

3279 Goldsmith, Raquel Rubio. La
Mexicana/Chicana. RENATO ROSALDO LECTURE
SERIES MONOGRAPH, Vol. 1, (Summer 1985), p.
1-67. English. DESCR: Clergy; House of the
Divine Providence [convent], Douglas, AZ;
*Social History and Conditions; Women; World
War II.

3280 Gonzalez, Rosalinda M. Chicanas and Mexican
immigrant families 1920-1940: women's
subordination and family exploitation. IN:
Scharf, Lois and Jensen, Joan M., eds.
DECADES OF DISCONTENT: THE WOMEN'S MOVEMENT,
1920-1940. Westport, CT: Greenwood Press,
1983, p. 59-84. English. DESCR: *Family;
Farm Workers; History; Immigrants; Labor;
Mexico; Pecan Shelling Worker's Union, San
Antonio, TX; Sex Roles; Strikes and
Lockouts; United Cannery Agricultural
Packing and Allied Workers of America
(UCAPAWA); Working Women.

3281 Green, George N. ILGWU in Texas, 1930-1970.
JOURNAL OF MEXICAN-AMERICAN HISTORY, Vol. 1,
no. 2 (Spring 1971) p. 144-169. English.
DESCR: History; International Ladies Garment
Workers Union (ILGWU); Texas.

3282 Iglesias, Norma. La flor mas bella de la
maquiladora: historias de vida de la mujer
obrera en Tijuana, B.C.N. Mexico, D.F.:
Secretaria de Educacion Publica, CEFNOMEX,
1985. 166 p.: ill. Spanish. DESCR:
Border Industrialization Program (BIP); *Border
Industries; Cultural Customs; Sindicato
Independiente Solidev; Solidev Mexicana,
S.A.; Tijuana, Baja California, Mexico;
*Women; Working Women.

3283 In the maquiladoras. CORRESPONDENCIA, no. 9
(December 1990), p. 3-9. English. DESCR:
*Border Industries; Tijuana, Baja
California, Mexico; Women; *Working Women.

3284 Jensen, Joan M. Commentary [on "And Miles to
Go": Mexican Women and Work, 1930-1985]. IN:
Schlissel, Lillian, et al., eds. WESTERN
WOMEN: THEIR LAND, THEIR LIVES. Albuquerque,
NM: University of New Mexico Press, 1988, p.
141-144. English. DESCR: "'And Miles to
Go...': Mexican Women and Work, 1930-1985";
California; Employment; Income; Public
Policy; Ruiz, Vicki L.; Women; *Working
Women.

3285 Keremitsis, Dawn. Del metate al molino: la
mujer mexicana de 1910 a 1940. HISTORIA
MEXICANA, Vol. 33, no. 2 (1983), p. 285-302.
Spanish. DESCR: Food Industry; History;
Mexico; Sex Roles; Strikes and Lockouts;
Women; *Working Women.

3286 Leonard, Jonathan S. The effect of unions on
the employment of Blacks, Hispanics, and
women. INDUSTRIAL AND LABOR RELATIONS
REVIEW, Vol. 39, no. 1 (October 1985), p.
115-132. English. DESCR: Blacks; Employment;
Women.

3287 Mendoza, Hope Schecter and Chall, Malca.
Activist in the labor movement, the
Democratic Party, and the Mexican-American
community: an interview. Berkeley, CA:
Regional Oral History Office, Bancroft
Library, University of California, Berkeley,
1980. xii, 170 p.: ill. English. DESCR:
*Biography; Chavez Ravine, Los Angeles, CA;
Church, Frank; Community Organizations;
Community Service Organization, Los Angeles,
(CSO); Democratic Party; Elections; Garment
Industry; Industrial Workers; Leadership;
Mendoza, Hope Schecter; Snyder, Elizabeth;
Warschaw, Carmen.

3288 Mirande, Alfredo and Enriquez, Evangelina.
Chicanas in the struggle for unions. IN:
Duran, Livie Isauro and Bernard, H. Russell,
eds. INTRODUCTION TO CHICANO STUDIES. 2nd.
ed. New York: Macmillan, 1973, p. 325-337.
English. DESCR: Gonzalez Parsons, Lucia;
Moreno, Luisa [union organizer]; Parsons,
Albert; Tenayuca, Emma; United Cannery
Agricultural Packing and Allied Workers of
America (UCAPAWA).

3289 Monroy, Douglas. La costura en Los Angeles,
1933-1939: the ILGWU and the politics of
domination. IN: Mora, Magdalena and Del
Castillo, Adelaida, eds. MEXICAN WOMEN IN
THE UNITED STATES: STRUGGLES PAST AND
PRESENT. Los Angeles, CA: Chicano Studies
Research Center, UCLA, 1980, p. 171-178.
English. DESCR: *Garment Industry; History;
International Ladies Garment Workers Union
(ILGWU); Los Angeles, CA.

3290 Mora, Magdalena. The Tolteca Strike: Mexican
women and the struggle for union
representation. IN: Rios-Bustamante,
Antonio, ed. MEXICAN IMMIGRANT WORKERS IN
THE U.S. Los Angeles, CA: Chicano Studies
Research Center Publications, University of
California, 1981, p. 111-117. English.
DESCR: Centro de Accion Social Autonomo
(CASA); Food Industry; *Strikes and
Lockouts; Toltec Foods, Richmond, CA.

Labor Unions (cont.)

3291 O'Connor, Mary I. Women's networks and the social needs of Mexican immigrants. URBAN ANTHROPOLOGY, Vol. 19, no. 1-2 (Spring, Summer, 1990), p. 81-98. English. **DESCR:** Employment; *Immigrants; *Natural Support Systems; *Sandyland Nursery, Carpinteria, CA; Undocumented Workers; United Farmworkers of America (UFW); Women.

3292 Pena, Devon Gerardo. Las maquiladoras: Mexican women in class struggle in the border industries. AZTLAN, Vol. 11, no. 2 (Fall 1980), p. 159-229. English. **DESCR:** Border Industries; *Economic History and Conditions; Labor; Mexico; Mexico-U.S. Border Development; Working Women.

3293 Rips, Geoffrey and Tenayuca, Emma. Living history: Emma Tenayuca tells her story. TEXAS OBSERVER, (October 28, 1983), p. 7-15. English. **DESCR:** *Autobiography; Communist Party; Food Industry; Leadership; Oral History; Pecan Shelling Worker's Union, San Antonio, TX; San Antonio, TX; Strikes and Lockouts; Tenayuca, Emma; United Cannery Agricultural Packing and Allied Workers of America (UCAPAWA); Worker's Alliance (WA), Los Angeles, CA; Working Women.

3294 Romero, Bertha. The exploitation of Mexican women in the canning industry and the effects of capital accumulation on striking workers. REVISTA MUJERES, Vol. 3, no. 2 (June 1986), p. 16-20. English. **DESCR:** Canneries; Capitalism; Industrial Workers; Strikes and Lockouts; *Watsonville Canning and Frozen Food Co.

3295 Rose, Margaret. Traditional and nontraditional patterns of female activism in the United Farm Workers of America, 1962-1980. FRONTIERS: A JOURNAL OF WOMEN STUDIES, Vol. 11, no. 1 (1990), p. [26]-32. English. **DESCR:** Boycotts; California; Chavez, Cesar E.; *Chavez, Helen; *Huerta, Dolores; Labor Disputes; National Farm Workers Association (NFWA); Sex Roles; Strikes and Lockouts; *United Farmworkers of America (UFW).

3296 Rose, Margaret. Women in the United Farm Workers: a study of Chicana Mexicana participation in a labor union, 1950-1980. Thesis (Ph.D.)--University of California, Los Angeles, 1988. 403p. English. **DESCR:** History; Huerta, Dolores; *Sex Roles; United Farmworkers of America (UFW); Working Women.

3297 Ruiz Funes, Concepcion and Tunon, Enriqueta. Panorama de las luchas de la mujer mexicana en el siglo XX. IN: Del Castillo, Adelaida R., ed. BETWEEN BORDERS: ESSAYS ON MEXICANA/CHICANA HISTORY. Encino, CA: Floricanto Press, 1990, p. 336-357. Spanish. **DESCR:** Coordinadora de Mujeres Trabajadoras; *Feminism; Frente Unido Pro Derechos de la Mujer; History; *Mexico; Sex Roles; *Women.

3298 Ruiz, Vicki L. "And miles to go...": Mexican women and work, 1930-1985. IN: Schlissel, Lillian, et al., eds. WESTERN WOMEN: THEIR LAND, THEIR LIVES. Albuquerque, NM: University of New Mexico Press, 1988, p. 117-136. English. **DESCR:** Education; El Paso Women's Employment and Education Project (EPWEE); *Employment; Farah Manufacturing Co., El Paso, TX; Farah Strike; *Income; Industrial Workers; Statistics; Undocumented Workers; United Cannery Agricultural Packing and Allied Workers of America (UCAPAWA); Women; *Working Women.

3299 Ruiz, Vicki L. Cannery women/cannery lives: Mexican women, unionization, and the California food processing industry, 1930-1950. Albuquerque, NM: University of New Mexico Press, 1987. xviii, 194 p.: ill. English. **DESCR:** Agricultural Labor Unions; California; *Canneries; Family; History; Industrial Workers; Labor Disputes; Trade Unions; United Cannery Agricultural Packing and Allied Workers of America (UCAPAWA); Women.

3300 Ruiz, Vicki L. Obreras y madres: labor activism among Mexican women and its impact on the family. RENATO ROSALDO LECTURE SERIES MONOGRAPH, Vol. 1, (Summer 1985), p. [19]-38. English. **DESCR:** Child Care Centers; Children; History; *Mexico; Sex Roles; Women; *Working Women.

3301 Ruiz, Vicki L. A promise fulfilled: Mexican cannery workers in Southern California. THE PACIFIC HISTORIAN, Vol. 30, no. 2 (Summer 1986), p. 51-61. English. **DESCR:** *California Sanitary Canning Company, Los Angeles, CA; *Canneries; Moreno, Luisa [union organizer]; Southern California; Strikes and Lockouts; *United Cannery Agricultural Packing and Allied Workers of America (UCAPAWA); Working Women.

3302 Ruiz, Vicki L. A promise fulfilled: Mexican cannery workers in Southern California. IN: DuBois, Ellen Carol and Ruiz, Vicki L., eds. UNEQUAL SISTERS: A MULTICULTURAL READER IN U.S. WOMEN'S HISTORY. New York: Routledge, 1990, p. 264-274. English. **DESCR:** *California Sanitary Canning Company, Los Angeles, CA; *Canneries; Moreno, Luisa [union organizer]; Southern California; Strikes and Lockouts; *United Cannery Agricultural Packing and Allied Workers of America (UCAPAWA); Working Women.

3303 Ruiz, Vicki L. A promise fulfilled: Mexican cannery workers in Southern California. IN: Del Castillo, Adelaida R., ed. BETWEEN BORDERS: ESSAYS ON MEXICANA/CHICANA HISTORY. Encino, CA: Floricanto Press, 1990, p. 281-298. English. **DESCR:** California Sanitary Canning Company, Los Angeles, CA; *Canneries; Moreno, Luisa [union organizer]; Southern California; Strikes and Lockouts; United Cannery Agricultural Packing and Allied Workers of America (UCAPAWA); Working Women.

3304 Ruiz, Vicki L. UCAPAWA, Chicanas, and the California food processing industry, 1937-1950. Thesis (Ph.D.)--Stanford University, 1982. x, 281 p. English. **DESCR:** *Canneries; Food Industry; Trade Unions; United Cannery Agricultural Packing and Allied Workers of America (UCAPAWA); Working Women.

3305 Ruiz, Vicki L. Working for wages: Mexican women in the Southwest, 1930-1980. Tucson, AZ: Southwest Institute for Research on Women, 1984. 24 p. English. **DESCR:** *Employment; History; *Income; *Women.

3306 Saavedra, Lupe. It is only fair that women be allowed to... AGENDA, (Winter 1976), p. 12-13. English. **DESCR:** Labor Disputes; SALT OF THE EARTH [film]; *Strikes and Lockouts.

3307 Shapiro, Peter. Watsonville shows "it can be done". GUARDIAN, Vol. 39, no. 24 (March 25, 1987), p. 1,9. English. **DESCR:** Canneries; NorCal Frozen Foods; *Strikes and Lockouts; *Watsonville Canning and Frozen Food Co.; Working Women.

Labor Unions (cont.)

3308 Spence, Mary Lee. Commentary [on "And Miles to Go": Mexican Women and Work, 1930-1985]. IN: Schlissel, Lilliar, et al., eds. WESTERN WOMEN: THEIR LAND, THEIR LIVES. Albuquerque, NM: University of New Mexico Press, 1988, p. 145-150. English. DESCR: "'And Miles to Go...': Mexican Women and Work, 1930-1985"; Food Industry; Income; Restaurants; Ruiz, Vicki L.; *Working Women.

3309 Vasquez, Mario F. The election day immigration raid at Lilli Diamond Originals and the response of the ILGWU. IN: Mora, Magdalena and Del Castillo, Adelaida, eds. MEXICAN WOMEN IN THE UNITED STATES: STRUGGLES PAST AND PRESENT. Los Angeles, CA: Chicano Studies Research Center, UCLA, 1980, p. 145-148. English. DESCR: Garment Industry; Immigration Regulation and Control; International Ladies Garment Workers Union (ILGWU); *Lilli Diamond Originals; Undocumented Workers; Women; Working Women.

3310 Vasquez, Mario F. Immigrant workers and the apparel manufacturing industry in Southern California. IN: Rios-Bustamante, Antonio, ed. MEXICAN IMMIGRANT WORKERS IN THE U.S. Los Angeles, CA: Chicano Studies Research Center Publications, University of California, 1981, p. 85-96. English. DESCR: AFL-CIO; California; Garment Industry; Immigrants; International Ladies Garment Workers Union (ILGWU); *Labor Supply and Market; Undocumented Workers; Women.

3311 Zavella, Patricia. "Abnormal intimacy": the varying work networks of Chicana cannery workers. FEMINIST STUDIES, Vol. 11, no. 3 (Fall 1985), p. 541-557. English. DESCR: Canneries; Discrimination in Employment; *Natural Support Systems; *Working Women.

3312 Zavella, Patricia. The politics of race and gender: organizing Chicana cannery workers in Northern California. IN: Bookman, Ann and Morgen, Sandra, eds. WOMEN AND THE POLITICS OF EMPOWERMENT. Philadelphia, PA: Temple University Press, 1988, p. 202-224. English. DESCR: Bay City Cannery Workers Committee *Canneries; Cannery Workers Committee (CWC); Discrimination; Garcia, Connie; Identity; Nationalism; Northern California; Santa Clara Valley, CA; Sex Roles; Sexism; *Working Women.

3313 Zavella, Patricia. Women, work and family in the Chicano community: cannery workers of the Santa Clara Valley. Thesis (Ph.D.)--University of California, Berkeley, 1982. ix, 254 p. English. DESCR: *Canneries; Employment; *Family; Industrial Workers; Santa Clara Valley, CA; *Sex Roles; *Working Women.

3314 Zavella, Patricia. Women's work and Chicano families: cannery workers of the Santa Clara Valley. Ithaca, NY: Cornell University Press, 1987. xviii, 191 p. English. DESCR: *Canneries; Employment; Family; Industrial Workers; Santa Clara Valley, CA; Sex Roles; *Working Women.

Laborers

3315 Friaz, Guadalupe. Chicanas in the workforce = Chicanas en la fuerza de trabajo: "Working 9 to 5". CAMINOS, Vol. 2, no. 3 (May 1981), p. 37-39, 61+. Bilingual. DESCR: Employment; Labor Unions; *Working Women.

3316 Pena, Manuel. Class, gender, and machismo:

the "treacherous-woman" folklore of Mexican male workers. GENDER & SOCIETY, Vol. 5, no. 1 (March 1991), p. 30-46. English. DESCR: *Folklore; *Machismo; Males; *Sex Roles; Sex Stereotypes; Social Classes; *Undocumented Workers; Women Men Relations.

3317 Tienda, Marta. Hispanics in the U.S. labor market: an overview of recent evidence. LA RED/THE NET, no. 50 (January 1982), p. 4-7. English. DESCR: *Labor Supply and Market; Working Women.

Laboring Classes

3318 Dixon, Marlene; Martinez, Elizabeth; and McCaughan, Ed. Chicanas and Mexicanas within a transnational working class: theoretical perspectives. REVIEW (Fernand Braudel Center), Vol. 7, no. 1 (1983), p. 109-150. English. DESCR: *Working Women.

3319 Dixon, Marlene; Martinez, Elizabeth; and McCaughan, Ed. Theoretical perspectives on Chicanas, Mexicanas and the transnational working class. CONTEMPORARY MARXISM, no. 11 (Fall 1985), p. 46-76. English. DESCR: Border Industries; Capitalism; Economic History and Conditions; History; *Immigration; *Labor Supply and Market; Mexico; Undocumented Workers; Women.

3320 Glenn, Evelyn Nakano. Racial ethnic women's labor: the intersection of race, gender and class oppression. REVIEW OF RADICAL POLITICAL ECONOMY, Vol. 17, no. 3 (Fall 1985), p. 86-108. English. DESCR: Asian Americans; Blacks; *Discrimination; *Feminism; *Marxism; Sexism; Social Classes; Women; Working Women.

3321 Lizarraga, Sylvia S. Hacia una teoria para la liberacion de la mujer. IN: Garcia, Juan R., ed. IN TIMES OF CHALLENGE: CHICANOS AND CHICANAS IN AMERICAN SOCIETY. Houston, TX: Mexican American Studies Program, University of Houston, 1988, p. 25-31. Spanish. DESCR: *Feminism; Social Classes; *Women; *Working Women.

3322 Martinez, Elizabeth and McCaughan, Ed. Chicanas and Mexicanas within a transnational working class: theoretical perspectives. IN: Del Castillo, Adelaida R., ed. BETWEEN BORDERS: ESSAYS ON MEXICANA/CHICANA HISTORY. Encino, CA: Floricanto Press, 1990, p. 31-60. English. DESCR: *Working Women.

3323 Segura, Denise. Chicana and Mexican immigrant women at work: the impact of class, race, and gender on occupational mobility. GENDER & SOCIETY, Vol. 3, no. 1 (March 1989), p. 37-52. English. DESCR: *Employment; *Immigrants; Labor Supply and Market; San Francisco Bay Area; *Social Mobility; Women; Working Women.

Lacayo, Carmela

3324 Espinosa, Ann. Hispanas: our resourses [sic] for the eighties. LA LUZ, Vol. 8, no. 4 (October, November, 1979), p. 10-13. English. DESCR: Baca Barragan, Polly; *Civil Rights; Comision Femenil Mexicana Nacional; DIRECTORY OF HISPANIC WOMEN; Discrimination in Education; Elected Officials; Hernandez, Irene; Lujan, Josie; Mexican American Women's National Association (MANA); Montanez Davis, Grace; Moreno, Olga; Mujeres Latinas en Accion (M.L.A.); National Conference of Puerto Rican Women, Inc. (NCOPRW); Organizations; Rangel, Irma.

Land Tenure

3325 Gonzalez, Deena J. The widowed women of Santa Fe: assessments on the lives of an unmarried population, 1850-80. IN: Scadron, Arlene, ed. ON THEIR OWN: WIDOWS AND WIDOWHOOD IN THE AMERICAN SOUTHWEST 1843-1939. Urbana, IL: University of Illinois Press, c1988, p. [65]-90. English. DESCR: Family; History; Income; *Santa Fe, NM; Sex Roles; Single Parents; *Widowhood; *Women.

3326 Gonzalez, Deena J. The widowed women of Santa Fe: assessments on the lives of an unmarried population, 1850-80. IN: DuBois, Ellen Carol and Ruiz, Vicki L., eds. UNEQUAL SISTERS: A MULTICULTURAL READER IN U.S. WOMEN'S HISTORY. New York: Routledge, 1990, p. 34-50. English. DESCR: Family; History; Income; *Santa Fe, NM; Sex Roles; Single Parents; *Widowhood; *Women.

Lane County, OR

3327 Ramirez, Carmen Cecilia. A study of the value orientation of Lane County, Oregon, Mexican American mothers with a special focus on family/school relationships. Thesis (Ph.D.)--University of Oregon, 1981. 183 p. English. DESCR: *Community School Relationships; Family; *Values.

Language

3328 Cota-Robles de Suarez, Cecilia. Sexual stereotypes--psychological and cultural survival: a description of child-rearing practices attributed to the Chicana (the Mexican American woman) and its psychological and cultural implications. REGENERACION, Vol. 2, no. 3 (1973), p. 17, 20-21. English. DESCR: Cultural Characteristics; Family; Folklore; Parenting; Sex Stereotypes; *Sexism; *Stereotypes.

Language Arts

3329 Trevathan, Wenda R. First conversations: verbal content of mother-newborn interaction. JOURNAL OF CROSS-CULTURAL PSYCHOLOGY, Vol. 19, no. 1 (March 1988), p. 65-77. English. DESCR: Cultural Characteristics; El Paso, TX; *Parent and Child Relationships.

Language Assessment

3330 Moore, Helen A. and Porter, Natalie K. Leadership and nonverbal behaviors of Hispanic females across school equity environments. PSYCHOLOGY OF WOMEN QUARTERLY, Vol. 12, no. 2 (June 1988), p. 147-163. English. DESCR: Assertiveness; *Leadership; Primary School Education.

Language Fluency
USE: Language Proficiency

Language Proficiency

3331 Tienda, Marta. Sex, ethnicity and Chicano status attainment. INTERNATIONAL MIGRATION REVIEW, Vol. 16, no. 2 (Summer 1982), p. 435-473. English. DESCR: Academic Achievement; Discrimination in Education; Discrimination in Employment; Identity; Income; Sexism; *Social Classes; Social Mobility.

Language Usage

3332 Aguilar-Henson, Marcella. The multi-faceted

poetic world of Angela de Hoyos. Austin, TX: Relampago Books Press, 1985, c1982. 81 p. English. DESCR: ARISE CHICANO; *Authors; CHICANO POEMS FOR THE BARRIO; de Hoyos, Angela; GATA POEMS; GOODBYE TO SILENCE; *Literary Criticism; *Poetry; SELECTED POEMS/SELECCIONES; YO, MUJER.

3333 Alarcon, Norma. Latina writers in the United States. IN: Marting, Diane E., ed. SPANISH AMERICAN WOMEN WRITERS: A BIO-BIBLIOGRAPHICAL SOURCE BOOK. New York: Greenwood Press, 1990, p. [557]-567. English. DESCR: *Authors; *Bibliography; BREAKING BOUNDARIES: LATINA WRITING AND CRITICAL READINGS; Cubanos; Intergroup Relations; *Literature Reviews; Puerto Ricans; THIRD WOMAN [journal]; *Women.

3334 Bach-y-Rita, George. The Mexican-American: religious and cultural influences. IN: Becerra, Rosina M., et al., eds. MENTAL HEALTH AND HISPANIC AMERICANS: CLINICAL PERSPECTIVES. New York: Grune & Stratton, 1982, p. 29-40. English. DESCR: Catholic Church; Cultural Characteristics; Culture; Machismo; *Mental Health; Psychotherapy; Religion.

3335 Bean, Frank D. and Swicegood, Gray. Mexican American fertility patterns. Austin, TX: University of Texas Press, 1985. x, 178 p. English. DESCR: Age Groups; Census; Education; *Fertility; *Population; Research Methodology; *Socioeconomic Factors; Statistics.

3336 Cuellar, Israel. Service delivery and mental health services for Chicano elders. IN: Miranda, Manuel and Ruiz, Rene A., eds. CHICANO AGING AND MENTAL HEALTH. Rockville, MD: U.S. Department of Health and Human Services, 1981, p. 185-211. English. DESCR: *Ancianos; Attitudes; Cultural Customs; Cultural Pluralism; Mental Health; Mental Health Clinics; Religion; Sex Roles; Spanish Language.

3337 Espin, Oliva M. Cultural and historical influences on sexuality in Hispanic/Latin women: implications for psychotherapy. IN: Vance, Carole S., ed. PLEASURE AND DANGER: EXPLORING FEMALE SEXUALITY. Boston, MA: Routledge & Kegan Paul, 1984, p. 149-164. English. DESCR: Immigration; Machismo; *Psychotherapy; Sex Roles; *Sexual Behavior; Social History and Conditions; Spanish Influence; *Women.

3338 Galindo, Letticia. Perceptions of pachuquismo and use of Calo/pachuco Spanish by various Chicana women. LA RED/THE NET, no. 48 (November 1981), p. 2,10. English. DESCR: Chicano Dialects; *Texas.

3339 Madrid, Sandra Emilia. The effects of socialization on goal actualization of public school Chicana principals and superintendents. Thesis (Ph.D.)--University of Washington, 1985. 253 p. English. DESCR: *Careers; *Educational Administration; *Socialization.

3340 Martinez, Marco Antonio. Conversational asymmetry between Mexican mothers and children. HISPANIC JOURNAL OF BEHAVIORAL SCIENCES, Vol. 3, no. 4 (December 1981), p. 329-346. English. DESCR: Anglo Americans; *Parent and Child Relationships.

Language Usage (cont.)

3341 Santillan, Richard. Rosita the riveter: Midwest Mexican American women during World War II, 1941-1945. PERSPECTIVES IN MEXICAN AMERICAN STUDIES, Vol. 2, (1989), p. 115-147. English. DESCR: History; Industrial Workers; Intergroup Relations; *Midwestern States; Military; Mutualistas; Sexism; War; *Working Women; *World War II.

3342 Sorenson, Ann Marie. The fertility and language characteristics of Mexican-American and non-Hispanic husbands and wives. SOCIOLOGICAL QUARTERLY, Vol. 29, no. 1 (March 1988), p. 111-130. English. DESCR: Anglo Americans; Fertility; Identity; Marriage; Sex Roles.

3343 Swicegood, Gray. Language opportunity costs and Mexican American fertility. Thesis (Ph.D.)--University of Texas, Austin, 1982. ix, 188 p. English. DESCR: *Fertility.

3344 Swicegood, Gray, et al. Language usage and fertility in the Mexican-origin population of the United States. DEMOGRAPHY, Vol. 25, no. 1 (February 1988), p. 17-33. English. DESCR: *Fertility; Immigrants; Population; Women.

3345 Tafolla, Carmen. Chicano literature: beyond beginnings. IN: Harris, Marie and Aguero, Kathleen, eds. A GIFT OF TONGUES: CRITICAL CHALLENGES IN CONTEMPORARY AMERICAN POETRY. Athens, GA: University of Georgia Press, 1987, p. 206-225. English. DESCR: *Authors; Cota-Cardenas, Margarita; *Literary Criticism; *Literature; Portillo Trambley, Estela; Sex Stereotypes; Symbolism; Tafolla, Carmen; Vigil-Pinon, Evangelina.

3346 Valdes, Guadalupe and Cardenas, Manuel. Positive speech accommodation in the language of Mexican American bilinguals: are women really more sensitive? HISPANIC JOURNAL OF BEHAVIORAL SCIENCES, Vol. 3, no. 4 (December 1981), p. 347-359. English. DESCR: Bilingualism; Spanish Language.

3347 Valdes, Guadalupe; Garcia, Herman; and Storment, Diamantina. Sex-related speech accommodations among Mexican-American bilinguals: a pilot study of language choice in customer-server interactions. IN: Barkin, Florence, et al., eds. BILINGUALISM AND LANGUAGE CONTACT: SPANISH, ENGLISH, AND NATIVE AMERICAN LANGUAGES. New York: Teachers College, 1982, p. 187-200. English. DESCR: Bilingualism; Las Cruces, NM; Surveys.

Lansing, MI

3348 Stark, Miriam. La Chicana: changing roles in a changing society. Thesis (B.A)--University of Michigan, 1984. ii, 157 leaves. English. DESCR: Acculturation; Identity; *Sex Roles; *Social History and Conditions.

Las Cruces, NM

3349 Valdes, Guadalupe; Garcia, Herman; and Storment, Diamantina. Sex-related speech accommodations among Mexican-American bilinguals: a pilot study of language choice in customer-server interactions. IN: Barkin, Florence, et al., eds. BILINGUALISM AND LANGUAGE CONTACT: SPANISH, ENGLISH, AND NATIVE AMERICAN LANGUAGES. New York: Teachers College, 1982, p. 187-200. English. DESCR: Bilingualism; *Language Usage; Surveys.

THE LAST OF THE MENU GIRLS

3350 Quintana, Alvina E. Chicana discourse: negations and mediations. Thesis (Ph.D.)--University of California, Santa Cruz, 1989. 226 p. English. DESCR: Authors; Castillo, Ana; Chavez, Denise; Chicano Movement; Cisneros, Sandra; Ethnology; Feminism; Literary Criticism; *Literature; NOVENA NARRATIVES; Oral Tradition; Political Ideology; THE HOUSE ON MANGO STREET; THE MIXQUIAHUALA LETTERS.

3351 Rosaldo, Renato. Fables of the fallen guy. IN: Calderon, Hector and Saldivar, Jose David, eds. CRITICISM IN THE BORDERLANDS: STUDIES IN CHICANO LITERATURE, CULTURE AND IDEOLOGY. Durham, NC: Duke University Press, 1991, p. [84]-93. English. DESCR: Chavez, Denise; Cisneros, Sandra; Fiction; Literary Characters; *Literary Criticism; Rios, Alberto; Sex Roles; THE HOUSE ON MANGO STREET; THE IGUANA KILLER: TWELVE STORIES OF THE HEART.

Latin America

3352 Bachu, Amara and O'Connell, Martin. Developing current fertility indicators for foreign-born women from the Current Population Survey. REVIEW OF PUBLIC DATA USE, Vol. 12, no. 3 (October 1984), p. 185-195. English. DESCR: Current Population Survey; *Fertility; Mexico; *Surveys; Vital Statistics; Women.

3353 Fennelly, Katherine; Kandiah, Vasantha; and Ortiz, Vilma. The cross-cultural study of fertility among Hispanic adolescents in the Americas. STUDIES IN FAMILY PLANNING, Vol. 20, no. 2 (March, April, 1989), p. 96-101. English. DESCR: Cultural Characteristics; Ethnic Groups; *Fertility; *Marriage; Youth.

Latin American Literature

3354 Spitta, Silvia D. Literary transculturation in Latin America. Thesis (Ph.D.)--University of Oregon, 1989. 184 p. English. DESCR: Anzaldua, Gloria; Arguedos, Jose Maria; Authors; Cultural Characteristics; Culture; *Intergroup Relations; Spanish Influence.

Latin Americans

3355 Cayer, Shirley. Chicago's new Hispanic health alliance. NUESTRO, Vol. 7, no. 5 (June, July, 1983), p. 44-48. English. DESCR: Alcoholism; Chicago Hispanic Health Alliance; Family Planning; *Health Education; *Medical Care.

3356 Espin, Oliva M. Perceptions of sexual discrimination among college women in Latin America and the United States. HISPANIC JOURNAL OF BEHAVIORAL SCIENCES, Vol. 2, no. 1 (March 1980), p. 1-19. English. DESCR: Colleges and Universities; CRITICAL INCIDENT TECHNIQUE; Feminism; *Sexism; Students; Women Men Relations.

3357 Jaech, Richard E. Latin American undocumented women in the United States. CURRENTS IN THEOLOGY AND MISSION, Vol. 9, no. 4 (August 1982), p. 196-211. English. DESCR: Garment Industry; Protestant Church; Socioeconomic Factors; *Undocumented Workers; *Women.

Latin Americans (cont.)

3358 Markides, Kyriakos S. Consequences of gender differentials in life expectancy for Black and Hispanic Americans. INTERNATIONAL JOURNAL OF AGING & HUMAN DEVELOPMENT, Vol. 29, no. 2 (1989), p. 95-102. English. DESCR: *Ancianos; Blacks; Census; Cubanos; Males; Population; Puerto Ricans; U.S. Bureau of the Census.

3359 Valtierra, Mary. Acculturation, social support, and reported stress of Latina physicians. Thesis (Ph.D.)--California School of Professional Psychology, 1989. 136 p. English. DESCR: *Acculturation; Careers; Cubanos; Immigration; *Medical Personnel; Puerto Ricans; *Stress; *Women.

3360 Yarbro-Bejarano, Yvonne. Primer encuentro de lesbianas feministas latinoamericanas y caribenas. THIRD WOMAN, Vol. 4, (1989), p. 143-146. English. DESCR: Caribbean Region; *Conferences and Meetings; First Meeting of Latin American and Caribbean Feminist Lesbians (October 14-17, 1987: Cuernavaca, Mexico); *Homosexuality; Sexual Behavior; *Women.

Latin Empresses

3361 Blanco, Gilbert M. Las Adelitas del Barrio. LATIN QUARTER, Vol. 1, no. 3 (January, February, 1975), p. 30-32. English. DESCR: City Terrace, CA; Community Development; Gangs; Youth.

The Latina Mother-Infant Project, Chicago, IL

3362 Stern, Gwen. Research, action, and social betterment. AMERICAN BEHAVIOR SCIENTISTS, Vol. 29, no. 2 (November, December, 1985), p. 229-248. English. DESCR: Chicago, IL; *Medical Care; Research Methodology.

Latinos in the Law [symposium] (1982: UCLA)

3363 Valadez, Esther. The role of the Latina. CHICANO LAW REVIEW, Vol. 6, (1983), p. 21-24. English. DESCR: *Voter Turnout.

Latins Anonymous [comedy review]

3364 Broyles-Gonzalez, Yolanda and Rodriguez, Diane. The living legacy of Chicana performers: preserving history through oral testimony. FRONTIERS: A JOURNAL OF WOMEN STUDIES, Vol. 11, no. 1 (1990), p. [46]-52. English. DESCR: *Actors and Actresses; El Teatro Campesino; Oral History; *Rodriguez, Diane; Sex Roles; Singers; Teatro.

Law

3365 Martinez, Virginia. Chicanas and the law. IN: LA CHICANA: BUILDING FOR THE FUTURE, AN ACTION PLAN FOR THE 80s. Oakland, CA: National Hispanic University, 1981, p. 134-146. English. DESCR: *Administration of Justice; Civil Rights; Feminism.

Leadership

3366 Adelante, mujer hispana. LATINO, Vol. 53, no. 2 (March, April, 1982), p. 26. English. DESCR: *Adelante Mujer Hispana Conference--Education and Employment Conference (January 11-12, 1980: Denver, CO); Conferences and Meetings.

3367 Aragon de Valdez, Theresa. Organizing as a political tool for the Chicana. FRONTIERS: A JOURNAL OF WOMEN STUDIES, Vol. 5, no. 2 (Summer 1980), p. 7-13. English. DESCR:

Discrimination; Feminism; Mexican American Legal Defense and Educational Fund (MALDEF); Social History and Conditions; Sterilization.

3368 Baca Barragan, Polly. La Chicana in politics. IN: LA CHICANA: BUILDING FOR THE FUTURE, AN ACTION PLAN FOR THE 80s. Oakland, CA: National Hispanic University, 1981, p. 21-31. English. DESCR: Elected Officials; Political Representation; *Politics.

3369 Braddom, Carolyn Lentz. The conceptualization of effective leadership as seen by women, Black and Hispanic superintendents. Thesis (Ed.D.)--University of Cincinnati, 1988. 232 p. English. DESCR: Anglo Americans; Blacks; *Educational Administration; Management; Women.

3370 Carr-Casanova, Rosario. Role-model history and demographic factors in the social composition of the family of forty Hispanic women leaders in four occupational groups. Thesis (Ph.D.)--Wright Institute, Berkeley, 1983. 136 p. English. DESCR: Family; San Francisco Bay Area.

3371 Del Castillo, Adelaida R. Mexican women in organization. IN: Mora, Magdalena and Del Castillo, Adelaida, eds. MEXICAN WOMEN IN THE UNITED STATES: STRUGGLES PAST AND PRESENT. Los Angeles, CA: Chicano Studies Research Center, UCLA, 1980, p. 7-16. English. DESCR: *Chicano Movement; Feminism; Student Organizations; Students.

3372 Duran, Isabelle Sandoval. Grounded theory study: Chicana administrators in Colorado and New Mexico. Thesis (Ed.D.)--University of Wyoming, Laramie, 1982. ix, 114 p. English. DESCR: Careers; Colorado; *Educational Administration; *Management; New Mexico.

3373 Enriquez-White, Celia. Attitudes of Hispanic and Anglo women managers toward women in management. Thesis (Ed.D.)--University of La Verne, 1982. 103 p. English. DESCR: Anglo Americans; *Attitudes; *Management; Women.

3374 Gallegos, Placida I. Emerging leadership among Hispanic women: the role of expressive behavior and nonverbal skill. Thesis (Ph.D.)--University of California, Riverside, 1987. 101 p. English. DESCR: Anglo Americans; Comparative Psychology; Corporations; *Management; Women.

3375 Gardea, Corina. A comparison of behavioral characteristics of Hispanic and Anglo female administrators in the resolution of critical incident situations. Thesis (Ph.D.)--University of Texas, Austin, 1984. 145 p. English. DESCR: Anglo Americans; *Community Colleges; *Educational Administration; Women.

3376 Gonzales, Sylvia Alicia. The Latina feminist: where we've been, where we're going. NUESTRO, Vol. 5, no. 6 (August, September, 1981), p. 45-47. English. DESCR: Conferences and Meetings; *Feminism; History; National Hispanic Feminist Conference (March 28-31, 1980: San Jose, CA).

3377 Jaramillo, Mari-Luci. Profile of Chicanas and international relations. IN: LA CHICANA: BUILDING FOR THE FUTURE, AN ACTION PLAN FOR THE 80s. Oakland, CA: National Hispanic University, 1981, p. 37-58. English. DESCR: Careers; Feminism; *International Relations.

Leadership (cont.)

3378 Lopez, Gloria Ann. Job satisfaction of the
Mexican American woman administrator in
higher education. Thesis (Ph.D.)--University
of Texas, Austin, 1984. 193 p. English.
DESCR: *Careers; *Educational
Administration; Higher Education.

3379 Martinez, Olivia. The three Rs of Chicana
leadership. IN: LA CHICANA: BUILDING FOR THE
FUTURE, AN ACTION PLAN FOR THE 80s. Oakland,
CA: National Hispanic University, 1981, p.
74-80. English.

3380 McClelland, Judith Raymond. The relationship
of independence to achievement: a
comparative study of Hispanic women. Thesis
(Ph.D.)--Fielding Institute, 1988. 164 p.
English. DESCR: *Assertiveness; Attitudes;
California Personality Inventory (CPI);
Careers; *Management; New Mexico;
Personality; *Working Women.

3381 Mendoza, Hope Schecter and Chall, Malca.
Activist in the labor movement, the
Democratic Party, and the Mexican-American
community: an interview. Berkeley, CA:
Regional Oral History Office, Bancroft
Library, University of California, Berkeley,
1980. xii, 170 p.: ill. English. DESCR:
*Biography; Chavez Ravine, Los Angeles, CA;
Church, Frank; Community Organizations;
Community Service Organization, Los Angeles,
(CSO); Democratic Party; Elections; Garment
Industry; Industrial Workers; *Labor Unions;
Mendoza, Hope Schecter; Snyder, Elizabeth;
Warschaw, Carmen.

3382 Mercado, Olivia. Chicanas: myths and roles.
COMADRE, no. 1 (Summer 1977), p. 26-32.
English. DESCR: Feminism; Gallo, Juana;
Huerta, Dolores; *Identity; Sex Roles.

3383 Moore, Helen A. and Porter, Natalie K.
Leadership and nonverbal behaviors of
Hispanic females across school equity
environments. PSYCHOLOGY OF WOMEN QUARTERLY,
Vol. 12, no. 2 (June 1988), p. 147-163.
English. DESCR: Assertiveness; Language
Assessment; Primary School Education.

3384 Oliveira, Annette. Remarkable Latinas. IN:
HISPANICS AND GRANTMAKERS: A SPECIAL REPORT
OF FOUNDATION NEWS. Washington, DC: Council
on Foundations, 1981, p. 34. English.
DESCR: Biography; *Puerto Ricans; Women.

3385 Rips, Geoffrey and Tenayuca, Emma. Living
history: Emma Tenayuca tells her story.
TEXAS OBSERVER, (October 28, 1983), p.
7-15. English. DESCR: *Autobiography;
Communist Party; Food Industry; Labor
Unions; Oral History; Pecan Shelling
Worker's Union, San Antonio, TX; San
Antonio, TX; Strikes and Lockouts; Tenayuca,
Emma; United Cannery Agricultural Packing
and Allied Workers of America (UCAPAWA);
Worker's Alliance (WA), Los Angeles, CA;
Working Women.

3386 Soto, Shirlene Ann. La Malinche: 16th
century leader. INTERCAMBIOS FEMENILES, Vol.
2, no. 6 (Spring 1987), p. 13. English.
DESCR: *Malinche.

3387 U.S. National Institute of Education.
Conference on the educational and
occupational needs of Hispanic women, June
29-30, 1976; December 10-12, 1976.
Washington, DC: U.S. Department of
Education, 1980. x, 301 p. English. DESCR:
Conference on the Educational and
Occupational Needs of Hispanic Women (1976:

Denver, CO); Conferences and Meetings;
*Education; *Employment; Higher Education;
Puerto Ricans; Sex Roles; *Women.

League of United Latin American Citizens (LULAC)

3388 Velasquez-Trevino, Gloria. Jovita Gonzalez,
una voz de resistencia cultural en la
temprana narrativa chicana. IN:
Lopez-Gonzalez, Aralia, et al., eds. MUJER Y
LITERATURA MEXICANA Y CHICANA: CULTURAS EN
CONTACTO. Mexico: Colegio de la Frontera
Norte, 1988, p. [77]-83. Spanish. DESCR:
Anglo Americans; Authors; Feminism;
Folklore; *Gonzalez, Jovita; Intergroup
Relations.

Legal Cases

3389 Velez-I., Carlos G. The nonconsenting
sterilization of Mexican women in Los
Angeles: issues of psychocultural rupture
and legal redress in paternalistic
behavioral environments. IN: Melville,
Margarita B., ed. TWICE A MINORITY. St.
Louis, MO: Mosby, 1980, p. 235-248. English.
DESCR: Dolores Madrigal, et al., Plaintiff,
v. E.J. Quilligan, et al.; Los Angeles, CA;
*Sterilization.

Legends
USE: Leyendas

Legislation

3390 Maymi, Carmen R. Fighting to open the doors
to opportunity. AGENDA, no. 4 (Spring 1974),
p. 8-10. English. DESCR: Business; Business
Enterprises; *Sexism.

3391 Sosa Riddell, Adaljiza. Synopsis on Senate
Concurrent Resolution 43: an example in
public policy making. IN: Sosa Riddell,
Adaljiza, ed. POLICY DEVELOPMENT:
CHICANA/LATINA SUMMER RESEARCH INSTITUTE.
Davis, CA: [Chicano Studies Program,
University of California, Davis, 1989?], p.
16-26. English. DESCR: *Public Policy;
Senate Concurrent Resolution 43, 1987;
University of California.

Lerma Bowerman, Liz

3392 Brown, Betty Ann. Chicanas speak out.
ARTWEEK, Vol. 15, no. 2 (January 14, 1984),
p. 1+. English. DESCR: *Art; Carrasco,
Barbara; Carrillo, Graciela; CHICANA VOICES
& VISIONS [exhibit]; Exhibits; Goldman,
Shifra M.; Hernandez, Ester; Rodriguez,
Carmen; Rodriguez, Sandra Maria; Social and
Public Art Resource Center, Venice, CA
(SPARC).

Lesbians
USE: Homosexuality

Lettuce Boycotts
USE: Boycotts

Leyendas

3393 Jones, Pamela. "There was a woman": La
Llorona in Oregon. WESTERN FOLKLORE, Vol.
47, no. 3 (July 1988), p. 195-211. English.
DESCR: Folklore; *La Llorona; Oregon;
Research Methodology.

Leyendas (cont.)

3394 Jordan, Rosan Augusta. The vaginal serpent and other themes from Mexican-American women's lore. IN: Jordan, Rosan A. and Kalcik, Susan J., eds. WOMEN'S FOLKLORE, WOMEN'S CULTURE. Philadelphia: University of Pennsylvania Press, 1985, p. 26-44. English. **DESCR:** Cuentos; Fertility; *Folklore; La Llorona; *Sex Roles; Sexism; Sexual Behavior.

3395 Limon, Jose E. [anthropologist]. La Llorona, the third legend of greater Mexico: cultural symbols, women, and the political unconscious. RENATO ROSALDO LECTURE SERIES MONOGRAPH, Vol. 2, (Spring 1986), p. [59]-93. English. **DESCR:** *Feminism; Folklore; *La Llorona; La Virgen de Guadalupe; Malinche; Mexico; *Symbolism; Women.

3396 Limon, Jose E. [anthropologist]. La Llorona, the third legend of greater Mexico: cultural symbols, women, and the political unconscious. IN: Del Castillo, Adelaida R. BETWEEN BORDERS: ESSAYS ON MEXICANA/CHICANA HISTORY. Encino, CA: Floricanto Press, 1990, p. 399-432. English. **DESCR:** *Feminism; Folklore; *La Llorona; La Virgen de Guadalupe; Malinche; Mexico; *Symbolism; Women.

Liberation Theology

3397 Isasi-Diaz, Ada Maria and Tarango, Yolanda. Hispanic women, prophetic voice in the Church: toward a Hispanic women's liberation theology. San Francisco, CA: Harper & Row, c1988. xx, 123 p. Bilingual. **DESCR:** Catholic Church; *Feminism; Religion; *Women.

LIFE IN CALIFORNIA

3398 Castaneda, Antonia I. The political economy of nineteenth century stereotypes of Californianas. IN: Del Castillo, Adelaida R., ed. BETWEEN BORDERS: ESSAYS ON MEXICANA/CHICANA HISTORY. Encino, CA: Floricanto Press, 1990, p. 213-236. English. **DESCR:** *California; *Californios; Dana, Richard Henry; Farnham, Thomas Jefferson; History; *Political Economy; Robinson, Alfred; *Sex Stereotypes; TRAVELS IN CALIFORNIA AND SCENES IN THE PACIFIC OCEAN; TWO YEARS BEFORE THE MAST; Women.

LIFE SPAN

3399 Ordonez, Elizabeth J. Body, spirit, and the text: Alma Villanueva's LIFE SPAN. IN: Calderon, Hector and Saldivar, Jose David, eds. CRITICISM IN THE BORDERLANDS: STUDIES IN CHICANO LITERATURE, CULTURE, AND IDEOLOGY. Durham, NC: Duke University Press, 1991, p. [61]-71. English. **DESCR:** Cixous, Helene; *Feminism; *Literary Criticism; Poetry; *Villanueva, Alma.

Lilli Diamond Originals

3400 Vasquez, Mario F. The election day immigration raid at Lilli Diamond Originals and the response of the ILGWU. IN: Mora, Magdalena and Del Castillo, Adelaida, eds. MEXICAN WOMEN IN THE UNITED STATES: STRUGGLES PAST AND PRESENT. Los Angeles, CA: Chicano Studies Research Center, UCLA, 1980, p. 145-148. English. **DESCR:** Garment Industry; Immigration Regulation and Control; International Ladies Garment Workers Union (ILGWU); Labor Unions; Undocumented Workers; Women; Working Women.

Literacy

3401 Pick, James B., et al. Socioeconomic influences on fertility in the Mexican borderlands region. MEXICAN STUDIES/ESTUDIOS MEXICANOS, Vol. 6, no. 1 (Winter 1990), p. 11-42. English. **DESCR:** *Border Region; *Employment; *Fertility; Labor Supply and Market; Socioeconomic Factors; Working Women.

3402 Rigg, Pat. Petra: learning to read at 45. JOURNAL OF EDUCATION, Vol. 167, no. 1 (1985), p. 129-139. English.

Literary Characters

3403 Dewey, Janice. Dona Josefa: bloodpulse of transition and change. IN: Horno-Delgado, Asuncion, et al., eds. BREAKING BOUNDARIES: LATINA WRITING AND CRITICAL READINGS. Amherst, MA: University of Massachusetts Press, c1989, p. 39-47. English. **DESCR:** *DAY OF THE SWALLOWS; Garcia-Lorca, Federico; LA CASA DE BERNARDA ALBA; Literary Criticism; *Portillo Trambley, Estela.

3404 Gutierrez Castillo, Dina. La imagen de la mujer en la novela fronteriza. IN: Lopez-Gonzalez, Aralia, et al., eds. MUJER Y LITERATURA MEXICANA Y CHICANA: CULTURAS EN CONTACTO. Mexico: Colegio de la Frontera Norte, 1988, p. [55]-63. Spanish. **DESCR:** *Border Region; Islas, Arturo; *Literary Criticism; Mendez M., Miguel; *Novel; PEREGRINOS DE AZTLAN; Sex Roles; Sex Stereotypes; THE RAIN GOD: A DESERT TALE; *Women.

3405 Herrera-Sobek, Maria. Women as metaphor in the patriarchal structure of HEART OF AZTLAN. IN: Gonzalez-T., Cesar A. RUDOLFO A. ANAYA: FOCUS ON CRITICISM. La Jolla, CA: Lalo Press, 1990, p. [165]-182. English. **DESCR:** Anaya, Rudolfo A.; *HEART OF AZTLAN; La Llorona; Literary Criticism; Sex Roles.

3406 Mondin, Sandra. The depiction of the Chicana in BLESS ME ULTIMA and THE MILAGRO BEANFIELD WAR: a study in contrasts. IN: Luna Lawhn, Juanita, et al., eds. MEXICO AND THE UNITED STATES: INTERCULTURAL RELATIONS IN THE HUMANITIES. San Antonio, TX: San Antonio College, 1984, p. 137-150. English. **DESCR:** Anaya, Rudolfo A.; BLESS ME, ULTIMA; Literary Criticism; Nichols, John; *Stereotypes; THE MILAGRO BEANFIELD WAR [novel].

3407 Ramirez, Genevieve M. and Salazar Parr, Carmen. The female hero in Chicano literature. IN: Herrera-Sobek, Maria, ed. BEYOND STEREOTYPES: THE CRITICAL ANALYSIS OF CHICANA LITERATURE. Binghamton, NY: Bilingual Press/Editorial Bilingue, 1985, p. 48-60. English. **DESCR:** Literary Criticism; Sex Roles.

3408 Rosaldo, Renato. Fables of the fallen guy. IN: Calderon, Hector and Saldivar, Jose David, eds. CRITICISM IN THE BORDERLANDS: STUDIES IN CHICANO LITERATURE, CULTURE AND IDEOLOGY. Durham, NC: Duke University Press, 1991, p. [84]-93. English. **DESCR:** Chavez, Denise; Cisneros, Sandra; Fiction; *Literary Criticism; Rios, Alberto; Sex Roles; THE HOUSE ON MANGO STREET; THE IGUANA KILLER: TWELVE STORIES OF THE HEART; THE LAST OF THE MENU GIRLS.

Literary Characters
(cont.)

3409 Salazar Parr, Carmen and Ramirez, Genevieve
M. The Chicana in Chicano literature. IN:
Martinez, Julio A. and Lomeli, Francisco A.,
eds. CHICANO LITERATURE: A REFERENCE GUIDE.
Westport, CT: Greenwood Press, 1985, p.
97-107. English. DESCR: Literary Criticism;
*Literature; *Stereotypes.

3410 Salazar Parr, Carmen. La Chicana in
literature. IN: Garcia, Eugene E., et al.,
eds. CHICANO STUDIES: A MULTIDISCIPLINARY
APPROACH. New York: Teachers College Press,
1984, p. 120-134. English. DESCR: DAY OF THE
SWALLOWS; Literary Criticism; *Literature;
Portillo Trambley, Estela; Stereotypes;
Teatro; "The Trees" [short story].

3411 Salinas, Judy. The image of woman in Chicano
literature. REVISTA CHICANO-RIQUENA, Vol. 4,
no. 4 (Fall 1976), p. 139-148. English.
DESCR: *Literature; *Stereotypes.

3412 Tatum, Charles M. Grappling with difference:
gender, race, class, and ethnicity in
contemporary Chicana/o literature. RENATO
ROSALDO LECTURE SERIES MONOGRAPH, Vol. 6,
(1988, 1989), p. 1-23. English. DESCR:
Anaya, Rudolfo A.; Authors; BLESS ME,
ULTIMA; *Feminism; Identity; *Literary
Criticism; Literature Reviews.

3413 Yarbro-Bejarano, Yvonne. The image of the
Chicana in teatro. IN: Cochran, Jo; Stewart,
J.T.; and Tsutakawa, Mayumi, eds. GATHERING
GROUND: NEW WRITING AND ART BY NORTHWEST
WOMEN OF COLOR. Seattle, WA: Seal Press,
1984, p. 90-96. English. DESCR: El Teatro de
la Esperanza; GUADALUFE [play]; HIJOS: ONCE
A FAMILY [play]; LA VICTIMA [play]; Sex
Roles; Sex Stereotypes; Stereotypes;
*Teatro; THE OCTOPUS [play]; Women Men
Relations.

3414 Zamora, Bernice. Mythopoeia of Chicano
poetry: an introduction to cultural
archetypes. Thesis (Ph.D.)--Stanford
University, 1986. 341 p. English. DESCR:
Literary Criticism; Literature; Malinche;
Pachucos; *Poetry; *Symbolism.

Literary Criticism

3415 Agosin, Marjorie. Elucubraciones y
antielucubraciones: critica feminista desde
perspectivas poeticas. THIRD WOMAN, Vol. 1,
no. 2 (1982), p. 65-69. Spanish. DESCR:
Essays; Feminism; *Literature.

3416 Aguilar-Henson, Marcella. The multi-faceted
poetic world of Angela de Hoyos. Austin, TX:
Relampago Books Press, 1985, c1982. 81 p.
English. DESCR: ARISE CHICANO; *Authors;
CHICANO POEMS FOR THE BARRIO; de Hoyos,
Angela; GATA POEMS; GOODBYE TO SILENCE;
Language Usage; *Poetry; SELECTED
POEMS/SELECCIONES; YO, MUJER.

3417 Alarcon, Justo S. and Martinez, Julio A.
[Bornstein-Somoza, Miriam]. IN: Martinez,
Julio A. and Lomeli, Francisco A., eds.
CHICANO LITERATURE: A REFERENCE GUIDE.
Westport, CT: Greenwood Press, 1985, p.
74-77. English. DESCR: *Authors; Biography;
Bornstein-Somoza, Miriam.

3418 Alarcon, Norma. Chicana writers and critics
in a social context : towards a contemporary
bibliography. THIRD WOMAN, Vol. 4, (1989),
p. 169-178. English. DESCR: *Bibliography;
*Literature.

3419 Alarcon, Norma. Making "familia" from
scratch: split subjectivities in the work of
Helena Maria Viramontes and Cherrie Moraga.
THE AMERICAS REVIEW, Vol. 15, no. 3-4 (Fall,
Winter, 1987), p. 147-159. English. DESCR:
GIVING UP THE GHOST; Moraga, Cherrie; *Sex
Roles; "Snapshots" [short story]; THE MOTHS
AND OTHER STORIES; Viramontes, Helena Maria.

3420 Alarcon, Norma. The sardonic powers of the
erotic in the work of Ana Castillo. IN:
Horro-Delgado, Asuncion, et al., eds.
BREAKING BOUNDARIES: LATINA WRITING AND
CRITICAL READINGS. Amherst, MA: University
of Massachusetts Press, c1989, p. 94-107.
English. DESCR: *Castillo, Ana; OTRO CANTO;
Poetry; Sex Roles; THE INVITATION; *THE
MIXQUIAHUALA LETTERS; WOMEN ARE NOT ROSES.

3421 Alarcon, Norma. The theoretical subject(s)
of THIS BRIDGE CALLED MY BACK and
Anglo-American feminism. IN: Anzaldua,
Gloria, ed. MAKING FACE, MAKING SOUL:
HACIENDO CARAS: CREATIVE AND CRITICAL
PERSPECTIVES BY WOMEN OF COLOR. San
Francisco, CA: Aunt Lute Foundation Books,
1990, p. 356-369. English. DESCR: *Anglo
Americans; Anzaldua, Gloria; *Feminism;
Moraga, Cherrie; THIS BRIDGE CALLED MY BACK;
*Women.

3422 Alarcon, Norma. What kind of lover have you
made me, Mother?: towards a theory of
Chicanas' feminism and cultural identity
through poetry. IN: McCluskey, Audrey T.,
ed. WOMEN OF COLOR: PERSPECTIVES ON FEMINISM
AND IDENTITY. Bloomington, IN: Women's
Studies Program, Indiana University, 1985,
p. 85-110. English. DESCR: Brinson-Pineda,
Barbara; Cervantes, Lorna Dee; Cisneros,
Sandra; Culture; *Feminism; Identity; Mora,
Pat; Moraga, Cherrie; *Poetry; Tafolla,
Carmen; Vigil-Pinon, Evangelina; Villanueva,
Alma.

3423 Anderson, Robert K. Marez y Luna and the
masculine-feminine dialectic. CRITICA
HISPANICA, Vol. 6, no. 2 (1984), p. 97-105.
English. DESCR: Anaya, Rudolfo A.; BLESS ME,
ULTIMA; Novel; *Women Men Relations.

3424 Anzaldua, Gloria. Border crossings. TRIVIA:
A JOURNAL OF IDEAS, no. 14 (Spring 1989), p.
46-51. English. DESCR: *Feminism;
Literature.

3425 [Bibliography of Special Issue: Chicana
Creativity and Criticism]. THE AMERICAS
REVIEW, Vol. 15, no. 3-4 (Fall, Winter,
1987), p. 182-188. English. DESCR:
*Bibliography; Literature.

3426 Billings, Linda M. and Alurista. In verbal
murals: a study of Chicana herstory and
poetry. CONFLUENCIA, Vol. 2, no. 1 (Fall
1986), p. 60-68. English. DESCR: Candelaria,
Cordelia; Cervantes, Lorna Dee; Cisneros,
Sandra; EMPLUMADA; *Feminism; History;
*Poetry; Xelina.

3427 Binder, Wolfgang. Mothers and grandmothers:
acts of mythification and remembrance in
Chicano poetry. IN: Bardeleben, Renate von,
et al., eds. MISSIONS IN CONFLICT: ESSAYS ON
U.S.-MEXICAN RELATIONS AND CHICANO CULTURE.
Tubingen, W. Germany: Gunter Narr Verlag,
1986, p. 133-143. English. DESCR:
Grandmothers; Poetry.

3428 Bornstein de Somoza, Miriam. La poetica
chicana: vision panoramica. LA PALABRA, Vol.
2, no. 2 (Fall 1980), p. 43-66. Spanish.
DESCR: Authors; Literary Influence; *Poetry.

Literary Criticism
(cont.)

3429 Bruce-Novoa, Juan. Bernice Zamora y Lorna Dee Cervantes: una estetica feminista. REVISTA IBEROAMERICANA, Vol. 51, (July, December, 1985), p. 565-573. English. DESCR: *Authors; *Cervantes, Lorna Dee; EMPLUMADA; Poetry; RESTLESS SERPENTS; *Zamora, Bernice.

3430 Bruce-Novoa, Juan. Deconstructing the dominant patriarchal text: Cecile Pineda's narratives. IN: Horno-Delgado, Asuncion, et al., eds. BREAKING BOUNDARIES: LATINA WRITING AND CRITICAL READINGS. Amherst, MA: University of Massachusetts Press, c1989, p. 72-81. English. DESCR: *FACE; *FRIEZE; Identity; Novel; *Pineda, Cecile.

3431 Cardenas de Dwyer, Carlota. Commentary. LA LUZ, Vol. 4, no. 8-9 (November, December, 1975), p. 8. English. DESCR: Sex Stereotypes; *Stereotypes.

3432 Cardenas de Dwyer, Carlota. Literary images of Mexican American women. LA LUZ, Vol. 6, no. 11 (November 1977), p. 11-12. English. DESCR: Sex Stereotypes.

3433 Castellano, Olivia. Of clarity and the moon: a study of two women in rebellion. DE COLORES, Vol. 3, no. 3 (1977), p. 25-30. English. DESCR: DAY OF THE SWALLOWS; Portillo Trambley, Estela; "The Apple Trees".

3434 Cisneros, Sandra. Cactus flowers: in search of Tejana feminist poetry. THIRD WOMAN, Vol. 3, no. 1-2 (1986), p. 73-80. English. DESCR: Authors; *Feminism; *Poetry; Texas.

3435 Crawford, John F. Notes toward a new multicultural criticism: three works by women of color. IN: Harris, Marie and Aguero, Kathleen, eds. A GIFT OF TONGUES: CRITICAL CHALLENGES IN CONTEMPORARY AMERICAN POETRY. Athens, GA: University of Georgia Press, 1987, p. 155-195. English. DESCR: AWAKE IN THE RIVER; Cervantes, Lorna Dee; EMPLUMADA; Harjo, Joy; Mirikitani, Janice; SHE HAD SOME HORSES.

3436 Dario Salaz, Ruben. The Chicana in American literature. LA LUZ, Vol. 4, no. 3 (June 1975), p. 28. English. DESCR: *Chicanos in American Literature; Sex Stereotypes.

3437 Dario Salaz, Ruben. The Chicana in American literature. LA LUZ, Vol. 6, no. 11 (November 1977), p. 15. English. DESCR: Chicanos in American Literature; Sex Stereotypes.

3438 de la Fuente, Patricia and Duke dos Santos, Maria I. The elliptic female presence as unifying force in the novels of Rolando Hinojosa. REVISTA CHICANO-RIQUENA, Vol. 12, no. 3-4 (Fall, Winter, 1984), p. 64-75. English. DESCR: ESTAMPAS DEL VALLE Y OTRAS OBRAS; GENERACIONES Y SEMBLANZAS; Hinojosa-Smith, Rolando R.; MI QUERIDO RAFA; RITES AND WITNESSES.

3439 de la Fuente, Patricia. Invisible women in the narrative of Tomas Rivera. REVISTA CHICANO-RIQUENA, Vol. 13, no. 3-4 (Fall, Winter, 1985), p. 81-89. English. DESCR: *Rivera, Tomas; Sex Stereotypes; Y NO SE LO TRAGO LA TIERRA/AND THE EARTH DID NOT PART.

3440 de Lotbiniere-Harwood, Susanne and Anzaldua, Gloria. Conversations at the Book Fair: interview with Gloria Anzaldua. TRIVIA: A JOURNAL OF IDEAS, no. 14 (Spring 1989), p. 37-45. English. DESCR: *Anzaldua, Gloria; *Authors; Biography; Feminism.

3441 Del Rio, Carmen M. Chicana poets: re-visions from the margin. REVISTA CANADIENSE DE ESTUDIOS HISPANICOS, Vol. 14, no. 3 (Spring 1990), p. 431-445. English. DESCR: Authors; *Feminism; *Poetry; Tafolla, Carmen; Villanueva, Alma.

3442 Desai, Parul and Zamora, Bernice. Interview with Bernice Zamora, a Chicana poet. IMAGINE, Vol. 2, no. 1 (Summer 1985), p. 26-39. English. DESCR: Literature; *Poetry; Zamora, Bernice.

3443 Dewey, Janice. Dona Josefa: bloodpulse of transition and change. IN: Horno-Delgado, Asuncion, et al., eds. BREAKING BOUNDARIES: LATINA WRITING AND CRITICAL READINGS. Amherst, MA: University of Massachusetts Press, c1989, p. 39-47. English. DESCR: *DAY OF THE SWALLOWS; Garcia-Lorca, Federico; LA CASA DE BERNARDA ALBA; Literary Characters; *Portillo Trambley, Estela.

3444 Eger, Ernestina. A bibliography of criticism of contemporary Chicano literature. Berkeley, CA: Chicano Studies Library Publications Unit, 1982. xxi, 295 p. English. DESCR: Authors; *Bibliography; Literature.

3445 Enriquez, Evangelina. Towards a definition of, and critical approaches to, Chicano(a) literature. Thesis (Ph.D.)--University of California, Riverside, 1982. viii, 182 p. English. DESCR: Feminism; Literary History; *Literature; Marxism.

3446 Gonzalez, LaVerne. [Portillo Trambley, Estela]. IN: Martinez, Julio A. and Lomeli, Francisco A., eds. CHICANO LITERATURE: A REFERENCE GUIDE. Westport, CT: Greenwood Press, 1985, p. 316-322. English. DESCR: Authors; Biography; *Portillo Trambley, Estela.

3447 Gonzalez-Berry, Erlinda and Rebolledo, Tey Diana. Growing up Chicano: Tomas Rivera and Sandra Cisneros. REVISTA CHICANO-RIQUENA, Vol. 13, no. 3-4 (Fall, Winter, 1985), p. 109-119. English. DESCR: Cisneros, Sandra; Cultural Characteristics; Rivera, Tomas; Sex Roles; THE HOUSE ON MANGO STREET; Y NO SE LO TRAGO LA TIERRA/AND THE EARTH DID NOT PART.

3448 Gutierrez Castillo, Dina. La imagen de la mujer en la novela fronteriza. IN: Lopez-Gonzalez, Aralia, et al., eds. MUJER Y LITERATURA MEXICANA Y CHICANA: CULTURAS EN CONTACTO. Mexico: Colegio de la Frontera Norte, 1988, p. [55]-63. Spanish. DESCR: *Border Region; Islas, Arturo; Literary Characters; Mendez M., Miguel; *Novel; PEREGRINOS DE AZTLAN; Sex Roles; Sex Stereotypes; THE RAIN GOD: A DESERT TALE; *Women.

3449 Harlow, Barbara. Sites of struggle: immigration, deportation, prison, and exile. IN: Calderon, Hector and Saldivar, Jose David, eds. CRITICISM IN THE BORDERLANDS: STUDIES IN CHICANO LITERATURE, CULTURE, AND IDEOLOGY. Durham, NC: Duke University Press, 1991, p. [149]-163. English. DESCR: Anzaldua, Gloria; BLACK GOLD; BORDERLANDS/LA FRONTERA: THE NEW MESTIZA; First, Ruth; Khalifeh, Sahar; *Political Ideology; Sanchez, Rosaura; Social Classes; "The Cariboo Cafe" [short story]; "The Ditch" [short story]; Viramontes, Helena Maria; WILD THORNS; *Women; Working Women.

Literary Criticism
(cont.)

3450 Heard, Martha E. The theatre of Denise Chavez: interior landscapes with SABOR NUEVOMEXICANO. THE AMERICAS REVIEW, Vol. 16, no. 2 (Summer 1988), p. 83-91. English. DESCR: *Chavez, Denise; EL CAMINO [play]; New Mexico; PLAZA [play]; *Teatro.

3451 Hernandez, Ines. Sara Estela Ramirez: the early twentieth century Texas-Mexican poet. Thesis (Ph.D.)--University of Houston, 1984. 94 p. English. DESCR: *Authors; *Biography; Feminism; Flores Magon, Ricardo; Journalism; Mexican Revolution - 1910-1920; Mexico; *Poetry; Ramirez, Sara Estela; Texas; Women.

3452 Hernandez, Lisa, ed. and Benitez, Tina, ed. Palabras chicanas: an undergraduate anthology. Berkeley, CA: Mujeres en Marcha, University of California, Berkeley, 1988. 91 p. Bilingual. DESCR: *Literature; Poems; Prose; *Students.

3453 Herrera-Sobek, Maria. Beyond stereotypes: the critical analysis of Chicana literature. Binghamton, NY: Bilingual Press, c1985. 152 p. English.

3454 Herrera-Sobek, Maria. The politics of rape: sexual transgression in Chicana fiction. THE AMERICAS REVIEW, Vol. 15, no. 3-4 (Fall, Winter, 1987), p. 171-181. English. DESCR: Cisneros, Sandra; *Feminism; Fiction; GIVING UP THE GHOST; Lizarraga, Sylvia; Moraga, Cherrie; *Rape; "Red Clowns" [short story]; Sex Roles; "Silver Lake Road" [short story].

3455 Herrera-Sobek, Maria. Women as metaphor in the patriarchal structure of HEART OF AZTLAN. IN: Gonzalez-T., Cesar A. RUDOLFO F. ANAYA: FOCUS ON CRITICISM. La Jolla, CA: Lalo Press, 1990, p. [165]-182. English. DESCR: Anaya, Rudolfo A.; *HEART OF AZTLAN; La Llorona; *Literary Characters; Sex Roles.

3456 Herrera-Sobek, Maria, ed. and Viramontes, Helena Maria, ed. Chicana creativity and criticism: charting new frontiers in American literature. Houston, TX: Arte Publico Press, 1988. 190 p. Bilingual. DESCR: Art; *Literature; Poems; Prose.

3457 Horno-Delgado, Asuncion, et al., eds. Breaking boundaries: Latina writing and critical readings. Amherst, MA: University of Massachusetts Press, c1989. xi, 268 p. English. DESCR: Women.

3458 Leal, Luis. Arquetipos femeninos en la literatura mexicana. IN: Leal, Luis. AZTLAN Y MEXICO: PERFILES LITERARIOS E HISTORICOS. Binghamton, NY: Bilingual Press/Editorial Bilingue, 1985, p. 168-176. Spanish. DESCR: La Virgen de Guadalupe; Malirche; Mexican Literature; Symbolism; Women.

3459 Leal, Luis. Female archetypes in Mexican literature. IN: Miller, Beth, ed. WOMEN IN HISPANIC LITERATURE: ICONS AND FALLEN IDOLS. Berkeley, CA: University of California Press, 1983, p. 227-242. English. DESCR: La Virgen de Guadalupe; Malinche; Mexican Literature; Symbolism; Women.

3460 Leal, Luis. La soldadera en la narrativa de la Revolucion. IN: Leal, Luis. AZTLAN Y MEXICO: PERFILES LITERARIOS E HISTORICOS. Binghamton, NY: Bilingual Press/Editorial Bilingue, 1985, p. 135-193. Spanish. DESCR: La Adelita; LA VOZ DEL PUEBLO; Mexican Literature; Mexican Revolution - 1910-1920; Women.

3461 Lindstrom, Naomi. Four representative Hispanic women poets of Central Texas: a portrait of plurality. THIRD WOMAN, Vol. 2, no. 1 (1984), p. 64-70. English. DESCR: Beltran, Beatriz; de Hoyos, Angela; Jimenez, Magali; Poetry; Tafolla, Carmen; Texas.

3462 Lizarraga, Sylvia S. "La mujer doblamente explotada: "On the Road to Texas: Pete Fonseca". AZTLAN, Vol. 16, no. 1-2 (1985), p. 197-215. Spanish. DESCR: "On the Road to Texas: Pete Fonseca" [short story]; Rivera, Tomas.

3463 Lizarraga, Sylvia S. La mujer ingeniosa. FEM, Vol. 8, no. 34 (June, July, 1984), p. 41. Spanish. DESCR: Novel; *THERE ARE NO MADMEN HERE; *Valdes, Gina.

3464 Lizarraga, Sylvia S. The patriarchal ideology in "La noche que se apagaron las luces". REVISTA CHICANO-RIQUENA, Vol. 13, no. 3-4 (Fall, Winter, 1985), p. 90-95. English. DESCR: "La noche que se apagaron las luces" [short story]; Rivera, Tomas; Sex Roles; Y NO SE LO TRAGO LA TIERRA/AND THE EARTH DID NOT PART.

3465 Lizarraga, Sylvia S. The resourceful woman in THERE ARE NO MADMEN HERE. THIRD WOMAN, Vol. 2, no. 1 (1984), p. 71-74. English. DESCR: THERE ARE NO MADMEN HERE; Valdes, Gina.

3466 Lomas, Clara. Libertad de no procrear: la voz de la mujer en "A una madre de nuestro tiempo" de Margarita Cota-Cardenas. IN: Cordova, Teresa, et al., eds. CHICANA VOICES. Austin, TX: Center for Mexican American Studies, 1986, p. 188-201. Bilingual. DESCR: "A una madre de nuestros tiempos" [poem]; *Cota-Cardenas, Margarita; Feminism; *Poetry; Sex Stereotypes.

3467 Lomas, Clara. Libertad de no procrear: la voz de la mujer en "A una madre de nuestro tiempo" de Margarita Cota-Cardenas. REVISTA MUJERES, Vol. 2, no. 1 (January 1985), p. 30-35. Spanish. DESCR: *"A una madre de nuestros tiempos" [poem]; *Cota-Cardenas, Margarita; Feminism; Poetry; Sex Stereotypes.

3468 Lomeli, Francisco A. Chicana novelists in the process of creating fictive voices. IN: Herrera-Sobek, Maria, ed. BEYOND STEREOTYPES: THE CRITICAL ANALYSIS OF CHICANA LITERATURE. Binghamton, NY: Bilingual Press/Editorial Bilingue, 1985, p. 29-46. English. DESCR: Authors; Literary History; *Novel.

3469 Lopez-Gonzalez, Aralia, et al., eds. Mujer y literatura mexicana y chicana: culturas en contacto. Mexico: Colegio de Mexico, Programa Interdisciplinario de Estudios de la Mujer; Tijuana, B.C., Mexico: Colegio de la Frontera Norte, 1988. 264 p. Spanish. DESCR: Mexican Literature; *Mexico; Sex Roles; *Women.

3470 Lucero, Marcela Christine. The socio-historical implication of the valley as a metaphor in three Colorado Chicana poets. Thesis (Ph.D.)--University of Minnesota, 1981. 176 p. English. DESCR: *Authors; Blea, Irene I.; Chicano Movement; Colorado; Feminism; Mondragon Valdez, Maria; Poetry; Zamora, Bernice.

Literary Criticism
(cont.)

3471 Luna-Lawhn, Juanita. Victorian attitudes affecting the Mexican woman writing in LA PRENSA during the early 1900s and the Chicana of the 1980s. IN: Bardeleben, Renate von, et al., eds. MISSIONS IN CONFLICT: ESSAYS ON U.S.-MEXICAN RELATIONS AND CHICANO CULTURE. Tubingen, W. Germany: Gunter Narr Verlag, 1986, p. 65-71. English. DESCR: Feminism; LA PRENSA, San Antonio, TX; *Newspapers; "Penitents" [poem]; Poetry; Zamora, Bernice.

3472 McCracken, Ellen. Latina narrative and politics of signification: articulation, antagonism, and populist rupture. CRITICA, Vol. 2, no. 2 (Fall 1990), p. 202-207. English. DESCR: *Cisneros, Sandra; IN NUEVA YORK; *Mohr, Nicolasa; Puerto Ricans; RITUALS OF SURVIVAL; Short Story; THE HOUSE ON MANGO STREET; Women.

3473 McCracken, Ellen. Sandra Cisneros' THE HOUSE ON MANGO STREET: community-oriented introspection and the demystification of patriarchal violence. IN: Horno-Delgado, Asuncion, et al., eds. BREAKING BOUNDARIES: LATINA WRITING AND CRITICAL READINGS. Amherst, MA: University of Massachusetts Press, c1989, p. 62-71. English. DESCR: *Cisneros, Sandra; *THE HOUSE ON MANGO STREET.

3474 Miller, Elaine N. and Sternbach, Nancy Saporta. Selected bibliography. IN: Horno-Delgado, Asuncion, et al., eds. BREAKING BOUNDARIES: LATINA WRITING AND CRITICAL READINGS. Amherst, MA: University of Massachusetts Press, c1989, p. 251-263. English. DESCR: *Bibliography; Cubanos; *Literature; Puerto Ricans; *Women.

3475 Mondin, Sandra. The depiction of the Chicana in BLESS ME ULTIMA and THE MILAGRO BEANFIELD WAR: a study in contrasts. IN: Luna Lawhn, Juanita, et al., eds. MEXICO AND THE UNITED STATES: INTERCULTURAL RELATIONS IN THE HUMANITIES. San Antonio, TX: San Antonio College, 1984, p. 137-150. English. DESCR: Anaya, Rudolfo A.; BLESS ME, ULTIMA; Literary Characters; Nichols, John; *Stereotypes; THE MILAGRO BEANFIELD WAR [novel].

3476 Monk, Janice and Norwood, Vera. Angles of vision: enhancing our perspectives on the Southwest. IN: Lensink, Judy Nolte, ed. OLD SOUTHWEST/NEW SOUTHWEST: ESSAYS ON A REGION AND ITS LITERATURE. Tucson, AZ: The Tucson Public Library, 1989, p. 39-47. English. DESCR: *Literature; Southwestern United States; *Women.

3477 Moraga, Cherrie, ed. and Castillo, Ana, ed. Esta [sic] puente, mi espalda: voces de mujeres tercermundistas en los Estados Unidos. San Francisco, CA: Ism Press, c1988. [19], 281 p.: ill. Spanish. DESCR: Ethnic Groups; *Feminism; *Poems; *Prose; *Women.

3478 Moraga, Cherrie, ed. and Anzaldua, Gloria, ed. This bridge called my back: writings by radical women of color. Watertown, MA: Persephone Press, c1981. xxvi, 261 p. English. DESCR: Ethnic Groups; *Feminism; *Poems; *Prose; *Women.

3479 Olivares, Julian. Sandra Cisneros' THE HOUSE ON MANGO STREET and the poetics of space. THE AMERICAS REVIEW, Vol. 15, no. 3-4 (Fall, Winter, 1987), p. 160-170. English. DESCR: Cisneros, Sandra; THE HOUSE ON MANGO STREET.

3480 Ordonez, Elizabeth J. Body, spirit, and the text: Alma Villanueva's LIFE SPAN. IN: Calderon, Hector and Saldivar, Jose David, eds. CRITICISM IN THE BORDERLANDS: STUDIES IN CHICANO LITERATURE, CULTURE, AND IDEOLOGY. Durham, NC: Duke University Press, 1991, p. [61]-71. English. DESCR: Cixous, Helene; *Feminism; *LIFE SPAN; Poetry; *Villanueva, Alma.

3481 Ordonez, Elizabeth J. The concept of cultural identity in Chicana poetry. THIRD WOMAN, Vol. 2, no. 1 (1984), p. 75-82. English. DESCR: Cervantes, Lorna Dee; Corpi, Lucha; Poetry; Tafolla, Carmen; Villanueva, Alma.

3482 Ordonez, Elizabeth J. Sexual politics and the theme of sexuality in Chicana poetry. IN: Miller, Beth, ed. WOMEN IN HISPANIC LITERATURE: ICONS AND FALLEN IDOLS. Berkeley, CA: University of California Press, 1983, p. 316-339. English. DESCR: Chicano Movement; Feminism; Poetry; Sexual Behavior.

3483 Ordonez, Elizabeth J. [Villanueva, Alma]. IN: Martinez, Julio A. and Lomeli, Francisco A., eds. CHICANO LITERATURE: A REFERENCE GUIDE. Westport, CT: Greenwood Press, 1985, p. 413-420. English. DESCR: Authors; Biography; *BLOODROOT; *Villanueva, Alma.

3484 Ortega, Eliana and Sternbach, Nancy Saporta. At the threshold of the unnamed: Latina literary discourse in the eighties. IN: Horno-Delgado, Asuncion, et al., eds. BREAKING BOUNDARIES: LATINA WRITING AND CRITICAL READINGS. Amherst, MA: University of Massachusetts Press, c1989, p. [2]-23. English. DESCR: Bilingualism; *Feminism; Literary History; Political Ideology; Sex Roles; *Women.

3485 Passman, Kristina. Demeter, Kore and the birth of the self: the quest for identity in the poetry of Alma Villanueva, Pat Mora y Cherrie Moraga. MONOGRAPHIC REVIEW, Vol. 6, (1990) p. 323-342. English. DESCR: Mora, Pat; Moraga, Cherrie; Mythology; Poetry; Villanueva, Alma.

3486 Quintana, Alvina E. Ana Castillo's THE MIXQUIAHUALA LETTERS: the novelist as ethnographer. IN: Calderon, Hector and Saldivar, Jose David, eds. CRITICISM IN THE BORDERLANDS: STUDIES IN CHICANO LITERATURE, CULTURE, AND IDEOLOGY. Durham, NC: Duke University Press, 1991, p. [72]-83. English. DESCR: Anthropology; Castillo, Ana; Cultural Studies; *Ethnology; Feminism; Geertz, Clifford; Novel; THE MIXQUIAHUALA LETTERS.

3487 Quintana, Alvina E. Challenge and counter challenge: Chicana literary motifs. AGAINST THE CURRENT, Vol. 2, no. 2 (March, April, 1987), p. 25,28-32. English. DESCR: Anglo Americans; Authors; Cervantes, Lorna Dee; Cultural Studies; *Feminism; Identity; *Literature; Moraga, Cherrie; THERE ARE NO MADMEN HERE; Valdes, Gina; Women.

3488 Quintana, Alvina E. Chicana discourse: negations and mediations. Thesis (Ph.D.)--University of California, Santa Cruz, 1989. 226 p. English. DESCR: Authors; Castillo, Ana; Chavez, Denise; Chicano Movement; Cisneros, Sandra; Ethnology; Feminism; *Literature; NOVENA NARRATIVES; Oral Tradition; Political Ideology; THE HOUSE ON MANGO STREET; THE LAST OF THE MENU GIRLS; THE MIXQUIAHUALA LETTERS.

Literary Criticism
(cont.)

3489 Quintana, Alvina E. Chicana literary motifs: challenge and counter-challenge. IMAGES: ETHNIC STUDIES OCCASIONAL PAPERS SERIES, (Fall 1986), p. 24-41. English. DESCR: Anglo Americans; Authors; Cervantes, Lorna Dee; Cultural Studies; *Feminism; *Identity; Literature; Moraga, Cherrie; THERE ARE NO MADMEN HERE; Valdes, Gina; Women.

3490 Quintana, Alvina E. Language, power, and women: a hermeneutic interpretation. CRITICAL PERSPECTIVES, Vol. 2, no. 1 (Fall 1984), p. 10-19. English. DESCR: *Feminism; Malinche.

3491 Quintana, Alvina E. O mama, with what's inside of me. REVISTA MUJERES, Vol. 3, no. 1 (January 1986), p. 38-40. English. DESCR: Alarcon, Norma; Feminism; Poetry; "What Kind of Lover Have You Made Me, Mother?: Towards a Theory of Chicanas' Feminism and Cultural Identity Through Poetry" [article].

3492 Quintana, Alvina E. Politics, representation and the emergence of a Chicana aesthetic. CULTURAL STUDIES, Vol. 4, no. 3 (October 1990), p. 257-263. English. DESCR: Anzaldua, Gloria; *Authors; Chavez, Denise; Chicana Studies; Cisneros, Sandra; Cultural Studies; Feminism.

3493 Quintana, Alvina E. Women: prisoners of the word. IN: Cordova, Teresa, et al., eds. CHICANA VOICES. Austin, TX: Center for Mexican American Studies, 1986, p. 208-219. English. DESCR: Women.

3494 Ramirez, Genevieve M. and Salazar Parr, Carmen. The female hero in Chicano literature. IN: Herrera-Sobek, Maria, ed. BEYOND STEREOTYPES: THE CRITICAL ANALYSIS OF CHICANA LITERATURE. Binghamton, NY: Bilingual Press/Editorial Bilingue, 1985, p. 48-60. English. DESCR: *Literary Characters; Sex Roles.

3495 Ramos, Luis Arturo. [Hoyos, Angela de]. IN: Martinez, Julio A. and Lomeli, Francisco A., eds. CHICANO LITERATURE: A REFERENCE GUIDE. Westport, CT: Greenwood Press, 1985, p. 260-265. English. DESCR: Authors; Biography; *de Hoyos, Angela.

3496 Rascon, Francisco. La caracterizacion de los personajes femeninos en ...Y NO SE LO TRAGO LA TIERRA. IN: Lattin, Vernon E., ed. CONTEMPORARY CHICANO FICTION: A CRITICAL SURVEY. Binghamton, NY: Bilingual Press/Editorial Bilingue, 1986, p. 141-148. Spanish. DESCR: Rivera, Tomas; Y NO SE LO TRAGO LA TIERRA/AND THE EARTH DID NOT PART.

3497 Rebolledo, Tey Diana. Abuelitas: mythology and integration in Chicana literature. REVISTA CHICANO-RIQUENA, Vol. 11, no. 3-4 (Fall 1983), p. 148-158. English. DESCR: Grandmothers; Poetry.

3498 Rebolledo, Tey Diana. The bittersweet nostalgia of childhood in the poetry of Margarita Cota-Cardenas. FRONTIERS: A JOURNAL OF WOMEN STUDIES, Vol. 5, no. 2 (Summer 1980), p. 31-35. English. DESCR: *Cota-Cardenas, Margarita; Poetry.

3499 Rebolledo, Tey Diana. Game theory in Chicana poetry. REVISTA CHICANO-RIQUENA, Vol. 11, no. 3-4 (Fall 1983), p. 159-168. English. DESCR: Poetry.

3500 Rebolledo, Tey Diana. The maturing of

Chicana poetry: the quiet revolution of the 1980s. IN: Treichler, Paula A., et al., eds. FOR ALMA MATER: THEORY AND PRACTICE IN FEMINIST SCHOLARSHIP. Urbana: University of Illinois Press, 1985, p. 143-158. English. DESCR: Identity; *Poetry; Sexual Behavior.

3501 Rebolledo, Tey Diana. Narrative strategies of resistance in Hispana writing. THE JOURNAL OF NARRATIVE TECHNIQUE, Vol. 20, no. 2 (Spring 1990), p. 134-146. English. DESCR: *Authors; Cabeza de Baca, Fabiola; Fiction; Jaramillo, Cleofas M.; Literature; New Mexico; OLD SPAIN IN OUR SOUTHWEST; *Oral Tradition; Otero Warren, Nina; ROMANCE OF A LITTLE VILLAGE GIRL; WE FED THEM CACTUS.

3502 Rebolledo, Tey Diana. The politics of poetics: or, what am I, a critic, doing in this text anyhow? THE AMERICAS REVIEW, Vol. 15, no. 3-4 (Fall, Winter, 1987), p. 129-138. English. DESCR: Literary History; Literature.

3503 Rebolledo, Tey Diana. The politics of poetics: or, what am I, a critic, doing in this text anyhow? IN: Anzaldua, Gloria, ed. MAKING FACE, MAKING SOUL: HACIENDO CARAS: CREATIVE AND CRITICAL PERSPECTIVES BY WOMEN OF COLOR. San Francisco, CA: Aunt Lute Foundation Books, 1990, p. 346-355. English. DESCR: Literary History; Literature.

3504 Rebolledo, Tey Diana. Soothing restless serpents: the dreaded creation and other inspirations in Chicana poetry. THIRD WOMAN, Vol. 2, no. 1 (1984), p. 83-102. English. DESCR: *Poetry.

3505 Rebolledo, Tey Diana. Tradition and mythology: signatures of landscape in Chicana literature. IN: Norwood, Vera and Monk, Janice, eds. THE DESERT IS NO LADY: SOUTHWESTERN LANDSCAPES IN WOMEN'S WRITING AND ART. New Haven, CT: Yale University Press, 1987, p. 96-124. English. DESCR: *Authors; Cabeza de Baca, Fabiola; Chavez, Denise; Jaramillo, Cleofas M.; *Literary History; Literature; Mora, Pat; Mythology; Otero Warren, Nina; Portillo Trambley, Estela; Silva, Beverly; Southwestern United States; WE FED THEM CACTUS.

3506 Rebolledo, Tey Diana. Walking the thin line: humor in Chicana literature. IN: Herrera-Sobek, Maria, ed. BEYOND STEREOTYPES: THE CRITICAL ANALYSIS OF CHICANA LITERATURE. Binghamton, NY: Bilingual Press/Editorial Bilingue, 1985, p. 91-107. English. DESCR: Chistes; *Humor; *Poetry.

3507 Rivero, Eliana S. Escritura chicana: la mujer. LA PALABRA, Vol. 2, no. 2 (Fall 1980), p. 2-9. Spanish.

3508 Rosaldo, Renato. Fables of the fallen guy. IN: Calderon, Hector and Saldivar, Jose David, eds. CRITICISM IN THE BORDERLANDS: STUDIES IN CHICANO LITERATURE, CULTURE AND IDEOLOGY. Durham, NC: Duke University Press, 1991, p. [84]-93. English. DESCR: Chavez, Denise; Cisneros, Sandra; Fiction; Literary Characters; Rios, Alberto; Sex Roles; THE HOUSE ON MANGO STREET; THE IGUANA KILLER: TWELVE STORIES OF THE HEART; THE LAST OF THE MENU GIRLS.

Literary Criticism
(cont.)

3509 Salazar Parr, Carmen and Ramirez, Genevieve M. The Chicana in Chicano literature. IN: Martinez, Julio A. and Lomeli, Francisco A., eds. CHICANO LITERATURE: A REFERENCE GUIDE. Westport, CT: Greenwood Press, 1985, p. 97-107. English. **DESCR:** Literary Characters; *Literature; *Stereotypes.

3510 Salazar Parr, Carmen. La Chicana in literature. IN: Garcia, Eugene E., et al., eds. CHICANO STUDIES: A MULTIDISCIPLINARY APPROACH. New York: Teachers College Press, 1984, p. 120-134. English. **DESCR:** DAY OF THE SWALLOWS; Literary Characters; *Literature; Portillo Trambley, Estela; Stereotypes; Teatro; "The Trees" [short story].

3511 Saldivar, Jose David. Towards a Chicano poetics: the making of the Chicano subject. CONFLUENCIA, Vol. 1, no. 2 (Spring 1986), p. 10-17. English. **DESCR:** Corridos; Feminism; "Los Vatos" [poem]; Montoya, Jose E.; *Poetry; RESTLESS SERPENTS; Rios, Alberto; WHISPERING TO FOOL THE WIND; Zamora, Bernice.

3512 Saldivar, Ramon. The dialectics of subjectivity: gender and difference in Isabella Rios, Sandra Cisneros, and Cherrie Moraga. IN: Saldivar, Ramon. CHICANO NARRATIVE: THE DIALECTICS OF DIFFERENCE. Madison, WI: University of Wisconsin Press, 1990, p. 171-199. English. **DESCR:** Authors; Autobiography; *Cisneros, Sandra; Feminism; Fiction; Literature; LOVING IN THE WAR YEARS; *Moraga, Cherrie; Political Ideology; *Rios, Isabella; THE HOUSE ON MANGO STREET; VICTUUM.

3513 Saldivar-Hull, Sonia. Feminism on the border: from gender politics to geopolitics. IN: Calderon, Hector and Saldivar, Jose David, eds. CRITICISM IN THE BORDERLANDS: STUDIES IN CHICANO LITERATURE, CULTURE, AND IDEOLOGY. Durham, NC: Duke University Press, 1991, p. [203]-220. English. **DESCR:** Anglo Americans; *Anzaldua, Gloria; *BORDERLANDS/LA FRONTERA: THE NEW MESTIZA; Feminism; Homosexuality; Mestizaje; Moraga, Cherrie; Sexism; "The Cariboo Cafe" [short story]; Viramontes, Helena Maria; Women.

3514 Salinas, Judy. The role of women in Chicano literature. IN: Jimenez, Francisco, ed. THE IDENTIFICATION AND ANALYSIS OF CHICANO LITERATURE. New York: Bilingual Press/Editorial Bilingue, 1979, p. 191-240. English.

3515 Sanchez, Elba R. La realidad a traves de la inocencia en el cuento: "Un Paseo". IN: Cordova, Teresa, et al., eds. CHICANA VOICES. Austin, TX: Center for Mexican American Studies, 1986, p. 202-207. Spanish. **DESCR:** *Garzon, Luz; Short Story; *"Un Paseo" [short story].

3516 Sanchez, Marta E. The birthing of the poetic "I" in Alma Villanueva's MOTHER MAY I?: the search for a feminine identity. IN: Herrera-Sobek, Maria, ed. BEYOND STEREOTYPES: THE CRITICAL ANALYSIS OF CHICANA LITERATURE. Binghamton, NY: Bilingual Press/Editorial Bilingue, 1985, p. 108-152. Also IN: Sanchez, Marta. CONTEMPORARY CHICANA POETRY. Berkeley, CA: University of California Press, 1985, p. 24-84. English. **DESCR:** *Identity; MOTHER MAY I?; Poetry; Villanueva, Alma.

3517 Sanchez, Marta E. Contemporary Chicana poetry. Berkeley, CA: University of California Press, c1985. xi, 377 p. English. **DESCR:** *Poetry.

3518 Sanchez, Marta E. Gender and ethnicity in contemporary Chicana poetry. CRITICAL PERSPECTIVES, Vol. 2, no. 1 (Fall 1984), p. 147-166. English. **DESCR:** MOTHER MAY I?; *Poetry; Villanueva, Alma.

3519 Sanchez, Marta E. Judy Lucero and Bernice Zamora: two dialectical statements in Chicana poetry. DE COLORES, Vol. 4, no. 3 (1978), p. 22-33. Bilingual. **DESCR:** Gomez-Quinones, Juan; Lucero, Judy A.; *Poetry; Zamora, Bernice.

3520 Sanchez, Marta E. Judy Lucero and Bernice Zamora: two dialectical statements in Chicana poetry. IN: Sommers, Joseph and Ybarra-Frausto, Tomas, eds. MODERN CHICANO WRITERS: A COLLECTION OF CRITICAL ESSAYS. Englewood Cliffs, NJ: Prentice-Hall, 1979, p. 141-149. English. **DESCR:** Gomez-Quinones, Juan; Lucero, Judy A.; *Poetry; Zamora, Bernice.

3521 Sanchez, Rita. Chicana writer breaking out of the silence. DE COLORES, Vol. 3, no. 3 (1977), p. 31-37. English. **DESCR:** Authors; Castaneda Shular, Antonia; Correa, Viola; Cunningham, Veronica; Hernandez, Barbara; Mendoza, Rita; *Poetry.

3522 Sanchez, Rosaura. Chicana prose writers: the case of Gina Valdes and Sylvia Lizarraga. IN: Herrera-Sobek, Maria, ed. BEYOND STEREOTYPES: THE CRITICAL ANALYSIS OF CHICANA LITERATURE. Binghamton, NY: Bilingual Press/Editorial Bilingue, 1985, p. 61-70. English. **DESCR:** *Authors; *Lizarraga, Sylvia; Prose; *Valdes, Gina.

3523 Sanchez, Rosaura. El discurso femenino en la literatura chicana. IN: Lopez-Gonzalez, Aralia, et al., eds. MUJER Y LITERATURA MEXICANA Y CHICANA: CULTURAS EN CONTACTO. Mexico: Colegio de la Frontera Norte, 1988, p. 37-43. Spanish. **DESCR:** *Feminism; Ruiz Burton, Maria Amparo.

3524 Sternbach, Nancy Saporta. "A deep racial memory of love": the Chicana feminism of Cherrie Moraga. IN: Horno-Delgado, Asuncion, et al., eds. BREAKING BOUNDARIES: LATINA WRITING AND CRITICAL READINGS. Amherst, MA: University of Massachusetts Press, c1989, p. 48-61. English. **DESCR:** Discrimination; Feminism; Homosexuality; *LOVING IN THE WAR YEARS; Machismo; Malinche; *Moraga, Cherrie; Sex Stereotypes; Sexism.

3525 Tafolla, Carmen. Chicano literature: beyond beginnings. IN: Harris, Marie and Aguero, Kathleen, eds. A GIFT OF TONGUES: CRITICAL CHALLENGES IN CONTEMPORARY AMERICAN POETRY. Athens, GA: University of Georgia Press, 1987, p. 206-225. English. **DESCR:** *Authors; Cota-Cardenas, Margarita; Language Usage; *Literature; Portillo Trambley, Estela; Sex Stereotypes; Symbolism; Tafolla, Carmen; Vigil-Pinon, Evangelina.

3526 Tatum, Charles M. Grappling with difference: gender, race, class, and ethnicity in contemporary Chicana/o literature. RENATO ROSALDO LECTURE SERIES MONOGRAPH, Vol. 6, (1988, 1989), p. 1-23. English. **DESCR:** Anaya, Rudolfo A.; Authors; BLESS ME, ULTIMA; *Feminism; Identity; Literary Characters; Literature Reviews.

Literary Criticism
(cont.)

3527 Tavera Rivera, Margarita. Autoridad in absentia: la censura patriarcal en la narrativa chicana. IN: Lopez-Gonzalez, Aralia, et al., eds. MUJER Y LITERATURA MEXICANA Y CHICANA: CULTURAS EN CONTACTO. Mexico: Colegio de la Frontera Norte, 1988, p. [65]-69. Spanish. DESCR: Feminism; Fiction; Sex Roles; *THE MOTHS AND OTHER STORIES; *Viramontes, Helena Maria.

3528 Treacy, Mary Jane. The ties that bind: women and community in Evangelina Vigil's THIRTY AN' SEEN A LOT. IN: Horno-Delgado, Asuncion, et al., eds. BREAKING BOUNDARIES: LATINA WRITING AND CRITICAL READINGS. Amherst, MA: University of Massachusetts Press, c1989, p. 82-93. English. DESCR: Identity; Poetry; Sexism; *THIRTY AN' SEEN A LOT; *Vigil-Pinon, Evangelina.

3529 Trujillo, Carla, ed. Chicana lesbians: the girls our mothers warned us about. Berkeley, CA: Third Woman Press, 1991. xii, 202 p.: ill. English. DESCR: *Homosexuality; Poems Prose.

3530 Trujillo Gaitan, Marcella. The dilemma of the modern Chicana artist and critic. DE COLORES, Vol. 3, no. 3 (1977), p. 38-48. Bilingual. DESCR: Art Criticism; Artists; *Chicano Movement; Gonzales, Sylvia Alicia; Machismo; Malinche; *Poetry; Symbolism.

3531 Trujillo Gaitan, Marcella. The dilemma of the modern Chicana artist and critic. HERESIES, Vol. 2, no. 4 (1979), p. 5-10. English. DESCR: Art Criticism; Artists; Authors; *Chicano Movement; Gonzales, Sylvia Alicia; Machismo; Malinche; *Poetry; Symbolism.

3532 Vallejos, Tomas. Estela Portillo Trambley's fictive search for paradise. FRONTIERS: A JOURNAL OF WOMEN STUDIES, Vol. 5, no. 2 (1980), p. 54-58. Also IN: Lattin, Vernon E., ed. CONTEMPORARY CHICANO FICTION. Binghamton, NY: Bilingual Press/Editorial Bilingue, 1986, p. 269-277. English. DESCR: DAY OF THE SWALLOWS; Novel; Portillo Trambley, Estela; RAIN OF SCORPIONS AND OTHER WRITINGS.

3533 Velasquez-Trevino, Gloria. Cultural ambivalence in early Chicana prose fiction. Thesis (Ph.D.)--Stanford University, 1985. 185 p. English. DESCR: Biculturalism; *Fiction; Gonzalez, Jovita; Mena, Maria Cristina; Niggli, Josephina; Prose; Sex Roles.

3534 Vigil, Evangelina, ed. Woman of her word: Hispanic women write. REVISTA CHICANO-RIQUENA, Vol. 11, no. 3-4 (Fall, Winter, 1983), p. [1]-180. Bilingual. DESCR: Art; *Literature; Poetry; Prose; *Women.

3535 Yarbro-Bejarano, Yvonne. Chicana literature from a Chicana feminist perspective. THE AMERICAS REVIEW, Vol. 15, no. 3-4 (Fall Winter, 1987), p. 139-145. English. DESCR: *Feminism; Literature.

3536 Yarbro-Bejarano, Yvonne. De-constructing the lesbian body: Cherrie Moraga's LOVING IN THE WAR YEARS. IN: Trujillo, Carla, ed. CHICANA LESBIANS: THE GIRLS OUR MOTHERS WARNED US ABOUT. Berkeley, CA: Third Woman Press, 1991, p. 143-155. English. DESCR: Homosexuality; *LOVING IN THE WAR YEARS; *Moraga, Cherrie; Skin Color.

3537 Zamora, Bernice. Archetypes in Chicana poetry. DE COLORES, Vol. 4, no. 3 (1978), p. 43-52. English. DESCR: Cervantes, Lorna Dee; Cunningham, Veronica; "Declaration on a Day of Little Inspiration" [poem]; Hernandez, Carlota; "I Speak in an Illusion" [poem]; Lucero, Judy A.; Macias, Margarita; Mendoza, Rita; "Para Mi Hijita" [poem]; *Poetry; "Rape Report" [poem]; "The White Line" [poem]; "Working Mother's Song" [poem]; "You Can Only Blame the System for So Long" [poem]; Zamora, Katarina.

3538 Zamora, Bernice. The Chicana as a literary critic. DE COLORES, Vol. 3, no. 3 (1977), p. 16-19. English.

3539 Zamora, Bernice. Mythopoeia of Chicano poetry: an introduction to cultural archetypes. Thesis (Ph.D.)--Stanford University, 1986. 341 p. English. DESCR: Literary Characters; Literature; Malinche; Pachucos; *Poetry; *Symbolism.

3540 Zamora, Emilio, Jr. Sara Estela Ramirez: una rosa roja en el movimiento. IN: Mora, Magdalena and Del Castillo, Adelaida, eds. MEXICAN WOMEN IN THE UNITED STATES: STRUGGLES PAST AND PRESENT. Los Angeles, CA: Chicano Studies Research Center, UCLA, 1980, p. 163-169. English. DESCR: *Biography; Poetry; *Ramirez, Sara Estela.

Literary History

3541 Enriquez, Evangelina. Towards a definition of, and critical approaches to, Chicano(a) literature. Thesis (Ph.D.)--University of California, Riverside, 1982. viii, 182 p. English. DESCR: Feminism; *Literary Criticism; *Literature; Marxism.

3542 Lomeli, Francisco A. Chicana novelists in the process of creating fictive voices. IN: Herrera-Sobek, Maria, ed. BEYOND STEREOTYPES: THE CRITICAL ANALYSIS OF CHICANA LITERATURE. Binghamton, NY: Bilingual Press/Editorial Bilingue, 1985, p. 29-46. English. DESCR: Authors; Literary Criticism; *Novel.

3543 Ortega, Eliana and Sternbach, Nancy Saporta. At the threshold of the unnamed: Latina literary discourse in the eighties. IN: Horno-Delgado, Asuncion, et al., eds. BREAKING BOUNDARIES: LATINA WRITING AND CRITICAL READINGS. Amherst, MA: University of Massachusetts Press, c1989, p. [2]-23. English. DESCR: Bilingualism; *Feminism; *Literary Criticism; Political Ideology; Sex Roles; *Women.

3544 Padilla, Genaro. Imprisoned narrative? Or lies, secrets, and silence in New Mexico women's autobiography. IN: Calderon, Hector and Saldivar, Jose David, eds. CRITICISM IN THE BORDERLANDS: STUDIES IN CHICANO LITERATURE, CULTURE, AND IDEOLOGY. Durham, NC: Duke University Press, 1991, p. [43]-60. English. DESCR: Authors; *Autobiography; *Cabeza de Baca, Fabiola; *Jaramillo, Cleofas M.; New Mexico; ROMANCE OF A LITTLE VILLAGE GIRL; WE FED THEM CACTUS.

3545 Padilla, Genaro. "Yo sola aprendi": contra-patriarchal containment in women's nineteenth-century California personal narratives. THE AMERICAS REVIEW, Vol. 16, no. 3-4 (Fall, Winter, 1988), p. 91-109. English. DESCR: Autobiography; California; *Women.

Literary History (cont.)

3546 Rebolledo, Tey Diana. Las escritoras: romances and realities. IN: Gonzales-Berry, Erlinda, ed. PASO POR AQUI: CRITICAL ESSAYS ON THE NEW MEXICAN LITERARY TRADITION. Albuquerque, NM: University of New Mexico Press, c1989, p. 199-214. English. **DESCR:** Authors; *Cabeza de Baca, Fabiola; *Jaramillo, Cleofas M.; New Mexico; OLD SPAIN IN OUR SOUTHWEST; *Otero Warren, Nina; ROMANCE OF A LITTLE VILLAGE GIRL; WE FED THEM CACTUS; Women.

3547 Rebolledo, Tey Diana. The politics of poetics: or, what am I, a critic, doing in this text anyhow? THE AMERICAS REVIEW, Vol. 15, no. 3-4 (Fall, Winter, 1987), p. 129-138. English. **DESCR:** *Literary Criticism; Literature.

3548 Rebolledo, Tey Diana. The politics of poetics: or, what am I, a critic, doing in this text anyhow? IN: Anzaldua, Gloria, ed. MAKING FACE, MAKING SOUL: HACIENDO CARAS: CREATIVE AND CRITICAL PERSPECTIVES BY WOMEN OF COLOR. San Francisco, CA: Aunt Lute Foundation Books, 1990, p. 346-355. English. **DESCR:** *Literary Criticism; Literature.

3549 Rebolledo, Tey Diana. Tradition and mythology: signatures of landscape in Chicana literature. IN: Norwood, Vera and Monk, Janice, eds. THE DESERT IS NO LADY: SOUTHWESTERN LANDSCAPES IN WOMEN'S WRITING AND ART. New Haven, CT: Yale University Press, 1987, p. 96-124. English. **DESCR:** *Authors; Cabeza de Baca, Fabiola; Chavez, Denise; Jaramillo, Cleofas M.; Literary Criticism; Literature; Mora, Pat; Mythology; Otero Warren, Nina; Portillo Trambley, Estela; Silva, Beverly; Southwestern United States; WE FED THEM CACTUS.

Literary Influence

3550 Bornstein de Somoza, Miriam. La poetica chicana: vision panoramica. LA PALABRA, Vol. 2, no. 2 (Fall 1980), p. 43-66. Spanish. **DESCR:** Authors; *Literary Criticism; *Poetry.

Literature

3551 Agosin, Marjorie. Elucubraciones y antielucubraciones: critica feminista desde perspectivas poeticas. THIRD WOMAN, Vol. 1, no. 2 (1982), p. 65-69. Spanish. **DESCR:** Essays; Feminism; Literary Criticism.

3552 Alarcon, Norma. Chicana writers and critics in a social context : towards a contemporary bibliography. THIRD WOMAN, Vol. 4, (1989), p. 169-178. English. **DESCR:** *Bibliography; *Literary Criticism.

3553 Alarcon, Norma. Chicana's feminist literature: a re-vision through Malintzinl or Malintzin: putting flesh back on the object. IN: Moraga, Cherrie and Anzaldua, Gloria, eds. THIS BRIDGE CALLED MY BACK: WRITINGS BY RADICAL WOMEN OF COLOR. Watertown, MA: Persephone Press, 1981, p. 182-190. English. **DESCR:** Feminism; Malinche; *Sex Roles; Stereotypes; Symbolism.

3554 Alarcon, Norma; Castillo, Ana; and Moraga, Cherrie. The sexuality of Latinas [special issue of THIRD WOMAN]. THIRD WOMAN, Vol. 4, (1989), p. 8-189. Bilingual. **DESCR:** Sex Roles; *Sexual Behavior; *Women.

3555 Anzaldua, Gloria. Border crossings. TRIVIA: A JOURNAL OF IDEAS, no. 14 (Spring 1989), p. 46-51. English. **DESCR:** *Feminism; *Literary Criticism.

3556 Anzaldua, Gloria, ed. Making face, making soul = Haciendo caras: creative and critical perspectives by women of color. San Francisco, CA: Aunt Lute Foundation Books, 1990. English. **DESCR:** Ethnic Groups; *Feminism; Women.

3557 [Bibliography of Special Issue: Chicana Creativity and Criticism]. THE AMERICAS REVIEW, Vol. 15, no. 3-4 (Fall, Winter, 1987), p. 182-188. English. **DESCR:** *Bibliography; *Literary Criticism.

3558 Desai, Parul and Zamora, Bernice. Interview with Bernice Zamora, a Chicana poet. IMAGINE, Vol. 2, no. 1 (Summer 1985), p. 26-39. English. **DESCR:** Literary Criticism; *Poetry; Zamora, Bernice.

3559 Domenella, Ana Rosa. Al margen de un coloquio fronterizo mujer y literatura mexicana y chicana. FEM, Vol. 14, no. 89 (May 1990), p. 32-34. Spanish. **DESCR:** *Border Region; Coloquio Fronterizo Mujer y Literatura Mexicana y Chicana (1987: Tijuana, Baja California, Mexico); *Conferences and Meetings; Mexican Literature; Mexico; Women.

3560 [Edicion feminista (Special Issue)]. IMAGINE, Vol. 2, no. 1 (Summer 1985), p. ii-159. Bilingual. **DESCR:** *Poems; Women.

3561 Eger, Ernestina. A bibliography of criticism of contemporary Chicano literature. Berkeley, CA: Chicano Studies Library Publications Unit, 1982. xxi, 295 p. English. **DESCR:** Authors; *Bibliography; *Literary Criticism.

3562 Enriquez, Evangelina. Towards a definition of, and critical approaches to, Chicano(a) literature. Thesis (Ph.D.)--University of California, Riverside, 1982. viii, 182 p. English. **DESCR:** Feminism; *Literary Criticism; Literary History; Marxism.

3563 Gonzales, Sylvia Alicia. The Chicana in literature. LA LUZ, Vol. 1, no. 9 (January 1973), p. 51-53. English. **DESCR:** *Essays.

3564 Hernandez, Lisa, ed. and Benitez, Tina, ed. Palabras chicanas: an undergraduate anthology. Berkeley, CA: Mujeres en Marcha, University of California, Berkeley, 1988. 97 p. Bilingual. **DESCR:** Literary Criticism; Poems; Prose; *Students.

3565 Herrera-Sobek, Maria, ed. and Viramontes, Helena Maria, ed. Chicana creativity and criticism: charting new frontiers in American literature. Houston, TX: Arte Publico Press, 1988. 190 p. Bilingual. **DESCR:** Art; Literary Criticism; Poems; Prose.

3566 Job, Peggy. La sexualidad en la narrativa femenina mexicana 1970-1987: una aproximacion. THIRD WOMAN, Vol. 4, (1989), p. 120-133. Spanish. **DESCR:** *Literature Reviews; Sex Roles; *Sexual Behavior; *Women.

3567 Lizarraga, Sylvia S. Chicana women writers and their audience. LECTOR, Vol. 1, no. 1 (June 1982), p. 15-16,18. English. **DESCR:** *Authors.

Literature (cont.)

3568 Lizarraga, Sylvia S. Images of women in Chicano literature by men. FEMINIST ISSUES, Vol. 5, no. 2 (Fall 1985), p. 69-88. English. DESCR: Morales, Alejandro; RETO EN EL PARAISO; Sexism; *Stereotypes.

3569 Lomas, Clara. Mexican precursors of Chicana feminist writing. IN: National Association for Chicano Studies. ESTUDIOS CHICANOS AND THE POLITICS OF COMMUNITY. [S.l.]: National Association for Chicano Studies, c1989, p. [149]-160. English. DESCR: Authors; de Cardenas, Isidra T.; *Feminism; Idar, Jovita; *Journalists; *Mexican Revolution - 1910-1920; Newspapers; Ramirez, Sara Estela; Villarreal, Andrea; Villegas de Magnon, Leonor.

3570 Luna-Lawhn, Juanita. EL REGIDOR and LA PRENSA: impediments to women's self-definition. THIRD WOMAN, Vol. 4, (1989), p. 134-142. English. DESCR: EL REGIDOR, San Antonio, TX; LA PRENSA, San Antonio, TX; *Newspapers; Sex Roles; *Sexism.

3571 Miller, Elaine N. and Sternbach, Nancy Saporta. Selected bibliography. IN: Horno-Delgado, Asuncion, et al., eds. BREAKING BOUNDARIES: LATINA WRITING AND CRITICAL READINGS. Amherst, MA: University of Massachusetts Press, c1989, p. 251-263. English. DESCR: *Bibliography; Cubanos; Literary Criticism; Puerto Ricans; *Women.

3572 Monk, Janice and Norwood, Vera. Angles of vision: enhancing our perspectives on the Southwest. IN: Lensirk, Judy Nolte, ed. OLD SOUTHWEST/NEW SOUTHWEST: ESSAYS ON A REGION AND ITS LITERATURE. Tucson, AZ: The Tucson Public Library, 1989, p. 39-47. English. DESCR: Literary Criticism; Southwestern United States; *Women.

3573 Navarro, Marta A. and Castillo, Ana. Interview with Ana Castillo. IN: Trujillo, Carla, ed. CHICANA LESBIANS: THE GIRLS OUR MOTHERS WARNED US ABOUT. Berkeley, CA: Third Woman Press, 1991, p. 113-132. English. DESCR: *Authors; Castillo, Ana; Homosexuality.

3574 Ordonez, Elizabeth J. Chicana literature and related sources: a selected and annotated bibliography. BILINGUAL REVIEW, Vol. 7, no. 2 (May, August, 1980), p. 143-164. English. DESCR: Bibliography.

3575 Perez-Erdelyi, Mireya and Corpi, Lucha. Entrevista con Lucha Corpi: poeta chicana. THE AMERICAS REVIEW, Vol. 17, no. 1 (Spring 1989), p. 72-82. Spanish. DESCR: Authors; *Corpi, Lucha.

3576 Quintana, Alvina E. Challenge and counter challenge: Chicana literary motifs. AGAINST THE CURRENT, Vol. 2, no. 2 (March, April, 1987), p. 25,28-32. English. DESCR: Anglo Americans; Authors; Cervantes, Lorna Dee; Cultural Studies; *Feminism; Identity; Literary Criticism; Moraga, Cherrie; THERE ARE NO MADMEN HERE; Valdes, Gina; Women.

3577 Quintana, Alvina E. Chicana discourse: negations and mediations. Thesis (Ph.D.)--University of California, Santa Cruz, 1989. 226 p. English. DESCR: Authors; Castillo, Ana; Chavez, Denise; Chicano Movement; Cisneros, Sandra; Ethnology; Feminism; Literary Criticism; NOVENA NARRATIVES; Oral Tradition; Political Ideology; THE HOUSE ON MANGO STREET; THE LAST OF THE MENU GIRLS; THE MIXQUIAHUALA LETTERS.

3578 Quintana, Alvina E. Chicana literary motifs: challenge and counter-challenge. IMAGES: ETHNIC STUDIES OCCASIONAL PAPERS SERIES, (Fall 1986), p. 24-41. English. DESCR: Anglo Americans; Authors; Cervantes, Lorna Dee; Cultural Studies; *Feminism; *Identity; *Literary Criticism; Moraga, Cherrie; THERE ARE NO MADMEN HERE; Valdes, Gina; Women.

3579 Ramos Escandon, Carmen. Alternative sources to women's history: literature. IN: Del Castillo, Adelaida R., ed. BETWEEN BORDERS: ESSAYS ON MEXICANA/CHICANA HISTORY. Encino, CA: Floricanto Press, 1990, p. 201-212. English. DESCR: *Sex Stereotypes; Stereotypes.

3580 Ramos, Juanita, ed. Companeras: Latina lesbians (an anthology). New York: Latina Lesbian History Project, 1987. xxix, 265 p. Bilingual. DESCR: *Homosexuality; Poetry; Prose; *Women.

3581 Rebolledo, Tey Diana. Hispanic women writers of the Southwest: tradition and innovation. IN: Lensink, Judy Nolte, ed. OLD SOUTHWEST/NEW SOUTHWEST: ESSAYS ON A REGION AND ITS LITERATURE. Tucson, AZ: The Tucson Public Library, 1987, p. 49-61. English. DESCR: *Authors; Cabeza de Baca, Fabiola; Jaramillo, Cleofas M.; Mora, Pat; OLD SPAIN IN OUR SOUTHWEST; Otero Warren, Nina; Preciado Martin, Patricia; Sex Roles; Sex Stereotypes; Silva, Beverly; *Southwestern United States; Vigil-Pinon, Evangelina; WE FED THEM CACTUS; *Women.

3582 Rebolledo, Tey Diana. Narrative strategies of resistance in Hispana writing. THE JOURNAL OF NARRATIVE TECHNIQUE, Vol. 20, no. 2 (Spring 1990), p. 134-146. English. DESCR: *Authors; Cabeza de Baca, Fabiola; Fiction; Jaramillo, Cleofas M.; *Literary Criticism; New Mexico; OLD SPAIN IN OUR SOUTHWEST; *Oral Tradition; Otero Warren, Nina; ROMANCE OF A LITTLE VILLAGE GIRL; WE FED THEM CACTUS.

3583 Rebolledo, Tey Diana. The politics of poetics: or, what am I, a critic, doing in this text anyhow? THE AMERICAS REVIEW, Vol. 15, no. 3-4 (Fall, Winter, 1987), p. 129-138. English. DESCR: *Literary Criticism; Literary History.

3584 Rebolledo, Tey Diana. The politics of poetics: or, what am I, a critic, doing in this text anyhow? IN: Anzaldua, Gloria, ed. MAKING FACE, MAKING SOUL: HACIENDO CARAS: CREATIVE AND CRITICAL PERSPECTIVES BY WOMEN OF COLOR. San Francisco, CA: Aunt Lute Foundation Books, 1990, p. 346-355. English. DESCR: *Literary Criticism; Literary History.

3585 Rebolledo, Tey Diana. Tradition and mythology: signatures of landscape in Chicana literature. IN: Norwood, Vera and Monk, Janice, eds. THE DESERT IS NO LADY: SOUTHWESTERN LANDSCAPES IN WOMEN'S WRITING AND ART. New Haven, CT: Yale University Press, 1987, p. 96-124. English. DESCR: *Authors; Cabeza de Baca, Fabiola; Chavez, Denise; Jaramillo, Cleofas M.; Literary Criticism; *Literary History; Mora, Pat; Mythology; Otero Warren, Nina; Portillo Trambley, Estela; Silva, Beverly; Southwestern United States; WE FED THEM CACTUS.

Literature (cont.)

3586 Rocard, Marcienne. The remembering voice in Chicana literature. THE AMERICAS REVIEW, Vol. 14, no. 3-4 (Fall, Winter, 1986), p. 150-159. English. DESCR: Culture.

3587 Rodriguez Aranda, Pilar E. and Cisneros, Sandra. On the solitary fate of being Mexican, female, wicked and thirty-three: an interview with writer Sandra Cisneros. THE AMERICAS REVIEW, Vol. 18, no. 1 (Spring 1990), p. 64-80. English. DESCR: *Artists; *Cisneros, Sandra; MY WICKED WICKED WAYS; THE HOUSE ON MANGO STREET.

3588 Salazar Parr, Carmen and Ramirez, Genevieve M. The Chicana in Chicano literature. IN: Martinez, Julio A. and Lomeli, Francisco A., eds. CHICANO LITERATURE: A REFERENCE GUIDE. Westport, CT: Greenwood Press, 1985, p. 97-107. English. DESCR: Literary Characters; Literary Criticism; *Stereotypes.

3589 Salazar Parr, Carmen. La Chicana in literature. IN: Garcia, Eugene E., et al., eds. CHICANO STUDIES: A MULTIDISCIPLINARY APPROACH. New York: Teachers College Press, 1984, p. 120-134. English. DESCR: DAY OF THE SWALLOWS; Literary Characters; Literary Criticism; Portillo Trambley, Estela; Stereotypes; Teatro; "The Trees" [short story].

3590 Saldivar, Ramon. The dialectics of subjectivity: gender and difference in Isabella Rios, Sandra Cisneros, and Cherrie Moraga. IN: Saldivar, Ramon. CHICANO NARRATIVE: THE DIALECTICS OF DIFFERENCE. Madison, WI: University of Wisconsin Press, 1990, p. 171-199. English. DESCR: Authors; Autobiography; *Cisneros, Sandra; Feminism; Fiction; *Literary Criticism; LOVING IN THE WAR YEARS; *Moraga, Cherrie; Political Ideology; *Rios, Isabella; THE HOUSE ON MANGO STREET; VICTUUM.

3591 Salinas, Judy. The image of woman in Chicano literature. REVISTA CHICANO-RIQUENA, Vol. 4, no. 4 (Fall 1976), p. 139-148. English. DESCR: Literary Characters; *Stereotypes.

3592 Tafolla, Carmen. Chicano literature: beyond beginnings. IN: Harris, Marie and Aguero, Kathleen, eds. A GIFT OF TONGUES: CRITICAL CHALLENGES IN CONTEMPORARY AMERICAN POETRY. Athens, GA: University of Georgia Press, 1987, p. 206-225. English. DESCR: *Authors; Cota-Cardenas, Margarita; Language Usage; *Literary Criticism; Portillo Trambley, Estela; Sex Stereotypes; Symbolism; Tafolla, Carmen; Vigil-Pinon, Evangelina.

3593 Vigil, Evangelina, ed. Woman of her word: Hispanic women write. REVISTA CHICANO-RIQUENA, Vol. 11, no. 3-4 (Fall, Winter, 1983), p. [1]-180. Bilingual. DESCR: Art; Literary Criticism; Poetry; Prose; *Women.

3594 Yarbro-Bejarano, Yvonne. Chicana literature from a Chicana feminist perspective. THE AMERICAS REVIEW, Vol. 15, no. 3-4 (Fall, Winter, 1987), p. 139-145. English. DESCR: *Feminism; *Literary Criticism.

3595 Zamora, Bernice. Mythopoeia of Chicano poetry: an introduction to cultural archetypes. Thesis (Ph.D.)--Stanford University, 1986. 341 p. English. DESCR: Literary Characters; Literary Criticism; Malinche; Pachucos; *Poetry; *Symbolism.

Literature Reviews

3596 Acuna, Rodolfo. The struggles of class and gender: current research in Chicano Studies [review essay]. JOURNAL OF AMERICAN ETHNIC HISTORY, Vol. 8, no. 2 (Spring 1989), p. 134-138. English. DESCR: *CANNERY WOMEN, CANNERY LIVES; *CHICANO ETHNICITY; Deutsch, Sarah; Keefe, Susan E.; *NO SEPARATE REFUGE; Padilla, Amado M.; Ruiz, Vicki L.; *WOMEN'S WORK AND CHICANO FAMILIES; Zavella, Pat.

3597 Alarcon, Norma. Latina writers in the United States. IN: Marting, Diane E., ed. SPANISH AMERICAN WOMEN WRITERS: A BIO-BIBLIOGRAPHICAL SOURCE BOOK. New York: Greenwood Press, 1990, p. [557]-567. English. DESCR: *Authors; *Bibliography; BREAKING BOUNDARIES: LATINA WRITING AND CRITICAL READINGS; Cubanos; Intergroup Relations; Language Usage; Puerto Ricans; THIRD WOMAN [journal]; *Women.

3598 Almaguer, Tomas. Urban Chicano workers in historical perspective: a review of recent literature. LA RED/THE NET, no. 68 (May 1983), p. 2-6. English. DESCR: *Labor; Working Women.

3599 Amaro, Hortensia. Abortion use and attitudes among Chicanas: the need for research. RESEARCH BULLETIN (SPANISH SPEAKING MENTAL HEALTH RES. CENTER), Vol. 4, no. 3 (March 1980), p. 1-5. English. DESCR: *Abortion; *Attitudes; Birth Control; Family Planning; Fertility; Mental Health.

3600 Amaro, Hortensia and Russo, Nancy Felipe. Hispanic women and mental health: an overview of contemporary issues in research and practice. PSYCHOLOGY OF WOMEN QUARTERLY, Vol. 11, no. 4 (December 1987), p. 393-407. English. DESCR: *Mental Health; *Women.

3601 Baca Zinn, Maxine. Mexican American women in the social sciences. SIGNS: JOURNAL OF WOMEN IN CULTURE AND SOCIETY, Vol. 8, no. 2 (Winter 1982), p. 259-272. English. DESCR: Social Science.

3602 Bridges, Julian C. Family life. IN: Stoddard, Ellwyn R., et al., eds. BORDERLANDS SOURCEBOOK: A GUIDE TO THE LITERATURE ON NORTHERN MEXICO AND THE AMERICAN SOUTHWEST. Norman, OK: University of Oklahoma Press, 1983, p. 259-262. English. DESCR: Border Region; *Family.

3603 Camarillo, Alberto M. The "new" Chicano history: historiography of Chicanos of the 1970s. IN: CHICANOS AND THE SOCIAL SCIENCES: A DECADE OF RESEARCH AND DEVELOPMENT (1970-1980) SYMPOSIUM WORKING PAPER. Santa Barbara, CA: Center for Chicano Studies, University of California, 1983, p. 9-17. English. DESCR: *Historiography; History; Urban Communities.

3604 Campos Carr, Irene. A survey of selected literature on La Chicana. NWSA JOURNAL, Vol. 1, (Winter 1988, 1989), p. 253-273. English. DESCR: Sexism; *Social Science.

Literature Reviews
(cont.)

3605 Candelaria, Cordelia. Six reference works on
Mexican-American women: a review essay.
FRONTIERS: A JOURNAL OF WOMEN STUDIES, Vol.
5, no. 2 (Summer 1980), p. 75-80. English.
DESCR: DIOSA Y HEMBRA: THE HISTORY AND
HERITAGE OF CHICANAS IN THE U.S.; ESSAYS ON
LA MUJER; LA CHICANA: THE MEXICAN AMERICAN
WOMAN; MEXICAN WOMEN IN THE UNITED STATES:
STRUGGLES PAST AND PRESENT; THE CHICANA: A
COMPREHENSIVE BIBLIOGRAPHIC STUDY; TWICE A
MINORITY: MEXICAN-AMERICAN WOMEN.

3606 Chabran, Richard. Chicana reference sources.
IN: Cordova, Teresa, et al., eds. CHICANA
VOICES. Austin, TX: Center for Mexican
American Studies, 1986, p. 146-156. English.
DESCR: Bibliography; *Reference Works.

3607 D'Andrea, Vaneeta-Marie. Ethnic women: a
critique of the literature, 1971-1981.
ETHNIC AND RACIAL STUDIES, Vol. 9, (April
1986), p. 235-246. English. DESCR:
Bibliography; Ethnic Groups; Periodical
Indexes; *Women.

3608 Del Castillo, Adelaida R. and Torres, Maria
The interdependency of educational
institutions and cultural norms: the Hispana
experience. IN: McKenna, Teresa and Ortiz,
Flora Ida, eds. THE BROKEN WEB: THE
EDUCATIONAL EXPERIENCE OF HISPANIC WOMEN.
Claremont, CA: Tomas Rivera Center;
Berkeley, CA: Floricanto Press, 1988, p.
39-60. English. DESCR: Academic Achievement;
Acculturation; *Cultural Characteristics;
*Education; Research Methodology; *Values;
Women.

3609 Flores, Estevan T. Chicanos and sociological
research: 1970-1980. IN: CHICANOS AND THE
SOCIAL SCIENCES: A DECADE OF RESEARCH AND
DEVELOPMENT (1970-1980) SYMPOSIUM WORKING
PAPER. Santa Barbara, CA: Center for Chicano
Studies, University of California, 1983, p.
19-45. English. DESCR: Bibliography; Family;
Internal Colony Model; Labor; Population;
Research Methodology; *Sociology.

3610 Garcia, Alma M. Studying Chicanas: bringing
women into the frame of Chicano Studies. IN:
Cordova, Teresa, et al., eds. CHICANA
VOICES. Austin, TX: Center for Mexican
American Studies, 1986, p. 19-29. English.
DESCR: Chicana Studies; *Chicano Studies;
Discrimination; Labor Supply and Market.

3611 Garcia, Mario T. Family and gender in
Chicano and border studies research. MEXICAN
STUDIES/ESTUDIOS MEXICANOS, Vol. 6, no. 1
(Winter 1990), p. 109-119. English. DESCR:
Alvarez, Robert R., Jr.; *Border Region;
CANNERY WOMEN, CANNERY LIVES; *Family; LA
FAMILIA: MIGRATION AND ADAPTATION IN BAJA
AND ALTA CALIFORNIA, 1800-1975; Ruiz, Vicki
L.; Tiano, Susan B.; Women; WOMEN ON THE
U.S.-MEXICO BORDER: RESPONSES TO CHANGE;
WOMEN'S WORK AND CHICANO FAMILIES; Zavella,
Pat.

3612 Job, Peggy. La sexualidad en la narrativa
femenina mexicana 1970-1987: una
aproximacion. THIRD WOMAN, Vol. 4, (1989),
p. 120-133. Spanish. DESCR: *Literature; Sex
Roles; *Sexual Behavior; *Women.

3613 Lavrin, Asuncion. El segundo sexo en Mexico:
experiencia, estudio e introspeccion,
1983-1987. MEXICAN STUDIES/ESTUDIOS
MEXICANOS, Vol. 5, no. 2 (Summer 1989), p.
297-312. Spanish. DESCR: Arenal, Sandra;
*Border Industries; Carrillo, Jorge;

Hernandez, Alberto; Iglesias, Norma; LA FLOR
MAS BELLA DE LA MAQUILADORA; Mexico; MUJERES
FRONTERIZAS EN LA INDUSTRIA MAQUILADORA;
SANGRE JOVEN: LAS MAQUILADORAS POR DENTRO;
Women.

3614 Lucero, Marcela Christine. Resources for the
Chicana feminist scholar. IN: Treichler,
Paula A., et al., eds. FOR ALMA MATER:
THEORY AND PRACTICE IN FEMINIST SCHOLARSHIP.
Urbana: University of Illinois Press, 1985,
p. 393-401. English. DESCR: *Chicana
Studies; *Feminism; Publishing Industry;
Research Methodology.

3615 Orozco, Cynthia. Getting started in Chicana
Studies. WOMEN'S STUDIES QUARTERLY, no. 1-2
(1990), p. 46-69. English. DESCR:
Bibliography; *Chicana Studies.

3616 Ramirez, Oscar and Arce, Carlos H. The
contemporary Chicano family: an empirically
based review. IN: Baron, Augustine, Jr., ed.
EXPLORATIONS IN CHICANO PSYCHOLOGY. New
York: Praeger, 1981, p. 3-28. English.
DESCR: *Family; Fertility; Machismo;
Population; Sex Roles.

3617 Solorzano-Torres, Rosalia. Female Mexican
immigrants in San Diego County. IN: Ruiz,
Vicki L. and Tiano, Susan, eds. WOMEN ON THE
U.S.-MEXICO BORDER: RESPONSES TO CHANGE.
Boston, MA: Allen & Unwin, 1987, p. 41-59.
English. DESCR: Employment; *Immigrants;
Immigration; San Diego County, CA; Surveys;
Undocumented Workers; Women.

3618 Soto, Shirlene Ann. The emerging Chicana: a
review of the journals. SOUTHWEST ECONOMY
AND SOCIETY, Vol. 2, no. 1 (October,
November, 1976), p. 39-45. English. DESCR:
Directories; Journals.

3619 Sweeney, Judith. Chicana history: a review
of the literature. IN: Sanchez, Rosaura and
Martinez Cruz, Rosa, eds. ESSAYS ON LA
MUJER. Los Angeles, CA: Chicano Studies
Center Publications, UCLA, 1977, p. 99-123.
English. DESCR: *History.

3620 Tatum, Charles M. Grappling with difference:
gender, race, class, and ethnicity in
contemporary Chicana/o literature. RENATO
ROSALDO LECTURE SERIES MONOGRAPH, Vol. 6,
(1988, 1989), p. 1-23. English. DESCR:
Anaya, Rudolfo A.; Authors; BLESS ME,
ULTIMA; *Feminism; Identity; Literary
Characters; *Literary Criticism.

3621 Vazquez-Nuttall, Ena; Romero-Garcia, Ivonne;
and De Leon, Brunilda. Sex roles and
perceptions of femininity and masculinity of
Hispanic women: a review of the literature.
PSYCHOLOGY OF WOMEN QUARTERLY, Vol. 11, no.
4 (December 1987), p. 409-425. English.
DESCR: Attitudes; *Chicanismo; Machismo;
Puerto Ricans; *Sex Roles; *Women.

Lizarraga, Sylvia

3622 Herrera-Sobek, Maria. The politics of rape:
sexual transgression in Chicana fiction. THE
AMERICAS REVIEW, Vol. 15, no. 3-4 (Fall,
Winter, 1987), p. 171-181. English. DESCR:
Cisneros, Sandra; *Feminism; Fiction; GIVING
UP THE GHOST; *Literary Criticism; Moraga,
Cherrie; *Rape; "Red Clowns" [short story];
Sex Roles; "Silver Lake Road" [short story].

Lizarraga, Sylvia
(cont.)

3623 Sanchez, Rosaura. Chicana prose writers: the case of Gina Valdes and Sylvia Lizarraga. IN: Herrera-Sobek, Maria, ed. BEYOND STEREOTYPES: THE CRITICAL ANALYSIS OF CHICANA LITERATURE. Binghamton, NY: Bilingual Press/Editorial Bilingue, 1985, p. 61-70. English. DESCR: *Authors; Literary Criticism; Prose; *Valdes, Gina.

La Llorona

3624 Fox, Linda C. Obedience and rebellion: re-vision of Chicana myths of motherhood. WOMEN'S STUDIES QUARTERLY, Vol. 11, no. 4 (Winter 1983), p. 20-22. English. DESCR: Feminism; Malinche; *Parent and Child Relationships.

3625 Herrera-Sobek, Maria. Women as metaphor in the patriarchal structure of HEART OF AZTLAN. IN: Gonzalez-T., Cesar A. RUDOLFO A. ANAYA: FOCUS ON CRITICISM. La Jolla, CA: Lalo Press, 1990, p. [165]-182. English. DESCR: Anaya, Rudolfo A.; *HEART OF AZTLAN; *Literary Characters; Literary Criticism; Sex Roles.

3626 Jones, Pamela. "There was a woman": La Llorona in Oregon. WESTERN FOLKLORE, Vol. 47, no. 3 (July 1988), p. 195-211. English. DESCR: Folklore; *Leyendas; Oregon; Research Methodology.

3627 Jordan, Rosan Augusta. The vaginal serpent and other themes from Mexican-American women's lore. IN: Jordan, Rosan A. and Kalcik, Susan J., eds. WOMEN'S FOLKLORE, WOMEN'S CULTURE. Philadelphia: University of Pennsylvania Press, 1985, p. 26-44. English. DESCR: Cuentos; Fertility; *Folklore; *Leyendas; *Sex Roles; Sexism; Sexual Behavior.

3628 Limon, Jose E. [anthropologist]. La Llorona, the third legend of greater Mexico: cultural symbols, women, and the political unconscious. RENATO ROSALDO LECTURE SERIES MONOGRAPH, Vol. 2, (Spring 1986), p. [59]-93. English. DESCR: *Feminism; Folklore; La Virgen de Guadalupe; *Leyendas; Malinche; Mexico; *Symbolism; Women.

3629 Limon, Jose E. [anthropologist]. La Llorona, the third legend of greater Mexico: cultural symbols, women, and the political unconscious. IN: Del Castillo, Adelaida R. BETWEEN BORDERS: ESSAYS ON MEXICANA/CHICANA HISTORY. Encino, CA: Floricanto Press, 1990, p. 399-432. English. DESCR: *Feminism; Folklore; La Virgen de Guadalupe; *Leyendas; Malinche; Mexico; *Symbolism; Women.

3630 Soto, Shirlene Ann. Tres modelos culturales: la Virgen de Guadalupe, la Malinche y la Llorona. FEM, Vol. 10, no. 48 (October, November, 1986), p. 13-16. Spanish. DESCR: Guadalupanismo; *La Virgen de Guadalupe; *Malinche; Symbolism; Women.

Loans (Student)
USE: Financial Aid

Local Government

3631 Karnig, Albert K.; Welch, Susan; and Eribes, Richard A. Employment of women by cities in the Southwest. SOCIAL SCIENCE JOURNAL, Vol. 21, no. 4 (October 1984), p. 41-48. English. DESCR: *Employment; Southwestern United States; Women.

Locus of Control

3632 Adams, Russell P. Predictors of self-esteem and locus-of-control in Mexican-American women. Thesis (Ph.D.)--Texas Tech University, 1989. 138 p. English. DESCR: *Identity; Mental Health; Research Methodology.

3633 Armas-Cardona, Regina. Anglo and Raza young women: a study of self-esteem, psychic distress and locus of control. Thesis (Ph.D.)--Wright Institute Graduate School of Psychology, 1985. 143 p. English. DESCR: *Anglo Americans; *Mental Health; Stress; *Women.

3634 Atkinson, Donald R.; Winzelberg, Andrew; and Holland, Abby. Ethnicity, locus of control for family planning, and pregnancy counselor credibility. JOURNAL OF COUNSELING PSYCHOLOGY, Vol. 32, no. 3 (July 1985), p. 417-421. English. DESCR: Anglo Americans; Counseling (Psychological); *Family Planning; Fertility; Identity; Women.

3635 Jackson, Laurie Elizabeth. Self-care agency and limitations with respect to contraceptive behavior of Mexican-American women. Thesis (M.S.N.)--Medical College of Ohio at Toledo, 1988. 198 p. English. DESCR: *Birth Control; *Fertility.

3636 Kluessendorf, Avonelle Donneeta. Role conflict in Mexican-American college women. Thesis (Ph.D.)--California School of Professional Psychology, Fresno, 1985. 111 p. English. DESCR: *Colleges and Universities; *Sex Roles; *Stress; Students.

3637 Melgoza, Bertha; Roll, Samuel; and Baker, Richard C. Conformity and cooperation in Chicanos: the case of the missing susceptibility to influence. JOURNAL OF COMMUNITY PSYCHOLOGY, Vol. 11, no. 4 (October 1983), p. 323-333. English. DESCR: *Comparative Psychology; *Cultural Characteristics; Socialization; Stereotypes; Women.

3638 Nyamathi, Adeline M. and Vasquez, Rose. Impact of poverty, homelessness, and drugs on Hispanic women at risk for HIV infection. HISPANIC JOURNAL OF BEHAVIORAL SCIENCES, Vol. 11, no. 4 (November 1989), p. 299-314. English. DESCR: *AIDS (Disease); Drug Use; Health Education; *Human Immunodeficiency Virus (HIV); Mental Health; Needle-Sharing; *Poverty.

Logos
USE: Symbolism

Lomas Garza, Carmen

3639 Goldman, Shifra M. Artistas en accion: conferencia de las mujeres chicanas. LA COMUNIDAD, (August 10, 1980), p. 15. Spanish. DESCR: *Artists; Chicano Studies; Conferences and Meetings; Flores, Gloriamalia.

Lomas Garza, Carmen
(cont.)

3640 Goldman, Shifra M. Mujeres de California:
Latin American women artists. IN: Moore,
Sylvia, ed. YESTERDAY AND TOMORROW:
CALIFORNIA WOMEN ARTISTS. New York, NY:
Midmarch Arts Press, c1989, p. 202-229.
English. DESCR: *Artists; Baca, Judith F.;
Biography; California; Carrasco, Barbara;
Cervantez, Yreina; de Larios, Dora;
Feminism; Hernandez, Judithe; Lopez, Yolanda
M.; Mesa-Bains, Amalia; Murillo, Patricia;
Sanchez, Olivia; Valdez, Patssi; Vallejo
Dillaway, Linda; Women; Zamora Lucero,
Linda.

3641 Lomas Garza, Carmen. Altares: arte
espiritual del hogar. HOJAS, (1976), p.
105-111. English. DESCR: *Altars; Artists;
Folk Art; Religious Art.

3642 Moreno, Jose Adan and Lomas Garza, Carmen.
Carmen Lomas Garza: traditional and
non-traditional. CAMINOS, Vol. 5, no. 10
(November 1984), p. 44-45,53. English.
DESCR: *Artists.

Lopez, Lexore

3643 Ordonez, Elizabeth J. La imagen de la mujer
en el nuevo cine chicanc. CARACOL, Vol. 5,
no. 2 (October 1978), p. 12-13. Spanish.
DESCR: Bonilla-Giannini, Roxanna; *Films;
ONLY ONCE IN A LIFETIME [film];
*Photography; RAICES DE SANGRE [film];
Robelo, Miguel; Sex Stereotypes.

Lopez, Tony

3644 Santillanes, Maria. Women in prison--C.I.W.:
an editorial. REGENERACION, Vol. 2, no. 4
(1975), p. 53. English. DESCR: Conferences
and Meetings; Garcia, Dolly; La Mesa College
Pinto and Pinta Program; Mares, Rene;
Martinez, Miguel; Pinto Conference (1973:
UCLA); Player; *Prisons; Salazar, Peggy.

Lopez, Yolanda M.

3645 Goldman, Shifra M. Mujeres de California:
Latin American women artists. IN: Moore,
Sylvia, ed. YESTERDAY AND TOMORROW:
CALIFORNIA WOMEN ARTISTS. New York, NY:
Midmarch Arts Press, c1989, p. 202-229.
English. DESCR: *Artists; Baca, Judith F ;
Biography; California; Carrasco, Barbara
Cervantez, Yreina; de Larios, Dora;
Feminism; Hernandez, Judithe; Lomas Garza,
Carmen; Mesa-Bains, Amalia; Murillo,
Patricia; Sanchez, Olivia; Valdez, Patssi;
Vallejo Dillaway, Linda; Women; Zamora
Lucero, Linda.

3646 Johnston Hernandez, Beatriz. Life as art.
VISTA, Vol. 3, no. 12 (August 7, 1988), p.
18,34. English. DESCR: *Artists; Paintings.

3647 La Duke, Betty. Trivial lives: artists
Yolanda Lopez and Patricia Rodriguez.
TRIVIA: A JOURNAL OF IDEAS, (Winter 1986),
p. 74-85. English. DESCR: Artists;
Biography; *Rodriguez, Patricia.

Los Angeles, CA

3648 Burnham, Linda. Patssi Valdez. HIGH
PERFORMANCE, Vol. 9, no. 3 (1986), p. 54.
English. DESCR: *Artists; ASCO [art group];
Los Angeles, CA; Performing Arts; Valdez,
Patssi.

3649 Engle, Patricia L. Prenatal and postnatal
anxiety in women giving birth in Los

Angeles. HEALTH PSYCHOLOGY, Vol. 9, no. 3
(1990), p. 285-299. English. DESCR:
*Fertility; Immigrants; *Maternal and Child
Welfare; Medical Care; *Prenatal Care;
*Stress; Women.

3650 Erickson, Pamela Irene. Pregnancy and
childbirth among Mexican origin teenagers in
Los Angeles. Thesis (Ph.D.)--UCLA, 1988.
xiii, 277 leaves. English. DESCR:
*Fertility; Medical Care; *Youth.

3651 Garcia, Chris; Guerro, Connie Destito; and
Mendez, Irene. La violacion sexual: the
reality of rape. AGENDA, Vol. 8, no. 5
(September, October, 1978), p. 10-11.
English. DESCR: Attitudes; *Rape.

3652 Harris, Mary G. Cholas: Latino girls and
gangs. New York: AMS Press, 1988. x, 220 p.
English. DESCR: Barrios; *Gangs; Juvenile
Delinquency; San Fernando Valley, CA;
*Youth.

3653 Monroy, Douglas. La costura en Los Angeles,
1933-1939: the ILGWU and the politics of
domination. IN: Mora, Magdalena and Del
Castillo, Adelaida, eds. MEXICAN WOMEN IN
THE UNITED STATES: STRUGGLES PAST AND
PRESENT. Los Angeles, CA: Chicano Studies
Research Center, UCLA, 1980, p. 171-178.
English. DESCR: *Garment Industry; History;
International Ladies Garment Workers Union
(ILGWU); Labor Unions.

3654 Powell, Douglas R.; Zambrana, Ruth E.; and
Silva-Palacios, Victor. Designing culturally
responsive parent programs: a comparison of
low-income Mexican and Mexican-American
mothers' preferences. FAMILY RELATIONS, Vol.
39, no. 3 (July 1990), p. 298-304. English.
DESCR: Acculturation; Children; Education;
Immigrants; Low Income; *Parent and Child
Relationships; *Parenting; Women.

3655 Richardson, Jean L., et al. Frequency and
adequacy of breast cancer screening among
elderly Hispanic women. PREVENTIVE MEDICINE,
Vol. 16, no. 6 (November 1987), p. 761-774.
English. DESCR: Ancianos; *Cancer; Diseases;
*Health Education; *Medical Care;
Preventative Medicine.

3656 Sabagh, Georges. Fertility expectations and
behavior among Mexican Americans in Los
Angeles, 1973-82. SOCIAL SCIENCE QUARTERLY,
Vol. 65, no. 2 (June 1984), p. 594-608.
English. DESCR: *Fertility; Immigrants.

3657 Salgado de Snyder, Nelly and Padilla, Amado
M. Interethnic marriages of Mexican
Americans after nearly two decades. [Los
Angeles, CA]: Spanish Speaking Mental Health
Research Center, 1985. 43 p. English.
DESCR: *Assimilation; Intergroup Relations;
*Intermarriage.

3658 Scrimshaw, Susan C.M., et al. Factors
affecting breastfeeding among women of
Mexican origin or descent in Los Angeles.
AMERICAN JOURNAL OF PUBLIC HEALTH, Vol. 77,
no. 4 (April 1987), p. 467-470. English.
DESCR: Acculturation; *Breastfeeding;
Immigrants; Working Women.

3659 Simon, Rita J. and DeLey, Margo. The work
experience of undocumented Mexican women
migrants in Los Angeles. INTERNATIONAL
MIGRATION REVIEW, Vol. 18, no. 4 (Winter
1984), p. 1212-1229. English. DESCR:
Immigrants; Income; Population;
Socioeconomic Factors; *Undocumented
Workers; *Working Women.

Los Angeles, CA (cont.)

3660 Sorenson, Susan B. and Telles, Cynthia A. Self-reports of spousal violence in a Mexican-American and non-Hispanic white population. VIOLENCE AND VICTIMS, Vol. 6, no. 1 (1991), p. 3-15. English. DESCR: Anglo Americans; *Battered Women; Los Angeles Epidemiologic Catchment Area Research Program (LAECA); Rape; Violence; Women; *Women Men Relations.

3661 Taylor, Paul S. Mexican women in Los Angeles industry in 1928. AZTLAN, Vol. 11, no. 1 (Spring 1980), p. 99-131. English. DESCR: Employment; History; Industrial Workers; *Working Women.

3662 Velez-I., Carlos G. The nonconsenting sterilization of Mexican women in Los Angeles: issues of psychocultural rupture and legal redress in paternalistic behavioral environments. IN: Melville, Margarita B., ed. TWICE A MINORITY. St. Louis, MO: Mosby, 1980, p. 235-248. English. DESCR: Dolores Madrigal, et al., Plaintiff, v. E.J. Quilligan, et al.; Legal Cases; *Sterilization.

3663 Velez-I., Carlos G. Se me acabo la cancion: an ethnography of non-consenting sterilizations among Mexican women in Los Angeles. IN: Mora, Magdalena and Del Castillo, Adelaida, eds. MEXICAN WOMEN IN THE UNITED STATES: STRUGGLES PAST AND PRESENT. Los Angeles, CA: Chicano Studies Research Center, UCLA, 1980, p. 71-91. English. DESCR: Ethnology; Madrigal v. Quilligan; *Sterilization.

3664 Zavala Martinez, Iris Zoraida. Depression among women of Mexican descent. Thesis (Ph.D.)--University of Massachusetts, 1984. 295 p. English. DESCR: *Depression (Psychological); Mental Health.

Los Angeles County, CA

3665 Aneshensel, Carol S., et al. Participation of Mexican American adolescents in a longitudinal panel survey. PUBLIC OPINION QUARTERLY, Vol. 53, no. 4 (Winter 1989), p. 548-562. English. DESCR: Age Groups; *Fertility; Social Science; *Surveys; *Women Men Relations; *Youth.

3666 Arguelles, Lourdes and Rivero, Anne M. HIV infection/AIDS and Latinas in Los Angeles County: considerations for prevention, treatment, and research practice. CALIFORNIA SOCIOLOGIST, Vol. 11, no. 1-2 (1988), p. 69-89. English. DESCR: *AIDS (Disease); Cultural Characteristics; Health Education; Homosexuality; Human Immunodeficiency Virus (HIV); Natural Support Systems; Parent and Child Relationships; Sexual Behavior; *Women.

3667 Balkwell, Carolyn Ann. Widowhood: its impact on morale and optimism among older persons of three ethnic groups. Thesis (Ph.D.)--University of Georgia, 1981. 170 p. English. DESCR: *Ancianos; Anglo Americans; Blacks; Depression (Psychological); Ethnic Groups; *Mental Health; Widowhood; *Women.

3668 Fernandez Kelly, Maria and Garcia, Anna M. The making of an underground economy: Hispanic women, home work, and the advanced capitalist state. URBAN ANTHROPOLOGY, Vol. 14, no. 1-3 (Spring, Fall, 1985), p. 59-90. English. DESCR: Capitalism; Cubanos; Employment; Garment Industry; Industrial Workers; International Economic Relations;

Labor Supply and Market; *Miami, FL; Women; Working Women.

3669 Flaskerud, Jacquelyn H. and Nyamathi, Adeline M. Black and Latina womens' AIDS related knowledge, attitudes, and practices. RESEARCH IN NURSING AND HEALTH, Vol. 12, no. 6 (December 1989), p. 339-346. English. DESCR: *AIDS (Disease); Attitudes; *Blacks; Health Education; Surveys; *Women.

3670 Gould, Jeffrey B.; Davey, Becky; and Stafford, Randall S. Socioeconomic differences in rates of cesarean section. THE NEW ENGLAND JOURNAL OF MEDICINE, Vol. 321, no. 4 (July 27, 1989), p. 233-239. English. DESCR: Anglo Americans; Asian Americans; Blacks; *Cesarean Section; *Fertility; *Socioeconomic Factors; Vital Statistics; Women.

3671 Peters, Ruth K., et al. Risk factors for invasive cervical cancer among Latinas and non-Latinas in Los Angeles County. JOURNAL OF THE NATIONAL CANCER INSTITUTE, Vol. 77, no. 5 (November 1986), p. 1063-1077. English. DESCR: *Cancer; Diseases; Educational Levels; *Public Health; Women.

3672 Radecki, Stephen E. and Bernstein, Gerald S. Use of clinic versus private family planning care by low-income women: access, cost and patient satisfaction. AMERICAN JOURNAL OF PUBLIC HEALTH, Vol. 79, no. 6 (June 1989), p. 692-697. English. DESCR: *Family Planning; *Low Income; Medical Care; *Medical Clinics; Medical Personnel.

3673 Remez, Lisa. Rates of adolescent pregnancy and childbearing are high among Mexican-born Mexican Americans. FAMILY PLANNING PERSPECTIVES, Vol. 23, no. 2 (March, April, 1991), p. 88-89. English. DESCR: *Fertility; *Immigrants; *Sexual Behavior; *Youth.

Los Angeles Epidemiologic Catchment Area Research Program (LAECA)

3674 Sorenson, Susan B. and Telles, Cynthia A. Self-reports of spousal violence in a Mexican-American and non-Hispanic white population. VIOLENCE AND VICTIMS, Vol. 6, no. 1 (1991), p. 3-15. English. DESCR: Anglo Americans; *Battered Women; Los Angeles, CA; Rape; Violence; Women; *Women Men Relations.

Los Robles, Cuernavaca, Morelos, Mexico

3675 LeVine, Sarah Ethel; Correa, Clara Sunderland; and Uribe, F. Medardo Tapia. The marital morality of Mexican women--an urban study. JOURNAL OF ANTHROPOLOGICAL RESEARCH, Vol. 42, no. 2 (Summer 1986), p. 183-202. English. DESCR: Family; *Machismo; Marriage; Parent and Child Relationships; *Sex Roles; Women; *Women Men Relations.

LOVING IN THE WAR YEARS

3676 Saldivar, Ramon. The dialectics of subjectivity: gender and difference in Isabella Rios, Sandra Cisneros, and Cherrie Moraga. IN: Saldivar, Ramon. CHICANO NARRATIVE: THE DIALECTICS OF DIFFERENCE. Madison, WI: University of Wisconsin Press, 1990, p. 171-199. English. DESCR: Authors; Autobiography; *Cisneros, Sandra; Feminism; Fiction; *Literary Criticism; Literature; *Moraga, Cherrie; Political Ideology; *Rios, Isabella; THE HOUSE ON MANGO STREET; VICTUUM.

LOVING IN THE WAR YEARS
(cont.)

3677 Sternbach, Nancy Saporta. "A deep racial memory of love": the Chicana feminism of Cherrie Moraga. IN: Horno-Delgado, Asuncion, et al., eds. BREAKING BOUNDARIES: LATINA WRITING AND CRITICAL READINGS. Amherst, MA: University of Massachusetts Press, c1989, p. 48-61. English. DESCR: Discrimination; Feminism; Homosexuality; Literary Criticism; Machismo; Malinche; *Moraga, Cherrie; Sex Stereotypes; Sexism.

3678 Yarbro-Bejarano, Yvonne. De-constructing the lesbian body: Cherrie Moraga's LOVING IN THE WAR YEARS. IN: Trujillo, Carla, ed. CHICANA LESBIANS: THE GIRLS OUR MOTHERS WARNED US ABOUT. Berkeley, CA: Third Woman Press, 1991, p. 143-155. English. DESCR: Homosexuality; Literary Criticism; *Moraga, Cherrie; Skin Color.

Low Income

3679 Carrasco, Frank F. Teaching strategies used by Chicano mothers with their Head Start children. Thesis (Ph.D.)--University of Colorado, Boulder, 1933. 177 p. English. DESCR: Bilingualism; Children; *Education; *Parent and Child Relationships; *Parenting.

3680 Cummings, Michele and Cummings, Scott. Family planning among the urban poor: sexual politics and social policy. FAMILY RELATIONS, Vol. 32, no. 1 (January 1983), p. 47-58. English. DESCR: Anglo Americans; Blacks; Discrimination; *Family Planning; *Stereotypes.

3681 Gonzalez, Judith Teresa. Factors relating to frequency of breast self-examination among low-income Mexican American women: implications for nursing practice. CANCER NURSING, Vol. 13, no 3 (June 1990), p. 134-142. English. DESCR: *Breast Cancer; Cancer; Medical Care; Medical Personnel; *Preventative Medicine.

3682 Gonzalez, Judith Teresa and Gonzalez, Virginia M. Initial validation of a scale measuring self-efficacy of breast self-examination among low-income Mexican American women. HISPANIC JOURNAL OF BEHAVIORAL SCIENCES, Vol. 12, no. 3 (August 1990), p. 277-291. English. DESCR: *Cancer; Medical Care; Medical Education; Preventative Medicine.

3683 Hendricks, Mary Lee. Factors relating to the continuation of breast feeding by low income Hispanic women. Thesis (M.S.)--California State University, Long Beach, 1986. 94 p. English. DESCR: *Breastfeeding.

3684 Hunt, Isabelle F., et al. Zinc supplementation during pregnancy: zinc concentration of serum and hair from low-income women of Mexican descent. AMERICAN JOURNAL OF CLINICAL NUTRITION, Vol. 37, no. 4 (April 1983) p. 572-582. English DESCR: Nutrition; *Prenatal Care; Surveys.

3685 Leblanc, Donna Marie. Quality of maternity care in rural Texas. Thesis (Dr. P.H.) --University of Texas H.S.C. at Houston School of Public Health, 1983. 266 p. English. DESCR: Fertility; *Maternal and Child Welfare; *Medical Care; Prenatal Care; *Rural Poor; Texas.

3686 Lopez-Trevino, Maria Elena. A radio model: a community strategy to address the problems and needs of Mexican-American women

farmworkers. Thesis (M.S.)--California State University, Long Beach, 1989. 179 p. English. DESCR: Coachella, CA; *Farm Workers; Income; Occupational Hazards; *Radio; *Sex Roles.

3687 Marin, Barbara Van Oss, et al. Health care utilization by low-income clients of a community clinic: an archival study. HISPANIC JOURNAL OF BEHAVIORAL SCIENCES, Vol. 3, no. 3 (September 1981), p. 257-273. English. DESCR: Family Planning; La Clinica Familiar del Barrio, Los Angeles, CA; *Medical Care; Medical Clinics.

3688 Ortiz, Sylvia and Casas, Jesus Manuel. Birth control and low-income Mexican-American women: the impact of three values. HISPANIC JOURNAL OF BEHAVIORAL SCIENCES, Vol. 12, no. 1 (February 1990), p. 83-92. English. DESCR: Acculturation; Attitudes; *Birth Control; Fertility; *Sex Roles; Values.

3689 Padgett, Deborah. Aging minority women. WOMEN & HEALTH, Vol. 14, no. 3-4 (1988), p. 213-225. English. DESCR: *Ancianos; Public Health; *Women.

3690 Powell, Douglas R.; Zambrana, Ruth E.; and Silva-Palacios, Victor. Designing culturally responsive parent programs: a comparison of low-income Mexican and Mexican-American mothers' preferences. FAMILY RELATIONS, Vol. 39, no. 3 (July 1990), p. 298-304. English. DESCR: Acculturation; Children; Education; Immigrants; Los Angeles, CA; *Parent and Child Relationships; *Parenting; Women.

3691 Radecki, Stephen E. and Bernstein, Gerald S. Use of clinic versus private family planning care by low-income women: access, cost and patient satisfaction. AMERICAN JOURNAL OF PUBLIC HEALTH, Vol. 79, no. 6 (June 1989), p. 692-697. English. DESCR: *Family Planning; Los Angeles County, CA; Medical Care; *Medical Clinics; Medical Personnel.

3692 Ramirez Boulette, Teresa. Assertive training with low income Mexican American women. IN: Miranda, Manuel R., ed. PSYCHOTHERAPY WITH THE SPANISH-SPEAKING: ISSUES IN RESEARCH AND SERVICE DELIVERY. Los Angeles, CA: Spanish Speaking Mental Health Research Center, University of California, 1976, p. 67-71. English. DESCR: *Assertiveness.

3693 Swinney, Gloria Luyas. The biocultural context of low-income Mexican-American women with type II non-insulin dependent diabetes and its implications for health care delivery. Thesis (Ph.D.)--University of Texas, Austin, 1988. 277 p. English. DESCR: *Diabetes; *Medical Care; Non-insulin Dependent Diabetes Mellitus (NIDDM).

3694 Vega, William A.; Kolody, Bohdan; and Valle, Juan Ramon. The relationship of marital status, confidant support, and depression among Mexican immigrant women. JOURNAL OF MARRIAGE AND THE FAMILY, Vol. 48, no. 3 (August 1986), p. 597-605. English. DESCR: *Depression (Psychological); *Immigrants; *Marriage; San Diego County, CA; Stress; Women.

3695 Zambrana, Ruth E., et al. Ethnic differences in the substance use patterns of low-income pregnant women. FAMILY & COMMUNITY HEALTH, Vol. 13, no. 4 (January 1991), p. 1-11. English. DESCR: Alcoholism; Blacks; *Drug Use; *Fertility; Immigrants; Smoking; Women.

Lower Class
USE: Social Classes

Lucero, Judy A.

3696 Sanchez, Marta E. Judy Lucero and Bernice Zamora: two dialectical statements in Chicana poetry. DE COLORES, Vol. 4, no. 3 (1978), p. 22-33. Bilingual. **DESCR:** Gomez-Quinones, Juan; *Literary Criticism; *Poetry; Zamora, Bernice.

3697 Sanchez, Marta E. Judy Lucero and Bernice Zamora: two dialectical statements in Chicana poetry. IN: Sommers, Joseph and Ybarra-Frausto, Tomas, eds. MODERN CHICANO WRITERS: A COLLECTION OF CRITICAL ESSAYS. Englewood Cliffs, NJ: Prentice-Hall, 1979, p. 141-149. English. **DESCR:** Gomez-Quinones, Juan; *Literary Criticism; *Poetry; Zamora, Bernice.

3698 Zamora, Bernice. Archetypes in Chicana poetry. DE COLORES, Vol. 4, no. 3 (1978), p. 43-52. English. **DESCR:** Cervantes, Lorna Dee; Cunningham, Veronica; "Declaration on a Day of Little Inspiration" [poem]; Hernandez, Carlota; "I Speak in an Illusion" [poem]; *Literary Criticism; Macias, Margarita; Mendoza, Rita; "Para Mi Hijita" [poem]; *Poetry; "Rape Report" [poem]; "The White Line" [poem]; "Working Mother's Song" [poem]; "You Can Only Blame the System for So Long" [poem]; Zamora, Katarina.

Lujan, Josie

3699 Espinosa, Ann. Hispanas: our resourses [sic] for the eighties. LA LUZ, Vol. 8, no. 4 (October, November, 1979), p. 10-13. English. **DESCR:** Baca Barragan, Polly; *Civil Rights; Comision Femenil Mexicana Nacional; DIRECTORY OF HISPANIC WOMEN; Discrimination in Education; Elected Officials; Hernandez, Irene; Lacayo, Carmela; Mexican American Women's National Association (MANA); Montanez Davis, Grace; Moreno, Olga; Mujeres Latinas en Accion (M.L.A.); National Conference of Puerto Rican Women, Inc. (NCOPRW); Organizations; Rangel, Irma.

Luna Mount, Julia

3700 Escalante, Virginia; Rivera, Nancy; and Valle, Victor Manuel. Inside the world of Latinas. IN: SOUTHERN CALIFORNIA'S LATINO COMMUNITY: A SERIES OF ARTICLES REPRINTED FROM THE LOS ANGELES TIMES. Los Angeles: Los Angeles Times, 1983, p. 82-91. English. **DESCR:** *Biography; Castillo Fierro, Catalina (Katie); Gaitan, Maria Elena; Gutierrez, Nancy; Ramirez, Cristina.

Machismo

3701 Abajo con los machos [letter to the editor]. LA RAZA, Vol. 1, no. 5 (1971), p. 3-4. English. **DESCR:** Chicano Movement; Women Men Relations.

3702 Alonso, Ana Maria and Koreck, Maria Teresa. Silences: "Hispanics", AIDS, and sexual practices. DIFFERENCES: A JOURNAL OF FEMINIST CULTURAL STUDIES, Vol. 1, no. 1 (Winter 1989), p. 101-124. English. **DESCR:** *AIDS (Disease); *Homosexuality; Human Immunodeficiency Virus (HIV); Mexico; *Self-Referents; Sex Roles; *Sexual Behavior.

3703 Baca Zinn, Maxine. Chicanas: power and control in the domestic sphere. DE COLORES, Vol. 2, no. 3 (1975), p. 19-31. English. **DESCR:** *Family; Immigration Regulation and Control; *Sex Roles; Stereotypes; *Women Men Relations.

3704 Baca Zinn, Maxine. Chicanas: power and control in the domestic sphere. IN: Cotera, Martha and Hufford, Larry, eds. BRIDGING TWO CULTURES. Austin, TX: National Educational Laboratory Publishers, 1980, p. 270-281. English. **DESCR:** Family; Immigration Regulation and Control; Sex Roles; *Stereotypes; Women Men Relations.

3705 Baca Zinn, Maxine. Chicano men and masculinity. JOURNAL OF ETHNIC STUDIES, Vol. 10, no. 2 (Summer 1982), p. 29-44. English. **DESCR:** Cultural Characteristics; Ethnic Stratification; Sex Roles; Sex Stereotypes; Socioeconomic Factors; Women Men Relations.

3706 Baca Zinn, Maxine. Political familism: toward sex role equality in Chicano families. AZTLAN, Vol. 6, no. 1 (Spring 1975), p. 13-26. English. **DESCR:** Acculturation; Chicano Movement; Family; *Sex Roles.

3707 Bach-y-Rita, George. The Mexican-American: religious and cultural influences. IN: Becerra, Rosina M. et al., eds. MENTAL HEALTH AND HISPANIC AMERICANS: CLINICAL PERSPECTIVES. New York: Grune & Stratton, 1982, p. 29-40. English. **DESCR:** Catholic Church; Cultural Characteristics; Culture; Language Usage; *Mental Health; Psychotherapy; Religion.

3708 Cardenas, Reyes. The machismo manifesto. CARACOL, Vol. 2, no. 8 (April 1976), p. 7. Bilingual. **DESCR:** Cotera, Marta P.; Malinche; Women Men Relations.

3709 Cordova, Marcella C. Women's rights: a Chicana's viewpoint. LA LUZ, Vol. 4, no. 2 (May 1975), p. 3. English. **DESCR:** Feminism; *Women Men Relations.

3710 Del Zotto, Augusta. Latinas with AIDS: life expectancy for Hispanic women is a startling 45 days after diagnosis. THIS WORLD, (April 9, 1989), p. 9. English. **DESCR:** Abortion; AIDS (Disease); Condom Use; Instituto Familiar de la Raza, San Francisco, CA; *Mano a Mano; Quintero, Juanita; Sex Roles; Women Men Relations.

3711 Delgado, Abelardo "Lalo". An open letter to Carolina... or relations between men and women. REVISTA CHICANO-RIQUENA, Vol. 10, no. 1-2 (Winter, Spring, 1982), p. 279-284. English. **DESCR:** *Essays; Sex Roles; Sex Stereotypes; Women Men Relations.

3712 Delgado, Sylvia. Young Chicana speaks up on problems faced by young girls. REGENERACION, Vol. 1, no. 10 (1971), p. 5-7. English. **DESCR:** Abortion; Feminism; Marriage; Sex Roles; *Women Men Relations.

3713 Duarte, Patricia. The post-lib tango: couples in chaos. NUESTRO, Vol. 3, no. 5 (June, July, 1979), p. 38-40. English. **DESCR:** Divorce; Marriage; *Sex Roles.

3714 Espin, Oliva M. Cultural and historical influences on sexuality in Hispanic/Latin women: implications for psychotherapy. IN: Vance, Carole S., ed. PLEASURE AND DANGER: EXPLORING FEMALE SEXUALITY. Boston, MA: Routledge & Kegan Paul, 1984, p. 149-164. English. **DESCR:** Immigration; Language Usage; *Psychotherapy; Sex Roles; *Sexual Behavior; Social History and Conditions; Spanish Influence; *Women.

---   ---
Machismo (cont.)

3715 Espinosa-Larsen, Anita. Machismo: another
     view. LA LUZ, Vol. 1, no. 4 (August 1972),
     p. 59. English.

3716 Flores, Francisca. Conference of Mexican
     women un remolino. REGENERACION, Vol. 1, no.
     10 (1971), p. 1-5. English. DESCR:
     Conferences and Meetings; Family; Feminism;
     First National Chicana Conference (May 1971:
     Houston, TX); National Mexican American
     Issues Conference (October 11, 1970:
     Sacramento, CA); Sex Roles; Sex Stereotypes;
     Statistics; *Women Men Relations.

3717 Flores, Francisca. Equality. REGENERACION,
     Vol. 2, no. 3 (1973), p. 4-5. English.
     DESCR: Anglo Americans; Chicano Movement;
     Discrimination; Elected Officials; Feminism;
     Income; *Working Women.

3718 Flores, Henry. Some different thoughts
     concerning "machismo". COMADRE, no. 3 (Fall
     1978), p. 7-9. English. DESCR: Sex Roles.

3719 Flores, Rosalie. The new Chicana and
     machismo. REGENERACION, Vol. 2, no. 4
     (1975), p. 55-56. English. DESCR: Identity.

3720 Gallegos y Chavez, Ester. The northern New
     Mexican woman: a changing silhouette. IN:
     Trejo, Arnulfo D., ed. THE CHICANOS: AS WE
     SEE OURSELVES. Tucson, AZ: University of
     Arizona Press, 1979, p. 67-79. English.
     DESCR: *Identity; New Mexico; Social History
     and Conditions.

3721 Garcia, Alma M. The development of Chicana
     feminist discourse, 1970-1980. GENDER &
     SOCIETY, Vol. 3, no. 2 (June 1989), p.
     217-238. English. DESCR: Anglo Americans;
     Chicana Studies; *Chicano Movement;
     *Feminism; Homosexuality; National
     Association for Chicano Studies (NACS);
     Organizations; *Sexism; Women.

3722 Garcia, Alma M. The development of Chicana
     feminist discourse, 1970-1980. IN: DuBois,
     Ellen Carol and Ruiz, Vicki L., eds. UNEQUAL
     SISTERS: A MULTICULTURAL READER IN U.S.
     WOMEN'S HISTORY. New York: Routledge, 1990,
     p. 418-431. English. DESCR: Anglo Americans;
     Chicana Studies; *Chicano Movement;
     *Feminism; Homosexuality; National
     Association for Chicano Studies (NACS);
     Organizations; *Sexism; Women.

3723 Gonzales, Sylvia Alicia. The Chicana
     perspective: a design for self-awareness.
     IN: Trejo, Arnulfo D., ed. THE CHICANOS: AS
     WE SEE OURSELVES. Tucson, AZ: University of
     Arizona Press, 1979, p. 81-99. English.
     DESCR: CHICANAS SPEAK OUT; Chicano Movement;
     Discrimination; Feminism; Identity; Madsen,
     William; *Mexican Revolution - 1910-1920;
     Mexico; Sex Roles; THE MEXICAN-AMERICANS OF
     SOUTH TEXAS; Vidal, Mirta.

3724 Gonzalez, Alex. Sex roles of the traditional
     Mexican family: a comparison of Chicano and
     Anglo students' attitudes. JOURNAL OF
     CROSS-CULTURAL PSYCHOLOGY, Vol. 13, no. 3
     (September 1982), p. 330-339. English.
     DESCR: Anglo Americans; Attitudes;
     Comparative Psychology; *Family; Hembrismo;
     Sex Roles; Students.

3725 Griswold del Castillo, Richard. La familia:
     Chicano families in the urban Southwest,
     1848 to the present. Notre Dame, IN:
     University of Notre Dame Press, c1984. xi,
     173 p. English. DESCR: *Family; History;
     Intermarriage; Parenting; *Sex Roles; Sexual

Behavior; *Social History and Conditions.

3726 Griswold del Castillo, Richard. Patriarchy
     and the status of women in the late
     nineteenth-century Southwest. IN: Rodriguez
     O., Jaime E., ed. THE MEXICAN AND MEXICAN
     AMERICAN EXPERIENCE IN THE 19TH CENTURY.
     Tempe, AZ: Bilingual Press/Editorial
     Bilingue, 1989, p. 85-99. English. DESCR:
     Family; *Feminism; History; *Sex Roles.

3727 Jensen, Evelyn E. The Hispanic perspective
     of the ideal woman: a correlational study.
     Thesis (Ph.D.)--Fuller Theological Seminary,
     School of World Mission, 1987. 163 p.
     English. DESCR: Family; *Hembrismo; *Sex
     Roles.

3728 Kantorowski Davis, Sharon and Chavez,
     Virginia. Hispanic househusbands. HISPANIC
     JOURNAL OF BEHAVIORAL SCIENCES, Vol. 7, no.
     4 (December 1985), p. 317-332. English.
     DESCR: Domestic Work; Marriage; *Sex Roles.

3729 Lara-Cantu, M. Asuncion. A sex role
     inventory with scales for "machismo" and
     "self-sacrificing woman". JOURNAL OF
     CROSS-CULTURAL PSYCHOLOGY, Vol. 20, no. 4
     (December 1989), p. 396-398. English.
     DESCR: *Masculine-Feminine Personality
     Traits Scale; *Personality; *Psychological
     Testing; *Sex Roles.

3730 Lawrence, Alberto Augusto. Traditional
     attitudes toward marriage, marital
     adjustment, acculturation, and self-esteem
     of Mexican-American and Mexican wives.
     Thesis (Ph.D.)--United States International
     University, San Diego, CA, 1982. ix, 191 p.
     English. DESCR: *Acculturation; *Attitudes;
     *Marriage; Mental Health; Psychological
     Testing; San Ysidro, CA; Sex Roles; Sex
     Stereotypes; Tijuana, Baja California,
     Mexico; Women.

3731 LeVine, Sarah Ethel; Correa, Clara
     Sunderland; and Uribe, F. Medardo Tapia. The
     marital morality of Mexican women--an urban
     study. JOURNAL OF ANTHROPOLOGICAL RESEARCH,
     Vol. 42, no. 2 (Summer 1986), p. 183-202.
     English. DESCR: Family; Los Robles,
     Cuernavaca, Morelos, Mexico; Marriage;
     Parent and Child Relationships; *Sex Roles;
     Women; *Women Men Relations.

3732 Longeaux y Vasquez, Enriqueta. The woman of
     La Raza. REGENERACION, Vol. 2, no. 4 (1975),
     p. 34-36. English. DESCR: Child Care
     Centers; Discrimination; Gallo, Juana;
     Housing; La Adelita; Sex Roles; *Social
     History and Conditions; Working Women.

3733 Longeaux y Vasquez, Enriqueta. The woman of
     La Raza. IN: Valdez, Luis and Steiner, Stan,
     eds. AZTLAN: AN ANTHOLOGY OF MEXICAN
     AMERICAN LITERATURE. New York: Vintage
     Books, 1972, p. 272-278. Also IN: Salinas,
     Luis Omar and Faderman, Lillian, compilers.
     FROM THE BARRIO: A CHICANO ANTHOLOGY. San
     Francisco, CA: Canfield Press, 1973, p.
     20-24. English. DESCR: Child Care Centers;
     Discrimination; Gallo, Juana; Housing; La
     Adelita; Sex Roles; *Social History and
     Conditions; Working Women.

3734 Lucero Trujillo, Marcela. The terminology of
     machismo. DE COLORES, Vol. 4, no. 3 (1978),
     p. 34-42. Bilingual. DESCR: *Chicanismo;
     *Sex Stereotypes; *Women Men Relations.

Machismo (cont.)

3735 Matsuda, Gema. La Chicana organizes: the Comision Femenil Mexicana in perspective. REGENERACION, Vol. 2, no. 4 (1975), p. 25-27. English. **DESCR:** Bojorquez, Frances; Chicano Movement; *Comision Femenil Mexicana Nacional; De la Cruz, Juana Ines; Flores, Francisca; History; Malinche; Prisons; Sex Stereotypes; *Sexism.

3736 Mirande, Alfredo. Machismo: rucas, chingasos, y chingaderas. DE COLORES, Vol. 6, no. 1-2 (1982), p. 17-31. English. **DESCR:** Sex Roles.

3737 Mirande, Alfredo. Que gacho es ser macho: it's a drag to be a macho man. AZTLAN, Vol. 17, no. 2 (Fall 1986), p. 63-89. English. **DESCR:** *Cultural Characteristics; Identity; Personality; Sex Roles; *Sex Stereotypes; Values.

3738 Monroy, Douglas. "They didn't call them 'padre' for nothing": patriarchy in Hispanic California. IN: Del Castillo, Adelaida R., ed. BETWEEN BORDERS: ESSAYS ON MEXICANA/CHICANA HISTORY. Encino, CA: Floricanto Press, 1990, p. 433-445. English. **DESCR:** *California; Clergy; History; Rape; *Sex Roles; *Sexism; Spanish Influence; Women Men Relations.

3739 Panitz, Daniel R., et al. The role of machismo and the Hispanic family in the etiology and treatment of alcoholism in the Hispanic American males. AMERICAN JOURNAL OF FAMILY THERAPY, Vol. 11, no. 1 (Spring 1983), p. 31-44. English. **DESCR:** *Alcoholism; Children; Family; Puerto Rico; Socioeconomic Factors.

3740 Pavich, Emma Guerrero. A Chicana perspective on Mexican culture and sexuality. JOURNAL OF SOCIAL WORK AND HUMAN SEXUALITY, Vol. 4, no. 3 (Spring 1986), p. 47-65. English. **DESCR:** California; Cultural Characteristics; Family; Feminism; Homosexuality; Sex Roles; Sex Stereotypes; *Sexual Behavior; Women Men Relations.

3741 Pena, Manuel. Class, gender, and machismo: the "treacherous-woman" folklore of Mexican male workers. GENDER & SOCIETY, Vol. 5, no. 1 (March 1991), p. 30-46. English. **DESCR:** *Folklore; Laborers; Males; *Sex Roles; Sex Stereotypes; Social Classes; *Undocumented Workers; Women Men Relations.

3742 Pierce, Jennifer. The implications of functionalism for Chicano family research. BERKELEY JOURNAL OF SOCIOLOGY, Vol. 29, (1984), p. 93-117. English. **DESCR:** Enriquez, Evangelina; *Family; LA CHICANA: THE MEXICAN AMERICAN WOMAN; Mirande, Alfredo; Research Methodology; Sex Roles.

3743 Poma, Pedro A. Pregnancy in Hispanic women. JOURNAL OF THE NATIONAL MEDICAL ASSOCIATION, Vol. 79, no. 9 (September 1987), p. 929-935. English. **DESCR:** *Cultural Characteristics; *Doctor Patient Relations; *Fertility; Preventative Medicine; Women.

3744 Ramirez, Oscar and Arce, Carlos H. The contemporary Chicano family: an empirically based review. IN: Baron, Augustine, Jr., ed. EXPLORATIONS IN CHICANO PSYCHOLOGY. New York: Praeger, 1981, p. 3-28. English. **DESCR:** *Family; Fertility; Literature Reviews; Population; Sex Roles.

3745 Segura, Denise. Familism and employment among Chicanas and Mexican immigrant women.

IN: Melville, Margarita, ed. MEXICANAS AT WORK IN THE UNITED STATES. Houston, TX: Mexican American Studies Program, University of Houston, 1988, p. 24-32. English. **DESCR:** *Employment; *Extended Family; Family; Immigrants; Income; Sex Roles; *Women; Working Women.

3746 Segura, Denise. The interplay of familism and patriarchy on employment among Chicana and Mexicana women. RENATO ROSALDO LECTURE SERIES MONOGRAPH, Vol. 5, (1989), p. 35-53. English. **DESCR:** Employment; *Family; Immigrants; *Sex Roles; Women; Women Men Relations; *Working Women.

3747 Sternbach, Nancy Saporta. "A deep racial memory of love": the Chicana feminism of Cherrie Moraga. IN: Horno-Delgado, Asuncion, et al., eds. BREAKING BOUNDARIES: LATINA WRITING AND CRITICAL READINGS. Amherst, MA: University of Massachusetts Press, c1989, p. 48-61. English. **DESCR:** Discrimination; Feminism; Homosexuality; Literary Criticism; *LOVING IN THE WAR YEARS; Malinche; *Moraga, Cherrie; Sex Stereotypes; Sexism.

3748 Terranes, Ed. Some thoughts of a macho on the Chicana Movement. AGENDA, Vol. 7, no. 6 (November, December, 1977), p. 35-36. English. **DESCR:** *Women Men Relations.

3749 Trujillo Gaitan, Marcella. The dilemma of the modern Chicana artist and critic. DE COLORES, Vol. 3, no. 3 (1977), p. 38-48. Bilingual. **DESCR:** Art Criticism; Artists; *Chicano Movement; Gonzales, Sylvia Alicia; *Literary Criticism; Malinche; *Poetry; Symbolism.

3750 Trujillo Gaitan, Marcella. The dilemma of the modern Chicana artist and critic. HERESIES, Vol. 2, no. 4 (1979), p. 5-10. English. **DESCR:** Art Criticism; Artists; Authors; *Chicano Movement; Gonzales, Sylvia Alicia; *Literary Criticism; Malinche; *Poetry; Symbolism.

3751 Urdaneta, Maria Luisa. Flesh pots, faith, or finances? Fertility rates among Mexican Americans. IN: West, Stanley A. and Macklin, June, eds. THE CHICANO EXPERIENCE. Boulder, CO: Westview Press, 1979, p. 191-206. English. **DESCR:** Catholic Church; *Fertility; Sex Roles.

3752 Vasquez, Melba J. T. and Gonzalez, Anna M. Sex roles among Chicanos: stereotypes, challenges and changes. IN: Baron, Augustine, Jr., ed. EXPLORATIONS IN CHICANO PSYCHOLOGY. New York: Praeger, 1981, p. 50-70. English. **DESCR:** Hembrismo; *Sex Roles; Social Science; Stereotypes.

3753 Vazquez-Nuttall, Ena; Romero-Garcia, Ivonne; and De Leon, Brunilda. Sex roles and perceptions of femininity and masculinity of Hispanic women: a review of the literature. PSYCHOLOGY OF WOMEN QUARTERLY, Vol. 11, no. 4 (December 1987), p. 409-425. English. **DESCR:** Attitudes; *Chicanismo; *Literature Reviews; Puerto Ricans; *Sex Roles; *Women.

3754 Ybarra, Lea. Marital decision-making and the role of machismo in the Chicano family. DE COLORES, Vol. 6, no. 1-2 (1982), p. 32-47. English. **DESCR:** Family; Marriage; Sex Roles.

Machismo (cont.)

3755 Ybarra, Lea. Separating a myth from reality: socio-economic and cultural influences on Chicanas and the world of work. IN: Melville, Margarita, ed. MEXICANAS AT WORK IN THE UNITED STATES. Houston, TX: Mexican American Studies Program, University of Houston, 1988, p. 12-23. English. DESCR: Attitudes; *Cultural Characteristics; Income; Sex Roles; *Socioeconomic Factors; Stereotypes; *Working Women.

Macias, Margarita

3756 Zamora, Bernice. Archetypes in Chicana poetry. DE COLORES, Vol. 4, no. 3 (1978), p. 43-52. English. DESCR: Cervantes, Lorna Dee; Cunningham, Veronica; "Declaration on a Day of Little Inspiration" [poem]; Hernandez, Carlota; "I Speak in an Illusion" [poem]; *Literary Criticism; Lucero, Judy A.; Mendoza, Rita; "Para Mi Hijita" [poem]; *Poetry; "Rape Report" [poem]; "The White Line" [poem]; "Working Mother's Song" [poem]; "You Can Only Blame the System for So Long" [poem]; Zamora, Katarina.

Macias, Ysidro

3757 Melville, Margarita B. Female and male in Chicano theatre. IN: Kanellos, Nicolas, ed. HISPANIC THEATRE IN THE UNITED STATES. Houston, TX: Arte Público Press, 1984, p. 71-79. English. DESCR: BERNABE; BRUJERIAS [play]; Cultural Characteristics; DAY OF THE SWALLOWS; Duarte-Clark, Rodrigo; EL JARDIN [play]; Family; Feminism; Morton, Carlos Portillo Trambley, Estela; RANCHO HOLLYWOOD [play]; *Sex Roles; *Teatro; THE ULTIMATE PENDEJADA [play]; Valdez, Luis; Women Men Relations.

Madrigal v. Quilligan

3758 Velez-I., Carlos G. Se me acabo la cancion: an ethnography of non-consenting sterilizations among Mexican women in Los Angeles. IN: Mora, Magdalena and Del Castillo, Adelaida, eds. MEXICAN WOMEN IN THE UNITED STATES: STRUGGLES PAST AND PRESENT. Los Angeles, CA: Chicano Studies Research Center, UCLA, 1980, p. 71-91. English. DESCR: Ethnology; Los Angeles, CA; *Sterilization.

Madsen, William

3759 Gonzales, Sylvia Alicia. The Chicana perspective: a design for self-awareness. IN: Trejo, Arnulfo D., ed. THE CHICANOS: AS WE SEE OURSELVES. Tucson, AZ: University of Arizona Press, 1979, p. 81-99. English. DESCR: CHICANAS SPEAK OUT; Chicano Movement; Discrimination; Feminism; Identity; Machismo; *Mexican Revolution - 1910-1920; Mexico; Sex Roles; THE MEXICAN-AMERICANS OF SOUTH TEXAS; Vidal, Mirta.

Male and Female Roles
USE: Sex Roles

Males

3760 Canales, Genevieve and Roberts, Robert E. Gender and mental health in the Mexican origin population of South Texas. IN: Rodriguez, Reymund and Coleman, Marion Tolbert, eds. MENTAL HEALTH ISSUES OF THE MEXICAN ORIGIN POPULATION IN TEXAS. Austin, TX: Hogg Foundation for Mental Health, University of Texas, 1987, p. 89-99. English. DESCR: Del Rio, TX; Depression (Psychological); Eagle Pass, TX; Health Education; *Mental Health; *Sex Roles; South Texas; Surveys.

3761 Fernandez Kelly, Maria. Mexican border industrialization, female labor force participation and migration. IN: Nash, June and Fernandez-Kelly, Patricia, eds. WOMEN, MEN, AND THE INTERNATIONAL DIVISION OF LABOR. Albany, NY: State University of New York Press, 1983, p. 205-223. English. DESCR: Border Industrialization Program (BIP); *Border Industries; Ciudad Juarez, Chihuahua, Mexico; Immigration; Industrial Workers; Labor Supply and Market; *Migration Patterns; Undocumented Workers; *Women; Working Women.

3762 Gonzalez, Judith Teresa. Dilemmas of the high achieving Chicana: the double bind factor in male/female relationships. Tucson, AZ: Mexican American Studies & Research Center, University of Arizona, 1987. 31 leaves. English. DESCR: *Academic Achievement; Higher Education; Identity; Marriage; *Sex Roles; *Sex Stereotypes; Women Men Relations.

3763 Gonzalez, Judith Teresa. Dilemmas of the high achieving Chicana: the double bind factor in male/female relationships. SEX ROLES, Vol. 18, no. 7-8 (April 1988), p. 367-380. English. DESCR: *Academic Achievement; Higher Education; Identity; Marriage; *Sex Roles; *Sex Stereotypes; Women Men Relations.

3764 Lucero, Aileen. Chicano sex role attitudes: a comparative study of sex differences in an urban barrio. Thesis (Ph.D.)--University of Colorado at Boulder, 1980. 160 p. English. DESCR: *Attitudes; Colorado; *Sex Roles.

3765 Marin, Gerardo; Perez-Stable, Eliseo J.; and Marin, Barbara Van Oss. Cigarette smoking among San Francisco Hispanics: the role of acculturation and gender. PUBLIC HEALTH BRIEFS, Vol. 79, no. 2 (February 1989), p. 196-198. English. DESCR: *Acculturation; Drug Use; San Francisco, CA; *Smoking; Women.

3766 Markides, Kyriakos S. Consequences of gender differentials in life expectancy for Black and Hispanic Americans. INTERNATIONAL JOURNAL OF AGING & HUMAN DEVELOPMENT, Vol. 29, no. 2 (1989), p. 95-102. English. DESCR: *Ancianos; Blacks; Census; Cubanos; Latin Americans; Population; Puerto Ricans; U.S. Bureau of the Census.

3767 Pena, Manuel. Class, gender, and machismo: the "treacherous-woman" folklore of Mexican male workers. GENDER & SOCIETY, Vol. 5, no. 1 (March 1991), p. 30-46. English. DESCR: *Folklore; Laborers; *Machismo; *Sex Roles; Sex Stereotypes; Social Classes; *Undocumented Workers; Women Men Relations.

3768 Powers, Stephen and Jones, Patricia. Factorial invariance of the California achievement tests across race and sex. EDUCATIONAL AND PSYCHOLOGICAL MEASUREMENT, Vol. 44, no. 4 (Winter 1984), p. 967-970. English. DESCR: Anglo Americans; Blacks; *California Achievement Test (CAT); Educational Tests and Measurements; Women.

Males (cont.)

3769 Reimers, Cordelia W. A comparative analysis of the wages of Hispanics, Blacks, and non-Hispanic whites. IN: Borjas, George J. and Tienda, Marta, eds. HISPANICS IN THE U.S. ECONOMY. Orlando, FL: Academic Press, 1985, p. 27-75. English. DESCR: Anglo Americans; Blacks; *Income; Labor Supply and Market; Survey of Income and Education (SIE).

3770 Sullivan, Teresa A. The occupational prestige of women immigrants: a comparison of Cubans and Mexicans. INTERNATIONAL MIGRATION REVIEW, Vol. 18, no. 4 (Winter 1984), p. 1045-1062. English. DESCR: Careers; Cubanos; Employment; *Immigrants; Mexico; Sex Roles; *Social Mobility; *Women; *Working Women.

3771 Valdez, Avelardo. Recent increases in intermarriage by Mexican American males: Bexar County, Texas from 1971 to 1980. SOCIAL SCIENCE QUARTERLY, Vol. 64, (March 1983), p. 136-144. English. DESCR: Bexar County, TX; *Intermarriage.

3772 Velasquez, Roberto J.; Callahan, Wendell J.; and Carrillo, Ricardo. MMPI differences among Mexican-American male and female psychiatric inpatients. PSYCHOLOGICAL REPORTS, Vol. 68, no. 1 (February 1991), p. 123-127. English. DESCR: Comparative Psychology; Minnesota Multiphasic Personality Inventory (MMPI); Personality; Psychiatry; *Psychological Testing; Sex Roles.

Malinche

3773 Alarcon, Norma. Chicana's feminist literature: a re-vision through Malintzinl or Malintzin: putting flesh back on the object. IN: Moraga, Cherrie and Anzaldua, Gloria, eds. THIS BRIDGE CALLED MY BACK: WRITINGS BY RADICAL WOMEN OF COLOR. Watertown, MA: Persephone Press, 1981, p. 182-190. English. DESCR: Feminism; Literature; *Sex Roles; Stereotypes; Symbolism.

3774 Alarcon, Norma. Traddutora, traditora: a paradigmatic figure of Chicana feminism. CULTURAL CRITIQUE, Vol. 13, (Fall 1989), p. 57-87. English. DESCR: *Feminism; Paz, Octavio; Sex Roles; Symbolism.

3775 Candelaria, Cordelia. La Malinche, feminist prototype. FRONTIERS: A JOURNAL OF WOMEN STUDIES, Vol. 5, no. 2 (Summer 1980), p. 1-6. English. DESCR: Aztecs; *Feminism; History.

3776 Cardenas, Reyes. The machismo manifesto. CARACOL, Vol. 2, no. 8 (April 1976), p. 7. Bilingual. DESCR: Cotera, Marta P.; *Machismo; Women Men Relations.

3777 Del Castillo, Adelaida R. Malintzin Tenepal: a preliminary look into a new perspective. ENCUENTRO FEMENIL, Vol. 1, no. 2 (1974), p. 58-77. English. DESCR: Aztecs; Biography; Cortes, Hernan; *History; Precolumbian Society.

3778 Del Castillo, Adelaida R. Malintzin Tenepal: a preliminary look into a new perspective. IN: Sanchez, Rosaura and Martinez Cruz, Rosa, eds. ESSAYS ON LA MUJER. Los Angeles, CA: Chicano Studies Center Publications, UCLA, 1977, p. 124-149. English. DESCR: Aztecs; Biography; Cortes, Hernan; *History; Precolumbian Society.

3779 Enriquez, Evangelina and Mirande, Alfredo. Liberation, Chicana style: colonial roots of feministas chicanas. DE COLORES, Vol. 4, no. 3 (1978), p. 7-21. Bilingual. DESCR: *Chicano Movement; Feminism; *Political History and Conditions; *Social History and Conditions.

3780 Fox, Linda C. Obedience and rebellion: re-vision of Chicana myths of motherhood. WOMEN'S STUDIES QUARTERLY, Vol. 11, no. 4 (Winter 1983), p. 20-22. English. DESCR: Feminism; La Llorona; *Parent and Child Relationships.

3781 Gonzales, Sylvia Alicia. La Chicana: Malinche or virgin? NUESTRO, Vol. 3, no. 5 (June, July, 1979), p. 41-45. English. DESCR: *La Virgen de Guadalupe; Paz, Octavio.

3782 Gonzales, Sylvia Alicia. Toward a feminist pedagogy for Chicana self-actualization. FRONTIERS: A JOURNAL OF WOMEN STUDIES, Vol. 5, no. 2 (Summer 1980), p. 48-51. English. DESCR: Chicano Movement; Education; *Feminism; Identity.

3783 Leal, Luis. Arquetipos femeninos en la literatura mexicana. IN: Leal, Luis. AZTLAN Y MEXICO: PERFILES LITERARIOS E HISTORICOS. Binghamton, NY: Bilingual Press/Editorial Bilingue, 1985, p. 168-176. Spanish. DESCR: La Virgen de Guadalupe; *Literary Criticism; Mexican Literature; Symbolism; Women.

3784 Leal, Luis. Female archetypes in Mexican literature. IN: Miller, Beth, ed. WOMEN IN HISPANIC LITERATURE: ICONS AND FALLEN IDOLS. Berkeley, CA: University of California Press, 1983, p. 227-242. English. DESCR: La Virgen de Guadalupe; *Literary Criticism; Mexican Literature; Symbolism; Women.

3785 Limon, Jose E. [anthropologist]. La Llorona, the third legend of greater Mexico: cultural symbols, women, and the political unconscious. RENATO ROSALDO LECTURE SERIES MONOGRAPH, Vol. 2, (Spring 1986), p. [59]-93. English. DESCR: *Feminism; Folklore; *La Llorona; La Virgen de Guadalupe; *Leyendas; Mexico; *Symbolism; Women.

3786 Limon, Jose E. [anthropologist]. La Llorona, the third legend of greater Mexico: cultural symbols, women, and the political unconscious. IN: Del Castillo, Adelaida R. BETWEEN BORDERS: ESSAYS ON MEXICANA/CHICANA HISTORY. Encino, CA: Floricanto Press, 1990, p. 399-432. English. DESCR: *Feminism; Folklore; *La Llorona; La Virgen de Guadalupe; *Leyendas; Mexico; *Symbolism; Women.

3787 Matsuda, Gema. La Chicana organizes: the Comision Femenil Mexicana in perspective. REGENERACION, Vol. 2, no. 4 (1975), p. 25-27. English. DESCR: Bojorquez, Frances; Chicano Movement; *Comision Femenil Mexicana Nacional; De la Cruz, Juana Ines; Flores, Francisca; History; Machismo; Prisons; Sex Stereotypes; *Sexism.

3788 Phillips, Rachel. Marina/Malinche: masks and shadows. IN: Miller, Beth, ed. WOMEN IN HISPANIC LITERATURE: ICONS AND FALLEN IDOLS. Berkeley, CA: University of California Press, 1983, p. 97-114. English. DESCR: Aztecs; History; Psychohistory; *Symbolism.

Malinche (cont.)

3789 Quintana, Alvina E. Language, power, and women: a hermeneutic interpretation. CRITICAL PERSPECTIVES, Vol. 2, no. 1 (Fall 1984), p. 10-19. English. DESCR: *Feminism; Literary Criticism.

3790 Quintanilla, Anita. Images of deceit. WOMANSPIRIT, Vol. 10, no. 37 (Fall 1983), p. 25-26. English. DESCR: Sexism.

3791 Soto, Shirlene Ann. La Malinche: 16th century leader. INTERCAMBIOS FEMENILES, Vol. 2, no. 6 (Spring 1987), p. 13. English. DESCR: Leadership.

3792 Soto, Shirlene Ann. Tres modelos culturales: la Virgen de Guadalupe, la Malinche y la Llorona. FEM, Vol. 10, no. 48 (October, November, 1986), p. 13-16. Spanish. DESCR: Guadalupanismo; *La Llorona; *La Virgen de Guadalupe; Symbolism; Women.

3793 Sternbach, Nancy Saporta. "A deep racial memory of love": the Chicana feminism of Cherrie Moraga. IN: Horno-Delgado, Asuncion, et al., eds. BREAKING BOUNDARIES: LATINA WRITING AND CRITICAL READINGS. Amherst, MA: University of Massachusetts Press, c1989, p. 48-61. English. DESCR: Discrimination; Feminism; Homosexuality; Literary Criticism; *LOVING IN THE WAR YEARS; Machismo; *Moraga, Cherrie; Sex Stereotypes; Sexism.

3794 Trujillo Gaitan, Marcella. The dilemma of the modern Chicana artist and critic. DE COLORES, Vol. 3, no. 3 (1977), p. 38-48. Bilingual. DESCR: Art Criticism; Artists; *Chicano Movement; Gonzales, Sylvia Alicia; *Literary Criticism; Machismo; *Poetry; Symbolism.

3795 Trujillo Gaitan, Marcella. The dilemma of the modern Chicana artist and critic. HERESIES, Vol. 2, no. 4 (1979), p. 5-10. English. DESCR: Art Criticism; Artists; Authors; *Chicano Movement; Gonzales, Sylvia Alicia; *Literary Criticism; Machismo; *Poetry; Symbolism.

3796 Yarbro-Bejarano, Yvonne. The female subject in Chicano theater: sexuality, race, and class. THEATRE JOURNAL, Vol. 38, no. 4 (December 1986), p. 389-407. English. DESCR: El Teatro Campesino; El Teatro de la Esperanza; El Teatro Nacional de Aztlan (TENAZ); Feminism; *Sex Roles; *Teatro; Women in Teatro (WIT).

3797 Zamora, Bernice. Mythopoeia of Chicano poetry: an introduction to cultural archetypes. Thesis (Ph.D.)--Stanford University, 1986. 341 p. English. DESCR: Literary Characters; Literary Criticism; Literature; Pachucos; *Poetry; *Symbolism.

Malintzin Tenepal
USE: Malinche

Management

3798 Ayers-Nackamkin, Beverly, et al. Sex and ethnic differences in the use of power. JOURNAL OF APPLIED PSYCHOLOGY, Vol. 67, no. 4 (August 1982), p. 464-471. English. DESCR: Anglo Americans; Ethnic Groups; *Personnel Management; Sex Roles; Social Psychology.

3799 Bauman, Raquel. A study of Mexican American women's perceptions of factors that influence academic and professional goal attainment. Thesis (Ed.D.)--University of Houston, 1984. 169 p. English. DESCR: *Careers; *Educational Administration; *Higher Education.

3800 Braddom, Carolyn Lentz. The conceptualization of effective leadership as seen by women, Black and Hispanic superintendents. Thesis (Ed.D.)--University of Cincinnati, 1988. 232 p. English. DESCR: Anglo Americans; Blacks; *Educational Administration; *Leadership; Women.

3801 Duran, Isabelle Sandoval. Grounded theory study: Chicana administrators in Colorado and New Mexico. Thesis (Ed.D.)--University of Wyoming, Laramie, 1982. ix, 114 p. English. DESCR: Careers; Colorado; *Educational Administration; Leadership; New Mexico.

3802 Enriquez-White, Celia. Attitudes of Hispanic and Anglo women managers toward women in management. Thesis (Ed.D.)--University of La Verne, 1982. 103 p. English. DESCR: Anglo Americans; *Attitudes; Leadership; Women.

3803 Gallegos, Placida I. Emerging leadership among Hispanic women: the role of expressive behavior and nonverbal skill. Thesis (Ph.D.)--University of California, Riverside, 1987. 101 p. English. DESCR: Anglo Americans; Comparative Psychology; Corporations; *Leadership; Women.

3804 Galloway, Irma Nell. Trends in the employment of minority women as administrators in Texas public schools--1976-1981. Thesis (Ed.D.)--Texas Southern University, 1986. 129 p. English. DESCR: Asian Americans; Blacks; Education; *Educational Administration; Native Americans; Texas; *Women.

3805 McClelland, Judith Raymond. The relationship of independence to achievement: a comparative study of Hispanic women. Thesis (Ph.D.)--Fielding Institute, 1988. 164 p. English. DESCR: *Assertiveness; Attitudes; California Personality Inventory (CPI); Careers; Leadership; New Mexico; Personality; *Working Women.

3806 Zambrana, Ruth E. Hispanic professional women: work, family and health. Los Angeles, CA: National Network of Hispanic Women, 1987. 75 leaves. English. DESCR: Business; *Careers; *Employment; Family; Mental Health; Social Classes; *Social Mobility; *Women.

Mano a Mano

3807 Del Zotto, Augusta. Latinas with AIDS: life expectancy for Hispanic women is a startling 45 days after diagnosis. THIS WORLD, (April 9, 1989), p. 9. English. DESCR: Abortion; AIDS (Disease); Condom Use; Instituto Familiar de la Raza, San Francisco, CA; Machismo; Quintero, Juanita; Sex Roles; Women Men Relations.

Maquiladoras
USE: Border Industries

MARCH (Movimiento Artistico Chicano)
USE: Movimiento Artistico Chicano (MARCH), Chicago, IL

Mares, Rene

3808 Santillanes, Maria. Women in prison--C.I.W.: an editorial. REGENERACION, Vol. 2, no. 4 (1975), p. 53. English. **DESCR:** Conferences and Meetings; Garcia, Dolly; La Mesa College Pinto and Pinta Program; Lopez, Tony; Martinez, Miguel; Pinto Conference (1973: UCLA); Player; *Prisons; Salazar, Peggy.

Marijuanos
USE: Drug Addicts

Marriage

3809 Baca Zinn, Maxine. Qualitative methods in family research: a look inside Chicano families. CALIFORNIA SOCIOLOGIST, Vol. 5, no. 2 (Summer 1982), p. 58-79. English. **DESCR:** *Family; *Research Methodology; *Sex Roles; Socioeconomic Factors.

3810 Balkwell, Carolyn Ann. An attitudinal correlate of the timing of a major life event: the case of morale in widowhood. FAMILY RELATIONS, Vol. 34, no. 4 (October 1985), p. 577-581. English. **DESCR:** *Ancianos; Counseling (Psychological); Mental Health; Natural Support Systems; Widowhood.

3811 Casas, Jesus Manuel and Ortiz, Sylvia. Exploring the applicability of the Dyadic Adjustment Scale for assessing level of marital adjustment with Mexican Americans. JOURNAL OF MARRIAGE AND THE FAMILY, Vol. 47, no. 4 (November 1985), p. 1023-1027. English. **DESCR:** Dyadic Adjustment Scale (DAS).

3812 Castaneda, Antonia I. Comparative frontiers: the migration of women to Alta California and New Zealand. IN: Schlissel, Lillian, et al., eds. WESTERN WOMEN: THEIR LAND, THEIR LIVES. Albuquerque, NM: University of New Mexico Press, 1988, p. 283-300. English. **DESCR:** Border Region; California; History; Immigrants; Immigration; Mexico; Missions; Native Americans; New Zealand; Social History and Conditions; *Women.

3813 Corbett, Kitty; Mora, Juana; and Ames, Genevieve. Drinking patterns and drinking-related problems of Mexican-American husbands and wives. JOURNAL OF STUDIES ON ALCOHOL, Vol. 52, no. 3 (May 1991), p. 215-223. English. **DESCR:** *Alcoholism; *Sex Roles.

3814 Curtis, Theodore T. and Baca Zinn, Maxine. Marital role orientation among Chicanos: an analysis of structural and cultural factors. LA RED/THE NET, no. 59 (October 1982), p. 2-4. English. **DESCR:** *Sex Roles.

3815 Delgado, Sylvia. Young Chicana speaks up on problems faced by young girls. REGENERACION, Vol. 1, no. 10 (1971), p. 5-7. English. **DESCR:** Abortion; Feminism; Machismo; Sex Roles; *Women Men Relations.

3816 Duarte, Patricia. The post-lib tango: couples in chaos. NUESTRO, Vol. 3, no. 5 (June, July, 1979), p. 38-40. English. **DESCR:** Divorce; Machismo; *Sex Roles.

3817 Farrell, Janice and Markides, Kyriakos S. Marriage and health: a three-generation study of Mexican Americans. JOURNAL OF MARRIAGE AND THE FAMILY, Vol. 47, no. 4 (November 1985), p. 1029-1036. English. **DESCR:** Public Health.

3818 Fennelly, Katherine; Kandiah, Vasantha; and

Ortiz, Vilma. The cross-cultural study of fertility among Hispanic adolescents in the Americas. STUDIES IN FAMILY PLANNING, Vol. 20, no. 2 (March, April, 1989), p. 96-101. English. **DESCR:** Cultural Characteristics; Ethnic Groups; *Fertility; Latin America; Youth.

3819 Frisbie, William Parker; Opitz, Wolfgang; and Kelly, William R. Marital instability trends among Mexican Americans as compared to Blacks and Anglos: new evidence. SOCIAL SCIENCE QUARTERLY, Vol. 66, no. 3 (September 1985), p. 587-601. English. **DESCR:** Anglo Americans; Blacks; Divorce.

3820 Frisbie, William Parker; Bean, Frank D.; and Eberstein, Isaac W. Patterns of marital instability among Mexican Americans, Blacks, and Anglos. IN: Bean, Frank D. and Frisbie, W. Parker, eds. THE DEMOGRAPHY OF RACIAL AND ETHNIC GROUPS. New York: Academic Press, 1978, p. 143-163. English. **DESCR:** Anglo Americans; Blacks; Divorce; Family.

3821 Frisbie, William Parker; Bean, Frank D.; and Eberstein, Isaac W. Recent changes in marital instability among Mexican Americans: convergence with Black and Anglo trends. SOCIAL FORCES, Vol. 58, no. 4 (June 1980), p. 1205-1220. English. **DESCR:** Age Groups; Anglo Americans; Blacks; *Divorce.

3822 Frisbie, William Parker. Variation in patterns of marital instability among Hispanics. JOURNAL OF MARRIAGE AND THE FAMILY, Vol. 48, no. 1 (February 1986), p. 99-106. English. **DESCR:** Cubanos; Puerto Ricans.

3823 Gonzalez, Judith Teresa. Dilemmas of the high achieving Chicana: the double bind factor in male/female relationships. Tucson, AZ: Mexican American Studies & Research Center, University of Arizona, 1987. 31 leaves. English. **DESCR:** *Academic Achievement; Higher Education; Identity; Males; *Sex Roles; *Sex Stereotypes; Women Men Relations.

3824 Gonzalez, Judith Teresa. Dilemmas of the high achieving Chicana: the double bind factor in male/female relationships. SEX ROLES, Vol. 18, no. 7-8 (April 1988), p. 367-380. English. **DESCR:** *Academic Achievement; Higher Education; Identity; Males; *Sex Roles; *Sex Stereotypes; Women Men Relations.

3825 Guendelman, Sylvia. The incorporation of Mexican women in seasonal migration: a study of gender differences. HISPANIC JOURNAL OF BEHAVIORAL SCIENCES, Vol. 9, no. 3 (September 1987), p. 245-264. English. **DESCR:** Immigrants; Mexico; *Migration Patterns; *Sex Roles; *Women; *Women Men Relations; Working Women.

3826 Gutierrez, Ramon A. From honor to love: transformations of the meaning of sexuality in colonial New Mexico. IN: Smith, Raymond T., ed. KINSHIP IDEOLOGY AND PRACTICE IN LATIN AMERICA. Chapel Hill, NC: University of North Carolina Press, 1984, p. [237]-263. English. **DESCR:** *Catholic Church; New Mexico; *Sexual Behavior; Social Classes; Social History and Conditions; Spanish Influence; Values; Women.

Marriage (cont.)

3827 Gutierrez, Ramon A. Honor ideology, marriage negotiation, and class-gender domination in New Mexico, 1690-1846. LATIN AMERICAN PERSPECTIVES, Vol. 12, no. 1 (Winter 1985), p. 81-104. English. **DESCR**: Sex Roles; *Social Classes; Social History and Conditions; Southwestern United States; Values; Women Men Relations.

3828 Gutierrez, Ramon A. Marriage and seduction in Colonial New Mexicc. IN: Del Castillo, Adelaida R., ed. BETWEEN BORDERS: ESSAYS ON MEXICANA/CHICANA HISTORY. Encino, CA: Floricanto Press, 1990, p. 447-457. English. **DESCR**: History; *New Mexico; Rape; *Sexual Behavior; Women.

3829 Gutierrez, Ramon A. When Jesus came, the corn mothers went away: marriage, sexuality, and power in New Mexico, 1500-1846. Stanford: Stanford University Pres, 1991. xxxi, 424 p. English. **DESCR**: Native Americans; *New Mexico; *Pueblo Indians; *Sex Roles; Sexual Behavior; Spanish Influence; Women.

3830 Hartzler, Kaye and Franco, Juan N. Ethnicity, division of household tasks and equity in marital roles: a comparison of Anglo and Mexican American couples. HISPANIC JOURNAL OF BEHAVIORAL SCIENCES, Vol. 7, no. 4 (December 1985), p. 333-344. English. **DESCR**: *Sex Roles.

3831 Hayghe, Howard. Married couples: work and income patterns. MONTHLY LABOR REVIEW, Vol. 106, no. 12 (December 1983), p. 26-29. English. **DESCR**: *Employment; *Income; *Sex Roles; Working Women.

3832 Hintz, Joy. Valiant migrant women = Las mujeres valerosas. Tiffin, OH: Sayger Printing, 1982. viii, 98 p. English. **DESCR**: Battered Women; *Farm Workers; Feminism; Florida; Migrant Children; Migrant Health Services; Migrant Housing; *Migrant Labor; Migration Patterns; Ohio; Sex Roles; Texas.

3833 Holscher, Louis M. Hispanic intermarriage: changing trends in New Mexico. AGENDA, Vol. 10, no. 6 (November, December, 1980), p. 8-10. English. **DESCR**: *Intermarriage; New Mexico.

3834 Jensen, Carol. Cleofas M. Jaramillo on marriage in territorial Northern New Mexico. NEW MEXICO HISTORICAL REVIEW, Vol. 58, no. 2 (April 1983), p. 153-171. English. **DESCR**: Jaramillo, Cleofas M.; New Mexico.

3835 Kantorowski Davis, Sharon and Chavez, Virginia. Hispanic househusbands. HISPANIC JOURNAL OF BEHAVIORAL SCIENCES, Vol. 7, no. 4 (December 1985), p. 317-332. English. **DESCR**: Domestic Work; Machismo; *Sex Roles.

3836 Kaplan, Celia Patricia. Critical factors affecting school dropout among Mexican-American women. Thesis (Doctor of Public Health)--UCLA, 1990. xviii, 256 p. English. **DESCR**: *Dropouts; Secondary School Education.

3837 Lawrence, Alberto Augusto. Traditional attitudes toward marriage, marital adjustment, acculturation, and self-esteem of Mexican-American and Mexican wives. Thesis (Ph.D.)--United States International University, San Diego, CA, 1982. ix, 191 p. English. **DESCR**: *Acculturation; *Attitudes; Machismo; Mental Health; Psychological Testing; San Ysidro, CA; Sex Roles; Sex

Stereotypes; Tijuana, Baja California, Mexico; Women.

3838 LeVine, Sarah Ethel; Correa, Clara Sunderland; and Uribe, F. Medardo Tapia. The marital morality of Mexican women--an urban study. JOURNAL OF ANTHROPOLOGICAL RESEARCH, Vol. 42, no. 2 (Summer 1986), p. 183-202. English. **DESCR**: Family; Los Robles, Cuernavaca, Morelos, Mexico; *Machismo; Parent and Child Relationships; *Sex Roles; Women; *Women Men Relations.

3839 Malvido, Elsa. El uso del cuerpo femenino en la epoca colonial mexicana a traves de los estudios de demografia historica. IN: Del Castillo, Adelaida R., ed. BETWEEN BORDERS: ESSAYS ON MEXICANA/CHICANA HISTORY. Encino, CA: Floricanto Press, 1990, p. 115-130. Spanish. **DESCR**: *Mexico; *Sex Roles; Sexual Behavior; *Vital Statistics; Widowhood; *Women.

3840 Markides, Kyriakos S. and Hoppe, Sue K. Marital satisfaction in three generations of Mexican Americans. SOCIAL SCIENCE QUARTERLY, Vol. 66, no. 1 (March 1985), p. 147-154. English. **DESCR**: *Age Groups.

3841 Markides, Kyriakos S. and Farrell, Janice. Marital status and depression among Mexican Americans. SOCIAL PSYCHIATRY, Vol. 20, no. 2 (1985), p. 86-91. English. **DESCR**: Depression (Psychological); Divorce; *Mental Health.

3842 Markides, Kyriakos S., et al. Sample representativeness in a three-generation study of Mexican Americans. JOURNAL OF MARRIAGE AND THE FAMILY, Vol. 45, no. 4 (November 1983), p. 911-916. English. **DESCR**: *Age Groups; Population; San Antonio, TX; *Socioeconomic Factors.

3843 Michael, Robert T. and Tuma, Nancy Brandon. Entry into marriage and parenthood by young men and women: the influence of family background. DEMOGRAPHY, Vol. 22, no. 4 (November 1985), p. 515-544. Magazine. English. **DESCR**: Anglo Americans; Blacks; *Cultural Characteristics; *Fertility; Population; Youth.

3844 Mosher, William D.; Johnson, David P.; and Horn, Marjorie C. Religion and fertility in the United States: the importance of marriage patterns and Hispanic origin. DEMOGRAPHY, Vol. 23, no. 3 (August 1986), p. 367-379. English. **DESCR**: *Catholic Church; *Fertility; Identity; Population; *Religion.

3845 Neff, James Alan; Gilbert, Kathleen R.; and Hoppe, Sue K. Divorce likelihood among Anglos and Mexican Americans. JOURNAL OF DIVORCE AND REMARRIAGE, Vol. 15, no. 1-2 (1991), p. 75-98. English. **DESCR**: *Anglo Americans; *Divorce; San Antonio, TX.

3846 Roberts, Robert E. and Roberts, Catharine Ramsay. Marriage, work and depressive symptoms among Mexican Americans. HISPANIC JOURNAL OF BEHAVIORAL SCIENCES, Vol. 4, no. 2 (June 1982), p. 199-221. English. **DESCR**: Depression (Psychological); Employment; *Mental Health.

3847 Saboonchi, Nasrin. The working women's reactions to the traditional marriage role: a crosscultural study within the symbolic interactionism framework. Thesis (Ph.D.)--United States International University, 1983. 173 p. English. **DESCR**: Immigrants; Iranians; *Sex Roles; Women; Working Women.

Marriage (cont.)

3848 Saenz, Rogelio; Goudy, Willis J.; and
     Lorenz, Frederick O. The effects of
     employment and marital relations on
     depression among Mexican American women.
     JOURNAL OF MARRIAGE AND THE FAMILY, Vol. 51,
     no. 1 (February 1989), p. 239-251. English.
     DESCR: *Depression (Psychological); Domestic
     Work; *Employment; Feminism; Women Men
     Relations; Working Women.

3849 Saenz, Rogelio. Traditional sex-roles,
     ethnic integration, marital satisfaction,
     and psychological distress among Chicanas.
     Thesis (Ph.D.)--Iowa State University, 1986.
     145 p. English. DESCR: *Mental Health; *Sex
     Roles; Stress.

3850 Schoen, Robert; Wooldredge, John; and
     Thomas, Barbara. Ethnic and educational
     effects on marriage choice. SOCIAL SCIENCE
     QUARTERLY, Vol. 70, no. 3 (September 1989),
     p. 617-630. English. DESCR: Education;
     Identity; *Intermarriage; Research
     Methodology; Social Classes.

3851 Sorenson, Ann Marie. The fertility and
     language characteristics of Mexican-American
     and non-Hispanic husbands and wives.
     SOCIOLOGICAL QUARTERLY, Vol. 29, no. 1
     (March 1988), p. 111-130. English. DESCR:
     Anglo Americans; Fertility; Identity;
     *Language Usage; Sex Roles.

3852 Torres Raines, Rosario. The Mexican American
     woman and work: intergenerational
     perspectives of comparative ethnic groups.
     IN: Melville, Margarita, ed. MEXICANAS AT
     WORK IN THE UNITED STATES. Houston, TX:
     Mexican American Studies Program, University
     of Houston, 1988, p. 33-46. English. DESCR:
     Age Groups; Anglo Americans; Employment;
     Feminism; Sex Roles; Social Classes;
     Socioeconomic Factors; *Working Women.

3853 Vega, William A.; Warheit, George; and
     Meinhardt, Kenneth. Marital disruption and
     the prevalence of depressive symptomatology
     among Anglos and Mexican Americans. JOURNAL
     OF MARRIAGE AND THE FAMILY, Vol. 46, no. 4
     (November 1984), p. 817-824. English.
     DESCR: Anglo Americans; Depression
     (Psychological); *Divorce; *Mental Health;
     Socioeconomic Factors.

3854 Vega, William A.; Kolody, Bohdan; and Valle,
     Juan Ramon. The relationship of marital
     status, confidant support, and depression
     among Mexican immigrant women. JOURNAL OF
     MARRIAGE AND THE FAMILY, Vol. 48, no. 3
     (August 1986), p. 597-605. English. DESCR:
     *Depression (Psychological); *Immigrants;
     Low Income; San Diego County, CA; Stress;
     Women.

3855 Williams, Norma. Role making among married
     Mexican American women: issues of class and
     ethnicity. JOURNAL OF APPLIED BEHAVIORAL
     SCIENCE, Vol. 24, no. 2 (1988), p. 203-217.
     English. DESCR: Austin, TX; Corpus Christi,
     TX; Identity; *Sex Roles; Social Classes.

3856 Ybarra, Lea. Marital decision-making and the
     role of machismo in the Chicano family. DE
     COLORES, Vol. 6, no. 1-2 (1982), p. 32-47.
     English. DESCR: Family; *Machismo; Sex
     Roles.

Martinez, Esperanza

3857 Three Latina artists = Tres artistas
     latinas. AMERICAS 2001, Vol. 1, no. 5
     (March, April, 1988), p. 21. Bilingual.

DESCR: *Artists; *Baca, Judith F.;
Biographical Notes; *Carrasco, Barbara.

Martinez, Joe L., Jr.

3858 Ramirez, Alex, et al. The relationship
     between sociocultural variables and Chicano
     and Anglo high school student responses on
     the Potency Dimension of the Semantic
     Differential. HISPANIC JOURNAL OF BEHAVIORAL
     SCIENCES, Vol. 3, no. 2 (June 1981), p.
     177-190. English. DESCR: Anglo Americans;
     Martinez, Sergio R.; MULTIVARIATE ANALYSIS
     OF VARIANCE (MANOVA); Olmedo, Esteban L.;
     *Parent and Child Relationships; Sex Roles;
     Sex Stereotypes; Students.

Martinez, Miguel

3859 Santillanes, Maria. Women in prison--C.I.W.:
     an editorial. REGENERACION, Vol. 2, no. 4
     (1975), p. 53. English. DESCR: Conferences
     and Meetings; Garcia, Dolly; La Mesa College
     Pinto and Pinta Program; Lopez, Tony; Mares,
     Rene; Pinto Conference (1973: UCLA); Player;
     *Prisons; Salazar, Peggy.

Martinez, Patrice

3860 Vega, Alicia. Three Latinas in Hollywood =
     Tres latinas en Hollywood. AMERICAS 2001,
     Vol. 1, no. 7 (July, August, 1988), p. 4-6.
     Bilingual. DESCR: *Actors and Actresses;
     Alonso, Maria Conchita; Ramos, Loyda.

Martinez, Sergio R.

3861 Ramirez, Alex, et al. The relationship
     between sociocultural variables and Chicano
     and Anglo high school student responses on
     the Potency Dimension of the Semantic
     Differential. HISPANIC JOURNAL OF BEHAVIORAL
     SCIENCES, Vol. 3, no. 2 (June 1981), p.
     177-190. English. DESCR: Anglo Americans;
     Martinez, Joe L., Jr.; MULTIVARIATE ANALYSIS
     OF VARIANCE (MANOVA); Olmedo, Esteban L.;
     *Parent and Child Relationships; Sex Roles;
     Sex Stereotypes; Students.

Marxism

3862 Apodaca, Maria Linda. The Chicana woman: a
     historical materialist perspective. IN:
     Bollinger, William, et al., eds. WOMEN IN
     LATIN AMERICA: AN ANTHOLOGY FROM LATIN
     AMERICAN PERSPECTIVES. Riverside, CA: Latin
     American Perspectives, c1979, p. 81-100.
     English. DESCR: Capitalism; *Historiography;
     Immigrants; Imperialism; Mexico; Oral
     History; Social Classes; Spanish Influence.

3863 Enriquez, Evangelina. Towards a definition
     of, and critical approaches to, Chicano(a)
     literature. Thesis (Ph.D.)--University of
     California, Riverside, 1982. viii, 182 p.
     English. DESCR: Feminism; *Literary
     Criticism; Literary History; *Literature.

3864 Glenn, Evelyn Nakano. Racial ethnic women's
     labor: the intersection of race, gender and
     class oppression. REVIEW OF RADICAL
     POLITICAL ECONOMY, Vol. 17, no. 3 (Fall
     1985), p. 86-108. English. DESCR: Asian
     Americans; Blacks; *Discrimination;
     *Feminism; Laboring Classes; Sexism; Social
     Classes; Women; Working Women.

Marxism (cont.)

3865 Pena, Devon Gerardo. Between the lines: a new perspective on the industrial sociology of women workers in transnational labor processes. IN: Cordova, Teresa, et al., eds. CHICANA VOICES. Austin, TX: Center for Mexican American Studies, 1986, p. 77-95. English. DESCR: Border Industries; *Labor; *Women; Working Women.

Masculine-Feminine Personality Traits Scale

3866 Lara-Cantu, M. Asuncion. A sex role inventory with scales for "machismo" and "self-sacrificing woman". JOURNAL OF CROSS-CULTURAL PSYCHOLOGY, Vol. 20, no. 4 (December 1989), p. 396-398. English. DESCR: Machismo; *Personality; *Psychological Testing; *Sex Roles.

Maternal and Child Welfare

3867 Acosta Johnson, Carmen. Breast-feeding and social class mobility: the case of Mexican migrant mothers in Houston, Texas. IN: Melville, Margarita B., ed. TWICE A MINORITY. St. Louis, MO: Mosby, 1980, p. 66-82. English. DESCR: *Breastfeeding; Herbal Medicine; *Social Classes; Social Mobility.

3868 de la Torre, Adela and Rush, Lynda. The determinants of breastfeeding for Mexican migrant women. INTERNATIONAL MIGRATION REVIEW, Vol. 21, no. 3 (Fall 1987), p. 728-742. English. DESCR: *Breastfeeding; Farm Workers; Migrant Health Services; Migrant Labor; Migration; Public Health; Working Women.

3869 Engle, Patricia L. Prenatal and postnatal anxiety in women giving birth in Los Angeles. HEALTH PSYCHOLOGY, Vol. 9, no. 3 (1990), p. 285-299. English. DESCR: *Fertility; Immigrants; Los Angeles, CA; Medical Care; *Prenatal Care; *Stress; Women.

3870 Fennelly, Katherine, et al. The effect of maternal age on the well-being of children. JOURNAL OF MARRIAGE AND THE FAMILY, Vol. 46, no. 4 (November 1984), p. 933-934. English. DESCR: *Age Groups; *Parenting; *Youth.

3871 Gunther Enriquez, Martha. Studying maternal-infant attachment: a Mexican-American example. IN: Kay, Margarita Artschwager, ed. ANTHROPOLOGY OF HUMAN BIRTH. Philadelphia, PA: F.A. Davis, 1982, p. 61-79. English. DESCR: Children; *Fertility; Immigrants; *Parent and Child Relationships.

3872 Hurtado, Aida. Midwife practices in Hidalgo County, Texas. TRABAJOS MONOGRAFICOS, Vol. 3, no. 1 (1987), p. 1-30. English. DESCR: Hidalgo County, TX; Midwives.

3873 Kay, Margarita Artschwager. Mexican, Mexican American, and Chicana childbirth. IN: Melville, Margarita B., ed. TWICE A MINORITY. St. Louis, MO: Mosby, 1980, p. 52-65. English. DESCR: *Cultural Characteristics; Herbal Medicine; Midwives; Sex Roles.

3874 Leblanc, Donna Marie. Quality of maternity care in rural Texas. Thesis (Dr. P.H.) --University of Texas H.S.C. at Houston School of Public Health, 1983. 266 p. English. DESCR: Fertility; Low Income; *Medical Care; Prenatal Care; *Rural Poor; Texas.

3875 Notzon, Francis Claude. Factors associated with low birth weight in Mexican-Americans and Mexicans. Thesis (Ph.D.)--John Hopkins University, 1989. 190 p. English. DESCR: Anglo Americans; Fertility; Mexico; *Prenatal Care; Public Health; *Women.

3876 Pletsch, Pamela K. Hispanics: at risk for adolescent pregnancy? PUBLIC HEALTH NURSING, Vol. 7, no. 2 (June 1990), p. 105-110. English. DESCR: *Fertility; *Youth.

3877 Smith, Jack C. Trends in the incidence of breastfeeding for Hispanics of Mexican origin and Anglos on the US-Mexican border. AMERICAN JOURNAL OF PUBLIC HEALTH, Vol. 72, no. 1 (January 1982), p. 59-61. English. DESCR: Anglo Americans; Border Region; Breastfeeding.

3878 Tajalli, Irene Queiro. Selected cultural, organizational, and economic factors related to prenatal care utilization by middle-income Hispanic women. Thesis (Ph.D.)--University of Illinois at Urbana-Champaign, 1984. 139 p. English. DESCR: *Fertility; Indiana; *Medical Care; Prenatal Care; Preventative Medicine.

3879 Ventura, Stephanie J. and Taffel, Selma M. Childbearing characteristics of U.S.- and foreign-born Hispanic mothers. PUBLIC HEALTH REPORTS, Vol. 100, no. 6 (November, December, 1985), p. 647-652. English. DESCR: *Fertility; Identity; Immigrants; *Statistics.

3880 Watkins, Elizabeth L.; Peoples, Mary D.; and Gates, Connie. Health and social needs of women farmworkers: receiving maternity care at a migrant health center. MIGRATION TODAY, Vol. 13, no. 2 (1985), p. 39-42. English. DESCR: Farm Workers; *Migrant Health Services; Women.

3881 Weller, Susan C. and Dungy, Claibourne I. Personal preferences and ethnic variations among Anglo and Hispanic breast and bottle feeders. SOCIAL SCIENCE & MEDICINE, Vol. 23, no. 6 (1986), p. 539-548. English. DESCR: Attitudes; *Breastfeeding; Orange, CA; Parenting; Socioeconomic Factors.

3882 Wolff, Cindy Brattan. Diet and pregnancy outcome in Mexican-American women. Thesis (Ph.D.)--Colorado State University, 1988. 257 p. English. DESCR: *Fertility; Food Practices; *Nutrition.

3883 Zambrana, Ruth E. Bibliography on maternal and child health across class, race and ethnicity. Memphis, TN: Distributed by the Memphis State University Center for Research on Women, c1990. 58 leaves. English. DESCR: *Bibliography; Ethnic Groups; *Medical Care; Social Classes; *Women.

3884 Zepeda, Marlene. Mother-infant behavior in Mexican and Mexican-American women: a study of the relationship of selected prenatal, perinatal and postnatal events. Thesis (Ph.D.)--University of California, Los Angeles, 1984, 429 p. English. DESCR: Children; *Fertility; *Parent and Child Relationships; Prenatal Care.

3885 Zepeda, Marlene. Selected maternal-infant care practices of Spanish-speaking women. JOGN NURSING, Vol. 11, no. 6 (November, December, 1982), p. 371-374. English. DESCR: Parenting.

Maternal Teaching Observation Technique (MTOT)

3886 Laosa, Luis M. Maternal teaching strategies in Chicano and Anglo-American families: the influence of culture and education on maternal behavior. CHILD DEVELOPMENT, Vol. 51, no. 3 (September 1980), p. 759-765. English. DESCR: Anglo Americans; Comparative Psychology; *Cultural Characteristics; *Education; Family; *Parent and Child Relationships; Parenting; Women.

3887 Martinez, Estella A. Child behavior in Mexican American/Chicano families: maternal teaching and child-rearing practices. FAMILY RELATIONS, Vol. 37, no. 3 (July 1988), p. 275-280. English. DESCR: *Acculturation; Family; Parent and Child Relationships; *Parenting; *Psychological Testing; Socioeconomic Factors; Values.

Mathematics

3888 Creswell, John L. and Exezidis, Roxane H. Research brief: sex and ethnic differences in mathematics achievement of Black and Mexican-American adolescents. TEXAS TECH JOURNAL OF EDUCATION, Vol. 9, no. 3 (Fall 1982), p. 219-222. English. DESCR: Blacks; Youth.

3889 Creswell, John L. Sex-related differences in the problem-solving abilities of rural Black, Anglo, and Chicano adolescents. TEXAS TECH JOURNAL OF EDUCATION, Vol. 10, no. 1 (Winter 1983), p. 29-33. English. DESCR: Aiken and Preger Revised Math Attitude Scale; Anglo Americans; Blacks; California Achievement Test (CAT); National Assessment of Educational Progress; National Council of Teachers of Mathematics (NCTM); Youth.

3890 MacCorquodale, Patricia. Mexican-American women and mathematics: participation, aspirations, and achievement. IN: Cocking, Rodney R. and Mestre, Jose P., eds. LINGUISTIC AND CULTURAL DIFFERENCES ON LEARNING MATHEMATICS. Hillsdale, NJ: Erlbaum, 1988, p. 137-160. English. DESCR: *Academic Achievement; Anglo Americans; Bilingualism; Family.

Matute-Bianchi, Maria Eugenia

3891 Matute-Bianchi, Maria Eugenia. A Chicana in academe. WOMEN'S STUDIES QUARTERLY, Vol. 10, no. 1 (Spring 1982), p. 14-17. English. DESCR: Discrimination; *Higher Education; Sex Roles; Sexism.

McAllen, TX

3892 Esparza, Mariana Ochoa. The impact of adult education on Mexican-American women. Thesis (Ed.D.)--Texas A & I University, 1981. 168 p. English. DESCR: *Adult Education; Careers; Sex Roles.

McGovern, George

3893 Huerta, Dolores. Dolores Huerta talks about Republicans, Cesar, children and her home town. REGENERACION, Vol. 2, no. 4 (1975), p. 20-24. English. DESCR: *Agricultural Labor Unions; *Biography; Chavez, Cesar E.; Community Service Organization, Los Angeles, (CSO); Democratic Party; Elected Officials; Flores, Art; Huerta, Dolores; *Politics; Ramirez, Henry M.; Ross, Fred; Sanchez, Philip V.; United Farmworkers of America (UFW); Working Women.

3894 Huerta, Dolores. Dolores Huerta talks about Republicans, Cesar, children and her home town. IN: Servin, Manuel P. ed. THE MEXICAN AMERICANS: AN AWAKENING MINORITY. 2nd ed. Beverly Hills, CA: Glencoe Press, 1974, p. 283-294. English. DESCR: *Agricultural Labor Unions; *Biography; Chavez, Cesar E.; Community Service Organization, Los Angeles, (CSO); Democratic Party; Elected Officials; Flores, Art; Huerta, Dolores; *Politics; Ramirez, Henry M.; Ross, Fred; Sanchez, Philip V.; United Farmworkers of America (UFW); Working Women.

MEChA

USE: Movimiento Estudiantil Chicano de Aztlan (MEChA)

Medi-Cal

3895 Hancock, Paula F. The effect of welfare eligibility on the labor force participation of women of Mexican origin in California. POPULATION RESEARCH AND POLICY REVIEW, Vol. 5, no. 2 (1986), p. 163-185. English. DESCR: Aid to Families with Dependent Children (AFDC); California; *Employment; Food Stamps; Immigrants; Single Parents; *Welfare; Women.

Medical Botany

USE: Herbal Medicine

Medical Care

3896 Aguilar, Marian Angela. Patterns of health care utilization of Mexican American women. Thesis (Ph.D.)--University of Illinois at Urbana-Champaign, 1983. v, 147 p. English. DESCR: Income; Insurance; *Public Health; Public Policy.

3897 Ainsworth, Diane. Cultural cross fires. IN: Duran, Livie Isauro and Bernard, H. Russell, eds. INTRODUCTION TO CHICANO STUDIES. 2nd ed. New York: Macmillan, c1982, p. 505-512. English. DESCR: Identity; *Sterilization; Velez Ibanez, Carlos.

3898 Alvarez-Amaya, Maria. Determinants of breast and cervical cancer behavior among Mexican American women. BORDER HEALTH/SALUD FRONTERIZA, Vol. 5, no. 3 (July, September, 1989), p. 22-27. Bilingual. DESCR: Border Region; *Breast Cancer; *Cancer; Diseases; Immigrants; *Preventative Medicine.

3899 Bauer, Richard L. Ethnic differences in hip fracture: a reduced incidence in Mexican-Americans. AMERICAN JOURNAL OF EPIDEMIOLOGY, Vol. 127, no. 1 (January 1988), p. 145-149. English. DESCR: Anglo Americans; Bexar County, TX; Blacks; Osteoporosis; *Public Health.

3900 Bauman, Raquel. The status of Chicanas in medicine. RESEARCH BULLETIN (SPANISH SPEAKING MENTAL HEALTH RES. CENTER), Vol. 4, no. 3 (March 1980), p. 6-7,12-13. English. DESCR: *Medical Education; *Medical Personnel; Precolumbian Medicine.

3901 Cayer, Shirley. Chicago's new Hispanic health alliance. NUESTRO, Vol. 7, no. 5 (June, July, 1983), p. 44-48. English. DESCR: Alcoholism; Chicago Hispanic Health Alliance; Family Planning; *Health Education; Latin Americans.

Medical Care (cont.)

3902 Cuellar, Israel, et al. Clinical psychiatric case presentation; culturally responsive diagnostic formulation and treatment in an Hispanic female. HISPANIC JOURNAL OF BEHAVIORAL SCIENCES, Vol. 5, no. 1 (March 1983), p. 93-103. English. DESCR: Acculturation Rating Scale for Mexican Americans (ARSMA); Case Studies; *Psychotherapy.

3903 Engle, Patricia L. Prenatal and postnatal anxiety in women giving birth in Los Angeles. HEALTH PSYCHOLOGY, Vol. 9, no. 3 (1990), p. 285-299. English. DESCR: *Fertility; Immigrants; Los Angeles, CA; *Maternal and Child Welfare; *Prenatal Care; *Stress; Women.

3904 Erickson, Pamela Irene. Pregnancy and childbirth among Mexican origin teenagers in Los Angeles. Thesis (Ph.D.)--UCLA, 1988. xiii, 277 leaves. English. DESCR: *Fertility; Los Angeles, CA; *Youth.

3905 Gonzalez, Judith Teresa. Factors relating to frequency of breast self-examination among low-income Mexican American women: implications for nursing practice. CANCER NURSING, Vol. 13, no. 3 (June 1990), p. 134-142. English. DESCR: *Breast Cancer; Cancer; Low Income; Medical Personnel; *Preventative Medicine.

3906 Gonzalez, Judith Teresa and Gonzalez, Virginia M. Initial validation of a scale measuring self-efficacy of breast self-examination among low-income Mexican American women. HISPANIC JOURNAL OF BEHAVIORAL SCIENCES, Vol. 12, no. 3 (August 1990), p. 277-291. English. DESCR: *Cancer; Low Income; Medical Education; Preventative Medicine.

3907 Henderson, Nancy. Perinatal service needs of Hispanic women with diabetes. Thesis (M.S.)--California State University, Long Beach, 1987. 79 p. English. DESCR: *Diabetes; Fertility; *Social Services; *Stress.

3908 Leblanc, Donna Marie. Quality of maternity care in rural Texas. Thesis (Dr. P.H.) --University of Texas H.S.C. at Houston School of Public Health, 1983. 266 p. English. DESCR: Fertility; Low Income; *Maternal and Child Welfare; Prenatal Care; *Rural Poor; Texas.

3909 Manzanedo, Hector Garcia; Walters, Esperanza Garcia; and Lorig, Kate R. Health and illness perceptions of the Chicana. IN: Melville, Margarita B., ed. TWICE A MINORITY. St. Louis, MO: Mosby, 1980, p. 191-207. English. DESCR: Cultural Characteristics; Culture; Public Health; Sex Roles; Values.

3910 Marin, Barbara Van Oss, et al. Health care utilization by low-income clients of a community clinic: an archival study. HISPANIC JOURNAL OF BEHAVIORAL SCIENCES, Vol. 3, no. 3 (September 1981), p. 257-273. English. DESCR: Family Planning; La Clinica Familiar del Barrio Los Angeles, CA; Low Income; Medical Clinics.

3911 Newton, Frank; Olmedo, Esteban L.; and Padilla, Amado M. Hispanic mental health research: a reference guide. Berkeley, CA: University of California Press, c1982. 685 p. English. DESCR: Anthropology; *Bibliography; Education; *Mental Health;

Psychology; Public Health; *Reference Works; Sociology.

3912 Ponce-Adame, Merrihelen. Women and cancer. CORAZON DE AZTLAN, Vol. 1, no. 2 (March, April, 1982), p. 32. English. DESCR: Cancer; Preventative Medicine.

3913 Queiro-Tajalli, Irene. Hispanic women's perceptions and use of prenatal health care services. AFFILIA: JOURNAL OF WOMEN AND SOCIAL WORK, Vol. 4, no. 2 (Summer 1989), p. 60-72. English. DESCR: Indianapolis, IN; *Prenatal Care; Surveys; Women.

3914 Radecki, Stephen E. and Bernstein, Gerald S. Use of clinic versus private family planning care by low-income women: access, cost and patient satisfaction. AMERICAN JOURNAL OF PUBLIC HEALTH, Vol. 79, no. 6 (June 1989), p. 692-697. English. DESCR: *Family Planning; Los Angeles County, CA; *Low Income; *Medical Clinics; Medical Personnel.

3915 Richardson, Jean L., et al. Frequency and adequacy of breast cancer screening among elderly Hispanic women. PREVENTIVE MEDICINE, Vol. 16, no. 6 (November 1987), p. 761-774. English. DESCR: Ancianos; *Cancer; Diseases; *Health Education; Los Angeles, CA; Preventative Medicine.

3916 Salazar, Sandra A. Chicanas as healers. IN: LA CHICANA: BUILDING FOR THE FUTURE, AN ACTION PLAN FOR THE 80s. Oakland, CA: National Hispanic University, 1981, p. 107-119. English. DESCR: Federal Aid; Public Health.

3917 Salazar, Sandra A. Reproductive choice for Hispanas. AGENDA, Vol. 9, no. 4 (July, August, 1979), p. 31-33, 36. English. DESCR: Abortion; *Public Health; Sterilization.

3918 Stern, Gwen. Research, action, and social betterment. AMERICAN BEHAVIOR SCIENTISTS, Vol. 29, no. 2 (November, December, 1985), p. 229-248. English. DESCR: Chicago, IL; Research Methodology; The Latina Mother-Infant Project, Chicago, IL.

3919 Swinney, Gloria Luyas. The biocultural context of low-income Mexican-American women with type II non-insulin dependent diabetes and its implications for health care delivery. Thesis (Ph.D.)--University of Texas, Austin, 1988. 277 p. English. DESCR: *Diabetes; Low Income; Non-insulin Dependent Diabetes Mellitus (NIDDM).

3920 Tajalli, Irene Queiro. Selected cultural, organizational, and economic factors related to prenatal care utilization by middle-income Hispanic women. Thesis (Ph.D.)--University of Illinois at Urbana-Champaign, 1984. 139 p. English. DESCR: *Fertility; Indiana; Maternal and Child Welfare; Prenatal Care; Preventative Medicine.

3921 Zambrana, Ruth E. Bibliography on maternal and child health across class, race and ethnicity. Memphis, TN: Distributed by the Memphis State University Center for Research on Women, c1990. 58 leaves. English. DESCR: *Bibliography; Ethnic Groups; *Maternal and Child Welfare; Social Classes; *Women.

Medical Care Laws and Legislation

3922 Talavera, Esther. Sterilization is not an alternative in family planning. AGENDA, Vol. 7, no. 6 (November, December, 1977), p. 8. English. DESCR: Discrimination; Family Planning; Feminism; *Fertility; Sterilization.

Medical Clinics

3923 Marin, Barbara Van Oss, et al. Health care utilization by low-income clients of a community clinic: an archival study. HISPANIC JOURNAL OF BEHAVIORAL SCIENCES, Vol. 3, no. 3 (September 1981), p. 257-273. English. DESCR: Family Planning; La Clinica Familiar del Barrio, Los Angeles, CA; Low Income; *Medical Care.

3924 Radecki, Stephen E. and Bernstein, Gerald S. Use of clinic versus private family planning care by low-income women: access, cost and patient satisfaction. AMERICAN JOURNAL OF PUBLIC HEALTH, Vol. 79, no. 6 (June 1989), p. 692-697. English. DESCR: *Family Planning; Los Angeles County, CA; *Low Income; Medical Care; Medical Personnel.

Medical Education

3925 Alvarado, Anita L. The status of Hispanic women in nursing. IN: Melville, Margarita B., ed. TWICE A MINORITY. St. Louis, MO: Mosby, 1980, p. 208-216. English. DESCR: Careers; *Medical Personnel.

3926 Bauman, Raquel. The status of Chicanas in medicine. RESEARCH BULLETIN (SPANISH SPEAKING MENTAL HEALTH RES. CENTER), Vol. 4, no. 3 (March 1980), p. 6-7,12-13. English. DESCR: *Medical Care; *Medical Personnel; Precolumbian Medicine.

3927 Fleming, Marilyn B. Problems experienced by Anglo, Hispanic and Navajo Indian women college students. JOURNAL OF AMERICAN INDIAN EDUCATION, Vol. 22, no. 1 (October 1982), p. 7-17. English. DESCR: Anglo Americans; Community Colleges; Ethnic Groups; *Higher Education; Identity; Native Americans; Students; Women.

3928 Gonzalez, Judith Teresa and Gonzalez, Virginia M. Initial validation of a scale measuring self-efficacy of breast self-examination among low-income Mexican American women. HISPANIC JOURNAL OF BEHAVIORAL SCIENCES, Vol. 12, no. 3 (August 1990), p. 277-291. English. DESCR: *Cancer; Low Income; Medical Care; Preventative Medicine.

3929 Hurtado, Aida. A view from within: midwife practices in South Texas. INTERNATIONAL QUARTERLY OF COMMUNITY HEALTH AND EDUCATION, Vol. 8, no. 4 (1987, 1988), p. 317-339. English. DESCR: Fertility; *Midwives; South Texas.

3930 Taylor, Elena. Conversations with a Chicana physician. REVISTA MUJERES, Vol. 1, no. 2 (June 1984), p. 44-46. English. DESCR: Medical Personnel; *Solinas, Lisa.

Medical Personnel

3931 Alvarado, Anita L. The status of Hispanic women in nursing. IN: Melville, Margarita B., ed. TWICE A MINORITY. St. Louis, MO: Mosby, 1980, p. 208-216. English. DESCR: Careers; Medical Education.

3932 Bauman, Raquel. The status of Chicanas in

medicine. RESEARCH BULLETIN (SPANISH SPEAKING MENTAL HEALTH RES. CENTER), Vol. 4, no. 3 (March 1980), p. 6-7,12-13. English. DESCR: *Medical Care; *Medical Education; Precolumbian Medicine.

3933 Floyd, Gloria Jo Wade. An exploration of the finding and seeking of meaning in life and the Mexican-American nurse's mood state. Thesis (Ph.D.)--Texas Women's University, 1980. 133 p. English. DESCR: *Mental Health; Stress.

3934 Gonzalez, Judith Teresa. Factors relating to frequency of breast self-examination among low-income Mexican American women: implications for nursing practice. CANCER NURSING, Vol. 13, no. 3 (June 1990), p. 134-142. English. DESCR: *Breast Cancer; Cancer; Low Income; Medical Care; *Preventative Medicine.

3935 Jorgensen, Stephen R. and Adams, Russell P. Family planning needs and behavior of Mexican American women: a study of health care professionals and their clientele. HISPANIC JOURNAL OF BEHAVIORAL SCIENCES, Vol. 9, no. 3 (September 1987), p. 265-286. English. DESCR: Acculturation; *Attitudes; Birth Control; *Cultural Characteristics; *Family Planning; Fertility; Stereotypes; Sterilization.

3936 La Monica, Grace; Gulino, Claire; and Ortiz Soto, Irma. A comparative study of female Mexican and American working nurses in the border corridor. BORDER HEALTH/SALUD FRONTERIZA, Vol. 5, no. 2 (April, June, 1989), p. 2-6. Bilingual. DESCR: Anglo Americans; *Border Region; Women; *Working Women.

3937 Ortega, E. Astrid. Moving Hispanics into nursing. CALIFORNIA NURSE, Vol. 83, no. 3 (April 1987), p. 8. English. DESCR: Careers.

3938 Perez, Robert. Stress and coping as determinants of adaptation to pregnancy in Hispanic women. Thesis (Ph.D.)--University of California, Los Angeles, 1982. 343 p. English. DESCR: *Fertility; Natural Support Systems; *Stress.

3939 Perrone, Bobette; Stockel, H. Henrietta; and Krueger, Victoria. Medicine women, curanderas, and women doctors. Norman, OK: University of Oklahoma Press, c1989. xix, 252 p.:ill. English. DESCR: Aragon, Jesusita, 1908-; *Curanderas; *Curanderismo; *Folk Medicine; Herbal Medicine; Herrera, Sabinita; Native Americans; *Oral History; Rodriguez, Gregorita; Women.

3940 Radecki, Stephen E. and Bernstein, Gerald S. Use of clinic versus private family planning care by low-income women: access, cost and patient satisfaction. AMERICAN JOURNAL OF PUBLIC HEALTH, Vol. 79, no. 6 (June 1989), p. 692-697. English. DESCR: *Family Planning; Los Angeles County, CA; *Low Income; Medical Care; *Medical Clinics.

3941 Solis, Faustina. Commentary on the Chicana and health services. IN: Sanchez, Rosaura and Martinez Cruz, Rosa, eds. ESSAYS ON LA MUJER. Los Angeles, CA: Chicano Studies Center Publications, UCLA, 1977, p. 82-90. English. DESCR: *Public Health; Sex Roles.

3942 Taylor, Elena. Conversations with a Chicana physician. REVISTA MUJERES, Vol. 1, no. 2 (June 1984), p. 44-46. English. DESCR: Medical Education; *Solinas, Lisa.

Medical Personnel
(cont.)

3943 Valtierra, Mary. Acculturation, social
support, and reported stress of Latina
physicians. Thesis (Ph.D.)--California
School of Professional Psychology, 1989. 136
p. English. **DESCR:** *Acculturation; Careers;
Cubanos; Immigration; Latin Americans;
Puerto Ricans; *Stress; *Women.

Medical Services
USE: Medical Care

Medicine
USE: Medical Care

Megatek, La Jolla, CA

3944 Fernandez Kelly, Maria and Garcia, Anna M.
Invisible amidst the glitter: Hispanic women
in the Southern California electronics
industry. IN: Statham, Anne; Miller, Eleanor
M.; and Mauksh, Hans O., eds. THE WORTH OF
WOMEN'S WORK: A QUALITATIVE SYNTHESIS.
Albany, NY: State University of New York
Press, 1988, p. 265-290. English. **DESCR:**
*Electronics Industry; Employment;
Immigrants; *Industrial Workers; Labor
Supply and Market; Nova-Tech, San Diego, CA;
Sex Roles; Southern California; *Working
Women.

Mena, Maria Cristina

3945 Velasquez-Trevino, Gloria. Cultural
ambivalence in early Chicana prose fiction.
Thesis (Ph.D.)--Stanford University, 1985.
185 p. English. **DESCR:** Biculturalism;
*Fiction; Gonzalez, Jovita; Literary
Criticism; Niggli, Josephina; Prose; Sex
Roles.

Mendez M., Miguel

3946 Gutierrez Castillo, Dina. La imagen de la
mujer en la novela fronteriza. IN:
Lopez-Gonzalez, Aralia, et al., eds. MUJER Y
LITERATURA MEXICANA Y CHICANA: CULTURAS EN
CONTACTO. Mexico: Colegio de la Frontera
Norte, 1988, p. [55]-63. Spanish. **DESCR:**
*Border Region; Islas, Arturo; Literary
Characters; *Literary Criticism; *Novel;
PEREGRINOS DE AZTLAN; Sex Roles; Sex
Stereotypes; THE RAIN GOD: A DESERT TALE;
*Women.

Mendoza, Hope Schecter

3947 Mendoza, Hope Schecter and Chall, Malca.
Activist in the labor movement, the
Democratic Party, and the Mexican-American
community: an interview. Berkeley, CA:
Regional Oral History Office, Bancroft
Library, University of California, Berkeley,
1980. xii, 170 p.: ill. English. **DESCR:**
*Biography; Chavez Ravine, Los Angeles, CA;
Church, Frank; Community Organizations;
Community Service Organization, Los Angeles,
(CSO); Democratic Party; Elections; Garment
Industry; Industrial Workers; *Labor Unions;
Leadership; Snyder, Elizabeth; Warschaw,
Carmen.

Mendoza, Lupe

3948 Mendoza, Lupe. Porque lo podemos hacer--a
poco no? REVISTA MUJERES, Vol. 1, no. 2
(June 1984), p. 33-37. Spanish. **DESCR:**
Autobiography; Higher Education.

Mendoza, Rita

3949 Sanchez, Rita. Chicana writer breaking out

of the silence. DE COLORES, Vol. 3, no. 3
(1977), p. 31-37. English. **DESCR:** Authors;
Castaneda Shular, Antonia; Correa, Viola;
Cunningham, Veronica; Hernandez, Barbara;
*Literary Criticism; *Poetry.

3950 Zamora, Bernice. Archetypes in Chicana
poetry. DE COLORES, Vol. 4, no. 3 (1978), p.
43-52. English. **DESCR:** Cervantes, Lorna Dee;
Cunningham, Veronica; "Declaration on a Day
of Little Inspiration" [poem]; Hernandez,
Carlota; "I Speak in an Illusion" [poem];
*Literary Criticism; Lucero, Judy A.;
Macias, Margarita; "Para Mi Hijita" [poem];
*Poetry; "Rape Report" [poem]; "The White
Line" [poem]; "Working Mother's Song"
[poem]; "You Can Only Blame the System for
So Long" [poem]; Zamora, Katarina.

Menopause

3951 Groessl, Patricia Ann. Depression and
anxiety in postmenopausal women: a study of
Black, white, and Hispanic women. Thesis
(Ed.D.)--Western Michigan University, 1987.
87 p. English. **DESCR:** Anglo Americans;
Blacks; *Depression (Psychological);
Michigan; Stress; Women.

Menstruation

3952 Finkelstein, Jordan W. and Von Eye,
Alexander. Sanitary product use by white,
Black, and Mexican American women. PUBLIC
HEALTH REPORTS, Vol. 105, no. 5 (September,
October, 1990), p. 491-496. English. **DESCR:**
Anglo Americans; Blacks; *Toxic Shock
Syndrome (TSS); *Women.

Mental Health

3953 Adams, Russell P. Predictors of self-esteem
and locus-of-control in Mexican-American
women. Thesis (Ph.D.)--Texas Tech
University, 1989. 138 p. English. **DESCR:**
*Identity; *Locus of Control; Research
Methodology.

3954 Amaro, Hortensia. Abortion use and attitudes
among Chicanas: the need for research.
RESEARCH BULLETIN (SPANISH SPEAKING MENTAL
HEALTH RES. CENTER), Vol. 4, no. 3 (March
1980), p. 1-5. English. **DESCR:** *Abortion;
*Attitudes; Birth Control; Family Planning;
Fertility; Literature Reviews.

3955 Amaro, Hortensia and Russo, Nancy Felipe.
Hispanic women and mental health: an
overview of contemporary issues in research
and practice. PSYCHOLOGY OF WOMEN QUARTERLY,
Vol. 11, no. 4 (December 1987), p. 393-407.
English. **DESCR:** *Literature Reviews; *Women.

3956 Andrade, Sally J., ed. Latino families in
the United States: a resource book for
family life education = Las familias latinas
en los Estados Unidos: recursos para la
capacitacion familiar. [S.l.]: Planned
Parenthood Federation of America, Inc.,
1983. ix, 79, 70, xi p. Bilingual. **DESCR:**
Bilingualism; Community Organizations;
Education; *Family; Public Health.

3957 Armas-Cardona, Regina. Anglo and Raza young
women: a study of self-esteem, psychic
distress and locus of control. Thesis
(Ph.D.)--Wright Institute Graduate School of
Psychology, 1985. 143 p. English. **DESCR:**
*Anglo Americans; Locus of Control; Stress;
*Women.

Mental Health (cont.)

3958 Bach-y-Rita, George. The Mexican-American: religious and cultural influences. IN: Becerra, Rosina M., et al., eds. MENTAL HEALTH AND HISPANIC AMERICANS: CLINICAL PERSPECTIVES. New York: Grune & Stratton, 1982, p. 29-40. English. **DESCR:** Catholic Church; Cultural Characteristics; Culture; Language Usage; Machismo; Psychotherapy; Religion.

3959 Balkwell, Carolyn Ann. An attitudinal correlate of the timing of a major life event: the case of morale in widowhood. FAMILY RELATIONS, Vol. 34, no. 4 (October 1985), p. 577-581. English. **DESCR:** *Ancianos; Counseling (Psychological); *Marriage; Natural Support Systems; Widowhood.

3960 Balkwell, Carolyn Ann. Widowhood: its impact on morale and optimism among older persons of three ethnic groups. Thesis (Ph.D.)--University of Georgia, 1981. 170 p. English. **DESCR:** *Ancianos; Anglo Americans; Blacks; Depression (Psychological); Ethnic Groups; Los Angeles County, CA; Widowhood; *Women.

3961 Belk, Sharyn S., et al. Impact of ethnicity, nationality, counseling orientation, and mental health standards on stereotypic beliefs about women. SEX ROLES, Vol. 21, no. 9-10 (November 1989), p. 671-695. English. **DESCR:** Anglo Americans; Beliefs About Women Scale (BAWS); *Comparative Psychology; *Counseling (Psychological); Cultural Characteristics; Identity; *Sex Stereotypes; Sexism; Women.

3962 Canales, Genevieve and Roberts, Robert E. Gender and mental health in the Mexican origin population of South Texas. IN: Rodriguez, Reymund and Coleman, Marion Tolbert, eds. MENTAL HEALTH ISSUES OF THE MEXICAN ORIGIN POPULATION IN TEXAS. Austin, TX: Hogg Foundation for Mental Health, University of Texas, 1987, p. 89-99. English. **DESCR:** Del Rio, TX; Depression (Psychological); Eagle Pass, TX; Health Education; *Males; *Sex Roles; South Texas; Surveys.

3963 Canino, Glorisa. The Hispanic woman: sociocultural influences on diagnoses and treatment. IN: Becerra, Rosina M., et al., eds. MENTAL HEALTH AND HISPANIC AMERICANS: CLINICAL PERSPECTIVES. New York: Grune & Stratton, 1982, p. 117-138. English. **DESCR:** Assimilation; Cultural Characteristics; Culture; *Depression (Psychological); Family; Feminism; Population; Sex Roles.

3964 Carrillo-Beron, Carmen. Raza mental health: perspectivas femeniles. IN: PERSPECTIVAS EN CHICANO STUDIES: PAPERS PRESENTED AT THE THIRD ANNUAL MEETING OF THE NATIONAL ASSOCIATION OF CHICANO SOCIAL SCIENCE, 1975. Los Angeles, CA: National Association of Chicano Social Science, 1977, p. 69-80. English. **DESCR:** Attitudes; Centro de Salud Mental, Oakland, CA; Conferences and Meetings; Mujeres de Hoy Conference (Oakland, CA).

3965 Cristo, Martha H. Stress and coping among Mexican women. Thesis (Ph.D.)--California School of Professional Psychology, Los Angeles, 1988. 336 p. English. **DESCR:** Cultural Characteristics; *Immigrants; Socioeconomic Factors; *Stress; *Women.

3966 Cuellar, Israel. Service delivery and mental health services for Chicano elders. IN: Miranda, Manuel and Ruiz, Rene A., eds. CHICANO AGING AND MENTAL HEALTH. Rockville, MD: U.S. Department of Health and Human Services, 1981, p. 185-211. English. **DESCR:** *Ancianos; Attitudes; Cultural Customs; Cultural Pluralism; Language Usage; Mental Health Clinics; Religion; Sex Roles; Spanish Language.

3967 Enguidanos-Clark, Gloria M. Acculturative stress and its contribution to the development of depression in Hispanic women. Thesis (Ph.D.)--Wright Institute, Berkeley, 1986. 198 p. English. **DESCR:** *Acculturation; *Depression (Psychological); Immigrants; *Stress.

3968 Falicov, Celia Jaes. Mexican families. IN: McGoldrick, Monica, et al., eds. ETHNICITY AND FAMILY THERAPY. New York: The Guilford Press, 1982, p. 134-163. English. **DESCR:** Acculturation; Cultural Customs; *Family; Sex Roles.

3969 Floyd, Gloria Jo Wade. An exploration of the finding and seeking of meaning in life and the Mexican-American nurse's mood state. Thesis (Ph.D.)--Texas Women's University, 1980. 133 p. English. **DESCR:** *Medical Personnel; Stress.

3970 Freier, Michelle Cyd. Psychosocial and physiological influences on birth outcomes among women of Mexican origin or descent. Thesis (Ph.D.)--UCLA, 1987. xiv, 197 leaves. English. **DESCR:** *Fertility.

3971 Gettman, Dawn and Pena, Devon Gerardo. Women, mental health, and the workplace in a transnational setting. SOCIAL WORK, Vol. 31, no. 1 (January, February, 1986), p. 5-11. English. **DESCR:** *Border Industries; Employment; Mexico; United States-Mexico Relations; Women; *Working Women.

3972 Gibson, Guadalupe. Hispanic women: stress and mental health issues. WOMEN AND THERAPY, Vol. 2, no. 2-3 (Summer, Fall, 1983), p. 113-133. English. **DESCR:** Cultural Characteristics; *Stress.

3973 Krause, Neal and Markides, Kyriakos S. Employment and psychological well-being in Mexican American women. JOURNAL OF HEALTH AND SOCIAL BEHAVIOR, Vol. 26, no. 1 (March 1985), p. 15-26. English. **DESCR:** *Attitudes; *Employment; Identity; Sex Roles; Working Women.

3974 Lawrence, Alberto Augusto. Traditional attitudes toward marriage, marital adjustment, acculturation, and self-esteem of Mexican-American and Mexican wives. Thesis (Ph.D.)--United States International University, San Diego, CA, 1982. ix, 191 p. English. **DESCR:** *Acculturation; *Attitudes; Machismo; *Marriage; Psychological Testing; San Ysidro, CA; Sex Roles; Sex Stereotypes; Tijuana, Baja California, Mexico; Women.

3975 Markides, Kyriakos S. and Vernon, Sally W. Aging, sex-role orientation and adjustment: a three-generations study of Mexican Americans. JOURNAL OF GERONTOLOGY, Vol. 39, no. 5 (September 1984), p. 586-591. English. **DESCR:** *Age Groups; *Ancianos; *Sex Roles.

3976 Markides, Kyriakos S. and Farrell, Janice. Marital status and depression among Mexican Americans. SOCIAL PSYCHIATRY, Vol. 20, no. 2 (1985), p. 86-91. English. **DESCR:** Depression (Psychological); Divorce; *Marriage.

Mental Health (cont.)

3977 Newton, Frank; Olmedo, Esteban L.; and
     Padilla, Amado M. Hispanic mental health
     research: a reference guide. Berkeley, CA:
     University of California Press, c1982. 685
     p. English. **DESCR:** Anthropology;
     *Bibliography; Education; Medical Care;
     Psychology; Public Health; *Reference Works;
     Sociology.

3978 Nyamathi, Adeline M. and Vasquez, Rose.
     Impact of poverty, homelessness, and drugs
     on Hispanic women at risk for HIV infection.
     HISPANIC JOURNAL OF BEHAVIORAL SCIENCES,
     Vol. 11, no. 4 (November 1989), p. 299-314.
     English. **DESCR:** *AIDS (Disease); Drug Use;
     Health Education; *Human Immunodeficiency
     Virus (HIV); Locus of Control;
     Needle-Sharing; *Poverty.

3979 Palacios, Maria and Franco, Juan N.
     Counseling Mexican-American women. JOURNAL
     OF MULTICULTURAL COUNSELING AND DEVELOPMENT,
     Vol. 14, (July 1986), p. 124-131. English.
     DESCR: *Counseling (Psychological); Cultural
     Characteristics.

3980 Rivera, George; Lucero, Aileen; and Regoli,
     Robert M. Contemporary curanderismo: a study
     of mental health agency and home clientele
     of a practicing curandera. ISSUES IN RADICAL
     THERAPY, Vol. 13, no. 1-2 (Winter, Spring,
     1988), p. 52-57. English. **DESCR:** Curanderas;
     *Curanderismo; Socioeconomic Factors.

3981 Roberts, Robert E. and Roberts, Catharine
     Ramsay. Marriage, work and depressive
     symptoms among Mexican Americans. HISPANIC
     JOURNAL OF BEHAVIORAL SCIENCES, Vol. 4, no.
     2 (June 1982), p. 199-221. English. **DESCR:**
     Depression (Psychological); Employment;
     Marriage.

3982 Rodriguez, Rogelio E. Psychological distress
     among Mexican-American women as a reaction
     to the new immigration law. Thesis
     (Ph.D.)--Loyola University of Chicago, 1989.
     87 p. English. **DESCR:** Depression
     (Psychological); Immigrants; *Immigration
     Law and Legislation; Immigration Reform and
     Control Act of 1986; Mexico; Stress;
     Undocumented Workers; Women.

3983 Saenz, Rogelio. Traditional sex-roles,
     ethnic integration, marital satisfaction,
     and psychological distress among Chicanas.
     Thesis (Ph.D.)--Iowa State University, 1986.
     145 p. English. **DESCR:** *Marriage; *Sex
     Roles; Stress.

3984 Salgado de Snyder, Nelly. Factors associated
     with acculturative stress and depressive
     symptomatology among married Mexican
     immigrant women. PSYCHOLOGY OF WOMEN
     QUARTERLY, Vol. 11, no. 4 (December 1987),
     p. 475-488. English. **DESCR:** *Acculturation;
     Depression (Psychological); *Immigrants;
     Mexico; *Stress; Women.

3985 Salgado de Snyder, Nelly. The role of ethnic
     loyalty among Mexican immigrant women.
     HISPANIC JOURNAL OF BEHAVIORAL SCIENCES,
     Vol. 9, no. 3 (September 1987), p. 287-298.
     English. **DESCR:** Acculturation; *Culture;
     *Identity; Immigrants; Mexico; *Women.

3986 Vargas-Willis, Gloria and Cervantes, Richard
     C. Consideration of psychosocial stress in
     the treatment of the Latina immigrant.
     HISPANIC JOURNAL OF BEHAVIORAL SCIENCES,
     Vol. 9, no. 3 (September 1987), p. 315-329.
     English. **DESCR:** Discrimination in
     Employment; *Immigrants; *Psychotherapy;
     *Stress.

3987 Vasquez, Melba J. T. Power and status of the
     Chicana: a social-psychological perspective.
     IN: Martinez, Joe L., Jr., ed. CHICANO
     PSYCHOLOGY. 2nd. ed. Orlando, FL: Academic
     Press, 1984, p. 269-287. English. **DESCR:**
     *Identity; Income; Psychology; *Sex Roles;
     Socialization; Working Women.

3988 Vega, William A.; Warheit, George; and
     Meinhardt, Kenneth. Marital disruption and
     the prevalence of depressive symptomatology
     among Anglos and Mexican Americans. JOURNAL
     OF MARRIAGE AND THE FAMILY, Vol. 46, no. 4
     (November 1984), p. 817-824. English.
     DESCR: Anglo Americans; Depression
     (Psychological); *Divorce; *Marriage;
     Socioeconomic Factors.

3989 Vega, William A.; Kolody, Bohdan; and Valle,
     Juan Ramon. Migration and mental health: an
     empirical test of depression risk factors
     among immigrant Mexican women. INTERNATIONAL
     MIGRATION REVIEW, Vol. 21, no. 3 (Fall
     1987), p. 512-530. English. **DESCR:**
     Acculturation; *Depression (Psychological);
     *Immigrants; Immigration; Migration; Stress;
     Undocumented Workers; Women.

3990 Vega, William A., et al. Depressive symptoms
     and their correlates among immigrant Mexican
     women in the United States. SOCIAL SCIENCE &
     MEDICINE, Vol. 22, no. 6 (1986), p. 645-652.
     English. **DESCR:** Depression (Psychological);
     *Immigrants; Public Health; San Diego, CA.

3991 White, Marni, et al. Perceived crime in the
     neighborhood and mental health of women and
     children. ENVIRONMENT AND BEHAVIOR, Vol. 19,
     no. 5 (September 1987), p. 588-613. English.
     DESCR: Attitudes; Children; Criminology;
     Housing; Women.

3992 Winter, Michael; Russo, Nancy Felipe; and
     Amaro, Hortensia. The use of inpatient
     mental health services by Hispanic women.
     PSYCHOLOGY OF WOMEN QUARTERLY, Vol. 11, no.
     4 (December 1987), p. 427-441. English.
     DESCR: *Mental Health Clinics; Social
     Services; *Women.

3993 Zambrana, Ruth E. Hispanic professional
     women: work, family and health. Los Angeles,
     CA: National Network of Hispanic Women,
     1987. 75 leaves. English. **DESCR:** Business;
     *Careers; *Employment; Family; Management;
     Social Classes; *Social Mobility; *Women.

3994 Zambrana, Ruth E. and Frith, Sandra.
     Mexican-American professional women: role
     satisfaction differences in single and
     multiple role lifestyles. JOURNAL OF SOCIAL
     BEHAVIOR AND PERSONALITY, Vol. 3, no. 4
     (1988), p. 347-361. English. **DESCR:**
     *Careers; Family; *Sex Roles; Working Women.

3995 Zavala Martinez, Iris Zoraida. Depression
     among women of Mexican descent. Thesis
     (Ph.D.)--University of Massachusetts, 1984.
     295 p. English. **DESCR:** *Depression
     (Psychological); Los Angeles, CA.

3996 Zayas, Luis H. Toward an understanding of
     suicide risks in young Hispanic females.
     JOURNAL OF ADOLESCENT RESEARCH, Vol. 2, no.
     1 (Spring 1987), p. 1-11. English. **DESCR:**
     Acculturation; Cubanos; Cultural
     Characteristics; Depression (Psychological);
     Puerto Ricans; *Suicide; *Women; *Youth.

Mental Health (cont.)

3997 Zuniga, Maria E. Assessment issues with Chicanas: practice implications. PSYCHOTHERAPY, Vol. 25, no. 2 (Summer 1988), p. 288-293. English. **DESCR:** Acculturation; Colleges and Universities; Family; Identity; Mexican-American Outreach Program, San Diego State University; *Psychotherapy; *Students.

Mental Health Clinics

3998 Cuellar, Israel. Service delivery and mental health services for Chicano elders. IN: Miranda, Manuel and Ruiz, Rene A., eds. CHICANO AGING AND MENTAL HEALTH. Rockville, MD: U.S. Department of Health and Human Services, 1981, p. 185-211. English. **DESCR:** *Ancianos; Attitudes; Cultural Customs; Cultural Pluralism; Language Usage; Mental Health; Religion; Sex Roles; Spanish Language.

3999 Leon, Ana M., et al. Self-help support groups for Hispanic mothers. CHILD WELFARE, Vol. 63, no. 3 (May, June, 1984), p. 261-268. English. **DESCR:** Family; *Natural Support Systems; *Parent and Child Relationships; Sex Roles.

4000 Winter, Michael; Russo, Nancy Felipe; and Amaro, Hortensia. The use of inpatient mental health services by Hispanic women. PSYCHOLOGY OF WOMEN QUARTERLY, Vol. 11, no. 4 (December 1987), p. 427-441. English. **DESCR:** Mental Health; Social Services; *Women.

Mental Hygiene
USE: Mental Health

Mental Illness

4001 Gonzalez del Valle, Amalia and Usher, Mary. Group therapy with aged Latino women: a pilot project and study. CLINICAL GERONTOLOGIST, Vol. 1, no. 1 (Fall 1982), p. 51-58. English. **DESCR:** *Ancianos; Cultural Characteristics; *Psychotherapy; San Mateo County, CA.

4002 Mullen, Julia Ann. Black, Anglo, and Chicana women's construction of mental illness. Thesis (Ph.D.)--University of California, Santa Barbara, 1985. 276 p. English. **DESCR:** Anglo Americans; Blacks; *Women.

Mentally Handicapped

4003 Mary, Nancy L. Reactions of Black, Hispanic, and white mothers to having a child with handicaps. MENTAL RETARDATION, Vol. 28, no. 1 (February 1990), p. 1-5. English. **DESCR:** Anglo Americans; *Attitudes; Blacks; *Children; Comparative Psychology; Parent and Child Relationships; *Women.

Mentoring

4004 Quezada, Rosa; Loheyde, Katherine Jones; and Kacmarczyk, Ronald. The Hispanic woman graduate student: barriers to mentoring in higher education. TEXAS TECH JOURNAL OF EDUCATION, Vol. 11, no. 3 (Fall 1984), p. 235-241. English. **DESCR:** Discrimination in Education; *Graduate Schools; *Higher Education; Students.

Mesa-Bains, Amalia

4005 Goldman, Shifra M. Mujeres de California: Latin American women artists. IN: Moore, Sylvia, ed. YESTERDAY AND TOMORROW: CALIFORNIA WOMEN ARTISTS. New York, NY: Midmarch Arts Press, c1989, p. 202-229. English. **DESCR:** *Artists; Baca, Judith F.; Biography; California; Carrasco, Barbara; Cervantez, Yreina; de Larios, Dora; Feminism; Hernandez, Judithe; Lomas Garza, Carmen; Lopez, Yolanda M.; Murillo, Patricia; Sanchez, Olivia; Valdez, Patssi; Vallejo Dillaway, Linda; Women; Zamora Lucero, Linda.

Mesilla Valley, NM

4006 Loustaunau, Martha Oehmke. Hispanic widows and their support systems in the Mesilla Valley of southern New Mexico, 1910-40. IN: Scadron, Arlene, ed. ON THEIR OWN: WIDOWS AND WIDOWHOOD IN THE AMERICAN SOUTHWEST 1843-1939. Urbana, IL: University of Illinois Press, c1988, p. [91]-116. English. **DESCR:** Cultural Customs; Extended Family; Natural Support Systems; Sex Roles; Single Parents; Widowhood; *Women.

Mestizaje

4007 Alarcon, Norma. Chicana feminism: in the tracks of 'the' native woman. CULTURAL STUDIES, Vol. 4, no. 3 (October 1990), p. 248-256. English. **DESCR:** Cultural Studies; *Feminism; *Identity; *Indigenismo; Women.

4008 Saldivar-Hull, Sonia. Feminism on the border: from gender politics to geopolitics. IN: Calderon, Hector and Saldivar, Jose David, eds. CRITICISM IN THE BORDERLANDS: STUDIES IN CHICANO LITERATURE, CULTURE, AND IDEOLOGY. Durham, NC: Duke University Press, 1991, p. [203]-220. English. **DESCR:** Anglo Americans; *Anzaldua, Gloria; *BORDERLANDS/LA FRONTERA: THE NEW MESTIZA; Feminism; Homosexuality; *Literary Criticism; Moraga, Cherrie; Sexism; "The Cariboo Cafe" [short story]; Viramontes, Helena Maria; Women.

Methodist Church

4009 Ruiz, Vicki L. Dead ends or gold mines?: using missionary records in Mexican-American women's history. FRONTIERS: A JOURNAL OF WOMEN STUDIES, Vol. 12, no. 1 (1991), p. 33-56. English. **DESCR:** Archives; Clergy; El Paso, TX; History; Protestant Church; *Research Methodology; *Rose Gregory Houchen Settlement House, El Paso, TX.

Methodology
USE: Research Methodology

Mexicali, Mexico

4010 Tiano, Susan B. Maquiladoras in Mexicali: integration or exploitation? IN: Ruiz, Vicki L. and Tiano, Susan, eds. WOMEN ON THE U.S.-MEXICO BORDER: RESPONSES TO CHANGE. Boston, MA: Allen & Unwin, 1987, p. 77-101. English. **DESCR:** Border Industrialization Program (BIP); *Border Industries; Border Region; Employment; Labor Supply and Market; Women; Working Women.

Mexican American Legal Defense and Educational Fund (MALDEF)

4011 Aragon de Valdez, Theresa. Organizing as a political tool for the Chicana. FRONTIERS: A JOURNAL OF WOMEN STUDIES, Vol. 5, no. 2 (Summer 1980), p. 7-13. English. **DESCR:** Discrimination; Feminism; *Leadership; Social History and Conditions; Sterilization.

Mexican American Legal Defense and Educational Fund (MALDEF) (cont.)

4012 Mexican American Legal Defense and Education Fund (MALDEF). Chicana rights: a major MALDEF issue (reprinted from MALDEF Newsletter, Fall 1977). COMADRE, no. 3 (Fall 1978), p. 31-35. English. DESCR: Chicana Rights Project; *Feminism; Statistics; Vasquez, Patricia.

Mexican American Research Association (MARA), California Institution for Women

4013 Vangie, Mary. Women at Frontera, CA. REGENERACION, Vol. 1, no. 10 (1971), p. 8. English. DESCR: Education; Prisons; Statistics.

Mexican American Women's National Association (MANA)

4014 Espinosa, Ann. Hispanas: our resources [sic] for the eighties. LA LUZ, Vol. 8, no. 4 (October, November, 1979), p. 10-13. English. DESCR: Baca Barragan, Polly; *Civil Rights; Comision Femeril Mexicana Nacional; DIRECTORY OF HISPANIC WOMEN; Discrimination in Education; Elected Officials; Hernandez, Irene; Lacayo, Carmela; Lujan, Josie; Montanez Davis, Grace; Moreno, Olga; Mujeres Latinas en Accion (M.L.A.); National Conference of Puerto Rican Women, Inc. (NCOPRW); Organizations; Rangel, Irma.

4015 Fostering the advancement of Latinas. NUESTRO, Vol. 6, no. 10 (December 1982), p. 48-49. English. DESCR: *Women Men Relations.

4016 Prida, Dolores. Looking for room of one's own. NUESTRO, Vol. 3, no. 5 (June, July, 1979), p. 24-29. English. DESCR: Comision Femenil Mexicana de California; *Feminism; National Association of Cuban American Women; National Conference of Puerto Rican Women, Inc. (NCOPRW); Organizations.

4017 Vivo, Paquita. Voces de Hispanas: Hispanic women and their concerns. IN: HISPANICS AND GRANTMAKERS: A SPECIAL REPORT OF FOUNDATION NEWS. Washington, DC: Council on Foundations, 1981, p. 35-39. English. DESCR: Puerto Ricans.

Mexican Border Industrialization Program USE: Border Industrialization Program (BIP)

Mexican Literature

4018 Domenella, Ana Rosa. Al margen de un coloquio fronterizo mujer y literatura mexicana y chicana. FEM, Vol. 14, no. 89 (May 1990), p. 32-34. Spanish. DESCR: *Border Region; Coloquio Fronterizo Mujer y Literatura Mexicana y Chicana (1987: Tijuana, Baja California, Mexico); *Conferences and Meetings; *Literature; Mexico; Women.

4019 Leal, Luis. Arquetipos femeninos en la literatura mexicana. IN: Leal, Luis. AZTLAN Y MEXICO: PERFILES LITERARIOS E HISTORICOS. Binghamton, NY: Bilingual Press/Editorial Bilingue, 1985, p. 168-176. Spanish. DESCR: La Virgen de Guadalupe; *Literary Criticism; Malinche; Symbolism; Women.

4020 Leal, Luis. Female archetypes in Mexican literature. IN: Miller, Beth, ed. WOMEN IN HISPANIC LITERATURE: ICONS AND FALLEN IDOLS. Berkeley, CA: University of California Press, 1983, p. 227-242. English. DESCR: La Virgen de Guadalupe; *Literary Criticism; Malinche; Symbolism; Women.

4021 Leal, Luis. La soldadera en la narrativa de la Revolucion. IN: Leal, Luis. AZTLAN Y MEXICO: PERFILES LITERARIOS E HISTORICOS. Binghamton, NY: Bilingual Press/Editorial Bilingue, 1985, p. 185-193. Spanish. DESCR: La Adelita; LA VOZ DEL PUEBLO; *Literary Criticism; Mexican Revolution - 1910-1920; Women.

4022 Lopez-Gonzalez, Aralia, et al., eds. Mujer y literatura mexicana y chicana: culturas en contacto. Mexico: Colegio de Mexico, Programa Interdisciplinario de Estudios de la Mujer; Tijuana, B.C., Mexico: Colegio de la Frontera Norte, 1988. 264 p. Spanish. DESCR: *Literary Criticism; *Mexico; Sex Roles; *Women.

Mexican Mothers' Club, Chicago, IL

4023 Ano Nuevo Kerr, Louise. Chicanas in the Great Depression. IN: Del Castillo, Adelaida R., ed. BETWEEN BORDERS: ESSAYS ON MEXICANA/CHICANA HISTORY. Encino, CA: Floricanto Press, 1990, p. 257-268. English. DESCR: *Chicago, IL; *Great Depression, 1929-1933; Historiography; *Working Women.

Mexican Revolution - 1910-1920

4024 Flores Magon, Ricardo. A la mujer = To women. IN: Mora, Magdalena and Del Castillo, Adelaida, eds. MEXICAN WOMEN IN THE UNITED STATES: STRUGGLES PAST AND PRESENT. Los Angeles, CA: Chicano Studies Research Center, UCLA, 1980, p. 159-162. English. DESCR: *Sexism.

4025 Gamio, Manuel. Senora Flores de Andrade. IN: Mora, Magdalena and Del Castillo, Adelaida, eds. MEXICAN WOMEN IN THE UNITED STATES: STRUGGLES PAST AND PRESENT. Los Angeles, CA: Chicano Studies Research Center, UCLA, 1980, p. 189-192. English. DESCR: Autobiography; Flores de Andrade, Senora; Immigrants; *Oral History.

4026 Gonzales, Sylvia Alicia. The Chicana perspective: a design for self-awareness. IN: Trejo, Arnulfo D., ed. THE CHICANOS: AS WE SEE OURSELVES. Tucson, AZ: University of Arizona Press, 1979, p. 81-99. English. DESCR: CHICANAS SPEAK OUT; Chicano Movement; Discrimination; Feminism; Identity; Machismo; Madsen, William; Mexico; Sex Roles; THE MEXICAN-AMERICANS OF SOUTH TEXAS; Vidal, Mirta.

4027 Hernandez, Ines. Sara Estela Ramirez: the early twentieth century Texas-Mexican poet. Thesis (Ph.D.)--University of Houston, 1984. 94 p. English. DESCR: *Authors; *Biography; Feminism; Flores Magon, Ricardo; Journalism; Literary Criticism; Mexico; *Poetry; Ramirez, Sara Estela; Texas; Women.

4028 Hernandez, Ines. Sara Estela Ramirez: sembradora. LEGACY: A JOURNAL OF NINETEENTH-CENTURY AMERICAN WOMEN WRITERS, Vol. 6, no. 1 (Spring 1989), p. 13-26. English. DESCR: Authors; *Biography; *Feminism; Flores Magon, Ricardo; *Journalism; LA CORREGIDORA [newspaper]; Mexico; Newspapers; Poetry; *Ramirez, Sara Estela; REGENERACION [newspaper].

Mexican Revolution - 1910-1920
    (cont.)

4029 Leal, Luis. La soldadera en la narrativa de
     la Revolucion. IN: Leal, Luis. AZTLAN Y
     MEXICO: PERFILES LITERARIOS E HISTORICOS.
     Binghamton, NY: Bilingual Press/Editorial
     Bilingue, 1985, p. 185-193. Spanish. DESCR:
     La Adelita; LA VOZ DEL PUEBLO; *Literary
     Criticism; Mexican Literature; Women.

4030 Lomas, Clara. Mexican precursors of Chicana
     feminist writing. IN: National Association
     for Chicano Studies. ESTUDIOS CHICANOS AND
     THE POLITICS OF COMMUNITY. [S.l.]: National
     Association for Chicano Studies, c1989, p.
     [149]-160. English. DESCR: Authors; de
     Cardenas, Isidra T.; *Feminism; Idar,
     Jovita; *Journalists; Literature;
     Newspapers; Ramirez, Sara Estela;
     Villarreal, Andrea; Villegas de Magnon,
     Leonor.

4031 Macias, Anna. Against all odds: the feminist
     movement in Mexico to 1940. Westport, CT:
     Greenwood Press, 1982. xv, 195 p. English.
     DESCR: Carrillo Puerto, Felipe; *Feminism;
     History; Mexico; *Women; Yucatan, Mexico.

4032 Perez, Emma. "A la mujer": a critique of the
     Partido Liberal Mexicano's gender ideology
     on women. IN: Del Castillo, Adelaida R., ed.
     BETWEEN BORDERS: ESSAYS ON MEXICANA/CHICANA
     HISTORY. Encino, CA: Floricanto Press, 1990,
     p. 459-482. English. DESCR: *"A La Mujer"
     [essay]; Essays; *Feminism; Flores Magon,
     Ricardo; Guerrero, Praxedis G.; Journalism;
     Mexico; Newspapers; *Partido Liberal
     Mexicano (PLM); Political Ideology;
     Political Parties and Organizations;
     *REGENERACION [newspaper]; Sex Roles; Women.

4033 Salas, Elizabeth. Soldaderas in the Mexican
     military: myth and history. Austin, TX:
     University of Texas Press, 1990. xiii, 163
     p., [12] p. of plates: ill. English. DESCR:
     Aztecs; History; *La Adelita; Mexico;
     *Military; Symbolism; War; *Women.

4034 Salas, Elizabeth. Soldaderas in the Mexican
     military: myth and history. Thesis
     (Ph.D.)--University of California, Los
     Angeles, 1987. 313p. English. DESCR: Aztecs;
     History; La Adelita; Mexico; Military;
     Symbolism; War; *Women.

4035 Soto, Shirlene Ann. Emergence of the modern
     Mexican woman: her participation in
     revolution and struggle for equality,
     1910-1940. Denver, CO: Arden Press, 1990.
     xvi, 199 p.: ill. English. DESCR: *Feminism;
     *Mexico; Political History and Conditions;
     *Women.

**MEXICAN WOMEN IN THE UNITED STATES: STRUGGLES PAST
AND PRESENT**

4036 Candelaria, Cordelia. Six reference works on
     Mexican-American women: a review essay.
     FRONTIERS: A JOURNAL OF WOMEN STUDIES, Vol.
     5, no. 2 (Summer 1980), p. 75-80. English.
     DESCR: DIOSA Y HEMBRA: THE HISTORY AND
     HERITAGE OF CHICANAS IN THE U.S.; ESSAYS ON
     LA MUJER; LA CHICANA: THE MEXICAN AMERICAN
     WOMAN; *Literature Reviews; THE CHICANA: A
     COMPREHENSIVE BIBLIOGRAPHIC STUDY; TWICE A
     MINORITY: MEXICAN-AMERICAN WOMEN.

**Mexican-American Outreach Program, San Diego State
University**

4037 Zuniga, Maria E. Assessment issues with
     Chicanas: practice implications.
     PSYCHOTHERAPY, Vol. 25, no. 2 (Summer 1988),

p. 288-293. English. DESCR: Acculturation;
Colleges and Universities; Family; Identity;
*Mental Health; *Psychotherapy; *Students.

THE MEXICAN-AMERICANS OF SOUTH TEXAS

4038 Gonzales, Sylvia Alicia. The Chicana
     perspective: a design for self-awareness.
     IN: Trejo, Arnulfo D., ed. THE CHICANOS: AS
     WE SEE OURSELVES. Tucson, AZ: University of
     Arizona Press, 1979, p. 81-99. English.
     DESCR: CHICANAS SPEAK OUT; Chicano Movement;
     Discrimination; Feminism; Identity;
     Machismo; Madsen, William; *Mexican
     Revolution - 1910-1920; Mexico; Sex Roles;
     Vidal, Mirta.

Mexicanism
    USE: Nationalism

Mexico

4039 Ahern, Susan; Bryan, Dexter Edward; and
     Baca, Reynaldo. Migration and la mujer
     fuerte. MIGRATION TODAY, Vol. 13, no. 1
     (1985), p. 14-20. English. DESCR:
     *Migration; *Sex Roles; *Women.

4040 Alba, Francisco. La fecundidad entre los
     Mexicano-Norteamericanos en relacion a los
     cambiantes patrones reproductivos en Mexico
     y los Estados Unidos. DEMOGRAFIA Y ECONOMIA,
     Vol. 16, no. 2 (1982), p. 236-249. Spanish.
     DESCR: *Fertility; Population.

4041 Alonso, Ana Maria and Koreck, Maria Teresa.
     Silences: "Hispanics", AIDS, and sexual
     practices. DIFFERENCES: A JOURNAL OF
     FEMINIST CULTURAL STUDIES, Vol. 1, no. 1
     (Winter 1989), p. 101-124. English. DESCR:
     *AIDS (Disease); *Homosexuality; Human
     Immunodeficiency Virus (HIV); Machismo;
     *Self-Referents; Sex Roles; *Sexual
     Behavior.

4042 Apodaca, Maria Linda. The Chicana woman: a
     historical materialist perspective. IN:
     Bollinger, William, et al., eds. WOMEN IN
     LATIN AMERICA: AN ANTHOLOGY FROM LATIN
     AMERICAN PERSPECTIVES. Riverside, CA: Latin
     American Perspectives, c1979, p. 81-100.
     English. DESCR: Capitalism; *Historiography;
     Immigrants; Imperialism; Marxism; Oral
     History; Social Classes; Spanish Influence.

4043 Arbelaez A., Marisol. Impacto social del
     sismo, Mexico 1985: las costureras. IN: Del
     Castillo, Adelaida R., ed. BETWEEN BORDERS:
     ESSAYS ON MEXICANA/CHICANA HISTORY. Encino,
     CA: Floricanto Press, 1990, p. 315-331.
     Spanish. DESCR: Earthquakes; Frente de
     Costureras, Mexico; *Garment Industry;
     *Industrial Workers; Labor Unions; Mexico
     City Earthquake, September 19, 1985; *Women;
     Working Women.

4044 Baca, Reynaldo and Bryan, Dexter Edward.
     Mexican women, migration and sex roles.
     MIGRATION TODAY, Vol. 13, no. 3 (1985), p.
     14-18. English. DESCR: *Migration; *Sex
     Roles; *Women.

4045 Bachu, Amara and O'Connell, Martin.
     Developing current fertility indicators for
     foreign-born women from the Current
     Population Survey. REVIEW OF PUBLIC DATA
     USE, Vol. 12, no. 3 (October 1984), p.
     185-195. English. DESCR: Current Population
     Survey; *Fertility; Latin America; *Surveys;
     Vital Statistics; Women.

THE CHICANA STUDIES INDEX - SUBJECTS
MEX-MEX

Mexico (cont.)

4046 Blanco, Iris. La mujer en los albores de la
conquista de Mexico. AZTLAN, Vol. 11, no. 2
(Fall 1980), p. 249-270. Spanish. **DESCR:**
*Aztecs; Sex Roles; Women.

4047 Blanco, Iris and Salorzano, Rosalia. O te
aclimatas o te aclimueres. FEM, Vol. 8, no.
34 (June, July, 1984), p. 20-22. Spanish.
DESCR: *Border Industries; *Immigration;
Women; Working Women.

4048 Blanco, Iris. Participacion de las mujeres
en la sociedad prehispanica. IN: Sanchez,
Rosaura and Martinez Cruz, Rosa, eds. ESSAYS
ON LA MUJER. Los Angeles, CA: Chicano
Studies Center Publications, UCLA, 1977, p.
48-81. Spanish. **DESCR:** Aztecs; Cultural
Customs; *History; Indigenismo; Precolumbian
Society; Women.

4049 Blanco, Iris. El sexo y su condicionamiento
cultural en el mundo prehispanico. IN: Del
Castillo, Adelaida R., ed. BETWEEN BORDERS:
ESSAYS ON MEXICANA/CHICANA HISTORY. Encino,
CA: Floricanto Press, 1990, p. 363-374.
Spanish. **DESCR:** *Precolumbian Society; *Sex
Roles; Sexual Behavior; Women.

4050 Bustamante, Jorge A. Maquiladoras: a new
face of international capitalism on Mexico's
northern frontier. IN: Nash, June and
Fernandez-Kelly, Patricia, eds. WOMEN, MEN,
AND THE INTERNATIONAL DIVISION OF LABOR.
Albany, NY: State University of New York
Press, 1983, p. 224-256. English. **DESCR:**
Banking Industry; Border Industrialization
Program (BIP); Border Industries; *Border
Region; Foreign Trade; Industrial Workers;
International Economic Relations;
Population; Programa Nacional Fronterizo
(PRONAF); United States-Mexico Relations;
Women; Working Women.

4051 Carrillo, Teresa. The women's movement and
the left in Mexico: the presidential
candidacy of Dona Rosario Ibarra. IN:
Cordova, Teresa, et al., eds. CHICANA
VOICES. Austin, TX: Center for Mexican
American Studies, 1986, p. 96-113. English.
DESCR: Biography; Ibarra, Rosario; Politics;
*Women.

4052 Castaneda, Antonia I. Comparative frontiers:
the migration of women to Alta California
and New Zealand. IN: Schlissel, Lillian, et
al., eds. WESTERN WOMEN: THEIR LAND, THEIR
LIVES. Albuquerque, NM: University of New
Mexico Press, 1988, p. 283-300. English.
DESCR: Border Region; California; History;
Immigrants; Immigration; Marriage; Missions;
Native Americans; New Zealand; Social
History and Conditions; *Women.

4053 Castaneda Garcia, Carmen. Fuentes para la
historia de la mujer en los archivos de
Guadalajara. IN: Del Castillo, Adelaida R.,
ed. BETWEEN BORDERS: ESSAYS ON
MEXICANA/CHICANA HISTORY. Encino, CA:
Floricanto Press, 1990, p. 102-112. Spanish.
DESCR: *Archives; *Guadalajara; History;
*Women.

4054 Curry Rodriguez, Julia E. Labor migration
and familial responsibilities: experiences
of Mexican women. IN: Melville, Margarita,
ed. MEXICANAS AT WORK IN THE UNITED STATES.
Houston, TX: Mexican American Studies
Program, University of Houston, 1988, p.
47-63. English. **DESCR:** Employment; Family;
*Immigrants; *Migrant Labor; Oral History;
Sex Roles; Undocumented Workers; *Women;
*Working Women.

4055 Curry Rodriguez, Julia E. Reconceptualizing
undocumented labor immigration: the causes,
impact and consequences in Mexican women's
lives. Thesis (Ph.D.)--University of Texas
at Austin, 1988. xiv, 329 p. English.
DESCR: Employment; *Immigrants; Oral
History; *Undocumented Workers; *Women.

4056 Del Castillo, Adelaida R., ed. Between
borders: essays on Mexicana/Chicana history.
Encino, CA: Floricanto Press, c1990. xv, 563
p. Bilingual. **DESCR:** Feminism;
Historiography; *History; *Women; Working
Women.

4057 Deutsch, Sarah. Women and intercultural
relations: the case of Hispanic New Mexico
and Colorado. SIGNS: JOURNAL OF WOMEN IN
CULTURE AND SOCIETY, Vol. 12, no. 4 (Summer
1987), p. 719-739. English. **DESCR:** Colorado;
Cultural Characteristics; Immigrants;
Intercultural Communication; New Mexico;
Rural Population; Sex Roles; Social History
and Conditions; *Women.

4058 Dixon, Marlene; Martinez, Elizabeth; and
McCaughan, Ed. Theoretical perspectives on
Chicanas, Mexicanas and the transnational
working class. CONTEMPORARY MARXISM, no. 11
(Fall 1985), p. 46-76. English. **DESCR:**
Border Industries; Capitalism; Economic
History and Conditions; History;
*Immigration; *Labor Supply and Market;
*Laboring Classes; Undocumented Workers;
Women.

4059 Domenella, Ana Rosa. Al margen de un
coloquio fronterizo mujer y literatura
mexicana y chicana. FEM, Vol. 14, no. 89
(May 1990), p. 32-34. Spanish. **DESCR:**
*Border Region; Coloquio Fronterizo Mujer y
Literatura Mexicana y Chicana (1987:
Tijuana, Baja California, Mexico);
*Conferences and Meetings; *Literature;
Mexican Literature; Women.

4060 Driscoll, Barbara A. Chicana historiography:
a research note regarding Mexican archival
sources. IN: Cordova, Teresa, et al., eds.
CHICANA VOICES. Austin, TX: Center for
Mexican American Studies, 1986, p. 136-145.
English. **DESCR:** Archives; *Historiography.

4061 Fernandez Kelly, Maria. "Chavalas de
maquiladora": a study of the female labor
force in Ciudad Juarez' offshore production
plants. Thesis (Ph.D.)--Rutgers University,
1980. xi, 391 leaves. English. **DESCR:**
*Border Industries; Ciudad Juarez,
Chihuahua, Mexico; Electronics Industry;
*Employment; Garment Industry; Industrial
Workers; Women; *Working Women.

4062 Gettman, Dawn and Pena, Devon Gerardo.
Women, mental health, and the workplace in a
transnational setting. SOCIAL WORK, Vol. 31,
no. 1 (January, February, 1986), p. 5-11.
English. **DESCR:** *Border Industries;
Employment; *Mental Health; United
States-Mexico Relations; Women; *Working
Women.

4063 Gilbert, M. Jean. Alcohol consumption
patterns in immigrant and later generation
Mexican American women. HISPANIC JOURNAL OF
BEHAVIORAL SCIENCES, Vol. 9, no. 3
(September 1987), p. 299-313. English.
DESCR: Acculturation; *Alcoholism;
*Attitudes; Cultural Characteristics;
*Immigrants.

225

Mexico (cont.)

4064 Gomez-Quinones, Juan. Questions within women's historiography. IN: Del Castillo, Adelaida R., ed. BETWEEN BORDERS: ESSAYS ON MEXICANA/CHICANA HISTORY. Encino, CA: Floricanto Press, 1990, p. 87-97. English. **DESCR:** *Historiography; *Women.

4065 Gonzales, Sylvia Alicia. The Chicana perspective: a design for self-awareness. IN: Trejo, Arnulfo D., ed. THE CHICANOS: AS WE SEE OURSELVES. Tucson, AZ: University of Arizona Press, 1979, p. 81-99. English. **DESCR:** CHICANAS SPEAK OUT; Chicano Movement; Discrimination; Feminism; Identity; Machismo; Madsen, William; *Mexican Revolution - 1910-1920; Sex Roles; THE MEXICAN-AMERICANS OF SOUTH TEXAS; Vidal, Mirta.

4066 Gonzalez, Maria R. El embrion nacionalista visto a traves de la obra de Sor Juana Ines de la Cruz. IN: Del Castillo, Adelaida R., ed. BETWEEN BORDERS: ESSAYS ON MEXICANA/CHICANA HISTORY. Encino, CA: Floricanto Press, 1990, p. 239-253. Spanish. **DESCR:** Authors; *Juana Ines de la Cruz, Sor; *Nationalism; Women.

4067 Gonzalez, Rosalinda M. Chicanas and Mexican immigrant families 1920-1940: women's subordination and family exploitation. IN: Scharf, Lois and Jensen, Joan M., eds. DECADES OF DISCONTENT: THE WOMEN'S MOVEMENT, 1920-1940. Westport, CT: Greenwood Press, 1983, p. 59-84. English. **DESCR:** *Family; Farm Workers; History; Immigrants; Labor; Labor Unions; Pecan Shelling Worker's Union, San Antonio, TX; Sex Roles; Strikes and Lockouts; United Cannery Agricultural Packing and Allied Workers of America (UCAPAWA); Working Women.

4068 Guendelman, Sylvia. The incorporation of Mexican women in seasonal migration: a study of gender differences. HISPANIC JOURNAL OF BEHAVIORAL SCIENCES, Vol. 9, no. 3 (September 1987), p. 245-264. English. **DESCR:** Immigrants; Marriage; *Migration Patterns; *Sex Roles; *Women; *Women Men Relations; Working Women.

4069 Hart, John M. Working-class women in nineteenth century Mexico. IN: Mora, Magdalena and Del Castillo, Adelaida, eds. MEXICAN WOMEN IN THE UNITED STATES: STRUGGLES PAST AND PRESENT. Los Angeles, CA: Chicano Studies Research Center, 1980, p. 151-157. English. **DESCR:** *Employment; History; Women; Working Women.

4070 Heathcote, Olivia D. Sex stereotyping in Mexican reading primers. READING TEACHER, Vol. 36, no. 2 (November 1982), p. 158-165. English. **DESCR:** Comparative Education; Curriculum Materials; Primary School Education; *Sex Stereotypes.

4071 Hernandez, Ines. Sara Estela Ramirez: the early twentieth century Texas-Mexican poet. Thesis (Ph.D.)--University of Houston, 1984. 94 p. English. **DESCR:** *Authors; *Biography; Feminism; Flores Magon, Ricardo; Journalism; Literary Criticism; Mexican Revolution - 1910-1920; *Poetry; Ramirez, Sara Estela; Texas; Women.

4072 Hernandez, Ines. Sara Estela Ramirez: sembradora. LEGACY: A JOURNAL OF NINETEENTH-CENTURY AMERICAN WOMEN WRITERS, Vol. 6, no. 1 (Spring 1989), p. 13-26. English. **DESCR:** Authors; *Biography; *Feminism; Flores Magon, Ricardo; *Journalism; LA CORREGIDORA [newspaper]; Mexican Revolution - 1910-1920; Newspapers; Poetry; *Ramirez, Sara Estela; REGENERACION [newspaper].

4073 Herrera-Sobek, Maria. The Mexican corrido: a feminist analysis. Bloomington, IN: Indiana University Press, 1990. xix, 151 p.: ill. English. **DESCR:** *Corridos; Military; *Sex Roles; Sex Stereotypes; Symbolism; *Women; Women Men Relations.

4074 Hovell, Melbourne F., et al. Occupational health risks for Mexican women: the case of the maquiladora along the Mexican-United States border. INTERNATIONAL JOURNAL OF HEALTH SERVICES, Vol. 18, no. 4 (1988), p. 617-627. English. **DESCR:** *Border Industries; Border Region; *Occupational Hazards; Project Concern International (PCI), San Diego, CA; Public Health; Surveys; Tijuana, Baja California, Mexico; Women; Working Women.

4075 Kay, Margarita Artschwager and Yoder, Marianne. Hot and cold in women's ethnotherapeutics: the American-Mexican West. SOCIAL SCIENCE & MEDICINE, Vol. 25, no. 4 (1987), p. 347-355. English. **DESCR:** *Diseases; *Folk Medicine; Herbal Medicine; Southwestern United States.

4076 Keremitsis, Dawn. Del metate al molino: la mujer mexicana de 1910 a 1940. HISTORIA MEXICANA, Vol. 33, no. 2 (1983), p. 285-302. Spanish. **DESCR:** Food Industry; History; Labor Unions; Sex Roles; Strikes and Lockouts; Women; *Working Women.

4077 Lara-Cantu, M. Asuncion and Navarro-Arias, Roberto. Positive and negative factors in the measurement of sex roles: findings from a Mexican sample. HISPANIC JOURNAL OF BEHAVIORAL SCIENCES, Vol. 8, no. 2 (June 1986), p. 143-155. English. **DESCR:** Bem Sex Role Inventory (BSRI); *Psychological Testing; *Sex Roles.

4078 Lavrin, Asuncion. El segundo sexo en Mexico: experiencia, estudio e introspeccion, 1983-1987. MEXICAN STUDIES/ESTUDIOS MEXICANOS, Vol. 5, no. 2 (Summer 1989), p. 297-312. Spanish. **DESCR:** Arenal, Sandra; *Border Industries; Carrillo, Jorge; Hernandez, Alberto; Iglesias, Norma; LA FLOR MAS BELLA DE LA MAQUILADORA; *Literature Reviews; MUJERES FRONTERIZAS EN LA INDUSTRIA MAQUILADORA; SANGRE JOVEN: LAS MAQUILADORAS POR DENTRO; Women.

4079 Lee, Bun Song and Pol, Louis G. A comparison of fertility adaptation between Mexican immigrants to the U.S. and internal migrants in Mexico. CONTEMPORARY POLICY ISSUES, Vol. 3, no. 3 (Spring, 1985), p. 91-101. English. **DESCR:** *Fertility; *Immigrants; Migration Patterns; *Rural Urban Migration; Women.

4080 Limon, Jose E. [anthropologist]. La Llorona, the third legend of greater Mexico: cultural symbols, women, and the political unconscious. RENATO ROSALDO LECTURE SERIES MONOGRAPH, Vol. 2, (Spring 1986), p. [59]-93. English. **DESCR:** *Feminism; Folklore; *La Llorona; La Virgen de Guadalupe; *Leyendas; Malinche; *Symbolism; Women.

Mexico (cont.)

4081 Limon, Jose E. [anthropologist]. La Llorona, the third legend of greater Mexico: cultural symbols, women, and the political unconscious. IN: Del Castillo, Adelaida R. BETWEEN BORDERS: ESSAYS ON MEXICANA/CHICANA HISTORY. Encino, CA: Floricanto Press, 1990 p. 399-432. English. DESCR: *Feminism; Folklore; *La Llorona; La Virgen de Guadalupe; *Leyendas; Malinche; *Symbolism; Women.

4082 Lopez-Garza, Maria C. Toward a reconceptualization of women's economic activities: the informal sector in urban Mexico. IN: Cordova, Teresa, et al., eds. CHICANA VOICES. Austin, TX: Center for Mexican American Studies, 1986, p. 66-76. English. DESCR: Employment; *Women.

4083 Lopez-Gonzalez, Aralia, et al., eds. Mujer y literatura mexicana y chicana: culturas en contacto. Mexico: Colegio de Mexico, Programa Interdisciplinario de Estudios de la Mujer; Tijuana, B.C., Mexico: Colegio de la Frontera Norte, 1988. 264 p. Spanish. DESCR: *Literary Criticism; Mexican Literature; Sex Roles; *Women.

4084 Macias, Anna. Against all odds: the feminist movement in Mexico to 1940. Westport, CT: Greenwood Press, 1982. xv, 195 p. English. DESCR: Carrillo Puerto, Felipe; *Feminism; History; Mexican Revolution - 1910-1920; *Women; Yucatan, Mexico.

4085 Malvido, Elsa. El uso del cuerpo femenino en la epoca colonial mexicana a traves de los estudios de demografia historica. IN: Del Castillo, Adelaida R., ed. BETWEEN BORDERS: ESSAYS ON MEXICANA/CHICANA HISTORY. Encino, CA: Floricanto Press, 1990, p. 115-130. Spanish. DESCR: Marriage; *Sex Roles; Sexual Behavior; *Vital Statistics; Widowhood; *Women.

4086 Notzon, Francis Claude. Factors associated with low birth weight in Mexican-Americans and Mexicans. Thesis (Ph.D.)--John Hopkins University, 1989. 190 p. English. DESCR: Anglo Americans; Fertility; *Maternal and Child Welfare; *Prenatal Care; Public Health; *Women.

4087 Pena, Devon Gerardo. Las maquiladoras: Mexican women in class struggle in the border industries. AZTLAN, Vol. 11, no. 2 (Fall 1980), p. 159-229. English. DESCR: Border Industries; *Economic History and Conditions; Labor; Labor Unions; Mexico-U.S. Border Development; Working Women.

4088 Perez, Emma. "A la mujer": a critique of the Partido Liberal Mexicano's gender ideology on women. IN: Del Castillo, Adelaida R., ed. BETWEEN BORDERS: ESSAYS ON MEXICANA/CHICANA HISTORY. Encino, CA: Floricanto Press, 1990, p. 459-482. English. DESCR: *"A La Mujer" [essay]; Essays; *Feminism; Flores Magon, Ricardo; Guerrero, Praxedis G.; Journalism; Mexican Revolution - 1910-1920; Newspapers; *Partido Liberal Mexicano (PLM); Political Ideology; Political Parties and Organizations; *REGENERACION [newspaper]; Sex Roles; Women.

4089 Rodriguez, Rogelio E. Psychological distress among Mexican-American women as a reaction to the new immigration law. Thesis (Ph.D.)--Loyola University of Chicago, 1989. 87 p. English. DESCR: Depression (Psychological); Immigrants; *Immigration Law and Legislation; Immigration Reform and Control Act of 1986; *Mental Health; Stress; Undocumented Workers; Women.

4090 Ruiz Funes, Concepcion and Tunon, Enriqueta. Panorama de las luchas de la mujer mexicana en el siglo XX. IN: Del Castillo, Adelaida R., ed. BETWEEN BORDERS: ESSAYS ON MEXICANA/CHICANA HISTORY. Encino, CA: Floricanto Press, 1990, p. 336-357. Spanish. DESCR: Coordinadora de Mujeres Trabajadoras; *Feminism; Frente Unido Pro Derechos de la Mujer; History; Labor Unions; Sex Roles; *Women.

4091 Ruiz, Vicki L. Obreras y madres: labor activism among Mexican women and its impact on the family. RENATO ROSALDO LECTURE SERIES MONOGRAPH, Vol. 1, (Summer 1985), p. [19]-38. English. DESCR: Child Care Centers; Children; History; *Labor Unions; Sex Roles; Women; *Working Women.

4092 Ruiz, Vicki L., ed. and Tiano, Susan B., ed. Women on the U.S.-Mexico border: responses to change. Boston, MA: Allen & Unwin, c1987. xi, 247 p. English. DESCR: *Border Industries; *Border Region; Employment; Feminism; Immigrants; Sex Roles; *Women.

4093 Salas, Elizabeth. Soldaderas in the Mexican military: myth and history. Austin, TX: University of Texas Press, 1990. xiii, 163 p., [12] p. of plates: ill. English. DESCR: Aztecs; History; *La Adelita; Mexican Revolution - 1910-1920; *Military; Symbolism; War; *Women.

4094 Salas, Elizabeth. Soldaderas in the Mexican military: myth and history. Thesis (Ph.D.)--University of California, Los Angeles, 1987. 313p. English. DESCR: Aztecs; History; La Adelita; Mexican Revolution - 1910-1920; Military; Symbolism; War; *Women.

4095 Salgado de Snyder, Nelly. Factors associated with acculturative stress and depressive symptomatology among married Mexican immigrant women. PSYCHOLOGY OF WOMEN QUARTERLY, Vol. 11, no. 4 (December 1987), p. 475-488. English. DESCR: *Acculturation; Depression (Psychological); *Immigrants; Mental Health; *Stress; Women.

4096 Salgado de Snyder, Nelly. The role of ethnic loyalty among Mexican immigrant women. HISPANIC JOURNAL OF BEHAVIORAL SCIENCES, Vol. 9, no. 3 (September 1987), p. 287-298. English. DESCR: Acculturation; *Culture; *Identity; Immigrants; Mental Health; *Women.

4097 Segura, Denise. Chicanas and Mexican immigrant women in the labor market: a study of occupational mobility and stratification. Thesis (Ph.D.)--University of California, Berkeley, 1986. iii, 282 p. English. DESCR: *Immigrants; *Labor Supply and Market; Women; *Working Women.

4098 Seligson, Mitchell A. and Williams, Edward J. Maquiladoras and migration workers in the Mexico-United States Border Industrialization Program. Austin, TX: Mexico-United States Border Research Program, University of Texas at Austin, 1981. xviii, 202 p. English. DESCR: Border Industrialization Program (BIP); *Border Region; Employment; Immigration; Industrial Workers; *Migration Patterns; Working Women.

Mexico (cont.)

4099 Sosa Riddell, Adaljiza. The status of women in Mexico: the impact of the "International Year of the Woman". IN: Iglitzin, Lynn B. and Ross, Ruth A., eds. WOMEN IN THE WORLD, 1975-1985. Santa Barbara, CA: ABC-Clio, Inc., 1986, p. 305-324. English. **DESCR:** Abortion; *Feminism; International Women's Year World Conference (1975: Mexico City); Political History and Conditions; Political Parties and Organizations; Rape; *Sexism; Social History and Conditions; *Women.

4100 Soto, Shirlene Ann. Emergence of the modern Mexican woman: her participation in revolution and struggle for equality, 1910-1940. Denver, CO: Arden Press, 1990. xvi, 199 p.: ill. English. **DESCR:** *Feminism; *Mexican Revolution - 1910-1920; Political History and Conditions; *Women.

4101 Soto, Shirlene Ann. The women's movement in Mexico: the first and second feminist congresses in Yucatan, 1916. IN: Del Castillo, Adelaida R., ed. BETWEEN BORDERS: ESSAYS ON MEXICANA/CHICANA HISTORY. Encino, CA: Floricanto Press, 1990, p. 483-491. English. **DESCR:** *Conferences and Meetings; *Feminism; *Feminist Congress (1916: Yucatan, Mexico); Women.

4102 Stoddard, Ellwyn R. Maquila: assembly plants in Northern Mexico. El Paso, TX: Texas Western Press, 1987. ix, 91 p., [4] p. of plates: ill. English. **DESCR:** Border Industrialization Program (BIP); *Border Industries; Immigration; Income; *Industrial Workers; Labor Supply and Market; Sexism; Undocumented Workers.

4103 Sullivan, Teresa A. The occupational prestige of women immigrants: a comparison of Cubans and Mexicans. INTERNATIONAL MIGRATION REVIEW, Vol. 18, no. 4 (Winter 1984), p. 1045-1062. English. **DESCR:** Careers; Cubanos; Employment; *Immigrants; Males; Sex Roles; *Social Mobility; *Women; *Working Women.

4104 Tiano, Susan B. Export processing, women's work, and the employment problem in developing countries: the case of the maquiladora program in Northern Mexico. El Paso, TX: Center for InterAmerican and Border Studies, UTEP, 1985. 32 p. English. **DESCR:** *Border Region; *Employment; Labor Supply and Market; *Sex Roles; Women; Working Women.

4105 Tiano, Susan B. Maquiladoras, women's work, and unemployment in northern Mexico. AZTLAN, Vol. 15, no. 2 (Fall 1984), p. 341-378. English. **DESCR:** *Border Industries; Employment; *Women; Working Women.

4106 Tiano, Susan B. Women's work and unemployment in northern Mexico. IN: Ruiz, Vicki L. and Tiano, Susan, eds. WOMEN ON THE U.S.-MEXICO BORDER: RESPONSES TO CHANGE. Boston, MA: Allen & Unwin, 1987, p. 17-39. English. **DESCR:** Border Industrialization Program (BIP); Border Industries; Border Region; Employment; Labor Supply and Market; Multinational Corporations; *Women.

4107 Vasquez, Josefina. Educacion y papel de la mujer en Mexico. IN: Del Castillo, Adelaida R., ed. BETWEEN BORDERS: ESSAYS ON MEXICANA/CHICANA HISTORY. Encino, CA: Floricanto Press, 1990, p. 377-398. Spanish. **DESCR:** *Education; History; *Sex Roles; *Women.

4108 Young, Gay. Women, border industrialization program, and human rights. El Paso, TX: Center for InterAmerican and Border Studies, UTEP, 1984. 33 p. English. **DESCR:** Border Industrialization Program (BIP); *Border Industries; Economic Development; Employment; Industrial Workers; Sex Roles; *Sexism; *Women; Working Women.

4109 Young, Gay. Women, development and human rights: issues in integrated transnational production. JOURNAL OF APPLIED BEHAVIORAL SCIENCE, Vol. 20, no. 4 (November 1984), p. 383-401. English. **DESCR:** Border Industrialization Program (BIP); *Border Industries; Feminism; Multinational Corporations; Women; Women Men Relations; *Working Women.

Mexico City

4110 Diehl, Paula and Saavedra, Lupe. Hispanas in the year of the woman: many voices. AGENDA, (Winter 1976), p. 14-21. English. **DESCR:** Discrimination; *Feminism; International Women's Year World Conference (1975: Mexico City).

Mexico City Earthquake, September 19, 1985

4111 Arbelaez A., Marisol. Impacto social del sismo, Mexico 1985: las costureras. IN: Del Castillo, Adelaida R., ed. BETWEEN BORDERS: ESSAYS ON MEXICANA/CHICANA HISTORY. Encino, CA: Floricanto Press, 1990, p. 315-331. Spanish. **DESCR:** Earthquakes; Frente de Costureras, Mexico; *Garment Industry; *Industrial Workers; Labor Unions; *Mexico; *Women; Working Women.

Mexico-U.S. Border Development

4112 Pena, Devon Gerardo. Las maquiladoras: Mexican women in class struggle in the border industries. AZTLAN, Vol. 11, no. 2 (Fall 1980), p. 159-229. English. **DESCR:** Border Industries; *Economic History and Conditions; Labor; Labor Unions; Mexico; Working Women.

Mexico-U.S. Lesbian Exchange

4113 Moraga, Cherrie. [Letter to Coordinadora Nacional de Lesbianas Feministas]. CORRESPONDENCIA, no. 9 (December 1990), p. 19-20. Bilingual. **DESCR:** Feminism; *Homosexuality; Identity.

MI QUERIDO RAFA

4114 de la Fuente, Patricia and Duke dos Santos, Maria I. The elliptic female presence as unifying force in the novels of Rolando Hinojosa. REVISTA CHICANO-RIQUENA, Vol. 12, no. 3-4 (Fall, Winter, 1984), p. 64-75. English. **DESCR:** ESTAMPAS DEL VALLE Y OTRAS OBRAS; GENERACIONES Y SEMBLANZAS; Hinojosa-Smith, Rolando R.; *Literary Criticism; RITES AND WITNESSES.

Miami, FL

4115 Fernandez Kelly, Maria and Garcia, Anna M. The making of an underground economy: Hispanic women, home work, and the advanced capitalist state. URBAN ANTHROPOLOGY, Vol. 14, no. 1-3 (Spring, Fall, 1985), p. 59-90. English. **DESCR:** Capitalism; Cubanos; Employment; Garment Industry; Industrial Workers; International Economic Relations; Labor Supply and Market; *Los Angeles County, CA; Women; Working Women.

Michigan

4116 Groessl, Patricia Ann. Depression and anxiety in postmenopausal women: a study of Black, white, and Hispanic women. Thesis (Ed.D.)--Western Michigan University, 1987. 87 p. English. DESCR: Anglo Americans; Blacks; *Depression (Psychological); Menopause; Stress; Women.

4117 Lockert, Lucia Fox. Chicanas: their voices, their lives. Lansing, MI: Michigan State Board of Education, 1988. xii, 36 p.: ill. English. DESCR: *Oral History; Working Women.

Middle Class
USE: Social Classes

Midwest Latina Writer's Workshop (1980: Chicago)

4118 Alarcon, Norma. Hay que inventarnos/we must invent ourselves. THIRD WOMAN, Vol. 1, no. 1 (1981), p. 4-6. English. DESCR: Art; Journals; Midwestern States; *THIRD WOMAN: OF LATINAS IN THE MIDWEST; Third World Literature (U.S.).

Midwestern States

4119 Alarcon, Norma. Hay que inventarnos/we must invent ourselves. THIRD WOMAN, Vol. 1, no. 1 (1981), p. 4-6. English. DESCR: Art; Journals; Midwest Latina Writer's Workshop (1980: Chicago); *THIRD WOMAN: OF LATINAS IN THE MIDWEST; Third World Literature (U.S.).

4120 Baca Zinn, Maxine. Urban kinship and Midwest Chicano families: evidence in support of revision. DE COLORES, Vol. 6, no. 1-2 (1982), p. 85-98. English. DESCR: Compadrazgo; *Extended Family; Family; Urban Communities.

4121 Chavira, Alicia. "Tienes que ser valiente": Mexicana migrants in a midwestern farm labor camp. IN: Melville, Margarita, ed. MEXICANAS AT WORK IN THE UNITED STATES. Houston, TX: Mexican American Studies Program, University of Houston, 1988, p. 64-74. English. DESCR: *Farm Workers; Immigrants; *Labor Camps; Migrant Health Services; *Migrant Labor; Sex Roles; *Women.

4122 Santillan, Richard. Rosita the riveter: Midwest Mexican American women during World War II, 1941-1945. PERSPECTIVES IN MEXICAN AMERICAN STUDIES, Vol. 2, (1989), p. 115-147. English. DESCR: History; Industrial Workers; Intergroup Relations; Language Usage; Military; Mutualistas; Sexism; War; *Working Women; *World War II.

Midwives

4123 Buss, Fran Leeper. La partera: story of a midwife. Ann Arbor, MI: University of Michigan Press, 1980. 140 p.: ill. English. DESCR: Aragon, Jesusita, 1908-; Cultural Customs; *Curanderas; Folk Medicine; Herbal Medicine; New Mexico; San Miguel County, NM.

4124 Hurtado, Aida. Midwife practices in Hidalgo County, Texas. TRABAJOS MONOGRAFICOS, Vol. 3, no. 1 (1987), p. 1-30. English. DESCR: Hidalgo County, TX; *Maternal and Child Welfare.

4125 Hurtado, Aida. A view from within: midwife practices in South Texas. INTERNATIONAL QUARTERLY OF COMMUNITY HEALTH AND EDUCATION, Vol. 8, no. 4 (1987, 1988), p. 317-339. English. DESCR: Fertility; Medical Education; South Texas.

4126 Kay, Margarita Artschwager. Mexican, Mexican American, and Chicana childbirth. IN: Melville, Margarita B., ed. TWICE A MINORITY. St. Louis, MO: Mosby, 1980, p. 52-65. English. DESCR: *Cultural Characteristics; Herbal Medicine; *Maternal and Child Welfare; Sex Roles.

La Migra
USE: Immigration Regulation and Control

Migrant Children

4127 de Leon Siantz, Mary Lou. Maternal acceptance/rejection of Mexican migrant mothers. PSYCHOLOGY OF WOMEN QUARTERLY, Vol. 14, no. 2 (June 1990), p. 245-254. English. DESCR: Child Study; Farm Workers; Migrant Labor; Natural Support Systems; *Parent and Child Relationships; Stress; Texas Migrant Council Headstart Program.

4128 Hintz, Joy. Valiant migrant women = Las mujeres valerosas. Tiffin, OH: Sayger Printing, 1982. viii, 98 p. English. DESCR: Battered Women; *Farm Workers; Feminism; Florida; Marriage; Migrant Health Services; Migrant Housing; *Migrant Labor; Migration Patterns; Ohio; Sex Roles; Texas.

Migrant Health Services

4129 Chavira, Alicia. "Tienes que ser valiente": Mexicana migrants in a midwestern farm labor camp. IN: Melville, Margarita, ed. MEXICANAS AT WORK IN THE UNITED STATES. Houston, TX: Mexican American Studies Program, University of Houston, 1988, p. 64-74. English. DESCR: *Farm Workers; Immigrants; *Labor Camps; Midwestern States; *Migrant Labor; Sex Roles; *Women.

4130 de la Torre, Adela and Rush, Lynda. The determinants of breastfeeding for Mexican migrant women. INTERNATIONAL MIGRATION REVIEW, Vol. 21, no. 3 (Fall 1987), p. 728-742. English. DESCR: *Breastfeeding; Farm Workers; Maternal and Child Welfare; Migrant Labor; Migration; Public Health; Working Women.

4131 Hintz, Joy. Valiant migrant women = Las mujeres valerosas. Tiffin, OH: Sayger Printing, 1982. viii, 98 p. English. DESCR: Battered Women; *Farm Workers; Feminism; Florida; Marriage; Migrant Children; Migrant Housing; *Migrant Labor; Migration Patterns; Ohio; Sex Roles; Texas.

4132 Watkins, Elizabeth L.; Peoples, Mary D.; and Gates, Connie. Health and social needs of women farmworkers: receiving maternity care at a migrant health center. MIGRATION TODAY, Vol. 13, no. 2 (1985), p. 39-42. English. DESCR: Farm Workers; *Maternal and Child Welfare; Women.

Migrant Housing

4133 Hintz, Joy. Valiant migrant women = Las mujeres valerosas. Tiffin, OH: Sayger Printing, 1982. viii, 98 p. English. DESCR: Battered Women; *Farm Workers; Feminism; Florida; Marriage; Migrant Children; Migrant Health Services; *Migrant Labor; Migration Patterns; Ohio; Sex Roles; Texas.

Migrant Labor

4134 Barton, Amy E. and California Commission on
     the Status of Women. Campesinas: women
     farmworkers in the California agricultural
     labor force, report of a study project.
     Sacramento, CA: The Commission, [1978], vii,
     23, 52 p. English. DESCR: California; *Farm
     Workers; Statistics; *Working Women.

4135 Chavira, Alicia. "Tienes que ser valiente":
     Mexicana migrants in a midwestern farm labor
     camp. IN: Melville, Margarita, ed. MEXICANAS
     AT WORK IN THE UNITED STATES. Houston, TX:
     Mexican American Studies Program, University
     of Houston, 1988, p. 64-74. English. DESCR:
     *Farm Workers; Immigrants; *Labor Camps;
     Midwestern States; Migrant Health Services;
     Sex Roles; *Women.

4136 Curry Rodriguez, Julia E. Labor migration
     and familial responsibilities: experiences
     of Mexican women. IN: Melville, Margarita,
     ed. MEXICANAS AT WORK IN THE UNITED STATES.
     Houston, TX: Mexican American Studies
     Program, University of Houston, 1988, p.
     47-63. English. DESCR: Employment; Family;
     *Immigrants; Mexico; Oral History; Sex
     Roles; Undocumented Workers; *Women;
     *Working Women.

4137 de la Torre, Adela and Rush, Lynda. The
     determinants of breastfeeding for Mexican
     migrant women. INTERNATIONAL MIGRATION
     REVIEW, Vol. 21, no. 3 (Fall 1987), p.
     728-742. English. DESCR: *Breastfeeding;
     Farm Workers; Maternal and Child Welfare;
     Migrant Health Services; Migration; Public
     Health; Working Women.

4138 de Leon Siantz, Mary Lou. Maternal
     acceptance/rejection of Mexican migrant
     mothers. PSYCHOLOGY OF WOMEN QUARTERLY, Vol.
     14, no. 2 (June 1990), p. 245-254. English.
     DESCR: Child Study; Farm Workers; *Migrant
     Children; Natural Support Systems; *Parent
     and Child Relationships; Stress; Texas
     Migrant Council Headstart Program.

4139 Garcia Castro, Mary. Migrant women: issues
     in organization and solidarity. MIGRATION
     WORLD MAGAZINE, Vol. 14, no. 1-2 (1986), p.
     15-19. English. DESCR: Labor Supply and
     Market; Organizations; Political Economy;
     Undocumented Workers; Women.

4140 Guttmacher, Sally. Women migrant workers in
     the U.S. CULTURAL SURVIVAL QUARTERLY, Vol.
     8, no. 2 (Summer 1984), p. 60-61. English.
     DESCR: Public Health; Undocumented Workers;
     *Women.

4141 Hintz, Joy. Valiant migrant women = Las
     mujeres valerosas. Tiffin, OH: Sayger
     Printing, 1982. viii, 98 p. English. DESCR:
     Battered Women; *Farm Workers; Feminism;
     Florida; Marriage; Migrant Children; Migrant
     Health Services; Migrant Housing; Migration
     Patterns; Ohio; Sex Roles; Texas.

4142 Kokinos, Mary and Dewey, Kathryn G. Infant
     feeding practices of migrant
     Mexican-American families in Northern
     California. ECOLOGY OF FOOD AND NUTRITION,
     Vol. 18, no. 3 (1986), p. 209-220. English.
     DESCR: *Breastfeeding; Farm Workers;
     Northern California; Nutrition.

4143 Kossoudji, Sherrie and Ranney, Susan. The
     labor market experience of female migrants:
     the case of temporary Mexican migration to
     the U.S. INTERNATIONAL MIGRATION REVIEW,
     Vol. 18, no. 4 (Winter 1984), p. 1120-1143.
     English. DESCR: Employment; Immigrants;

Income; *Labor Supply and Market; Sex Roles;
*Women; Working Women.

4144 Melville, Margarita B., ed. Mexicanas at
     work in the United States. Houston, TX:
     Mexican American Studies Program, University
     of Houston, 1988. 83 p. English. DESCR:
     Border Region; *Employment; Family; *Labor;
     *Women; Working Women.

4145 Melville, Margarita B. Selective
     acculturation of female Mexican migrants.
     IN: Melville, Margarita B., ed. TWICE A
     MINORITY. St. Louis, MO: Mosby, 1980, p.
     155-163. English. DESCR: *Acculturation;
     Identity; Working Women.

4146 Whiteford, Linda. Mexican American women as
     innovators. IN: Melville, Margarita B., ed.
     TWICE A MINORITY. St. Louis, MO: Mosby,
     1980, p. 109-126. English. DESCR: Border
     Region; Farm Workers; *Working Women.

4147 Williams, Brett. Why migrant women feed
     their husbands tamales: foodways as a basis
     for a revisionist view of Tejano family
     life. IN: Brown, Linda Keller and Mussell,
     Kay, eds. ETHNIC AND REGIONAL FOODWAYS IN
     THE UNITED STATES: THE PERFORMANCE OF GROUP
     IDENTITY. Knoxville, TN: University of
     Tennessee Press, 1984, p. 113-126. English.
     DESCR: Cultural Customs; Extended Family;
     Family; *Food Practices; Illinois; Sex
     Roles; Tamales; Texas.

Migration

4148 Ahern, Susan; Bryan, Dexter Edward; and
     Baca, Reynaldo. Migration and la mujer
     fuerte. MIGRATION TODAY, Vol. 13, no. 1
     (1985), p. 14-20. English. DESCR: Mexico;
     *Sex Roles; *Women.

4149 Alcalay, Rina. Hispanic women in the United
     States: family & work relations. MIGRATION
     TODAY, Vol. 12, no. 3 (1984), p. 13-20.
     English. DESCR: Extended Family;
     *Immigrants; *Women.

4150 Baca, Reynaldo and Bryan, Dexter Edward.
     Mexican women, migration and sex roles.
     MIGRATION TODAY, Vol. 13, no. 3 (1985), p.
     14-18. English. DESCR: Mexico; *Sex Roles;
     *Women.

4151 de la Torre, Adela and Rush, Lynda. The
     determinants of breastfeeding for Mexican
     migrant women. INTERNATIONAL MIGRATION
     REVIEW, Vol. 21, no. 3 (Fall 1987), p.
     728-742. English. DESCR: *Breastfeeding;
     Farm Workers; Maternal and Child Welfare;
     Migrant Health Services; Migrant Labor;
     Public Health; Working Women.

4152 Vega, William A.; Kolody, Bohdan; and Valle,
     Juan Ramon. Migration and mental health: an
     empirical test of depression risk factors
     among immigrant Mexican women. INTERNATIONAL
     MIGRATION REVIEW, Vol. 21, no. 3 (Fall
     1987), p. 512-530. English. DESCR:
     Acculturation; *Depression (Psychological);
     *Immigrants; Immigration; *Mental Health;
     Stress; Undocumented Workers; Women.

Migration Patterns

4153 Cardenas, Gilbert and Flores, Estevan T. The
     migration and settlement of undocumented
     women. Austin, TX: CMAS Publications, 1986.
     69 p. English. DESCR: Employment; Houston,
     TX; *Immigration; Income; Labor Supply and
     Market; Public Policy; Socioeconomic
     Factors; *Undocumented Workers.

Migration Patterns
(cont.)

4154 Fernandez Kelly, Maria. Mexican border industrialization, female labor force participation and migration. IN: Nash, June and Fernandez-Kelly, Patricia, eds. WOMEN, MEN, AND THE INTERNATIONAL DIVISION OF LABOR. Albany, NY: State University of New York Press, 1983, p. 205-223. English. DESCR: Border Industrialization Program (BIP); *Border Industries; Ciudad Juarez, Chihuahua, Mexico; Immigration; Industrial Workers; Labor Supply and Market; Males; Undocumented Workers; *Women; Working Women.

4155 Guendelman, Sylvia. The incorporation of Mexican women in seasonal migration: a study of gender differences. HISPANIC JOURNAL OF BEHAVIORAL SCIENCES, Vol. 9, no. 3 (September 1987), p. 245-264. English. DESCR: Immigrants; Marriage; Mexico; *Sex Roles; *Women; *Women Men Relations; Working Women.

4156 Hintz, Joy. Valiant migrant women = Las mujeres valerosas. Tiffin, OH: Sayger Printing, 1982. viii, 98 p. English. DESCR: Battered Women; *Farm Workers; Feminism; Florida; Marriage; Migrant Children; Migrant Health Services; Migrant Housing; *Migrant Labor; Ohio; Sex Roles; Texas.

4157 Lee, Bun Song and Pol, Louis G. A comparison of fertility adaptation between Mexican immigrants to the U.S. and internal migrants in Mexico. CONTEMPORARY POLICY ISSUES, Vol. 3, no. 3 (Spring, 1985), p. 91-101. English. DESCR: *Fertility; *Immigrants; Mexico; *Rural Urban Migration; Women.

4158 Lindemann, Constance and Scott, Wilbur. The fertility related behavior of Mexican American adolescents. JOURNAL OF EARLY ADOLESCENCE, Vol. 2, no. 1 (Spring 1982), p. 31-38. English. DESCR: *Fertility; Youth.

4159 Macklin, June and Teniente de Costilla, Alvina. Virgen de Guadalupe and the American dream: the melting pot bubbles on in Toledo, Ohio. IN: West, Stanley A. and Macklin, June, eds. THE CHICANO EXPERIENCE. Boulder, CO: Westview Press, 1979, p. 111-143. English. DESCR: Assimilation; Catholic Church; *Identity; Intermarriage; La Virgen de Guadalupe; Quinceaneras; Toledo, OH.

4160 Seligson, Mitchell A. and Williams, Edward J. Maquiladoras and migration workers in the Mexico-United States Border Industrialization Program. Austin, TX: Mexico-United States Border Research Program, University of Texas at Austin, 1981. xviii, 202 p. English. DESCR: Border Industrialization Program (BIP); *Border Region; Employment; Immigration; Industrial Workers; Mexico; Working Women.

Migratory Labor
USE: Migrant Labor

THE MILAGRO BEANFIELD WAR [novel]

4161 Mondin, Sandra. The depiction of the Chicana in BLESS ME ULTIMA and THE MILAGRO BEANFIELD WAR: a study in contrasts. IN: Luna Lawhn, Juanita, et al., eds. MEXICO AND THE UNITED STATES: INTERCULTURAL RELATIONS IN THE HUMANITIES. San Antonio, TX: San Antonio College, 1984, p. 137-150. English. DESCR: Anaya, Rudolfo A.; BLESS ME, ULTIMA; Literary Characters; Literary Criticism; Nichols, John; *Stereotypes.

Military

4162 Campbell, Julie A. Madres y esposas: Tucson's Spanish-American Mothers and Wives Association. JOURNAL OF ARIZONA HISTORY, Vol. 31, no. 2 (Summer 1990), p. 161-182. English. DESCR: History; Organizations; *Spanish-American Mothers and Wives Association, Tucson, AZ; Tucson, AZ; World War II.

4163 Herrera-Sobek, Maria. The Mexican corrido: a feminist analysis. Bloomington, IN: Indiana University Press, 1990. xix, 151 p.: ill. English. DESCR: *Corridos; Mexico; *Sex Roles; Sex Stereotypes; Symbolism; *Women; Women Men Relations.

4164 Murguia, Edward. Chicano intermarriage: a theoretical and empirical study. San Antonio, TX: Trinity University Press, 1982. xiv, 134 p. English. DESCR: Assimilation; Attitudes; Ethnic Groups; *Intermarriage; Social Classes; Weddings.

4165 Salas, Elizabeth. Soldaderas in the Mexican military: myth and history. Austin, TX: University of Texas Press, 1990. xiii, 163 p., [12] p. of plates: ill. English. DESCR: Aztecs; History; *La Adelita; Mexican Revolution - 1910-1920; Mexico; Symbolism; War; *Women.

4166 Salas, Elizabeth. Soldaderas in the Mexican military: myth and history. Thesis (Ph.D.)--University of California, Los Angeles, 1987. 313p. English. DESCR: Aztecs; History; La Adelita; Mexican Revolution - 1910-1920; Mexico; Symbolism; War; *Women.

4167 Santillan, Richard. Rosita the riveter: Midwest Mexican American women during World War II, 1941-1945. PERSPECTIVES IN MEXICAN AMERICAN STUDIES, Vol. 2, (1989), p. 115-147. English. DESCR: History; Industrial Workers; Intergroup Relations; Language Usage; *Midwestern States; Mutualistas; Sexism; War; *Working Women; *World War II.

Mining Industry

4168 Deutsch, Sarah. No separate refuge: culture, class, and gender on an Anglo-Hispanic frontier in the American Southwest, 1880-1940. New York: Oxford University Press, 1987. vi, 356 p. English. DESCR: Anglo Americans; Colorado; Immigrants; Immigration; Missions; New Mexico; *Sex Roles; *Social Classes; *Social History and Conditions; Women; Working Women; World War I.

Minnesota Multiphasic Personality Inventory (MMPI)

4169 Velasquez, Roberto J.; Callahan, Wendell J.; and Carrillo, Ricardo. MMPI differences among Mexican-American male and female psychiatric inpatients. PSYCHOLOGICAL REPORTS, Vol. 68, no. 1 (February 1991), p. 123-127. English. DESCR: Comparative Psychology; Males; Personality; Psychiatry; *Psychological Testing; Sex Roles.

Minorities
USE: Ethnic Groups

Minority Business Development Agency (MBDA)

4170 Padilla, Steve. You've come a long way, baby. Or have you? NUESTRO, Vol. 7, no. 6 (August 1983), p. 38-41. English. DESCR: *Business Enterprises; National Alliance of Homebased Businesswomen.

Minority Literature
USE: Third World Literature (U.S.)

Mirande, Alfredo

4171 Pierce, Jennifer. The implications of functionalism for Chicano family research. BERKELEY JOURNAL OF SOCIOLOGY, Vol. 29, (1984), p. 93-117. English. DESCR: Enriquez, Evangelina; *Family; LA CHICANA: THE MEXICAN AMERICAN WOMAN; Machismo; Research Methodology; Sex Roles.

Mirikitani, Janice

4172 Crawford, John F. Notes toward a new multicultural criticism: three works by women of color. IN: Harris, Marie and Aguero, Kathleen, eds. A GIFT OF TONGUES: CRITICAL CHALLENGES IN CONTEMPORARY AMERICAN POETRY. Athens, GA: University of Georgia Press, 1987, p. 155-195. English. DESCR: AWAKE IN THE RIVER; Cervantes, Lorna Dee; EMPLUMADA; Harjo, Joy; *Literary Criticism; SHE HAD SOME HORSES.

Miscegenation
USE: Intermarriage

La Mission Media Arts, San Francisco, CA

4173 Soberon, Mercedes. La revolucion se trata de amor: Mercedes Soberon. CHISMEARTE, Vol. 1, no. 1 (Fall 1976), p. 14-18. Spanish. DESCR: Art Criticism; Concilio de Arte Popular, Los Angeles, CA; Cultural Organizations; San Francisco, CA; *Sex Roles; Soberon, Mercedes.

Mission of Santa Clara

4174 Lara-Cea, Helen. Notes on the use of parish registers in the reconstruction of Chicana history in California prior to 1850. IN: Del Castillo, Adelaida R., ed. BETWEEN BORDERS: ESSAYS ON MEXICANA/CHICANA HISTORY. Encino, CA: Floricanto Press, 1990, p. 131-159. English. DESCR: *California; Catholic Church; History; Indigenismo; Population; *San Jose, CA; *Vital Statistics.

Missions

4175 Castaneda, Antonia I. Comparative frontiers: the migration of women to Alta California and New Zealand. IN: Schlissel, Lillian, et al., eds. WESTERN WOMEN: THEIR LAND, THEIR LIVES. Albuquerque, NM: University of New Mexico Press, 1988, p. 283-300. English. DESCR: Border Region; California; History; Immigrants; Immigration; Marriage; Mexico; Native Americans; New Zealand; Social History and Conditions; *Women.

4176 Deutsch, Sarah. No separate refuge: culture, class, and gender on an Anglo-Hispanic frontier in the American Southwest, 1880-1940. New York: Oxford University Press, 1987. vi, 356 p. English. DESCR: Anglo Americans; Colorado; Immigrants; Immigration; Mining Industry; New Mexico; *Sex Roles; *Social Classes; *Social History and Conditions; Women; Working Women; World War I.

Mistral, Gabriela

4177 De Ortego y Gasca, Felipe. The Hispanic woman: a humanistic perspective. LA LUZ, Vol. 6, no. 11 (November 1977), p. 7-10. English. DESCR: De la Cruz, Juana Ines; Dona Ximena; *Essays; History; Ortiz de Dominguez, Josefa; *Women Men Relations; *Women's Suffrage.

4178 De Ortego y Gasca, Felipe. The Hispanic woman: a humanistic perspective. LA LUZ, Vol. 8, no. 8 (October, November, 1980), p. 6-9. English. DESCR: De la Cruz, Juana Ines; Dona Ximena; *Essays; History; Ortiz de Dominguez, Josefa; *Women Men Relations; *Women's Suffrage.

THE MIXQUIAHUALA LETTERS

4179 Alarcon, Norma. The sardonic powers of the erotic in the work of Ana Castillo. IN: Horno-Delgado, Asuncion, et al., eds. BREAKING BOUNDARIES: LATINA WRITING AND CRITICAL READINGS. Amherst, MA: University of Massachusetts Press, c1989, p. 94-107. English. DESCR: *Castillo, Ana; Literary Criticism; OTRO CANTO; Poetry; Sex Roles; THE INVITATION; WOMEN ARE NOT ROSES.

4180 Quintana, Alvina E. Ana Castillo's THE MIXQUIAHUALA LETTERS: the novelist as ethnographer. IN: Calderon, Hector and Saldivar, Jose David, eds. CRITICISM IN THE BORDERLANDS: STUDIES IN CHICANO LITERATURE, CULTURE, AND IDEOLOGY. Durham, NC: Duke University Press, 1991, p. [72]-83. English. DESCR: Anthropology; Castillo, Ana; Cultural Studies; *Ethnology; Feminism; Geertz, Clifford; *Literary Criticism; Novel.

4181 Quintana, Alvina E. Chicana discourse: negations and mediations. Thesis (Ph.D.)--University of California, Santa Cruz, 1989. 226 p. English. DESCR: Authors; Castillo, Ana; Chavez, Denise; Chicano Movement; Cisneros, Sandra; Ethnology; Feminism; Literary Criticism; *Literature; NOVENA NARRATIVES; Oral Tradition; Political Ideology; THE HOUSE ON MANGO STREET; THE LAST OF THE MENU GIRLS.

Mohr, Nicolasa

4182 McCracken, Ellen. Latina narrative and politics of signification: articulation, antagonism, and populist rupture. CRITICA, Vol. 2, no. 2 (Fall 1990), p. 202-207. English. DESCR: *Cisneros, Sandra; IN NUEVA YORK; *Literary Criticism; Puerto Ricans; RITUALS OF SURVIVAL; Short Story; THE HOUSE ON MANGO STREET; Women.

4183 Olivera, Mercedes. The new Hispanic women. VISTA, Vol. 2, no. 11 (July 5, 1987), p. 6-8. English. DESCR: Alvarez, Linda; Esquiroz, Margarita; Garcia, Juliet; *Hernandez, Antonia A.; Molina, Gloria; Pabon, Maria; Working Women.

Mojados
USE: Undocumented Workers

Molina, Gloria

4184 Olivera, Mercedes. The new Hispanic women. VISTA, Vol. 2, no. 11 (July 5, 1987), p. 6-8. English. DESCR: Alvarez, Linda; Esquiroz, Margarita; Garcia, Juliet; *Hernandez, Antonia A.; Mohr, Nicolasa; Pabon, Maria; Working Women.

Mondragon Valdez, Maria

4185 Lucero, Marcela Christine. The socio-historical implication of the valley as a metaphor in three Colorado Chicana poets. Thesis (Ph.D.)--University of Minnesota, 1981. 176 p. English. DESCR: *Authors; Blea, Irene I.; Chicano Movement; Colorado; Feminism; Literary Criticism; Poetry; Zamora, Bernice.

Montanez Davis, Grace

4186 Espinosa, Ann. Hispanas: our resources [sic] for the eighties. LA LUZ, Vol. 8, no. 4 (October, November, 1979), p. 10-13. English. DESCR: Baca Barragan, Polly; *Civil Rights; Comision Femenil Mexicana Nacional; DIRECTORY OF HISPANIC WOMEN; Discrimination in Education; Elected Officials; Hernandez, Irene; Lacayo, Carmela; Lujan, Josie; Mexican American Women's National Association (MANA); Moreno, Olga; Mujeres Latinas en Accion (M.L.A.); National Conference of Puerto Rican Women, Inc. (NCOPRW); Organizations; Rangel, Irma.

Montijo, Manuel

4187 Sheridan, Thomas E. From Luisa Espinel to Lalo Guerrero: Tucson's Mexican musicians before World War II. JOURNAL OF ARIZONA HISTORY, Vol. 25, no. 3 (Fall 1984), p. 285-300. English. DESCR: Biography; Espinel, Luisa Ronstadt; Guerrero, Eduardo "Lalo"; History; *Musicians; Rebeil, Julia; Singers; *Tucson, AZ.

Montoya, Jose E.

4188 Saldivar, Jose David. Towards a Chicano poetics: the making of the Chicano subject. CONFLUENCIA, Vol. 1, no. 2 (Spring 1986), p. 10-17. English. DESCR: Corridos; Feminism; *Literary Criticism; "Los Vatos" [poem]; *Poetry; RESTLESS SERPENTS; Rios, Alberto; WHISPERING TO FOOL THE WIND; Zamora, Bernice.

Mora, Pat

4189 Alarcon, Norma and Mora, Pat. Interview with Pat Mora. THIRD WOMAN, Vol. 3, no. 1-2 (1986), p. 121-126. English. DESCR: Authors; Biography.

4190 Alarcon, Norma. What kind of lover have you made me, Mother?: towards a theory of Chicanas' feminism and cultural identity through poetry. IN: McCluskey, Audrey T., ed. WOMEN OF COLOR: PERSPECTIVES ON FEMINISM AND IDENTITY. Bloomington, IN: Women's Studies Program, Indiana University, 1985, p. 85-110. English. DESCR: Brinson-Pineda, Barbara; Cervantes, Lorna Dee; Cisneros, Sandra; Culture; *Feminism; Identity; *Literary Criticism; Moraga, Cherrie; *Poetry; Tafolla, Carmen; Vigil-Pinon, Evangelina; Villanueva, Alma.

4191 Mora, Pat and Alarcon, Norma. A poet analyzes her craft. NUESTRO, Vol. 11, no. 2 (March 1987), p. 25-27. English. DESCR: *Authors; BORDERS; CHANTS; *Poetry.

4192 Passman, Kristina. Demeter, Kore and the birth of the self: the quest for identity in the poetry of Alma Villanueva, Pat Mora y Cherrie Moraga. MONOGRAPHIC REVIEW, Vol. 6, (1990), p. 323-342. English. DESCR: *Literary Criticism; Moraga, Cherrie; Mythology; Poetry; Villanueva, Alma.

4193 Rebolledo, Tey Diana. Hispanic women writers

of the Southwest: tradition and innovation. IN: Lensink, Judy Nolte, ed. OLD SOUTHWEST/NEW SOUTHWEST: ESSAYS ON A REGION AND ITS LITERATURE. Tucson, AZ: The Tucson Public Library, 1987, p. 49-61. English. DESCR: *Authors; Cabeza de Baca, Fabiola; Jaramillo, Cleofas M.; Literature; OLD SPAIN IN OUR SOUTHWEST; Otero Warren, Nina; Preciado Martin, Patricia; Sex Roles; Sex Stereotypes; Silva, Beverly; *Southwestern United States; Vigil-Pinon, Evangelina; WE FED THEM CACTUS; *Women.

4194 Rebolledo, Tey Diana. Tradition and mythology: signatures of landscape in Chicana literature. IN: Norwood, Vera and Monk, Janice, eds. THE DESERT IS NO LADY: SOUTHWESTERN LANDSCAPES IN WOMEN'S WRITING AND ART. New Haven, CT: Yale University Press, 1987, p. 96-124. English. DESCR: *Authors; Cabeza de Baca, Fabiola; Chavez, Denise; Jaramillo, Cleofas M.; Literary Criticism; *Literary History; Literature; Mythology; Otero Warren, Nina; Portillo Trambley, Estela; Silva, Beverly; Southwestern United States; WE FED THEM CACTUS.

Moraga, Cherrie

4195 Alarcon, Norma and Moraga, Cherrie. Interview with Cherrie Moraga. THIRD WOMAN, Vol. 3, no. 1-2 (1986), p. 127-134. English. DESCR: Authors; Biography; Homosexuality; Sex Roles.

4196 Alarcon, Norma. Making "familia" from scratch: split subjectivities in the work of Helena Maria Viramontes and Cherrie Moraga. THE AMERICAS REVIEW, Vol. 15, no. 3-4 (Fall, Winter, 1987), p. 147-159. English. DESCR: GIVING UP THE GHOST; *Literary Criticism; *Sex Roles; "Snapshots" [short story]; THE MOTHS AND OTHER STORIES; Viramontes, Helena Maria.

4197 Alarcon, Norma. The theoretical subject(s) of THIS BRIDGE CALLED MY BACK and Anglo-American feminism. IN: Calderon, Hector and Saldivar, Jose David, eds. CRITICISM IN THE BORDERLANDS: STUDIES IN CHICANO LITERATURE, CULTURE, AND IDEOLOGY. Durham, NC: Duke University Press, 1991, p. [28]-39. English. DESCR: *Anglo Americans; Anzaldua, Gloria; *Feminism; THIS BRIDGE CALLED MY BACK; *Women.

4198 Alarcon, Norma. The theoretical subject(s) of THIS BRIDGE CALLED MY BACK and Anglo-American feminism. IN: Anzaldua, Gloria, ed. MAKING FACE, MAKING SOUL: HACIENDO CARAS: CREATIVE AND CRITICAL PERSPECTIVES BY WOMEN OF COLOR. San Francisco, CA: Aunt Lute Foundation Books, 1990, p. 356-369. English. DESCR: *Anglo Americans; Anzaldua, Gloria; *Feminism; Literary Criticism; THIS BRIDGE CALLED MY BACK; *Women.

4199 Alarcon, Norma. What kind of lover have you made me, Mother?: towards a theory of Chicanas' feminism and cultural identity through poetry. IN: McCluskey, Audrey T., ed. WOMEN OF COLOR: PERSPECTIVES ON FEMINISM AND IDENTITY. Bloomington, IN: Women's Studies Program, Indiana University, 1985, p. 85-110. English. DESCR: Brinson-Pineda, Barbara; Cervantes, Lorna Dee; Cisneros, Sandra; Culture; *Feminism; Identity; *Literary Criticism; Mora, Pat; *Poetry; Tafolla, Carmen; Vigil-Pinon, Evangelina; Villanueva, Alma.

Moraga, Cherrie (cont.)

4200 Herrera-Sobek, Maria. The politics of rape: sexual transgression in Chicana fiction. THE AMERICAS REVIEW, Vol. 15, no. 3-4 (Fall, Winter, 1987), p. 171-181. English. **DESCR:** Cisneros, Sandra; *Feminism; Fiction; GIVING UP THE GHOST; *Literary Criticism; Lizarraga, Sylvia; *Rape; "Red Clowns" [short story]; Sex Roles; "Silver Lake Road" [short story].

4201 Moraga, Cherrie. Loving in the war years: lo que nunca paso por sus labios. Boston, MA: South End Press, c1983. viii, 152 p. English. **DESCR:** *Autobiography; Homosexuality; *Poems.

4202 Passman, Kristina. Demeter, Kore and the birth of the self: the quest for identity in the poetry of Alma Villanueva, Pat Mora y Cherrie Moraga. MONOGRAPHIC REVIEW, Vol. 6, (1990), p. 323-342. English. **DESCR:** *Literary Criticism; Mora, Pat; Mythology; Poetry; Villanueva, Alma.

4203 Quintana, Alvina E. Challenge and counter challenge: Chicana literary motifs. AGAINST THE CURRENT, Vol. 2, no. 2 (March, April, 1987), p. 25,28-32. English. **DESCR:** Anglo Americans; Authors; Cervantes, Lorna Dee; Cultural Studies; *Feminism; Identity; Literary Criticism; *Literature; THERE ARE NO MADMEN HERE; Valdes, Gina; Women.

4204 Quintana, Alvina E. Chicana literary motifs: challenge and counter-challenge. IMAGES: ETHNIC STUDIES OCCASIONAL PAPERS SERIES, (Fall 1986), p. 24-41. English. **DESCR:** Anglo Americans; Authors; Cervantes, Lorna Dee; Cultural Studies; *Feminism; *Identity; *Literary Criticism; Literature; THERE ARE NO MADMEN HERE; Valdes, Gina; Women.

4205 Saldivar, Ramon. The dialectics of subjectivity: gender and difference in Isabella Rios, Sandra Cisneros, and Cherrie Moraga. IN: Saldivar, Ramon. CHICANO NARRATIVE: THE DIALECTICS OF DIFFERENCE. Madison, WI: University of Wisconsin Press, 1990, p. 171-199. English. **DESCR:** Authors; Autobiography; *Cisneros, Sandra; Feminism; Fiction; *Literary Criticism; Literature; LOVING IN THE WAR YEARS; Political Ideology; *Rios, Isabella; THE HOUSE ON MANGO STREET; VICTUUM.

4206 Saldivar-Hull, Sonia. Feminism on the border: from gender politics to geopolitics. IN: Calderon, Hector and Saldivar, Jose David, eds. CRITICISM IN THE BORDERLANDS: STUDIES IN CHICANO LITERATURE, CULTURE, AND IDEOLOGY. Durham, NC: Duke University Press, 1991, p. [203]-220. English. **DESCR:** Anglo Americans; *Anzaldua, Gloria; *BORDERLANDS/LA FRONTERA: THE NEW MESTIZA; Feminism; Homosexuality; *Literary Criticism; Mestizaje; Sexism; "The Cariboo Cafe" [short story]; Viramontes, Helena Maria; Women.

4207 Sternbach, Nancy Saporta. "A deep racial memory of love": the Chicana feminism of Cherrie Moraga. IN: Horno-Delgado, Asuncion, et al., eds. BREAKING BOUNDARIES: LATINA WRITING AND CRITICAL READINGS. Amherst, MA: University of Massachusetts Press, c1989, p. 48-61. English. **DESCR:** Discrimination; Feminism; Homosexuality; Literary Criticism; *LOVING IN THE WAR YEARS; Machismo; Malinche; Sex Stereotypes; Sexism.

4208 Yarbro-Bejarano, Yvonne. Cherrie Moraga's GIVING UP THE GHOST: the representation of

female desire. THIRD WOMAN, Vol. 3, no. 1-2 (1986), p. 113-120. English. **DESCR:** *GIVING UP THE GHOST; Homosexuality; Teatro.

4209 Yarbro-Bejarano, Yvonne. De-constructing the lesbian body: Cherrie Moraga's LOVING IN THE WAR YEARS. IN: Trujillo, Carla, ed. CHICANA LESBIANS: THE GIRLS OUR MOTHERS WARNED US ABOUT. Berkeley, CA: Third Woman Press, 1991, p. 143-155. English. **DESCR:** Homosexuality; Literary Criticism; *LOVING IN THE WAR YEARS; Skin Color.

Morales, Alejandro

4210 Lizarraga, Sylvia S. Images of women in Chicano literature by men. FEMINIST ISSUES, Vol. 5, no. 2 (Fall 1985), p. 69-88. English. **DESCR:** *Literature; RETO EN EL PARAISO; Sexism; *Stereotypes.

Morales, Sylvia

4211 Fregoso, Rosa Linda. La quinceanera of Chicana counter aesthetics. CENTRO BULLETIN, Vol. 3, no. 1 (Winter 1990, 1991), p. [87]-91. English. **DESCR:** *AGUEDA MARTINEZ [film]; ANIMA [film]; *CHICANA! [film]; *DESPUES DEL TERREMOTO [film]; Espana, Frances Salome; Feminism; *Films; Portillo, Lourdes; Vasquez, Esperanza.

4212 Sanchez, Rosaura. The history of Chicanas: a proposal for a materialist perspective. IN: Del Castillo, Adelaida R., ed. BETWEEN BORDERS: ESSAYS ON MEXICANA/CHICANA HISTORY. Encino, CA: Floricanto Press, 1990, p. 1-29. English. **DESCR:** Apodaca, Maria Linda; *Chicana Studies; Del Castillo, Adelaida R.; Feminism; Historiography; History; Ruiz, Vicki L.

Morenci Miners Women's Auxiliary (MMWA)

4213 Aulette, Judy and Mills, Trudy. Something old, something new: auxiliary work in the 1983-1986 copper strike. FEMINIST STUDIES, Vol. 14, no. 2 (Summer 1988), p. 251-268. English. **DESCR:** Arizona; Clifton-Morenci Copper Strike, 1983-1986; Clifton-Morenci District, Arizona; Feminism; Labor Unions; Mutualistas; Phelps Dodge Corporation, Morenci, AZ; SALT OF THE EARTH [film]; Sex Roles; *Strikes and Lockouts.

Moreno, Luisa [union organizer]

4214 Delgado Campbell, Dolores. Shattering the stereotype: Chicanas as labor union organizers. BERKELEY WOMEN OF COLOR, no. 11 (Summer 1983), p. 20-23. English. **DESCR:** Farah Manufacturing Co., El Paso, TX; Farah Strike; *Gonzalez Parsons, Lucia; Huerta, Dolores; *Labor Unions; Tenayuca, Emma; Working Women.

4215 Goldman, Shifra M. Trabajadoras mexicanas y chicanas en las artes visuales. IN: Leal, Salvador, ed. A TRAVES DE LA FRONTERA. Mexico, D.F.: Centro de Estudios Economicos y Sociales del Tercer Mundo, A.C.; Instituto de Investigaciones Esteticas, U.N.A.M., 1983, p. 153-161. Spanish. **DESCR:** Art; Gonzalez Parsons, Lucia; Huerta, Dolores; SALT OF THE EARTH [film]; Tenayuca, Emma; *Working Women.

Moreno, Luisa [union organizer]
(cont.)

4216 Mirande, Alfredo and Enriquez, Evangelina.
Chicanas in the struggle for unions. IN:
Duran, Livie Isauro and Bernard, H. Russell,
eds. INTRODUCTION TO CHICANO STUDIES. 2nd.
ed. New York: Macmillan, 1973, p. 325-337.
English. DESCR: Gonzalez Parsons, Lucia;
*Labor Unions; Parsons, Albert; Tenayuca,
Emma; United Cannery Agricultural Packing
and Allied Workers of America (UCAPAWA).

4217 Ruiz, Vicki L. A promise fulfilled: Mexican
cannery workers in Southern California. THE
PACIFIC HISTORIAN, Vol. 30, no. 2 (Summer
1986), p. 51-61. English. DESCR: *California
Sanitary Canning Company, Los Angeles, CA;
*Canneries; Labor Unions; Southern
California; Strikes and Lockouts; *United
Cannery Agricultural Packing and Allied
Workers of America (UCAPAWA); Working Women.

4218 Ruiz, Vicki L. A promise fulfilled: Mexican
cannery workers in Southern California. IN:
DuBois, Ellen Carol and Ruiz, Vicki L., eds.
UNEQUAL SISTERS: A MULTICULTURAL READER IN
U.S. WOMEN'S HISTORY. New York: Routledge,
1990, p. 264-274. English. DESCR:
*California Sanitary Canning Company, Los
Angeles, CA; *Canneries; Labor Unions;
Southern California; Strikes and Lockouts;
*United Cannery Agricultural Packing and
Allied Workers of America (UCAPAWA); Working
Women.

4219 Ruiz, Vicki L. A promise fulfilled: Mexican
cannery workers in Southern California. IN:
Del Castillo, Adelaida R., ed. BETWEEN
BORDERS: ESSAYS ON MEXICANA/CHICANA HISTORY.
Encino, CA: Floricanto Press, 1990, p.
281-298. English. DESCR: California Sanitary
Canning Company, Los Angeles, CA;
*Canneries; Labor Unions; Southern
California; Strikes and Lockouts; United
Cannery Agricultural Packing and Allied
Workers of America (UCAPAWA); Working Women.

Moreno, Maria

4220 Moreno, Maria. I'm talking for justice. IN:
Mora, Magdalena and Del Castillo, Adelaida,
eds. MEXICAN WOMEN IN THE UNITED STATES:
STRUGGLES PAST AND PRESENT. Los Angeles, CA:
Chicano Studies Research Center, UCLA, 1980,
p. 181-182. English. DESCR: *Biography.

Moreno, Olga

4221 Espinosa, Ann. Hispanas: our resourses [sic]
for the eighties. LA LUZ, Vol. 8, no. 4
(October, November, 1979), p. 10-13.
English. DESCR: Baca Barragan, Polly; *Civil
Rights; Comision Femenil Mexicana Nacional;
DIRECTORY OF HISPANIC WOMEN; Discrimination
in Education; Elected Officials; Hernandez,
Irene; Lacayo, Carmela; Lujan, Josie;
Mexican American Women's National
Association (MANA); Montanez Davis, Grace;
Mujeres Latinas en Accion (M.L.A.); National
Conference of Puerto Rican Women, Inc.
(NCOPRW); Organizations; Rangel, Irma.

Morton, Carlos

4222 Melville, Margarita B. Female and male in
Chicano theatre. IN: Kanellos, Nicolas, ed.
HISPANIC THEATRE IN THE UNITED STATES.
Houston, TX: Arte Publico Press, 1984, p.
71-79. English. DESCR: BERNABE; BRUJERIAS
[play]; Cultural Characteristics; DAY OF THE
SWALLOWS; Duarte-Clark, Rodrigo; EL JARDIN
[play]; Family; Feminism; Macias, Ysidro;

Portillo Trambley, Estela; RANCHO HOLLYWOOD
[play]; *Sex Roles; *Teatro; THE ULTIMATE
PENDEJADA [play]; Valdez, Luis; Women Men
Relations.

MOTHER MAY I?

4223 Sanchez, Marta E. The birthing of the poetic
"I" in Alma Villanueva's MOTHER MAY I?: the
search for a feminine identity. IN:
Herrera-Sobek, Maria, ed. BEYOND
STEREOTYPES: THE CRITICAL ANALYSIS OF
CHICANA LITERATURE. Binghamton, NY:
Bilingual Press/Editorial Bilingue, 1985, p.
108-152. Also IN: Sanchez, Marta.
CONTEMPORARY CHICANA POETRY. Berkeley, CA:
University of California Press, 1985, p.
24-84. English. DESCR: *Identity; Literary
Criticism; Poetry; Villanueva, Alma.

4224 Sanchez, Marta E. Gender and ethnicity in
contemporary Chicana poetry. CRITICAL
PERSPECTIVES, Vol. 2, no. 1 (Fall 1984), p.
147-166. English. DESCR: *Literary
Criticism; *Poetry; Villanueva, Alma.

Mothers of East L.A. (MELA)

4225 Pardo, Mary. Mexican American women
grassroots community activists: "Mothers of
East Los Angeles". FRONTIERS: A JOURNAL OF
WOMEN STUDIES, Vol. 11, no. 1 (1990), p.
[1]-7. English. DESCR: Coalition Against the
Prison, East Los Angeles, CA; *Community
Organizations; East Los Angeles, CA; Family;
*Feminism; Organizations; Political Parties
and Organizations; Politics; Sex Roles.

THE MOTHS AND OTHER STORIES

4226 Alarcon, Norma. Making "familia" from
scratch: split subjectivities in the work of
Helena Maria Viramontes and Cherrie Moraga.
THE AMERICAS REVIEW, Vol. 15, no. 3-4 (Fall,
Winter, 1987), p. 147-159. English. DESCR:
GIVING UP THE GHOST; *Literary Criticism;
Moraga, Cherrie; *Sex Roles; "Snapshots"
[short story]; Viramontes, Helena Maria.

4227 Tavera Rivera, Margarita. Autoridad in
absentia: la censura patriarcal en la
narrativa chicana. IN: Lopez-Gonzalez,
Aralia, et al., eds. MUJER Y LITERATURA
MEXICANA Y CHICANA: CULTURAS EN CONTACTO.
Mexico: Colegio de la Frontera Norte, 1988,
p. [65]-69. Spanish. DESCR: Feminism;
Fiction; *Literary Criticism; Sex Roles;
*Viramontes, Helena Maria.

Motion Pictures
USE: Films

Movimiento Artistico Chicano (MARCH), Chicago, IL

4228 Allen, Jane and Guthrie, Derek. La mujer: a
visual dialogue. NEW ART EXAMINER, Vol. 5,
no. 10 (July 1978), p. 14. English. DESCR:
California; Chicago, IL; *Feminism;
Stereotypes.

Movimiento Estudiantil Chicano de Aztlan (MEChA)

4229 Hernandez, Patricia. Lives of Chicana
activists: the Chicano student movement (a
case study). IN: Mora, Magdalena and Del
Castillo, Adelaida, eds. MEXICAN WOMEN IN
THE UNITED STATES: STRUGGLES PAST AND
PRESENT. Los Angeles, CA: Chicano Studies
Research Center, UCLA, 1980, p. 17-25.
English. DESCR: California State University,
San Diego; Case Studies; *Chicano Movement;
Colleges and Universities; Student
Movements; Student Organizations.

Mujeres Artistas del Suroeste (MAS), Austin, TX

4230 Goldman, Shifra M. Artistas chicanas texanas. FEM, Vol. 8, no. 34 (June, July, 1984), p. 29-31. Spanish. DESCR: *Artists; Texas.

4231 Goldman, Shifra M. Women artists of Texas: MAS = More + Artists + Women = MAS. CHISMEARTE, no. 7 (January 1981), p. 21-22. English. DESCR: Arredondo, Alicia; Art Organizations and Groups; Barraza, Santa; Exhibits; Feminism; Flores, Maria; Folk Art; Gonzalez Dodson, Nora; Photography; Texas; Trevino, Modesta Barbina; WOMEN & THEIR WORK [festival] (Austin, TX: 1977).

4232 Orozco, Sylvia. Las mujeres--Chicana artists come into their own. MOVING ON, Vol. 2, no. 3 (May 1978), p. 14-16. English. DESCR: Art Organizations and Groups; Artists; Barraza, Santa; Flores, Maria; Gonzalez Dodson, Nora; Trevino, Modesta Barbina.

Mujeres de Hoy Conference (Oakland, CA)

4233 Carrillo-Beron, Carmen. Raza mental health: perspectivas femeniles. IN: PERSPECTIVAS EN CHICANO STUDIES: PAPERS PRESENTED AT THE THIRD ANNUAL MEETING OF THE NATIONAL ASSOCIATION OF CHICANO SOCIAL SCIENCE, 1975. Los Angeles, CA: National Association of Chicano Social Science, 1977, p. 69-80. English. DESCR: Attitudes; Centro de Salud Mental, Oakland, CA; Conferences and Meetings; *Mental Health.

MUJERES FRONTERIZAS EN LA INDUSTRIA MAQUILADORA

4234 Lavrin, Asuncion. El segundo sexo en Mexico: experiencia, estudio e introspeccion, 1983-1987. MEXICAN STUDIES/ESTUDIOS MEXICANOS, Vol. 5, no. 2 (Summer 1989), p. 297-312. Spanish. DESCR: Arenal, Sandra; *Border Industries; Carrillo, Jorge; Hernandez, Alberto; Iglesias, Norma; LA FLOR MAS BELLA DE LA MAQUILADORA; *Literature Reviews; Mexico; SANGRE JOVEN: LAS MAQUILADORAS POR DENTRO; Women.

Mujeres Latinas en Accion (M.L.A.)

4235 Espinosa, Ann. Hispanas: our resourses [sic] for the eighties. LA LUZ, Vol. 8, no. 4 (October, November, 1979), p. 10-13. English. DESCR: Baca Barragan, Polly; *Civil Rights; Comision Femenil Mexicana Nacional; DIRECTORY OF HISPANIC WOMEN; Discrimination in Education; Elected Officials; Hernandez, Irene; Lacayo, Carmela; Lujan, Josie; Mexican American Women's National Association (MANA); Montanez Davis, Grace; Moreno, Olga; National Conference of Puerto Rican Women, Inc. (NCOPRW); Organizations; Rangel, Irma.

Las Mujeres Muralistas, San Francisco, CA

4236 Venegas, Sybil. The artists and their work--the role of the Chicana artist. CHISMEARTE, Vol. 1, no. 4 (Fall, Winter, 1977), p. 3, 5. English. DESCR: Art Criticism; *Artists; Carrasco, Barbara; Delgado, Etta; Hernandez, Ester; Mural Art.

Las Mujeres, University of California, Santa Cruz

4237 Carrillo, Ana, et al. History of Las Mujeres. REVISTA MUJERES, Vol. 1, no. 1 (January 1984), p. 4-5. English. DESCR: *Organizations.

Multicultural Education
USE: Cultural Pluralism

Multinational Corporations

4238 Tiano, Susan B. Women's work and unemployment in northern Mexico. IN: Ruiz, Vicki L. and Tiano, Susan, eds. WOMEN ON THE U.S.-MEXICO BORDER: RESPONSES TO CHANGE. Boston, MA: Allen & Unwin, 1987, p. 17-39. English. DESCR: Border Industrialization Program (BIP); Border Industries; Border Region; Employment; Labor Supply and Market; Mexico; *Women.

4239 Young, Gay. Women, development and human rights: issues in integrated transnational production. JOURNAL OF APPLIED BEHAVIORAL SCIENCE, Vol. 20, no. 4 (November 1984), p. 383-401. English. DESCR: Border Industrialization Program (BIP); *Border Industries; Feminism; Mexico; Women; Women Men Relations; *Working Women.

MULTIVARIATE ANALYSIS OF VARIANCE (MANOVA)

4240 Ramirez, Alex, et al. The relationship between sociocultural variables and Chicano and Anglo high school student responses on the Potency Dimension of the Semantic Differential. HISPANIC JOURNAL OF BEHAVIORAL SCIENCES, Vol. 3, no. 2 (June 1981), p. 177-190. English. DESCR: Anglo Americans; Martinez, Joe L., Jr.; Martinez, Sergio R.; Olmedo, Esteban L.; *Parent and Child Relationships; Sex Roles; Sex Stereotypes; Students.

Municipal Government
USE: Local Government

Mural Art

4241 Burnham, Linda. Barbara Carrasco and public activist art. HIGH PERFORMANCE, Vol. 9, no. 3 (1986), p. 48. English. DESCR: *Artists; Carrasco, Barbara; Politics.

4242 Mesa-Bains, Amalia. Quest for identity: profile of two Chicana muralists: based on interviews with Judith F. Baca and Patricia Rodriguez. IN: Cockcroft, Eva Sperling and Barnet-Sanchez, Holly, eds. SIGNS FROM THE HEART: CALIFORNIA CHICANO MURALS. Venice, CA: Social and Public Art Resource Center, 1990, p. [68-83]. English. DESCR: Artists; Baca, Judith F.; Chicano Movement; GREAT WALL OF LOS ANGELES [mural]; Rodriguez, Patricia.

4243 Pohl, Frances K. and Baca, Judith F. THE WORLD WALL: A VISION OF THE FUTURE WITHOUT FEAR: an interview with Judith F. Baca. FRONTIERS: A JOURNAL OF WOMEN STUDIES, Vol. 11, no. 1 (1990), p. [33]-43. English. DESCR: Art Organizations and Groups; *Artists; *Baca, Judith F.; Social and Public Art Resource Center, Venice, CA (SPARC); *THE WORLD WALL: A VISION OF THE FUTURE WITHOUT FEAR [mural].

4244 Venegas, Sybil. The artists and their work--the role of the Chicana artist. CHISMEARTE, Vol. 1, no. 4 (Fall, Winter, 1977), p. 3, 5. English. DESCR: Art Criticism; *Artists; Carrasco, Barbara; Delgado, Etta; Hernandez, Ester; Las Mujeres Muralistas, San Francisco, CA.

Murillo, Patricia

4245 Goldman, Shifra M. Mujeres de California:
Latin American women artists. IN: Moore,
Sylvia, ed. YESTERDAY AND TOMORROW:
CALIFORNIA WOMEN ARTISTS. New York, NY:
Midmarch Arts Press, c1989, p. 202-229.
English. DESCR: *Artists; Baca, Judith F.;
Biography; California; Carrasco, Barbara;
Cervantez, Yreina; de Larios, Dora;
Feminism; Hernandez, Judithe; Lomas Garza,
Carmen; Lopez, Yolanda M.; Mesa-Bains,
Amalia; Sanchez, Olivia; Valdez, Patssi;
Vallejo Dillaway, Linda; Women; Zamora
Lucero, Linda.

Music

4246 Herrera-Sobek, Maria. The treacherous woman
archetype: a structuring agent in the
corrido. AZTLAN, Vol. 13, no. 1-2 (Spring,
Fall, 1982), p. 135-148. English. DESCR:
*Corridos; Folk Songs.

Musical Lyrics

4247 Fajardo, Ramon. Liberacion femenil: cancion
corrido. XALMAN, Vol. 3, no. 2 (Fall 1980),
p. 97-98. Spanish. DESCR: *Corridos;
Feminism.

4248 Fajardo, Ramon. Liberacion femenil: cancior
corrido. IN: Bardeleben, Renate von, et al.,
eds. MISSIONS IN CONFLICT: ESSAYS ON
U.S.-MEXICAN RELATIONS AND CHICANO CULTURE.
Tubingen, W. Germany: Gunter Narr Verlag,
1986, p. 108-109. Spanish. DESCR: *Corridos;
*Feminism.

4249 Herrera-Sobek, Maria. The acculturation
process of the Chicana in the corrido.
PROCEEDINGS OF THE PACIFIC COAST COUNCIL OF
LATIN AMER STUDIES, Vol. 9, (1982), p.
25-34. English. DESCR: *Acculturation;
*Corridos; *Women Men Relations.

Musicians

4250 Sheridan, Thomas E. From Luisa Espinel to
Lalo Guerrero: Tucson s Mexican musicians
before World War II. JOURNAL OF ARIZONA
HISTORY, Vol. 25, no. 3 (Fall 1984), p.
285-300. English. DESCR: Biography; Espinel,
Luisa Ronstadt; Guerrero, Eduardo "Lalo";
History; Montijo, Manuel; Rebeil, Julia;
Singers; *Tucson, AZ.

Mutual Aid Societies
USE: Mutualistas

Mutualistas

4251 Aulette, Judy and Mills, Trudy. Something
old, something new: auxiliary work in the
1983-1986 copper strike. FEMINIST STUDIES,
Vol. 14, no. 2 (Summer 1988), p. 251-268.
English. DESCR: Arizona; Clifton-Morenci
Copper Strike, 1983-1986; Clifton-Morenci
District, Arizona; Feminism; Labor Unions;
Morenci Miners Women's Auxiliary (MMWA);
Phelps Dodge Corporation, Morenci, AZ; SALT
OF THE EARTH [film]; Sex Roles; *Strikes and
Lockouts.

4252 Santillan, Richard. Rosita the riveter:
Midwest Mexican American women during World
War II, 1941-1945. PERSPECTIVES IN MEXICAN
AMERICAN STUDIES, Vol. 2, (1989), p.
115-147. English. DESCR: History; Industrial
Workers; Intergroup Relations; Language
Usage; *Midwestern States; Military; Sexism;
War; *Working Women; *World War II.

MY WICKED WICKED WAYS

4253 Rodriguez Aranda, Pilar E. and Cisneros,
Sandra. On the solitary fate of being
Mexican, female, wicked and thirty-three: an
interview with writer Sandra Cisneros. THE
AMERICAS REVIEW, Vol. 18, no. 1 (Spring
1990), p. 64-80. English. DESCR: *Artists;
*Cisneros, Sandra; Literature; THE HOUSE ON
MANGO STREET.

Mythology

4254 Anzaldua, Gloria. Borderlands/La frontera:
the new mestiza. San Francisco, CA:
Spinsters/Aunt Lute, 1987. 203 p. Bilingual.
DESCR: Aztecs; Border Region; *Identity;
Poems; Prose; Sex Roles.

4255 Passman, Kristina. Demeter, Kore and the
birth of the self: the quest for identity in
the poetry of Alma Villanueva, Pat Mora y
Cherrie Moraga. MONOGRAPHIC REVIEW, Vol. 6,
(1990), p. 323-342. English. DESCR:
*Literary Criticism; Mora, Pat; Moraga,
Cherrie; Poetry; Villanueva, Alma.

4256 Rebolledo, Tey Diana. Tradition and
mythology: signatures of landscape in
Chicana literature. IN: Norwood, Vera and
Monk, Janice, eds. THE DESERT IS NO LADY:
SOUTHWESTERN LANDSCAPES IN WOMEN'S WRITING
AND ART. New Haven, CT: Yale University
Press, 1987, p. 96-124. English. DESCR:
*Authors; Cabeza de Baca, Fabiola; Chavez,
Denise; Jaramillo, Cleofas M.; Literary
Criticism; *Literary History; Literature;
Mora, Pat; Otero Warren, Nina; Portillo
Trambley, Estela; Silva, Beverly;
Southwestern United States; WE FED THEM
CACTUS.

Narcissistic Personality Inventory

4257 Smith, Bradford M. The measurement of
narcissism in Asian, Caucasian, and Hispanic
American women. PSYCHOLOGICAL REPORTS, Vol.
67, no. 3 (December 1990), p. 779-785.
English. DESCR: Anglo Americans; Asian
Americans; Comparative Psychology; Cultural
Characteristics; *Personality;
*Psychological Testing; *Women.

Narcotic Addicts
USE: Drug Addicts

Narcotic Traffic
USE: Drug Traffic

National Alliance of Homebased Businesswomen

4258 Padilla, Steve. You've come a long way,
baby. Or have you? NUESTRO, Vol. 7, no. 6
(August 1983), p. 38-41. English. DESCR:
*Business Enterprises; Minority Business
Development Agency (MBDA).

National Assessment of Educational Progress

4259 Creswell, John L. Sex-related differences in
the problem-solving abilities of rural
Black, Anglo, and Chicano adolescents. TEXAS
TECH JOURNAL OF EDUCATION, Vol. 10, no. 1
(Winter 1983), p. 29-33. English. DESCR:
Aiken and Preger Revised Math Attitude
Scale; Anglo Americans; Blacks; California
Achievement Test (CAT); *Mathematics;
National Council of Teachers of Mathematics
(NCTM); Youth.

National Association for Chicano Studies (NACS)

4260 Garcia, Alma M. The development of Chicana feminist discourse, 1970-1980. GENDER & SOCIETY, Vol. 3, no. 2 (June 1989), p. 217-238. English. DESCR: Anglo Americans; Chicana Studies; *Chicano Movement; *Feminism; Homosexuality; Machismo; Organizations; *Sexism; Women.

4261 Garcia, Alma M. The development of Chicana feminist discourse, 1970-1980. IN: DuBois, Ellen Carol and Ruiz, Vicki L., eds. UNEQUAL SISTERS: A MULTICULTURAL READER IN U.S. WOMEN'S HISTORY. New York: Routledge, 1990, p. 418-431. English. DESCR: Anglo Americans; Chicana Studies; *Chicano Movement; *Feminism; Homosexuality; Machismo; Organizations; *Sexism; Women.

4262 Mujeres en Marcha, University of California, Berkeley. Chicanas in the 80s: unsettled issues. Berkeley, CA: Chicano Studies Library Publications Unit, 1983. 31 p. English. DESCR: Conferences and Meetings; Feminism; National Association for Chicano Studies Annual Conference (1982: Tempe, AZ); *Sexism.

National Association of Cuban American Women

4263 Prida, Dolores. Looking for room of one's own. NUESTRO, Vol. 3, no. 5 (June, July, 1979), p. 24-29. English. DESCR: Comision Femenil Mexicana de California; *Feminism; Mexican American Women's National Association (MANA); National Conference of Puerto Rican Women, Inc. (NCOPRW); Organizations.

National Association for Chicano Studies Annual Conference (1982: Tempe, AZ)

4264 Mujeres en Marcha, University of California, Berkeley. Chicanas in the 80s: unsettled issues. Berkeley, CA: Chicano Studies Library Publications Unit, 1983. 31 p. English. DESCR: Conferences and Meetings; Feminism; National Association for Chicano Studies (NACS); *Sexism.

National Chicana Coalition

4265 Robinson, Bea Vasquez. Are we racist? Are we sexist? AGENDA, (Winter 1976), p. 23-24. English. DESCR: Conferences and Meetings; Discrimination; Feminism; International Women's Year World Conference (1975: Mexico City); *Sexism.

National Conference of Puerto Rican Women, Inc. (NCOPRW)

4266 Espinosa, Ann. Hispanas: our resourses [sic] for the eighties. LA LUZ, Vol. 8, no. 4 (October, November, 1979), p. 10-13. English. DESCR: Baca Barragan, Polly; *Civil Rights; Comision Femenil Mexicana Nacional; DIRECTORY OF HISPANIC WOMEN; Discrimination in Education; Elected Officials; Hernandez, Irene; Lacayo, Carmela; Lujan, Josie; Mexican American Women's National Association (MANA); Montanez Davis, Grace; Moreno, Olga; Mujeres Latinas en Accion (M.L.A.); Organizations; Rangel, Irma.

4267 Prida, Dolores. Looking for room of one's own. NUESTRO, Vol. 3, no. 5 (June, July, 1979), p. 24-29. English. DESCR: Comision Femenil Mexicana de California; *Feminism; Mexican American Women's National Association (MANA); National Association of Cuban American Women; Organizations.

National Council of Teachers of Mathematics (NCTM)

4268 Creswell, John L. Sex-related differences in the problem-solving abilities of rural Black, Anglo, and Chicano adolescents. TEXAS TECH JOURNAL OF EDUCATION, Vol. 10, no. 1 (Winter 1983), p. 29-33. English. DESCR: Aiken and Preger Revised Math Attitude Scale; Anglo Americans; Blacks; California Achievement Test (CAT); *Mathematics; National Assessment of Educational Progress; Youth.

National Farm Workers Association (NFWA)

4269 Rose, Margaret. Traditional and nontraditional patterns of female activism in the United Farm Workers of America, 1962-1980. FRONTIERS: A JOURNAL OF WOMEN STUDIES, Vol. 11, no. 1 (1990), p. [26]-32. English. DESCR: Boycotts; California; Chavez, Cesar E.; *Chavez, Helen; *Huerta, Dolores; Labor Disputes; Labor Unions; Sex Roles; Strikes and Lockouts; *United Farmworkers of America (UFW).

National Hispanic Feminist Conference (March 28-31, 1980: San Jose, CA)

4270 Estrada, Iliad. Hispanic feminists meet--it's a trip. LA LUZ, Vol. 8, no. 7 (August, September, 1980), p. 35. English. DESCR: Conferences and Meetings; Feminism; *Puerto Ricans.

4271 Gonzales, Sylvia Alicia. The Latina feminist: where we've been, where we're going. NUESTRO, Vol. 5, no. 6 (August, September, 1981), p. 45-47. English. DESCR: Conferences and Meetings; *Feminism; History; Leadership.

National Mexican American Issues Conference (October 11, 1970: Sacramento, CA)

4272 Flores, Francisca. Conference of Mexican women un remolino. REGENERACION, Vol. 1, no. 10 (1971), p. 1-5. English. DESCR: Conferences and Meetings; Family; Feminism; First National Chicana Conference (May 1971: Houston, TX); Machismo; Sex Roles; Sex Stereotypes; Statistics; *Women Men Relations.

National Women's Conference (November, 1977: Houston, TX)

4273 Burciaga, Cecilia P. The 1977 National Women's Conference in Houston: gains and disappointments for Hispanics. LA LUZ, Vol. 7, no. 11 (November 1978), p. 8-9. English. DESCR: Conferences and Meetings.

4274 Saavedra-Vela, Pilar. Hispanic women in double jeopardy. AGENDA, Vol. 7, no. 6 (November, December, 1977), p. 4-7. English. DESCR: Conferences and Meetings; Discrimination; Houston, TX; *Sexism.

4275 Saavedra-Vela, Pilar. Nosotras in Houston. AGENDA, Vol. 8, no. 2 (March, April, 1978), p. 26-31. English. DESCR: Conferences and Meetings; *Feminism; Houston, TX.

National Women's Political Caucus (February 9-11, 1973: Houston, TX)

4276 Avila, Consuelo. Ecos de una convencion. MAGAZIN, Vol. 1, no. 9 (September 1973), p. 33-36. Spanish. DESCR: Conferences and Meetings; *Feminism.

National Women's Political Caucus (February 9-11, 1973: Houston, TX) (cont.)

4277 Chapa, Olivia Evey. Report from the National Women's Political Caucus. MAGAZIN, Vol. 1, no. 9 (September 1973), p. 37-39. English. DESCR: Conferences and Meetings; *Feminism.

4278 Nieto Gomez de Lazarin, Anna. La femenista [sic]. ENCUENTRO FEMENIL, Vol. 1, no. 2 (1974), p. 34-47. English. DESCR: Anglo Americans; Chicana Caucus, National Women's Political Caucus; Chicano Movement; Conferences and Meetings; Discrimination; *Feminism; *Sexism; Women.

Nationalism

4279 Gonzalez, Maria R. El embrion nacionalista visto a traves de la obra de Sor Juana Ines de la Cruz. IN: Del Castillo, Adelaida R., ed. BETWEEN BORDERS: ESSAYS ON MEXICANA/CHICANA HISTORY. Encino, CA: Floricanto Press, 1990, p. 239-253. Spanish. DESCR: Authors; *Juana Ines de la Cruz, Sor; Mexico; Women.

4280 Zavella, Patricia. The politics of race and gender: organizing Chicana cannery workers in Northern California. IN: Bockman, Ann and Morgen, Sandra, eds. WOMEN AND THE POLITICS OF EMPOWERMENT. Philadelphia, PA: Temple University Press, 1988, p. 202-224. English. DESCR: Bay City Cannery Workers Committee; *Canneries; Cannery Workers Committee (CWC); Discrimination; Garcia, Connie; Identity; *Labor Unions; Northern California; Santa Clara Valley, CA; Sex Roles; Sexism; *Working Women.

Native Americans

4281 Castaneda, Antonia I. Comparative frontiers: the migration of women to Alta California and New Zealand. IN: Schlissel, Lillian, et al., eds. WESTERN WOMEN: THEIR LAND, THEIR LIVES. Albuquerque, NM: University of New Mexico Press, 1988, p. 283-300. English. DESCR: Border Region; California; History; Immigrants; Immigration; Marriage; Mexico; Missions; New Zealand; Social History and Conditions; *Women.

4282 Cochran, Jo, et al., eds. Bearing witness/Sobreviviendo: an anthology of Native American/Latina art and literature. CALYX: A JOURNAL OF ART AND LITERATURE BY WOMEN, Vol. 8, no. 2 (Spring 1984), p. [1]-128. English. DESCR: *Art; Drawings; *Fiction; *Poems; Women.

4283 Fleming, Marilyn B. Problems experienced by Anglo, Hispanic and Navajo Indian women college students. JOURNAL OF AMERICAN INDIAN EDUCATION, Vol. 22, no. 1 (October 1982), p. 7-17. English. DESCR: Anglo Americans; Community Colleges; Ethnic Groups; *Higher Education; Identity; Medical Education; Students; Women.

4284 Galloway, Irma Nell. Trends in the employment of minority women as administrators in Texas public schools--1976-1981. Thesis (Ed.D.)--Texas Southern University, 1986. 129 p. English. DESCR: Asian Americans; Blacks; Education; *Educational Administration; *Management; Texas; *Women.

4285 Gutierrez, Ramon A. When Jesus came, the corn mothers went away: marriage, sexuality, and power in New Mexico, 1500-1846. Stanford: Stanford University Pres, 1991.

xxxi, 424 p. English. DESCR: *Marriage; *New Mexico; *Pueblo Indians; *Sex Roles; Sexual Behavior; Spanish Influence; Women.

4286 Hunter, Kathleen I.; Linn, Margaret W.; and Stein, Shayna R. Sterilization among American Indian and Chicano mothers. INTERNATIONAL QUARTERLY OF COMMUNITY HEALTH AND EDUCATION, Vol. 4, no. 4 (1983, 1984), p. 343-352. English. DESCR: *Sterilization.

4287 Perrone, Bobette; Stockel, H. Henrietta; and Krueger, Victoria. Medicine women, curanderas, and women doctors. Norman, OK: University of Oklahoma Press, c1989. xix, 252 p.: ill. English. DESCR: Aragon, Jesusita, 1908-; *Curanderas; *Curanderismo; *Folk Medicine; Herbal Medicine; Herrera, Sabinita; Medical Personnel; *Oral History; Rodriguez, Gregorita; Women.

4288 Ruiz, Vicki L., ed. and DuBois, Ellen Carol, ed. Unequal sisters: a multicultural reader in U.S. women's history. New York: Routledge, 1990. xvi, 473 p. English. DESCR: Anglo Americans; Asian Americans; Blacks; Feminism; *History; *Women.

4289 Schlissel, Lillian, ed.; Ruiz, Vicki L., ed.; and Monk, Janice, ed. Western women: their land, their lives. Albuquerque, NM: University of New Mexico Press, c1988. vi, 354 p. English. DESCR: Anglo Americans; History; Immigration; Intermarriage; Labor; *Social History and Conditions; Southwestern United States; *Women.

Nativism
USE: Assimilation

Natural Support Systems

4290 Arevalo, Rodolfo, ed. and Minor, Marianne, ed. Chicanas and alcoholism: a sociocultural perspective of women. San Jose, CA: School of Social Work, San Jose State University, c1981. 55 p. English. DESCR: *Alcoholism; Drug Abuse Programs; Family; Feminism; Preventative Medicine; Psychotherapy.

4291 Arguelles, Lourdes and Rivero, Anne M. HIV infection/AIDS and Latinas in Los Angeles County: considerations for prevention, treatment, and research practice. CALIFORNIA SOCIOLOGIST, Vol. 11, no. 1-2 (1988), p. 69-89. English. DESCR: *AIDS (Disease); Cultural Characteristics; Health Education; Homosexuality; Human Immunodeficiency Virus (HIV); Los Angeles County, CA; Parent and Child Relationships; Sexual Behavior; *Women.

4292 Balkwell, Carolyn Ann. An attitudinal correlate of the timing of a major life event: the case of morale in widowhood. FAMILY RELATIONS, Vol. 34, no. 4 (October 1985), p. 577-581. English. DESCR: *Ancianos; Counseling (Psychological); *Marriage; Mental Health; Widowhood.

4293 Becerra, Rosina M. and de Anda, Diane. Pregnancy and motherhood among Mexican American adolescents. HEALTH AND SOCIAL WORK, Vol. 9, no. 2 (Spring 1984), p. 106-23. English. DESCR: Acculturation; Anglo Americans; Attitudes; Birth Control; *Fertility; *Youth.

Natural Support Systems
(cont.)

4294 de Anda, Diane and Becerra, Rosina M. Support networks for adolescent mothers. SOCIAL CASEWORK: JOURNAL OF CONTEMPORARY SOCIAL WORK, Vol. 65, no. 3 (March 1984), p. 172-181. English. DESCR: California; *Fertility; Spanish Language; *Youth.

4295 de Leon Siantz, Mary Lou. Maternal acceptance/rejection of Mexican migrant mothers. PSYCHOLOGY OF WOMEN QUARTERLY, Vol. 14, no. 2 (June 1990), p. 245-254. English. DESCR: Child Study; Farm Workers; *Migrant Children; Migrant Labor; *Parent and Child Relationships; Stress; Texas Migrant Council Headstart Program.

4296 Dugan, Anna Baziak. Kin, social supports, and depression among women of Mexican heritage who are single parents. Thesis (Ph.D.)--Bryn Mawr College, 1982. vii, 188 p. English. DESCR: *Depression (Psychological); Detroit, MI; Family; *Single Parents.

4297 Gondolf, Edward W.; Fisher, Ellen; and McFerron, J. Richard. Racial differences among shelter residents: a comparison of Anglo, Black, and Hispanic battered. JOURNAL OF FAMILY VIOLENCE, Vol. 3, no. 1 (March 1988), p. 39-51. English. DESCR: Anglo Americans; Battered Women; Blacks; Comparative Psychology; Cultural Characteristics; Socioeconomic Factors; *Violence; *Women.

4298 Jaramillo, Mari-Luci. How to suceed in business and remain Chicana. LA LUZ, Vol. 8, no. 7 (August, September, 1980), p. 33-35. English. DESCR: Assertiveness; Cultural Characteristics; Family; Identity; *Working Women.

4299 Leon, Ana M., et al. Self-help support groups for Hispanic mothers. CHILD WELFARE, Vol. 63, no. 3 (May, June, 1984), p. 261-268. English. DESCR: Family; Mental Health Clinics; *Parent and Child Relationships; Sex Roles.

4300 Loustaunau, Martha Oehmke. Hispanic widows and their support systems in the Mesilla Valley of southern New Mexico, 1910-40. IN: Scadron, Arlene, ed. ON THEIR OWN: WIDOWS AND WIDOWHOOD IN THE AMERICAN SOUTHWEST 1843-1939. Urbana, IL: University of Illinois Press, c1988. p. [91]-116. English. DESCR: Cultural Customs; Extended Family; Mesilla Valley, NM; Sex Roles; Single Parents; Widowhood; *Women.

4301 Lozano-Bull, Irma. Acculturative stress in Mexican-American women. Thesis (Ph.D.)--California School of Professional Psychology, Los Angeles, 1987. 201 p. English. DESCR: *Acculturation; *Stress.

4302 Mata, Alberto Guardiola and Castillo, Valerie. Rural female adolescent dissatisfaction, support and helpseeking. FREE INQUIRY IN CREATIVE SOCIOLOGY, Vol. 14, no. 2 (November 1986), p. 135-138. English. DESCR: Alcoholism; *Drug Use; Interpersonal Relations; Parent and Child Relationships; Rural Population; *Youth.

4303 Mink, Diane Leslie. Early grandmotherhood: an exploratory study. Thesis (Ph.D.)--California School of Professional Psychology, Los Angeles, 1987. 190 p. English. DESCR: Age Groups; *Ancianos; Assertiveness; Family; Fertility; Grandmothers; *Sex Roles; Surveys; Youth.

4304 Morales, Aida G. Barriers, critical events, and support systems affecting Chicanas in their pursuit of an academic doctorate. Thesis (Ph.D.)--East Texas State University, 1988. 184 p. English. DESCR: *Academic Achievement; *Higher Education.

4305 O'Connor, Mary I. Women's networks and the social needs of Mexican immigrants. URBAN ANTHROPOLOGY, Vol. 19, no. 1-2 (Spring, Summer, 1990), p. 81-98. English. DESCR: Employment; *Immigrants; Labor Unions; *Sandyland Nursery, Carpinteria, CA; Undocumented Workers; United Farmworkers of America (UFW); Women.

4306 Perez, Robert. Effects of stress, social support and coping style on adjustment to pregnancy among Hispanic women. HISPANIC JOURNAL OF BEHAVIORAL SCIENCES, Vol. 5, no. 2 (June 1983), p. 141-161. English. DESCR: Fertility; *Stress.

4307 Perez, Robert. Stress and coping as determinants of adaptation to pregnancy in Hispanic women. Thesis (Ph.D.)--University of California, Los Angeles, 1982. 343 p. English. DESCR: *Fertility; Medical Personnel; *Stress.

4308 Rodriguez, Rogelio E. and DeWolfe, Alan. Psychological distress among Mexican-American and Mexican women as related to status on the new immigration law. JOURNAL OF CONSULTING AND CLINICAL PSYCHOLOGY, Vol. 58, no. 5 (October 1990), p. 548-553. English. DESCR: *Immigrants; Immigration Law and Legislation; Immigration Reform and Control Act of 1986; *Stress; Undocumented Workers; Women.

4309 Romero, Mary. Day work in the suburbs: the work experience of Chicana private housekeepers. IN: Statham, Anne; Miller, Eleanor M; and Mauksch, Hans O., eds. THE WORTH OF WOMEN'S WORK: A QUALITATIVE SYNTHESIS. Albany, NY: State University of New York Press, 1988. p. 77-91. English. DESCR: Domestic Work; Employment; Interpersonal Relations; Social Mobility; Working Women.

4310 Sabogal, Fabio, et al. Hispanic familism and acculturation: what changes and what doesn't? HISPANIC JOURNAL OF BEHAVIORAL SCIENCES, Vol. 9, no. 4 (December 1987), p. 397-412. English. DESCR: *Acculturation; Attitudes; Cultural Characteristics; Ethnic Groups; Extended Family; *Family; Values.

4311 Salgado de Snyder, Nelly. Mexican immigrant women: the relationship of ethnic loyalty and social support to acculturative stress and depressive symptomatology. Los Angeles, CA: Spanish Speaking Mental Health Research Center, 1987. 73 p. English. DESCR: *Acculturation; Depression (Psychological); Identity; *Immigrants; *Stress; Women.

4312 Vallez, Andrea. Acculturation, social support, stress and adjustment of the Mexican American college woman. Thesis (Ph.D.)--University of Colorado at Boulder, 1984. 121 p. English. DESCR: *Acculturation; *Colleges and Universities; Depression (Psychological); Higher Education; Southern California; Stress; *Students.

Natural Support Systems
(cont.)

4313 Wagner, Roland M. Changes in extended family relationships for Mexican American and Anglo single mothers. JOURNAL OF DIVORCE, Vol. 11, no. 2 (Winter 1987), p. 69-87. English. DESCR: Anglo Americans *Divorce; *Extended Family; San Jose, CA; *Single Parents; Women.

4314 Wagner, Roland M. Changes in the friend network during the first year of single parenthood for Mexican American and Anglo women. JOURNAL OF DIVORCE, Vol. 11, no. 2 (Winter 1987), p. 89-109. English. DESCR: Anglo Americans; Divorce; *Single Parents; Widowhood; Women.

4315 Wagner, Roland M. and Schaffer, Diane M. Social networks and survival strategies: an exploratory study of Mexican American, Black, and Anglo female family heads in San Jose, California. IN: Melville, Margarita B., ed. TWICE A MINORITY. St. Louis, MO: Mosby, 1980, p. 173-190. English. DESCR: Anglo Americans; Blacks; Identity; San Jose, CA; *Single Parents; Stress.

4316 Walker, Todd. The relationship of nativity social support and depression to the home environment among Mexican-American women. Thesis (Ph.D.)--University of Houston, 1980. 123 p. English. DESCR: Acculturation; Avance Parent-Child Education Program, San Antonio, TX; Children; Depression (Psychological); *Immigrants; *Parenting; Women.

4317 Williams, Joyce E. Secondary victimization: confronting public attitudes about rape. VICTIMOLOGY, Vol. 9, no. 1 (1984), p. 66-81. English. DESCR: *Attitudes; *Rape; San Antonio, TX.

4318 Worth, Dooley and Rodriguez, Ruth. Latina women and AIDS. SIECUS REPORT, (January, February, 1986), p. 5-7. English. DESCR: Cultural Characteristics; Drug Addicts; Drug Use; Health Education; New York; Preventative Medicine; Puerto Ricans; Sex Roles; *Vital Statistics; Women.

4319 Zambrano, Myrna. Mejor sola que mal acompanada: para la mujer golpeada. Seattle, WA: Seal Press, 1985. 241 p. Bilingual. DESCR: Battered Women; *Women.

4320 Zavella, Patricia. "Abnormal intimacy": the varying work networks of Chicana cannery workers. FEMINIST STUDIES, Vol. 11, no. 3 (Fall 1985), p. 541-557. English. DESCR: Canneries; Discrimination in Employment; Labor Unions; *Working Women.

4321 Zavella, Patricia. Work related networks and household organization among Chicana cannery workers. Stanford, CA: Stanford Center for Chicano Research, 1984. 12 leaves. English. DESCR: *Canneries; Industrial Workers; *Working Women.

Naturalization

4322 Alvarez, Robert R. A profile of the citizenship process among Hispanics in the United States. INTERNATIONAL MIGRATION REVIEW, Vol. 21, no. 2 (Summer 1987), p. 327-351. English. DESCR: Identity; Immigration and Naturalization Service (INS).

Nava, Yolanda

4323 Nieto Gomez de Lazarin, Anna. Un proposito

para estudios femeniles de la chicana. REGENERACION, Vol. 2, no. 4 (1975), p. 30, 31-32. English. DESCR: Chicano Studies; Curriculum; *Education; History; Sexism.

Needle-Sharing

4324 Nyamathi, Adeline M. and Vasquez, Rose. Impact of poverty, homelessness, and drugs on Hispanic women at risk for HIV infection. HISPANIC JOURNAL OF BEHAVIORAL SCIENCES, Vol. 11, no. 4 (November 1989), p. 299-314. English. DESCR: *AIDS (Disease); Drug Use; Health Education; *Human Immunodeficiency Virus (HIV); Locus of Control; Mental Health; *Poverty.

New Mexico

4325 Blea, Irene I. Brujeria: a sociological analysis of Mexican American witches. IN: Barrera, Mario, et al., eds. WORK, FAMILY, SEX ROLES, LANGUAGE: SELECTED PAPERS, 1979. Berkeley, CA: Tonatiuh-Quinto Sol, 1980, p. 177-193. English. DESCR: *Brujas; Colorado; Folklore; Kiev, Ari.

4326 Buss, Fran Leeper. La partera: story of a midwife. Ann Arbor, MI: University of Michigan Press, 1980. 140 p.: ill. English. DESCR: Aragon, Jesusita, 1908-; Cultural Customs; *Curanderas; Folk Medicine; Herbal Medicine; *Midwives; San Miguel County, NM.

4327 Craver, Rebecca McDowell. The impact of intimacy: Mexican-Anglo intermarriage in New Mexico 1821-1846. SOUTHWESTERN STUDIES, no. 66 (1982), p. 1-79. English. DESCR: Acculturation; Anglo Americans; Assimilation; History; *Intermarriage; Rio Arriba Valley, NM.

4328 Craver, Rebecca McDowell. The impact of intimacy: Mexican-Anglo intermarriage in New Mexico 1821-1846. El Paso, TX: Texas Western Press, University of Texas at El Paso, 1982. 79 p. English. DESCR: Acculturation; Anglo Americans; Assimilation; History; *Intermarriage; Rio Arriba Valley, NM.

4329 Deutsch, Sarah. Culture, class, and gender: Chicanas and Chicanos in Colorado and New Mexico, 1900-1940. Thesis (Ph.D.)--Yale University, 1985. xii, 510 p. English. DESCR: Anglo Americans; Colorado; Immigrants; *Sex Roles; *Social Classes; Social History and Conditions; Women; *Working Women.

4330 Deutsch, Sarah. No separate refuge: culture, class, and gender on an Anglo-Hispanic frontier in the American Southwest, 1880-1940. New York: Oxford University Press, 1987. vi, 356 p. English. DESCR: Anglo Americans; Colorado; Immigrants; Immigration; Mining Industry; Missions; *Sex Roles; *Social Classes; *Social History and Conditions; Women; Working Women; World War I.

4331 Deutsch, Sarah. Women and intercultural relations: the case of Hispanic New Mexico and Colorado. SIGNS: JOURNAL OF WOMEN IN CULTURE AND SOCIETY, Vol. 12, no. 4 (Summer 1987), p. 719-739. English. DESCR: Colorado; Cultural Characteristics; Immigrants; Intercultural Communication; Mexico; Rural Population; Sex Roles; Social History and Conditions; *Women.

New Mexico (cont.)

4332 Duran, Isabelle Sandoval. Grounded theory study: Chicana administrators in Colorado and New Mexico. Thesis (Ed.D.)--University of Wyoming, Laramie, 1982. ix, 114 p. English. **DESCR:** Careers; Colorado; *Educational Administration; Leadership; *Management.

4333 Elsasser, Nan; MacKenzie, Kyle; and Tixier y Vigil, Yvonne. Las mujeres: conversations from a Hispanic community. Old Wesbury, NY: Feminist Press; New York: McGraw-Hill, 1980. xxv, 163 p.: ill. English. **DESCR:** Biography; Oral History.

4334 Gallegos y Chavez, Ester. The northern New Mexican woman: a changing silhouette. IN: Trejo, Arnulfo D., ed. THE CHICANOS: AS WE SEE OURSELVES. Tucson, AZ: University of Arizona Press, 1979, p. 67-79. English. **DESCR:** *Identity; Machismo; Social History and Conditions.

4335 Gutierrez, Ramon A. From honor to love: transformations of the meaning of sexuality in colonial New Mexico. IN: Smith, Raymond T., ed. KINSHIP IDEOLOGY AND PRACTICE IN LATIN AMERICA. Chapel Hill, NC: University of North Carolina Press, 1984, p. [237]-263. English. **DESCR:** *Catholic Church; *Marriage; *Sexual Behavior; Social Classes; Social History and Conditions; Spanish Influence; Values; Women.

4336 Gutierrez, Ramon A. Marriage and seduction in Colonial New Mexico. IN: Del Castillo, Adelaida R., ed. BETWEEN BORDERS: ESSAYS ON MEXICANA/CHICANA HISTORY. Encino, CA: Floricanto Press, 1990, p. 447-457. English. **DESCR:** History; *Marriage; Rape; *Sexual Behavior; Women.

4337 Gutierrez, Ramon A. When Jesus came, the corn mothers went away: marriage, sexuality, and power in New Mexico, 1500-1846. Stanford: Stanford University Pres, 1991. xxxi, 424 p. English. **DESCR:** *Marriage; Native Americans; *Pueblo Indians; *Sex Roles; Sexual Behavior; Spanish Influence; Women.

4338 Heard, Martha E. The theatre of Denise Chavez: interior landscapes with SABOR NUEVOMEXICANO. THE AMERICAS REVIEW, Vol. 16, no. 2 (Summer 1988), p. 83-91. English. **DESCR:** *Chavez, Denise; EL CAMINO [play]; Literary Criticism; PLAZA [play]; *Teatro.

4339 Holscher, Louis M. Hispanic intermarriage: changing trends in New Mexico. AGENDA, Vol. 10, no. 6 (November, December, 1980), p. 8-10. English. **DESCR:** *Intermarriage; *Marriage.

4340 Jensen, Carol. Cleofas M. Jaramillo on marriage in territorial Northern New Mexico. NEW MEXICO HISTORICAL REVIEW, Vol. 58, no. 2 (April 1983), p. 153-171. English. **DESCR:** Jaramillo, Cleofas M.; *Marriage.

4341 Jensen, Joan M. Canning comes to New Mexico: women and the agricultural extension service, 1914-1919. NEW MEXICO HISTORICAL REVIEW, Vol. 57, no. 4 (October 1982), p. 361-386. English. **DESCR:** *Canneries; Food Industry; New Mexico Agricultural Extension Service.

4342 Jensen, Joan M. Crossing ethnic barriers in the Southwest: women's agricultural extension education, 1914-1940. AGRICULTURAL HISTORY, Vol. 60, no. 2 (Spring 1986), p.

169-181. English. **DESCR:** *Agricultural Extension Service; Agriculture; Cabeza de Baca, Fabiola; History; *Rural Education.

4343 Jensen, Joan M. "I've worked, I'm not afraid of work": farm women in New Mexico, 1920-1940. NEW MEXICO HISTORICAL REVIEW, Vol. 61, no. 1 (January 1986), p. 27-52. English. **DESCR:** *Farm Workers; History; *Rural Economics; *Working Women.

4344 McClelland, Judith Raymond. The relationship of independence to achievement: a comparative study of Hispanic women. Thesis (Ph.D.)--Fielding Institute, 1988. 164 p. English. **DESCR:** *Assertiveness; Attitudes; California Personality Inventory (CPI); Careers; Leadership; *Management; Personality; *Working Women.

4345 Miller, Darlis A. Cross-cultural marriages in the Southwest: the New Mexico experience, 1846-1900. NEW MEXICO HISTORICAL REVIEW, Vol. 57, no. 4 (October 1982), p. 335-359. English. **DESCR:** Assimilation; Attitudes; Ethnic Groups; *Intermarriage; Social History and Conditions.

4346 Padilla, Genaro. Imprisoned narrative? Or lies, secrets, and silence in New Mexico women's autobiography. IN: Calderon, Hector and Saldivar, Jose David, eds. CRITICISM IN THE BORDERLANDS: STUDIES IN CHICANO LITERATURE, CULTURE, AND IDEOLOGY. Durham, NC: Duke University Press, 1991, p. [43]-60. English. **DESCR:** *Authors; *Autobiography; *Cabeza de Baca, Fabiola; *Jaramillo, Cleofas M.; Literary History; ROMANCE OF A LITTLE VILLAGE GIRL; WE FED THEM CACTUS.

4347 Rebolledo, Tey Diana. Las escritoras: romances and realities. IN: Gonzales-Berry, Erlinda, ed. PASO POR AQUI: CRITICAL ESSAYS ON THE NEW MEXICAN LITERARY TRADITION. Albuquerque, NM: University of New Mexico Press, c1989, p. 199-214. English. **DESCR:** Authors; *Cabeza de Baca, Fabiola; *Jaramillo, Cleofas M.; Literary History; OLD SPAIN IN OUR SOUTHWEST; *Otero Warren, Nina; ROMANCE OF A LITTLE VILLAGE GIRL; WE FED THEM CACTUS; Women.

4348 Rebolledo, Tey Diana, ed.; Gonzales-Berry, Erlinda, ed.; and Marquez, Maria Teresa, ed. Las mujeres hablan: an anthology of Nuevo Mexicana writers. Albuquerque, NM: El Norte Publications, c1988. xiv, 210 p.: ill. English. **DESCR:** *Poems; *Prose; *Short Story.

4349 Rebolledo, Tey Diana. Narrative strategies of resistance in Hispana writing. THE JOURNAL OF NARRATIVE TECHNIQUE, Vol. 20, no. 2 (Spring 1990), p. 134-146. English. **DESCR:** *Authors; Cabeza de Baca, Fabiola; Fiction; Jaramillo, Cleofas M.; *Literary Criticism; Literature; OLD SPAIN IN OUR SOUTHWEST; *Oral Tradition; Otero Warren, Nina; ROMANCE OF A LITTLE VILLAGE GIRL; WE FED THEM CACTUS.

4350 Stevens, Joanne Darsey. Santos by twentieth-century santeras: continuation of a traditional art form. Thesis (Ph.D.)--University of Texas at Dallas, 1986. 259 p. English. **DESCR:** Art History; *Artists; Dallas Museum of Art; *Santos.

4351 Stoller, Marianne L. The Hispanic women artists of New Mexico: present and past. PALACIO, Vol. 92, no. 1 (1986), p. 21-25. English. **DESCR:** *Artists; *Santeros.

New Mexico (cont.)

4352 Veyna, Angelina F. Una vista al pasado: la mujer en Nuevo Mexico, 1744-1767. TRABAJOS MONOGRAFICOS, Vol. 1, no. 1 (1985), p. 28-42. English. DESCR: History; Sex Roles.

4353 Veyna, Angelina F. Women in early New Mexico: a preliminary view. IN: Cordova, Teresa, et al., eds. CHICANA VOICES. Austin TX: Center for Mexican American Studies, 1986, p. 120-135. English. DESCR: Administration of Justice; History; *Women.

New Mexico Agricultural Extension Service

4354 Jensen, Joan M. Canning comes to New Mexico: women and the agricultural extension service, 1914-1919. NEW MEXICO HISTORICAL REVIEW, Vol. 57, no. 4 (October 1982), p. 361-386. English. DESCR: *Canneries; Food Industry; New Mexico.

New Mexico State University

4355 De Blassie, Richard R. and Franco, Juan N. The differences between personality inventory scores and self-rating in a sample of Hispanic subjects. JOURNAL OF NON-WHITE CONCERNS IN PERSONNEL AND GUIDANCE, Vol. 11, no. 2 (January 1983), p. 43-46. English. DESCR: Higher Education; Hispanic Education [program]; *Personality; Sixteen Personality Factor Questionnaire; Students.

New York

4356 Worth, Dooley and Rodriguez, Ruth. Latina women and AIDS. SIECUS REPORT, (January, February, 1986), p. 5-7. English. DESCR: Cultural Characteristics; Drug Addicts; Drug Use; Health Education; Natural Support Systems; Preventative Medicine; Puerto Ricans; Sex Roles; *Vital Statistics; Women.

New Zealand

4357 Castaneda, Antonia I. Comparative frontiers: the migration of women to Alta California and New Zealand. IN: Schlissel, Lillian, et al., eds. WESTERN WOMEN: THEIR LAND, THEIR LIVES. Albuquerque, NM: University of New Mexico Press, 1988, p. 283-300. English. DESCR: Border Region; California; History; Immigrants; Immigration; Marriage; Mexico; Missions; Native Americans; Social History and Conditions; *Women.

Newspapers

4358 Hernandez, Ines. Sara Estela Ramirez: sembradora. LEGACY: A JOURNAL OF NINETEENTH-CENTURY AMERICAN WOMEN WRITERS, Vol. 6, no. 1 (Spring 1989), p. 13-26. English. DESCR: Authors; *Biography; *Feminism; Flores Magon, Ricardo; *Journalism; LA CORREGIDORA [newspaper]; Mexican Revolution - 1910-1920; Mexico; Poetry; *Ramirez, Sara Estela; REGENERACION [newspaper].

4359 Lomas, Clara. Mexican precursors of Chicana feminist writing. IN: National Association for Chicano Studies. ESTUDIOS CHICANOS AND THE POLITICS OF COMMUNITY. [S.l.]: National Association for Chicano Studies, c1989, p. [149]-160. English. DESCR: Authors; de Cardenas, Isidra T.; *Feminism; Idar, Jovita; *Journalists; Literature; *Mexican Revolution - 1910-1920; Ramirez, Sara Estela; Villarreal, Andrea; Villegas de Magnon, Leonor.

4360 Luna-Lawhn, Juanita. EL REGIDOR and LA PRENSA: impediments to women's self-definition. THIRD WOMAN, Vol. 4, (1989), p. 134-142. English. DESCR: EL REGIDOR, San Antonio, TX; LA PRENSA, San Antonio, TX; Literature; Sex Roles; *Sexism.

4361 Luna-Lawhn, Juanita. Victorian attitudes affecting the Mexican woman writing in LA PRENSA during the early 1900s and the Chicana of the 1980s. IN: Bardeleben, Renate von, et al., eds. MISSIONS IN CONFLICT: ESSAYS ON U.S.-MEXICAN RELATIONS AND CHICANO CULTURE. Tubingen, W. Germany: Gunter Narr Verlag, 1986, p. 65-71. English. DESCR: Feminism; LA PRENSA, San Antonio, TX; Literary Criticism; "Penitents" [poem]; Poetry; Zamora, Bernice.

4362 Perez, Emma. "A la mujer": a critique of the Partido Liberal Mexicano's gender ideology on women. IN: Del Castillo, Adelaida R., ed. BETWEEN BORDERS: ESSAYS ON MEXICANA/CHICANA HISTORY. Encino, CA: Floricanto Press, 1990, p. 459-482. English. DESCR: *"A La Mujer" [essay]; Essays; *Feminism; Flores Magon, Ricardo; Guerrero, Praxedis G.; Journalism; Mexican Revolution - 1910-1920; Mexico; *Partido Liberal Mexicano (PLM); Political Ideology; Political Parties and Organizations; *REGENERACION [newspaper]; Sex Roles; Women.

Nichols, John

4363 Mondin, Sandra. The depiction of the Chicana in BLESS ME ULTIMA and THE MILAGRO BEANFIELD WAR: a study in contrasts. IN: Luna Lawhn, Juanita, et al., eds. MEXICO AND THE UNITED STATES: INTERCULTURAL RELATIONS IN THE HUMANITIES. San Antonio, TX: San Antonio College, 1984, p. 137-150. English. DESCR: Anaya, Rudolfo A.; BLESS ME, ULTIMA; Literary Characters; Literary Criticism; *Stereotypes; THE MILAGRO BEANFIELD WAR [novel].

Niggli, Josephina

4364 Velasquez-Trevino, Gloria. Cultural ambivalence in early Chicana prose fiction. Thesis (Ph.D.)--Stanford University, 1985. 185 p. English. DESCR: Biculturalism; *Fiction; Gonzalez, Jovita; Literary Criticism; Mena, Maria Cristina; Prose; Sex Roles.

La Nina de Cabora
  USE: Urrea, Teresa

Nixon, Richard

4365 Nieto Gomez de Lazarin, Anna. What is the Talmadge Amendment?: justicia para las madres. REGENERACION, Vol. 2, no. 3 (1973), p. 14-15. English. DESCR: Chicana Welfare Rights Organization; *Child Care Centers; Community Work Experience Program (C.W.E.F.); Discrimination in Employment; Employment Tests; Escalante, Alicia; *Feminism; Working Women.

NO SEPARATE REFUGE

4366 Acuna, Rodolfo. The struggles of class and gender: current research in Chicano Studies [review essay]. JOURNAL OF AMERICAN ETHNIC HISTORY, Vol. 8, no. 2 (Spring 1989), p. 134-138. English. DESCR: *CANNERY WOMEN, CANNERY LIVES; *CHICANO ETHNICITY; Deutsch, Sarah; Keefe, Susan E.; Literature Reviews; Padilla, Amado M.; Ruiz, Vicki L.; *WOMEN'S WORK AND CHICANO FAMILIES; Zavella, Pat.

"La noche que se apagaron las luces" [short story]

4367 Lizarraga, Sylvia S. The patriarchal ideology in "La noche que se apagaron las luces". REVISTA CHICANO-RIQUENA, Vol. 13, no. 3-4 (Fall, Winter, 1985), p. 90-95. English. DESCR: *Literary Criticism; Rivera, Tomas; Sex Roles; Y NO SE LO TRAGO LA TIERRA/AND THE EARTH DID NOT PART.

Non-insulin Dependent Diabetes Mellitus (NIDDM)

4368 Swinney, Gloria Luyas. The biocultural context of low-income Mexican-American women with type II non-insulin dependent diabetes and its implications for health care delivery. Thesis (Ph.D.)--University of Texas, Austin, 1988. 277 p. English. DESCR: *Diabetes; Low Income; *Medical Care.

NorCal Frozen Foods

4369 Shapiro, Peter. Watsonville shows "it can be done". GUARDIAN, Vol. 39, no. 24 (March 25, 1987), p. 1,9. English. DESCR: Canneries; Labor Unions; *Strikes and Lockouts; *Watsonville Canning and Frozen Food Co.; Working Women.

Northern California

4370 Kokinos, Mary and Dewey, Kathryn G. Infant feeding practices of migrant Mexican-American families in Northern California. ECOLOGY OF FOOD AND NUTRITION, Vol. 18, no. 3 (1986), p. 209-220. English. DESCR: *Breastfeeding; Farm Workers; Migrant Labor; Nutrition.

4371 Zavella, Patricia. The politics of race and gender: organizing Chicana cannery workers in Northern California. IN: Bookman, Ann and Morgen, Sandra, eds. WOMEN AND THE POLITICS OF EMPOWERMENT. Philadelphia, PA: Temple University Press, 1988, p. 202-224. English. DESCR: Bay City Cannery Workers Committee; *Canneries; Cannery Workers Committee (CWC); Discrimination; Garcia, Connie; Identity; *Labor Unions; Nationalism; Santa Clara Valley, CA; Sex Roles; Sexism; *Working Women.

Northwestern United States

4372 Cook, Annabel Kirschner. Diversity among Northwest Hispanics. SOCIAL SCIENCE JOURNAL, Vol. 23, no. 2 (April 1986), p. 205-216. English. DESCR: *Population; Socioeconomic Factors.

Nova-Tech, San Diego, CA

4373 Fernandez Kelly, Maria and Garcia, Anna M. Invisible amidst the glitter: Hispanic women in the Southern California electronics industry. IN: Statham, Anne; Miller, Eleanor M.; and Mauksh, Hans O., eds. THE WORTH OF WOMEN'S WORK: A QUALITATIVE SYNTHESIS. Albany, NY: State University of New York Press, 1988, p. 265-290. English. DESCR: *Electronics Industry; Employment; Immigrants; *Industrial Workers; Labor Supply and Market; Megatek, La Jolla, CA; Sex Roles; Southern California; *Working Women.

Novel

4374 Anderson, Robert K. Marez y Luna and the masculine-feminine dialectic. CRITICA HISPANICA, Vol. 6, no. 2 (1984), p. 97-105. English. DESCR: Anaya, Rudolfo A.; BLESS ME, ULTIMA; Literary Criticism; *Women Men Relations.

4375 Bruce-Novoa, Juan. Deconstructing the dominant patriarchal text: Cecile Pineda's narratives. IN: Horno-Delgado, Asuncion, et al., eds. BREAKING BOUNDARIES: LATINA WRITING AND CRITICAL READINGS. Amherst, MA: University of Massachusetts Press, c1989, p. 72-81. English. DESCR: *FACE; *FRIEZE; Identity; Literary Criticism; *Pineda, Cecile.

4376 Gutierrez Castillo, Dina. La imagen de la mujer en la novela fronteriza. IN: Lopez-Gonzalez, Aralia, et al., eds. MUJER Y LITERATURA MEXICANA Y CHICANA: CULTURAS EN CONTACTO. Mexico: Colegio de la Frontera Norte, 1988, p. [55]-63. Spanish. DESCR: *Border Region; Islas, Arturo; Literary Characters; *Literary Criticism; Mendez M., Miguel; PEREGRINOS DE AZTLAN; Sex Roles; Sex Stereotypes; THE RAIN GOD: A DESERT TALE; *Women.

4377 Lizarraga, Sylvia S. La mujer ingeniosa. FEM, Vol. 8, no. 34 (June, July, 1984), p. 41. Spanish. DESCR: Literary Criticism; *THERE ARE NO MADMEN HERE; *Valdes, Gina.

4378 Lomeli, Francisco A. Chicana novelists in the process of creating fictive voices. IN: Herrera-Sobek, Maria, ed. BEYOND STEREOTYPES: THE CRITICAL ANALYSIS OF CHICANA LITERATURE. Binghamton, NY: Bilingual Press/Editorial Bilingue, 1985, p. 29-46. English. DESCR: Authors; Literary Criticism; Literary History.

4379 Quintana, Alvina E. Ana Castillo's THE MIXQUIAHUALA LETTERS: the novelist as ethnographer. IN: Calderon, Hector and Saldivar, Jose David, eds. CRITICISM IN THE BORDERLANDS: STUDIES IN CHICANO LITERATURE, CULTURE, AND IDEOLOGY. Durham, NC: Duke University Press, 1991, p. [72]-83. English. DESCR: Anthropology; Castillo, Ana; Cultural Studies; *Ethnology; Feminism; Geertz, Clifford; *Literary Criticism; THE MIXQUIAHUALA LETTERS.

4380 Vallejos, Tomas. Estela Portillo Trambley's fictive search for paradise. FRONTIERS: A JOURNAL OF WOMEN STUDIES, Vol. 5, no. 2 (1980),p. 54-58. Also IN: Lattin, Vernon E., ed. CONTEMPORARY CHICANO FICTION. Binghamton, NY: Bilingual Press/Editorial Bilingue, 1986, p. 269-277. English. DESCR: DAY OF THE SWALLOWS; *Literary Criticism; Portillo Trambley, Estela; RAIN OF SCORPIONS AND OTHER WRITINGS.

Novelists
   USE: Authors

NOVENA NARRATIVES

4381 Quintana, Alvina E. Chicana discourse: negations and mediations. Thesis (Ph.D.)--University of California, Santa Cruz, 1989. 226 p. English. DESCR: Authors; Castillo, Ana; Chavez, Denise; Chicano Movement; Cisneros, Sandra; Ethnology; Feminism; Literary Criticism; *Literature; Oral Tradition; Political Ideology; THE HOUSE ON MANGO STREET; THE LAST OF THE MENU GIRLS; THE MIXQUIAHUALA LETTERS.

Nurseries (Children)
   USE: Child Care Centers

Nursery School
   USE: Child Care Centers

Nutrition

4382 Fanelli-Kuczmarski, Marie T., et al. Folate status of Mexican American, Cuban, and Puerto Rican women. AMERICAN JOURNAL OF CLINICAL NUTRITION, Vol. 52, no. 2 (August 1990), p. 368-372. English. DESCR: Cubanos; *Folic Acid Deficiency; Hispanic Health and Nutrition Examination Survey (HHANES); Puerto Ricans; *Women.

4383 Garn, Stanley M. and LaVelle, Marquisa. Reproductive histories of low weight girls and women. AMERICAN JOURNAL OF CLINICAL NUTRITION, Vol. 37, no. 5 (May 1983), p. 862-866. English. DESCR: *Fertility; Youth.

4384 Hazuda, Helen P., et al. Employment status and women's protection against coronary heart disease. AMERICAN JOURNAL OF EPIDEMIOLOGY, Vol. 123, no. 4 (April 1986), p. 623-640. English. DESCR: Anglo Americans; Diseases; Employment; *Heart Disease; *Public Health; San Antonio, TX.

4385 Hunt, Isabelle F., et al. Zinc supplementation during pregnancy: zinc concentration of serum and hair from low-income women of Mexican descent. AMERICAN JOURNAL OF CLINICAL NUTRITION, Vol. 37, no. 4 (April 1983), p. 572-582. English. DESCR: Low Income; *Prenatal Care; Surveys.

4386 Hunt, Isabelle F., et al. Zinc supplementation during pregnancy in low-income teenagers of Mexican descent: effects on selected blood constituents and on progress and outcome of pregnancy. AMERICAN JOURNAL OF CLINICAL NUTRITION, Vol. 42, no. 5 (November 1985), p. 815-828. English. DESCR: *Fertility; *Youth.

4387 Joos, Sandra Kay. Social, attitudinal and behavioral correlates of weight change among Mexican American women. Thesis (Ph.D.)--University of Texas H.S.C. at Houston School of Public Health, 1984. 235 p. English. DESCR: *Obesity.

4388 Kokinos, Mary and Dewey, Kathryn G. Infant feeding practices of migrant Mexican-American families in Northern California. ECOLOGY OF FOOD AND NUTRITION, Vol. 18, no. 3 (1986), p. 209-220. English. DESCR: *Breastfeeding; Farm Workers; Migrant Labor; Northern California.

4389 Olvera-Ezzell, Norma; Power, Thomas G.; and Cousins, Jennifer H. Maternal socialization of children's eating habits: strategies used by obese Mexican-American mothers. CHILD DEVELOPMENT, Vol. 61, no. 2 (April 1990), p. 395-400. English. DESCR: Children; Food Practices; *Obesity; *Parent and Child Relationships; *Socialization.

4390 Pumariega, Andres J. Acculturation and eating attitudes in adolescent girls: a comparative and correlational study. JOURNAL OF THE AMERICAN ACADEMY OF CHILD PSYCHIATRY, Vol. 25, no. 2 (March 1986), p. 276-279. English. DESCR: *Acculturation; Anorexia Nervosa; Cultural Characteristics; Eating Attitudes Test (EAT); Socioeconomic Factors; Youth.

4391 Wolff, Cindy Brattan. Diet and pregnancy outcome in Mexican-American women. Thesis (Ph.D.)--Colorado State University, 1986. 257 p. English. DESCR: *Fertility; Food Practices; *Maternal and Child Welfare.

Obesity

4392 Joos, Sandra Kay. Social, attitudinal and behavioral correlates of weight change among Mexican American women. Thesis (Ph.D.)--University of Texas H.S.C. at Houston School of Public Health, 1984. 235 p. English. DESCR: *Nutrition.

4393 Olvera-Ezzell, Norma; Power, Thomas G.; and Cousins, Jennifer H. Maternal socialization of children's eating habits: strategies used by obese Mexican-American mothers. CHILD DEVELOPMENT, Vol. 61, no. 2 (April 1990), p. 395-400. English. DESCR: Children; Food Practices; *Nutrition; *Parent and Child Relationships; *Socialization.

Occupational Aspirations
USE: Careers

Occupational Hazards

4394 Hovell, Melbourne F., et al. Occupational health risks for Mexican women: the case of the maquiladora along the Mexican-United States border. INTERNATIONAL JOURNAL OF HEALTH SERVICES, Vol. 18, no. 4 (1988), p. 617-627. English. DESCR: *Border Industries; Border Region; Mexico; Project Concern International (PCI), San Diego, CA; Public Health; Surveys; Tijuana, Baja California, Mexico; Women; Working Women.

4395 Lopez-Trevino, Maria Elena. A radio model: a community strategy to address the problems and needs of Mexican-American women farmworkers. Thesis (M.S.)--California State University, Long Beach, 1989. 179 p. English. DESCR: Coachella, CA; *Farm Workers; Income; Low Income; *Radio; *Sex Roles.

Occupational Training
USE: Vocational Education

OCCUPIED AMERICA

4396 Orozco, Cynthia. Sexism in Chicano Studies and the community. IN: Cordova, Teresa, et al., eds. CHICANA VOICES. Austin, TX: Center for Mexican American Studies, 1986, p. 11-18. English. DESCR: Acuna, Rodolfo; Chicano Studies; Feminism; *Sexism.

THE OCTOPUS [play]

4397 Yarbro-Bejarano, Yvonne. The image of the Chicana in teatro. IN: Cochran, Jo; Stewart, J.T.; and Tsutakawa, Mayumi, eds. GATHERING GROUND: NEW WRITING AND ART BY NORTHWEST WOMEN OF COLOR. Seattle, WA: Seal Press, 1984, p. 90-96. English. DESCR: El Teatro de la Esperanza; GUADALUPE [play]; HIJOS: ONCE A FAMILY [play]; LA VICTIMA [play]; *Literary Characters; Sex Roles; Sex Stereotypes; Stereotypes; *Teatro; Women Men Relations.

Ohio

4398 Hintz, Joy. Valiant migrant women = Las mujeres valerosas. Tiffin, OH: Sayger Printing, 1982. viii, 98 p. English. DESCR: Battered Women; *Farm Workers; Feminism; Florida; Marriage; Migrant Children; Migrant Health Services; Migrant Housing; *Migrant Labor; Migration Patterns; Sex Roles; Texas.

Old Age
USE: Ancianos

OLD SPAIN IN OUR SOUTHWEST

4399 Rebolledo, Tey Diana. Las escritoras: romances and realities. IN: Gonzales-Berry, Erlinda, ed. PASO POR AQUI: CRITICAL ESSAYS ON THE NEW MEXICAN LITERARY TRADITION. Albuquerque, NM: University of New Mexico Press, c1989, p. 199-214. English. **DESCR:** Authors; *Cabeza de Baca, Fabiola; *Jaramillo, Cleofas M.; Literary History; New Mexico; *Otero Warren, Nina; ROMANCE OF A LITTLE VILLAGE GIRL; WE FED THEM CACTUS; Women.

4400 Rebolledo, Tey Diana. Hispanic women writers of the Southwest: tradition and innovation. IN: Lensink, Judy Nolte, ed. OLD SOUTHWEST/NEW SOUTHWEST: ESSAYS ON A REGION AND ITS LITERATURE. Tucson, AZ: The Tucson Public Library, 1987, p. 49-61. English. **DESCR:** *Authors; Cabeza de Baca, Fabiola; Jaramillo, Cleofas M.; Literature; Mora, Pat; Otero Warren, Nina; Preciado Martin, Patricia; Sex Roles; Sex Stereotypes; Silva, Beverly; *Southwestern United States; Vigil-Pinon, Evangelina; WE FED THEM CACTUS; *Women.

4401 Rebolledo, Tey Diana. Narrative strategies of resistance in Hispana writing. THE JOURNAL OF NARRATIVE TECHNIQUE, Vol. 20, no. 2 (Spring 1990), p. 134-146. English. **DESCR:** *Authors; Cabeza de Baca, Fabiola; Fiction; Jaramillo, Cleofas M.; *Literary Criticism; Literature; New Mexico; *Oral Tradition; Otero Warren, Nina; ROMANCE OF A LITTLE VILLAGE GIRL; WE FED THEM CACTUS.

Olmedo, Esteban L.

4402 Ramirez, Alex, et al. The relationship between sociocultural variables and Chicano and Anglo high school student responses on the Potency Dimension of the Semantic Differential. HISPANIC JOURNAL OF BEHAVIORAL SCIENCES, Vol. 3, no. 2 (June 1981), p. 177-190. English. **DESCR:** Anglo Americans; Martinez, Joe L., Jr.; Martinez, Sergio R.; MULTIVARIATE ANALYSIS OF VARIANCE (MANOVA); *Parent and Child Relationships; Sex Roles; Sex Stereotypes; Students.

Olsen, Tillie

4403 Woodward, Carolyn. Dare to write: Virginia Woolf, Tillie Olsen, Gloria Anzaldua. IN: Cochran, Jo Whitehorse, et al., eds. CHANGING OUR POWER: AN INTRODUCTION TO WOMEN STUDIES. Dubuque, IA: Kendall/Hunt Publishing Co., 1988, p. 336-349. English. **DESCR:** Anzaldua, Gloria; *Authors; Feminism; Women; Woolf, Virginia.

"On the Road to Texas: Pete Fonseca" [short story]

4404 Lizarraga, Sylvia S. "La mujer doblamente explotada: "On the Road to Texas: Pete Fonseca". AZTLAN, Vol. 16, no. 1-2 (1985), p. 197-215. Spanish. **DESCR:** *Literary Criticism; Rivera, Tomas.

ONLY ONCE IN A LIFETIME [film]

4405 Ordonez, Elizabeth J. La imagen de la mujer en el nuevo cine chicano. CARACOL, Vol. 5, no. 2 (October 1978), p. 12-13. Spanish. **DESCR:** Bonilla-Giannini, Roxanna; *Films; Lopez, Lexore; *Photography; RAICES DE SANGRE [film]; Robelo, Miguel; Sex Stereotypes.

Oral History

4406 Apodaca, Maria Linda. The Chicana woman: a

historical materialist perspective. IN: Bollinger, William, et al., eds. WOMEN IN LATIN AMERICA: AN ANTHOLOGY FROM LATIN AMERICAN PERSPECTIVES. Riverside, CA: Latin American Perspectives, c1979, p. 81-100. English. **DESCR:** Capitalism; *Historiography; Immigrants; Imperialism; Marxism; Mexico; Social Classes; Spanish Influence.

4407 Arenal, Sandra. Sangre joven: las maquiladoras por dentro. Mexico, D.F.: Editorial Nuestro Tiempo, 1986. 130 p.: ill. Spanish. **DESCR:** *Border Industries; *Border Region; Employment; Women; Working Women.

4408 Broyles-Gonzalez, Yolanda and Rodriguez, Diane. The living legacy of Chicana performers: preserving history through oral testimony. FRONTIERS: A JOURNAL OF WOMEN STUDIES, Vol. 11, no. 1 (1990), p. [46]-52. English. **DESCR:** *Actors and Actresses; El Teatro Campesino; Latins Anonymous [comedy review]; *Rodriguez, Diane; Sex Roles; Singers; Teatro.

4409 Cantarow, Ellen and De la Cruz, Jessie Lopez. Jessie Lopez De la Cruz: the battle for farmworkers' rights. IN: Cantarow, Ellen. MOVING THE MOUNTAIN: WOMEN WORKING FOR SOCIAL CHANGE. Old Westbury, NY: Feminist Press, 1980, p. 94-151. English. **DESCR:** Agricultural Labor Unions; Chavez, Cesar E.; *De la Cruz, Jessie Lopez; *Farm Workers; Labor Disputes; Parlier, CA; Sex Roles; Strikes and Lockouts; *United Farmworkers of America (UFW).

4410 Curry Rodriguez, Julia E. Labor migration and familial responsibilities: experiences of Mexican women. IN: Melville, Margarita, ed. MEXICANAS AT WORK IN THE UNITED STATES. Houston, TX: Mexican American Studies Program, University of Houston, 1988, p. 47-63. English. **DESCR:** Employment; Family; *Immigrants; Mexico; *Migrant Labor; Sex Roles; Undocumented Workers; *Women; *Working Women.

4411 Curry Rodriguez, Julia E. Reconceptualizing undocumented labor immigration: the causes, impact and consequences in Mexican women's lives. Thesis (Ph.D.)--University of Texas at Austin, 1988. xiv, 329 p. English. **DESCR:** Employment; *Immigrants; Mexico; *Undocumented Workers; *Women.

4412 Duran Apodaca, Maria. North from Mexico. IN: Jensen, Joan M. ed. WITH THESE HANDS: WOMEN WORKING ON THE LAND. New York: McGraw-Hill, 1981, p. 120-122. English. **DESCR:** *Biography; Duran Apodaca, Maria.

4413 Elsasser, Nan; MacKenzie, Kyle; and Tixier y Vigil, Yvonne. Las mujeres: conversations from a Hispanic community. Old Wesbury, NY: Feminist Press; New York: McGraw-Hill, 1980. xxv, 163 p.: ill. English. **DESCR:** Biography; *New Mexico.

4414 Gamio, Manuel. Senora Flores de Andrade. IN: Mora, Magdalena and Del Castillo, Adelaida, eds. MEXICAN WOMEN IN THE UNITED STATES: STRUGGLES PAST AND PRESENT. Los Angeles, CA: Chicano Studies Research Center, UCLA, 1980, p. 189-192. English. **DESCR:** Autobiography; Flores de Andrade, Senora; Immigrants; Mexican Revolution - 1910-1920.

4415 Iglesias, Norma and Carrillo, Jorge. Que me dejo el trabajo?: mi vida se pregunta. TRABAJOS MONOGRAFICOS, Vol. 2, no. 1 (1986), p. 10-18. Spanish. **DESCR:** Border Industries; *Working Women.

Oral History (cont.)

4416 Lockert, Lucia Fox. Chicanas: their voices, their lives. Lansing, MI: Michigan State Board of Education, 1938. xii, 36 p.: ill. English. DESCR: Michigan; Working Women.

4417 Perrone, Bobette; Stockel, H. Henrietta; and Krueger, Victoria. Medicine women, curanderas, and women doctors. Norman, OK: University of Oklahoma Press, c1989. xix, 252 p.:ill. English. DESCR: Aragon, Jesusita, 1908-; *Curanderas; *Curanderismo; *Folk Medicine; Herbal Medicine; Herrera, Sabinita; Medical Personnel; Native Americans; Rodriguez, Gregorita; Women.

4418 Preciado Martin, Patricia. Images and conversations: Mexican Americans recall a Southwestern past. Tucson, AZ: University of Arizona Press, 1983. 110 p.: ill. English. DESCR: Photography; Social History and Conditions; Tucson, AZ.

4419 Quintana, Alvina E. Her story. REVISTA MUJERES, Vol. 4, no. 1 (January 1987), p. 44-47. English.

4420 Rips, Geoffrey and Tenayuca, Emma. Living history: Emma Tenayuca tells her story. TEXAS OBSERVER, (October 28, 1983), p. 7-15. English. DESCR: *Autobiography; Communist Party; Food Industry; Labor Unions; Leadership; Pecan Shelling Worker's Union, San Antonio, TX; San Antonio, TX; Strikes and Lockouts; Tenayuca, Emma; United Cannery Agricultural Packing and Allied Workers of America (UCAPAWA); Worker's Alliance (WA), Los Angeles, CA; Working Women.

4421 Rubio Goldsmith, Raquel. Oral history: considerations and problems for its use in the history of Mexicanas in the United States. IN: Del Castillo, Adelaida R., ed. BETWEEN BORDERS: ESSAYS ON MEXICANA/CHICANA HISTORY. Encino, CA: Floricanto Press, 1990, p. 161-173. English. DESCR: History; *Research Methodology.

4422 Weber, Devra Anne. Mexican women on strike: memory, history and oral narratives. IN: Del Castillo, Adelaida R., ed. BETWEEN BORDERS: ESSAYS ON MEXICANA/CHICANA HISTORY. Encino, CA: Floricanto Press, 1990, p. 175-200. English. DESCR: *1933 Cotton Strike; Cotton Industry; History; San Joaquin Valley, CA; Strikes and Lockouts; *Valdez, Rosaura; Working Women.

Oral Tradition

4423 Quintana, Alvina E. Chicana discourse: negations and mediations. Thesis (Ph.D.)--University of California, Santa Cruz, 1989. 226 p. English. DESCR: Authors; Castillo, Ana; Chavez, Denise; Chicano Movement; Cisneros, Sandra; Ethnology; Feminism; Literary Criticism; *Literature; NOVENA NARRATIVES; Political Ideology; THE HOUSE ON MANGO STREET; THE LAST OF THE MENU GIRLS; THE MIXQUIAHUALA LETTERS.

4424 Rebolledo, Tey Diana. Narrative strategies of resistance in Hispana writing. THE JOURNAL OF NARRATIVE TECHNIQUE, Vol. 20, no. 2 (Spring 1990), p. 134-145. English. DESCR: *Authors; Cabeza de Baca, Fabiola; Fiction; Jaramillo, Cleofas M.; *Literary Criticism; Literature; New Mexico; OLD SPAIN IN OUR SOUTHWEST; Otero Warren, Nina; ROMANCE OF A LITTLE VILLAGE GIRL; WE FED THEM CACTUS.

Orange, CA

4425 Weller, Susan C. and Dungy, Claibourne I. Personal preferences and ethnic variations among Anglo and Hispanic breast and bottle feeders. SOCIAL SCIENCE & MEDICINE, Vol. 23, no. 6 (1985), p. 539-548. English. DESCR: Attitudes; *Breastfeeding; *Maternal and Child Welfare; Parenting; Socioeconomic Factors.

Oregon

4426 Jones, Pamela. "There was a woman": La Llorona in Oregon. WESTERN FOLKLORE, Vol. 47, no. 3 (July 1988), p. 195-211. English. DESCR: Folklore; *La Llorona; *Leyendas; Research Methodology.

Organizations

4427 Campbell, Julie A. Madres y esposas: Tucson's Spanish-American Mothers and Wives Association. JOURNAL OF ARIZONA HISTORY, Vol. 31, no. 2 (Summer 1990), p. 161-182. English. DESCR: History; Military; *Spanish-American Mothers and Wives Association, Tucson, AZ; Tucson, AZ; World War II.

4428 Carrillo, Ana, et al. History of Las Mujeres. REVISTA MUJERES, Vol. 1, no. 1 (January 1984), p. 4-5. English. DESCR: *Las Mujeres, University of California, Santa Cruz.

4429 Castillo, Sylvia. A guide to Hispanic women's resources: a perspective on networking among Hispanic women. CALIFORNIA WOMEN, (December 1983), p. 2-6. English. DESCR: *Directories; Professional Organizations; Women.

4430 Cotera, Marta P. Feminism: the Chicana and Anglo versions: a historical analysis. IN: Melville, Margarita B., ed. TWICE A MINORITY. St. Louis, MO: Mosby, 1980, p. 217-234. English. DESCR: *Anglo Americans; Chicano Movement; Conferences and Meetings; *Feminism; Social History and Conditions; Voting Rights; *Women.

4431 Espinosa, Ann. Hispanas: our resourses [sic] for the eighties. LA LUZ, Vol. 8, no. 4 (October, November, 1979), p. 10-13. English. DESCR: Baca Barragan, Polly; *Civil Rights; Comision Femenil Mexicana Nacional; DIRECTORY OF HISPANIC WOMEN; Discrimination in Education; Elected Officials; Hernandez, Irene; Lacayo, Carmela; Lujan, Josie; Mexican American Women's National Association (MANA); Montanez Davis, Grace; Moreno, Olga; Mujeres Latinas en Accion (M.L.A.); National Conference of Puerto Rican Women, Inc. (NCOPRW); Rangel, Irma.

4432 Flores, Francisca. Comision Femenil Mexicana. REGENERACION, Vol. 2, no. 1 (1971), p. 6. English. DESCR: Abortion; Children; Comision Femenil Mexicana Nacional; *Family Planning; Feminism; Politics.

4433 Garcia, Alma M. The development of Chicana feminist discourse, 1970-1980. GENDER & SOCIETY, Vol. 3, no. 2 (June 1989), p. 217-238. English. DESCR: Anglo Americans; Chicana Studies; *Chicano Movement; *Feminism; Homosexuality; Machismo; National Association for Chicano Studies (NACS); *Sexism; Women.

Organizations (cont.)

4434 Garcia, Alma M. The development of Chicana feminist discourse, 1970-1980. IN: DuBois, Ellen Carol and Ruiz, Vicki L., eds. UNEQUAL SISTERS: A MULTICULTURAL READER IN U.S. WOMEN'S HISTORY. New York: Routledge, 1990, p. 418-431. English. **DESCR:** Anglo Americans; Chicana Studies; *Chicano Movement; *Feminism; Homosexuality; Machismo; National Association for Chicano Studies (NACS); *Sexism; Women.

4435 Garcia Castro, Mary. Migrant women: issues in organization and solidarity. MIGRATION WORLD MAGAZINE, Vol. 14, no. 1-2 (1986), p. 15-19. English. **DESCR:** Labor Supply and Market; *Migrant Labor; Political Economy; Undocumented Workers; Women.

4436 Gonzales, Sylvia Alicia. Hispanic American voluntary organizations. Westport, CT: Greenwood Press, 1985. xx, 267 p. English. **DESCR:** Art Organizations and Groups; *Community Organizations; Cultural Organizations; *Directories; Educational Organizations; Political Parties and Organizations; Professional Organizations.

4437 Iglesias, Maria and Hernandez, Maria Luz. Hermanas. IN: Stevens Arroyo, Antonio M., ed. PROPHETS DENIED HONOR: AN ANTHOLOGY ON THE HISPANO CHURCH OF THE UNITED STATES. Maryknoll, NY: Orbis Books, 1980, p. 141-142. English. **DESCR:** *Catholic Church; Clergy; Las Hermanas [organization].

4438 Introduction. ENCUENTRO FEMENIL, Vol. 1, no. 2 (1974), p. 3-7. English. **DESCR:** Books; ENCUENTRO FEMENIL; Hijas de Cuauhtemoc; *Periodicals.

4439 Marin, Christine. La Asociacion Hispano-Americana de Madres y Esposas: Tucson's Mexican American women in World War II. RENATO ROSALDO LECTURE SERIES MONOGRAPH, Vol. 1, (Summer 1985), p. [5]-18. English. **DESCR:** Cultural Organizations; History; *La Asociacion Hispano-Americana de Madres y Esposas, Tucson, AZ; *Tucson, AZ; World War II.

4440 Pardo, Mary. Mexican American women grassroots community activists: "Mothers of East Los Angeles". FRONTIERS: A JOURNAL OF WOMEN STUDIES, Vol. 11, no. 1 (1990), p. [1]-7. English. **DESCR:** Coalition Against the Prison, East Los Angeles, CA; *Community Organizations; East Los Angeles, CA; Family; *Feminism; *Mothers of East L.A. (MELA); Political Parties and Organizations; Politics; Sex Roles.

4441 Prida, Dolores. Looking for room of one's own. NUESTRO, Vol. 3, no. 5 (June, July, 1979), p. 24-29. English. **DESCR:** Comision Femenil Mexicana de California; *Feminism; Mexican American Women's National Association (MANA); National Association of Cuban American Women; National Conference of Puerto Rican Women, Inc. (NCOPRW).

4442 Rivera, Yvette. Hispanic women's organizations and periodicals needed to communicate new options: Yvette Rivera report. MEDIA REPORT TO WOMEN, Vol. 12, no. 5 (September, October, 1984), p. 15. English. **DESCR:** Periodicals.

4443 Staudt, Kathleen. Programming women's empowerment: a case from northern Mexico. IN: Ruiz, Vicki L. and Tiano, Susan, eds. WOMEN ON THE U.S.-MEXICO BORDER: RESPONSES TO CHANGE. Boston, MA: Allen & Unwin, 1987, p. 155-173. English. **DESCR:** Alternative Education; Border Region; Ciudad Juarez, Chihuahua, Mexico; Curriculum; Employment; *Feminism; Women.

4444 Varela, Vivian. Hispanic women's resource guide. COMMONGROUND MAGAZINE, Vol. 1, no. 3 (May 1983), p. 14-15. English. **DESCR:** *Directories.

Orozco, Cynthia

4445 Acuna, Rodolfo. Response to Cynthia Orozco. LA RED/THE NET, no. 79 (April 1984), p. 13-15. English. **DESCR:** Sexism.

Ortega y Gasset, Jose

4446 Oeste, Marcia. Mujeres arriba y adelante. LA LUZ, Vol. 1, no. 2 (May 1972), p. 39-40. English. **DESCR:** *Feminism; *Women Men Relations; Working Women.

Ortiz de Dominguez, Josefa

4447 De Ortego y Gasca, Felipe. The Hispanic woman: a humanistic perspective. LA LUZ, Vol. 6, no. 11 (November 1977), p. 7-10. English. **DESCR:** De la Cruz, Juana Ines; Dona Ximena; *Essays; History; Mistral, Gabriela; *Women Men Relations; *Women's Suffrage.

4448 De Ortego y Gasca, Felipe. The Hispanic woman: a humanistic perspective. LA LUZ, Vol. 8, no. 8 (October, November, 1980), p. 6-9. English. **DESCR:** De la Cruz, Juana Ines; Dona Ximena; *Essays; History; Mistral, Gabriela; *Women Men Relations; *Women's Suffrage.

Osteopathy
USE: Curanderismo

Osteoporosis

4449 Bauer, Richard L. Ethnic differences in hip fracture: a reduced incidence in Mexican-Americans. AMERICAN JOURNAL OF EPIDEMIOLOGY, Vol. 127, no. 1 (January 1988), p. 145-149. English. **DESCR:** Anglo Americans; Bexar County, TX; Blacks; Medical Care; *Public Health.

4450 Bauer, Richard L. and Deyo, Richard A. Low risk of vertebral fracture in Mexican American women. ARCHIVES OF INTERNAL MEDICINE, Vol. 147, no. 8 (August 1987), p. 1437-1439. English. **DESCR:** Anglo Americans; Preventative Medicine; Women.

Otero Warren, Nina

4451 Rebolledo, Tey Diana. Las escritoras: romances and realities. IN: Gonzales-Berry, Erlinda, ed. PASO POR AQUI: CRITICAL ESSAYS ON THE NEW MEXICAN LITERARY TRADITION. Albuquerque, NM: University of New Mexico Press, c1989, p. 199-214. English. **DESCR:** Authors; *Cabeza de Baca, Fabiola; *Jaramillo, Cleofas M.; Literary History; New Mexico; OLD SPAIN IN OUR SOUTHWEST; ROMANCE OF A LITTLE VILLAGE GIRL; WE FED THEM CACTUS; Women.

Otero Warren, Nina
(cont.)

4452 Rebolledo, Tey Diana. Hispanic women writers of the Southwest: tradition and innovation. IN: Lensink, Judy Nolte, ed. OLD SOUTHWEST/NEW SOUTHWEST: ESSAYS ON A REGION AND ITS LITERATURE. Tucson, AZ: The Tucson Public Library, 1987, p. 49-61. English. DESCR: *Authors; Cabeza de Baca, Fabiola; Jaramillo, Cleofas M.; Literature; Mora, Pat; OLD SPAIN IN OUR SOUTHWEST; Preciado Martin, Patricia; Sex Roles; Sex Stereotypes; Silva, Beverly; *Southwestern United States; Vigil-Pinon, Evangelina; WE FED THEM CACTUS; *Women.

4453 Rebolledo, Tey Diana. Narrative strategies of resistance in Hispana writing. THE JOURNAL OF NARRATIVE TECHNIQUE, Vol. 20, no. 2 (Spring 1990), p. 134-146. English. DESCR: *Authors; Cabeza de Baca, Fabiola; Fiction; Jaramillo, Cleofas M.; *Literary Criticism; Literature; New Mexico; OLD SPAIN IN OUR SOUTHWEST; *Oral Tradition; ROMANCE OF A LITTLE VILLAGE GIRL; WE FED THEM CACTUS.

4454 Rebolledo, Tey Diana. Tradition and mythology: signatures of landscape in Chicana literature. IN: Norwood, Vera and Monk, Janice, eds. THE DESERT IS NO LADY: SOUTHWESTERN LANDSCAPES IN WOMEN'S WRITING AND ART. New Haven, CT: Yale University Press, 1987, p. 96-124. English. DESCR: *Authors; Cabeza de Baca, Fabiola; Chavez, Denise; Jaramillo, Cleofas M.; Literary Criticism; *Literary History; Literature; Mora, Pat; Mythology; Portillo Trambley, Estela; Silva, Beverly; Southwestern United States; WE FED THEM CACTUS.

OTRO CANTO

4455 Alarcon, Norma. The sardonic powers of the erotic in the work of Ana Castillo. IN: Horno-Delgado, Asuncion, et al., eds. BREAKING BOUNDARIES: LATINA WRITING AND CRITICAL READINGS. Amherst, MA: University of Massachusetts Press, c1989, p. 94-107. English. DESCR: *Castillo, Ana; Literary Criticism; Poetry; Sex Roles; THE INVITATION; *THE MIXQUIAHUALA LETTERS; WOMEN ARE NOT ROSES.

Pabon, Maria

4456 Olivera, Mercedes. The new Hispanic women. VISTA, Vol. 2, no. 11 (July 5, 1987), p. 6-8. English. DESCR: Alvarez, Linda; Esquiroz, Margarita; Garcia, Juliet; *Hernandez, Antonia A.; Mohr, Nicolasa; Molina, Gloria; Working Women.

Pachucos

4457 Moore, Joan W. Mexican-American women addicts: the influence of family background. IN: Glick, Ronald and Moore, Joan, eds. DRUGS IN HISPANIC COMMUNITIES. New Brunswick, NJ: Rutgers University Press, c1990, p. 127-153. English. DESCR: Barrios; *Drug Addicts; Drug Use; East Los Angeles, CA; *Family; *Gangs; Heroin; Hoyo-Mara Gang, East Los Angeles, CA; Sex Roles; Socialization; White Fence Gang; Youth.

4458 Zamora, Bernice. Mythopoeia of Chicano poetry: an introduction to cultural archetypes. Thesis (Ph.D.)--Stanford University, 1986. 341 p. English. DESCR: Literary Characters; Literary Criticism; Literature; Malinche; *Poetry; *Symbolism.

Pachuquismos
USE: Chicano Dialects

Padilla, Amado M.

4459 Acuna, Rodolfo. The struggles of class and gender: current research in Chicano Studies [review essay]. JOURNAL OF AMERICAN ETHNIC HISTORY, Vol. 8, no. 2 (Spring 1989), p. 134-138. English. DESCR: *CANNERY WOMEN, CANNERY LIVES; *CHICANO ETHNICITY; Deutsch, Sarah; Keefe, Susan E.; Literature Reviews; *NO SEPARATE REFUGE; Ruiz, Vicki L.; *WOMEN'S WORK AND CHICANO FAMILIES; Zavella, Pat.

Padilla, Esther

4460 Rose, Margaret. From the fields to the picket line: Huelga women and the boycott, 1965-1975. LABOR HISTORY, Vol. 31, no. 3 (1990), p. 271-293. English. DESCR: *Boycotts; Family; Farm Workers; Padilla, Gilbert; Rodriguez, Conrado; Rodriguez, Herminia; *United Farmworkers of America (UFW); Washington, D.C.

Padilla, Gilbert

4461 Rose, Margaret. From the fields to the picket line: Huelga women and the boycott, 1965-1975. LABOR HISTORY, Vol. 31, no. 3 (1990), p. 271-293. English. DESCR: *Boycotts; Family; Farm Workers; Padilla, Esther; Rodriguez, Conrado; Rodriguez, Herminia; *United Farmworkers of America (UFW); Washington, D.C.

Painters
USE: Artists

Paintings

4462 Johnston Hernandez, Beatriz. Life as art. VISTA, Vol. 3, no. 12 (August 7, 1988), p. 18,34. English. DESCR: *Artists; *Lopez, Yolanda M.

"Para Mi Hijita" [poem]

4463 Zamora, Bernice. Archetypes in Chicana poetry. DE COLORES, Vol. 4, no. 3 (1978), p. 43-52. English. DESCR: Cervantes, Lorna Dee; Cunningham, Veronica; "Declaration on a Day of Little Inspiration" [poem]; Hernandez, Carlota; "I Speak in an Illusion" [poem]; *Literary Criticism; Lucero, Judy A.; Macias, Margarita; Mendoza, Rita; *Poetry; "Rape Report" [poem]; "The White Line" [poem]; "Working Mother's Song" [poem]; "You Can Only Blame the System for So Long" [poem]; Zamora, Katarina.

Parent and Child Relationships

4464 Arguelles, Lourdes and Rivero, Anne M. HIV infection/AIDS and Latinas in Los Angeles County: considerations for prevention, treatment, and research practice. CALIFORNIA SOCIOLOGIST, Vol. 11, no. 1-2 (1988), p. 69-89. English. DESCR: *AIDS (Disease); Cultural Characteristics; Health Education; Homosexuality; Human Immunodeficiency Virus (HIV); Los Angeles County, CA; Natural Support Systems; Sexual Behavior; *Women.

Parent and Child Relationships
(cont.)

4465 Buriel, Raymond, et al. Mexican-American disciplinary practices and attitudes toward child maltreatment:a comparison of foreign and native-born mothers. HISPANIC JOURNAL OF BEHAVIORAL SCIENCES, Vol. 13, no. 1 (February 1991), p. 78-94. English. DESCR: *Attitudes; *Child Abuse; Immigrants; *Parenting; Values; Violence.

4466 Carrasco, Frank F. Teaching strategies used by Chicano mothers with their Head Start children. Thesis (Ph.D.)--University of Colorado, Boulder, 1983. 177 p. English. DESCR: Bilingualism; Children; *Education; Low Income; *Parenting.

4467 de Leon Siantz, Mary Lou. Maternal acceptance/rejection of Mexican migrant mothers. PSYCHOLOGY OF WOMEN QUARTERLY, Vol. 14, no. 2 (June 1990), p. 245-254. English. DESCR: Child Study; Farm Workers; *Migrant Children; Migrant Labor; Natural Support Systems; Stress; Texas Migrant Council Headstart Program.

4468 Fox, Linda C. Obedience and rebellion: re-vision of Chicana myths of motherhood. WOMEN'S STUDIES QUARTERLY, Vol. 11, no. 4 (Winter 1983), p. 20-22. English. DESCR: Feminism; La Llorona; Malinche.

4469 Gunther Enriquez, Martha. Studying maternal-infant attachment: a Mexican-American example. IN: Kay, Margarita Artschwager, ed. ANTHROPOLOGY OF HUMAN BIRTH. Philadelphia, PA: F.A. Davis, 1982, p. 61-79. English. DESCR: Children; *Fertility; Immigrants; *Maternal and Child Welfare.

4470 Laosa, Luis M. Maternal teaching strategies and cognitive styles in Chicano families. IN: Duran, Richard P., ed. LATINO LANGUAGE AND COMMUNICATIVE BEHAVIOR. Norwood, NJ: ABLEX Publishing Corp., 1981, p. 295-310. English. DESCR: *Cognition; *Education; *Parenting.

4471 Laosa, Luis M. Maternal teaching strategies in Chicano and Anglo-American families: the influence of culture and education on maternal behavior. CHILD DEVELOPMENT, Vol. 51, no. 3 (September 1980), p. 759-765. English. DESCR: Anglo Americans; Comparative Psychology; *Cultural Characteristics; *Education; Family; Maternal Teaching Observation Technique (MTOT); Parenting; Women.

4472 Leon, Ana M., et al. Self-help support groups for Hispanic mothers. CHILD WELFARE, Vol. 63, no. 3 (May, June, 1984), p. 261-268. English. DESCR: Family; Mental Health Clinics; *Natural Support Systems; Sex Roles.

4473 LeVine, Sarah Ethel; Correa, Clara Sunderland; and Uribe, F. Medardo Tapia. The marital morality of Mexican women--an urban study. JOURNAL OF ANTHROPOLOGICAL RESEARCH, Vol. 42, no. 2 (Summer 1986), p. 183-202. English. DESCR: Family; Los Robles, Cuernavaca, Morelos, Mexico; *Machismo; Marriage; *Sex Roles; Women; *Women Men Relations.

4474 Martinez, Estella A. Child behavior in Mexican American/Chicano families: maternal teaching and child-rearing practices. FAMILY RELATIONS, Vol. 37, no. 3 (July 1988), p. 275-280. English. DESCR: *Acculturation; Family; Maternal Teaching Observation Technique (MTOT); *Parenting; *Psychological Testing; Socioeconomic Factors; Values.

4475 Martinez, Marco Antonio. Conversational asymmetry between Mexican mothers and children. HISPANIC JOURNAL OF BEHAVIORAL SCIENCES, Vol. 3, no. 4 (December 1981), p. 329-346. English. DESCR: Anglo Americans; Language Usage.

4476 Mary, Nancy L. Reactions of Black, Hispanic, and white mothers to having a child with handicaps. MENTAL RETARDATION, Vol. 28, no. 1 (February 1990), p. 1-5. English. DESCR: Anglo Americans; *Attitudes; Blacks; *Children; Comparative Psychology; *Mentally Handicapped; *Women.

4477 Mata, Alberto Guardiola and Castillo, Valerie. Rural female adolescent dissatisfaction, support and helpseeking. FREE INQUIRY IN CREATIVE SOCIOLOGY, Vol. 14, no. 2 (November 1986), p. 135-138. English. DESCR: Alcoholism; *Drug Use; Interpersonal Relations; *Natural Support Systems; Rural Population; *Youth.

4478 Olvera-Ezzell, Norma; Power, Thomas G.; and Cousins, Jennifer H. Maternal socialization of children's eating habits: strategies used by obese Mexican-American mothers. CHILD DEVELOPMENT, Vol. 61, no. 2 (April 1990), p. 395-400. English. DESCR: Children; Food Practices; *Nutrition; *Obesity; *Socialization.

4479 Powell, Douglas R.; Zambrana, Ruth E.; and Silva-Palacios, Victor. Designing culturally responsive parent programs: a comparison of low-income Mexican and Mexican-American mothers' preferences. FAMILY RELATIONS, Vol. 39, no. 3 (July 1990), p. 298-304. English. DESCR: Acculturation; Children; Education; Immigrants; Los Angeles, CA; Low Income; *Parenting; Women.

4480 Ramirez, Alex, et al. The relationship between sociocultural variables and Chicano and Anglo high school student responses on the Potency Dimension of the Semantic Differential. HISPANIC JOURNAL OF BEHAVIORAL SCIENCES, Vol. 3, no. 2 (June 1981), p. 177-190. English. DESCR: Anglo Americans; Martinez, Joe L., Jr.; Martinez, Sergio R.; MULTIVARIATE ANALYSIS OF VARIANCE (MANOVA); Olmedo, Esteban L.; Sex Roles; Sex Stereotypes; Students.

4481 Ramos, Maria. A micro-ethnographic study of Chicana mother and daughter socialization practices. Thesis (Ph.D.)--University of Colorado at Boulder, 1982. 292 p. English. DESCR: Ethnology; *Interpersonal Relations; Parenting; *Socialization.

4482 Rogers, Linda Perkowski and Markides, Kyriakos S. Well-being in the postparental stage in Mexican-American women. RESEARCH ON AGING, Vol. 11, no. 4 (December 1989), p. 508-516. English. DESCR: *Age Groups; Ancianos; Children; *"Empty Nest" Syndrome; San Antonio, TX.

4483 Shapiro, Johanna and Tittle, Ken. Maternal adaptation to child disability in a Hispanic population. FAMILY RELATIONS, Vol. 39, no. 2 (April 1990), p. 179-185. English. DESCR: Children; *Handicapped; Psychological Testing; *Stress.

Parent and Child Relationships
(cont.)

4484 Stroup-Benham, Christine A.; Trevino, Fernando M.; and Trevino, Dorothy B. Alcohol consumption patterns among Mexican American mothers and among children from single- and dual-headed households: findings from HHANES 1982-84. AMERICAN JOURNAL OF PUBLIC HEALTH, Vol. 80, (December 1990), p. 36-41. English. DESCR: *Alcoholism; *Children; Hispanic Health and Nutrition Examination Survey (HHANES); *Single Parents.

4485 Trevathan, Wenda R. First conversations: verbal content of mother-newborn interaction. JOURNAL OF CROSS-CULTURAL PSYCHOLOGY, Vol. 19, no. 1 (March 1988), p. 65-77. English. DESCR: Cultural Characteristics; El Paso, TX; Language Arts.

4486 Triandis, Harry C. Role perceptions of Hispanic young adults. JOURNAL OF CROSS-CULTURAL PSYCHOLOGY, Vol. 15, no. 3 (September 1984), p. 297-320. English. DESCR: *Cultural Characteristics; *Family; *Sex Roles; Social Psychology; Values; Youth.

4487 Zapata, Jesse T. and Jaramillo, Pat T. The Mexican American family: an Adlerian perspective. HISPANIC JOURNAL OF BEHAVIORAL SCIENCES, Vol. 3, no. 3 (September 1981), p. 275-290. English. DESCR: Adlerian "Life Style Inventory"; *Family; Sex Roles; Stereotypes.

4488 Zepeda, Marlene. Mother-infant behavior in Mexican and Mexican-American women: a study of the relationship of selected prenatal, perinatal and postnatal events. Thesis (Ph.D.)--University of California, Los Angeles, 1984, 429 p. English. DESCR: Children; *Fertility; *Maternal and Child Welfare; Prenatal Care.

Parenting

4489 Buriel, Raymond, et al. Mexican-American disciplinary practices and attitudes toward child maltreatment:a comparison of foreign and native-born mothers. HISPANIC JOURNAL OF BEHAVIORAL SCIENCES, Vol. 13, no. 1 (February 1991), p. 78-94. English. DESCR: *Attitudes; *Child Abuse; Immigrants; *Parent and Child Relationships; Values; Violence.

4490 Carrasco, Frank F. Teaching strategies used by Chicano mothers with their Head Start children. Thesis (Ph.D.)--University of Colorado, Boulder, 1983. 177 p. English. DESCR: Bilingualism; Children; *Education; Low Income; *Parent and Child Relationships.

4491 Chavez, John M. and Buriel, Raymond. Reinforcing children's effort: a comparison of immigrant, native-born Mexican American and Euro-American mothers. HISPANIC JOURNAL OF BEHAVIORAL SCIENCES, Vol. 8, no. 2 (June 1986), p. 127-142. English. DESCR: Acculturation; Immigrants.

4492 Cota-Robles de Suarez, Cecilia. Sexual stereotypes--psychological and cultural survival: a description of child-rearing practices attributed to the Chicana (the Mexican American woman) and its psychological and cultural implications. REGENERACION, Vol. 2, no. 3 (1973), p. 17, 20-21. English. DESCR: Cultural Characteristics; Family; Folklore; Language; Sex Stereotypes; *Sexism; *Stereotypes.

4493 Fennelly, Katherine, et al. The effect of maternal age on the well-being of children. JOURNAL OF MARRIAGE AND THE FAMILY, Vol. 46, no. 4 (November 1984), p. 933-934. English. DESCR: *Age Groups; *Maternal and Child Welfare; *Youth.

4494 Griswold del Castillo, Richard. La familia: Chicano families in the urban Southwest, 1848 to the present. Notre Dame, IN: University of Notre Dame Press, c1984. xv, 173 p. English. DESCR: *Family; History; Intermarriage; Machismo; *Sex Roles; Sexual Behavior; *Social History and Conditions.

4495 Gutierrez, Jeannie and Sameroff, Arnold. Determinants of complexity in Mexican-American and Anglo-American mothers' conceptions of child development. CHILD DEVELOPMENT, Vol. 61, no. 2 (April 1990), p. 384-394. English. DESCR: Acculturation; *Anglo Americans; Children; Cultural Characteristics; Values; *Women.

4496 Laosa, Luis M. Maternal teaching strategies and cognitive styles in Chicano families. IN: Duran, Richard P., ed. LATINO LANGUAGE AND COMMUNICATIVE BEHAVIOR. Norwood, NJ: ABLEX Publishing Corp., 1981, p. 295-310. English. DESCR: *Cognition; *Education; *Parent and Child Relationships.

4497 Laosa, Luis M. Maternal teaching strategies in Chicano and Anglo-American families: the influence of culture and education on maternal behavior. CHILD DEVELOPMENT, Vol. 51, no. 3 (September 1980), p. 759-765. English. DESCR: Anglo Americans; Comparative Psychology; *Cultural Characteristics; *Education; Family; Maternal Teaching Observation Technique (MTOT); *Parent and Child Relationships; Women.

4498 Maez, Angelita. The effects of two parent training programs on parental attitudes and self-concepts of Mexican American mothers. Thesis (Ph.D.)--UCLA, 1987. xiv, 184 leaves. English. DESCR: *Attitudes; Family.

4499 Martinez, Estella A. Child behavior in Mexican American/Chicano families: maternal teaching and child-rearing practices. FAMILY RELATIONS, Vol. 37, no. 3 (July 1988), p. 275-280. English. DESCR: *Acculturation; Family; Maternal Teaching Observation Technique (MTOT); Parent and Child Relationships; *Psychological Testing; Socioeconomic Factors; Values.

4500 Miranda, Gloria E. Hispano-Mexican childrearing practices in pre-American Santa Barbara. SOUTHERN CALIFORNIA QUARTERLY, Vol. 65, no. 4 (Winter 1983), p. 307-320. English. DESCR: *Children; Cultural Characteristics; *Family; History; Santa Barbara, CA; Socialization.

4501 Moore, Joan W. and Devitt, Mary. The paradox of deviance in addicted Mexican American mothers. GENDER & SOCIETY, Vol. 3, no. 1 (March 1989), p. 53-70. English. DESCR: Children; *Drug Addicts; *Drug Use; Family; *Fertility; Gangs; Sex Roles.

4502 Parra, Elena and Henderson, Ronald W. Mexican American perceptions of parent and teacher roles in child development. IN: Fishman, Joshua A. and Keller, Gary D., eds. BILINGUAL EDUCATION FOR HISPANIC STUDENTS IN THE UNITED STATES. New York: Teachers College Press, 1982, p. 289-299. English. DESCR: *Children; Family; Sex Roles; Teacher Attitudes.

Parenting (cont.)

4503 Powell, Douglas R.; Zambrana, Ruth E.; and
Silva-Palacios, Victor. Designing culturally
responsive parent programs: a comparison of
low-income Mexican and Mexican-American
mothers' preferences. FAMILY RELATIONS, Vol.
39, no. 3 (July 1990). p. 298-304. English.
DESCR: Acculturation; Children; Education;
Immigrants; Los Angeles, CA; Low Income;
*Parent and Child Relationships; Women.

4504 Ramos, Maria. A micro-ethnographic study of
Chicana mother and daughter socialization
practices. Thesis (Ph.D.)--University of
Colorado at Boulder, 1982. 292 p. English.
DESCR: Ethnology; *Interpersonal Relations;
*Parent and Child Relationships;
*Socialization.

4505 Walker, Todd. The relationship of nativity,
social support and depression to the home
environment among Mexican-American women.
Thesis (Ph.D.)--University of Houston, 1989.
123 p. English. DESCR: Acculturation; Avance
Parent-Child Education Program, San Antonio,
TX; Children; Depression (Psychological);
*Immigrants; Natural Support Systems; Women.

4506 Weller, Susan C. and Dungy, Claibourne I.
Personal preferences and ethnic variations
among Anglo and Hispanic breast and bottle
feeders. SOCIAL SCIENCE & MEDICINE, Vol. 23,
no. 6 (1986), p. 539-548. English. DESCR:
Attitudes; *Breastfeeding; *Maternal and
Child Welfare; Orange, CA; Socioeconomic
Factors.

4507 Zepeda, Marlene. Selected maternal-infant
care practices of Spanish-speaking women.
JOGN NURSING, Vol. 11, no. 6 (November,
December, 1982), p. 371-374. English.
DESCR: *Maternal and Child Welfare.

Parlier, CA

4508 Cantarow, Ellen and De la Cruz, Jessie
Lopez. Jessie Lopez De la Cruz: the battle
for farmworkers' rights. IN: Cantarow,
Ellen. MOVING THE MOUNTAIN: WOMEN WORKING
FOR SOCIAL CHANGE. Old Westbury, NY:
Feminist Press, 1980, p. 94-151. English.
DESCR: Agricultural Labor Unions; Chavez,
Cesar E.; *De la Cruz, Jessie Lopez; *Farm
Workers; Labor Disputes; Oral History; Sex
Roles; Strikes and Lockouts; *United
Farmworkers of America (UFW).

Parsons, Albert

4509 Mirande, Alfredo and Enriquez, Evangelina.
Chicanas in the struggle for unions. IN:
Duran, Livie Isauro and Bernard, H. Russell,
eds. INTRODUCTION TO CHICANO STUDIES. 2nd.
ed. New York: Macmillan, 1973, p. 325-337.
English. DESCR: Gonzalez Parsons, Lucia;
*Labor Unions; Moreno, Luisa [union
organizer]; Tenayuca, Emma; United Cannery
Agricultural Packing and Allied Workers of
America (UCAPAWA).

Parsons, Lucia Gonzalez
USE: Gonzalez Parsons, Lucia

Partido Liberal Mexicano (PLM)

4510 Perez, Emma. "A la mujer": a critique of the
Partido Liberal Mexicano's gender ideology
on women. IN: Del Castillo, Adelaida R., ed.
BETWEEN BORDERS: ESSAYS ON MEXICANA/CHICANA
HISTORY. Encino, CA: Floricanto Press, 1990,
p. 459-482. English. DESCR: *"A La Mujer"
[essay]; Essays; *Feminism; Flores Magon,
Ricardo; Guerrero, Praxedis G.; Journalism;

Mexican Revolution - 1910-1920; Mexico;
Newspapers; Political Ideology; Political
Parties and Organizations; *REGENERACION
[newspaper]; Sex Roles; Women.

"Un Paseo" [short story]

4511 Sanchez, Elba R. La realidad a traves de la
inocencia en el cuento: "Un Paseo". IN:
Cordova, Teresa, et al., eds. CHICANA
VOICES. Austin, TX: Center for Mexican
American Studies, 1986, p. 202-207. Spanish.
DESCR: *Garzon, Luz; Literary Criticism;
Short Story.

Patssi
USE: Valdez, Patssi

Paz, Octavio

4512 Alarcon, Norma. Traddutora, traditora: a
paradigmatic figure of Chicana feminism.
CULTURAL CRITIQUE, Vol. 13, (Fall 1989), p.
57-87. English. DESCR: *Feminism; *Malinche;
Sex Roles; Symbolism.

4513 Gonzales, Sylvia Alicia. La Chicana:
Malinche or virgin? NUESTRO, Vol. 3, no. 5
(June, July, 1979), p. 41-45. English.
DESCR: *La Virgen de Guadalupe; *Malinche.

4514 Perez, Emma. Sexuality and discourse: notes
from a Chicana survivor. IN: Trujillo,
Carla, ed. CHICANA LESBIANS: THE GIRLS OUR
MOTHERS WARNED US ABOUT. Berkeley, CA: Third
Woman Press, 1991, p. 159-184. English.
DESCR: *Feminism; Homosexuality; Intergroup
Relations; *Sex Roles; *Sexism; Skin Color.

Pecan Shelling Worker's Union, San Antonio, TX

4515 Gonzalez, Rosalinda M. Chicanas and Mexican
immigrant families 1920-1940: women's
subordination and family exploitation. IN:
Scharf, Lois and Jensen, Joan M., eds.
DECADES OF DISCONTENT: THE WOMEN'S MOVEMENT,
1920-1940. Westport, CT: Greenwood Press,
1983, p. 59-84. English. DESCR: *Family;
Farm Workers; History; Immigrants; Labor;
Labor Unions; Mexico; Sex Roles; Strikes and
Lockouts; United Cannery Agricultural
Packing and Allied Workers of America
(UCAPAWA); Working Women.

4516 Rips, Geoffrey and Tenayuca, Emma. Living
history: Emma Tenayuca tells her story.
TEXAS OBSERVER, (October 28, 1983), p.
7-15. English. DESCR: *Autobiography;
Communist Party; Food Industry; Labor
Unions; Leadership; Oral History; San
Antonio, TX; Strikes and Lockouts; Tenayuca,
Emma; United Cannery Agricultural Packing
and Allied Workers of America (UCAPAWA);
Worker's Alliance (WA), Los Angeles, CA;
Working Women.

Pecos County, TX

4517 Cazares, Ralph B.; Murguia, Edward; and
Frisbie, William Parker. Mexican American
intermarriage in a nonmetropolitan context.
SOCIAL SCIENCE QUARTERLY, Vol. 65, no. 2
(June 1984), p. 626-634. English. DESCR: Age
Groups; *Intermarriage; Social Classes;
Texas.

Pecos County, TX (cont.)

4518 Cazares, Ralph B.; Murguia, Edward; and Frisbie, William Parker. Mexican American intermarriage in a nonmetropolitan context. IN: O. de la Garza, Rodolfo, et al., eds. THE MEXICAN AMERICAN EXPERIENCE: AN INTERDISCIPLINARY ANTHOLOGY. Austin, TX: University of Texas Press, 1985, p. 393-401 English. DESCR: Age Groups; *Intermarriage; Social Classes; Texas.

"Penitents" [poem]

4519 Luna-Lawhn, Juanita. Victorian attitudes affecting the Mexican woman writing in LA PRENSA during the early 1900s and the Chicana of the 1980s. IN: Bardeleben, Renate von, et al., eds. MISSIONS IN CONFLICT: ESSAYS ON U.S.-MEXICAN RELATIONS AND CHICANO CULTURE. Tubingen, W. Germany: Gunter Narr Verlag, 1986, p. 65-71. English. DESCR: Feminism; LA PRENSA, San Antonio, TX; Literary Criticism; *Newspapers; Poetry; Zamora, Bernice.

PEREGRINOS DE AZTLAN

4520 Gutierrez Castillo, Dina. La imagen de la mujer en la novela fronteriza. IN: Lopez-Gonzalez, Aralia, et al., eds. MUJER Y LITERATURA MEXICANA Y CHICANA: CULTURAS EN CONTACTO. Mexico: Colegio de la Frontera Norte, 1988, p. [55]-63. Spanish. DESCR: *Border Region; Islas, Arturo; Literary Characters; *Literary Criticism; Mendez M. Miguel; *Novel; Sex Roles; Sex Stereotypes; THE RAIN GOD: A DESERT TALE; *Women.

Performing Arts

4521 Burnham, Linda. Patssi Valdez. HIGH PERFORMANCE, Vol. 9, no. 3 (1986), p. 54. English. DESCR: *Artists; ASCO [art group], Los Angeles, CA; Los Angeles, CA; Valdez, Patssi.

Periodical Indexes

4522 Castillo-Speed, Lillian, ed.; Chabran, Richard, ed.; and Garcia-Ayvers, Francisco, ed. The Chicano index: a comprehensive subject, author, and title index to Chicano materials. Berkeley, CA: Chicano Studies Library Publications Unit, 1989-. English. DESCR: *Indexes.

4523 Castillo-Speed, Lillian, ed.; Chabran, Richard, ed.; and Garcia-Ayvens, Francisco, ed. Chicano Periodical Index: a cumulative index to selected Chicano periodicals between 1967 and 1978. Berkeley, CA: Chicano Studies Library Publications Unit, 1985-1988. English.

4524 Committee for the Development of Subject Access to Chicano Literatures. Chicano Periodical Index: a cumulative index to selected Chicano periodicals between 1967 and 1978. Boston, MA: G.K. Hall, 1981-1983. English.

4525 D'Andrea, Vaneeta-Marie. Ethnic women: a critique of the literature, 1971-1981. ETHNIC AND RACIAL STUDIES, Vol. 9, (April 1986), p. 235-246. English. DESCR: Bibliography; Ethnic Groups; *Literature Reviews; *Women.

Periodicals

4526 Introduction. ENCUENTRO FEMENIL, Vol. 1, no. 2 (1974), p. 3-7. English. DESCR: Books; ENCUENTRO FEMENIL; Hijas de Cuauhtemoc;

Organizations.

4527 Rivera, Yvette. Hispanic women's organizations and periodicals needed to communicate new options: Yvette Rivera report. MEDIA REPORT TO WOMEN, Vol. 12, no. 5 (September, October, 1984), p. 15. English. DESCR: *Organizations.

Personal Narrative
USE: Oral History

Personality

4528 De Blassie, Richard R. and Franco, Juan N. The differences between personality inventory scores and self-rating in a sample of Hispanic subjects. JOURNAL OF NON-WHITE CONCERNS IN PERSONNEL AND GUIDANCE, Vol. 11, no. 2 (January 1983), p. 43-46. English. DESCR: Higher Education; Hispanic Education [program]; New Mexico State University; Sixteen Personality Factor Questionnaire; Students.

4529 Gibbs, Jewelle Taylor. Personality patterns of delinquent females: ethnic and sociocultural variations. JOURNAL OF CLINICAL PSYCHOLOGY, Vol. 38, no. 1 (January 1982), p. 198-206. English. DESCR: Ethnic Groups; Identity; *Juvenile Delinquency; Psychological Testing; Socioeconomic Factors.

4530 Lara-Cantu, M. Asuncion. A sex role inventory with scales for "machismo" and "self-sacrificing woman". JOURNAL OF CROSS-CULTURAL PSYCHOLOGY, Vol. 20, no. 4 (December 1989), p. 396-398. English. DESCR: Machismo; *Masculine-Feminine Personality Traits Scale; *Psychological Testing; *Sex Roles.

4531 McClelland, Judith Raymond. The relationship of independence to achievement: a comparative study of Hispanic women. Thesis (Ph.D.)--Fielding Institute, 1988. 164 p. English. DESCR: *Assertiveness; Attitudes; California Personality Inventory (CPI); Careers; Leadership; *Management; New Mexico; *Working Women.

4532 Mirande, Alfredo. Que gacho es ser macho: it's a drag to be a macho man. AZTLAN, Vol. 17, no. 2 (Fall 1986), p. 63-89. English. DESCR: *Cultural Characteristics; Identity; *Machismo; Sex Roles; *Sex Stereotypes; Values.

4533 Smith, Bradford M. The measurement of narcissism in Asian, Caucasian, and Hispanic American women. PSYCHOLOGICAL REPORTS, Vol. 67, no. 3 (December 1990), p. 779-785. English. DESCR: Anglo Americans; Asian Americans; Comparative Psychology; Cultural Characteristics; *Narcissistic Personality Inventory; *Psychological Testing; *Women.

4534 Velasquez, Roberto J.; Callahan, Wendell J.; and Carrillo, Ricardo. MMPI differences among Mexican-American male and female psychiatric inpatients. PSYCHOLOGICAL REPORTS, Vol. 68, no. 1 (February 1991), p. 123-127. English. DESCR: Comparative Psychology; Males; Minnesota Multiphasic Personality Inventory (MMPI); Psychiatry; *Psychological Testing; Sex Roles.

Personnel Management

4535 Ayers-Nackamkin, Beverly, et al. Sex and
ethnic differences in the use of power.
JOURNAL OF APPLIED PSYCHOLOGY, Vol. 67, no.
4 (August 1982), p. 464-471. English.
DESCR: Anglo Americans; Ethnic Groups;
Management; Sex Roles; Social Psychology.

4536 Pena, Devon Gerardo. Tortuosidad: shop floor
struggles of female maquiladora workers. IN:
Ruiz, Vicki L. and Tiano, Susan, eds. WOMEN
ON THE U.S.-MEXICO BORDER: RESPONSES TO
CHANGE. Boston, MA: Allen & Unwin, 1987, p.
129-154. English. **DESCR:** Border Industries;
Ciudad Juarez, Chihuahua, Mexico;
Employment; Population; Surveys; *Women;
Working Women.

4537 Williams, Edward J. and Passe-Smith, John T.
Turnover and recruitment in the maquila
industry: causes and solutions. Las Cruces,
NM: Joint Border Research Institute, New
Mexico State University, 1989. ii, 59 p.
English. **DESCR:** *Border Industries;
*Employment; Income; *Labor Supply and
Market; Surveys; Women; *Working Women.

Phelps Dodge Corporation, Morenci, AZ

4538 Aulette, Judy and Mills, Trudy. Something
old, something new: auxiliary work in the
1983-1986 copper strike. FEMINIST STUDIES,
Vol. 14, no. 2 (Summer 1988), p. 251-268.
English. **DESCR:** Arizona; Clifton-Morenci
Copper Strike, 1983-1986; Clifton-Morenci
District, Arizona; Feminism; Labor Unions;
Morenci Miners Women's Auxiliary (MMWA);
Mutualistas; SALT OF THE EARTH [film]; Sex
Roles; *Strikes and Lockouts.

Photography

4539 Benardo, Margot L. and Anthony, Darius.
Hispanic women and their men. LATINA, Vol.
1, no. 3 (1983), p. 24-29. English. **DESCR:**
*Women Men Relations.

4540 Goldman, Shifra M. Women artists of Texas:
MAS = More + Artists + Women = MAS.
CHISMEARTE, no. 7 (January 1981), p. 21-22.
English. **DESCR:** Arredondo, Alicia; Art
Organizations and Groups; Barraza, Santa;
Exhibits; Feminism; Flores, Maria; Folk Art;
Gonzalez Dodson, Nora; *Mujeres Artistas del
Suroeste (MAS), Austin, TX; Texas; Trevino,
Modesta Barbina; WOMEN & THEIR WORK
[festival] (Austin, TX: 1977).

4541 Ordonez, Elizabeth J. La imagen de la mujer
en el nuevo cine chicano. CARACOL, Vol. 5,
no. 2 (October 1978), p. 12-13. Spanish.
DESCR: Bonilla-Giannini, Roxanna; *Films;
Lopez, Lexore; ONLY ONCE IN A LIFETIME
[film]; RAICES DE SANGRE [film]; Robelo,
Miguel; Sex Stereotypes.

4542 Preciado Martin, Patricia. Images and
conversations: Mexican Americans recall a
Southwestern past. Tucson, AZ: University of
Arizona Press, 1983. 110 p.: ill. English.
DESCR: *Oral History; Social History and
Conditions; Tucson, AZ.

Picardias
USE: Chistes

Pineda, Cecile

4543 Bruce-Novoa, Juan. Deconstructing the
dominant patriarchal text: Cecile Pineda's
narratives. IN: Horno-Delgado, Asuncion, et
al., eds. BREAKING BOUNDARIES: LATINA
WRITING AND CRITICAL READINGS. Amherst, MA:

University of Massachusetts Press, c1989, p.
72-81. English. **DESCR:** *FACE; *FRIEZE;
Identity; Literary Criticism; Novel.

Pinto Conference (1973: UCLA)

4544 Santillanes, Maria. Women in prison--C.I.W.:
an editorial. REGENERACION, Vol. 2, no. 4
(1975), p. 53. English. **DESCR:** Conferences
and Meetings; Garcia, Dolly; La Mesa College
Pinto and Pinta Program; Lopez, Tony; Mares,
Rene; Martinez, Miguel; Player; *Prisons;
Salazar, Peggy.

Player

4545 Santillanes, Maria. Women in prison--C.I.W.:
an editorial. REGENERACION, Vol. 2, no. 4
(1975), p. 53. English. **DESCR:** Conferences
and Meetings; Garcia, Dolly; La Mesa College
Pinto and Pinta Program; Lopez, Tony; Mares,
Rene; Martinez, Miguel; Pinto Conference
(1973: UCLA); *Prisons; Salazar, Peggy.

Plays
USE: Teatro

PLAZA [play]

4546 Heard, Martha E. The theatre of Denise
Chavez: interior landscapes with SABOR
NUEVOMEXICANO. THE AMERICAS REVIEW, Vol. 16,
no. 2 (Summer 1988), p. 83-91. English.
DESCR: *Chavez, Denise; EL CAMINO [play];
Literary Criticism; New Mexico; *Teatro.

Pluralism
USE: Cultural Pluralism

Pocho
USE: Chicano Dialects

Poems

4547 Anzaldua, Gloria. Borderlands/La frontera:
the new mestiza. San Francisco, CA:
Spinsters/Aunt Lute, 1987. 203 p. Bilingual.
DESCR: Aztecs; Border Region; *Identity;
Mythology; Prose; Sex Roles.

4548 Boza, Maria del Carmen, ed.; Silva, Beverly,
ed.; and Valle, Carmen, ed. Nosotras: Latina
literature today. Binghamton, NY: Bilingual
Review Press, 1986. 93 p. Bilingual. **DESCR:**
*Short Story; Women.

4549 Cochran, Jo, et al., eds. Bearing
witness/Sobreviviendo: an anthology of
Native American/Latina art and literature.
CALYX: A JOURNAL OF ART AND LITERATURE BY
WOMEN, Vol. 8, no. 2 (Spring 1984), p.
[1]-128. English. **DESCR:** *Art; Drawings;
*Fiction; Native Americans; Women.

4550 [Edicion feminista (Special Issue)].
IMAGINE, Vol. 2, no. 1 (Summer 1985), p.
ii-159. Bilingual. **DESCR:** Literature; Women.

4551 Gaspar de Alba, Alice; Herrera-Sobek, Maria;
and Martinez, Demetria. Three times a woman:
Chicana poetry. Tempe, AZ: Bilingual
Press/Editorial Bilingue, c1989. 156 p.
English.

4552 Hernandez, Lisa, ed. and Benitez, Tina, ed.
Palabras chicanas: an undergraduate
anthology. Berkeley, CA: Mujeres en Marcha,
University of California, Berkeley, 1988. 97
p. Bilingual. **DESCR:** Literary Criticism;
*Literature; Prose; *Students.

Poems (cont.)

4553 Herrera-Sobek, Maria, ed. and Viramontes, Helena Maria, ed. Chicana creativity and criticism: charting new frontiers in American literature. Houston, TX: Arte Publico Press, 1988. 190 p. Bilingual. **DESCR:** Art; Literary Criticism; *Literature Prose.

4554 Moraga, Cherrie. Loving in the war years: lo que nunca paso por sus labios. Boston, MA: South End Press, c1983. viii, 152 p. English. **DESCR:** *Autobiography; Homosexuality; Moraga, Cherrie.

4555 Moraga, Cherrie, ed. and Castillo, Ana, ed. Esta [sic] puente, mi espalda: voces de mujeres tercermundistas en los Estados Unidos. San Francisco, CA: Ism Press, c1988. [19], 281 p.: ill. Spanish. **DESCR:** Ethnic Groups; *Feminism; Literary Criticism; *Prose; *Women.

4556 Moraga, Cherrie, ed. and Anzaldua, Gloria, ed. This bridge called my back: writings by radical women of color. Watertown, MA: Persephone Press, c1981. xxvi, 261 p. English. **DESCR:** Ethnic Groups; *Feminism; Literary Criticism; *Prose; *Women.

4557 Rebolledo, Tey Diana, ed.; Gonzales-Berry, Erlinda, ed.; and Marquez, Maria Teresa, ed. Las mujeres hablan: an anthology of Nuevo Mexicana writers. Albuquerque, NM: El Norte Publications, c1988. xiv, 210 p.: ill. English. **DESCR:** *New Mexico; *Prose; *Short Story.

4558 Rios-C., Herminio; Romano-V., Octavio Ignacio; and Portillo Trambley, Estela. Chicanas en la literatura y el arte (El Grito Book Series: Book 1, September 1973). EL GRITO, Vol. 7, no. 1 (Fall 1973), p. 1-84. Bilingual. **DESCR:** *Art; Authors; Teatro.

4559 Trujillo, Carla, ed. Chicana lesbians: the girls our mothers warned us about. Berkeley, CA: Third Woman Press, 1991. xii, 202 p.: ill. English. **DESCR:** *Homosexuality; Literary Criticism; Prose.

4560 Yarbro-Bejarano, Yvonne. Teatropoesia by Chicanas in the Bay Area: TONGUES OF FIRE. REVISTA CHICANO-RIQUENA, Vol. 11, no. 1 (Spring 1983), p. 78-94. English. **DESCR:** El Teatro Nacional de Aztlan (TENAZ); San Francisco Bay Area; *Teatro; TONGUES OF FIRE.

Poetry

4561 Aguilar-Henson, Marcella. The multi-faceted poetic world of Angela de Hoyos. Austin, TX: Relampago Books Press, 1985, c1982. 81 p. English. **DESCR:** ARISE CHICANO; *Authors; CHICANO POEMS FOR THE BARRIO; de Hoyos, Angela; GATA POEMS; GOODBYE TO SILENCE; Language Usage; *Literary Criticism; SELECTED POEMS/SELECCIONES; YO, MUJER.

4562 Alarcon, Norma. The sardonic powers of the erotic in the work of Ana Castillo. IN: Horno-Delgado, Asuncion, et al., eds. BREAKING BOUNDARIES: LATINA WRITING AND CRITICAL READINGS. Amherst, MA: University of Massachusetts Press, c1989, p. 94-107. English. **DESCR:** *Castillo, Ana; Literary Criticism; OTRO CANTO; Sex Roles; THE INVITATION; *THE MIXQUIAHUALA LETTERS; WOMEN ARE NOT ROSES.

4563 Alarcon, Norma. What kind of lover have you

made me, Mother?: towards a theory of Chicanas' feminism and cultural identity through poetry. IN: McCluskey, Audrey T., ed. WOMEN OF COLOR: PERSPECTIVES ON FEMINISM AND IDENTITY. Bloomington, IN: Women's Studies Program, Indiana University, 1985, p. 85-110. English. **DESCR:** Brinson-Pineda, Barbara; Cervantes, Lorna Dee; Cisneros, Sandra; Culture; *Feminism; Identity; *Literary Criticism; Mora, Pat; Moraga, Cherrie; Tafolla, Carmen; Vigil-Pinon, Evangelina; Villanueva, Alma.

4564 Billings, Linda M. and Alurista. In verbal murals: a study of Chicana herstory and poetry. CONFLUENCIA, Vol. 2, no. 1 (Fall 1986), p. 60-68. English. **DESCR:** Candelaria, Cordelia; Cervantes, Lorna Dee; Cisneros, Sandra; EMPLUMADA; *Feminism; History; Literary Criticism; Xelina.

4565 Binder, Wolfgang. Mothers and grandmothers: acts of mythification and remembrance in Chicano poetry. IN: Bardeleben, Renate von, et al., eds. MISSIONS IN CONFLICT: ESSAYS ON U.S.-MEXICAN RELATIONS AND CHICANO CULTURE. Tubingen, W. Germany: Gunter Narr Verlag, 1986, p. 133-143. English. **DESCR:** Grandmothers; *Literary Criticism.

4566 Binder, Wolfgang, ed. Partial autobiographies: interviews with twenty Chicano poets. Erlangen: Verlag Palm & Enke, 1985. xviii, 263 p. English. **DESCR:** *Authors; *Autobiography.

4567 Bornstein de Somoza, Miriam. La poetica chicana: vision panoramica. LA PALABRA, Vol. 2, no. 2 (Fall 1980), p. 43-66. Spanish. **DESCR:** Authors; *Literary Criticism; Literary Influence.

4568 Brinson-Pineda, Barbara and Binder, Wolfgang. [Interview with] Barbara Brinson-Pineda. IN: Binder, Wolfgang, ed. PARTIAL AUTOBIOGRAPHIES: INTERVIEWS WITH TWENTY CHICANO POETS. Erlangen, W. Germany: Verlag Palm & Enke, 1985, p. 16-27. English. **DESCR:** Authors; Autobiography; *Brinson-Pineda, Barbara.

4569 Bruce-Novoa, Juan. Bernice Zamora y Lorna Dee Cervantes: una estetica feminista. REVISTA IBEROAMERICANA, Vol. 51, (July, December, 1985), p. 565-573. English. **DESCR:** *Authors; *Cervantes, Lorna Dee; EMPLUMADA; Literary Criticism; RESTLESS SERPENTS; *Zamora, Bernice.

4570 Campos Carr, Irene. Proyecto La Mujer: Latina women shaping consciousness. WOMEN'S STUDIES INTERNATIONAL FORUM, Vol. 12, no. 1 (1989), p. 45-49. English. **DESCR:** Artists; Aurora, IL; Authors; Barrios; Conferences and Meetings; Elgin, IL; *Feminism; Joliet, IL; Proyecto La Mujer Conference (Spring, 1982: Northern Illinois); Women.

4571 Castillo, Ana and Binder, Wolfgang. [Interview with] Ana Castillo. IN: Binder, Wolfgang, ed. PARTIAL AUTOBIOGRAPHIES: INTERVIEWS WITH TWENTY CHICANO POETS. Erlangen, W. Germany: Verlag Palm & Enke, 1985, p. 28-38. English. **DESCR:** Authors; Autobiography; *Castillo, Ana.

Poetry (cont.)

4572 Cervantes, Lorna Dee and Binder, Wolfgang. [Interview with] Lorna Dee Cervantes. IN: Binder, Wolfgang, ed. PARTIAL AUTOBIOGRAPHIES: INTERVIEWS WITH TWENTY CHICANO POETS. Erlangen, W. Germany: Verlag Palm & Enke, 1985, p. 39-53. English. **DESCR:** Authors; Autobiography; *Cervantes, Lorna Dee.

4573 Cisneros, Sandra. Cactus flowers: in search of Tejana feminist poetry. THIRD WOMAN, Vol. 3, no. 1-2 (1986), p. 73-80. English. **DESCR:** Authors; *Feminism; Literary Criticism; Texas.

4574 Cisneros, Sandra and Binder, Wolfgang. [Interview with] Sandra Cisneros. IN: Binder, Wolfgang, ed. PARTIAL AUTOBIOGRAPHIES: INTERVIEWS WITH TWENTY CHICANO POETS. Erlangen, W. Germany: Verlag Palm & Enke, 1985, p. 54-74. English. **DESCR:** Authors; Autobiography; *Cisneros, Sandra.

4575 Corpi, Lucha and Binder, Wolfgang. [Interview with] Lucha Corpi. IN: Binder, Wolfgang, ed. PARTIAL AUTOBIOGRAPHIES: INTERVIEWS WITH TWENTY CHICANO POETS. Erlangen, W. Germany: Verlag Palm & Enke, 1985, p. 75-85. English. **DESCR:** Authors; Autobiography; *Corpi, Lucha.

4576 Cunningham, Veronica and Binder, Wolfgang. [Interview with] Veronica Cunningham. IN: Binder, Wolfgang, ed. PARTIAL AUTOBIOGRAPHIES: INTERVIEWS WITH TWENTY CHICANO POETS. Erlangen, W. Germany: Verlag Palm & Enke, 1985, p. 86-92. English. **DESCR:** Authors; Autobiography; *Cunningham, Veronica.

4577 de Hoyos, Angela and Binder, Wolfgang. [Interview with] Angela de Hoyos. IN: Binder, Wolfgang, ed. PARTIAL AUTOBIOGRAPHIES: INTERVIEWS WITH TWENTY CHICANO POETS. Erlangen, W. Germany: Verlag Palm & Enke, 1985, p. 109-116. English. **DESCR:** Authors; Autobiography; *de Hoyos, Angela.

4578 Del Rio, Carmen M. Chicana poets: re-visions from the margin. REVISTA CANADIENSE DE ESTUDIOS HISPANICOS, Vol. 14, no. 3 (Spring 1990), p. 431-445. English. **DESCR:** Authors; *Feminism; *Literary Criticism; Tafolla, Carmen; Villanueva, Alma.

4579 Desai, Parul and Zamora, Bernice. Interview with Bernice Zamora, a Chicana poet. IMAGINE, Vol. 2, no. 1 (Summer 1985), p. 26-39. English. **DESCR:** Literary Criticism; Literature; Zamora, Bernice.

4580 Gonzales, Rebecca and Binder, Wolfgang. [Interview with] Rebecca Gonzales. IN: Binder, Wolfgang, ed. PARTIAL AUTOBIOGRAPHIES: INTERVIEWS WITH TWENTY CHICANO POETS. Erlangen, W. Germany: Verlag Palm & Enke, 1985, p. 93-94. English. **DESCR:** Authors; Autobiography; *Gonzales, Rebecca.

4581 Hernandez, Ines. Sara Estela Ramirez: the early twentieth century Texas-Mexican poet. Thesis (Ph.D.)--University of Houston, 1984. 94 p. English. **DESCR:** *Authors; *Biography; Feminism; Flores Magon, Ricardo; Journalism; Literary Criticism; Mexican Revolution - 1910-1920; Mexico; Ramirez, Sara Estela; Texas; Women.

4582 Hernandez, Ines. Sara Estela Ramirez:

sembradora. LEGACY: A JOURNAL OF NINETEENTH-CENTURY AMERICAN WOMEN WRITERS, Vol. 6, no. 1 (Spring 1989), p. 13-26. English. **DESCR:** Authors; *Biography; *Feminism; Flores Magon, Ricardo; *Journalism; LA CORREGIDORA [newspaper]; Mexican Revolution - 1910-1920; Mexico; Newspapers; *Ramirez, Sara Estela; REGENERACIÓN [newspaper].

4583 Lindstrom, Naomi. Four representative Hispanic women poets of Central Texas: a portrait of plurality. THIRD WOMAN, Vol. 2, no. 1 (1984), p. 64-70. English. **DESCR:** Beltran, Beatriz; de Hoyos, Angela; Jimenez, Magali; *Literary Criticism; Tafolla, Carmen; Texas.

4584 Lomas, Clara. Libertad de no procrear: la voz de la mujer en "A una madre de nuestro tiempo" de Margarita Cota-Cardenas. IN: Cordova, Teresa, et al., eds. CHICANA VOICES. Austin, TX: Center for Mexican American Studies, 1986, p. 188-201. Bilingual. **DESCR:** "A una madre de nuestros tiempos" [poem]; *Cota-Cardenas, Margarita; Feminism; Literary Criticism; Sex Stereotypes.

4585 Lomas, Clara. Libertad de no procrear: la voz de la mujer en "A una madre de nuestro tiempo" de Margarita Cota-Cardenas. REVISTA MUJERES, Vol. 2, no. 1 (January 1985), p. 30-35. Spanish. **DESCR:** *"A una madre de nuestros tiempos" [poem]; *Cota-Cardenas, Margarita; Feminism; Literary Criticism; Sex Stereotypes.

4586 Lucero, Marcela Christine. The socio-historical implication of the valley as a metaphor in three Colorado Chicana poets. Thesis (Ph.D.)--University of Minnesota, 1981. 176 p. English. **DESCR:** *Authors; Blea, Irene I.; Chicano Movement; Colorado; Feminism; Literary Criticism; Mondragon Valdez, Maria; Zamora, Bernice.

4587 Luna-Lawhn, Juanita. Victorian attitudes affecting the Mexican woman writing in LA PRENSA during the early 1900s and the Chicana of the 1980s. IN: Bardeleben, Renate von, et al., eds. MISSIONS IN CONFLICT: ESSAYS ON U.S.-MEXICAN RELATIONS AND CHICANO CULTURE. Tubingen, W. Germany: Gunter Narr Verlag, 1986, p. 65-71. English. **DESCR:** Feminism; LA PRENSA, San Antonio, TX; Literary Criticism; *Newspapers; "Penitents" [poem]; Zamora, Bernice.

4588 Mora, Pat and Alarcon, Norma. A poet analyzes her craft. NUESTRO, Vol. 11, no. 2 (March 1987), p. 25-27. English. **DESCR:** *Authors; BORDERS; CHANTS; *Mora, Pat.

4589 Ordonez, Elizabeth J. Body, spirit, and the text: Alma Villanueva's LIFE SPAN. IN: Calderon, Hector and Saldivar, Jose David, eds. CRITICISM IN THE BORDERLANDS: STUDIES IN CHICANO LITERATURE, CULTURE, AND IDEOLOGY. Durham, NC: Duke University Press, 1991, p. [61]-71. English. **DESCR:** Cixous, Helene; *Feminism; *LIFE SPAN; *Literary Criticism; *Villanueva, Alma.

4590 Ordonez, Elizabeth J. The concept of cultural identity in Chicana poetry. THIRD WOMAN, Vol. 2, no. 1 (1984), p. 75-82. English. **DESCR:** Cervantes, Lorna Dee; Corpi, Lucha; *Literary Criticism; Tafolla, Carmen; Villanueva, Alma.

Poetry (cont.)

4591 Ordonez, Elizabeth J. Sexual politics and the theme of sexuality in Chicana poetry. IN: Miller, Beth, ed. WOMEN IN HISPANIC LITERATURE: ICONS AND FALLEN IDOLS. Berkeley, CA: University of California Press, 1983, p. 316-339. English. DESCR: Chicano Movement; Feminism; *Literary Criticism; Sexual Behavior.

4592 Passman, Kristina. Demeter, Kore and the birth of the self: the quest for identity in the poetry of Alma Villanueva, Pat Mora y Cherrie Moraga. MONOGRAPHIC REVIEW, Vol. 6, (1990), p. 323-342. English. DESCR: *Literary Criticism; Mora, Pat; Moraga, Cherrie; Mythology; Villanueva, Alma.

4593 Quintana, Alvina E. O mama, with what's inside of me. REVISTA MUJERES, Vol. 3, no. 1 (January 1986), p. 38-40. English. DESCR: Alarcon, Norma; Feminism; *Literary Criticism; "What Kind of Lover Have You Made Me, Mother?: Towards a Theory of Chicanas' Feminism and Cultural Identity Through Poetry" [article].

4594 Ramos, Juanita, ed. Companeras: Latina lesbians (an anthology). New York: Latina Lesbian History Project, 1987. xxix, 265 p. Bilingual. DESCR: *Homosexuality; *Literature; Prose; *Women.

4595 Rebolledo, Tey Diana. Abuelitas: mythology and integration in Chicana literature. REVISTA CHICANO-RIQUENA, Vol. 11, no. 3-4 (Fall 1983), p. 148-158. English. DESCR: Grandmothers; *Literary Criticism.

4596 Rebolledo, Tey Diana. The bittersweet nostalgia of childhood in the poetry of Margarita Cota-Cardenas. FRONTIERS: A JOURNAL OF WOMEN STUDIES, Vol. 5, no. 2 (Summer 1980), p. 31-35. English. DESCR: *Cota-Cardenas, Margarita; *Literary Criticism.

4597 Rebolledo, Tey Diana. Game theory in Chicana poetry. REVISTA CHICANO-RIQUENA, Vol. 11, no. 3-4 (Fall 1983), p. 159-168. English. DESCR: *Literary Criticism.

4598 Rebolledo, Tey Diana. The maturing of Chicana poetry: the quiet revolution of the 1980s. IN: Treichler, Paula A., et al., eds. FOR ALMA MATER: THEORY AND PRACTICE IN FEMINIST SCHOLARSHIP. Urbana: University of Illinois Press, 1985, p. 143-158. English. DESCR: Identity; *Literary Criticism; Sexual Behavior.

4599 Rebolledo, Tey Diana. Soothing restless serpents: the dreaded creation and other inspirations in Chicana poetry. THIRD WOMAN, Vol. 2, no. 1 (1984), p. 83-102. English. DESCR: *Literary Criticism.

4600 Rebolledo, Tey Diana. Walking the thin line: humor in Chicana literature. IN: Herrera-Sobek, Maria, ed. BEYOND STEREOTYPES: THE CRITICAL ANALYSIS OF CHICANA LITERATURE. Binghamton, NY: Bilingual Press/Editorial Bilingue, 1985, p. 91-107. English. DESCR: Chistes; *Humor; Literary Criticism.

4601 Saldivar, Jose David. Towards a Chicano poetics: the making of the Chicano subject. CONFLUENCIA, Vol. 1, no. 2 (Spring 1986), p. 10-17. English. DESCR: Corridos; Feminism; *Literary Criticism; "Los Vatos" [poem]; Montoya, Jose E.; RESTLESS SERPENTS; Rios, Alberto; WHISPERING TO FOOL THE WIND; Zamora, Bernice.

4602 Sanchez, Marta E. The birthing of the poetic "I" in Alma Villanueva's MOTHER MAY I?: the search for a feminine identity. IN: Herrera-Sobek, Maria, ed. BEYOND STEREOTYPES: THE CRITICAL ANALYSIS OF CHICANA LITERATURE. Binghamton, NY: Bilingual Press/Editorial Bilingue, 1985, p. 108-152. Also IN: Sanchez, Marta. CONTEMPORARY CHICANA POETRY. Berkeley, CA: University of California Press, 1985, p. 24-84. English. DESCR: *Identity; Literary Criticism; MOTHER MAY I?; Villanueva, Alma.

4603 Sanchez, Marta E. Contemporary Chicana poetry. Berkeley, CA: University of California Press, c1985. xi, 377 p. English. DESCR: *Literary Criticism.

4604 Sanchez, Marta E. Gender and ethnicity in contemporary Chicana poetry. CRITICAL PERSPECTIVES, Vol. 2, no. 1 (Fall 1984), p. 147-166. English. DESCR: *Literary Criticism; MOTHER MAY I?; Villanueva, Alma.

4605 Sanchez, Marta E. Judy Lucero and Bernice Zamora: two dialectical statements in Chicana poetry. DE COLORES, Vol. 4, no. 3 (1978), p. 22-33. Bilingual. DESCR: Gomez-Quinones, Juan; *Literary Criticism; Lucero, Judy A.; Zamora, Bernice.

4606 Sanchez, Marta E. Judy Lucero and Bernice Zamora: two dialectical statements in Chicana poetry. IN: Sommers, Joseph and Ybarra-Frausto, Tomas, eds. MODERN CHICANO WRITERS: A COLLECTION OF CRITICAL ESSAYS. Englewood Cliffs, NJ: Prentice-Hall, 1979, p. 141-149. English. DESCR: Gomez-Quinones, Juan; *Literary Criticism; Lucero, Judy A.; Zamora, Bernice.

4607 Sanchez, Rita. Chicana writer breaking out of the silence. DE COLORES, Vol. 3, no. 3 (1977), p. 31-37. English. DESCR: Authors; Castaneda Shular, Antonia; Correa, Viola; Cunningham, Veronica; Hernandez, Barbara; *Literary Criticism; Mendoza, Rita.

4608 Sonntag, Iliana. Hacia una bibliografia de poesia femenina chicana. LA PALABRA, Vol. 2, no. 2 (Fall 1980), p. 91-109. Spanish. DESCR: *Bibliography.

4609 Treacy, Mary Jane. The ties that bind: women and community in Evangelina Vigil's THIRTY AN' SEEN A LOT. IN: Horno-Delgado, Asuncion, et al., eds. BREAKING BOUNDARIES: LATINA WRITING AND CRITICAL READINGS. Amherst, MA: University of Massachusetts Press, c1989, p. 82-93. English. DESCR: Identity; Literary Criticism; Sexism; *THIRTY AN' SEEN A LOT; *Vigil-Pinon, Evangelina.

4610 Trujillo Gaitan, Marcella. The dilemma of the modern Chicana artist and critic. DE COLORES, Vol. 3, no. 3 (1977), p. 38-48. Bilingual. DESCR: Art Criticism; Artists; *Chicano Movement; Gonzales, Sylvia Alicia; *Literary Criticism; Machismo; Malinche; Symbolism.

4611 Trujillo Gaitan, Marcella. The dilemma of the modern Chicana artist and critic. HERESIES, Vol. 2, no. 4 (1979), p. 5-10. English. DESCR: Art Criticism; Artists; Authors; *Chicano Movement; Gonzales, Sylvia Alicia; *Literary Criticism; Machismo; Malinche; Symbolism.

Poetry (cont.)

4612 Vigil, Evangelina, ed. Woman of her word: Hispanic women write. REVISTA CHICANO-RIQUENA, Vol. 11, no. 3-4 (Fall, Winter, 1983), p. [1]-180. Bilingual. DESCR: Art; Literary Criticism; *Literature; Prose; *Women.

4613 Villanueva, Alma and Binder, Wolfgang. [Interview with] Alma Villanueva. IN: Binder, Wolfgang, ed. PARTIAL AUTOBIOGRAPHIES: INTERVIEWS WITH TWENTY CHICANO POETS. Erlangen, W. Germany: Verlag Palm & Enke, 1985, p. 201-202. English. DESCR: Authors; Autobiography; *Villanueva, Alma.

4614 Zamora, Bernice. Archetypes in Chicana poetry. DE COLORES, Vol. 4, no. 3 (1978), p. 43-52. English. DESCR: Cervantes, Lorna Dee; Cunningham, Veronica; "Declaration on a Day of Little Inspiration" [poem]; Hernandez, Carlota; "I Speak in an Illusion" [poem]; *Literary Criticism; Lucero, Judy A.; Macias, Margarita; Mendoza, Rita; "Para Mi Hijita" [poem]; "Rape Report" [poem]; "The White Line" [poem]; "Working Mother's Song" [poem]; "You Can Only Blame the System for So Long" [poem]; Zamora, Katarina.

4615 Zamora, Bernice and Binder, Wolfgang. [Interview with] Bernice Zamora. IN: Binder, Wolfgang, ed. PARTIAL AUTOBIOGRAPHIES: INTERVIEWS WITH TWENTY CHICANO POETS. Erlangen, W. Germany: Verlag Palm & Enke, 1985, p. 221-229. English. DESCR: Authors; Autobiography; *Zamora, Bernice.

4616 Zamora, Bernice. Mythopoeia of Chicano poetry: an introduction to cultural archetypes. Thesis (Ph.D.)--Stanford University, 1986. 341 p. English. DESCR: Literary Characters; Literary Criticism; Literature; Malinche; Pachucos; *Symbolism.

4617 Zamora, Emilio, Jr. Sara Estela Ramirez: una rosa roja en el movimiento. IN: Mora, Magdalena and Del Castillo, Adelaida, eds. MEXICAN WOMEN IN THE UNITED STATES: STRUGGLES PAST AND PRESENT. Los Angeles, CA: Chicano Studies Research Center, UCLA, 1980, p. 163-169. English. DESCR: *Biography; Literary Criticism; *Ramirez, Sara Estela.

Poets
USE: Authors

Police

4618 Miller, George A. Latinas on border patrol. VISTA, Vol. 4, no. 18 (January 1, 1989), p. 8-10. English. DESCR: *Border Patrol; Border Region; Statistics.

Policy
USE: Public Policy

Political Economy

4619 Castaneda, Antonia I. The political economy of nineteenth century stereotypes of Californianas. IN: Del Castillo, Adelaida R., ed. BETWEEN BORDERS: ESSAYS ON MEXICANA/CHICANA HISTORY. Encino, CA: Floricanto Press, 1990, p. 213-236. English. DESCR: *California; *Californios; Dana, Richard Henry; Farnham, Thomas Jefferson; History; LIFE IN CALIFORNIA; Robinson, Alfred; *Sex Stereotypes; TRAVELS IN CALIFORNIA AND SCENES IN THE PACIFIC OCEAN; TWO YEARS BEFORE THE MAST; Women.

4620 Garcia Castro, Mary. Migrant women: issues in organization and solidarity. MIGRATION WORLD MAGAZINE, Vol. 14, no. 1-2 (1986), p. 15-19. English. DESCR: Labor Supply and Market; *Migrant Labor; Organizations; Undocumented Workers; Women.

Political History and Conditions

4621 Camarillo, Alberto M., ed. Latinos in the United States: a historical bibliography. Santa Barbara, CA: ABC-CLIO, 1986. x, 332 p.. English. DESCR: *Bibliography; Social History and Conditions.

4622 Cordova, Teresa, et al., eds. and National Association for Chicano Studies. Chicana voices: intersections of class, race, and gender. Austin, TX: Center for Mexican American Studies Publications, 1986. xi, 223 p. English. DESCR: Chicana Studies; Labor; *Social History and Conditions.

4623 Enriquez, Evangelina and Mirande, Alfredo. Liberation, Chicana style: colonial roots of feministas chicanas. DE COLORES, Vol. 4, no. 3 (1978), p. 7-21. Bilingual. DESCR: *Chicano Movement; Feminism; Malinche; *Social History and Conditions.

4624 Sosa Riddell, Adaljiza. The status of women in Mexico: the impact of the "International Year of the Woman". IN: Iglitzin, Lynn B. and Ross, Ruth A., eds. WOMEN IN THE WORLD, 1975-1985. Santa Barbara, CA: ABC-Clio, Inc., 1986, p. 305-324. English. DESCR: Abortion; *Feminism; International Women's Year World Conference (1975: Mexico City); *Mexico; Political Parties and Organizations; Rape; *Sexism; Social History and Conditions; *Women.

4625 Soto, Shirlene Ann. Emergence of the modern Mexican woman: her participation in revolution and struggle for equality, 1910-1940. Denver, CO: Arden Press, 1990. xvi, 199 p.: ill. English. DESCR: *Feminism; *Mexican Revolution - 1910-1920; *Mexico; *Women.

Political Ideology

4626 Harlow, Barbara. Sites of struggle: immigration, deportation, prison, and exile. IN: Calderon, Hector and Saldivar, Jose David, eds. CRITICISM IN THE BORDERLANDS: STUDIES IN CHICANO LITERATURE, CULTURE, AND IDEOLOGY. Durham, NC: Duke University Press, 1991, p. [149]-163. English. DESCR: Anzaldua, Gloria; BLACK GOLD; BORDERLANDS/LA FRONTERA: THE NEW MESTIZA; First, Ruth; Khalifeh, Sahar; *Literary Criticism; Sanchez, Rosaura; Social Classes; "The Cariboo Cafe" [short story]; "The Ditch" [short story]; Viramontes, Helena Maria; WILD THORNS; *Women; Working Women.

4627 Hurtado, Aida. Relating to privilege: seduction and rejection in the subordination of white women and women of color. SIGNS: JOURNAL OF WOMEN IN CULTURE AND SOCIETY, Vol. 14, no. 4 (Summer 1989), p. 833-855. English. DESCR: *Anglo Americans; Asian Americans; Blacks; Ethnic Groups; *Feminism; Political Socialization; *Women.

Political Ideology
(cont.)

4628 Ortega, Eliana and Sternbach, Nancy Saporta
At the threshold of the unnamed: Latina
literary discourse in the eighties. IN:
Horno-Delgado, Asuncion, et al., eds.
BREAKING BOUNDARIES: LATINA WRITING AND
CRITICAL READINGS. Amherst, MA: University
of Massachusetts Press, c1989, p. [2]-23.
English. DESCR: Bilingualism; *Feminism;
*Literary Criticism; Literary History; Sex
Roles; *Women.

4629 Perez, Emma. "A la mujer": a critique of the
Partido Liberal Mexicano's gender ideology
on women. IN: Del Castillo, Adelaida R., ed.
BETWEEN BORDERS: ESSAYS ON MEXICANA/CHICANA
HISTORY. Encino, CA: Floricanto Press, 199C,
p. 459-482. English. DESCR: *"A La Mujer"
[essay]; Essays; *Feminism; Flores Magon,
Ricardo; Guerrero, Praxedis G.; Journalism;
Mexican Revolution - 1910-1920; Mexico;
Newspapers; *Partido Liberal Mexicano (PLM);
Political Parties and Organizations;
*REGENERACION [newspaper]; Sex Roles; Women.

4630 Quintana, Alvina E. Chicana discourse:
negations and mediations. Thesis
(Ph.D.)--University of California, Santa
Cruz, 1989. 226 p. English. DESCR: Authors;
Castillo, Ana; Chavez, Denise; Chicano
Movement; Cisneros, Sandra; Ethnology;
Feminism; Literary Criticism; *Literature;
NOVENA NARRATIVES; Oral Tradition; THE HOUSE
ON MANGO STREET; THE LAST OF THE MENU GIRLS;
THE MIXQUIAHUALA LETTERS.

4631 Saldivar, Ramon. The dialectics of
subjectivity: gender and difference in
Isabella Rios, Sandra Cisneros, and Cherrie
Moraga. IN: Saldivar, Ramon. CHICANO
NARRATIVE: THE DIALECTICS OF DIFFERENCE.
Madison, WI: University of Wisconsin Press,
1990, p. 171-199. English. DESCR: Authors;
Autobiography; *Cisneros, Sandra; Feminism;
Fiction; *Literary Criticism; Literature;
LOVING IN THE WAR YEARS; *Moraga, Cherrie;
*Rios, Isabella; THE HOUSE ON MANGO STREET;
VICTUUM.

4632 Yarbro-Bejarano, Yvonne. Chicana's
experience in collective theatre: ideology
and form. WOMEN AND PERFORMANCE, Vol. 2, no.
2 (1985), p. 45-58. English. DESCR: Actors
and Actresses; Careers; El Teatro Campesino;
El Teatro de la Esperanza; *San Francisco
Mime Troupe; Sex Roles; Teatro; Teatro
Libertad; Valentina Productions; Women.

Political Participation
USE: Voter Turnout

Political Parties and Organizations

4633 Baca Barragan, Polly; Hamner, Richard; and
Guerrero, Lena. [Untitled interview with
State Senators (Colorado) Polly
Baca-Barragan and Lena Guerrero]. NATIONAL
HISPANIC JOURNAL, Vol. 1, no. 2 (Winter
1982), p. 8-11. English. DESCR: Baca
Barragan, Polly; Carter, Jimmy (President);
Democratic Party; Elected Officials;
Guerrero, Lena.

4634 Chapa, Olivia Evey. Mujeres por la Raza
unida. CARACOL, Vol. 1, no. 2 (October
1974), p. 3-5. English. DESCR: Canales,
Alma; Cotera, Marta P.; Diaz, Elena; La Raza
Unida Party; REPORT OF FIRST CONFERENCIA DE
MUJERES POR LA RAZA UNIDA PARTY.

4635 Gonzales, Sylvia Alicia. Hispanic American
voluntary organizations. Westport, CT:

Greenwood Press, 1985. xx, 267 p. English.
DESCR: Art Organizations and Groups;
*Community Organizations; Cultural
Organizations; *Directories; Educational
Organizations; *Organizations; Professional
Organizations.

4636 Marquez, Evelina and Ramirez, Margarita.
Women's task is to gain liberation. IN:
Sanchez, Rosaura and Martinez Cruz, Rosa,
eds. ESSAYS ON LA MUJER. Los Angeles, CA:
Chicano Studies Center Publications, UCLA,
1977, p. 188-194. English. DESCR: Centro de
Accion Social Autonomo (CASA); *Feminism.

4637 Pardo, Mary. Mexican American women
grassroots community activists: "Mothers of
East Los Angeles". FRONTIERS: A JOURNAL OF
WOMEN STUDIES, Vol. 11, no. 1 (1990), p.
[1]-7. English. DESCR: Coalition Against the
Prison, East Los Angeles, CA; *Community
Organizations; East Los Angeles, CA; Family;
*Feminism; *Mothers of East L.A. (MELA);
Organizations; Politics; Sex Roles.

4638 Perez, Emma. "A la mujer": a critique of the
Partido Liberal Mexicano's gender ideology
on women. IN: Del Castillo, Adelaida R., ed.
BETWEEN BORDERS: ESSAYS ON MEXICANA/CHICANA
HISTORY. Encino, CA: Floricanto Press, 1990,
p. 459-482. English. DESCR: *"A La Mujer"
[essay]; Essays; *Feminism; Flores Magon,
Ricardo; Guerrero, Praxedis G.; Journalism;
Mexican Revolution - 1910-1920; Mexico;
Newspapers; *Partido Liberal Mexicano (PLM);
Political Ideology; *REGENERACION
[newspaper]; Sex Roles; Women.

4639 Sosa Riddell, Adaljiza. The status of women
in Mexico: the impact of the "International
Year of the Woman". IN: Iglitzin, Lynn B.
and Ross, Ruth A., eds. WOMEN IN THE WORLD,
1975-1985. Santa Barbara, CA: ABC-Clio,
Inc., 1986, p. 305-324. English. DESCR:
Abortion; *Feminism; International Women's
Year World Conference (1975: Mexico City);
*Mexico; Political History and Conditions;
Rape; *Sexism; Social History and
Conditions; *Women.

Political Representation

4640 Baca Barragan, Polly. La Chicana in
politics. IN: LA CHICANA: BUILDING FOR THE
FUTURE, AN ACTION PLAN FOR THE 80s. Oakland,
CA: National Hispanic University, 1981, p.
21-31. English. DESCR: Elected Officials;
Leadership; *Politics.

4641 Chacon, Peter. Chicanas and political
representation. IN: LA CHICANA: BUILDING FOR
THE FUTURE, AN ACTION PLAN FOR THE 80s.
Oakland, CA: National Hispanic University,
1981, p. 32-36. English. DESCR: Elected
Officials; Politics; Voter Turnout.

Political Socialization

4642 Howell-Martinez, Vicky. The influence of
gender roles on political socialization: an
experimental study of Mexican-American
children. WOMEN & POLITICS, Vol. 2, no. 3
(Fall 1982), p. 33-46. English. DESCR: *Sex
Roles; Sex Stereotypes.

4643 Hurtado, Aida. Relating to privilege:
seduction and rejection in the subordination
of white women and women of color. SIGNS:
JOURNAL OF WOMEN IN CULTURE AND SOCIETY,
Vol. 14, no. 4 (Summer 1989), p. 833-855.
English. DESCR: *Anglo Americans; Asian
Americans; Blacks; Ethnic Groups; *Feminism;
Political Ideology; *Women.

Politicos
    USE: Elected Officials

Politics

4644 Baca Barragan, Polly. La Chicana in
     politics. IN: LA CHICANA: BUILDING FOR THE
     FUTURE, AN ACTION PLAN FOR THE 80s. Oakland,
     CA: National Hispanic University, 1981, p.
     21-31. English. **DESCR**: Elected Officials;
     Leadership; Political Representation.

4645 Burnham, Linda. Barbara Carrasco and public
     activist art. HIGH PERFORMANCE, Vol. 9, no.
     3 (1986), p. 48. English. **DESCR**: *Artists;
     Carrasco, Barbara; Mural Art.

4646 Campoamor, Diana. Gender gap in politics: no
     laughing matter. VISTA, Vol. 4, no. 8
     (October 24, 1988), p. 14. English. **DESCR**:
     Attitudes; Essays; *Women Men Relations.

4647 Carrillo, Teresa. The women's movement and
     the left in Mexico: the presidential
     candidacy of Dona Rosario Ibarra. IN:
     Cordova, Teresa, et al., eds. CHICANA
     VOICES. Austin, TX: Center for Mexican
     American Studies, 1986, p. 96-113. English.
     DESCR: Biography; Ibarra, Rosario; Mexico;
     *Women.

4648 Chacon, Peter. Chicanas and political
     representation. IN: LA CHICANA: BUILDING FOR
     THE FUTURE, AN ACTION PLAN FOR THE80s.
     Oakland, CA: National Hispanic University,
     1981, p. 32-36. English. **DESCR**: Elected
     Officials; *Political Representation; Voter
     Turnout.

4649 Flores, Francisca. Comision Femenil
     Mexicana. REGENERACION, Vol. 2, no. 1
     (1971), p. 6. English. **DESCR**: Abortion;
     Children; Comision Femenil Mexicana
     Nacional; *Family Planning; Feminism;
     Organizations.

4650 Huerta, Dolores. Dolores Huerta talks about
     Republicans, Cesar, children and her home
     town. REGENERACION, Vol. 2, no. 4 (1975), p.
     20-24. English. **DESCR**: *Agricultural Labor
     Unions; *Biography; Chavez, Cesar E.;
     Community Service Organization, Los Angeles,
     (CSO); Democratic Party; Elected Officials;
     Flores, Art; Huerta, Dolores; McGovern,
     George; Ramirez, Henry M.; Ross, Fred;
     Sanchez, Philip V.; United Farmworkers of
     America (UFW); Working Women.

4651 Huerta, Dolores. Dolores Huerta talks about
     Republicans, Cesar, children and her home
     town. IN: Servin, Manuel P. ed. THE MEXICAN
     AMERICANS: AN AWAKENING MINORITY. 2nd ed.
     Beverly Hills, CA: Glencoe Press, 1974, p.
     283-294. English. **DESCR**: *Agricultural Labor
     Unions; *Biography; Chavez, Cesar E.;
     Community Service Organization, Los Angeles,
     (CSO); Democratic Party; Elected Officials;
     Flores, Art; Huerta, Dolores; McGovern,
     George; Ramirez, Henry M.; Ross, Fred;
     Sanchez, Philip V.; United Farmworkers of
     America (UFW); Working Women.

4652 Olivarez, Elizabeth. Women's rights and the
     Mexican American woman. REGENERACION, Vol.
     2, no. 4 (1975), p. 40-42. English. **DESCR**:
     Education; *Feminism; Identity; Psychology;
     Religion; Sex Roles.

4653 Pardo, Mary. Mexican American women
     grassroots community activists: "Mothers of
     East Los Angeles". FRONTIERS: A JOURNAL OF
     WOMEN STUDIES, Vol. 11, no. 1 (1990), p.
     [1]-7. English. **DESCR**: Coalition Against the
     Prison, East Los Angeles, CA; *Community

Organizations; East Los Angeles, CA; Family;
*Feminism; *Mothers of East L.A. (MELA);
Organizations; Political Parties and
Organizations; Sex Roles.

Population

4654 Alba, Francisco. La fecundidad entre los
     Mexicano-Norteamericanos en relacion a los
     cambiantes patrones reproductivos en Mexico
     y los Estados Unidos. DEMOGRAFIA Y ECONOMIA,
     Vol. 16, no. 2 (1982), p. 236-249. Spanish.
     DESCR: *Fertility; Mexico.

4655 Amaro, Hortensia. Considerations for
     prevention of HIV infection among Hispanic
     women. PSYCHOLOGY OF WOMEN QUARTERLY, Vol.
     12, no. 4 (December 1988), p. 429-443.
     English. **DESCR**: *AIDS (Disease); Attitudes;
     *Women.

4656 Arce, Carlos H. and Abney-Guardado, Armando
     J. Demographic and cultural correlates of
     Chicano intermarriage. CALIFORNIA
     SOCIOLOGIST, Vol. 5, no. 2 (Summer 1982), p.
     41-58. English. **DESCR**: Cultural
     Characteristics; Culture; *Intermarriage;
     Social Psychology.

4657 Bean, Frank D. and Tienda, Marta. The
     Hispanic population of the United States.
     New York: Russell Sage Foundation, 1987.
     xxiv, 456 p. English. **DESCR**: *Census;
     Education; Employment; Fertility; Identity;
     Immigration; Income; Self-Referents;
     *Statistics.

4658 Bean, Frank D. and Bradshaw, Benjamin S.
     Mexican American fertility. IN: Teller,
     Charles H., et al., eds. CUANTOS SOMOS: A
     DEMOGRAPHIC STUDY OF THE MEXICAN AMERICAN
     POPULATION. Austin, TX: Center for Mexican
     American Studies, University of Texas at
     Austin, 1977, p. 101-130. English. **DESCR**:
     Attitudes; Birth Control; *Fertility;
     Income; Religion.

4659 Bean, Frank D. and Swicegood, Gray. Mexican
     American fertility patterns. Austin, TX:
     University of Texas Press, 1985. x, 178 p.
     English. **DESCR**: Age Groups; Census;
     Education; *Fertility; Language Usage;
     Research Methodology; *Socioeconomic
     Factors; Statistics.

4660 Bean, Frank D.; Stephen, Elizabeth H.; and
     Opitz, Wolfgang. The Mexican origin
     population in the United States: a
     demographic overview. IN: O. de la Garza,
     Rodolfo, et al., eds. THE MEXICAN AMERICAN
     EXPERIENCE: AN INTERDISCIPLINARY ANTHOLOGY.
     Austin, TX: University of Texas Press, 1985,
     p. 57-75. English. **DESCR**: Employment;
     Fertility; Income; Vital Statistics.

4661 Bustamante, Jorge A. Maquiladoras: a new
     face of international capitalism on Mexico's
     northern frontier. IN: Nash, June and
     Fernandez-Kelly, Patricia, eds. WOMEN, MEN,
     AND THE INTERNATIONAL DIVISION OF LABOR.
     Albany, NY: State University of New York
     Press, 1983, p. 224-256. English. **DESCR**:
     Banking Industry; Border Industrialization
     Program (BIP); Border Industries; *Border
     Region; Foreign Trade; Industrial Workers;
     International Economic Relations; Mexico;
     Programa Nacional Fronterizo (PRONAF);
     United States-Mexico Relations; Women;
     Working Women.

Population (cont.)

4662 Canino, Glorisa. The Hispanic woman: sociocultural influences on diagnoses and treatment. IN: Becerra Rosina M., et al., eds. MENTAL HEALTH AND HISPANIC AMERICANS: CLINICAL PERSPECTIVES. New York: Grune & Stratton, 1982, p. 117-138. English. DESCR: Assimilation; Cultural Characteristics; Culture; *Depression (Psychological); Family; Feminism; Mental Health; Sex Roles.

4663 Cook, Annabel Kirschner. Diversity among Northwest Hispanics. SOCIAL SCIENCE JOURNAL, Vol. 23, no. 2 (April 1986), p. 205-216. English. DESCR: Northwestern United States; Socioeconomic Factors.

4664 Davis, Cary; Haub, Carl; and Willette, JoAnne. U.S. Hispanics: changing the face of America. POPULATION BULLETIN, Vol. 38, no. 3 (June 1983), p. 1-43. English. DESCR: Education; Employment; Fertility; Immigration; Income; Statistics; Vital Statistics.

4665 Flores, Estevan T. Chicanos and sociological research: 1970-1980. IN: CHICANOS AND THE SOCIAL SCIENCES: A DECADE OF RESEARCH AND DEVELOPMENT (1970-1980) SYMPOSIUM WORKING PAPER. Santa Barbara, CA: Center for Chicano Studies, University of California, 1983, p. 19-45. English. DESCR: Bibliography; Family; Internal Colony Model; Labor; Literature Reviews; Research Methodology; *Sociology.

4666 Griswold del Castillo, Richard. "Only for my family...": historical dimensions of Chicano family solidarity--the case of San Antonio in 1860. AZTLAN, Vol. 16, no. 1-2 (1985), p. 145-176. English. DESCR: Extended Family; *Family; History; San Antonio, TX.

4667 Gurak, Douglas T. Assimilation and fertility: a comparison of Mexican American and Japanese American women. HISPANIC JOURNAL OF BEHAVIORAL SCIENCES, Vol. 2, no. 3 (September 1980), p. 219-239. English. DESCR: Asian Americans; Assimilation; *Fertility; Japanese; Women.

4668 Hedderson, John J. Fertility and mortality. IN: Stoddard, Ellwyn R., et al., eds. BORDERLANDS SOURCEBOOK: A GUIDE TO THE LITERATURE ON NORTHERN MEXICO AND THE AMERICAN SOUTHWEST. Norman, OK: University of Oklahoma Press, 1983, p. 232-236. English. DESCR: Border Region; *Fertility; *Vital Statistics.

4669 Kranau, Edgar J.; Green, Vicki; and Valencia-Weber, Gloria. Acculturation and the Hispanic woman: attitudes toward women, sex-role attribution, sex-role behavior, and demographics. HISPANIC JOURNAL OF BEHAVIORAL SCIENCES, Vol. 4, no. 1 (March 1982), p. 21-40. English. DESCR: Acculturation; *Sex Roles.

4670 Lara-Cea, Helen. Notes on the use of parish registers in the reconstruction of Chicana history in California prior to 1850. IN: Del Castillo, Adelaida R., ed. BETWEEN BORDERS: ESSAYS ON MEXICANA/CHICANA HISTORY. Encino, CA: Floricanto Press, 1990, p. 131-159. English. DESCR: *California; Catholic Church; History; Indigenismo; Mission of Santa Clara; *San Jose, CA; *Vital Statistics.

4671 Lorenzana, Noemi. La Chicana: transcending the old and carving out a new life and self-image. DE COLORES, Vol. 2, no. 3 (1975), p. 6-14. English. DESCR: *Census;

Identity; *Social History and Conditions.

4672 Markides, Kyriakos S. Consequences of gender differentials in life expectancy for Black and Hispanic Americans. INTERNATIONAL JOURNAL OF AGING & HUMAN DEVELOPMENT, Vol. 29, no. 2 (1989), p. 95-102. English. DESCR: *Ancianos; Blacks; Census; Cubanos; Latin Americans; Males; Puerto Ricans; U.S. Bureau of the Census.

4673 Markides, Kyriakos S., et al. Sample representativeness in a three-generation study of Mexican Americans. JOURNAL OF MARRIAGE AND THE FAMILY, Vol. 45, no. 4 (November 1983), p. 911-916. English. DESCR: *Age Groups; *Marriage; San Antonio, TX; *Socioeconomic Factors.

4674 Martinez, Douglas R. Hispanic origin women in the U.S. LA LUZ, Vol. 8, no. 8 (October, November, 1980), p. 11-12. English. DESCR: *Educational Statistics; Statistics.

4675 Michael, Robert T. and Tuma, Nancy Brandon. Entry into marriage and parenthood by young men and women: the influence of family background. DEMOGRAPHY, Vol. 22, no. 4 (November 1985), p. 515-544. Magazine. English. DESCR: Anglo Americans; Blacks; *Cultural Characteristics; *Fertility; *Marriage; Youth.

4676 Mosher, William D.; Johnson, David P.; and Horn, Marjorie C. Religion and fertility in the United States: the importance of marriage patterns and Hispanic origin. DEMOGRAPHY, Vol. 23, no. 3 (August 1986), p. 367-379. English. DESCR: *Catholic Church; *Fertility; Identity; Marriage; *Religion.

4677 One birth in four. AMERICAN DEMOGRAPHICS, Vol. 6, no. 1 (January 1984), p. 15. English. DESCR: Fertility; *Vital Statistics.

4678 Pena, Devon Gerardo. Tortuosidad: shop floor struggles of female maquiladora workers. IN: Ruiz, Vicki L. and Tiano, Susan, eds. WOMEN ON THE U.S.-MEXICO BORDER: RESPONSES TO CHANGE. Boston, MA: Allen & Unwin, 1987, p. 129-154. English. DESCR: Border Industries; Ciudad Juarez, Chihuahua, Mexico; Employment; Personnel Management; Surveys; *Women; Working Women.

4679 Ramirez, Oscar and Arce, Carlos H. The contemporary Chicano family: an empirically based review. IN: Baron, Augustine, Jr., ed. EXPLORATIONS IN CHICANO PSYCHOLOGY. New York: Praeger, 1981, p. 3-28. English. DESCR: *Family; Fertility; Literature Reviews; Machismo; Sex Roles.

4680 Rincon, Bernice. Chicanas on the move. REGENERACION, Vol. 2, no. 4 (1975), p. 52. English. DESCR: Flores, Francisca; *Sexism.

4681 Romero-Cachinero, M. Carmen. Hispanic women in Canada: a framework for analysis. RESOURCES FOR FEMINIST RESEARCH, Vol. 16, no. 1 (March 1987), p. 19-20. English. DESCR: *Canada; Social History and Conditions; Women.

4682 Simon, Rita J. and DeLey, Margo. The work experience of undocumented Mexican women migrants in Los Angeles. INTERNATIONAL MIGRATION REVIEW, Vol. 18, no. 4 (Winter 1984), p. 1212-1229. English. DESCR: Immigrants; Income; *Los Angeles, CA; Socioeconomic Factors; *Undocumented Workers; *Working Women.

Population (cont.)

4683 Stephen, Elizabeth H. At the crossroads: fertility of Mexican-American women. New York: Garland Publishers, 1989. v, 184 p.: ill. English. **DESCR:** Assimilation; *Fertility; Immigration.

4684 Swicegood, Gray, et al. Language usage and fertility in the Mexican-origin population of the United States. DEMOGRAPHY, Vol. 25, no. 1 (February 1988), p. 17-33. English. **DESCR:** *Fertility; Immigrants; *Language Usage; Women.

4685 Waldman, Elizabeth. Profile of the Chicana: a statistical fact sheet. IN: Mora, Magdalena and Del Castillo, Adelaida, eds. MEXICAN WOMEN IN THE UNITED STATES: STRUGGLES PAST AND PRESENT. Los Angeles, CA: Chicano Studies Research Center, UCLA, 1980, p. 195-204. English. **DESCR:** Employment; Family; *Statistics.

Population Distribution
USE: Population

Population Trends
USE: Population

Portillo, Lourdes

4686 Fregoso, Rosa Linda. La quinceanera of Chicana counter aesthetics. CENTRO BULLETIN, Vol. 3, no. 1 (Winter 1990, 1991), p. [87]-91. English. **DESCR:** *AGUEDA MARTINEZ [film]; ANIMA [film]; *CHICANA! [film]; *DESPUES DEL TERREMOTO [film]; Espana, Frances Salome; Feminism; *Films; Morales, Sylvia; Vasquez, Esperanza.

Portillo Trambley, Estela

4687 Castellano, Olivia. Of clarity and the moon: a study of two women in rebellion. DE COLORES, Vol. 3, no. 3 (1977), p. 25-30. English. **DESCR:** DAY OF THE SWALLOWS; *Literary Criticism; "The Apple Trees".

4688 Dewey, Janice. Dona Josefa: bloodpulse of transition and change. IN: Horno-Delgado, Asuncion, et al., eds. BREAKING BOUNDARIES: LATINA WRITING AND CRITICAL READINGS. Amherst, MA: University of Massachusetts Press, c1989, p. 39-47. English. **DESCR:** *DAY OF THE SWALLOWS; Garcia-Lorca, Federico; LA CASA DE BERNARDA ALBA; Literary Characters; Literary Criticism.

4689 Gonzalez, LaVerne. [Portillo Trambley, Estela]. IN: Martinez, Julio A. and Lomeli, Francisco A., eds. CHICANO LITERATURE: A REFERENCE GUIDE. Westport, CT: Greenwood Press, 1985, p. 316-322. English. **DESCR:** Authors; Biography; Literary Criticism.

4690 Melville, Margarita B. Female and male in Chicano theatre. IN: Kanellos, Nicolas, ed. HISPANIC THEATRE IN THE UNITED STATES. Houston, TX: Arte Publico Press, 1984, p. 71-79. English. **DESCR:** BERNABE; BRUJERIAS [play]; Cultural Characteristics; DAY OF THE SWALLOWS; Duarte-Clark, Rodrigo; EL JARDIN [play]; Family; Feminism; Macias, Ysidro; Morton, Carlos; RANCHO HOLLYWOOD [play]; *Sex Roles; *Teatro; THE ULTIMATE PENDEJADA [play]; Valdez, Luis; Women Men Relations.

4691 Rebolledo, Tey Diana. Tradition and mythology: signatures of landscape in Chicana literature. IN: Norwood, Vera and Monk, Janice, eds. THE DESERT IS NO LADY: SOUTHWESTERN LANDSCAPES IN WOMEN'S WRITING AND ART. New Haven, CT: Yale University Press, 1987, p. 96-124. English. **DESCR:** *Authors; Cabeza de Baca, Fabiola; Chavez, Denise; Jaramillo, Cleofas M.; Literary Criticism; *Literary History; Literature; Mora, Pat; Mythology; Otero Warren, Nina; Silva, Beverly; Southwestern United States; WE FED THEM CACTUS.

4692 Salazar Parr, Carmen. La Chicana in literature. IN: Garcia, Eugene E., et al., eds. CHICANO STUDIES: A MULTIDISCIPLINARY APPROACH. New York: Teachers College Press, 1984, p. 120-134. English. **DESCR:** DAY OF THE SWALLOWS; Literary Characters; Literary Criticism; *Literature; Stereotypes; Teatro; "The Trees" [short story].

4693 Tafolla, Carmen. Chicano literature: beyond beginnings. IN: Harris, Marie and Aguero, Kathleen, eds. A GIFT OF TONGUES: CRITICAL CHALLENGES IN CONTEMPORARY AMERICAN POETRY. Athens, GA: University of Georgia Press, 1987, p. 206-225. English. **DESCR:** *Authors; Cota-Cardenas, Margarita; Language Usage; *Literary Criticism; *Literature; Sex Stereotypes; Symbolism; Tafolla, Carmen; Vigil-Pinon, Evangelina.

4694 Vallejos, Tomas. Estela Portillo Trambley's fictive search for paradise. FRONTIERS: A JOURNAL OF WOMEN STUDIES, Vol. 5, no. 2 (1980),p. 54-58. Also IN: Lattin, Vernon E., ed. CONTEMPORARY CHICANO FICTION. Binghamton, NY: Bilingual Press/Editorial Bilingue, 1986, p. 269-277. English. **DESCR:** DAY OF THE SWALLOWS; *Literary Criticism; Novel; RAIN OF SCORPIONS AND OTHER WRITINGS.

Post Secondary Education
USE: Higher Education

Poverty

4695 Chavez, Henri. Unsung heroine of La Causa. REGENERACION, Vol. 1, no. 10 (1971), p. 20. English. **DESCR:** AFL-CIO United Farmworkers Organizing Committee; Agricultural Labor Unions; Community Service Organization, Los Angeles, (CSO); Family; Farm Workers; *Huerta, Dolores; Working Women.

4696 Facio, Elisa "Linda". Constraints, resources, and self-definition: a case study of Chicano older women. Thesis (Ph.D.)--University of California, Berkeley, 1988. 246 p. English. **DESCR:** *Ancianos; *Family; Grandmothers; Sex Roles; Widowhood.

4697 Facio, Elisa "Linda". The interaction of age and gender in Chicana older lives: a case study of Chicana elderly in a senior citizen center. RENATO ROSALDO LECTURE SERIES MONOGRAPH, Vol. 4, (1988), p. 21-38. English. **DESCR:** Age Groups; *Ancianos; Social Classes.

4698 Jensen, Leif. Secondary earner strategies and family poverty: immigrant-native differentials, 1960-1980. INTERNATIONAL MIGRATION REVIEW, Vol. 25, no. 1 (Spring 1991), p. 113-140. English. **DESCR:** Anglo Americans; *Asian Americans; Blacks; Family; Immigrants; Immigration; Income; Women; Working Women.

Poverty (cont.)

4699 Nyamathi, Adeline M. and Vasquez, Rose. Impact of poverty, homelessness, and drugs on Hispanic women at risk for HIV infection. HISPANIC JOURNAL OF BEHAVIORAL SCIENCES, Vol. 11, no. 4 (November 1989), p. 299-314. English. DESCR: *AIDS (Disease); Drug Use; Health Education; *Human Immunodeficiency Virus (HIV); Locus of Control; Mental Health; Needle-Sharing.

4700 Weiner, Raine. The needs of poverty women heading households: a return to postsecondary education. Thesis (Ph.D.)--California School of Professional Psychology, Los Angeles, 1986. 180 p. English. DESCR: Anglo Americans; Blacks; *Employment Training; Ethnic Groups; *Single Parents; Vocational Education; Welfare; Women.

Preciado Martin, Patricia

4701 Rebolledo, Tey Diana. Hispanic women writers of the Southwest: tradition and innovation. IN: Lensink, Judy Nolte, ed. OLD SOUTHWEST/NEW SOUTHWEST: ESSAYS ON A REGION AND ITS LITERATURE. Tucson, AZ: The Tucson Public Library, 1987, p. 49-61. English. DESCR: *Authors; Cabeza de Baca, Fabiola; Jaramillo, Cleofas M.; Literature; Mora, Pat; OLD SPAIN IN OUR SOUTHWEST; Otero Warren, Nina; Sex Roles; Sex Stereotypes; Silva, Beverly; *Southwestern United States; Vigil-Pinon, Evangelina; WE FED THEM CACTUS; *Women.

Precolumbian Medicine

4702 Bauman, Raquel. The status of Chicanas in medicine. RESEARCH BULLETIN (SPANISH SPEAKING MENTAL HEALTH RES. CENTER), Vol. 4, no. 3 (March 1980), p. 6-7,12-13. English. DESCR: *Medical Care; *Medical Education; *Medical Personnel.

Precolumbian Society

4703 Blanco, Iris. Participacion de las mujeres en la sociedad prehispanica. IN: Sanchez, Rosaura and Martinez Cruz, Rosa, eds. ESSAYS ON LA MUJER. Los Angeles, CA: Chicano Studies Center Publications, UCLA, 1977, p 48-81. Spanish. DESCR: Aztecs; Cultural Customs; *History; Indigenismo; Mexico; Women.

4704 Blanco, Iris. El sexo y su condicionamiento cultural en el mundo prehispanico. IN: Del Castillo, Adelaida R., ed. BETWEEN BORDERS: ESSAYS ON MEXICANA/CHICANA HISTORY. Encino, CA: Floricanto Press, 1990, p. 363-374. Spanish. DESCR: Mexico; *Sex Roles; Sexual Behavior; Women.

4705 Del Castillo, Adelaida R. Malintzin Tenepal: a preliminary look into a new perspective. ENCUENTRO FEMENIL, Vol. 1, no. 2 (1974), p. 58-77. English. DESCR: Aztecs; Biography; Cortes, Hernan; *History; *Malinche.

4706 Del Castillo, Adelaida R. Malintzin Tenepal: a preliminary look into a new perspective. IN: Sanchez, Rosaura and Martinez Cruz, Rosa, eds. ESSAYS ON LA MUJER. Los Angeles, CA: Chicano Studies Center Publications, UCLA, 1977, p. 124-149. English. DESCR: Aztecs; Biography; Cortes, Hernan; *History; *Malinche.

Pregnancy
USE: Fertility

Prejudice (Social)
USE: Discrimination

Prenatal Care

4707 Dowling, Patrick T. and Fisher, Michael. Maternal factors and low birthweight infants: a comparison of Blacks with Mexican-Americans. JOURNAL OF FAMILY PRACTICE, Vol. 25, no. 2 (August 1987), p. 153-158. English. DESCR: Blacks; Cook County, IL; *Infant Mortality; *Public Health; *Socioeconomic Factors.

4708 Engle, Patricia L. Prenatal and postnatal anxiety in women giving birth in Los Angeles. HEALTH PSYCHOLOGY, Vol. 9, no. 3 (1990), p. 285-299. English. DESCR: *Fertility; Immigrants; Los Angeles, CA; *Maternal and Child Welfare; Medical Care; *Stress; Women.

4709 Felice, Marianne E., et al. Clinical observations of Mexican-American, Caucasian, and Black pregnant teenagers. JOURNAL OF ADOLESCENT HEALTH CARE, Vol. 7, no. 5 (September 1986), p. 305-310. English. DESCR: Anglo Americans; Blacks; *Fertility; San Diego, CA; Youth.

4710 Fenster, Laura and Coye, Molly J. Birthweight of infants born to Hispanic women employed in agriculture. ARCHIVES OF ENVIRONMENTAL HEALTH, Vol. 45, no. 1 (January, February, 1990), p. 46-52. English. DESCR: *Farm Workers; Women.

4711 Hunt, Isabelle F., et al. Zinc supplementation during pregnancy: zinc concentration of serum and hair from low-income women of Mexican descent. AMERICAN JOURNAL OF CLINICAL NUTRITION, Vol. 37, no. 4 (April 1983), p. 572-582. English. DESCR: Low Income; Nutrition; Surveys.

4712 Leblanc, Donna Marie. Quality of maternity care in rural Texas. Thesis (Dr. P.H.) --University of Texas H.S.C. at Houston School of Public Health, 1983. 266 p. English. DESCR: Fertility; Low Income; *Maternal and Child Welfare; *Medical Care; *Rural Poor; Texas.

4713 Notzon, Francis Claude. Factors associated with low birth weight in Mexican-Americans and Mexicans. Thesis (Ph.D.)--John Hopkins University, 1989. 190 p. English. DESCR: Anglo Americans; Fertility; *Maternal and Child Welfare; Mexico; Public Health; *Women.

4714 Queiro-Tajalli, Irene. Hispanic women's perceptions and use of prenatal health care services. AFFILIA: JOURNAL OF WOMEN AND SOCIAL WORK, Vol. 4, no. 2 (Summer 1989), p. 60-72. English. DESCR: Indianapolis, IN; *Medical Care; Surveys; Women.

4715 Tajalli, Irene Queiro. Selected cultural, organizational, and economic factors related to prenatal care utilization by middle-income Hispanic women. Thesis (Ph.D.)--University of Illinois at Urbana-Champaign, 1984. 139 p. English. DESCR: *Fertility; Indiana; Maternal and Child Welfare; *Medical Care; Preventative Medicine.

Prenatal Care (cont.)

4716 Zepeda, Marlene. Mother-infant behavior in Mexican and Mexican-American women: a study of the relationship of selected prenatal, perinatal and postnatal events. Thesis (Ph.D.)--University of California, Los Angeles, 1984, 429 p. English. **DESCR:** Children; *Fertility; *Maternal and Child Welfare; *Parent and Child Relationships.

Prenatal Influence
USE: Prenatal Care

LA PRENSA, San Antonio, TX

4717 Luna-Lawhn, Juanita. EL REGIDOR and LA PRENSA: impediments to women's self-definition. THIRD WOMAN, Vol. 4, (1989), p. 134-142. English. **DESCR:** EL REGIDOR, San Antonio, TX; Literature; *Newspapers; Sex Roles; *Sexism.

4718 Luna-Lawhn, Juanita. Victorian attitudes affecting the Mexican woman writing in LA PRENSA during the early 1900s and the Chicana of the 1980s. IN: Bardeleben, Renate von, et al., eds. MISSIONS IN CONFLICT: ESSAYS ON U.S.-MEXICAN RELATIONS AND CHICANO CULTURE. Tubingen, W. Germany: Gunter Narr Verlag, 1986, p. 65-71. English. **DESCR:** Feminism; Literary Criticism; *Newspapers; "Penitents" [poem]; Poetry; Zamora, Bernice.

Presbyterian Church

4719 McRipley, Bernadine G. Racial/ethnic Presbyterian women: in search of community. CHURCH AND SOCIETY, Vol. 76, no. 4 (March, April, 1986), p. 47-53. English. **DESCR:** Religion; Sex Roles; *Women.

Preventative Medicine

4720 Alvarez-Amaya, Maria. Determinants of breast and cervical cancer behavior among Mexican American women. BORDER HEALTH/SALUD FRONTERIZA, Vol. 5, no. 3 (July, September, 1989), p. 22-27. Bilingual. **DESCR:** Border Region; *Breast Cancer; *Cancer; Diseases; Immigrants; Medical Care.

4721 Arevalo, Rodolfo, ed. and Minor, Marianne, ed. Chicanas and alcoholism: a sociocultural perspective of women. San Jose, CA: School of Social Work, San Jose State University, c1981. 55 p. English. **DESCR:** *Alcoholism; Drug Abuse Programs; Family; Feminism; Natural Support Systems; Psychotherapy.

4722 Bauer, Richard L. and Deyo, Richard A. Low risk of vertebral fracture in Mexican American women. ARCHIVES OF INTERNAL MEDICINE, Vol. 147, no. 8 (August 1987), p. 1437-1439. English. **DESCR:** Anglo Americans; *Osteoporosis; Women.

4723 Gonzalez, Judith Teresa. Factors relating to frequency of breast self-examination among low-income Mexican American women: implications for nursing practice. CANCER NURSING, Vol. 13, no. 3 (June 1990), p. 134-142. English. **DESCR:** *Breast Cancer; Cancer; Low Income; Medical Care; Medical Personnel.

4724 Gonzalez, Judith Teresa and Gonzalez, Virginia M. Initial validation of a scale measuring self-efficacy of breast self-examination among low-income Mexican American women. HISPANIC JOURNAL OF BEHAVIORAL SCIENCES, Vol. 12, no. 3 (August 1990), p. 277-291. English. **DESCR:** *Cancer; Low Income; Medical Care; Medical Education.

4725 Mays, Vicki M. and Cochran, Susan D. Issues in the perception of AIDS risk and risk reduction activities by Black and Hispanic/Latina women. AMERICAN PSYCHOLOGIST, Vol. 43, no. 11 (November 1988), p. 949-957. English. **DESCR:** *AIDS (Disease); Blacks; Condom Use; Fertility; Health Education; *Sexual Behavior; Women.

4726 Norris, Henry E. AIDS, women and reproductive rights. MULTICULTURAL INQUIRY AND RESEARCH ON AIDS (MIRA) NEWSLETTER, Vol. 1, no. 3 (Summer 1987), p. [2-3]. English. **DESCR:** Abortion; *AIDS (Disease); Center for Constitutional Rights; Discrimination; Women.

4727 Poma, Pedro A. Pregnancy in Hispanic women. JOURNAL OF THE NATIONAL MEDICAL ASSOCIATION, Vol. 79, no. 9 (September 1987), p. 929-935. English. **DESCR:** *Cultural Characteristics; *Doctor Patient Relations; *Fertility; Machismo; Women.

4728 Ponce-Adame, Merrihelen. Women and cancer. CORAZON DE AZTLAN, Vol. 1, no. 2 (March, April, 1982), p. 32. English. **DESCR:** Cancer; *Medical Care.

4729 Richardson, Jean L., et al. Frequency and adequacy of breast cancer screening among elderly Hispanic women. PREVENTIVE MEDICINE, Vol. 16, no. 6 (November 1987), p. 761-774. English. **DESCR:** Ancianos; *Cancer; Diseases; *Health Education; Los Angeles, CA; *Medical Care.

4730 Tajalli, Irene Queiro. Selected cultural, organizational, and economic factors related to prenatal care utilization by middle-income Hispanic women. Thesis (Ph.D.)--University of Illinois at Urbana-Champaign, 1984. 139 p. English. **DESCR:** *Fertility; Indiana; Maternal and Child Welfare; *Medical Care; Prenatal Care.

4731 Worth, Dooley and Rodriguez, Ruth. Latina women and AIDS. SIECUS REPORT, (January, February, 1986), p. 5-7. English. **DESCR:** Cultural Characteristics; Drug Addicts; Drug Use; Health Education; Natural Support Systems; New York; Puerto Ricans; Sex Roles; *Vital Statistics; Women.

Primary School Education

4732 Heathcote, Olivia D. Sex stereotyping in Mexican reading primers. READING TEACHER, Vol. 36, no. 2 (November 1982), p. 158-165. English. **DESCR:** Comparative Education; Curriculum Materials; Mexico; *Sex Stereotypes.

4733 Moore, Helen A. and Porter, Natalie K. Leadership and nonverbal behaviors of Hispanic females across school equity environments. PSYCHOLOGY OF WOMEN QUARTERLY, Vol. 12, no. 2 (June 1988), p. 147-163. English. **DESCR:** Assertiveness; Language Assessment; *Leadership.

Prisons

4734 Jurado, Marlo. Lack of communication. REGENERACION, Vol. 1, no. 10 (1971), p. 8. English. **DESCR:** Drug Addicts.

4735 Mares, Renee. La pinta: the myth of rehabilitation. ENCUENTRO FEMENIL, Vol. 1, no. 2 (1974), p. 20-27. English.

Prisons (cont.)

4736 Matsuda, Gema. La Chicana organizes: the
Comision Femenil Mexicana in perspective.
REGENERACION, Vol. 2, no. 4 (1975), p.
25-27. English. DESCR: Bojorquez, Frances;
Chicano Movement; *Comision Femenil Mexicana
Nacional; De la Cruz, Juana Ines; Flores,
Francisca; History; Machismo; Malinche; Sex
Stereotypes; *Sexism.

4737 Santillanes, Maria. Women in prison--C.I.W.:
an editorial. REGENERACION, Vol. 2, no. 4
(1975), p. 53. English. DESCR: Conferences
and Meetings; Garcia, Colly; La Mesa College
Pinto and Pinta Program; Lopez, Tony; Mares,
Rene; Martinez, Miguel; Pinto Conference
(1973: UCLA); Player; Salazar, Peggy.

4738 Vangie, Mary. Women at Frontera, CA.
REGENERACION, Vol. 1, no. 10 (1971), p. 8.
English. DESCR: Education; *Mexican American
Research Association (MARA), California
Institution for Women; Statistics.

Private Education

4739 Lee, Valerie. Achievement and educational
aspirations among Hispanic female high
school students: comparison between public
and Catholic schools. IN: McKenna, Teresa
and Ortiz, Flora Ida, eds. THE BROKEN WEB:
THE EDUCATIONAL EXPERIENCE OF HISPANIC
WOMEN. Claremont, CA: Tomas Rivera Center;
Berkeley, CA: Floricanto Press, 1988. p.
137-192. English. DESCR: *Academic
Achievement; Anglo Americans; Catholic
Church; Education; Educational Statistics;
Religious Education; *Secondary School
Education; *Women.

Professional Organizations

4740 Castillo, Sylvia. A guide to Hispanic
women's resources: a perspective on
networking among Hispanic women. CALIFORNIA
WOMEN, (December 1983), p. 2-6. English.
DESCR: *Directories; *Organizations; Women

4741 Gonzales, Sylvia Alicia. Hispanic American
voluntary organizations. Westport, CT:
Greenwood Press, 1985. xx, 267 p. English.
DESCR: Art Organizations and Groups;
*Community Organizations; Cultural
Organizations; *Directories; Educational
Organizations; *Organizations; Political
Parties and Organizations.

Programa Nacional Fronterizo (PRONAF)

4742 Bustamante, Jorge A. Maquiladoras: a new
face of international capitalism on Mexico's
northern frontier. IN: Nash, June and
Fernandez-Kelly, Patricia, eds. WOMEN, MEN,
AND THE INTERNATIONAL DIVISION OF LABOR.
Albany, NY: State University of New York
Press, 1983, p. 224-256. English. DESCR:
Banking Industry; Border Industrialization
Program (BIP); Border Industries; *Border
Region; Foreign Trade; Industrial Workers;
International Economic Relations; Mexico;
Population; United States-Mexico Relations;
Women; Working Women.

Project Concern International (PCI), San Diego, CA

4743 Hovell, Melbourne F. et al. Occupational
health risks for Mexican women: the case of
the maquiladora along the Mexican-United
States border. INTERNATIONAL JOURNAL OF
HEALTH SERVICES, Vol. 18, no. 4 (1988), p.
617-627. English. DESCR: *Border Industries;
Border Region; Mexico; *Occupational
Hazards; Public Health; Surveys; Tijuana,

Baja California, Mexico; Women; Working
Women.

Prose

4744 Anzaldua, Gloria. Borderlands/La frontera:
the new mestiza. San Francisco, CA:
Spinsters/Aunt Lute, 1987. 203 p. Bilingual.
DESCR: Aztecs; Border Region; *Identity;
Mythology; Poems; Sex Roles.

4745 Cisneros, Sandra. Do you know me?: I wrote
THE HOUSE ON MANGO STREET. THE AMERICAS
REVIEW, Vol. 15, no. 1 (Spring 1987), p.
77-79. English. DESCR: Authors;
Autobiography; Cisneros, Sandra; THE HOUSE
ON MANGO STREET.

4746 Cisneros, Sandra. Ghosts and voices: writing
from obsession. THE AMERICAS REVIEW, Vol.
15, no. 1 (Spring 1987), p. 69-73. English.
DESCR: *Authors; Autobiography; Cisneros,
Sandra.

4747 Cisneros, Sandra. Notes to a young(er)
writer. THE AMERICAS REVIEW, Vol. 15, no. 1
(Spring 1987), p. 74-76. English. DESCR:
*Authors; Autobiography; Cisneros, Sandra.

4748 Herrandez, Lisa, ed. and Benitez, Tina, ed.
Palabras chicanas: an undergraduate
anthology. Berkeley, CA: Mujeres en Marcha,
University of California, Berkeley, 1988. 97
p. Bilingual. DESCR: Literary Criticism;
*Literature; Poems; *Students.

4749 Herrera-Sobek, Maria, ed. and Viramontes,
Helena Maria, ed. Chicana creativity and
criticism: charting new frontiers in
American literature. Houston, TX: Arte
Publico Press, 1988. 190 p. Bilingual.
DESCR: Art; Literary Criticism; *Literature;
Poems.

4750 Moraga, Cherrie, ed. and Castillo, Ana, ed.
Esta [sic] puente, mi espalda: voces de
mujeres tercermundistas en los Estados
Unidos. San Francisco, CA: Ism Press, c1988.
[19], 281 p.: ill. Spanish. DESCR: Ethnic
Groups; *Feminism; Literary Criticism;
*Poems; *Women.

4751 Moraga, Cherrie, ed. and Anzaldua, Gloria,
ed. This bridge called my back: writings by
radical women of color. Watertown, MA:
Persephone Press, c1981. xxvi, 261 p.
English. DESCR: Ethnic Groups; *Feminism;
Literary Criticism; *Poems; *Women.

4752 Ramos, Juanita, ed. Companeras: Latina
lesbians (an anthology). New York: Latina
Lesbian History Project, 1987. xxix, 265 p.
Bilingual. DESCR: *Homosexuality;
*Literature; Poetry; *Women.

4753 Rebolledo, Tey Diana, ed.; Gonzales-Berry,
Erlinda, ed.; and Marquez, Maria Teresa, ed.
Las mujeres hablan: an anthology of Nuevo
Mexicana writers. Albuquerque, NM: El Norte
Publications, c1988. xiv, 210 p.: ill.
English. DESCR: *New Mexico; *Poems; *Short
Story.

4754 Sanchez, Rosaura. Chicana prose writers: the
case of Gina Valdes and Sylvia Lizarraga.
IN: Herrera-Sobek, Maria, ed. BEYOND
STEREOTYPES: THE CRITICAL ANALYSIS OF
CHICANA LITERATURE. Binghamton, NY:
Bilingual Press/Editorial Bilingue, 1985, p.
61-70. English. DESCR: *Authors; Literary
Criticism; *Lizarraga, Sylvia; *Valdes,
Gina.

Prose (cont.)

4755 Trujillo, Carla, ed. Chicana lesbians: the girls our mothers warned us about. Berkeley, CA: Third Woman Press, 1991. xii, 202 p.: ill. English. DESCR: *Homosexuality; Literary Criticism; Poems.

4756 Velasquez-Trevino, Gloria. Cultural ambivalence in early Chicana prose fiction. Thesis (Ph.D.)--Stanford University, 1985. 185 p. English. DESCR: Biculturalism; *Fiction; Gonzalez, Jovita; Literary Criticism; Mena, Maria Cristina; Niggli, Josephina; Sex Roles.

4757 Vigil, Evangelina, ed. Woman of her word: Hispanic women write. REVISTA CHICANO-RIQUENA, Vol. 11, no. 3-4 (Fall, Winter, 1983), p. [1]-180. Bilingual. DESCR: Art; Literary Criticism; *Literature; Poetry; *Women.

Prostitution

4758 Blackwelder, Julia Kirk. Women of the depression: caste and culture in San Antonio, 1929-1939. College Station, TX: Texas A&M University Press, 1984. xviii, 279 p.: ill. English. DESCR: Criminal Justice System; Cultural Characteristics; Employment; Family; Great Depression, 1929-1933; Labor Supply and Market; Labor Unions; San Antonio, TX; *Social Classes; *Women.

4759 Hser, Yih-Ing; Chou, Chih-Ping; and Anglin, M. Douglas. The criminality of female narcotics addicts: a causal modeling approach. JOURNAL OF QUANTITATIVE CRIMINOLOGY, Vol. 6, no. 2 (June 1990), p. 207-228. English. DESCR: Anglo Americans; Criminal Acts; *Drug Addicts; Drug Traffic; Women.

Protestant Church

4760 Jaech, Richard E. Latin American undocumented women in the United States. CURRENTS IN THEOLOGY AND MISSION, Vol. 9, no. 4 (August 1982), p. 196-211. English. DESCR: Garment Industry; Latin Americans; Socioeconomic Factors; *Undocumented Workers; *Women.

4761 Ruiz, Vicki L. Dead ends or gold mines?: using missionary records in Mexican-American women's history. FRONTIERS: A JOURNAL OF WOMEN STUDIES, Vol. 12, no. 1 (1991), p. 33-56. English. DESCR: Archives; Clergy; El Paso, TX; History; *Methodist Church; *Research Methodology; *Rose Gregory Houchen Settlement House, El Paso, TX.

Proyecto La Mujer Conference (Spring, 1982: Northern Illinois)

4762 Campos Carr, Irene. Proyecto La Mujer: Latina women shaping consciousness. WOMEN'S STUDIES INTERNATIONAL FORUM, Vol. 12, no. 1 (1989), p. 45-49. English. DESCR: Artists; Aurora, IL; Authors; Barrios; Conferences and Meetings; Elgin, IL; *Feminism; Joliet, IL; Poetry; Women.

Psychiatry

4763 Velasquez, Roberto J.; Callahan, Wendell J.; and Carrillo, Ricardo. MMPI differences among Mexican-American male and female psychiatric inpatients. PSYCHOLOGICAL REPORTS, Vol. 68, no. 1 (February 1991), p. 123-127. English. DESCR: Comparative Psychology; Males; Minnesota Multiphasic Personality Inventory (MMPI); Personality; *Psychological Testing; Sex Roles.

Psychohistory

4764 Phillips, Rachel. Marina/Malinche: masks and shadows. IN: Miller, Beth, ed. WOMEN IN HISPANIC LITERATURE: ICONS AND FALLEN IDOLS. Berkeley, CA: University of California Press, 1983, p. 97-114. English. DESCR: Aztecs; History; Malinche; *Symbolism.

Psychological Testing

4765 Buriel, Raymond and Saenz, Evangelina. Psychocultural characteristics of college-bound and noncollege-bound Chicanas. JOURNAL OF SOCIAL PSYCHOLOGY, Vol. 110, (April 1980), p. 245-251. English. DESCR: Biculturalism; *Biculturalism Inventory for Mexican American Students (BIMAS); Higher Education; Identity; Income; Sex Roles; Social Psychology.

4766 Gibbs, Jewelle Taylor. Personality patterns of delinquent females: ethnic and sociocultural variations. JOURNAL OF CLINICAL PSYCHOLOGY, Vol. 38, no. 1 (January 1982), p. 198-206. English. DESCR: Ethnic Groups; Identity; *Juvenile Delinquency; Personality; Socioeconomic Factors.

4767 Hawley, Peggy and Even, Brenda. Work and sex-role attitudes in relation to education and other characteristics. VOCATIONAL GUIDANCE QUARTERLY, Vol. 31, no. 2 (December 1982), p. 101-108. English. DESCR: Attitudes; Careers; Education; Ethnic Groups; *Sex Roles; Working Women.

4768 Lara-Cantu, M. Asuncion and Navarro-Arias, Roberto. Positive and negative factors in the measurement of sex roles: findings from a Mexican sample. HISPANIC JOURNAL OF BEHAVIORAL SCIENCES, Vol. 8, no. 2 (June 1986), p. 143-155. English. DESCR: Bem Sex Role Inventory (BSRI); Mexico; *Sex Roles.

4769 Lara-Cantu, M. Asuncion. A sex role inventory with scales for "machismo" and "self-sacrificing woman". JOURNAL OF CROSS-CULTURAL PSYCHOLOGY, Vol. 20, no. 4 (December 1989), p. 396-398. English. DESCR: Machismo; *Masculine-Feminine Personality Traits Scale; *Personality; *Sex Roles.

4770 Lawrence, Alberto Augusto. Traditional attitudes toward marriage, marital adjustment, acculturation, and self-esteem of Mexican-American and Mexican wives. Thesis (Ph.D.)--United States International University, San Diego, CA, 1982. ix, 191 p. English. DESCR: *Acculturation; *Attitudes; Machismo; *Marriage; Mental Health; San Ysidro, CA; Sex Roles; Sex Stereotypes; Tijuana, Baja California, Mexico; Women.

4771 Long, John M. and Vigil, James Diego. Cultural styles and adolescent sex role perceptions: an exploration of responses to a value picture projective test. IN: Melville, Margarita B., ed. TWICE A MINORITY. St. Louis, MO: Mosby, 1980, p. 164-172. English. DESCR: *Sex Roles; Youth.

Psychological Testing
      (cont.)

4772 Martinez, Estella A. Child behavior in
     Mexican American/Chicano families: maternal
     teaching and child-rearing practices. FAMILY
     RELATIONS, Vol. 37, no. 3 (July 1988), p.
     275-280. English. DESCR: *Acculturation;
     Family; Maternal Teaching Observation
     Technique (MTOT); Parent and Child
     Relationships; *Parenting; Socioeconomic
     Factors; Values.

4773 Shapiro, Johanna and Tittle, Ken. Maternal
     adaptation to child disability in a Hispanic
     population. FAMILY RELATIONS, Vol. 39, no. 2
     (April 1990), p. 179-185. English. DESCR:
     Children; *Handicapped; *Parent and Child
     Relationships; *Stress.

4774 Smith, Bradford M. The measurement of
     narcissism in Asian, Caucasian, and Hispanic
     American women. PSYCHOLOGICAL REPORTS, Vol.
     67, no. 3 (December 1990), p. 779-785.
     English. DESCR: Anglo Americans; Asian
     Americans; Comparative Psychology; Cultural
     Characteristics; *Narcissistic Personality
     Inventory; *Personality; *Women.

4775 Terrazas, Olga Esperanza. The self-concept
     of Mexican-American adolescent females.
     Thesis (Ph.D.)--Wright Institute, 1980. 262
     p. English. DESCR: *Identity; *Youth.

4776 Velasquez, Roberto J.; Callahan, Wendell C.;
     and Carrillo, Ricardo. MMPI differences
     among Mexican-American male and female
     psychiatric inpatients. PSYCHOLOGICAL
     REPORTS, Vol. 68, no. 1 (February 1991), p.
     123-127. English. DESCR: Comparative
     Psychology; Males; Minnesota Multiphasic
     Personality Inventory (MMPI); Personality
     Psychiatry; Sex Roles.

Psychology

4777 Amaro, Hortensia; Russo, Nancy Felipe; and
     Pares-Avila, Jose A. Contemporary research
     on Hispanic women: a selected bibliography
     of the social science literature. PSYCHOLOGY
     OF WOMEN QUARTERLY, Vol. 11, no. 4 (December
     1987), p. 523-532. English. DESCR:
     *Bibliography; Social Science; *Women.

4778 Amaro, Hortensia. Hispanic women in
     psychology: a resource directory.
     Washington, DC: American Psychological
     Association, 1984. ii, 41 p. English.
     DESCR: *Directories; *Women.

4779 Navar, Isabelle. La Mexicana: an image of
     strength. AGENDA, no. 4 (Spring 1974), p.
     3-5. English. DESCR: Family; Feminism;
     *Identity; Sexism; Working Women.

4780 Navar, Isabelle. La Mexicana: an image of
     strength. REGENERACION, Vol. 2, no. 4
     (1974), p. 4-6. English. DESCR: Family;
     Feminism; *Identity; Sexism; Working Women.

4781 Newton, Frank; Olmedo, Esteban L.; and
     Padilla, Amado M. Hispanic mental health
     research: a reference guide. Berkeley, CA:
     University of California Press, c1982. 685
     p. English. DESCR: Anthropology;
     *Bibliography; Education; Medical Care;
     *Mental Health; Public Health; *Reference
     Works; Sociology.

4782 Nieto Senour, Maria. Psychology of the
     Chicana. IN: Martinez, Joe L., Jr., ed.
     CHICANO PSYCHOLOGY. New York: Academic
     Press, 1977, p. 329-342. English. DESCR:
     Academic Achievement; Acculturation;

Cultural Customs; Identity; Sex Roles.

4783 Olivarez, Elizabeth. Women's rights and the
     Mexican American woman. REGENERACION, Vol.
     2, no. 4 (1975), p. 40-42. English. DESCR:
     Education; *Feminism; Identity; Politics;
     Religion; Sex Roles.

4784 Vasquez, Melba J. T. Power and status of the
     Chicana: a social-psychological perspective.
     IN: Martinez, Joe L., Jr., ed. CHICANO
     PSYCHOLOGY. 2nd. ed. Orlando, FL: Academic
     Press, 1984, p. 269-287. English. DESCR:
     *Identity; Income; *Mental Health; *Sex
     Roles; Socialization; Working Women.

Psychotherapy

4785 Arevalo, Rodolfo, ed. and Minor, Marianne,
     ed. Chicanas and alcoholism: a sociocultural
     perspective of women. San Jose, CA: School
     of Social Work, San Jose State University,
     c1981. 55 p. English. DESCR: *Alcoholism;
     Drug Abuse Programs; Family; Feminism;
     Natural Support Systems; Preventative
     Medicine.

4786 Bach-y-Rita, George. The Mexican-American:
     religious and cultural influences. IN:
     Becerra, Rosina M., et al., eds. MENTAL
     HEALTH AND HISPANIC AMERICANS: CLINICAL
     PERSPECTIVES. New York: Grune & Stratton,
     1982, p. 29-40. English. DESCR: Catholic
     Church; Cultural Characteristics; Culture;
     Language Usage; Machismo; *Mental Health;
     Religion.

4787 Cuellar, Israel, et al. Clinical psychiatric
     case presentation; culturally responsive
     diagnostic formulation and treatment in an
     Hispanic female. HISPANIC JOURNAL OF
     BEHAVIORAL SCIENCES, Vol. 5, no. 1 (March
     1983), p. 93-103. English. DESCR:
     Acculturation Rating Scale for Mexican
     Americans (ARSMA); Case Studies; Medical
     Care.

4788 Espin, Oliva M. Cultural and historical
     influences on sexuality in Hispanic/Latin
     women: implications for psychotherapy. IN:
     Vance, Carole S., ed. PLEASURE AND DANGER:
     EXPLORING FEMALE SEXUALITY. Boston, MA:
     Routledge & Kegan Paul, 1984, p. 149-164.
     English. DESCR: Immigration; Language Usage;
     Machismo; Sex Roles; *Sexual Behavior;
     Social History and Conditions; Spanish
     Influence; *Women.

4789 Franklin, Gerald S. and Kaufman, Karen S.
     Group psychotherapy for elderly female
     Hispanic outpatients. HOSPITAL AND COMMUNITY
     PSYCHIATRY, Vol. 33, no. 5 (May 1982), p.
     335-387. English. DESCR: Ancianos.

4790 Gonzalez del Valle, Amalia and Usher, Mary.
     Group therapy with aged Latino women: a
     pilot project and study. CLINICAL
     GERONTOLOGIST, Vol. 1, no. 1 (Fall 1982), p.
     51-58. English. DESCR: *Ancianos; Cultural
     Characteristics; Mental Illness; San Mateo
     County, CA.

4791 Hardy-Fanta, Carol and Montana, Priscila.
     The Hispanic female adolescent: a group
     therapy model. INTERNATIONAL JOURNAL OF
     GROUP PSYCHOTHERAPY, Vol. 32, no. 3 (July
     1982), p. 351-366. English. DESCR: Puerto
     Ricans; *Women; Youth.

Psychotherapy (cont.)

4792 Juarez, Reina Maria. Evaluation of three treatment modalities with preorgasmic Hispanic women treated without partners. Thesis (Ph.D.)--California School of Professional Psychology, Los Angeles, 1982. 236 p. English. **DESCR**: *Sexual Behavior.

4793 Vargas-Willis, Gloria and Cervantes, Richard C. Consideration of psychosocial stress in the treatment of the Latina immigrant. HISPANIC JOURNAL OF BEHAVIORAL SCIENCES, Vol. 9, no. 3 (September 1987), p. 315-329. English. **DESCR**: Discrimination in Employment; *Immigrants; Mental Health; *Stress.

4794 Zuniga, Maria E. Assessment issues with Chicanas: practice implications. PSYCHOTHERAPY, Vol. 25, no. 2 (Summer 1988), p. 288-293. English. **DESCR**: Acculturation; Colleges and Universities; Family; Identity; *Mental Health; Mexican-American Outreach Program, San Diego State University; *Students.

Public Education
USE: Education

Public Health

4795 Aguilar, Marian Angela. Patterns of health care utilization of Mexican American women. Thesis (Ph.D.)--University of Illinois at Urbana-Champaign, 1983. v, 147 p. English. **DESCR**: Income; Insurance; *Medical Care; Public Policy.

4796 Andrade, Sally J., ed. Latino families in the United States: a resource book for family life education = Las familias latinas en los Estados Unidos: recursos para la capacitacion familiar. [S.l.]: Planned Parenthood Federation of America, Inc., 1983. ix, 79, 70, xi p. Bilingual. **DESCR**: Bilingualism; Community Organizations; Education; *Family; Mental Health.

4797 Bauer, Richard L. Ethnic differences in hip fracture: a reduced incidence in Mexican-Americans. AMERICAN JOURNAL OF EPIDEMIOLOGY, Vol. 127, no. 1 (January 1988), p. 145-149. English. **DESCR**: Anglo Americans; Bexar County, TX; Blacks; Medical Care; Osteoporosis.

4798 Bauer, Richard L., et al. Risk of postmenopausal hip fracture in Mexican-American women. AMERICAN JOURNAL OF PUBLIC HEALTH, Vol. 76, no. 8 (August 1986), p. 1020-1021. English. **DESCR**: *Ancianos.

4799 Castro, Felipe G.; Furth, Pauline; and Karlow, Herbert. The health beliefs of Mexican, Mexican American and Anglo American women. HISPANIC JOURNAL OF BEHAVIORAL SCIENCES, Vol. 6, no. 4 (December 1984), p. 365-383. English. **DESCR**: Anglo Americans.

4800 de la Torre, Adela and Rush, Lynda. The determinants of breastfeeding for Mexican migrant women. INTERNATIONAL MIGRATION REVIEW, Vol. 21, no. 3 (Fall 1987), p. 728-742. English. **DESCR**: *Breastfeeding; Farm Workers; Maternal and Child Welfare; Migrant Health Services; Migrant Labor; Migration; Working Women.

4801 Dowling, Patrick T. and Fisher, Michael. Maternal factors and low birthweight infants: a comparison of Blacks with Mexican-Americans. JOURNAL OF FAMILY PRACTICE, Vol. 25, no. 2 (August 1987), p.

153-158. English. **DESCR**: Blacks; Cook County, IL; *Infant Mortality; *Prenatal Care; *Socioeconomic Factors.

4802 Farrell, Janice and Markides, Kyriakos S. Marriage and health: a three-generation study of Mexican Americans. JOURNAL OF MARRIAGE AND THE FAMILY, Vol. 47, no. 4 (November 1985), p. 1029-1036. English. **DESCR**: *Marriage.

4803 Franks, Adele L.; Binkin, Nancy J.; and Snider, Dixie E. Isoniazid hepatitis among pregnant and postpartum Hispanic patients. PUBLIC HEALTH REPORTS, Vol. 104, no. 2 (March, April, 1989), p. 151-155. English. **DESCR**: Fertility; *Hepatitis; Vital Statistics.

4804 Guttmacher, Sally. Women migrant workers in the U.S. CULTURAL SURVIVAL QUARTERLY, Vol. 8, no. 2 (Summer 1984), p. 60-61. English. **DESCR**: *Migrant Labor; Undocumented Workers; *Women.

4805 Hazuda, Helen P., et al. Employment status and women's protection against coronary heart disease. AMERICAN JOURNAL OF EPIDEMIOLOGY, Vol. 123, no. 4 (April 1986), p. 623-640. English. **DESCR**: Anglo Americans; Diseases; Employment; *Heart Disease; Nutrition; San Antonio, TX.

4806 Holck, Susan E. Lung cancer mortality and smoking habits: Mexican-American women. AMERICAN JOURNAL OF PUBLIC HEALTH, Vol. 72, no. 1 (January 1982), p. 38-42. English. **DESCR**: Anglo Americans; Cancer; *Smoking.

4807 Hovell, Melbourne F., et al. Occupational health risks for Mexican women: the case of the maquiladora along the Mexican-United States border. INTERNATIONAL JOURNAL OF HEALTH SERVICES, Vol. 18, no. 4 (1988), p. 617-627. English. **DESCR**: *Border Industries; Border Region; Mexico; *Occupational Hazards; Project Concern International (PCI), San Diego, CA; Surveys; Tijuana, Baja California, Mexico; Women; Working Women.

4808 Krause, Neal and Markides, Kyriakos S. Gender roles, illness, and illness behavior in a Mexican American population. SOCIAL SCIENCE QUARTERLY, Vol. 68, no. 1 (March 1987), p. 102-121. English. **DESCR**: Family; San Antonio, TX; *Sex Roles.

4809 Manzanedo, Hector Garcia; Walters, Esperanza Garcia; and Lorig, Kate R. Health and illness perceptions of the Chicana. IN: Melville, Margarita B., ed. TWICE A MINORITY. St. Louis, MO: Mosby, 1980, p. 191-207. English. **DESCR**: Cultural Characteristics; Culture; *Medical Care; Sex Roles; Values.

4810 Newton, Frank; Olmedo, Esteban L.; and Padilla, Amado M. Hispanic mental health research: a reference guide. Berkeley, CA: University of California Press, c1982. 685 p. English. **DESCR**: Anthropology; *Bibliography; Education; Medical Care; *Mental Health; Psychology; *Reference Works; Sociology.

4811 Notzon, Francis Claude. Factors associated with low birth weight in Mexican-Americans and Mexicans. Thesis (Ph.D.)--John Hopkins University, 1989. 190 p. English. **DESCR**: Anglo Americans; Fertility; *Maternal and Child Welfare; Mexico; *Prenatal Care; *Women.

Public Health (cont.)

4812 Olivares, Yvette. The sweatshop: the garment industry's reborn child. REVISTA MUJERES, Vol. 3, no. 2 (June 1986), p. 55-62. English. DESCR: Garment Industry; Labor; Third World; *Undocumented Workers; *Women; Working Women.

4813 Padgett, Deborah. Aging minority women. WOMEN & HEALTH, Vol. 14, no. 3-4 (1988), p. 213-225. English. DESCR: *Ancianos; Low Income; *Women.

4814 Peters, Ruth K., et al. Risk factors for invasive cervical cancer among Latinas and non-Latinas in Los Angeles County. JOURNAL OF THE NATIONAL CANCER INSTITUTE, Vol. 77, no. 5 (November 1986), p. 1063-1077. English. DESCR: *Cancer; Diseases; Educational Levels; Los Angeles County, CA; Women.

4815 Ponce-Adame, Merrihelen. Latinas and breast cancer. NUESTRO, Vol. 6, no. 8 (October 1982), p. 30-31. English. DESCR: Cancer.

4816 Salazar, Sandra A. Chicanas as healers. IN: LA CHICANA: BUILDING FOR THE FUTURE, AN ACTION PLAN FOR THE 80s. Oakland, CA: National Hispanic University, 1981, p. 107-119. English. DESCR: Federal Aid; *Medical Care.

4817 Salazar, Sandra A. Reproductive choice for Hispanas. AGENDA, Vol. 9, no. 4 (July, August, 1979), p. 31-33, 36. English. DESCR: Abortion; Medical Care; Sterilization.

4818 Solis, Faustina. Commentary on the Chicana and health services. IN: Sanchez, Rosaura and Martinez Cruz, Rosa, eds. ESSAYS ON LA MUJER. Los Angeles, CA: Chicano Studies Center Publications, UCLA, 1977, p. 82-90. English. DESCR: Medical Personnel; Sex Roles.

4819 Sorel, Janet Elaine. The relationship between gender role incongruity on measures of coping and material resources and blood pressure among Mexican-American women. Thesis (Ph.D.)--University of North Carolina at Chapel Hill, 1988. 268 p. English. DESCR: High Blood Pressure; Hispanic Health and Nutrition Examination Survey (HHANES); Hypertension; *Sex Roles; *Stress.

4820 Sweeny, Mary Anne and Gulino, Claire. The health belief model as an explanation for breast-feeding practices in a Hispanic population. ANS: ADVANCES IN NURSING SCIENCE, Vol. 9, no. 4 (July 1987), p. 35-50. English. DESCR: *Breastfeeding; *Cultural Customs; San Diego, CA; Tijuana, Baja California, Mexico; Women.

4821 Vega, William A., et al. Depressive symptoms and their correlates among immigrant Mexican women in the United States. SOCIAL SCIENCE & MEDICINE, Vol. 22, no. 6 (1986), p. 645-652. English. DESCR: Depression (Psychological); *Immigrants; *Mental Health; San Diego, CA.

Public Hygiene
    USE: Public Health

Public Policy

4822 Aguilar, Marian Angela. Patterns of health care utilization of Mexican American women. Thesis (Ph.D.)--University of Illinois at Urbana-Champaign, 1983. v, 147 p. English. DESCR: Income; Insurance; *Medical Care;

*Public Health.

4823 Carcenas, Gilbert and Flores, Estevan T. The migration and settlement of undocumented women. Austin, TX: CMAS Publications, 1986. 69 p. English. DESCR: Employment; Houston, TX; *Immigration; Income; Labor Supply and Market; *Migration Patterns; Socioeconomic Factors; *Undocumented Workers.

4824 Chacon, Maria A., et al. Chicanas in postsecondary education. Stanford, CA: Center for Research on Women, Stanford University, 1982. iii, 106, [68] p. English. DESCR: Colleges and Universities; *Higher Education; *Surveys.

4825 Del Castillo, Adelaida R., et al. An assessment of the status of the education of Hispanic American women. IN: McKenna, Teresa and Ortiz, Flora Ida, eds. THE BROKEN WEB: THE EDUCATIONAL EXPERIENCE OF HISPANIC WOMEN. Claremont, CA: Tomas Rivera Center; Berkeley, CA: Floricanto Press, 1988, p. 3-24. English. DESCR: Academic Achievement; Conferences and Meetings; Discrimination in Education; Dropouts; *Education; Higher Education; Research Methodology; The Educational Experience of Hispanic American Women [symposium] (1985: Claremont, CA); *Women.

4826 Delgado, Jane L. Adolescent pregnancy: an overview. IN: National Hispanic Center for Advanced Studies and Policy Analysis and National Hispanic University. THE STATE OF HISPANIC AMERICA. VOL. VI. Oakland, CA: National Hispanic University, c1987, p. 37-49. English. DESCR: Family Planning; *Fertility; *Youth.

4827 Gonzalez, Francisca. Steps for developing an idea into a public policy. IN: Sosa Riddell, Adaljiza, ed. POLICY DEVELOPMENT: CHICANA/LATINA SUMMER RESEARCH INSTITUTE. Davis, CA: [Chicano Studies Program, University of California, Davis, 1989?], p. 9-11. English.

4828 Jensen, Joan M. Commentary [on "And Miles to Go": Mexican Women and Work, 1930-1985]. IN: Schlissel, Lillian, et al., eds. WESTERN WOMEN: THEIR LAND, THEIR LIVES. Albuquerque, NM: University of New Mexico Press, 1988, p. 141-144. English. DESCR: "'And Miles to Go...': Mexican Women and Work, 1930-1985"; California; Employment; Income; Labor Unions; Ruiz, Vicki L.; Women; *Working Women.

4829 Menchaca, Luisa. Translating ideas of public policy into public institutions. IN: Sosa Riddell, Adaljiza, ed. POLICY DEVELOPMENT: CHICANA/LATINA SUMMER RESEARCH INSTITUTE. Davis, CA: [Chicano Studies Program, University of California, Davis, 1989?], p. 12, 15. English.

4830 Sosa Riddell, Adaljiza. Background: a critical overview on Chicanas/Latinas and public policies. IN: Sosa Riddell, Adaljiza, ed. POLICY DEVELOPMENT: CHICANA/LATINA SUMMER RESEARCH INSTITUTE. Davis, CA: [Chicano Studies Program, University of California, Davis, 1989?], p. 2-8. English. DESCR: Discrimination; Educational Administration; Sexism.

Public Policy (cont.)

4831 Sosa Riddell, Adaljiza. Bibliography on Chicanas and public policy. IN: Sosa Riddell, Adaljiza, ed. POLICY DEVELOPMENT: CHICANA/LATINA SUMMER RESEARCH INSTITUTE. Davis, CA: [Chicano Studies Program, University of California, Davis, 1989?], p. 27-29. English. **DESCR:** *Bibliography.

4832 Sosa Riddell, Adaljiza, ed. Policy development: Chicana/Latina Summer Research Institute [handbook]. Davis, CA: [Chicano Studies Program, UC Davis, 1989?]. 29 p. English. **DESCR:** *Chicana/Latina Summer Research Institute (August 19, 1989: Santa Clara University); Conferences and Meetings.

4833 Sosa Riddell, Adaljiza. Synopsis on Senate Concurrent Resolution 43: an example in public policy making. IN: Sosa Riddell, Adaljiza, ed. POLICY DEVELOPMENT: CHICANA/LATINA SUMMER RESEARCH INSTITUTE. Davis, CA: [Chicano Studies Program, University of California, Davis, 1989?], p. 16-26. English. **DESCR:** Legislation; Senate Concurrent Resolution 43, 1987; University of California.

Public Welfare
USE: Welfare

Publications
USE: Books

Publishing Industry

4834 Lucero, Marcela Christine. Resources for the Chicana feminist scholar. IN: Treichler, Paula A., et al., eds. FOR ALMA MATER: THEORY AND PRACTICE IN FEMINIST SCHOLARSHIP. Urbana: University of Illinois Press, 1985, p. 393-401. English. **DESCR:** *Chicana Studies; *Feminism; Literature Reviews; Research Methodology.

Pueblo Indians

4835 Gutierrez, Ramon A. When Jesus came, the corn mothers went away: marriage, sexuality, and power in New Mexico, 1500-1846. Stanford: Stanford University Pres, 1991. xxxi, 424 p. English. **DESCR:** *Marriage; Native Americans; *New Mexico; *Sex Roles; Sexual Behavior; Spanish Influence; Women.

Pueblos
USE: Barrios

Puerto Ricans

4836 Alarcon, Norma. Latina writers in the United States. IN: Marting, Diane E., ed. SPANISH AMERICAN WOMEN WRITERS: A BIO-BIBLIOGRAPHICAL SOURCE BOOK. New York: Greenwood Press, 1990, p. [557]-567. English. **DESCR:** *Authors; *Bibliography; BREAKING BOUNDARIES: LATINA WRITING AND CRITICAL READINGS; Cubanos; Intergroup Relations; Language Usage; *Literature Reviews; THIRD WOMAN [journal]; *Women.

4837 Andrade, Sally J. Family roles of Hispanic women: stereotypes, empirical findings, and implications for research. IN: Zambrana, Ruth E., ed. WORK, FAMILY, AND HEALTH: LATINA WOMEN IN TRANSITION. Bronx, NY: Hispanic Research Center, Fordham University, 1982, p. 95-106. English. **DESCR:** *Family; *Research Methodology; *Sex Roles; Sex Stereotypes; Women.

4838 Bean, Frank D.; Swicegood, Gray; and King, Allan G. Role incompatibility and the relationship between fertility and labor supply among Hispanic women. IN: Borjas, George J. and Tienda, Marta, eds. HISPANICS IN THE U.S. ECONOMY. Orlando, FL: Academic Press, 1985, p. 221-242. English. **DESCR:** Cubanos; *Employment; Fertility; Labor Supply and Market.

4839 Del Castillo, Adelaida R. Sterilization: an overview. IN: Mora, Magdalena and Del Castillo, Adelaida, eds. MEXICAN WOMEN IN THE UNITED STATES: STRUGGLES PAST AND PRESENT. Los Angeles, CA: Chicano Studies Research Center, UCLA, 1980, p. 65-70. English. **DESCR:** *Sterilization; Women.

4840 Estrada, Iliad. Hispanic feminists meet--it's a trip. LA LUZ, Vol. 8, no. 7 (August, September, 1980), p. 35. English. **DESCR:** Conferences and Meetings; Feminism; National Hispanic Feminist Conference (March 28-31, 1980: San Jose, CA).

4841 Fanelli-Kuczmarski, Marie T., et al. Folate status of Mexican American, Cuban, and Puerto Rican women. AMERICAN JOURNAL OF CLINICAL NUTRITION, Vol. 52, no. 2 (August 1990), p. 368-372. English. **DESCR:** Cubanos; *Folic Acid Deficiency; Hispanic Health and Nutrition Examination Survey (HHANES); *Nutrition; *Women.

4842 Fennelly, Katherine and Ortiz, Vilma. Childbearing among young Latino women in the United States. AMERICAN JOURNAL OF PUBLIC HEALTH, Vol. 77, no. 1 (January 1987), p. 25-28. English. **DESCR:** *Ethnic Groups; *Fertility; Women; *Youth.

4843 Frisbie, William Parker. Variation in patterns of marital instability among Hispanics. JOURNAL OF MARRIAGE AND THE FAMILY, Vol. 48, no. 1 (February 1986), p. 99-106. English. **DESCR:** Cubanos; *Marriage.

4844 Hadley-Freydberg, Elizabeth. Prostitutes, concubines, whores and bitches: Black and Hispanic women in contemporary American film. IN: McCluskey, Audrey T., ed. WOMEN OF COLOR: PERSPECTIVES ON FEMINISM AND IDENTITY. Bloomington, IN: Women's Studies Program, Indiana University, 1985, p. 46-65. English. **DESCR:** *Actors and Actresses; Blacks; *Films; *Sex Stereotypes; Stereotypes; Women.

4845 Hardy-Fanta, Carol and Montana, Priscila. The Hispanic female adolescent: a group therapy model. INTERNATIONAL JOURNAL OF GROUP PSYCHOTHERAPY, Vol. 32, no. 3 (July 1982), p. 351-366. English. **DESCR:** Psychotherapy; *Women; Youth.

4846 Markides, Kyriakos S. Consequences of gender differentials in life expectancy for Black and Hispanic Americans. INTERNATIONAL JOURNAL OF AGING & HUMAN DEVELOPMENT, Vol. 29, no. 2 (1989), p. 95-102. English. **DESCR:** *Ancianos; Blacks; Census; Cubanos; Latin Americans; Males; Population; U.S. Bureau of the Census.

4847 McCracken, Ellen. Latina narrative and politics of signification: articulation, antagonism, and populist rupture. CRITICA, Vol. 2, no. 2 (Fall 1990), p. 202-207. English. **DESCR:** *Cisneros, Sandra; IN NUEVA YORK; *Literary Criticism; *Mohr, Nicolasa; RITUALS OF SURVIVAL; Short Story; THE HOUSE ON MANGO STREET; Women.

Puerto Ricans (cont.)

4848 Miller, Elaine N. and Sternbach, Nancy
Saporta. Selected bibliography. IN:
Horno-Delgado, Asuncion, et al., eds.
BREAKING BOUNDARIES: LATINA WRITING AND
CRITICAL READINGS. Amherst, MA: University
of Massachusetts Press, c1989, p. 251-263.
English. DESCR: *Bibliography; Cubanos;
Literary Criticism; *Literature; *Women.

4849 Nieves-Squires, Sarah. Hispanic women:
making their presence on campus less
tenuous. Washington, DC: Association of
American Colleges, c1991. 14 p. English.
DESCR: Afro-Hispanics; Colleges and
Universities; Cubanos; *Discrimination in
Education; *Higher Education; *Women.

4850 Oliveira, Annette. Remarkable Latinas. IN:
HISPANICS AND GRANTMAKERS: A SPECIAL REPORT
OF FOUNDATION NEWS. Washington, DC: Council
on Foundations, 1981, p. 34. English.
DESCR: Biography; Leadership; Women.

4851 Romero-Gwynn, Eunice and Carias, Lucia.
Breast-feeding intentions and practice among
Hispanic mothers in Southern California.
PEDIATRICS, Vol. 84, no. 4 (October 1989),
p. 626-632. English. DESCR: *Breastfeeding
Cubanos; Expanded Food and Nutrition
Education Program; Immigrants; Southern
California; Women.

4852 Stroup-Benham, Christine A. and Trevino,
Fernando M. Reproductive characteristics of
Mexican-American, mainland Puerto Rican, and
Cuban-American women: data from the Hispanic
Health and Nutrition Examination Survey.
JAMA: JOURNAL OF THE AMERICAN MEDICAL
ASSOCIATION, Vol. 265, no. 2 (January 9,
1991), p. 222-226. English. DESCR: *Birth
Control; Breastfeeding; Cubanos; *Fertility;
Hispanic Health and Nutrition Examination
Survey (HHANES); *Women.

4853 Tienda, Marta and Angel, Ronald J. Headship
and household composition among Blacks,
Hispanics and other whites. SOCIAL FORCES,
Vol. 61, no. 2 (December 1982), p. 508-531.
English. DESCR: Anglo Americans; Blacks;
Cultural Characteristics; Extended Family;
*Family; Single Parents.

4854 Tienda, Marta and Guhleman, Patricia. The
occupational position of employed Hispanic
women. IN: Borjas, George J. and Tienda,
Marta, eds. HISPANICS IN THE U.S. ECONOMY
Orlando, FL: Academic Press, 1985, p.
243-273. English. DESCR: *Employment;
Identity.

4855 U.S. National Institute of Education.
Conference on the educational and
occupational needs of Hispanic women, June
29-30, 1976; December 10-12, 1976.
Washington, DC: U.S. Department of
Education, 1980. x, 301 p. English. DESCR:
Conference on the Educational and
Occupational Needs of Hispanic Women (1976:
Denver, CO); Conferences and Meetings;
*Education; *Employment; Higher Education;
Leadership; Sex Roles; *Women.

4856 Valtierra, Mary. Acculturation, social
support, and reported stress of Latina
physicians. Thesis (Ph.D.)--California
School of Professional Psychology, 1989. 136
p. English. DESCR: *Acculturation; Careers;
Cubanos; Immigration; Latin Americans;
*Medical Personnel; *Stress; *Women.

4857 Vazquez-Nuttall, Ena; Romero-Garcia, Ivonne;
and De Leon, Brunilda. Sex roles and
perceptions of femininity and masculinity of
Hispanic women: a review of the literature.
PSYCHOLOGY OF WOMEN QUARTERLY, Vol. 11, no.
4 (December 1987), p. 409-425. English.
DESCR: Attitudes; *Chicanismo; *Literature
Reviews; Machismo; *Sex Roles; *Women.

4858 Vivo, Paquita. Voces de Hispanas: Hispanic
women and their concerns. IN: HISPANICS AND
GRANTMAKERS: A SPECIAL REPORT OF FOUNDATION
NEWS. Washington, DC: Council on
Foundations, 1981, p. 35-39. English.
DESCR: *Mexican American Women's National
Association (MANA).

4859 Worth, Dooley and Rodriguez, Ruth. Latina
women and AIDS. SIECUS REPORT, (January,
February, 1986), p. 5-7. English. DESCR:
Cultural Characteristics; Drug Addicts; Drug
Use; Health Education; Natural Support
Systems; New York; Preventative Medicine;
Sex Roles; *Vital Statistics; Women.

4860 Zayas, Luis H. Toward an understanding of
suicide risks in young Hispanic females.
JOURNAL OF ADOLESCENT RESEARCH, Vol. 2, no.
1 (Spring 1987), p. 1-11. English. DESCR:
Acculturation; Cubanos; Cultural
Characteristics; Depression (Psychological);
Mental Health; *Suicide; *Women; *Youth.

Puerto Rico

4861 Paritz, Daniel R., et al. The role of
machismo and the Hispanic family in the
etiology and treatment of alcoholism in the
Hispanic American males. AMERICAN JOURNAL OF
FAMILY THERAPY, Vol. 11, no. 1 (Spring
1983), p. 31-44. English. DESCR:
*Alcoholism; Children; Family; *Machismo;
Socioeconomic Factors.

Quinceaneras

4862 Erevia, Angela. Quinceanera. San Antonio,
TX: Mexican American Cultural Center, 1980.
xiii, 73 p. English. DESCR: Catholic Church;
*Cultural Customs.

4863 Macklin, June and Teniente de Costilla,
Alvina. Virgen de Guadalupe and the American
dream: the melting pot bubbles on in Toledo,
Ohio. IN: West, Stanley A. and Macklin,
June, eds. THE CHICANO EXPERIENCE. Boulder,
CO: Westview Press, 1979, p. 111-143.
English. DESCR: Assimilation; Catholic
Church; *Identity; Intermarriage; La Virgen
de Guadalupe; Migration Patterns; Toledo,
OH.

Quintero, Juanita

4864 Del Zotto, Augusta. Latinas with AIDS: life
expectancy for Hispanic women is a startling
45 days after diagnosis. THIS WORLD, (April
9, 1989), p. 9. English. DESCR: Abortion;
AIDS (Disease); Condom Use; Instituto
Familiar de la Raza, San Francisco, CA;
Machismo; *Mano a Mano; Sex Roles; Women Men
Relations.

Race Awareness
USE: Identity

Race Identity
USE: Identity

Race Relations
USE: Intergroup Relations

Racism
USE: Discrimination

Radio

4865 Lopez-Trevino, Maria Elena. A radio model: a community strategy to address the problems and needs of Mexican-American women farmworkers. Thesis (M.S.)--California State University, Long Beach, 1989. 179 p. English. DESCR: Coachella, CA; *Farm Workers; Income; Low Income; Occupational Hazards; *Sex Roles.

RAICES DE SANGRE [film]

4866 Morales, Sylvia. Chicano-produced celluloid mujeres. BILINGUAL REVIEW, Vol. 10, no. 2-3 (May, December, 1983), p. 89-93. English. DESCR: BALLAD OF GREGORIO CORTEZ [film]; Film Reviews; *Films; SEGUIN [movie]; *Stereotypes; ZOOT SUIT [film].

4867 Ordonez, Elizabeth J. La imagen de la mujer en el nuevo cine chicano. CARACOL, Vol. 5, no. 2 (October 1978), p. 12-13. Spanish. DESCR: Bonilla-Giannini, Roxanna; *Films; Lopez, Lexore; ONLY ONCE IN A LIFETIME [film]; *Photography; Robelo, Miguel; Sex Stereotypes.

THE RAIN GOD: A DESERT TALE

4868 Gutierrez Castillo, Dina. La imagen de la mujer en la novela fronteriza. IN: Lopez-Gonzalez, Aralia, et al., eds. MUJER Y LITERATURA MEXICANA Y CHICANA: CULTURAS EN CONTACTO. Mexico: Colegio de la Frontera Norte, 1988, p. [55]-63. Spanish. DESCR: *Border Region; Islas, Arturo; Literary Characters; *Literary Criticism; Mendez M., Miguel; *Novel; PEREGRINOS DE AZTLAN; Sex Roles; Sex Stereotypes; *Women.

RAIN OF SCORPIONS AND OTHER WRITINGS

4869 Vallejos, Tomas. Estela Portillo Trambley's fictive search for paradise. FRONTIERS: A JOURNAL OF WOMEN STUDIES, Vol. 5, no. 2 (1980), p. 54-58. Also IN: Lattin, Vernon E., ed. CONTEMPORARY CHICANO FICTION. Binghamton, NY: Bilingual Press/Editorial Bilingue, 1986. p. 269-277. English. DESCR: DAY OF THE SWALLOWS; *Literary Criticism; Novel; Portillo Trambley, Estela.

Ramirez, Cristina

4870 Escalante, Virginia; Rivera, Nancy; and Valle, Victor Manuel. Inside the world of Latinas. IN: SOUTHERN CALIFORNIA'S LATINO COMMUNITY: A SERIES OF ARTICLES REPRINTED FROM THE LOS ANGELES TIMES. Los Angeles: Los Angeles Times, 1983, p. 82-91. English. DESCR: *Biography; Castillo Fierro, Catalina (Katie); Gaitan, Maria Elena; Gutierrez, Nancy; Luna Mount, Julia.

Ramirez, Henry M.

4871 Huerta, Dolores. Dolores Huerta talks about Republicans, Cesar, children and her home town. REGENERACION, Vol. 2, no. 4 (1975), p. 20-24. English. DESCR: *Agricultural Labor Unions; *Biography; Chavez, Cesar E.; Community Service Organization, Los Angeles, (CSO); Democratic Party; Elected Officials; Flores, Art; Huerta, Dolores; McGovern, George; *Politics; Ross, Fred; Sanchez, Philip V.; United Farmworkers of America (UFW); Working Women.

4872 Huerta, Dolores. Dolores Huerta talks about Republicans, Cesar, children and her home town. IN: Servin, Manuel P. ed. THE MEXICAN AMERICANS: AN AWAKENING MINORITY. 2nd ed. Beverly Hills, CA: Glencoe Press, 1974, p.

283-294. English. DESCR: *Agricultural Labor Unions; *Biography; Chavez, Cesar E.; Community Service Organization, Los Angeles, (CSO); Democratic Party; Elected Officials; Flores, Art; Huerta, Dolores; McGovern, George; *Politics; Ross, Fred; Sanchez, Philip V.; United Farmworkers of America (UFW); Working Women.

Ramirez, Sara Estela

4873 Hernandez, Ines. Sara Estela Ramirez: the early twentieth century Texas-Mexican poet. Thesis (Ph.D.)--University of Houston, 1984. 94 p. English. DESCR: *Authors; *Biography; Feminism; Flores Magon, Ricardo; Journalism; Literary Criticism; Mexican Revolution - 1910-1920; Mexico; *Poetry; Texas; Women.

4874 Hernandez, Ines. Sara Estela Ramirez: sembradora. LEGACY: A JOURNAL OF NINETEENTH-CENTURY AMERICAN WOMEN WRITERS, Vol. 6, no. 1 (Spring 1989), p. 13-26. English. DESCR: Authors; *Biography; *Feminism; Flores Magon, Ricardo; *Journalism; LA CORREGIDORA [newspaper]; Mexican Revolution - 1910-1920; Mexico; Newspapers; Poetry; REGENERACION [newspaper].

4875 Lomas, Clara. Mexican precursors of Chicana feminist writing. IN: National Association for Chicano Studies. ESTUDIOS CHICANOS AND THE POLITICS OF COMMUNITY. [S.l.]: National Association for Chicano Studies, c1989, p. [149]-160. English. DESCR: Authors; de Cardenas, Isidra T.; *Feminism; Idar, Jovita; *Journalists; Literature; *Mexican Revolution - 1910-1920; Newspapers; Villarreal, Andrea; Villegas de Magnon, Leonor.

4876 Zamora, Emilio, Jr. Sara Estela Ramirez: una rosa roja en el movimiento. IN: Mora, Magdalena and Del Castillo, Adelaida, eds. MEXICAN WOMEN IN THE UNITED STATES: STRUGGLES PAST AND PRESENT. Los Angeles, CA: Chicano Studies Research Center, UCLA, 1980, p. 163-169. English. DESCR: *Biography; Literary Criticism; Poetry.

Ramos, Loyda

4877 Vega, Alicia. Three Latinas in Hollywood = Tres latinas en Hollywood. AMERICAS 2001, Vol. 1, no. 7 (July, August, 1988), p. 4-6. Bilingual. DESCR: *Actors and Actresses; Alonso, Maria Conchita; Martinez, Patrice.

RANCHO HOLLYWOOD [play]

4878 Melville, Margarita B. Female and male in Chicano theatre. IN: Kanellos, Nicolas, ed. HISPANIC THEATRE IN THE UNITED STATES. Houston, TX: Arte Publico Press, 1984, p. 71-79. English. DESCR: BERNABE; BRUJERIAS [play]; Cultural Characteristics; DAY OF THE SWALLOWS; Duarte-Clark, Rodrigo; EL JARDIN [play]; Family; Feminism; Macias, Ysidro; Morton, Carlos; Portillo Trambley, Estela; *Sex Roles; *Teatro; THE ULTIMATE PENDEJADA [play]; Valdez, Luis; Women Men Relations.

Rangel, Irma

4879 Espinosa, Ann. Hispanas: our resourses [sic] for the eighties. LA LUZ, Vol. 8, no. 4 (October, November, 1979), p. 10-13. English. DESCR: Baca Barragan, Polly; *Civil Rights; Comision Femenil Mexicana Nacional; DIRECTORY OF HISPANIC WOMEN; Discrimination in Education; Elected Officials; Hernandez, Irene; Lacayo, Carmela; Lujan, Josie; Mexican American Women's National Association (MANA); Montanez Davis, Grace; Moreno, Olga; Mujeres Latinas en Accion (M.L.A.); National Conference of Puerto Rican Women, Inc. (NCCPRW); Organizations.

Rape

4880 Garcia, Chris; Guerro, Connie Destito; and Mendez, Irene. La violacion sexual: the reality of rape. AGENDA, Vol. 8, no. 5 (September, October, 1978), p. 10-11. English. DESCR: Attitudes; Los Angeles, CA.

4881 Gutierrez, Ramon A. Marriage and seduction in Colonial New Mexico. IN: Del Castillo, Adelaida R., ed. BETWEEN BORDERS: ESSAYS ON MEXICANA/CHICANA HISTORY. Encino, CA: Floricanto Press, 1990, p. 447-457. English. DESCR: History; *Marriage; *New Mexico; *Sexual Behavior; Women.

4882 Herrera-Sobek, Maria. The politics of rape: sexual transgression in Chicana fiction. THE AMERICAS REVIEW, Vol. 15, no. 3-4 (Fall, Winter, 1987), p. 171-181. English. DESCR: Cisneros, Sandra; *Feminism; Fiction; GIVING UP THE GHOST; *Literary Criticism; Lizarraga, Sylvia; Moraga, Cherrie; "Red Clowns" [short story]; Sex Roles; "Silver Lake Road" [short story].

4883 Monroy, Douglas. "They didn't call them 'padre' for nothing": patriarchy in Hispanic California. IN: Del Castillo, Adelaida R., ed. BETWEEN BORDERS: ESSAYS ON MEXICANA/CHICANA HISTORY. Encino, CA: Floricanto Press, 1990, p. 433-445. English. DESCR: *California; Clergy; History; *Machismo; *Sex Roles; *Sexism; Spanish Influence; Women Men Relations.

4884 Sanford, Judy, et al. Patterns of reported rape in a tri-ethnic population: Houston, Texas, 1974-1975. AMERICAN JOURNAL OF PUBLIC HEALTH, Vol. 69, no. 5 (May 1979), p. 480-484. English. DESCR: Anglo Americans; Blacks; Criminology; *Ethnic Groups; *Houston, TX; Statistics; Women.

4885 Silva, Helga. The unspeakable crime. NUESTRO, Vol. 1, no. 2 (May 1977), p. 48-49. English.

4886 Sorenson, Susan B. and Telles, Cynthia A. Self-reports of spousal violence in a Mexican-American and non-Hispanic white population. VIOLENCE AND VICTIMS, Vol. 6, no. 1 (1991), p. 3-15. English. DESCR: Anglo Americans; *Battered Women; Los Angeles, CA; Los Angeles Epidemiologic Catchment Area Research Program (LAECA); Violence; Women; *Women Men Relations.

4887 Sosa Riddell, Adaljiza. The status of women in Mexico: the impact of the "International Year of the Woman". IN: Iglitzin, Lynn B. and Ross, Ruth A., eds. WOMEN IN THE WORLD, 1975-1985. Santa Barbara, CA: ABC-Clio, Inc., 1986, p. 305-324. English. DESCR: Abortion; *Feminism; International Women's Year World Conference (1975: Mexico City); *Mexico; Political History and Conditions; Political Parties and Organizations; *Sexism; Social History and Conditions; *Women.

4888 Williams, Joyce E. Mexican American and Anglo attitudes about sex roles and rape. FREE INQUIRY IN CREATIVE SOCIOLOGY, Vol. 13, no. 1 (May 1985), p. 15-20. English. DESCR: Anglo Americans; Attitudes; *Feminism; *Sex Roles; Women.

4889 Williams, Joyce E. Secondary victimization: confronting public attitudes about rape. VICTIMOLOGY, Vol. 9, no. 1 (1984), p. 66-81. English. DESCR: *Attitudes; Natural Support Systems; San Antonio, TX.

"Rape Report" [poem]

4890 Zamora, Bernice. Archetypes in Chicana poetry. DE COLORES, Vol. 4, no. 3 (1978), p. 43-52. English. DESCR: Cervantes, Lorna Dee; Cunningham, Veronica; "Declaration on a Day of Little Inspiration" [poem]; Hernandez, Carlota; "I Speak in an Illusion" [poem]; *Literary Criticism; Lucero, Judy A.; Macias, Margarita; Mendoza, Rita; "Para Mi Hijita" [poem]; *Poetry; "The White Line" [poem]; "Working Mother's Song" [poem]; "You Can Only Blame the System for So Long" [poem]; Zamora, Katarina.

La Raza Unida Party

4891 Chapa, Olivia Evey. Mujeres por la Raza unida. CARACOL, Vol. 1, no. 2 (October 1974), p. 3-5. English. DESCR: Canales, Alma; Cotera, Marta P.; Diaz, Elena; *Political Parties and Organizations; REPORT OF FIRST CONFERENCIA DE MUJERES POR LA RAZA UNIDA PARTY.

La Raza Unida Party, Texas

4892 Cotera, Marta P. Chicana caucus. MAGAZIN, Vol. 1, no. 6 (August 1972), p. 24-26. English. DESCR: *Chicano Movement.

Rebeil, Julia

4893 Sheridan, Thomas E. From Luisa Espinel to Lalo Guerrero: Tucson's Mexican musicians before World War II. JOURNAL OF ARIZONA HISTORY, Vol. 25, no. 3 (Fall 1984), p. 285-300. English. DESCR: Biography; Espinel, Luisa Ronstadt; Guerrero, Eduardo "Lalo"; History; Montijo, Manuel; *Musicians; Singers; *Tucson, AZ.

"Red Clowns" [short story]

4894 Herrera-Sobek, Maria. The politics of rape: sexual transgression in Chicana fiction. THE AMERICAS REVIEW, Vol. 15, no. 3-4 (Fall, Winter, 1987), p. 171-181. English. DESCR: Cisneros, Sandra; *Feminism; Fiction; GIVING UP THE GHOST; *Literary Criticism; Lizarraga, Sylvia; Moraga, Cherrie; *Rape; Sex Roles; "Silver Lake Road" [short story].

Reference Books
USE: Reference Works

Reference Works

4895 Chabran, Richard. Chicana reference sources. IN: Cordova, Teresa, et al., eds. CHICANA VOICES. Austin, TX: Center for Mexican American Studies, 1986, p. 146-156. English. DESCR: Bibliography; Literature Reviews.

Reference Works (cont.)

4896 Newton, Frank; Olmedo, Esteban L.; and Padilla, Amado M. Hispanic mental health research: a reference guide. Berkeley, CA: University of California Press, c1982. 685 p. English. DESCR: Anthropology; *Bibliography; Education; Medical Care; *Mental Health; Psychology; Public Health; Sociology.

REGENERACION [newspaper]

4897 Hernandez, Ines. Sara Estela Ramirez: sembradora. LEGACY: A JOURNAL OF NINETEENTH-CENTURY AMERICAN WOMEN WRITERS, Vol. 6, no. 1 (Spring 1989), p. 13-26. English. DESCR: Authors; *Biography; *Feminism; Flores Magon, Ricardo; *Journalism; LA CORREGIDORA [newspaper]; Mexican Revolution - 1910-1920; Mexico; Newspapers; Poetry; *Ramirez, Sara Estela.

4898 Perez, Emma. "A la mujer": a critique of the Partido Liberal Mexicano's gender ideology on women. IN: Del Castillo, Adelaida R., ed. BETWEEN BORDERS: ESSAYS ON MEXICANA/CHICANA HISTORY. Encino, CA: Floricanto Press, 1990, p. 459-482. English. DESCR: *"A La Mujer" [essay]; Essays; *Feminism; Flores Magon, Ricardo; Guerrero, Praxedis G.; Journalism; Mexican Revolution - 1910-1920; Mexico; Newspapers; *Partido Liberal Mexicano (PLM); Political Ideology; Political Parties and Organizations; Sex Roles; Women.

EL REGIDOR, San Antonio, TX

4899 Luna-Lawhn, Juanita. EL REGIDOR and LA PRENSA: impediments to women's self-definition. THIRD WOMAN, Vol. 4, (1989), p. 134-142. English. DESCR: LA PRENSA, San Antonio, TX; Literature; *Newspapers; Sex Roles; *Sexism.

Religion

4900 Abrahamse, Allan F.; Morrison, Peter A.; and Waite, Linda J. Beyond stereotypes: who becomes a single teenage mother? Santa Monica, CA: RAND Corp., 1988. xv, 88 p. English. DESCR: *Fertility; Secondary School Education; *Single Parents; Statistics; *Women; *Youth.

4901 Amaro, Hortensia. Women in the Mexican-American community: religion, culture, and reproductive attitudes and experiences. JOURNAL OF COMMUNITY PSYCHOLOGY, Vol. 16, no. 1 (January 1988), p. 6-20. English. DESCR: Abortion; *Attitudes; Birth Control; Family Planning; *Fertility.

4902 Bach-y-Rita, George. The Mexican-American: religious and cultural influences. IN: Becerra, Rosina M., et al., eds. MENTAL HEALTH AND HISPANIC AMERICANS: CLINICAL PERSPECTIVES. New York: Grune & Stratton, 1982, p. 29-40. English. DESCR: Catholic Church; Cultural Characteristics; Culture; Language Usage; Machismo; *Mental Health; Psychotherapy.

4903 Bean, Frank D. and Bradshaw, Benjamin S. Mexican American fertility. IN: Teller, Charles H., et al., eds. CUANTOS SOMOS: A DEMOGRAPHIC STUDY OF THE MEXICAN AMERICAN POPULATION. Austin, TX: Center for Mexican American Studies, University of Texas at Austin, 1977, p. 101-130. English. DESCR: Attitudes; Birth Control; *Fertility; Income; Population.

4904 Cuellar, Israel. Service delivery and mental health services for Chicano elders. IN: Miranda, Manuel and Ruiz, Rene A., eds. CHICANO AGING AND MENTAL HEALTH. Rockville, MD: U.S. Department of Health and Human Services, 1981, p. 185-211. English. DESCR: *Ancianos; Attitudes; Cultural Customs; Cultural Pluralism; Language Usage; Mental Health; Mental Health Clinics; Sex Roles; Spanish Language.

4905 Isasi-Diaz, Ada Maria and Tarango, Yolanda. Hispanic women, prophetic voice in the Church: toward a Hispanic women's liberation theology. San Francisco, CA: Harper & Row, c1988. xx, 123 p. Bilingual. DESCR: Catholic Church; *Feminism; Liberation Theology; *Women.

4906 McRipley, Bernadine G. Racial/ethnic Presbyterian women: in search of community. CHURCH AND SOCIETY, Vol. 76, no. 4 (March, April, 1986), p. 47-53. English. DESCR: *Presbyterian Church; Sex Roles; *Women.

4907 Mercado, Olivia; Corrales, Ramona; and Segovia, Sara. Las hermanas. COMADRE, no. 2 (Spring 1978), p. 34-41. English. DESCR: *Clergy.

4908 Mosher, William D.; Johnson, David P.; and Horn, Marjorie C. Religion and fertility in the United States: the importance of marriage patterns and Hispanic origin. DEMOGRAPHY, Vol. 23, no. 3 (August 1986), p. 367-379. English. DESCR: *Catholic Church; *Fertility; Identity; Marriage; Population.

4909 Olivarez, Elizabeth. Women's rights and the Mexican American woman. REGENERACION, Vol. 2, no. 4 (1975), p. 40-42. English. DESCR: Education; *Feminism; Identity; Politics; Psychology; Sex Roles.

4910 Ortiz, Carmen G. The influence of religious images on perceptions of femininity among women of Mexican origin. Thesis (Ph.D.)--California School of Professional Psychology, Berkeley, 1988. 210 p. English. DESCR: Catholic Church; *Identity; *Sexual Behavior; Symbolism.

4911 Padilla, Eligio R. and O'Grady, Kevin E. Sexuality among Mexican Americans: a case of sexual stereotyping. JOURNAL OF PERSONALITY AND SOCIAL PSYCHOLOGY, Vol. 52, no. 1 (1987), p. 5-10. English. DESCR: Age Groups; Anglo Americans; Attitudes; California; *Sex Roles; *Sex Stereotypes; Sexual Behavior; Sexual Knowledge and Attitude Test; *Stereotypes; Students; Values.

4912 Rosenhouse-Persson, Sandra and Sabagh, Georges. Attitudes toward abortion among Catholic Mexican-American women: the effects of religiosity and education. DEMOGRAPHY, Vol. 20, no. 1 (February 1983), p. 87-98. English. DESCR: Abortion; Attitudes; *Catholic Church; Education.

4913 Sabagh, Georges and Lopez, David. Religiosity and fertility: the case of Chicanas. SOCIAL FORCES, Vol. 59, no. 2 (December 1980), p. 431-439. English. DESCR: Catholic Church; *Family Planning; *Fertility; Immigrants; Women.

4914 Williams, Norma. The Mexican American family: tradition and change. Dix Hills, NY: General Hall, Inc., c1990. x, 170 p. English. DESCR: Cultural Characteristics; *Cultural Customs; *Family; *Sex Roles; Working Women.

Religious Art

4915 Altars as folk art. ARRIBA, Vol. 1, no. 1 (July 1980), p. 4. English. DESCR: *Altars; Artists; De Leon, Josefina; Folk Art.

4916 Lomas Garza, Carmen. Altares: arte espiritual del hogar. HOJAS, (1976), p. 105-111. English. DESCR: *Altars; Artists; Folk Art; Lomas Garza, Carmen.

4917 Navar, M. Margarita. La vela prendida: home altars. ARRIBA, Vol. 1, no. 5 (February 1980), p. 12. English. DESCR: *Altars; Artists; Exhibits; Folk Art.

Religious Education

4918 Lee, Valerie. Achievement and educational aspirations among Hispanic female high school students: comparison between public and Catholic schools. IN: McKenna, Teresa and Ortiz, Flora Ida, eds. THE BROKEN WEB: THE EDUCATIONAL EXPERIENCE OF HISPANIC WOMEN. Claremont, CA: Tomas Rivera Center; Berkeley, CA: Floricanto Press, 1988, p. 137-192. English. DESCR: *Academic Achievement; Anglo Americans; Catholic Church; Education; Educational Statistics; Private Education; *Secondary School Education; *Women.

REPORT OF FIRST CONFERENCIA DE MUJERES POR LA RAZA UNIDA PARTY

4919 Chapa, Olivia Evey. Mujeres por la Raza unida. CARACOL, Vol. 1, no. 2 (October 1974), p. 3-5. English. DESCR: Canales, Alma; Cotera, Marta P.; Diaz, Elena; La Raza Unida Party; *Political Parties and Organizations.

Reports and Reporting
USE: Journalism

Research Methodology

4920 Adams, Russell P. Predictors of self-esteem and locus-of-control in Mexican-American women. Thesis (Ph.D.)--Texas Tech University, 1989. 138 p. English. DESCR: *Identity; *Locus of Control; Mental Health.

4921 Alba, Richard D. A comment on Schoen and Cohen. AMERICAN JOURNAL OF SOCIOLOGY, Vol 87, no. 4 (January 1982), p. 935-939. English. DESCR: Cohen, Lawrence E.; ETHNIC ENDOGAMY AMONG MEXICAN AMERICAN GROOMS; Intermarriage; Schoen, Robert.

4922 Andrade, Sally J. Family roles of Hispanic women: stereotypes, empirical findings, and implications for research. IN: Zambrana, Ruth E., ed. WORK, FAMILY, AND HEALTH: LATINA WOMEN IN TRANSITION. Bronx, NY: Hispanic Research Center, Fordham University, 1982, p. 95-106. English. DESCR: *Family; Puerto Ricans; *Sex Roles; Sex Stereotypes; Women.

4923 Baca Zinn, Maxine. Chicano family research: conceptual distortions and alternative directions. JOURNAL OF ETHNIC STUDIES, Vol. 7, no. 3 (Fall 1979), p. 59-71. English. DESCR: Cultural Characteristics; Culture *Family; Stereotypes.

4924 Baca Zinn, Maxine. Ongoing questions in the study of Chicano families. IN: Valdez, Armando, et al., eds. THE STATE OF CHICANO RESEARCH ON FAMILY, LABOR, AND MIGRATION. Stanford, CA: Stanford Center for Chicano Research, 1983, p. 139-146. English. DESCR: *Family.

4925 Baca Zinn, Maxine. Qualitative methods in family research: a look inside Chicano families. CALIFORNIA SOCIOLOGIST, Vol. 5, no. 2 (Summer 1982), p. 58-79. English. DESCR: *Family; Marriage; *Sex Roles; Socioeconomic Factors.

4926 Bean, Frank D. and Swicegood, Gray. Mexican American fertility patterns. Austin, TX: University of Texas Press, 1985. x, 178 p. English. DESCR: Age Groups; Census; Education; *Fertility; Language Usage; *Population; *Socioeconomic Factors; Statistics.

4927 Del Castillo, Adelaida R., et al. An assessment of the status of the education of Hispanic American women. IN: McKenna, Teresa and Ortiz, Flora Ida, eds. THE BROKEN WEB: THE EDUCATIONAL EXPERIENCE OF HISPANIC WOMEN. Claremont, CA: Tomas Rivera Center; Berkeley, CA: Floricanto Press, 1988, p. 3-24. English. DESCR: Academic Achievement; Conferences and Meetings; Discrimination in Education; Dropouts; *Education; Higher Education; Public Policy; The Educational Experience of Hispanic American Women [symposium] (1985: Claremont, CA); *Women.

4928 Del Castillo, Adelaida R. and Torres, Maria. The interdependency of educational institutions and cultural norms: the Hispana experience. IN: McKenna, Teresa and Ortiz, Flora Ida, eds. THE BROKEN WEB: THE EDUCATIONAL EXPERIENCE OF HISPANIC WOMEN. Claremont, CA: Tomas Rivera Center; Berkeley, CA: Floricanto Press, 1988, p. 39-60. English. DESCR: Academic Achievement; Acculturation; *Cultural Characteristics; *Education; *Literature Reviews; *Values; Women.

4929 Flores, Estevan T. Chicanos and sociological research: 1970-1980. IN: CHICANOS AND THE SOCIAL SCIENCES: A DECADE OF RESEARCH AND DEVELOPMENT (1970-1980) SYMPOSIUM WORKING PAPER. Santa Barbara, CA: Center for Chicano Studies, University of California, 1983, p. 19-45. English. DESCR: Bibliography; Family; Internal Colony Model; Labor; Literature Reviews; Population; *Sociology.

4930 Jones, Pamela. "There was a woman": La Llorona in Oregon. WESTERN FOLKLORE, Vol. 47, no. 3 (July 1988), p. 195-211. English. DESCR: Folklore; *La Llorona; *Leyendas; Oregon.

4931 Lucero, Marcela Christine. Resources for the Chicana feminist scholar. IN: Treichler, Paula A., et al., eds. FOR ALMA MATER: THEORY AND PRACTICE IN FEMINIST SCHOLARSHIP. Urbana: University of Illinois Press, 1985, p. 393-401. English. DESCR: *Chicana Studies; *Feminism; Literature Reviews; Publishing Industry.

4932 Mindiola, Tatcho, Jr. and Gutierrez, Armando. Education and discrimination against Mexican Americans in the Southwest. CALIFORNIA SOCIOLOGIST, Vol. 5, no. 2 (Summer 1982), p. 80-97. English. DESCR: *Discrimination in Education; Social Classes.

4933 Pierce, Jennifer. The implications of functionalism for Chicano family research. BERKELEY JOURNAL OF SOCIOLOGY, Vol. 29, (1984), p. 93-117. English. DESCR: Enriquez, Evangelina; *Family; LA CHICANA: THE MEXICAN AMERICAN WOMAN; Machismo; Mirande, Alfredo; Sex Roles.

Research Methodology
(cont.)

4934 Ramos, Reyes. Discovering the production of
Mexican American family structure. DE
COLORES, Vol. 6, no. 1-2 (1982), p. 120-134.
English. **DESCR:** *Family.

4935 Rubio Goldsmith, Raquel. Oral history:
considerations and problems for its use in
the history of Mexicanas in the United
States. IN: Del Castillo, Adelaida R., ed.
BETWEEN BORDERS: ESSAYS ON MEXICANA/CHICANA
HISTORY. Encino, CA: Floricanto Press, 1990,
p. 161-173. English. **DESCR:** History; *Oral
History.

4936 Ruiz, Vicki L. Dead ends or gold mines?:
using missionary records in Mexican-American
women's history. FRONTIERS: A JOURNAL OF
WOMEN STUDIES, Vol. 12, no. 1 (1991), p.
33-56. English. **DESCR:** Archives; Clergy; El
Paso, TX; History; *Methodist Church;
Protestant Church; *Rose Gregory Houchen
Settlement House, El Paso, TX.

4937 Schoen, Robert; Wooldredge, John; and
Thomas, Barbara. Ethnic and educational
effects on marriage choice. SOCIAL SCIENCE
QUARTERLY, Vol. 70, no. 3 (September 1989),
p. 617-630. English. **DESCR:** Education;
Identity; *Intermarriage; Marriage; Social
Classes.

4938 Stern, Gwen. Research, action, and social
betterment. AMERICAN BEHAVIOR SCIENTISTS,
Vol. 29, no. 2 (November, December, 1985),
p. 229-248. English. **DESCR:** Chicago, IL;
*Medical Care; The Latina Mother-Infant
Project, Chicago, IL.

4939 Valdez, Diana. Mexican American family
research: a critical review and conceptual
framework. DE COLORES, Vol. 6, no. 1-2
(1982), p. 48-63. English. **DESCR:** *Family.

4940 Ybarra, Lea. Empirical and theoretical
developments in the study of Chicano
families. IN: Valdez, Armando, et al., eds.
THE STATE OF CHICANO RESEARCH ON FAMILY,
LABOR, AND MIGRATION. Stanford, CA: Stanford
Center for Chicano Research, 1983, p.
91-110. English. **DESCR:** *Family; Sex Roles;
Social Science; *Stereotypes.

4941 Zambrana, Ruth E. Toward understanding the
educational trajectory and socialization of
Latina women. IN: McKenna, Teresa and Ortiz,
Flora Ida, eds. THE BROKEN WEB: THE
EDUCATIONAL EXPERIENCE OF HISPANIC WOMEN.
Claremont, CA: Tomas Rivera Center;
Berkeley, CA: Floricanto Press, 1988, p.
61-77. English. **DESCR:** Academic Achievement;
Anglo Americans; *Education; Feminism;
Identity; *Socialization; *Women.

Restaurants

4942 Spence, Mary Lee. Commentary [on "And Miles
to Go": Mexican Women and Work, 1930-1985].
IN: Schlissel, Lillian, et al., eds. WESTERN
WOMEN: THEIR LAND, THEIR LIVES. Albuquerque,
NM: University of New Mexico Press, 1988, p.
145-150. English. **DESCR:** "'And Miles to
Go...': Mexican Women and Work, 1930-1985";
Food Industry; Income; Labor Unions; Ruiz,
Vicki L.; *Working Women.

RESTLESS SERPENTS

4943 Bruce-Novoa, Juan. Bernice Zamora y Lorna
Dee Cervantes: una estetica feminista.
REVISTA IBEROAMERICANA, Vol. 51, (July,
December, 1985), p. 565-573. English.

DESCR: *Authors; *Cervantes, Lorna Dee;
EMPLUMADA; Literary Criticism; Poetry;
*Zamora, Bernice.

4944 Saldivar, Jose David. Towards a Chicano
poetics: the making of the Chicano subject.
CONFLUENCIA, Vol. 1, no. 2 (Spring 1986), p.
10-17. English. **DESCR:** Corridos; Feminism;
*Literary Criticism; "Los Vatos" [poem];
Montoya, Jose E.; *Poetry; Rios, Alberto;
WHISPERING TO FOOL THE WIND; Zamora,
Bernice.

RETO EN EL PARAISO

4945 Lizarraga, Sylvia S. Images of women in
Chicano literature by men. FEMINIST ISSUES,
Vol. 5, no. 2 (Fall 1985), p. 69-88.
English. **DESCR:** *Literature; Morales,
Alejandro; Sexism; *Stereotypes.

Rio Arriba Valley, NM

4946 Craver, Rebecca McDowell. The impact of
intimacy: Mexican-Anglo intermarriage in New
Mexico 1821-1846. SOUTHWESTERN STUDIES, no.
66 (1982), p. 1-79. English. **DESCR:**
Acculturation; Anglo Americans;
Assimilation; History; *Intermarriage; New
Mexico.

4947 Craver, Rebecca McDowell. The impact of
intimacy: Mexican-Anglo intermarriage in New
Mexico 1821-1846. El Paso, TX: Texas Western
Press, University of Texas at El Paso, 1982.
79 p. English. **DESCR:** Acculturation; Anglo
Americans; Assimilation; History;
*Intermarriage; New Mexico.

Rios, Alberto

4948 Rosaldo, Renato. Fables of the fallen guy.
IN: Calderon, Hector and Saldivar, Jose
David, eds. CRITICISM IN THE BORDERLANDS:
STUDIES IN CHICANO LITERATURE, CULTURE AND
IDEOLOGY. Durham, NC: Duke University Press,
1991, p. [84]-93. English. **DESCR:** Chavez,
Denise; Cisneros, Sandra; Fiction; Literary
Characters; *Literary Criticism; Sex Roles;
THE HOUSE ON MANGO STREET; THE IGUANA
KILLER: TWELVE STORIES OF THE HEART; THE
LAST OF THE MENU GIRLS.

4949 Saldivar, Jose David. Towards a Chicano
poetics: the making of the Chicano subject.
CONFLUENCIA, Vol. 1, no. 2 (Spring 1986), p.
10-17. English. **DESCR:** Corridos; Feminism;
*Literary Criticism; "Los Vatos" [poem];
Montoya, Jose E.; *Poetry; RESTLESS
SERPENTS; WHISPERING TO FOOL THE WIND;
Zamora, Bernice.

Rios, Isabella

4950 Saldivar, Ramon. The dialectics of
subjectivity: gender and difference in
Isabella Rios, Sandra Cisneros, and Cherrie
Moraga. IN: Saldivar, Ramon. CHICANO
NARRATIVE: THE DIALECTICS OF DIFFERENCE.
Madison, WI: University of Wisconsin Press,
1990, p. 171-199. English. **DESCR:** Authors;
Autobiography; *Cisneros, Sandra; Feminism;
Fiction; *Literary Criticism; Literature;
LOVING IN THE WAR YEARS; *Moraga, Cherrie;
Political Ideology; THE HOUSE ON MANGO
STREET; VICTUUM.

RITES AND WITNESSES

4951 de la Fuente, Patricia and Duke dos Santos, Maria I. The elliptic female presence as unifying force in the novels of Rolando Hinojosa. REVISTA CHICANO-RIQUENA, Vol. 12, no. 3-4 (Fall, Winter, 1984), p. 64-75. English. DESCR: ESTAMPAS DEL VALLE Y OTRAS OBRAS; GENERACIONES Y SEMBLANZAS; Hinojosa-Smith, Rolando R.; *Literary Criticism; MI QUERIDO RAFA.

RITUALS OF SURVIVAL

4952 McCracken, Ellen. Latina narrative and politics of signification: articulation, antagonism, and populist rupture. CRITICA, Vol. 2, no. 2 (Fall 1990), p. 202-207. English. DESCR: *Cisneros, Sandra; IN NUEVA YORK; *Literary Criticism; *Mohr, Nicolasa; Puerto Ricans; Short Story; THE HOUSE ON MANGO STREET; Women.

Rivera, Tomas

4953 de la Fuente, Patricia. Invisible women in the narrative of Tomas Rivera. REVISTA CHICANO-RIQUENA, Vol. 13, no. 3-4 (Fall, Winter, 1985), p. 81-89. English. DESCR: Literary Criticism; Sex Stereotypes; Y NO SE LO TRAGO LA TIERRA/AND THE EARTH DID NOT PART.

4954 Gonzalez-Berry, Erlinda and Rebolledo, Tey Diana. Growing up Chicano: Tomas Rivera and Sandra Cisneros. REVISTA CHICANO-RIQUENA, Vol. 13, no. 3-4 (Fall, Winter, 1985), p. 109-119. English. DESCR: Cisneros, Sandra; Cultural Characteristics; *Literary Criticism; Sex Roles; THE HOUSE ON MANGO STREET; Y NO SE LO TRAGO LA TIERRA/AND THE EARTH DID NOT PART.

4955 Lizarraga, Sylvia S. "La mujer doblamente explotada: "On the Road to Texas: Pete Fonseca". AZTLAN, Vol. 16, no. 1-2 (1985), p. 197-215. Spanish. DESCR: *Literary Criticism; "On the Road to Texas: Pete Fonseca" [short story].

4956 Lizarraga, Sylvia S. The patriarchal ideology in "La noche que se apagaron las luces". REVISTA CHICANO-RIQUENA, Vol. 13, no. 3-4 (Fall, Winter, 1985), p. 90-95. English. DESCR: "La noche que se apagaron las luces" [short story]; *Literary Criticism; Sex Roles; Y NO SE LO TRAGO LA TIERRA/AND THE EARTH DID NOT PART.

4957 Rascon, Francisco. La caracterizacion de los personajes femeninos en ...Y NO SE LO TRAGO LA TIERRA. IN: Lattin, Vernon E., ed. CONTEMPORARY CHICANO FICTION: A CRITICAL SURVEY. Binghamton, NY: Bilingual Press/Editorial Bilingue, 1986, p. 141-148. Spanish. DESCR: *Literary Criticism; Y NO SE LO TRAGO LA TIERRA/AND THE EARTH DID NOT PART.

Robelo, Miguel

4958 Ordonez, Elizabeth J. La imagen de la mujer en el nuevo cine chicano. CARACOL, Vol. 5, no. 2 (October 1978), p. 12-13. Spanish. DESCR: Bonilla-Giannini, Roxanna; *Films; Lopez, Lexore; ONLY ONCE IN A LIFETIME [film]; *Photography; RAICES DE SANGRE [film]; Sex Stereotypes.

Robinson, Alfred

4959 Castaneda, Antonia I. The political economy of nineteenth century stereotypes of Californianas. IN: Del Castillo, Adelaida R., ed. BETWEEN BORDERS: ESSAYS ON MEXICANA/CHICANA HISTORY. Encino, CA: Floricanto Press, 1990, p. 213-236. English. DESCR: *California; *Californios; Dana, Richard Henry; Farnham, Thomas Jefferson; History; LIFE IN CALIFORNIA; *Political Economy; *Sex Stereotypes; TRAVELS IN CALIFORNIA AND SCENES IN THE PACIFIC OCEAN; TWO YEARS BEFORE THE MAST; Women.

Robledo, Refugio

4960 Mirande, Alfredo and Enriquez, Evangelina. Chicanas in the history of the Southwest. IN: Duran, Livie Isauro and Bernard, H. Russell, eds. INTRODUCTION TO CHICANO STUDIES. 2nd ed. New York: Macmillan, 1982, p. 156-179. English. DESCR: Arguello, Concepcion; Barcelo, Gertrudes "La Tules"; Fages, Eulalia; *History; "Juanita of Downieville"; Urrea, Teresa.

Rodriguez, Carmen

4961 Brown, Betty Ann. Chicanas speak out. ARTWEEK, Vol. 15, no. 2 (January 14, 1984), p. 1+. English. DESCR: *Art; Carrasco, Barbara; Carrillo, Graciela; CHICANA VOICES & VISIONS [exhibit]; Exhibits; Goldman, Shifra M.; Hernandez, Ester; Lerma Bowerman, Liz; Rodriguez, Sandra Maria; Social and Public Art Resource Center, Venice, CA (SPARC).

Rodriguez, Conrado

4962 Rose, Margaret. From the fields to the picket line: Huelga women and the boycott, 1965-1975. LABOR HISTORY, Vol. 31, no. 3 (1990), p. 271-293. English. DESCR: *Boycotts; Family; Farm Workers; Padilla, Esther; Padilla, Gilbert; Rodriguez, Herminia; *United Farmworkers of America (UFW); Washington, D.C.

Rodriguez, Diane

4963 Broyles-Gonzalez, Yolanda and Rodriguez, Diane. The living legacy of Chicana performers: preserving history through oral testimony. FRONTIERS: A JOURNAL OF WOMEN STUDIES, Vol. 11, no. 1 (1990), p. [46]-52. English. DESCR: *Actors and Actresses; El Teatro Campesino; Latins Anonymous [comedy review]; Oral History; Sex Roles; Singers; Teatro.

Rodriguez, Gregorita

4964 Perrone, Bobette; Stockel, H. Henrietta; and Krueger, Victoria. Medicine women, curanderas, and women doctors. Norman, OK: University of Oklahoma Press, c1989. xix, 252 p.:ill. English. DESCR: Aragon, Jesusita, 1908-; *Curanderas; *Curanderismo; *Folk Medicine; Herbal Medicine; Herrera, Sabinita; Medical Personnel; Native Americans; *Oral History; Women.

Rodriguez, Herminia

4965 Rose, Margaret. From the fields to the picket line: Huelga women and the boycott, 1965-1975. LABOR HISTORY, Vol. 31, no. 3 (1990), p. 271-293. English. DESCR: *Boycotts; Family; Farm Workers; Padilla, Esther; Padilla, Gilbert; Rodriguez, Conrado; *United Farmworkers of America (UFW); Washington, D.C.

Rodriguez, Patricia

4966 La Duke, Betty. Trivial lives: artists
Yolanda Lopez and Patricia Rodriguez.
TRIVIA: A JOURNAL OF IDEAS, (Winter 1986),
p. 74-85. English. **DESCR:** Artists;
Biography; *Lopez, Yolanda M.

4967 Mesa-Bains, Amalia. Quest for identity:
profile of two Chicana muralists: based on
interviews with Judith F. Baca and Patricia
Rodriguez. IN: Cockcroft, Eva Sperling and
Barnet-Sanchez, Holly, eds. SIGNS FROM THE
HEART: CALIFORNIA CHICANO MURALS. Venice,
CA: Social and Public Art Resource Center,
1990, p. [68-83]. English. **DESCR:** Artists;
Baca, Judith F.; Chicano Movement; GREAT
WALL OF LOS ANGELES [mural]; *Mural Art.

Rodriguez, Sandra Maria

4968 Brown, Betty Ann. Chicanas speak out.
ARTWEEK, Vol. 15, no. 2 (January 14, 1984),
p. 1+. English. **DESCR:** *Art; Carrasco,
Barbara; Carrillo, Graciela; CHICANA VOICES
& VISIONS [exhibit]; Exhibits; Goldman,
Shifra M.; Hernandez, Ester; Lerma Bowerman,
Liz; Rodriguez, Carmen; Social and Public
Art Resource Center, Venice, CA (SPARC).

ROMANCE OF A LITTLE VILLAGE GIRL

4969 Padilla, Genaro. Imprisoned narrative? Or
lies, secrets, and silence in New Mexico
women's autobiography. IN: Calderon, Hector
and Saldivar, Jose David, eds. CRITICISM IN
THE BORDERLANDS: STUDIES IN CHICANO
LITERATURE, CULTURE, AND IDEOLOGY. Durham,
NC: Duke University Press, 1991, p. [43]-60.
English. **DESCR:** Authors; *Autobiography;
*Cabeza de Baca, Fabiola; *Jaramillo,
Cleofas M.; Literary History; New Mexico; WE
FED THEM CACTUS.

4970 Rebolledo, Tey Diana. Las escritoras:
romances and realities. IN: Gonzales-Berry,
Erlinda, ed. PASO POR AQUI: CRITICAL ESSAYS
ON THE NEW MEXICAN LITERARY TRADITION.
Albuquerque, NM: University of New Mexico
Press, c1989, p. 199-214. English. **DESCR:**
Authors; *Cabeza de Baca, Fabiola;
*Jaramillo, Cleofas M.; Literary History;
New Mexico; OLD SPAIN IN OUR SOUTHWEST;
*Otero Warren, Nina; WE FED THEM CACTUS;
Women.

4971 Rebolledo, Tey Diana. Narrative strategies
of resistance in Hispana writing. THE
JOURNAL OF NARRATIVE TECHNIQUE, Vol. 20, no.
2 (Spring 1990), p. 134-146. English.
DESCR: *Authors; Cabeza de Baca, Fabiola;
Fiction; Jaramillo, Cleofas M.; *Literary
Criticism; Literature; New Mexico; OLD SPAIN
IN OUR SOUTHWEST; *Oral Tradition; Otero
Warren, Nina; WE FED THEM CACTUS.

ROOSTERS [play]

4972 Bouknight, Jon. Language as a cure: an
interview with Milcha Sanchez-Scott. LATIN
AMERICAN THEATRE REVIEW, Vol. 23, no. 2
(Spring 1990), p. 63-74. English. **DESCR:**
Actos; *Authors; Sanchez-Scott, Milcha;
*Teatro.

Rose Gregory Houchen Settlement House, El Paso, TX

4973 Ruiz, Vicki L. Dead ends or gold mines?:
using missionary records in Mexican-American
women's history. FRONTIERS: A JOURNAL OF
WOMEN STUDIES, Vol. 12, no. 1 (1991), p.
33-56. English. **DESCR:** Archives; Clergy; El
Paso, TX; History; *Methodist Church;
Protestant Church; *Research Methodology.

Ross, Fred

4974 Huerta, Dolores. Dolores Huerta talks about
Republicans, Cesar, children and her home
town. REGENERACION, Vol. 2, no. 4 (1975), p.
20-24. English. **DESCR:** *Agricultural Labor
Unions; *Biography; Chavez, Cesar E.;
Community Service Organization, Los Angeles,
(CSO); Democratic Party; Elected Officials;
Flores, Art; Huerta, Dolores; McGovern,
George; *Politics; Ramirez, Henry M.;
Sanchez, Philip V.; United Farmworkers of
America (UFW); Working Women.

4975 Huerta, Dolores. Dolores Huerta talks about
Republicans, Cesar, children and her home
town. IN: Servin, Manuel P. ed. THE MEXICAN
AMERICANS: AN AWAKENING MINORITY. 2nd ed.
Beverly Hills, CA: Glencoe Press, 1974, p.
283-294. English. **DESCR:** *Agricultural Labor
Unions; *Biography; Chavez, Cesar E.;
Community Service Organization, Los Angeles,
(CSO); Democratic Party; Elected Officials;
Flores, Art; Huerta, Dolores; McGovern,
George; *Politics; Ramirez, Henry M.;
Sanchez, Philip V.; United Farmworkers of
America (UFW); Working Women.

Ruelas, J. Oshi

4976 Ruelas, J. Oshi. Moments of change. REVISTA
MUJERES, Vol. 4, no. 1 (January 1987), p.
23-33. English. **DESCR:** *Autobiography;
Essays; Sex Roles; Sexism.

Ruiz Burton, Maria Amparo

4977 Ruiz, Vicki L. California's early pioneers:
Spanish/Mexican women. SOCIAL STUDIES
REVIEW, Vol. 29, no. 1 (Fall 1989), p.
24-30. English. **DESCR:** *California;
*History; Sex Roles; *Women.

4978 Sanchez, Rosaura. El discurso femenino en la
literatura chicana. IN: Lopez-Gonzalez,
Aralia, et al., eds. MUJER Y LITERATURA
MEXICANA Y CHICANA: CULTURAS EN CONTACTO.
Mexico: Colegio de la Frontera Norte, 1988,
p. 37-43. Spanish. **DESCR:** *Feminism;
*Literary Criticism.

Ruiz, Vicki L.

4979 Acuna, Rodolfo. The struggles of class and
gender: current research in Chicano Studies
[review essay]. JOURNAL OF AMERICAN ETHNIC
HISTORY, Vol. 8, no. 2 (Spring 1989), p.
134-138. English. **DESCR:** *CANNERY WOMEN,
CANNERY LIVES; *CHICANO ETHNICITY; Deutsch,
Sarah; Keefe, Susan E.; Literature Reviews;
*NO SEPARATE REFUGE; Padilla, Amado M.;
*WOMEN'S WORK AND CHICANO FAMILIES; Zavella,
Pat.

4980 Dublin, Thomas. Commentary [on "And Miles to
Go": Mexican Women and Work, 1930-1985]. IN:
Schlissel, Lillian, et al., eds. WESTERN
WOMEN: THEIR LAND, THEIR LIVES. Albuquerque,
NM: University of New Mexico Press, 1988, p.
137-140. English. **DESCR:** "'And Miles to
Go...': Mexican Women and Work, 1930-1985";
Employment; Income; Labor Unions;
Undocumented Workers; Women; *Working Women.

Ruiz, Vicki L. (cont.)

4981 Garcia, Mario T. Family and gender in Chicano and border studies research. MEXICAN STUDIES/ESTUDIOS MEXICANOS, Vol. 6, no. 1 (Winter 1990), p. 109-119. English. DESCR: Alvarez, Robert R., Jr.; *Border Region; CANNERY WOMEN, CANNERY LIVES; *Family; LA FAMILIA: MIGRATION AND ADAPTATION IN BAJA AND ALTA CALIFORNIA, 1800-1975; *Literature Reviews; Tiano, Susan B.; Women; WOMEN ON THE U.S.-MEXICO BORDER: RESPONSES TO CHANGE; WOMEN'S WORK AND CHICANO FAMILIES; Zavella, Pat.

4982 Jensen, Joan M. Commentary [on "And Miles to Go": Mexican Women and Work, 1930-1985]. IN: Schlissel, Lillian, et al., eds. WESTERN WOMEN: THEIR LAND, THEIR LIVES. Albuquerque, NM: University of New Mexico Press, 1988, p. 141-144. English. DESCR: "'And Miles to Go...': Mexican Women and Work, 1930-1985"; California; Employment; Income; Labor Unions; Public Policy; Women; *Working Women.

4983 Sanchez, Rosaura. The history of Chicanas: a proposal for a materialist perspective. IN: Del Castillo, Adelaida R., ed. BETWEEN BORDERS: ESSAYS ON MEXICANA/CHICANA HISTORY. Encino, CA: Floricanto Press, 1990, p. 1-29. English. DESCR: Apodaca, Maria Linda; *Chicana Studies; Del Castillo, Adelaida R.; Feminism; Historiography; History; Morales, Sylvia.

4984 Spence, Mary Lee. Commentary [on "And Miles to Go": Mexican Women and Work, 1930-1985]. IN: Schlissel, Lillian, et al., eds. WESTERN WOMEN: THEIR LAND, THEIR LIVES. Albuquerque, NM: University of New Mexico Press, 1988, p. 145-150. English. DESCR: "'And Miles to Go...': Mexican Women and Work, 1930-1985"; Food Industry; Income; Labor Unions; Restaurants; *Working Women.

4985 Winkler, Karen J. Scholars say issues of diversity have "revolutionized" field of Chicano Studies. CHRONICLE OF HIGHER EDUCATION, Vol. 37, no. 4 (September 26, 1990), p. A4-A9. English. DESCR: Chicana Studies; Chicano Studies; Curriculum; *Feminism; Higher Education; Saragoza, Alex M.

Rural Economics

4986 Jensen, Joan M. "I've worked, I'm not afraid of work": farm women in New Mexico, 1920-1940. NEW MEXICO HISTORICAL REVIEW, Vol. 61, no. 1 (January 1986), p. 27-52. English. DESCR: *Farm Workers; History; New Mexico; *Working Women.

Rural Education

4987 Jensen, Joan M. Crossing ethnic barriers in the Southwest: women's agricultural extension education, 1914-1940. AGRICULTURAL HISTORY, Vol. 60, no. 2 (Spring 1986), p. 169-181. English. DESCR: *Agricultural Extension Service; Agriculture; Cabeza de Baca, Fabiola; History; New Mexico.

Rural Poor

4988 Leblanc, Donna Marie. Quality of maternity care in rural Texas. Thesis (Dr. P.H.) --University of Texas H.S.C. at Houston School of Public Health, 1983. 266 p. English. DESCR: Fertility; Low Income; *Maternal and Child Welfare; *Medical Care; Prenatal Care; Texas.

Rural Population

4989 Amodeo, Luiza B.; Edelson, Rosalyn; and Martin, Jeanette. The triple bias: rural, minority and female. RURAL EDUCATOR, Vol. 3, no. 3 (Spring 1982), p. 1-6. English. DESCR: *Education; Social History and Conditions; Women.

4990 Chavez, Ernest; Beauvais, Fred; and Oetting, E.R. Drug use by small town Mexican American youth: a pilot study. HISPANIC JOURNAL OF BEHAVIORAL SCIENCES, Vol. 8, no. 3 (September 1986), p. 243-258. English. DESCR: Anglo Americans; *Drug Use; Youth.

4991 Davis, Sally M. and Harris, Mary B. Sexual knowledge, sexual interests, and sources of sexual information of rural and urban adolescents from three cultures. ADOLESCENCE, Vol. 17, no. 66 (Summer 1982), p. 471-492. English. DESCR: Birth Control; Cultural Characteristics; Identity; *Sex Education; Sex Roles; Urban Communities; Youth.

4992 Deutsch, Sarah. Women and intercultural relations: the case of Hispanic New Mexico and Colorado. SIGNS: JOURNAL OF WOMEN IN CULTURE AND SOCIETY, Vol. 12, no. 4 (Summer 1987), p. 719-739. English. DESCR: Colorado; Cultural Characteristics; Immigrants; Intercultural Communication; Mexico; New Mexico; Sex Roles; Social History and Conditions; *Women.

4993 Mata, Alberto Guardiola and Castillo, Valerie. Rural female adolescent dissatisfaction, support and helpseeking. FREE INQUIRY IN CREATIVE SOCIOLOGY, Vol. 14, no. 2 (November 1986), p. 135-138. English. DESCR: Alcoholism; *Drug Use; Interpersonal Relations; *Natural Support Systems; Parent and Child Relationships; *Youth.

4994 Romero, Mary. Domestic service in the transition from rural to urban life: the case of la Chicana. WOMEN'S STUDIES QUARTERLY, Vol. 13, no. 3 (February 1987), p. 199-222. English. DESCR: *Domestic Work; Employment; Interpersonal Relations; Social Mobility; Sociology; Urban Communities; Working Women.

Rural Urban Migration

4995 Lee, Bun Song and Pol, Louis G. A comparison of fertility adaptation between Mexican immigrants to the U.S. and internal migrants in Mexico. CONTEMPORARY POLICY ISSUES, Vol. 3, no. 3 (Spring, 1985), p. 91-101. English. DESCR: *Fertility; *Immigrants; Mexico; Migration Patterns; Women.

Sacramento County, CA

4996 Bourque, Linda B.; Kraus, Jess F.; and Cosand, Beverly J. Attributes of suicide in females. SUICIDE AND LIFE-THREATENING BEHAVIOR, Vol. 13, no. 2 (Summer 1983), p. 123-138. English. DESCR: Anglo Americans; *Suicide; Women.

Saint of Cabora
USE: Urrea, Teresa

Saints
USE: Santos

Salazar, Peggy

4997 Santillanes, Maria. Women in prison--C.I.W.: an editorial. REGENERACION, Vol. 2, no. 4 (1975), p. 53. English. DESCR: Conferences and Meetings; Garcia, Dolly; La Mesa College Pinto and Pinta Program; Lopez, Tony; Mares, Rene; Martinez, Miguel; Pinto Conference (1973: UCLA); Player; *Prisons.

SALT OF THE EARTH [film]

4998 Aulette, Judy and Mills, Trudy. Something old, something new: auxiliary work in the 1983-1986 copper strike. FEMINIST STUDIES, Vol. 14, no. 2 (Summer 1988), p. 251-268. English. DESCR: Arizona; Clifton-Morenci Copper Strike, 1983-1986; Clifton-Morenci District, Arizona; Feminism; Labor Unions; Morenci Miners Women's Auxiliary (MMWA); Mutualistas; Phelps Dodge Corporation, Morenci, AZ; Sex Roles; *Strikes and Lockouts.

4999 Goldman, Shifra M. Trabajadoras mexicanas y chicanas en las artes visuales. IN: Leal, Salvador, ed. A TRAVES DE LA FRONTERA. Mexico, D.F.: Centro de Estudios Economicos y Sociales del Tercer Mundo, A.C.; Instituto de Investigaciones Esteticas, U.N.A.M., 1983, p. 153-161. Spanish. DESCR: Art; Gonzalez Parsons, Lucia; Huerta, Dolores; Moreno, Luisa [union organizer]; Tenayuca, Emma; *Working Women.

5000 Kernan, Lisa. Keep marching sisters: the second generation looks at SALT OF THE EARTH. NUESTRO, Vol. 9, no. 4 (May 1985), p. 23-25. English. DESCR: Films; Strikes and Lockouts.

5001 Saavedra, Lupe. It is only fair that women be allowed to... AGENDA, (Winter 1976), p. 12-13. English. DESCR: Labor Disputes; Labor Unions; *Strikes and Lockouts.

San Antonio, TX

5002 Blackwelder, Julia Kirk. Women of the depression: caste and culture in San Antonio, 1929-1939. College Station, TX: Texas A&M University Press, 1984. xviii, 279 p.: ill. English. DESCR: Criminal Justice System; Cultural Characteristics; Employment; Family; Great Depression, 1929-1933; Labor Supply and Market; Labor Unions; Prostitution; *Social Classes; *Women.

5003 Griswold del Castillo, Richard. "Only for my family...": historical dimensions of Chicano family solidarity--the case of San Antonio in 1860. AZTLAN, Vol. 16, no. 1-2 (1985), p. 145-176. English. DESCR: Extended Family; *Family; History; Population.

5004 Hazuda, Helen P., et al. Employment status and women's protection against coronary heart disease. AMERICAN JOURNAL OF EPIDEMIOLOGY, Vol. 123, no. 4 (April 1986), p. 623-640. English. DESCR: Anglo Americans; Diseases; Employment; *Heart Disease; Nutrition; *Public Health.

5005 Krause, Neal and Markides, Kyriakos S. Gender roles, illness, and illness behavior in a Mexican American population. SOCIAL SCIENCE QUARTERLY, Vol. 68, no. 1 (March 1987), p. 102-121. English. DESCR: Family; Public Health; *Sex Roles.

5006 Markides, Kyriakos S., et al. Sample representativeness in a three-generation study of Mexican Americans. JOURNAL OF

MARRIAGE AND THE FAMILY, Vol. 45, no. 4 (November 1983), p. 911-916. English. DESCR: *Age Groups; *Marriage; Population; *Socioeconomic Factors.

5007 McDuff, Mary Ann. Mexican-American women: a three-generational study of attitudes and behaviors. Thesis (M.A.)--Texas Women's University, 1989. 200 p. English. DESCR: *Acculturation; *Age Groups; Family; *Sex Roles.

5008 Neff, James Alan; Gilbert, Kathleen R.; and Hoppe, Sue K. Divorce likelihood among Anglos and Mexican Americans. JOURNAL OF DIVORCE AND REMARRIAGE, Vol. 15, no. 1-2 (1991), p. 75-98. English. DESCR: *Anglo Americans; *Divorce; *Marriage.

5009 Rips, Geoffrey and Tenayuca, Emma. Living history: Emma Tenayuca tells her story. TEXAS OBSERVER, (October 28, 1983), p. 7-15. English. DESCR: *Autobiography; Communist Party; Food Industry; Labor Unions; Leadership; Oral History; Pecan Shelling Worker's Union, San Antonio, TX; Strikes and Lockouts; Tenayuca, Emma; United Cannery Agricultural Packing and Allied Workers of America (UCAPAWA); Worker's Alliance (WA), Los Angeles, CA; Working Women.

5010 Rogers, Linda Perkowski and Markides, Kyriakos S. Well-being in the postparental stage in Mexican-American women. RESEARCH ON AGING, Vol. 11, no. 4 (December 1989), p. 508-516. English. DESCR: *Age Groups; Ancianos; Children; *"Empty Nest" Syndrome; *Parent and Child Relationships.

5011 Williams, Joyce E. Secondary victimization: confronting public attitudes about rape. VICTIMOLOGY, Vol. 9, no. 1 (1984), p. 66-81. English. DESCR: *Attitudes; Natural Support Systems; *Rape.

San Diego, CA

5012 Felice, Marianne E., et al. Clinical observations of Mexican-American, Caucasian, and Black pregnant teenagers. JOURNAL OF ADOLESCENT HEALTH CARE, Vol. 7, no. 5 (September 1986), p. 305-310. English. DESCR: Anglo Americans; Blacks; *Fertility; *Prenatal Care; Youth.

5013 Sweeny, Mary Anne and Gulino, Claire. The health belief model as an explanation for breast-feeding practices in a Hispanic population. ANS: ADVANCES IN NURSING SCIENCE, Vol. 9, no. 4 (July 1987), p. 35-50. English. DESCR: *Breastfeeding; *Cultural Customs; *Public Health; Tijuana, Baja California, Mexico; Women.

5014 Vega, William A., et al. Depressive symptoms and their correlates among immigrant Mexican women in the United States. SOCIAL SCIENCE & MEDICINE, Vol. 22, no. 6 (1986), p. 645-652. English. DESCR: Depression (Psychological); *Immigrants; *Mental Health; Public Health.

San Diego County, CA

5015 Solorzano-Torres, Rosalia. Female Mexican immigrants in San Diego County. IN: Ruiz, Vicki L. and Tiano, Susan, eds. WOMEN ON THE U.S.-MEXICO BORDER: RESPONSES TO CHANGE. Boston, MA: Allen & Unwin, 1987, p. 41-59. English. DESCR: Employment; *Immigrants; Immigration; Literature Reviews; Surveys; Undocumented Workers; Women.

San Diego County, CA
(cont.)

5016 Vega, William A.; Kolody, Bohdan; and Valle,
Juan Ramon. The relationship of marital
status, confidant support, and depression
among Mexican immigrant women. JOURNAL OF
MARRIAGE AND THE FAMILY, Vol. 48, no. 3
(August 1986), p. 597-605. English. DESCR:
*Depression (Psychological); *Immigrants;
Low Income; *Marriage; Stress; Women.

San Diego State University
USE: California State University, San Diego

San Fernando Valley, CA

5017 Harris, Mary G. Cholas: Latino girls and
gangs. New York: AMS Press, 1988. x, 220 p
English. DESCR: Barrios; *Gangs; Juvenile
Delinquency; Los Angeles, CA; *Youth.

San Francisco Bay Area

5018 Carr-Casanova, Rosario. Role-model history
and demographic factors in the social
composition of the family of forty Hispanic
women leaders in four occupational groups.
Thesis (Ph.D.)--Wright Institute, Berkeley,
1983. 136 p. English. DESCR: Family;
*Leadership.

5019 Chase, Charlotte Fay. Alcohol-related
problems of Mexican-American women in the
San Francisco Bay Area. Thesis
(M.S.)--University of California, San
Francisco, 1988. ix, 121 leaves. English.
DESCR: *Alcoholism.

5020 Hogeland, Chris and Rosen, Karen. Dreams
lost, dreams found: undocumented women in
the land of opportunity. San Francisco, CA:
Coalition for Immigrant and Refugee Rights
and Services, c1991. 153 p. English. DESCR:
*Battered Women; *Coalition for Immigrant
and Refugee Rights and Services, Immigrant
Woman's Task Force; Discrimination;
Immigrants; Sex Roles; Sexism; Social
Services; Undocumented Workers; Violence;
Women; Women Men Relations.

5021 Segura, Denise. Chicana and Mexican
immigrant women at work: the impact of
class, race, and gender on occupational
mobility. GENDER & SOCIETY, Vol. 3, no.
(March 1989), p. 37-52. English. DESCR:
*Employment; *Immigrants; Labor Supply and
Market; Laboring Classes; *Social Mobility;
Women; Working Women.

5022 Yarbro-Bejarano, Yvonne. Teatropoesia by
Chicanas in the Bay Area: TONGUES OF FIRE.
REVISTA CHICANO-RIQUENA, Vol. 11, no. 1
(Spring 1983), p. 78-94. English. DESCR: El
Teatro Nacional de Aztlan (TENAZ); Poems;
*Teatro; TONGUES OF FIRE.

San Francisco, CA

5023 Marin, Gerardo; Perez-Stable, Eliseo J. and
Marin, Barbara Van Oss. Cigarette smoking
among San Francisco Hispanics: the role of
acculturation and gender. PUBLIC HEALTH
BRIEFS, Vol. 79, no. 2 (February 1989), p.
196-198. English. DESCR: *Acculturation;
Drug Use; Males; *Smoking; Women.

5024 Soberon, Mercedes. La revolucion se trata de
amor: Mercedes Soberon. CHISMEARTE, Vol. 1,
no. 1 (Fall 1976), p. 14-18. Spanish.
DESCR: Art Criticism; Concilio de Arte
Popular, Los Angeles, CA; Cultural
Organizations; La Mission Media Arts, San
Francisco, CA; *Sex Roles; Soberon,
Mercedes.

San Francisco Mime Troupe

5025 Yarbro-Bejarano, Yvonne. Chicana's
experience in collective theatre: ideology
and form. WOMEN AND PERFORMANCE, Vol. 2, no.
2 (1985), p. 45-58. English. DESCR: Actors
and Actresses; Careers; El Teatro Campesino;
El Teatro de la Esperanza; Political
Ideology; Sex Roles; Teatro; Teatro
Libertad; Valentina Productions; Women.

San Joaquin Valley, CA

5026 Weber, Devra Anne. Mexican women on strike:
memory, history and oral narratives. IN: Del
Castillo, Adelaida R., ed. BETWEEN BORDERS:
ESSAYS ON MEXICANA/CHICANA HISTORY. Encino,
CA: Floricanto Press, 1990, p. 175-200.
English. DESCR: *1933 Cotton Strike; Cotton
Industry; History; *Oral History; Strikes
and Lockouts; *Valdez, Rosaura; Working
Women.

San Jose, CA

5027 Lara-Cea, Helen. Notes on the use of parish
registers in the reconstruction of Chicana
history in California prior to 1850. IN: Del
Castillo, Adelaida R., ed. BETWEEN BORDERS:
ESSAYS ON MEXICANA/CHICANA HISTORY. Encino,
CA: Floricanto Press, 1990, p. 131-159.
English. DESCR: *California; Catholic
Church; History; Indigenismo; Mission of
Santa Clara; Population; *Vital Statistics.

5028 Wagner, Roland M. Changes in extended family
relationships for Mexican American and Anglo
single mothers. JOURNAL OF DIVORCE, Vol. 11,
no. 2 (Winter 1987), p. 69-87. English.
DESCR: Anglo Americans; *Divorce; *Extended
Family; Natural Support Systems; *Single
Parents; Women.

5029 Wagner, Roland M. and Schaffer, Diane M.
Social networks and survival strategies: an
exploratory study of Mexican American,
Black, and Anglo female family heads in San
Jose, California. IN: Melville, Margarita
B., ed. TWICE A MINORITY. St. Louis, MO:
Mosby, 1980, p. 173-190. English. DESCR:
Anglo Americans; Blacks; Identity; *Natural
Support Systems; *Single Parents; Stress.

San Luis Valley, CO

5030 Nelson, Kathryn J. Excerpts from los
testamentos: Hispanic women folk artists of
the San Luis Valley, Colorado. FRONTIERS: A
JOURNAL OF WOMEN STUDIES, Vol. 5, no. 3
(Fall 1980), p. 34-43. English. DESCR:
*Archuleta, Eppie; Artists; Biography; Folk
Art.

San Mateo County, CA

5031 Gonzalez del Valle, Amalia and Usher, Mary.
Group therapy with aged Latino women: a
pilot project and study. CLINICAL
GERONTOLOGIST, Vol. 1, no. 1 (Fall 1982), p.
51-58. English. DESCR: *Ancianos; Cultural
Characteristics; Mental Illness;
*Psychotherapy.

San Miguel County, NM

5032 Buss, Fran Leeper. La partera: story of a
midwife. Ann Arbor, MI: University of
Michigan Press, 1980. 140 p.: ill. English.
DESCR: Aragon, Jesusita, 1908- ; Cultural
Customs; *Curanderas; Folk Medicine; Herbal
Medicine; *Midwives; New Mexico.

San Ysidro, CA

5033 Lawrence, Alberto Augusto. Traditional attitudes toward marriage, marital adjustment, acculturation, and self-esteem of Mexican-American and Mexican wives. Thesis (Ph.D.)--United States International University, San Diego, CA, 1982. ix, 191 p. English. DESCR: *Acculturation; *Attitudes; Machismo; *Marriage; Mental Health; Psychological Testing; Sex Roles; Sex Stereotypes; Tijuana, Baja California, Mexico; Women.

Sanchez, Olivia

5034 Goldman, Shifra M. Mujeres de California: Latin American women artists. IN: Moore, Sylvia, ed. YESTERDAY AND TOMORROW: CALIFORNIA WOMEN ARTISTS. New York, NY: Midmarch Arts Press, c1989, p. 202-229. English. DESCR: *Artists; Baca, Judith F.; Biography; California; Carrasco, Barbara; Cervantez, Yreina; de Larios, Dora; Feminism; Hernandez, Judithe; Lomas Garza, Carmen; Lopez, Yolanda M.; Mesa-Bains, Amalia; Murillo, Patricia; Valdez, Patssi; Vallejo Dillaway, Linda; Women; Zamora Lucero, Linda.

Sanchez, Philip V.

5035 Huerta, Dolores. Dolores Huerta talks about Republicans, Cesar, children and her home town. REGENERACION, Vol. 2, no. 4 (1975), p. 20-24. English. DESCR: *Agricultural Labor Unions; *Biography; Chavez, Cesar E.; Community Service Organization, Los Angeles, (CSO); Democratic Party; Elected Officials; Flores, Art; Huerta, Dolores; McGovern, George; *Politics; Ramirez, Henry M.; Ross, Fred; United Farmworkers of America (UFW); Working Women.

5036 Huerta, Dolores. Dolores Huerta talks about Republicans, Cesar, children and her home town. IN: Servin, Manuel P. ed. THE MEXICAN AMERICANS: AN AWAKENING MINORITY. 2nd ed. Beverly Hills, CA: Glencoe Press, 1974, p. 283-294. English. DESCR: *Agricultural Labor Unions; *Biography; Chavez, Cesar E.; Community Service Organization, Los Angeles, (CSO); Democratic Party; Elected Officials; Flores, Art; Huerta, Dolores; McGovern, George; *Politics; Ramirez, Henry M.; Ross, Fred; United Farmworkers of America (UFW); Working Women.

Sanchez, Rosaura

5037 Harlow, Barbara. Sites of struggle: immigration, deportation, prison, and exile. IN: Calderon, Hector and Saldivar, Jose David, eds. CRITICISM IN THE BORDERLANDS: STUDIES IN CHICANO LITERATURE, CULTURE, AND IDEOLOGY. Durham, NC: Duke University Press, 1991, p. [149]-163. English. DESCR: Anzaldua, Gloria; BLACK GOLD; BORDERLANDS/LA FRONTERA: THE NEW MESTIZA; First, Ruth; Khalifeh, Sahar; *Literary Criticism; *Political Ideology; Social Classes; "The Cariboo Cafe" [short story]; "The Ditch" [short story]; Viramontes, Helena Maria; WILD THORNS; *Women; Working Women.

5038 Hispanic women writers: an interview with Rosaura Sanchez. LECTOR, Vol. 2, no. 3 (November, December, 1983), p. 5,7. English. DESCR: *Authors.

Sanchez-Scott, Milcha

5039 Bouknight, Jon. Language as a cure: an interview with Milcha Sanchez-Scott. LATIN

AMERICAN THEATRE REVIEW, Vol. 23, no. 2 (Spring 1990), p. 63-74. English. DESCR: Actos; *Authors; ROOSTERS [play]; *Teatro.

Sandyland Nursery, Carpinteria, CA

5040 O'Connor, Mary I. Women's networks and the social needs of Mexican immigrants. URBAN ANTHROPOLOGY, Vol. 19, no. 1-2 (Spring, Summer, 1990), p. 81-98. English. DESCR: Employment; *Immigrants; Labor Unions; *Natural Support Systems; Undocumented Workers; United Farmworkers of America (UFW); Women.

SANGRE JOVEN: LAS MAQUILADORAS POR DENTRO

5041 Lavrin, Asuncion. El segundo sexo en Mexico: experiencia, estudio e introspeccion, 1983-1987. MEXICAN STUDIES/ESTUDIOS MEXICANOS, Vol. 5, no. 2 (Summer 1989), p. 297-312. Spanish. DESCR: Arenal, Sandra; *Border Industries; Carrillo, Jorge; Hernandez, Alberto; Iglesias, Norma; LA FLOR MAS BELLA DE LA MAQUILADORA; *Literature Reviews; Mexico; MUJERES FRONTERIZAS EN LA INDUSTRIA MAQUILADORA; Women.

Santa Barbara, CA

5042 Miranda, Gloria E. Hispano-Mexican childrearing practices in pre-American Santa Barbara. SOUTHERN CALIFORNIA QUARTERLY, Vol. 65, no. 4 (Winter 1983), p. 307-320. English. DESCR: *Children; Cultural Characteristics; *Family; History; *Parenting; Socialization.

Santa Clara Valley, CA

5043 Zavella, Patricia. The politics of race and gender: organizing Chicana cannery workers in Northern California. IN: Bookman, Ann and Morgen, Sandra, eds. WOMEN AND THE POLITICS OF EMPOWERMENT. Philadelphia, PA: Temple University Press, 1988, p. 202-224. English. DESCR: Bay City Cannery Workers Committee; *Canneries; Cannery Workers Committee (CWC); Discrimination; Garcia, Connie; Identity; *Labor Unions; Nationalism; Northern California; Sex Roles; Sexism; *Working Women.

5044 Zavella, Patricia. Women, work and family in the Chicano community: cannery workers of the Santa Clara Valley. Thesis (Ph.D.)--University of California, Berkeley, 1982. ix, 254 p. English. DESCR: *Canneries; Employment; *Family; Industrial Workers; Labor Unions; *Sex Roles; *Working Women.

5045 Zavella, Patricia. Women's work and Chicano families: cannery workers of the Santa Clara Valley. Ithaca, NY: Cornell University Press, 1987. xviii, 191 p. English. DESCR: *Canneries; Employment; Family; Industrial Workers; Labor Unions; Sex Roles; *Working Women.

Santa Fe, NM

5046 Gonzalez, Deena J. The widowed women of Santa Fe: assessments on the lives of an unmarried population, 1850-80. IN: Scadron, Arlene, ed. ON THEIR OWN: WIDOWS AND WIDOWHOOD IN THE AMERICAN SOUTHWEST 1843-1939. Urbana, IL: University of Illinois Press, c1988, p. [65]-90. English. DESCR: Family; History; Income; Land Tenure; Sex Roles; Single Parents; *Widowhood; *Women.

Santa Fe, NM (cont.)

5047 Gonzalez, Deena J. The widowed women of Santa Fe: assessments on the lives of an unmarried population, 1850-80. IN: DuBois, Ellen Carol and Ruiz, Vicki L., eds. UNEQUAL SISTERS: A MULTICULTURAL READER IN U.S. WOMEN'S HISTORY. New York: Routledge, 1990, p. 34-50. English. DESCR: Family; History; Income; Land Tenure; Sex Roles; Single Parents; *Widowhood; *Women.

Santa Teresa de Cabora
USE: Urrea, Teresa

Santeros

5048 Stoller, Marianne L. The Hispanic women artists of New Mexico: present and past. PALACIO, Vol. 92, no. 1 (1986), p. 21-25. English. DESCR: *Artists; *New Mexico.

Santos

5049 Stevens, Joanne Darsey. Santos by twentieth-century santeras: continuation of a traditional art form. Thesis (Ph.D.)--University of Texas at Dallas, 1986. 259 p. English. DESCR: Art History; *Artists; Dallas Museum of Art; New Mexico.

Saragoza, Alex M.

5050 Winkler, Karen J. Scholars say issues of diversity have "revolutionized" field of Chicano Studies. CHRONICLE OF HIGHER EDUCATION, Vol. 37, no. 4 (September 26, 1990), p. A4-A9. English. DESCR: Chicana Studies; Chicano Studies; Curriculum; *Feminism; Higher Education; Ruiz, Vicki L.

Schoen, Robert

5051 Alba, Richard D. A comment on Schoen and Cohen. AMERICAN JOURNAL OF SOCIOLOGY, Vol. 87, no. 4 (January 1982), p. 935-939. English. DESCR: Cohen, Lawrence E.; ETHNIC ENDOGAMY AMONG MEXICAN AMERICAN GROOMS; Intermarriage; *Research Methodology.

Scholarship
USE: Financial Aid

Schooling
USE: Education

Science as a Profession

5052 MacCorquodale, Patricia. Social influences on the participation of Mexican-American women in science: final report. Unpublished report of study conducted at the Dept. of Sociology at the University of Arizona at Tucson and sponsored by the National Institute of Education. 1983, 81 p. (Eric Document: ED234944. English. DESCR: Arizona; Careers.

Sculptors
USE: Artists

Seasonal Labor
USE: Migrant Labor

Secondary School Education

5053 Abrahamse, Allan F.; Morrison, Peter A.; and Waite, Linda J. Beyond stereotypes: who becomes a single teenage mother? Santa Monica, CA: RAND Corp., 1988. xv, 88 p. English. DESCR: *Fertility; Religion; *Single Parents; Statistics; *Women; *Youth.

5054 Daggett, Andrea Stuhlman. A comparison of occupational goal orientations of female Mexican-Americans and Anglo high-school seniors of the classes of 1972 and 1980. Thesis (Ph.D.)--University of Arizona, Tucson, 1983. xii, 134 p. English. DESCR: Academic Achievement; Anglo Americans; *Careers; Sexism; Students; Women.

5055 Guajardo, Maria Resendez. Educational attainment of Chicana adolescents. Thesis (Ph.D.)--University of Denver, 1988. 266 p. English. DESCR: Academic Achievement; *Dropouts; *Youth.

5056 Isaacs, Barbara Gail. Anglo, Black, and Latin adolescents' participation in sports. Thesis (Ph.D.)--California School of Professional Psychology, Los Angeles, 1984. 283 p. English. DESCR: Anglo Americans; Blacks; Cultural Characteristics; *Sports; *Women; Youth.

5057 Kaplan, Celia Patricia. Critical factors affecting school dropout among Mexican-American women. Thesis (Doctor of Public Health)--UCLA, 1990. xviii, 256 p. English. DESCR: *Dropouts; Marriage.

5058 Lee, Valerie. Achievement and educational aspirations among Hispanic female high school students: comparison between public and Catholic schools. IN: McKenna, Teresa and Ortiz, Flora Ida, eds. THE BROKEN WEB: THE EDUCATIONAL EXPERIENCE OF HISPANIC WOMEN. Claremont, CA: Tomas Rivera Center; Berkeley, CA: Floricanto Press, 1988, p. 137-192. English. DESCR: *Academic Achievement; Anglo Americans; Catholic Church; Education; Educational Statistics; Private Education; Religious Education; *Women.

5059 Vigil, James Diego. The nexus of class, culture and gender in the education of Mexican American females. IN: McKenna, Teresa and Ortiz, Flora Ida, eds. THE BROKEN WEB: THE EDUCATIONAL EXPERIENCE OF HISPANIC WOMEN. Claremont, CA: Tomas Rivera Center; Berkeley, CA: Floricanto Press, 1988, p. 79-103. English. DESCR: Academic Achievement; Acculturation; Discrimination in Education; *Education; Identity; Sex Roles; Social Classes; Students.

SEGUIN [movie]

5060 Morales, Sylvia. Chicano-produced celluloid mujeres. BILINGUAL REVIEW, Vol. 10, no. 2-3 (May, December, 1983), p. 89-93. English. DESCR: BALLAD OF GREGORIO CORTEZ [film]; Film Reviews; *Films; RAICES DE SANGRE [film]; *Stereotypes; ZOOT SUIT [film].

SELECTED POEMS/SELECCIONES

5061 Aguilar-Henson, Marcella. The multi-faceted poetic world of Angela de Hoyos. Austin, TX: Relampago Books Press, 1985, c1982. 81 p. English. DESCR: ARISE CHICANO; *Authors; CHICANO POEMS FOR THE BARRIO; de Hoyos, Angela; GATA POEMS; GOODBYE TO SILENCE; Language Usage; *Literary Criticism; *Poetry; YO, MUJER.

Self Concept
USE: Identity

Self Perception
USE: Identity

Self-Concept Self Report Scale

5062 Fu, Victoria R.; Hinkle, Dennis E.; and Korslund, Mary K. A development study of ethnic self-concept among pre-adolescent girls. JOURNAL OF GENETIC PSYCHOLOGY, Vol. 14, (March 1983), p. 67-73. English. DESCR: Comparative Psychology; *Identity; Junior High School; Students; Youth.

Self-Help Groups
USE: Mutualistas

Self-Referents

5063 Alonso, Ana Maria and Koreck, Maria Teresa. Silences: "Hispanics", AIDS, and sexual practices. DIFFERENCES: A JOURNAL OF FEMINIST CULTURAL STUDIES, Vol. 1, no. 1 (Winter 1989), p. 101-124. English. DESCR: *AIDS (Disease); *Homosexuality; Human Immunodeficiency Virus (HIV); Machismo; Mexico; Sex Roles; *Sexual Behavior.

5064 Bean, Frank D. and Tienda, Marta. The Hispanic population of the United States. New York: Russell Sage Foundation, 1987. xxiv, 456 p. English. DESCR: *Census; Education; Employment; Fertility; Identity; Immigration; Income; *Population; *Statistics.

5065 Bello, Ruth T. Being Hispanic in Houston: a matter of identity. THE AMERICAS REVIEW, Vol. 16, no. 1 (Spring 1988), p. 31-43. English. DESCR: Autobiography; *Essays; *Houston, TX; *Identity.

5066 Estrada, Esther R. The importance of the 1980 census. IN: LA CHICANA: BUILDING FOR THE FUTURE, AN ACTION PLAN FOR THE'80s. Oakland, CA: National Hispanic University, 1981, p. 2-7. English. DESCR: *Census; Ethnic Groups.

5067 Rivero, Eliana S. La mujer y La Raza: Latinas y Chicanas [part I]. CARACOL, Vol. 4, no. 1 (September 1977), p. 8-9. Spanish. DESCR: *Chicano Movement.

Senate Concurrent Resolution 43, 1987

5068 Sosa Riddell, Adaljiza. Synopsis on Senate Concurrent Resolution 43: an example in public policy making. IN: Sosa Riddell, Adaljiza, ed. POLICY DEVELOPMENT: CHICANA/LATINA SUMMER RESEARCH INSTITUTE. Davis, CA: [Chicano Studies Program, University of California, Davis, 1989?], p. 16-26. English. DESCR: Legislation; *Public Policy; University of California.

Sex Discrimination
USE: Sexism

Sex Education

5069 Davis, Sally M. and Harris, Mary B. Sexual knowledge, sexual interests, and sources of sexual information of rural and urban adolescents from three cultures. ADOLESCENCE, Vol. 17, no. 66 (Summer 1982), p. 471-492. English. DESCR: Birth Control; Cultural Characteristics; Identity; Rural Population; Sex Roles; Urban Communities; Youth.

5070 de Anda, Diane; Becerra, Rosina M.; and Fielder, Eve P. Sexuality, pregnancy, and motherhood among Mexican-American adolescents. JOURNAL OF ADOLESCENT RESEARCH, Vol. 3, no. 3-4 (Fall, Winter, 1988), p. 403-411. English. DESCR: Anglo Americans; Attitudes; Birth Control; *Fertility;

*Sexual Behavior; Women; *Youth.

5071 Forste, Renata T. and Heaton, Tim B. Initiation of sexual activity among female adolescents. YOUTH AND SOCIETY, Vol. 19, no. 3 (March 1988), p. 250-268. English. DESCR: Anglo Americans; Blacks; Family; *Sexual Behavior; Women; *Youth.

5072 Hutchison, James. Teenagers and contraception in Cameron and Willacy Counties. BORDERLANDS JOURNAL, Vol. 7, no. 1 (Fall 1983), p. 75-90. English. DESCR: *Birth Control; Cameron County, TX; *Family Planning; Fertility; Willacy County, TX; Youth.

5073 Martinez, Ruben. AIDS in the Latino community. AMERICAS 2001, Vol. 1, no. 5 (March, April, 1988), p. [14-18]. Bilingual. DESCR: *AIDS (Disease).

5074 Sex education, abortion views of Mexican Americans typical of U.S. beliefs. FAMILY PLANNING PERSPECTIVES, Vol. 15, (July, August, 1983), p. 197-201. English. DESCR: *Abortion; *Attitudes; Birth Control; Family Planning.

Sex Roles

5075 Ahern, Susan; Bryan, Dexter Edward; and Baca, Reynaldo. Migration and la mujer fuerte. MIGRATION TODAY, Vol. 13, no. 1 (1985), p. 14-20. English. DESCR: Mexico; *Migration; *Women.

5076 Alanis, Elsa. The relationship between state and trait anxiety and acculturation in Mexican-American women homemakers and Mexican-American community college female students. Thesis (Ph.D.)--United States International University, 1989. 161 p. English. DESCR: *Acculturation; *Community Colleges; Family; *Stress; Students.

5077 Alarcon, Norma. Chicana's feminist literature: a re-vision through Malintzinl or Malintzin: putting flesh back on the object. IN: Moraga, Cherrie and Anzaldua, Gloria, eds. THIS BRIDGE CALLED MY BACK: WRITINGS BY RADICAL WOMEN OF COLOR. Watertown, MA: Persephone Press, 1981, p. 182-190. English. DESCR: Feminism; Literature; Malinche; Stereotypes; Symbolism.

5078 Alarcon, Norma and Moraga, Cherrie. Interview with Cherrie Moraga. THIRD WOMAN, Vol. 3, no. 1-2 (1986), p. 127-134. English. DESCR: Authors; Biography; Homosexuality; *Moraga, Cherrie.

5079 Alarcon, Norma. Making "familia" from scratch: split subjectivities in the work of Helena Maria Viramontes and Cherrie Moraga. THE AMERICAS REVIEW, Vol. 15, no. 3-4 (Fall, Winter, 1987), p. 147-159. English. DESCR: GIVING UP THE GHOST; *Literary Criticism; Moraga, Cherrie; "Snapshots" [short story]; THE MOTHS AND OTHER STORIES; Viramontes, Helena Maria.

5080 Alarcon, Norma. The sardonic powers of the erotic in the work of Ana Castillo. IN: Horno-Delgado, Asuncion, et al., eds. BREAKING BOUNDARIES: LATINA WRITING AND CRITICAL READINGS. Amherst, MA: University of Massachusetts Press, c1989, p. 94-107. English. DESCR: *Castillo, Ana; Literary Criticism; OTRO CANTO; Poetry; THE INVITATION; *THE MIXQUIAHUALA LETTERS; WOMEN ARE NOT ROSES.

Sex Roles (cont.)

5081 Alarcon, Norma; Castillo, Ana; and Moraga, Cherrie. The sexuality of Latinas [special issue of THIRD WOMAN]. THIRD WOMAN, Vol. 4, (1989), p. 8-189. Bilingual. DESCR: *Literature; *Sexual Behavior; *Women.

5082 Alarcon, Norma. Traddutora, traditora: a paradigmatic figure of Chicana feminism. CULTURAL CRITIQUE, Vol. 13, (Fall 1989), p. 57-87. English. DESCR: *Feminism; *Malinche; Paz, Octavio; Symbolism.

5083 Alba, Isabel Catherine. Achievement conflicts, sex-role orientation, and performance on sex-role appropriate and sex-role inappropriate tasks in women of three ethnic groups. Thesis (Ph.D.)--University of California, Riverside, 1987. 129 p English. DESCR: Anglo Americans; *Assertiveness; Blacks; Ethnic Groups; Fear of Success Scale (FOSS) Women.

5084 Alonso, Ana Maria and Koreck, Maria Teresa. Silences: "Hispanics", AIDS, and sexual practices. DIFFERENCES: A JOURNAL OF FEMINIST CULTURAL STUDIES, Vol. 1, no. 1 (Winter 1989), p. 101-124. English. DESCR: *AIDS (Disease); *Homosexuality; Human Immunodeficiency Virus (HIV); Machismo; Mexico; *Self-Referents; *Sexual Behavior.

5085 Andrade, Sally J. Family roles of Hispanic women: stereotypes, empirical findings, and implications for research. IN: Zambrana, Ruth E., ed. WORK, FAMILY, AND HEALTH: LATINA WOMEN IN TRANSITION. Bronx, NY: Hispanic Research Center, Fordham University, 1982, p. 95-106. English. DESCR: *Family; Puerto Ricans; *Research Methodology; Sex Stereotypes; Women.

5086 Andrade, Sally J. Social science stereotypes of the Mexican American woman: policy implications for research. HISPANIC JOURNAL OF BEHAVIORAL SCIENCES, Vol. 4, no. 2 (June 1982), p. 223-244. English. DESCR: Social Science; Stereotypes.

5087 Anzaldua, Gloria. Borderlands/La frontera: the new mestiza. San Francisco, CA: Spinsters/Aunt Lute, 1987. 203 p. Bilingual. DESCR: Aztecs; Border Region; *Identity; Mythology; Poems; Prose.

5088 Ashley, Laurel Maria. Self, family and community: the social process of aging among urban Mexican-American women. Thesis (Ph.D.)--University of California, Los Angeles, 1985. 306 p. English. DESCR: Acculturation; *Ancianos; *Family; Grandmothers; Southern California.

5089 Aulette, Judy and Mills, Trudy. Something old, something new: auxiliary work in the 1983-1986 copper strike. FEMINIST STUDIES, Vol. 14, no. 2 (Summer 1988), p. 251-268 English. DESCR: Arizona; Clifton-Morenci Copper Strike, 1983-1986; Clifton-Morenci District, Arizona; Feminism; Labor Unions; Morenci Miners Women's Auxiliary (MMWA); Mutualistas; Phelps Dodge Corporation, Morenci, AZ; SALT OF THE EARTH [film]; *Strikes and Lockouts.

5090 Ayers-Nackamkin, Beverly, et al. Sex and ethnic differences in the use of power. JOURNAL OF APPLIED PSYCHOLOGY, Vol. 67, no. 4 (August 1982), p. 464-471. English. DESCR: Anglo Americans; Ethnic Groups; Management; *Personnel Management; Social Psychology.

5091 Baca, Reynaldo and Bryan, Dexter Edward. Mexican women, migration and sex roles. MIGRATION TODAY, Vol. 13, no. 3 (1985), p. 14-18. English. DESCR: Mexico; *Migration; *Women.

5092 Baca Zinn, Maxine. Chicanas: power and control in the domestic sphere. DE COLORES, Vol. 2, no. 3 (1975), p. 19-31. English. DESCR: *Family; Immigration Regulation and Control; Machismo; Stereotypes; *Women Men Relations.

5093 Baca Zinn, Maxine. Chicanas: power and control in the domestic sphere. IN: Cotera, Martha and Hufford, Larry, eds. BRIDGING TWO CULTURES. Austin, TX: National Educational Laboratory Publishers, 1980, p. 270-281. English. DESCR: Family; Immigration Regulation and Control; Machismo; *Stereotypes; Women Men Relations.

5094 Baca Zinn, Maxine. Chicano men and masculinity. JOURNAL OF ETHNIC STUDIES, Vol. 10, no. 2 (Summer 1982), p. 29-44. English. DESCR: Cultural Characteristics; Ethnic Stratification; *Machismo; Sex Stereotypes; Socioeconomic Factors; Women Men Relations.

5095 Baca Zinn, Maxine. Employment and education of Mexican-American women: the interplay of modernity and ethnicity in eight families. HARVARD EDUCATIONAL REVIEW, Vol. 50, no. 1 (February 1980), p. 47-62. English. DESCR: Acculturation; Decision Making; *Education; *Employment; *Family; Identity; Social Classes; Values.

5096 Baca Zinn, Maxine. Gender and ethnic identity among Chicanos. FRONTIERS: A JOURNAL OF WOMEN STUDIES, Vol. 5, no. 2 (Summer 1980), p. 18-24. English. DESCR: *Identity.

5097 Baca Zinn, Maxine. Political familism: toward sex role equality in Chicano families. AZTLAN, Vol. 6, no. 1 (Spring 1975), p. 13-26. English. DESCR: Acculturation; Chicano Movement; Family; Machismo.

5098 Baca Zinn, Maxine. Qualitative methods in family research: a look inside Chicano families. CALIFORNIA SOCIOLOGIST, Vol. 5, no. 2 (Summer 1982), p. 58-79. English. DESCR: *Family; Marriage; *Research Methodology; Socioeconomic Factors.

5099 Berger, Peggy S. Differences in importance of and satisfaction from job characteristics by sex and occupational type among Mexican-American employees. JOURNAL OF VOCATIONAL BEHAVIOR, Vol. 28, no. 3 (June 1986), p. 203-213. English. DESCR: *Attitudes; *Employment.

5100 Blanco, Iris. La mujer en los albores de la conquista de Mexico. AZTLAN, Vol. 11, no. 2 (Fall 1980), p. 249-270. Spanish. DESCR: *Aztecs; Mexico; Women.

5101 Blanco, Iris. El sexo y su condicionamiento cultural en el mundo prehispanico. IN: Del Castillo, Adelaida R., ed. BETWEEN BORDERS: ESSAYS ON MEXICANA/CHICANA HISTORY. Encino, CA: Floricanto Press, 1990, p. 363-374. Spanish. DESCR: Mexico; *Precolumbian Society; Sexual Behavior; Women.

Sex Roles (cont.)

5102 Blea, Irene I. Mexican American female experience. IN: Blea, Irene I. TOWARD A CHICANO SOCIAL SCIENCE. New York: Praeger, 1988, p. [67]-89. English. **DESCR:** Chicano Movement; *Feminism; Sexism.

5103 Borland, Dolores C. A cohort analysis approach to the empty nest syndrome among three ethnic groups of women: a theoretical position. JOURNAL OF MARRIAGE AND THE FAMILY, Vol. 44, no. 1 (February 1982), p. 117-129. English. **DESCR:** "Empty Nest" Syndrome; Ethnic Groups; Social Psychology; Women.

5104 Bova, Breda Murphy and Phillips, Rebecca R. Hispanic women at midlife: implications for higher and adult education. JOURNAL OF ADULT EDUCATION, Vol. 18, no. 1 (Fall 1989), p. 9-15. English. **DESCR:** *Adult Education; Cultural Characteristics; *Higher Education; Identity.

5105 Briody, Elizabeth K. Patterns of household immigration into South Texas. INTERNATIONAL MIGRATION REVIEW, Vol. 21, no. 1 (Spring 1987), p. 27-47. English. **DESCR:** *Family; *Immigrants; *Social Mobility; *South Texas.

5106 Broyles-Gonzalez, Yolanda and Rodriguez, Diane. The living legacy of Chicana performers: preserving history through oral testimony. FRONTIERS: A JOURNAL OF WOMEN STUDIES, Vol. 11, no. 1 (1990), p. [46]-52. English. **DESCR:** *Actors and Actresses; El Teatro Campesino; Latins Anonymous [comedy review]; Oral History; *Rodriguez, Diane; Singers; Teatro.

5107 Buriel, Raymond and Saenz, Evangelina. Psychocultural characteristics of college-bound and noncollege-bound Chicanas. JOURNAL OF SOCIAL PSYCHOLOGY, Vol. 110, (April 1980), p. 245-251. English. **DESCR:** Biculturalism; *Biculturalism Inventory for Mexican American Students (BIMAS); Higher Education; Identity; Income; Psychological Testing; Social Psychology.

5108 Canales, Genevieve and Roberts, Robert E. Gender and mental health in the Mexican origin population of South Texas. IN: Rodriguez, Reymund and Coleman, Marion Tolbert, eds. MENTAL HEALTH ISSUES OF THE MEXICAN ORIGIN POPULATION IN TEXAS. Austin, TX: Hogg Foundation for Mental Health, University of Texas, 1987, p. 89-99. English. **DESCR:** Del Rio, TX; Depression (Psychological); Eagle Pass, TX; Health Education; *Males; *Mental Health; South Texas; Surveys.

5109 Canino, Glorisa. The Hispanic woman: sociocultural influences on diagnoses and treatment. IN: Becerra, Rosina M., et al., eds. MENTAL HEALTH AND HISPANIC AMERICANS: CLINICAL PERSPECTIVES. New York: Grune & Stratton, 1982, p. 117-138. English. **DESCR:** Assimilation; Cultural Characteristics; Culture; *Depression (Psychological); Family; Feminism; Mental Health; Population.

5110 Cantarow, Ellen and De la Cruz, Jessie Lopez. Jessie Lopez De la Cruz: the battle for farmworkers' rights. IN: Cantarow, Ellen. MOVING THE MOUNTAIN: WOMEN WORKING FOR SOCIAL CHANGE. Old Westbury, NY: Feminist Press, 1980, p. 94-151. English. **DESCR:** Agricultural Labor Unions; Chavez, Cesar E.; *De la Cruz, Jessie Lopez; *Farm Workers; Labor Disputes; Oral History; Parlier, CA; Strikes and Lockouts; *United Farmworkers of America (UFW).

5111 Cardoza, Desdemona. College attendance and persistence among Hispanic women: an examination of some contributing factors. SEX ROLES, Vol. 24, no. 3-4 (January 1991), p. 133-147. English. **DESCR:** Academic Achievement; College Preparation; *Enrollment; High School and Beyond Project (HS&B); *Higher Education; Socialization; Socioeconomic Factors.

5112 Chavira, Alicia. "Tienes que ser valiente": Mexicana migrants in a midwestern farm labor camp. IN: Melville, Margarita, ed. MEXICANAS AT WORK IN THE UNITED STATES. Houston, TX: Mexican American Studies Program, University of Houston, 1988, p. 64-74. English. **DESCR:** *Farm Workers; Immigrants; *Labor Camps; Midwestern States; Migrant Health Services; *Migrant Labor; *Women.

5113 Corbett, Kitty; Mora, Juana; and Ames, Genevieve. Drinking patterns and drinking-related problems of Mexican-American husbands and wives. JOURNAL OF STUDIES ON ALCOHOL, Vol. 52, no. 3 (May 1991), p. 215-223. English. **DESCR:** *Alcoholism; *Marriage.

5114 Corrales, Ramona. Undocumented Hispanas in America. IN: LA CHICANA: BUILDING FOR THE FUTURE, AN ACTION PLAN FOR THE 80s. Oakland, CA: National Hispanic University, 1981, p. 59-73. Also IN: THE STATE OF HISPANIC AMERICA II. Oakland, CA: National Hispanic Center Advanced Studies and Policy Analysis, 1982, p. 100-107. English. **DESCR:** Immigration; Immigration Law and Legislation; *Undocumented Workers.

5115 Cotera, Marta P. Sexism in bilingual bicultural education. IN: Cotera, Martha and Hufford, Larry, eds. BRIDGING TWO CULTURES. Austin, TX: National Educational Laboratory Publishers, 1980, p. 181-190. English. **DESCR:** *Bilingual Bicultural Education; Sexism; Stereotypes; Textbooks.

5116 Cuellar, Israel. Service delivery and mental health services for Chicano elders. IN: Miranda, Manuel and Ruiz, Rene A., eds. CHICANO AGING AND MENTAL HEALTH. Rockville, MD: U.S. Department of Health and Human Services, 1981, p. 185-211. English. **DESCR:** *Ancianos; Attitudes; Cultural Customs; Cultural Pluralism; Language Usage; Mental Health; Mental Health Clinics; Religion; Spanish Language.

5117 Curry Rodriguez, Julia E. Labor migration and familial responsibilities: experiences of Mexican women. IN: Melville, Margarita, ed. MEXICANAS AT WORK IN THE UNITED STATES. Houston, TX: Mexican American Studies Program, University of Houston, 1988, p. 47-63. English. **DESCR:** Employment; Family; *Immigrants; Mexico; *Migrant Labor; Oral History; Undocumented Workers; *Women; *Working Women.

5118 Curtis, Theodore T. and Baca Zinn, Maxine. Marital role orientation among Chicanos: an analysis of structural and cultural factors. LA RED/THE NET, no. 59 (October 1982), p. 2-4. English. **DESCR:** *Marriage.

Sex Roles (cont.)

5119 Davis, Sally M. and Harris, Mary B. Sexual knowledge, sexual interests, and sources of sexual information of rural and urban adolescents from three cultures. ADOLESCENCE, Vol. 17, no. 66 (Summer 1982), p. 471-492. English. DESCR: Birth Control; Cultural Characteristics; Identity; Rural Population; *Sex Education; Urban Communities; Youth.

5120 Del Zotto, Augusta. Latinas with AIDS: life expectancy for Hispanic women is a startling 45 days after diagnosis. THIS WORLD, (April 9, 1989), p. 9. English. DESCR: Abortion; AIDS (Disease); Condom Use; Instituto Familiar de la Raza, San Francisco, CA; Machismo; *Mano a Mano; Quintero, Juanita; Women Men Relations.

5121 Delgado, Abelardo "Lalo". An open letter to Carolina... or relations between men and women. REVISTA CHICANO-RIQUENA, Vol. 10, no. 1-2 (Winter, Spring, 1982), p. 279-284. English. DESCR: *Essays; Machismo; Sex Stereotypes; Women Men Relations.

5122 Delgado, Sylvia. Young Chicana speaks up or problems faced by young girls. REGENERACION, Vol. 1, no. 10 (1971), p. 5-7. English. DESCR: Abortion; Feminism; Machismo; Marriage; *Women Men Relations.

5123 Deutsch, Sarah. Culture, class, and gender Chicanas and Chicanos in Colorado and New Mexico, 1900-1940. Thesis (Ph.D.)--Yale University, 1985. xii, 510 p. English. DESCR: Anglo Americans; Colorado; Immigrants; New Mexico; *Social Classes; Social History and Conditions; Women; *Working Women.

5124 Deutsch, Sarah. No separate refuge: culture, class, and gender on an Anglo-Hispanic frontier in the American Southwest, 1880-1940. New York: Oxford University Press, 1987. vi, 356 p. English. DESCR: Anglo Americans; Colorado; Immigrants; Immigration; Mining Industry; Missions; New Mexico; *Social Classes; *Social History and Conditions; Women; Working Women; World War I.

5125 Deutsch, Sarah. Women and intercultural relations: the case of Hispanic New Mexico and Colorado. SIGNS: JOURNAL OF WOMEN IN CULTURE AND SOCIETY, Vol. 12, no. 4 (Summer 1987), p. 719-739. English. DESCR: Colorado; Cultural Characteristics; Immigrants; Intercultural Communication; Mexico; New Mexico; Rural Population; Social History and Conditions; *Women.

5126 Dill, Bonnie Thornton. Our mothers' grief: racial ethnic women and the maintenance of families. JOURNAL OF FAMILY HISTORY, Vol. 13, no. 4 (October 1988), p. 415-431. English. DESCR: Asian Americans; Blacks; Domestic Work; *Family; Fertility; *Women; *Working Women.

5127 Duarte, Patricia. The post-lib tango: couples in chaos. NUESTRO, Vol. 3, no. 5 (June, July, 1979), p. 38-40. English. DESCR: Divorce; Machismo; Marriage.

5128 Esparza, Mariana Ochoa. The impact of adult education on Mexican-American women. Thesis (Ed.D.)--Texas A & I University, 1981. 68 p. English. DESCR: *Adult Education; Careers; McAllen, TX.

5129 Espin, Oliva M. Cultural and historical influences on sexuality in Hispanic/Latin women: implications for psychotherapy. IN: Vance, Carole S., ed. PLEASURE AND DANGER: EXPLORING FEMALE SEXUALITY. Boston, MA: Routledge & Kegan Paul, 1984, p. 149-164. English. DESCR: Immigration; Language Usage; Machismo; *Psychotherapy; *Sexual Behavior; Social History and Conditions; Spanish Influence; *Women.

5130 Facio, Elisa "Linda". Constraints, resources, and self-definition: a case study of Chicano older women. Thesis (Ph.D.)--University of California, Berkeley, 1988. 246 p. English. DESCR: *Ancianos; *Family; Grandmothers; *Poverty; Widowhood.

5131 Falicov, Celia Jaes. Mexican families. IN: McGoldrick, Monica, et al., eds. ETHNICITY AND FAMILY THERAPY. New York: The Guilford Press, 1982, p. 134-163. English. DESCR: Acculturation; Cultural Customs; *Family; Mental Health.

5132 Ferrandez Kelly, Maria and Garcia, Anna M. Invisible amidst the glitter: Hispanic women in the Southern California electronics industry. IN: Statham, Anne; Miller, Eleanor M.; and Mauksh, Hans O., eds. THE WORTH OF WOMEN'S WORK: A QUALITATIVE SYNTHESIS. Albany, NY: State University of New York Press, 1988, p. 265-290. English. DESCR: *Electronics Industry; Employment; Immigrants; *Industrial Workers; Labor Supply and Market; Megatek, La Jolla, CA; Nova-Tech, San Diego, CA; Southern California; *Working Women.

5133 Flores, Francisca. Conference of Mexican women un remolino. REGENERACION, Vol. 1, no. 10 (1971), p. 1-5. English. DESCR: Conferences and Meetings; Family; Feminism; First National Chicana Conference (May 1971: Houston, TX); Machismo; National Mexican American Issues Conference (October 11, 1970: Sacramento, CA); Sex Stereotypes; Statistics; *Women Men Relations.

5134 Flores, Henry. Some different thoughts concerning "machismo". COMADRE, no. 3 (Fall 1978), p. 7-9. English. DESCR: *Machismo.

5135 Garcia, Mario T. The Chicana in American history: the Mexican women of El Paso, 1880-1920 - a case study. PACIFIC HISTORICAL REVIEW, Vol. 49, no. 2 (May 1980), p. 315-337. English. DESCR: Acme Laundry, El Paso, TX; American Federation of Labor (AFL); Case Studies; Central Labor Union; Domestic Work; *El Paso, TX; Employment; *History; Immigrants; Income; Labor Unions; Strikes and Lockouts; *Working Women.

5136 Garcia, Mario T. La familia: the Mexican immigrant family, 1900-1930. IN: Barrera, Mario, et al., eds. WORK, FAMILY, SEX ROLES, LANGUAGE: SELECTED PAPERS, 1979. Berkeley, CA: Toratiuh-Quinto Sol, 1980, p. 117-139. English. DESCR: Assimilation; Cultural Customs; El Paso, TX; Family; *Historiography; History; Immigration; Labor.

5137 Garcia-Bahne, Betty. La Chicana and the Chicano family. IN: Sanchez, Rosaura and Martinez Cruz, Rosa, eds. ESSAYS ON LA MUJER. Los Angeles, CA: Chicano Studies Center Publications, UCLA, 1977, p. 30-47. English. DESCR: Cultural Customs; *Family; Social Classes; Socialization; Stereotypes.

Sex Roles (cont.)

5138 Golding, Jacqueline M. Division of household labor, strain, and depressive symptoms among Mexican Americans and non-Hispanic whites. PSYCHOLOGY OF WOMEN QUARTERLY, Vol. 14, no. 1 (March 1990), p. 103-117. English. DESCR: Anglo Americans; Comparative Psychology; *Depression (Psychological); Domestic Work; Employment; Identity; Women.

5139 Gonzales, Sylvia Alicia. The Chicana perspective: a design for self-awareness. IN: Trejo, Arnulfo D., ed. THE CHICANOS: AS WE SEE OURSELVES. Tucson, AZ: University of Arizona Press, 1979, p. 81-99. English. DESCR: CHICANAS SPEAK OUT; Chicano Movement; Discrimination; Feminism; Identity; Machismo; Madsen, William; *Mexican Revolution - 1910-1920; Mexico; THE MEXICAN-AMERICANS OF SOUTH TEXAS; Vidal, Mirta.

5140 Gonzalez, Alex. Sex roles of the traditional Mexican family: a comparison of Chicano and Anglo students' attitudes. JOURNAL OF CROSS-CULTURAL PSYCHOLOGY, Vol. 13, no. 3 (September 1982), p. 330-339. English. DESCR: Anglo Americans; Attitudes; Comparative Psychology; *Family; Hembrismo; Machismo; Students.

5141 Gonzalez, Deena J. The widowed women of Santa Fe: assessments on the lives of an unmarried population, 1850-80. IN: Scadron, Arlene, ed. ON THEIR OWN: WIDOWS AND WIDOWHOOD IN THE AMERICAN SOUTHWEST 1843-1939. Urbana, IL: University of Illinois Press, c1988, p. [65]-90. English. DESCR: Family; History; Income; Land Tenure; *Santa Fe, NM; Single Parents; *Widowhood; *Women.

5142 Gonzalez, Deena J. The widowed women of Santa Fe: assessments on the lives of an unmarried population, 1850-80. IN: DuBois, Ellen Carol and Ruiz, Vicki L., eds. UNEQUAL SISTERS: A MULTICULTURAL READER IN U.S. WOMEN'S HISTORY. New York: Routledge, 1990, p. 34-50. English. DESCR: Family; History; Income; Land Tenure; *Santa Fe, NM; Single Parents; *Widowhood; *Women.

5143 Gonzalez, Judith Teresa. Dilemmas of the high achieving Chicana: the double bind factor in male/female relationships. Tucson, AZ: Mexican American Studies & Research Center, University of Arizona, 1987. 31 leaves. English. DESCR: *Academic Achievement; Higher Education; Identity; Males; Marriage; *Sex Stereotypes; Women Men Relations.

5144 Gonzalez, Judith Teresa. Dilemmas of the high achieving Chicana: the double bind factor in male/female relationships. SEX ROLES, Vol. 18, no. 7-8 (April 1988), p. 367-380. English. DESCR: *Academic Achievement; Higher Education; Identity; Males; Marriage; *Sex Stereotypes; Women Men Relations.

5145 Gonzalez, Rosalinda M. Chicanas and Mexican immigrant families 1920-1940: women's subordination and family exploitation. IN: Scharf, Lois and Jensen, Joan M., eds. DECADES OF DISCONTENT: THE WOMEN'S MOVEMENT, 1920-1940. Westport, CT: Greenwood Press, 1983, p. 59-84. English. DESCR: *Family; Farm Workers; History; Immigrants; Labor; Labor Unions; Mexico; Pecan Shelling Worker's Union, San Antonio, TX; Strikes and Lockouts; United Cannery Agricultural Packing and Allied Workers of America

(UCAPAWA); Working Women.

5146 Gonzalez-Berry, Erlinda and Rebolledo, Tey Diana. Growing up Chicano: Tomas Rivera and Sandra Cisneros. REVISTA CHICANO-RIQUENA, Vol. 13, no. 3-4 (Fall, Winter, 1985), p. 109-119. English. DESCR: Cisneros, Sandra; Cultural Characteristics; *Literary Criticism; Rivera, Tomas; THE HOUSE ON MANGO STREET; Y NO SE LO TRAGO LA TIERRA/AND THE EARTH DID NOT PART.

5147 Griswold del Castillo, Richard. La familia: Chicano families in the urban Southwest, 1848 to the present. Notre Dame, IN: University of Notre Dame Press, c1984. xv, 173 p. English. DESCR: *Family; History; Intermarriage; Machismo; Parenting; Sexual Behavior; *Social History and Conditions.

5148 Griswold del Castillo, Richard. Patriarchy and the status of women in the late nineteenth-century Southwest. IN: Rodriguez O., Jaime E., ed. THE MEXICAN AND MEXICAN AMERICAN EXPERIENCE IN THE 19TH CENTURY. Tempe, AZ: Bilingual Press/Editorial Bilingue, 1989, p. 85-99. English. DESCR: Family; *Feminism; History; *Machismo.

5149 Guendelman, Sylvia. The incorporation of Mexican women in seasonal migration: a study of gender differences. HISPANIC JOURNAL OF BEHAVIORAL SCIENCES, Vol. 9, no. 3 (September 1987), p. 245-264. English. DESCR: Immigrants; Marriage; Mexico; *Migration Patterns; *Women; *Women Men Relations; Working Women.

5150 Gutierrez Castillo, Dina. La imagen de la mujer en la novela fronteriza. IN: Lopez-Gonzalez, Aralia, et al., eds. MUJER Y LITERATURA MEXICANA Y CHICANA: CULTURAS EN CONTACTO. Mexico: Colegio de la Frontera Norte, 1988, p. [55]-63. Spanish. DESCR: *Border Region; Islas, Arturo; Literary Characters; *Literary Criticism; Mendez M., Miguel; *Novel; PEREGRINOS DE AZTLAN; Sex Stereotypes; THE RAIN GOD: A DESERT TALE; *Women.

5151 Gutierrez, Ramon A. Honor ideology, marriage negotiation, and class-gender domination in New Mexico, 1690-1846. LATIN AMERICAN PERSPECTIVES, Vol. 12, no. 1 (Winter 1985), p. 81-104. English. DESCR: Marriage; *Social Classes; Social History and Conditions; Southwestern United States; Values; Women Men Relations.

5152 Gutierrez, Ramon A. When Jesus came, the corn mothers went away: marriage, sexuality, and power in New Mexico, 1500-1846. Stanford: Stanford University Pres, 1991. xxxi, 424 p. English. DESCR: *Marriage; Native Americans; *New Mexico; *Pueblo Indians; Sexual Behavior; Spanish Influence; Women.

5153 Hartzler, Kaye and Franco, Juan N. Ethnicity, division of household tasks and equity in marital roles: a comparison of Anglo and Mexican American couples. HISPANIC JOURNAL OF BEHAVIORAL SCIENCES, Vol. 7, no. 4 (December 1985), p. 333-344. English. DESCR: Marriage.

Sex Roles (cont.)

5154 Hawley, Peggy and Even, Brenda. Work and sex-role attitudes in relation to education and other characteristics. VOCATIONAL GUIDANCE QUARTERLY, Vol. 31, no. 2 (December 1982), p. 101-108. English. DESCR: Attitudes; Careers; Education; Ethnic Groups; Psychological Testing; Working Women.

5155 Hayghe, Howard. Married couples: work and income patterns. MONTHLY LABOR REVIEW, Vol. 106, no. 12 (December 1983), p. 26-29. English. DESCR: *Employment; *Income; *Marriage; Working Women.

5156 Herrera-Sobek, Maria. The acculturation process of the Chicana in the corrido. DE COLORES, Vol. 6, no. 1-2 (1982), p. 7-16. English. DESCR: *Acculturation; Corridos.

5157 Herrera-Sobek, Maria. The Mexican corrido: a feminist analysis. Bloomington, IN: Indiana University Press, 1990. xix, 151 p.: ill. English. DESCR: *Corridos; Mexico; Military; Sex Stereotypes; Symbolism; *Women; Women Men Relations.

5158 Herrera-Sobek, Maria. The politics of rape: sexual transgression in Chicana fiction. THE AMERICAS REVIEW, Vol. 15, no. 3-4 (Fall, Winter, 1987), p. 171-181. English. DESCR: Cisneros, Sandra; *Feminism; Fiction; GIVING UP THE GHOST; *Literary Criticism; Lizarraga, Sylvia; Moraga, Cherrie; *Rape; "Red Clowns" [short story]; "Silver Lake Road" [short story].

5159 Herrera-Sobek, Maria. Women as metaphor in the patriarchal structure of HEART OF AZTLAN. IN: Gonzalez-T., Cesar A. RUDOLFO A. ANAYA: FOCUS ON CRITICISM. La Jolla, CA: Lalo Press, 1990, p. [165]-182. English. DESCR: Anaya, Rudolfo A.; *HEART OF AZTLAN; La Llorona; *Literary Characters; Literary Criticism.

5160 Hintz, Joy. Valiant migrant women = Las mujeres valerosas. Tiffin, OH: Sayger Printing, 1982. viii, 98 p. English. DESCR: Battered Women; *Farm Workers; Feminism; Florida; Marriage; Migrant Children; Migrant Health Services; Migrant Housing; *Migrant Labor; Migration Patterns; Ohio; Texas.

5161 Hogeland, Chris and Rosen, Karen. Dreams lost, dreams found: undocumented women in the land of opportunity. San Francisco, CA: Coalition for Immigrant and Refugee Rights and Services, c1991. 153 p. English. DESCR: *Battered Women; *Coalition for Immigrant and Refugee Rights and Services, Immigrant Woman's Task Force; Discrimination; Immigrants; *San Francisco Bay Area; Sexism; Social Services; Undocumented Workers; Violence; Women; Women Men Relations.

5162 Horowitz, Ruth. Femininity and womanhood: virginity, unwed motherhood, and violence. IN: Horowitz, Ruth. HONOR AND THE AMERICAN DREAM: CULTURE AND IDENTITY IN A CHICANO COMMUNITY. New Brunswick, NJ: Rutgers University Press, 1983, p. 114-136. English DESCR: *Birth Control; *Fertility; Identity *Sexual Behavior; Single Parents; Violence; Women Men Relations; Youth.

5163 Horowitz, Ruth. Passion, submission and motherhood: the negotiation of identity by unmarried innercity Chicanas. SOCIOLOGICAL QUARTERLY, Vol. 22, no. 2 (Spring 1981), p. 241-252. English. DESCR: Barrios; Birth Control; *Fertility; Identity; *Sexual

Behavior; Single Parents; Youth.

5164 Howell-Martinez, Vicky. The influence of gender roles on political socialization: an experimental study of Mexican-American children. WOMEN & POLITICS, Vol. 2, no. 3 (Fall 1982), p. 33-46. English. DESCR: Political Socialization; Sex Stereotypes.

5165 Jenoveva. La Chicana: principle of life, survival and endurance. CALMECAC, Vol. 1, (Summer 1980), p. 7-10. English. DESCR: Identity.

5166 Jensen, Evelyn E. The Hispanic perspective of the ideal woman: a correlational study. Thesis (Ph.D.)--Fuller Theological Seminary, School of World Mission, 1987. 163 p. English. DESCR: Family; *Hembrismo; *Machismo.

5167 Job, Peggy. La sexualidad en la narrativa femenina mexicana 1970-1987: una aproximacion. THIRD WOMAN, Vol. 4, (1989), p. 120-133. Spanish. DESCR: *Literature; *Literature Reviews; *Sexual Behavior; *Women.

5168 Johnson, Susan L. Sharing bed and board: cohabitation and cultural difference in central Arizona mining towns. FRONTIERS: A JOURNAL OF WOMEN STUDIES, Vol. 7, no. 3 (1984), p. 36-42. English. DESCR: Arizona; *Intermarriage.

5169 Jordan, Rosan Augusta. The vaginal serpent and other themes from Mexican-American women's lore. IN: Jordan, Rosan A. and Kalcik, Susan J., eds. WOMEN'S FOLKLORE, WOMEN'S CULTURE. Philadelphia: University of Pennsylvania Press, 1985, p. 26-44. English. DESCR: Cuentos; Fertility; *Folklore; La Llorona; *Leyendas; Sexism; Sexual Behavior.

5170 Kantorowski Davis, Sharon and Chavez, Virginia. Hispanic househusbands. HISPANIC JOURNAL OF BEHAVIORAL SCIENCES, Vol. 7, no. 4 (December 1985), p. 317-332. English. DESCR: Domestic Work; Machismo; Marriage.

5171 Kay, Margarita Artschwager. Mexican, Mexican American, and Chicana childbirth. IN: Melville, Margarita B., ed. TWICE A MINORITY. St. Louis, MO: Mosby, 1980, p. 52-65. English. DESCR: *Cultural Characteristics; Herbal Medicine; *Maternal and Child Welfare; Midwives.

5172 Keremitsis, Dawn. Del metate al molino: la mujer mexicana de 1910 a 1940. HISTORIA MEXICANA, Vol. 33, no. 2 (1983), p. 285-302. Spanish. DESCR: Food Industry; History; Labor Unions; Mexico; Strikes and Lockouts; Women; *Working Women.

5173 Kimbel, Charles E.; Marsh, Nancy B.; and Kiska, Andrew C. Sex, age, and cultural differences in self-reported assertiveness. PSYCHOLOGICAL REPORTS, Vol. 55, no. 2 (October 1984), p. 419-422. English. DESCR: *Assertiveness; Cultural Characteristics; Identity.

5174 Kluessendorf, Avonelle Donneeta. Role conflict in Mexican-American college women. Thesis (Ph.D.)--California School of Professional Psychology, Fresno, 1985. 111 p. English. DESCR: *Colleges and Universities; Locus of Control; *Stress; Students.

Sex Roles (cont.)

5175 Kossoudji, Sherrie and Ranney, Susan. The labor market experience of female migrants: the case of temporary Mexican migration to the U.S. INTERNATIONAL MIGRATION REVIEW, Vol. 18, no. 4 (Winter 1984), p. 1120-1143. English. **DESCR:** Employment; Immigrants; Income; *Labor Supply and Market; *Migrant Labor; *Women; Working Women.

5176 Kranau, Edgar J.; Green, Vicki; and Valencia-Weber, Gloria. Acculturation and the Hispanic woman: attitudes toward women, sex-role attribution, sex-role behavior, and demographics. HISPANIC JOURNAL OF BEHAVIORAL SCIENCES, Vol. 4, no. 1 (March 1982), p. 21-40. English. **DESCR:** Acculturation; Population.

5177 Krause, Neal and Markides, Kyriakos S. Employment and psychological well-being in Mexican American women. JOURNAL OF HEALTH AND SOCIAL BEHAVIOR, Vol. 26, no. 1 (March 1985), p. 15-26. English. **DESCR:** *Attitudes; *Employment; Identity; Mental Health; Working Women.

5178 Krause, Neal and Markides, Kyriakos S. Gender roles, illness, and illness behavior in a Mexican American population. SOCIAL SCIENCE QUARTERLY, Vol. 68, no. 1 (March 1987), p. 102-121. English. **DESCR:** Family; Public Health; San Antonio, TX.

5179 Lara-Cantu, M. Asuncion and Navarro-Arias, Roberto. Positive and negative factors in the measurement of sex roles: findings from a Mexican sample. HISPANIC JOURNAL OF BEHAVIORAL SCIENCES, Vol. 8, no. 2 (June 1986), p. 143-155. English. **DESCR:** Bem Sex Role Inventory (BSRI); Mexico; *Psychological Testing.

5180 Lara-Cantu, M. Asuncion. A sex role inventory with scales for "machismo" and "self-sacrificing woman". JOURNAL OF CROSS-CULTURAL PSYCHOLOGY, Vol. 20, no. 4 (December 1989), p. 396-398. English. **DESCR:** Machismo; *Masculine-Feminine Personality Traits Scale; *Personality; *Psychological Testing.

5181 Larguia, Isabel and Dumoulin, John. Toward a science of women's liberation. IN: Mora, Magdalena and Del Castillo, Adelaida, eds. MEXICAN WOMEN IN THE UNITED STATES: STRUGGLES PAST AND PRESENT. Los Angeles, CA: Chicano Studies Research Center, 1980, p. 45-61. English. **DESCR:** *Feminism; Labor; Social Classes.

5182 Lawrence, Alberto Augusto. Traditional attitudes toward marriage, marital adjustment, acculturation, and self-esteem of Mexican-American and Mexican wives. Thesis (Ph.D.)--United States International University, San Diego, CA, 1982. ix, 191 p. English. **DESCR:** *Acculturation; *Attitudes; Machismo; *Marriage; Mental Health; Psychological Testing; San Ysidro, CA; Sex Stereotypes; Tijuana, Baja California, Mexico; Women.

5183 Leon, Ana M., et al. Self-help support groups for Hispanic mothers. CHILD WELFARE, Vol. 63, no. 3 (May, June, 1984), p. 261-268. English. **DESCR:** Family; Mental Health Clinics; *Natural Support Systems; *Parent and Child Relationships.

5184 LeVine, Sarah Ethel; Correa, Clara Sunderland; and Uribe, F. Medardo Tapia. The marital morality of Mexican women--an urban study. JOURNAL OF ANTHROPOLOGICAL RESEARCH, Vol. 42, no. 2 (Summer 1986), p. 183-202. English. **DESCR:** Family; Los Robles, Cuernavaca, Morelos, Mexico; *Machismo; Marriage; Parent and Child Relationships; Women; *Women Men Relations.

5185 Limon, Jose E. [anthropologist]. "La vieja Ines," a Mexican folkgame: a research note. IN: Melville, Margarita B., ed. TWICE A MINORITY. St. Louis, MO: Mosby, 1980, p. 88-94. English. **DESCR:** Children; *Folklore; *Games.

5186 Lizarraga, Sylvia S. The patriarchal ideology in "La noche que se apagaron las luces". REVISTA CHICANO-RIQUENA, Vol. 13, no. 3-4 (Fall, Winter, 1985), p. 90-95. English. **DESCR:** "La noche que se apagaron las luces" [short story]; *Literary Criticism; Rivera, Tomas; Y NO SE LO TRAGO LA TIERRA/AND THE EARTH DID NOT PART.

5187 Long, John M. and Vigil, James Diego. Cultural styles and adolescent sex role perceptions: an exploration of responses to a value picture projective test. IN: Melville, Margarita B., ed. TWICE A MINORITY. St. Louis, MO: Mosby, 1980, p. 164-172. English. **DESCR:** Psychological Testing; Youth.

5188 Longeaux y Vasquez, Enriqueta. The woman of La Raza. REGENERACION, Vol. 2, no. 4 (1975), p. 34-36. English. **DESCR:** Child Care Centers; Discrimination; Gallo, Juana; Housing; La Adelita; Machismo; *Social History and Conditions; Working Women.

5189 Longeaux y Vasquez, Enriqueta. The woman of La Raza. IN: Valdez, Luis and Steiner, Stan, eds. AZTLAN: AN ANTHOLOGY OF MEXICAN AMERICAN LITERATURE. New York: Vintage Books, 1972, p. 272-278. Also IN: Salinas, Luis Omar and Faderman, Lillian, compilers. FROM THE BARRIO: A CHICANO ANTHOLOGY. San Francisco, CA: Canfield Press, 1973, p. 20-24. English. **DESCR:** Child Care Centers; Discrimination; Gallo, Juana; Housing; La Adelita; Machismo; *Social History and Conditions; Working Women.

5190 Lopez-Gonzalez, Aralia, et al., eds. Mujer y literatura mexicana y chicana: culturas en contacto. Mexico: Colegio de Mexico, Programa Interdisciplinario de Estudios de la Mujer; Tijuana, B.C., Mexico: Colegio de la Frontera Norte, 1988. 264 p. Spanish. **DESCR:** *Literary Criticism; Mexican Literature; *Mexico; *Women.

5191 Lopez-Trevino, Maria Elena. A radio model: a community strategy to address the problems and needs of Mexican-American women farmworkers. Thesis (M.S.)--California State University, Long Beach, 1989. 179 p. English. **DESCR:** Coachella, CA; *Farm Workers; Income; Low Income; Occupational Hazards; *Radio.

5192 Loustaunau, Martha Oehmke. Hispanic widows and their support systems in the Mesilla Valley of southern New Mexico, 1910-40. IN: Scadron, Arlene, ed. ON THEIR OWN: WIDOWS AND WIDOWHOOD IN THE AMERICAN SOUTHWEST 1843-1939. Urbana, IL: University of Illinois Press, c1988, p. [91]-116. English. **DESCR:** Cultural Customs; Extended Family; Mesilla Valley, NM; Natural Support Systems; Single Parents; Widowhood; *Women.

Sex Roles (cont.)

5193 Lucero, Aileen. Chicano sex role attitudes: a comparative study of sex differences in an urban barrio. Thesis (Ph.D.)--University of Colorado at Boulder, 1980. 160 p. English. **DESCR:** *Attitudes; Colorado; Males.

5194 Luna-Lawhn, Juanita. EL REGIDOR and LA PRENSA: impediments to women's self-definition. THIRD WOMAN, Vol. 4, (1989), p. 134-142. English. **DESCR:** EL REGIDOR, San Antonio, TX; LA PRENSA, San Antonio, TX; Literature; *Newspapers; *Sexism.

5195 Macklin, June. "All the good and bad in this world": women, traditional medicine, and Mexican American culture. IN: Melville, Margarita B., ed. TWICE A MINORITY. St. Louis, MO: Mosby, 1980, p. 127-148. English. **DESCR:** *Curanderismo; Folk Medicine.

5196 Malvido, Elsa. El uso del cuerpo femenino en la epoca colonial mexicana a traves de los estudios de demografia historica. IN: Del Castillo, Adelaida R. ed. BETWEEN BORDERS ESSAYS ON MEXICANA/CHICANA HISTORY. Encino, CA: Floricanto Press, 1990, p. 115-130. Spanish. **DESCR:** Marriage; *Mexico; Sexual Behavior; *Vital Statistics; Widowhood; *Women.

5197 Manzanedo, Hector Garcia; Walters, Esperanza Garcia; and Lorig, Kate R. Health and illness perceptions of the Chicana. IN: Melville, Margarita B., ed. TWICE A MINORITY. St. Louis, MO: Mosby, 1980, p. 191-207. English. **DESCR:** Cultural Characteristics; Culture; *Medical Care; Public Health; Values.

5198 Markides, Kyriakos S. and Vernon, Sally W. Aging, sex-role orientation and adjustment: a three-generations study of Mexican Americans. JOURNAL OF GERONTOLOGY, Vol. 39, no. 5 (September 1984), p. 586-591. English. **DESCR:** *Age Groups; *Ancianos; Mental Health.

5199 Martinez, Ruben and Dukes, Richard L. Race, gender and self-esteem among youth. HISPANIC JOURNAL OF BEHAVIORAL SCIENCES, Vol. 9, no. 4 (December 1987), p. 427-443. English. **DESCR:** *Comparative Psychology; *Identity; *Youth.

5200 Mason, Theresa Hope. Experience and meaning: an interpretive study of family and gender ideologies among a sample of Mexican-American women of two generations. Thesis (Ph.D.)--University of Texas, Austin. 1987. 406 p. English. **DESCR:** *Age Groups; Culture; Extended Family; *Family.

5201 Matute-Bianchi, Maria Eugenia. A Chicana in academe. WOMEN'S STUDIES QUARTERLY, Vol. 10, no. 1 (Spring 1982), p. 14-17. English. **DESCR:** Discrimination; *Higher Education; Matute-Bianchi, Maria Eugenia; Sexism.

5202 McDuff, Mary Ann. Mexican-American women: a three-generational study of attitudes and behaviors. Thesis (M.A.)--Texas Women's University, 1989. 200 p. English. **DESCR:** *Acculturation; *Age Groups; Family; San Antonio, TX.

5203 McRipley, Bernadine G. Racial/ethnic Presbyterian women: in search of community. CHURCH AND SOCIETY, Vol. 76, no. 4 (March, April, 1986), p. 47-53. English. **DESCR:** *Presbyterian Church; Religion; *Women.

5204 Melville, Margarita B. Female and male in Chicano theatre. IN: Kanellos, Nicolas, ed. HISPANIC THEATRE IN THE UNITED STATES. Houston, TX: Arte Publico Press, 1984, p. 71-79. English. **DESCR:** BERNABE; BRUJERIAS [play]; Cultural Characteristics; DAY OF THE SWALLOWS; Duarte-Clark, Rodrigo; EL JARDIN [play]; Family; Feminism; Macias, Ysidro; Morton, Carlos; Portillo Trambley, Estela; RANCHO HOLLYWOOD [play]; *Teatro; THE ULTIMATE PENDEJADA [play]; Valdez, Luis; Women Men Relations.

5205 Melville, Margarita B. Gender roles. IN: Melville, Margarita B., ed. TWICE A MINORITY. St. Louis, MO: Mosby, 1980, p. 83-87. English.

5206 Melville, Margarita B. Matrescence. IN: Melville, Margarita B., ed. TWICE A MINORITY. St. Louis, MO: Mosby, 1980, p. 11-16. English. **DESCR:** Family.

5207 Melville, Margarita B. Mexican women adapt to migration. IN: Rios-Bustamante, Antonio, ed. MEXICAN IMMIGRANT WORKERS IN THE U.S. Los Angeles, CA: Chicano Studies Research Center Publications, University of California, 1981, p. 119-124. English. **DESCR:** Acculturation; Attitudes; Immigrants; Stress; *Undocumented Workers.

5208 Mercado, Olivia. Chicanas: myths and roles. COMADRE, no. 1 (Summer 1977), p. 26-32. English. **DESCR:** Feminism; Gallo, Juana; Huerta, Dolores; *Identity; Leadership.

5209 Miller, Michael V. Variations in Mexican American family life: a review synthesis of empirical research. AZTLAN, Vol. 9, no. 1 (1978), p. 209-231. Bibliography. English. **DESCR:** Acculturation; Compadrazgo; *Family; Intermarriage; Stereotypes.

5210 Mink, Diane Leslie. Early grandmotherhood: an exploratory study. Thesis (Ph.D.)--California School of Professional Psychology, Los Angeles, 1987. 190 p. English. **DESCR:** Age Groups; *Ancianos; Assertiveness; Family; Fertility; Grandmothers; Natural Support Systems; Surveys Youth.

5211 Mirande, Alfredo. The Chicano family and sex roles: an overview and introduction. DE COLORES, Vol. 6, no. 1-2 (1982), p. 1-6. English. **DESCR:** *Family.

5212 Mirande, Alfredo. Machismo: rucas, chingasos, y chingaderas. DE COLORES, Vol. 6, no. 1-2 (1982), p. 17-31. English. **DESCR:** *Machismo.

5213 Mirande, Alfredo. Que gacho es ser macho: it's a drag to be a macho man. AZTLAN, Vol. 17, no. 2 (Fall 1986), p. 63-89. English. **DESCR:** *Cultural Characteristics; Identity; *Machismo; Personality; *Sex Stereotypes; Values.

5214 Monroy, Douglas. "They didn't call them 'padre' for nothing": patriarchy in Hispanic California. IN: Del Castillo, Adelaida R., ed. BETWEEN BORDERS: ESSAYS ON MEXICANA/CHICANA HISTORY. Encino, CA: Floricanto Press, 1990, p. 433-445. English. **DESCR:** *California; Clergy; History; *Machismo; Rape; *Sexism; Spanish Influence; Women Men Relations.

Sex Roles (cont.)

5215 Moore, Joan W. Mexican-American women addicts: the influence of family background. IN: Glick, Ronald and Moore, Joan, eds. DRUGS IN HISPANIC COMMUNITIES. New Brunswick, NJ: Rutgers University Press, c1990, p. 127-153. English. **DESCR:** Barrios; *Drug Addicts; Drug Use; East Los Angeles, CA; *Family; *Gangs; Heroin; Hoyo-Mara Gang, East Los Angeles, CA; Pachucos; Socialization; White Fence Gang; Youth.

5216 Moore, Joan W. and Devitt, Mary. The paradox of deviance in addicted Mexican American mothers. GENDER & SOCIETY, Vol. 3, no. 1 (March 1989), p. 53-70. English. **DESCR:** Children; *Drug Addicts; *Drug Use; Family; *Fertility; Gangs; Parenting.

5217 Nieto Gomez de Lazarin, Anna. Ana Nieto Gomez: sexism in the Movimiento. LA GENTE DE AZTLAN, Vol. 6, no. 4 (March 1976), p. 10. English. **DESCR:** *Chicano Movement; Feminism; *Sexism.

5218 Nieto Senour, Maria. Psychology of the Chicana. IN: Martinez, Joe L., Jr., ed. CHICANO PSYCHOLOGY. New York: Academic Press, 1977, p. 329-342. English. **DESCR:** Academic Achievement; Acculturation; Cultural Customs; Identity; *Psychology.

5219 Norinsky, Margaret Elaine. The relationship between sex-role identity and ethnicity to styles of assertiveness and aggression in women. Thesis (Ed.D.)--University of San Francisco, 1987. 164 p. English. **DESCR:** Anglo Americans; *Assertiveness; Blacks; Ethnic Groups; *Identity; *Women.

5220 O'Guinn, Thomas C.; Imperia, Giovanna; and MacAdams, Elizabeth A. Acculturation and perceived family decision-making input among Mexican American wives. JOURNAL OF CROSS-CULTURAL PSYCHOLOGY, Vol. 18, no. 1 (March 1987), p. 78-92. English. **DESCR:** *Acculturation; Attitudes; Consumers; Family.

5221 Olivarez, Elizabeth. Women's rights and the Mexican American woman. REGENERACION, Vol. 2, no. 4 (1975), p. 40-42. English. **DESCR:** Education; *Feminism; Identity; Politics; Psychology; Religion.

5222 Ortega, Eliana and Sternbach, Nancy Saporta. At the threshold of the unnamed: Latina literary discourse in the eighties. IN: Horno-Delgado, Asuncion, et al., eds. BREAKING BOUNDARIES: LATINA WRITING AND CRITICAL READINGS. Amherst, MA: University of Massachusetts Press, c1989, p. [2]-23. English. **DESCR:** Bilingualism; *Feminism; *Literary Criticism; Literary History; Political Ideology; *Women.

5223 Ortiz, Flora Ida. Hispanic American women in higher education: a consideration of the socialization process. AZTLAN, Vol. 17, no. 2 (Fall 1986), p. 125-152. English. **DESCR:** *Academic Achievement; Counseling (Educational); Enrollment; *Higher Education; *Sexism; Socialization; Students; University of California.

5224 Ortiz, Sylvia and Casas, Jesus Manuel. Birth control and low-income Mexican-American women: the impact of three values. HISPANIC JOURNAL OF BEHAVIORAL SCIENCES, Vol. 12, no. 1 (February 1990), p. 83-92. English. **DESCR:** Acculturation; Attitudes; *Birth Control; Fertility; *Low Income; Values.

5225 Ortiz, Vilma and Cooney, Rosemary Santana. Sex-role attitudes and labor force participation among young Hispanic females and non-Hispanic white females. SOCIAL SCIENCE QUARTERLY, Vol. 65, no. 2 (June 1984), p. 392-400. English. **DESCR:** Anglo Americans; Attitudes; Employment; Working Women.

5226 Ortiz, Vilma and Cooney, Rosemary Santana. Sex-role attitudes and labor force participation among young Hispanic females and non-Hispanic white females. IN: O. de la Garza, Rodolfo, et al., eds. THE MEXICAN AMERICAN EXPERIENCE: AN INTERDISCIPLINARY ANTHOLOGY. Austin, TX: University of Texas Press, 1985, p. 174-182. English. **DESCR:** Anglo Americans; Attitudes; Employment; Working Women.

5227 Padilla, Amado M. and Baird, Traci L. Mexican-American adolescent sexuality and sexual knowledge: an exploratory study. HISPANIC JOURNAL OF BEHAVIORAL SCIENCES, Vol. 13, no. 1 (February 1991), p. 95-104. English. **DESCR:** *Attitudes; *Birth Control; *Sexual Behavior; Surveys; *Youth.

5228 Padilla, Eligio R. and O'Grady, Kevin E. Sexuality among Mexican Americans: a case of sexual stereotyping. JOURNAL OF PERSONALITY AND SOCIAL PSYCHOLOGY, Vol. 52, no. 1 (1987), p. 5-10. English. **DESCR:** Age Groups; Anglo Americans; Attitudes; California; Religion; *Sex Stereotypes; Sexual Behavior; Sexual Knowledge and Attitude Test; *Stereotypes; Students; Values.

5229 Palacios, Maria. Fear of success: Mexican-American women in two work environments. Thesis (Ph.D.)--New Mexico State University, 1988. 163 p. English. **DESCR:** Academic Achievement; *Assertiveness; *Careers; Income; *Working Women.

5230 Pallais, Maria L. The myth of the vanishing virgin. NUESTRO, Vol. 4, no. 7 (October 1980), p. 57-58. English. **DESCR:** *Sex Stereotypes.

5231 Pardo, Mary. Mexican American women grassroots community activists: "Mothers of East Los Angeles". FRONTIERS: A JOURNAL OF WOMEN STUDIES, Vol. 11, no. 1 (1990), p. [1]-7. English. **DESCR:** Coalition Against the Prison, East Los Angeles, CA; *Community Organizations; East Los Angeles, CA; Family; *Feminism; *Mothers of East L.A. (MELA); Organizations; Political Parties and Organizations; Politics.

5232 Parra, Elena and Henderson, Ronald W. Mexican American perceptions of parent and teacher roles in child development. IN: Fishman, Joshua A. and Keller, Gary D., eds. BILINGUAL EDUCATION FOR HISPANIC STUDENTS IN THE UNITED STATES. New York: Teachers College Press, 1982, p. 289-299. English. **DESCR:** *Children; Family; *Parenting; Teacher Attitudes.

5233 Pavich, Emma Guerrero. A Chicana perspective on Mexican culture and sexuality. JOURNAL OF SOCIAL WORK AND HUMAN SEXUALITY, Vol. 4, no. 3 (Spring 1986), p. 47-65. English. **DESCR:** California; Cultural Characteristics; Family; Feminism; Homosexuality; Machismo; Sex Stereotypes; *Sexual Behavior; Women Men Relations.

Sex Roles (cont.)

5234 Pena, Manuel. Class, gender, and machismo: the "treacherous-woman" folklore of Mexican male workers. GENDER & SOCIETY, Vol. 5, no. 1 (March 1991), p. 30-45. English. DESCR: *Folklore; Laborers; *Machismo; Males; Sex Stereotypes; Social Classes; *Undocumented Workers; Women Men Relations.

5235 Perez, Emma. "A la mujer": a critique of the Partido Liberal Mexicano's gender ideology on women. IN: Del Castillo, Adelaida R., ed. BETWEEN BORDERS: ESSAYS ON MEXICANA/CHICANA HISTORY. Encino, CA: Floricanto Press, 1990, p. 459-482. English. DESCR: *"A La Mujer" [essay]; Essays; *Feminism; Flores Magon, Ricardo; Guerrero, Praxedis G.; Journalism; Mexican Revolution - 1910-1920; Mexico; Newspapers; *Partido Liberal Mexicano (PLM); Political Ideology; Political Parties and Organizations; *REGENERACION [newspaper]; Women.

5236 Perez, Emma. Sexuality and discourse: notes from a Chicana survivor. IN: Trujillo, Carla, ed. CHICANA LESBIANS: THE GIRLS OUR MOTHERS WARNED US ABOUT. Berkeley, CA: Third Woman Press, 1991, p. 159-184. English. DESCR: *Feminism; Homosexuality; Intergroup Relations; Paz, Octavio; *Sexism; Skin Color.

5237 Pesquera, Beatriz M. Work and family: a comparative analysis of professional, clerical and blue-collar Chicana workers. Thesis (Ph.D.)--University of California, Berkeley, 1985. i, 212 p. English. DESCR: *Family; *Working Women.

5238 Pierce, Jennifer. The implications of functionalism for Chicano family research. BERKELEY JOURNAL OF SOCIOLOGY, Vol. 29, (1984), p. 93-117. English. DESCR: Enriquez, Evangelina; *Family; LA CHICANA: THE MEXICAN AMERICAN WOMAN; Machismo; Mirande, Alfredo; Research Methodology.

5239 Ramirez, Alex, et al. The relationship between sociocultural variables and Chicano and Anglo high school student responses on the Potency Dimension of the Semantic Differential. HISPANIC JOURNAL OF BEHAVIORAL SCIENCES, Vol. 3, no. 2 (June 1981), p. 177-190. English. DESCR: Anglo Americans; Martinez, Joe L., Jr.; Martinez, Sergio R.; MULTIVARIATE ANALYSIS OF VARIANCE (MANOVA); Olmedo, Esteban L.; *Parent and Child Relationships; Sex Stereotypes; Students.

5240 Ramirez, Genevieve M. and Salazar Parr, Carmen. The female hero in Chicano literature. IN: Herrera-Sobek, Maria, ed. BEYOND STEREOTYPES: THE CRITICAL ANALYSIS OF CHICANA LITERATURE. Binghamton, NY: Bilingual Press/Editorial Bilingue, 1985, p. 48-60. English. DESCR: *Literary Characters; Literary Criticism.

5241 Ramirez, Oscar and Arce, Carlos H. The contemporary Chicano family: an empirically based review. IN: Baron, Augustine, Jr., ed. EXPLORATIONS IN CHICANO PSYCHOLOGY. New York: Praeger, 1981, p. 3-28. English. DESCR: *Family; Fertility; Literature Reviews; Machismo; Population.

5242 Rebolledo, Tey Diana. Hispanic women writers of the Southwest: tradition and innovation. IN: Lensink, Judy Nolte, ed. OLD SOUTHWEST/NEW SOUTHWEST: ESSAYS ON A REGION AND ITS LITERATURE. Tucson, AZ: The Tucson Public Library, 1987, p. 49-61. English. DESCR: *Authors; Cabeza de Baca, Fabiola; Jaramillo, Cleofas M.; Literature; Mora, Pat; OLD SPAIN IN OUR SOUTHWEST; Otero Warren, Nina; Preciado Martin, Patricia; Sex Stereotypes; Silva, Beverly; *Southwestern United States; Vigil-Pinon, Evangelina; WE FED THEM CACTUS; *Women.

5243 Reed-Sanders, Delores; Dodder, Richard A.; and Webster, Lucia. The Bem Sex-Role Inventory across three cultures. JOURNAL OF SOCIAL PSYCHOLOGY, Vol. 125, no. 4 (August 1985), p. 523-525. English. DESCR: Bem Sex Role Inventory (BSRI); Comparative Psychology.

5244 Rider, Kennon V. Relationship satisfaction of the Mexican American woman: effects of acculturation, socioeconomic status, and interaction structures. Thesis (Ph.D.)--Texas Tech University, 1988. 145 p. English. DESCR: *Acculturation; *Interpersonal Relations; *Socioeconomic Factors.

5245 Rivero, Eliana S. La mujer y La Raza: Latinas y Chicanas [part II]. CARACOL, Vol. 4, no. 2 (October 1977), p. 21-22. Spanish. DESCR: *Sex Stereotypes.

5246 Rosaldo, Renato. Fables of the fallen guy. IN: Calderon, Hector and Saldivar, Jose David, eds. CRITICISM IN THE BORDERLANDS: STUDIES IN CHICANO LITERATURE, CULTURE AND IDEOLOGY. Durham, NC: Duke University Press, 1991, p. [84]-93. English. DESCR: Chavez, Denise; Cisneros, Sandra; Fiction; Literary Characters; *Literary Criticism; Rios, Alberto; THE HOUSE ON MANGO STREET; THE IGUANA KILLER: TWELVE STORIES OF THE HEART; THE LAST OF THE MENU GIRLS.

5247 Rose, Margaret. Traditional and nontraditional patterns of female activism in the United Farm Workers of America, 1962-1980. FRONTIERS: A JOURNAL OF WOMEN STUDIES, Vol. 11, no. 1 (1990), p. [26]-32. English. DESCR: Boycotts; California; Chavez, Cesar E.; *Chavez, Helen; *Huerta, Dolores; Labor Disputes; Labor Unions; National Farm Workers Association (NFWA); Strikes and Lockouts; *United Farmworkers of America (UFW).

5248 Rose, Margaret. Women in the United Farm Workers: a study of Chicana Mexicana participation in a labor union, 1950-1980. Thesis (Ph.D.)--University of California, Los Angeles, 1988. 403p. English. DESCR: History; Huerta, Dolores; *Labor Unions; United Farmworkers of America (UFW); Working Women.

5249 Ross, Catherine E.; Mirowsky, John; and Ulbrich, Patricia. Distress and the traditional female role: a comparison of Mexicans and Anglos. AMERICAN JOURNAL OF SOCIOLOGY, Vol. 89, no. 3 (November 1983), p. 670-682. English. DESCR: Anglo Americans; Comparative Psychology; Stress; Women.

5250 Ruelas, J. Oshi. Moments of change. REVISTA MUJERES, Vol. 4, no. 1 (January 1987), p. 23-33. English. DESCR: *Autobiography; Essays; *Ruelas, J. Oshi; Sexism.

Sex Roles (cont.)

5251 Ruiz Funes, Concepcion and Tunon, Enriqueta. Panorama de las luchas de la mujer mexicana en el siglo XX. IN: Del Castillo, Adelaida R., ed. BETWEEN BORDERS: ESSAYS ON MEXICANA/CHICANA HISTORY. Encino, CA: Floricanto Press, 1990, p. 336-357. Spanish. DESCR: Coordinadora de Mujeres Trabajadoras; *Feminism; Frente Unido Pro Derechos de la Mujer; History; Labor Unions; *Mexico; *Women.

5252 Ruiz, Vicki L. California's early pioneers: Spanish/Mexican women. SOCIAL STUDIES REVIEW, Vol. 29, no. 1 (Fall 1989), p. 24-30. English. DESCR: *California; *History; Ruiz Burton, Maria Amparo; *Women.

5253 Ruiz, Vicki L. Obreras y madres: labor activism among Mexican women and its impact on the family. RENATO ROSALDO LECTURE SERIES MONOGRAPH, Vol. 1, (Summer 1985), p. [19]-38. English. DESCR: Child Care Centers; Children; History; *Labor Unions; *Mexico; Women; *Working Women.

5254 Ruiz, Vicki L., ed. and Tiano, Susan B., ed. Women on the U.S.-Mexico border: responses to change. Boston, MA: Allen & Unwin, c1987. xi, 247 p. English. DESCR: *Border Industries; *Border Region; Employment; Feminism; Immigrants; Mexico; *Women.

5255 Saboonchi, Nasrin. The working women's reactions to the traditional marriage role: a crosscultural study within the symbolic interactionism framework. Thesis (Ph.D.)--United States International University, 1983. 173 p. English. DESCR: Immigrants; Iranians; *Marriage; Women; Working Women.

5256 Saenz, Rogelio. Traditional sex-roles, ethnic integration, marital satisfaction, and psychological distress among Chicanas. Thesis (Ph.D.)--Iowa State University, 1986. 145 p. English. DESCR: *Marriage; *Mental Health; Stress.

5257 Salgado de Snyder, Nelly; Cervantes, Richard C.; and Padilla, Amado M. Gender and ethnic differences in psychosocial stress and generalized distress among Hispanics. SEX ROLES, Vol. 22, no. 7-8 (April, 1990), p. 441-453. English. DESCR: Anglo Americans; Central Americans; *Comparative Psychology; Depression (Psychological); Hispanic Stress Inventory (HSI); *Immigrants; Immigration; *Stress; Women.

5258 Saracho, Olivia N. Women and education: sex role modifications of Mexican American women. EDUCATION, Vol. 109, no. 3 (Spring 1989), p. 295-301. English. DESCR: Acculturation; *Education.

5259 Segura, Denise. Familism and employment among Chicanas and Mexican immigrant women. IN: Melville, Margarita, ed. MEXICANAS AT WORK IN THE UNITED STATES. Houston, TX: Mexican American Studies Program, University of Houston, 1988, p. 24-32. English. DESCR: *Employment; *Extended Family; Family; Immigrants; Income; Machismo; *Women; Working Women.

5260 Segura, Denise. The interplay of familism and patriarchy on employment among Chicana and Mexicana women. RENATO ROSALDO LECTURE SERIES MONOGRAPH, Vol. 5, (1989), p. 35-53. English. DESCR: Employment; *Family; Immigrants; Machismo; Women; Women Men Relations; *Working Women.

5261 Soberon, Mercedes. La revolucion se trata de amor: Mercedes Soberon. CHISMEARTE, Vol. 1, no. 1 (Fall 1976), p. 14-18. Spanish. DESCR: Art Criticism; Concilio de Arte Popular, Los Angeles, CA; Cultural Organizations; La Mission Media Arts, San Francisco, CA; San Francisco, CA; Soberon, Mercedes.

5262 Solis, Faustina. Commentary on the Chicana and health services. IN: Sanchez, Rosaura and Martinez Cruz, Rosa, eds. ESSAYS ON LA MUJER. Los Angeles, CA: Chicano Studies Center Publications, UCLA, 1977, p. 82-90. English. DESCR: Medical Personnel; *Public Health.

5263 Sorel, Janet Elaine. The relationship between gender role incongruity on measures of coping and material resources and blood pressure among Mexican-American women. Thesis (Ph.D.)--University of North Carolina at Chapel Hill, 1988. 268 p. English. DESCR: High Blood Pressure; Hispanic Health and Nutrition Examination Survey (HHANES); Hypertension; Public Health; *Stress.

5264 Sorenson, Ann Marie. The fertility and language characteristics of Mexican-American and non-Hispanic husbands and wives. SOCIOLOGICAL QUARTERLY, Vol. 29, no. 1 (March 1988), p. 111-130. English. DESCR: Anglo Americans; Fertility; Identity; *Language Usage; Marriage.

5265 Stark, Miriam. La Chicana: changing roles in a changing society. Thesis (B.A)--University of Michigan, 1984. ii, 157 leaves. English. DESCR: Acculturation; Identity; Lansing, MI; *Social History and Conditions.

5266 Sullivan, Teresa A. The occupational prestige of women immigrants: a comparison of Cubans and Mexicans. INTERNATIONAL MIGRATION REVIEW, Vol. 18, no. 4 (Winter 1984), p. 1045-1062. English. DESCR: Careers; Cubanos; Employment; *Immigrants; Males; Mexico; *Social Mobility; *Women; *Working Women.

5267 Tafolla, Carmen. To split a human: mitos, machos y la mujer chicana. San Antonio, TX: Mexican American Cultural Center, 1985. 115 p.: ill. English. DESCR: Discrimination; Education; *Feminism; Films; Sex Stereotypes; *Sexism.

5268 Tavera Rivera, Margarita. Autoridad in absentia: la censura patriarcal en la narrativa chicana. IN: Lopez-Gonzalez, Aralia, et al., eds. MUJER Y LITERATURA MEXICANA Y CHICANA: CULTURAS EN CONTACTO. Mexico: Colegio de la Frontera Norte, 1988, p. [65]-69. Spanish. DESCR: Feminism; Fiction; *Literary Criticism; *THE MOTHS AND OTHER STORIES; *Viramontes, Helena Maria.

5269 Tiano, Susan B. Export processing, women's work, and the employment problem in developing countries: the case of the maquiladora program in Northern Mexico. El Paso, TX: Center for InterAmerican and Border Studies, UTEP, 1985. 32 p. English. DESCR: *Border Region; *Employment; Labor Supply and Market; Mexico; Women; Working Women.

Sex Roles (cont.)

5270 Tienda, Marta and Glass, Jennifer. Household structure and labor-force participation of Black, Hispanic, and white mothers. DEMOGRAPHY, Vol. 22, no. 3 (August 1985), p. 381-394. English. DESCR: Anglo Americans; Blacks; *Extended Family; *Family; *Working Women.

5271 Torres Raines, Rosario. The Mexican American woman and work: intergenerational perspectives of comparative ethnic groups. IN: Melville, Margarita. ed. MEXICANAS AT WORK IN THE UNITED STATES. Houston, TX: Mexican American Studies Program, University of Houston, 1988, p. 33-45. English. DESCR: Age Groups; Anglo Americans; Employment; Feminism; Marriage; Social Classes; Socioeconomic Factors; *Working Women.

5272 Triandis, Harry C. Role perceptions of Hispanic young adults. JOURNAL OF CROSS-CULTURAL PSYCHOLOGY, Vol. 15, no. 3 (September 1984), p. 297-320. English. DESCR: *Cultural Characteristics; *Family; Parent and Child Relationships; Social Psychology; Values; Youth.

5273 Trotter, Robert T. Ethnic and sexual patterns of alcohol use: Anglo and Mexican American college students. ADOLESCENCE, Vol. 17, no. 66 (Summer 1982), p. 305-325. English. DESCR: *Alcoholism; Anglo Americans; Colleges and Universities; Cultural Characteristics; Ethnic Groups; Students; Youth.

5274 Trujillo, Carla. Chicana lesbians: fear and loathing in the Chicano community. IN: Trujillo, Carla, ed. CHICANA LESBIANS: THE GIRLS OUR MOTHERS WARNED US ABOUT. Berkeley CA: Third Woman Press, 1991, p. 186-194. English. DESCR: Essays; *Homosexuality; Sexual Behavior.

5275 Urdaneta, Maria Luisa. Flesh pots, faith, or finances? Fertility rates among Mexican Americans. IN: West, Stanley A. and Macklin, June, eds. THE CHICANO EXPERIENCE. Boulder, CO: Westview Press, 1979, p. 191-206. English. DESCR: Catholic Church; *Fertility; Machismo.

5276 U.S. National Institute of Education. Conference on the educational and occupational needs of Hispanic women, June 29-30, 1976; December 10-12, 1976. Washington, DC: U.S. Department of Education, 1980. x, 301 p. English. DESCR: Conference on the Educational and Occupational Needs of Hispanic Women (1976: Denver, CO); Conferences and Meetings; *Education; *Employment; Higher Education; Leadership; Puerto Ricans; *Women.

5277 Valdes-Fallis, Guadalupe. A liberated Chicana: a struggle against tradition. WOMEN: A JOURNAL OF LIBERATION, Vol. 3, no 4 (1974), p. 20-21. English. DESCR: Essays Feminism; *Sexism.

5278 Vasquez, Josefina. Educacion y papel de la mujer en Mexico. IN: Del Castillo, Adelaida R., ed. BETWEEN BORDERS: ESSAYS ON MEXICANA/CHICANA HISTORY. Encino, CA: Floricanto Press, 1990, p. 377-398. Spanish. DESCR: *Education; History; *Mexico; *Women.

5279 Vasquez, Melba J. T. Confronting barriers to the participation of Mexican American women in higher education. HISPANIC JOURNAL OF BEHAVIORAL SCIENCES, Vol. 4, no. 2 (June 1982), p. 147-165. English. DESCR: Academic Achievement; Higher Education; Socioeconomic Factors.

5280 Vasquez, Melba J. T. Power and status of the Chicana: a social-psychological perspective. IN: Martinez Joe L., Jr., ed. CHICANO PSYCHOLOGY. 2nd. ed. Orlando, FL: Academic Press, 1984, p. 269-287. English. DESCR: *Identity; Income; *Mental Health; Psychology; Socialization; Working Women.

5281 Vasquez, Melba J. T. and Gonzalez, Anna M. Sex roles among Chicanos: stereotypes, challenges and changes. IN: Baron, Augustine, Jr., ed. EXPLORATIONS IN CHICANO PSYCHOLOGY. New York: Praeger, 1981, p. 50-70. English. DESCR: Hembrismo; Machismo; Social Science; Stereotypes.

5282 Vazquez-Nuttall, Ena; Romero-Garcia, Ivonne; and De Leon, Brunilda. Sex roles and perceptions of femininity and masculinity of Hispanic women: a review of the literature. PSYCHOLOGY OF WOMEN QUARTERLY, Vol. 11, no. 4 (December 1987), p. 409-425. English. DESCR: Attitudes; *Chicanismo; *Literature Reviews; Machismo; Puerto Ricans; *Women.

5283 Velasquez, Roberto J.; Callahan, Wendell J.; and Carrillo, Ricardo. MMPI differences among Mexican-American male and female psychiatric inpatients. PSYCHOLOGICAL REPORTS, Vol. 68, no. 1 (February 1991), p. 123-127. English. DESCR: Comparative Psychology; Males; Minnesota Multiphasic Personality Inventory (MMPI); Personality; Psychiatry; *Psychological Testing.

5284 Velasquez-Trevino, Gloria. Cultural ambivalence in early Chicana prose fiction. Thesis (Ph.D.)--Stanford University, 1985. 185 p. English. DESCR: Biculturalism; *Fiction; Gonzalez, Jovita; Literary Criticism; Mena, Maria Cristina; Niggli, Josephina; Prose.

5285 Veloz, Josefina Estrada. Chicana identity: gender and ethnicity. Thesis (Ph.D.)--New Mexico State University, 1981. 239 p. English. DESCR: *Identity.

5286 Veyna, Angelina F. Una vista al pasado: la mujer en Nuevo Mexico, 1744-1767. TRABAJOS MONOGRAFICOS, Vol. 1, no. 1 (1985), p. 28-42. English. DESCR: History; *New Mexico.

5287 Vigil, James Diego. The nexus of class, culture and gender in the education of Mexican American females. IN: McKenna, Teresa and Ortiz, Flora Ida, eds. THE BROKEN WEB: THE EDUCATIONAL EXPERIENCE OF HISPANIC WOMEN. Claremont, CA: Tomas Rivera Center; Berkeley, CA: Floricanto Press, 1988, p. 79-103. English. DESCR: Academic Achievement; Acculturation; Discrimination in Education; *Education; Identity; Secondary School Education; Social Classes; Students.

5288 Whiteford, Linda. Migrants no longer: changing family structure of Mexican Americans in South Texas. DE COLORES, Vol. 6, no. 1-2 (1982), p. 99-108. English. DESCR: *Family; South Texas.

Sex Roles (cont.)

5289 Williams, Brett. Why migrant women feed their husbands tamales: foodways as a basis for a revisionist view of Tejano family life. IN: Brown, Linda Keller and Mussell, Kay, eds. ETHNIC AND REGIONAL FOODWAYS IN THE UNITED STATES: THE PERFORMANCE OF GROUP IDENTITY. Knoxville, TN: University of Tennessee Press, 1984, p. 113-126. English. **DESCR:** Cultural Customs; Extended Family; Family; *Food Practices; Illinois; *Migrant Labor; Tamales; Texas.

5290 Williams, Joyce E. Mexican American and Anglo attitudes about sex roles and rape. FREE INQUIRY IN CREATIVE SOCIOLOGY, Vol. 13, no. 1 (May 1985), p. 15-20. English. **DESCR:** Anglo Americans; Attitudes; *Feminism; *Rape; Women.

5291 Williams, Norma. Changes in funeral patterns and gender roles among Mexican Americans. IN: Ruiz, Vicki L. and Tiano, Susan, eds. WOMEN ON THE U.S.-MEXICO BORDER: RESPONSES TO CHANGE. Boston, MA: Allen & Unwin, 1987, p. 197-217. English. **DESCR:** Assimilation; Austin, TX; Cultural Customs; *Funerals.

5292 Williams, Norma. The Mexican American family: tradition and change. Dix Hills, NY: General Hall, Inc., c1990. x, 170 p. English. **DESCR:** Cultural Characteristics; *Cultural Customs; *Family; Religion; Working Women.

5293 Williams, Norma. Role making among married Mexican American women: issues of class and ethnicity. JOURNAL OF APPLIED BEHAVIORAL SCIENCE, Vol. 24, no. 2 (1988), p. 203-217. English. **DESCR:** Austin, TX; Corpus Christi, TX; Identity; Marriage; Social Classes.

5294 Worth, Dooley and Rodriguez, Ruth. Latina women and AIDS. SIECUS REPORT, (January, February, 1986), p. 5-7. English. **DESCR:** Cultural Characteristics; Drug Addicts; Drug Use; Health Education; Natural Support Systems; New York; Preventative Medicine; Puerto Ricans; *Vital Statistics; Women.

5295 Yarbro-Bejarano, Yvonne. Chicana's experience in collective theatre: ideology and form. WOMEN AND PERFORMANCE, Vol. 2, no. 2 (1985), p. 45-58. English. **DESCR:** Actors and Actresses; Careers; El Teatro Campesino; El Teatro de la Esperanza; Political Ideology; *San Francisco Mime Troupe; Teatro; Teatro Libertad; Valentina Productions; Women.

5296 Yarbro-Bejarano, Yvonne. The female subject in Chicano theater: sexuality, race, and class. THEATRE JOURNAL, Vol. 38, no. 4 (December 1986), p. 389-407. English. **DESCR:** El Teatro Campesino; El Teatro de la Esperanza; El Teatro Nacional de Aztlan (TENAZ); Feminism; *Malinche; *Teatro; Women in Teatro (WIT).

5297 Yarbro-Bejarano, Yvonne. The image of the Chicana in teatro. IN: Cochran, Jo; Stewart, J.T.; and Tsutakawa, Mayumi, eds. GATHERING GROUND: NEW WRITING AND ART BY NORTHWEST WOMEN OF COLOR. Seattle, WA: Seal Press, 1984, p. 90-96. English. **DESCR:** El Teatro de la Esperanza; GUADALUPE [play]; HIJOS: ONCE A FAMILY [play]; LA VICTIMA [play]; *Literary Characters; Sex Stereotypes; Stereotypes; *Teatro; THE OCTOPUS [play]; Women Men Relations.

5298 Ybarra, Lea. Empirical and theoretical developments in the study of Chicano

families. IN: Valdez, Armando, et al., eds. THE STATE OF CHICANO RESEARCH ON FAMILY, LABOR, AND MIGRATION. Stanford, CA: Stanford Center for Chicano Research, 1983, p. 91-110. English. **DESCR:** *Family; *Research Methodology; Social Science; *Stereotypes.

5299 Ybarra, Lea. Marital decision-making and the role of machismo in the Chicano family. DE COLORES, Vol. 6, no. 1-2 (1982), p. 32-47. English. **DESCR:** Family; *Machismo; Marriage.

5300 Ybarra, Lea. Separating a myth from reality: socio-economic and cultural influences on Chicanas and the world of work. IN: Melville, Margarita, ed. MEXICANAS AT WORK IN THE UNITED STATES. Houston, TX: Mexican American Studies Program, University of Houston, 1988, p. 12-23. English. **DESCR:** Attitudes; *Cultural Characteristics; Income; Machismo; *Socioeconomic Factors; Stereotypes; *Working Women.

5301 Young, Gay. Gender identification and working-class solidarity among maquila workers in Ciudad Juarez: stereotypes and realities. IN: Ruiz, Vicki L. and Tiano, Susan, eds. WOMEN ON THE U.S.-MEXICO BORDER: RESPONSES TO CHANGE. Boston, MA: Allen & Unwin, 1987, p. 105-127. English. **DESCR:** Assertiveness; Attitudes; Border Industrialization Program (BIP); *Border Industries; Border Region; Ciudad Juarez, Chihuahua, Mexico; Employment; Garment Industry; Surveys; Working Women.

5302 Young, Gay. Women, border industrialization program, and human rights. El Paso, TX: Center for InterAmerican and Border Studies, UTEP, 1984. 33 p. English. **DESCR:** Border Industrialization Program (BIP); *Border Industries; Economic Development; Employment; Industrial Workers; Mexico; *Sexism; *Women; Working Women.

5303 Zambrana, Ruth E. and Frith, Sandra. Mexican-American professional women: role satisfaction differences in single and multiple role lifestyles. JOURNAL OF SOCIAL BEHAVIOR AND PERSONALITY, Vol. 3, no. 4 (1988), p. 347-361. English. **DESCR:** *Careers; Family; *Mental Health; Working Women.

5304 Zapata, Jesse T. and Jaramillo, Pat T. The Mexican American family: an Adlerian perspective. HISPANIC JOURNAL OF BEHAVIORAL SCIENCES, Vol. 3, no. 3 (September 1981), p. 275-290. English. **DESCR:** Adlerian "Life Style Inventory"; *Family; Parent and Child Relationships; Stereotypes.

5305 Zavella, Patricia. The politics of race and gender: organizing Chicana cannery workers in Northern California. IN: Bookman, Ann and Morgen, Sandra, eds. WOMEN AND THE POLITICS OF EMPOWERMENT. Philadelphia, PA: Temple University Press, 1988, p. 202-224. English. **DESCR:** Bay City Cannery Workers Committee; *Canneries; Cannery Workers Committee (CWC); Discrimination; Garcia, Connie; Identity; *Labor Unions; Nationalism; Northern California; Santa Clara Valley, CA; Sexism; *Working Women.

5306 Zavella, Patricia. Women, work and family in the Chicano community: cannery workers of the Santa Clara Valley. Thesis (Ph.D.)--University of California, Berkeley, 1982. ix, 254 p. English. **DESCR:** *Canneries; Employment; *Family; Industrial Workers; Labor Unions; Santa Clara Valley, CA; *Working Women.

Sex Roles (cont.)

5307 Zavella, Patricia. Women's work and Chicano families: cannery workers of the Santa Clara Valley. Ithaca, NY: Cornell University Press, 1987. xviii, 191 p. English. DESCR: *Canneries; Employment; Family; Industrial Workers; Labor Unions; Santa Clara Valley, CA; *Working Women.

5308 Zeff, Shirley B. A cross-cultural study of Mexican American, Black American and white American women of a large urban university. HISPANIC JOURNAL OF BEHAVIORAL SCIENCES, Vol. 4, no. 2 (June 1982), p. 245-261. English. DESCR: Anglo Americans; Blacks; *Higher Education; Students.

Sex Stereotypes

5309 Andrade, Sally J. Family roles of Hispanic women: stereotypes, empirical findings, and implications for research. IN: Zambrana, Ruth E., ed. WORK, FAMILY, AND HEALTH: LATINA WOMEN IN TRANSITION. Bronx, NY: Hispanic Research Center, Fordham University, 1982, p. 95-106. English. DESCR: *Family; Puerto Ricans; *Research Methodology; *Sex Roles; Women.

5310 Baca Zinn, Maxine. Chicano men and masculinity. JOURNAL OF ETHNIC STUDIES, Vol. 10, no. 2 (Summer 1982), p. 29-44. English. DESCR: Cultural Characteristics; Ethnic Stratification; *Machismo; Sex Roles; Socioeconomic Factors; Women Men Relations.

5311 Belk, Sharyn S., et al. Impact of ethnicity, nationality, counseling orientation, and mental health standards on stereotypic beliefs about women. SEX ROLES, Vol. 21, no. 9-10 (November 1989), p. 671-695. English. DESCR: Anglo Americans; Beliefs About Women Scale (BAWS); *Comparative Psychology; *Counseling (Psychological); Cultural Characteristics; Identity; Mental Health; Sexism; Women.

5312 Cardenas de Dwyer, Carlota. Commentary. LA LUZ, Vol. 4, no. 8-9 (November, December, 1975), p. 8. English. DESCR: Literary Criticism; *Stereotypes.

5313 Cardenas de Dwyer, Carlota. Literary images of Mexican American women. LA LUZ, Vol. 6, no. 11 (November 1977), p. 11-12. English. DESCR: *Literary Criticism.

5314 Castaneda, Antonia I. Gender, race, and culture: Spanish-Mexican women in the historiography of frontier California. FRONTIERS: A JOURNAL OF WOMEN STUDIES, Vol. 11, no. 1 (1990), p. [8]-20. English. DESCR: Bancroft, Hubert Howe; Bolton, Herbert Eugene; *California; Californios; *Historiography; History; Intermarriage; Spanish Borderlands Theory; Spanish Influence; Stereotypes; Turner, Frederick Jackson; Women.

5315 Castaneda, Antonia I. The political economy of nineteenth century stereotypes of Californianas. IN: Del Castillo, Adelaida R., ed. BETWEEN BORDERS: ESSAYS ON MEXICANA/CHICANA HISTORY. Encino, CA: Floricanto Press, 1990, p. 213-236. English. DESCR: *California; *Californios; Dana, Richard Henry; Farnham, Thomas Jefferson; History; LIFE IN CALIFORNIA; *Political Economy; Robinson, Alfred; TRAVELS IN CALIFORNIA AND SCENES IN THE PACIFIC OCEAN TWO YEARS BEFORE THE MAST; Women.

5316 Cota-Robles de Suarez, Cecilia. Sexual

stereotypes--psychological and cultural survival: a description of child-rearing practices attributed to the Chicana (the Mexican American woman) and its psychological and cultural implications. REGENERACION, Vol. 2, no. 3 (1973), p. 17, 20-21. English. DESCR: Cultural Characteristics; Family; Folklore; Language; Parenting; *Sexism; *Stereotypes.

5317 Dario Salaz, Ruben. The Chicana in American literature. LA LUZ, Vol. 4, no. 3 (June 1975), p. 28. English. DESCR: *Chicanos in American Literature; Literary Criticism.

5318 Dario Salaz, Ruben. The Chicana in American literature. LA LUZ, Vol. 6, no. 11 (November 1977), p. 15. English. DESCR: Chicanos in American Literature; *Literary Criticism.

5319 de la Fuente, Patricia. Invisible women in the narrative of Tomas Rivera. REVISTA CHICANO-RIQUENA, Vol. 13, no. 3-4 (Fall, Winter, 1985), p. 81-89. English. DESCR: Literary Criticism; *Rivera, Tomas; Y NO SE LO TRAGO LA TIERRA/AND THE EARTH DID NOT PART.

5320 Delgado, Abelardo "Lalo". An open letter to Carolina... or relations between men and women. REVISTA CHICANO-RIQUENA, Vol. 10, no. 1-2 (Winter Spring, 1982), p. 279-284. English. DESCR: *Essays; Machismo; Sex Roles; Women Men Relations.

5321 Flores, Francisca. Conference of Mexican women un remolino. REGENERACION, Vol. 1, no. 10 (1971), p. 1-5. English. DESCR: Conferences and Meetings; Family; Feminism; First National Chicana Conference (May 1971: Houston, TX); Machismo; National Mexican American Issues Conference (October 11, 1970: Sacramento, CA); Sex Roles; Statistics; *Women Men Relations.

5322 Gonzalez, Judith Teresa. Dilemmas of the high achieving Chicana: the double bind factor in male/female relationships. Tucson, AZ: Mexican American Studies & Research Center, University of Arizona, 1987. 31 leaves. English. DESCR: *Academic Achievement; Higher Education; Identity; Males; Marriage; *Sex Roles; Women Men Relations.

5323 Gonzalez, Judith Teresa. Dilemmas of the high achieving Chicana: the double bind factor in male/female relationships. SEX ROLES, Vol. 18, no. 7-8 (April 1988), p. 367-380. English. DESCR: *Academic Achievement; Higher Education; Identity; Males; Marriage; *Sex Roles; Women Men Relations.

5324 Gutierrez Castillo, Dina. La imagen de la mujer en la novela fronteriza. IN: Lopez-Gonzalez, Aralia, et al., eds. MUJER Y LITERATURA MEXICANA Y CHICANA: CULTURAS EN CONTACTO. Mexico: Colegio de la Frontera Norte, 1988, p. [55]-63. Spanish. DESCR: *Border Region; Islas, Arturo; Literary Characters; *Literary Criticism; Mendez M., Miguel; *Novel; PEREGRINOS DE AZTLAN; Sex Roles; THE RAIN GOD: A DESERT TALE; *Women.

Sex Stereotypes (cont.)

5325 Hadley-Freydberg, Elizabeth. Prostitutes, concubines, whores and bitches: Black and Hispanic women in contemporary American film. IN: McCluskey, Audrey T., ed. WOMEN OF COLOR: PERSPECTIVES ON FEMINISM AND IDENTITY. Bloomington, IN: Women's Studies Program, Indiana University, 1985, p. 46-65. English. DESCR: *Actors and Actresses; Blacks; *Films; Puerto Ricans; Stereotypes; Women.

5326 Heathcote, Olivia D. Sex stereotyping in Mexican reading primers. READING TEACHER, Vol. 36, no. 2 (November 1982), p. 158-165. English. DESCR: Comparative Education; Curriculum Materials; Mexico; Primary School Education.

5327 Herrera-Sobek, Maria. The Mexican corrido: a feminist analysis. Bloomington, IN: Indiana University Press, 1990. xix, 151 p.: ill. English. DESCR: *Corridos; Mexico; Military; *Sex Roles; Symbolism; *Women; Women Men Relations.

5328 Howell-Martinez, Vicky. The influence of gender roles on political socialization: an experimental study of Mexican-American children. WOMEN & POLITICS, Vol. 2, no. 3 (Fall 1982), p. 33-46. English. DESCR: Political Socialization; *Sex Roles.

5329 Lawrence, Alberto Augusto. Traditional attitudes toward marriage, marital adjustment, acculturation, and self-esteem of Mexican-American and Mexican wives. Thesis (Ph.D.)--United States International University, San Diego, CA, 1982. ix, 191 p. English. DESCR: *Acculturation; *Attitudes; Machismo; *Marriage; Mental Health; Psychological Testing; San Ysidro, CA; Sex Roles; Tijuana, Baja California, Mexico; Women.

5330 Lomas, Clara. Libertad de no procrear: la voz de la mujer en "A una madre de nuestro tiempo" de Margarita Cota-Cardenas. IN: Cordova, Teresa, et al., eds. CHICANA VOICES. Austin, TX: Center for Mexican American Studies, 1986, p. 188-201. Bilingual. DESCR: "A una madre de nuestros tiempos" [poem]; *Cota-Cardenas, Margarita; Feminism; Literary Criticism; *Poetry.

5331 Lomas, Clara. Libertad de no procrear: la voz de la mujer en "A una madre de nuestro tiempo" de Margarita Cota-Cardenas. REVISTA MUJERES, Vol. 2, no. 1 (January 1985), p. 30-35. Spanish. DESCR: *"A una madre de nuestros tiempos" [poem]; *Cota-Cardenas, Margarita; Feminism; Literary Criticism; Poetry.

5332 Lucero Trujillo, Marcela. The terminology of machismo. DE COLORES, Vol. 4, no. 3 (1978), p. 34-42. Bilingual. DESCR: *Chicanismo; *Machismo; *Women Men Relations.

5333 Matsuda, Gema. La Chicana organizes: the Comision Femenil Mexicana in perspective. REGENERACION, Vol. 2, no. 4 (1975), p. 25-27. English. DESCR: Bojorquez, Frances; Chicano Movement; *Comision Femenil Mexicana Nacional; De la Cruz, Juana Ines; Flores, Francisca; History; Machismo; Malinche; Prisons; *Sexism.

5334 Melville, Margarita B. Mexican women in the U.S. wage labor force. IN: Melville, Margarita, ed. MEXICANAS AT WORK IN THE UNITED STATES. Houston, TX: Mexican American Studies Program, University of Houston, 1988, p. 1-11. English. DESCR: Feminism; *Women; *Working Women.

5335 Mirande, Alfredo. Que gacho es ser macho: it's a drag to be a macho man. AZTLAN, Vol. 17, no. 2 (Fall 1986), p. 63-89. English. DESCR: *Cultural Characteristics; Identity; *Machismo; Personality; Sex Roles; Values.

5336 Ordonez, Elizabeth J. La imagen de la mujer en el nuevo cine chicano. CARACOL, Vol. 5, no. 2 (October 1978), p. 12-13. Spanish. DESCR: Bonilla-Giannini, Roxanna; *Films; Lopez, Lexore; ONLY ONCE IN A LIFETIME [film]; *Photography; RAICES DE SANGRE [film]; Robelo, Miguel.

5337 Padilla, Eligio R. and O'Grady, Kevin E. Sexuality among Mexican Americans: a case of sexual stereotyping. JOURNAL OF PERSONALITY AND SOCIAL PSYCHOLOGY, Vol. 52, no. 1 (1987), p. 5-10. English. DESCR: Age Groups; Anglo Americans; Attitudes; California; Religion; *Sex Roles; Sexual Behavior; Sexual Knowledge and Attitude Test; *Stereotypes; Students; Values.

5338 Pallais, Maria L. The myth of the vanishing virgin. NUESTRO, Vol. 4, no. 7 (October 1980), p. 57-58. English. DESCR: Sex Roles.

5339 Pavich, Emma Guerrero. A Chicana perspective on Mexican culture and sexuality. JOURNAL OF SOCIAL WORK AND HUMAN SEXUALITY, Vol. 4, no. 3 (Spring 1986), p. 47-65. English. DESCR: California; Cultural Characteristics; Family; Feminism; Homosexuality; Machismo; Sex Roles; *Sexual Behavior; Women Men Relations.

5340 Pena, Manuel. Class, gender, and machismo: the "treacherous-woman" folklore of Mexican male workers. GENDER & SOCIETY, Vol. 5, no. 1 (March 1991), p. 30-46. English. DESCR: *Folklore; Laborers; *Machismo; Males; *Sex Roles; Social Classes; *Undocumented Workers; Women Men Relations.

5341 Ramirez, Alex, et al. The relationship between sociocultural variables and Chicano and Anglo high school student responses on the Potency Dimension of the Semantic Differential. HISPANIC JOURNAL OF BEHAVIORAL SCIENCES, Vol. 3, no. 2 (June 1981), p. 177-190. English. DESCR: Anglo Americans; Martinez, Joe L., Jr.; Martinez, Sergio R.; MULTIVARIATE ANALYSIS OF VARIANCE (MANOVA); Olmedo, Esteban L.; *Parent and Child Relationships; Sex Roles; Students.

5342 Ramos Escandon, Carmen. Alternative sources to women's history: literature. IN: Del Castillo, Adelaida R., ed. BETWEEN BORDERS: ESSAYS ON MEXICANA/CHICANA HISTORY. Encino, CA: Floricanto Press, 1990, p. 201-212. English. DESCR: *Literature; Stereotypes.

5343 Rebolledo, Tey Diana. Hispanic women writers of the Southwest: tradition and innovation. IN: Lensink, Judy Nolte, ed. OLD SOUTHWEST/NEW SOUTHWEST: ESSAYS ON A REGION AND ITS LITERATURE. Tucson, AZ: The Tucson Public Library, 1987, p. 49-61. English. DESCR: *Authors; Cabeza de Baca, Fabiola; Jaramillo, Cleofas M.; Literature; Mora, Pat; OLD SPAIN IN OUR SOUTHWEST; Otero Warren, Nina; Preciado Martin, Patricia; Sex Roles; Silva, Beverly; *Southwestern United States; Vigil-Pinon, Evangelina; WE FED THEM CACTUS; *Women.

Sex Stereotypes (cont.)

5344 Riccatelli, Ralph. The sexual stereotypes of the Chicana in literature. ENCUENTRO FEMENIL, Vol. 1, no. 2 (1974), p. 48-56. English. DESCR: *Sexism; Stereotypes.

5345 Rivero, Eliana S. La mujer y La Raza: Latinas y Chicanas [part II]. CARACOL, Vol. 4, no. 2 (October 1977), p. 21-22. Spanish. DESCR: Sex Roles.

5346 Simoniello, Katina. On investigating the attitudes toward achievement and success in eight professional U.S. Mexican women. AZTLAN, Vol. 12, no. 1 (Spring 1981), p. 121-137. English. DESCR: Attitudes.

5347 Sternbach, Nancy Saporta. "A deep racial memory of love": the Chicana feminism of Cherrie Moraga. IN: Horno-Delgado, Asuncion, et al., eds. BREAKING BOUNDARIES: LATINA WRITING AND CRITICAL READINGS. Amherst, MA: University of Massachusetts Press, c1989, p. 48-61. English. DESCR: Discrimination; Feminism; Homosexuality; Literary Criticism; *LOVING IN THE WAR YEARS; Machismo; Malinche; *Moraga, Cherrie; Sexism.

5348 Tafolla, Carmen. Chicano literature: beyond beginnings. IN: Harris, Marie and Aguero, Kathleen, eds. A GIFT OF TONGUES: CRITICAL CHALLENGES IN CONTEMPORARY AMERICAN POETRY. Athens, GA: University of Georgia Press, 1987, p. 206-225. English. DESCR: *Authors; Cota-Cardenas, Margarita; Language Usage; *Literary Criticism; *Literature; Portillo Trambley, Estela; Symbolism; Tafolla, Carmen; Vigil-Pinon, Evangelina.

5349 Tafolla, Carmen. To split a human: mitos, machos y la mujer chicana. San Antonio, TX Mexican American Cultural Center, 1985. 115 p.: ill. English. DESCR: Discrimination; Education; *Feminism; Films; *Sex Roles; *Sexism.

5350 Tiano, Susan B. Labor composition and gender stereotypes in the maquila. JOURNAL OF BORDERLAND STUDIES, Vol. 5, no. 1 (Spring 1990), p. 20-24. English. DESCR: *Border Industries; Industrial Workers; Labor Supply and Market; Women; *Working Women.

5351 Yarbro-Bejarano, Yvonne. The image of the Chicana in teatro. IN: Cochran, Jo; Stewart, J.T.; and Tsutakawa, Mayumi, eds. GATHERING GROUND: NEW WRITING AND ART BY NORTHWEST WOMEN OF COLOR. Seattle, WA: Seal Press, 1984, p. 90-96. English. DESCR: El Teatro de la Esperanza; GUADALUPE [play]; HIJOS: ONCE A FAMILY [play]; LA VICTIMA [play]; *Literary Characters; Sex Roles; Stereotypes; *Teatro; THE OCTOPUS [play]; Women Men Relations.

Sexism

5352 Acuna, Rodolfo. Response to Cynthia Orozco. LA RED/THE NET, no. 79 (April 1984), p. 13-15. English. DESCR: *Orozco, Cynthia.

5353 Asuncion-Lande, Nobleza C. Problems and strategies for sexual identity and cultural integration: Mexican-American women on the move. IN: Newmark, Eileen, ed. WOMEN'S ROLES: A CROSS-CULTURAL PERSPECTIVE. New York, NY: Pergamon Press, 1980, p. 497-506. English. DESCR: Chicano Movement; *Feminism; *Identity.

5354 Barton, Amy E. Women farmworkers: their workplace and capitalist patriarchy. REVISTA MUJERES, Vol. 3, no. 2 (June 1986), p. 11-13. English. DESCR: Capitalism; Discrimination; *Farm Workers.

5355 Belk, Sharyn S., et al. Impact of ethnicity, nationality, counseling orientation, and mental health standards on stereotypic beliefs about women. SEX ROLES, Vol. 21, no. 9-10 (November 1989), p. 671-695. English. DESCR: Anglo Americans; Beliefs About Women Scale (BAWS); *Comparative Psychology; *Counseling (Psychological); Cultural Characteristics; Identity; Mental Health; *Sex Stereotypes; Women.

5356 Blea, Irene I. Mexican American female experience. IN: Blea, Irene I. TOWARD A CHICANO SOCIAL SCIENCE. New York: Praeger, 1988, p. [67]-89. English. DESCR: Chicano Movement; *Feminism; Sex Roles.

5357 Campos Carr, Irene. A survey of selected literature on La Chicana. NWSA JOURNAL, Vol. 1, (Winter 1988, 1989), p. 253-273. English. DESCR: *Literature Reviews; *Social Science.

5358 Chavez, Henri. Las Chicanas/The Chicanas. REGENERACION, Vol. 1, no. 10 (1971), p. 14. Bilingual. DESCR: *Chicano Movement; *Women Men Relations.

5359 Cota-Robles de Suarez, Cecilia. Sexual stereotypes--psychological and cultural survival: a description of child-rearing practices attributed to the Chicana (the Mexican American woman) and its psychological and cultural implications. REGENERACION, Vol. 2, no. 3 (1973), p. 17, 20-21. English. DESCR: Cultural Characteristics; Family; Folklore; Language; Parenting; Sex Stereotypes; *Stereotypes.

5360 Cotera, Marta P. Sexism in bilingual bicultural education. IN: Cotera, Martha and Hufford, Larry, eds. BRIDGING TWO CULTURES. Austin, TX: National Educational Laboratory Publishers, 1980, p. 181-190. English. DESCR: *Bilingual Bicultural Education; Sex Roles; Stereotypes; Textbooks.

5361 Daggett, Andrea Stuhlman. A comparison of occupational goal orientations of female Mexican-Americans and Anglo high-school seniors of the classes of 1972 and 1980. Thesis (Ph.D.)--University of Arizona, Tucson, 1983. xii, 134 p. English. DESCR: Academic Achievement; Anglo Americans; *Careers; *Secondary School Education; Students; Women.

5362 Dixon, Marlene. The rise and demise of women's liberation: a class analysis. IN: Mora, Magdalena and Del Castillo, Adelaida, eds. MEXICAN WOMEN IN THE UNITED STATES: STRUGGLES PAST AND PRESENT. Los Angeles, CA: Chicano Studies Research Center, 1980, p. 37-43. English. DESCR: *Feminism; Social Classes.

5363 Dunbar Ortiz, Roxanne. Toward a democratic women's movement in the United States. IN: Mora, Magdalena and Del Castillo, Adelaida, eds. MEXICAN WOMEN IN THE UNITED STATES: STRUGGLES PAST AND PRESENT. Los Angeles, CA: Chicano Studies Research Center, UCLA, 1980, p. 29-35. English. DESCR: *Feminism.

Sexism (cont.)

Alejandro; RETO EN EL PARAISO; *Stereotypes.

5364 Espin, Oliva M. Perceptions of sexual discrimination among college women in Latin America and the United States. HISPANIC JOURNAL OF BEHAVIORAL SCIENCES, Vol. 2, no. 1 (March 1980), p. 1-19. English. DESCR: Colleges and Universities; CRITICAL INCIDENT TECHNIQUE; Feminism; Latin Americans; Students; Women Men Relations.

5365 Flores Magon, Ricardo. A la mujer = To women. IN: Mora, Magdalena and Del Castillo, Adelaida, eds. MEXICAN WOMEN IN THE UNITED STATES: STRUGGLES PAST AND PRESENT. Los Angeles, CA: Chicano Studies Research Center, UCLA, 1980, p. 159-162. English. DESCR: Mexican Revolution - 1910-1920.

5366 Garcia, Alma M. The development of Chicana feminist discourse, 1970-1980. GENDER & SOCIETY, Vol. 3, no. 2 (June 1989), p. 217-238. English. DESCR: Anglo Americans; Chicana Studies; *Chicano Movement; *Feminism; Homosexuality; Machismo; National Association for Chicano Studies (NACS); Organizations; Women.

5367 Garcia, Alma M. The development of Chicana feminist discourse, 1970-1980. IN: DuBois, Ellen Carol and Ruiz, Vicki L., eds. UNEQUAL SISTERS: A MULTICULTURAL READER IN U.S. WOMEN'S HISTORY. New York: Routledge, 1990, p. 418-431. English. DESCR: Anglo Americans; Chicana Studies; *Chicano Movement; *Feminism; Homosexuality; Machismo; National Association for Chicano Studies (NACS); Organizations; Women.

5368 Glenn, Evelyn Nakano. Racial ethnic women's labor: the intersection of race, gender and class oppression. REVIEW OF RADICAL POLITICAL ECONOMY, Vol. 17, no. 3 (Fall 1985), p. 86-108. English. DESCR: Asian Americans; Blacks; *Discrimination; *Feminism; Laboring Classes; *Marxism; Social Classes; Women; Working Women.

5369 Hogeland, Chris and Rosen, Karen. Dreams lost, dreams found: undocumented women in the land of opportunity. San Francisco, CA: Coalition for Immigrant and Refugee Rights and Services, c1991. 153 p. English. DESCR: *Battered Women; *Coalition for Immigrant and Refugee Rights and Services, Immigrant Woman's Task Force; Discrimination; Immigrants; *San Francisco Bay Area; Sex Roles; Social Services; Undocumented Workers; Violence; Women; Women Men Relations.

5370 Jordan, Rosan Augusta. The vaginal serpent and other themes from Mexican-American women's lore. IN: Jordan, Rosan A. and Kalcik, Susan J., eds. WOMEN'S FOLKLORE, WOMEN'S CULTURE. Philadelphia: University of Pennsylvania Press, 1985, p. 26-44. English. DESCR: Cuentos; Fertility; *Folklore; La Llorona; *Leyendas; *Sex Roles; Sexual Behavior.

5371 Klor de Alva, J. Jorge. Chicana history and historical significance: some theoretical considerations. IN: Del Castillo, Adelaida R., ed. BETWEEN BORDERS: ESSAYS ON MEXICANA/CHICANA HISTORY. Encino, CA: Floricanto Press, 1990, p. 61-86. English. DESCR: Chicana Studies; *Historiography; *History.

5372 Lizarraga, Sylvia S. Images of women in Chicano literature by men. FEMINIST ISSUES, Vol. 5, no. 2 (Fall 1985), p. 69-88. English. DESCR: *Literature; Morales,

5373 Longeaux y Vasquez, Enriqueta. The Mexican American woman. IN: Meier, Matt S. and Rivera, Feliciano, eds. READINGS ON LA RAZA: THE TWENTIETH CENTURY. New York: Hill and Wang, [1974], p. 254-258. English. DESCR: *Social History and Conditions.

5374 Luna-Lawhn, Juanita. EL REGIDOR and LA PRENSA: impediments to women's self-definition. THIRD WOMAN, Vol. 4, (1989), p. 134-142. English. DESCR: EL REGIDOR, San Antonio, TX; LA PRENSA, San Antonio, TX; Literature; *Newspapers; Sex Roles.

5375 Martinez, Diana. The double bind. AGENDA, (Summer 1976), p. 10-11. English. DESCR: Careers; Discrimination.

5376 Matsuda, Gema. La Chicana organizes: the Comision Femenil Mexicana in perspective. REGENERACION, Vol. 2, no. 4 (1975), p. 25-27. English. DESCR: Bojorquez, Frances; Chicano Movement; *Comision Femenil Mexicana Nacional; De la Cruz, Juana Ines; Flores, Francisca; History; Machismo; Malinche; Prisons; Sex Stereotypes.

5377 Matute-Bianchi, Maria Eugenia. A Chicana in academe. WOMEN'S STUDIES QUARTERLY, Vol. 10, no. 1 (Spring 1982), p. 14-17. English. DESCR: Discrimination; *Higher Education; Matute-Bianchi, Maria Eugenia; Sex Roles.

5378 Maymi, Carmen R. Fighting to open the doors to opportunity. AGENDA, no. 4 (Spring 1974), p. 8-10. English. DESCR: Business; Business Enterprises; Legislation.

5379 Medina Gonzales, Esther. Sisterhood. LA LUZ, Vol. 4, no. 5 (September, October, 1975), p. 7. English. DESCR: *Attitudes; *Discrimination.

5380 Molina de Pick, Gracia. Reflexiones sobre el feminismo y la Raza. LA LUZ, Vol. 1, no. 4 (August 1972), p. 58. Spanish. DESCR: *Feminism; *Stereotypes.

5381 Molina de Pick, Gracia. Reflexiones sobre el feminismo y la Raza. REGENERACION, Vol. 2, no. 4 (1975), p. 33-34. Spanish. DESCR: Feminism; Stereotypes.

5382 Monroy, Douglas. "They didn't call them 'padre' for nothing": patriarchy in Hispanic California. IN: Del Castillo, Adelaida R., ed. BETWEEN BORDERS: ESSAYS ON MEXICANA/CHICANA HISTORY. Encino, CA: Floricanto Press, 1990, p. 433-445. English. DESCR: *California; Clergy; History; *Machismo; Rape; *Sex Roles; Spanish Influence; Women Men Relations.

5383 Mujeres en Marcha, University of California, Berkeley. Chicanas in the 80s: unsettled issues. Berkeley, CA: Chicano Studies Library Publications Unit, 1983. 31 p. English. DESCR: Conferences and Meetings; Feminism; National Association for Chicano Studies (NACS); National Association for Chicano Studies Annual Conference (1982: Tempe, AZ).

Sexism (cont.)

5384 Nava, Yolanda. The Chicana and employment: needs analysis and recommendations for legislation. REGENERACION, Vol. 2, no. 3 (1973), p. 7-9. English. DESCR: California Commission on the Status of Women; Child Care Centers; Comision Femenil Mexicana Nacional; *Discrimination in Employment; Employment Tests; Employment Training; Equal Rights Amendment (ERA); Statistics; Stereotypes; Working Women.

5385 Nava, Yolanda. Employment counseling and the Chicana. ENCUENTRO FEMENIL, Vol. 1, no. 1 (Spring 1973), p. 20-26. English. DESCR: *Employment; Employment Training.

5386 Navar, Isabelle. La Mexicana: an image of strength. AGENDA, no. 2 (Spring 1974), p. 3-5. English. DESCR: Family; Feminism; *Identity; Psychology; Working Women.

5387 Navar, Isabelle. La Mexicana: an image of strength. REGENERACION Vol. 2, no. 4 (1974), p. 4-6. English. DESCR: Family; Feminism; *Identity; Psychology; Working Women.

5388 Nieto Gomez de Lazarin, Anna. Ana Nieto Gomez: sexism in the Movimiento. LA GENTE DE AZTLAN, Vol. 6, no. 4 (March 1976), p. 10. English. DESCR: *Chicano Movement; Feminism; Sex Roles.

5389 Nieto Gomez de Lazarin, Anna. The Chicana: perspectives for education. ENCUENTRO FEMENIL, Vol. 1, no. 1 (Spring 1973), p. 34-61. English. DESCR: Colleges and Universities; Discrimination; Discrimination in Education; *Education; Family; Identity.

5390 Nieto Gomez de Lazarin, Anna. La femenista [sic]. ENCUENTRO FEMENIL, Vol. 1, no. 2 (1974), p. 34-47. English. DESCR: Anglo Americans; Chicana Caucus, National Women's Political Caucus; Chicano Movement; Conferences and Meetings; Discrimination; *Feminism; National Women's Political Caucus (February 9-11, 1973: Houston, TX); Women.

5391 Nieto Gomez de Lazarin, Anna. Un proposito para estudios femeniles de la chicana. REGENERACION, Vol. 2, no. 4 (1975), p. 30, 31-32. English. DESCR: Chicano Studies; Curriculum; *Education; History; Nava, Yolanda.

5392 Orozco, Cynthia. Chicana labor history: a critique of male consciousness in historical writing. LA RED/THE NET, no. 77 (January 1984), p. 2-5. English. DESCR: *Historiography; Labor; Working Women.

5393 Orozco, Cynthia. Sexism in Chicano Studies and the community. IN: Cordova, Teresa, et al., eds. CHICANA VOICES. Austin, TX: Center for Mexican American Studies, 1986, p. 11-18. English. DESCR: Acuna, Rodolfo; Chicano Studies; Feminism; OCCUPIED AMERICA.

5394 Ortiz, Flora Ida. Hispanic American women in higher education: a consideration of the socialization process. AZTLAN, Vol. 17, no. 2 (Fall 1986), p. 125-152. English. DESCR: *Academic Achievement; Counseling (Educational); Enrollment; *Higher Education; Sex Roles; Socialization; Students; University of California.

5395 Perez, Emma. Sexuality and discourse: notes from a Chicana survivor. IN: Trujillo, Carla, ed. CHICANA LESBIANS: THE GIRLS OUR MOTHERS WARNED US ABOUT. Berkeley, CA: Third

Woman Press, 1991, p. 159-184. English. DESCR: *Feminism; Homosexuality; Intergroup Relations; Paz, Octavio; *Sex Roles; Skin Color.

5396 Phillips, Melody. The Chicana: her attitudes towards the woman's liberation movement. COMADRE, no. 2 (Spring 1978), p. 42-50. English. DESCR: Attitudes; *Feminism.

5397 Quintanilla Anita. Images of deceit. WOMANSPIRIT Vol. 10, no. 37 (Fall 1983), p. 25-26. English. DESCR: *Malinche.

5398 Riccatelli, Ralph. The sexual stereotypes of the Chicana in literature. ENCUENTRO FEMENIL, Vol. 1, no. 2 (1974), p. 48-56. English. DESCR: Sex Stereotypes; Stereotypes.

5399 Rincon, Bernice. Chicanas on the move. REGENERACION, Vol. 2, no. 4 (1975), p. 52. English. DESCR: Flores, Francisca; Population.

5400 Robinson, Bea Vasquez. Are we racist? Are we sexist? AGENDA, (Winter 1976), p. 23-24. English. DESCR: Conferences and Meetings; Discrimination; Feminism; International Women's Year World Conference (1975: Mexico City); National Chicana Coalition.

5401 Ruelas, J. Oshi. Moments of change. REVISTA MUJERES, Vol. 4, no. 1 (January 1987), p. 23-33. English. DESCR: *Autobiography; Essays; *Ruelas, J. Oshi; Sex Roles.

5402 Saavedra-Vela, Pilar. Hispanic women in double jeopardy. AGENDA, Vol. 7, no. 6 (November, December, 1977), p. 4-7. English. DESCR: Conferences and Meetings; Discrimination; Houston, TX; National Women's Conference (November, 1977: Houston, TX).

5403 Saldivar-Hull, Sonia. Feminism on the border: from gender politics to geopolitics. IN: Calderon, Hector and Saldivar, Jose David, eds. CRITICISM IN THE BORDERLANDS: STUDIES IN CHICANO LITERATURE, CULTURE, AND IDEOLOGY. Durham, NC: Duke University Press, 1991, p. [203]-220. English. DESCR: Anglo Americans; *Anzaldua, Gloria; *BORDERLANDS/LA FRONTERA: THE NEW MESTIZA; Feminism; Homosexuality; *Literary Criticism; Mestizaje; Moraga, Cherrie; "The Cariboo Cafe" [short story]; Viramontes, Helena Maria; Women.

5404 Sanchez, Corina. Higher education y la Chicana? ENCUENTRO FEMENIL, Vol. 1, no. 1 (Spring 1973), p. 27-33. English. DESCR: Discrimination; Discrimination in Education; *Higher Education; Identity.

5405 Sartillan, Richard. Rosita the riveter: Midwest Mexican American women during World War II, 1941-1945. PERSPECTIVES IN MEXICAN AMERICAN STUDIES, Vol. 2, (1989), p. 115-147. English. DESCR: History; Industrial Workers; Intergroup Relations; Language Usage; *Midwestern States; Military; Mutualistas; War; *Working Women; *World War II.

Sexism (cont.)

5406 Sosa Riddell, Adaljiza. Background: a critical overview on Chicanas/Latinas and public policies. IN: Sosa Riddell, Adaljiza, ed. POLICY DEVELOPMENT: CHICANA/LATINA SUMMER RESEARCH INSTITUTE. Davis, CA: [Chicano Studies Program, University of California, Davis, 1989?], p. 2-8. English. **DESCR:** Discrimination; Educational Administration; *Public Policy.

5407 Sosa Riddell, Adaljiza. The status of women in Mexico: the impact of the "International Year of the Woman". IN: Iglitzin, Lynn B. and Ross, Ruth A., eds. WOMEN IN THE WORLD, 1975-1985. Santa Barbara, CA: ABC-Clio, Inc., 1986, p. 305-324. English. **DESCR:** Abortion; *Feminism; International Women's Year World Conference (1975: Mexico City); *Mexico; Political History and Conditions; Political Parties and Organizations; Rape; Social History and Conditions; *Women.

5408 Sternbach, Nancy Saporta. "A deep racial memory of love": the Chicana feminism of Cherrie Moraga. IN: Horno-Delgado, Asuncion, et al., eds. BREAKING BOUNDARIES: LATINA WRITING AND CRITICAL READINGS. Amherst, MA: University of Massachusetts Press, c1989, p. 48-61. English. **DESCR:** Discrimination; Feminism; Homosexuality; Literary Criticism; *LOVING IN THE WAR YEARS; Machismo; Malinche; *Moraga, Cherrie; Sex Stereotypes.

5409 Stoddard, Ellwyn R. Maquila: assembly plants in Northern Mexico. El Paso, TX: Texas Western Press, 1987. ix, 91 p., [4] p. of plates: ill. English. **DESCR:** Border Industrialization Program (BIP); *Border Industries; Immigration; Income; *Industrial Workers; Labor Supply and Market; Mexico; Undocumented Workers.

5410 Tafolla, Carmen. To split a human: mitos, machos y la mujer chicana. San Antonio, TX: Mexican American Cultural Center, 1985. 115 p.: ill. English. **DESCR:** Discrimination; Education; *Feminism; Films; *Sex Roles; Sex Stereotypes.

5411 Tienda, Marta. Sex, ethnicity and Chicano status attainment. INTERNATIONAL MIGRATION REVIEW, Vol. 16, no. 2 (Summer 1982), p. 435-473. English. **DESCR:** Academic Achievement; Discrimination in Education; Discrimination in Employment; Identity; Income; Language Proficiency; *Social Classes; Social Mobility.

5412 Treacy, Mary Jane. The ties that bind: women and community in Evangelina Vigil's THIRTY AN' SEEN A LOT. IN: Horno-Delgado, Asuncion, et al., eds. BREAKING BOUNDARIES: LATINA WRITING AND CRITICAL READINGS. Amherst, MA: University of Massachusetts Press, c1989, p. 82-93. English. **DESCR:** Identity; Literary Criticism; Poetry; *THIRTY AN' SEEN A LOT; *Vigil-Pinon, Evangelina.

5413 Valdes-Fallis, Guadalupe. A liberated Chicana: a struggle against tradition. WOMEN: A JOURNAL OF LIBERATION, Vol. 3, no. 4 (1974), p. 20-21. English. **DESCR:** Essays; Feminism; Sex Roles.

5414 Williams, Norma. A Mexican American woman encounters sociology: an autobiographical perspective. AMERICAN SOCIOLOGIST, Vol. 19, no. 4 (Winter 1988), p. 340-346. English. **DESCR:** Autobiography; Social Science; *Sociology; Williams, Norma.

5415 Young, Gay. Women, border industrialization program, and human rights. El Paso, TX: Center for InterAmerican and Border Studies, UTEP, 1984. 33 p. English. **DESCR:** Border Industrialization Program (BIP); *Border Industries; Economic Development; Employment; Industrial Workers; Mexico; Sex Roles; *Women; Working Women.

5416 Zavella, Patricia. The politics of race and gender: organizing Chicana cannery workers in Northern California. IN: Bookman, Ann and Morgen, Sandra, eds. WOMEN AND THE POLITICS OF EMPOWERMENT. Philadelphia, PA: Temple University Press, 1988, p. 202-224. English. **DESCR:** Bay City Cannery Workers Committee; *Canneries; Cannery Workers Committee (CWC); Discrimination; Garcia, Connie; Identity; *Labor Unions; Nationalism; Northern California; Santa Clara Valley, CA; Sex Roles; *Working Women.

Sexual Behavior

5417 Alarcon, Norma; Castillo, Ana; and Moraga, Cherrie. The sexuality of Latinas [special issue of THIRD WOMAN]. THIRD WOMAN, Vol. 4, (1989), p. 8-189. Bilingual. **DESCR:** *Literature; Sex Roles; *Women.

5418 Alonso, Ana Maria and Koreck, Maria Teresa. Silences: "Hispanics", AIDS, and sexual practices. DIFFERENCES: A JOURNAL OF FEMINIST CULTURAL STUDIES, Vol. 1, no. 1 (Winter 1989), p. 101-124. English. **DESCR:** *AIDS (Disease); *Homosexuality; Human Immunodeficiency Virus (HIV); Machismo; Mexico; *Self-Referents; Sex Roles.

5419 Aneshensel, Carol S., et al. Onset of fertility-related events during adolescence: a prospective comparison of Mexican American and non-Hispanic white females. AMERICAN JOURNAL OF PUBLIC HEALTH, Vol. 80, no. 8 (August 1990), p. 959-963. English. **DESCR:** Abortion; Anglo Americans; Birth Control; *Fertility; Women; *Youth.

5420 Arguelles, Lourdes and Rivero, Anne M. HIV infection/AIDS and Latinas in Los Angeles County: considerations for prevention, treatment, and research practice. CALIFORNIA SOCIOLOGIST, Vol. 11, no. 1-2 (1988), p. 69-89. English. **DESCR:** *AIDS (Disease); Cultural Characteristics; Health Education; Homosexuality; Human Immunodeficiency Virus (HIV); Los Angeles County, CA; Natural Support Systems; Parent and Child Relationships; *Women.

5421 Bassoff, Betty Z. and Ortiz, Elizabeth Thompson. Teen women: disparity between cognitive values and anticipated life events. CHILD WELFARE, Vol. 63, no. 2 (March, April, 1984), p. 125-138. English. **DESCR:** *Values; Women; *Youth.

5422 Blanco, Iris. El sexo y su condicionamiento cultural en el mundo prehispanico. IN: Del Castillo, Adelaida R., ed. BETWEEN BORDERS: ESSAYS ON MEXICANA/CHICANA HISTORY. Encino, CA: Floricanto Press, 1990, p. 363-374. Spanish. **DESCR:** Mexico; *Precolumbian Society; *Sex Roles; Women.

5423 Castillo, Ana. La macha: toward a beautiful whole self. IN: Trujillo, Carla, ed. CHICANA LESBIANS: THE GIRLS OUR MOTHERS WARNED US ABOUT. Berkeley, CA: Third Woman Press, 1991, p. 24-48. English. **DESCR:** *Homosexuality.

Sexual Behavior (cont.)

5424 Castro, Rafaela. Mexican women's sexual jokes. AZTLAN, Vol. 13, no. 1-2 (Spring, Fall, 1982), p. 275-293. English. DESCR: *Chistes; Humor.

5425 de Anda, Diane; Becerra, Rosina M.; and Fielder, Eve P. In their own words: the life experiences of Mexican-American and white pregnant adolescents and adolescent mothers CHILD AND ADOLESCENT SOCIAL WORK, Vol. 7, no. 4 (August 1990), p. 301-318. English. DESCR: Anglo Americans; *Fertility; Women; *Youth.

5426 de Anda, Diane; Becerra, Rosina M.; and Fielder, Eve P. Sexuality, pregnancy, and motherhood among Mexican-American adolescents. JOURNAL OF ADOLESCENT RESEARCH, Vol. 3, no. 3-4 (Fall, Winter, 1988), p. 403-411. English. DESCR: Anglo Americans; Attitudes; Birth Control; *Fertility; Sex Education; Women; *Youth.

5427 Espin, Oliva M. Cultural and historical influences on sexuality in Hispanic/Latin women: implications for psychotherapy. IN: Vance, Carole S., ed. PLEASURE AND DANGER: EXPLORING FEMALE SEXUALITY. Boston, MA: Routledge & Kegan Paul, 1984, p. 149-164. English. DESCR: Immigration; Language Usage; Machismo; *Psychotherapy; Sex Roles; Social History and Conditions; Spanish Influence; *Women.

5428 Forste, Renata T. and Heaton, Tim B. Initiation of sexual activity among female adolescents. YOUTH AND SOCIETY, Vol. 19, no. 3 (March 1988), p. 250-268. English. DESCR: Anglo Americans; Blacks; Family; Sex Education; Women; *Youth.

5429 Griswold del Castillo, Richard. La familia: Chicano families in the urban Southwest, 1848 to the present. Notre Dame, IN: University of Notre Dame Press, c1984. xv, 173 p. English. DESCR: *Family; History; Intermarriage; Machismo; Parenting; *Sex Roles; *Social History and Conditions.

5430 Gutierrez, Ramon A. From honor to love: transformations of the meaning of sexuality in colonial New Mexico. IN: Smith, Raymond T., ed. KINSHIP IDEOLOGY AND PRACTICE IN LATIN AMERICA. Chapel Hill, NC: University of North Carolina Press, 1984, p. [237]-263. English. DESCR: *Catholic Church; *Marriage; New Mexico; Social Classes; Social History and Conditions; Spanish Influence; Values; Women.

5431 Gutierrez, Ramon A. Marriage and seduction in Colonial New Mexico. IN: Del Castillo, Adelaida R., ed. BETWEEN BORDERS: ESSAYS ON MEXICANA/CHICANA HISTORY. Encino, CA: Floricanto Press, 1990, p. 447-457. English. DESCR: History; *Marriage; *New Mexico; Rape; Women.

5432 Gutierrez, Ramon A. When Jesus came, the corn mothers went away: marriage, sexuality, and power in New Mexico, 1500-1846. Stanford: Stanford University Press, 1991. xxxi, 424 p. English. DESCR: *Marriage Native Americans; *New Mexico; *Pueblo Indians; *Sex Roles; Spanish Influence; Women.

5433 Horowitz, Ruth. Femininity and womanhood: virginity, unwed motherhood, and violence. IN: Horowitz, Ruth. HONOR AND THE AMERICAN DREAM: CULTURE AND IDENTITY IN A CHICANO COMMUNITY. New Brunswick, NJ: Rutgers University Press, 1983, p. 114-136. English. DESCR: *Birth Control; *Fertility; Identity; Sex Roles; Single Parents; Violence; Women Men Relations; Youth.

5434 Horowitz, Ruth. Passion, submission and motherhood: the negotiation of identity by unmarried innercity Chicanas. SOCIOLOGICAL QUARTERLY, Vol. 22, no. 2 (Spring 1981), p. 241-252. English. DESCR: Barrios; Birth Control; *Fertility; Identity; *Sex Roles; Single Parents; Youth.

5435 Job, Peggy. La sexualidad en la narrativa femenina mexicana 1970-1987: una aproximacion. THIRD WOMAN, Vol. 4, (1989), p. 120-133 Spanish. DESCR: *Literature; *Literature Reviews; Sex Roles; *Women.

5436 Jordan, Rosan Augusta. The vaginal serpent and other themes from Mexican-American women's lore. IN: Jordan, Rosan A. and Kalcik, Susan J., eds. WOMEN'S FOLKLORE, WOMEN'S CULTURE. Philadelphia: University of Pennsylvania Press, 1985, p. 26-44. English. DESCR: Cuentos; Fertility; *Folklore; La Llorona; *Leyendas; *Sex Roles; Sexism.

5437 Juarez, Reina Maria. Evaluation of three treatment modalities with preorgasmic Hispanic women treated without partners. Thesis (Ph.D.)--California School of Professional Psychology, Los Angeles, 1982. 236 p. English. DESCR: *Psychotherapy.

5438 Malvido, Elsa. El uso del cuerpo femenino en la epoca colonial mexicana a traves de los estudios de demografia historica. IN: Del Castillo, Adelaida R., ed. BETWEEN BORDERS: ESSAYS ON MEXICANA/CHICANA HISTORY. Encino, CA: Floricanto Press, 1990, p. 115-130. Spanish. DESCR: Marriage; *Mexico; *Sex Roles; *Vital Statistics; Widowhood; *Women.

5439 Mays, Vicki M. and Cochran, Susan D. Issues in the perception of AIDS risk and risk reduction activities by Black and Hispanic/Latina women. AMERICAN PSYCHOLOGIST, Vol. 43, no. 11 (November 1988), p. 949-957. English. DESCR: *AIDS (Disease); Blacks; Condom Use; Fertility; Health Education; Preventative Medicine; Women.

5440 Ordonez Elizabeth J. Sexual politics and the theme of sexuality in Chicana poetry. IN: Miller, Beth, ed. WOMEN IN HISPANIC LITERATURE: ICONS AND FALLEN IDOLS. Berkeley, CA: University of California Press, 1983, p. 316-339. English. DESCR: Chicano Movement; Feminism; *Literary Criticism; Poetry.

5441 Ortiz, Carmen G. The influence of religious images on perceptions of femininity among women of Mexican origin. Thesis (Ph.D.)--California School of Professional Psychology, Berkeley, 1988. 210 p. English. DESCR: Catholic Church; *Identity; *Religion; Symbolism.

5442 Ortiz, Sylvia. An analysis of the relationship between the values of sexual regulation, male dominance, and motherhood, and Mexican-American women's attitudes, knowledge, and usage of birth control. Thesis (Ph.D.)--University of California, Santa Barbara, 1987. 128 p. English. DESCR: Acculturation; *Attitudes; *Birth Control; *Family Planning.

Sexual Behavior (cont.)

5443 Padilla, Amado M. and Baird, Traci L.
Mexican-American adolescent sexuality and
sexual knowledge: an exploratory study.
HISPANIC JOURNAL OF BEHAVIORAL SCIENCES,
Vol. 13, no. 1 (February 1991), p. 95-104.
English. DESCR: *Attitudes; *Birth Control;
Sex Roles; Surveys; *Youth.

5444 Padilla, Eligio R. and O'Grady, Kevin E.
Sexuality among Mexican Americans: a case of
sexual stereotyping. JOURNAL OF PERSONALITY
AND SOCIAL PSYCHOLOGY, Vol. 52, no. 1
(1987), p. 5-10. English. DESCR: Age Groups;
Anglo Americans; Attitudes; California;
Religion; *Sex Roles; *Sex Stereotypes;
Sexual Knowledge and Attitude Test;
*Stereotypes; Students; Values.

5445 Pavich, Emma Guerrero. A Chicana perspective
on Mexican culture and sexuality. JOURNAL OF
SOCIAL WORK AND HUMAN SEXUALITY, Vol. 4, no.
3 (Spring 1986), p. 47-65. English. DESCR:
California; Cultural Characteristics;
Family; Feminism; Homosexuality; Machismo;
Sex Roles; Sex Stereotypes; Women Men
Relations.

5446 Rebolledo, Tey Diana. The maturing of
Chicana poetry: the quiet revolution of the
1980s. IN: Treichler, Paula A., et al., eds.
FOR ALMA MATER: THEORY AND PRACTICE IN
FEMINIST SCHOLARSHIP. Urbana: University of
Illinois Press, 1985, p. 143-158. English.
DESCR: Identity; *Literary Criticism;
*Poetry.

5447 Remez, Lisa. Rates of adolescent pregnancy
and childbearing are high among Mexican-born
Mexican Americans. FAMILY PLANNING
PERSPECTIVES, Vol. 23, no. 2 (March, April,
1991), p. 88-89. English. DESCR: *Fertility;
*Immigrants; Los Angeles County, CA; *Youth.

5448 Trujillo, Carla. Chicana lesbians: fear and
loathing in the Chicano community. IN:
Trujillo, Carla, ed. CHICANA LESBIANS: THE
GIRLS OUR MOTHERS WARNED US ABOUT. Berkeley,
CA: Third Woman Press, 1991, p. 186-194.
English. DESCR: Essays; *Homosexuality; *Sex
Roles.

5449 Yarbro-Bejarano, Yvonne. Primer encuentro de
lesbianas feministas latinoamericanas y
caribenas. THIRD WOMAN, Vol. 4, (1989), p.
143-146. English. DESCR: Caribbean Region;
*Conferences and Meetings; First Meeting of
Latin American and Caribbean Feminist
Lesbians (October 14-17, 1987: Cuernavaca,
Mexico); *Homosexuality; Latin Americans;
*Women.

Sexual Harassment
USE: Sexism

Sexual Knowledge and Attitude Test

5450 Padilla, Eligio R. and O'Grady, Kevin E.
Sexuality among Mexican Americans: a case of
sexual stereotyping. JOURNAL OF PERSONALITY
AND SOCIAL PSYCHOLOGY, Vol. 52, no. 1
(1987), p. 5-10. English. DESCR: Age Groups;
Anglo Americans; Attitudes; California;
Religion; *Sex Roles; *Sex Stereotypes;
Sexual Behavior; *Stereotypes; Students;
Values.

SHE HAD SOME HORSES

5451 Crawford, John F. Notes toward a new
multicultural criticism: three works by
women of color. IN: Harris, Marie and
Aguero, Kathleen, eds. A GIFT OF TONGUES:

CRITICAL CHALLENGES IN CONTEMPORARY AMERICAN
POETRY. Athens, GA: University of Georgia
Press, 1987, p. 155-195. English. DESCR:
AWAKE IN THE RIVER; Cervantes, Lorna Dee;
EMPLUMADA; Harjo, Joy; *Literary Criticism;
Mirikitani, Janice.

Short Story

5452 Boza, Maria del Carmen, ed.; Silva, Beverly,
ed.; and Valle, Carmen, ed. Nosotras: Latina
literature today. Binghamton, NY: Bilingual
Review Press, 1986. 93 p. Bilingual. DESCR:
*Poems; Women.

5453 Gomez, Alma, ed.; Moraga, Cherrie, ed.; and
Romo-Carmona, Mariana, ed. Cuentos: stories
by Latinas. New York: Kitchen Table, Women
of Color Press, 1983. xx, 241 p. Bilingual.
DESCR: Women.

5454 McCracken, Ellen. Latina narrative and
politics of signification: articulation,
antagonism, and populist rupture. CRITICA,
Vol. 2, no. 2 (Fall 1990), p. 202-207.
English. DESCR: *Cisneros, Sandra; IN NUEVA
YORK; *Literary Criticism; *Mohr, Nicolasa;
Puerto Ricans; RITUALS OF SURVIVAL; THE
HOUSE ON MANGO STREET; Women.

5455 Rebolledo, Tey Diana, ed.; Gonzales-Berry,
Erlinda, ed.; and Marquez, Maria Teresa, ed.
Las mujeres hablan: an anthology of Nuevo
Mexicana writers. Albuquerque, NM: El Norte
Publications, c1988. xiv, 210 p.: ill.
English. DESCR: *New Mexico; *Poems; *Prose.

5456 Sanchez, Elba R. La realidad a traves de la
inocencia en el cuento: "Un Paseo". IN:
Cordova, Teresa, et al., eds. CHICANA
VOICES. Austin, TX: Center for Mexican
American Studies, 1986, p. 202-207. Spanish.
DESCR: *Garzon, Luz; Literary Criticism;
*"Un Paseo" [short story].

Silva, Beverly

5457 Rebolledo, Tey Diana. Hispanic women writers
of the Southwest: tradition and innovation.
IN: Lensink, Judy Nolte, ed. OLD
SOUTHWEST/NEW SOUTHWEST: ESSAYS ON A REGION
AND ITS LITERATURE. Tucson, AZ: The Tucson
Public Library, 1987, p. 49-61. English.
DESCR: *Authors; Cabeza de Baca, Fabiola;
Jaramillo, Cleofas M.; Literature; Mora,
Pat; OLD SPAIN IN OUR SOUTHWEST; Otero
Warren, Nina; Preciado Martin, Patricia; Sex
Roles; Sex Stereotypes; *Southwestern United
States; Vigil-Pinon, Evangelina; WE FED THEM
CACTUS; *Women.

5458 Rebolledo, Tey Diana. Tradition and
mythology: signatures of landscape in
Chicana literature. IN: Norwood, Vera and
Monk, Janice, eds. THE DESERT IS NO LADY:
SOUTHWESTERN LANDSCAPES IN WOMEN'S WRITING
AND ART. New Haven, CT: Yale University
Press, 1987, p. 96-124. English. DESCR:
*Authors; Cabeza de Baca, Fabiola; Chavez,
Denise; Jaramillo, Cleofas M.; Literary
Criticism; *Literary History; Literature;
Mora, Pat; Mythology; Otero Warren, Nina;
Portillo Trambley, Estela; Southwestern
United States; WE FED THEM CACTUS.

"Silver Lake Road" [short story]

5459 Herrera-Sobek, Maria. The politics of rape: sexual transgression in Chicana fiction. THE AMERICAS REVIEW, Vol. 15, no. 3-4 (Fall, Winter, 1987), p. 171-131. English. DESCR: Cisneros, Sandra; *Feminism; Fiction; GIVING UP THE GHOST; *Literary Criticism; Lizarraga, Sylvia; Moraga, Cherrie; *Rape; "Red Clowns" [short story]; Sex Roles.

Sindicato Independiente Solicev

5460 Iglesias, Norma. La flor mas bella de la maquiladora: historias de vida de la mujer obrera en Tijuana, B.C.N. Mexico, D.F.: Secretaria de Educacion Publica, CEFNOMEX, 1985. 166 p.: ill. Spanish. DESCR: Border Industrialization Program (BIP); *Border Industries; Cultural Customs; Labor Unions; Solidev Mexicana, S.A.; Tijuana, Baja California, Mexico; *Women; Working Women.

Singers

5461 Broyles-Gonzalez, Yolanda and Rodriguez, Diane. The living legacy of Chicana performers: preserving history through oral testimony. FRONTIERS: A JOURNAL OF WOMEN STUDIES, Vol. 11, no. 1 (1990), p. [46]-52. English. DESCR: *Actors and Actresses; El Teatro Campesino; Latins Anonymous [comedy review]; Oral History; *Rodriguez, Diane; Sex Roles; Teatro.

5462 Sheridan, Thomas E. From Luisa Espinel to Lalo Guerrero: Tucson's Mexican musicians before World War II. JOURNAL OF ARIZONA HISTORY, Vol. 25, no. 3 (Fall 1984), p. 285-300. English. DESCR: Biography; Espinel, Luisa Ronstadt; Guerrero, Eduardo "Lalo"; History; Montijo, Manuel; *Musicians; Rebeil, Julia; *Tucson, AZ.

Single Parents

5463 Abrahamse, Allan F.; Morrison, Peter A.; and Waite, Linda J. Beyond stereotypes: who becomes a single teenage mother? Santa Monica, CA: RAND Corp., 1988. xv, 88 p. English. DESCR: *Fertility; Religion; Secondary School Education; Statistics; *Women; *Youth.

5464 Abrahamse, Allan F.; Morrison, Peter A.; and Waite, Linda J. Teenagers willing to consider single parenthood: who is at greatest risk? FAMILY PLANNING PERSPECTIVES, Vol. 20, no. 1 (January, February, 1988), p. 13-18. English. DESCR: Blacks; Family Planning; *Fertility; High School and Beyond Project (HS&B); Women; *Youth.

5465 Dugan, Anna Baziak. Kin, social supports and depression among women of Mexican heritage who are single parents. Thesis (Ph.D.)--Bryn Mawr College, 1982. vii, 138 p. English. DESCR: *Depression (Psychological); Detroit, MI; Family; *Natural Support Systems.

5466 Eisen, Marvin. Factors discriminating pregnancy resolution decisions of unmarried adolescents. GENETIC PSYCHOLOGY MONOGRAPHS, Vol. 108, no. 1 (August 1983), p. 69-95. English. DESCR: Abortion; Attitudes; Decision Making; *Fertility; *Youth.

5467 Gonzalez, Deena J. The widowed women of Santa Fe: assessments on the lives of an unmarried population, 1850-80. IN: Scadron, Arlene, ed. ON THEIR OWN: WIDOWS AND WIDOWHOOD IN THE AMERICAN SOUTHWEST 1843-1939. Urbana, IL: University of

Illinois Press, c1988, p. [65]-90. English. DESCR: Family; History; Income; Land Tenure; *Santa Fe, NM; Sex Roles; *Widowhood; *Women.

5468 Gonzalez, Deena J. The widowed women of Santa Fe: assessments on the lives of an unmarried population, 1850-80. IN: DuBois, Ellen Carol and Ruiz, Vicki L., eds. UNEQUAL SISTERS: A MULTICULTURAL READER IN U.S. WOMEN'S HISTORY. New York: Routledge, 1990, p. 34-50. English. DESCR: Family; History; Income; Land Tenure; *Santa Fe, NM; Sex Roles; *Widowhood; *Women.

5469 Hancock, Paula F. The effect of welfare eligibility on the labor force participation of women of Mexican origin in California. POPULATION RESEARCH AND POLICY REVIEW, Vol. 5, no. 2 (1986), p. 163-185. English. DESCR: Aid to Families with Dependent Children (AFDC); California; *Employment; Food Stamps; Immigrants; Medi-Cal; *Welfare; Women.

5470 Horowitz, Ruth. Femininity and womanhood: virginity, unwed motherhood, and violence. IN: Horowitz, Ruth. HONOR AND THE AMERICAN DREAM: CULTURE AND IDENTITY IN A CHICANO COMMUNITY. New Brunswick, NJ: Rutgers University Press, 1983, p. 114-136. English. DESCR: *Birth Control; *Fertility; Identity; Sex Roles; *Sexual Behavior; Violence; Women Men Relations; Youth.

5471 Horowitz, Ruth. Passion, submission and motherhood: the negotiation of identity by unmarried innercity Chicanas. SOCIOLOGICAL QUARTERLY, Vol. 22, no. 2 (Spring 1981), p. 241-252. English. DESCR: Barrios; Birth Control; *Fertility; Identity; *Sex Roles; *Sexual Behavior; Youth.

5472 Loustaunau, Martha Oehmke. Hispanic widows and their support systems in the Mesilla Valley of southern New Mexico, 1910-40. IN: Scadron, Arlene, ed. ON THEIR OWN: WIDOWS AND WIDOWHOOD IN THE AMERICAN SOUTHWEST 1843-1939. Urbana, IL: University of Illinois Press, c1988, p. [91]-116. English. DESCR: Cultural Customs; Extended Family; Mesilla Valley, NM; Natural Support Systems; Sex Roles; Widowhood; *Women.

5473 Stroup-Benham, Christine A.; Trevino, Fernando M.; and Trevino, Dorothy B. Alcohol consumption patterns among Mexican American mothers and among children from single- and dual-headed households: findings from HHANES 1982-84. AMERICAN JOURNAL OF PUBLIC HEALTH, Vol. 80, (December 1990), p. 36-41. English. DESCR: *Alcoholism; *Children; Hispanic Health and Nutrition Examination Survey (HHANES); Parent and Child Relationships.

5474 Tienda, Marta and Angel, Ronald J. Headship and household composition among Blacks, Hispanics and other whites. SOCIAL FORCES, Vol. 61, no. 2 (December 1982), p. 508-531. English. DESCR: Anglo Americans; Blacks; Cultural Characteristics; Extended Family; *Family; Puerto Ricans.

5475 Wagner, Roland M. Changes in extended family relationships for Mexican American and Anglo single mothers. JOURNAL OF DIVORCE, Vol. 11, no. 2 (Winter 1987), p. 69-87. English. DESCR: Anglo Americans; *Divorce; *Extended Family; Natural Support Systems; San Jose, CA; Women.

Single Parents (cont.)

5476 Wagner, Roland M. Changes in the friend network during the first year of single parenthood for Mexican American and Anglo women. JOURNAL OF DIVORCE, Vol. 11, no. 2 (Winter 1987), p. 89-109. English. DESCR: Anglo Americans; Divorce; *Natural Support Systems; Widowhood; Women.

5477 Wagner, Roland M. and Schaffer, Diane M. Social networks and survival strategies: an exploratory study of Mexican American, Black, and Anglo female family heads in San Jose, California. IN: Melville, Margarita B., ed. TWICE A MINORITY. St. Louis, MO: Mosby, 1980, p. 173-190. English. DESCR: Anglo Americans; Blacks; Identity; *Natural Support Systems; San Jose, CA; Stress.

5478 Weiner, Raine. The needs of poverty women heading households: a return to postsecondary education. Thesis (Ph.D.)--California School of Professional Psychology, Los Angeles, 1986. 180 p. English. DESCR: Anglo Americans; Blacks; *Employment Training; Ethnic Groups; *Poverty; Vocational Education; Welfare; Women.

Sixteen Personality Factor Questionnaire

5479 De Blassie, Richard R. and Franco, Juan N. The differences between personality inventory scores and self-rating in a sample of Hispanic subjects. JOURNAL OF NON-WHITE CONCERNS IN PERSONNEL AND GUIDANCE, Vol. 11, no. 2 (January 1983), p. 43-46. English. DESCR: Higher Education; Hispanic Education [program]; New Mexico State University; *Personality; Students.

Skin Color

5480 Perez, Emma. Sexuality and discourse: notes from a Chicana survivor. IN: Trujillo, Carla, ed. CHICANA LESBIANS: THE GIRLS OUR MOTHERS WARNED US ABOUT. Berkeley, CA: Third Woman Press, 1991, p. 159-184. English. DESCR: *Feminism; Homosexuality; Intergroup Relations; Paz, Octavio; *Sex Roles; *Sexism.

5481 Yarbro-Bejarano, Yvonne. De-constructing the lesbian body: Cherrie Moraga's LOVING IN THE WAR YEARS. IN: Trujillo, Carla, ed. CHICANA LESBIANS: THE GIRLS OUR MOTHERS WARNED US ABOUT. Berkeley, CA: Third Woman Press, 1991, p. 143-155. English. DESCR: Homosexuality; Literary Criticism; *LOVING IN THE WAR YEARS; *Moraga, Cherrie.

Smoking

5482 Holck, Susan E. Lung cancer mortality and smoking habits: Mexican-American women. AMERICAN JOURNAL OF PUBLIC HEALTH, Vol. 72, no. 1 (January 1982), p. 38-42. English. DESCR: Anglo Americans; Cancer; *Public Health.

5483 Marin, Gerardo; Perez-Stable, Eliseo J.; and Marin, Barbara Van Oss. Cigarette smoking among San Francisco Hispanics: the role of acculturation and gender. PUBLIC HEALTH BRIEFS, Vol. 79, no. 2 (February 1989), p. 196-198. English. DESCR: *Acculturation; Drug Use; Males; San Francisco, CA; Women.

5484 Zambrana, Ruth E., et al. Ethnic differences in the substance use patterns of low-income pregnant women. FAMILY & COMMUNITY HEALTH, Vol. 13, no. 4 (January 1991), p. 1-11. English. DESCR: Alcoholism; Blacks; *Drug Use; *Fertility; Immigrants; *Low Income; Women.

"Snapshots" [short story]

5485 Alarcon, Norma. Making "familia" from scratch: split subjectivities in the work of Helena Maria Viramontes and Cherrie Moraga. THE AMERICAS REVIEW, Vol. 15, no. 3-4 (Fall, Winter, 1987), p. 147-159. English. DESCR: GIVING UP THE GHOST; *Literary Criticism; Moraga, Cherrie; *Sex Roles; THE MOTHS AND OTHER STORIES; Viramontes, Helena Maria.

Snyder, Elizabeth

5486 Mendoza, Hope Schecter and Chall, Malca. Activist in the labor movement, the Democratic Party, and the Mexican-American community: an interview. Berkeley, CA: Regional Oral History Office, Bancroft Library, University of California, Berkeley, 1980. xii, 170 p.: ill. English. DESCR: *Biography; Chavez Ravine, Los Angeles, CA; Church, Frank; Community Organizations; Community Service Organization, Los Angeles, (CSO); Democratic Party; Elections; Garment Industry; Industrial Workers; *Labor Unions; Leadership; Mendoza, Hope Schecter; Warschaw, Carmen.

Soberon, Mercedes

5487 Soberon, Mercedes. La revolucion se trata de amor: Mercedes Soberon. CHISMEARTE, Vol. 1, no. 1 (Fall 1976), p. 14-18. Spanish. DESCR: Art Criticism; Concilio de Arte Popular, Los Angeles, CA; Cultural Organizations; La Mission Media Arts, San Francisco, CA; San Francisco, CA; *Sex Roles.

Social and Public Art Resource Center, Venice, CA (SPARC)

5488 Brown, Betty Ann. Chicanas speak out. ARTWEEK, Vol. 15, no. 2 (January 14, 1984), p. 1+. English. DESCR: *Art; Carrasco, Barbara; Carrillo, Graciela; CHICANA VOICES & VISIONS [exhibit]; Exhibits; Goldman, Shifra M.; Hernandez, Ester; Lerma Bowerman, Liz; Rodriguez, Carmen; Rodriguez, Sandra Maria.

5489 Pohl, Frances K. and Baca, Judith F. THE WORLD WALL: A VISION OF THE FUTURE WITHOUT FEAR: an interview with Judith F. Baca. FRONTIERS: A JOURNAL OF WOMEN STUDIES, Vol. 11, no. 1 (1990), p. [33]-43. English. DESCR: Art Organizations and Groups; *Artists; *Baca, Judith F.; *Mural Art; *THE WORLD WALL: A VISION OF THE FUTURE WITHOUT FEAR [mural].

Social Classes

5490 Acosta Johnson, Carmen. Breast-feeding and social class mobility: the case of Mexican migrant mothers in Houston, Texas. IN: Melville, Margarita B., ed. TWICE A MINORITY. St. Louis, MO: Mosby, 1980, p. 66-82. English. DESCR: *Breastfeeding; Herbal Medicine; Maternal and Child Welfare; Social Mobility.

Social Classes (cont.)

5491 Apodaca, Maria Linda. The Chicana woman: a historical materialist perspective. IN: Bollinger, William, et al., eds. WOMEN IN LATIN AMERICA: AN ANTHOLOGY FROM LATIN AMERICAN PERSPECTIVES. Riverside, CA: Latin American Perspectives, c1979, p. 81-100. English. DESCR: Capitalism; *Historiography; Immigrants; Imperialism; Marxism; Mexico; Oral History; Spanish Influence.

5492 Baca Zinn, Maxine. Employment and education of Mexican-American women: the interplay of modernity and ethnicity in eight families. HARVARD EDUCATIONAL REVIEW, Vol. 50, no. 1 (February 1980), p. 47-62. English. DESCR: Acculturation; Decision Making; *Education; *Employment; *Family; Identity; Sex Roles; Values.

5493 Blackwelder, Julia Kirk. Women of the depression: caste and culture in San Antonio, 1929-1939. College Station, TX: Texas A&M University Press, 1984. xviii, 279 p.: ill. English. DESCR: Criminal Justice System; Cultural Characteristics; Employment; Family; Great Depression, 1929-1933; Labor Supply and Market; Labor Unions; Prostitution; San Antonio, TX; *Women.

5494 Cazares, Ralph B.; Murguia, Edward; and Frisbie, William Parker. Mexican American intermarriage in a nonmetropolitan context. SOCIAL SCIENCE QUARTERLY, Vol. 65, no. 2 (June 1984), p. 626-634. English. DESCR: Age Groups; *Intermarriage; Pecos County, TX; Texas.

5495 Cazares, Ralph B.; Murguia, Edward; and Frisbie, William Parker. Mexican American intermarriage in a nonmetropolitan context. IN: O. de la Garza, Rodolfo, et al., eds. THE MEXICAN AMERICAN EXPERIENCE: AN INTERDISCIPLINARY ANTHOLOGY. Austin, TX: University of Texas Press, 1985, p. 393-401. English. DESCR: Age Groups; *Intermarriage; Pecos County, TX; Texas.

5496 Deutsch, Sarah. Culture, class, and gender: Chicanas and Chicanos in Colorado and New Mexico, 1900-1940. Thesis (Ph.D.)--Yale University, 1985. xii, 510 p. English. DESCR: Anglo Americans; Colorado; Immigrants; New Mexico; *Sex Roles; Social History and Conditions; Women; *Working Women.

5497 Deutsch, Sarah. No separate refuge: culture, class, and gender on an Anglo-Hispanic frontier in the American Southwest, 1880-1940. New York: Oxford University Press, 1987. vi, 356 p. English. DESCR: Anglo Americans; Colorado; Immigrants; Immigration; Mining Industry; Missions; New Mexico; *Sex Roles; *Social History and Conditions; Women; Working Women; World War I.

5498 Dixon, Marlene. The rise and demise of women's liberation: a class analysis. IN: Mora, Magdalena and Del Castillo, Adelaida, eds. MEXICAN WOMEN IN THE UNITED STATES: STRUGGLES PAST AND PRESENT. Los Angeles, CA: Chicano Studies Research Center, 1980, p. 37-43. English. DESCR: *Feminism; Sexism.

5499 Facio, Elisa "Linda". The interaction of age and gender in Chicana older lives: a case study of Chicana elderly in a senior citizen center. RENATO ROSALDO LECTURE SERIES MONOGRAPH, Vol. 4, (1988), p. 21-38. English. DESCR: Age Groups; *Ancianos; Poverty.

5500 Garcia-Bahne, Betty. La Chicana and the Chicano family. IN: Sanchez, Rosaura and Martinez Cruz, Rosa, eds. ESSAYS ON LA MUJER. Los Angeles, CA: Chicano Studies Center Publications, UCLA, 1977, p. 30-47. English. DESCR: Cultural Customs; *Family; Sex Roles; Socialization; Stereotypes.

5501 Glenn, Evelyn Nakano. Racial ethnic women's labor: the intersection of race, gender and class oppression. REVIEW OF RADICAL POLITICAL ECONOMY, Vol. 17, no. 3 (Fall 1985), p. 86-108. English. DESCR: Asian Americans; Blacks; *Discrimination; *Feminism; Laboring Classes; *Marxism; Sexism; Women; Working Women.

5502 Gutierrez, Ramon A. From honor to love: transformations of the meaning of sexuality in colonial New Mexico. IN: Smith, Raymond T., ed. KINSHIP IDEOLOGY AND PRACTICE IN LATIN AMERICA. Chapel Hill, NC: University of North Carolina Press, 1984, p. [237]-263. English. DESCR: *Catholic Church; *Marriage; New Mexico; *Sexual Behavior; Social History and Conditions; Spanish Influence; Values; Women.

5503 Gutierrez, Ramon A. Honor ideology, marriage negotiation, and class-gender domination in New Mexico, 1690-1846. LATIN AMERICAN PERSPECTIVES, Vol. 12, no. 1 (Winter 1985), p. 81-104. English. DESCR: Marriage; Sex Roles; Social History and Conditions; Southwestern United States; Values; Women Men Relations.

5504 Harlow, Barbara. Sites of struggle: immigration, deportation, prison, and exile. IN: Calderon, Hector and Saldivar, Jose David, eds. CRITICISM IN THE BORDERLANDS: STUDIES IN CHICANO LITERATURE, CULTURE, AND IDEOLOGY. Durham, NC: Duke University Press, 1991, p. [149]-163. English. DESCR: Anzaldua, Gloria; BLACK GOLD; BORDERLANDS/LA FRONTERA: THE NEW MESTIZA; First, Ruth; Khalifeh, Sahar; *Literary Criticism; *Political Ideology; Sanchez, Rosaura; "The Cariboo Cafe" [short story]; "The Ditch" [short story]; Viramontes, Helena Maria; WILD THORNS; *Women; Working Women.

5505 Larguia, Isabel and Dumoulin, John. Toward a science of women's liberation. IN: Mora, Magdalena and Del Castillo, Adelaida, eds. MEXICAN WOMEN IN THE UNITED STATES: STRUGGLES PAST AND PRESENT. Los Angeles, CA: Chicano Studies Research Center, 1980, p. 45-61. English. DESCR: *Feminism; Labor; Sex Roles.

5506 Lizarraga, Sylvia S. Hacia una teoria para la liberacion de la mujer. IN: Garcia, Juan R., ed. IN TIMES OF CHALLENGE: CHICANOS AND CHICANAS IN AMERICAN SOCIETY. Houston, TX: Mexican American Studies Program, University of Houston, 1988, p. 25-31. Spanish. DESCR: *Feminism; Laboring Classes; *Women; *Working Women.

5507 Marquez, Evelina and Ramirez, Margarita. La tarea de la mujer es la liberacion. IN: Maciel, David R., compiler. LA OTRA CARA DE MEXICO: EL PUEBLO CHICANO. Mexico, D.F.: Ediciones "El Caballito," 1977, p. 173-181. Spanish. DESCR: *Feminism.

Social Classes (cont.)

5508 Mindiola, Tatcho, Jr. and Gutierrez, Armando. Education and discrimination against Mexican Americans in the Southwest. CALIFORNIA SOCIOLOGIST, Vol. 5, no. 2 (Summer 1982), p. 80-97. English. DESCR: *Discrimination in Education; Research Methodology.

5509 Murguia, Edward. Chicano intermarriage: a theoretical and empirical study. San Antonio, TX: Trinity University Press, 1982. xiv, 134 p. English. DESCR: Assimilation; Attitudes; Ethnic Groups; *Intermarriage; Military; Weddings.

5510 Pena, Manuel. Class, gender, and machismo: the "treacherous-woman" folklore of Mexican male workers. GENDER & SOCIETY, Vol. 5, no. 1 (March 1991), p. 30-46. English. DESCR: *Folklore; Laborers; *Machismo; Males; *Sex Roles; Sex Stereotypes; *Undocumented Workers; Women Men Relations.

5511 Sanchez, Rosaura. The Chicana labor force. IN: Sanchez, Rosaura and Martinez Cruz, Rosa, eds. ESSAYS ON LA MUJER. Los Angeles, CA: Chicano Studies Center Publications, UCLA, 1977, p. 3-15. English. DESCR: *Employment; Income.

5512 Schoen, Robert; Wooldredge, John; and Thomas, Barbara. Ethnic and educational effects on marriage choice. SOCIAL SCIENCE QUARTERLY, Vol. 70, no. 3 (September 1989), p. 617-630. English. DESCR: Education; Identity; *Intermarriage; Marriage; Research Methodology.

5513 Segura, Denise. Conflict in social relations at work: a Chicana perspective. IN: National Association for Chicano Studies. ESTUDIOS CHICANOS AND THE POLITICS OF COMMUNITY. [S.l.]: National Association for Chicano Studies, c1989, p. [110]-131. English. DESCR: *Discrimination in Employment; Employment Training; Immigrants; *Interpersonal Relations; Women; *Working Women.

5514 Tienda, Marta. Sex, ethnicity and Chicano status attainment. INTERNATIONAL MIGRATION REVIEW, Vol. 16, no. 2 (Summer 1982), p. 435-473. English. DESCR: Academic Achievement; Discrimination in Education; Discrimination in Employment; Identity; Income; Language Proficiency; Sexism; Social Mobility.

5515 Torres Raines, Rosario. The Mexican American woman and work: intergenerational perspectives of comparative ethnic groups. IN: Melville, Margarita, ed. MEXICANAS AT WORK IN THE UNITED STATES. Houston, TX: Mexican American Studies Program, University of Houston, 1988, p. 33-46. English. DESCR: Age Groups; Anglo Americans; Employment; Feminism; Marriage; Sex Roles; Socioeconomic Factors; *Working Women.

5516 Vigil, James Diego. The nexus of class, culture and gender in the education of Mexican American females. IN: McKenna, Teresa and Ortiz, Flora Ida, eds. THE BROKEN WEB: THE EDUCATIONAL EXPERIENCE OF HISPANIC WOMEN. Claremont, CA: Tomas Rivera Center; Berkeley, CA: Floricanto Press, 1988, p. 79-103. English. DESCR: Academic Achievement; Acculturation; Discrimination in Education; *Education; Identity; Secondary School Education; Sex Roles; Students.

5517 Williams, Norma. Role making among married Mexican American women: issues of class and ethnicity. JOURNAL OF APPLIED BEHAVIORAL SCIENCE, Vol. 24, no. 2 (1988), p. 203-217. English. DESCR: Austin, TX; Corpus Christi, TX; Identity; Marriage; *Sex Roles.

5518 Zambrana, Ruth E. Bibliography on maternal and child health across class, race and ethnicity. Memphis, TN: Distributed by the Memphis State University Center for Research on Women, c1990. 58 leaves. English. DESCR: *Bibliography; Ethnic Groups; *Maternal and Child Welfare; *Medical Care; *Women.

5519 Zambrana, Ruth E. Hispanic professional women: work, family and health. Los Angeles, CA: National Network of Hispanic Women, 1987. 75 leaves. English. DESCR: Business; *Careers; *Employment; Family; Management; Mental Health; *Social Mobility; *Women.

Social History and Conditions

5520 Amodeo, Luiza B.; Edelson, Rosalyn; and Martin, Jeanette. The triple bias: rural, minority and female. RURAL EDUCATOR, Vol. 3, no. 3 (Spring 1982), p. 1-6. English. DESCR: *Education; Rural Population; Women.

5521 Aragon de Valdez, Theresa. Organizing as a political tool for the Chicana. FRONTIERS: A JOURNAL OF WOMEN STUDIES, Vol. 5, no. 2 (Summer 1980), p. 7-13. English. DESCR: Discrimination; Feminism; *Leadership; Mexican American Legal Defense and Educational Fund (MALDEF); Sterilization.

5522 Camarillo, Alberto M., ed. Latinos in the United States: a historical bibliography. Santa Barbara, CA: ABC-CLIO, 1986. x, 332 p.. English. DESCR: *Bibliography; Political History and Conditions.

5523 Castaneda, Antonia I. Comparative frontiers: the migration of women to Alta California and New Zealand. IN: Schlissel, Lillian, et al., eds. WESTERN WOMEN: THEIR LAND, THEIR LIVES. Albuquerque, NM: University of New Mexico Press, 1988, p. 283-300. English. DESCR: Border Region; California; History; Immigrants; Immigration; Marriage; Mexico; Missions; Native Americans; New Zealand; *Women.

5524 Cordova, Teresa, et al., eds. and National Association for Chicano Studies. Chicana voices: intersections of class, race, and gender. Austin, TX: Center for Mexican American Studies Publications, 1986. xi, 223 p. English. DESCR: Chicana Studies; Labor; Political History and Conditions.

5525 Cotera, Marta P. The Chicana feminist. Austin, TX: Information Systems Development, c1977. 68 p.: port. English. DESCR: *Feminism.

5526 Cotera, Marta P. Diosa y hembra, the history and heritage of Chicanas in the United States. Austin, TX: Information Systems Development, 1976. 202 p. English. DESCR: History.

5527 Cotera, Marta P. Feminism: the Chicana and Anglo versions: a historical analysis. IN: Melville, Margarita B., ed. TWICE A MINORITY. St. Louis, MO: Mosby, 1980, p. 217-234. English. DESCR: *Anglo Americans; Chicano Movement; Conferences and Meetings; *Feminism; Organizations; Voting Rights; *Women.

Social History and Conditions
(cont.)

5528 Cotera, Marta P. Profile on the Mexican
American woman. Austin, TX: National
Educational Laboratory Publishers, 1976. v,
264 p. English. **DESCR:** History.

5529 Deutsch, Sarah. Culture, class, and gender:
Chicanas and Chicanos in Colorado and New
Mexico, 1900-1940. Thesis (Ph.D.)--Yale
University, 1985. xii, 510 p. English.
DESCR: Anglo Americans; Colorado;
Immigrants; New Mexico; *Sex Roles; *Social
Classes; Women; *Working Women.

5530 Deutsch, Sarah. No separate refuge: culture
class, and gender on an Anglo-Hispanic
frontier in the American Southwest,
1880-1940. New York: Oxford University
Press, 1987. vi, 356 p. English. **DESCR:**
Anglo Americans; Colorado; Immigrants;
Immigration; Mining Industry; Missions; New
Mexico; *Sex Roles; *Social Classes; Women;
Working Women; World War I.

5531 Deutsch, Sarah. Women and intercultural
relations: the case of Hispanic New Mexico
and Colorado. SIGNS: JOURNAL OF WOMEN IN
CULTURE AND SOCIETY, Vol. 12, no. 4 (Summer
1987), p. 719-739. English. **DESCR:** Colorado;
Cultural Characteristics; Immigrants;
Intercultural Communication; Mexico; New
Mexico; Rural Population; Sex Roles; *Women.

5532 Enriquez, Evangelina and Mirande, Alfredo.
Liberation, Chicana style: colonial roots of
feministas chicanas. DE COLORES, Vol. 4, no.
3 (1978), p. 7-21. Bilingual. **DESCR:**
*Chicano Movement; Feminism; Malinche;
*Political History and Conditions.

5533 Escobedo, Theresa Herrera, ed. Thematic
issue: Chicana issues. HISPANIC JOURNAL OF
BEHAVIORAL SCIENCES, Vol. 4, no. 2 (June
1982), p. 145-286. English. **DESCR:**
Education; Higher Education.

5534 Espin, Oliva M. Cultural and historical
influences on sexuality in Hispanic/Latin
women: implications for psychotherapy. IN:
Vance, Carole S., ed. PLEASURE AND DANGER:
EXPLORING FEMALE SEXUALITY. Boston, MA:
Routledge & Kegan Paul, 1984, p. 149-164.
English. **DESCR:** Immigration; Language Usage;
Machismo; *Psychotherapy; Sex Roles; *Sexual
Behavior; Spanish Influence; *Women.

5535 Gallegos y Chavez, Ester. The northern New
Mexican woman: a charging silhouette. IN:
Trejo, Arnulfo D., ed. THE CHICANOS: AS WE
SEE OURSELVES. Tucson, AZ: University of
Arizona Press, 1979, p. 67-79. English.
DESCR: *Identity; Machismo; New Mexico.

5536 Goldsmith, Raquel Rubio. La
Mexicana/Chicana. RENATO ROSALDO LECTURE
SERIES MONOGRAPH, Vol. 1, (Summer 1985), p.
1-67. English. **DESCR:** Clergy; House of the
Divine Providence [convent], Douglas, AZ;
Labor Unions; Women; World War II.

5537 Gonzales, Erlinda. La muerte de un refran.
DE COLORES, Vol. 2, no. 3 (1975), p. 15-13.
Spanish. **DESCR:** *Higher Education;
*Identity; Socialization.

5538 Griswold del Castillo, Richard. La familia:
Chicano families in the urban Southwest,
1848 to the present. Notre Dame, IN:
University of Notre Dame Press, c1984. xv,
173 p. English. **DESCR:** *Family; History;
Intermarriage; Machismo; Parenting; *Sex
Roles; Sexual Behavior.

5539 Gutierrez, Ramon A. From honor to love:
transformations of the meaning of sexuality
in colonial New Mexico. IN: Smith, Raymond
T., ed. KINSHIP IDEOLOGY AND PRACTICE IN
LATIN AMERICA. Chapel Hill, NC: University
of North Carolina Press, 1984, p. [237]-263.
English. **DESCR:** *Catholic Church; *Marriage;
New Mexico; *Sexual Behavior; Social
Classes; Spanish Influence; Values; Women.

5540 Gutierrez, Ramon A. Honor ideology, marriage
negotiation, and class-gender domination in
New Mexico, 1690-1846. LATIN AMERICAN
PERSPECTIVES, Vol. 12, no. 1 (Winter 1985),
p. 81-104. English. **DESCR:** Marriage; Sex
Roles; *Social Classes; Southwestern United
States; Values; Women Men Relations.

5541 Longeaux y Vasquez, Enriqueta. The Mexican
American woman. IN: Meier, Matt S. and
Rivera, Feliciano, eds. READINGS ON LA RAZA:
THE TWENTIETH CENTURY. New York: Hill and
Wang, [1974], p. 254-258. English. **DESCR:**
Sexism.

5542 Longeaux y Vasquez, Enriqueta. The woman of
La Raza. REGENERACION, Vol. 2, no. 4 (1975),
p. 34-36. English. **DESCR:** Child Care
Centers; Discrimination; Gallo, Juana;
Housing; La Adelita; Machismo; Sex Roles;
Working Women.

5543 Longeaux y Vasquez, Enriqueta. The woman of
La Raza. IN: Valdez, Luis and Steiner, Stan,
eds. AZTLAN: AN ANTHOLOGY OF MEXICAN
AMERICAN LITERATURE. New York: Vintage
Books, 1972, p. 272-278. Also IN: Salinas,
Luis Omar and Faderman, Lillian, compilers.
FROM THE BARRIO: A CHICANO ANTHOLOGY. San
Francisco, CA: Canfield Press, 1973, p.
20-24. English. **DESCR:** Child Care Centers;
Discrimination; Gallo, Juana; Housing; La
Adelita; Machismo; Sex Roles; Working Women.

5544 Lorenzana, Noemi. La Chicana: transcending
the old and carving out a new life and
self-image. DE COLORES, Vol. 2, no. 3
(1975), p. 6-14. English. **DESCR:** *Census;
Identity; Population.

5545 Miller, Darlis A. Cross-cultural marriages
in the Southwest: the New Mexico experience,
1846-1900. NEW MEXICO HISTORICAL REVIEW,
Vol. 57, no. 4 (October 1982), p. 335-359.
English. **DESCR:** Assimilation; Attitudes;
Ethnic Groups; *Intermarriage; New Mexico.

5546 Mirande, Alfredo and Enriquez, Evangelina.
La Chicana: the Mexican-American woman.
Chicago: University of Chicago Press, 1979.
x, 283 p.: ill. English. **DESCR:** Family;
Feminism.

5547 Mora, Magdalena and Del Castillo, Adelaida
R. Mexican women in the United States:
struggles past and present. Los Angeles, CA:
Chicano Studies Research Center
Publications, c1980. 204 p. English. **DESCR:**
Feminism; *Working Women.

5548 Myres, Sandra Lynn. Mexican Americans and
westering Anglos: a feminine perspective.
NEW MEXICO HISTORICAL REVIEW, Vol. 57, no. 4
(October 1982), p. 317-333. English. **DESCR:**
Anglo Americans; *Attitudes; *Ethnic Groups;
Southwestern United States; Stereotypes.

5549 Ortiz Ortega, Adriana. Un camino por
transitar. FEM, Vol. 8, no. 34 (June, July,
1984), p. 25-26. Spanish.

Social History and Conditions
(cont.)

5550 Preciado Martin, Patricia. Images and conversations: Mexican Americans recall a Southwestern past. Tucson, AZ: University of Arizona Press, 1983. 110 p.: ill. English. **DESCR:** *Oral History; Photography; Tucson, AZ.

5551 Romero-Cachinero, M. Carmen. Hispanic women in Canada: a framework for analysis. RESOURCES FOR FEMINIST RESEARCH, Vol. 16, no. 1 (March 1987), p. 19-20. English. **DESCR:** *Canada; Population; Women.

5552 Sanchez, George J. "Go after the women": Americanization and the Mexican immigrant woman, 1915-1929. Stanford, CA: Stanford Center for Chicano Research [1984?]. [32] leaves. English. **DESCR:** Acculturation; *Assimilation; Biculturalism; *Immigrants; Values; Women.

5553 Sanchez, George J. "Go after the women": Americanization and the Mexican immigrant woman, 1915-1929. IN: DuBois, Ellen Carol and Ruiz, Vicki L., eds. UNEQUAL SISTERS: A MULTICULTURAL READER IN U.S. WOMEN'S HISTORY. New York: Routledge, 1990, p. 250-263. English. **DESCR:** Acculturation; *Assimilation; Biculturalism; *Immigrants; Values; Women.

5554 Sanchez, Rosaura, ed. and Martinez Cruz, Rosa, ed. Essays on la mujer. Los Angeles, CA: Chicano Studies Center Publications, c1977. vi, 194 p. Bilingual.

5555 Saragoza, Alex M. The conceptualization of the history of the Chicano family. IN: Valdez, Armando, et al., eds. THE STATE OF CHICANO RESEARCH ON FAMILY, LABOR AND MIGRATION. Stanford, CA: Stanford Center for Chicano Research, 1983, p. 111-138. English. **DESCR:** *Family.

5556 Schlissel, Lillian, ed.; Ruiz, Vicki L., ed.; and Monk, Janice, ed. Western women: their land, their lives. Albuquerque, NM: University of New Mexico Press, c1988. vi, 354 p. English. **DESCR:** Anglo Americans; History; Immigration; Intermarriage; Labor; Native Americans; Southwestern United States; *Women.

5557 Sosa Riddell, Adaljiza. The status of women in Mexico: the impact of the "International Year of the Woman". IN: Iglitzin, Lynn B. and Ross, Ruth A., eds. WOMEN IN THE WORLD, 1975-1985. Santa Barbara, CA: ABC-Clio, Inc., 1986, p. 305-324. English. **DESCR:** Abortion; *Feminism; International Women's Year World Conference (1975: Mexico City); *Mexico; Political History and Conditions; Political Parties and Organizations; Rape; *Sexism; *Women.

5558 Stark, Miriam. La Chicana: changing roles in a changing society. Thesis (B.A)--University of Michigan, 1984. ii, 157 leaves. English. **DESCR:** Acculturation; Identity; Lansing, MI; *Sex Roles.

5559 Torano, Maria Elena and Alvarez, Lourdes. Hispanas: success in America. IN: THE STATE OF HISPANIC AMERICA II. Oakland, CA: National Hispanic Center for Advanced Studies and Policy Analysis, 1982, p. 151-167. English. **DESCR:** *Biographical Notes.

Social Mobility

5560 Acosta Johnson, Carmen. Breast-feeding and social class mobility: the case of Mexican migrant mothers in Houston, Texas. IN: Melville, Margarita B., ed. TWICE A MINORITY. St. Louis, MO: Mosby, 1980, p. 66-82. English. **DESCR:** *Breastfeeding; Herbal Medicine; Maternal and Child Welfare; *Social Classes.

5561 Briody, Elizabeth K. Patterns of household immigration into South Texas. INTERNATIONAL MIGRATION REVIEW, Vol. 21, no. 1 (Spring 1987), p. 27-47. English. **DESCR:** *Family; *Immigrants; Sex Roles; *South Texas.

5562 Murguia, Edward and Cazares, Ralph B. Intermarriage of Mexican Americans. MARRIAGE & FAMILY REVIEW, Vol. 5, no. 1 (Spring 1982), p. 91-100. English. **DESCR:** Acculturation; Anglo Americans; *Intermarriage.

5563 Romero, Mary. Day work in the suburbs: the work experience of Chicana private housekeepers. IN: Statham, Anne; Miller, Eleanor M; and Mauksch, Hans O., eds. THE WORTH OF WOMEN'S WORK: A QUALITATIVE SYNTHESIS. Albany, NY: State University of New York Press, 1988, p. 77-91. English. **DESCR:** Domestic Work; Employment; Interpersonal Relations; *Natural Support Systems; Working Women.

5564 Romero, Mary. Domestic service in the transition from rural to urban life: the case of la Chicana. WOMEN'S STUDIES QUARTERLY, Vol. 13, no. 3 (February 1987), p. 199-222. English. **DESCR:** *Domestic Work; Employment; Interpersonal Relations; Rural Population; Sociology; Urban Communities; Working Women.

5565 Segura, Denise. Chicana and Mexican immigrant women at work: the impact of class, race, and gender on occupational mobility. GENDER & SOCIETY, Vol. 3, no. 1 (March 1989), p. 37-52. English. **DESCR:** *Employment; *Immigrants; Labor Supply and Market; Laboring Classes; San Francisco Bay Area; Women; Working Women.

5566 Sullivan, Teresa A. The occupational prestige of women immigrants: a comparison of Cubans and Mexicans. INTERNATIONAL MIGRATION REVIEW, Vol. 18, no. 4 (Winter 1984), p. 1045-1062. English. **DESCR:** Careers; Cubanos; Employment; *Immigrants; Males; Mexico; Sex Roles; *Women; *Working Women.

5567 Tienda, Marta. Sex, ethnicity and Chicano status attainment. INTERNATIONAL MIGRATION REVIEW, Vol. 16, no. 2 (Summer 1982), p. 435-473. English. **DESCR:** Academic Achievement; Discrimination in Education; Discrimination in Employment; Identity; Income; Language Proficiency; Sexism; *Social Classes.

5568 Zambrana, Ruth E. Hispanic professional women: work, family and health. Los Angeles, CA: National Network of Hispanic Women, 1987. 75 leaves. English. **DESCR:** Business; *Careers; *Employment; Family; Management; Mental Health; Social Classes; *Women.

Social Organizations
USE: Cultural Organizations

Social Psychology

5569 Arce, Carlos H. and Abney-Guardado, Armando J. Demographic and cultural correlates of Chicano intermarriage. CALIFORNIA SOCIOLOGIST, Vol. 5, no. 2 (Summer 1982), p. 41-58. English. DESCR: Cultural Characteristics; Culture; *Intermarriage; Population.

5570 Ayers-Nackamkin, Beverly, et al. Sex and ethnic differences in the use of power. JOURNAL OF APPLIED PSYCHOLOGY, Vol. 67, no. 4 (August 1982), p. 464-471. English. DESCR: Anglo Americans; Ethnic Groups; Management; *Personnel Management; Sex Roles.

5571 Borland, Dolores C. A cohort analysis approach to the empty nest syndrome among three ethnic groups of women: a theoretical position. JOURNAL OF MARRIAGE AND THE FAMILY, Vol. 44, no. 1 (February 1982), p. 117-129. English. DESCR: "Empty Nest" Syndrome; Ethnic Groups; *Sex Roles; Women.

5572 Buriel, Raymond and Saenz, Evangelina. Psychocultural characteristics of college-bound and noncollege-bound Chicanas. JOURNAL OF SOCIAL PSYCHOLOGY, Vol. 110, (April 1980), p. 245-251. English. DESCR: Biculturalism; *Biculturalism Inventory for Mexican American Students (BIMAS); Higher Education; Identity; Income; Psychological Testing; Sex Roles.

5573 Triandis, Harry C. Role perceptions of Hispanic young adults. JOURNAL OF CROSS-CULTURAL PSYCHOLOGY, Vol. 15, no. 3 (September 1984), p. 297-320. English. DESCR: *Cultural Characteristics; *Family; Parent and Child Relationships; *Sex Roles; Values; Youth.

Social Science

5574 Amaro, Hortensia; Russo, Nancy Felipe; and Pares-Avila, Jose A. Contemporary research on Hispanic women: a selected bibliography of the social science literature. PSYCHOLOGY OF WOMEN QUARTERLY, Vol. 11, no. 4 (December 1987), p. 523-532. English. DESCR: *Bibliography; *Psychology; *Women.

5575 Andrade, Sally J. Social science stereotypes of the Mexican American woman: policy implications for research. HISPANIC JOURNAL OF BEHAVIORAL SCIENCES, Vol. 4, no. 2 (June 1982), p. 223-244. English. DESCR: *Sex Roles; Stereotypes.

5576 Aneshensel, Carol S., et al. Participation of Mexican American adolescents in a longitudinal panel survey. PUBLIC OPINION QUARTERLY, Vol. 53, no. 4 (Winter 1989), p. 548-562. English. DESCR: Age Groups; *Fertility; Los Angeles County, CA; *Surveys; *Women Men Relations; *Youth.

5577 Baca Zinn, Maxine. Mexican American women in the social sciences. SIGNS: JOURNAL OF WOMEN IN CULTURE AND SOCIETY, Vol. 8, no. 2 (Winter 1982), p. 259-272. English. DESCR: *Literature Reviews.

5578 Campos Carr, Irene. A survey of selected literature on La Chicana. NWSA JOURNAL, Vol. 1, (Winter 1988, 1989), p. 253-273. English. DESCR: *Literature Reviews; Sexism.

5579 Timberlake, Andrea, et al. Women of color and southern women: a bibliography of social science research, 1975 to 1988. Memphis, TN: Center for Research on Women, Memphis State University, 1988. vii, 264 p. English. DESCR: *Bibliography; Blacks; *Women.

5580 Vasquez, Melba J. T. and Gonzalez, Anna M. Sex roles among Chicanos: stereotypes, challenges and changes. IN: Baron, Augustine, Jr., ed. EXPLORATIONS IN CHICANO PSYCHOLOGY. New York: Praeger, 1981, p. 50-70. English. DESCR: Hembrismo; Machismo; *Sex Roles; Stereotypes.

5581 Williams, Norma. A Mexican American woman encounters sociology: an autobiographical perspective. AMERICAN SOCIOLOGIST, Vol. 19, no. 4 (Winter 1988), p. 340-346. English. DESCR: Autobiography; Sexism; *Sociology; Williams, Norma.

5582 Ybarra, Lea. Empirical and theoretical developments in the study of Chicano families. IN: Valdez, Armando, et al., eds. THE STATE OF CHICANO RESEARCH ON FAMILY, LABOR, AND MIGRATION. Stanford, CA: Stanford Center for Chicano Research, 1983, p. 91-110. English. DESCR: *Family; *Research Methodology; Sex Roles; *Stereotypes.

Social Security

5583 Bergdolt-Munzer, Sara L. Homemakers and retirement income benefits: the other home security issue. CHICANO LAW REVIEW, Vol. 8, (1985), p. 61-80. English. DESCR: Ancianos; Domestic Work; Feminism; *Women.

Social Security Act

5584 Flores, Francisca. A reaction to discussions on the Talmadge Amendment to the Social Security Act. ENCUENTRO FEMENIL, Vol. 1, no. 2 (1974), p. 13-14. English. DESCR: *Chicana Welfare Rights Organization; Child Care Centers; Discrimination; Feminism; Income; Social Services; *Talmadge Amendment to the Social Security Act, 1971; Welfare; Working Women.

5585 Flores, Francisca. A reaction to discussions on the Talmadge Amendment to the Social Security Act. REGENERACION, Vol. 2, no. 3 (1973), p. 16. English. DESCR: *Chicana Welfare Rights Organization; Child Care Centers; Discrimination; Feminism; Income; Social Services; *Talmadge Amendment to the Social Security Act, 1971; Welfare; Working Women.

Social Services

5586 Chicana Welfare Rights challenges Talmadge amendment. REGENERACION, Vol. 2, no. 3 (1973), p. 14. English. DESCR: Chicana Welfare Rights Organization; *Feminism; Talmadge Amendment to the Social Security Act, 1971; *Welfare.

5587 Flores, Francisca. A reaction to discussions on the Talmadge Amendment to the Social Security Act. ENCUENTRO FEMENIL, Vol. 1, no. 2 (1974), p. 13-14. English. DESCR: *Chicana Welfare Rights Organization; Child Care Centers; Discrimination; Feminism; Income; *Social Security Act; *Talmadge Amendment to the Social Security Act, 1971; Welfare; Working Women.

Social Services (cont.)

5588 Flores, Francisca. A reaction to discussions on the Talmadge Amendment to the Social Security Act. REGENERACION, Vol. 2, no. 3 (1973), p. 16. English. DESCR: *Chicana Welfare Rights Organization; Child Care Centers; Discrimination; Feminism; Income; *Social Security Act; *Talmadge Amendment to the Social Security Act, 1971; Welfare; Working Women.

5589 Henderson, Nancy. Perinatal service needs of Hispanic women with diabetes. Thesis (M.S.)--California State University, Long Beach, 1987. 79 p. English. DESCR: *Diabetes; Fertility; Medical Care; *Stress.

5590 Hogeland, Chris and Rosen, Karen. Dreams lost, dreams found: undocumented women in the land of opportunity. San Francisco, CA: Coalition for Immigrant and Refugee Rights and Services, c1991. 153 p. English. DESCR: *Battered Women; *Coalition for Immigrant and Refugee Rights and Services, Immigrant Woman's Task Force; Discrimination; Immigrants; *San Francisco Bay Area; Sex Roles; Sexism; Undocumented Workers; Violence; Women; Women Men Relations.

5591 Winter, Michael; Russo, Nancy Felipe; and Amaro, Hortensia. The use of inpatient mental health services by Hispanic women. PSYCHOLOGY OF WOMEN QUARTERLY, Vol. 11, no. 4 (December 1987), p. 427-441. English. DESCR: Mental Health; *Mental Health Clinics; *Women.

Social Stratification
USE: Social Classes

Social Studies
USE: Social Science

Social Work

5592 Gutierrez, Lorraine M. Working with women of color: an empowerment perspective. SOCIAL WORK, Vol. 35, no. 2 (March 1990), p. 149-153. English. DESCR: *Assertiveness; Ethnic Groups; Feminism; Intergroup Relations; *Interpersonal Relations; *Women.

Socialization

5593 Cardoza, Desdemona. College attendance and persistence among Hispanic women: an examination of some contributing factors. SEX ROLES, Vol. 24, no. 3-4 (January 1991), p. 133-147. English. DESCR: Academic Achievement; College Preparation; *Enrollment; High School and Beyond Project (HS&B); *Higher Education; *Sex Roles; Socioeconomic Factors.

5594 Garcia-Bahne, Betty. La Chicana and the Chicano family. IN: Sanchez, Rosaura and Martinez Cruz, Rosa, eds. ESSAYS ON LA MUJER. Los Angeles, CA: Chicano Studies Center Publications, UCLA, 1977, p. 30-47. English. DESCR: Cultural Customs; *Family; Sex Roles; Social Classes; Stereotypes.

5595 Gonzales, Erlinda. La muerte de un refran. DE COLORES, Vol. 2, no. 3 (1975), p. 15-18. Spanish. DESCR: *Higher Education; *Identity; *Social History and Conditions.

5596 Hernandez, Leodoro. The socialization of a Chicano family. DE COLORES, Vol. 6, no. 1-2 (1982), p. 75-84. English. DESCR: Acculturation; Family.

5597 Madrid, Sandra Emilia. The effects of socialization on goal actualization of public school Chicana principals and superintendents. Thesis (Ph.D.)--University of Washington, 1985. 253 p. English. DESCR: *Careers; *Educational Administration; Language Usage.

5598 Melgoza, Bertha; Roll, Samuel; and Baker, Richard C. Conformity and cooperation in Chicanos: the case of the missing susceptibility to influence. JOURNAL OF COMMUNITY PSYCHOLOGY, Vol. 11, no. 4 (October 1983), p. 323-333. English. DESCR: *Comparative Psychology; *Cultural Characteristics; *Locus of Control; Stereotypes; Women.

5599 Miranda, Gloria E. Hispano-Mexican childrearing practices in pre-American Santa Barbara. SOUTHERN CALIFORNIA QUARTERLY, Vol. 65, no. 4 (Winter 1983), p. 307-320. English. DESCR: *Children; Cultural Characteristics; *Family; History; *Parenting; Santa Barbara, CA.

5600 Moore, Joan W. Mexican-American women addicts: the influence of family background. IN: Glick, Ronald and Moore, Joan, eds. DRUGS IN HISPANIC COMMUNITIES. New Brunswick, NJ: Rutgers University Press, c1990, p. 127-153. English. DESCR: Barrios; *Drug Addicts; Drug Use; East Los Angeles, CA; *Family; *Gangs; Heroin; Hoyo-Mara Gang, East Los Angeles, CA; Pachucos; Sex Roles; White Fence Gang; Youth.

5601 Olvera-Ezzell, Norma; Power, Thomas G.; and Cousins, Jennifer H. Maternal socialization of children's eating habits: strategies used by obese Mexican-American mothers. CHILD DEVELOPMENT, Vol. 61, no. 2 (April 1990), p. 395-400. English. DESCR: Children; Food Practices; *Nutrition; *Obesity; *Parent and Child Relationships.

5602 Ortiz, Flora Ida. Hispanic American women in higher education: a consideration of the socialization process. AZTLAN, Vol. 17, no. 2 (Fall 1986), p. 125-152. English. DESCR: *Academic Achievement; Counseling (Educational); Enrollment; *Higher Education; Sex Roles; *Sexism; Students; University of California.

5603 Ramos, Maria. A micro-ethnographic study of Chicana mother and daughter socialization practices. Thesis (Ph.D.)--University of Colorado at Boulder, 1982. 292 p. English. DESCR: Ethnology; *Interpersonal Relations; *Parent and Child Relationships; Parenting.

5604 Vasquez, Melba J. T. Power and status of the Chicana: a social-psychological perspective. IN: Martinez, Joe L., Jr., ed. CHICANO PSYCHOLOGY. 2nd. ed. Orlando, FL: Academic Press, 1984, p. 269-287. English. DESCR: *Identity; Income; *Mental Health; Psychology; *Sex Roles; Working Women.

5605 Zambrana, Ruth E. Toward understanding the educational trajectory and socialization of Latina women. IN: McKenna, Teresa and Ortiz, Flora Ida, eds. THE BROKEN WEB: THE EDUCATIONAL EXPERIENCE OF HISPANIC WOMEN. Claremont, CA: Tomas Rivera Center; Berkeley, CA: Floricanto Press, 1988, p. 61-77. English. DESCR: Academic Achievement; Anglo Americans; *Education; Feminism; Identity; Research Methodology; *Women.

Socioeconomic Factors

5606 Aneshensel, Carol S.; Fielder, Eve P.; and Becerra, Rosina M. Fertility and fertility-related behavior among Mexican-American and non-Hispanic white female adolescents. JOURNAL OF HEALTH AND SOCIAL BEHAVIOR, Vol. 30, no. 1 (March 1989), p. 56-76. English. DESCR: Anglo Americans; *Fertility; Youth.

5607 Baca Zinn, Maxine. Chicano men and masculinity. JOURNAL OF ETHNIC STUDIES, Vol. 10, no. 2 (Summer 1982), p. 29-44. English. DESCR: Cultural Characteristics; Ethnic Stratification; *Machismo; Sex Roles; Sex Stereotypes; Women Men Relations.

5608 Baca Zinn, Maxine. Qualitative methods in family research: a look inside Chicano families. CALIFORNIA SOCIOLOGIST, Vol. 5, no. 2 (Summer 1982), p. 58-79. English. DESCR: *Family; Marriage; *Research Methodology; *Sex Roles.

5609 Bean, Frank D. and Swicegood, Gray. Mexican American fertility patterns. Austin, TX: University of Texas Press, 1985. x, 178 p. English. DESCR: Age Groups; Census; Education; *Fertility; Language Usage; *Population; Research Methodology; Statistics.

5610 Cardenas, Gilbert and Flores, Estevan T. The migration and settlement of uncocumented women. Austin, TX: CMAS Publications, 1986. 69 p. English. DESCR: Employment; Houston, TX; *Immigration; Income; Labor Supply and Market; *Migration Patterns; Public Policy; *Undocumented Workers.

5611 Cardoza, Desdemona. College attendance and persistence among Hispanic women: an examination of some contributing factors. SEX ROLES, Vol. 24, no. 3-4 (January 1991) p. 133-147. English. DESCR: Academic Achievement; College Preparation; *Enrollment; High School and Beyond Project (HS&B); *Higher Education; *Sex Roles; Socialization.

5612 Cook, Annabel Kirschner. Diversity among Northwest Hispanics. SOCIAL SCIENCE JOURNAL, Vol. 23, no. 2 (April 1986), p. 205-216. English. DESCR: Northwestern United States; *Population.

5613 Cristo, Martha H. Stress and coping among Mexican women. Thesis (Ph.D.)--California School of Professional Psychology, Los Angeles, 1988. 336 p. English. DESCR: Cultural Characteristics; *Immigrants; Mental Health; *Stress; *Women.

5614 Dowling, Patrick T. and Fisher, Michael. Maternal factors and low birthweight infants: a comparison of Blacks with Mexican-Americans. JOURNAL OF FAMILY PRACTICE, Vol. 25, no. 2 (August 1987), p. 153-158. English. DESCR: Blacks; Cook County, IL; *Infant Mortality; *Prenatal Care; *Public Health.

5615 Fischer, Nancy A. and Marcum, John P. Ethnic integration, socioeconomic status, and fertility among Mexican Americans. SOCIAL SCIENCE QUARTERLY, Vol. 65, no. 2 (June 1984), p. 583-593. English. DESCR: Assimilation; *Fertility; Identity.

5616 Gibbs, Jewelle Taylor. Personality patterns of delinquent females: ethnic and sociocultural variations. JOURNAL OF CLINICAL PSYCHOLOGY, Vol. 38, no. 1 (January 1982), p. 198-206. English. DESCR: Ethnic Groups; Identity; *Juvenile Delinquency; Personality; Psychological Testing.

5617 Gondolf, Edward W.; Fisher, Ellen; and McFerron, J. Richard. Racial differences among shelter residents: a comparison of Anglo, Black, and Hispanic battered. JOURNAL OF FAMILY VIOLENCE, Vol. 3, no. 1 (March 1988), p. 39-51. English. DESCR: Anglo Americans; Battered Women; Blacks; Comparative Psychology; Cultural Characteristics; Natural Support Systems; *Violence; *Women.

5618 Gould, Jeffrey B.; Davey, Becky; and Stafford, Randall S. Socioeconomic differences in rates of cesarean section. THE NEW ENGLAND JOURNAL OF MEDICINE, Vol. 321, no. 4 (July 27, 1989), p. 233-239. English. DESCR: Anglo Americans; Asian Americans; Blacks; *Cesarean Section; *Fertility; Los Angeles County, CA; Vital Statistics; Women.

5619 Jaech, Richard E. Latin American undocumented women in the United States. CURRENTS IN THEOLOGY AND MISSION, Vol. 9, no. 4 (August 1982), p. 196-211. English. DESCR: Garment Industry; Latin Americans; Protestant Church; *Undocumented Workers; *Women.

5620 Markides, Kyriakos S., et al. Sample representativeness in a three-generation study of Mexican Americans. JOURNAL OF MARRIAGE AND THE FAMILY, Vol. 45, no. 4 (November 1983), p. 911-916. English. DESCR: *Age Groups; *Marriage; Population; San Antonio, TX.

5621 Martinez, Estella A. Child behavior in Mexican American/Chicano families: maternal teaching and child-rearing practices. FAMILY RELATIONS, Vol. 37, no. 3 (July 1988), p. 275-280. English. DESCR: *Acculturation; Family; Maternal Teaching Observation Technique (MTOT); Parent and Child Relationships; *Parenting; *Psychological Testing; Values.

5622 Panitz, Daniel R., et al. The role of machismo and the Hispanic family in the etiology and treatment of alcoholism in the Hispanic American males. AMERICAN JOURNAL OF FAMILY THERAPY, Vol. 11, no. 1 (Spring 1983), p. 31-44. English. DESCR: *Alcoholism; Children; Family; *Machismo; Puerto Rico.

5623 Pick, James B., et al. Socioeconomic influences on fertility in the Mexican borderlands region. MEXICAN STUDIES/ESTUDIOS MEXICANOS, Vol. 6, no. 1 (Winter 1990), p. 11-42. English. DESCR: *Border Region; *Employment; *Fertility; Labor Supply and Market; Literacy; Working Women.

5624 Pumariega, Andres J. Acculturation and eating attitudes in adolescent girls: a comparative and correlational study. JOURNAL OF THE AMERICAN ACADEMY OF CHILD PSYCHIATRY, Vol. 25, no. 2 (March 1986), p. 276-279. English. DESCR: *Acculturation; Anorexia Nervosa; Cultural Characteristics; Eating Attitudes Test (EAT); Nutrition; Youth.

Socioeconomic Factors
(cont.)

5625 Rider, Kennon V. Relationship satisfaction of the Mexican American woman: effects of acculturation, socioeconomic status, and interaction structures. Thesis (Ph.D.)--Texas Tech University, 1988. 145 p. English. **DESCR:** *Acculturation; *Interpersonal Relations; Sex Roles.

5626 Rivera, George; Lucero, Aileen; and Regoli, Robert M. Contemporary curanderismo: a study of mental health agency and home clientele of a practicing curandera. ISSUES IN RADICAL THERAPY, Vol. 13, no. 1-2 (Winter, Spring, 1988), p. 52-57. English. **DESCR:** Curanderas; *Curanderismo; Mental Health.

5627 Segura, Denise. Labor market stratification: the Chicana experience. BERKELEY JOURNAL OF SOCIOLOGY, Vol. 29, (1984), p. 57-91. English. **DESCR:** *Discrimination in Employment; Employment; *Labor Supply and Market; *Working Women.

5628 Simon, Rita J. and DeLey, Margo. The work experience of undocumented Mexican women migrants in Los Angeles. INTERNATIONAL MIGRATION REVIEW, Vol. 18, no. 4 (Winter 1984), p. 1212-1229. English. **DESCR:** Immigrants; Income; *Los Angeles, CA; Population; *Undocumented Workers; *Working Women.

5629 Torres Raines, Rosario. The Mexican American woman and work: intergenerational perspectives of comparative ethnic groups. IN: Melville, Margarita, ed. MEXICANAS AT WORK IN THE UNITED STATES. Houston, TX: Mexican American Studies Program, University of Houston, 1988, p. 33-46. English. **DESCR:** Age Groups; Anglo Americans; Employment; Feminism; Marriage; Sex Roles; Social Classes; *Working Women.

5630 Vasquez, Melba J. T. Confronting barriers to the participation of Mexican American women in higher education. HISPANIC JOURNAL OF BEHAVIORAL SCIENCES, Vol. 4, no. 2 (June 1982), p. 147-165. English. **DESCR:** Academic Achievement; Higher Education; *Sex Roles.

5631 Vega, William A.; Warheit, George; and Meinhardt, Kenneth. Marital disruption and the prevalence of depressive symptomatology among Anglos and Mexican Americans. JOURNAL OF MARRIAGE AND THE FAMILY, Vol. 46, no. 4 (November 1984), p. 817-824. English. **DESCR:** Anglo Americans; Depression (Psychological); *Divorce; *Marriage; *Mental Health.

5632 Weller, Susan C. and Dungy, Claibourne I. Personal preferences and ethnic variations among Anglo and Hispanic breast and bottle feeders. SOCIAL SCIENCE & MEDICINE, Vol. 23, no. 6 (1986), p. 539-548. English. **DESCR:** Attitudes; *Breastfeeding; *Maternal and Child Welfare; Orange, CA; Parenting.

5633 Ybarra, Lea. Separating a myth from reality: socio-economic and cultural influences on Chicanas and the world of work. IN: Melville, Margarita, ed. MEXICANAS AT WORK IN THE UNITED STATES. Houston, TX: Mexican American Studies Program, University of Houston, 1988, p. 12-23. English. **DESCR:** Attitudes; *Cultural Characteristics; Income; Machismo; Sex Roles; Stereotypes; *Working Women.

Sociolinguistics

5634 Yanez, Rosa H. The complimenting speech act among Chicano women. IN: Bergen, John J., ed. SPANISH IN THE UNITED STATES: SOCIOLINGUISTIC ISSUES. Washington, DC: Georgetown University Press, 1990, p. 79-85. English. **DESCR:** Interpersonal Relations.

Sociology

5635 Flores, Estevan T. Chicanos and sociological research: 1970-1980. IN: CHICANOS AND THE SOCIAL SCIENCES: A DECADE OF RESEARCH AND DEVELOPMENT (1970-1980) SYMPOSIUM WORKING PAPER. Santa Barbara, CA: Center for Chicano Studies, University of California, 1983, p. 19-45. English. **DESCR:** Bibliography; Family; Internal Colony Model; Labor; Literature Reviews; Population; Research Methodology.

5636 Newton, Frank; Olmedo, Esteban L.; and Padilla, Amado M. Hispanic mental health research: a reference guide. Berkeley, CA: University of California Press, c1982. 685 p. English. **DESCR:** Anthropology; *Bibliography; Education; Medical Care; *Mental Health; Psychology; Public Health; *Reference Works.

5637 Romero, Gloria J. and Garza, Raymond T. Attributions for the occupational success/failure of ethnic minority and nonminority women. SEX ROLES, Vol. 14, no. 7-8 (April 1986), p. 445-452. English. **DESCR:** Anglo Americans; *Attitudes; Careers; Identity; Women.

5638 Romero, Mary. Domestic service in the transition from rural to urban life: the case of la Chicana. WOMEN'S STUDIES QUARTERLY, Vol. 13, no. 3 (February 1987), p. 199-222. English. **DESCR:** *Domestic Work; Employment; Interpersonal Relations; Rural Population; Social Mobility; Urban Communities; Working Women.

5639 Williams, Norma. A Mexican American woman encounters sociology: an autobiographical perspective. AMERICAN SOCIOLOGIST, Vol. 19, no. 4 (Winter 1988), p. 340-346. English. **DESCR:** Autobiography; Sexism; Social Science; Williams, Norma.

Solidev Mexicana, S.A.

5640 Iglesias, Norma. La flor mas bella de la maquiladora: historias de vida de la mujer obrera en Tijuana, B.C.N. Mexico, D.F.: Secretaria de Educacion Publica, CEFNOMEX, 1985. 166 p.: ill. Spanish. **DESCR:** Border Industrialization Program (BIP); *Border Industries; Cultural Customs; Labor Unions; Sindicato Independiente Solidev; Tijuana, Baja California, Mexico; *Women; Working Women.

Solinas, Lisa

5641 Taylor, Elena. Conversations with a Chicana physician. REVISTA MUJERES, Vol. 1, no. 2 (June 1984), p. 44-46. English. **DESCR:** Medical Education; Medical Personnel.

Solis Sager, Manuela

5642 Calderon, Roberto R. and Zamora, Emilio, Jr.
Manuela Solis Sager and Emma Tenayuca: a
tribute. IN: Cordova, Teresa, et al., eds.
CHICANA VOICES. Austin, TX: Center for
Mexican American Studies, 1986, p. 30-41.
English. DESCR: Agricultural Labor Unions;
Biography; History; Labor; South Texas
Agricultural Worker's Union (STAWU);
*Tenayuca, Emma; United Cannery Agricultural
Packing and Allied Workers of America
(UCAPAWA).

5643 Calderon, Roberto R. and Zamora, Emilio, Jr.
Manuela Solis Sager and Emma Tenayuca: a
tribute. IN: Del Castillo, Adelaida R., ed.
BETWEEN BORDERS: ESSAYS ON MEXICANA/CHICANA
HISTORY. Encino, CA: Floricanto Press, 1990,
p. 269-279. English. DESCR: Agricultural
Labor Unions; Biography; History; Labor;
South Texas Agricultural Worker's Union
(STAWU); *Tenayuca, Emma; United Cannery
Agricultural Packing and Allied Workers of
America (UCAPAWA).

South Platte Valley, CO

5644 Romero, Mary and Margolis, Eric. Tending the
beets: campesinas and the Great Western
Sugar Company. REVISTA MUJERES, Vol. 2, no.
2 (June 1985), p. 17-27. English. DESCR:
*Farm Workers; Food Industry; Great Western
Sugar Company, Hudson, CO.

South Texas

5645 Briody, Elizabeth K. Patterns of household
immigration into South Texas. INTERNATIONAL
MIGRATION REVIEW, Vol. 21, no. 1 (Spring
1987), p. 27-47. English. DESCR: *Family;
*Immigrants; Sex Roles; *Social Mobility.

5646 Canales, Genevieve and Roberts, Robert E.
Gender and mental health in the Mexican
origin population of South Texas. IN:
Rodriguez, Reymund and Coleman, Marion
Tolbert, eds. MENTAL HEALTH ISSUES OF THE
MEXICAN ORIGIN POPULATION IN TEXAS. Austin
TX: Hogg Foundation for Mental Health,
University of Texas, 1987, p. 89-99.
English. DESCR: Del Rio, TX; Depression
(Psychological); Eagle Pass, TX; Health
Education; *Males; *Mental Health; *Sex
Roles; Surveys.

5647 Hurtado, Aida. A view from within: midwife
practices in South Texas. INTERNATIONAL
QUARTERLY OF COMMUNITY HEALTH AND EDUCATION,
Vol. 8, no. 4 (1987, 1988), p. 317-339.
English. DESCR: Fertility; Medical
Education; *Midwives.

5648 Whiteford, Linda. Migrants no longer:
changing family structure of Mexican
Americans in South Texas. DE COLORES, Vol.
6, no. 1-2 (1982), p. 99-108. English.
DESCR: *Family; Sex Roles.

South Texas Agricultural Worker's Union (STAWU)

5649 Calderon, Roberto R. and Zamora, Emilio, Jr.
Manuela Solis Sager and Emma Tenayuca: a
tribute. IN: Cordova, Teresa, et al., eds.
CHICANA VOICES. Austin, TX: Center for
Mexican American Studies, 1986, p. 30-41.
English. DESCR: Agricultural Labor Unions;
Biography; History; Labor; *Solis Sager,
Manuela; *Tenayuca, Emma; United Cannery
Agricultural Packing and Allied Workers of
America (UCAPAWA).

5650 Calderon, Roberto R. and Zamora, Emilio, Jr.
Manuela Solis Sager and Emma Tenayuca: a
tribute. IN: Del Castillo, Adelaida R., ed.
BETWEEN BORDERS: ESSAYS ON MEXICANA/CHICANA
HISTORY. Encino, CA: Floricanto Press, 1990,
p. 269-279. English. DESCR: Agricultural
Labor Unions; Biography; History; Labor;
*Solis Sager, Manuela; *Tenayuca, Emma;
United Cannery Agricultural Packing and
Allied Workers of America (UCAPAWA).

Southern California

5651 Ashley, Laurel Maria. Self, family and
community: the social process of aging among
urban Mexican-American women. Thesis
(Ph.D.)--University of California, Los
Angeles, 1985. 306 p. English. DESCR:
Acculturation; *Ancianos; *Family;
Grandmothers; *Sex Roles.

5652 Ferrandez Kelly, Maria and Garcia, Anna M.
Invisible amidst the glitter: Hispanic women
in the Southern California electronics
industry. IN: Statham, Anne; Miller, Eleanor
M.; and Mauksh, Hans O., eds. THE WORTH OF
WOMEN'S WORK: A QUALITATIVE SYNTHESIS.
Albany, NY: State University of New York
Press, 1988, p. 265-290. English. DESCR:
*Electronics Industry; Employment;
Immigrants; *Industrial Workers; Labor
Supply and Market; Megatek, La Jolla, CA;
Nova-Tech, San Diego, CA; Sex Roles;
*Working Women.

5653 Romero-Gwynn, Eunice and Carias, Lucia.
Breast-feeding intentions and practice among
Hispanic mothers in Southern California.
PEDIATRICS, Vol. 84, no. 4 (October 1989),
p. 626-632. English. DESCR: *Breastfeeding;
Cubanos; Expanded Food and Nutrition
Education Program; Immigrants; Puerto
Ricans; Women.

5654 Ruiz, Vicki L. A promise fulfilled: Mexican
cannery workers in Southern California. THE
PACIFIC HISTORIAN, Vol. 30, no. 2 (Summer
1986), p. 51-61. English. DESCR: *California
Sanitary Canning Company, Los Angeles, CA;
*Canneries; Labor Unions; Moreno, Luisa
[union organizer]; Strikes and Lockouts;
*United Cannery Agricultural Packing and
Allied Workers of America (UCAPAWA); Working
Women.

5655 Ruiz, Vicki L. A promise fulfilled: Mexican
cannery workers in Southern California. IN:
DuBois, Ellen Carol and Ruiz, Vicki L., eds.
UNEQUAL SISTERS: A MULTICULTURAL READER IN
U.S. WOMEN'S HISTORY. New York: Routledge,
1990, p. 264-274. English. DESCR:
*California Sanitary Canning Company, Los
Angeles, CA; *Canneries; Labor Unions;
Moreno, Luisa [union organizer]; Strikes and
Lockouts; *United Cannery Agricultural
Packing and Allied Workers of America
(UCAPAWA); Working Women.

5656 Ruiz, Vicki L. A promise fulfilled: Mexican
cannery workers in Southern California. IN:
Del Castillo, Adelaida R., ed. BETWEEN
BORDERS: ESSAYS ON MEXICANA/CHICANA HISTORY.
Encino, CA: Floricanto Press, 1990, p.
281-298. English. DESCR: California Sanitary
Canning Company, Los Angeles, CA;
*Canneries; Labor Unions; Moreno, Luisa
[union organizer]; Strikes and Lockouts;
United Cannery Agricultural Packing and
Allied Workers of America (UCAPAWA); Working
Women.

Southern California
   (cont.)

5657 Vallez, Andrea. Acculturation, social
      support, stress and adjustment of the
      Mexican American college woman. Thesis
      (Ph.D.)--University of Colorado at Boulder,
      1984. 121 p. English. DESCR: *Acculturation;
      *Colleges and Universities; Depression
      (Psychological); Higher Education; Natural
      Support Systems; Stress; *Students.

Southwestern United States

5658 Gutierrez, Ramon A. Honor ideology, marriage
      negotiation, and class-gender domination in
      New Mexico, 1690-1846. LATIN AMERICAN
      PERSPECTIVES, Vol. 12, no. 1 (Winter 1985),
      p. 81-104. English. DESCR: Marriage; Sex
      Roles; *Social Classes; Social History and
      Conditions; Values; Women Men Relations.

5659 Karnig, Albert K.; Welch, Susan; and Eribes,
      Richard A. Employment of women by cities in
      the Southwest. SOCIAL SCIENCE JOURNAL, Vol.
      21, no. 4 (October 1984), p. 41-48. English.
      DESCR: *Employment; Local Government; Women.

5660 Kay, Margarita Artschwager and Yoder,
      Marianne. Hot and cold in women's
      ethnotherapeutics: the American-Mexican
      West. SOCIAL SCIENCE & MEDICINE, Vol. 25,
      no. 4 (1987), p. 347-355. English. DESCR:
      *Diseases; *Folk Medicine; Herbal Medicine;
      Mexico.

5661 Monk, Janice and Norwood, Vera. Angles of
      vision: enhancing our perspectives on the
      Southwest. IN: Lensink, Judy Nolte, ed. OLD
      SOUTHWEST/NEW SOUTHWEST: ESSAYS ON A REGION
      AND ITS LITERATURE. Tucson, AZ: The Tucson
      Public Library, 1989, p. 39-47. English.
      DESCR: Literary Criticism; *Literature;
      *Women.

5662 Myres, Sandra Lynn. Mexican Americans and
      westering Anglos: a feminine perspective.
      NEW MEXICO HISTORICAL REVIEW, Vol. 57, no. 4
      (October 1982), p. 317-333. English. DESCR:
      Anglo Americans; *Attitudes; *Ethnic Groups;
      Social History and Conditions; Stereotypes.

5663 Rebolledo, Tey Diana. Hispanic women writers
      of the Southwest: tradition and innovation.
      IN: Lensink, Judy Nolte, ed. OLD
      SOUTHWEST/NEW SOUTHWEST: ESSAYS ON A REGION
      AND ITS LITERATURE. Tucson, AZ: The Tucson
      Public Library, 1987, p. 49-61. English.
      DESCR: *Authors; Cabeza de Baca, Fabiola;
      Jaramillo, Cleofas M.; Literature; Mora,
      Pat; OLD SPAIN IN OUR SOUTHWEST; Otero
      Warren, Nina; Preciado Martin, Patricia; Sex
      Roles; Sex Stereotypes; Silva, Beverly;
      Vigil-Pinon, Evangelina; WE FED THEM CACTUS;
      *Women.

5664 Rebolledo, Tey Diana. Tradition and
      mythology: signatures of landscape in
      Chicana literature. IN: Norwood, Vera and
      Monk, Janice, eds. THE DESERT IS NO LADY:
      SOUTHWESTERN LANDSCAPES IN WOMEN'S WRITING
      AND ART. New Haven, CT: Yale University
      Press, 1987, p. 96-124. English. DESCR:
      *Authors; Cabeza de Baca, Fabiola; Chavez,
      Denise; Jaramillo, Cleofas M.; Literary
      Criticism; *Literary History; Literature;
      Mora, Pat; Mythology; Otero Warren, Nina;
      Portillo Trambley, Estela; Silva, Beverly;
      WE FED THEM CACTUS.

5665 Schlissel, Lillian, ed.; Ruiz, Vicki L.,
      ed.; and Monk, Janice, ed. Western women:
      their land, their lives. Albuquerque, NM:
      University of New Mexico Press, c1988. vi,

354 p. English. DESCR: Anglo Americans;
History; Immigration; Intermarriage; Labor;
Native Americans; *Social History and
Conditions; *Women.

Spanish Borderlands Theory

5666 Castaneda, Antonia I. Gender, race, and
      culture: Spanish-Mexican women in the
      historiography of frontier California.
      FRONTIERS: A JOURNAL OF WOMEN STUDIES, Vol.
      11, no. 1 (1990), p. [8]-20. English.
      DESCR: Bancroft, Hubert Howe; Bolton,
      Herbert Eugene; *California; Californios;
      *Historiography; History; Intermarriage;
      *Sex Stereotypes; Spanish Influence;
      Stereotypes; Turner, Frederick Jackson;
      Women.

Spanish Influence

5667 Apodaca, Maria Linda. The Chicana woman: a
      historical materialist perspective. IN:
      Bollinger, William, et al., eds. WOMEN IN
      LATIN AMERICA: AN ANTHOLOGY FROM LATIN
      AMERICAN PERSPECTIVES. Riverside, CA: Latin
      American Perspectives, c1979, p. 81-100.
      English. DESCR: Capitalism; *Historiography;
      Immigrants; Imperialism; Marxism; Mexico;
      Oral History; Social Classes.

5668 Castaneda, Antonia I. Gender, race, and
      culture: Spanish-Mexican women in the
      historiography of frontier California.
      FRONTIERS: A JOURNAL OF WOMEN STUDIES, Vol.
      11, no. 1 (1990), p. [8]-20. English.
      DESCR: Bancroft, Hubert Howe; Bolton,
      Herbert Eugene; *California; Californios;
      *Historiography; History; Intermarriage;
      *Sex Stereotypes; Spanish Borderlands
      Theory; Stereotypes; Turner, Frederick
      Jackson; Women.

5669 Espin, Oliva M. Cultural and historical
      influences on sexuality in Hispanic/Latin
      women: implications for psychotherapy. IN:
      Vance, Carole S., ed. PLEASURE AND DANGER:
      EXPLORING FEMALE SEXUALITY. Boston, MA:
      Routledge & Kegan Paul, 1984, p. 149-164.
      English. DESCR: Immigration; Language Usage;
      Machismo; *Psychotherapy; Sex Roles; *Sexual
      Behavior; Social History and Conditions;
      *Women.

5670 Gutierrez, Ramon A. From honor to love:
      transformations of the meaning of sexuality
      in colonial New Mexico. IN: Smith, Raymond
      T., ed. KINSHIP IDEOLOGY AND PRACTICE IN
      LATIN AMERICA. Chapel Hill, NC: University
      of North Carolina Press, 1984, p. [237]-263.
      English. DESCR: *Catholic Church; *Marriage;
      New Mexico; *Sexual Behavior; Social
      Classes; Social History and Conditions;
      Values; Women.

5671 Gutierrez, Ramon A. When Jesus came, the
      corn mothers went away: marriage, sexuality,
      and power in New Mexico, 1500-1846.
      Stanford: Stanford University Pres, 1991.
      xxxi, 424 p. English. DESCR: *Marriage;
      Native Americans; *New Mexico; *Pueblo
      Indians; *Sex Roles; Sexual Behavior; Women.

5672 Monroy, Douglas. "They didn't call them
      'padre' for nothing": patriarchy in Hispanic
      California. IN: Del Castillo, Adelaida R.,
      ed. BETWEEN BORDERS: ESSAYS ON
      MEXICANA/CHICANA HISTORY. Encino, CA:
      Floricanto Press, 1990, p. 433-445. English.
      DESCR: *California; Clergy; History;
      *Machismo; Rape; *Sex Roles; *Sexism; Women
      Men Relations.

Spanish Influence
(cont.)

5673 Spitta, Silvia D. Literary transculturation in Latin America. Thesis (Ph.D.)--University of Oregon, 1989. 184 p. English. DESCR: Anzaldua, Gloria; Arguecos, Jose Maria; Authors; Cultural Characteristics; Culture; *Intergroup Relations; *Latin American Literature.

Spanish Language

5674 Cuellar, Israel. Service delivery and mental health services for Chicano elders. IN: Miranda, Manuel and Ruiz, Rene A., eds. CHICANO AGING AND MENTAL HEALTH. Rockville, MD: U.S. Department of Health and Human Services, 1981, p. 185-211. English. DESCR: *Ancianos; Attitudes; Cultural Customs; Cultural Pluralism; Language Usage; Mental Health; Mental Health Clinics; Religion; Sex Roles.

5675 de Anda, Diane and Becerra, Rosina M. Support networks for adolescent mothers. SOCIAL CASEWORK: JOURNAL OF CONTEMPORARY SOCIAL WORK, Vol. 65, no. 3 (March 1984), p. 172-181. English. DESCR: California; *Fertility; *Natural Support Systems; *Youth.

5676 Valdes, Guadalupe and Cardenas, Manuel. Positive speech accommodation in the language of Mexican American bilinguals: are women really more sensitive? HISPANIC JOURNAL OF BEHAVIORAL SCIENCES, Vol. 3, no. 4 (December 1981), p. 347-359. English. DESCR: Bilingualism; *Language Usage.

Spanish-American Mothers and Wives Association, Tucson, AZ

5677 Campbell, Julie A. Madres y esposas: Tucson's Spanish-American Mothers and Wives Association. JOURNAL OF ARIZONA HISTORY, Vol. 31, no. 2 (Summer 1990), p. 161-182. English. DESCR: History; Military; Organizations; Tucson, AZ; World War II.

Sports

5678 Isaacs, Barbara Gail. Anglo, Black, and Latin adolescents' participation in sports. Thesis (Ph.D.)--California School of Professional Psychology, Los Angeles, 1984. 283 p. English. DESCR: Anglo Americans; Blacks; Cultural Characteristics; *Secondary School Education; *Women; Youth.

Standard of Living
USE: Economic History and Conditions

Stanford University, Stanford, CA

5679 Chacon, Maria A. An overdue study of the Chicana undergraduate college experience. LA LUZ, Vol. 8, no. 8 (October, November, 1980), p. 27. English. DESCR: Colleges and Universities; *Educational Statistics; Higher Education; Students.

Starkist Tuna Cannery, Wilmington, CA

5680 Romero, Gloria J.; Castro, Felipe G.; and Cervantes, Richard C. Latinas without work: family, occupational, and economic stress following unemployment. PSYCHOLOGY OF WOMEN QUARTERLY, Vol. 12, no. 3 (September 1988), p. 281-297. English. DESCR: *Employment; Family; *Stress.

Statistics

5681 Abrahamse, Allan F.; Morrison, Peter A.; and Waite, Linda J. Beyond stereotypes: who becomes a single teenage mother? Santa Monica, CA: RAND Corp., 1988. xv, 88 p. English. DESCR: *Fertility; Religion; Secondary School Education; *Single Parents; *Women; *Youth.

5682 Anglin, M. Douglas and Hser, Yih-Ing. Addicted women and crime. CRIMINOLOGY: AN INTERDISCIPLINARY JOURNAL, Vol. 25, no. 2 (1987), p. 359-397. English. DESCR: Criminal Acts; Drug Abuse Programs; *Drug Addicts.

5683 Barton, Amy E. and California Commission on the Status of Women. Campesinas: women farmworkers in the California agricultural labor force, report of a study project. Sacramento, CA: The Commission, [1978], vii, 23, 52 p. English. DESCR: California; *Farm Workers; Migrant Labor; *Working Women.

5684 Bean, Frank D. and Tienda, Marta. The Hispanic population of the United States. New York: Russell Sage Foundation, 1987. xxiv, 456 p. English. DESCR: *Census; Education; Employment; Fertility; Identity; Immigration; Income; *Population; Self-Referents.

5685 Bean, Frank D. and Swicegood, Gray. Mexican American fertility patterns. Austin, TX: University of Texas Press, 1985. x, 178 p. English. DESCR: Age Groups; Census; Education; *Fertility; Language Usage; *Population; Research Methodology; *Socioeconomic Factors.

5686 Davis, Cary; Haub, Carl; and Willette, JoAnne. U.S. Hispanics: changing the face of America. POPULATION BULLETIN, Vol. 38, no. 3 (June 1983), p. 1-43. English. DESCR: Education; Employment; Fertility; Immigration; Income; *Population; Vital Statistics.

5687 Flores, Francisca. Conference of Mexican women un remolino. REGENERACION, Vol. 1, no. 10 (1971), p. 1-5. English. DESCR: Conferences and Meetings; Family; Feminism; First National Chicana Conference (May 1971: Houston, TX); Machismo; National Mexican American Issues Conference (October 11, 1970: Sacramento, CA); Sex Roles; Sex Stereotypes; *Women Men Relations.

5688 Lopez, Norma Y. Hispanic teenage pregnancy: overview and implications. Washington, DC: National Council of La Raza, 1987. 17 leaves. English. DESCR: *Fertility; Women; *Youth.

5689 Martinez, Douglas R. Hispanic origin women in the U.S. LA LUZ, Vol. 8, no. 8 (October, November, 1980), p. 11-12. English. DESCR: *Educational Statistics; *Population.

5690 Mexican American Legal Defense and Education Fund (MALDEF). Chicana rights: a major MALDEF issue (reprinted from MALDEF Newsletter, Fall 1977). COMADRE, no. 3 (Fall 1978), p. 31-35. English. DESCR: Chicana Rights Project; *Feminism; Mexican American Legal Defense and Educational Fund (MALDEF); Vasquez, Patricia.

5691 Miller, George A. Latinas on border patrol. VISTA, Vol. 4, no. 18 (January 1, 1989), p. 8-10. English. DESCR: *Border Patrol; Border Region; Police.

Statistics (cont.)

5692 Nava, Yolanda. The Chicana and employment: needs analysis and recommendations for legislation. REGENERACION, Vol. 2, no. 3 (1973), p. 7-9. English. DESCR: California Commission on the Status of Women; Child Care Centers; Comision Femenil Mexicana Nacional; *Discrimination in Employment; Employment Tests; Employment Training; Equal Rights Amendment (ERA); Sexism; Stereotypes; Working Women.

5693 Romero, Fred E. The labor market status of Chicanas. IN: Romero, Fred. CHICANO WORKERS: THEIR UTILIZATION AND DEVELOPMENT. Los Angeles: Chicano Studies Center Publications, UCLA, 1979, p. 82-95. English. DESCR: *Employment; Income; Labor Supply and Market; *Working Women.

5694 Romero, Mary. Twice protected?: assessing the impact of affirmative action on Mexican-American women. JOURNAL OF HISPANIC POLICY, Vol. 3, (1988, 1989), p. 83-101. English. DESCR: *Affirmative Action; Careers; *Discrimination in Employment.

5695 Ruiz, Vicki L. "And miles to go...": Mexican women and work, 1930-1985. IN: Schlissel, Lillian, et al., eds. WESTERN WOMEN: THEIR LAND, THEIR LIVES. Albuquerque, NM: University of New Mexico Press, 1988, p. 117-136. English. DESCR: Education; El Paso Women's Employment and Education Project (EPWEE); *Employment; Farah Manufacturing Co., El Paso, TX; Farah Strike; *Income; Industrial Workers; Labor Unions; Undocumented Workers; United Cannery Agricultural Packing and Allied Workers of America (UCAPAWA); Women; *Working Women.

5696 Sanford, Judy, et al. Patterns of reported rape in a tri-ethnic population: Houston, Texas, 1974-1975. AMERICAN JOURNAL OF PUBLIC HEALTH, Vol. 69, no. 5 (May 1979), p. 480-484. English. DESCR: Anglo Americans; Blacks; Criminology; *Ethnic Groups; *Houston, TX; *Rape; Women.

5697 Vangie, Mary. Women at Frontera, CA. REGENERACION, Vol. 1, no. 10 (1971), p. 8. English. DESCR: Education; *Mexican American Research Association (MARA), California Institution for Women; Prisons.

5698 Ventura, Stephanie J. and Taffel, Selma M. Childbearing characteristics of U.S.- and foreign-born Hispanic mothers. PUBLIC HEALTH REPORTS, Vol. 100, no. 6 (November, December, 1985), p. 647-652. English. DESCR: *Fertility; Identity; Immigrants; *Maternal and Child Welfare.

5699 Waldman, Elizabeth. Profile of the Chicana: a statistical fact sheet. IN: Mora, Magdalena and Del Castillo, Adelaida, eds. MEXICAN WOMEN IN THE UNITED STATES: STRUGGLES PAST AND PRESENT. Los Angeles, CA: Chicano Studies Research Center, UCLA, 1980, p. 195-204. English. DESCR: Employment; Family; Population.

Stereotypes

5700 Alarcon, Norma. Chicana's feminist literature: a re-vision through Malintzinl or Malintzin: putting flesh back on the object. IN: Moraga, Cherrie and Anzaldua, Gloria, eds. THIS BRIDGE CALLED MY BACK: WRITINGS BY RADICAL WOMEN OF COLOR. Watertown, MA: Persephone Press, 1981, p. 182-190. English. DESCR: Feminism; Literature; Malinche; *Sex Roles; Symbolism.

5701 Allen, Jane and Guthrie, Derek. La mujer: a visual dialogue. NEW ART EXAMINER, Vol. 5, no. 10 (July 1978), p. 14. English. DESCR: California; Chicago, IL; *Feminism; Movimiento Artistico Chicano (MARCH), Chicago, IL.

5702 Andrade, Sally J. Social science stereotypes of the Mexican American woman: policy implications for research. HISPANIC JOURNAL OF BEHAVIORAL SCIENCES, Vol. 4, no. 2 (June 1982), p. 223-244. English. DESCR: *Sex Roles; Social Science.

5703 Baca Zinn, Maxine. Chicanas: power and control in the domestic sphere. DE COLORES, Vol. 2, no. 3 (1975), p. 19-31. English. DESCR: *Family; Immigration Regulation and Control; Machismo; *Sex Roles; *Women Men Relations.

5704 Baca Zinn, Maxine. Chicanas: power and control in the domestic sphere. IN: Cotera, Martha and Hufford, Larry, eds. BRIDGING TWO CULTURES. Austin, TX: National Educational Laboratory Publishers, 1980, p. 270-281. English. DESCR: Family; Immigration Regulation and Control; Machismo; Sex Roles; Women Men Relations.

5705 Baca Zinn, Maxine. Chicano family research: conceptual distortions and alternative directions. JOURNAL OF ETHNIC STUDIES, Vol. 7, no. 3 (Fall 1979), p. 59-71. English. DESCR: Cultural Characteristics; Culture; *Family; Research Methodology.

5706 Broyles-Gonzalez, Yolanda. Women in El Teatro Campesino: "A poco estaba molacha la Virgen de Guadalupe?". IN: Cordova, Teresa, et al., eds. CHICANA VOICES. Austin, TX: Center for Mexican American Studies, 1986, p. 162-187. English. DESCR: Actors and Actresses; CORRIDOS [play]; *El Teatro Campesino; Teatro; Valdez, Socorro.

5707 Candelaria, Cordelia. Film portrayals of La Mujer Hispana. AGENDA, Vol. 11, no. 3 (May, June, 1981), p. 32-36. English. DESCR: *Films.

5708 Candelaria, Cordelia. Social equity in film criticism. BILINGUAL REVIEW, Vol. 10, no. 2-3 (May, December, 1983), p. 64-70. English. DESCR: *Film Reviews.

5709 Cantu, Norma. Women then and now: an analysis of the Adelita image versus the Chicana as political writer and philosopher. IN: Cordova, Teresa, et al., eds. CHICANA VOICES. Austin, TX: Center for Mexican American Studies, 1986, p. 8-10. English. DESCR: Chicano Studies; Discrimination; Higher Education; *La Adelita.

5710 Cardenas de Dwyer, Carlota. Commentary. LA LUZ, Vol. 4, no. 8-9 (November, December, 1975), p. 8. English. DESCR: Literary Criticism; Sex Stereotypes.

5711 Cardenas de Dwyer, Carlota. Mexican American women: images and realities. IN: Cotera, Martha and Hufford, Larry, eds. BRIDGING TWO CULTURES. Austin, TX: National Educational Laboratory Publishers, 1980, p. 294-296. English. DESCR: Historiography.

Stereotypes (cont.)

5712 Castaneda, Antonia I. Gender, race, and culture: Spanish-Mexican women in the historiography of frontier California. FRONTIERS: A JOURNAL OF WOMEN STUDIES, Vol. 11, no. 1 (1990), p. [8]-20. English. DESCR: Bancroft, Hubert Howe; Bolton, Herbert Eugene; *California; Californios; *Historiography; History; Intermarriage; *Sex Stereotypes; Spanish Borderlands Theory; Spanish Influence; Turner, Frederick Jackson; Women.

5713 Cortes, Carlos E. Chicanas in film: history of an image. BILINGUAL REVIEW, Vol. 10, no. 2-3 (May, December, 1983), p. 94-108. English. DESCR: Film Reviews; *Films.

5714 Cota-Robles de Suarez, Cecilia. Sexual stereotypes--psychological and cultural survival: a description of child-rearing practices attributed to the Chicana (the Mexican American woman) and its psychological and cultural implications. REGENERACION, Vol. 2, no. 3 (1973), p. 17, 20-21. English. DESCR: Cultural Characteristics; Family; Folklore; Language; Parenting; Sex Stereotypes; *Sexism.

5715 Cotera, Marta P. Sexism in bilingual bicultural education. IN: Cotera, Martha and Hufford, Larry, eds. BRIDGING TWO CULTURES. Austin, TX: National Educational Laboratory Publishers, 1980, p. 181-190. English. DESCR: *Bilingual Bicultural Education; Sex Roles; Sexism; Textbooks.

5716 Cummings, Michele and Cummings, Scott. Family planning among the urban poor: sexual politics and social policy. FAMILY RELATIONS, Vol. 32, no. 1 (January 1983), p. 47-58. English. DESCR: Anglo Americans; Blacks; Discrimination; *Family Planning; Low Income.

5717 Fernandez Kelly, Maria. The 'maquila' women. NACLA: REPORT ON THE AMERICAS, Vol. 14, no. 5 (September, October, 1980), p. 14-19. English. DESCR: *Border Industries; Feminism; Industrial Workers; Women; *Working Women.

5718 Garcia-Bahne, Betty. La Chicana and the Chicano family. IN: Sanchez, Rosaura and Martinez Cruz, Rosa, eds. ESSAYS ON LA MUJER. Los Angeles, CA: Chicano Studies Center Publications, UCLA, 1977, p. 30-47. English. DESCR: Cultural Customs; *Family; Sex Roles; Social Classes; Socialization.

5719 Hadley-Freydberg, Elizabeth. Prostitutes, concubines, whores and bitches: Black and Hispanic women in contemporary American film. IN: McCluskey, Audrey T., ed. WOMEN OF COLOR: PERSPECTIVES ON FEMINISM AND IDENTITY. Bloomington, IN: Women's Studies Program, Indiana University, 1985, p. 46-65. English. DESCR: *Actors and Actresses; Blacks; *Films; Puerto Ricans; *Sex Stereotypes; Women.

5720 Jorgensen, Stephen R. and Adams, Russell P. Family planning needs and behavior of Mexican American women: a study of health care professionals and their clientele. HISPANIC JOURNAL OF BEHAVIORAL SCIENCES, Vol. 9, no. 3 (September 1987), p. 265-286. English. DESCR: Acculturation; *Attitudes; Birth Control; *Cultural Characteristics; *Family Planning; Fertility; Medical Personnel; Sterilization.

5721 Lizarraga, Sylvia S. Images of women in Chicano literature by men. FEMINIST ISSUES, Vol. 5, no. 2 (Fall 1985), p. 69-88. English. DESCR: *Literature; Morales, Alejandro; RETO EN EL PARAISO; Sexism.

5722 Melgoza, Bertha; Roll, Samuel; and Baker, Richard C. Conformity and cooperation in Chicanos: the case of the missing susceptibility to influence. JOURNAL OF COMMUNITY PSYCHOLOGY, Vol. 11, no. 4 (October 1983), p. 323-333. English. DESCR: *Comparative Psychology; *Cultural Characteristics; *Locus of Control; Socialization; Women.

5723 Miller, Michael V. Variations in Mexican American family life: a review synthesis of empirical research. AZTLAN, Vol. 9, no. 1 (1978), p. 209-231. Bibliography. English. DESCR: Acculturation; Compadrazgo; *Family; Intermarriage; Sex Roles.

5724 Molina de Pick, Gracia. Reflexiones sobre el feminismo y la Raza. LA LUZ, Vol. 1, no. 4 (August 1972), p. 58. Spanish. DESCR: *Feminism; Sexism.

5725 Molina de Pick, Gracia. Reflexiones sobre el feminismo y la Raza. REGENERACION, Vol. 2, no. 4 (1975), p. 33-34. Spanish. DESCR: Feminism; *Sexism.

5726 Moncin, Sandra. The depiction of the Chicana in BLESS ME ULTIMA and THE MILAGRO BEANFIELD WAR: a study in contrasts. IN: Luna Lawhn, Juanita, et al., eds. MEXICO AND THE UNITED STATES: INTERCULTURAL RELATIONS IN THE HUMANITIES. San Antonio, TX: San Antonio College, 1984, p. 137-150. English. DESCR: Anaya, Rudolfo A.; BLESS ME, ULTIMA; Literary Characters; Literary Criticism; Nichols, John; THE MILAGRO BEANFIELD WAR [novel].

5727 Morales, Sylvia. Chicano-produced celluloid mujeres. BILINGUAL REVIEW, Vol. 10, no. 2-3 (May, December, 1983), p. 89-93. English. DESCR: BALLAD OF GREGORIO CORTEZ [film]; Film Reviews; *Films; RAICES DE SANGRE [film]; SEGUIN [movie]; ZOOT SUIT [film].

5728 El Movimiento and the Chicana. LA RAZA, Vol. 1, no. 6 (1971), p. 40-42. English. DESCR: *Chicano Movement.

5729 Myres, Sandra Lynn. Mexican Americans and westering Anglos: a feminine perspective. NEW MEXICO HISTORICAL REVIEW, Vol. 57, no. 4 (October 1982), p. 317-333. English. DESCR: Anglo Americans; *Attitudes; *Ethnic Groups; Social History and Conditions; Southwestern United States.

5730 Nava, Yolanda. The Chicana and employment: needs analysis and recommendations for legislation. REGENERACION, Vol. 2, no. 3 (1973), p. 7-9. English. DESCR: California Commission on the Status of Women; Child Care Centers; Comision Femenil Mexicana Nacional; *Discrimination in Employment; Employment Tests; Employment Training; Equal Rights Amendment (ERA); Sexism; Statistics; Working Women.

5731 Nava, Yolanda. Chicanas in the television media. IN: LA CHICANA: BUILDING FOR THE FUTURE, AN ACTION PLAN FOR THE 80s. Oakland, CA: National Hispanic University, 1981, p. 120-133. English. DESCR: Careers; Employment; *Television.

Stereotypes (cont.)

5732 Padilla, Eligio R. and O'Grady, Kevin E. Sexuality among Mexican Americans: a case of sexual stereotyping. JOURNAL OF PERSONALITY AND SOCIAL PSYCHOLOGY, Vol. 52, no. 1 (1987), p. 5-10. English. **DESCR:** Age Groups; Anglo Americans; Attitudes; California; Religion; *Sex Roles; *Sex Stereotypes; Sexual Behavior; Sexual Knowledge and Attitude Test; Students; Values.

5733 Ramos Escandon, Carmen. Alternative sources to women's history: literature. IN: Del Castillo, Adelaida R., ed. BETWEEN BORDERS: ESSAYS ON MEXICANA/CHICANA HISTORY. Encino, CA: Floricanto Press, 1990, p. 201-212. English. **DESCR:** *Literature; *Sex Stereotypes.

5734 Riccatelli, Ralph. The sexual stereotypes of the Chicana in literature. ENCUENTRO FEMENIL, Vol. 1, no. 2 (1974), p. 48-56. English. **DESCR:** Sex Stereotypes; *Sexism.

5735 Salazar Parr, Carmen and Ramirez, Genevieve M. The Chicana in Chicano literature. IN: Martinez, Julio A. and Lomeli, Francisco A., eds. CHICANO LITERATURE: A REFERENCE GUIDE. Westport, CT: Greenwood Press, 1985, p. 97-107. English. **DESCR:** Literary Characters; Literary Criticism; *Literature.

5736 Salazar Parr, Carmen. La Chicana in literature. IN: Garcia, Eugene E., et al., eds. CHICANO STUDIES: A MULTIDISCIPLINARY APPROACH. New York: Teachers College Press, 1984, p. 120-134. English. **DESCR:** DAY OF THE SWALLOWS; Literary Characters; Literary Criticism; *Literature; Portillo Trambley, Estela; Teatro; "The Trees" [short story].

5737 Salinas, Judy. The image of woman in Chicano literature. REVISTA CHICANO-RIQUENA, Vol. 4, no. 4 (Fall 1976), p. 139-148. English. **DESCR:** Literary Characters; *Literature.

5738 Sosa Riddell, Adaljiza. Chicanas and el Movimiento. AZTLAN, Vol. 5, no. 1 (Spring 1974), p. 155-165. English. **DESCR:** *Chicano Movement.

5739 Vasquez, Melba J. T. and Gonzalez, Anna M. Sex roles among Chicanos: stereotypes, challenges and changes. IN: Baron, Augustine, Jr., ed. EXPLORATIONS IN CHICANO PSYCHOLOGY. New York: Praeger, 1981, p. 50-70. English. **DESCR:** Hembrismo; Machismo; *Sex Roles; Social Science.

5740 Yarbro-Bejarano, Yvonne. The image of the Chicana in teatro. IN: Cochran, Jo; Stewart, J.T.; and Tsutakawa, Mayumi, eds. GATHERING GROUND: NEW WRITING AND ART BY NORTHWEST WOMEN OF COLOR. Seattle, WA: Seal Press, 1984, p. 90-96. English. **DESCR:** El Teatro de la Esperanza; GUADALUPE [play]; HIJOS: ONCE A FAMILY [play]; LA VICTIMA [play]; *Literary Characters; Sex Roles; Sex Stereotypes; *Teatro; THE OCTOPUS [play]; Women Men Relations.

5741 Ybarra, Lea. Empirical and theoretical developments in the study of Chicano families. IN: Valdez, Armando, et al., eds. THE STATE OF CHICANO RESEARCH ON FAMILY, LABOR, AND MIGRATION. Stanford, CA: Stanford Center for Chicano Research, 1983, p. 91-110. English. **DESCR:** *Family; *Research Methodology; Sex Roles; Social Science.

5742 Ybarra, Lea. Separating a myth from reality: socio-economic and cultural influences on Chicanas and the world of work. IN:

Melville, Margarita, ed. MEXICANAS AT WORK IN THE UNITED STATES. Houston, TX: Mexican American Studies Program, University of Houston, 1988, p. 12-23. English. **DESCR:** Attitudes; *Cultural Characteristics; Income; Machismo; Sex Roles; *Socioeconomic Factors; *Working Women.

5743 Zapata, Jesse T. and Jaramillo, Pat T. The Mexican American family: an Adlerian perspective. HISPANIC JOURNAL OF BEHAVIORAL SCIENCES, Vol. 3, no. 3 (September 1981), p. 275-290. English. **DESCR:** Adlerian "Life Style Inventory"; *Family; Parent and Child Relationships; Sex Roles.

5744 Zavella, Patricia. Reflections on diversity among Chicanas. FRONTIERS: A JOURNAL OF WOMEN STUDIES, Vol. 12, no. 2 (1991), p. 73-85. English. **DESCR:** *Cultural Pluralism; Culture; *Feminism; Identity.

Sterilization

5745 Ainsworth, Diane. Cultural cross fires. IN: Duran, Livie Isauro and Bernard, H. Russell, eds. INTRODUCTION TO CHICANO STUDIES. 2nd ed. New York: Macmillan, c1982, p. 505-512. English. **DESCR:** Identity; Medical Care; Velez Ibanez, Carlos.

5746 Aragon de Valdez, Theresa. Organizing as a political tool for the Chicana. FRONTIERS: A JOURNAL OF WOMEN STUDIES, Vol. 5, no. 2 (Summer 1980), p. 7-13. English. **DESCR:** Discrimination; Feminism; *Leadership; Mexican American Legal Defense and Educational Fund (MALDEF); Social History and Conditions.

5747 Del Castillo, Adelaida R. Sterilization: an overview. IN: Mora, Magdalena and Del Castillo, Adelaida, eds. MEXICAN WOMEN IN THE UNITED STATES: STRUGGLES PAST AND PRESENT. Los Angeles, CA: Chicano Studies Research Center, UCLA, 1980, p. 65-70. English. **DESCR:** Puerto Ricans; Women.

5748 Fennelly, Katherine. Childbearing among Hispanics in the United States: an annotated bibliography. New York: Greenwood Press, 1987. xii, 167 p. English. **DESCR:** Abortion; *Bibliography; Birth Control; *Fertility; *Women; Youth.

5749 Hernandez, Antonia A. Chicanas and the issue of involuntary sterilization: reforms needed to protect informed consent. CHICANO LAW REVIEW, Vol. 3, (1976), p. 3-37. Bibliography. English. **DESCR:** *Birth Control.

5750 Hunter, Kathleen I.; Linn, Margaret W.; and Stein, Shayna R. Sterilization among American Indian and Chicano mothers. INTERNATIONAL QUARTERLY OF COMMUNITY HEALTH AND EDUCATION, Vol. 4, no. 4 (1983, 1984), p. 343-352. English. **DESCR:** Native Americans.

5751 Jorgensen, Stephen R. and Adams, Russell P. Family planning needs and behavior of Mexican American women: a study of health care professionals and their clientele. HISPANIC JOURNAL OF BEHAVIORAL SCIENCES, Vol. 9, no. 3 (September 1987), p. 265-286. English. **DESCR:** Acculturation; *Attitudes; Birth Control; *Cultural Characteristics; *Family Planning; Fertility; Medical Personnel; Stereotypes.

Sterilization (cont.)

5752 Salazar, Sandra A. Reproductive choice for Hispanas. AGENDA, Vol. 9, no. 4 (July, August, 1979), p. 31-33, 36. English. DESCR: Abortion; Medical Care; *Public Health.

5753 Talavera, Esther. Sterilization is not an alternative in family planning. AGENDA, Vol. 7, no. 6 (November, December, 1977), p. 8. English. DESCR: Discrimination; Family Planning; Feminism; *Fertility; Medical Care Laws and Legislation.

5754 Velez-I., Carlos G. The nonconsenting sterilization of Mexican women in Los Angeles: issues of psychocultural rupture and legal redress in paternalistic behavioral environments. IN: Melville, Margarita B., ed. TWICE A MINORITY. St. Louis, MO: Mosby, 1980, p. 235-248. English. DESCR: Dolores Madrigal, et al., Plaintiff, v. E.J. Quilligan, et al.; Legal Cases; Los Angeles, CA.

5755 Velez-I., Carlos G. Se me acabo la cancion: an ethnography of non-consenting sterilizations among Mexican women in Los Angeles. IN: Mora, Magdalena and Del Castillo, Adelaida, eds. MEXICAN WOMEN IN THE UNITED STATES: STRUGGLES PAST AND PRESENT. Los Angeles, CA: Chicano Studies Research Center, UCLA, 1980, p. 71-91. English. DESCR: Ethnology; Los Angeles, CA; Madrigal v. Quilligan.

Street Theater
USE: Teatro

Stress

5756 Alanis, Elsa. The relationship between state and trait anxiety and acculturation in Mexican-American women homemakers and Mexican-American community college female students. Thesis (Ph.D.)--United States International University, 1989. 161 p. English. DESCR: *Acculturation; *Community Colleges; Family; Sex Roles; Students.

5757 Armas-Cardona, Regina. Anglo and Raza young women: a study of self-esteem, psychic distress and locus of control. Thesis (Ph.D.)--Wright Institute Graduate School of Psychology, 1985. 143 p. English. DESCR: *Anglo Americans; Locus of Control; *Mental Health; *Women.

5758 Chacon, Maria A.; Cohen, Elizabeth G.; and Strover, Sharon. Chicanas and Chicanos: barriers to progress in higher education. IN: Olivas, Michael A., ed. LATINO COLLEGE STUDENTS. New York: Teachers College Press, 1986, p. 296-324. English. DESCR: Community Colleges; Discrimination; Dropouts; *Higher Education; Surveys.

5759 Codega, Susan A.; Pasley, B. Kay; and Kreutzer, Jill. Coping behaviors of adolescent mothers: an exploratory study and comparison of Mexican-Americans and Anglos. JOURNAL OF ADOLESCENT RESEARCH, Vol. 5, no. 1 (January 1990), p. 34-53. English. DESCR: Anglo Americans; Colorado; *Fertility; Women; *Youth.

5760 Cristo, Martha H. Stress and coping among Mexican women. Thesis (Ph.D.)--California School of Professional Psychology, Los Angeles, 1988. 336 p. English. DESCR: Cultural Characteristics; *Immigrants; Mental Health; Socioeconomic Factors; *Women.

5761 de Leon Siantz, Mary Lou. Maternal acceptance/rejection of Mexican migrant mothers. PSYCHOLOGY OF WOMEN QUARTERLY, Vol. 14, no. 2 (June 1990), p. 245-254. English. DESCR: Child Study; Farm Workers; *Migrant Children; Migrant Labor; Natural Support Systems; *Parent and Child Relationships; Texas Migrant Council Headstart Program.

5762 Engle, Patricia L. Prenatal and postnatal anxiety in women giving birth in Los Angeles. HEALTH PSYCHOLOGY, Vol. 9, no. 3 (1990), p. 285-299. English. DESCR: *Fertility; Immigrants; Los Angeles, CA; *Maternal and Child Welfare; Medical Care; *Prenatal Care; Women.

5763 Enguidanos-Clark, Gloria M. Acculturative stress and its contribution to the development of depression in Hispanic women. Thesis (Ph.D.)--Wright Institute, Berkeley, 1986. 198 p. English. DESCR: *Acculturation; *Depression (Psychological); Immigrants; Mental Health.

5764 Floyd, Gloria Jo Wade. An exploration of the finding and seeking of meaning in life and the Mexican-American nurse's mood state. Thesis (Ph.D.)--Texas Women's University, 1980. 133 p. English. DESCR: *Medical Personnel; *Mental Health.

5765 Gibson, Guadalupe. Hispanic women: stress and mental health issues. WOMEN AND THERAPY, Vol. 2, no. 2-3 (Summer, Fall, 1983), p. 113-133. English. DESCR: Cultural Characteristics; *Mental Health.

5766 Groessl, Patricia Ann. Depression and anxiety in postmenopausal women: a study of Black, white, and Hispanic women. Thesis (Ed.D.)--Western Michigan University, 1987. 87 p. English. DESCR: Anglo Americans; Blacks; *Depression (Psychological); Menopause; Michigan; Women.

5767 Henderson, Nancy. Perinatal service needs of Hispanic women with diabetes. Thesis (M.S.)--California State University, Long Beach, 1987. 79 p. English. DESCR: *Diabetes; Fertility; Medical Care; *Social Services.

5768 Kluessendorf, Avonelle Donneeta. Role conflict in Mexican-American college women. Thesis (Ph.D.)--California School of Professional Psychology, Fresno, 1985. 111 p. English. DESCR: *Colleges and Universities; Locus of Control; *Sex Roles; Students.

5769 Lozano-Bull, Irma. Acculturative stress in Mexican-American women. Thesis (Ph.D.)--California School of Professional Psychology, Los Angeles, 1987. 201 p. English. DESCR: *Acculturation; Natural Support Systems.

5770 Melville, Margarita B. Mexican women adapt to migration. IN: Rios-Bustamante, Antonio, ed. MEXICAN IMMIGRANT WORKERS IN THE U.S. Los Angeles, CA: Chicano Studies Research Center Publications, University of California, 1981, p. 119-124. English. DESCR: Acculturation; Attitudes; Immigrants; Sex Roles; *Undocumented Workers.

Stress (cont.)

5771 Munoz, Daniel G. Identifying areas of stress for Chicano undergraduates. IN: Olivas, Michael A., ed. LATINO COLLEGE STUDENTS. New York: Teachers College Press, 1986, p. 131-156. English. DESCR: Academic Achievement; *Attitudes; Colleges and Universities; Financial Aid; Surveys.

5772 Perez, Robert. Effects of stress, social support and coping style on adjustment to pregnancy among Hispanic women. HISPANIC JOURNAL OF BEHAVIORAL SCIENCES, Vol. 5, no. 2 (June 1983), p. 141-161. English. DESCR: Fertility; Natural Support Systems.

5773 Perez, Robert. Stress and coping as determinants of adaptation to pregnancy in Hispanic women. Thesis (Ph.D.)--University of California, Los Angeles, 1982. 343 p. English. DESCR: *Fertility; Medical Personnel; Natural Support Systems.

5774 Rodriguez, Rogelio E. Psychological distress among Mexican-American women as a reaction to the new immigration law. Thesis (Ph.D.)--Loyola University of Chicago, 1989. 87 p. English. DESCR: Depression (Psychological); Immigrants; *Immigration Law and Legislation; Immigration Reform and Control Act of 1986; *Mental Health; Mexico; Undocumented Workers; Women.

5775 Rodriguez, Rogelio E. and DeWolfe, Alan. Psychological distress among Mexican-American and Mexican women as related to status on the new immigration law. JOURNAL OF CONSULTING AND CLINICAL PSYCHOLOGY, Vol. 58, no. 5 (October 1990), p. 548-553. English. DESCR: *Immigrants; Immigration Law and Legislation; Immigration Reform and Control Act of 1986; Natural Support Systems; Undocumented Workers; Women.

5776 Romero, Gloria J.; Castro, Felipe G.; and Cervantes, Richard C. Latinas without work: family, occupational, and economic stress following unemployment. PSYCHOLOGY OF WOMEN QUARTERLY, Vol. 12, no. 3 (September 1988), p. 281-297. English. DESCR: *Employment; Family; Starkist Tuna Cannery, Wilmington, CA.

5777 Romero, Gloria J.; Cervantes, Richard C.; and Castro, Felipe G. Long-term stress among Latino women after a plant closure. SOCIOLOGY & SOCIAL RESEARCH, Vol. 71, no. 2 (January 1987), p. 85-88. English. DESCR: Attitudes; Employment; Family; Wilmington, CA.

5778 Ross, Catherine E.; Mirowsky, John; and Ulbrich, Patricia. Distress and the traditional female role: a comparison of Mexicans and Anglos. AMERICAN JOURNAL OF SOCIOLOGY, Vol. 89, no. 3 (November 1983), p. 670-682. English. DESCR: Anglo Americans; Comparative Psychology; *Sex Roles; Women.

5779 Saenz, Rogelio. Traditional sex-roles, ethnic integration, marital satisfaction, and psychological distress among Chicanas. Thesis (Ph.D.)--Iowa State University, 1986. 145 p. English. DESCR: *Marriage; *Mental Health; *Sex Roles.

5780 Salgado de Snyder, Nelly. Factors associated with acculturative stress and depressive symptomatology among married Mexican immigrant women. PSYCHOLOGY OF WOMEN QUARTERLY, Vol. 11, no. 4 (December 1987), p. 475-488. English. DESCR: *Acculturation; Depression (Psychological); *Immigrants; Mental Health; Mexico; Women.

5781 Salgado de Snyder, Nelly; Cervantes, Richard C.; and Padilla, Amado M. Gender and ethnic differences in psychosocial stress and generalized distress among Hispanics. SEX ROLES, Vol. 22, no. 7-8 (April, 1990), p. 441-453. English. DESCR: Anglo Americans; Central Americans; *Comparative Psychology; Depression (Psychological); Hispanic Stress Inventory (HSI); *Immigrants; Immigration; *Sex Roles; Women.

5782 Salgado de Snyder, Nelly. Mexican immigrant women: the relationship of ethnic loyalty and social support to acculturative stress and depressive symptomatology. Los Angeles, CA: Spanish Speaking Mental Health Research Center, 1987. 73 p. English. DESCR: *Acculturation; Depression (Psychological); Identity; *Immigrants; Natural Support Systems; Women.

5783 Shapiro, Johanna and Tittle, Ken. Maternal adaptation to child disability in a Hispanic population. FAMILY RELATIONS, Vol. 39, no. 2 (April 1990), p. 179-185. English. DESCR: Children; *Handicapped; *Parent and Child Relationships; Psychological Testing.

5784 Sorel, Janet Elaine. The relationship between gender role incongruity on measures of coping and material resources and blood pressure among Mexican-American women. Thesis (Ph.D.)--University of North Carolina at Chapel Hill, 1988. 268 p. English. DESCR: High Blood Pressure; Hispanic Health and Nutrition Examination Survey (HHANES); Hypertension; Public Health; *Sex Roles.

5785 Vallez, Andrea. Acculturation, social support, stress and adjustment of the Mexican American college woman. Thesis (Ph.D.)--University of Colorado at Boulder, 1984. 121 p. English. DESCR: *Acculturation; *Colleges and Universities; Depression (Psychological); Higher Education; Natural Support Systems; Southern California; *Students.

5786 Valtierra, Mary. Acculturation, social support, and reported stress of Latina physicians. Thesis (Ph.D.)--California School of Professional Psychology, 1989. 136 p. English. DESCR: *Acculturation; Careers; Cubanos; Immigration; Latin Americans; *Medical Personnel; Puerto Ricans; *Women.

5787 Vargas-Willis, Gloria and Cervantes, Richard C. Consideration of psychosocial stress in the treatment of the Latina immigrant. HISPANIC JOURNAL OF BEHAVIORAL SCIENCES, Vol. 9, no. 3 (September 1987), p. 315-329. English. DESCR: Discrimination in Employment; *Immigrants; Mental Health; *Psychotherapy.

5788 Vega, William A.; Kolody, Bohdan; and Valle, Juan Ramon. Migration and mental health: an empirical test of depression risk factors among immigrant Mexican women. INTERNATIONAL MIGRATION REVIEW, Vol. 21, no. 3 (Fall 1987), p. 512-530. English. DESCR: Acculturation; *Depression (Psychological); *Immigrants; Immigration; *Mental Health; Migration; Undocumented Workers; Women.

Stress (cont.)

5789 Vega, William A.; Kolody, Bohdan; and Valle, Juan Ramon. The relationship of marital status, confidant support, and depression among Mexican immigrant women. JOURNAL OF MARRIAGE AND THE FAMILY Vol. 48, no. 3 (August 1986), p. 597-605. English. DESCR: *Depression (Psychological); *Immigrants; Low Income; *Marriage; San Diego County, CA; Women.

5790 Wagner, Roland M. and Schaffer, Diane M. Social networks and survival strategies: an exploratory study of Mexican American, Black, and Anglo female family heads in San Jose, California. IN: Melville, Margarita B., ed. TWICE A MINORITY. St. Louis, MO: Mosby, 1980, p. 173-190. English. DESCR: Anglo Americans; Blacks; Identity; *Natural Support Systems; San Jose, CA; *Single Parents.

Strikes and Lockouts

5791 Arroyo, Laura E. Industrial and occupational distribution of Chicana workers. AZTLAN, Vol. 4, no. 2 (Fall 1973), p. 343-382. English. DESCR: California; *Employment; Farah Manufacturing Co., El Paso, TX; Farah Strike; Garment Industry; Industrial Workers; Texas.

5792 Arroyo, Laura E. Industrial and occupational distribution of Chicana workers. IN: Sanchez, Rosaura and Martinez Cruz, Rosa, eds. ESSAYS ON LA MUJER. Los Angeles, CA: Chicano Studies Center Publications, UCLA, 1977, p. 150-187. English. DESCR: California; *Employment; Farah Manufacturing Co., El Paso, TX; Farah Strike; Garment Industry; Industrial Workers; Texas.

5793 Aulette, Judy and Mills, Trudy. Something old, something new: auxiliary work in the 1983-1986 copper strike. FEMINIST STUDIES, Vol. 14, no. 2 (Summer 1988), p. 251-268. English. DESCR: Arizona; Clifton-Morenci Copper Strike, 1983-1986; Clifton-Morenci District, Arizona; Feminism; Labor Unions; Morenci Miners Women's Auxiliary (MMWA); Mutualistas; Phelps Dodge Corporation, Morenci, AZ; SALT OF THE EARTH [film]; Sex Roles.

5794 Cantarow, Ellen and De la Cruz, Jessie Lopez. Jessie Lopez De la Cruz: the battle for farmworkers' rights. IN: Cantarow, Ellen. MOVING THE MOUNTAIN: WOMEN WORKING FOR SOCIAL CHANGE. Old Westbury, NY: Feminist Press, 1980, p. 94-151. English. DESCR: Agricultural Labor Unions; Chavez, Cesar E.; *De la Cruz, Jessie Lopez; *Farm Workers; Labor Disputes; Oral History; Parlier, CA; Sex Roles; *United Farmworkers of America (UFW).

5795 Coyle, Laurie; Hershatter, Gail; and Honig, Emily. Women at Farah: an unfinished story. IN: Mora, Magdalena and Del Castillo, Adelaida, eds. MEXICAN WOMEN IN THE UNITED STATES: STRUGGLES PAST AND PRESENT. Los Angeles, CA: Chicano Studies Research Center, UCLA, 1980, p. 117-143. English. DESCR: Farah Manufacturing Co., El Paso, TX; Farah Strike; Garment Industry; Labor Unions.

5796 Duron, Clementina. Mexican women and labor conflict in Los Angeles: the ILGWU dressmakers' strike of 1933. AZTLAN, Vol. 15, no. 1 (Spring 1984), p. 145-161. English. DESCR: Garment Industry; International Ladies Garment Workers Union (ILGWU); Labor Unions.

5797 Garcia, Mario T. The Chicana in American history: the Mexican women of El Paso, 1880-1920 - a case study. PACIFIC HISTORICAL REVIEW, Vol. 49, no. 2 (May 1980), p. 315-337. English. DESCR: Acme Laundry, El Paso, TX; American Federation of Labor (AFL); Case Studies; Central Labor Union; Domestic Work; *El Paso, TX; Employment; *History; Immigrants; Income; Labor Unions; Sex Roles; *Working Women.

5798 Gonzalez, Rosalinda M. Chicanas and Mexican immigrant families 1920-1940: women's subordination and family exploitation. IN: Scharf, Lois and Jensen, Joan M., eds. DECADES OF DISCONTENT: THE WOMEN'S MOVEMENT, 1920-1940. Westport, CT: Greenwood Press, 1983, p. 59-84. English. DESCR: *Family; Farm Workers; History; Immigrants; Labor; Labor Unions; Mexico; Pecan Shelling Worker's Union, San Antonio, TX; Sex Roles; United Cannery Agricultural Packing and Allied Workers of America (UCAPAWA); Working Women.

5799 Keremitsis, Dawn. Del metate al molino: la mujer mexicana de 1910 a 1940. HISTORIA MEXICANA, Vol. 33, no. 2 (1983), p. 285-302. Spanish. DESCR: Food Industry; History; Labor Unions; Mexico; Sex Roles; Women; *Working Women.

5800 Kernan, Lisa. Keep marching sisters: the second generation looks at SALT OF THE EARTH. NUESTRO, Vol. 9, no. 4 (May 1985), p. 23-25. English. DESCR: Films; *SALT OF THE EARTH [film].

5801 Mora, Magdalena. The Tolteca Strike: Mexican women and the struggle for union representation. IN: Rios-Bustamante, Antonio, ed. MEXICAN IMMIGRANT WORKERS IN THE U.S. Los Angeles, CA: Chicano Studies Research Center Publications, University of California, 1981, p. 111-117. English. DESCR: Centro de Accion Social Autonomo (CASA); Food Industry; *Labor Unions; Toltec Foods, Richmond, CA.

5802 Rips, Geoffrey and Tenayuca, Emma. Living history: Emma Tenayuca tells her story. TEXAS OBSERVER, (October 28, 1983), p. 7-15. English. DESCR: *Autobiography; Communist Party; Food Industry; Labor Unions; Leadership; Oral History; Pecan Shelling Worker's Union, San Antonio, TX; San Antonio, TX; Tenayuca, Emma; United Cannery Agricultural Packing and Allied Workers of America (UCAPAWA); Worker's Alliance (WA), Los Angeles, CA; Working Women.

5803 Romero, Bertha. The exploitation of Mexican women in the canning industry and the effects of capital accumulation on striking workers. REVISTA MUJERES, Vol. 3, no. 2 (June 1986), p. 16-20. English. DESCR: Canneries; Capitalism; Industrial Workers; Labor Unions; *Watsonville Canning and Frozen Food Co.

Strikes and Lockouts
(cont.)

5804 Rose, Margaret. Traditional and nontraditional patterns of female activism in the United Farm Workers of America, 1962-1980. FRONTIERS: A JOURNAL OF WOMEN STUDIES, Vol. 11, no. 1 (1990), p. [26]-32. English. DESCR: Boycotts; California; Chavez, Cesar E.; *Chavez, Helen; *Huerta, Dolores; Labor Disputes; Labor Unions; National Farm Workers Association (NFWA); Sex Roles; *United Farmworkers of America (UFW).

5805 Ruiz, Vicki L. A promise fulfilled: Mexican cannery workers in Southern California. THE PACIFIC HISTORIAN, Vol. 30, no. 2 (Summer 1986), p. 51-61. English. DESCR: *California Sanitary Canning Company, Los Angeles, CA; *Canneries; Labor Unions; Moreno, Luisa [union organizer]; Southern California; *United Cannery Agricultural Packing and Allied Workers of America (UCAPAWA); Working Women.

5806 Ruiz, Vicki L. A promise fulfilled: Mexican cannery workers in Southern California. IN: DuBois, Ellen Carol and Ruiz, Vicki L., eds. UNEQUAL SISTERS: A MULTICULTURAL READER IN U.S. WOMEN'S HISTORY. New York: Routledge, 1990, p. 264-274. English. DESCR: *California Sanitary Canning Company, Los Angeles, CA; *Canneries; Labor Unions; Moreno, Luisa [union organizer]; Southern California; *United Cannery Agricultural Packing and Allied Workers of America (UCAPAWA); Working Women.

5807 Ruiz, Vicki L. A promise fulfilled: Mexican cannery workers in Southern California. IN: Del Castillo, Adelaida R., ed. BETWEEN BORDERS: ESSAYS ON MEXICANA/CHICANA HISTORY. Encino, CA: Floricanto Press, 1990, p. 281-298. English. DESCR: California Sanitary Canning Company, Los Angeles, CA; *Canneries; Labor Unions; Moreno, Luisa [union organizer]; Southern California; United Cannery Agricultural Packing and Allied Workers of America (UCAPAWA); Working Women.

5808 Saavedra, Lupe. It is only fair that women be allowed to... AGENDA, (Winter 1976), p. 12-13. English. DESCR: Labor Disputes; Labor Unions; SALT OF THE EARTH [film].

5809 Shapiro, Peter. Watsonville shows "it can be done". GUARDIAN, Vol. 39, no. 24 (March 25, 1987), p. 1,9. English. DESCR: Canneries; Labor Unions; NorCal Frozen Foods; *Watsonville Canning and Frozen Food Co.; Working Women.

5810 Weber, Devra Anne. Mexican women on strike: memory, history and oral narratives. IN: Del Castillo, Adelaida R., ed. BETWEEN BORDERS: ESSAYS ON MEXICANA/CHICANA HISTORY. Encino, CA: Floricanto Press, 1990, p. 175-200. English. DESCR: *1933 Cotton Strike; Cotton Industry; History; *Oral History; San Joaquin Valley, CA; *Valdez, Rosaura; Working Women.

Student Movements

5811 Hernandez, Patricia. Lives of Chicana activists: the Chicano student movement (a case study). IN: Mora, Magdalena and Del Castillo, Adelaida, eds. MEXICAN WOMEN IN THE UNITED STATES: STRUGGLES PAST AND PRESENT. Los Angeles, CA: Chicano Studies Research Center, UCLA, 1980, p. 17-25. English. DESCR: California State University,

San Diego; Case Studies; *Chicano Movement; Colleges and Universities; Movimiento Estudiantil Chicano de Aztlan (MEChA); Student Organizations.

5812 Lopez, Sonia A. The role of the Chicana within the student movement. IN: Sanchez, Rosaura and Martinez Cruz, Rosa, eds. ESSAYS ON LA MUJER. Los Angeles, CA: Chicano Studies Center Publications, UCLA, 1977, p. 16-29. English. DESCR: Chicano Movement; Conferences and Meetings; Feminism; First National Chicana Conference (May 1971: Houston, TX).

Student Organizations

5813 Del Castillo, Adelaida R. Mexican women in organization. IN: Mora, Magdalena and Del Castillo, Adelaida, eds. MEXICAN WOMEN IN THE UNITED STATES: STRUGGLES PAST AND PRESENT. Los Angeles, CA: Chicano Studies Research Center, UCLA, 1980, p. 7-16. English. DESCR: *Chicano Movement; Feminism; Leadership; Students.

5814 Hernandez, Patricia. Lives of Chicana activists: the Chicano student movement (a case study). IN: Mora, Magdalena and Del Castillo, Adelaida, eds. MEXICAN WOMEN IN THE UNITED STATES: STRUGGLES PAST AND PRESENT. Los Angeles, CA: Chicano Studies Research Center, UCLA, 1980, p. 17-25. English. DESCR: California State University, San Diego; Case Studies; *Chicano Movement; Colleges and Universities; Movimiento Estudiantil Chicano de Aztlan (MEChA); Student Movements.

Students

5815 Alanis, Elsa. The relationship between state and trait anxiety and acculturation in Mexican-American women homemakers and Mexican-American community college female students. Thesis (Ph.D.)--United States International University, 1989. 161 p. English. DESCR: *Acculturation; *Community Colleges; Family; Sex Roles; *Stress.

5816 Chacon, Maria A. An overdue study of the Chicana undergraduate college experience. LA LUZ, Vol. 8, no. 8 (October, November, 1980), p. 27. English. DESCR: Colleges and Universities; *Educational Statistics; Higher Education; Stanford University, Stanford, CA.

5817 Chacon, Maria A., et al. Chicanas in California post secondary education: a comparative study of barriers to the program progress. Stanford, CA: Stanford Center for Chicano Research, 1985. viii, 217 p. English. DESCR: *Academic Achievement; Colleges and Universities; Counseling (Educational); Educational Statistics; Enrollment; *Higher Education; Surveys.

5818 Daggett, Andrea Stuhlman. A comparison of occupational goal orientations of female Mexican-Americans and Anglo high-school seniors of the classes of 1972 and 1980. Thesis (Ph.D.)--University of Arizona, Tucson, 1983. xii, 134 p. English. DESCR: Academic Achievement; Anglo Americans; *Careers; *Secondary School Education; Sexism; Women.

Students (cont.)

5819 De Blassie, Richard R. and Frarco, Juan N.
The differences between personality
inventory scores and self-rating in a sample
of Hispanic subjects. JOURNAL OF NON-WHITE
CONCERNS IN PERSONNEL AND GUIDANCE, Vol. 11,
no. 2 (January 1983), p. 43-45. English.
DESCR: Higher Education; Hispanic Education
[program]; New Mexico State University;
*Personality; Sixteen Personality Factor
Questionnaire.

5820 De Llano, Carmen. Comparisons of the
psychocultural characteristics of graduate
school-bound and nongraduate school-bound
Mexican American and Anglo American college
women. Thesis (Ph.D.)--California School of
Professional Psychology, 1986. 223 p.
English. DESCR: *Anglo Americans; Colleges
and Universities; Comparative Psychology;
Cultural Characteristics; *Graduate Schools;
Higher Education; *Women.

5821 Del Castillo, Adelaida R. Mexican women in
organization. IN: Mora, Magdalena and Del
Castillo, Adelaida, eds. MEXICAN WOMEN IN
THE UNITED STATES: STRUGGLES PAST AND
PRESENT. Los Angeles, CA: Chicano Studies
Research Center, UCLA, 1980, p. 7-16.
English. DESCR: *Chicano Movement; Feminism;
Leadership; Student Organizations.

5822 Espin, Oliva M. Perceptions of sexual
discrimination among college women in Latin
America and the United States. HISPANIC
JOURNAL OF BEHAVIORAL SCIENCES, Vol. 2, no.
1 (March 1980), p. 1-19. English. DESCR:
Colleges and Universities; CRITICAL INCIDENT
TECHNIQUE; Feminism; Latin Americans;
*Sexism; Women Men Relations.

5823 Fleming, Marilyn B. Problems experienced by
Anglo, Hispanic and Navajo Indian women
college students. JOURNAL OF AMERICAN INDIAN
EDUCATION, Vol. 22, no. 1 (October 1982), p.
7-17. English. DESCR: Anglo Americans;
Community Colleges; Ethnic Groups; *Higher
Education; Identity; Medical Education;
Native Americans; Women.

5824 Fu, Victoria R.; Hinkle, Dennis E.; and
Korslund, Mary K. A development study of
ethnic self-concept among pre-adolescent
girls. JOURNAL OF GENETIC PSYCHOLOGY, Vol.
14, (March 1983), p. 67-73. English.
DESCR: Comparative Psychology; *Identity;
Junior High School; Self-Concept Self Report
Scale; Youth.

5825 Gonzalez, Alex. Sex roles of the traditional
Mexican family: a comparison of Chicano and
Anglo students' attitudes. JOURNAL OF
CROSS-CULTURAL PSYCHOLOGY, Vol. 13, no. 3
(September 1982), p. 330-339. English.
DESCR: Anglo Americans; Attitudes;
Comparative Psychology; *Family; Hembrismo;
Machismo; Sex Roles.

5826 Hernandez, Lisa, ed. and Benitez, Tina, ed.
Palabras chicanas: an undergraduate
anthology. Berkeley, CA: Mujeres en Marcha,
University of California, Berkeley, 1988. 97
p. Bilingual. DESCR: Literary Criticism;
*Literature; Poems; Prose.

5827 Jaramillo, Mari-Luci. Institutional
responsibility in the provision of
educational experiences to the Hispanic
American female student. IN: McKenna, Teresa
and Ortiz, Flora Ida, eds. THE BROKEN WEB:
THE EDUCATIONAL EXPERIENCE OF HISPANIC
WOMEN. Claremont, CA: Tomaas Rivera Center;
Berkeley, CA: Floricanto Press, 1988, p.

25-35. English. DESCR: Academic Achievement;
*Discrimination in Education; Dropouts;
*Education; Educational Administration;
Enrollment; Higher Education; *Women.

5828 Kluessendorf, Avonelle Donneeta. Role
conflict in Mexican-American college women.
Thesis (Ph.D.)--California School of
Professional Psychology, Fresno, 1985. 111
p. English. DESCR: *Colleges and
Universities; Locus of Control; *Sex Roles;
*Stress.

5829 Martinez-Metcalf, Rosario. Concerns of
Hispanic community college women. Thesis
(Ph.D.)--North Texas State University, 1985.
153 p. English. DESCR: *Community Colleges.

5830 Ortiz, Flora Ida. Hispanic American women in
higher education: a consideration of the
socialization process. AZTLAN, Vol. 17, no.
2 (Fall 1986), p. 125-152. English. DESCR:
*Academic Achievement; Counseling
(Educational); Enrollment; *Higher
Education; Sex Roles; *Sexism;
Socialization; University of California.

5831 Padilla, Eligio R. and O'Grady, Kevin E.
Sexuality among Mexican Americans: a case of
sexual stereotyping. JOURNAL OF PERSONALITY
AND SOCIAL PSYCHOLOGY, Vol. 52, no. 1
(1987), p. 5-10. English. DESCR: Age Groups;
Anglo Americans; Attitudes; California;
Religion; *Sex Roles; *Sex Stereotypes;
Sexual Behavior; Sexual Knowledge and
Attitude Test; *Stereotypes; Values.

5832 Quezada, Rosa; Loheyde, Katherine Jones; and
Kacmarczyk, Ronald. The Hispanic woman
graduate student: barriers to mentoring in
higher education. TEXAS TECH JOURNAL OF
EDUCATION, Vol. 11, no. 3 (Fall 1984), p.
235-241. English. DESCR: Discrimination in
Education; *Graduate Schools; *Higher
Education; *Mentoring.

5833 Ramirez, Alex, et al. The relationship
between sociocultural variables and Chicano
and Anglo high school student responses on
the Potency Dimension of the Semantic
Differential. HISPANIC JOURNAL OF BEHAVIORAL
SCIENCES, Vol. 3, no. 2 (June 1981), p.
177-190. English. DESCR: Anglo Americans;
Martinez, Joe L., Jr.; Martinez, Sergio R.;
MULTIVARIATE ANALYSIS OF VARIANCE (MANOVA);
Olmedo, Esteban L.; *Parent and Child
Relationships; Sex Roles; Sex Stereotypes.

5834 Trotter, Robert T. Ethnic and sexual
patterns of alcohol use: Anglo and Mexican
American college students. ADOLESCENCE, Vol.
17, no. 66 (Summer 1982), p. 305-325.
English. DESCR: *Alcoholism; Anglo
Americans; Colleges and Universities;
Cultural Characteristics; Ethnic Groups; Sex
Roles; Youth.

5835 Vallez, Andrea. Acculturation, social
support, stress and adjustment of the
Mexican American college woman. Thesis
(Ph.D.)--University of Colorado at Boulder,
1984. 121 p. English. DESCR: *Acculturation;
*Colleges and Universities; Depression
(Psychological); Higher Education; Natural
Support Systems; Southern California;
Stress.

Students (cont.)

5836 Vigil, James Diego. The nexus of class, culture and gender in the education of Mexican American females. IN: McKenna, Teresa and Ortiz, Flora Ida, eds. THE BROKEN WEB: THE EDUCATIONAL EXPERIENCE OF HISPANIC WOMEN. Claremont, CA: Tomas Rivera Center; Berkeley, CA: Floricanto Press, 1988, p. 79-103. English. DESCR: Academic Achievement; Acculturation; Discrimination in Education; *Education; Identity; Secondary School Education; Sex Roles; Social Classes.

5837 Zeff, Shirley B. A cross-cultural study of Mexican American, Black American and white American women of a large urban university. HISPANIC JOURNAL OF BEHAVIORAL SCIENCES, Vol. 4, no. 2 (June 1982), p. 245-261. English. DESCR: Anglo Americans; Blacks; *Higher Education; Sex Roles.

5838 Zuniga, Maria E. Assessment issues with Chicanas: practice implications. PSYCHOTHERAPY, Vol. 25, no. 2 (Summer 1988), p. 288-293. English. DESCR: Acculturation; Colleges and Universities; Family; Identity; *Mental Health; Mexican-American Outreach Program, San Diego State University; *Psychotherapy.

Suffrage
USE: Voting Rights

Suicide

5839 Bourque, Linda B.; Kraus, Jess F.; and Cosand, Beverly J. Attributes of suicide in females. SUICIDE AND LIFE-THREATENING BEHAVIOR, Vol. 13, no. 2 (Summer 1983), p. 123-138. English. DESCR: Anglo Americans; Sacramento County, CA; Women.

5840 Zayas, Luis H. Toward an understanding of suicide risks in young Hispanic females. JOURNAL OF ADOLESCENT RESEARCH, Vol. 2, no. 1 (Spring 1987), p. 1-11. English. DESCR: Acculturation; Cubanos; Cultural Characteristics; Depression (Psychological); Mental Health; Puerto Ricans; *Women; *Youth.

Support Groups
USE: Natural Support Systems

Survey of Income and Education (SIE)

5841 Reimers, Cordelia W. A comparative analysis of the wages of Hispanics, Blacks, and non-Hispanic whites. IN: Borjas, George J. and Tienda, Marta, eds. HISPANICS IN THE U.S. ECONOMY. Orlando, FL: Academic Press, 1985, p. 27-75. English. DESCR: Anglo Americans; Blacks; *Income; Labor Supply and Market; Males.

Surveys

5842 Achor, Shirley and Morales, Aida G. Chicanas holding doctoral degrees: social reproduction and cultural ecological approaches. ANTHROPOLOGY AND EDUCATION QUARTERLY, Vol. 21, no. 3 (September 1990), p. 269-287. English. DESCR: *Academic Achievement; *Discrimination in Education; Graduate Schools; *Higher Education.

5843 Aneshensel, Carol S., et al. Participation of Mexican American adolescents in a longitudinal panel survey. PUBLIC OPINION QUARTERLY, Vol. 53, no. 4 (Winter 1989), p. 548-562. English. DESCR: Age Groups; *Fertility; Los Angeles County, CA; Social

Science; *Women Men Relations; *Youth.

5844 Bachu, Amara and O'Connell, Martin. Developing current fertility indicators for foreign-born women from the Current Population Survey. REVIEW OF PUBLIC DATA USE, Vol. 12, no. 3 (October 1984), p. 185-195. English. DESCR: Current Population Survey; *Fertility; Latin America; Mexico; Vital Statistics; Women.

5845 Canales, Genevieve and Roberts, Robert E. Gender and mental health in the Mexican origin population of South Texas. IN: Rodriguez, Reymund and Coleman, Marion Tolbert, eds. MENTAL HEALTH ISSUES OF THE MEXICAN ORIGIN POPULATION IN TEXAS. Austin, TX: Hogg Foundation for Mental Health, University of Texas, 1987, p. 89-99. English. DESCR: Del Rio, TX; Depression (Psychological); Eagle Pass, TX; Health Education; *Males; *Mental Health; *Sex Roles; South Texas.

5846 Chacon, Maria A.; Cohen, Elizabeth G.; and Strover, Sharon. Chicanas and Chicanos: barriers to progress in higher education. IN: Olivas, Michael A., ed. LATINO COLLEGE STUDENTS. New York: Teachers College Press, 1986, p. 296-324. English. DESCR: Community Colleges; Discrimination; Dropouts; *Higher Education; Stress.

5847 Chacon, Maria A., et al. Chicanas in California post secondary education: a comparative study of barriers to the program progress. Stanford, CA: Stanford Center for Chicano Research, 1985. viii, 217 p. English. DESCR: *Academic Achievement; Colleges and Universities; Counseling (Educational); Educational Statistics; Enrollment; *Higher Education; Students.

5848 Chacon, Maria A., et al. Chicanas in postsecondary education. Stanford, CA: Center for Research on Women, Stanford University, 1982. iii, 106, [68] p. English. DESCR: Colleges and Universities; *Higher Education; Public Policy.

5849 Flaskerud, Jacquelyn H. and Nyamathi, Adeline M. Black and Latina womens' AIDS related knowledge, attitudes, and practices. RESEARCH IN NURSING AND HEALTH, Vol. 12, no. 6 (December 1989), p. 339-346. English. DESCR: *AIDS (Disease); Attitudes; *Blacks; Health Education; Los Angeles County, CA; *Women.

5850 Holck, Susan E., et al. Alcohol consumption among Mexican American and Anglo women: results of a survey along the U.S.-Mexico border. JOURNAL OF STUDIES ON ALCOHOL, Vol. 45, no. 2 (March 1984), p. 149-154. English. DESCR: *Alcoholism; Anglo Americans; Border Region.

5851 Hovell, Melbourne F., et al. Occupational health risks for Mexican women: the case of the maquiladora along the Mexican-United States border. INTERNATIONAL JOURNAL OF HEALTH SERVICES, Vol. 18, no. 4 (1988), p. 617-627. English. DESCR: *Border Industries; Border Region; Mexico; *Occupational Hazards; Project Concern International (PCI), San Diego, CA; Public Health; Tijuana, Baja California, Mexico; Women; Working Women.

Surveys (cont.)

5852 Hunt, Isabelle F., et al. Zinc
supplementation during pregnancy: zinc
concentration of serum and hair from
low-income women of Mexican descent.
AMERICAN JOURNAL OF CLINICAL NUTRITION, Vol.
37, no. 4 (April 1983), p. 572-582. English.
DESCR: Low Income; Nutrition; *Prenatal
Care.

5853 Mink, Diane Leslie. Early grandmotherhood:
an exploratory study. Thesis
(Ph.D.)--California School of Professional
Psychology, Los Angeles, 1987. 190 p.
English. DESCR: Age Groups; *Ancianos;
Assertiveness; Family; Fertility;
Grandmothers; Natural Support Systems; *Sex
Roles; Youth.

5854 Munoz, Daniel G. Identifying areas of stress
for Chicano undergraduates. IN: Olivas,
Michael A., ed. LATINO COLLEGE STUDENTS. New
York: Teachers College Press, 1986, p.
131-156. English. DESCR: Academic
Achievement; *Attitudes; Colleges and
Universities; Financial Aid; *Stress.

5855 Padilla, Amado M. and Baird, Traci L.
Mexican-American adolescent sexuality and
sexual knowledge: an exploratory study.
HISPANIC JOURNAL OF BEHAVIORAL SCIENCES,
Vol. 13, no. 1 (February 1991), p. 95-104.
English. DESCR: *Attitudes; *Birth Control;
Sex Roles; *Sexual Behavior; *Youth.

5856 Pena, Devon Gerardo. Tortuosidad: shop floor
struggles of female maquiladora workers. IN:
Ruiz, Vicki L. and Tiano, Susan, eds. WOMEN
ON THE U.S.-MEXICO BORDER: RESPONSES TO
CHANGE. Boston, MA: Allen & Unwin, 1987, p.
129-154. English. DESCR: Border Industries;
Ciudad Juarez, Chihuahua, Mexico;
Employment; Personnel Management;
Population; *Women; Working Women.

5857 Queiro-Tajalli, Irene. Hispanic women's
perceptions and use of prenatal health care
services. AFFILIA: JOURNAL OF WOMEN AND
SOCIAL WORK, Vol. 4, no. 2 (Summer 1989), p.
60-72. English. DESCR: Indianapolis, IN;
*Medical Care; *Prenatal Care; Women.

5858 Solorzano-Torres, Rosalia. Female Mexican
immigrants in San Diego County. IN: Ruiz,
Vicki L. and Tiano, Susan, eds. WOMEN ON THE
U.S.-MEXICO BORDER: RESPONSES TO CHANGE.
Boston, MA: Allen & Unwin, 1987, p. 41-59.
English. DESCR: Employment; *Immigrants;
Immigration; Literature Reviews; San Diego
County, CA; Undocumented Workers; Women.

5859 Valdes, Guadalupe; Garcia, Herman; and
Storment, Diamantina. Sex-related speech
accommodations among Mexican-American
bilinguals: a pilot study of language choice
in customer-server interactions. IN: Barkin,
Florence, et al., eds. BILINGUALISM AND
LANGUAGE CONTACT: SPANISH, ENGLISH, AND
NATIVE AMERICAN LANGUAGES. New York:
Teachers College, 1982, p. 187-200. English.
DESCR: Bilingualism; *Language Usage; Las
Cruces, NM.

5860 Williams, Edward J. and Passe-Smith, John T.
Turnover and recruitment in the maquila
industry: causes and solutions. Las Cruces,
NM: Joint Border Research Institute, New
Mexico State University, 1989. ii, 59 p.
English. DESCR: *Border Industries;
*Employment; Income; *Labor Supply and
Market; Personnel Management; Women;
*Working Women.

5861 Young, Gay. Gender identification and
working-class solidarity among maquila
workers in Ciudad Juarez: stereotypes and
realities. IN: Ruiz, Vicki L. and Tiano,
Susan, eds. WOMEN ON THE U.S.-MEXICO BORDER:
RESPONSES TO CHANGE. Boston, MA: Allen &
Unwin, 1987, p. 105-127. English. DESCR:
Assertiveness; Attitudes; Border
Industrialization Program (BIP); *Border
Industries; Border Region; Ciudad Juarez,
Chihuahua, Mexico; Employment; Garment
Industry; Sex Roles; Working Women.

Symbolism

5862 Alarcon, Norma. Chicana's feminist
literature: a re-vision through Malintzinl
or Malintzin: putting flesh back on the
object. IN: Moraga, Cherrie and Anzaldua,
Gloria, eds. THIS BRIDGE CALLED MY BACK:
WRITINGS BY RADICAL WOMEN OF COLOR.
Watertown, MA: Persephone Press, 1981, p.
182-190. English. DESCR: Feminism;
Literature; Malinche; *Sex Roles;
Stereotypes.

5863 Alarcon, Norma. Traddutora, traditora: a
paradigmatic figure of Chicana feminism.
CULTURAL CRITIQUE, Vol. 13, (Fall 1989), p.
57-87. English. DESCR: *Feminism; *Malinche;
Paz, Octavio; Sex Roles.

5864 Herrera-Sobek, Maria. The Mexican corrido: a
feminist analysis. Bloomington, IN: Indiana
University Press, 1990. xix, 151 p.: ill.
English. DESCR: *Corridos; Mexico; Military;
*Sex Roles; Sex Stereotypes; *Women; Women
Men Relations.

5865 Leal, Luis. Arquetipos femeninos en la
literatura mexicana. IN: Leal, Luis. AZTLAN
Y MEXICO: PERFILES LITERARIOS E HISTORICOS.
Binghamton, NY: Bilingual Press/Editorial
Bilingue, 1985, p. 168-176. Spanish. DESCR:
La Virgen de Guadalupe; *Literary Criticism;
Malinche; Mexican Literature; Women.

5866 Leal, Luis. Female archetypes in Mexican
literature. IN: Miller, Beth, ed. WOMEN IN
HISPANIC LITERATURE: ICONS AND FALLEN IDOLS.
Berkeley, CA: University of California
Press, 1983, p. 227-242. English. DESCR: La
Virgen de Guadalupe; *Literary Criticism;
Malinche; Mexican Literature; Women.

5867 Limon, Jose E. [anthropologist]. La Llorona,
the third legend of greater Mexico: cultural
symbols, women, and the political
unconscious. RENATO ROSALDO LECTURE SERIES
MONOGRAPH, Vol. 2, (Spring 1986), p.
[59]-93. English. DESCR: *Feminism;
Folklore; *La Llorona; La Virgen de
Guadalupe; *Leyendas; Malinche; Mexico;
Women.

5868 Limon, Jose E. [anthropologist]. La Llorona,
the third legend of greater Mexico: cultural
symbols, women, and the political
unconscious. IN: Del Castillo, Adelaida R.
BETWEEN BORDERS: ESSAYS ON MEXICANA/CHICANA
HISTORY. Encino, CA: Floricanto Press, 1990,
p. 399-432. English. DESCR: *Feminism;
Folklore; *La Llorona; La Virgen de
Guadalupe; *Leyendas; Malinche; Mexico;
Women.

5869 Ortiz, Carmen G. The influence of religious
images on perceptions of femininity among
women of Mexican origin. Thesis
(Ph.D.)--California School of Professional
Psychology, Berkeley, 1988. 210 p. English.
DESCR: Catholic Church; *Identity;
*Religion; *Sexual Behavior.

Symbolism (cont.)

5870 Phillips, Rachel. Marina/Malinche: masks and shadows. IN: Miller, Beth, ed. WOMEN IN HISPANIC LITERATURE: ICONS AND FALLEN IDOLS. Berkeley, CA: University of California Press, 1983, p. 97-114. English. **DESCR:** Aztecs; History; Malinche; Psychohistory.

5871 Salas, Elizabeth. Soldaderas in the Mexican military: myth and history. Austin, TX: University of Texas Press, 1990. xiii, 163 p., [12] p. of plates: ill. English. **DESCR:** Aztecs; History; *La Adelita; Mexican Revolution - 1910-1920; Mexico; *Military; War; *Women.

5872 Salas, Elizabeth. Soldaderas in the Mexican military: myth and history. Thesis (Ph.D.)--University of California, Los Angeles, 1987. 313p. English. **DESCR:** Aztecs; History; La Adelita; Mexican Revolution - 1910-1920; Mexico; Military; War; *Women.

5873 Soto, Shirlene Ann. Tres modelos culturales: la Virgen de Guadalupe, la Malinche y la Llorona. FEM, Vol. 10, no. 48 (October, November, 1986), p. 13-16. Spanish. **DESCR:** Guadalupanismo; *La Llorona; *La Virgen de Guadalupe; *Malinche; Women.

5874 Tafolla, Carmen. Chicano literature: beyond beginnings. IN: Harris, Marie and Aguero, Kathleen, eds. A GIFT OF TONGUES: CRITICAL CHALLENGES IN CONTEMPORARY AMERICAN POETRY. Athens, GA: University of Georgia Press, 1987, p. 206-225. English. **DESCR:** *Authors; Cota-Cardenas, Margarita; Language Usage; *Literary Criticism; *Literature; Portillo Trambley, Estela; Sex Stereotypes; Tafolla, Carmen; Vigil-Pinon, Evangelina.

5875 Trujillo Gaitan, Marcella. The dilemma of the modern Chicana artist and critic. DE COLORES, Vol. 3, no. 3 (1977), p. 38-48. Bilingual. **DESCR:** Art Criticism; Artists; *Chicano Movement; Gonzales, Sylvia Alicia; *Literary Criticism; Machismo; Malinche; *Poetry.

5876 Trujillo Gaitan, Marcella. The dilemma of the modern Chicana artist and critic. HERESIES, Vol. 2, no. 4 (1979), p. 5-10. English. **DESCR:** Art Criticism; Artists; Authors; *Chicano Movement; Gonzales, Sylvia Alicia; *Literary Criticism; Machismo; Malinche; *Poetry.

5877 Zamora, Bernice. Mythopoeia of Chicano poetry: an introduction to cultural archetypes. Thesis (Ph.D.)--Stanford University, 1986. 341 p. English. **DESCR:** Literary Characters; Literary Criticism; Literature; Malinche; Pachucos; *Poetry.

Tafolla, Carmen

5878 Alarcon, Norma. What kind of lover have you made me, Mother?: towards a theory of Chicanas' feminism and cultural identity through poetry. IN: McCluskey, Audrey T., ed. WOMEN OF COLOR: PERSPECTIVES ON FEMINISM AND IDENTITY. Bloomington, IN: Women's Studies Program, Indiana University, 1985, p. 85-110. English. **DESCR:** Brinson-Pineda, Barbara; Cervantes, Lorna Dee; Cisneros, Sandra; Culture; *Feminism; Identity; *Literary Criticism; Mora, Pat; Moraga, Cherrie; *Poetry; Vigil-Pinon, Evangelina; Villanueva, Alma.

5879 Del Rio, Carmen M. Chicana poets: re-visions from the margin. REVISTA CANADIENSE DE ESTUDIOS HISPANICOS, Vol. 14, no. 3 (Spring 1990), p. 431-445. English. **DESCR:** Authors; *Feminism; *Literary Criticism; *Poetry; Villanueva, Alma.

5880 Lindstrom, Naomi. Four representative Hispanic women poets of Central Texas: a portrait of plurality. THIRD WOMAN, Vol. 2, no. 1 (1984), p. 64-70. English. **DESCR:** Beltran, Beatriz; de Hoyos, Angela; Jimenez, Magali; *Literary Criticism; Poetry; Texas.

5881 Ordonez, Elizabeth J. The concept of cultural identity in Chicana poetry. THIRD WOMAN, Vol. 2, no. 1 (1984), p. 75-82. English. **DESCR:** Cervantes, Lorna Dee; Corpi, Lucha; *Literary Criticism; Poetry; Villanueva, Alma.

5882 Tafolla, Carmen. Chicano literature: beyond beginnings. IN: Harris, Marie and Aguero, Kathleen, eds. A GIFT OF TONGUES: CRITICAL CHALLENGES IN CONTEMPORARY AMERICAN POETRY. Athens, GA: University of Georgia Press, 1987, p. 206-225. English. **DESCR:** *Authors; Cota-Cardenas, Margarita; Language Usage; *Literary Criticism; *Literature; Portillo Trambley, Estela; Sex Stereotypes; Symbolism; Vigil-Pinon, Evangelina.

Talmadge Amendment to the Social Security Act, 1971

5883 Chicana Welfare Rights challenges Talmadge amendment. REGENERACION, Vol. 2, no. 3 (1973), p. 14. English. **DESCR:** Chicana Welfare Rights Organization; *Feminism; Social Services; *Welfare.

5884 Escalante, Alicia. Chicana Welfare Rights vs. the Talmadge amendment. LA RAZA, Vol. 2, no. 1 (February 1974), p. 20-21. English. **DESCR:** Chicana Welfare Rights Organization; Flores, Francisca; *Welfare.

5885 Escalante, Alicia. A letter from the Chicana Welfare Rights organization. ENCUENTRO FEMENIL, Vol. 1, no. 2 (1974), p. 15-19. English. **DESCR:** *Chicana Welfare Rights Organization; Child Care Centers; Welfare; Working Women.

5886 Flores, Francisca. A reaction to discussions on the Talmadge Amendment to the Social Security Act. ENCUENTRO FEMENIL, Vol. 1, no. 2 (1974), p. 13-14. English. **DESCR:** *Chicana Welfare Rights Organization; Child Care Centers; Discrimination; Feminism; Income; *Social Security Act; Social Services; Welfare; Working Women.

5887 Flores, Francisca. A reaction to discussions on the Talmadge Amendment to the Social Security Act. REGENERACION, Vol. 2, no. 3 (1973), p. 16. English. **DESCR:** *Chicana Welfare Rights Organization; Child Care Centers; Discrimination; Feminism; Income; *Social Security Act; Social Services; Welfare; Working Women.

5888 Nieto Gomez de Lazarin, Anna. Madres por justicia! ENCUENTRO FEMENIL, Vol. 1, no. 1 (Spring 1973), p. 12-19. English. **DESCR:** Chicana Welfare Rights Organization; Employment; *Welfare.

Tamales

5889 Williams, Brett. Why migrant women feed their husbands tamales: Foodways as a basis for a revisionist view of Tejano family life. IN: Brown, Linda Keller and Mussell, Kay, eds. ETHNIC AND REGIONAL FOODWAYS IN THE UNITED STATES: THE PERFORMANCE OF GROUP IDENTITY. Knoxville, TN: University of Tennessee Press, 1984, p. 113-125. English. DESCR: Cultural Customs; Extended Family; Family; *Food Practices; Illinois; *Migrant Labor; Sex Roles; Texas.

Teacher Attitudes

5890 Parra, Elena and Henderson, Ronald W. Mexican American perceptions of parent and teacher roles in child development. IN: Fishman, Joshua A. and Keller, Gary D., eds. BILINGUAL EDUCATION FOR HISPANIC STUDENTS IN THE UNITED STATES. New York: Teachers College Press, 1982, p. 289-299. English. DESCR: *Children; Family; *Parenting; Sex Roles.

Teacher-Pupil Interaction

5891 de Anda, Diane. A study of the interaction of Hispanic junior high school students and their teachers. HISPANIC JOURNAL OF BEHAVIORAL SCIENCES, Vol. 4, no. 1 (March 1982), p. 57-74. English. DESCR: Dropouts; Junior High School.

Teaching
USE: Education

Teaching Profession

5892 Ortiz, Flora Ida. The distribution of Mexican American women in school organizations. HISPANIC JOURNAL OF BEHAVIORAL SCIENCES, Vol. 4, no. 2 (June 1982), p. 181-198. English. DESCR: Educational Administration; Educational Organizations.

Teatro

5893 Arizmendi, Yareli. La mujer y el teatro chicano. IN: Lopez-Gonzalez, Aralia, et al., eds. MUJER Y LITERATURA MEXICANA Y CHICANA: CULTURAS EN CONTACTO. Mexico: Colegio de la Frontera Norte, 1988, p. [85]-91. Spanish. DESCR: Chicano Movement.

5894 Bouknight, Jon. Language as a cure: an interview with Milcha Sanchez-Scott. LATIN AMERICAN THEATRE REVIEW, Vol. 23, no. 2 (Spring 1990), p. 63-74. English. DESCR: Actos; *Authors; ROOSTERS [play]; Sanchez-Scott, Milcha.

5895 Broyles-Gonzalez, Yolanda and Rodriguez, Diane. The living legacy of Chicana performers: preserving history through oral testimony. FRONTIERS: A JOURNAL OF WOMEN STUDIES, Vol. 11, no. 1 (1990), p. [46]-52. English. DESCR: *Actors and Actresses; El Teatro Campesino; Latins Anonymous [comedy review]; Oral History; *Rodriguez, Diane; Sex Roles; Singers.

5896 Broyles-Gonzalez, Yolanda. Women in El Teatro Campesino: "A poco estaba molacha la Virgen de Guadalupe?". IN: Cordova, Teresa, et al., eds. CHICANA VOICES. Austin, TX: Center for Mexican American Studies, 1986, p. 162-187. English. DESCR: Actors and Actresses; CORRIDOS [play]; *El Teatro Campesino; Stereotypes; Valdez, Socorro.

5897 Heard, Martha E. The theatre of Denise Chavez: interior landscapes with SABOR NUEVOMEXICANO. THE AMERICAS REVIEW, Vol. 16, no. 2 (Summer 1988), p. 83-91. English. DESCR: *Chavez, Denise; EL CAMINO [play]; Literary Criticism; New Mexico; PLAZA [play].

5898 Mason, Terry. Symbolic strategies for change: a discussion of the Chicana women's movement. IN: Melville, Margarita B., ed. TWICE A MINORITY. St. Louis, MO: Mosby, 1980, p. 95-108. English. DESCR: Actos; Anglo Americans; *Feminism; Women.

5899 Melville, Margarita B. Female and male in Chicano theatre. IN: Kanellos, Nicolas, ed. HISPANIC THEATRE IN THE UNITED STATES. Houston, TX: Arte Publico Press, 1984, p. 71-79. English. DESCR: BERNABE; BRUJERIAS [play]; Cultural Characteristics; DAY OF THE SWALLOWS; Duarte-Clark, Rodrigo; EL JARDIN [play]; Family; Feminism; Macias, Ysidro; Morton, Carlos; Portillo Trambley, Estela; RANCHO HOLLYWOOD [play]; *Sex Roles; THE ULTIMATE PENDEJADA [play]; Valdez, Luis; Women Men Relations.

5900 Rios-C., Herminio; Romano-V., Octavio Ignacio; and Portillo Trambley, Estela. Chicanas en la literatura y el arte (El Grito Book Series: Book 1, September 1973). EL GRITO, Vol. 7, no. 1 (Fall 1973), p. 1-84. Bilingual. DESCR: *Art; Authors; *Poems.

5901 Salazar Parr, Carmen. La Chicana in literature. IN: Garcia, Eugene E., et al., eds. CHICANO STUDIES: A MULTIDISCIPLINARY APPROACH. New York: Teachers College Press, 1984, p. 120-134. English. DESCR: DAY OF THE SWALLOWS; Literary Characters; Literary Criticism; *Literature; Portillo Trambley, Estela; Stereotypes; "The Trees" [short story].

5902 Yarbro-Bejarano, Yvonne. Cherrie Moraga's GIVING UP THE GHOST: the representation of female desire. THIRD WOMAN, Vol. 3, no. 1-2 (1986), p. 113-120. English. DESCR: *GIVING UP THE GHOST; Homosexuality; Moraga, Cherrie.

5903 Yarbro-Bejarano, Yvonne. Chicana's experience in collective theatre: ideology and form. WOMEN AND PERFORMANCE, Vol. 2, no. 2 (1985), p. 45-58. English. DESCR: Actors and Actresses; Careers; El Teatro Campesino; El Teatro de la Esperanza; Political Ideology; *San Francisco Mime Troupe; Sex Roles; Teatro Libertad; Valentina Productions; Women.

5904 Yarbro-Bejarano, Yvonne. The female subject in Chicano theater: sexuality, race, and class. THEATRE JOURNAL, Vol. 38, no. 4 (December 1986), p. 389-407. English. DESCR: El Teatro Campesino; El Teatro de la Esperanza; El Teatro Nacional de Aztlan (TENAZ); Feminism; *Malinche; *Sex Roles; Women in Teatro (WIT).

5905 Yarbro-Bejarano, Yvonne. The image of the Chicana in teatro. IN: Cochran, Jo; Stewart, J.T.; and Tsutakawa, Mayumi, eds. GATHERING GROUND: NEW WRITING AND ART BY NORTHWEST WOMEN OF COLOR. Seattle, WA: Seal Press, 1984, p. 90-96. English. DESCR: El Teatro de la Esperanza; GUADALUPE [play]; HIJOS: ONCE A FAMILY [play]; LA VICTIMA [play]; *Literary Characters; Sex Roles; Sex Stereotypes; Stereotypes; THE OCTOPUS [play]; Women Men Relations.

Teatro (cont.)

5906 Yarbro-Bejarano, Yvonne. Teatropoesia by Chicanas in the Bay Area: TONGUES OF FIRE. REVISTA CHICANO-RIQUENA, Vol. 11, no. 1 (Spring 1983), p. 78-94. English. **DESCR:** El Teatro Nacional de Aztlan (TENAZ); Poems; San Francisco Bay Area; TONGUES OF FIRE.

El Teatro Campesino

5907 Broyles-Gonzalez, Yolanda and Rodriguez, Diane. The living legacy of Chicana performers: preserving history through oral testimony. FRONTIERS: A JOURNAL OF WOMEN STUDIES, Vol. 11, no. 1 (1990), p. [46]-52. English. **DESCR:** *Actors and Actresses; Latins Anonymous [comedy review]; Oral History; *Rodriguez, Diane; Sex Roles; Singers; Teatro.

5908 Broyles-Gonzalez, Yolanda. Women in El Teatro Campesino: "A poco estaba molacha la Virgen de Guadalupe?". IN: Cordova, Teresa, et al., eds. CHICANA VOICES. Austin, TX: Center for Mexican American Studies, 1986, p. 162-187. English. **DESCR:** Actors and Actresses; CORRIDOS [play]; Stereotypes; Teatro; Valdez, Socorro.

5909 Yarbro-Bejarano, Yvonne. Chicana's experience in collective theatre: ideology and form. WOMEN AND PERFORMANCE, Vol. 2, no. 2 (1985), p. 45-58. English. **DESCR:** Actors and Actresses; Careers; El Teatro de la Esperanza; Political Ideology; *San Francisco Mime Troupe; Sex Roles; Teatro; Teatro Libertad; Valentina Productions; Women.

5910 Yarbro-Bejarano, Yvonne. The female subject in Chicano theater: sexuality, race, and class. THEATRE JOURNAL, Vol. 38, no. 4 (December 1986), p. 389-407. English. **DESCR:** El Teatro de la Esperanza; El Teatro Nacional de Aztlan (TENAZ); Feminism; *Malinche; *Sex Roles; *Teatro; Women in Teatro (WIT).

El Teatro de la Esperanza

5911 Yarbro-Bejarano, Yvonne. Chicana's experience in collective theatre: ideology and form. WOMEN AND PERFORMANCE, Vol. 2, no. 2 (1985), p. 45-58. English. **DESCR:** Actors and Actresses; Careers; El Teatro Campesino; Political Ideology; *San Francisco Mime Troupe; Sex Roles; Teatro; Teatro Libertad; Valentina Productions; Women.

5912 Yarbro-Bejarano, Yvonne. The female subject in Chicano theater: sexuality, race, and class. THEATRE JOURNAL, Vol. 38, no. 4 (December 1986), p. 389-407. English. **DESCR:** El Teatro Campesino; El Teatro Nacional de Aztlan (TENAZ); Feminism; *Malinche; *Sex Roles; *Teatro; Women in Teatro (WIT).

Teatro Libertad

5914 Yarbro-Bejarano, Yvonne. Chicana's

5913 Yarbro-Bejarano, Yvonne. The image of the Chicana in teatro. IN: Cochran, Jo; Stewart, J.T.; and Tsutakawa, Mayumi, eds. GATHERING GROUND: NEW WRITING AND ART BY NORTHWEST WOMEN OF COLOR. Seattle, WA: Seal Press, 1984, p. 90-96. English. **DESCR:** GUADALUPE [play]; HIJOS: ONCE A FAMILY [play]; LA VICTIMA [play]; *Literary Characters; Sex Roles; Sex Stereotypes; Stereotypes; *Teatro; THE OCTOPUS [play]; Women Men Relations.

experience in collective theatre: ideology and form. WOMEN AND PERFORMANCE, Vol. 2, no. 2 (1985), p. 45-58. English. **DESCR:** Actors and Actresses; Careers; El Teatro Campesino; El Teatro de la Esperanza; Political Ideology; *San Francisco Mime Troupe; Sex Roles; Teatro; Valentina Productions; Women.

El Teatro Nacional de Aztlan (TENAZ)

5915 Yarbro-Bejarano, Yvonne. The female subject in Chicano theater: sexuality, race, and class. THEATRE JOURNAL, Vol. 38, no. 4 (December 1986), p. 389-407. English. **DESCR:** El Teatro Campesino; El Teatro de la Esperanza; Feminism; *Malinche; *Sex Roles; *Teatro; Women in Teatro (WIT).

5916 Yarbro-Bejarano, Yvonne. Teatropoesia by Chicanas in the Bay Area: TONGUES OF FIRE. REVISTA CHICANO-RIQUENA, Vol. 11, no. 1 (Spring 1983), p. 78-94. English. **DESCR:** Poems; San Francisco Bay Area; *Teatro; TONGUES OF FIRE.

Tecatos
USE: Drug Addicts

Television

5917 Nava, Yolanda. Chicanas in the television media. IN: LA CHICANA: BUILDING FOR THE FUTURE, AN ACTION PLAN FOR THE 80s. Oakland, CA: National Hispanic University, 1981, p. 120-133. English. **DESCR:** Careers; Employment; Stereotypes.

Tenayuca, Emma

5918 Calderon, Roberto R. and Zamora, Emilio, Jr. Manuela Solis Sager and Emma Tenayuca: a tribute. IN: Cordova, Teresa, et al., eds. CHICANA VOICES. Austin, TX: Center for Mexican American Studies, 1986, p. 30-41. English. **DESCR:** Agricultural Labor Unions; Biography; History; Labor; *Solis Sager, Manuela; South Texas Agricultural Worker's Union (STAWU); United Cannery Agricultural Packing and Allied Workers of America (UCAPAWA).

5919 Calderon, Roberto R. and Zamora, Emilio, Jr. Manuela Solis Sager and Emma Tenayuca: a tribute. IN: Del Castillo, Adelaida R., ed. BETWEEN BORDERS: ESSAYS ON MEXICANA/CHICANA HISTORY. Encino, CA: Floricanto Press, 1990, p. 269-279. English. **DESCR:** Agricultural Labor Unions; Biography; History; Labor; *Solis Sager, Manuela; South Texas Agricultural Worker's Union (STAWU); United Cannery Agricultural Packing and Allied Workers of America (UCAPAWA).

5920 Delgado Campbell, Dolores. Shattering the stereotype: Chicanas as labor union organizers. BERKELEY WOMEN OF COLOR, no. 11 (Summer 1983), p. 20-23. English. **DESCR:** Farah Manufacturing Co., El Paso, TX; Farah Strike; *Gonzalez Parsons, Lucia; Huerta, Dolores; *Labor Unions; Moreno, Luisa [union organizer]; Working Women.

5921 Goldman, Shifra M. Trabajadoras mexicanas y chicanas en las artes visuales. IN: Leal, Salvador, ed. A TRAVES DE LA FRONTERA. Mexico, D.F.: Centro de Estudios Economicos y Sociales del Tercer Mundo, A.C.; Instituto de Investigaciones Esteticas, U.N.A.M., 1983, p. 153-161. Spanish. **DESCR:** Art; Gonzalez Parsons, Lucia; Huerta, Dolores; Moreno, Luisa [union organizer]; SALT OF THE EARTH [film]; *Working Women.

Tenayuca, Emma (cont.)

5922 Mirande, Alfredo and Enriquez, Evangelina. Chicanas in the struggle for unions. IN: Duran, Livie Isauro and Bernard, H. Russell, eds. INTRODUCTION TO CHICANO STUDIES. 2nd. ed. New York: Macmillan, 1973, p. 325-337. English. DESCR: Gonzalez Parsons, Lucia; *Labor Unions; Moreno, Luisa [union organizer]; Parsons, Albert; United Cannery Agricultural Packing and Allied Workers of America (UCAPAWA).

5923 Rips, Geoffrey and Tenayuca, Emma. Living history: Emma Tenayuca tells her story. TEXAS OBSERVER, (October 28, 1983), p. 7-15. English. DESCR: Autobiography; Communist Party; Food Industry; Labor Unions; Leadership; Oral History; Pecan Shelling Worker's Union, San Antonio, TX; San Antonio, TX; Strikes and Lockouts; United Cannery Agricultural Packing and Allied Workers of America (UCAPAWA); Worker's Alliance (WA), Los Angeles, CA; Working Women.

Tenepal, Malintzin
   USE: Malinche

Texas

5924 Arroyo, Laura E. Industrial and occupational distribution of Chicana workers. AZTLAN, Vol. 4, no. 2 (Fall 1973), p. 343-382. English. DESCR: California; *Employment; Farah Manufacturing Co., El Paso, TX; Farah Strike; Garment Industry; Industrial Workers; Strikes and Lockouts.

5925 Arroyo, Laura E. Industrial and occupational distribution of Chicana workers. IN: Sanchez, Rosaura and Martinez Cruz, Rosa, eds. ESSAYS ON LA MUJER. Los Angeles, CA: Chicano Studies Center Publications, UCLA, 1977, p. 150-187. English. DESCR: California; *Employment; Farah Manufacturing Co., El Paso, TX; Farah Strike; Garment Industry; Industrial Workers; Strikes and Lockouts.

5926 Cazares, Ralph B.; Murguia, Edward; and Frisbie, William Parker. Mexican American intermarriage in a nonmetropolitan context. SOCIAL SCIENCE QUARTERLY, Vol. 65, no. 2 (June 1984), p. 626-634. English. DESCR: Age Groups; *Intermarriage; Pecos County, TX; Social Classes.

5927 Cazares, Ralph B.; Murguia, Edward; and Frisbie, William Parker. Mexican American intermarriage in a nonmetropolitan context. IN: O. de la Garza, Rodolfo, et al., eds. THE MEXICAN AMERICAN EXPERIENCE: AN INTERDISCIPLINARY ANTHOLOGY. Austin, TX: University of Texas Press, 1985, p. 393-401. English. DESCR: Age Groups; *Intermarriage; Pecos County, TX; Social Classes.

5928 Cisneros, Sandra. Cactus flowers: in search of Tejana feminist poetry. THIRD WOMAN, Vol. 3, no. 1-2 (1986), p. 73-80. English. DESCR: Authors; *Feminism; Literary Criticism; *Poetry.

5929 Estrada, Rosa Omega. A study of the attitudes of Texas Mexican American women toward higher education. Thesis (Ed.D.)--Baylor University, 1985. 280 p. English. DESCR: *Attitudes; Education; *Higher Education.

5930 Galindo, Letticia. Perceptions of pachuquismo and use of Calo/pachuco Spanish by various Chicana women. LA RED/THE NET,

no. 48 (November 1981), p. 2,10. English. DESCR: Chicano Dialects; Language Usage.

5931 Galloway, Irma Nell. Trends in the employment of minority women as administrators in Texas public schools--1976-1981. Thesis (Ed.D.)--Texas Southern University, 1986. 129 p. English. DESCR: Asian Americans; Blacks; Education; *Educational Administration; *Management; Native Americans; *Women.

5932 Goldman, Shifra M. Artistas chicanas texanas. FEM, Vol. 8, no. 34 (June, July, 1984), p. 29-31. Spanish. DESCR: *Artists; Mujeres Artistas del Suroeste (MAS), Austin, TX.

5933 Goldman, Shifra M. Women artists of Texas: MAS = More + Artists + Women = MAS. CHISMEARTE, no. 7 (January 1981), p. 21-22. English. DESCR: Arredondo, Alicia; Art Organizations and Groups; Barraza, Santa; Exhibits; Feminism; Flores, Maria; Folk Art; Gonzalez Dodson, Nora; *Mujeres Artistas del Suroeste (MAS), Austin, TX; Photography; Trevino, Modesta Barbina; WOMEN & THEIR WORK [festival] (Austin, TX: 1977).

5934 Green, George N. ILGWU in Texas, 1930-1970. JOURNAL OF MEXICAN-AMERICAN HISTORY, Vol. 1, no. 2 (Spring 1971), p. 144-169. English. DESCR: History; International Ladies Garment Workers Union (ILGWU); *Labor Unions.

5935 Hernandez, Ines. Sara Estela Ramirez: the early twentieth century Texas-Mexican poet. Thesis (Ph.D.)--University of Houston, 1984. 94 p. English. DESCR: *Authors; *Biography; Feminism; Flores Magon, Ricardo; Journalism; Literary Criticism; Mexican Revolution - 1910-1920; Mexico; *Poetry; Ramirez, Sara Estela; Women.

5936 Hintz, Joy. Valiant migrant women = Las mujeres valerosas. Tiffin, OH: Sayger Printing, 1982. viii, 98 p. English. DESCR: Battered Women; *Farm Workers; Feminism; Florida; Marriage; Migrant Children; Migrant Health Services; Migrant Housing; *Migrant Labor; Migration Patterns; Ohio; Sex Roles.

5937 Leblanc, Donna Marie. Quality of maternity care in rural Texas. Thesis (Dr. P.H.) --University of Texas H.S.C. at Houston School of Public Health, 1983. 266 p. English. DESCR: Fertility; Low Income; *Maternal and Child Welfare; *Medical Care; Prenatal Care; *Rural Poor.

5938 Lindstrom, Naomi. Four representative Hispanic women poets of Central Texas: a portrait of plurality. THIRD WOMAN, Vol. 2, no. 1 (1984), p. 64-70. English. DESCR: Beltran, Beatriz; de Hoyos, Angela; Jimenez, Magali; *Literary Criticism; Poetry; Tafolla, Carmen.

5939 MacManus, Susan A.; Bullock, Charles S.; and Grothe, Barbara P. A longitudinal examination of political participation rates of Mexican-American females. SOCIAL SCIENCE QUARTERLY, Vol. 67, no. 3 (1986), p. 604-612. English. DESCR: *Voter Turnout.

5940 Stewart, Kenneth L. and de Leon, Arnoldo. Fertility among Mexican Americans and Anglos in Texas, 1900. BORDERLANDS JOURNAL, Vol. 9, no. 1 (Spring 1986), p. 61-67. English. DESCR: Anglo Americans; *Fertility; Women.

Texas (cont.)

5941 Stewart, Kenneth L. and de Leon, Arnoldo. Work force participation among Mexican immigrant women in Texas, 1900. BORDERLANDS JOURNAL, Vol. 9, no. 1 (Spring 1986), p. 69-74. English. DESCR: Employment; History; *Immigrants; Women; *Working Women.

5942 Williams, Brett. Why migrant women feed their husbands tamales: foodways as a basis for a revisionist view of Tejano family life. IN: Brown, Linda Keller and Mussell, Kay, eds. ETHNIC AND REGIONAL FOODWAYS IN THE UNITED STATES: THE PERFORMANCE OF GROUP IDENTITY. Knoxville, TN: University of Tennessee Press, 1984, p. 113-126. English. DESCR: Cultural Customs; Extended Family; Family; *Food Practices; Illinois; *Migrant Labor; Sex Roles; Tamales.

Texas Migrant Council Headstart Program

5943 de Leon Siantz, Mary Lou. Maternal acceptance/rejection of Mexican migrant mothers. PSYCHOLOGY OF WOMEN QUARTERLY, Vol. 14, no. 2 (June 1990), p. 245-254. English. DESCR: Child Study; Farm Workers; *Migrant Children; Migrant Labor; Natural Support Systems; *Parent and Child Relationships; Stress.

Textbooks

5944 Cotera, Marta P. Sexism in bilingual bicultural education. IN: Cotera, Martha and Hufford, Larry, eds. BRIDGING TWO CULTURES. Austin, TX: National Educational Laboratory Publishers, 1980, p. 181-190. English. DESCR: *Bilingual Bicultural Education; Sex Roles; Sexism; Stereotypes.

Theater
USE: Teatro

THERE ARE NO MADMEN HERE

5945 Lizarraga, Sylvia S. La mujer ingeniosa. FEM, Vol. 8, no. 34 (June, July, 1984), p. 41. Spanish. DESCR: Literary Criticism; Novel; *Valdes, Gina.

5946 Lizarraga, Sylvia S. The resourceful woman in THERE ARE NO MADMEN HERE. THIRD WOMAN, Vol. 2, no. 1 (1984), p. 71-74. English. DESCR: *Literary Criticism; Valdes, Gina.

5947 Quintana, Alvina E. Challenge and counter challenge: Chicana literary motifs. AGAINST THE CURRENT, Vol. 2, no. 2 (March, April, 1987), p. 25,28-32. English. DESCR: Anglo Americans; Authors; Cervantes, Lorna Dee; Cultural Studies; *Feminism; Identity; Literary Criticism; *Literature; Moraga, Cherrie; Valdes, Gina; Women.

5948 Quintana, Alvina E. Chicana literary motifs: challenge and counter-challenge. IMAGES: ETHNIC STUDIES OCCASIONAL PAPERS SERIES, (Fall 1986), p. 24-41. English. DESCR: Anglo Americans; Authors; Cervantes, Lorna Dee; Cultural Studies; *Feminism; *Identity; *Literary Criticism; Literature; Moraga, Cherrie; Valdes, Gina; Women.

THIRD WOMAN [journal]

5949 Alarcon, Norma. Latina writers in the United States. IN: Marting, Diane E., ed. SPANISH AMERICAN WOMEN WRITERS: A BIO-BIBLIOGRAPHICAL SOURCE BOOK. New York: Greenwood Press, 1990, p. [557]-567. English. DESCR: *Authors; *Bibliography; BREAKING BOUNDARIES: LATINA WRITING AND CRITICAL READINGS; Cubanos; Intergroup Relations; Language Usage; *Literature Reviews; Puerto Ricans; *Women.

THIRD WOMAN: OF LATINAS IN THE MIDWEST

5950 Alarcon, Norma. Hay que inventarnos/we must invent ourselves. THIRD WOMAN, Vol. 1, no. 1 (1981), p. 4-6. English. DESCR: Art; Journals; Midwest Latina Writer's Workshop (1980: Chicago); Midwestern States; Third World Literature (U.S.).

Third World

5951 Olivares, Yvette. The sweatshop: the garment industry's reborn child. REVISTA MUJERES, Vol. 3, no. 2 (June 1986), p. 55-62. English. DESCR: Garment Industry; Labor; Public Health; *Undocumented Workers; *Women; Working Women.

Third World Literature (U.S.)

5952 Alarcon, Norma. Hay que inventarnos/we must invent ourselves. THIRD WOMAN, Vol. 1, no. 1 (1981), p. 4-6. English. DESCR: Art; Journals; Midwest Latina Writer's Workshop (1980: Chicago); Midwestern States; *THIRD WOMAN: OF LATINAS IN THE MIDWEST.

THIRTY AN' SEEN A LOT

5953 Treacy, Mary Jane. The ties that bind: women and community in Evangelina Vigil's THIRTY AN' SEEN A LOT. IN: Horno-Delgado, Asuncion, et al., eds. BREAKING BOUNDARIES: LATINA WRITING AND CRITICAL READINGS. Amherst, MA: University of Massachusetts Press, c1989, p. 82-93. English. DESCR: Identity; Literary Criticism; Poetry; Sexism; *Vigil-Pinon, Evangelina.

THIS BRIDGE CALLED MY BACK

5954 Alarcon, Norma. The theoretical subject(s) of THIS BRIDGE CALLED MY BACK and Anglo-American feminism. IN: Calderon, Hector and Saldivar, Jose David, eds. CRITICISM IN THE BORDERLANDS: STUDIES IN CHICANO LITERATURE, CULTURE, AND IDEOLOGY. Durham, NC: Duke University Press, 1991, p. [28]-39. English. DESCR: *Anglo Americans; Anzaldua, Gloria; *Feminism; Moraga, Cherrie; *Women.

5955 Alarcon, Norma. The theoretical subject(s) of THIS BRIDGE CALLED MY BACK and Anglo-American feminism. IN: Anzaldua, Gloria, ed. MAKING FACE, MAKING SOUL: HACIENDO CARAS: CREATIVE AND CRITICAL PERSPECTIVES BY WOMEN OF COLOR. San Francisco, CA: Aunt Lute Foundation Books, 1990, p. 356-369. English. DESCR: *Anglo Americans; Anzaldua, Gloria; *Feminism; Literary Criticism; Moraga, Cherrie; *Women.

Tiano, Susan B.

5956 Garcia, Mario T. Family and gender in Chicano and border studies research. MEXICAN STUDIES/ESTUDIOS MEXICANOS, Vol. 6, no. 1 (Winter 1990), p. 109-119. English. DESCR: Alvarez, Robert R., Jr.; *Border Region; CANNERY WOMEN, CANNERY LIVES; *Family; LA FAMILIA: MIGRATION AND ADAPTATION IN BAJA AND ALTA CALIFORNIA, 1800-1975; *Literature Reviews; Ruiz, Vicki L.; Women; WOMEN ON THE U.S.-MEXICO BORDER: RESPONSES TO CHANGE; WOMEN'S WORK AND CHICANO FAMILIES; Zavella, Pat.

Tijuana, Baja California, Mexico

5957 Hovell, Melbourne F., et al. Occupational health risks for Mexican women: the case of the maquiladora along the Mexican-United States border. INTERNATIONAL JOURNAL OF HEALTH SERVICES, Vol. 18, no. 4 (1988), p. 617-627. English. DESCR: *Border Industries; Border Region; Mexico; *Occupational Hazards; Project Concern International (PCI), San Diego, CA; Public Health; Surveys; Women; Working Women.

5958 Iglesias, Norma. La flor mas bella de la maquiladora: historias de vida de la mujer obrera en Tijuana, B.C.N. Mexico, D.F.: Secretaria de Educacion Publica, CEFNOMEX, 1985. 166 p.: ill. Spanish. DESCR: Border Industrialization Program (BIP); *Border Industries; Cultural Customs; Labor Unions; Sindicato Independiente Solidev; Solidev Mexicana, S.A.; *Women; Working Women.

5959 In the maquiladoras. CORRESPONDENCIA, no. 9 (December 1990), p. 3-9. English. DESCR: *Border Industries; Labor Unions; Women; *Working Women.

5960 Lawrence, Alberto Augusto. Traditional attitudes toward marriage, marital adjustment, acculturation, and self-esteem of Mexican-American and Mexican wives. Thesis (Ph.D.)--United States International University, San Diego, CA, 1982. ix, 191 p. English. DESCR: *Acculturation; *Attitudes; Machismo; *Marriage; Mental Health; Psychological Testing; San Ysidro, CA; Sex Roles; Sex Stereotypes; Women.

5961 Sweeny, Mary Anne and Gulino, Claire. The health belief model as an explanation for breast-feeding practices in a Hispanic population. ANS: ADVANCES IN NURSING SCIENCE, Vol. 9, no. 4 (July 1987), p. 35-50. English. DESCR: *Breastfeeding; *Cultural Customs; *Public Health; San Diego, CA; Women.

Title VII Bilingual Education Doctoral Fellowship Program

5962 Flores, Laura Jane. A study of successful completion and attrition among Chicana Title VII Bilingual Education Doctoral Fellows at selected Southwestern universities. Thesis (Ed.D.)--New Mexico State University, 1984. 145 p. English. DESCR: Academic Achievement; Colleges and Universities; Graduate Schools; *Higher Education.

Toledo, OH

5963 Macklin, June and Teniente de Costilla, Alvina. Virgen de Guadalupe and the American dream: the melting pot bubbles on in Toledo, Ohio. IN: West, Stanley A. and Macklin, June, eds. THE CHICANO EXPERIENCE. Boulder, CO: Westview Press, 1979, p. 111-143. English. DESCR: Assimilation; Catholic Church; *Identity; Intermarriage; La Virgen de Guadalupe; Migration Patterns; Quinceaneras.

Toltec Foods, Richmond, CA

5964 Mora, Magdalena. The Tolteca Strike: Mexican women and the struggle for union representation. IN: Rios-Bustamante, Antonio, ed. MEXICAN IMMIGRANT WORKERS IN THE U.S. Los Angeles, CA: Chicano Studies Research Center Publications, University of California, 1981, p. 111-117. English. DESCR: Centro de Accion Social Autonomo (CASA); Food Industry; *Labor Unions; *Strikes and Lockouts.

TONGUES OF FIRE

5965 Yarbro-Bejarano, Yvonne. Teatropoesia by Chicanas in the Bay Area: TONGUES OF FIRE. REVISTA CHICANO-RIQUENA, Vol. 11, no. 1 (Spring 1983), p. 78-94. English. DESCR: El Teatro Nacional de Aztlan (TENAZ); Poems; San Francisco Bay Area; *Teatro.

Toxic Shock Syndrome (TSS)

5966 Finkelstein, Jordan W. and Von Eye, Alexander. Sanitary product use by white, Black, and Mexican American women. PUBLIC HEALTH REPORTS, Vol. 105, no. 5 (September, October, 1990), p. 491-496. English. DESCR: Anglo Americans; Blacks; *Menstruation; *Women.

Trade Unions

5967 Pena, Devon Gerardo. The class politics of abstract labor: organizational forms and industrial relations in the Mexican maquiladoras. Thesis (Ph.D.)--University of Texas, Austin, 1983. xix, 587 p. English. DESCR: *Border Industries; Border Region; International Economic Relations; Women; Working Women.

5968 Ruiz, Vicki L. Cannery women/cannery lives: Mexican women, unionization, and the California food processing industry, 1930-1950. Albuquerque, NM: University of New Mexico Press, 1987. xviii, 194 p.: ill. English. DESCR: Agricultural Labor Unions; California; *Canneries; Family; History; Industrial Workers; Labor Disputes; *Labor Unions; United Cannery Agricultural Packing and Allied Workers of America (UCAPAWA); Women.

5969 Ruiz, Vicki L. UCAPAWA, Chicanas, and the California food processing industry, 1937-1950. Thesis (Ph.D.)--Stanford University, 1982. x, 281 p. English. DESCR: *Canneries; Food Industry; *Labor Unions; United Cannery Agricultural Packing and Allied Workers of America (UCAPAWA); Working Women.

Training Programs
USE: Employment Training

Trambley, Estela Portillo
USE: Portillo Trambley, Estela

TRAVELS IN CALIFORNIA AND SCENES IN THE PACIFIC OCEAN

5970 Castaneda, Antonia I. The political economy of nineteenth century stereotypes of Californianas. IN: Del Castillo, Adelaida R., ed. BETWEEN BORDERS: ESSAYS ON MEXICANA/CHICANA HISTORY. Encino, CA: Floricanto Press, 1990, p. 213-236. English. DESCR: *California; *Californios; Dana, Richard Henry; Farnham, Thomas Jefferson; History; LIFE IN CALIFORNIA; *Political Economy; Robinson, Alfred; *Sex Stereotypes; TWO YEARS BEFORE THE MAST; Women.

"The Trees" [short story]

5971 Salazar Parr, Carmen. La Chicana in literature. IN: Garcia, Eugene E., et al., eds. CHICANO STUDIES: A MULTIDISCIPLINARY APPROACH. New York: Teachers College Press, 1984, p. 120-134. English. DESCR: DAY OF THE SWALLOWS; Literary Characters; Literary Criticism; *Literature; Portillo Trambley, Estela; Stereotypes; Teatro.

Trevino, Modesta Barbina

5972 Goldman, Shifra M. Women artists of Texas: MAS = More + Artists + Women = MAS. CHISMEARTE, no. 7 (January 1981), p. 21-22. English. DESCR: Arredondo, Alicia; Art Organizations and Groups; Barraza, Santa; Exhibits; Feminism; Flores, Maria; Folk Art; Gonzalez Dodson, Nora; *Mujeres Artistas del Suroeste (MAS), Austin, TX; Photography; Texas; WOMEN & THEIR WORK [festival] (Austin, TX: 1977).

5973 Orozco, Sylvia. Las mujeres--Chicana artists come into their own. MOVING ON, Vol. 2, no. 3 (May 1978), p. 14-16. English. DESCR: Art Organizations and Groups; Artists; Barraza, Santa; Flores, Maria; Gonzalez Dodson, Nora; *Mujeres Artistas del Suroeste (MAS), Austin, TX.

Tucson, AZ

5974 Campbell, Julie A. Madres y esposas: Tucson's Spanish-American Mothers and Wives Association. JOURNAL OF ARIZONA HISTORY, Vol. 31, no. 2 (Summer 1990), p. 161-182. English. DESCR: History; Military; Organizations; *Spanish-American Mothers and Wives Association, Tucson, AZ; World War II.

5975 Marin, Christine. La Asociacion Hispano-Americana de Madres y Esposas: Tucson's Mexican American women in World War II. RENATO ROSALDO LECTURE SERIES MONOGRAPH, Vol. 1, (Summer 1985), p. [5]-18. English. DESCR: Cultural Organizations; History; *La Asociacion Hispano-Americana de Madres y Esposas, Tucson, AZ; Organizations; World War II.

5976 Preciado Martin, Patricia. Images and conversations: Mexican Americans recall a Southwestern past. Tucson, AZ: University of Arizona Press, 1983. 110 p.: ill. English. DESCR: *Oral History; Photography; Social History and Conditions.

5977 Sheridan, Thomas E. From Luisa Espinel to Lalo Guerrero: Tucson's Mexican musicians before World War II. JOURNAL OF ARIZONA HISTORY, Vol. 25, no. 3 (Fall 1984), p. 285-300. English. DESCR: Biography; Espinel, Luisa Ronstadt; Guerrero, Eduardo "Lalo"; History; Montijo, Manuel; *Musicians; Rebeil, Julia; Singers.

Tujunga Wash Mural, Los Angeles, CA
USE: GREAT WALL OF LOS ANGELES [mural]

Turner, Frederick Jackson

5978 Castaneda, Antonia I. Gender, race, and culture: Spanish-Mexican women in the historiography of frontier California. FRONTIERS: A JOURNAL OF WOMEN STUDIES, Vol. 11, no. 1 (1990), p. [8]-20. English. DESCR: Bancroft, Hubert Howe; Bolton, Herbert Eugene; *California; Californios; *Historiography; History; Intermarriage; *Sex Stereotypes; Spanish Borderlands Theory; Spanish Influence; Stereotypes; Women.

TWICE A MINORITY: MEXICAN-AMERICAN WOMEN

5979 Candelaria, Cordelia. Six reference works on Mexican-American women: a review essay. FRONTIERS: A JOURNAL OF WOMEN STUDIES, Vol. 5, no. 2 (Summer 1980), p. 75-80. English. DESCR: DIOSA Y HEMBRA: THE HISTORY AND HERITAGE OF CHICANAS IN THE U.S.; ESSAYS ON LA MUJER; LA CHICANA: THE MEXICAN AMERICAN WOMAN; *Literature Reviews; MEXICAN WOMEN IN THE UNITED STATES: STRUGGLES PAST AND PRESENT; THE CHICANA: A COMPREHENSIVE BIBLIOGRAPHIC STUDY.

TWO YEARS BEFORE THE MAST

5980 Castaneda, Antonia I. The political economy of nineteenth century stereotypes of Californianas. IN: Del Castillo, Adelaida R., ed. BETWEEN BORDERS: ESSAYS ON MEXICANA/CHICANA HISTORY. Encino, CA: Floricanto Press, 1990, p. 213-236. English. DESCR: *California; *Californios; Dana, Richard Henry; Farnham, Thomas Jefferson; History; LIFE IN CALIFORNIA; *Political Economy; Robinson, Alfred; *Sex Stereotypes; TRAVELS IN CALIFORNIA AND SCENES IN THE PACIFIC OCEAN; Women.

Ulibarri, Sabine R.

5981 Irizarry, Estelle. La abuelita in literature. NUESTRO, Vol. 7, no. 7 (September 1983), p. 50. English. DESCR: Alonso, Luis Ricardo; *Ancianos; Cotto-Thorner, Guillermo; Family; Grandmothers; Valero, Robert.

THE ULTIMATE PENDEJADA [play]

5982 Melville, Margarita B. Female and male in Chicano theatre. IN: Kanellos, Nicolas, ed. HISPANIC THEATRE IN THE UNITED STATES. Houston, TX: Arte Publico Press, 1984, p. 71-79. English. DESCR: BERNABE; BRUJERIAS [play]; Cultural Characteristics; DAY OF THE SWALLOWS; Duarte-Clark, Rodrigo; EL JARDIN [play]; Family; Feminism; Macias, Ysidro; Morton, Carlos; Portillo Trambley, Estela; RANCHO HOLLYWOOD [play]; *Sex Roles; *Teatro; Valdez, Luis; Women Men Relations.

Undocumented Workers

5983 Arguelles, Lourdes. Undocumented female labor in the United States Southwest: an essay on migration, consciousness, oppression and struggle. IN: Del Castillo, Adelaida R., ed. BETWEEN BORDERS: ESSAYS ON MEXICANA/CHICANA HISTORY. Encino, CA: Floricanto Press, 1990, p. 299-312. English. DESCR: Arizona Farm Workers (AFW); Immigrants; Immigration; Working Women.

5984 Baker, Susan Gonzalez. Many rivers to cross: Mexican immigrants, women workers, and the structure of labor markets in the urban Southwest. Thesis (Ph.D.)--University of Texas, Austin, 1989. 163 p. English. DESCR: *Immigrants; Immigration Reform and Control Act of 1986; *Labor Supply and Market; Women; *Working Women.

5985 Cardenas, Gilbert and Flores, Estevan T. The migration and settlement of undocumented women. Austin, TX: CMAS Publications, 1986. 69 p. English. DESCR: Employment; Houston, TX; *Immigration; Income; Labor Supply and Market; *Migration Patterns; Public Policy; Socioeconomic Factors.

Undocumented Workers
(cont.)

5986 Cardenas, Gilbert; Shelton, Beth Anne; and Pena, Devon Gerardo. Undocumented immigrant women in the Houston labor force. CALIFORNIA SOCIOLOGIST, Vol. 5, no. 2 (Summer 1982), p. 98-118. English. DESCR: Employment; Houston, TX; *Immigrants; *Labor Supply and Market.

5987 Corrales, Ramona. Undocumented Hispanas in America. IN: LA CHICANA: BUILDING FOR THE FUTURE, AN ACTION PLAN FOR THE 80s. Oakland CA: National Hispanic University, 1981, p. 59-73. Also IN: THE STATE OF HISPANIC AMERICA II. Oakland, CA: National Hispanic Center Advanced Studies and Policy Analysis, 1982, p. 100-107. English. DESCR: Immigration; Immigration Law and Legislation; Sex Roles.

5988 Curry Rodriguez, Julia E. Labor migration and familial responsibilities: experiences of Mexican women. IN: Melville, Margarita, ed. MEXICANAS AT WORK IN THE UNITED STATES. Houston, TX: Mexican American Studies Program, University of Houston, 1988, p. 47-63. English. DESCR: Employment; Family; *Immigrants; Mexico; *Migrant Labor; Oral History; Sex Roles; *Women; *Working Women.

5989 Curry Rodriguez, Julia E. Reconceptualizing undocumented labor immigration: the causes, impact and consequences in Mexican women's lives. Thesis (Ph.D.)--University of Texas at Austin, 1988. xiv, 329 p. English. DESCR: Employment; *Immigrants; Mexico; Oral History; *Women.

5990 Dixon, Marlene; Martinez, Elizabeth; and McCaughan, Ed. Theoretical perspectives on Chicanas, Mexicanas and the transnational working class. CONTEMPORARY MARXISM, no. 11 (Fall 1985), p. 46-73. English. DESCR: Border Industries; Capitalism; Economic History and Conditions; History; *Immigration; *Labor Supply and Market; *Laboring Classes; Mexico; Women.

5991 Dublin, Thomas. Commentary [on "And Miles to Go": Mexican Women and Work, 1930-1985]. IN: Schlissel, Lillian, et al., eds. WESTERN WOMEN: THEIR LAND, THEIR LIVES. Albuquerque, NM: University of New Mexico Press, 1988, p. 137-140. English. DESCR: "'And Miles to Go...': Mexican Women and Work, 1930-1985"; Employment; Income; Labor Unions; Ruiz, Vicki L.; Women; *Working Women.

5992 Falasco, Dee and Heer, David. Economic and fertility differences between legal and undocumented migrant Mexican families: possible effects of immigration policy changes. SOCIAL SCIENCE QUARTERLY, Vol. 65, no. 2 (June 1984), p. 495-504. English. DESCR: *Economic History and Conditions; *Fertility; *Immigration Law and Legislation; Immigration Regulation and Control; Income.

5993 Fernandez Kelly, Maria. Mexican border industrialization, female labor force participation and migration. IN: Nash, June and Fernandez-Kelly, Patricia, eds. WOMEN, MEN, AND THE INTERNATIONAL DIVISION OF LABOR. Albany, NY: State University of New York Press, 1983, p. 205-223. English. DESCR: Border Industrialization Program (BIP); *Border Industries; Ciudad Juarez, Chihuahua, Mexico; Immigration; Industrial Workers; Labor Supply and Market; Males; *Migration Patterns; *Women; Working Women.

5994 Garcia Castro, Mary. Migrant women: issues in organization and solidarity. MIGRATION WORLD MAGAZINE, Vol. 14, no. 1-2 (1986), p. 15-19. English. DESCR: Labor Supply and Market; *Migrant Labor; Organizations; Political Economy; Women.

5995 Guttmacher, Sally. Women migrant workers in the U.S. CULTURAL SURVIVAL QUARTERLY, Vol. 8, no. 2 (Summer 1984), p. 60-61. English. DESCR: *Migrant Labor; Public Health; *Women.

5996 Hancock, Paula F. The effects of nativity, legal status and welfare eligibility on the labor force participation of women of Mexican origin in California. Thesis (Ph.D.)--University of Southern California, 1985. English. DESCR: *Employment; *Immigrants; *Welfare.

5997 Hogeland, Chris and Rosen, Karen. Dreams lost, dreams found: undocumented women in the land of opportunity. San Francisco, CA: Coalition for Immigrant and Refugee Rights and Services, c1991. 153 p. English. DESCR: *Battered Women; *Coalition for Immigrant and Refugee Rights and Services, Immigrant Woman's Task Force; Discrimination; Immigrants; *San Francisco Bay Area; Sex Roles; Sexism; Social Services; Violence; Women; Women Men Relations.

5998 Jaech, Richard E. Latin American undocumented women in the United States. CURRENTS IN THEOLOGY AND MISSION, Vol. 9, no. 4 (August 1982), p. 196-211. English. DESCR: Garment Industry; Latin Americans; Protestant Church; Socioeconomic Factors; *Women.

5999 Melville, Margarita B. Mexican women adapt to migration. IN: Rios-Bustamante, Antonio, ed. MEXICAN IMMIGRANT WORKERS IN THE U.S. Los Angeles, CA: Chicano Studies Research Center Publications, University of California, 1981, p. 119-124. English. DESCR: Acculturation; Attitudes; Immigrants; Sex Roles; Stress.

6000 O'Connor, Mary I. Women's networks and the social needs of Mexican immigrants. URBAN ANTHROPOLOGY, Vol. 19, no. 1-2 (Spring, Summer, 1990), p. 81-98. English. DESCR: Employment; *Immigrants; Labor Unions; *Natural Support Systems; *Sandyland Nursery, Carpinteria, CA; United Farmworkers of America (UFW); Women.

6001 Olivares, Yvette. The sweatshop: the garment industry's reborn child. REVISTA MUJERES, Vol. 3, no. 2 (June 1986), p. 55-62. English. DESCR: Garment Industry; Labor; Public Health; Third World; *Women; Working Women.

6002 Pena, Manuel. Class, gender, and machismo: the "treacherous-woman" folklore of Mexican male workers. GENDER & SOCIETY, Vol. 5, no. 1 (March 1991), p. 30-46. English. DESCR: *Folklore; Laborers; *Machismo; Males; *Sex Roles; Sex Stereotypes; Social Classes; Women Men Relations.

6003 Rodriguez, Rogelio E. Psychological distress among Mexican-American women as a reaction to the new immigration law. Thesis (Ph.D.)--Loyola University of Chicago, 1989. 87 p. English. DESCR: Depression (Psychological); Immigrants; *Immigration Law and Legislation; Immigration Reform and Control Act of 1986; *Mental Health; Mexico; Stress; Women.

Undocumented Workers
(cont.)

6004 Rodriguez, Rogelio E. and DeWolfe, Alan. Psychological distress among Mexican-American and Mexican women as related to status on the new immigration law. JOURNAL OF CONSULTING AND CLINICAL PSYCHOLOGY, Vol. 58, no. 5 (October 1990), p. 548-553. English. DESCR: *Immigrants; Immigration Law and Legislation; Immigration Reform and Control Act of 1986; Natural Support Systems; *Stress; Women.

6005 Ruiz, Vicki L. "And miles to go...": Mexican women and work, 1930-1985. IN: Schlissel, Lillian, et al., eds. WESTERN WOMEN: THEIR LAND, THEIR LIVES. Albuquerque, NM: University of New Mexico Press, 1988, p. 117-136. English. DESCR: Education; El Paso Women's Employment and Education Project (EPWEE); *Employment; Farah Manufacturing Co., El Paso, TX; Farah Strike; *Income; Industrial Workers; Labor Unions; Statistics; United Cannery Agricultural Packing and Allied Workers of America (UCAPAWA); Women; *Working Women.

6006 Simon, Rita J. and DeLey, Margo. The work experience of undocumented Mexican women migrants in Los Angeles. INTERNATIONAL MIGRATION REVIEW, Vol. 18, no. 4 (Winter 1984), p. 1212-1229. English. DESCR: Immigrants; Income; *Los Angeles, CA; Population; Socioeconomic Factors; *Working Women.

6007 Solorzano-Torres, Rosalia. Female Mexican immigrants in San Diego County. IN: Ruiz, Vicki L. and Tiano, Susan, eds. WOMEN ON THE U.S.-MEXICO BORDER: RESPONSES TO CHANGE. Boston, MA: Allen & Unwin, 1987, p. 41-59. English. DESCR: Employment; *Immigrants; Immigration; Literature Reviews; San Diego County, CA; Surveys; Women.

6008 Solorzano-Torres, Rosalia. Women, labor, and the U.S.-Mexico border: Mexican maids in El Paso, Texas. IN: Melville, Margarita, ed. MEXICANAS AT WORK IN THE UNITED STATES. Houston, TX: Mexican American Studies Program, University of Houston, 1988, p. 75-83. English. DESCR: Border Patrol; *Border Region; Domestic Work; El Paso, TX; Immigrants; Immigration and Naturalization Service (INS); Immigration Regulation and Control; *Labor Supply and Market; *Women; *Working Women.

6009 Stoddard, Ellwyn R. Maquila: assembly plants in Northern Mexico. El Paso, TX: Texas Western Press, 1987. ix, 91 p., [4] p. of plates: ill. English. DESCR: Border Industrialization Program (BIP); *Border Industries; Immigration; Income; *Industrial Workers; Labor Supply and Market; Mexico; Sexism.

6010 Vasquez, Mario F. The election day immigration raid at Lilli Diamond Originals and the response of the ILGWU. IN: Mora, Magdalena and Del Castillo, Adelaida, eds. MEXICAN WOMEN IN THE UNITED STATES: STRUGGLES PAST AND PRESENT. Los Angeles, CA: Chicano Studies Research Center, UCLA, 1980, p. 145-148. English. DESCR: Garment Industry; Immigration Regulation and Control; International Ladies Garment Workers Union (ILGWU); Labor Unions; *Lilli Diamond Originals; Women; Working Women.

6011 Vasquez, Mario F. Immigrant workers and the apparel manufacturing industry in Southern California. IN: Rios-Bustamante, Antonio,

ed. MEXICAN IMMIGRANT WORKERS IN THE U.S. Los Angeles, CA: Chicano Studies Research Center Publications, University of California, 1981, p. 85-96. English. DESCR: AFL-CIO; California; Garment Industry; Immigrants; International Ladies Garment Workers Union (ILGWU); *Labor Supply and Market; Labor Unions; Women.

6012 Vega, William A.; Kolody, Bohdan; and Valle, Juan Ramon. Migration and mental health: an empirical test of depression risk factors among immigrant Mexican women. INTERNATIONAL MIGRATION REVIEW, Vol. 21, no. 3 (Fall 1987), p. 512-530. English. DESCR: Acculturation; *Depression (Psychological); *Immigrants; Immigration; *Mental Health; Migration; Stress; Women.

Unemployment
USE: Employment

Unemployment Insurance
USE: Employment

United Cannery Agricultural Packing and Allied Workers of America (UCAPAWA)

6013 Calderon, Roberto R. and Zamora, Emilio, Jr. Manuela Solis Sager and Emma Tenayuca: a tribute. IN: Cordova, Teresa, et al., eds. CHICANA VOICES. Austin, TX: Center for Mexican American Studies, 1986, p. 30-41. English. DESCR: Agricultural Labor Unions; Biography; History; Labor; *Solis Sager, Manuela; South Texas Agricultural Worker's Union (STAWU); *Tenayuca, Emma.

6014 Calderon, Roberto R. and Zamora, Emilio, Jr. Manuela Solis Sager and Emma Tenayuca: a tribute. IN: Del Castillo, Adelaida R., ed. BETWEEN BORDERS: ESSAYS ON MEXICANA/CHICANA HISTORY. Encino, CA: Floricanto Press, 1990, p. 269-279. English. DESCR: Agricultural Labor Unions; Biography; History; Labor; *Solis Sager, Manuela; South Texas Agricultural Worker's Union (STAWU); *Tenayuca, Emma.

6015 Gonzalez, Rosalinda M. Chicanas and Mexican immigrant families 1920-1940: women's subordination and family exploitation. IN: Scharf, Lois and Jensen, Joan M., eds. DECADES OF DISCONTENT: THE WOMEN'S MOVEMENT, 1920-1940. Westport, CT: Greenwood Press, 1983, p. 59-84. English. DESCR: *Family; Farm Workers; History; Immigrants; Labor; Labor Unions; Mexico; Pecan Shelling Worker's Union, San Antonio, TX; Sex Roles; Strikes and Lockouts; Working Women.

6016 Mirande, Alfredo and Enriquez, Evangelina. Chicanas in the struggle for unions. IN: Duran, Livie Isauro and Bernard, H. Russell, eds. INTRODUCTION TO CHICANO STUDIES. 2nd. ed. New York: Macmillan, 1973, p. 325-337. English. DESCR: Gonzalez Parsons, Lucia; *Labor Unions; Moreno, Luisa [union organizer]; Parsons, Albert; Tenayuca, Emma.

6017 Rips, Geoffrey and Tenayuca, Emma. Living history: Emma Tenayuca tells her story. TEXAS OBSERVER, (October 28, 1983), p. 7-15. English. DESCR: *Autobiography; Communist Party; Food Industry; Labor Unions; Leadership; Oral History; Pecan Shelling Worker's Union, San Antonio, TX; San Antonio, TX; Strikes and Lockouts; Tenayuca, Emma; Worker's Alliance (WA), Los Angeles, CA; Working Women.

United Cannery Agricultural Packing and Allied Workers of America (UCAPAWA) (cont.)

6018 Ruiz, Vicki L. "And miles to go...": Mexican women and work, 1930-1985. IN: Schlissel, Lillian, et al., eds. WESTERN WOMEN: THEIR LAND, THEIR LIVES. Albuquerque, NM: University of New Mexico Press, 1988, p. 117-136. English. DESCR: Education; El Paso Women's Employment and Education Project (EPWEE); *Employment; Farah Manufacturing Co., El Paso, TX; Farah Strike; *Income; Industrial Workers; Labor Unions; Statistics; Undocumented Workers; Women; *Working Women.

6019 Ruiz, Vicki L. Cannery women/cannery lives: Mexican women, unionization, and the California food processing industry, 1930-1950. Albuquerque, NM: University of New Mexico Press, 1987. xviii, 194 p.: ill. English. DESCR: Agricultural Labor Unions; California; *Canneries; Family; History; Industrial Workers; Labor Disputes; *Labor Unions; Trade Unions; Women.

6020 Ruiz, Vicki L. A promise fulfilled: Mexican cannery workers in Southern California. THE PACIFIC HISTORIAN, Vol. 30, no. 2 (Summer 1986), p. 51-61. English. DESCR: *California Sanitary Canning Company, Los Angeles, CA; *Canneries; Labor Unions; Moreno, Luisa [union organizer]; Southern California; Strikes and Lockouts; Working Women.

6021 Ruiz, Vicki L. A promise fulfilled: Mexican cannery workers in Southern California. IN: DuBois, Ellen Carol and Ruiz, Vicki L., eds. UNEQUAL SISTERS: A MULTICULTURAL READER IN U.S. WOMEN'S HISTORY. New York: Routledge, 1990, p. 264-274. English. DESCR: *California Sanitary Canning Company, Los Angeles, CA; *Canneries; Labor Unions; Moreno, Luisa [union organizer]; Southern California; Strikes and Lockouts; Working Women.

6022 Ruiz, Vicki L. A promise fulfilled: Mexican cannery workers in Southern California. IN: Del Castillo, Adelaida R., ed. BETWEEN BORDERS: ESSAYS ON MEXICANA/CHICANA HISTORY. Encino, CA: Floricanto Press, 1990, p. 281-298. English. DESCR: California Sanitary Canning Company, Los Angeles, CA; *Canneries; Labor Unions; Moreno, Luisa [union organizer]; Southern California; Strikes and Lockouts; Working Women.

6023 Ruiz, Vicki L. UCAPAWA, Chicanas, and the California food processing industry, 1937-1950. Thesis (Ph.D.)--Stanford University, 1982. x, 281 p. English. DESCR: *Canneries; Food Industry; *Labor Unions; Trade Unions; Working Women.

United Farmworkers of America (UFW)

6024 Cantarow, Ellen and De la Cruz, Jessie Lopez. Jessie Lopez De la Cruz: the battle for farmworkers' rights. IN: Cantarow, Ellen. MOVING THE MOUNTAIN: WOMEN WORKING FOR SOCIAL CHANGE. Old Westbury, NY: Feminist Press, 1980, p. 94-151. English. DESCR: Agricultural Labor Unions; Chavez, Cesar E.; *De la Cruz, Jessie Lopez; *Farm Workers; Labor Disputes; Oral History; Parlier, CA; Sex Roles; Strikes and Lockouts.

6025 Echaveste, Beatrice and Huerta, Dolores. In the shadow of the eagle: Huerta = A la sombra del aguila: Huerta. AMERICAS 2001, Vol. 1, no. 3 (November, December, 1987), p.

26-30. Bilingual. DESCR: Agricultural Labor Unions; Boycotts; *Farm Workers; Huerta, Dolores.

6026 Huerta, Dolores. Dolores Huerta talks about Republicans, Cesar, children and her home town. REGENERACION, Vol. 2, no. 4 (1975), p. 20-24. English. DESCR: *Agricultural Labor Unions; *Biography; Chavez, Cesar E.; Community Service Organization, Los Angeles, (CSO); Democratic Party; Elected Officials; Flores, Art; Huerta, Dolores; McGovern, George; *Politics; Ramirez, Henry M.; Ross, Fred; Sanchez, Philip V.; Working Women.

6027 Huerta, Dolores. Dolores Huerta talks about Republicans, Cesar, children and her home town. IN: Servin, Manuel P. ed. THE MEXICAN AMERICANS: AN AWAKENING MINORITY. 2nd ed. Beverly Hills, CA: Glencoe Press, 1974, p. 283-294. English. DESCR: *Agricultural Labor Unions; *Biography; Chavez, Cesar E.; Community Service Organization, Los Angeles, (CSO); Democratic Party; Elected Officials; Flores, Art; Huerta, Dolores; McGovern, George; *Politics; Ramirez, Henry M.; Ross, Fred; Sanchez, Philip V.; Working Women.

6028 O'Connor, Mary I. Women's networks and the social needs of Mexican immigrants. URBAN ANTHROPOLOGY, Vol. 19, no. 1-2 (Spring, Summer, 1990), p. 81-98. English. DESCR: Employment; *Immigrants; Labor Unions; *Natural Support Systems; *Sandyland Nursery, Carpinteria, CA; Undocumented Workers; Women.

6029 Rose, Margaret. From the fields to the picket line: Huelga women and the boycott, 1965-1975. LABOR HISTORY, Vol. 31, no. 3 (1990), p. 271-293. English. DESCR: *Boycotts; Family; Farm Workers; Padilla, Esther; Padilla, Gilbert; Rodriguez, Conrado; Rodriguez, Herminia; Washington, D.C.

6030 Rose, Margaret. Traditional and nontraditional patterns of female activism in the United Farm Workers of America, 1962-1980. FRONTIERS: A JOURNAL OF WOMEN STUDIES, Vol. 11, no. 1 (1990), p. [26]-32. English. DESCR: Boycotts; California; Chavez, Cesar E.; *Chavez, Helen; *Huerta, Dolores; Labor Disputes; Labor Unions; National Farm Workers Association (NFWA); Sex Roles; Strikes and Lockouts.

6031 Rose, Margaret. Women in the United Farm Workers: a study of Chicana Mexicana participation in a labor union, 1950-1980. Thesis (Ph.D.)--University of California, Los Angeles, 1988. 403p. English. DESCR: History; Huerta, Dolores; *Labor Unions; *Sex Roles; Working Women.

United States-Mexico Relations

6032 Bustamante, Jorge A. Maquiladoras: a new face of international capitalism on Mexico's northern frontier. IN: Nash, June and Fernandez-Kelly, Patricia, eds. WOMEN, MEN, AND THE INTERNATIONAL DIVISION OF LABOR. Albany, NY: State University of New York Press, 1983, p. 224-256. English. DESCR: Banking Industry; Border Industrialization Program (BIP); Border Industries; *Border Region; Foreign Trade; Industrial Workers; International Economic Relations; Mexico; Population; Programa Nacional Fronterizo (PRONAF); Women; Working Women.

United States-Mexico Relations
(cont.)

6033 Gettman, Dawn and Pena, Devon Gerardo. Women, mental health, and the workplace in a transnational setting. SOCIAL WORK, Vol. 31, no. 1 (January, February, 1986), p. 5-11. English. DESCR: *Border Industries; Employment; *Mental Health; Mexico; Women; *Working Women.

6034 Levy Oved, Albert and Alcocer Marban, Sonia. Las maquiladoras en Mexico. Mexico: Fondo de Cultura Economica, 1984. 125 p.: ill. Spanish. DESCR: *Border Industries; *Border Region; International Economic Relations; Women.

Universities
USE: Colleges and Universities

University of California

6035 Ortiz, Flora Ida. Hispanic American women in higher education: a consideration of the socialization process. AZTLAN, Vol. 17, no. 2 (Fall 1986), p. 125-152. English. DESCR: *Academic Achievement; Counseling (Educational); Enrollment; *Higher Education; Sex Roles; *Sexism; Socialization; Students.

6036 Sosa Riddell, Adaljiza. Synopsis on Senate Concurrent Resolution 43: an example in public policy making. IN: Sosa Riddell, Adaljiza, ed. POLICY DEVELOPMENT: CHICANA/LATINA SUMMER RESEARCH INSTITUTE. Davis, CA: [Chicano Studies Program, University of California, Davis, 1989?], p. 16-26. English. DESCR: Legislation; *Public Policy; Senate Concurrent Resolution 43, 1987.

University of California, San Diego

6037 Orozco, Yolanda. La Chicana and "women's liberation". LA RAZA HABLA, Vol. 1, no. 5 (August 1976), p. 3-4. English. DESCR: *Feminism.

Upper Class
USE: Social Classes

Urban Communities

6038 Baca Zinn, Maxine. Urban kinship and Midwest Chicano families: evidence in support of revision. DE COLORES, Vol. 6, no. 1-2 (1982), p. 85-98. English. DESCR: Compadrazgo; *Extended Family; Family; Midwestern States.

6039 Camarillo, Alberto M. The "new" Chicano history: historiography of Chicanos of the 1970s. IN: CHICANOS AND THE SOCIAL SCIENCES: A DECADE OF RESEARCH AND DEVELOPMENT (1970-1980) SYMPOSIUM WORKING PAPER. Santa Barbara, CA: Center for Chicano Studies, University of California, 1983, p. 9-17. English. DESCR: *Historiography; History; Literature Reviews.

6040 Davis, Sally M. and Harris, Mary B. Sexual knowledge, sexual interests, and sources of sexual information of rural and urban adolescents from three cultures. ADOLESCENCE, Vol. 17, no. 66 (Summer 1982), p. 471-492. English. DESCR: Birth Control; Cultural Characteristics; Identity; Rural Population; *Sex Education; Sex Roles; Youth.

6041 Espin, Oliva M. Spiritual power and the mundane world: Hispanic female healers in urban U.S. communities. WOMEN'S STUDIES QUARTERLY, Vol. 16, no. 3 (Fall 1988), p. 33-47. English. DESCR: *Curanderas.

6042 Farkas, George; Barton, Margaret; and Kushner, Kathy. White, Black, and Hispanic female youths in central city labor markets. SOCIOLOGICAL QUARTERLY, Vol. 29, no. 4 (Winter 1988), p. 605-621. English. DESCR: Anglo Americans; Blacks; Employment; *Income; *Labor Supply and Market; Women; *Youth.

6043 Romero, Mary. Domestic service in the transition from rural to urban life: the case of la Chicana. WOMEN'S STUDIES QUARTERLY, Vol. 13, no. 3 (February 1987), p. 199-222. English. DESCR: *Domestic Work; Employment; Interpersonal Relations; Rural Population; Social Mobility; Sociology; Working Women.

Urbanization
USE: Urban Communities

Urrea, Teresa

6044 Mirande, Alfredo and Enriquez, Evangelina. Chicanas in the history of the Southwest. IN: Duran, Livie Isauro and Bernard, H. Russell, eds. INTRODUCTION TO CHICANO STUDIES. 2nd ed. New York: Macmillan, 1982, p. 156-179. English. DESCR: Arguello, Concepcion; Barcelo, Gertrudes "La Tules"; Fages, Eulalia; *History; "Juanita of Downieville"; Robledo, Refugio.

U.S. Bureau of the Census

6045 Markides, Kyriakos S. Consequences of gender differentials in life expectancy for Black and Hispanic Americans. INTERNATIONAL JOURNAL OF AGING & HUMAN DEVELOPMENT, Vol. 29, no. 2 (1989), p. 95-102. English. DESCR: *Ancianos; Blacks; Census; Cubanos; Latin Americans; Males; Population; Puerto Ricans.

Valdes, Gina

6046 Lizarraga, Sylvia S. La mujer ingeniosa. FEM, Vol. 8, no. 34 (June, July, 1984), p. 41. Spanish. DESCR: Literary Criticism; Novel; *THERE ARE NO MADMEN HERE.

6047 Lizarraga, Sylvia S. The resourceful woman in THERE ARE NO MADMEN HERE. THIRD WOMAN, Vol. 2, no. 1 (1984), p. 71-74. English. DESCR: *Literary Criticism; THERE ARE NO MADMEN HERE.

6048 Quintana, Alvina E. Challenge and counter challenge: Chicana literary motifs. AGAINST THE CURRENT, Vol. 2, no. 2 (March, April, 1987), p. 25,28-32. English. DESCR: Anglo Americans; Authors; Cervantes, Lorna Dee; Cultural Studies; *Feminism; Identity; Literary Criticism; *Literature; Moraga, Cherrie; THERE ARE NO MADMEN HERE; Women.

6049 Quintana, Alvina E. Chicana literary motifs: challenge and counter-challenge. IMAGES: ETHNIC STUDIES OCCASIONAL PAPERS SERIES, (Fall 1986), p. 24-41. English. DESCR: Anglo Americans; Authors; Cervantes, Lorna Dee; Cultural Studies; *Feminism; *Identity; *Literary Criticism; Literature; Moraga, Cherrie; THERE ARE NO MADMEN HERE; Women.

Valdes, Gina (cont.)

6050 Sanchez, Rosaura. Chicana prose writers: the case of Gina Valdes and Sylvia Lizarraga. IN: Herrera-Sobek, Maria, ed. BEYOND STEREOTYPES: THE CRITICAL ANALYSIS OF CHICANA LITERATURE. Binghamton, NY: Bilingual Press/Editorial Bilingue, 1985, p. 61-70. English. DESCR: *Authors; Literary Criticism; *Lizarraga, Sylvia; Prose.

Valdez, Luis

6051 Melville, Margarita B. Female and male in Chicano theatre. IN: Kanellos, Nicolas, ed. HISPANIC THEATRE IN THE UNITED STATES. Houston, TX: Arte Publico Press, 1984, p. 71-79. English. DESCR: BERNABE; BRUJERIAS [play]; Cultural Characteristics; DAY OF THE SWALLOWS; Duarte-Clark, Rodrigo; EL JARDIN [play]; Family; Feminism; Macias, Ysidro; Morton, Carlos; Portillo Trambley, Estela; RANCHO HOLLYWOOD [play]; *Sex Roles; *Teatro; THE ULTIMATE PENDEJADA [play]; Women Men Relations.

Valdez, Patssi

6052 Burnham, Linda. Patssi Valdez. HIGH PERFORMANCE, Vol. 9, no. 3 (1986), p. 54. English. DESCR: *Artists; ASCO [art group]; Los Angeles, CA; Los Angeles, CA; Performing Arts.

6053 Goldman, Shifra M. Mujeres de California: Latin American women artists. IN: Moore, Sylvia, ed. YESTERDAY AND TOMORROW: CALIFORNIA WOMEN ARTISTS. New York, NY: Midmarch Arts Press, c1989, p. 202-229. English. DESCR: *Artists; Baca, Judith F.; Biography; California; Carrasco, Barbara; Cervantez, Yreina; de Larios, Dora; Feminism; Hernandez, Judithe; Lomas Garza, Carmen; Lopez, Yolanda M.; Mesa-Bains, Amalia; Murillo, Patricia; Sanchez, Olivia; Vallejo Dillaway, Linda; Women; Zamora Lucero, Linda.

Valdez, Rosaura

6054 Weber, Devra Anne. Mexican women on strike: memory, history and oral narratives. IN: Del Castillo, Adelaida R., ed. BETWEEN BORDERS: ESSAYS ON MEXICANA/CHICANA HISTORY. Encino, CA: Floricanto Press, 1990, p. 175-200. English. DESCR: *1933 Cotton Strike; Cotton Industry; History; *Oral History; San Joaquin Valley, CA; Strikes and Lockouts; Working Women.

Valdez, Socorro

6055 Broyles-Gonzalez, Yolanda. Women in El Teatro Campesino: "¿A poco estaba molacha la Virgen de Guadalupe?". IN: Cordova, Teresa, et al., eds. CHICANA VOICES. Austin, TX: Center for Mexican American Studies, 1986, p. 162-187. English. DESCR: Actors and Actresses; CORRIDOS [play]; *El Teatro Campesino; Stereotypes; Teatro.

Valentina Productions

6056 Yarbro-Bejarano, Yvonne. Chicana's experience in collective theatre: ideology and form. WOMEN AND PERFORMANCE, Vol. 2, no. 2 (1985), p. 45-58. English. DESCR: Actors and Actresses; Careers; El Teatro Campesino; El Teatro de la Esperanza; Political Ideology; *San Francisco Mime Troupe; Sex Roles; Teatro; Teatro Libertad; Women.

Valero, Robert

6057 Irizarry, Estelle. La abuelita in literature. NUESTRO, Vol. 7, no. 7 (September 1983), p. 50. English. DESCR: Alonso, Luis Ricardo; *Ancianos; Cotto-Thorner, Guillermo; Family; Grandmothers; Ulibarri, Sabine R.

Vallejo Dillaway, Linda

6058 Goldman, Shifra M. Mujeres de California: Latin American women artists. IN: Moore, Sylvia, ed. YESTERDAY AND TOMORROW: CALIFORNIA WOMEN ARTISTS. New York, NY: Midmarch Arts Press, c1989, p. 202-229. English. DESCR: *Artists; Baca, Judith F.; Biography; California; Carrasco, Barbara; Cervantez, Yreina; de Larios, Dora; Feminism; Hernandez, Judithe; Lomas Garza, Carmen; Lopez, Yolanda M.; Mesa-Bains, Amalia; Murillo, Patricia; Sanchez, Olivia; Valdez, Patssi; Women; Zamora Lucero, Linda.

Vallejo, Linda
USE: Vallejo Dillaway, Linda

Values

6059 Baca Zinn, Maxine. Employment and education of Mexican-American women: the interplay of modernity and ethnicity in eight families. HARVARD EDUCATIONAL REVIEW, Vol. 50, no. 1 (February 1980), p. 47-62. English. DESCR: Acculturation; Decision Making; *Education; *Employment; *Family; Identity; Sex Roles; Social Classes.

6060 Bassoff, Betty Z. and Ortiz, Elizabeth Thompson. Teen women: disparity between cognitive values and anticipated life events. CHILD WELFARE, Vol. 63, no. 2 (March, April, 1984), p. 125-138. English. DESCR: Sexual Behavior; Women; *Youth.

6061 Buriel, Raymond, et al. Mexican-American disciplinary practices and attitudes toward child maltreatment:a comparison of foreign and native-born mothers. HISPANIC JOURNAL OF BEHAVIORAL SCIENCES, Vol. 13, no. 1 (February 1991), p. 78-94. English. DESCR: *Attitudes; *Child Abuse; Immigrants; *Parent and Child Relationships; *Parenting; Violence.

6062 Del Castillo, Adelaida R. and Torres, Maria. The interdependency of educational institutions and cultural norms: the Hispana experience. IN: McKenna, Teresa and Ortiz, Flora Ida, eds. THE BROKEN WEB: THE EDUCATIONAL EXPERIENCE OF HISPANIC WOMEN. Claremont, CA: Tomas Rivera Center; Berkeley, CA: Floricanto Press, 1988, p. 39-60. English. DESCR: Academic Achievement; Acculturation; *Cultural Characteristics; *Education; *Literature Reviews; Research Methodology; Women.

6063 Gutierrez, Jeannie and Sameroff, Arnold. Determinants of complexity in Mexican-American and Anglo-American mothers' conceptions of child development. CHILD DEVELOPMENT, Vol. 61, no. 2 (April 1990), p. 384-394. English. DESCR: Acculturation; *Anglo Americans; Children; Cultural Characteristics; *Parenting; *Women.

Values (cont.)

6064 Gutierrez, Ramon A. From honor to love: transformations of the meaning of sexuality in colonial New Mexico. IN: Smith, Raymond T., ed. KINSHIP IDEOLOGY AND PRACTICE IN LATIN AMERICA. Chapel Hill, NC: University of North Carolina Press, 1984, p. [237]-263. English. **DESCR:** *Catholic Church; *Marriage; New Mexico; *Sexual Behavior; Social Classes; Social History and Conditions; Spanish Influence; Women.

6065 Gutierrez, Ramon A. Honor ideology, marriage negotiation, and class-gender domination in New Mexico, 1690-1846. LATIN AMERICAN PERSPECTIVES, Vol. 12, no. 1 (Winter 1985), p. 81-104. English. **DESCR:** Marriage; Sex Roles; *Social Classes; Social History and Conditions; Southwestern United States; Women Men Relations.

6066 Manzanedo, Hector Garcia; Walters, Esperanza Garcia; and Lorig, Kate R. Health and illness perceptions of the Chicana. IN: Melville, Margarita B., ed. TWICE A MINORITY. St. Louis, MO: Mosby, 1980, p. 191-207. English. **DESCR:** Cultural Characteristics; Culture; *Medical Care; Public Health; Sex Roles.

6067 Martinez, Estella A. Child behavior in Mexican American/Chicano families: maternal teaching and child-rearing practices. FAMILY RELATIONS, Vol. 37, no. 3 (July 1988), p. 275-280. English. **DESCR:** *Acculturation; Family; Maternal Teaching Observation Technique (MTOT); Parent and Child Relationships; *Parenting; *Psychological Testing; Socioeconomic Factors.

6068 Mirande, Alfredo. Que gacho es ser macho: it's a drag to be a macho man. AZTLAN, Vol. 17, no. 2 (Fall 1986), p. 63-89. English. **DESCR:** *Cultural Characteristics; Identity; *Machismo; Personality; Sex Roles; *Sex Stereotypes.

6069 Ortiz, Sylvia and Casas, Jesus Manuel. Birth control and low-income Mexican-American women: the impact of three values. HISPANIC JOURNAL OF BEHAVIORAL SCIENCES, Vol. 12, no. 1 (February 1990), p. 83-92. English. **DESCR:** Acculturation; Attitudes; *Birth Control; Fertility; *Low Income; *Sex Roles.

6070 Padilla, Eligio R. and O'Grady, Kevin E. Sexuality among Mexican Americans: a case of sexual stereotyping. JOURNAL OF PERSONALITY AND SOCIAL PSYCHOLOGY, Vol. 52, no. 1 (1987), p. 5-10. English. **DESCR:** Age Groups; Anglo Americans; Attitudes; California; Religion; *Sex Roles; *Sex Stereotypes; Sexual Behavior; Sexual Knowledge and Attitude Test; *Stereotypes; Students.

6071 Ramirez, Carmen Cecilia. A study of the value orientation of Lane County, Oregon, Mexican American mothers with a special focus on family/school relationships. Thesis (Ph.D.)--University of Oregon, 1981. 183 p. English. **DESCR:** *Community School Relationships; Family; Lane County, OR.

6072 Sabogal, Fabio, et al. Hispanic familism and acculturation: what changes and what doesn't? HISPANIC JOURNAL OF BEHAVIORAL SCIENCES, Vol. 9, no. 4 (December 1987), p. 397-412. English. **DESCR:** *Acculturation; Attitudes; Cultural Characteristics; Ethnic Groups; Extended Family; *Family; Natural Support Systems.

6073 Sanchez, George J. "Go after the women": Americanization and the Mexican immigrant woman, 1915-1929. Stanford, CA: Stanford Center for Chicano Research [1984?]. [32] leaves. English. **DESCR:** Acculturation; *Assimilation; Biculturalism; *Immigrants; Social History and Conditions; Women.

6074 Sanchez, George J. "Go after the women": Americanization and the Mexican immigrant woman, 1915-1929. IN: DuBois, Ellen Carol and Ruiz, Vicki L., eds. UNEQUAL SISTERS: A MULTICULTURAL READER IN U.S. WOMEN'S HISTORY. New York: Routledge, 1990, p. 250-263. English. **DESCR:** Acculturation; *Assimilation; Biculturalism; *Immigrants; Social History and Conditions; Women.

6075 Sorenson, Ann Marie. Fertility, expectations and ethnic identity among Mexican-American adolescents: an expression of cultural ideals. SOCIOLOGICAL PERSPECTIVES, Vol. 28, no. 3 (July 1985), p. 339-360. English. **DESCR:** Acculturation; Anglo Americans; Cultural Characteristics; *Fertility; Identity; Youth.

6076 Triandis, Harry C. Role perceptions of Hispanic young adults. JOURNAL OF CROSS-CULTURAL PSYCHOLOGY, Vol. 15, no. 3 (September 1984), p. 297-320. English. **DESCR:** *Cultural Characteristics; *Family; Parent and Child Relationships; *Sex Roles; Social Psychology; Youth.

6077 Votaw, Carmen Delgado. Cultural influences on Hispanic feminism. AGENDA, Vol. 11, no. 4 (1981), p. 44-49. Bilingual. **DESCR:** Culture; *Feminism; Identity.

Vasquez, Esperanza

6078 Fregoso, Rosa Linda. La quinceanera of Chicana counter aesthetics. CENTRO BULLETIN, Vol. 3, no. 1 (Winter 1990, 1991), p. [87]-91. English. **DESCR:** *AGUEDA MARTINEZ [film]; ANIMA [film]; *CHICANA! [film]; *DESPUES DEL TERREMOTO [film]; Espana, Frances Salome; Feminism; *Films; Morales, Sylvia; Portillo, Lourdes.

Vasquez, Patricia

6079 Mexican American Legal Defense and Education Fund (MALDEF). Chicana rights: a major MALDEF issue (reprinted from MALDEF Newsletter, Fall 1977). COMADRE, no. 3 (Fall 1978), p. 31-35. English. **DESCR:** Chicana Rights Project; *Feminism; Mexican American Legal Defense and Educational Fund (MALDEF); Statistics.

"Los Vatos" [poem]

6080 Saldivar, Jose David. Towards a Chicano poetics: the making of the Chicano subject. CONFLUENCIA, Vol. 1, no. 2 (Spring 1986), p. 10-17. English. **DESCR:** Corridos; Feminism; *Literary Criticism; Montoya, Jose E.; *Poetry; RESTLESS SERPENTS; Rios, Alberto; WHISPERING TO FOOL THE WIND; Zamora, Bernice.

Velez Ibanez, Carlos

6081 Ainsworth, Diane. Cultural cross fires. IN: Duran, Livie Isauro and Bernard, H. Russell, eds. INTRODUCTION TO CHICANO STUDIES. 2nd ed. New York: Macmillan, c1982, p. 505-512. English. **DESCR:** Identity; Medical Care; *Sterilization.

Vice

USE: Criminal Acts

LA VICTIMA [play]

6082 Yarbro-Bejarano, Yvonne. The image of the Chicana in teatro. IN: Cochran, Jo; Stewart, J.T.; and Tsutakawa, Mayumi, eds. GATHERING GROUND: NEW WRITING AND ART BY NORTHWEST WOMEN OF COLOR. Seattle, WA: Seal Press, 1984, p. 90-96. English. DESCR: El Teatro de la Esperanza; GUADALUPE [play]; HIJOS: ONCE A FAMILY [play]; *Literary Characters; Sex Roles; Sex Stereotypes; Stereotypes; *Teatro; THE OCTOPUS [play]; Women Men Relations.

VICTUUM

6083 Saldivar, Ramon. The dialectics of subjectivity: gender and difference in Isabella Rios, Sandra Cisneros, and Cherrie Moraga. IN: Saldivar, Ramon. CHICANO NARRATIVE: THE DIALECTICS OF DIFFERENCE. Madison, WI: University of Wisconsin Press, 1990, p. 171-199. English. DESCR: Authors; Autobiography; *Cisneros, Sandra; Feminism; Fiction; *Literary Criticism; Literature; LOVING IN THE WAR YEARS; *Moraga, Cherrie; Political Ideology; *Rios, Isabella; THE HOUSE ON MANGO STREET.

Vidal, Mirta

6084 Gonzales, Sylvia Alicia. The Chicana perspective: a design for self-awareness. IN: Trejo, Arnulfo D. ed. THE CHICANOS: AS WE SEE OURSELVES. Tucson, AZ: University of Arizona Press, 1979, p. 81-99. English. DESCR: CHICANAS SPEAK OUT; Chicano Movement; Discrimination; Feminism; Identity; Machismo; Madsen, William; *Mexican Revolution - 1910-1920; Mexico; Sex Roles; THE MEXICAN-AMERICANS OF SOUTH TEXAS.

Vigil-Pinon, Evangelina

6085 Alarcon, Norma. What kind of lover have you made me, Mother?: towards a theory of Chicanas' feminism and cultural identity through poetry. IN: McCluskey, Audrey T., ed. WOMEN OF COLOR: PERSPECTIVES ON FEMINISM AND IDENTITY. Bloomington, IN: Women's Studies Program, Indiana University, 1985, p. 85-110. English. DESCR: Brinson-Pineda, Barbara; Cervantes, Lorna Dee; Cisneros, Sandra; Culture; *Feminism; Identity; *Literary Criticism; Mora, Pat; Moraga, Cherrie; *Poetry; Tafolla, Carmen; Villanueva, Alma.

6086 Rebolledo, Tey Diana. Hispanic women writers of the Southwest: tradition and innovation. IN: Lensink, Judy Nolte, ed. OLD SOUTHWEST/NEW SOUTHWEST: ESSAYS ON A REGION AND ITS LITERATURE. Tucson, AZ: The Tucson Public Library, 1987, p. 49-61. English. DESCR: *Authors; Cabeza de Baca, Fabiola; Jaramillo, Cleofas M.; Literature; Mora, Pat; OLD SPAIN IN OUR SOUTHWEST; Otero Warren, Nina; Preciado Martin, Patricia; Sex Roles; Sex Stereotypes; Silva, Beverly; *Southwestern United States; WE FED THEM CACTUS; *Women.

6087 Tafolla, Carmen. Chicano literature: beyond beginnings. IN: Harris, Marie and Aguero, Kathleen, eds. A GIFT OF TONGUES: CRITICAL CHALLENGES IN CONTEMPORARY AMERICAN POETRY. Athens, GA: University of Georgia Press, 1987, p. 206-225. English. DESCR: *Authors; Cota-Cardenas, Margarita; Language Usage; *Literary Criticism; *Literature; Portillo Trambley, Estela; Sex Stereotypes; Symbolism; Tafolla, Carmen.

6088 Treacy, Mary Jane. The ties that bind: women

and community in Evangelina Vigil's THIRTY AN' SEEN A LOT. IN: Horno-Delgado, Asuncion, et al., eds. BREAKING BOUNDARIES: LATINA WRITING AND CRITICAL READINGS. Amherst, MA: University of Massachusetts Press, c1989, p. 82-93. English. DESCR: Identity; Literary Criticism; Poetry; Sexism; *THIRTY AN' SEEN A LOT.

Villanueva, Alma

6089 Alarcon, Norma. What kind of lover have you made me, Mother?: towards a theory of Chicanas' feminism and cultural identity through poetry. IN: McCluskey, Audrey T., ed. WOMEN OF COLOR: PERSPECTIVES ON FEMINISM AND IDENTITY. Bloomington, IN: Women's Studies Program, Indiana University, 1985, p. 85-110. English. DESCR: Brinson-Pineda, Barbara; Cervantes, Lorna Dee; Cisneros, Sandra; Culture; *Feminism; Identity; *Literary Criticism; Mora, Pat; Moraga, Cherrie; *Poetry; Tafolla, Carmen; Vigil-Pinon, Evangelina.

6090 Del Rio, Carmen M. Chicana poets: re-visions from the margin. REVISTA CANADIENSE DE ESTUDIOS HISPANICOS, Vol. 14, no. 3 (Spring 1990), p. 431-445. English. DESCR: Authors; *Feminism; *Literary Criticism; *Poetry; Tafolla, Carmen.

6091 Ordonez, Elizabeth J. Body, spirit, and the text: Alma Villanueva's LIFE SPAN. IN: Calderon, Hector and Saldivar, Jose David, eds. CRITICISM IN THE BORDERLANDS: STUDIES IN CHICANO LITERATURE, CULTURE, AND IDEOLOGY. Durham, NC: Duke University Press, 1991, p. [61]-71. English. DESCR: Cixous, Helene; *Feminism; *LIFE SPAN; *Literary Criticism; Poetry.

6092 Ordonez, Elizabeth J. The concept of cultural identity in Chicana poetry. THIRD WOMAN, Vol. 2, no. 1 (1984), p. 75-82. English. DESCR: Cervantes, Lorna Dee; Corpi, Lucha; *Literary Criticism; Poetry; Tafolla, Carmen.

6093 Ordonez, Elizabeth J. [Villanueva, Alma]. IN: Martinez, Julio A. and Lomeli, Francisco A., eds. CHICANO LITERATURE: A REFERENCE GUIDE. Westport, CT: Greenwood Press, 1985, p. 413-420. English. DESCR: Authors; Biography; *BLOODROOT; Literary Criticism.

5094 Passman, Kristina. Demeter, Kore and the birth of the self: the quest for identity in the poetry of Alma Villanueva, Pat Mora y Cherrie Moraga. MONOGRAPHIC REVIEW, Vol. 6, (1990), p. 323-342. English. DESCR: *Literary Criticism; Mora, Pat; Moraga, Cherrie; Mythology; Poetry.

6095 Sanchez, Marta E. The birthing of the poetic 'I' in Alma Villanueva's MOTHER MAY I?: the search for a feminine identity. IN: Herrera-Sobek, Maria, ed. BEYOND STEREOTYPES: THE CRITICAL ANALYSIS OF CHICANA LITERATURE. Binghamton, NY: Bilingual Press/Editorial Bilingue, 1985, p. 108-152. Also IN: Sanchez, Marta. CONTEMPORARY CHICANA POETRY. Berkeley, CA: University of California Press, 1985, p. 24-84. English. DESCR: *Identity; Literary Criticism; MOTHER MAY I?; Poetry.

6096 Sanchez, Marta E. Gender and ethnicity in contemporary Chicana poetry. CRITICAL PERSPECTIVES, Vol. 2, no. 1 (Fall 1984), p. 147-166. English. DESCR: *Literary Criticism; MOTHER MAY I?; *Poetry.

Villanueva, Alma (cont.)

6097 Villanueva, Alma and Binder, Wolfgang.
[Interview with] Alma Villanueva. IN:
Binder, Wolfgang, ed. PARTIAL
AUTOBIOGRAPHIES: INTERVIEWS WITH TWENTY
CHICANO POETS. Erlangen, W. Germany: Verlag
Palm & Enke, 1985, p. 201-202. English.
DESCR: Authors; Autobiography; Poetry.

Villarreal, Andrea

6098 Lomas, Clara. Mexican precursors of Chicana
feminist writing. IN: National Association
for Chicano Studies. ESTUDIOS CHICANOS AND
THE POLITICS OF COMMUNITY. [S.l.]: National
Association for Chicano Studies, c1989, p.
[149]-160. English. DESCR: Authors; de
Cardenas, Isidra T.; *Feminism; Idar,
Jovita; *Journalists; Literature; *Mexican
Revolution - 1910-1920; Newspapers; Ramirez,
Sara Estela; Villegas de Magnon, Leonor.

Villegas de Magnon, Leonor

6099 Lomas, Clara. Mexican precursors of Chicana
feminist writing. IN: National Association
for Chicano Studies. ESTUDIOS CHICANOS AND
THE POLITICS OF COMMUNITY. [S.l.]: National
Association for Chicano Studies, c1989, p.
[149]-160. English. DESCR: Authors; de
Cardenas, Isidra T.; *Feminism; Idar,
Jovita; *Journalists; Literature; *Mexican
Revolution - 1910-1920; Newspapers; Ramirez,
Sara Estela; Villarreal, Andrea.

Violence

6100 Buriel, Raymond, et al. Mexican-American
disciplinary practices and attitudes toward
child maltreatment:a comparison of foreign
and native-born mothers. HISPANIC JOURNAL OF
BEHAVIORAL SCIENCES, Vol. 13, no. 1
(February 1991), p. 78-94. English. DESCR:
*Attitudes; *Child Abuse; Immigrants;
*Parent and Child Relationships; *Parenting;
Values.

6101 Gondolf, Edward W.; Fisher, Ellen; and
McFerron, J. Richard. Racial differences
among shelter residents: a comparison of
Anglo, Black, and Hispanic battered. JOURNAL
OF FAMILY VIOLENCE, Vol. 3, no. 1 (March
1988), p. 39-51. English. DESCR: Anglo
Americans; Battered Women; Blacks;
Comparative Psychology; Cultural
Characteristics; Natural Support Systems;
Socioeconomic Factors; *Women.

6102 Hogeland, Chris and Rosen, Karen. Dreams
lost, dreams found: undocumented women in
the land of opportunity. San Francisco, CA:
Coalition for Immigrant and Refugee Rights
and Services, c1991. 153 p. English. DESCR:
*Battered Women; *Coalition for Immigrant
and Refugee Rights and Services, Immigrant
Woman's Task Force; Discrimination;
Immigrants; *San Francisco Bay Area; Sex
Roles; Sexism; Social Services; Undocumented
Workers; Women; Women Men Relations.

6103 Horowitz, Ruth. Femininity and womanhood:
virginity, unwed motherhood, and violence.
IN: Horowitz, Ruth. HONOR AND THE AMERICAN
DREAM: CULTURE AND IDENTITY IN A CHICANO
COMMUNITY. New Brunswick, NJ: Rutgers
University Press, 1983, p. 114-136. English.
DESCR: *Birth Control; *Fertility; Identity;
Sex Roles; *Sexual Behavior; Single Parents;
Women Men Relations; Youth.

6104 Sorenson, Susan B. and Telles, Cynthia A.
Self-reports of spousal violence in a
Mexican-American and non-Hispanic white
population. VIOLENCE AND VICTIMS, Vol. 6,
no. 1 (1991), p. 3-15. English. DESCR: Anglo
Americans; *Battered Women; Los Angeles, CA;
Los Angeles Epidemiologic Catchment Area
Research Program (LAECA); Rape; Women;
*Women Men Relations.

6105 Torres, Sara. A comparative analysis of wife
abuse among Anglo-American and
Mexican-American battered women: attitudes,
nature, severity, frequency and response to
the abuse. Thesis (Ph.D.)--University of
Texas, Austin, 1986. 265 p. English. DESCR:
Anglo Americans; Attitudes; Battered Women;
Family; *Women.

Viramontes, Helena Maria

6106 Alarcon, Norma. Making "familia" from
scratch: split subjectivities in the work of
Helena Maria Viramontes and Cherrie Moraga.
THE AMERICAS REVIEW, Vol. 15, no. 3-4 (Fall,
Winter, 1987), p. 147-159. English. DESCR:
GIVING UP THE GHOST; *Literary Criticism;
Moraga, Cherrie; *Sex Roles; "Snapshots"
[short story]; THE MOTHS AND OTHER STORIES.

6107 Harlow, Barbara. Sites of struggle:
immigration, deportation, prison, and exile.
IN: Calderon, Hector and Saldivar, Jose
David, eds. CRITICISM IN THE BORDERLANDS:
STUDIES IN CHICANO LITERATURE, CULTURE, AND
IDEOLOGY. Durham, NC: Duke University Press,
1991, p. [149]-163. English. DESCR:
Anzaldua, Gloria; BLACK GOLD; BORDERLANDS/LA
FRONTERA: THE NEW MESTIZA; First, Ruth;
Khalifeh, Sahar; *Literary Criticism;
*Political Ideology; Sanchez, Rosaura;
Social Classes; "The Cariboo Cafe" [short
story]; "The Ditch" [short story]; WILD
THORNS; *Women; Working Women.

6108 Saldivar-Hull, Sonia. Feminism on the
border: from gender politics to geopolitics.
IN: Calderon, Hector and Saldivar, Jose
David, eds. CRITICISM IN THE BORDERLANDS:
STUDIES IN CHICANO LITERATURE, CULTURE, AND
IDEOLOGY. Durham, NC: Duke University Press,
1991, p. [203]-220. English. DESCR: Anglo
Americans; *Anzaldua, Gloria;
*BORDERLANDS/LA FRONTERA: THE NEW MESTIZA;
Feminism; Homosexuality; *Literary
Criticism; Mestizaje; Moraga, Cherrie;
Sexism; "The Cariboo Cafe" [short story];
Women.

6109 Tavera Rivera, Margarita. Autoridad in
absentia: la censura patriarcal en la
narrativa chicana. IN: Lopez-Gonzalez,
Aralia, et al., eds. MUJER Y LITERATURA
MEXICANA Y CHICANA: CULTURAS EN CONTACTO.
Mexico: Colegio de la Frontera Norte, 1988,
p. [65]-69. Spanish. DESCR: Feminism;
Fiction; *Literary Criticism; Sex Roles;
*THE MOTHS AND OTHER STORIES.

6110 Viramontes, Helena Maria. "Nopalitos": the
making of fiction. IN: Horno-Delgado,
Asuncion, et al., eds. BREAKING BOUNDARIES:
LATINA WRITING AND CRITICAL READINGS.
Amherst, MA: University of Massachusetts
Press, c1989, p. 33-38. English. DESCR:
*Authors; *Autobiography; Essays.

La Virgen de Guadalupe

6111 Gonzales, Sylvia Alicia. La Chicana:
Malinche or virgin? NUESTRO, Vol. 3, no. 5
(June, July, 1979), p. 41-45. English.
DESCR: *Malinche; Paz, Octavio.

La Virgen de Guadalupe
(cont.)

6112 Leal, Luis. Arquetipos femeninos en la literatura mexicana. IN: Leal, Luis. AZTLAN Y MEXICO: PERFILES LITERARIOS E HISTORICOS. Binghamton, NY: Bilingual Press/Editorial Bilingue, 1985, p. 168-176. Spanish. DESCR: *Literary Criticism; Malinche; Mexican Literature; Symbolism; Women.

6113 Leal, Luis. Female archetypes in Mexican literature. IN: Miller Beth, ed. WOMEN IN HISPANIC LITERATURE: ICONS AND FALLEN IDOLS Berkeley, CA: University of California Press, 1983, p. 227-242. English. DESCR: *Literary Criticism; Malinche; Mexican Literature; Symbolism; Women.

6114 Limon, Jose E. [anthropologist]. La Llorona, the third legend of greater Mexico: cultural symbols, women, and the political unconscious. RENATO ROSALDO LECTURE SERIES MONOGRAPH, Vol. 2, (Spring 1986), p. [59]-93. English. DESCR: *Feminism; Folklore; *La Llorona; *Leyendas; Malinche; Mexico; *Symbolism; Women.

6115 Limon, Jose E. [anthropologist]. La Llorona, the third legend of greater Mexico: cultural symbols, women, and the political unconscious. IN: Del Castillo, Adelaida R. BETWEEN BORDERS: ESSAYS ON MEXICANA/CHICANA HISTORY. Encino, CA: Floricanto Press, 1990, p. 399-432. English. DESCR: *Feminism; Folklore; *La Llorona; *Leyendas; Malinche; Mexico; *Symbolism; Women.

6116 Macklin, June and Teniente de Costilla, Alvina. Virgen de Guadalupe and the American dream: the melting pot bubbles on in Toledo, Ohio. IN: West, Stanley A. and Macklin, June, eds. THE CHICANO EXPERIENCE. Boulder, CO: Westview Press, 1979, p. 111-143. English. DESCR: Assimilation; Catholic Church; *Identity; Intermarriage; Migration Patterns; Quinceaneras; Toledo, OH.

6117 Soto, Shirlene Ann. Tres modelos culturales: la Virgen de Guadalupe, la Malinche y la Llorona. FEM, Vol. 10, no. 48 (October, November, 1986), p. 13-16. Spanish. DESCR: Guadalupanismo; *La Llorona; *Malinche; Symbolism; Women.

Vital Statistics

6118 Bachu, Amara and O'Connell, Martin. Developing current fertility indicators for foreign-born women from the Current Population Survey. REVIEW OF PUBLIC DATA USE, Vol. 12, no. 3 (October 1984), p. 185-195. English. DESCR: Current Population Survey; *Fertility; Latin America; Mexico; *Surveys; Women.

6119 Bean, Frank D.; Stephen, Elizabeth H.; and Opitz, Wolfgang. The Mexican origin population in the United States: a demographic overview. IN: O. de la Garza, Rodolfo, et al., eds. THE MEXICAN AMERICAN EXPERIENCE: AN INTERDISCIPLINARY ANTHOLOGY. Austin, TX: University of Texas Press, 1985, p. 57-75. English. DESCR: Employment; Fertility; Income; *Population.

6120 Bean, Frank D., et al. Generational differences in fertility among Mexican Americans: implications for assessing the effects of immigration. SOCIAL SCIENCE QUARTERLY, Vol. 65, no. 2 (June 1984), p. 573-582. English. DESCR: Age Groups; *Fertility; Immigration.

6121 Davis, Cary; Haub, Carl; and Willette, JoAnne. U.S. Hispanics: changing the face of America. POPULATION BULLETIN, Vol. 38, no. 3 (June 1983), p. 1-43. English. DESCR: Education; Employment; Fertility; Immigration; Income; *Population; Statistics.

6122 Franks, Adele L.; Binkin, Nancy J.; and Snider, Dixie E. Isoniazid hepatitis among pregnant and postpartum Hispanic patients. PUBLIC HEALTH REPORTS, Vol. 104, no. 2 (March, April, 1989), p. 151-155. English. DESCR: Fertility; *Hepatitis; Public Health.

6123 Gould, Jeffrey B.; Davey, Becky; and Stafford, Randall S. Socioeconomic differences in rates of cesarean section. THE NEW ENGLAND JOURNAL OF MEDICINE, Vol. 321, no. 4 (July 27, 1989), p. 233-239. English. DESCR: Anglo Americans; Asian Americans; Blacks; *Cesarean Section; *Fertility; Los Angeles County, CA; *Socioeconomic Factors; Women.

6124 Henderson, John J. Fertility and mortality. IN: Stoddard, Ellwyn R., et al., eds. BORDERLANDS SOURCEBOOK: A GUIDE TO THE LITERATURE ON NORTHERN MEXICO AND THE AMERICAN SOUTHWEST. Norman, OK: University of Oklahoma Press, 1983, p. 232-236. English. DESCR: Border Region; *Fertility; Population.

6125 Lara-Cea, Helen. Notes on the use of parish registers in the reconstruction of Chicana history in California prior to 1850. IN: Del Castillo, Adelaida R., ed. BETWEEN BORDERS: ESSAYS ON MEXICANA/CHICANA HISTORY. Encino, CA: Floricanto Press, 1990, p. 131-159. English. DESCR: *California; Catholic Church; History; Indigenismo; Mission of Santa Clara; Population; *San Jose, CA.

6126 Malvido, Elsa. El uso del cuerpo femenino en la epoca colonial mexicana a traves de los estudios de demografia historica. IN: Del Castillo, Adelaida R., ed. BETWEEN BORDERS: ESSAYS ON MEXICANA/CHICANA HISTORY. Encino, CA: Floricanto Press, 1990, p. 115-130. Spanish. DESCR: Marriage; *Mexico; *Sex Roles; Sexual Behavior; Widowhood; *Women.

6127 One birth in four. AMERICAN DEMOGRAPHICS, Vol. 6, no. 1 (January 1984), p. 15. English. DESCR: Fertility; Population.

6128 Worth, Dooley and Rodriguez, Ruth. Latina women and AIDS. SIECUS REPORT, (January, February, 1986), p. 5-7. English. DESCR: Cultural Characteristics; Drug Addicts; Drug Use; Health Education; Natural Support Systems; New York; Preventative Medicine; Puerto Ricans; Sex Roles; Women.

Vocalists
USE: Singers

Vocational Aspirations
USE: Vocational Education

Vocational Education

6129 Weiner, Raine. The needs of poverty women heading households: a return to postsecondary education. Thesis (Ph.D.)--California School of Professional Psychology, Los Angeles, 1986. 180 p. English. DESCR: Anglo Americans; Blacks; *Employment Training; Ethnic Groups; *Poverty; *Single Parents; Welfare; Women.

Volunteer Associations
USE: Mutualistas

Voter Turnout

6130 Chacon, Peter. Chicanas and political representation. IN: LA CHICANA: BUILDING FOR THE FUTURE, AN ACTION PLAN FOR THE80s. Oakland, CA: National Hispanic University, 1981, p. 32-36. English. DESCR: Elected Officials; *Political Representation; Politics.

6131 MacManus, Susan A.; Bullock, Charles S.; and Grothe, Barbara P. A longitudinal examination of political participation rates of Mexican-American females. SOCIAL SCIENCE QUARTERLY, Vol. 67, no. 3 (1986), p. 604-612. English. DESCR: Texas.

6132 Valadez, Esther. The role of the Latina. CHICANO LAW REVIEW, Vol. 6, (1983), p. 21-24. English. DESCR: Latinos in the Law [symposium] (1982: UCLA).

Voting Rights

6133 Cotera, Marta P. Feminism: the Chicana and Anglo versions: a historical analysis. IN: Melville, Margarita B., ed. TWICE A MINORITY. St. Louis, MO: Mosby, 1980, p. 217-234. English. DESCR: *Anglo Americans; Chicano Movement; Conferences and Meetings; *Feminism; Organizations; Social History and Conditions; *Women.

6134 Valenzuela-Crocker, Elvira. Women, power and the vote. NUESTRO, Vol. 8, no. 6 (August 1984), p. 43-44. English. DESCR: Women; *Women's Suffrage.

LA VOZ DEL PUEBLO

6135 Leal, Luis. La soldadera en la narrativa de la Revolucion. IN: Leal, Luis. AZTLAN Y MEXICO: PERFILES LITERARIOS E HISTORICOS. Binghamton, NY: Bilingual Press/Editorial Bilingue, 1985, p. 185-193. Spanish. DESCR: La Adelita; *Literary Criticism; Mexican Literature; Mexican Revolution - 1910-1920; Women.

Wages
USE: Income

War

6136 Salas, Elizabeth. Soldaderas in the Mexican military: myth and history. Austin, TX: University of Texas Press, 1990. xiii, 163 p., [12] p. of plates: ill. English. DESCR: Aztecs; History; *La Adelita; Mexican Revolution - 1910-1920; Mexico; *Military; Symbolism; *Women.

6137 Salas, Elizabeth. Soldaderas in the Mexican military: myth and history. Thesis (Ph.D.)--University of California, Los Angeles, 1987. 313p. English. DESCR: Aztecs; History; La Adelita; Mexican Revolution - 1910-1920; Mexico; Military; Symbolism; *Women.

6138 Santillan, Richard. Rosita the riveter: Midwest Mexican American women during World War II, 1941-1945. PERSPECTIVES IN MEXICAN AMERICAN STUDIES, Vol. 2, (1989), p. 115-147. English. DESCR: History; Industrial Workers; Intergroup Relations; Language Usage; *Midwestern States; Military; Mutualistas; Sexism; *Working Women; *World War II.

Warschaw, Carmen

6139 Mendoza, Hope Schecter and Chall, Malca. Activist in the labor movement, the Democratic Party, and the Mexican-American community: an interview. Berkeley, CA: Regional Oral History Office, Bancroft Library, University of California, Berkeley, 1980. xii, 170 p.: ill. English. DESCR: *Biography; Chavez Ravine, Los Angeles, CA; Church, Frank; Community Organizations; Community Service Organization, Los Angeles, (CSO); Democratic Party; Elections; Garment Industry; Industrial Workers; *Labor Unions; Leadership; Mendoza, Hope Schecter; Snyder, Elizabeth.

Washington, D.C.

6140 Rose, Margaret. From the fields to the picket line: Huelga women and the boycott, 1965-1975. LABOR HISTORY, Vol. 31, no. 3 (1990), p. 271-293. English. DESCR: *Boycotts; Family; Farm Workers; Padilla, Esther; Padilla, Gilbert; Rodriguez, Conrado; Rodriguez, Herminia; *United Farmworkers of America (UFW).

Watsonville Canning and Frozen Food Co.

6141 Romero, Bertha. The exploitation of Mexican women in the canning industry and the effects of capital accumulation on striking workers. REVISTA MUJERES, Vol. 3, no. 2 (June 1986), p. 16-20. English. DESCR: Canneries; Capitalism; Industrial Workers; Labor Unions; Strikes and Lockouts.

6142 Shapiro, Peter. Watsonville shows "it can be done". GUARDIAN, Vol. 39, no. 24 (March 25, 1987), p. 1,9. English. DESCR: Canneries; Labor Unions; NorCal Frozen Foods; *Strikes and Lockouts; Working Women.

WE FED THEM CACTUS

6143 Padilla, Genaro. Imprisoned narrative? Or lies, secrets, and silence in New Mexico women's autobiography. IN: Calderon, Hector and Saldivar, Jose David, eds. CRITICISM IN THE BORDERLANDS: STUDIES IN CHICANO LITERATURE, CULTURE, AND IDEOLOGY. Durham, NC: Duke University Press, 1991, p. [43]-60. English. DESCR: Authors; *Autobiography; *Cabeza de Baca, Fabiola; *Jaramillo, Cleofas M.; Literary History; New Mexico; ROMANCE OF A LITTLE VILLAGE GIRL.

6144 Rebolledo, Tey Diana. Las escritoras: romances and realities. IN: Gonzales-Berry, Erlinda, ed. PASO POR AQUI: CRITICAL ESSAYS ON THE NEW MEXICAN LITERARY TRADITION. Albuquerque, NM: University of New Mexico Press, c1989, p. 199-214. English. DESCR: Authors; *Cabeza de Baca, Fabiola; *Jaramillo, Cleofas M.; Literary History; New Mexico; OLD SPAIN IN OUR SOUTHWEST; *Otero Warren, Nina; ROMANCE OF A LITTLE VILLAGE GIRL; Women.

WE FED THEM CACTUS
    (cont.)

6145 Rebolledo, Tey Diana. Hispanic women writers
     of the Southwest: tradition and innovation.
     IN: Lensink, Judy Nolte, ed. OLD
     SOUTHWEST/NEW SOUTHWEST: ESSAYS ON A REGION
     AND ITS LITERATURE. Tucson, AZ: The Tucson
     Public Library, 1987, p. 49-61. English.
     DESCR: *Authors; Cabeza de Baca, Fabiola;
     Jaramillo, Cleofas M.; Literature; Mora,
     Pat; OLD SPAIN IN OUR SOUTHWEST; Otero
     Warren, Nina; Preciado Martin, Patricia; Sex
     Roles; Sex Stereotypes; Silva, Beverly;
     *Southwestern United States; Vigil-Pinon,
     Evangelina; *Women.

6146 Rebolledo, Tey Diana. Narrative strategies
     of resistance in Hispana writing. THE
     JOURNAL OF NARRATIVE TECHNIQUE, Vol. 20, no.
     2 (Spring 1990), p. 134-146. English.
     DESCR: *Authors; Cabeza de Baca, Fabiola;
     Fiction; Jaramillo, Cleofas M.; *Literary
     Criticism; Literature; New Mexico; OLD SPAIN
     IN OUR SOUTHWEST; *Oral Tradition; Otero
     Warren, Nina; ROMANCE OF A LITTLE VILLAGE
     GIRL.

6147 Rebolledo, Tey Diana. Tradition and
     mythology: signatures of landscape in
     Chicana literature. IN: Norwood, Vera and
     Monk, Janice, eds. THE DESERT IS NO LADY:
     SOUTHWESTERN LANDSCAPES IN WOMEN'S WRITING
     AND ART. New Haven, CT: Yale University
     Press, 1987, p. 96-124. English. **DESCR:**
     *Authors; Cabeza de Baca, Fabiola; Chavez,
     Denise; Jaramillo, Cleofas M.; Literary
     Criticism; *Literary History; Literature;
     Mora, Pat; Mythology; Otero Warren, Nina;
     Portillo Trambley, Estela; Silva, Beverly;
     Southwestern United States.

Weddings

6148 Murguia, Edward. Chicano intermarriage: a
     theoretical and empirical study. San
     Antonio, TX: Trinity University Press, 1982.
     xiv, 134 p. English. **DESCR:** Assimilation;
     Attitudes; Ethnic Groups; *Intermarriage;
     Military; Social Classes.

Welfare

6149 Chicana Welfare Rights challenges Talmadge
     amendment. REGENERACION, Vol. 2, no. 3
     (1973), p. 14. English. **DESCR:** Chicana
     Welfare Rights Organization; *Feminism;
     Social Services; Talmadge Amendment to the
     Social Security Act, 1971.

6150 Escalante, Alicia. Chicana Welfare Rights
     vs. the Talmadge amendment. LA RAZA, Vol. 2,
     no. 1 (February 1974), p. 20-21. English.
     DESCR: Chicana Welfare Rights Organization;
     Flores, Francisca; Talmadge Amendment to the
     Social Security Act, 1971.

6151 Escalante, Alicia. A letter from the Chicana
     Welfare Rights organization. ENCUENTRO
     FEMENIL, Vol. 1, no. 2 (1974), p. 15-19.
     English. **DESCR:** *Chicana Welfare Rights
     Organization; Child Care Centers; *Talmadge
     Amendment to the Social Security Act, 1971;
     Working Women.

6152 Flores, Francisca. A reaction to discussions
     on the Talmadge Amendment to the Social
     Security Act. ENCUENTRO FEMENIL, Vol. 1, no.
     2 (1974), p. 13-14. English. **DESCR:** *Chicana
     Welfare Rights Organization; Child Care
     Centers; Discrimination; Feminism; Income;
     *Social Security Act; Social Services;
     *Talmadge Amendment to the Social Security
     Act, 1971; Working Women.

6153 Flores, Francisca. A reaction to discussions
     on the Talmadge Amendment to the Social
     Security Act. REGENERACION, Vol. 2, no. 3
     (1973), p. 16. English. **DESCR:** *Chicana
     Welfare Rights Organization; Child Care
     Centers; Discrimination; Feminism; Income;
     *Social Security Act; Social Services;
     *Talmadge Amendment to the Social Security
     Act, 1971; Working Women.

6154 Hancock, Paula F. The effect of welfare
     eligibility on the labor force participation
     of women of Mexican origin in California.
     POPULATION RESEARCH AND POLICY REVIEW, Vol.
     5, no. 2 (1986), p. 163-185. English.
     DESCR: Aid to Families with Dependent
     Children (AFDC); California; *Employment;
     Food Stamps; Immigrants; Medi-Cal; Single
     Parents; Women.

6155 Hancock, Paula F. The effects of nativity,
     legal status and welfare eligibility on the
     labor force participation of women of
     Mexican origin in California. Thesis
     (Ph.D.)--University of Southern California,
     1985. English. **DESCR:** *Employment;
     *Immigrants; Undocumented Workers.

6156 Nieto Gomez de Lazarin, Anna. Madres por
     justicia! ENCUENTRO FEMENIL, Vol. 1, no. 1
     (Spring 1973), p. 12-19. English. **DESCR:**
     Chicana Welfare Rights Organization;
     Employment; Talmadge Amendment to the Social
     Security Act, 1971.

6157 Weiner, Raine. The needs of poverty women
     heading households: a return to
     postsecondary education. Thesis
     (Ph.D.)--California School of Professional
     Psychology, Los Angeles, 1986. 180 p.
     English. **DESCR:** Anglo Americans; Blacks;
     *Employment Training; Ethnic Groups;
     *Poverty; *Single Parents; Vocational
     Education; Women.

**"What Kind of Lover Have You Made Me, Mother?:
Towards a Theory of Chicanas' Feminism and
Cultural Identity Through Poetry" [article]**

6158 Quintana, Alvina E. O mama, with what's
     inside of me. REVISTA MUJERES, Vol. 3, no. 1
     (January 1986), p. 38-40. English. **DESCR:**
     Alarcon, Norma; Feminism; *Literary
     Criticism; Poetry.

WHISPERING TO FOOL THE WIND

6159 Saldivar, Jose David. Towards a Chicano
     poetics: the making of the Chicano subject.
     CONFLUENCIA, Vol. 1, no. 2 (Spring 1986), p.
     10-17. English. **DESCR:** Corridos; Feminism;
     *Literary Criticism; "Los Vatos" [poem];
     Montoya, Jose E.; *Poetry; RESTLESS
     SERPENTS; Rios, Alberto; Zamora, Bernice.

White Fence Gang

6160 Moore, Joan W. Mexican-American women
     addicts: the influence of family background.
     IN: Glick, Ronald and Moore, Joan, eds.
     DRUGS IN HISPANIC COMMUNITIES. New
     Brunswick, NJ: Rutgers University Press,
     c1990, p. 127-153. English. **DESCR:** Barrios;
     *Drug Addicts; Drug Use; East Los Angeles,
     CA; *Family; *Gangs; Heroin; Hoyo-Mara Gang,
     East Los Angeles, CA; Pachucos; Sex Roles;
     Socialization; Youth.

"The White Line" [poem]

6161 Zamora, Bernice. Archetypes in Chicana
poetry. DE COLORES, Vol. 4, no. 3 (1978), p.
43-52. English. DESCR: Cervantes, Lorna Dee;
Cunningham, Veronica; "Declaration on a Day
of Little Inspiration" [poem]; Hernandez,
Carlota; "I Speak in an Illusion" [poem];
*Literary Criticism; Lucero, Judy A.;
Macias, Margarita; Mendoza, Rita; "Para Mi
Hijita" [poem]; *Poetry; "Rape Report"
[poem]; "Working Mother's Song" [poem]; "You
Can Only Blame the System for So Long"
[poem]; Zamora, Katarina.

Widowhood

6162 Balkwell, Carolyn Ann. An attitudinal
correlate of the timing of a major life
event: the case of morale in widowhood.
FAMILY RELATIONS, Vol. 34, no. 4 (October
1985), p. 577-581. English. DESCR:
*Ancianos; Counseling (Psychological);
*Marriage; Mental Health; Natural Support
Systems.

6163 Balkwell, Carolyn Ann. Widowhood: its impact
on morale and optimism among older persons
of three ethnic groups. Thesis
(Ph.D.)--University of Georgia, 1981. 170 p.
English. DESCR: *Ancianos; Anglo Americans;
Blacks; Depression (Psychological); Ethnic
Groups; Los Angeles County, CA; *Mental
Health; *Women.

6164 Facio, Elisa "Linda". Constraints,
resources, and self-definition: a case study
of Chicano older women. Thesis
(Ph.D.)--University of California, Berkeley,
1988. 246 p. English. DESCR: *Ancianos;
*Family; Grandmothers; *Poverty; Sex Roles.

6165 Gonzalez, Deena J. The widowed women of
Santa Fe: assessments on the lives of an
unmarried population, 1850-80. IN: Scadron,
Arlene, ed. ON THEIR OWN: WIDOWS AND
WIDOWHOOD IN THE AMERICAN SOUTHWEST
1843-1939. Urbana, IL: University of
Illinois Press, c1988, p. [65]-90. English.
DESCR: Family; History; Income; Land Tenure;
*Santa Fe, NM; Sex Roles; Single Parents;
*Women.

6166 Gonzalez, Deena J. The widowed women of
Santa Fe: assessments on the lives of an
unmarried population, 1850-80. IN: DuBois,
Ellen Carol and Ruiz, Vicki L., eds. UNEQUAL
SISTERS: A MULTICULTURAL READER IN U.S.
WOMEN'S HISTORY. New York: Routledge, 1990,
p. 34-50. English. DESCR: Family; History;
Income; Land Tenure; *Santa Fe, NM; Sex
Roles; Single Parents; *Women.

6167 Loustaunau, Martha Oehmke. Hispanic widows
and their support systems in the Mesilla
Valley of southern New Mexico, 1910-40. IN:
Scadron, Arlene, ed. ON THEIR OWN: WIDOWS
AND WIDOWHOOD IN THE AMERICAN SOUTHWEST
1843-1939. Urbana, IL: University of
Illinois Press, c1988, p. [91]-116. English.
DESCR: Cultural Customs; Extended Family;
Mesilla Valley, NM; Natural Support Systems;
Sex Roles; Single Parents; *Women.

6168 Malvido, Elsa. El uso del cuerpo femenino en
la epoca colonial mexicana a traves de los
estudios de demografia historica. IN: Del
Castillo, Adelaida R., ed. BETWEEN BORDERS:
ESSAYS ON MEXICANA/CHICANA HISTORY. Encino,
CA: Floricanto Press, 1990, p. 115-130.
Spanish. DESCR: Marriage; *Mexico; *Sex
Roles; Sexual Behavior; *Vital Statistics;
*Women.

6169 Wagner, Roland M. Changes in the friend
network during the first year of single
parenthood for Mexican American and Anglo
women. JOURNAL OF DIVORCE, Vol. 11, no. 2
(Winter 1987), p. 89-109. English. DESCR:
Anglo Americans; Divorce; *Natural Support
Systems; *Single Parents; Women.

WILD THORNS

6170 Harlow, Barbara. Sites of struggle:
immigration, deportation, prison, and exile.
IN: Calderon, Hector and Saldivar, Jose
David, eds. CRITICISM IN THE BORDERLANDS:
STUDIES IN CHICANO LITERATURE, CULTURE, AND
IDEOLOGY. Durham, NC: Duke University Press,
1991, p. [149]-163. English. DESCR:
Anzaldua, Gloria; BLACK GOLD; BORDERLANDS/LA
FRONTERA: THE NEW MESTIZA; First, Ruth;
Khalifeh, Sahar; *Literary Criticism;
*Political Ideology; Sanchez, Rosaura;
Social Classes; "The Cariboo Cafe" [short
story]; "The Ditch" [short story];
Viramontes, Helena Maria; *Women; Working
Women.

Willacy County, TX

6171 Hutchison, James. Teenagers and
contraception in Cameron and Willacy
Counties. BORDERLANDS JOURNAL, Vol. 7, no. 1
(Fall 1983), p. 75-90. English. DESCR:
*Birth Control; Cameron County, TX; *Family
Planning; Fertility; Sex Education; Youth.

Williams, Norma

6172 Williams, Norma. A Mexican American woman
encounters sociology: an autobiographical
perspective. AMERICAN SOCIOLOGIST, Vol. 19,
no. 4 (Winter 1988), p. 340-346. English.
DESCR: Autobiography; Sexism; Social
Science; *Sociology.

Wilmington, CA

6173 Romero, Gloria J.; Cervantes, Richard C.;
and Castro, Felipe G. Long-term stress among
Latino women after a plant closure.
SOCIOLOGY & SOCIAL RESEARCH, Vol. 71, no. 2
(January 1987), p. 85-88. English. DESCR:
Attitudes; Employment; Family; *Stress.

Witchcraft
USE: Brujas

Women Here are entered works about non-Chicanas.
For Mexican-American women USE Chicanas

6174 Abrahamse, Allan F.; Morrison, Peter A.; and
Waite, Linda J. Beyond stereotypes: who
becomes a single teenage mother? Santa
Monica, CA: RAND Corp., 1988. xv, 88 p.
English. DESCR: *Fertility; Religion;
Secondary School Education; *Single Parents;
Statistics; *Youth.

6175 Abrahamse, Allan F.; Morrison, Peter A.; and
Waite, Linda J. Teenagers willing to
consider single parenthood: who is at
greatest risk? FAMILY PLANNING PERSPECTIVES,
Vol. 20, no. 1 (January, February, 1988), p.
13-18. English. DESCR: Blacks; Family
Planning; *Fertility; High School and Beyond
Project (HS&B); *Single Parents; *Youth.

6176 Ahern, Susan; Bryan, Dexter Edward; and
Baca, Reynaldo. Migration and la mujer
fuerte. MIGRATION TODAY, Vol. 13, no. 1
(1985), p. 14-20. English. DESCR: Mexico;
*Migration; *Sex Roles.

Women (cont.)

6177 Alarcon, Norma. Chicana feminism: in the tracks of 'the' native woman. CULTURAL STUDIES, Vol. 4, no. 3 (October 1990), p. 248-256. English. DESCR: Cultural Studies; *Feminism; *Identity; *Indigenismo; Mestizaje.

6178 Alarcon, Norma. Latina writers in the United States. IN: Marting, Diane E., ed. SPANISH AMERICAN WOMEN WRITERS: A BIO-BIBLIOGRAPHICAL SOURCE BOOK. New York: Greenwood Press, 1990, p. [557]-567. English. DESCR: *Authors; *Bibliography; BREAKING BOUNDARIES: LATINA WRITING AND CRITICAL READINGS; Cubanos; Intergroup Relations; Language Usage; *Literature Reviews; Puerto Ricans; THIRD WOMAN [journal].

6179 Alarcon, Norma; Castillo, Ana; and Moraga, Cherrie. The sexuality of Latinas [special issue of THIRD WOMAN]. THIRD WOMAN, Vol. 4, (1989), p. 8-189. Bilingual. DESCR: *Literature; Sex Roles; *Sexual Behavior.

6180 Alarcon, Norma. The theoretical subject(s) of THIS BRIDGE CALLED MY BACK and Anglo-American feminism. IN: Calderon, Hector and Saldivar, Jose David, eds. CRITICISM IN THE BORDERLANDS: STUDIES IN CHICANO LITERATURE, CULTURE, AND IDEOLOGY. Durham, NC: Duke University Press, 1991, p. [28]-39. English. DESCR: *Anglo Americans; Anzaldua, Gloria; *Feminism; Moraga, Cherrie; THIS BRIDGE CALLED MY BACK.

6181 Alarcon, Norma. The theoretical subject(s) of THIS BRIDGE CALLED MY BACK and Anglo-American feminism. IN: Anzaldua, Gloria, ed. MAKING FACE, MAKING SOUL: HACIENDO CARAS: CREATIVE AND CRITICAL PERSPECTIVES BY WOMEN OF COLOR. San Francisco, CA: Aunt Lute Foundation Books, 1990, p. 356-369. English. DESCR: *Anglo Americans; Anzaldua, Gloria; *Feminism; Literary Criticism; Moraga, Cherrie; THIS BRIDGE CALLED MY BACK.

6182 Alba, Isabel Catherine. Achievement conflicts, sex-role orientation, and performance on sex-role appropriate and sex-role inappropriate tasks in women of three ethnic groups. Thesis (Ph.D.)--University of California, Riverside, 1987. 129 p. English. DESCR: Anglo Americans; *Assertiveness; Blacks; Ethnic Groups; Fear of Success Scale (FOSS); *Sex Roles.

6183 Alcalay, Rina. Hispanic women in the United States: family & work relations. MIGRATION TODAY, Vol. 12, no. 3 (1984), p. 13-20. English. DESCR: Extended Family; *Immigrants; Migration.

6184 Amaro, Hortensia. Considerations for prevention of HIV infection among Hispanic women. PSYCHOLOGY OF WOMEN QUARTERLY, Vol 12, no. 4 (December 1988), p. 429-443. English. DESCR: *AIDS (Disease); Attitudes; Population.

6185 Amaro, Hortensia; Russo, Nancy Felipe; and Pares-Avila, Jose A. Contemporary research on Hispanic women: a selected bibliography of the social science literature. PSYCHOLOGY OF WOMEN QUARTERLY, Vol. 11, no. 4 (December 1987), p. 523-532. English. DESCR: *Bibliography; *Psychology; Social Science.

6186 Amaro, Hortensia and Russo, Nancy Felipe. Hispanic women and mental health: an

overview of contemporary issues in research and practice. PSYCHOLOGY OF WOMEN QUARTERLY, Vol. 11, no. 4 (December 1987), p. 393-407. English. DESCR: *Literature Reviews; *Mental Health.

6187 Amaro, Hortensia. Hispanic women in psychology: a resource directory. Washington, DC: American Psychological Association, 1984. ii, 41 p. English. DESCR: *Directories; *Psychology.

6188 Amodeo, Luiza B.; Edelson, Rosalyn; and Martin, Jeanette. The triple bias: rural, minority and female. RURAL EDUCATOR, Vol. 3, no. 3 (Spring 1982), p. 1-6. English. DESCR: *Education; Rural Population; Social History and Conditions.

6189 Andrade, Sally J. Family roles of Hispanic women: stereotypes, empirical findings, and implications for research. IN: Zambrana, Ruth E., ed. WORK, FAMILY, AND HEALTH: LATINA WOMEN IN TRANSITION. Bronx, NY: Hispanic Research Center, Fordham University, 1982, p. 95-106. English. DESCR: *Family; Puerto Ricans; *Research Methodology; *Sex Roles; Sex Stereotypes.

6190 Aneshensel, Carol S., et al. Onset of fertility-related events during adolescence: a prospective comparison of Mexican American and non-Hispanic white females. AMERICAN JOURNAL OF PUBLIC HEALTH, Vol. 80, no. 8 (August 1990), p. 959-963. English. DESCR: Abortion; Anglo Americans; Birth Control; *Fertility; *Sexual Behavior; *Youth.

6191 Anzaldua, Gloria, ed. Making face, making soul = Haciendo caras: creative and critical perspectives by women of color. San Francisco, CA: Aunt Lute Foundation Books, 1990. English. DESCR: Ethnic Groups; *Feminism; *Literature.

6192 Apodaca, Maria Linda. A double edge sword: Hispanas and liberal feminism. CRITICA, Vol. 1, no. 3 (Fall 1986), p. 96-114. English. DESCR: *Feminism; History.

6193 Arbelaez A., Marisol. Impacto social del sismo, Mexico 1985: las costureras. IN: Del Castillo, Adelaida R., ed. BETWEEN BORDERS: ESSAYS ON MEXICANA/CHICANA HISTORY. Encino, CA: Floricanto Press, 1990, p. 315-331. Spanish. DESCR: Earthquakes; Frente de Costureras, Mexico; *Garment Industry; *Industrial Workers; Labor Unions; *Mexico; Mexico City Earthquake, September 19, 1985; Working Women.

6194 Arenal, Sandra. Sangre joven: las maquiladoras por dentro. Mexico, D.F.: Editorial Nuestro Tiempo, 1986. 130 p.: ill. Spanish. DESCR: *Border Industries; *Border Region; Employment; *Oral History; Working Women.

6195 Arguelles, Lourdes and Rivero, Anne M. HIV infection/AIDS and Latinas in Los Angeles County: considerations for prevention, treatment, and research practice. CALIFORNIA SOCIOLOGIST, Vol. 11, no. 1-2 (1988), p. 69-89. English. DESCR: *AIDS (Disease); Cultural Characteristics; Health Education; Homosexuality; Human Immunodeficiency Virus (HIV); Los Angeles County, CA; Natural Support Systems; Parent and Child Relationships; Sexual Behavior.

Women (cont.)

6196 Armas-Cardona, Regina. Anglo and Raza young women: a study of self-esteem, psychic distress and locus of control. Thesis (Ph.D.)--Wright Institute Graduate School of Psychology, 1985. 143 p. English. DESCR: *Anglo Americans; Locus of Control; *Mental Health; Stress.

6197 Atkinson, Donald R.; Winzelberg, Andrew; and Holland, Abby. Ethnicity, locus of control for family planning, and pregnancy counselor credibility. JOURNAL OF COUNSELING PSYCHOLOGY, Vol. 32, no. 3 (July 1985), p. 417-421. English. DESCR: Anglo Americans; Counseling (Psychological); *Family Planning; Fertility; Identity; *Locus of Control.

6198 Baca, Reynaldo and Bryan, Dexter Edward. Mexican women, migration and sex roles. MIGRATION TODAY, Vol. 13, no. 3 (1985), p. 14-18. English. DESCR: Mexico; *Migration; *Sex Roles.

6199 Bachu, Amara and O'Connell, Martin. Developing current fertility indicators for foreign-born women from the Current Population Survey. REVIEW OF PUBLIC DATA USE, Vol. 12, no. 3 (October 1984), p. 185-195. English. DESCR: Current Population Survey; *Fertility; Latin America; Mexico; *Surveys; Vital Statistics.

6200 Baezconde-Garbanati, Lourdes and Salgado de Snyder, Nelly. Mexican immigrant women: a selected bibliography. HISPANIC JOURNAL OF BEHAVIORAL SCIENCES, Vol. 9, no. 3 (September 1987), p. 331-358. English. DESCR: *Bibliography; *Immigrants.

6201 Baker, Susan Gonzalez. Many rivers to cross: Mexican immigrants, women workers, and the structure of labor markets in the urban Southwest. Thesis (Ph.D.)--University of Texas, Austin, 1989. 163 p. English. DESCR: *Immigrants; Immigration Reform and Control Act of 1986; *Labor Supply and Market; Undocumented Workers; *Working Women.

6202 Balkwell, Carolyn Ann. Widowhood: its impact on morale and optimism among older persons of three ethnic groups. Thesis (Ph.D.)--University of Georgia, 1981. 170 p. English. DESCR: *Ancianos; Anglo Americans; Blacks; Depression (Psychological); Ethnic Groups; Los Angeles County, CA; *Mental Health; Widowhood.

6203 Bassoff, Betty Z. and Ortiz, Elizabeth Thompson. Teen women: disparity between cognitive values and anticipated life events. CHILD WELFARE, Vol. 63, no. 2 (March, April, 1984), p. 125-138. English. DESCR: Sexual Behavior; *Values; *Youth.

6204 Bauer, Richard L. and Deyo, Richard A. Low risk of vertebral fracture in Mexican American women. ARCHIVES OF INTERNAL MEDICINE, Vol. 147, no. 8 (August 1987), p. 1437-1439. English. DESCR: Anglo Americans; *Osteoporosis; Preventative Medicine.

6205 Belk, Sharyn S., et al. Impact of ethnicity, nationality, counseling orientation, and mental health standards on stereotypic beliefs about women. SEX ROLES, Vol. 21, no. 9-10 (November 1989), p. 671-695. English. DESCR: Anglo Americans; Beliefs About Women Scale (BAWS); *Comparative Psychology; *Counseling (Psychological); Cultural Characteristics; Identity; Mental Health; *Sex Stereotypes; Sexism.

6206 Bergdolt-Munzer, Sara L. Homemakers and retirement income benefits: the other home security issue. CHICANO LAW REVIEW, Vol. 8, (1985), p. 61-80. English. DESCR: Ancianos; Domestic Work; Feminism; Social Security.

6207 Blackwelder, Julia Kirk. Women of the depression: caste and culture in San Antonio, 1929-1939. College Station, TX: Texas A&M University Press, 1984. xviii, 279 p.: ill. English. DESCR: Criminal Justice System; Cultural Characteristics; Employment; Family; Great Depression, 1929-1933; Labor Supply and Market; Labor Unions; Prostitution; San Antonio, TX; *Social Classes.

6208 Blanco, Iris. La mujer en los albores de la conquista de Mexico. AZTLAN, Vol. 11, no. 2 (Fall 1980), p. 249-270. Spanish. DESCR: *Aztecs; Mexico; Sex Roles.

6209 Blanco, Iris and Salorzano, Rosalia. O te aclimatas o te aclimueres. FEM, Vol. 8, no. 34 (June, July, 1984), p. 20-22. Spanish. DESCR: *Border Industries; *Immigration; Mexico; Working Women.

6210 Blanco, Iris. Participacion de las mujeres en la sociedad prehispanica. IN: Sanchez, Rosaura and Martinez Cruz, Rosa, eds. ESSAYS ON LA MUJER. Los Angeles, CA: Chicano Studies Center Publications, UCLA, 1977, p. 48-81. Spanish. DESCR: Aztecs; Cultural Customs; *History; Indigenismo; Mexico; Precolumbian Society.

6211 Blanco, Iris. El sexo y su condicionamiento cultural en el mundo prehispanico. IN: Del Castillo, Adelaida R., ed. BETWEEN BORDERS: ESSAYS ON MEXICANA/CHICANA HISTORY. Encino, CA: Floricanto Press, 1990, p. 363-374. Spanish. DESCR: Mexico; *Precolumbian Society; *Sex Roles; Sexual Behavior.

6212 Borland, Dolores C. A cohort analysis approach to the empty nest syndrome among three ethnic groups of women: a theoretical position. JOURNAL OF MARRIAGE AND THE FAMILY, Vol. 44, no. 1 (February 1982), p. 117-129. English. DESCR: "Empty Nest" Syndrome; Ethnic Groups; *Sex Roles; Social Psychology.

6213 Bourque, Linda B.; Kraus, Jess F.; and Cosand, Beverly J. Attributes of suicide in females. SUICIDE AND LIFE-THREATENING BEHAVIOR, Vol. 13, no. 2 (Summer 1983), p. 123-138. English. DESCR: Anglo Americans; Sacramento County, CA; *Suicide.

6214 Boza, Maria del Carmen, ed.; Silva, Beverly, ed.; and Valle, Carmen, ed. Nosotras: Latina literature today. Binghamton, NY: Bilingual Review Press, 1986. 93 p. Bilingual. DESCR: *Poems; *Short Story.

6215 Braddom, Carolyn Lentz. The conceptualization of effective leadership as seen by women, Black and Hispanic superintendents. Thesis (Ed.D.)--University of Cincinnati, 1988. 232 p. English. DESCR: Anglo Americans; Blacks; *Educational Administration; *Leadership; Management.

Women (cont.)

6216 Bustamante, Jorge A. Maquiladoras: a new face of international capitalism on Mexico's northern frontier. IN: Nash, June and Fernandez-Kelly, Patricia, eds. WOMEN, MEN, AND THE INTERNATIONAL DIVISION OF LABOR. Albany, NY: State University of New York Press, 1983, p. 224-256. English. DESCR: Banking Industry; Border Industrialization Program (BIP); Border Industries; *Border Region; Foreign Trade; Industrial Workers; International Economic Relations; Mexico; Population; Programa Nacional Fronterizo (PRONAF); United States-Mexico Relations; Working Women.

6217 Calderon, Vivian. Maternal employment and career orientation of young Chicana, Black, and white women. Thesis (Ph.D.)--University of California, Santa Cruz, 1984. 150 p. English. DESCR: Anglo Americans; Blacks; *Careers; *Employment; *Youth.

6218 Campos Carr, Irene. Proyecto La Mujer: Latina women shaping consciousness. WOMEN'S STUDIES INTERNATIONAL FORUM, Vol. 12, no. 1 (1989), p. 45-49. English. DESCR: Artists; Aurora, IL; Authors; Barrios; Conferences and Meetings; Elgin, IL; *Feminism; Joliet, IL; Poetry; Proyecto La Mujer Conference (Spring, 1982: Northern Illinois).

6219 Carrillo, Teresa. The women's movement and the left in Mexico: the presidential candidacy of Dona Rosario Ibarra. IN: Cordova, Teresa, et al., eds. CHICANA VOICES. Austin, TX: Center for Mexican American Studies, 1986, p. 96-113. English. DESCR: Biography; Ibarra, Rosario; Mexico; Politics.

6220 Carrillo V., Jorge and Hernandez H., Alberto. Mujeres fronterizas en la industria maquiladora. Mexico, D.F.: Secretaria de Educacion Publica; Tijuana, B.C.N.: Centro de Estudios Fronterizos del Norte de Mexico, 1985. 216 p. Spanish. DESCR: *Border Industries; *Employment; Working Women.

6221 Castaneda, Antonia I. Comparative frontiers: the migration of women to Alta California and New Zealand. IN: Schlissel, Lillian, et al., eds. WESTERN WOMEN: THEIR LAND, THEIR LIVES. Albuquerque, NM: University of New Mexico Press, 1988, p. 283-300. English. DESCR: Border Region; California; History; Immigrants; Immigration; Marriage; Mexico; Missions; Native Americans; New Zealand; Social History and Conditions.

6222 Castaneda, Antonia I. Gender, race, and culture: Spanish-Mexican women in the historiography of frontier California. FRONTIERS: A JOURNAL OF WOMEN STUDIES, Vol. 11, no. 1 (1990), p. [8]-20. English. DESCR: Bancroft, Hubert Howe; Bolton, Herbert Eugene; *California; Californios; *Historiography; History; Intermarriage; *Sex Stereotypes; Spanish Borderlands Theory; Spanish Influence; Stereotypes; Turner, Frederick Jackson.

6223 Castaneda, Antonia I. The political economy of nineteenth century stereotypes of Californianas. IN: Del Castillo, Adelaida R., ed. BETWEEN BORDERS: ESSAYS ON MEXICANA/CHICANA HISTORY. Encino, CA: Floricanto Press, 1990, p. 213-236. English. DESCR: *California; *Californios; Dana, Richard Henry; Farnham, Thomas Jefferson; History; LIFE IN CALIFORNIA; *Political Economy; Robinson, Alfred; *Sex Stereotypes; TRAVELS IN CALIFORNIA AND SCENES IN THE PACIFIC OCEAN; TWO YEARS BEFORE THE MAST.

6224 Castaneda Garcia, Carmen. Fuentes para la historia de la mujer en los archivos de Guadalajara. IN: Del Castillo, Adelaida R., ed. BETWEEN BORDERS: ESSAYS ON MEXICANA/CHICANA HISTORY. Encino, CA: Floricanto Press, 1990, p. 102-112. Spanish. DESCR: *Archives; *Guadalajara; History; *Mexico.

6225 Castillo, Sylvia. A guide to Hispanic women's resources: a perspective on networking among Hispanic women. CALIFORNIA WOMEN, (December 1983), p. 2-6. English. DESCR: *Directories; *Organizations; Professional Organizations.

6226 Chavira, Alicia. "Tienes que ser valiente": Mexicana migrants in a midwestern farm labor camp. IN: Melville, Margarita, ed. MEXICANAS AT WORK IN THE UNITED STATES. Houston, TX: Mexican American Studies Program, University of Houston, 1988, p. 64-74. English. DESCR: *Farm Workers; Immigrants; *Labor Camps; Midwestern States; Migrant Health Services; *Migrant Labor; Sex Roles.

6227 Cochran, Jo, et al., eds. Bearing witness/Sobreviviendo: an anthology of Native American/Latina art and literature. CALYX: A JOURNAL OF ART AND LITERATURE BY WOMEN, Vol. 8, no. 2 (Spring 1984), p. [1]-128. English. DESCR: *Art; Drawings; *Fiction; Native Americans; *Poems.

6228 Codega, Susan A.; Pasley, B. Kay; and Kreutzer, Jill. Coping behaviors of adolescent mothers: an exploratory study and comparison of Mexican-Americans and Anglos. JOURNAL OF ADOLESCENT RESEARCH, Vol. 5, no. 1 (January 1990), p. 34-53. English. DESCR: Anglo Americans; Colorado; *Fertility; *Stress; *Youth.

6229 Cooney, Rosemary Santana and Ortiz, Vilma. Nativity, national origin, and Hispanic female participation in the labor force. SOCIAL SCIENCE QUARTERLY, Vol. 64, (September 1983), p. 510-523. English. DESCR: Immigrants; *Working Women.

6230 Cotera, Marta P. Feminism: the Chicana and Anglo versions: a historical analysis. IN: Melville, Margarita B., ed. TWICE A MINORITY. St. Louis, MO: Mosby, 1980, p. 217-234. English. DESCR: *Anglo Americans; Chicano Movement; Conferences and Meetings; *Feminism; Organizations; Social History and Conditions; Voting Rights.

6231 Cristo, Martha H. Stress and coping among Mexican women. Thesis (Ph.D.)--California School of Professional Psychology, Los Angeles, 1988. 336 p. English. DESCR: Cultural Characteristics; *Immigrants; Mental Health; Socioeconomic Factors; *Stress.

6232 Curry Rodriguez, Julia E. Labor migration and familial responsibilities: experiences of Mexican women. IN: Melville, Margarita, ed. MEXICANAS AT WORK IN THE UNITED STATES. Houston, TX: Mexican American Studies Program, University of Houston, 1988, p. 47-63. English. DESCR: Employment; Family; *Immigrants; Mexico; *Migrant Labor; Oral History; Sex Roles; Undocumented Workers; *Working Women.

Women (cont.)

6233 Curry Rodriguez, Julia E. Reconceptualizing undocumented labor immigration: the causes, impact and consequences in Mexican women's lives. Thesis (Ph.D.)--University of Texas at Austin, 1988. xiv, 329 p. English. **DESCR:** Employment; *Immigrants; Mexico; Oral History; *Undocumented Workers.

6234 Daggett, Andrea Stuhlman. A comparison of occupational goal orientations of female Mexican-Americans and Anglo high-school seniors of the classes of 1972 and 1980. Thesis (Ph.D.)--University of Arizona, Tucson, 1983. xii, 134 p. English. **DESCR:** Academic Achievement; Anglo Americans; *Careers; *Secondary School Education; Sexism; Students.

6235 Daly, Mary B.; Clark, Gary M.; and McGuire, William L. Breast cancer prognosis in a mixed Caucasian-Hispanic population. JNCI: JOURNAL OF THE NATIONAL CANCER INSTITUTE, Vol. 74, no. 4 (April 1985), p. 753-757. English. **DESCR:** Anglo Americans; *Cancer.

6236 D'Andrea, Vaneeta-Marie. Ethnic women: a critique of the literature, 1971-1981. ETHNIC AND RACIAL STUDIES, Vol. 9, (April 1986), p. 235-246. English. **DESCR:** Bibliography; Ethnic Groups; *Literature Reviews; Periodical Indexes.

6237 de Anda, Diane; Becerra, Rosina M.; and Fielder, Eve P. In their own words: the life experiences of Mexican-American and white pregnant adolescents and adolescent mothers. CHILD AND ADOLESCENT SOCIAL WORK, Vol. 7, no. 4 (August 1990), p. 301-318. English. **DESCR:** Anglo Americans; *Fertility; *Sexual Behavior; *Youth.

6238 de Anda, Diane; Becerra, Rosina M.; and Fielder, Eve P. Sexuality, pregnancy, and motherhood among Mexican-American adolescents. JOURNAL OF ADOLESCENT RESEARCH, Vol. 3, no. 3-4 (Fall, Winter, 1988), p. 403-411. English. **DESCR:** Anglo Americans; Attitudes; Birth Control; *Fertility; Sex Education; *Sexual Behavior; *Youth.

6239 De Llano, Carmen. Comparisons of the psychocultural characteristics of graduate school-bound and nongraduate school-bound Mexican American and Anglo American college women. Thesis (Ph.D.)--California School of Professional Psychology, 1986. 223 p. English. **DESCR:** *Anglo Americans; Colleges and Universities; Comparative Psychology; Cultural Characteristics; *Graduate Schools; Higher Education; Students.

6240 Del Castillo, Adelaida R., et al. An assessment of the status of the education of Hispanic American women. IN: McKenna, Teresa and Ortiz, Flora Ida, eds. THE BROKEN WEB: THE EDUCATIONAL EXPERIENCE OF HISPANIC WOMEN. Claremont, CA: Tomas Rivera Center; Berkeley, CA: Floricanto Press, 1988, p. 3-24. English. **DESCR:** Academic Achievement; Conferences and Meetings; Discrimination in Education; Dropouts; *Education; Higher Education; Public Policy; Research Methodology; The Educational Experience of Hispanic American Women [symposium] (1985: Claremont, CA).

6241 Del Castillo, Adelaida R., ed. Between borders: essays on Mexicana/Chicana history. Encino, CA: Floricanto Press, c1990. xv, 563 p. Bilingual. **DESCR:** Feminism; Historiography; *History; Mexico; Working Women.

6242 Del Castillo, Adelaida R. and Torres, Maria. The interdependency of educational institutions and cultural norms: the Hispana experience. IN: McKenna, Teresa and Ortiz, Flora Ida, eds. THE BROKEN WEB: THE EDUCATIONAL EXPERIENCE OF HISPANIC WOMEN. Claremont, CA: Tomas Rivera Center; Berkeley, CA: Floricanto Press, 1988, p. 39-60. English. **DESCR:** Academic Achievement; Acculturation; *Cultural Characteristics; *Education; *Literature Reviews; Research Methodology; *Values.

6243 Del Castillo, Adelaida R. Sterilization: an overview. IN: Mora, Magdalena and Del Castillo, Adelaida, eds. MEXICAN WOMEN IN THE UNITED STATES: STRUGGLES PAST AND PRESENT. Los Angeles, CA: Chicano Studies Research Center, UCLA, 1980, p. 65-70. English. **DESCR:** Puerto Ricans; *Sterilization.

6244 Del Castillo, Adelaida R. La vision chicana. REGENERACION, Vol. 2, no. 4 (1975), p. 46-48. English. **DESCR:** Anglo Americans; *Feminism.

6245 Deutsch, Sarah. Culture, class, and gender: Chicanas and Chicanos in Colorado and New Mexico, 1900-1940. Thesis (Ph.D.)--Yale University, 1985. xii, 510 p. English. **DESCR:** Anglo Americans; Colorado; Immigrants; New Mexico; *Sex Roles; *Social Classes; Social History and Conditions; *Working Women.

6246 Deutsch, Sarah. No separate refuge: culture, class, and gender on an Anglo-Hispanic frontier in the American Southwest, 1880-1940. New York: Oxford University Press, 1987. vi, 356 p. English. **DESCR:** Anglo Americans; Colorado; Immigrants; Immigration; Mining Industry; Missions; New Mexico; *Sex Roles; *Social Classes; *Social History and Conditions; Working Women; World War I.

6247 Deutsch, Sarah. Women and intercultural relations: the case of Hispanic New Mexico and Colorado. SIGNS: JOURNAL OF WOMEN IN CULTURE AND SOCIETY, Vol. 12, no. 4 (Summer 1987), p. 719-739. English. **DESCR:** Colorado; Cultural Characteristics; Immigrants; Intercultural Communication; Mexico; New Mexico; Rural Population; Sex Roles; Social History and Conditions.

6248 Dill, Bonnie Thornton. Our mothers' grief: racial ethnic women and the maintenance of families. JOURNAL OF FAMILY HISTORY, Vol. 13, no. 4 (October 1988), p. 415-431. English. **DESCR:** Asian Americans; Blacks; Domestic Work; *Family; Fertility; *Sex Roles; *Working Women.

6249 Dixon, Marlene; Martinez, Elizabeth; and McCaughan, Ed. Theoretical perspectives on Chicanas, Mexicanas and the transnational working class. CONTEMPORARY MARXISM, no. 11 (Fall 1985), p. 46-76. English. **DESCR:** Border Industries; Capitalism; Economic History and Conditions; History; *Immigration; *Labor Supply and Market; *Laboring Classes; Mexico; Undocumented Workers.

Women (cont.)

6250 Domenella, Ana Rosa. Al margen de un coloquio fronterizo mujer y literatura mexicana y chicana. FEM, Vol. 14, no. 89 (May 1990), p. 32-34. Spanish. DESCR: *Border Region; Coloquio Fronterizo Mujer y Literatura Mexicana y Chicana (1987: Tijuana, Baja California, Mexico); *Conferences and Meetings; *Literature; Mexican Literature; Mexico.

6251 Dressel, Paula. Symposium. Civil rights, affirmative action, and the aged of the future: will life chances be different for Blacks, Hispanics, and women? An overview of the issues. GERONTOLOGIST, Vol. 26, no. 2 (April 1986), p. 128-131. English. DESCR: Affirmative Action; *Ancianos; Blacks; *Civil Rights.

6252 Dublin, Thomas. Commentary [on "And Miles to Go": Mexican Women and Work, 1930-1985]. IN: Schlissel, Lillian, et al., eds. WESTERN WOMEN: THEIR LAND, THEIR LIVES. Albuquerque, NM: University of New Mexico Press, 1988, p. 137-140. English. DESCR: "'And Miles to Go...': Mexican Women and Work, 1930-1985"; Employment; Income; Labor Unions; Ruiz, Vicki L.; Undocumented Workers; *Working Women.

6253 Dungy, Claibourne I. Breast feeding preference of Hispanic and Anglo women. CLINICAL PEDIATRICS, Vol. 28, no. 2 (February 1989), p. 92-94. English. DESCR: Anglo Americans; Attitudes; *Breastfeeding.

6254 [Edicion feminista (Special Issue)]. IMAGINE, Vol. 2, no. 1 (Summer 1985), p. ii-159. Bilingual. DESCR: Literature; *Poems.

6255 Engle, Patricia L. Prenatal and postnatal anxiety in women giving birth in Los Angeles. HEALTH PSYCHOLOGY, Vol. 9, no. 3 (1990), p. 285-299. English. DESCR: *Fertility; Immigrants; Los Angeles, CA; *Maternal and Child Welfare; Medical Care; *Prenatal Care; *Stress.

6256 Enriquez-White, Celia. Attitudes of Hispanic and Anglo women managers toward women in management. Thesis (Ed.D.)--University of La Verne, 1982. 103 p. English. DESCR: Anglo Americans; *Attitudes; Leadership; *Management.

6257 Espin, Oliva M. Cultural and historical influences on sexuality in Hispanic/Latin women: implications for psychotherapy. IN: Vance, Carole S., ed. PLEASURE AND DANGER: EXPLORING FEMALE SEXUALITY. Boston, MA: Routledge & Kegan Paul, 1984, p. 149-164. English. DESCR: Immigration; Language Usage; Machismo; *Psychotherapy; Sex Roles; *Sexual Behavior; Social History and Conditions; Spanish Influence.

6258 Fanelli-Kuczmarski, Marie T., et al. Folate status of Mexican American, Cuban, and Puerto Rican women. AMERICAN JOURNAL OF CLINICAL NUTRITION, Vol. 52, no. 2 (August 1990), p. 368-372. English. DESCR: Cubanos; *Folic Acid Deficiency; Hispanic Health and Nutrition Examination Survey (HHANES); *Nutrition; Puerto Ricans.

6259 Farkas, George; Barton, Margaret; and Kushner, Kathy. White, Black, and Hispanic female youths in central city labor markets. SOCIOLOGICAL QUARTERLY, Vol. 29, no. 4 (Winter 1988), p. 605-621. English. DESCR: Anglo Americans; Blacks; Employment; *Income; *Labor Supply and Market; Urban Communities; *Youth.

6260 Fennelly, Katherine. Childbearing among Hispanics in the United States: an annotated bibliography. New York: Greenwood Press, 1987. xii, 157 p. English. DESCR: Abortion; *Bibliography; Birth Control; *Fertility; Sterilization; Youth.

6261 Fennelly, Katherine and Ortiz, Vilma. Childbearing among young Latino women in the United States. AMERICAN JOURNAL OF PUBLIC HEALTH, Vol. 77, no. 1 (January 1987), p. 25-28. English. DESCR: *Ethnic Groups; *Fertility; Puerto Ricans; *Youth.

6262 Fennelly, Katherine. El embarazo precoz: childbearing among Hispanic teenagers in the United States. New York, NY: School of Public Health, Columbia University, c1988. 36 p.: ill. Bilingual. DESCR: *Fertility; Youth.

6263 Fenster, Laura and Coye, Molly J. Birthweight of infants born to Hispanic women employed in agriculture. ARCHIVES OF ENVIRONMENTAL HEALTH, Vol. 45, no. 1 (January, February, 1990), p. 46-52. English. DESCR: *Farm Workers; *Prenatal Care.

6264 Fernandez Kelly, Maria. "Chavalas de maquiladora": a study of the female labor force in Ciudad Juarez' offshore production plants. Thesis (Ph.D.)--Rutgers University, 1980. xi, 391 leaves. English. DESCR: *Border Industries; Ciudad Juarez, Chihuahua, Mexico; Electronics Industry; *Employment; Garment Industry; Industrial Workers; Mexico; *Working Women.

6265 Fernandez Kelly, Maria and Garcia, Anna M. The making of an underground economy: Hispanic women, home work, and the advanced capitalist state. URBAN ANTHROPOLOGY, Vol. 14, no. 1-3 (Spring, Fall, 1985), p. 59-90. English. DESCR: Capitalism; Cubanos; Employment; Garment Industry; Industrial Workers; International Economic Relations; Labor Supply and Market; *Los Angeles County, CA; *Miami, FL; Working Women.

6266 Fernandez Kelly, Maria. The 'maquila' women. NACLA: REPORT ON THE AMERICAS, Vol. 14, no. 5 (September, October, 1980), p. 14-19. English. DESCR: *Border Industries; Feminism; Industrial Workers; Stereotypes; *Working Women.

6267 Fernandez Kelly, Maria. Mexican border industrialization, female labor force participation and migration. IN: Nash, June and Fernandez-Kelly, Patricia, eds. WOMEN, MEN, AND THE INTERNATIONAL DIVISION OF LABOR. Albany, NY: State University of New York Press, 1983, p. 205-223. English. DESCR: Border Industrialization Program (BIP); *Border Industries; Ciudad Juarez, Chihuahua, Mexico; Immigration; Industrial Workers; Labor Supply and Market; Males; *Migration Patterns; Undocumented Workers; Working Women.

6268 Finkelstein, Jordan W. and Von Eye, Alexander. Sanitary product use by white, Black, and Mexican American women. PUBLIC HEALTH REPORTS, Vol. 105, no. 5 (September, October, 1990), p. 491-496. English. DESCR: Anglo Americans; Blacks; *Menstruation; *Toxic Shock Syndrome (TSS).

Women (cont.)

6269 Flaskerud, Jacquelyn H. and Nyamathi, Adeline M. Black and Latina womens' AIDS related knowledge, attitudes, and practices. RESEARCH IN NURSING AND HEALTH, Vol. 12, no. 6 (December 1989), p. 339-346. English. **DESCR:** *AIDS (Disease); Attitudes; *Blacks; Health Education; Los Angeles County, CA; Surveys.

6270 Fleming, Marilyn B. Problems experienced by Anglo, Hispanic and Navajo Indian women college students. JOURNAL OF AMERICAN INDIAN EDUCATION, Vol. 22, no. 1 (October 1982), p. 7-17. English. **DESCR:** Anglo Americans; Community Colleges; Ethnic Groups; *Higher Education; Identity; Medical Education; Native Americans; Students.

6271 Forste, Renata T. and Heaton, Tim B. Initiation of sexual activity among female adolescents. YOUTH AND SOCIETY, Vol. 19, no. 3 (March 1988), p. 250-268. English. **DESCR:** Anglo Americans; Blacks; Family; Sex Education; *Sexual Behavior; *Youth.

6272 Fuentes, Annette and Ehrenreich, Barbara. Women in the global factory. New York: Institute for New Communications; Boston: South End Press, 1983. 64 p.: ill. English. **DESCR:** *Border Industries; Industrial Workers; *International Economic Relations; *Working Women.

6273 Gallegos, Placida I. Emerging leadership among Hispanic women: the role of expressive behavior and nonverbal skill. Thesis (Ph.D.)--University of California, Riverside, 1987. 101 p. English. **DESCR:** Anglo Americans; Comparative Psychology; Corporations; *Leadership; *Management.

6274 Galloway, Irma Nell. Trends in the employment of minority women as administrators in Texas public schools--1976-1981. Thesis (Ed.D.)--Texas Southern University, 1986. 129 p. English. **DESCR:** Asian Americans; Blacks; Education; *Educational Administration; *Management; Native Americans; Texas.

6275 Garcia, Alma M. The development of Chicana feminist discourse, 1970-1980. GENDER & SOCIETY, Vol. 3, no. 2 (June 1989), p. 217-238. English. **DESCR:** Anglo Americans; Chicana Studies; *Chicano Movement; *Feminism; Homosexuality; Machismo; National Association for Chicano Studies (NACS); Organizations; *Sexism.

6276 Garcia, Alma M. The development of Chicana feminist discourse, 1970-1980. IN: DuBois, Ellen Carol and Ruiz, Vicki L., eds. UNEQUAL SISTERS: A MULTICULTURAL READER IN U.S. WOMEN'S HISTORY. New York: Routledge, 1990, p. 418-431. English. **DESCR:** Anglo Americans; Chicana Studies; *Chicano Movement; *Feminism; Homosexuality; Machismo; National Association for Chicano Studies (NACS); Organizations; *Sexism.

6277 Garcia Castro, Mary. Migrant women: issues in organization and solidarity. MIGRATION WORLD MAGAZINE, Vol. 14, no. 1-2 (1986), p. 15-19. English. **DESCR:** Labor Supply and Market; *Migrant Labor; Organizations; Political Economy; Undocumented Workers.

6278 Garcia, Mario T. Family and gender in Chicano and border studies research. MEXICAN STUDIES/ESTUDIOS MEXICANOS, Vol. 6, no. 1 (Winter 1990), p. 109-119. English. **DESCR:** Alvarez, Robert R., Jr.; *Border Region; CANNERY WOMEN, CANNERY LIVES; *Family; LA FAMILIA: MIGRATION AND ADAPTATION IN BAJA AND ALTA CALIFORNIA, 1800-1975; *Literature Reviews; Ruiz, Vicki L.; Tiano, Susan B.; WOMEN ON THE U.S.-MEXICO BORDER: RESPONSES TO CHANGE; WOMEN'S WORK AND CHICANO FAMILIES; Zavella, Pat.

6279 Gardea, Corina. A comparison of behavioral characteristics of Hispanic and Anglo female administrators in the resolution of critical incident situations. Thesis (Ph.D.)--University of Texas, Austin, 1984. 145 p. English. **DESCR:** Anglo Americans; *Community Colleges; *Educational Administration; Leadership.

6280 Gettman, Dawn and Pena, Devon Gerardo. Women, mental health, and the workplace in a transnational setting. SOCIAL WORK, Vol. 31, no. 1 (January, February, 1986), p. 5-11. English. **DESCR:** *Border Industries; Employment; *Mental Health; Mexico; United States-Mexico Relations; *Working Women.

6281 Glenn, Evelyn Nakano. Racial ethnic women's labor: the intersection of race, gender and class oppression. REVIEW OF RADICAL POLITICAL ECONOMY, Vol. 17, no. 3 (Fall 1985), p. 86-108. English. **DESCR:** Asian Americans; Blacks; *Discrimination; *Feminism; Laboring Classes; *Marxism; Sexism; Social Classes; Working Women.

6282 Golding, Jacqueline M. Division of household labor, strain, and depressive symptoms among Mexican Americans and non-Hispanic whites. PSYCHOLOGY OF WOMEN QUARTERLY, Vol. 14, no. 1 (March 1990), p. 103-117. English. **DESCR:** Anglo Americans; Comparative Psychology; *Depression (Psychological); Domestic Work; Employment; Identity; *Sex Roles.

6283 Goldman, Shifra M. Mujeres de California: Latin American women artists. IN: Moore, Sylvia, ed. YESTERDAY AND TOMORROW: CALIFORNIA WOMEN ARTISTS. New York, NY: Midmarch Arts Press, c1989, p. 202-229. English. **DESCR:** *Artists; Baca, Judith F.; Biography; California; Carrasco, Barbara; Cervantez, Yreina; de Larios, Dora; Feminism; Hernandez, Judithe; Lomas Garza, Carmen; Lopez, Yolanda M.; Mesa-Bains, Amalia; Murillo, Patricia; Sanchez, Olivia; Valdez, Patssi; Vallejo Dillaway, Linda; Zamora Lucero, Linda.

6284 Goldsmith, Raquel Rubio. La Mexicana/Chicana. RENATO ROSALDO LECTURE SERIES MONOGRAPH, Vol. 1, (Summer 1985), p. 1-67. English. **DESCR:** Clergy; House of the Divine Providence [convent], Douglas, AZ; Labor Unions; *Social History and Conditions; World War II.

6285 Goldsmith, Raquel Rubio. Shipwrecked in the desert: a short history of the adventures and struggles for survival of the Mexican Sisters of the House of the Providence in Douglas, Arizona during their first twenty-two years of existence (1927-1949). RENATO ROSALDO LECTURE SERIES MONOGRAPH, Vol. 1, (Summer 1985), p. [39]-67. English. **DESCR:** Catholic Church; Clergy; Douglas, AZ; History; *House of the Divine Providence [convent], Douglas, AZ.

6286 Gomez, Alma, ed.; Moraga, Cherrie, ed.; and Romo-Carmona, Mariana, ed. Cuentos: stories by Latinas. New York: Kitchen Table, Women of Color Press, 1983. xx, 241 p. Bilingual. **DESCR:** *Short Story.

Women (cont.)

6287 Gomez-Quinones, Juan. Questions within women's historiography. IN: Del Castillo, Adelaida R., ed. BETWEEN BORDERS: ESSAYS ON MEXICANA/CHICANA HISTORY. Encino, CA: Floricanto Press, 1990, p. 87-97. English. **DESCR:** *Historiography; *Mexico.

6288 Gondolf, Edward W.; Fisher, Ellen; and McFerron, J. Richard. Racial differences among shelter residents: a comparison of Anglo, Black, and Hispanic battered. JOURNAL OF FAMILY VIOLENCE, Vol. 3, no. 1 (March 1988), p. 39-51. English. **DESCR:** Anglo Americans; Battered Women; Blacks; Comparative Psychology; Cultural Characteristics; Natural Support Systems; Socioeconomic Factors; *Violence.

6289 Gonzalez, Deena J. The widowed women of Santa Fe: assessments on the lives of an unmarried population, 1850-80. IN: Scadron, Arlene, ed. ON THEIR OWN: WIDOWS AND WIDOWHOOD IN THE AMERICAN SOUTHWEST 1843-1939. Urbana, IL: University of Illinois Press, c1988, p. [65]-90. English. **DESCR:** Family; History; Income; Land Tenure; *Santa Fe, NM; Sex Roles; Single Parents; *Widowhood.

6290 Gonzalez, Deena J. The widowed women of Santa Fe: assessments on the lives of an unmarried population, 1850-80. IN: DuBois, Ellen Carol and Ruiz, Vicki L., eds. UNEQUAL SISTERS: A MULTICULTURAL READER IN U.S. WOMEN'S HISTORY. New York: Routledge, 1990, p. 34-50. English. **DESCR:** Family; History; Income; Land Tenure; *Santa Fe, NM; Sex Roles; Single Parents; *Widowhood.

6291 Gonzalez, Maria R. El embrion nacionalista visto a traves de la obra de Sor Juana Ines de la Cruz. IN: Del Castillo, Adelaida R., ed. BETWEEN BORDERS: ESSAYS ON MEXICANA/CHICANA HISTORY. Encino, CA: Floricanto Press, 1990, p. 239-253. Spanish. **DESCR:** Authors; *Juana Ines de la Cruz, Sor; Mexico; *Nationalism.

6292 Gould, Jeffrey B.; Davey, Becky; and Stafford, Randall S. Socioeconomic differences in rates of cesarean section. THE NEW ENGLAND JOURNAL OF MEDICINE, Vol. 321, no. 4 (July 27, 1989), p. 233-239. English. **DESCR:** Anglo Americans; Asian Americans; Blacks; *Cesarean Section; *Fertility; Los Angeles County, CA; *Socioeconomic Factors; Vital Statistics.

6293 Groessl, Patricia Ann. Depression and anxiety in postmenopausal women: a study of Black, white, and Hispanic women. Thesis (Ed.D.)--Western Michigan University, 1987. 87 p. English. **DESCR:** Anglo Americans; Blacks; *Depression (Psychological); Menopause; Michigan; Stress.

6294 Guendelman, Sylvia. The incorporation of Mexican women in seasonal migration: a study of gender differences. HISPANIC JOURNAL OF BEHAVIORAL SCIENCES, Vol. 9, no. 3 (September 1987), p. 245-264. English. **DESCR:** Immigrants; Marriage; Mexico; *Migration Patterns; *Sex Roles; *Women Men Relations; Working Women.

6295 Gurak, Douglas T. Assimilation and fertility: a comparison of Mexican American and Japanese American women. HISPANIC JOURNAL OF BEHAVIORAL SCIENCES, Vol. 2, no. 3 (September 1980), p. 219-239. English. **DESCR:** Asian Americans; Assimilation; *Fertility; Japanese; Population.

6296 Gutierrez Castillo, Dina. La imagen de la mujer en la novela fronteriza. IN: Lopez-Gonzalez, Aralia, et al., eds. MUJER Y LITERATURA MEXICANA Y CHICANA: CULTURAS EN CONTACTO. Mexico: Colegio de la Frontera Norte, 1988, p. [55]-63. Spanish. **DESCR:** *Border Region; Islas, Arturo; Literary Characters; *Literary Criticism; Mendez M., Miguel; *Novel; PEREGRINOS DE AZTLAN; Sex Roles; Sex Stereotypes; THE RAIN GOD: A DESERT TALE.

6297 Gutierrez, Jeannie and Sameroff, Arnold. Determinants of complexity in Mexican-American and Anglo-American mothers' conceptions of child development. CHILD DEVELOPMENT, Vol. 61, no. 2 (April 1990), p. 384-394. English. **DESCR:** Acculturation; *Anglo Americans; Children; Cultural Characteristics; *Parenting; Values.

6298 Gutierrez, Lorraine M. Working with women of color: an empowerment perspective. SOCIAL WORK, Vol. 35, no. 2 (March 1990), p. 149-153. English. **DESCR:** *Assertiveness; Ethnic Groups; Feminism; Intergroup Relations; *Interpersonal Relations; *Social Work.

6299 Gutierrez, Ramon A. From honor to love: transformations of the meaning of sexuality in colonial New Mexico. IN: Smith, Raymond T., ed. KINSHIP IDEOLOGY AND PRACTICE IN LATIN AMERICA. Chapel Hill, NC: University of North Carolina Press, 1984, p. [237]-263. English. **DESCR:** *Catholic Church; *Marriage; New Mexico; *Sexual Behavior; Social Classes; Social History and Conditions; Spanish Influence; Values.

6300 Gutierrez, Ramon A. Marriage and seduction in Colonial New Mexico. IN: Del Castillo, Adelaida R., ed. BETWEEN BORDERS: ESSAYS ON MEXICANA/CHICANA HISTORY. Encino, CA: Floricanto Press, 1990, p. 447-457. English. **DESCR:** History; *Marriage; *New Mexico; Rape; *Sexual Behavior.

6301 Gutierrez, Ramon A. When Jesus came, the corn mothers went away: marriage, sexuality, and power in New Mexico, 1500-1846. Stanford: Stanford University Pres, 1991. xxxi, 424 p. English. **DESCR:** *Marriage; Native Americans; *New Mexico; *Pueblo Indians; *Sex Roles; Sexual Behavior; Spanish Influence.

6302 Guttmacher, Sally. Women migrant workers in the U.S. CULTURAL SURVIVAL QUARTERLY, Vol. 8, no. 2 (Summer 1984), p. 60-61. English. **DESCR:** *Migrant Labor; Public Health; Undocumented Workers.

6303 Hadley-Freydberg, Elizabeth. Prostitutes, concubines, whores and bitches: Black and Hispanic women in contemporary American film. IN: McCluskey, Audrey T., ed. WOMEN OF COLOR: PERSPECTIVES ON FEMINISM AND IDENTITY. Bloomington, IN: Women's Studies Program, Indiana University, 1985, p. 46-65. English. **DESCR:** *Actors and Actresses; Blacks; *Films; Puerto Ricans; *Sex Stereotypes; Stereotypes.

Women (cont.)

English. **DESCR:** *Literary Criticism.

6304 Hancock, Paula F. The effect of welfare
eligibility on the labor force participation
of women of Mexican origin in California.
POPULATION RESEARCH AND POLICY REVIEW, Vol.
5, no. 2 (1986), p. 163-185. English.
DESCR: Aid to Families with Dependent
Children (AFDC); California; *Employment;
Food Stamps; Immigrants; Medi-Cal; Single
Parents; *Welfare.

6305 Hardy-Fanta, Carol and Montana, Priscila.
The Hispanic female adolescent: a group
therapy model. INTERNATIONAL JOURNAL OF
GROUP PSYCHOTHERAPY, Vol. 32, no. 3 (July
1982), p. 351-366. English. **DESCR:**
Psychotherapy; Puerto Ricans; Youth.

6306 Harlow, Barbara. Sites of struggle:
immigration, deportation, prison, and exile.
IN: Calderon, Hector and Saldivar, Jose
David, eds. CRITICISM IN THE BORDERLANDS:
STUDIES IN CHICANO LITERATURE, CULTURE, AND
IDEOLOGY. Durham, NC: Duke University Press,
1991, p. [149]-163. English. **DESCR:**
Anzaldua, Gloria; BLACK GOLD; BORDERLANDS/LA
FRONTERA: THE NEW MESTIZA; First, Ruth;
Khalifeh, Sahar; *Literary Criticism;
*Political Ideology; Sanchez, Rosaura;
Social Classes; "The Cariboo Cafe" [short
story]; "The Ditch" [short story];
Viramontes, Helena Maria; WILD THORNS;
Working Women.

6307 Hart, John M. Working-class women in
nineteenth century Mexico. IN: Mora,
Magdalena and Del Castillo, Adelaida, eds.
MEXICAN WOMEN IN THE UNITED STATES:
STRUGGLES PAST AND PRESENT. Los Angeles, CA:
Chicano Studies Research Center, 1980, p.
151-157. English. **DESCR:** *Employment;
History; Mexico; Working Women.

6308 Hernandez, Ines. Sara Estela Ramirez: the
early twentieth century Texas-Mexican poet.
Thesis (Ph.D.)--University of Houston, 1984.
94 p. English. **DESCR:** *Authors; *Biography;
Feminism; Flores Magon, Ricardo; Journalism;
Literary Criticism; Mexican Revolution -
1910-1920; Mexico; *Poetry; Ramirez, Sara
Estela; Texas.

6309 Herrera-Sobek, Maria. The Mexican corrido: a
feminist analysis. Bloomington, IN: Indiana
University Press, 1990. xix, 151 p.: ill.
English. **DESCR:** *Corridos; Mexico; Military;
*Sex Roles; Sex Stereotypes; Symbolism;
Women Men Relations.

6310 Hogeland, Chris and Rosen, Karen. Dreams
lost, dreams found: undocumented women in
the land of opportunity. San Francisco, CA:
Coalition for Immigrant and Refugee Rights
and Services, c1991. 153 p. English. **DESCR:**
*Battered Women; *Coalition for Immigrant
and Refugee Rights and Services, Immigrant
Woman's Task Force; Discrimination;
Immigrants; *San Francisco Bay Area; Sex
Roles; Sexism; Social Services; Undocumented
Workers; Violence; Women Men Relations.

6311 Holck, Susan E., et al. Need for family
planning services among Anglo and Hispanic
women in the United States counties
bordering Mexico. FAMILY PLANNING
PERSPECTIVES, Vol. 14, no. 3 (May, June,
1982), p. 155-159. English. **DESCR:** Anglo
Americans; Border Region; *Family Planning.

6312 Horno-Delgado, Asuncion, et al., eds.
Breaking boundaries: Latina writing and
critical readings. Amherst, MA: University
of Massachusetts Press, c1989. xi, 268 p.

6313 Hovell, Melbourne F., et al. Occupational
health risks for Mexican women: the case of
the maquiladora along the Mexican-United
States border. INTERNATIONAL JOURNAL OF
HEALTH SERVICES, Vol. 18, no. 4 (1988), p.
617-627. English. **DESCR:** *Border Industries;
Border Region; Mexico; *Occupational
Hazards; Project Concern International
(PCI), San Diego, CA; Public Health;
Surveys; Tijuana, Baja California, Mexico;
Working Women.

6314 Hser, Yih-Ing; Chou, Chih-Ping; and Anglin,
M. Douglas. The criminality of female
narcotics addicts: a causal modeling
approach. JOURNAL OF QUANTITATIVE
CRIMINOLOGY, Vol. 6, no. 2 (June 1990), p.
207-228. English. **DESCR:** Anglo Americans;
Criminal Acts; *Drug Addicts; Drug Traffic;
Prostitution.

6315 Hurtado, Aida. Relating to privilege:
seduction and rejection in the subordination
of white women and women of color. SIGNS:
JOURNAL OF WOMEN IN CULTURE AND SOCIETY,
Vol. 14, no. 4 (Summer 1989), p. 833-855.
English. **DESCR:** *Anglo Americans; Asian
Americans; Blacks; Ethnic Groups; *Feminism;
Political Ideology; Political Socialization.

6316 Iglesias, Norma. La flor mas bella de la
maquiladora: historias de vida de la mujer
obrera en Tijuana, B.C.N. Mexico, D.F.:
Secretaria de Educacion Publica, CEFNOMEX,
1985. 166 p.: ill. Spanish. **DESCR:** Border
Industrialization Program (BIP); *Border
Industries; Cultural Customs; Labor Unions;
Sindicato Independiente Solidev; Solidev
Mexicana, S.A.; Tijuana, Baja California,
Mexico; Working Women.

6317 Iglesias, Norma. "Las mujeres somos mas
responsables": la utilizacion de mano de
obra femenina en las maquiladoras
fronterizas. TRABAJOS MONOGRAFICOS, Vol. 2,
no. 1 (1986), p. 19-30. Spanish. **DESCR:**
*Border Industries; *Working Women.

6318 Iglesias, Norma and Carrillo, Jorge. Que me
dejo el trabajo? FEM, Vol. 10, no. 48
(October, November, 1986), p. 43-45.
Spanish. **DESCR:** Border Industries; *Working
Women.

6319 In the maquiladoras. CORRESPONDENCIA, no. 9
(December 1990), p. 3-9. English. **DESCR:**
*Border Industries; Labor Unions; Tijuana,
Baja California, Mexico; *Working Women.

6320 Isaacs, Barbara Gail. Anglo, Black, and
Latin adolescents' participation in sports.
Thesis (Ph.D.)--California School of
Professional Psychology, Los Angeles, 1984.
283 p. English. **DESCR:** Anglo Americans;
Blacks; Cultural Characteristics; *Secondary
School Education; *Sports; Youth.

6321 Isasi-Diaz, Ada Maria and Tarango, Yolanda.
Hispanic women, prophetic voice in the
Church: toward a Hispanic women's liberation
theology. San Francisco, CA: Harper & Row,
c1988. xx, 123 p. Bilingual. **DESCR:** Catholic
Church; *Feminism; Liberation Theology;
Religion.

Women (cont.)

6322 Jaech, Richard E. Latin American undocumented women in the United States. CURRENTS IN THEOLOGY AND MISSION, Vol. 9, no. 4 (August 1982), p. 195-211. English. DESCR: Garment Industry; Latin Americans; Protestant Church; Socioeconomic Factors; *Undocumented Workers.

6323 Jaramillo, Mari-Luci. Institutional responsibility in the provision of educational experiences to the Hispanic American female student. IN: McKenna, Teresa and Ortiz, Flora Ida, eds. THE BROKEN WEB: THE EDUCATIONAL EXPERIENCE OF HISPANIC WOMEN. Claremont, CA: Tomaas Rivera Center; Berkeley, CA: Floricanto Press, 1988, p. 25-35. English. DESCR: Academic Achievement; *Discrimination in Education; Dropouts; *Education; Educational Administration; Enrollment; Higher Education; Students.

6324 Jaramillo, Mari-Luci. To serve Hispanic American female students: challenges and responsibilities for educational institutions. Claremont, CA: Tomas Rivera Center, c1987. 11 p. English. DESCR: Dropouts; *Education; Higher Education.

6325 Jensen, Joan M. Commentary [on "And Miles to Go": Mexican Women and Work, 1930-1985]. IN: Schlissel, Lillian, et al., eds. WESTERN WOMEN: THEIR LAND, THEIR LIVES. Albuquerque, NM: University of New Mexico Press, 1988, p. 141-144. English. DESCR: "'And Miles to Go...': Mexican Women and Work, 1930-1985"; California; Employment; Income; Labor Unions; Public Policy; Ruiz, Vicki L.; *Working Women.

6326 Jensen, Leif. Secondary earner strategies and family poverty: immigrant-native differentials, 1960-1980. INTERNATIONAL MIGRATION REVIEW, Vol. 25, no. 1 (Spring 1991), p. 113-140. English. DESCR: Anglo Americans; *Asian Americans; Blacks; Family; Immigrants; Immigration; Income; Poverty; Working Women.

6327 Job, Peggy. La sexualidad en la narrativa femenina mexicana 1970-1987: una aproximacion. THIRD WOMAN, Vol. 4, (1989), p. 120-133. Spanish. DESCR: *Literature; *Literature Reviews; Sex Roles; *Sexual Behavior.

6328 Karnig, Albert K.; Welch, Susan; and Eribes, Richard A. Employment of women by cities in the Southwest. SOCIAL SCIENCE JOURNAL, Vol. 21, no. 4 (October 1984), p. 41-48. English. DESCR: *Employment; Local Government; Southwestern United States.

6329 Keremitsis, Dawn. Del metate al molino: la mujer mexicana de 1910 a 1940. HISTORIA MEXICANA, Vol. 33, no. 2 (1983), p. 285-302. Spanish. DESCR: Food Industry; History; Labor Unions; Mexico; Sex Roles; Strikes and Lockouts; *Working Women.

6330 Kossoudji, Sherrie and Ranney, Susan. The labor market experience of female migrants: the case of temporary Mexican migration to the U.S. INTERNATIONAL MIGRATION REVIEW, Vol. 18, no. 4 (Winter 1984), p. 1120-1143. English. DESCR: Employment; Immigrants; Income; *Labor Supply and Market; *Migrant Labor; Sex Roles; Working Women.

6331 La Monica, Grace; Gulino, Claire; and Ortiz Soto, Irma. A comparative study of female Mexican and American working nurses in the border corridor. BORDER HEALTH/SALUD FRONTERIZA, Vol. 5, no. 2 (April, June, 1989), p. 2-6. Bilingual. DESCR: Anglo Americans; =Border Region; *Medical Personnel; =Working Women.

6332 Laosa, Luis M. Maternal teaching strategies in Chicano and Anglo-American families: the influence of culture and education on maternal behavior. CHILD DEVELOPMENT, Vol. 51, no. 3 (September 1980), p. 759-765. English. DESCR: Anglo Americans; Comparative Psychology; *Cultural Characteristics; *Education; Family; Maternal Teaching Observation Technique (MTOT); *Parent and Child Relationships; Parenting.

6333 Lavrin, Asuncion. El segundo sexo en Mexico: experiencia, estudio e introspeccion, 1983-1987. MEXICAN STUDIES/ESTUDIOS MEXICANOS, Vol. 5, no. 2 (Summer 1989), p. 297-312. Spanish. DESCR: Arenal, Sandra; *Border Industries; Carrillo, Jorge; Hernandez, Alberto; Iglesias, Norma; LA FLOR MAS BELLA DE LA MAQUILADORA; *Literature Reviews; Mexico; MUJERES FRONTERIZAS EN LA INDUSTRIA MAQUILADORA; SANGRE JOVEN: LAS MAQUILADORAS POR DENTRO.

6334 Lawrence, Alberto Augusto. Traditional attitudes toward marriage, marital adjustment, acculturation, and self-esteem of Mexican-American and Mexican wives. Thesis (Ph.D.)--United States International University, San Diego, CA, 1982. ix, 191 p. English. DESCR: *Acculturation; *Attitudes; Machismo; *Marriage; Mental Health; Psychological Testing; San Ysidro, CA; Sex Roles; Sex Stereotypes; Tijuana, Baja California, Mexico.

6335 Leal, Luis. Arquetipos femeninos en la literatura mexicana. IN: Leal, Luis. AZTLAN Y MEXICO: PERFILES LITERARIOS E HISTORICOS. Binghamton, NY: Bilingual Press/Editorial Bilingue, 1985, p. 168-176. Spanish. DESCR: La Virgen de Guadalupe; *Literary Criticism; Malinche; Mexican Literature; Symbolism.

6336 Leal, Luis. Female archetypes in Mexican literature. IN: Miller, Beth, ed. WOMEN IN HISPANIC LITERATURE: ICONS AND FALLEN IDOLS. Berkeley, CA: University of California Press, 1983, p. 227-242. English. DESCR: La Virgen de Guadalupe; *Literary Criticism; Malinche; Mexican Literature; Symbolism.

6337 Leal, Luis. La soldadera en la narrativa de la Revolucion. IN: Leal, Luis. AZTLAN Y MEXICO: PERFILES LITERARIOS E HISTORICOS. Binghamton, NY: Bilingual Press/Editorial Bilingue, 1985, p. 185-193. Spanish. DESCR: La Adelita; LA VOZ DEL PUEBLO; *Literary Criticism; Mexican Literature; Mexican Revolution - 1910-1920.

6338 Lee, Bun Song and Pol, Louis G. A comparison of fertility adaptation between Mexican immigrants to the U.S. and internal migrants in Mexico. CONTEMPORARY POLICY ISSUES, Vol. 3, no. 3 (Spring, 1985), p. 91-101. English. DESCR: *Fertility; *Immigrants; Mexico; Migration Patterns; *Rural Urban Migration.

--   --

Women (cont.)

6339 Lee, Valerie. Achievement and educational
     aspirations among Hispanic female high
     school students: comparison between public
     and Catholic schools. IN: McKenna, Teresa
     and Ortiz, Flora Ida, eds. THE BROKEN WEB:
     THE EDUCATIONAL EXPERIENCE OF HISPANIC
     WOMEN. Claremont, CA: Tomas Rivera Center;
     Berkeley, CA: Floricanto Press, 1988, p.
     137-192. English. **DESCR:** *Academic
     Achievement; Anglo Americans; Catholic
     Church; Education; Educational Statistics;
     Private Education; Religious Education;
     *Secondary School Education.

6340 Leonard, Jonathan S. The effect of unions on
     the employment of Blacks, Hispanics, and
     women. INDUSTRIAL AND LABOR RELATIONS
     REVIEW, Vol. 39, no. 1 (October 1985), p.
     115-132. English. **DESCR:** Blacks; Employment;
     *Labor Unions.

6341 LeVine, Sarah Ethel; Correa, Clara
     Sunderland; and Uribe, F. Medardo Tapia. The
     marital morality of Mexican women--an urban
     study. JOURNAL OF ANTHROPOLOGICAL RESEARCH,
     Vol. 42, no. 2 (Summer 1986), p. 183-202.
     English. **DESCR:** Family; Los Robles,
     Cuernavaca, Morelos, Mexico; *Machismo;
     Marriage; Parent and Child Relationships;
     *Sex Roles; *Women Men Relations.

6342 Levy Oved, Albert and Alcocer Marban, Sonia.
     Las maquiladoras en Mexico. Mexico: Fondo de
     Cultura Economica, 1984. 125 p.: ill.
     Spanish. **DESCR:** *Border Industries; *Border
     Region; International Economic Relations;
     United States-Mexico Relations.

6343 Limon, Jose E. [anthropologist]. La Llorona,
     the third legend of greater Mexico: cultural
     symbols, women, and the political
     unconscious. RENATO ROSALDO LECTURE SERIES
     MONOGRAPH, Vol. 2, (Spring 1986), p.
     [59]-93. English. **DESCR:** *Feminism;
     Folklore; *La Llorona; La Virgen de
     Guadalupe; *Leyendas; Malinche; Mexico;
     *Symbolism.

6344 Limon, Jose E. [anthropologist]. La Llorona,
     the third legend of greater Mexico: cultural
     symbols, women, and the political
     unconscious. IN: Del Castillo, Adelaida R.
     BETWEEN BORDERS: ESSAYS ON MEXICANA/CHICANA
     HISTORY. Encino, CA: Floricanto Press, 1990,
     p. 399-432. English. **DESCR:** *Feminism;
     Folklore; *La Llorona; La Virgen de
     Guadalupe; *Leyendas; Malinche; Mexico;
     *Symbolism.

6345 Lizarraga, Sylvia S. Hacia una teoria para
     la liberacion de la mujer. IN: Garcia, Juan
     R., ed. IN TIMES OF CHALLENGE: CHICANOS AND
     CHICANAS IN AMERICAN SOCIETY. Houston, TX:
     Mexican American Studies Program, University
     of Houston, 1988, p. 25-31. Spanish. **DESCR:**
     *Feminism; Laboring Classes; Social Classes;
     *Working Women.

6346 Lopez, Norma Y. Hispanic teenage pregnancy:
     overview and implications. Washington, DC:
     National Council of La Raza, 1987. 17
     leaves. English. **DESCR:** *Fertility;
     Statistics; *Youth.

6347 Lopez-Garza, Maria C. Toward a
     reconceptualization of women's economic
     activities: the informal sector in urban
     Mexico. IN: Cordova, Teresa, et al., eds.
     CHICANA VOICES. Austin, TX: Center for
     Mexican American Studies, 1986, p. 66-76.
     English. **DESCR:** Employment; Mexico.

6348 Lopez-Gonzalez, Aralia, et al., eds. Mujer y
     literatura mexicana y chicana: culturas en
     contacto. Mexico: Colegio de Mexico,
     Programa Interdisciplinario de Estudios de
     la Mujer; Tijuana, B.C., Mexico: Colegio de
     la Frontera Norte, 1988. 264 p. Spanish.
     DESCR: *Literary Criticism; Mexican
     Literature; *Mexico; Sex Roles.

6349 Loustaunau, Martha Oehmke. Hispanic widows
     and their support systems in the Mesilla
     Valley of southern New Mexico, 1910-40. IN:
     Scadron, Arlene, ed. ON THEIR OWN: WIDOWS
     AND WIDOWHOOD IN THE AMERICAN SOUTHWEST
     1843-1939. Urbana, IL: University of
     Illinois Press, c1988, p. [91]-116. English.
     DESCR: Cultural Customs; Extended Family;
     Mesilla Valley, NM; Natural Support Systems;
     Sex Roles; Single Parents; Widowhood.

6350 Macias, Anna. Against all odds: the feminist
     movement in Mexico to 1940. Westport, CT:
     Greenwood Press, 1982. xv, 195 p. English.
     DESCR: Carrillo Puerto, Felipe; *Feminism;
     History; Mexican Revolution - 1910-1920;
     Mexico; Yucatan, Mexico.

6351 Malvido, Elsa. El uso del cuerpo femenino en
     la epoca colonial mexicana a traves de los
     estudios de demografia historica. IN: Del
     Castillo, Adelaida R., ed. BETWEEN BORDERS:
     ESSAYS ON MEXICANA/CHICANA HISTORY. Encino,
     CA: Floricanto Press, 1990, p. 115-130.
     Spanish. **DESCR:** Marriage; *Mexico; *Sex
     Roles; Sexual Behavior; *Vital Statistics;
     Widowhood.

6352 Marin, Gerardo; Perez-Stable, Eliseo J.; and
     Marin, Barbara Van Oss. Cigarette smoking
     among San Francisco Hispanics: the role of
     acculturation and gender. PUBLIC HEALTH
     BRIEFS, Vol. 79, no. 2 (February 1989), p.
     196-198. English. **DESCR:** *Acculturation;
     Drug Use; Males; San Francisco, CA;
     *Smoking.

6353 Mary, Nancy L. Reactions of Black, Hispanic,
     and white mothers to having a child with
     handicaps. MENTAL RETARDATION, Vol. 28, no.
     1 (February 1990), p. 1-5. English. **DESCR:**
     Anglo Americans; *Attitudes; Blacks;
     *Children; Comparative Psychology; *Mentally
     Handicapped; Parent and Child Relationships.

6354 Mason, Terry. Symbolic strategies for
     change: a discussion of the Chicana women's
     movement. IN: Melville, Margarita B., ed.
     TWICE A MINORITY. St. Louis, MO: Mosby,
     1980, p. 95-108. English. **DESCR:** Actos;
     Anglo Americans; *Feminism; Teatro.

6355 Mays, Vicki M. and Cochran, Susan D. Issues
     in the perception of AIDS risk and risk
     reduction activities by Black and
     Hispanic/Latina women. AMERICAN
     PSYCHOLOGIST, Vol. 43, no. 11 (November
     1988), p. 949-957. English. **DESCR:** *AIDS
     (Disease); Blacks; Condom Use; Fertility;
     Health Education; Preventative Medicine;
     *Sexual Behavior.

6356 McCracken, Ellen. Latina narrative and
     politics of signification: articulation,
     antagonism, and populist rupture. CRITICA,
     Vol. 2, no. 2 (Fall 1990), p. 202-207.
     English. **DESCR:** *Cisneros, Sandra; IN NUEVA
     YORK; *Literary Criticism; *Mohr, Nicolasa;
     Puerto Ricans; RITUALS OF SURVIVAL; Short
     Story; THE HOUSE ON MANGO STREET.

Women (cont.)

6357 McKenna, Teresa and Ortiz, Flora Ida. Facts and figures on Hispanic Americans, women, and education. IN: McKenna, Teresa and Ortiz, Flora Ida, eds. THE BROKEN WEB: THE EDUCATIONAL EXPERIENCE OF HISPANIC WOMEN. Claremont, CA: Tomas Rivera Center; Berkeley, CA: Floricanto Press 1988, p. 195-217. English. DESCR: *Education; *Educational Statistics.

6358 McKenna, Teresa and Ortiz, Flora Ida. Select bibliography on Hispanic women and education. IN: McKenna, Teresa and Ortiz, Flora Ida, eds. THE BROKEN WEB: THE EDUCATIONAL EXPERIENCE OF HISPANIC WOMEN. Claremont, CA: Tomas Rivera Center; Berkeley, CA: Floricanto Press, 1988, p. 221-254. English. DESCR: *Bibliography; *Education.

6359 McKenna, Teresa, ed. and Ortiz, Flora Ida, ed. The broken web: the educational experience of Hispanic American women. Claremont, CA: Tomas Rivera Center; Berkeley, CA: Floricanto Press, 1988. iii, 262 p. English. DESCR: *Academic Achievement; *Education; Educational Statistics; The Educational Experience of Hispanic American Women [symposium] (1985: Claremont, CA).

6360 McRipley, Bernadine G. Racial/ethnic Presbyterian women: in search of community. CHURCH AND SOCIETY, Vol. 76, no. 4 (March, April, 1986), p. 47-53. English. DESCR: *Presbyterian Church; Religion; Sex Roles.

6361 Melgoza, Bertha; Roll, Samuel; and Baker, Richard C. Conformity and cooperation in Chicanos: the case of the missing susceptibility to influence. JOURNAL OF COMMUNITY PSYCHOLOGY, Vol. 11, no. 4 (October 1983), p. 323-333. English. DESCR: *Comparative Psychology; *Cultural Characteristics; *Locus of Control; Socialization; Stereotypes.

6362 Melville, Margarita B. Mexican women in the U.S. wage labor force. IN: Melville, Margarita, ed. MEXICANAS AT WORK IN THE UNITED STATES. Houston, TX: Mexican American Studies Program, University of Houston, 1988, p. 1-11. English. DESCR: Feminism; Sex Stereotypes; *Working Women.

6363 Melville, Margarita B., ed. Mexicanas at work in the United States. Houston, TX: Mexican American Studies Program, University of Houston, 1988. 83 p. English. DESCR: Border Region; *Employment; Family; *Labor; Migrant Labor; Working Women.

6364 Miller, Elaine N. and Sterrbach, Nancy Saporta. Selected bibliography. IN: Horno-Delgado, Asuncion, et al., eds. BREAKING BOUNDARIES: LATINA WRITING AND CRITICAL READINGS. Amherst, MA: University of Massachusetts Press, c1989, p. 251-263. English. DESCR: *Bibliography; Cubanos; Literary Criticism; *Literature; Puerto Ricans.

6365 Monk, Janice and Norwood, Vera. Angles of vision: enhancing our perspectives on the Southwest. IN: Lensink, Judy Nolte, ed. OLD SOUTHWEST/NEW SOUTHWEST: ESSAYS ON A REGION AND ITS LITERATURE. Tucson, AZ: The Tucson Public Library, 1989, p. 39-47. English. DESCR: Literary Criticism; *Literature; Southwestern United States.

6366 Moraga, Cherrie. Third World women in the

United States--by and about us: a selected bibliography. IN: Moraga, Cherrie and Anzaldua, Gloria, eds. THIS BRIDGE CALLED MY BACK: WRITINGS BY RADICAL WOMEN OF COLOR. Watertown, MA: Persephone Press, 1981, p. 251-261. English. DESCR: Bibliography; *Feminism.

6367 Moraga, Cherrie, ed. and Castillo, Ana, ed. Esta [sic] puente, mi espalda: voces de mujeres tercermundistas en los Estados Unidos. San Francisco, CA: Ism Press, c1988. [19], 281 p.: ill. Spanish. DESCR: Ethnic Groups; *Feminism; Literary Criticism; *Poems; *Prose.

6368 Moraga, Cherrie, ed. and Anzaldua, Gloria, ed. This bridge called my back: writings by radical women of color. Watertown, MA: Persephone Press, c1981. xxvi, 261 p. English. DESCR: Ethnic Groups; *Feminism; Literary Criticism; *Poems; *Prose.

6369 Mullen, Julia Ann. Black, Anglo, and Chicana women's construction of mental illness. Thesis (Ph.D.)--University of California, Santa Barbara, 1985. 276 p. English. DESCR: Anglo Americans; Blacks; *Mental Illness.

6370 Nieto Gomez de Lazarin, Anna. La femenista [sic]. ENCUENTRO FEMENIL, Vol. 1, no. 2 (1974), p. 34-47. English. DESCR: Anglo Americans; Chicana Caucus, National Women's Political Caucus; Chicano Movement; Conferences and Meetings; Discrimination; *Feminism; National Women's Political Caucus (February 9-11, 1973: Houston, TX); *Sexism.

6371 Nieves-Squires, Sarah. Hispanic women: making their presence on campus less tenuous. Washington, DC: Association of American Colleges, c1991. 14 p. English. DESCR: Afro-Hispanics; Colleges and Universities; Cubanos; *Discrimination in Education; *Higher Education; Puerto Ricans.

6372 Norirsky, Margaret Elaine. The relationship between sex-role identity and ethnicity to styles of assertiveness and aggression in women. Thesis (Ed.D.)--University of San Francisco, 1987. 164 p. English. DESCR: Anglo Americans; *Assertiveness; Blacks; Ethnic Groups; *Identity; *Sex Roles.

6373 Norris, Henry E. AIDS, women and reproductive rights. MULTICULTURAL INQUIRY AND RESEARCH ON AIDS (MIRA) NEWSLETTER, Vol. 1, no. 3 (Summer 1987), p. [2-3]. English. DESCR: Abortion; *AIDS (Disease); Center for Constitutional Rights; Discrimination; Preventative Medicine.

6374 Notzon, Francis Claude. Factors associated with low birth weight in Mexican-Americans and Mexicans. Thesis (Ph.D.)--John Hopkins University, 1989. 190 p. English. DESCR: Anglo Americans; Fertility; *Maternal and Child Welfare; Mexico; *Prenatal Care; Public Health.

6375 O'Connor, Mary I. Women's networks and the social needs of Mexican immigrants. URBAN ANTHROPOLOGY, Vol. 19, no. 1-2 (Spring, Summer, 1990), p. 81-98. English. DESCR: Employment; *Immigrants; Labor Unions; *Natural Support Systems; *Sandyland Nursery, Carpinteria, CA; Undocumented Workers; United Farmworkers of America (UFW).

Women (cont.)

6376 Olivares, Yvette. The sweatshop: the garment industry's reborn child. REVISTA MUJERES, Vol. 3, no. 2 (June 1986), p. 55-62. English. **DESCR:** Garment Industry; Labor; Public Health; Third World; *Undocumented Workers; Working Women.

6377 Oliveira, Annette. Remarkable Latinas. IN: HISPANICS AND GRANTMAKERS: A SPECIAL REPORT OF FOUNDATION NEWS. Washington, DC: Council on Foundations, 1981, p. 34. English. **DESCR:** Biography; Leadership; *Puerto Ricans.

6378 Ortega, Eliana and Sternbach, Nancy Saporta. At the threshold of the unnamed: Latina literary discourse in the eighties. IN: Horno-Delgado, Asuncion, et al., eds. BREAKING BOUNDARIES: LATINA WRITING AND CRITICAL READINGS. Amherst, MA: University of Massachusetts Press, c1989, p. [2]-23. English. **DESCR:** Bilingualism; *Feminism; *Literary Criticism; Literary History; Political Ideology; Sex Roles.

6379 Ortiz, Vilma and Fennelly, Katherine. Early childbearing and employment among young Mexican origin, Black, and white women. SOCIAL SCIENCE QUARTERLY, Vol. 69, no. 4 (December 1988), p. 987-995. English. **DESCR:** Anglo Americans; Blacks; *Employment; *Fertility; *Youth.

6380 Padgett, Deborah. Aging minority women. WOMEN & HEALTH, Vol. 14, no. 3-4 (1988), p. 213-225. English. **DESCR:** *Ancianos; Low Income; Public Health.

6381 Padilla, Genaro. "Yo sola aprendi": contra-patriarchal containment in women's nineteenth-century California personal narratives. THE AMERICAS REVIEW, Vol. 16, no. 3-4 (Fall, Winter, 1988), p. 91-109. English. **DESCR:** Autobiography; California; *Literary History.

6382 Pena, Devon Gerardo. Between the lines: a new perspective on the industrial sociology of women workers in transnational labor processes. IN: Cordova, Teresa, et al., eds. CHICANA VOICES. Austin, TX: Center for Mexican American Studies, 1986, p. 77-95. English. **DESCR:** Border Industries; *Labor; Marxism; Working Women.

6383 Pena, Devon Gerardo. The class politics of abstract labor: organizational forms and industrial relations in the Mexican maquiladoras. Thesis (Ph.D.)--University of Texas, Austin, 1983. xix, 587 p. English. **DESCR:** *Border Industries; Border Region; International Economic Relations; *Trade Unions; Working Women.

6384 Pena, Devon Gerardo. Tortuosidad: shop floor struggles of female maquiladora workers. IN: Ruiz, Vicki L. and Tiano, Susan, eds. WOMEN ON THE U.S.-MEXICO BORDER: RESPONSES TO CHANGE. Boston, MA: Allen & Unwin, 1987, p. 129-154. English. **DESCR:** Border Industries; Ciudad Juarez, Chihuahua, Mexico; Employment; Personnel Management; Population; Surveys; Working Women.

6385 Perez, Emma. "A la mujer": a critique of the Partido Liberal Mexicano's gender ideology on women. IN: Del Castillo, Adelaida R., ed. BETWEEN BORDERS: ESSAYS ON MEXICANA/CHICANA HISTORY. Encino, CA: Floricanto Press, 1990, p. 459-482. English. **DESCR:** *"A La Mujer" [essay]; Essays; *Feminism; Flores Magon, Ricardo; Guerrero, Praxedis G.; Journalism;

Mexican Revolution - 1910-1920; Mexico; Newspapers; *Partido Liberal Mexicano (PLM); Political Ideology; Political Parties and Organizations; *REGENERACION [newspaper]; Sex Roles.

6386 Perrone, Bobette; Stockel, H. Henrietta; and Krueger, Victoria. Medicine women, curanderas, and women doctors. Norman, OK: University of Oklahoma Press, c1989. xix, 252 p.:ill. English. **DESCR:** Aragon, Jesusita, 1908-; *Curanderas; *Curanderismo; *Folk Medicine; Herbal Medicine; Herrera, Sabinita; Medical Personnel; Native Americans; *Oral History; Rodriguez, Gregorita.

6387 Peters, Ruth K., et al. Risk factors for invasive cervical cancer among Latinas and non-Latinas in Los Angeles County. JOURNAL OF THE NATIONAL CANCER INSTITUTE, Vol. 77, no. 5 (November 1986), p. 1063-1077. English. **DESCR:** *Cancer; Diseases; Educational Levels; Los Angeles County, CA; *Public Health.

6388 Poma, Pedro A. Pregnancy in Hispanic women. JOURNAL OF THE NATIONAL MEDICAL ASSOCIATION, Vol. 79, no. 9 (September 1987), p. 929-935. English. **DESCR:** *Cultural Characteristics; *Doctor Patient Relations; *Fertility; Machismo; Preventative Medicine.

6389 Popp, Gary E. and Muhs, William F. Fears of success and women employees. HUMAN RELATIONS, Vol. 35, no. 7 (July 1982), p. 511-519. English. **DESCR:** *Employment.

6390 Powell, Douglas R.; Zambrana, Ruth E.; and Silva-Palacios, Victor. Designing culturally responsive parent programs: a comparison of low-income Mexican and Mexican-American mothers' preferences. FAMILY RELATIONS, Vol. 39, no. 3 (July 1990), p. 298-304. English. **DESCR:** Acculturation; Children; Education; Immigrants; Los Angeles, CA; Low Income; *Parent and Child Relationships; *Parenting.

6391 Powers, Stephen and Jones, Patricia. Factorial invariance of the California achievement tests across race and sex. EDUCATIONAL AND PSYCHOLOGICAL MEASUREMENT, Vol. 44, no. 4 (Winter 1984), p. 967-970. English. **DESCR:** Anglo Americans; Blacks; *California Achievement Test (CAT); Educational Tests and Measurements; Males.

6392 Queiro-Tajalli, Irene. Hispanic women's perceptions and use of prenatal health care services. AFFILIA: JOURNAL OF WOMEN AND SOCIAL WORK, Vol. 4, no. 2 (Summer 1989), p. 60-72. English. **DESCR:** Indianapolis, IN; *Medical Care; *Prenatal Care; Surveys.

6393 Quintana, Alvina E. Challenge and counter challenge: Chicana literary motifs. AGAINST THE CURRENT, Vol. 2, no. 2 (March, April, 1987), p. 25,28-32. English. **DESCR:** Anglo Americans; Authors; Cervantes, Lorna Dee; Cultural Studies; *Feminism; Identity; Literary Criticism; *Literature; Moraga, Cherrie; THERE ARE NO MADMEN HERE; Valdes, Gina.

6394 Quintana, Alvina E. Chicana literary motifs: challenge and counter-challenge. IMAGES: ETHNIC STUDIES OCCASIONAL PAPERS SERIES, (Fall 1986), p. 24-41. English. **DESCR:** Anglo Americans; Authors; Cervantes, Lorna Dee; Cultural Studies; *Feminism; *Identity; *Literary Criticism; Literature; Moraga, Cherrie; THERE ARE NO MADMEN HERE; Valdes, Gina.

Women (cont.)

6395 Quintana, Alvina E. Women: prisoners of the word. IN: Cordova, Teresa, et al., eds. CHICANA VOICES. Austin, TX: Center for Mexican American Studies, 1986, p. 208-219. English. DESCR: *Literary Criticism.

6396 Ramos, Juanita, ed. Companeras: Latina lesbians (an anthology). New York: Latina Lesbian History Project, 1987. xxix, 265 p. Bilingual. DESCR: *Homosexuality; *Literature; Poetry; Prose.

6397 Rebolledo, Tey Diana. Las escritoras: romances and realities. IN: Gonzales-Berry, Erlinda, ed. PASO POR AQUI: CRITICAL ESSAYS ON THE NEW MEXICAN LITERARY TRADITION. Albuquerque, NM: University of New Mexico Press, c1989, p. 199-214. English. DESCR: Authors; *Cabeza de Baca, Fabiola; *Jaramillo, Cleofas M.; Literary History; New Mexico; OLD SPAIN IN OUR SOUTHWEST; *Otero Warren, Nina; ROMANCE OF A LITTLE VILLAGE GIRL; WE FED THEM CACTUS.

6398 Rebolledo, Tey Diana. Hispanic women writers of the Southwest: tradition and innovation. IN: Lensink, Judy Nolte, ed. OLD SOUTHWEST/NEW SOUTHWEST: ESSAYS ON A REGION AND ITS LITERATURE. Tucson, AZ: The Tucson Public Library, 1987, p. 49-61. English. DESCR: *Authors; Cabeza de Baca, Fabiola; Jaramillo, Cleofas M.; Literature; Mora, Pat; OLD SPAIN IN OUR SOUTHWEST; Otero Warren, Nina; Preciado Martin, Patricia; Sex Roles; Sex Stereotypes; Silva, Beverly; *Southwestern United States; Vigil-Pinon, Evangelina; WE FED THEM CACTUS.

6399 Rodriguez, Rogelio E. Psychological distress among Mexican-American women as a reaction to the new immigration law. Thesis (Ph.D.)--Loyola University of Chicago, 1989. 87 p. English. DESCR: Depression (Psychological); Immigrants; *Immigration Law and Legislation; Immigration Reform and Control Act of 1986; *Mental Health; Mexico; Stress; Undocumented Workers.

6400 Rodriguez, Rogelio E. and DeWolfe, Alan. Psychological distress among Mexican-American and Mexican women as related to status on the new immigration law. JOURNAL OF CONSULTING AND CLINICAL PSYCHOLOGY, Vol. 58, no. 5 (October 1990), p. 548-553. English. DESCR: *Immigrants; Immigration Law and Legislation; Immigration Reform and Control Act of 1986; Natural Support Systems; *Stress; Undocumented Workers.

6401 Romero, Gloria J. and Garza, Raymond T. Attributions for the occupational success/failure of ethnic minority and nonminority women. SEX ROLES, Vol. 14, no. 7-8 (April 1986), p. 445-452. English. DESCR: Anglo Americans; *Attitudes; Careers; Identity; Sociology.

6402 Romero-Cachinero, M. Carmen. Hispanic women in Canada: a framework for analysis. RESOURCES FOR FEMINIST RESEARCH, Vol. 16, no. 1 (March 1987), p. 19-20. English. DESCR: *Canada; Population; Social History and Conditions.

6403 Romero-Gwynn, Eunice and Carias, Lucia. Breast-feeding intentions and practice among Hispanic mothers in Southern California PEDIATRICS, Vol. 84, no. 4 (October 1989), p. 626-632. English. DESCR: *Breastfeeding; Cubanos; Expanded Food and Nutrition Education Program; Immigrants; Puerto Ricans; Southern California.

6404 Roraback, Rosanne Lisa. The effects of occupational type, educational level, marital status, and race/ethnicity on women's attitudes towards feminist issues. Thesis (M.A.)--Michigan State University, 1988. 62 p. English. DESCR: Abortion; *Attitudes; Equal Rights Amendment (ERA); *Feminism; Identity.

6405 Ross, Catherine E.; Mirowsky, John; and Ulbrich, Patricia. Distress and the traditional female role: a comparison of Mexicans and Anglos. AMERICAN JOURNAL OF SOCIOLOGY, Vol. 89, no. 3 (November 1983), p. 670-682. English. DESCR: Anglo Americans; Comparative Psychology; *Sex Roles; Stress.

6406 Ruiz Funes, Concepcion and Tunon, Enriqueta. Panorama de las luchas de la mujer mexicana en el siglo XX. IN: Del Castillo, Adelaida R., ed. BETWEEN BORDERS: ESSAYS ON MEXICANA/CHICANA HISTORY. Encino, CA: Floricanto Press, 1990, p. 336-357. Spanish. DESCR: Coordinadora de Mujeres Trabajadoras; *Feminism; Frente Unido Pro Derechos de la Mujer; History; Labor Unions; *Mexico; Sex Roles.

6407 Ruiz, Vicki L. "And miles to go...": Mexican women and work, 1930-1985. IN: Schlissel, Lillian, et al., eds. WESTERN WOMEN: THEIR LAND, THEIR LIVES. Albuquerque, NM: University of New Mexico Press, 1988, p. 117-136. English. DESCR: Education; El Paso Women's Employment and Education Project (EPWEE); *Employment; Farah Manufacturing Co., El Paso, TX; Farah Strike; *Income; Industrial Workers; Labor Unions; Statistics; Undocumented Workers; United Cannery Agricultural Packing and Allied Workers of America (UCAPAWA); *Working Women.

6408 Ruiz, Vicki L. California's early pioneers: Spanish/Mexican women. SOCIAL STUDIES REVIEW, Vol. 29, no. 1 (Fall 1989), p. 24-30. English. DESCR: *California; *History; Ruiz Burton, Maria Amparo; Sex Roles.

6409 Ruiz, Vicki L. Cannery women/cannery lives: Mexican women, unionization, and the California food processing industry, 1930-1950. Albuquerque, NM: University of New Mexico Press, 1987. xviii, 194 p.: ill. English. DESCR: Agricultural Labor Unions; California; *Canneries; Family; History; Industrial Workers; Labor Disputes; *Labor Unions; Trade Unions; United Cannery Agricultural Packing and Allied Workers of America (UCAPAWA).

6410 Ruiz, Vicki L. Obreras y madres: labor activism among Mexican women and its impact on the family. RENATO ROSALDO LECTURE SERIES MONOGRAPH, Vol. 1, (Summer 1985), p. [19]-38. English. DESCR: Child Care Centers; Children; History; *Labor Unions; *Mexico; Sex Roles; *Working Women.

6411 Ruiz, Vicki L. Working for wages: Mexican women in the Southwest, 1930-1980. Tucson, AZ: Southwest Institute for Research on Women, 1984. 24 p. English. DESCR: *Employment; History; *Income; Labor Unions.

Women (cont.)

6412 Ruiz, Vicki L., ed. and DuBois, Ellen Carol, ed. Unequal sisters: a multicultural reader in U.S. women's history. New York: Routledge, 1990. xvi, 473 p. English. DESCR: Anglo Americans; Asian Americans; Blacks; Feminism; *History; Native Americans.

6413 Ruiz, Vicki L., ed. and Tiano, Susan B., ed. Women on the U.S.-Mexico border: responses to change. Boston, MA: Allen & Unwin, c1987. xi, 247 p. English. DESCR: *Border Industries; *Border Region; Employment; Feminism; Immigrants; Mexico; Sex Roles.

6414 Sabagh, Georges and Lopez, David. Religiosity and fertility: the case of Chicanas. SOCIAL FORCES, Vol. 59, no. 2 (December 1980), p. 431-439. English. DESCR: Catholic Church; *Family Planning; *Fertility; Immigrants; *Religion.

6415 Saboonchi, Nasrin. The working women's reactions to the traditional marriage role: a crosscultural study within the symbolic interactionism framework. Thesis (Ph.D.)--United States International University, 1983. 173 p. English. DESCR: Immigrants; Iranians; *Marriage; *Sex Roles; Working Women.

6416 Salas, Elizabeth. Soldaderas in the Mexican military: myth and history. Austin, TX: University of Texas Press, 1990. xiii, 163 p., [12] p. of plates: ill. English. DESCR: Aztecs; History; *La Adelita; Mexican Revolution - 1910-1920; Mexico; *Military; Symbolism; War.

6417 Salas, Elizabeth. Soldaderas in the Mexican military: myth and history. Thesis (Ph.D.)--University of California, Los Angeles, 1987. 313p. English. DESCR: Aztecs; History; La Adelita; Mexican Revolution - 1910-1920; Mexico; Military; Symbolism; War.

6418 Saldivar-Hull, Sonia. Feminism on the border: from gender politics to geopolitics. IN: Calderon, Hector and Saldivar, Jose David, eds. CRITICISM IN THE BORDERLANDS: STUDIES IN CHICANO LITERATURE, CULTURE, AND IDEOLOGY. Durham, NC: Duke University Press, 1991, p. [203]-220. English. DESCR: Anglo Americans; *Anzaldua, Gloria; *BORDERLANDS/LA FRONTERA: THE NEW MESTIZA; Feminism; Homosexuality; *Literary Criticism; Mestizaje; Moraga, Cherrie; Sexism; "The Cariboo Cafe" [short story]; Viramontes, Helena Maria.

6419 Salgado de Snyder, Nelly. Factors associated with acculturative stress and depressive symptomatology among married Mexican immigrant women. PSYCHOLOGY OF WOMEN QUARTERLY, Vol. 11, no. 4 (December 1987), p. 475-488. English. DESCR: *Acculturation; Depression (Psychological); *Immigrants; Mental Health; Mexico; *Stress.

6420 Salgado de Snyder, Nelly; Cervantes, Richard C.; and Padilla, Amado M. Gender and ethnic differences in psychosocial stress and generalized distress among Hispanics. SEX ROLES, Vol. 22, no. 7-8 (April, 1990), p. 441-453. English. DESCR: Anglo Americans; Central Americans; *Comparative Psychology; Depression (Psychological); Hispanic Stress Inventory (HSI); *Immigrants; Immigration; *Sex Roles; *Stress.

6421 Salgado de Snyder, Nelly. Mexican immigrant women: the relationship of ethnic loyalty and social support to acculturative stress and depressive symptomatology. Los Angeles, CA: Spanish Speaking Mental Health Research Center, 1987. 73 p. English. DESCR: *Acculturation; Depression (Psychological); Identity; *Immigrants; Natural Support Systems; *Stress.

6422 Salgado de Snyder, Nelly. The role of ethnic loyalty among Mexican immigrant women. HISPANIC JOURNAL OF BEHAVIORAL SCIENCES, Vol. 9, no. 3 (September 1987), p. 287-298. English. DESCR: Acculturation; *Culture; *Identity; Immigrants; Mental Health; Mexico.

6423 Sanchez, George J. "Go after the women": Americanization and the Mexican immigrant woman, 1915-1929. Stanford, CA: Stanford Center for Chicano Research [1984?]. [32] leaves. English. DESCR: Acculturation; *Assimilation; Biculturalism; *Immigrants; Social History and Conditions; Values.

6424 Sanchez, George J. "Go after the women": Americanization and the Mexican immigrant woman, 1915-1929. IN: DuBois, Ellen Carol and Ruiz, Vicki L., eds. UNEQUAL SISTERS: A MULTICULTURAL READER IN U.S. WOMEN'S HISTORY. New York: Routledge, 1990, p. 250-263. English. DESCR: Acculturation; *Assimilation; Biculturalism; *Immigrants; Social History and Conditions; Values.

6425 Sanford, Judy, et al. Patterns of reported rape in a tri-ethnic population: Houston, Texas, 1974-1975. AMERICAN JOURNAL OF PUBLIC HEALTH, Vol. 69, no. 5 (May 1979), p. 480-484. English. DESCR: Anglo Americans; Blacks; Criminology; *Ethnic Groups; *Houston, TX; *Rape; Statistics.

6426 Schlissel, Lillian, ed.; Ruiz, Vicki L., ed.; and Monk, Janice, ed. Western women: their land, their lives. Albuquerque, NM: University of New Mexico Press, c1988. vi, 354 p. English. DESCR: Anglo Americans; History; Immigration; Intermarriage; Labor; Native Americans; *Social History and Conditions; Southwestern United States.

6427 Segura, Denise. Chicana and Mexican immigrant women at work: the impact of class, race, and gender on occupational mobility. GENDER & SOCIETY, Vol. 3, no. 1 (March 1989), p. 37-52. English. DESCR: *Employment; *Immigrants; Labor Supply and Market; Laboring Classes; San Francisco Bay Area; *Social Mobility; Working Women.

6428 Segura, Denise. Chicanas and Mexican immigrant women in the labor market: a study of occupational mobility and stratification. Thesis (Ph.D.)--University of California, Berkeley, 1986. iii, 282 p. English. DESCR: *Immigrants; *Labor Supply and Market; Mexico; *Working Women.

6429 Segura, Denise. Conflict in social relations at work: a Chicana perspective. IN: National Association for Chicano Studies. ESTUDIOS CHICANOS AND THE POLITICS OF COMMUNITY. [S.l.]: National Association for Chicano Studies, c1989, p. [110]-131. English. DESCR: *Discrimination in Employment; Employment Training; Immigrants; *Interpersonal Relations; Social Classes; *Working Women.

Women (cont.)

6430 Segura, Denise. Familism and employment
among Chicanas and Mexican immigrant women.
IN: Melville, Margarita, ed. MEXICANAS AT
WORK IN THE UNITED STATES. Houston, TX:
Mexican American Studies Program, University
of Houston, 1988, p. 24-32. English. DESCR:
*Employment; *Extended Family; Family;
Immigrants; Income; Machismo; Sex Roles;
Working Women.

6431 Segura, Denise. The interplay of familism
and patriarchy on employment among Chicana
and Mexicana women. RENATO ROSALDO LECTURE
SERIES MONOGRAPH, Vol. 5, (1989), p. 35-53.
English. DESCR: Employment; *Family;
Immigrants; Machismo; *Sex Roles; Women Men
Relations; *Working Women.

6432 Smith, Bradford M. The measurement of
narcissism in Asian, Caucasian, and Hispanic
American women. PSYCHOLOGICAL REPORTS, Vol.
67, no. 3 (December 1990), p. 779-785.
English. DESCR: Anglo Americans; Asian
Americans; Comparative Psychology; Cultural
Characteristics; *Narcissistic Personality
Inventory; *Personality; *Psychological
Testing.

6433 Solorzano-Torres, Rosalia. Female Mexican
immigrants in San Diego County. IN: Ruiz,
Vicki L. and Tiano, Susan, eds. WOMEN ON THE
U.S.-MEXICO BORDER: RESPONSES TO CHANGE.
Boston, MA: Allen & Unwin, 1987, p. 41-59.
English. DESCR: Employment; *Immigrants;
Immigration; Literature Reviews; San Diego
County, CA; Surveys; Undocumented Workers.

6434 Solorzano-Torres, Rosalia. Women, labor, and
the U.S.-Mexico border: Mexican maids in El
Paso, Texas. IN: Melville, Margarita, ed.
MEXICANAS AT WORK IN THE UNITED STATES.
Houston, TX: Mexican American Studies
Program, University of Houston, 1988, p.
75-83. English. DESCR: Border Patrol;
*Border Region; Domestic Work; El Paso, TX;
Immigrants; Immigration and Naturalization
Service (INS); Immigration Regulation and
Control; *Labor Supply and Market;
Undocumented Workers; *Working Women.

6435 Sorenson, Susan B. and Telles, Cynthia A.
Self-reports of spousal violence in a
Mexican-American and non-Hispanic white
population. VIOLENCE AND VICTIMS, Vol. 6,
no. 1 (1991), p. 3-15. English. DESCR: Anglo
Americans; *Battered Women; Los Angeles, CA;
Los Angeles Epidemiologic Catchment Area
Research Program (LAECA); Rape; Violence;
*Women Men Relations.

6436 Sosa Riddell, Adaljiza. The status of women
in Mexico: the impact of the "International
Year of the Woman". IN: Iglitzin, Lynn B.
and Ross, Ruth A., eds. WOMEN IN THE WORLD,
1975-1985. Santa Barbara, CA: ABC-Clio,
Inc., 1986, p. 305-324. English. DESCR:
Abortion; *Feminism; International Women s
Year World Conference (1975: Mexico City);
*Mexico; Political History and Conditions;
Political Parties and Organizations; Rape;
*Sexism; Social History and Conditions.

6437 Soto, Shirlene Ann. Emergence of the modern
Mexican woman: her participation in
revolution and struggle for equality,
1910-1940. Denver, CO: Arden Press, 1990.
xvi, 199 p.: ill. English. DESCR: *Feminism;
*Mexican Revolution - 1910-1920; *Mexico;
Political History and Conditions.

6438 Soto, Shirlene Ann. Tres modelos culturales:
la Virgen de Guadalupe, la Malinche y la

Llorona. FEM, Vol. 10, no. 48 (October,
November, 1986), p. 13-16. Spanish. DESCR:
Guadalupanismo; *La Llorona; *La Virgen de
Guadalupe; *Malinche; Symbolism.

6439 Soto, Shirlene Ann. The women's movement in
Mexico: the first and second feminist
congresses in Yucatan, 1916. IN: Del
Castillo, Adelaida R., ed. BETWEEN BORDERS:
ESSAYS ON MEXICANA/CHICANA HISTORY. Encino,
CA: Floricanto Press, 1990, p. 483-491.
English. DESCR: *Conferences and Meetings;
*Feminism; *Feminist Congress (1916:
Yucatan, Mexico); Mexico.

6440 Staudt, Kathleen. Programming women's
empowerment: a case from northern Mexico.
IN: Ruiz, Vicki L. and Tiano, Susan, eds.
WOMEN ON THE U.S.-MEXICO BORDER: RESPONSES
TO CHANGE. Boston, MA: Allen & Unwin, 1987,
p. 155-173. English. DESCR: Alternative
Education; Border Region; Ciudad Juarez,
Chihuahua, Mexico; Curriculum; Employment;
*Feminism; Organizations.

6441 Stewart, Kenneth L. and de Leon, Arnoldo.
Fertility among Mexican Americans and Anglos
in Texas, 1900. BORDERLANDS JOURNAL, Vol. 9,
no. 1 (Spring 1986), p. 61-67. English.
DESCR: Anglo Americans; *Fertility; Texas.

6442 Stewart, Kenneth L. and de Leon, Arnoldo.
Work force participation among Mexican
immigrant women in Texas, 1900. BORDERLANDS
JOURNAL, Vol. 9, no. 1 (Spring 1986), p.
69-74. English. DESCR: Employment; History;
*Immigrants; Texas; *Working Women.

6443 Stroup-Benham, Christine A. and Trevino,
Fernando M. Reproductive characteristics of
Mexican-American, mainland Puerto Rican, and
Cuban-American women: data from the Hispanic
Health and Nutrition Examination Survey.
JAMA: JOURNAL OF THE AMERICAN MEDICAL
ASSOCIATION, Vol. 265, no. 2 (January 9,
1991), p. 222-226. English. DESCR: *Birth
Control; Breastfeeding; Cubanos; *Fertility;
Hispanic Health and Nutrition Examination
Survey (HHANES); Puerto Ricans.

6444 Sullivan, Teresa A. The occupational
prestige of women immigrants: a comparison
of Cubans and Mexicans. INTERNATIONAL
MIGRATION REVIEW, Vol. 18, no. 4 (Winter
1984), p. 1045-1062. English. DESCR:
Careers; Cubanos; Employment; *Immigrants;
Males; Mexico; Sex Roles; *Social Mobility;
*Working Women.

6445 Sweeny, Mary Anne and Gulino, Claire. The
health belief model as an explanation for
breast-feeding practices in a Hispanic
population. ANS: ADVANCES IN NURSING
SCIENCE, Vol. 9, no. 4 (July 1987), p.
35-50. English. DESCR: *Breastfeeding;
*Cultural Customs; *Public Health; San
Diego, CA; Tijuana, Baja California, Mexico.

6446 Swicegood, Gray, et al. Language usage and
fertility in the Mexican-origin population
of the United States. DEMOGRAPHY, Vol. 25,
no. 1 (February 1988), p. 17-33. English.
DESCR: *Fertility; Immigrants; *Language
Usage; Population.

--   --

Women (cont.)

6447 Tiano, Susan B. Export processing, women's
     work, and the employment problem in
     developing countries: the case of the
     maquiladora program in Northern Mexico. El
     Paso, TX: Center for InterAmerican and
     Border Studies, UTEP, 1985. 32 p. English.
     DESCR: *Border Region; *Employment; Labor
     Supply and Market; Mexico; *Sex Roles;
     Working Women.

6448 Tiano, Susan B. Labor composition and gender
     stereotypes in the maquila. JOURNAL OF
     BORDERLAND STUDIES, Vol. 5, no. 1 (Spring
     1990), p. 20-24. English. **DESCR:** *Border
     Industries; Industrial Workers; Labor Supply
     and Market; *Sex Stereotypes; *Working
     Women.

6449 Tiano, Susan B. Maquiladoras in Mexicali:
     integration or exploitation? IN: Ruiz, Vicki
     L. and Tiano, Susan, eds. WOMEN ON THE
     U.S.-MEXICO BORDER: RESPONSES TO CHANGE.
     Boston, MA: Allen & Unwin, 1987, p. 77-101.
     English. **DESCR:** Border Industrialization
     Program (BIP); *Border Industries; Border
     Region; Employment; Labor Supply and Market;
     Mexicali, Mexico; Working Women.

6450 Tiano, Susan B. Maquiladoras, women's work,
     and unemployment in northern Mexico. AZTLAN,
     Vol. 15, no. 2 (Fall 1984), p. 341-378.
     English. **DESCR:** *Border Industries;
     Employment; Mexico; Working Women.

6451 Tiano, Susan B. Women's work and
     unemployment in northern Mexico. IN: Ruiz,
     Vicki L. and Tiano, Susan, eds. WOMEN ON THE
     U.S.-MEXICO BORDER: RESPONSES TO CHANGE.
     Boston, MA: Allen & Unwin, 1987, p. 17-39.
     English. **DESCR:** Border Industrialization
     Program (BIP); Border Industries; Border
     Region; Employment; Labor Supply and Market;
     Mexico; Multinational Corporations.

6452 Timberlake, Andrea, et al. Women of color
     and southern women: a bibliography of social
     science research, 1975 to 1988. Memphis, TN:
     Center for Research on Women, Memphis State
     University, 1988. vii, 264 p. English.
     DESCR: *Bibliography; Blacks; *Social
     Science.

6453 Torres, Sara. A comparative analysis of wife
     abuse among Anglo-American and
     Mexican-American battered women: attitudes,
     nature, severity, frequency and response to
     the abuse. Thesis (Ph.D.)--University of
     Texas, Austin, 1986. 265 p. English. **DESCR:**
     Anglo Americans; Attitudes; Battered Women;
     Family; *Violence.

6454 U.S. Department of Labor, Women's Bureau.
     Adelante mujer hispana: a conference model
     for Hispanic women. Washington, DC: The
     Bureau, 1980. 39 p.: ill. English. **DESCR:**
     *Adelante Mujer Hispana
     Conference--Education and Employment
     Conference (January 11-12, 1980: Denver,
     CO); *Conferences and Meetings.

6455 U.S. National Institute of Education.
     Conference on the educational and
     occupational needs of Hispanic women, June
     29-30, 1976; December 10-12, 1976.
     Washington, DC: U.S. Department of
     Education, 1980. x, 301 p. English. **DESCR:**
     Conference on the Educational and
     Occupational Needs of Hispanic Women (1976:
     Denver, CO); Conferences and Meetings;
     *Education; *Employment; Higher Education;
     Leadership; Puerto Ricans; Sex Roles.

6456 Valenzuela-Crocker, Elvira. Women, power and
     the vote. NUESTRO, Vol. 8, no. 6 (August
     1984), p. 43-44. English. **DESCR:** Voting
     Rights; *Women's Suffrage.

6457 Valtierra, Mary. Acculturation, social
     support, and reported stress of Latina
     physicians. Thesis (Ph.D.)--California
     School of Professional Psychology, 1989. 136
     p. English. **DESCR:** *Acculturation; Careers;
     Cubanos; Immigration; Latin Americans;
     *Medical Personnel; Puerto Ricans; *Stress.

6458 Vasquez, Josefina. Educacion y papel de la
     mujer en Mexico. IN: Del Castillo, Adelaida
     R., ed. BETWEEN BORDERS: ESSAYS ON
     MEXICANA/CHICANA HISTORY. Encino, CA:
     Floricanto Press, 1990, p. 377-398. Spanish.
     DESCR: *Education; History; *Mexico; *Sex
     Roles.

6459 Vasquez, Mario F. The election day
     immigration raid at Lilli Diamond Originals
     and the response of the ILGWU. IN: Mora,
     Magdalena and Del Castillo, Adelaida, eds.
     MEXICAN WOMEN IN THE UNITED STATES:
     STRUGGLES PAST AND PRESENT. Los Angeles, CA:
     Chicano Studies Research Center, UCLA, 1980,
     p. 145-148. English. **DESCR:** Garment
     Industry; Immigration Regulation and
     Control; International Ladies Garment
     Workers Union (ILGWU); Labor Unions; *Lilli
     Diamond Originals; Undocumented Workers;
     Working Women.

6460 Vasquez, Mario F. Immigrant workers and the
     apparel manufacturing industry in Southern
     California. IN: Rios-Bustamante, Antonio,
     ed. MEXICAN IMMIGRANT WORKERS IN THE U.S.
     Los Angeles, CA: Chicano Studies Research
     Center Publications, University of
     California, 1981, p. 85-96. English. **DESCR:**
     AFL-CIO; California; Garment Industry;
     Immigrants; International Ladies Garment
     Workers Union (ILGWU); *Labor Supply and
     Market; Labor Unions; Undocumented Workers.

6461 Vazquez-Nuttall, Ena; Romero-Garcia, Ivonne;
     and De Leon, Brunilda. Sex roles and
     perceptions of femininity and masculinity of
     Hispanic women: a review of the literature.
     PSYCHOLOGY OF WOMEN QUARTERLY, Vol. 11, no.
     4 (December 1987), p. 409-425. English.
     DESCR: Attitudes; *Chicanismo; *Literature
     Reviews; Machismo; Puerto Ricans; *Sex
     Roles.

6462 Vega, William A.; Kolody, Bohdan; and Valle,
     Juan Ramon. Migration and mental health: an
     empirical test of depression risk factors
     among immigrant Mexican women. INTERNATIONAL
     MIGRATION REVIEW, Vol. 21, no. 3 (Fall
     1987), p. 512-530. English. **DESCR:**
     Acculturation; *Depression (Psychological);
     *Immigrants; Immigration; *Mental Health;
     Migration; Stress; Undocumented Workers.

6463 Vega, William A.; Kolody, Bohdan; and Valle,
     Juan Ramon. The relationship of marital
     status, confidant support, and depression
     among Mexican immigrant women. JOURNAL OF
     MARRIAGE AND THE FAMILY, Vol. 48, no. 3
     (August 1986), p. 597-605. English. **DESCR:**
     *Depression (Psychological); *Immigrants;
     Low Income; *Marriage; San Diego County, CA;
     Stress.

Women (cont.)

6464 Veyna, Angelina F. Women in early New Mexico: a preliminary view. IN: Cordova, Teresa, et al., eds. CHICANA VOICES. Austin, TX: Center for Mexican American Studies, 1986, p. 120-135. English. DESCR: Administration of Justice; History; New Mexico.

6465 Vigil, Evangelina, ed. Woman of her word: Hispanic women write. REVISTA CHICANO-RIQUENA, Vol. 11, no. 3-4 (Fall, Winter, 1983), p. [1]-180. Bilingual. DESCR: Art; Literary Criticism; *Literature; Poetry; Prose.

6466 Wagner, Roland M. Changes in extended family relationships for Mexican American and Anglo single mothers. JOURNAL OF DIVORCE, Vol. 11, no. 2 (Winter 1987), p. 69-87. English. DESCR: Anglo Americans; *Divorce; *Extended Family; Natural Support Systems; San Jose, CA; *Single Parents.

6467 Wagner, Roland M. Changes in the friend network during the first year of single parenthood for Mexican American and Anglo women. JOURNAL OF DIVORCE, Vol. 11, no. 2 (Winter 1987), p. 89-109. English. DESCR: Anglo Americans; Divorce; *Natural Support Systems; *Single Parents; Widowhood.

6468 Walker, Todd. The relationship of nativity, social support and depression to the home environment among Mexican-American women. Thesis (Ph.D.)--University of Houston, 1989. 123 p. English. DESCR: Acculturation; Avance Parent-Child Education Program, San Antonio, TX; Children; Depression (Psychological); *Immigrants; Natural Support Systems; *Parenting.

6469 Warren, Charles W.; Smith, Jack C.; and Rochat, Roger W. Differentials in the planning status of the most recent live birth to Mexican Americans and Anglos. PUBLIC HEALTH REPORTS, Vol. 98, no. 2 (March, April, 1983), p. 152-160. English. DESCR: Anglo Americans; *Family Planning; Fertility.

6470 Watkins, Elizabeth L.; Peoples, Mary D.; and Gates, Connie. Health and social needs of women farmworkers: receiving maternity care at a migrant health center. MIGRATION TODAY, Vol. 13, no. 2 (1985), p. 39-42. English. DESCR: Farm Workers; *Maternal and Child Welfare; *Migrant Health Services.

6471 Weiner, Raine. The needs of poverty women heading households: a return to postsecondary education. Thesis (Ph.D.)--California School of Professional Psychology, Los Angeles, 1986. 180 p. English. DESCR: Anglo Americans; Blacks; *Employment Training; Ethnic Groups; *Poverty; *Single Parents; Vocational Education; Welfare.

6472 White, Marni, et al. Perceived crime in the neighborhood and mental health of women and children. ENVIRONMENT AND BEHAVIOR, Vol. 19, no. 5 (September 1987), p. 588-613. English. DESCR: Attitudes; Children; Criminology; Housing; *Mental Health.

6473 Williams, Edward J. and Passe-Smith, John T. Turnover and recruitment in the maquila industry: causes and solutions. Las Cruces, NM: Joint Border Research Institute, New Mexico State University, 1989. ii, 59 p. English. DESCR: *Border Industries; *Employment; Income; *Labor Supply and Market; Personnel Management; Surveys; *Working Women.

6474 Williams, Joyce E. Mexican American and Anglo attitudes about sex roles and rape. FREE INQUIRY IN CREATIVE SOCIOLOGY, Vol. 13, no. 1 (May 1985), p. 15-20. English. DESCR: Anglo Americans; Attitudes; *Feminism; *Rape; *Sex Roles.

6475 Winter, Michael; Russo, Nancy Felipe; and Amaro, Hortensia. The use of inpatient mental health services by Hispanic women. PSYCHOLOGY OF WOMEN QUARTERLY, Vol. 11, no. 4 (December 1987), p. 427-441. English. DESCR: Mental Health; *Mental Health Clinics; Social Services.

6476 Woodward, Carolyn. Dare to write: Virginia Woolf, Tillie Olsen, Gloria Anzaldua. IN: Cochran, Jo Whitehorse, et al., eds. CHANGING OUR POWER: AN INTRODUCTION TO WOMEN STUDIES. Dubuque, IA: Kendall/Hunt Publishing Co., 1988, p. 336-349. English. DESCR: Anzaldua, Gloria; *Authors; Feminism; Olsen, Tillie; Woolf, Virginia.

6477 Worth, Dooley and Rodriguez, Ruth. Latina women and AIDS. SIECUS REPORT, (January, February, 1986), p. 5-7. English. DESCR: Cultural Characteristics; Drug Addicts; Drug Use; Health Education; Natural Support Systems; New York; Preventative Medicine; Puerto Ricans; Sex Roles; *Vital Statistics.

6478 Yarbro-Bejarano, Yvonne. Chicana's experience in collective theatre: ideology and form. WOMEN AND PERFORMANCE, Vol. 2, no. 2 (1985), p. 45-58. English. DESCR: Actors and Actresses; Careers; El Teatro Campesino; El Teatro de la Esperanza; Political Ideology; *San Francisco Mime Troupe; Sex Roles; Teatro; Teatro Libertad; Valentina Productions.

6479 Yarbro-Bejarano, Yvonne. Primer encuentro de lesbianas feministas latinoamericanas y caribenas. THIRD WOMAN, Vol. 4, (1989), p. 143-146. English. DESCR: Caribbean Region; *Conferences and Meetings; First Meeting of Latin American and Caribbean Feminist Lesbians (October 14-17, 1987: Cuernavaca, Mexico); *Homosexuality; Latin Americans; Sexual Behavior.

6480 Young, Gay. Women, border industrialization program, and human rights. El Paso, TX: Center for InterAmerican and Border Studies, UTEP, 1984. 33 p. English. DESCR: Border Industrialization Program (BIP); *Border Industries; Economic Development; Employment; Industrial Workers; Mexico; Sex Roles; *Sexism; Working Women.

6481 Young, Gay. Women, development and human rights: issues in integrated transnational production. JOURNAL OF APPLIED BEHAVIORAL SCIENCE, Vol. 20, no. 4 (November 1984), p. 383-401. English. DESCR: Border Industrialization Program (BIP); *Border Industries; Feminism; Mexico; Multinational Corporations; Women Men Relations; *Working Women.

6482 Zambrana, Ruth E. Bibliography on maternal and child health across class, race and ethnicity. Memphis, TN: Distributed by the Memphis State University Center for Research on Women, c1990. 58 leaves. English. DESCR: *Bibliography; Ethnic Groups; *Maternal and Child Welfare; *Medical Care; Social Classes.

Women (cont.)

6483 Zambrana, Ruth E. Hispanic professional women: work, family and health. Los Angeles, CA: National Network of Hispanic Women, 1987. 75 leaves. English. DESCR: Business; *Careers; *Employment; Family; Management; Mental Health; Social Classes; *Social Mobility.

6484 Zambrana, Ruth E. Toward understanding the educational trajectory and socialization of Latina women. IN: McKenna, Teresa and Ortiz, Flora Ida, eds. THE BROKEN WEB: THE EDUCATIONAL EXPERIENCE OF HISPANIC WOMEN. Claremont, CA: Tomas Rivera Center; Berkeley, CA: Floricanto Press, 1988, p. 61-77. English. DESCR: Academic Achievement; Anglo Americans; *Education; Feminism; Identity; Research Methodology; *Socialization.

6485 Zambrana, Ruth E., et al. Ethnic differences in the substance use patterns of low-income pregnant women. FAMILY & COMMUNITY HEALTH, Vol. 13, no. 4 (January 1991), p. 1-11. English. DESCR: Alcoholism; Blacks; *Drug Use; *Fertility; Immigrants; *Low Income; Smoking.

6486 Zambrano, Myrna. Mejor sola que mal acompanada: para la mujer golpeada. Seattle, WA: Seal Press, 1985. 241 p. Bilingual. DESCR: Battered Women; Natural Support Systems.

6487 Zavella, Patricia. The problematic relationship of feminism and Chicana Studies. WOMEN'S STUDIES QUARTERLY, Vol. 17, no. 1-2 (1989), p. 25-36. English. DESCR: Chicana Studies; *Feminism.

6488 Zayas, Luis H. Toward an understanding of suicide risks in young Hispanic females. JOURNAL OF ADOLESCENT RESEARCH, Vol. 2, no. 1 (Spring 1987), p. 1-11. English. DESCR: Acculturation; Cubanos; Cultural Characteristics; Depression (Psychological); Mental Health; Puerto Ricans; *Suicide; *Youth.

WOMEN & THEIR WORK [festival] (Austin, TX: 1977)

6489 Goldman, Shifra M. Women artists of Texas: MAS = More + Artists + Women = MAS. CHISMEARTE, no. 7 (January 1981), p. 21-22. English. DESCR: Arredondo, Alicia; Art Organizations and Groups; Barraza, Santa; Exhibits; Feminism; Flores, Maria; Folk Art; Gonzalez Dodson, Nora; *Mujeres Artistas del Suroeste (MAS), Austin, TX; Photography; Texas; Trevino, Modesta Barbina.

WOMEN ARE NOT ROSES

6490 Alarcon, Norma. The sardonic powers of the erotic in the work of Ana Castillo. IN: Horno-Delgado, Asuncion, et al., eds. BREAKING BOUNDARIES: LATINA WRITING AND CRITICAL READINGS. Amherst, MA: University of Massachusetts Press, c1989, p. 94-107. English. DESCR: *Castillo, Ana; Literary Criticism; OTRO CANTO; Poetry; Sex Roles; THE INVITATION; *THE MIXQUIAHUALA LETTERS.

Women in Teatro (WIT)

6491 Yarbro-Bejarano, Yvonne. The female subject in Chicano theater: sexuality, race, and class. THEATRE JOURNAL, Vol. 38, no. 4 (December 1986), p. 389-407. English. DESCR: El Teatro Campesino; El Teatro de la Esperanza; El Teatro Nacional de Aztlan (TENAZ); Feminism; *Malinche; *Sex Roles;

*Teatro.

Women Men Relations

6492 Abajo con los machos [letter to the editor]. LA RAZA, Vol. 1, no. 5 (1971), p. 3-4. English. DESCR: Chicano Movement; *Machismo.

6493 Anderson, Robert K. Marez y Luna and the masculine-feminine dialectic. CRITICA HISPANICA, Vol. 6, no. 2 (1984), p. 97-105. English. DESCR: Anaya, Rudolfo A.; BLESS ME, ULTIMA; Literary Criticism; Novel.

6494 Aneshensel, Carol S., et al. Participation of Mexican American adolescents in a longitudinal panel survey. PUBLIC OPINION QUARTERLY, Vol. 53, no. 4 (Winter 1989), p. 548-562. English. DESCR: Age Groups; *Fertility; Los Angeles County, CA; Social Science; *Surveys; *Youth.

6495 Baca Zinn, Maxine. Chicanas: power and control in the domestic sphere. DE COLORES, Vol. 2, no. 3 (1975), p. 19-31. English. DESCR: *Family; Immigration Regulation and Control; Machismo; *Sex Roles; Stereotypes.

6496 Baca Zinn, Maxine. Chicanas: power and control in the domestic sphere. IN: Cotera, Martha and Hufford, Larry, eds. BRIDGING TWO CULTURES. Austin, TX: National Educational Laboratory Publishers, 1980, p. 270-281. English. DESCR: Family; Immigration Regulation and Control; Machismo; Sex Roles; *Stereotypes.

6497 Baca Zinn, Maxine. Chicano men and masculinity. JOURNAL OF ETHNIC STUDIES, Vol. 10, no. 2 (Summer 1982), p. 29-44. English. DESCR: Cultural Characteristics; Ethnic Stratification; *Machismo; Sex Roles; Sex Stereotypes; Socioeconomic Factors.

6498 Benardo, Margot L. and Anthony, Darius. Hispanic women and their men. LATINA, Vol. 1, no. 3 (1983), p. 24-29. English. DESCR: Photography.

6499 Campoamor, Diana. Gender gap in politics: no laughing matter. VISTA, Vol. 4, no. 8 (October 24, 1988), p. 14. English. DESCR: Attitudes; Essays; Politics.

6500 Cardenas, Reyes. The machismo manifesto. CARACOL, Vol. 2, no. 8 (April 1976), p. 7. Bilingual. DESCR: Cotera, Marta P.; *Machismo; Malinche.

6501 Chavez, Henri. Las Chicanas/The Chicanas. REGENERACION, Vol. 1, no. 10 (1971), p. 14. Bilingual. DESCR: *Chicano Movement; Sexism.

6502 Chicana regional conference. LA RAZA, Vol. 1, no. 6 (1971), p. 43-45. English. DESCR: Chicana Regional Conference (May 8, 1971: Los Angeles, CA); *Chicano Movement; Conferences and Meetings; Feminism.

6503 Cordova, Marcella C. Women's rights: a Chicana's viewpoint. LA LUZ, Vol. 4, no. 2 (May 1975), p. 3. English. DESCR: Feminism; *Machismo.

6504 Cotera, Marta P. Chicana identity. CARACOL, Vol. 2, no. 6 (February 1976), p. 14-15, 17. English.

6505 Cotera, Marta P. ERA: the Latina challenge. NUESTRO, Vol. 5, no. 8 (November 1981), p. 47-48. English. DESCR: Equal Rights Amendment (ERA); Feminism.

Women Men Relations
(cont.)

6506 Cotera, Marta P. La nueva hispana y [sic] hispanidad. LA LUZ, Vol. 8, no. 4 (October, November, 1979), p. 8-10. English. DESCR: *Civil Rights; *Feminism.

6507 De Ortego y Gasca, Felipe. The Hispanic woman: a humanistic perspective. LA LUZ, Vol. 6, no. 11 (November 1977), p. 7-10. English. DESCR: De la Cruz, Juana Ines; Dona Ximena; *Essays; History; Mistral, Gabriela; Ortiz de Dominguez, Josefa; *Women's Suffrage.

6508 De Ortego y Gasca, Felipe. The Hispanic woman: a humanistic perspective. LA LUZ, Vol. 8, no. 8 (October November, 1980), p. 6-9. English. DESCR: De la Cruz, Juana Ines Dona Ximena; *Essays; History; Mistral, Gabriela; Ortiz de Dominguez, Josefa; *Women's Suffrage.

6509 Del Zotto, Augusta. Latinas with AIDS: life expectancy for Hispanic women is a startling 45 days after diagnosis. THIS WORLD, (April 9, 1989), p. 9. English. DESCR: Abortion; AIDS (Disease); Condom Use; Instituto Familiar de la Raza, San Francisco, CA; Machismo; *Mano a Mano; Quintero, Juanita; Sex Roles.

6510 Delgado, Abelardo "Lalo". An open letter to Carolina... or relations between men and women. REVISTA CHICANO-RIQUENA, Vol. 10, no. 1-2 (Winter, Spring, 1982), p. 279-284. English. DESCR: *Essays; Machismo; Sex Roles; Sex Stereotypes.

6511 Delgado, Sylvia. Chicana: the forgotten woman. REGENERACION, Vol. 2, no. 1 (1971), p. 2-4. English. DESCR: *Abortion; Free Clinics; Working Women.

6512 Delgado, Sylvia. Young Chicana speaks up on problems faced by young girls. REGENERACION, Vol. 1, no. 10 (1971), p. 5-7. English. DESCR: Abortion; Feminism; Machismo; Marriage; Sex Roles

6513 Espin, Oliva M. Perceptions of sexual discrimination among college women in Latin America and the United States. HISPANIC JOURNAL OF BEHAVIORAL SCIENCES, Vol. 2, no. 1 (March 1980), p. 1-19. English. DESCR: Colleges and Universities; CRITICAL INCIDENT TECHNIQUE; Feminism; Latin Americans; *Sexism; Students.

6514 Flores, Francisca. Conference of Mexican women un remolino. REGENERACION, Vol. 1, no. 10 (1971), p. 1-5. English. DESCR: Conferences and Meetings; Family; Feminism; First National Chicana Conference (May 1971: Houston, TX); Machismo; National Mexican American Issues Conference (October 11, 1970: Sacramento, CA); Sex Roles; Sex Stereotypes; Statistics.

6515 Fostering the advancement of Latinas. NUESTRO, Vol. 6, no. 10 (December 1982), p. 48-49. English. DESCR: Mexican American Women's National Association (MANA).

6516 Gonzalez, Judith Teresa. Dilemmas of the high achieving Chicana: the double bind factor in male/female relationships. Tucson, AZ: Mexican American Studies & Research Center, University of Arizona, 1987. 31 leaves. English. DESCR: *Academic Achievement; Higher Education; Identity; Males; Marriage; *Sex Roles; *Sex Stereotypes.

6517 Gonzalez, Judith Teresa. Dilemmas of the high achieving Chicana: the double bind factor in male/female relationships. SEX ROLES, Vol. 18, no. 7-8 (April 1988), p. 367-380. English. DESCR: *Academic Achievement; Higher Education; Identity; Males; Marriage; *Sex Roles; *Sex Stereotypes.

6518 Guendelman, Sylvia. The incorporation of Mexican women in seasonal migration: a study of gender differences. HISPANIC JOURNAL OF BEHAVIORAL SCIENCES, Vol. 9, no. 3 (September 1987), p. 245-264. English. DESCR: Immigrants; Marriage; Mexico; *Migration Patterns; *Sex Roles; *Women; Working Women.

6519 Gutierrez, Ramon A. Honor ideology, marriage negotiation, and class-gender domination in New Mexico, 1690-1846. LATIN AMERICAN PERSPECTIVES, Vol. 12, no. 1 (Winter 1985), p. 81-104. English. DESCR: Marriage; Sex Roles; *Social Classes; Social History and Conditions; Southwestern United States; Values.

6520 Herrera-Sobek, Maria. The acculturation process of the Chicana in the corrido. PROCEEDINGS OF THE PACIFIC COAST COUNCIL ON LATIN AMER STUDIES, Vol. 9, (1982), p. 25-34. English. DESCR: *Acculturation; *Corridos; Musical Lyrics.

6521 Herrera-Sobek, Maria. The Mexican corrido: a feminist analysis. Bloomington, IN: Indiana University Press, 1990. xix, 151 p.: ill. English. DESCR: *Corridos; Mexico; Military; *Sex Roles; Sex Stereotypes; Symbolism; *Women.

6522 Hogeland, Chris and Rosen, Karen. Dreams lost, dreams found: undocumented women in the land of opportunity. San Francisco, CA: Coalition for Immigrant and Refugee Rights and Services, c1991. 153 p. English. DESCR: *Battered Women; *Coalition for Immigrant and Refugee Rights and Services, Immigrant Woman's Task Force; Discrimination; Immigrants; *San Francisco Bay Area; Sex Roles; Sexism; Social Services; Undocumented Workers; Violence; Women.

6523 Horowitz, Ruth. Femininity and womanhood: virginity, unwed motherhood, and violence. IN: Horowitz, Ruth. HONOR AND THE AMERICAN DREAM: CULTURE AND IDENTITY IN A CHICANO COMMUNITY. New Brunswick, NJ: Rutgers University Press, 1983, p. 114-136. English. DESCR: *Birth Control; *Fertility; Identity; Sex Roles; *Sexual Behavior; Single Parents; Violence; Youth.

6524 LeVine, Sarah Ethel; Correa, Clara Sunderland; and Uribe, F. Medardo Tapia. The marital morality of Mexican women--an urban study. JOURNAL OF ANTHROPOLOGICAL RESEARCH, Vol. 42, no. 2 (Summer 1986), p. 183-202. English. DESCR: Family; Los Robles, Cuernavaca, Morelos, Mexico; *Machismo; Marriage; Parent and Child Relationships; *Sex Roles; Women.

6525 Lucero Trujillo, Marcela. The terminology of machismo. DE COLORES, Vol. 4, no. 3 (1978), p. 34-42. Bilingual. DESCR: *Chicanismo; *Machismo; *Sex Stereotypes.

Women Men Relations
(cont.)

6526 Melville, Margarita B. Female and male in Chicano theatre. IN: Kanellos, Nicolas, ed. HISPANIC THEATRE IN THE UNITED STATES. Houston, TX: Arte Publico Press, 1984, p. 71-79. English. **DESCR**: BERNABE; BRUJERIAS [play]; Cultural Characteristics; DAY OF THE SWALLOWS; Duarte-Clark, Rodrigo; EL JARDIN [play]; Family; Feminism; Macias, Ysidro; Morton, Carlos; Portillo Trambley, Estela; RANCHO HOLLYWOOD [play]; *Sex Roles; *Teatro; THE ULTIMATE PENDEJADA [play]; Valdez, Luis.

6527 Monroy, Douglas. "They didn't call them 'padre' for nothing": patriarchy in Hispanic California. IN: Del Castillo, Adelaida R., ed. BETWEEN BORDERS: ESSAYS ON MEXICANA/CHICANA HISTORY. Encino, CA: Floricanto Press, 1990, p. 433-445. English. **DESCR**: *California; Clergy; History; *Machismo; Rape; *Sex Roles; *Sexism; Spanish Influence.

6528 Oeste, Marcia. Mujeres arriba y adelante. LA LUZ, Vol. 1, no. 2 (May 1972), p. 39-40. English. **DESCR**: *Feminism; Ortega y Gasset, Jose; Working Women.

6529 Pavich, Emma Guerrero. A Chicana perspective on Mexican culture and sexuality. JOURNAL OF SOCIAL WORK AND HUMAN SEXUALITY, Vol. 4, no. 3 (Spring 1986), p. 47-65. English. **DESCR**: California; Cultural Characteristics; Family; Feminism; Homosexuality; Machismo; Sex Roles; Sex Stereotypes; *Sexual Behavior.

6530 Pena, Manuel. Class, gender, and machismo: the "treacherous-woman" folklore of Mexican male workers. GENDER & SOCIETY, Vol. 5, no. 1 (March 1991), p. 30-46. English. **DESCR**: *Folklore; Laborers; *Machismo; Males; *Sex Roles; Sex Stereotypes; Social Classes; *Undocumented Workers.

6531 Rincon, Bernice. La Chicana: her role in the past and her search for a new role in the future. REGENERACION, Vol. 1, no. 10 (1971), p. 15-18. English. **DESCR**: Feminism.

6532 Rincon, Bernice. La Chicana: her role in the past and her search for a new role in the future. REGENERACION, Vol. 2, no. 4 (1975), p. 36-39. English. **DESCR**: Feminism.

6533 Saenz, Rogelio; Goudy, Willis J.; and Lorenz, Frederick O. The effects of employment and marital relations on depression among Mexican American women. JOURNAL OF MARRIAGE AND THE FAMILY, Vol. 51, no. 1 (February 1989), p. 239-251. English. **DESCR**: *Depression (Psychological); Domestic Work; *Employment; Feminism; *Marriage; Working Women.

6534 Segura, Denise. The interplay of familism and patriarchy on employment among Chicana and Mexicana women. RENATO ROSALDO LECTURE SERIES MONOGRAPH, Vol. 5, (1989), p. 35-53. English. **DESCR**: Employment; *Family; Immigrants; Machismo; *Sex Roles; Women; *Working Women.

6535 Sorenson, Susan B. and Telles, Cynthia A. Self-reports of spousal violence in a Mexican-American and non-Hispanic white population. VIOLENCE AND VICTIMS, Vol. 6, no. 1 (1991), p. 3-15. English. **DESCR**: Anglo Americans; *Battered Women; Los Angeles, CA; Los Angeles Epidemiologic Catchment Area Research Program (LAECA); Rape; Violence;

Women.

6536 Terranes, Ed. Some thoughts of a macho on the Chicana Movement. AGENDA, Vol. 7, no. 6 (November, December, 1977), p. 35-36. English. **DESCR**: Machismo.

6537 Yarbro-Bejarano, Yvonne. The image of the Chicana in teatro. IN: Cochran, Jo; Stewart, J.T.; and Tsutakawa, Mayumi, eds. GATHERING GROUND: NEW WRITING AND ART BY NORTHWEST WOMEN OF COLOR. Seattle, WA: Seal Press, 1984, p. 90-96. English. **DESCR**: El Teatro de la Esperanza; GUADALUPE [play]; HIJOS: ONCE A FAMILY [play]; LA VICTIMA [play]; *Literary Characters; Sex Roles; Sex Stereotypes; Stereotypes; *Teatro; THE OCTOPUS [play].

6538 Young, Gay. Women, development and human rights: issues in integrated transnational production. JOURNAL OF APPLIED BEHAVIORAL SCIENCE, Vol. 20, no. 4 (November 1984), p. 383-401. English. **DESCR**: Border Industrialization Program (BIP); *Border Industries; Feminism; Mexico; Multinational Corporations; Women; *Working Women.

WOMEN ON THE U.S.-MEXICO BORDER: RESPONSES TO CHANGE

6539 Garcia, Mario T. Family and gender in Chicano and border studies research. MEXICAN STUDIES/ESTUDIOS MEXICANOS, Vol. 6, no. 1 (Winter 1990), p. 109-119. English. **DESCR**: Alvarez, Robert R., Jr.; *Border Region; CANNERY WOMEN, CANNERY LIVES; *Family; LA FAMILIA: MIGRATION AND ADAPTATION IN BAJA AND ALTA CALIFORNIA, 1800-1975; *Literature Reviews; Ruiz, Vicki L.; Tiano, Susan B.; Women; WOMEN'S WORK AND CHICANO FAMILIES; Zavella, Pat.

Women's Rights
USE: Feminism

Women's Suffrage

6540 De Ortego y Gasca, Felipe. The Hispanic woman: a humanistic perspective. LA LUZ, Vol. 6, no. 11 (November 1977), p. 7-10. English. **DESCR**: De la Cruz, Juana Ines; Dona Ximena; *Essays; History; Mistral, Gabriela; Ortiz de Dominguez, Josefa; *Women Men Relations.

6541 De Ortego y Gasca, Felipe. The Hispanic woman: a humanistic perspective. LA LUZ, Vol. 8, no. 8 (October, November, 1980), p. 6-9. English. **DESCR**: De la Cruz, Juana Ines; Dona Ximena; *Essays; History; Mistral, Gabriela; Ortiz de Dominguez, Josefa; *Women Men Relations.

6542 Valenzuela-Crocker, Elvira. Women, power and the vote. NUESTRO, Vol. 8, no. 6 (August 1984), p. 43-44. English. **DESCR**: Voting Rights; Women.

WOMEN'S WORK AND CHICANO FAMILIES

6543 Acuna, Rodolfo. The struggles of class and gender: current research in Chicano Studies [review essay]. JOURNAL OF AMERICAN ETHNIC HISTORY, Vol. 8, no. 2 (Spring 1989), p. 134-138. English. **DESCR**: *CANNERY WOMEN, CANNERY LIVES; *CHICANO ETHNICITY; Deutsch, Sarah; Keefe, Susan E.; Literature Reviews; *NO SEPARATE REFUGE; Padilla, Amado M.; Ruiz, Vicki L.; Zavella, Pat.

WOMEN'S WORK AND CHICANO FAMILIES
(cont.)

6544 Garcia, Mario T. Family and gender in Chicano and border studies research. MEXICAN STUDIES/ESTUDIOS MEXICANOS, Vol. 6, no. 1 (Winter 1990), p. 109-119. English. DESCR: Alvarez, Robert R., Jr.; *Border Region; CANNERY WOMEN, CANNERY LIVES; *Family; LA FAMILIA: MIGRATION AND ADAPTATION IN BAJA AND ALTA CALIFORNIA, 1800-1975; *Literature Reviews; Ruiz, Vicki L.; Tiano, Susan B.; Women; WOMEN ON THE U.S.-MEXICO BORDER: RESPONSES TO CHANGE; Zavella, Pat.

Woodlake, CA

6545 Bays, Sharon Arlene. Women of the Valley of the Sun: women and family work culture in Woodlake, California. Thesis (M.A.)--UCLA, 1988. 89 leaves. English. DESCR: Family; *Farm Workers; Working Women.

Woolf, Virginia

6546 Woodward, Carolyn. Dare to write: Virginia Woolf, Tillie Olsen, Gloria Anzaldua. IN: Cochran, Jo Whitehorse, et al., eds. CHANGING OUR POWER: AN INTRODUCTION TO WOMEN STUDIES. Dubuque, IA: Kendall/Hunt Publishing Co., 1988, p. 336-349. English. DESCR: Anzaldua, Gloria; *Authors; Feminism; Olsen, Tillie; Women.

Workers
USE: Laborers

Worker's Alliance (WA), Los Angeles, CA

6547 Rips, Geoffrey and Tenayuca, Emma. Living history: Emma Tenayuca tells her story. TEXAS OBSERVER, (October 28, 1983), p. 7-15. English. DESCR: *Autobiography; Communist Party; Food Industry; Labor Unions; Leadership; Oral History; Pecan Shelling Worker's Union, San Antonio, TX; San Antonio, TX; Strikes and Lockouts; Tenayuca, Emma; United Cannery Agricultural Packing and Allied Workers of America (UCAPAWA); Working Women.

Working Force
USE: Laborers

"Working Mother's Song" [poem]

6548 Zamora, Bernice. Archetypes in Chicana poetry. DE COLORES, Vol. 4, no. 3 (1978), p. 43-52. English. DESCR: Cervantes, Lorna Dee; Cunningham, Veronica; "Declaration on a Day of Little Inspiration" [poem]; Hernandez, Carlota; "I Speak in an Illusion" [poem]; *Literary Criticism; Lucero, Judy A.; Macias, Margarita; Mendoza, Rita; "Para Mi Hijita" [poem]; *Poetry; "Rape Report" [poem]; "The White Line" [poem]; "You Can Only Blame the System for So Long" [poem]; Zamora, Katarina.

Working Women

6549 Almaguer, Tomas. Urban Chicano workers in historical perspective: a review of recent literature. LA RED/THE NET, no. 68 (May 1983), p. 2-6. English. DESCR: *Labor; *Literature Reviews.

6550 Ano Nuevo Kerr, Louise. Chicanas in the Great Depression. IN: Del Castillo, Adelaida R., ed. BETWEEN BORDERS: ESSAYS ON MEXICANA/CHICANA HISTORY. Encino, CA: Floricanto Press, 1990, p. 257-268. English. DESCR: *Chicago, IL; *Great Depression, 1929-1933; Historiography; Mexican Mothers'

Club, Chicago, IL.

6551 Arbelaez A., Marisol. Impacto social del sismo, Mexico 1985: las costureras. IN: Del Castillo, Adelaida R., ed. BETWEEN BORDERS: ESSAYS ON MEXICANA/CHICANA HISTORY. Encino, CA: Floricanto Press, 1990, p. 315-331. Spanish. DESCR: Earthquakes; Frente de Costureras, Mexico; *Garment Industry; *Industrial Workers; Labor Unions; *Mexico; Mexico City Earthquake, September 19, 1985; *Women.

6552 Arenal, Sandra. Sangre joven: las maquiladoras por dentro. Mexico, D.F.: Editorial Nuestro Tiempo, 1986. 130 p.: ill. Spanish. DESCR: *Border Industries; *Border Region; Employment; *Oral History; Women.

6553 Arguelles, Lourdes. Undocumented female labor in the United States Southwest: an essay on migration, consciousness, oppression and struggle. IN: Del Castillo, Adelaida R., ed. BETWEEN BORDERS: ESSAYS ON MEXICANA/CHICANA HISTORY. Encino, CA: Floricanto Press, 1990, p. 299-312. English. DESCR: Arizona Farm Workers (AFW); Immigrants; Immigration; *Undocumented Workers.

6554 Baker, Susan Gonzalez. Many rivers to cross: Mexican immigrants, women workers, and the structure of labor markets in the urban Southwest. Thesis (Ph.D.)--University of Texas, Austin, 1989. 163 p. English. DESCR: *Immigrants; Immigration Reform and Control Act of 1986; *Labor Supply and Market; Undocumented Workers; Women.

6555 Barton, Amy E. and California Commission on the Status of Women. Campesinas: women farmworkers in the California agricultural labor force, report of a study project. Sacramento, CA: The Commission, [1978], vii, 23, 52 p. English. DESCR: California; *Farm Workers; Migrant Labor; Statistics.

6556 Bays, Sharon Arlene. Women of the Valley of the Sun: women and family work culture in Woodlake, California. Thesis (M.A.)--UCLA, 1988. 89 leaves. English. DESCR: Family; *Farm Workers; Woodlake, CA.

6557 Blanco, Iris and Salorzano, Rosalia. O te aclimatas o te aclimueres. FEM, Vol. 8, no. 34 (June, July, 1984), p. 20-22. Spanish. DESCR: *Border Industries; *Immigration; Mexico; Women.

6558 Bustamante, Jorge A. Maquiladoras: a new face of international capitalism on Mexico's northern frontier. IN: Nash, June and Fernandez-Kelly, Patricia, eds. WOMEN, MEN, AND THE INTERNATIONAL DIVISION OF LABOR. Albany, NY: State University of New York Press, 1983, p. 224-256. English. DESCR: Banking Industry; Border Industrialization Program (BIP); Border Industries; *Border Region; Foreign Trade; Industrial Workers; International Economic Relations; Mexico; Population; Programa Nacional Fronterizo (PRONAF); United States-Mexico Relations; Women.

6559 Carrillo V., Jorge and Hernandez H., Alberto. Mujeres fronterizas en la industria maquiladora. Mexico, D.F.: Secretaria de Educacion Publica; Tijuana, B.C.N.: Centro de Estudios Fronterizos del Norte de Mexico, 1985. 216 p. Spanish. DESCR: *Border Industries; *Employment; *Women.

Working Women (cont.)

6560 Chavez, Henri. Unsung heroine of La Causa. REGENERACION, Vol. 1, no. 10 (1971), p. 20. English. **DESCR:** AFL-CIO United Farmworkers Organizing Committee; Agricultural Labor Unions; Community Service Organization, Los Angeles, (CSO); Family; Farm Workers; *Huerta, Dolores; Poverty.

6561 Cooney, Rosemary Santana and Ortiz, Vilma. Nativity, national origin, and Hispanic female participation in the labor force. SOCIAL SCIENCE QUARTERLY, Vol. 64, (September 1983), p. 510-523. English. **DESCR:** Immigrants; Women.

6562 Curry Rodriguez, Julia E. Labor migration and familial responsibilities: experiences of Mexican women. IN: Melville, Margarita, ed. MEXICANAS AT WORK IN THE UNITED STATES. Houston, TX: Mexican American Studies Program, University of Houston, 1988, p. 47-63. English. **DESCR:** Employment; Family; *Immigrants; Mexico; *Migrant Labor; Oral History; Sex Roles; Undocumented Workers; *Women.

6563 de la Torre, Adela and Rush, Lynda. The determinants of breastfeeding for Mexican migrant women. INTERNATIONAL MIGRATION REVIEW, Vol. 21, no. 3 (Fall 1987), p. 728-742. English. **DESCR:** *Breastfeeding; Farm Workers; Maternal and Child Welfare; Migrant Health Services; Migrant Labor; Migration; Public Health.

6564 Del Castillo, Adelaida R., ed. Between borders: essays on Mexicana/Chicana history. Encino, CA: Floricanto Press, c1990. xv, 563 p. Bilingual. **DESCR:** Feminism; Historiography; *History; Mexico; *Women.

6565 Delgado Campbell, Dolores. Shattering the stereotype: Chicanas as labor union organizers. BERKELEY WOMEN OF COLOR, no. 11 (Summer 1983), p. 20-23. English. **DESCR:** Farah Manufacturing Co., El Paso, TX; Farah Strike; *Gonzalez Parsons, Lucia; Huerta, Dolores; *Labor Unions; Moreno, Luisa [union organizer]; Tenayuca, Emma.

6566 Delgado, Sylvia. Chicana: the forgotten woman. REGENERACION, Vol. 2, no. 1 (1971), p. 2-4. English. **DESCR:** *Abortion; Free Clinics; *Women Men Relations.

6567 Deutsch, Sarah. Culture, class, and gender: Chicanas and Chicanos in Colorado and New Mexico, 1900-1940. Thesis (Ph.D.)--Yale University, 1985. xii, 510 p. English. **DESCR:** Anglo Americans; Colorado; Immigrants; New Mexico; *Sex Roles; *Social Classes; Social History and Conditions; Women.

6568 Deutsch, Sarah. No separate refuge: culture, class, and gender on an Anglo-Hispanic frontier in the American Southwest, 1880-1940. New York: Oxford University Press, 1987. vi, 356 p. English. **DESCR:** Anglo Americans; Colorado; Immigrants; Immigration; Mining Industry; Missions; New Mexico; *Sex Roles; *Social Classes; *Social History and Conditions; Women; World War I.

6569 Dill, Bonnie Thornton. Our mothers' grief: racial ethnic women and the maintenance of families. JOURNAL OF FAMILY HISTORY, Vol. 13, no. 4 (October 1988), p. 415-431. English. **DESCR:** Asian Americans; Blacks; Domestic Work; *Family; Fertility; *Sex Roles; *Women.

6570 Dixon, Marlene; Martinez, Elizabeth; and McCaughan, Ed. Chicanas and Mexicanas within a transnational working class: theoretical perspectives. REVIEW (Fernand Braudel Center), Vol. 7, no. 1 (1983), p. 109-150. English. **DESCR:** Laboring Classes.

6571 Dublin, Thomas. Commentary [on "And Miles to Go": Mexican Women and Work, 1930-1985]. IN: Schlissel, Lillian, et al., eds. WESTERN WOMEN: THEIR LAND, THEIR LIVES. Albuquerque, NM: University of New Mexico Press, 1988, p. 137-140. English. **DESCR:** "'And Miles to Go...': Mexican Women and Work, 1930-1985"; Employment; Income; Labor Unions; Ruiz, Vicki L.; Undocumented Workers; Women.

6572 Duran, Lucy. Lucy Duran--wife, mother, and organizer. IN: Mora, Magdalena and Del Castillo, Adelaida, eds. MEXICAN WOMEN IN THE UNITED STATES: STRUGGLES PAST AND PRESENT. Los Angeles, CA: Chicano Studies Research Center, UCLA, 1980, p. 183-184. English. **DESCR:** Agricultural Labor Unions; *Biography; Duran, Lucy; Farm Labor Organizing Commmittee (FLOC); Farm Workers.

6573 Escalante, Alicia. A letter from the Chicana Welfare Rights organization. ENCUENTRO FEMENIL, Vol. 1, no. 2 (1974), p. 15-19. English. **DESCR:** *Chicana Welfare Rights Organization; Child Care Centers; *Talmadge Amendment to the Social Security Act, 1971; Welfare.

6574 Fernandez Kelly, Maria. "Chavalas de maquiladora": a study of the female labor force in Ciudad Juarez' offshore production plants. Thesis (Ph.D.)--Rutgers University, 1980. xi, 391 leaves. English. **DESCR:** *Border Industries; Ciudad Juarez, Chihuahua, Mexico; Electronics Industry; *Employment; Garment Industry; Industrial Workers; Mexico; Women.

6575 Fernandez Kelly, Maria and Garcia, Anna M. Economic restructuring in the United States: Hispanic women in the garment and electronics industries. WOMEN AND WORK, Vol. 3, (1988), p. 49-65. English. **DESCR:** Business Enterprises; Businesspeople; *Electronics Industry; *Garment Industry; Industrial Workers; *International Economic Relations.

6576 Fernandez Kelly, Maria. For we are sold, I and my people: women and industry in Mexico's frontier. Albany, NY: State University of New York Press, 1983. vii, 217 p. English. **DESCR:** Border Industries; *Border Region; Ciudad Juarez, Chihuahua, Mexico; *Electronics Industry; *Garment Industry; Industrial Workers.

6577 Fernandez Kelly, Maria and Garcia, Anna M. Invisible amidst the glitter: Hispanic women in the Southern California electronics industry. IN: Statham, Anne; Miller, Eleanor M.; and Mauksh, Hans O., eds. THE WORTH OF WOMEN'S WORK: A QUALITATIVE SYNTHESIS. Albany, NY: State University of New York Press, 1988, p. 265-290. English. **DESCR:** *Electronics Industry; Employment; Immigrants; *Industrial Workers; Labor Supply and Market; Megatek, La Jolla, CA; Nova-Tech, San Diego, CA; Sex Roles; Southern California.

Working Women (cont.)

6578 Fernandez Kelly, Maria and Garcia, Anna M. The making of an underground economy: Hispanic women, home work, and the advanced capitalist state. URBAN ANTHROPOLOGY, Vol. 14, no. 1-3 (Spring, Fall, 1985), p. 59-90. English. DESCR: Capitalism; Cubanos; Employment; Garment Industry; Industrial Workers; International Economic Relations; Labor Supply and Market; *Los Angeles County, CA; *Miami, FL; Women.

6579 Fernandez Kelly, Maria. The 'maquila' women. NACLA: REPORT ON THE AMERICAS, Vol. 14, no. 5 (September, October, 1980), p. 14-19. English. DESCR: *Border Industries; Feminism; Industrial Workers; Stereotypes; Women.

6580 Fernandez Kelly, Maria. Mexican border industrialization, female labor force participation and migration. IN: Nash, June and Fernandez-Kelly, Patricia, eds. WOMEN, MEN, AND THE INTERNATIONAL DIVISION OF LABOR. Albany, NY: State University of New York Press, 1983, p. 205-223. English. DESCR: Border Industrialization Program (BIP); *Border Industries; Ciudad Juarez, Chihuahua, Mexico; Immigration; Industrial Workers; Labor Supply and Market; Males; *Migration Patterns; Undocumented Workers; *Women.

6581 Flores, Francisca. Comision Femenil Mexicana. REGENERACION, Vol. 2, no. 4 (1975), p. 24-25. English. DESCR: *Abortion; Child Care Centers; Comision Femenil Mexicana Nacional; Identity.

6582 Flores, Francisca. Equality. REGENERACION, Vol. 2, no. 3 (1973), p. 4-5. English. DESCR: Anglo Americans; Chicano Movement; Discrimination; Elected Officials; Feminism; Income; *Machismo.

6583 Flores, Francisca. A reaction to discussions on the Talmadge Amendment to the Social Security Act. ENCUENTRO FEMENIL, Vol. 1, no. 2 (1974), p. 13-14. English. DESCR: *Chicana Welfare Rights Organization; Child Care Centers; Discrimination; Feminism; Income; *Social Security Act; Social Services; *Talmadge Amendment to the Social Security Act, 1971; Welfare.

6584 Flores, Francisca. A reaction to discussions on the Talmadge Amendment to the Social Security Act. REGENERACION, Vol. 2, no. 3 (1973), p. 16. English. DESCR: *Chicana Welfare Rights Organization; Child Care Centers; Discrimination; Feminism; Income; *Social Security Act; Social Services; *Talmadge Amendment to the Social Security Act, 1971; Welfare.

6585 Friaz, Guadalupe. Chicanas in the workforce = Chicanas en la fuerza de trabajo: "Working 9 to 5". CAMINOS, Vol. 2, no. 3 (May 1981), p. 37-39, 61+. Bilingual. DESCR: Employment; Labor Unions; Laborers.

6586 Fuentes, Annette and Ehrenreich, Barbara. Women in the global factory. New York: Institute for New Communications; Boston: South End Press, 1983. 64 p.: ill. English. DESCR: *Border Industries; Industrial Workers; *International Economic Relations; *Women.

6587 Garcia, Mario T. The Chicana in American history: the Mexican women of El Paso, 1880-1920 - a case study. PACIFIC HISTORICAL REVIEW, Vol. 49, no. 2 (May 1980), p.

315-337. English. DESCR: Acme Laundry, El Paso, TX; American Federation of Labor (AFL); Case Studies; Central Labor Union; Domestic Work; *El Paso, TX; Employment; *History; Immigrants; Income; Labor Unions; Sex Roles; Strikes and Lockouts.

6588 Gettman, Dawn and Pena, Devon Gerardo. Women, mental health, and the workplace in a transnational setting. SOCIAL WORK, Vol. 31, no. 1 (January, February, 1986), p. 5-11. English. DESCR: *Border Industries; Employment; *Mental Health; Mexico; United States-Mexico Relations; Women.

6589 Glenn, Evelyn Nakano. Racial ethnic women's labor: the intersection of race, gender and class oppression. REVIEW OF RADICAL POLITICAL ECONOMY, Vol. 17, no. 3 (Fall 1985), p. 86-108. English. DESCR: Asian Americans; Blacks; *Discrimination; *Feminism; Laboring Classes; *Marxism; Sexism; Social Classes; Women.

6590 Goldman, Shifra M. Trabajadoras mexicanas y chicanas en las artes visuales. IN: Leal, Salvador, ed. A TRAVES DE LA FRONTERA. Mexico, D.F.: Centro de Estudios Economicos y Sociales del Tercer Mundo, A.C.; Instituto de Investigaciones Esteticas, U.N.A.M., 1983, p. 153-161. Spanish. DESCR: Art; Gonzalez Parsons, Lucia; Huerta, Dolores; Moreno, Luisa [union organizer]; SALT OF THE EARTH [film]; Tenayuca, Emma.

6591 Gonzalez, Rosalinda M. Chicanas and Mexican immigrant families 1920-1940: women's subordination and family exploitation. IN: Scharf, Lois and Jensen, Joan M., eds. DECADES OF DISCONTENT: THE WOMEN'S MOVEMENT, 1920-1940. Westport, CT: Greenwood Press, 1983, p. 59-84. English. DESCR: *Family; Farm Workers; History; Immigrants; Labor; Labor Unions; Mexico; Pecan Shelling Worker's Union, San Antonio, TX; Sex Roles; Strikes and Lockouts; United Cannery Agricultural Packing and Allied Workers of America (UCAPAWA).

6592 Guendelman, Sylvia. The incorporation of Mexican women in seasonal migration: a study of gender differences. HISPANIC JOURNAL OF BEHAVIORAL SCIENCES, Vol. 9, no. 3 (September 1987), p. 245-264. English. DESCR: Immigrants; Marriage; Mexico; *Migration Patterns; *Sex Roles; *Women; *Women Men Relations.

6593 Harlow, Barbara. Sites of struggle: immigration, deportation, prison, and exile. IN: Calderon, Hector and Saldivar, Jose David, eds. CRITICISM IN THE BORDERLANDS: STUDIES IN CHICANO LITERATURE, CULTURE, AND IDEOLOGY. Durham, NC: Duke University Press, 1991, p. [149]-163. English. DESCR: Anzaldua, Gloria; BLACK GOLD; BORDERLANDS/LA FRONTERA: THE NEW MESTIZA; First, Ruth; Khalifeh, Sahar; *Literary Criticism; *Political Ideology; Sanchez, Rosaura; Social Classes; "The Cariboo Cafe" [short story]; "The Ditch" [short story]; Viramontes, Helena Maria; WILD THORNS; *Women.

6594 Hart, John M. Working-class women in nineteenth century Mexico. IN: Mora, Magdalena and Del Castillo, Adelaida, eds. MEXICAN WOMEN IN THE UNITED STATES: STRUGGLES PAST AND PRESENT. Los Angeles, CA: Chicano Studies Research Center, 1980, p. 151-157. English. DESCR: *Employment; History; Mexico; Women.

Working Women (cont.)

6595 Hawley, Peggy and Even, Brenda. Work and sex-role attitudes in relation to education and other characteristics. VOCATIONAL GUIDANCE QUARTERLY, Vol. 31, no. 2 (December 1982), p. 101-108. English. **DESCR:** Attitudes; Careers; Education; Ethnic Groups; Psychological Testing; *Sex Roles.

6596 Hayghe, Howard. Married couples: work and income patterns. MONTHLY LABOR REVIEW, Vol. 106, no. 12 (December 1983), p. 26-29. English. **DESCR:** *Employment; *Income; *Marriage; *Sex Roles.

6597 Hovell, Melbourne F., et al. Occupational health risks for Mexican women: the case of the maquiladora along the Mexican-United States border. INTERNATIONAL JOURNAL OF HEALTH SERVICES, Vol. 18, no. 4 (1988), p. 617-627. English. **DESCR:** *Border Industries; Border Region; Mexico; *Occupational Hazards; Project Concern International (PCI), San Diego, CA; Public Health; Surveys; Tijuana, Baja California, Mexico; Women.

6598 Huerta, Dolores. Dolores Huerta talks about Republicans, Cesar, children and her home town. REGENERACION, Vol. 2, no. 4 (1975), p. 20-24. English. **DESCR:** *Agricultural Labor Unions; *Biography; Chavez, Cesar E.; Community Service Organization, Los Angeles, (CSO); Democratic Party; Elected Officials; Flores, Art; Huerta, Dolores; McGovern, George; *Politics; Ramirez, Henry M.; Ross, Fred; Sanchez, Philip V.; United Farmworkers of America (UFW).

6599 Huerta, Dolores. Dolores Huerta talks about Republicans, Cesar, children and her home town. IN: Servin, Manuel P. ed. THE MEXICAN AMERICANS: AN AWAKENING MINORITY. 2nd ed. Beverly Hills, CA: Glencoe Press, 1974, p. 283-294. English. **DESCR:** *Agricultural Labor Unions; *Biography; Chavez, Cesar E.; Community Service Organization, Los Angeles, (CSO); Democratic Party; Elected Officials; Flores, Art; Huerta, Dolores; McGovern, George; *Politics; Ramirez, Henry M.; Ross, Fred; Sanchez, Philip V.; United Farmworkers of America (UFW).

6600 Iglesias, Norma. La flor mas bella de la maquiladora: historias de vida de la mujer obrera en Tijuana, B.C.N. Mexico, D.F.: Secretaria de Educacion Publica, CEFNOMEX, 1985. 166 p.: ill. Spanish. **DESCR:** Border Industrialization Program (BIP); *Border Industries; Cultural Customs; Labor Unions; Sindicato Independiente Solidev; Solidev Mexicana, S.A.; Tijuana, Baja California, Mexico; *Women.

6601 Iglesias, Norma. "Las mujeres somos mas responsables": la utilizacion de mano de obra femenina en las maquiladoras fronterizas. TRABAJOS MONOGRAFICOS, Vol. 2, no. 1 (1986), p. 19-30. Spanish. **DESCR:** *Border Industries; Women.

6602 Iglesias, Norma and Carrillo, Jorge. Que me dejo el trabajo? FEM, Vol. 10, no. 48 (October, November, 1986), p. 43-45. Spanish. **DESCR:** Border Industries; Women.

6603 Iglesias, Norma and Carrillo, Jorge. Que me dejo el trabajo?: mi vida se pregunta. TRABAJOS MONOGRAFICOS, Vol. 2, no. 1 (1986), p. 10-18. Spanish. **DESCR:** Border Industries; *Oral History.

6604 In the maquiladoras. CORRESPONDENCIA, no. 9

(December 1990), p. 3-9. English. **DESCR:** *Border Industries; Labor Unions; Tijuana, Baja California, Mexico; Women.

6605 Jaramillo, Mari-Luci. How to suceed in business and remain Chicana. LA LUZ, Vol. 8, no. 7 (August, September, 1980), p. 33-35. English. **DESCR:** Assertiveness; Cultural Characteristics; Family; Identity; *Natural Support Systems.

6606 Jensen, Joan M. Commentary [on "And Miles to Go": Mexican Women and Work, 1930-1985]. IN: Schlissel, Lillian, et al., eds. WESTERN WOMEN: THEIR LAND, THEIR LIVES. Albuquerque, NM: University of New Mexico Press, 1988, p. 141-144. English. **DESCR:** "'And Miles to Go...': Mexican Women and Work, 1930-1985"; California; Employment; Income; Labor Unions; Public Policy; Ruiz, Vicki L.; Women.

6607 Jensen, Joan M. "I've worked, I'm not afraid of work": farm women in New Mexico, 1920-1940. NEW MEXICO HISTORICAL REVIEW, Vol. 61, no. 1 (January 1986), p. 27-52. English. **DESCR:** *Farm Workers; History; New Mexico; *Rural Economics.

6608 Jensen, Leif. Secondary earner strategies and family poverty: immigrant-native differentials, 1960-1980. INTERNATIONAL MIGRATION REVIEW, Vol. 25, no. 1 (Spring 1991), p. 113-140. English. **DESCR:** Anglo Americans; *Asian Americans; Blacks; Family; Immigrants; Immigration; Income; Poverty; Women.

6609 Keremitsis, Dawn. Del metate al molino: la mujer mexicana de 1910 a 1940. HISTORIA MEXICANA, Vol. 33, no. 2 (1983), p. 285-302. Spanish. **DESCR:** Food Industry; History; Labor Unions; Mexico; Sex Roles; Strikes and Lockouts; Women.

6610 Kossoudji, Sherrie and Ranney, Susan. The labor market experience of female migrants: the case of temporary Mexican migration to the U.S. INTERNATIONAL MIGRATION REVIEW, Vol. 18, no. 4 (Winter 1984), p. 1120-1143. English. **DESCR:** Employment; Immigrants; Income; *Labor Supply and Market; *Migrant Labor; Sex Roles; *Women.

6611 Krause, Neal and Markides, Kyriakos S. Employment and psychological well-being in Mexican American women. JOURNAL OF HEALTH AND SOCIAL BEHAVIOR, Vol. 26, no. 1 (March 1985), p. 15-26. English. **DESCR:** *Attitudes; *Employment; Identity; Mental Health; Sex Roles.

6612 La Monica, Grace; Gulino, Claire; and Ortiz Soto, Irma. A comparative study of female Mexican and American working nurses in the border corridor. BORDER HEALTH/SALUD FRONTERIZA, Vol. 5, no. 2 (April, June, 1989), p. 2-6. Bilingual. **DESCR:** Anglo Americans; *Border Region; *Medical Personnel; Women.

6613 Lizarraga, Sylvia S. Hacia una teoria para la liberacion de la mujer. IN: Garcia, Juan R., ed. IN TIMES OF CHALLENGE: CHICANOS AND CHICANAS IN AMERICAN SOCIETY. Houston, TX: Mexican American Studies Program, University of Houston, 1988, p. 25-31. Spanish. **DESCR:** *Feminism; Laboring Classes; Social Classes; *Women.

Working Women (cont.)

6614 Lockert, Lucia Fox. Chicanas: their voices, their lives. Lansing, MI: Michigan State Board of Education, 1988. xii, 36 p.: ill. English. DESCR: Michigan; *Oral History.

6615 Longeaux y Vasquez, Enriqueta. The woman of La Raza. REGENERACION, Vol. 2, no. 4 (1975) p. 34-36. English. DESCR: Child Care Centers; Discrimination; Gallo, Juana; Housing; La Adelita; Machismo; Sex Roles; *Social History and Conditions.

6616 Longeaux y Vasquez, Enriqueta. The woman of La Raza. IN: Valdez, Luis and Steiner, Stan, eds. AZTLAN: AN ANTHOLOGY OF MEXICAN AMERICAN LITERATURE. New York: Vintage Books, 1972, p. 272-278. Also IN: Salinas, Luis Omar and Faderman, Lillian, compilers. FROM THE BARRIO: A CHICANO ANTHOLOGY. San Francisco, CA: Canfield Press, 1973, p. 20-24. English. DESCR: Child Care Centers Discrimination; Gallo, Juana; Housing; La Adelita; Machismo; Sex Roles; *Social History and Conditions.

6617 Martinez, Elizabeth and McCaughan, Ed. Chicanas and Mexicanas within a transnational working class: theoretical perspectives. IN: Del Castillo, Adelaida R., ed. BETWEEN BORDERS: ESSAYS ON MEXICANA/CHICANA HISTORY. Encino, CA: Floricanto Press, 1990, p. 31-60. English. DESCR: Laboring Classes.

6618 McClelland, Judith Raymond. The relationship of independence to achievement: a comparative study of Hispanic women. Thesis (Ph.D.)--Fielding Institute, 1988. 164 p. English. DESCR: *Assertiveness; Attitudes; California Personality Inventory (CPI); Careers; Leadership; *Management; New Mexico; Personality.

6619 Melville, Margarita B. Mexican women in the U.S. wage labor force. IN: Melville, Margarita, ed. MEXICANAS AT WORK IN THE UNITED STATES. Houston, TX: Mexican American Studies Program, University of Houston, 1988, p. 1-11. English. DESCR: Feminism; Sex Stereotypes; *Women.

6620 Melville, Margarita B., ed. Mexicanas at work in the United States. Houston, TX: Mexican American Studies Program, University of Houston, 1988. 83 p. English. DESCR: Border Region; *Employment; Family; *Labor; Migrant Labor; =Women.

6621 Melville, Margarita B. Selective acculturation of female Mexican migrants. IN: Melville, Margarita B., ed. TWICE A MINORITY. St. Louis, MO: Mosby, 1980, p. 155-163. English. DESCR: *Acculturation; Identity; Migrant Labor.

6622 Mindiola, Tatcho, Jr. The cost of being a Mexican female worker in the 1970 Houston labor market. AZTLAN, Vol. 11, no. 2 (Fall 1980), p. 231-247. English. DESCR: Discrimination; *Discrimination in Employment; Houston, TX; Labor Supply and Market.

6623 Mora, Magdalena and Del Castillo, Adelaida R. Mexican women in the United States: struggles past and present. Los Angeles, CA: Chicano Studies Research Center Publications, c1980. 204 p. English. DESCR: Feminism; *Social History and Conditions.

6624 Nava, Yolanda. The Chicana and employment: needs analysis and recommendations for

legislation. REGENERACION, Vol. 2, no. 3 (1973), p. 7-9. English. DESCR: California Commission on the Status of Women; Child Care Centers; Comision Femenil Mexicana Nacional; *Discrimination in Employment; Employment Tests; Employment Training; Equal Rights Amendment (ERA); Sexism; Statistics; Stereotypes.

6625 Navar, Isabelle. La Mexicana: an image of strength. AGENDA, no. 4 (Spring 1974), p. 3-5. English. DESCR: Family; Feminism; *Identity; Psychology; Sexism.

6626 Navar, Isabelle. La Mexicana: an image of strength. REGENERACION, Vol. 2, no. 4 (1974), p. 4-6. English. DESCR: Family; Feminism; *Identity; Psychology; Sexism.

6627 Nieto Gomez de Lazarin, Anna. Chicanas in the labor force. ENCUENTRO FEMENIL, Vol. 1, no. 2 (1974), p. 28-33. English. DESCR: Discrimination in Employment; Employment.

6628 Nieto Gomez de Lazarin, Anna. What is the Talmadge Amendment?: justicia para las madres. REGENERACION, Vol. 2, no. 3 (1973), p. 14-15. English. DESCR: Chicana Welfare Rights Organization; *Child Care Centers; Community Work Experience Program (C.W.E.P.); Discrimination in Employment; Employment Tests; Escalante, Alicia; *Feminism; Nixon, Richard.

6629 Oeste, Marcia. Mujeres arriba y adelante. LA LUZ, Vol. 1, no. 2 (May 1972), p. 39-40. English. DESCR: *Feminism; Ortega y Gasset, Jose; *Women Men Relations.

6630 Olivares, Yvette. The sweatshop: the garment industry's reborn child. REVISTA MUJERES, Vol. 3, no. 2 (June 1986), p. 55-62. English. DESCR: Garment Industry; Labor; Public Health; Third World; *Undocumented Workers; *Women.

6631 Olivera, Mercedes. The new Hispanic women. VISTA, Vol. 2, no. 11 (July 5, 1987), p. 6-8. English. DESCR: Alvarez, Linda; Esquiroz, Margarita; Garcia, Juliet; *Hernandez, Antonia A.; Mohr, Nicolasa; Molina, Gloria; Pabon, Maria.

6632 Orozco, Cynthia. Chicana labor history: a critique of male consciousness in historical writing. LA RED/THE NET, no. 77 (January 1984), p. 2-5. English. DESCR: *Historiography; Labor; *Sexism.

6633 Ortiz, Vilma and Cooney, Rosemary Santana. Sex-role attitudes and labor force participation among young Hispanic females and non-Hispanic white females. SOCIAL SCIENCE QUARTERLY, Vol. 65, no. 2 (June 1984), p. 392-400. English. DESCR: Anglo Americans; Attitudes; Employment; *Sex Roles.

6634 Ortiz, Vilma and Cooney, Rosemary Santana. Sex-role attitudes and labor force participation among young Hispanic females and non-Hispanic white females. IN: O. de la Garza, Rodolfo, et al., eds. THE MEXICAN AMERICAN EXPERIENCE: AN INTERDISCIPLINARY ANTHOLOGY. Austin, TX: University of Texas Press, 1985, p. 174-182. English. DESCR: Anglo Americans; Attitudes; Employment; *Sex Roles.

Working Women (cont.)

6635 Palacios, Maria. Fear of success:
Mexican-American women in two work
environments. Thesis (Ph.D.)--New Mexico
State University, 1988. 163 p. English.
DESCR: Academic Achievement; *Assertiveness;
*Careers; Income; Sex Roles.

6636 Pena, Devon Gerardo. Between the lines: a
new perspective on the industrial sociology
of women workers in transnational labor
processes. IN: Cordova, Teresa, et al., eds.
CHICANA VOICES. Austin, TX: Center for
Mexican American Studies, 1986, p. 77-95.
English. **DESCR:** Border Industries; *Labor;
Marxism; *Women.

6637 Pena, Devon Gerardo. The class politics of
abstract labor: organizational forms and
industrial relations in the Mexican
maquiladoras. Thesis (Ph.D.)--University of
Texas, Austin, 1983. xix, 587 p. English.
DESCR: *Border Industries; Border Region;
International Economic Relations; *Trade
Unions; Women.

6638 Pena, Devon Gerardo. Las maquiladoras:
Mexican women in class struggle in the
border industries. AZTLAN, Vol. 11, no. 2
(Fall 1980), p. 159-229. English. **DESCR:**
Border Industries; *Economic History and
Conditions; Labor; Labor Unions; Mexico;
Mexico-U.S. Border Development.

6639 Pena, Devon Gerardo. Tortuosidad: shop floor
struggles of female maquiladora workers. IN:
Ruiz, Vicki L. and Tiano, Susan, eds. WOMEN
ON THE U.S.-MEXICO BORDER: RESPONSES TO
CHANGE. Boston, MA: Allen & Unwin, 1987, p.
129-154. English. **DESCR:** Border Industries;
Ciudad Juarez, Chihuahua, Mexico;
Employment; Personnel Management;
Population; Surveys; *Women.

6640 Pesquera, Beatriz M. and Duran, Flo. Having
a job gives you some sort of power:
reflections of a Chicana working woman.
FEMINIST ISSUES, Vol. 4, no. 2 (Fall 1984),
p. 79-96. English. **DESCR:** Duran, Flo;
Feminism.

6641 Pesquera, Beatriz M. Work and family: a
comparative analysis of professional,
clerical and blue-collar Chicana workers.
Thesis (Ph.D.)--University of California,
Berkeley, 1985. i, 212 p. English. **DESCR:**
*Family; *Sex Roles.

6642 Pick, James B., et al. Socioeconomic
influences on fertility in the Mexican
borderlands region. MEXICAN STUDIES/ESTUDIOS
MEXICANOS, Vol. 6, no. 1 (Winter 1990), p.
11-42. English. **DESCR:** *Border Region;
*Employment; *Fertility; Labor Supply and
Market; Literacy; Socioeconomic Factors.

6643 Preuss, Sabine. Die Frauen von Acapulco
Fashion: Weiblicher Lebenszusammenhang und
Industrialisierung in den Weltmarktfabriken
Mexikos. Berlin: Express, c1985. 133 p.:
ill. Other. **DESCR:** *Acapulco Fashion, Ciudad
Juarez, Mexico; *Border Industries;
*Employment.

6644 Rips, Geoffrey and Tenayuca, Emma. Living
history: Emma Tenayuca tells her story.
TEXAS OBSERVER, (October 28, 1983), p.
7-15. English. **DESCR:** *Autobiography;
Communist Party; Food Industry; Labor
Unions; Leadership; Oral History; Pecan
Shelling Worker's Union, San Antonio, TX;
San Antonio, TX; Strikes and Lockouts;
Tenayuca, Emma; United Cannery Agricultural

Packing and Allied Workers of America
(UCAPAWA); Worker's Alliance (WA), Los
Angeles, CA.

6645 Romero, Fred E. The labor market status of
Chicanas. IN: Romero, Fred. CHICANO WORKERS:
THEIR UTILIZATION AND DEVELOPMENT. Los
Angeles: Chicano Studies Center
Publications, UCLA, 1979, p. 82-95. English.
DESCR: *Employment; Income; Labor Supply and
Market; *Statistics.

6646 Romero, Mary. Chicanas modernize domestic
service. QUALITATIVE SOCIOLOGY, Vol. 11, no.
4 (Winter 1988), p. 319-334. English.
DESCR: *Domestic Work; *Employment; Income;
*Interpersonal Relations.

6647 Romero, Mary. Day work in the suburbs: the
work experience of Chicana private
housekeepers. IN: Statham, Anne; Miller,
Eleanor M; and Mauksch, Hans O., eds. THE
WORTH OF WOMEN'S WORK: A QUALITATIVE
SYNTHESIS. Albany, NY: State University of
New York Press, 1988, p. 77-91. English.
DESCR: Domestic Work; Employment;
Interpersonal Relations; *Natural Support
Systems; Social Mobility.

6648 Romero, Mary. Domestic service in the
transition from rural to urban life: the
case of la Chicana. WOMEN'S STUDIES
QUARTERLY, Vol. 13, no. 3 (February 1987),
p. 199-222. English. **DESCR:** *Domestic Work;
Employment; Interpersonal Relations; Rural
Population; Social Mobility; Sociology;
Urban Communities.

6649 Rose, Margaret. Women in the United Farm
Workers: a study of Chicana Mexicana
participation in a labor union, 1950-1980.
Thesis (Ph.D.)--University of California,
Los Angeles, 1988. 403p. English. **DESCR:**
History; Huerta, Dolores; *Labor Unions;
*Sex Roles; United Farmworkers of America
(UFW).

6650 Ruiz, Vicki L. "And miles to go...": Mexican
women and work, 1930-1985. IN: Schlissel,
Lillian, et al., eds. WESTERN WOMEN: THEIR
LAND, THEIR LIVES. Albuquerque, NM:
University of New Mexico Press, 1988, p.
117-136. English. **DESCR:** Education; El Paso
Women's Employment and Education Project
(EPWEE); *Employment; Farah Manufacturing
Co., El Paso, TX; Farah Strike; *Income;
Industrial Workers; Labor Unions;
Statistics; Undocumented Workers; United
Cannery Agricultural Packing and Allied
Workers of America (UCAPAWA); Women.

6651 Ruiz, Vicki L. By the day or week: Mexicana
domestic workers in El Paso. TRABAJOS
MONOGRAFICOS, Vol. 2, no. 1 (1986), p.
35-58. English. **DESCR:** *Domestic Work; El
Paso, TX; Employment; Labor Supply and
Market.

6652 Ruiz, Vicki L. Obreras y madres: labor
activism among Mexican women and its impact
on the family. RENATO ROSALDO LECTURE SERIES
MONOGRAPH, Vol. 1, (Summer 1985), p.
[19]-38. English. **DESCR:** Child Care Centers;
Children; History; *Labor Unions; *Mexico;
Sex Roles; Women.

Working Women (cont.)

6653 Ruiz, Vicki L. A promise fulfilled: Mexican cannery workers in Southern California. THE PACIFIC HISTORIAN, Vol. 30, no. 2 (Summer 1986), p. 51-61. English. DESCR: *California Sanitary Canning Company, Los Angeles, CA; *Canneries; Labor Unions; Moreno, Luisa [union organizer]; Southern California; Strikes and Lockouts; *United Cannery Agricultural Packing and Allied Workers of America (UCAPAWA).

6654 Ruiz, Vicki L. A promise fulfilled: Mexican cannery workers in Southern California. IN: DuBois, Ellen Carol and Ruiz, Vicki L., eds. UNEQUAL SISTERS: A MULTICULTURAL READER IN U.S. WOMEN'S HISTORY. New York: Routledge, 1990, p. 264-274. English. DESCR: *California Sanitary Canning Company, Los Angeles, CA; *Canneries; Labor Unions; Moreno, Luisa [union organizer]; Southern California; Strikes and Lockouts; *United Cannery Agricultural Packing and Allied Workers of America (UCAPAWA).

6655 Ruiz, Vicki L. A promise fulfilled: Mexican cannery workers in Southern California. IN: Del Castillo, Adelaida R., ed. BETWEEN BORDERS: ESSAYS ON MEXICANA/CHICANA HISTORY. Encino, CA: Floricanto Press, 1990, p. 281-298. English. DESCR: California Sanitary Canning Company, Los Angeles, CA; *Canneries; Labor Unions; Moreno, Luisa [union organizer]; Southern California; Strikes and Lockouts; United Cannery Agricultural Packing and Allied Workers of America (UCAPAWA).

6656 Ruiz, Vicki L. UCAPAWA, Chicanas, and the California food processing industry, 1937-1950. Thesis (Ph.D.)--Stanford University, 1982. x, 281 p. English. DESCR: *Canneries; Food Industry; *Labor Unions; Trade Unions; United Cannery Agricultural Packing and Allied Workers of America (UCAPAWA).

6657 Saboonchi, Nasrin. The working women's reactions to the traditional marriage role: a crosscultural study within the symbolic interactionism framework. Thesis (Ph.D.)--United States International University, 1983. 173 p. English. DESCR: Immigrants; Iranians; *Marriage; *Sex Roles; Women.

6658 Saenz, Rogelio; Goudy, Willis J.; and Lorenz, Frederick O. The effects of employment and marital relations on depression among Mexican American women. JOURNAL OF MARRIAGE AND THE FAMILY, Vol. 51, no. 1 (February 1989), p. 239-251. English. DESCR: *Depression (Psychological); Domestic Work; *Employment; Feminism; *Marriage; Women Men Relations.

6659 Santillan, Richard. Rosita the riveter: Midwest Mexican American women during World War II, 1941-1945. PERSPECTIVES IN MEXICAN AMERICAN STUDIES. Vol. 2, (1989), p. 115-147. English. DESCR: History; Industrial Workers; Intergroup Relations; Language Usage; *Midwestern States; Military; Mutualistas; Sexism; War; *World War II.

6660 Scrimshaw, Susan C.M., et al. Factors affecting breastfeeding among women of Mexican origin or descent in Los Angeles. AMERICAN JOURNAL OF PUBLIC HEALTH, Vol. 77, no. 4 (April 1987), p. 467-470. English. DESCR: Acculturation; *Breastfeeding; Immigrants; Los Angeles, CA.

6661 Segura, Denise. Chicana and Mexican immigrant women at work: the impact of class, race, and gender on occupational mobility. GENDER & SOCIETY, Vol. 3, no. 1 (March 1989), p. 37-52. English. DESCR: *Employment; *Immigrants; Labor Supply and Market; Laboring Classes; San Francisco Bay Area; *Social Mobility; Women.

6662 Segura, Denise. Chicanas and Mexican immigrant women in the labor market: a study of occupational mobility and stratification. Thesis (Ph.D.)--University of California, Berkeley, 1986. iii, 282 p. English. DESCR: *Immigrants; *Labor Supply and Market; Mexico; Women.

6663 Segura, Denise. Conflict in social relations at work: a Chicana perspective. IN: National Association for Chicano Studies. ESTUDIOS CHICANOS AND THE POLITICS OF COMMUNITY. [S.l.]: National Association for Chicano Studies, c1989, p. [110]-131. English. DESCR: *Discrimination in Employment; Employment Training; Immigrants; *Interpersonal Relations; Social Classes; Women.

6664 Segura, Denise. Familism and employment among Chicanas and Mexican immigrant women. IN: Melville, Margarita, ed. MEXICANAS AT WORK IN THE UNITED STATES. Houston, TX: Mexican American Studies Program, University of Houston, 1988, p. 24-32. English. DESCR: *Employment; *Extended Family; Family; Immigrants; Income; Machismo; Sex Roles; *Women.

6665 Segura, Denise. The interplay of familism and patriarchy on employment among Chicana and Mexicana women. RENATO ROSALDO LECTURE SERIES MONOGRAPH, Vol. 5, (1989), p. 35-53. English. DESCR: Employment; *Family; Immigrants; Machismo; *Sex Roles; Women; Women Men Relations.

6666 Segura, Denise. Labor market stratification: the Chicana experience. BERKELEY JOURNAL OF SOCIOLOGY, Vol. 29, (1984), p. 57-91. English. DESCR: *Discrimination in Employment; Employment; *Labor Supply and Market; Socioeconomic Factors.

6667 Seligson, Mitchell A. and Williams, Edward J. Maquiladoras and migration workers in the Mexico-United States Border Industrialization Program. Austin, TX: Mexico-United States Border Research Program, University of Texas at Austin, 1981. xviii, 202 p. English. DESCR: Border Industrialization Program (BIP); *Border Region; Employment; Immigration; Industrial Workers; Mexico; *Migration Patterns.

6668 Shapiro, Peter. Watsonville shows "it can be done". GUARDIAN, Vol. 39, no. 24 (March 25, 1987), p. 1,9. English. DESCR: Canneries; Labor Unions; NorCal Frozen Foods; *Strikes and Lockouts; *Watsonville Canning and Frozen Food Co.

6669 Simon, Rita J. and DeLey, Margo. The work experience of undocumented Mexican women migrants in Los Angeles. INTERNATIONAL MIGRATION REVIEW, Vol. 18, no. 4 (Winter 1984), p. 1212-1229. English. DESCR: Immigrants; Income; *Los Angeles, CA; Population; Socioeconomic Factors; *Undocumented Workers.

Working Women (cont.)

6670 Solorzano-Torres, Rosalia. Women, labor, and the U.S.-Mexico border: Mexican maids in El Paso, Texas. IN: Melville, Margarita, ed. MEXICANAS AT WORK IN THE UNITED STATES. Houston, TX: Mexican American Studies Program, University of Houston, 1988, p. 75-83. English. **DESCR:** Border Patrol; *Border Region; Domestic Work; El Paso, TX; Immigrants; Immigration and Naturalization Service (INS); Immigration Regulation and Control; *Labor Supply and Market; Undocumented Workers; *Women.

6671 Spence, Mary Lee. Commentary [on "And Miles to Go": Mexican Women and Work, 1930-1985]. IN: Schlissel, Lillian, et al., eds. WESTERN WOMEN: THEIR LAND, THEIR LIVES. Albuquerque, NM: University of New Mexico Press, 1988, p. 145-150. English. **DESCR:** "'And Miles to Go...': Mexican Women and Work, 1930-1985"; Food Industry; Income; Labor Unions; Restaurants; Ruiz, Vicki L.

6672 Stewart, Kenneth L. and de Leon, Arnoldo. Work force participation among Mexican immigrant women in Texas, 1900. BORDERLANDS JOURNAL, Vol. 9, no. 1 (Spring 1986), p. 69-74. English. **DESCR:** Employment; History; *Immigrants; Texas; Women.

6673 Sullivan, Teresa A. The occupational prestige of women immigrants: a comparison of Cubans and Mexicans. INTERNATIONAL MIGRATION REVIEW, Vol. 18, no. 4 (Winter 1984), p. 1045-1062. English. **DESCR:** Careers; Cubanos; Employment; *Immigrants; Males; Mexico; Sex Roles; *Social Mobility; *Women.

6674 Taylor, Paul S. Mexican women in Los Angeles industry in 1928. AZTLAN, Vol. 11, no. 1 (Spring 1980), p. 99-131. English. **DESCR:** Employment; History; Industrial Workers; Los Angeles, CA.

6675 Tiano, Susan B. Export processing, women's work, and the employment problem in developing countries: the case of the maquiladora program in Northern Mexico. El Paso, TX: Center for InterAmerican and Border Studies, UTEP, 1985. 32 p. English. **DESCR:** *Border Region; *Employment; Labor Supply and Market; Mexico; *Sex Roles; Women.

6676 Tiano, Susan B. Labor composition and gender stereotypes in the maquila. JOURNAL OF BORDERLAND STUDIES, Vol. 5, no. 1 (Spring 1990), p. 20-24. English. **DESCR:** *Border Industries; Industrial Workers; Labor Supply and Market; *Sex Stereotypes; Women.

6677 Tiano, Susan B. Maquiladoras in Mexicali: integration or exploitation? IN: Ruiz, Vicki L. and Tiano, Susan, eds. WOMEN ON THE U.S.-MEXICO BORDER: RESPONSES TO CHANGE. Boston, MA: Allen & Unwin, 1987, p. 77-101. English. **DESCR:** Border Industrialization Program (BIP); *Border Industries; Border Region; Employment; Labor Supply and Market; Mexicali, Mexico; Women.

6678 Tiano, Susan B. Maquiladoras, women's work, and unemployment in northern Mexico. AZTLAN, Vol. 15, no. 2 (Fall 1984), p. 341-378. English. **DESCR:** *Border Industries; Employment; Mexico; *Women.

6679 Tienda, Marta. Hispanics in the U.S. labor market: an overview of recent evidence. LA RED/THE NET, no. 50 (January 1982), p. 4-7. English. **DESCR:** *Labor Supply and Market; Laborers.

6680 Tienda, Marta and Glass, Jennifer. Household structure and labor-force participation of Black, Hispanic, and white mothers. DEMOGRAPHY, Vol. 22, no. 3 (August 1985), p. 381-394. English. **DESCR:** Anglo Americans; Blacks; *Extended Family; *Family; *Sex Roles.

6681 Torres Raines, Rosario. The Mexican American woman and work: intergenerational perspectives of comparative ethnic groups. IN: Melville, Margarita, ed. MEXICANAS AT WORK IN THE UNITED STATES. Houston, TX: Mexican American Studies Program, University of Houston, 1988, p. 33-46. English. **DESCR:** Age Groups; Anglo Americans; Employment; Feminism; Marriage; Sex Roles; Social Classes; Socioeconomic Factors.

6682 Vasquez, Enriqueta L. La Chicana. MAGAZIN, Vol. 1, no. 4 (April 1972), p. 66-68+. English. **DESCR:** *Chicano Movement; Family.

6683 Vasquez, Mario F. The election day immigration raid at Lilli Diamond Originals and the response of the ILGWU. IN: Mora, Magdalena and Del Castillo, Adelaida, eds. MEXICAN WOMEN IN THE UNITED STATES: STRUGGLES PAST AND PRESENT. Los Angeles, CA: Chicano Studies Research Center, UCLA, 1980, p. 145-148. English. **DESCR:** Garment Industry; Immigration Regulation and Control; International Ladies Garment Workers Union (ILGWU); Labor Unions; *Lilli Diamond Originals; Undocumented Workers; Women.

6684 Vasquez, Melba J. T. Power and status of the Chicana: a social-psychological perspective. IN: Martinez, Joe L., Jr., ed. CHICANO PSYCHOLOGY. 2nd. ed. Orlando, FL: Academic Press, 1984, p. 269-287. English. **DESCR:** *Identity; Income; *Mental Health; Psychology; *Sex Roles; Socialization.

6685 Weber, Devra Anne. Mexican women on strike: memory, history and oral narratives. IN: Del Castillo, Adelaida R., ed. BETWEEN BORDERS: ESSAYS ON MEXICANA/CHICANA HISTORY. Encino, CA: Floricanto Press, 1990, p. 175-200. English. **DESCR:** *1933 Cotton Strike; Cotton Industry; History; *Oral History; San Joaquin Valley, CA; Strikes and Lockouts; *Valdez, Rosaura.

6686 Whiteford, Linda. Mexican American women as innovators. IN: Melville, Margarita B., ed. TWICE A MINORITY. St. Louis, MO: Mosby, 1980, p. 109-126. English. **DESCR:** Border Region; Farm Workers; Migrant Labor.

6687 Williams, Edward J. and Passe-Smith, John T. Turnover and recruitment in the maquila industry: causes and solutions. Las Cruces, NM: Joint Border Research Institute, New Mexico State University, 1989. ii, 59 p. English. **DESCR:** *Border Industries; *Employment; Income; *Labor Supply and Market; Personnel Management; Surveys; Women.

6688 Williams, Norma. The Mexican American family: tradition and change. Dix Hills, NY: General Hall, Inc., c1990. x, 170 p. English. **DESCR:** Cultural Characteristics; *Cultural Customs; *Family; Religion; *Sex Roles.

Working Women (cont.)

6689 Ybarra, Lea. Separating a myth from reality: socio-economic and cultural influences on Chicanas and the world of work. IN: Melville, Margarita, ed. MEXICANAS AT WORK IN THE UNITED STATES. Houston, TX: Mexican American Studies Program, University of Houston, 1988, p. 12-23. English. DESCR: Attitudes; *Cultural Characteristics; Income; Machismo; Sex Roles; *Socioeconomic Factors; Stereotypes.

6690 Ybarra, Lea. When wives work: the impact or the Chicano family. JOURNAL OF MARRIAGE AND THE FAMILY, Vol. 44, (February 1982), p. 169-178. English. DESCR: Family.

6691 Young, Gay. Gender identification and working-class solidarity among maquila workers in Ciudad Juarez: stereotypes and realities. IN: Ruiz, Vicki L. and Tiano, Susan, eds. WOMEN ON THE U.S.-MEXICO BORDER: RESPONSES TO CHANGE. Boston, MA: Allen & Unwin, 1987, p. 105-127. English. DESCR: Assertiveness; Attitudes; Border Industrialization Program (BIP); *Border Industries; Border Region; Ciudad Juarez, Chihuahua, Mexico; Employment; Garment Industry; Sex Roles; Surveys.

6692 Young, Gay. Women, border industrialization program, and human rights. El Paso, TX: Center for InterAmerican and Border Studies, UTEP, 1984. 33 p. English. DESCR: Border Industrialization Program (BIP); *Border Industries; Economic Development; Employment; Industrial Workers; Mexico; Sex Roles; *Sexism; *Women.

6693 Young, Gay. Women, development and human rights: issues in integrated transnational production. JOURNAL OF APPLIED BEHAVIORAL SCIENCE, Vol. 20, no. 4 (November 1984), p. 383-401. English. DESCR: Border Industrialization Program (BIP); *Border Industries; Feminism; Mexico; Multinational Corporations; Women; Women Men Relations.

6694 Zambrana, Ruth E. and Frith, Sandra. Mexican-American professional women: role satisfaction differences in single and multiple role lifestyles. JOURNAL OF SOCIAL BEHAVIOR AND PERSONALITY, Vol. 3, no. 4 (1988), p. 347-361. English. DESCR: *Careers; Family; *Mental Health; *Sex Roles.

6695 Zavella, Patricia. "Abnormal intimacy": the varying work networks of Chicana cannery workers. FEMINIST STUDIES, Vol. 11, no. 3 (Fall 1985), p. 541-557. English. DESCR: Canneries; Discrimination in Employment; Labor Unions; *Natural Support Systems.

6696 Zavella, Patricia. The impact of "sun belt industrialization" on Chicanas. FRONTIERS: A JOURNAL OF WOMEN STUDIES, Vol. 8, no. 1 (1984), p. 21-27. English. DESCR: Albuquerque, NM; Employment; *Industrial Workers; Industrialization.

6697 Zavella, Patricia. The impact of "sun belt industrialization" on Chicanas. Stanford, CA: Stanford Center for Chicano Research, 1984. 25 leaves. English. DESCR: Albuquerque, NM; Employment; *Industrial Workers; Industrialization.

6698 Zavella, Patricia. The politics of race and gender: organizing Chicana cannery workers in Northern California. IN: Bookman, Ann and Morgen, Sandra, eds. WOMEN AND THE POLITICS OF EMPOWERMENT. Philadelphia, PA: Temple University Press, 1988, p. 202-224. English. DESCR: Bay City Cannery Workers Committee; *Canneries; Cannery Workers Committee (CWC); Discrimination; Garcia, Connie; Identity; *Labor Unions; Nationalism; Northern California; Santa Clara Valley, CA; Sex Roles; Sexism.

6699 Zavella, Patricia. Women, work and family in the Chicano community: cannery workers of the Santa Clara Valley. Thesis (Ph.D.)--University of California, Berkeley, 1982. ix, 254 p. English. DESCR: *Canneries; Employment; *Family; Industrial Workers; Labor Unions; Santa Clara Valley, CA; *Sex Roles.

6700 Zavella, Patricia. Women's work and Chicano families: cannery workers of the Santa Clara Valley. Ithaca, NY: Cornell University Press, 1987. xviii, 191 p. English. DESCR: *Canneries; Employment; Family; Industrial Workers; Labor Unions; Santa Clara Valley, CA; Sex Roles.

6701 Zavella, Patricia. Work related networks and household organization among Chicana cannery workers. Stanford, CA: Stanford Center for Chicano Research, 1984. 12 leaves. English. DESCR: *Canneries; Industrial Workers; Natural Support Systems.

THE WORLD WALL: A VISION OF THE FUTURE WITHOUT FEAR [mural]

6702 Pohl, Frances K. and Baca, Judith F. THE WORLD WALL: A VISION OF THE FUTURE WITHOUT FEAR: an interview with Judith F. Baca. FRONTIERS: A JOURNAL OF WOMEN STUDIES, Vol. 11, no. 1 (1990), p. [33]-43. English. DESCR: Art Organizations and Groups; *Artists; *Baca, Judith F.; *Mural Art; Social and Public Art Resource Center, Venice, CA (SPARC).

World War I

6703 Deutsch, Sarah. No separate refuge: culture, class, and gender on an Anglo-Hispanic frontier in the American Southwest, 1880-1940. New York: Oxford University Press, 1987. vi, 356 p. English. DESCR: Anglo Americans; Colorado; Immigrants; Immigration; Mining Industry; Missions; New Mexico; *Sex Roles; *Social Classes; *Social History and Conditions; Women; Working Women.

World War II

6704 Campbell, Julie A. Madres y esposas: Tucson's Spanish-American Mothers and Wives Association. JOURNAL OF ARIZONA HISTORY, Vol. 31, no. 2 (Summer 1990), p. 161-182. English. DESCR: History; Military; Organizations; *Spanish-American Mothers and Wives Association, Tucson, AZ; Tucson, AZ.

6705 Goldsmith, Raquel Rubio. La Mexicana/Chicana. RENATO ROSALDO LECTURE SERIES MONOGRAPH, Vol. 1, (Summer 1985), p. 1-67. English. DESCR: Clergy; House of the Divine Providence [convent], Douglas, AZ; Labor Unions; *Social History and Conditions; Women.

World War II (cont.)

6706 Marin, Christine. La Asociacion
Hispano-Americana de Madres y Esposas:
Tucson's Mexican American women in World War
II. RENATO ROSALDO LECTURE SERIES MONOGRAPH,
Vol. 1, (Summer 1985), p. [5]-18. English.
DESCR: Cultural Organizations; History; *La
Asociacion Hispano-Americana de Madres y
Esposas, Tucson, AZ; Organizations; *Tucson,
AZ.

6707 Santillan, Richard. Rosita the riveter:
Midwest Mexican American women during World
War II, 1941-1945. PERSPECTIVES IN MEXICAN
AMERICAN STUDIES, Vol. 2, (1989), p.
115-147. English. DESCR: History; Industrial
Workers; Intergroup Relations; Language
Usage; *Midwestern States; Military;
Mutualistas; Sexism; War; *Working Women.

Writers
USE: Authors

Xelina

6708 Billings, Linda M. and Alurista. In verbal
murals: a study of Chicana herstory and
poetry. CONFLUENCIA, Vol. 2, no. 1 (Fall
1986), p. 60-68. English. DESCR: Candelaria,
Cordelia; Cervantes, Lorna Dee; Cisneros,
Sandra; EMPLUMADA; *Feminism; History;
Literary Criticism; *Poetry.

**Y NO SE LO TRAGO LA TIERRA/AND THE EARTH DID NOT
PART**

6709 de la Fuente, Patricia. Invisible women in
the narrative of Tomas Rivera. REVISTA
CHICANO-RIQUENA, Vol. 13, no. 3-4 (Fall,
Winter, 1985), p. 81-89. English. DESCR:
Literary Criticism; *Rivera, Tomas; Sex
Stereotypes.

6710 Gonzalez-Berry, Erlinda and Rebolledo, Tey
Diana. Growing up Chicano: Tomas Rivera and
Sandra Cisneros. REVISTA CHICANO-RIQUENA,
Vol. 13, no. 3-4 (Fall, Winter, 1985), p.
109-119. English. DESCR: Cisneros, Sandra;
Cultural Characteristics; *Literary
Criticism; Rivera, Tomas; Sex Roles; THE
HOUSE ON MANGO STREET.

6711 Lizarraga, Sylvia S. The patriarchal
ideology in "La noche que se apagaron las
luces". REVISTA CHICANO-RIQUENA, Vol. 13,
no. 3-4 (Fall, Winter, 1985), p. 90-95.
English. DESCR: "La noche que se apagaron
las luces" [short story]; *Literary
Criticism; Rivera, Tomas; Sex Roles.

6712 Rascon, Francisco. La caracterizacion de los
personajes femeninos en ...Y NO SE LO TRAGO
LA TIERRA. IN: Lattin, Vernon E., ed.
CONTEMPORARY CHICANO FICTION: A CRITICAL
SURVEY. Binghamton, NY: Bilingual
Press/Editorial Bilingue, 1986, p. 141-148.
Spanish. DESCR: *Literary Criticism; Rivera,
Tomas.

YO, MUJER

6713 Aguilar-Henson, Marcella. The multi-faceted
poetic world of Angela de Hoyos. Austin, TX:
Relampago Books Press, 1985, c1982. 81 p.
English. DESCR: ARISE CHICANO; *Authors;
CHICANO POEMS FOR THE BARRIO; de Hoyos,
Angela; GATA POEMS; GOODBYE TO SILENCE;
Language Usage; *Literary Criticism;
*Poetry; SELECTED POEMS/SELECCIONES.

"You Can Only Blame the System for So Long" [poem]

6714 Zamora, Bernice. Archetypes in Chicana
poetry. DE COLORES, Vol. 4, no. 3 (1978), p.
43-52. English. DESCR: Cervantes, Lorna Dee;
Cunningham, Veronica; "Declaration on a Day
of Little Inspiration" [poem]; Hernandez,
Carlota; "I Speak in an Illusion" [poem];
*Literary Criticism; Lucero, Judy A.;
Macias, Margarita; Mendoza, Rita; "Para Mi
Hijita" [poem]; *Poetry; "Rape Report"
[poem]; "The White Line" [poem]; "Working
Mother's Song" [poem]; Zamora, Katarina.

Youth

6715 Abrahamse, Allan F.; Morrison, Peter A.; and
Waite, Linda J. Beyond stereotypes: who
becomes a single teenage mother? Santa
Monica, CA: RAND Corp., 1988. xv, 88 p.
English. DESCR: *Fertility; Religion;
Secondary School Education; *Single Parents;
Statistics; *Women.

6716 Abrahamse, Allan F.; Morrison, Peter A.; and
Waite, Linda J. Teenagers willing to
consider single parenthood: who is at
greatest risk? FAMILY PLANNING PERSPECTIVES,
Vol. 20, no. 1 (January, February, 1988), p.
13-18. English. DESCR: Blacks; Family
Planning; *Fertility; High School and Beyond
Project (HS&B); *Single Parents; Women.

6717 Andrade, Sally J. Chicana adolescents and
contraception issues. LA RED/THE NET, no. 35
(October 1980), p. 2,14. English. DESCR:
*Birth Control.

6718 Aneshensel, Carol S.; Fielder, Eve P.; and
Becerra, Rosina M. Fertility and
fertility-related behavior among
Mexican-American and non-Hispanic white
female adolescents. JOURNAL OF HEALTH AND
SOCIAL BEHAVIOR, Vol. 30, no. 1 (March
1989), p. 56-76. English. DESCR: Anglo
Americans; *Fertility; Socioeconomic
Factors.

6719 Aneshensel, Carol S., et al. Onset of
fertility-related events during adolescence:
a prospective comparison of Mexican American
and non-Hispanic white females. AMERICAN
JOURNAL OF PUBLIC HEALTH, Vol. 80, no. 8
(August 1990), p. 959-963. English. DESCR:
Abortion; Anglo Americans; Birth Control;
*Fertility; *Sexual Behavior; Women.

6720 Aneshensel, Carol S., et al. Participation
of Mexican American adolescents in a
longitudinal panel survey. PUBLIC OPINION
QUARTERLY, Vol. 53, no. 4 (Winter 1989), p.
548-562. English. DESCR: Age Groups;
*Fertility; Los Angeles County, CA; Social
Science; *Surveys; *Women Men Relations.

6721 Bassoff, Betty Z. and Ortiz, Elizabeth
Thompson. Teen women: disparity between
cognitive values and anticipated life
events. CHILD WELFARE, Vol. 63, no. 2
(March, April, 1984), p. 125-138. English.
DESCR: Sexual Behavior; *Values; Women.

6722 Becerra, Rosina M. and de Anda, Diane.
Pregnancy and motherhood among Mexican
American adolescents. HEALTH AND SOCIAL
WORK, Vol. 9, no. 2 (Spring 1984), p.
106-23. English. DESCR: Acculturation; Anglo
Americans; Attitudes; Birth Control;
*Fertility; Natural Support Systems.

Youth (cont.)

6723 Blanco, Gilbert M. Las Adelitas del Barrio. LATIN QUARTER, Vol. 1, no. 3 (January, February, 1975), p. 30-32. English. DESCR: City Terrace, CA; Community Development; Gangs; *Latin Empresses.

6724 Calderon, Vivian. Maternal employment and career orientation of young Chicana, Black, and white women. Thesis (Ph.D.)--University of California, Santa Cruz, 1984. 150 p. English. DESCR: Anglo Americans; Blacks; *Careers; *Employment; Women.

6725 Chavez, Ernest; Beauvais, Fred; and Oetting, E.R. Drug use by small town Mexican American youth: a pilot study. HISPANIC JOURNAL OF BEHAVIORAL SCIENCES, Vol. 8, no. 3 (September 1986), p. 243-258. English. DESCR: Anglo Americans; *Drug Use; Rural Population.

6726 Codega, Susan A.; Pasley, B. Kay; and Kreutzer, Jill. Coping behaviors of adolescent mothers: an exploratory study and comparison of Mexican-Americans and Anglos. JOURNAL OF ADOLESCENT RESEARCH, Vol. 5, no. 1 (January 1990), p. 34-53. English. DESCR: Anglo Americans; Colorado; *Fertility; *Stress; Women.

6727 Creswell, John L. and Exezidis, Roxane H. Research brief: sex and ethnic differences in mathematics achievement of Black and Mexican-American adolescents. TEXAS TECH JOURNAL OF EDUCATION, Vol. 9, no. 3 (Fall 1982), p. 219-222. English. DESCR: Blacks; *Mathematics.

6728 Creswell, John L. Sex-related differences in the problem-solving abilities of rural Black, Anglo, and Chicano adolescents. TEXAS TECH JOURNAL OF EDUCATION, Vol. 10, no. 1 (Winter 1983), p. 29-33. English. DESCR: Aiken and Preger Revised Math Attitude Scale; Anglo Americans; Blacks; California Achievement Test (CAT); *Mathematics; National Assessment of Educational Progress; National Council of Teachers of Mathematics (NCTM).

6729 Davis, Sally M. and Harris, Mary B. Sexual knowledge, sexual interests, and sources of sexual information of rural and urban adolescents from three cultures. ADOLESCENCE, Vol. 17, no. 66 (Summer 1982), p. 471-492. English. DESCR: Birth Control; Cultural Characteristics; Identity; Rural Population; *Sex Education; Sex Roles; Urban Communities.

6730 de Anda, Diane; Becerra, Rosina M.; and Fielder, Eve P. In their own words: the life experiences of Mexican-American and white pregnant adolescents and adolescent mothers. CHILD AND ADOLESCENT SOCIAL WORK, Vol. 7, no. 4 (August 1990), p. 301-318. English. DESCR: Anglo Americans; *Fertility; *Sexual Behavior; Women.

6731 de Anda, Diane; Becerra, Rosina M.; and Fielder, Eve P. Sexuality, pregnancy, and motherhood among Mexican-American adolescents. JOURNAL OF ADOLESCENT RESEARCH, Vol. 3, no. 3-4 (Fall, Winter, 1988), p. 403-411. English. DESCR: Anglo Americans; Attitudes; Birth Control; *Fertility Sex Education; *Sexual Behavior; Women.

6732 de Anda, Diane and Becerra, Rosina M. Support networks for adolescent mothers. SOCIAL CASEWORK: JOURNAL OF CONTEMPORARY SOCIAL WORK, Vol. 65, no. 3 (March 1984), p. 172-181. English. DESCR: California; *Fertility; *Natural Support Systems; Spanish Language.

6733 Delgado, Jane L. Adolescent pregnancy: an overview. IN: National Hispanic Center for Advanced Studies and Policy Analysis and National Hispanic University. THE STATE OF HISPANIC AMERICA. VOL. VI. Oakland, CA: National Hispanic University, c1987, p. 37-49. English. DESCR: Family Planning; *Fertility; Public Policy.

6734 Eisen, Marvin. Factors discriminating pregnancy resolution decisions of unmarried adolescents. GENETIC PSYCHOLOGY MONOGRAPHS, Vol. 103, no. 1 (August 1983), p. 69-95. English. DESCR: Abortion; Attitudes; Decision Making; *Fertility; *Single Parents.

6735 Eisen, Marvin and Zellman, Gail L. Factors predicting pregnancy resolution decision satisfaction of unmarried adolescents. JOURNAL OF GENETIC PSYCHOLOGY, Vol. 145, no. 2 (December 1984), p. 231-239. English. DESCR: Abortion; Anglo Americans; Attitudes; Counseling (Psychological); Family Planning; *Fertility.

6736 Erickson, Pamela Irene. Pregnancy and childbirth among Mexican origin teenagers in Los Angeles. Thesis (Ph.D.)--UCLA, 1988. xiii, 277 leaves. English. DESCR: *Fertility; Los Angeles, CA; Medical Care.

6737 Farkas, George; Barton, Margaret; and Kushner, Kathy. White, Black, and Hispanic female youths in central city labor markets. SOCIOLOGICAL QUARTERLY, Vol. 29, no. 4 (Winter 1988), p. 605-621. English. DESCR: Anglo Americans; Blacks; Employment; *Income; *Labor Supply and Market; Urban Communities; Women.

6738 Felice, Marianne E., et al. Clinical observations of Mexican-American, Caucasian, and Black pregnant teenagers. JOURNAL OF ADOLESCENT HEALTH CARE, Vol. 7, no. 5 (September 1986), p. 305-310. English. DESCR: Anglo Americans; Blacks; *Fertility; *Prenatal Care; San Diego, CA.

6739 Fennelly, Katherine. Childbearing among Hispanics in the United States: an annotated bibliography. New York: Greenwood Press, 1987. xii, 167 p. English. DESCR: Abortion; *Bibliography; Birth Control; *Fertility; Sterilization; *Women.

6740 Fennelly, Katherine and Ortiz, Vilma. Childbearing among young Latino women in the United States. AMERICAN JOURNAL OF PUBLIC HEALTH, Vol. 77, no. 1 (January 1987), p. 25-28. English. DESCR: *Ethnic Groups; *Fertility; Puerto Ricans; Women.

6741 Fennelly, Katherine; Kandiah, Vasantha; and Ortiz, Vilma. The cross-cultural study of fertility among Hispanic adolescents in the Americas. STUDIES IN FAMILY PLANNING, Vol. 20, no. 2 (March, April, 1989), p. 96-101. English. DESCR: Cultural Characteristics; Ethnic Groups; *Fertility; Latin America; *Marriage.

6742 Fennelly, Katherine. El embarazo precoz: childbearing among Hispanic teenagers in the United States. New York, NY: School of Public Health, Columbia University, c1988. 56 p.: ill. Bilingual. DESCR: *Fertility; Women.

Youth (cont.)

6743 Fennelly, Katherine; Dryfoos, Joy; and
Schwartz, Dana. Hispanic adolescent
fertility. HISPANIC JOURNAL OF BEHAVIORAL
SCIENCES, Vol. 8, no. 2 (June 1986), p.
157-171. English. **DESCR:** *Fertility.

6744 Fennelly, Katherine, et al. The effect of
maternal age on the well-being of children.
JOURNAL OF MARRIAGE AND THE FAMILY, Vol. 46,
no. 4 (November 1984), p. 933-934. English.
DESCR: *Age Groups; *Maternal and Child
Welfare; *Parenting.

6745 Forste, Renata T. and Heaton, Tim B.
Initiation of sexual activity among female
adolescents. YOUTH AND SOCIETY, Vol. 19, no.
3 (March 1988), p. 250-268. English. **DESCR:**
Anglo Americans; Blacks; Family; Sex
Education; *Sexual Behavior; Women.

6746 Fu, Victoria R.; Hinkle, Dennis E.; and
Korslund, Mary K. A development study of
ethnic self-concept among pre-adolescent
girls. JOURNAL OF GENETIC PSYCHOLOGY, Vol.
14, (March 1983), p. 67-73. English.
DESCR: Comparative Psychology; *Identity;
Junior High School; Self-Concept Self Report
Scale; Students.

6747 Garn, Stanley M. and LaVelle, Marquisa.
Reproductive histories of low weight girls
and women. AMERICAN JOURNAL OF CLINICAL
NUTRITION, Vol. 37, no. 5 (May 1983), p.
862-866. English. **DESCR:** *Fertility;
Nutrition.

6748 Guajardo, Maria Resendez. Educational
attainment of Chicana adolescents. Thesis
(Ph.D.)--University of Denver, 1988. 266 p.
English. **DESCR:** Academic Achievement;
*Dropouts; *Secondary School Education.

6749 Hardy-Fanta, Carol and Montana, Priscila.
The Hispanic female adolescent: a group
therapy model. INTERNATIONAL JOURNAL OF
GROUP PSYCHOTHERAPY, Vol. 32, no. 3 (July
1982), p. 351-366. English. **DESCR:**
Psychotherapy; Puerto Ricans; *Women.

6750 Harris, Mary G. Cholas: Latino girls and
gangs. New York: AMS Press, 1988. x, 220 p.
English. **DESCR:** Barrios; *Gangs; Juvenile
Delinquency; Los Angeles, CA; San Fernando
Valley, CA.

6751 Horowitz, Ruth. Femininity and womanhood:
virginity, unwed motherhood, and violence.
IN: Horowitz, Ruth. HONOR AND THE AMERICAN
DREAM: CULTURE AND IDENTITY IN A CHICANO
COMMUNITY. New Brunswick, NJ: Rutgers
University Press, 1983, p. 114-136. English.
DESCR: *Birth Control; *Fertility; Identity;
Sex Roles; *Sexual Behavior; Single Parents;
Violence; Women Men Relations.

6752 Horowitz, Ruth. Passion, submission and
motherhood: the negotiation of identity by
unmarried innercity Chicanas. SOCIOLOGICAL
QUARTERLY, Vol. 22, no. 2 (Spring 1981), p.
241-252. English. **DESCR:** Barrios; Birth
Control; *Fertility; Identity; *Sex Roles;
*Sexual Behavior; Single Parents.

6753 Hunt, Isabelle F., et al. Zinc
supplementation during pregnancy in
low-income teenagers of Mexican descent:
effects on selected blood constituents and
on progress and outcome of pregnancy.
AMERICAN JOURNAL OF CLINICAL NUTRITION, Vol.
42, no. 5 (November 1985), p. 815-828.
English. **DESCR:** *Fertility; *Nutrition.

6754 Hutchison, James. Teenagers and
contraception in Cameron and Willacy
Counties. BORDERLANDS JOURNAL, Vol. 7, no. 1
(Fall 1983), p. 75-90. English. **DESCR:**
*Birth Control; Cameron County, TX; *Family
Planning; Fertility; Sex Education; Willacy
County, TX.

6755 Isaacs, Barbara Gail. Anglo, Black, and
Latin adolescents' participation in sports.
Thesis (Ph.D.)--California School of
Professional Psychology, Los Angeles, 1984.
283 p. English. **DESCR:** Anglo Americans;
Blacks; Cultural Characteristics; *Secondary
School Education; *Sports; *Women.

6756 Lindemann, Constance and Scott, Wilbur. The
fertility related behavior of Mexican
American adolescents. JOURNAL OF EARLY
ADOLESCENCE, Vol. 2, no. 1 (Spring 1982), p.
31-38. English. **DESCR:** *Fertility; Migration
Patterns.

6757 Long, John M. and Vigil, James Diego.
Cultural styles and adolescent sex role
perceptions: an exploration of responses to
a value picture projective test. IN:
Melville, Margarita B., ed. TWICE A
MINORITY. St. Louis, MO: Mosby, 1980, p.
164-172. English. **DESCR:** Psychological
Testing; *Sex Roles.

6758 Lopez, Norma Y. Hispanic teenage pregnancy:
overview and implications. Washington, DC:
National Council of La Raza, 1987. 17
leaves. English. **DESCR:** *Fertility;
Statistics; Women.

6759 Marshall, Maria Sandra Gonzalez. The
childbearing beliefs and practices of
pregnant Mexican-American adolescents living
in Southwest border regions. Thesis
(M.S.)--University of Arizona, 1987. 117 p.
English. **DESCR:** *Acculturation; Border
Region; *Fertility.

6760 Martinez, Ruben and Dukes, Richard L. Race,
gender and self-esteem among youth. HISPANIC
JOURNAL OF BEHAVIORAL SCIENCES, Vol. 9, no.
4 (December 1987), p. 427-443. English.
DESCR: *Comparative Psychology; *Identity;
*Sex Roles.

6761 Mata, Alberto Guardiola and Castillo,
Valerie. Rural female adolescent
dissatisfaction, support and helpseeking.
FREE INQUIRY IN CREATIVE SOCIOLOGY, Vol. 14,
no. 2 (November 1986), p. 135-138. English.
DESCR: Alcoholism; *Drug Use; Interpersonal
Relations; *Natural Support Systems; Parent
and Child Relationships; Rural Population.

6762 Michael, Robert T. and Tuma, Nancy Brandon.
Entry into marriage and parenthood by young
men and women: the influence of family
background. DEMOGRAPHY, Vol. 22, no. 4
(November 1985), p. 515-544. Magazine.
English. **DESCR:** Anglo Americans; Blacks;
*Cultural Characteristics; *Fertility;
*Marriage; Population.

6763 Mink, Diane Leslie. Early grandmotherhood:
an exploratory study. Thesis
(Ph.D.)--California School of Professional
Psychology, Los Angeles, 1987. 190 p.
English. **DESCR:** Age Groups; *Ancianos;
Assertiveness; Family; Fertility;
Grandmothers; Natural Support Systems; *Sex
Roles; Surveys.

Youth (cont.)

6764 Moore, Joan W. Mexican-American women addicts: the influence of family background. IN: Glick, Ronald and Moore, Joan, eds. DRUGS IN HISPANIC COMMUNITIES. New Brunswick, NJ: Rutgers University Press, c1990, p. 127-153. English. DESCR: Barrios; *Drug Addicts; Drug Use; East Los Angeles, CA; *Family; *Gangs; Heroin; Hoyo-Mara Gang, East Los Angeles, CA; Pachucos; Sex Roles; Socialization; White Fence Gang.

6765 Ochoa, Mariaelena Lopez. Group counseling Chicana troubled youth: an exploratory group counseling project. Thesis (Ed.D.) --University of Massachusetts, 1981. 326 p. English. DESCR: *Counseling (Educational).

6766 Ortiz, Vilma and Fennelly, Katherine. Early childbearing and employment among young Mexican origin, Black, and white women. SOCIAL SCIENCE QUARTERLY, Vol. 69, no. 4 (December 1988), p. 987-995. English. DESCR: Anglo Americans; Blacks; *Employment; *Fertility; *Women.

6767 Padilla, Amado M. and Baird, Traci L. Mexican-American adolescent sexuality and sexual knowledge: an exploratory study. HISPANIC JOURNAL OF BEHAVIORAL SCIENCES, Vol. 13, no. 1 (February 1991), p. 95-104. English. DESCR: *Attitudes; *Birth Control; Sex Roles; *Sexual Behavior; Surveys.

6768 Pletsch, Pamela K. Hispanics: at risk for adolescent pregnancy? PUBLIC HEALTH NURSING, Vol. 7, no. 2 (June 1990), p. 105-110. English. DESCR: *Fertility; *Maternal and Child Welfare.

6769 Pumariega, Andres J. Acculturation and eating attitudes in adolescent girls: a comparative and correlational study. JOURNAL OF THE AMERICAN ACADEMY OF CHILD PSYCHIATRY, Vol. 25, no. 2 (March 1986), p. 276-279. English. DESCR: *Acculturation; Anorexia Nervosa; Cultural Characteristics; Eating Attitudes Test (EAT); Nutrition; Socioeconomic Factors.

6770 Remez, Lisa. Rates of adolescent pregnancy and childbearing are high among Mexican-born Mexican Americans. FAMILY PLANNING PERSPECTIVES, Vol. 23, no. 2 (March, April, 1991), p. 88-89. English. DESCR: *Fertility; *Immigrants; Los Angeles County, CA; *Sexual Behavior.

6771 Ridgely, Julia S. Health means jobs. WORLD HEALTH, (January, February, 1985), p. 18-20. English. DESCR: Employment Training; *Family Planning.

6772 Salgado de Snyder, Nelly; Lopez, Cynthia M.; and Padilla, Amado M. Ethnic identity and cultural awareness among the offspring of Mexican interethnic marriages. JOURNAL OF EARLY ADOLESCENCE, Vol. 2, no. 3 (Fall 1982), p. 277-282. English. DESCR: *Acculturation; Children; *Identity; *Intermarriage.

6773 Sorenson, Ann Marie. Fertility, expectations and ethnic identity among Mexican-American adolescents: an expression of cultural ideals. SOCIOLOGICAL PERSPECTIVES, Vol. 28, no. 3 (July 1985), p. 339-360. English. DESCR: Acculturation; Anglo Americans; Cultural Characteristics; *Fertility; Identity; Values.

6774 Terrazas, Olga Esperanza. The self-concept of Mexican-American adolescent females.

Thesis (Ph.D.)--Wright Institute, 1980. 262 p. English. DESCR: *Identity; Psychological Testing.

6775 Torres, Aida and Singh, Susheela. Contraceptive practice among Hispanic adolescents. FAMILY PLANNING PERSPECTIVES, Vol. 18, no. 4 (July, August, 1986), p. 193-194. English. DESCR: Birth Control; *Family Planning.

6776 Triandis, Harry C. Role perceptions of Hispanic young adults. JOURNAL OF CROSS-CULTURAL PSYCHOLOGY, Vol. 15, no. 3 (September 1984), p. 297-320. English. DESCR: *Cultural Characteristics; *Family; Parent and Child Relationships; *Sex Roles; Social Psychology; Values.

6777 Trotter, Robert T. Ethnic and sexual patterns of alcohol use: Anglo and Mexican American college students. ADOLESCENCE, Vol. 17, no. 66 (Summer 1982), p. 305-325. English. DESCR: *Alcoholism; Anglo Americans; Colleges and Universities; Cultural Characteristics; Ethnic Groups; Sex Roles; Students.

6778 Zayas, Luis H. Toward an understanding of suicide risks in young Hispanic females. JOURNAL OF ADOLESCENT RESEARCH, Vol. 2, no. 1 (Spring 1987), p. 1-11. English. DESCR: Acculturation; Cubanos; Cultural Characteristics; Depression (Psychological); Mental Health; Puerto Ricans; *Suicide; *Women.

Youth Offenders
    USE: Juvenile Delinquency

Yucatan, Mexico

6779 Macias, Anna. Against all odds: the feminist movement in Mexico to 1940. Westport, CT: Greenwood Press, 1982. xv, 195 p. English. DESCR: Carrillo Puerto, Felipe; *Feminism; History; Mexican Revolution - 1910-1920; Mexico; *Women.

Zamora, Bernice

6780 Bruce-Novoa, Juan. Bernice Zamora y Lorna Dee Cervantes: una estetica feminista. REVISTA IBEROAMERICANA, Vol. 51, (July, December, 1985), p. 565-573. English. DESCR: *Authors; *Cervantes, Lorna Dee; EMPLUMADA; Literary Criticism; Poetry; RESTLESS SERPENTS.

6781 Desai, Parul and Zamora, Bernice. Interview with Bernice Zamora, a Chicana poet. IMAGINE, Vol. 2, no. 1 (Summer 1985), p. 26-39. English. DESCR: Literary Criticism; Literature; *Poetry.

6782 Lucero, Marcela Christine. The socio-historical implication of the valley as a metaphor in three Colorado Chicana poets. Thesis (Ph.D.)--University of Minnesota, 1981. 176 p. English. DESCR: *Authors; Blea, Irene I.; Chicano Movement; Colorado; Feminism; Literary Criticism; Mondragon Valdez, Maria; Poetry.

Zamora, Bernice (cont.)

6783 Luna-Lawhn, Juanita. Victorian attitudes
     affecting the Mexican woman writing in LA
     PRENSA during the early 1900s and the
     Chicana of the 1980s. IN: Bardeleben, Renate
     von, et al., eds. MISSIONS IN CONFLICT:
     ESSAYS ON U.S.-MEXICAN RELATIONS AND CHICANO
     CULTURE. Tubingen, W. Germany: Gunter Narr
     Verlag, 1986, p. 65-71. English. **DESCR:**
     Feminism; LA PRENSA, San Antonio, TX;
     Literary Criticism; *Newspapers; "Penitents"
     [poem]; Poetry.

6784 Saldivar, Jose David. Towards a Chicano
     poetics: the making of the Chicano subject.
     CONFLUENCIA, Vol. 1, no. 2 (Spring 1986), p.
     10-17. English. **DESCR:** Corridos; Feminism;
     *Literary Criticism; "Los Vatos" [poem];
     Montoya, Jose E.; *Poetry; RESTLESS
     SERPENTS; Rios, Alberto; WHISPERING TO FOOL
     THE WIND.

6785 Sanchez, Marta E. Judy Lucero and Bernice
     Zamora: two dialectical statements in
     Chicana poetry. DE COLORES, Vol. 4, no. 3
     (1978), p. 22-33. Bilingual. **DESCR:**
     Gomez-Quinones, Juan; *Literary Criticism;
     Lucero, Judy A.; *Poetry.

6786 Sanchez, Marta E. Judy Lucero and Bernice
     Zamora: two dialectical statements in
     Chicana poetry. IN: Sommers, Joseph and
     Ybarra-Frausto, Tomas, eds. MODERN CHICANO
     WRITERS: A COLLECTION OF CRITICAL ESSAYS.
     Englewood Cliffs, NJ: Prentice-Hall, 1979,
     p. 141-149. English. **DESCR:** Gomez-Quinones,
     Juan; *Literary Criticism; Lucero, Judy A.;
     *Poetry.

6787 Zamora, Bernice and Binder, Wolfgang.
     [Interview with] Bernice Zamora. IN: Binder,
     Wolfgang, ed. PARTIAL AUTOBIOGRAPHIES:
     INTERVIEWS WITH TWENTY CHICANO POETS.
     Erlangen, W. Germany: Verlag Palm & Enke,
     1985, p. 221-229. English. **DESCR:** Authors;
     Autobiography; Poetry.

Zamora, Katarina

6788 Zamora, Bernice. Archetypes in Chicana
     poetry. DE COLORES, Vol. 4, no. 3 (1978), p.
     43-52. English. **DESCR:** Cervantes, Lorna Dee;
     Cunningham, Veronica; "Declaration on a Day
     of Little Inspiration" [poem]; Hernandez,
     Carlota; "I Speak in an Illusion" [poem];
     *Literary Criticism; Lucero, Judy A.;
     Macias, Margarita; Mendoza, Rita; "Para Mi
     Hijita" [poem]; *Poetry; "Rape Report"
     [poem]; "The White Line" [poem]; "Working
     Mother's Song" [poem]; "You Can Only Blame
     the System for So Long" [poem].

Zamora Lucero, Linda

6789 Goldman, Shifra M. Mujeres de California:
     Latin American women artists. IN: Moore,
     Sylvia, ed. YESTERDAY AND TOMORROW:
     CALIFORNIA WOMEN ARTISTS. New York, NY:
     Midmarch Arts Press, c1989, p. 202-229.
     English. **DESCR:** *Artists; Baca, Judith F.;
     Biography; California; Carrasco, Barbara;
     Cervantez, Yreina; de Larios, Dora;
     Feminism; Hernandez, Judithe; Lomas Garza,
     Carmen; Lopez, Yolanda M.; Mesa-Bains,
     Amalia; Murillo, Patricia; Sanchez, Olivia;
     Valdez, Patssi; Vallejo Dillaway, Linda;
     Women.

Zavella, Pat

6790 Acuna, Rodolfo. The struggles of class and
     gender: current research in Chicano Studies
     [review essay]. JOURNAL OF AMERICAN ETHNIC
     HISTORY, Vol. 8, no. 2 (Spring 1989), p.
     134-138. English. **DESCR:** *CANNERY WOMEN,
     CANNERY LIVES; *CHICANO ETHNICITY; Deutsch,
     Sarah; Keefe, Susan E.; Literature Reviews;
     *NO SEPARATE REFUGE; Padilla, Amado M.;
     Ruiz, Vicki L.; *WOMEN'S WORK AND CHICANO
     FAMILIES.

6791 Garcia, Mario T. Family and gender in
     Chicano and border studies research. MEXICAN
     STUDIES/ESTUDIOS MEXICANOS, Vol. 6, no. 1
     (Winter 1990), p. 109-119. English. **DESCR:**
     Alvarez, Robert R., Jr.; *Border Region;
     CANNERY WOMEN, CANNERY LIVES; *Family; LA
     FAMILIA: MIGRATION AND ADAPTATION IN BAJA
     AND ALTA CALIFORNIA, 1800-1975; *Literature
     Reviews; Ruiz, Vicki L.; Tiano, Susan B.;
     Women; WOMEN ON THE U.S.-MEXICO BORDER:
     RESPONSES TO CHANGE; WOMEN'S WORK AND
     CHICANO FAMILIES.

ZOOT SUIT [film]

6792 Morales, Sylvia. Chicano-produced celluloid
     mujeres. BILINGUAL REVIEW, Vol. 10, no. 2-3
     (May, December, 1983), p. 89-93. English.
     DESCR: BALLAD OF GREGORIO CORTEZ [film];
     Film Reviews; *Films; RAICES DE SANGRE
     [film]; SEGUIN [movie]; *Stereotypes.

Zoot Suiter
     USE: Pachucos

AUTHOR INDEX

Abelardo
USE: Delgado, Abelardo "Lalo"

Abney-Guardado, Armando J.
Chicano intermarriage in the United States: a
sociocultural analysis, 52.
Demographic and cultural correlates of Chicano
intermarriage, 1429.

Abrahamse, Allan F.
Beyond stereotypes: who becomes a single
teenage mother?, 2368.
Teenagers willing to consider single
parenthood: who is at greatest risk?, 762.

Achor, Shirley
Chicanas holding doctoral degrees: social
reproduction and cultural ecological
approaches, 24.

Acosta Johnson, Carmen
Breast-feeding and social class mobility: the
case of Mexican migrant mothers in Houston,
Texas, 909.

Acuna, Rodolfo
Response to Cynthia Orozco, 4445.
The struggles of class and gender: current
research in Chicano Studies [review essay],
998.

Adams, Russell P.
Family planning needs and behavior of Mexican
American women: a study of health care
professionals and their clientele, 69.
Predictors of self-esteem and locus-of-control
in Mexican-American women, 2848.

Agosin, Marjorie
Elucubraciones y antielucubraciones: critica
feminista desde perspectivas poeticas, 1948.

Aguilar, Marian Angela
Patterns of health care utilization of Mexican
American women, 3054.

Aguilar-Henson, Marcella
The multi-faceted poetic world of Angela de
Hoyos, 372.

Ahern, Susan
Migration and la mujer fuerte, 4039.

Ainsworth, Diane
Cultural cross fires, 2849.

Alanis, Elsa
The relationship between state and trait
anxiety and acculturation in
Mexican-American women homemakers and
Mexican-American community college female
students, 53.

Alarcon, Justo S.
[Bornstein-Somoza, Miriam], 529.

Alarcon, Norma
Chicana feminism: in the tracks of 'the'
native woman, 1503.
Chicana writers and critics in a social
context : towards a contemporary
bibliography, 664.
Chicana's feminist literature: a re-vision
through Malintzinl or Malintzin: putting
flesh back on the object, 2185.
Hay que inventarnos/we must invent ourselves,
380.
Interview with Cherrie Moraga, 530.
Interview with Pat Mora, 531.
Latina writers in the United States, 532.
Making "familia" from scratch: split
subjectivities in the work of Helena Maria
Viramontes and Cherrie Moraga, 2575.
A poet analyzes her craft, 564.
The sardonic powers of the erotic in the work
of Ana Castillo, 1053.
The sexuality of Latinas [special issue of
THIRD WOMAN], 3554.
The theoretical subject(s) of THIS BRIDGE
CALLED MY BACK and Anglo-American feminism,
235.
The theoretical subject(s) of THIS BRIDGE
CALLED MY BACK and Anglo-American feminism,
236.
Traddutora, traditora: a paradigmatic figure
of Chicana feminism, 2188.
What kind of lover have you made me, Mother?:
towards a theory of Chicanas' feminism and

cultural identity through poetry, 923.

Alba, Francisco
La fecundidad entre los
Mexicano-Norteamericanos en relacion a los
cambiantes patrones reproductivos en Mexico
y los Estados Unidos, 2370.

Alba, Isabel Catherine
Achievement conflicts, sex-role orientation,
and performance on sex-role appropriate and
sex-role inappropriate tasks in women of
three ethnic groups, 237.

Alba, Richard D.
A comment on Schoen and Cohen, 1270.

Alcalay, Rina
Hispanic women in the United States: family &
work relations, 2001.

Alcocer Marban, Sonia
Las maquiladoras en Mexico, 848.

Allen, Jane
La mujer: a visual dialogue, 941.

Almaguer, Tomas
Urban Chicano workers in historical
perspective: a review of recent literature,
3219.

Alonso, Ana Maria
Silences: "Hispanics", AIDS, and sexual
practices, 171.

Alurista
In verbal murals: a study of Chicana herstory
and poetry, 984.

Alvarado, Anita L.
The status of Hispanic women in nursing, 1008.

Alvarez, Lourdes
Hispanas: success in America, 708.

Alvarez, Robert R.
A profile of the citizenship process among
Hispanics in the United States, 2852.

Alvarez-Amaya, Maria
Determinants of breast and cervical cancer
behavior among Mexican American women, 868.

Amaro, Hortensia
Abortion use and attitudes among Chicanas: the
need for research, 5.
Considerations for prevention of HIV infection
among Hispanic women, 172.
Contemporary research on Hispanic women: a
selected bibliography of the social science
literature, 666.
Hispanic women and mental health: an overview
of contemporary issues in research and
practice, 3600.
Hispanic women in psychology: a resource
directory, 1598.
Psychosocial determinants of abortion
attitudes among Mexican American women, 6.
The use of inpatient mental health services by
Hispanic women, 3992.
Women in the Mexican-American community:
religion, culture, and reproductive
attitudes and experiences, 7.

Ames, Genevieve
Drinking patterns and drinking-related
problems of Mexican-American husbands and
wives, 188.

Amodeo, Luiza B.
The triple bias: rural, minority and female,
1740.

Anderson, Robert K.
Marez y Luna and the masculine-feminine
dialectic, 206.

Andrade, Sally J.
Chicana adolescents and contraception issues,
741.
Family planning practices of Mexican
Americans, 742.
Family roles of Hispanic women: stereotypes,
empirical findings, and implications for
research, 2018.
Social science stereotypes of the Mexican
American woman: policy implications for
research, 5086.

Andrade, Sally J., ed.
Latino families in the United States: a
resource book for family life education =

Las familias latinas en los Estados Unidos:
recursos para la capacitacion familiar, 701.

Aneshensel, Carol S.
Fertility and fertility-related behavior among
Mexican-American and non-Hispanic white
female adolescents, 238.

Aneshensel, Carol S., et al.
Onset of fertility-related events during
adolescence: a prospective comparison of
Mexican American and non-Hispanic white
females, 8.
Participation of Mexican American adolescents
in a longitudinal panel survey, 137.

Angel, Ronald J.
Determinants of extended household structure:
cultural pattern or economical need?, 2002.
Headship and household composition among
Blacks, Hispanics and other whites, 334.

Anglin, M. Douglas
Addicted women and crime, 1409.
The criminality of female narcotics addicts: a
causal modeling approach, 293.

Anguiano, Lupe, ed.
Every woman's right: the right to quality
education and economic independence, 1251.

Ano Nuevo Kerr, Louise
Chicanas in the Great Depression, 1111.

Anonymous
Workshop resolutions - First National Chicana
Conference, May 1971, 1343.

Anthony, Darius
Hispanic women and their men, 4539.

Anzaldua, Gloria
Border crossings, 2192.
Borderlands/La frontera: the new mestiza, 624.
Conversations at the Book Fair: interview with
Gloria Anzaldua, 355.
La prieta, 712.

Anzaldua, Gloria, ed.
Making face, making soul = Haciendo caras:
creative and critical perspectives by women
of color, 1967.
This bridge called my back: writings by
radical women of color, 1982.

Apodaca, Maria Linda
The Chicana woman: a historical materialist
perspective, 1001.
A double edge sword: Hispanas and liberal
feminism, 2195.

Aragon de Valdez, Theresa
Organizing as a political tool for the
Chicana, 1604.

Arbelaez A., Marisol
Impacto social del sismo, Mexico 1985: las
costureras, 1732.

Arce, Carlos H.
The contemporary Chicano family: an
empirically based review, 2096.
Demographic and cultural correlates of Chicano
intermarriage, 1429.

Arenal, Sandra
Sangre joven: las maquiladoras por dentro,
829.

Arevalo, Rodolfo, ed.
Chicanas and alcoholism: a sociocultural
perspective of women, 185.

Arguelles, Lourdes
HIV infection/AIDS and Latinas in Los Angeles
County: considerations for prevention,
treatment, and research practice, 173.
Undocumented female labor in the United States
Southwest: an essay on migration,
consciousness, oppression and struggle, 378.

Arizmendi, Yareli
La mujer y el teatro chicano, 1148.

Armas-Cardona, Regina
Anglo and Raza young women: a study of
self-esteem, psychic distress and locus of
control, 240.

Arroyo, Laura E.
Industrial and occupational distribution of
Chicana workers, 942.
Industrial and occupational distribution of
Chicana workers, 943.

Ashley, Laurel Maria
Self, family and community: the social process
of aging among urban Mexican-American women,
54.

Asuncion-Lande, Nobleza C.
Problems and strategies for sexual identity
and cultural integration: Mexican-American
women on the move, 1149.

Atkinson, Donald R.
Ethnicity, locus of control for family
planning, and pregnancy counselor
credibility, 241.

Aulette, Judy
Something old, something new: auxiliary work
in the 1983-1986 copper strike, 373.

Avila, Consuelo
Ecos de una convencion, 1344.

Ayers-Nackamkin, Beverly, et al.
Sex and ethnic differences in the use of
power, 242.

Baca Barragan, Polly
La Chicana in politics, 1815.
[Untitled interview with State Senators
(Colorado) Polly Baca-Barragan and Lena
Guerrero], 633.

Baca, Judith F.
THE WORLD WALL: A VISION OF THE FUTURE WITHOUT
FEAR: an interview with Judith F. Baca, 398.

Baca, Reynaldo
Mexican women, migration and sex roles, 4044.
Migration and la mujer fuerte, 4039.

Baca Zinn, Maxine
Chicanas: power and control in the domestic
sphere, 2022.
Chicanas: power and control in the domestic
sphere, 2023.
Chicano family research: conceptual
distortions and alternative directions,
1431.
Chicano men and masculinity, 1432.
Employment and education of Mexican-American
women: the interplay of modernity and
ethnicity in eight families, 55.
Gender and ethnic identity among Chicanos,
2857.
Marital role orientation among Chicanos: an
analysis of structural and cultural factors,
3814.
Mexican American women in the social sciences,
3601.
Ongoing questions in the study of Chicano
families, 2026.
Political familism: toward sex role equality
in Chicano families, 56.
Qualitative methods in family research: a look
inside Chicano families, 2028.
Urban kinship and Midwest Chicano families:
evidence in support of revision, 1319.

Bachu, Amara
Developing current fertility indicators for
foreign-born women from the Current
Population Survey, 1534.

Bach-y-Rita, George
The Mexican-American: religious and cultural
influences, 1060.

Baezconde-Garbanati, Lourdes
Mexican immigrant women: a selected
bibliography, 667.

Baird, Traci L.
Mexican-American adolescent sexuality and
sexual knowledge: an exploratory study, 506.

Baker, Richard C.
Conformity and cooperation in Chicanos: the
case of the missing susceptibility to
influence, 1332.

Baker, Susan Gonzalez
Many rivers to cross: Mexican immigrants,
women workers, and the structure of labor
markets in the urban Southwest, 2950.

Balkwell, Carolyn Ann
An attitudinal correlate of the timing of a
major life event: the case of morale in
widowhood, 211.
Widowhood: its impact on morale and optimism

among older persons of three ethnic groups, 212.

Barton, Amy E.
Campesinas: women farmworkers in the California agricultural labor force, report of a study project, 944.
Women farmworkers: their workplace and capitalist patriarchy, 1002.

Barton, Margaret
White, Black, and Hispanic female youths in central city labor markets, 270.

Bassoff, Betty Z.
Teen women: disparity between cognitive values and anticipated life events, 5421.

Bauer, Richard L.
Ethnic differences in hip fracture: a reduced incidence in Mexican-Americans, 244.
Low risk of vertebral fracture in Mexican American women, 245.

Bauer, Richard L., et al.
Risk of postmenopausal hip fracture in Mexican-American women, 213.

Bauman, Raquel
The status of Chicanas in medicine, 3900.
A study of Mexican American women's perceptions of factors that influence academic and professional goal attainment, 1009.

Bays, Sharon Arlene
Women of the Valley of the Sun: women and family work culture in Woodlake, California, 2030.

Bean, Frank D.
Generation, female education and Mexican American fertility, 138.
The Hispanic population of the United States, 1074.
Mexican American fertility, 469.
Mexican American fertility patterns, 139.
The Mexican origin population in the United States: a demographic overview, 1834.
Patterns of marital instability among Mexican Americans, Blacks, and Anglos, 277.
Recent changes in marital instability among Mexican Americans: convergence with Black and Anglo trends, 145.
Role incompatibility and the relationship between fertility and labor supply among Hispanic women, 1416.

Bean, Frank D., et al.
Generational differences in fertility among Mexican Americans: implications for assessing the effects of immigration, 140.

Beauvais, Fred
Drug use by small town Mexican American youth: a pilot study, 252.

Becerra, Gloria V.
Chicana employment--options for the future, 1836.

Becerra, Rosina M.
Fertility and fertility-related behavior among Mexican-American and non-Hispanic white female adolescents, 238.
In their own words: the life experiences of Mexican-American and white pregnant adolescents and adolescent mothers, 261.
Pregnancy and motherhood among Mexican American adolescents, 57.
Sexuality, pregnancy, and motherhood among Mexican-American adolescents, 262.
Support networks for adolescent mothers, 948.

Belk, Sharyn S., et al.
Impact of ethnicity, nationality, counseling orientation, and mental health standards on stereotypic beliefs about women, 247.

Bello, Ruth T.
Being Hispanic in Houston: a matter of identity, 591.

Benardo, Margot L.
Hispanic women and their men, 4539.

Benitez, Tina, ed.
Palabras chicanas: an undergraduate anthology, 3452.

Bergdolt-Munzer, Sara L.

Homemakers and retirement income benefits: the other home security issue, 214.

Berger, Peggy S.
Differences in importance of and satisfaction from job characteristics by sex and occupational type among Mexican-American employees, 471.

Bernstein, Gerald S.
Use of clinic versus private family planning care by low-income women: access, cost and patient satisfaction, 2142.

Billings, Linda M.
In verbal murals: a study of Chicana herstory and poetry, 984.

Binder, Wolfgang
[Interview with] Alma Villanueva, 587.
[Interview with] Ana Castillo, 539.
[Interview with] Angela de Hoyos, 550.
[Interview with] Barbara Brinson-Pineda, 536.
[Interview with] Bernice Zamora, 590.
[Interview with] Lorna Dee Cervantes, 540.
[Interview with] Lucha Corpi, 548.
[Interview with] Rebecca Gonzales, 554.
[Interview with] Sandra Cisneros, 545.
[Interview with] Veronica Cunningham, 549.
Mothers and grandmothers: acts of mythification and remembrance in Chicano poetry, 2597.

Binder, Wolfgang, ed.
Partial autobiographies: interviews with twenty Chicano poets, 533.

Binkin, Nancy J.
Isoniazid hepatitis among pregnant and postpartum Hispanic patients, 2407.

Blackwelder, Julia Kirk
Women of the depression: caste and culture in San Antonio, 1929-1939, 1411.

Blair, Leita Mae
Characteristics of professional and traditional Mexican American women related to family of origin, role models, and conflicts: a case study, 1010.

Blanco, Gilbert M.
Las Adelitas del Barrio, 1244.

Blanco, Iris
La mujer en los albores de la conquista de Mexico, 625.
O te aclimatas o te aclimueres, 830.
Participacion de las mujeres en la sociedad prehispanica, 626.
El sexo y su condicionamiento cultural en el mundo prehispanico, 4049.

Blau, Zena Smith
To be aged, Hispanic, and female: the triple risk, 230.

Blea, Irene I.
Brujeria: a sociological analysis of Mexican American witches, 925.
Mexican American female experience, 1151.

Borland, Dolores C.
A cohort analysis approach to the empty nest syndrome among three ethnic groups of women: a theoretical position, 1933.

Bornstein de Somoza, Miriam
La poetica chicana: vision panoramica, 534.

Bouknight, Jon
Language as a cure: an interview with Milcha Sanchez-Scott, 116.

Bourque, Linda B.
Attributes of suicide in females, 248.

Bova, Breda Murphy
Hispanic women at midlife: implications for higher and adult education, 130.

Boza, Maria del Carmen, ed.
Nosotras: Latina literature today, 4548.

Braddom, Carolyn Lentz
The conceptualization of effective leadership as seen by women, Black and Hispanic superintendents, 249.

Bradshaw, Benjamin S.
Mexican American fertility, 469.

Bridges, Julian C.
Family life, 871.

Brinson-Pineda, Barbara

Exploring the applicability of the Dyadic Adjustment Scale for assessing level of marital adjustment with Mexican Americans, 1730.

Profiling an invisible minority in higher education: the Chicana, 2656.

Castaneda, Antonia I.
Comparative frontiers: the migration of women to Alta California and New Zealand, 873.
Gender, race, and culture: Spanish-Mexican women in the historiography of frontier California, 640.
The political economy of nineteenth century stereotypes of Californianas, 947.

Castaneda Garcia, Carmen
Fuentes para la historia de la mujer en los archivos de Guadalajara, 365.

Castellano, Olivia
Of clarity and the moon: a study of two women in rebellion, 362.

Castillo, Ana
[Interview with] Ana Castillo, 539.
Interview with Ana Castillo, 565.
La macha: toward a beautiful whole self, 2791.
The sexuality of Latinas [special issue of THIRD WOMAN], 3554.

Castillo, Ana, ed.
Esta [sic] puente, mi espalca: voces de mujeres tercermundistas en los Estados Unidos, 1981.

Castillo, Sylvia
A guide to Hispanic women's resources: a perspective on networking among Hispanic women, 1599.

Castillo, Valerie
Rural female adolescent dissatisfaction, support and helpseeking, 191.

Castillo-Speed, Lillian
Chicana Studies: a selected list of materials since 1980, 671.

Castillo-Speed, Lillian, ed.
The Chicano index: a comprehensive subject, author, and title index to Chicano materials, 3092.
Chicano Periodical Index: a cumulative index to selected Chicano periodicals between 1967 and 1978, 4523.

Castro, Felipe G.
The health beliefs of Mexican, Mexican American and Anglo American women, 251.
Latinas without work: family, occupational, and economic stress following unemployment, 1885.
Long-term stress among Latino women after a plant closure, 510.

Castro, Rafaela
Mexican women's sexual jokes, 1224.

Cayer, Shirley
Chicago's new Hispanic health alliance, 186.

Cazares, Ralph B.
Intermarriage of Mexican Americans, 81.
Mexican American intermarriage in a nonmetropolitan context, 141.
Mexican American intermarriage in a nonmetropolitan context, 142.

Cervantes, Lorna Dee
[Interview with] Lorna Dee Cervantes, 540.

Cervantes, Richard C.
Consideration of psychosocial stress in the treatment of the Latina immigrant, 1663.
Gender and ethnic differences in psychosocial stress and generalized distress among Hispanics, 325.
Latinas without work: family, occupational, and economic stress following unemployment, 1885.
Long-term stress among Latino women after a plant closure, 510.

Chabran, Richard
Chicana reference sources, 672.

Chabran, Richard, ed.
The Chicano index: a comprehensive subject, author, and title index to Chicano materials, 3092.

Chicano Periodical Index: a cumulative index to selected Chicano periodicals between 1967 and 1978, 4523.

Chacon, Maria A.
Chicanas and Chicanos: barriers to progress in higher education, 1304.
An overdue study of the Chicana undergraduate college experience, 1272.

Chacon, Maria A., et al.
Chicanas in California post secondary education: a comparative study of barriers to the program progress, 26.
Chicanas in postsecondary education, 1274.

Chacon, Peter
Chicanas and political representation, 1817.

Chall, Malca
Activist in the labor movement, the Democratic Party, and the Mexican-American community: an interview, 731.

Chapa, Evey
USE: Chapa, Olivia Evey

Chapa, Olivia Evey
Mujeres por la Raza unida, 974.
Report from the National Women's Political Caucus, 1348.

Chase, Charlotte Fay
Alcohol-related problems of Mexican-American women in the San Francisco Bay Area, 187.

Chavez, Denise
Heat and rain (testimonio), 541.

Chavez, Ernest
Drug use by small town Mexican American youth: a pilot study, 252.

Chavez, Henri
Las Chicanas/The Chicanas, 1152.
Unsung heroine of La Causa, 135.

Chavez, John M.
Reinforcing children's effort: a comparison of immigrant, native-born Mexican American and Euro-American mothers, 58.

Chavez, Virginia
Hispanic househusbands, 1687.

Chavira, Alicia
"Tienes que ser valiente": Mexicana migrants in a midwestern farm labor camp, 2165.

Chou, Chih-Ping
The criminality of female narcotics addicts: a causal modeling approach, 293.

Cisneros, Sandra
Cactus flowers: in search of Tejana feminist poetry, 542.
Do you know me?: I wrote THE HOUSE ON MANGO STREET, 543.
Ghosts and voices: writing from obsession, 544.
[Interview with] Sandra Cisneros, 545.
Living as a writer: choice and circumstance, 546.
Notes to a young(er) writer, 547.
On the solitary fate of being Mexican, female, wicked and thirty-three: an interview with writer Sandra Cisneros, 417.

Clark, Gary M.
Breast cancer prognosis in a mixed Caucasian-Hispanic population, 260.

Cochran, Jo, et al., eds.
Bearing witness/Sobreviviendo: an anthology of Native American/Latina art and literature, 383.

Cochran, Susan D.
Issues in the perception of AIDS risk and risk reduction activities by Black and Hispanic/Latina women, 177.

Codega, Susan A.
Coping behaviors of adolescent mothers: an exploratory study and comparison of Mexican-Americans and Anglos, 253.

Cohen, Elizabeth G.
Chicanas and Chicanos: barriers to progress in higher education, 1304.

Committee for the Development of Subject Access to Chicano Literatures
Chicano Periodical Index: a cumulative index to selected Chicano periodicals between 1967

--   --

and 1978, 4524.
Cook, Annabel Kirschner
    Diversity among Northwest Hispanics, 4372.
Cooney, Rosemary Santana
    The Mexican American female in the labor
        force, 1843.
    Nativity, national origin, and Hispanic female
        participation in the labor force, 2957.
    Sex-role attitudes and labor force
        participation among young Hispanic females
        and non-Hispanic white females, 313.
    Sex-role attitudes and labor force
        participation among young Hispanic females
        and non-Hispanic white females, 314.
Corbett, Kitty
    Drinking patterns and drinking-related
        problems of Mexican-American husbands and
        wives, 188.
Cordova, Marcella C.
    Women's rights: a Chicana's viewpoint, 2212.
Cordova, Teresa, et al., eds.
    Chicana voices: intersections of class, race,
        and gender, 1120.
Corpi, Lucha
    Entrevista con Lucha Corpi: poeta chicana,
        568.
    [Interview with] Lucha Corpi, 548.
Corrales, Ramona
    Las hermanas, 1260.
    Undocumented Hispanas in America, 3022.
Correa, Clara Sunderland
    The marital morality of Mexican women--an
        urban study, 2068.
Cortes, Carlos E.
    Chicanas in film: history of an image, 2471.
Cosand, Beverly J.
    Attributes of suicide in females, 248.
Cota-Robles de Suarez, Cecilia
    Sexual stereotypes--psychological and cultural
        survival: a description of child-rearing
        practices attributed to the Chicana (the
        Mexican American woman) and its
        psychological and cultural implications,
        1438.
Cota-Robles de Suarez, Cecilia, ed.
    Every woman's right: the right to quality
        education and economic independence, 1251.
Cotera, Marta P.
    Chicana caucus, 1154.
    The Chicana feminist, 2214.
    Chicana identity, 6504.
    Diosa y hembra, the history and heritage of
        Chicanas in the United States, 2727.
    ERA: the Latina challenge, 1941.
    Feminism: the Chicana and Anglo versions: a
        historical analysis, 254.
    Mexicano feminism, 2217.
    La nueva hispana y [sic] hispanidad, 1252.
    Profile on the Mexican American woman, 2728.
    Sexism in bilingual bicultural education, 700.
Cousins, Jennifer H.
    Maternal socialization of children's eating
        habits: strategies used by obese
        Mexican-American mothers, 1212.
Coye, Molly J.
    Birthweight of infants born to Hispanic women
        employed in agriculture, 2170.
Coyle, Laurie
    Women at Farah: an unfinished story, 2151.
Craver, Rebecca McDowell
    The impact of intimacy: Mexican-Anglo
        intermarriage in New Mexico 1821-1846, 59.
    The impact of intimacy: Mexican-Anglo
        intermarriage in New Mexico 1821-1846, 60.
Crawford, John F.
    Notes toward a new multicultural criticism:
        three works by women of color, 623.
Creswell, John L.
    Research brief: sex and ethnic differences in
        mathematics achievement of Black and
        Mexican-American adolescents, 768.
    Sex-related differences in the problem-solving
        abilities of rural Black, Anglo, and Chicano
        adolescents, 180.

Cristo, Martha H.
    Stress and coping among Mexican women, 1439.
Crocker, Elvira Valenzuela
    USE: Valenzuela-Crocker, Elvira
Cuellar, Israel
    Service delivery and mental health services
        for Chicano elders, 215.
Cuellar, Israel, et al.
    Clinical psychiatric case presentation;
        culturally responsive diagnostic formulation
        and treatment in an Hispanic female, 109.
Cummings, Michele
    Family planning among the urban poor: sexual
        politics and social policy, 258.
Cummings, Scott
    Family planning among the urban poor: sexual
        politics and social policy, 258.
Cunningham, Veronica
    [Interview with] Veronica Cunningham, 549.
Curiel, Barbara Brinson
    USE: Brinson-Pineda, Barbara
Curry Rodriguez, Julia E.
    Labor migration and familial responsibilities:
        experiences of Mexican women, 1844.
    Reconceptualizing undocumented labor
        immigration: the causes, impact and
        consequences in Mexican women's lives, 1845.
Curtis, Theodore T.
    Marital role orientation among Chicanos: an
        analysis of structural and cultural factors,
        3814.
Daggett, Andrea Stuhlman
    A comparison of occupational goal orientations
        of female Mexican-Americans and Anglo
        high-school seniors of the classes of 1972
        and 1980, 27.
Daly, Mary B.
    Breast cancer prognosis in a mixed
        Caucasian-Hispanic population, 260.
D'Andrea, Vaneeta-Marie
    Ethnic women: a critique of the literature,
        1971-1981, 673.
Darabi, Katherine F.
    USE: Fennelly, Katherine
Darabi, Katherine F., et al.
    USE: Fennelly, Katherine, et al.
Dario Salaz, Ruben
    The Chicana in American literature, 1191.
    The Chicana in American literature, 1192.
Davey, Becky
    Socioeconomic differences in rates of cesarean
        section, 286.
Davis, Cary
    U.S. Hispanics: changing the face of America,
        1749.
Davis, Sally M.
    Sexual knowledge, sexual interests, and
        sources of sexual information of rural and
        urban adolescents from three cultures, 746.
de Anda, Diane
    In their own words: the life experiences of
        Mexican-American and white pregnant
        adolescents and adolescent mothers, 261.
    Pregnancy and motherhood among Mexican
        American adolescents, 57.
    Sexuality, pregnancy, and motherhood among
        Mexican-American adolescents, 262.
    A study of the interaction of Hispanic junior
        high school students and their teachers,
        1700.
    Support networks for adolescent mothers, 948.
De Blassie, Richard R.
    The differences between personality inventory
        scores and self-rating in a sample of
        Hispanic subjects, 2661.
de Hoyos, Angela
    [Interview with] Angela de Hoyos, 550.
    Mujeres en el movimiento: platica de las
        mujeres de CARACOL, 1006.
De la Cruz, Jessie Lopez
    Jessie Lopez De la Cruz: the battle for
        farmworkers' rights, 161.
de la Fuente, Patricia
    The elliptic female presence as unifying force

Toward a democratic women's movement in the
United States, 2229.
Dungy, Claibourne I.
Breast feeding preference of Hispanic and
Anglo women, 267.
Personal preferences and ethnic variations
among Anglo and Hispanic breast and bottle
feeders, 519.
Duran Apodaca, Maria
North from Mexico, 719.
Duran, Flo
Having a job gives you some sort of power:
reflections of a Chicana working woman,
1728.
Duran, Isabelle Sandoval
Grounded theory study: Chicana administrators
in Colorado and New Mexico, 1013.
Duran, Lucy
Lucy Duran--wife, mother, and organizer, 163.
Duron, Clementina
Mexican women and labor conflict in Los
Angeles: the ILGWU dressmakers' strike of
1933, 2559.
Eberstein, Isaac W.
Patterns of marital instability among Mexican
Americans, Blacks, and Anglos, 277.
Recent changes in marital instability among
Mexican Americans: convergence with Black
and Anglo trends, 145.
Echaveste, Beatrice
In the shadow of the eagle: Huerta = A la
sombra del aguila: Huerta, 164.
Edelson, Rosalyn
The triple bias: rural, minority and female,
1740.
Eger, Ernestina
A bibliography of criticism of contemporary
Chicano literature, 553.
Ehrenreich, Barbara
Women in the global factory, 839.
Eisen, Marvin
Factors discriminating pregnancy resolution
decisions of unmarried adolescents, 12.
Factors predicting pregnancy resolution
decision satisfaction of unmarried
adolescents, 13.
Elsasser, Nan
Las mujeres: conversations from a Hispanic
community, 721.
Engle, Patricia L.
Prenatal and postnatal anxiety in women giving
birth in Los Angeles, 2397.
Enguidanos-Clark, Gloria M.
Acculturative stress and its contribution to
the development of depression in Hispanic
women, 62.
Enriquez, Evangelina
La Chicana: the Mexican-American woman, 2080.
Chicanas in the history of the Southwest, 371.
Chicanas in the struggle for unions, 2590.
Liberation, Chicana style: colonial roots of
feministas chicanas, 1157.
Towards a definition of, and critical
approaches to, Chicano(a) literature, 2231.
Enriquez-White, Celia
Attitudes of Hispanic and Anglo women managers
toward women in management, 269.
Erevia, Angela
Quinceanera, 1061.
Eribes, Richard A.
Employment of women by cities in the
Southwest, 1862.
Erickson, Pamela Irene
Pregnancy and childbirth among Mexican origin
teenagers in Los Angeles, 2398.
Escalante, Alicia
Chicana Welfare Rights vs. the Talmadge
amendment, 1135.
A letter from the Chicana Welfare Rights
organization, 1136.
Escalante, Virginia
Inside the world of Latinas, 722.
Escobedo, Theresa Herrera, ed.
Thematic issue: Chicana issues, 1753.

Esparza, Mariana Ochoa
The impact of adult education on
Mexican-American women, 131.
Espin, Oliva M.
Cultural and historical influences on
sexuality in Hispanic/Latin women:
implications for psychotherapy, 3026.
Perceptions of sexual discrimination among
college women in Latin America and the
United States, 1276.
Spiritual power and the mundane world:
Hispanic female healers in urban U.S.
communities, 1526.
Espinosa, Ann
Hispanas: our resourses [sic] for the
eighties, 634.
Espinosa-Larsen, Anita
Machismo: another view, 3715.
Estrada, Esther R.
The importance of the 1980 census, 1076.
Estrada, Iliad
Hispanic feminists meet--it's a trip, 1353.
Estrada, Rosa Omega
A study of the attitudes of Texas Mexican
American women toward higher education, 481.
Even, Brenda
Work and sex-role attitudes in relation to
education and other characteristics, 486.
Exezidis, Roxane H.
Research brief: sex and ethnic differences in
mathematics achievement of Black and
Mexican-American adolescents, 768.
Facio, Elisa "Linda"
Constraints, resources, and self-definition: a
case study of Chicano older women, 217.
Gender and aging: a case of Mexicana/Chicana
elderly, 218.
The interaction of age and gender in Chicana
older lives: a case study of Chicana elderly
in a senior citizen center, 143.
Fajardo, Ramon
Liberacion femenil: cancion corrido, 1381.
Liberacion femenil: cancion corrido, 1382.
Falasco, Dee
Economic and fertility differences between
legal and undocumented migrant Mexican
families: possible effects of immigration
policy changes, 1738.
Falicov, Celia Jaes
Mexican families, 63.
Fanelli-Kuczmarski, Marie T., et al.
Folate status of Mexican American, Cuban, and
Puerto Rican women, 1417.
Farkas, George
White, Black, and Hispanic female youths in
central city labor markets, 270.
Farrell, Janice
Marital status and depression among Mexican
Americans, 1575.
Marriage and health: a three-generation study
of Mexican Americans, 3817.
Felice, Marianne E., et al.
Clinical observations of Mexican-American,
Caucasian, and Black pregnant teenagers,
271.
Fennelly, Katherine
Childbearing among Hispanics in the United
States: an annotated bibliography, 14.
Childbearing among young Latino women in the
United States, 1973.
The cross-cultural study of fertility among
Hispanic adolescents in the Americas, 1444.
Early childbearing and employment among young
Mexican origin, Black, and white women, 312.
El embarazo precoz: childbearing among
Hispanic teenagers in the United States,
2404.
Hispanic adolescent fertility, 2405.
Fennelly, Katherine, et al.
The effect of maternal age on the well-being
of children, 144.
Fenster, Laura
Birthweight of infants born to Hispanic women
employed in agriculture, 2170.

Fernandez, Celestino
  Chicano-Anglo intermarriage in Arizona,
    1960-1980: an exploratory study of eight
    counties, 375.
Fernandez Kelly, Maria
  "Chavalas de maquiladora": a study of the
    female labor force in Ciudad Juarez'
    offshore production plants, 835.
  Economic restructuring in the United States:
    Hispanic women in the garment and
    electronics industries, 929.
  For we are sold, I and my people: women and
    industry in Mexico's frontier, 836.
  Invisible amidst the glitter: Hispanic women
    in the Southern California electronics
    industry, 1827.
  The making of an underground economy: Hispanic
    women, home work, and the advanced
    capitalist state, 1004.
  The 'maquila' women, 837.
  Mexican border industrialization, female labor
    force participation and migration, 820.
Fielder, Eve P.
  Fertility and fertility-related behavior among
    Mexican-American and non-Hispanic white
    female adolescents, 238.
  In their own words: the life experiences of
    Mexican-American and white pregnant
    adolescents and adolescent mothers, 261.
  Sexuality, pregnancy, and motherhood among
    Mexican-American adolescents, 262.
Finkelstein, Jordan W.
  Sanitary product use by white, Black, and
    Mexican American women, 272.
Fischer, Nancy A.
  Ethnic integration, socioeconomic status, and
    fertility among Mexican Americans, 451.
Fisher, Ellen
  Racial differences among shelter residents: a
    comparison of Anglo, Black, and Hispanic
    battered, 284.
Fisher, Michael
  Maternal factors and low birthweight infants:
    a comparison of Blacks with
    Mexican-Americans, 772.
Flaskerud, Jacquelyn H.
  Black and Latina womens' AIDS related
    knowledge, attitudes, and practices, 175.
Fleming, Marilyn B.
  Problems experienced by Anglo, Hispanic and
    Navajo Indian women college students, 273.
Flores, Estevan T.
  Chicanos and sociological research: 1970-1980,
    676.
  The migration and settlement of undocumented
    women, 1840.
Flores, Francisca
  Comision Femenil Mexicana, 15.
  Comision Femenil Mexicana, 16.
  Conference of Mexican women un remolino, 1554.
  Equality, 274.
  A reaction to discussions on the Talmadge
    Amendment to the Social Security Act, 1137.
  A reaction to discussions on the Talmadge
    Amendment to the Social Security Act, 1138.
Flores, Henry
  Some different thoughts concerning "machismo",
    3718.
Flores, Laura Jane
  A study of successful completion and attrition
    among Chicana Title VII Bilingual Education
    Doctoral Fellows at selected Southwestern
    universities, 31.
Flores Magon, Ricardo
  A la mujer = To women, 4024.
Flores, Rosalie
  The new Chicana and machismo, 2870.
Floyd, Gloria Jo Wade
  An exploration of the finding and seeking of
    meaning in life and the Mexican-American
    nurse's mood state, 3933.
Forste, Renata T.
  Initiation of sexual activity among female
    adolescents, 275.

Fox, Linda C.
  Obedience and rebellion: re-vision of Chicana
    myths of motherhood, 2242.
Franco, Juan N.
  Counseling Mexican-American women, 1407.
  The differences between personality inventory
    scores and self-rating in a sample of
    Hispanic subjects, 2661.
  Ethnicity, division of household tasks and
    equity in marital roles: a comparison of
    Anglo and Mexican American couples, 3830.
Franklin, Gerald S.
  Group psychotherapy for elderly female
    Hispanic outpatients, 220.
Franks, Adele L.
  Isoniazid hepatitis among pregnant and
    postpartum Hispanic patients, 2407.
Fregoso, Rosa Linda
  La quinceanera of Chicana counter aesthetics,
    169.
Freier, Michelle Cyd
  Psychosocial and physiological influences on
    birth outcomes among women of Mexican origin
    or descent, 2408.
Friaz, Guadalupe
  Chicanas in the workforce = Chicanas en la
    fuerza de trabajo: "Working 9 to 5", 1852.
Frisbie, William Parker
  Marital instability trends among Mexican
    Americans as compared to Blacks and Anglos:
    new evidence, 276.
  Mexican American intermarriage in a
    nonmetropolitan context, 141.
  Mexican American intermarriage in a
    nonmetropolitan context, 142.
  Patterns of marital instability among Mexican
    Americans, Blacks, and Anglos, 277.
  Recent changes in marital instability among
    Mexican Americans: convergence with Black
    and Anglo trends, 145.
  Variation in patterns of marital instability
    among Hispanics, 1419.
Frith, Sandra
  Mexican-American professional women: role
    satisfaction differences in single and
    multiple role lifestyles, 1034.
Fu, Victoria R.
  A development study of ethnic self-concept
    among pre-adolescent girls, 1324.
Fuentes, Annette
  Women in the global factory, 839.
Furth, Pauline
  The health beliefs of Mexican, Mexican
    American and Anglo American women, 251.
Galindo, Letticia
  Perceptions of pachuquismo and use of
    Calo/pachuco Spanish by various Chicana
    women, 1145.
Gallegos, Placida I.
  Emerging leadership among Hispanic women: the
    role of expressive behavior and nonverbal
    skill, 279.
Gallegos y Chavez, Ester
  The northern New Mexican woman: a changing
    silhouette, 2872.
Galloway, Irma Nell
  Trends in the employment of minority women as
    administrators in Texas public
    schools--1976-1981, 427.
Gamio, Manuel
  Senora Flores de Andrade, 605.
Gandara, Patricia
  Passing through the eye of the needle:
    high-achieving Chicanas, 32.
Garcia, Alma M.
  The development of Chicana feminist discourse,
    1970-1980, 280.
  The development of Chicana feminist discourse,
    1970-1980, 281.
  El femenismo [sic] chicano: un panorama
    historico, 2246.
  Studying Chicanas: bringing women into the
    frame of Chicano Studies, 1123.
Garcia, Anna M.

Economic restructuring in the United States: Hispanic women in the garment and electronics industries, 929.

Invisible amidst the glitter: Hispanic women in the Southern California electronics industry, 1827.

The making of an underground economy: Hispanic women, home work, and the advanced capitalist state, 1004.

Garcia Castro, Mary
Migrant women: issues in organization and solidarity, 3250.

Garcia, Chris
La violacion sexual: the reality of rape, 483.

Garcia, Herman
Sex-related speech accommodations among Mexican-American bilinguals: a pilot study of language choice in customer-server interactions, 706.

Garcia, Mario T.
The Chicana in American history: the Mexican women of El Paso, 1880-1920 - a case study, 110.
La familia: the Mexican immigrant family, 1900-1930, 452.
Family and gender in Chicano and border studies research, 204.

Garcia, Norma Varisto de
Education and the Spanish-speaking woman: a sad reality, 1641.

Garcia-Ayvens, Francisco, ed.
The Chicano index: a comprehensive subject, author, and title index to Chicano materials, 3092.
Chicano Periodical Index: a cumulative index to selected Chicano periodicals between 1967 and 1978, 4523.

Garcia-Bahne, Betty
La Chicana and the Chicano family, 1489.

Garcia-Camarillo, Mia
Mujeres en el movimiento: platica de las mujeres de CARACOL, 1007.

Gardea, Corina
A comparison of behavioral characteristics of Hispanic and Anglo female administrators in the resolution of critical incident situations, 282.

Garn, Stanley M.
Reproductive histories of low weight girls and women, 2409.

Garza, M'Liss
USE: Garza-Livingston, M'Liss

Garza, M'Liss, ed.
USE: Garza-Livingston, M'Liss, ed.

Garza, Raymond T.
Attributions for the occupational success/failure of ethnic minority and nonminority women, 321.

Garza-Livingston, M'Liss
Annotated bibliography of selected materials on la mujer y la Chicana, 677.
Annotated bibliography of selected materials on la mujer y la Chicana, 678.

Garza-Livingston, M'Liss, ed.
Chicana journals, 3207.

Gaspar de Alba, Alice
Three times a woman: Chicana poetry, 4551.

Gates, Connie
Health and social needs of women farmworkers: receiving maternity care at a migrant health center, 2178.

Gettman, Dawn
Women, mental health, and the workplace in a transnational setting, 840.

Gibbs, Jewelle Taylor
Personality patterns of delinquent females: ethnic and sociocultural variations, 1976.

Gibbs, Ronald S.
Prevalence of asymptomatic hepatitis-B infection in pregnant Mexican-American women, 1666.

Gibson, Guadalupe
Hispanic women: stress and mental health issues, 1445.

Gilbert, Kathleen R.
Divorce likelihood among Anglos and Mexican Americans, 308.

Gilbert, M. Jean
Alcohol consumption patterns in immigrant and later generation Mexican American women, 64.

Glass, Jennifer
Household structure and labor-force participation of Black, Hispanic, and white mothers, 335.

Glenn, Evelyn Nakano
Racial ethnic women's labor: the intersection of race, gender and class oppression, 428.

Golding, Jacqueline M.
Division of household labor, strain, and depressive symptoms among Mexican Americans and non-Hispanic whites, 283.

Goldman, Shifra M.
Arte Chicano: a comprehensive annotated bibliography of Chicano art, 1965-1981, 384.
Artistas chicanas texanas, 404.
Artistas en accion: conferencia de las mujeres chicanas, 405.
Mujeres de California: Latin American women artists, 406.
Trabajadoras mexicanas y chicanas en las artes visuales, 385.
Women artists of Texas: MAS = More + Artists + Women = MAS, 379.

Goldsmith, Raquel Rubio
La Mexicana/Chicana, 1257.
Shipwrecked in the desert: a short history of the adventures and struggles for survival of the Mexican Sisters of the House of the Providence in Douglas, Arizona during their first twenty-two years of existence (1927-1949), 1062.

Gomez, Alma, ed.
Cuentos: stories by Latinas, 5453.

Gomez, Ana Nieto
USE: Nieto Gomez de Lazarin, Anna

Gomez-Quinones, Juan
Questions within women's historiography, 2709.

Gondolf, Edward W.
Racial differences among shelter residents: a comparison of Anglo, Black, and Hispanic battered, 284.

Gonzales, Erlinda
La muerte de un refran, 2669.

Gonzales, Rebecca
[Interview with] Rebecca Gonzales, 554.

Gonzales, Sylvia Alicia
The Chicana in literature, 1955.
La Chicana: Malinche or virgin?, 3781.
The Chicana perspective: a design for self-awareness, 1142.
Hispanic American voluntary organizations, 396.
The Latina feminist: where we've been, where we're going, 1356.
Toward a feminist pedagogy for Chicana self-actualization, 1163.

Gonzales-Berry, Erlinda, ed.
Las mujeres hablan: an anthology of Nuevo Mexicana writers, 4348.

Gonzalez, Alex
Sex roles of the traditional Mexican family: a comparison of Chicano and Anglo students' attitudes, 285.

Gonzalez, Anna M.
Sex roles among Chicanos: stereotypes, challenges and changes, 2627.

Gonzalez, Deena J.
The widowed women of Santa Fe: assessments on the lives of an unmarried population, 1850-80, 2053.
The widowed women of Santa Fe: assessments on the lives of an unmarried population, 1850-80, 2054.

Gonzalez del Valle, Amalia
Group therapy with aged Latino women: a pilot project and study, 221.

Gonzalez, Francisca
Steps for developing an idea into a public

U.S. Hispanics: changing the face of America, 1749.
Hawley, Peggy
Work and sex-role attitudes in relation to education and other characteristics, 486.
Hayghe, Howard
Married couples: work and income patterns, 1859.
Hazuda, Helen P., et al.
Employment status and women's protection against coronary heart disease, 289.
Heard, Martha E.
The theatre of Denise Chavez: interior landscapes with SABOR NUEVOMEXICANO, 972.
Heathcote, Olivia D.
Sex stereotyping in Mexican reading primers, 1321.
Heaton, Tim B.
Initiation of sexual activity among female adolescents, 275.
Hedderson, John J.
Fertility and mortality, 878.
Heer, David
Economic and fertility differences between legal and undocumented migrant Mexican families: possible effects of immigration policy changes, 1738.
Henderson, Nancy
Perinatal service needs of Hispanic women with diabetes, 1593.
Henderson, Ronald W.
Mexican American perceptions of parent and teacher roles in child development, 1214.
Hendricks, Mary Lee
Factors relating to the continuation of breast feeding by low income Hispanic women, 912.
Hernandez, Antonia A.
Chicanas and the issue of involuntary sterilization: reforms needed to protect informed consent, 749.
Hernandez, Beatriz Johnston
USE: Johnston Hernandez, Beatriz
Hernandez H., Alberto
La industria maquiladora en Mexico: bibliografia, directorio e investigaciones recientes = Border assembly industry and recent research, 670.
Mujeres fronterizas en la industria maquiladora, 833.
Hernandez, Ines
Sara Estela Ramirez: the early twentieth century Texas-Mexican poet, 557.
Sara Estela Ramirez: sembradora, 558.
Hernandez, Leodoro
The socialization of a Chicano family, 66.
Hernandez, Lisa, ed.
Palabras chicanas: an undergraduate anthology, 3452.
Hernandez, Lucha Corpi
USE: Corpi, Lucha
Hernandez, Maria Luz
Hermanas, 1064.
Hernandez, Patricia
Lives of Chicana activists: the Chicano student movement (a case study), 968.
Herrera-Sobek, Maria
The acculturation process of the Chicana in the corrido, 67.
The acculturation process of the Chicana in the corrido, 68.
Beyond stereotypes: the critical analysis of Chicana literature, 3453.
The Mexican corrido: a feminist analysis, 1385.
The politics of rape: sexual transgression in Chicana fiction, 1235.
Three times a woman: Chicana poetry, 4551.
The treacherous woman archetype: a structuring agent in the corrido, 1386.
Women as metaphor in the patriarchal structure of HEART OF AZTLAN, 207.
Herrera-Sobek, Maria, ed.
Chicana creativity and criticism: charting new frontiers in American literature, 386.

Hershatter, Gail
Women at Farah: an unfinished story, 2151.
Hinkle, Dennis E.
A development study of ethnic self-concept among pre-adolescent girls, 1324.
Hintz, Joy
Valiant migrant women = Las mujeres valerosas, 650.
Hogeland, Chris
Dreams lost, dreams found: undocumented women in the land of opportunity, 651.
Holck, Susan E.
Lung cancer mortality and smoking habits: Mexican-American women, 290.
Holck, Susan E., et al.
Alcohol consumption among Mexican American and Anglo women: results of a survey along the U.S.-Mexico border, 190.
Need for family planning services among Anglo and Hispanic women in the United States counties bordering Mexico, 292.
Holland, Abby
Ethnicity, locus of control for family planning, and pregnancy counselor credibility, 241.
Holscher, Louis M.
Chicano-Anglo intermarriage in Arizona, 1960-1980: an exploratory study of eight counties, 375.
Hispanic intermarriage: changing trends in New Mexico, 3149.
Honig, Emily
Women at Farah: an unfinished story, 2151.
Hoppe, Sue K.
Divorce likelihood among Anglos and Mexican Americans, 308.
Marital satisfaction in three generations of Mexican Americans, 149.
Horn, Marjorie C.
Religion and fertility in the United States: the importance of marriage patterns and Hispanic origin, 1069.
Horno-Delgado, Asuncion, et al., eds
Breaking boundaries: Latina writing and critical readings, 3457.
Horowitz, Ruth
Femininity and womanhood: virginity, unwed motherhood, and violence, 750.
Passion, submission and motherhood: the negotiation of identity by unmarried innercity Chicanas, 647.
Hovell, Melbourne F., et al.
Occupational health risks for Mexican women: the case of the maquiladora along the Mexican-United States border, 841.
Howell-Martinez, Vicky
The influence of gender roles on political socialization: an experimental study of Mexican-American children, 4642.
Hser, Yih-Ing
Addicted women and crime, 1409.
The criminality of female narcotics addicts: a causal modeling approach, 293.
Huerta, Dolores
Dolores Huerta talks about Republicans, Cesar, children and her home town, 165.
Dolores Huerta talks about Republicans, Cesar, children and her home town, 166.
In the shadow of the eagle: Huerta = A la sombra del aguila: Huerta, 164.
Hunt, Isabelle F., et al.
Zinc supplementation during pregnancy: zinc concentration of serum and hair from low-income women of Mexican descent, 3684.
Zinc supplementation during pregnancy in low-income teenagers of Mexican descent: effects on selected blood constituents and on progress and outcome of pregnancy, 2417.
Hunter, Kathleen I.
Sterilization among American Indian and Chicano mothers, 4286.
Hurtado, Aida
Midwife practices in Hidalgo County, Texas, 2646.

self-reported assertiveness, 439.
Klor de Alva, J. Jorge
Chicana history and historical significance:
some theoretical considerations, 1124.
Kluessendorf, Avonelle Donneeta
Role conflict in Mexican-American college
women, 1279.
Kokinos, Mary
Infant feeding practices of migrant
Mexican-American families in Northern
California, 914.
Kolody, Bohdan
Migration and mental health: an empirical test
of depression risk factors among immigrant
Mexican women, 103.
The relationship of marital status, confidant
support, and depression among Mexican
immigrant women, 1585.
Koreck, Maria Teresa
Silences: "Hispanics", AIDS, and sexual
practices, 171.
Korslund, Mary K.
A development study of ethnic self-concept
among pre-adolescent girls, 1324.
Kossoudji, Sherrie
The labor market experience of female
migrants: the case of temporary Mexican
migration to the U.S., 1863.
Kranau, Edgar J.
Acculturation and the Hispanic woman:
attitudes toward women, sex-role
attribution, sex-role behavior, and
demographics, 70.
Kraus, Jess F.
Attributes of suicide in females, 248.
Krause, Neal
Employment and psychological well-being in
Mexican American women, 488.
Gender roles, illness, and illness behavior in
a Mexican American population, 2065.
Kreutzer, Jill
Coping behaviors of adolescent mothers: an
exploratory study and comparison of
Mexican-Americans and Anglos, 253.
Krueger, Victoria
Medicine women, curanderas, and women doctors,
364.
Kushner, Kathy
White, Black, and Hispanic female youths in
central city labor markets, 270.
La Duke, Betty
Trivial lives: artists Yolanda Lopez and
Patricia Rodriguez, 408.
La Monica, Grace
A comparative study of female Mexican and
American working nurses in the border
corridor, 297.
Lampe, Philip E.
Female Mexican Americans: minority within a
minority, 455.
Laosa, Luis M.
Maternal teaching strategies and cognitive
styles in Chicano families, 1269.
Maternal teaching strategies in Chicano and
Anglo-American families: the influence of
culture and education on maternal behavior,
298.
Lara-Cantu, M. Asuncion
Positive and negative factors in the
measurement of sex roles: findings from a
Mexican sample, 659.
A sex role inventory with scales for
"machismo" and "self-sacrificing woman",
3729.
Lara-Cea, Helen
Notes on the use of parish registers in the
reconstruction of Chicana history in
California prior to 1850, 952.
Larguia, Isabel
Toward a science of women's liberation, 2262.
LaVelle, Marquisa
Reproductive histories of low weight girls and
women, 2409.
Lavrin, Asuncion

El segundo sexo en Mexico: experiencia,
estudio e introspeccion, 1983-1987, 369.
Lawhn, Juanita
USE: Luna-Lawhn, Juanita
Lawrence, Alberto Augusto
Traditional attitudes toward marriage, marital
adjustment, acculturation, and self-esteem
of Mexican-American and Mexican wives, 71.
Leal, Luis
Arquetipos femeninos en la literatura
mexicana, 3458.
Female archetypes in Mexican literature, 3459.
La soldadera en la narrativa de la Revolucion,
122.
Leblanc, Donna Marie
Quality of maternity care in rural Texas,
2423.
Lee, Bun Song
A comparison of fertility adaptation between
Mexican immigrants to the U.S. and internal
migrants in Mexico, 2424.
Lee, Valerie
Achievement and educational aspirations among
Hispanic female high school students:
comparison between public and Catholic
schools, 37.
Leon, Ana M., et al.
Self-help support groups for Hispanic mothers,
2067.
Leonard, Jonathan S.
The effect of unions on the employment of
Blacks, Hispanics, and women, 791.
LeVine, Sarah Ethel
The marital morality of Mexican women--an
urban study, 2068.
Levy Oved, Albert
Las maquiladoras en Mexico, 848.
Limon, Jose E. [anthropologist]
La Llorona, the third legend of greater
Mexico: cultural symbols, women, and the
political unconscious, 2263.
La Llorona, the third legend of greater
Mexico: cultural symbols, women, and the
political unconscious, 2264.
"La vieja Ines," a Mexican folkgame: a
research note, 1208.
Lindemann, Constance
The fertility related behavior of Mexican
American adolescents, 2425.
Lindstrom, Naomi
Four representative Hispanic women poets of
Central Texas: a portrait of plurality, 658.
Linn, Margaret W.
Sterilization among American Indian and
Chicano mothers, 4286.
Lizarraga, Sylvia S.
Chicana women writers and their audience, 560.
Hacia una teoria para la liberacion de la
mujer, 2265.
Images of women in Chicano literature by men,
3568.
"La mujer doblamente explotada: "On the Road
to Texas: Pete Fonseca", 3462.
La mujer ingeniosa, 3463.
The patriarchal ideology in "La noche que se
apagaron las luces", 3464.
The resourceful woman in THERE ARE NO MADMEN
HERE, 3465.
Lockert, Lucia Fox
Chicanas: their voices, their lives, 4117.
Loeb, Catherine
La Chicana: a bibliographic survey, 680.
Loheyde, Katherine Jones
The Hispanic woman graduate student: barriers
to mentoring in higher education, 1646.
Lomas, Clara
Libertad de no procrear: la voz de la mujer en
"A una madre de nuestro tiempo" de Margarita
Cota-Cardenas, 3.
Libertad de no procrear: la voz de la mujer en
"A una madre de nuestro tiempo" de Margarita
Cota-Cardenas, 4.
Mexican precursors of Chicana feminist
writing, 561.

Lomas Garza, Carmen
  Altares: arte espiritual del hogar, 199.
  Carmen Lomas Garza: traditional and
    non-traditional, 412.
Lomeli, Francisco A.
  Chicana novelists in the process of creating
    fictive voices, 562.
Long, John M.
  Cultural styles and adolescent sex role
    perceptions: an exploration of responses to
    a value picture projective test, 4771.
Longeaux y Vasquez, Enriqueta
  The Mexican American woman, 5373.
  Soy Chicana primero, 1165.
  Soy Chicana primero, 1166.
  The woman of La Raza, 123.
  The woman of La Raza, 124.
Lopez, Cynthia M.
  Ethnic identity and cultural awareness among
    the offspring of Mexican interethnic
    marriages, 91.
Lopez, David
  Religiosity and fertility: the case of
    Chicanas, 1072.
Lopez, Gloria Ann
  Job satisfaction of the Mexican American woman
    administrator in higher education, 1017.
Lopez, Martha
  Chicana employment--options for the future,
    1836.
Lopez, Norma Y.
  Hispanic teenage pregnancy: overview and
    implications, 2426.
Lopez, Sonia A.
  The role of the Chicana within the student
    movement, 1167.
Lopez-Garza, Maria C.
  Toward a reconceptualization of women's
    economic activities: the informal sector in
    urban Mexico, 1866.
Lopez-Gonzalez, Aralia, et al., eds.
  Mujer y literatura mexicana y chicana:
    culturas en contacto, 3469.
Lopez-Trevino, Maria Elena
  A radio model: a community strategy to address
    the problems and needs of Mexican-American
    women farmworkers, 1266.
Lorenz, Frederick O.
  The effects of employment and marital
    relations on depression among Mexican
    American women, 1578.
Lorenzana, Noemi
  La Chicana: transcending the old and carving
    out a new life and self-image, 1077.
  Hijas de Aztlan, 2890.
Lorig, Kate R.
  Health and illness perceptions of the Chicana,
    1457.
Loustaunau, Martha Oehmke
  Hispanic widows and their support systems in
    the Mesilla Valley of southern New Mexico,
    1910-40, 1491.
Lozano-Bull, Irma
  Acculturative stress in Mexican-American
    women, 72.
Lucero, Aileen
  Chicano sex role attitudes: a comparative
    study of sex differences in an urban barrio,
    490.
  Contemporary curanderismo: a study of mental
    health agency and home clientele of a
    practicing curandera, 1529.
Lucero, Marcela Christine
  Resources for the Chicana feminist scholar,
    1125.
  The socio-historical implication of the valley
    as a metaphor in three Colorado Chicana
    poets, 563.
Lucero Trujillo, Marcela
  The terminology of machismo, 1143.
Luna-Lawhn, Juanita
  EL REGIDOR and LA PRENSA: impediments to
    women's self-definition, 3570.
  Victorian attitudes affecting the Mexican

woman writing in LA PRENSA during the early
  1900s and the Chicana of the 1980s, 2274.
Lyson, Thomas A.
  The fotonovela as a cultural bridge of
    Hispanic women in the United States, 2536.
MacAdams, Elizabeth A.
  Acculturation and perceived family
    decision-making input among Mexican American
    wives, 83.
MacCorquodale, Patricia
  Mexican-American women and mathematics:
    participation, aspirations, and achievement,
    38.
  Social influences on the participation of
    Mexican-American women in science: final
    report, 377.
Macias, Anna
  Against all odds: the feminist movement in
    Mexico to 1940, 1045.
MacKenzie, Kyle
  Las mujeres: conversations from a Hispanic
    community, 721.
Macklin, June
  "All the good and bad in this world": women,
    traditional medicine, and Mexican American
    culture, 1530.
  Virgen de Guadalupe and the American dream:
    the melting pot bubbles on in Toledo, Ohio,
    456.
MacManus, Susan A.
  A longitudinal examination of political
    participation rates of Mexican-American
    females, 5939.
Madrid, Sandra Emilia
  The effects of socialization on goal
    actualization of public school Chicana
    principals and superintendents, 1019.
Maez, Angelita
  The effects of two parent training programs on
    parental attitudes and self-concepts of
    Mexican American mothers, 491.
Magnus, Peter D.
  Breastfeeding among Hispanics [letter], 915.
Major, Linda Borsch
  The psyche: changing role creates Latina's
    world of conflict, 492.
MALDEF
  USE: Mexican American Legal Defense and
    Education Fund (MALDEF)
Malvido, Elsa
  El uso del cuerpo femenino en la epoca
    colonial mexicana a traves de los estudios
    de demografia historica, 3839.
Manzanedo, Hector Garcia
  Health and illness perceptions of the Chicana,
    1457.
Marcum, John P.
  Ethnic integration, socioeconomic status, and
    fertility among Mexican Americans, 451.
Mares, Renee
  La pinta: the myth of rehabilitation, 4735.
Margolis, Eric
  Tending the beets: campesinas and the Great
    Western Sugar Company, 2176.
Marin, Barbara Van Oss
  Cigarette smoking among San Francisco
    Hispanics: the role of acculturation and
    gender, 73.
Marin, Barbara Van Oss, et al.
  Health care utilization by low-income clients
    of a community clinic: an archival study,
    1265.
Marin, Christine
  La Asociacion Hispano-Americana de Madres y
    Esposas: Tucson's Mexican American women in
    World War II, 435.
Marin, Gerardo
  Cigarette smoking among San Francisco
    Hispanics: the role of acculturation and
    gender, 73.
Markides, Kyriakos S.
  Aging, sex-role orientation and adjustment: a
    three-generations study of Mexican
    Americans, 148.

Consequences of gender differentials in life expectancy for Black and Hispanic Americans, 224.

Employment and psychological well-being in Mexican American women, 488.

Gender roles, illness, and illness behavior in a Mexican American population, 2065.

Marital satisfaction in three generations of Mexican Americans, 149.

Marital status and depression among Mexican Americans, 1575.

Marriage and health: a three-generation study of Mexican Americans, 3817.

Well-being in the postparental stage in Mexican-American women, 156.

Markides, Kyriakos S., et al.
Sample representativeness in a three-generation study of Mexican Americans, 150.

Marquez, Evelina
La tarea de la mujer es la liberacion, 2276.
Women's task is to gain liberation, 1082.

Marquez, Maria Teresa, ed.
Las mujeres hablan: an anthology of Nuevo Mexicana writers, 4348.

Marsh, Nancy B.
Sex, age, and cultural differences in self-reported assertiveness, 439.

Marshall, Maria Sandra Gonzalez
The childbearing beliefs and practices of pregnant Mexican-American adolescents living in Southwest border regions, 74.

Martin, Jeanette
The triple bias: rural, minority and female, 1740.

Martin, Patricia Preciado
USE: Preciado Martin, Patricia

Martinez Cruz, Rosa, ed.
Essays on la mujer, 5554.

Martinez, Demetria
Three times a woman: Chicana poetry, 4551.

Martinez, Diana
The double bind, 1020.

Martinez, Douglas R.
Hispanic origin women in the U.S., 1803.

Martinez, Elisa A.
Sharing her tiny pieces of the past, 608.

Martinez, Elizabeth
Chicanas and Mexicanas within a transnational working class: theoretical perspectives, 3318.
Chicanas and Mexicanas within a transnational working class: theoretical perspectives, 3322.
Theoretical perspectives on Chicanas, Mexicanas and the transnational working class, 834.

Martinez, Estella A.
Child behavior in Mexican American/Chicano families: maternal teaching and child-rearing practices, 75.

Martinez, Julio A.
[Bornstein-Somoza, Miriam], 529.

Martinez, Marco Antonio
Conversational asymmetry between Mexican mothers and children, 301.

Martinez, Olivia
The three Rs of Chicana leadership, 3379.

Martinez, Ruben
AIDS in the Latino community, 176.
Race, gender and self-esteem among youth, 1330.

Martinez, Thomas M.
Alicia in Wonderland: Chicana drug addicts, 1708.

Martinez, Virginia
Chicanas and the law, 128.

Martinez-Metcalf, Rosario
Concerns of Hispanic community college women, 1307.

Martorell, Reynaldo
Incidence and duration of breast-feeding in Mexican-American infants, 1970-1982, 913.

Mary, Nancy L.
Reactions of Black, Hispanic, and white mothers to having a child with handicaps, 302.

Mason, Terry
Symbolic strategies for change: a discussion of the Chicana women's movement, 117.

Mason, Theresa Hope
Experience and meaning: an interpretive study of family and gender ideologies among a sample of Mexican-American women of two generations, 151.

Mata, Alberto Guardiola
Rural female adolescent dissatisfaction, support and helpseeking, 191.

Matsuda, Gema
La Chicana organizes: the Comision Femenil Mexicana in perspective, 815.

Matute-Bianchi, Maria Eugenia
A Chicana in academe, 1620.

Mayers, Raymond Sanchez
Use of folk medicine by elderly Mexican-American women, 152.

Maymi, Carmen R.
Fighting to open the doors to opportunity, 927.

Mays, Vicki M.
Issues in the perception of AIDS risk and risk reduction activities by Black and Hispanic/Latina women, 177.

McCaughan, Ed
Chicanas and Mexicanas within a transnational working class: theoretical perspectives, 3318.
Chicanas and Mexicanas within a transnational working class: theoretical perspectives, 3322.
Theoretical perspectives on Chicanas, Mexicanas and the transnational working class, 834.

McClelland, Judith Raymond
The relationship of independence to achievement: a comparative study of Hispanic women, 440.

McCracken, Ellen
Latina narrative and politics of signification: articulation, antagonism, and populist rupture, 1236.
Sandra Cisneros' THE HOUSE ON MANGO STREET: community-oriented introspection and the demystification of patriarchal violence, 1237.

McDuff, Mary Ann
Mexican-American women: a three-generational study of attitudes and behaviors, 76.

McFerron, J. Richard
Racial differences among shelter residents: a comparison of Anglo, Black, and Hispanic battered, 284.

McGuire, William L.
Breast cancer prognosis in a mixed Caucasian-Hispanic population, 260.

McKenna, Teresa
Facts and figures on Hispanic Americans, women, and education, 1765.
Select bibliography on Hispanic women and education, 681.

McKenna, Teresa, ed.
The broken web: the educational experience of Hispanic American women, 39.

McRipley, Bernadine G.
Racial/ethnic Presbyterian women: in search of community, 4719.

Medina, Cecilia
Chicanas live in Aztlan also, 2280.

Medina Gonzales, Esther
Sisterhood, 495.

Meier, Matt S.
Mexican American biographies: a historical dictionary, 1836-1987, 730.

Meinhardt, Kenneth
Marital disruption and the prevalence of depressive symptomatology among Anglos and Mexican Americans, 339.

Melgoza, Bertha

Moreno, Dorinda
    The image of the Chicana and the La Raza
        woman, 2762.
Moreno, Jose Adan
    Carmen Lomas Garza: traditional and
        non-traditional, 412.
Moreno, Maria
    I'm talking for justice, 732.
Morrison, Peter A.
    Beyond stereotypes: who becomes a single
        teenage mother?, 2368.
    Teenagers willing to consider single
        parenthood: who is at greatest risk?, 762.
Mosher, William D.
    Religion and fertility in the United States:
        the importance of marriage patterns and
        Hispanic origin, 1069.
Muhs, William F.
    Fears of success and women employees, 1881.
Mujeres en Marcha, University of California,
    Berkeley
    Chicanas in the 80s: unsettled issues, 1359.
Mullen, Julia Ann
    Black, Anglo, and Chicana women's construction
        of mental illness, 305.
Munoz, Daniel G.
    Identifying areas of stress for Chicano
        undergraduates, 42.
Murguia, Edward
    Age differences of spouses in Mexican American
        intermarriage: exploring the cost of
        minority assimilation, 147.
    Chicano intermarriage: a theoretical and
        empirical study, 458.
    Intermarriage of Mexican Americans, 81.
    Mexican American intermarriage in a
        nonmetropolitan context, 141.
    Mexican American intermarriage in a
        nonmetropolitan context, 142.
Myres, Sandra Lynn
    Mexican Americans and westering Anglos: a
        feminine perspective, 307.
National Association for Chicano Studies
    Chicana voices: intersections of class, race,
        and gender, 1120.
Nava, Yolanda
    The Chicana and employment: needs analysis and
        recommendations for legislation, 963.
    Chicanas in the television media, 1022.
    Employment counseling and the Chicana, 1869.
Navar, Isabelle
    Como Chicana mi madre, 2901.
    La Mexicana: an image of strength, 2084.
    La Mexicana: an image of strength, 2085.
Navar, M. Margarita
    La vela prendida: home altars, 200.
Navarro, Marta A.
    Interview with Ana Castillo, 565.
Navarro-Arias, Roberto
    Positive and negative factors in the
        measurement of sex roles: findings from a
        Mexican sample, 659.
Neff, James Alan
    Divorce likelihood among Anglos and Mexican
        Americans, 308.
Nelson, Kathryn J.
    Excerpts from los testamentos: Hispanic women
        folk artists of the San Luis Valley,
        Colorado, 368.
Newton, Frank
    Hispanic mental health research: a reference
        guide, 351.
Nieto, Consuelo
    The Chicana and the women's rights movement,
        2297.
Nieto Gomez de Lazarin, Anna
    Ana Nieto Gomez: sexism in the Movimiento,
        1172.
    Chicana feminism, 2299.
    The Chicana: perspectives for education, 1281.
    Chicanas identify, 1173.
    Chicanas in the labor force, 1653.
    La femenista [sic], 309.
    Madres por justicia!, 1139.

    Un proposito para estudios femeniles de la
        chicana, 1188.
    What is the Talmadge Amendment?: justicia para
        las madres, 1140.
Nieto Senour, Maria
    Psychology of the Chicana, 43.
Nieto-Gomez, Anna
    USE: Nieto Gomez de Lazarin, Anna
Nieves-Squires, Sarah
    Hispanic women: making their presence on
        campus less tenuous, 136.
Norinsky, Margaret Elaine
    The relationship between sex-role identity and
        ethnicity to styles of assertiveness and
        aggression in women, 310.
Norris, Henry E.
    AIDS, women and reproductive rights, 17.
Norwood, Vera
    Angles of vision: enhancing our perspectives
        on the Southwest, 3476.
Notzon, Francis Claude
    Factors associated with low birth weight in
        Mexican-Americans and Mexicans, 311.
Novoa, Juan Bruce
    USE: Bruce-Novoa, Juan
Nyamathi, Adeline M.
    Black and Latina womens' AIDS related
        knowledge, attitudes, and practices, 175.
    Impact of poverty, homelessness, and drugs on
        Hispanic women at risk for HIV infection,
        179.
Ochoa, Mariaelena Lopez
    Group counseling Chicana troubled youth: an
        exploratory group counseling project, 1400.
O'Connell, Martin
    Developing current fertility indicators for
        foreign-born women from the Current
        Population Survey, 1534.
O'Connor, Mary I.
    Women's networks and the social needs of
        Mexican immigrants, 1872.
Oeste, Marcia
    Mujeres arriba y adelante, 2302.
Oetting, E.R.
    Drug use by small town Mexican American youth:
        a pilot study, 252.
O'Grady, Kevin E.
    Sexuality among Mexican Americans: a case of
        sexual stereotyping, 155.
O'Guinn, Thomas C.
    Acculturation and perceived family
        decision-making input among Mexican American
        wives, 83.
Olivares, Julian
    Sandra Cisneros' THE HOUSE ON MANGO STREET and
        the poetics of space, 1238.
Olivares, Yvette
    The sweatshop: the garment industry's reborn
        child, 2567.
Olivarez, Elizabeth
    Women's rights and the Mexican American woman,
        1772.
Oliveira, Annette
    Remarkable Latinas, 734.
Olivera, Mercedes
    The new Hispanic women, 203.
Olivero, Magaly
    Career Latinas: facing the challenges of a
        family and a career, 1023.
Olmedo, Esteban L.
    Hispanic mental health research: a reference
        guide, 351.
Olvera-Ezzell, Norma
    Maternal socialization of children's eating
        habits: strategies used by obese
        Mexican-American mothers, 1212.
Opitz, Wolfgang
    Marital instability trends among Mexican
        Americans as compared to Blacks and Anglos:
        new evidence, 276.
    The Mexican origin population in the United
        States: a demographic overview, 1834.
Ordonez, Elizabeth J.
    Body, spirit, and the text: Alma Villanueva's

Latinas without work: family, occupational, and economic stress following unemployment, 1885.

Long-term stress among Latino women after a plant closure, 510.

Romero, Mary
Chicanas modernize domestic service, 1688.

Day work in the suburbs: the work experience of Chicana private housekeepers, 1689.

Domestic service in the transition from rural to urban life: the case of la Chicana, 1690.

Tending the beets: campesinas and the Great Western Sugar Company, 2176.

Twice protected?: assessing the impact of affirmative action on Mexican-American women, 133.

Romero-Cachinero, M. Carmen
Hispanic women in Canada: a framework for analysis, 973.

Romero-Garcia, Ivonne
Sex roles and perceptions of femininity and masculinity of Hispanic women: a review of the literature, 518.

Romero-Gwynn, Eunice
Breast-feeding intentions and practice among Hispanic mothers in Southern California, 916.

Romo-Carmona, Mariana, ed.
Cuentos: stories by Latinas, 5453.

Roraback, Rosanne Lisa
The effects of occupational type, educational level, marital status, and race/ethnicity on women's attitudes towards feminist issues, 18.

Rosaldo, Renato
Fables of the fallen guy, 1106.

Rose, Margaret
From the fields to the picket line: Huelga women and the boycott, 1965-1975, 904.

Traditional and nontraditional patterns of female activism in the United Farm Workers of America, 1962-1980, 905.

Women in the United Farm Workers: a study of Chicana Mexicana participation in a labor union, 1950-1980, 2765.

Rosen, Karen
Dreams lost, dreams found: undocumented women in the land of opportunity, 651.

Rosenhouse-Persson, Sandra
Attitudes toward abortion among Catholic Mexican-American women: the effects of religiosity and education, 19.

Ross, Catherine E.
Distress and the traditional female role: a comparison of Mexicans and Anglos, 322.

Rubio Goldsmith, Raquel
Oral history: considerations and problems for its use in the history of Mexicanas in the United States, 2766.

Ruelas, J. Oshi
Moments of change, 614.

Ruiz Funes, Concepcion
Panorama de las luchas de la mujer mexicana en el siglo XX, 1373.

Ruiz, Vicki L.
"And miles to go...": Mexican women and work, 1930-1985, 1775.

By the day or week: Mexicana domestic workers in El Paso, 1691.

By the day or week: Mexicana domestic workers in El Paso, 1692.

California's early pioneers: Spanish/Mexican women, 958.

Cannery women/cannery lives: Mexican women, unionization, and the California food processing industry, 1930-1950, 167.

Dead ends or gold mines?: using missionary records in Mexican-American women's history, 367.

Obreras y madres: labor activism among Mexican women and its impact on the family, 1202.

A promise fulfilled: Mexican cannery workers in Southern California, 965.

A promise fulfilled: Mexican cannery workers

in Southern California, 966.

A promise fulfilled: Mexican cannery workers in Southern California, 967.

UCAPAWA, Chicanas, and the California food processing industry, 1937-1950, 991.

Working for wages: Mexican women in the Southwest, 1930-1980, 1893.

Ruiz, Vicki L., ed.
Unequal sisters: a multicultural reader in U.S. women's history, 323.

Western women: their land, their lives, 327.

Women on the U.S.-Mexico border: responses to change, 854.

Rush, Lynda
The determinants of breastfeeding for Mexican migrant women, 910.

Russo, Nancy Felipe
Contemporary research on Hispanic women: a selected bibliography of the social science literature, 666.

Hispanic women and mental health: an overview of contemporary issues in research and practice, 3600.

The use of inpatient mental health services by Hispanic women, 3992.

Saavedra, Lupe
Hispanas in the year of the woman: many voices, 1609.

It is only fair that women be allowed to..., 3237.

Saavedra-Vela, Pilar
The dark side of Hispanic women's education, 1028.

Hispanic women in double jeopardy, 1362.

Nosotras in Houston, 1363.

Sabagh, Georges
Attitudes toward abortion among Catholic Mexican-American women: the effects of religiosity and education, 19.

Fertility expectations and behavior among Mexican Americans in Los Angeles, 1973-82, 2444.

Religiosity and fertility: the case of Chicanas, 1072.

Sable, Martin H.
Las maquiladoras: assembly and manufacturing plants on the United States-Mexico border: an international guide, 687.

Sabogal, Fabio, et al.
Hispanic familism and acculturation: what changes and what doesn't?, 89.

Saboonchi, Nasrin
The working women's reactions to the traditional marriage role: a crosscultural study within the symbolic interactionism framework, 2989.

Saenz, Evangelina
Psychocultural characteristics of college-bound and noncollege-bound Chicanas, 693.

Saenz, Rogelio
The effects of employment and marital relations on depression among Mexican American women, 1578.

Traditional sex-roles, ethnic integration, marital satisfaction, and psychological distress among Chicanas, 3849.

Salas, Elizabeth
Soldaderas in the Mexican military: myth and history, 125.

Soldaderas in the Mexican military: myth and history, 126.

Salazar Parr, Carmen
The Chicana in Chicano literature, 3409.

La Chicana in literature, 1544.

The female hero in Chicano literature, 3407.

Salazar, Sandra A.
Chicanas as healers, 2182.

Reproductive choice for Hispanas, 20.

Saldivar, Jose David
Towards a Chicano poetics: the making of the Chicano subject, 1387.

Saldivar, Ramon
The dialectics of subjectivity: gender and

difference in Isabella Rios, Sandra
Cisneros, and Cherrie Moraga, 579.
Saldivar-Hull, Sonia
Feminism on the border: from gender politics
to geopolitics, 324.
Salgado de Snyder, Nelly
Cultural and ethnic maintenance of
interethnically married Mexican-Americans,
90.
Ethnic identity and cultural awareness among
the offspring of Mexican interethnic
marriages, 91.
Factors associated with acculturative stress
and depressive symptomatology among married
Mexican immigrant women, 92.
Gender and ethnic differences in psychosocial
stress and generalized distress among
Hispanics, 325.
Interethnic marriages of Mexican Americans
after nearly two decades, 459.
Mexican immigrant women: a selected
bibliography, 667.
Mexican immigrant women: the relationship of
ethnic loyalty and social support to
acculturative stress and depressive
symptomatology, 93.
The role of ethnic loyalty among Mexican
immigrant women, 94.
Salinas, Judy
The image of woman in Chicano literature,
3411.
The role of women in Chicano literature, 3514.
Salorzano, Rosalia
O te aclimatas o te aclimueres, 830.
Saltzer, Eleanor B.
Attitudes toward breast-feeding among
Mexican-American women, 515.
Sameroff, Arnold
Determinants of complexity in Mexican-American
and Anglo-American mothers' conceptions of
child development, 65.
San Miguel, Rachel
Being Hispanic in Houston: my name is Carmen
Quezada, 616.
Sanchez, Corina
Higher education y la Chicana?, 1631.
Sanchez, Elba R.
La realidad a traves de la inocencia en el
cuento: "Un Paseo", 2571.
Sanchez, George J.
"Go after the women": Americanization and the
Mexican immigrant woman, 1915-1929, 95.
"Go after the women": Americanization and the
Mexican immigrant woman, 1915-1929, 96.
Sanchez, Joaquin John
An investigation of the initial experience of
a Chicana with higher education, 696.
Sanchez, Marta E.
The birthing of the poetic "I" in Alma
Villanueva's MOTHER MAY I?: the search for a
feminine identity, 2919.
Contemporary Chicana poetry, 3517.
Gender and ethnicity in contemporary Chicana
poetry, 3518.
Judy Lucero and Bernice Zamora: two
dialectical statements in Chicana poetry,
2579.
Judy Lucero and Bernice Zamora: two
dialectical statements in Chicana poetry,
2580.
Sanchez, Rita
Chicana writer breaking out of the silence,
580.
Sanchez, Rosaura
The Chicana labor force, 1896.
Chicana prose writers: the case of Gina Valdes
and Sylvia Lizarraga, 581.
El discurso femenino en la literatura chicana,
2339.
The history of Chicanas: a proposal for a
materialist perspective, 361.
Sanchez, Rosaura, ed.
Essays on la mujer, 5554.
Sanford, Judy, et al.

Patterns of reported rape in a tri-ethnic
population: Houston, Texas, 1974-1975, 326.
Santiago, Myrna I
La Chicana, 1178.
Santillan, Richard
Rosita the riveter: Midwest Mexican American
women during World War II, 1941-1945, 2778.
Santillanes, Maria
Women in prison--C.I.W.: an editorial, 1364.
Saracho, Olivia N.
Women and education: sex role modifications of
Mexican American women, 97.
Saragoza, Alex M.
The conceptualization of the history of the
Chicano family, 2103.
Schaffer, Diane M.
Social networks and survival strategies: an
exploratory study of Mexican American,
Black, and Anglo female family heads in San
Jose, California, 343.
Schlissel, Lillian, ed.
Western women: their land, their lives, 327.
Schoen, Robert
Ethnic and educational effects on marriage
choice, 1778.
Schwartz, Dana
Hispanic adolescent fertility, 2405.
Scott, Wilbur
The fertility related behavior of Mexican
American adolescents, 2425.
Scrimshaw, Susan C.M., et al.
Factors affecting breastfeeding among women of
Mexican origin or descent in Los Angeles,
98.
Segovia, Sara
Las hermanas, 1260.
Segura, Denise
Chicana and Mexican immigrant women at work:
the impact of class, race, and gender on
occupational mobility, 1897.
Chicanas and Mexican immigrant women in the
labor market: a study of occupational
mobility and stratification, 2998.
Conflict in social relations at work: a
Chicana perspective, 1659.
Familism and employment among Chicanas and
Mexican immigrant women, 1898.
The interplay of familism and patriarchy on
employment among Chicana and Mexicana women,
1899.
Labor market stratification: the Chicana
experience, 1660.
Seligson, Mitchell A.
Maquiladoras and migration workers in the
Mexico-United States Border
Industrialization Program, 822.
Sepulveda, Betty R.
The Hispanic woman responding to the
challenges that affect us all, 2342.
Shapiro, Johanna
Attitudes toward breast-feeding among
Mexican-American women, 515.
Maternal adaptation to child disability in a
Hispanic population, 1219.
Shapiro, Peter
Watsonville shows "it can be done", 992.
Shelton, Beth Anne
Undocumented immigrant women in the Houston
labor force, 1841.
Sheridan, Thomas E.
From Luisa Espinel to Lalo Guerrero: Tucson's
Mexican musicians before World War II, 737.
Sierra, Christine Marie
The university setting reinforces inequality,
1632.
Silva, Beverly, ed.
Nosotras: Latina literature today, 4548.
Silva, Helga
The unspeakable crime, 4885.
Silva-Palacios, Victor
Designing culturally responsive parent
programs: a comparison of low-income Mexican
and Mexican-American mothers' preferences,
86.

Simon, Rita J.
  The work experience of undocumented Mexican
    women migrants in Los Angeles, 3002.
Simoniello, Katina
  On investigating the attitudes toward
    achievement and success in eight
    professional U.S. Mexican women, 516.
Singh, Susheela
  Contraceptive practice among Hispanic
    adolescents, 760.
Smith, Bradford M.
  The measurement of narcissism in Asian,
    Caucasian, and Hispanic American women, 328.
Smith, Jack C.
  Differentials in the planning status of the
    most recent live birth to Mexican Americans
    and Anglos, 344.
  Trends in the incidence of breastfeeding for
    Hispanics of Mexican origin and Anglos on
    the US-Mexican border, 329.
Snider, Dixie E.
  Isoniazid hepatitis among pregnant and
    postpartum Hispanic patients, 2407.
Soberon, Mercedes
  La revolucion se trata de amor: Mercedes
    Soberon, 389.
Solis, Faustina
  Commentary on the Chicana and health services,
    3941.
Solorzano-Torres, Rosalia
  Female Mexican immigrants in San Diego County,
    1902.
  Women, labor, and the U.S.-Mexico border:
    Mexican maids in El Paso, Texas, 867.
Sonntag, Iliana
  Hacia una bibliografia de poesia femenina
    chicana, 688.
Sorel, Janet Elaine
  The relationship between gender role
    incongruity on measures of coping and
    material resources and blood pressure among
    Mexican-American women, 2647.
Sorenson, Ann Marie
  The fertility and language characteristics of
    Mexican-American and non-Hispanic husbands
    and wives, 330.
  Fertility, expectations and ethnic identity
    among Mexican-American adolescents: an
    expression of cultural ideals, 99.
Sorenson, Susan B.
  Self-reports of spousal violence in a
    Mexican-American and non-Hispanic white
    population, 332.
Sosa Riddell, Adaljiza
  Background: a critical overview on
    Chicanas/Latinas and public policies, 1633.
  Bibliography on Chicanas and public policy,
    689.
  Chicanas and el Movimiento, 1179.
  The status of women in Mexico: the impact of
    the "International Year of the Woman", 22.
  Synopsis on Senate Concurrent Resolution 43:
    an example in public policy making, 3391.
Sosa Riddell, Adaljiza, ed.
  Policy development: Chicana/Latina Summer
    Research Institute [handbook], 1141.
Soto, Shirlene Ann
  Emergence of the modern Mexican woman: her
    participation in revolution and struggle for
    equality, 1910-1940, 2344.
  The emerging Chicana: a review of the
    journals, 1601.
  La Malinche: 16th century leader, 3386.
  Tres modelos culturales: la Virgen de
    Guadalupe, la Malinche y la Llorona, 2607.
  The women's movement in Mexico: the first and
    second feminist congresses in Yucatan, 1916,
    1366.
Spence, Mary Lee
  Commentary [on "And Miles to Go": Mexican
    Women and Work, 1930-1985], 234.
Spitta, Silvia D.
  Literary transculturation in Latin America,
    359.

Stafford, Randall S.
  Socioeconomic differences in rates of cesarean
    section, 286.
Stark, Miriam
  La Chicana: changing roles in a changing
    society, 100.
Staudt, Kathleen
  Programming women's empowerment: a case from
    northern Mexico, 202.
Stein, Shayna R.
  Sterilization among American Indian and
    Chicano mothers, 4286.
Stephen, Elizabeth H.
  At the crossroads: fertility of
    Mexican-American women, 462.
  The Mexican origin population in the United
    States: a demographic overview, 1834.
Stephens, Richard C.
  To be aged, Hispanic, and female: the triple
    risk, 230.
Stern, Gwen
  Research, action, and social betterment, 1112.
Sternbach, Nancy Saporta
  At the threshold of the unnamed: Latina
    literary discourse in the eighties, 704.
  "A deep racial memory of love": the Chicana
    feminism of Cherrie Moraga, 1634.
  Selected bibliography, 682.
Stevens, Joanne Darsey
  Santos by twentieth-century santeras:
    continuation of a traditional art form, 394.
Stewart, Kenneth L.
  Fertility among Mexican Americans and Anglos
    in Texas, 1900, 333.
  Work force participation among Mexican
    immigrant women in Texas, 1900, 1904.
Stockel, H. Henrietta
  Medicine women, curanderas, and women doctors,
    364.
Stoddard, Ellwyn R.
  Maquila: assembly plants in Northern Mexico,
    823.
Stoller, Marianne L.
  The Hispanic women artists of New Mexico:
    present and past, 419.
Storment, Diamantina
  Sex-related speech accommodations among
    Mexican-American bilinguals: a pilot study
    of language choice in customer-server
    interactions, 706.
Stroup-Benham, Christine A.
  Alcohol consumption patterns among Mexican
    American mothers and among children from
    single- and dual-headed households: findings
    from HHANES 1982-84, 193.
  Reproductive characteristics of
    Mexican-American, mainland Puerto Rican, and
    Cuban-American women: data from the Hispanic
    Health and Nutrition Examination Survey,
    759.
Strover, Sharon
  Chicanas and Chicanos: barriers to progress in
    higher education, 1304.
Suarez, Cecilia C.R.
  USE: Cota-Robles de Suarez, Cecilia
Sullivan, Teresa A.
  The occupational prestige of women immigrants:
    a comparison of Cubans and Mexicans, 1029.
Sutton, Arlene Vigil
  La mujer en el ochenta, 1501.
Sweeney, Judith
  Chicana history: a review of the literature,
    2782.
Sweeny, Mary Anne
  The health belief model as an explanation for
    breast-feeding practices in a Hispanic
    population, 921.
Swicegood, Gray
  Generation, female education and Mexican
    American fertility, 138.
  Language opportunity costs and Mexican
    American fertility, 2451.
  Mexican American fertility patterns, 139.
  Role incompatibility and the relationship

--   --

between fertility and labor supply among
Hispanic women, 1416.

Swicegood, Gray, et al.
Language usage and fertility in the
Mexican-origin population of the United
States, 2452.

Swinney, Gloria Luyas
The biocultural context of low-income
Mexican-American women with type II
non-insulin dependent diabetes and its
implications for health care delivery, 1594.

Taffel, Selma M.
Childbearing characteristics of U.S.- and
foreign-born Hispanic mothers, 2457.

Tafolla, Carmen
Chicano literature: beyond beginnings, 583.
To split a human: mitos, machos y la mujer
chicana, 1635.

Tajalli, Irene Queiro
Selected cultural, organizational, and
economic factors related to prenatal care
utilization by middle-income Hispanic women,
2453.

Talavera, Esther
Sterilization is not an alternative in family
planning, 1636.

Tarango, Yolanda
Hispanic women, prophetic voice in the Church:
toward a Hispanic women's liberation
theology, 1065.

Tatum, Charles M.
Grappling with difference: gender, race,
class, and ethnicity in contemporary
Chicana/o literature, 209.

Tavera Rivera, Margarita
Autoridad in absentia: la censura patriarcal
en la narrativa chicana, 2351.

Taylor, Elena
Conversations with a Chicana physician, 3030.

Taylor, Paul S.
Mexican women in Los Angeles industry in 1928,
1906.

Telles, Cynthia A.
Self-reports of spousal violence in a
Mexican-American and non-Hispanic white
population, 332.

Tenayuca, Emma
Living history: Emma Tenayuca tells her story,
613.

Teniente de Costilla, Alvina
Virgen de Guadalupe and the American dream:
the melting pot bubbles on in Toledo, Ohio,
456.

Terranes, Ed
Some thoughts of a macho on the Chicana
Movement, 3748.

Terrazas, Olga Esperanza
The self-concept of Mexican-American
adolescent females, 2926.

Texas Memorial Museum, University of Texas,
Austin, TX
La vela prendida: Mexican-American women's
home altars, 201.

Thomas, Barbara
Ethnic and educational effects on marriage
choice, 1778.

Tiano, Susan B.
Export processing, women's work, and the
employment problem in developing countries:
the case of the maquiladora program in
Northern Mexico, 894.
Labor composition and gender stereotypes in
the maquila, 857.
Maquiladoras in Mexicali: integration or
exploitation?, 824.
Maquiladoras, women's work, and unemployment
in northern Mexico, 859.
Women's work and unemployment in northern
Mexico, 825.

Tiano, Susan B., ed.
Women on the U.S.-Mexico border: responses to
change, 854.

Tienda, Marta
Determinants of extended household structure:

cultural pattern or economical need?, 2002.
Headship and household composition among
Blacks, Hispanics and other whites, 334.
The Hispanic population of the United States,
1074.
Hispanics in the U.S. labor market: an
overview of recent evidence, 3267.
Household structure and labor-force
participation of Black, Hispanic, and white
mothers, 335.
The occupational position of employed Hispanic
women, 1911.
Sex, ethnicity and Chicano status attainment,
47.

Timberlake, Andrea, et al.
Women of color and southern women: a
bibliography of social science research,
1975 to 1988, 690.

Tittle, Ken
Maternal adaptation to child disability in a
Hispanic population, 1219.

Tixier y Vigil, Yvonne
Las mujeres: conversations from a Hispanic
community, 721.

Torano, Maria Elena
Hispanas: success in America, 708.

Torres, Aida
Contraceptive practice among Hispanic
adolescents, 760.

Torres, Cynthia
Cultural and psychological attributes and
their implications for career choice and
aspirations among Mexican American females,
697.

Torres, Maria
The interdependency of educational
institutions and cultural norms: the Hispana
experience, 29.

Torres Raines, Rosario
The Mexican American woman and work:
intergenerational perspectives of
comparative ethnic groups, 157.

Torres, Sara
A comparative analysis of wife abuse among
Anglo-American and Mexican-American battered
women: attitudes, nature, severity,
frequency and response to the abuse, 337.
Hispanic-American battered women: why consider
cultural differences?, 654.

Treacy, Mary Jane
The ties that bind: women and community in
Evangelina Vigil's THIRTY AN' SEEN A LOT,
2929.

Trevathan, Wenda R.
First conversations: verbal content of
mother-newborn interaction, 1475.

Trevino, Dorothy B.
Alcohol consumption patterns among Mexican
American mothers and among children from
single- and dual-headed households: findings
from HHANES 1982-84, 193.

Trevino, Fernando M.
Alcohol consumption patterns among Mexican
American mothers and among children from
single- and dual-headed households: findings
from HHANES 1982-84, 193.
Reproductive characteristics of
Mexican-American, mainland Puerto Rican, and
Cuban-American women: data from the Hispanic
Health and Nutrition Examination Survey,
759.

Triandis, Harry C.
Role perceptions of Hispanic young adults,
1476.

Trotter, Robert T.
Ethnic and sexual patterns of alcohol use:
Anglo and Mexican American college students,
194.

Trujillo, Carla
Chicana lesbians: fear and loathing in the
Chicano community, 1959.

Trujillo, Carla, ed.
Chicana lesbians: the girls our mothers warned
us about, 2803.

Trujillo Gaitan, Marcella
    The dilemma of the modern Chicana artist and
        critic, 390.
    The dilemma of the modern Chicana artist and
        critic, 391.
Tuma, Nancy Brandon
    Entry into marriage and parenthood by young
        men and women: the influence of family
        background, 304.
Tunon, Enriqueta
    Panorama de las luchas de la mujer mexicana en
        el siglo XX, 1373.
Ulbrich, Patricia
    Distress and the traditional female role: a
        comparison of Mexicans and Anglos, 322.
Urdaneta, Maria Luisa
    Chicana use of abortion: the case of Alcala,
        23.
    Flesh pots, faith, or finances? Fertility
        rates among Mexican Americans, 1073.
Uribe, F. Medardo Tapia
    The marital morality of Mexican women--an
        urban study, 2068.
U.S. Department of Labor, Women's Bureau
    Adelante mujer hispana: a conference model for
        Hispanic women, 120.
U.S. National Institute of Education
    Conference on the educational and occupational
        needs of Hispanic women, June 29-30, 1976;
        December 10-12, 1976, 1341.
Usher, Mary
    Group therapy with aged Latino women: a pilot
        project and study, 221.
Valadez, Esther
    The role of the Latina, 3363.
Valdes, Guadalupe
    Positive speech accommodation in the language
        of Mexican American bilinguals: are women
        really more sensitive?, 705.
    Sex-related speech accommodations among
        Mexican-American bilinguals: a pilot study
        of language choice in customer-server
        interactions, 706.
Valdes-Fallis, Guadalupe
    A liberated Chicana: a struggle against
        tradition, 1960.
Valdez, Avelardo
    Recent increases in intermarriage by Mexican
        American males: Bexar County, Texas from
        1971 to 1980, 663.
Valdez, Diana
    Mexican American family research: a critical
        review and conceptual framework, 2110.
Valencia-Weber, Gloria
    Acculturation and the Hispanic woman:
        attitudes toward women, sex-role
        attribution, sex-role behavior, and
        demographics, 70.
Valenzuela-Crocker, Elvira
    Forging paths in power and profit, 932.
    Women, power and the vote, 6134.
Valladolid-Cuaron, Alicia V.
    La mujer en el ochenta, 1501.
Valle, Carmen, ed.
    Nosotras: Latina literature today, 4548.
Valle, Juan Ramon
    Migration and mental health: an empirical test
        of depression risk factors among immigrant
        Mexican women, 103.
    The relationship of marital status, confidant
        support, and depression among Mexican
        immigrant women, 1585.
Valle, Ramon
    USE: Valle, Juan Ramon
Valle, Victor Manuel
    Inside the world of Latinas, 722.
Vallejos, Tomas
    Estela Portillo Trambley's fictive search for
        paradise, 1545.
Vallez, Andrea
    Acculturation, social support, stress and
        adjustment of the Mexican American college
        woman, 101.
Valtierra, Mary

Acculturation, social support, and reported
    stress of Latina physicians, 102.
Vangie, Mary
    Women at Frontera, CA, 1781.
Varela, Vivian
    Hispanic women's resource guide, 1602.
Vargas-Willis, Gloria
    Consideration of psychosocial stress in the
        treatment of the Latina immigrant, 1663.
Vasquez, Carlos
    Women in the Chicano Movement, 1182.
Vasquez, Enriqueta L.
    La Chicana, 1183.
Vasquez, Josefina
    Educacion y papel de la mujer en Mexico, 1782.
Vasquez, Mario F.
    The election day immigration raid at Lilli
        Diamond Originals and the response of the
        ILGWU, 2568.
    Immigrant workers and the apparel
        manufacturing industry in Southern
        California, 134.
Vasquez, Melba J. T.
    Confronting barriers to the participation of
        Mexican American women in higher education,
        48.
    Power and status of the Chicana: a
        social-psychological perspective, 2930.
    Sex roles among Chicanos: stereotypes,
        challenges and changes, 2627.
Vasquez, Rose
    Impact of poverty, homelessness, and drugs on
        Hispanic women at risk for HIV infection,
        179.
Vazquez-Nuttall, Ena
    Sex roles and perceptions of femininity and
        masculinity of Hispanic women: a review of
        the literature, 518.
Vega, Alicia
    Three Latinas in Hollywood = Tres latinas en
        Hollywood, 114.
Vega, William A.
    Marital disruption and the prevalence of
        depressive symptomatology among Anglos and
        Mexican Americans, 339.
    Migration and mental health: an empirical test
        of depression risk factors among immigrant
        Mexican women, 103.
    The relationship of marital status, confidant
        support, and depression among Mexican
        immigrant women, 1585.
Vega, William A., et al.
    Depressive symptoms and their correlates among
        immigrant Mexican women in the United
        States, 1586.
Velasquez, Roberto J.
    MMPI differences among Mexican-American male
        and female psychiatric inpatients, 1337.
Velasquez-Trevino, Gloria
    Cultural ambivalence in early Chicana prose
        fiction, 698.
    Jovita Gonzalez, una voz de resistencia
        cultural en la temprana narrativa chicana,
        340.
Velazquez Trevino, Gloria
    USE: Velasquez-Trevino, Gloria
Velez-I., Carlos G.
    The nonconsenting sterilization of Mexican
        women in Los Angeles: issues of
        psychocultural rupture and legal redress in
        paternalistic behavioral environments, 1682.
    Se me acabo la cancion: an ethnography of
        non-consenting sterilizations among Mexican
        women in Los Angeles, 1995.
Veloz, Josefina Estrada
    Chicana identity: gender and ethnicity, 2931.
Venegas, Sybil
    The artists and their work--the role of the
        Chicana artist, 392.
Ventura, Stephanie J.
    Childbearing characteristics of U.S.- and
        foreign-born Hispanic mothers, 2457.
Vernon, Sally W.
    Aging, sex-role orientation and adjustment: a

three-generations study of Mexican
Americans, 148.
Veyna, Angelina F.
Una vista al pasado: la mujer en Nuevo Mexico,
1744-1767, 2785.
Women in early New Mexico: a preliminary view,
129.
Vidal, Mirta
Women: new voice of La Raza, 369.
Vigil, Evangelina, ed.
Woman of her word: Hispanic women write, 388.
Vigil, James Diego
Cultural styles and adolescent sex role
perceptions: an exploration of responses to
a value picture projective test, 4771.
The nexus of class, culture and gender in the
education of Mexican American females, 49.
Villalobos, Rolando M.
Research guide to the literature on Northern
Mexico's maquiladora assembly industry, 691.
Villanueva, Alma
[Interview with] Alma Villanueva, 587.
Viramontes, Helena Maria
"Nopalitos": the making of fiction, 588.
Viramontes, Helena Maria, ed.
Chicana creativity and criticism: charting new
frontiers in American literature, 386.
Vivo, Paquita
Voces de Hispanas: Hispanic women and their
concerns, 4017.
Von Eye, Alexander
Sanitary product use by white, Black, and
Mexican American women, 272.
Votaw, Carmen Delgado
Cultural influences on Hispanic feminism,
1519.
Wagner, Roland M.
Changes in extended family relationships for
Mexican American and Anglo single mothers,
341.
Changes in the friend network during the first
year of single parenthood for Mexican
American and Anglo women, 342.
Social networks and survival strategies: an
exploratory study of Mexican American,
Black, and Anglo female family heads in San
Jose, California, 343
Waite, Linda J.
Beyond stereotypes: who becomes a single
teenage mother?, 2368.
Teenagers willing to consider single
parenthood: who is at greatest risk?, 762.
Waldman, Elizabeth
Profile of the Chicana: a statistical fact
sheet, 1914.
Walker, Todd
The relationship of nativity, social support
and depression to the home environment among
Mexican-American women, 105.
Walters, Esperanza Garcia
Health and illness perceptions of the Chicana,
1457.
Warheit, George
Marital disruption and the prevalence of
depressive symptomatology among Anglos and
Mexican Americans, 339.
Warren, Charles W.
Differentials in the planning status of the
most recent live birth to Mexican Americans
and Anglos, 344.
Watkins, Elizabeth L.
Health and social needs of women farmworkers:
receiving maternity care at a migrant health
center, 2178.
Weber, Devra Anne
Mexican women on strike: memory, history and
oral narratives, 1.
Webster, Lucia
The Bem Sex-Role Inventory across three
cultures, 660.
Weiner, Raine
The needs of poverty women heading households:
a return to postsecondary education 345.
Welch, Susan

Employment of women by cities in the
Southwest, 1862.
Weller, Susan C.
Personal preferences and ethnic variations
among Anglo and Hispanic breast and bottle
feeders, 519.
White, Marni, et al.
Perceived crime in the neighborhood and mental
health of women and children, 520.
Whiteford, Linda
Mexican American women as innovators, 897.
Migrants no longer: changing family structure
of Mexican Americans in South Texas, 2113.
Willette, JoAnne
U.S. Hispanics: changing the face of America,
1749.
Williams, Brett
Why migrant women feed their husbands tamales:
foodways as a basis for a revisionist view
of Tejano family life, 1494.
Williams, Edward J.
Maquiladoras and migration workers in the
Mexico-United States Border
Industrialization Program, 822.
Turnover and recruitment in the maquila
industry: causes and solutions, 862.
Williams, Joyce E.
Mexican American and Anglo attitudes about sex
roles and rape, 346.
Secondary victimization: confronting public
attitudes about rape, 522.
Williams, Norma
Changes in funeral patterns and gender roles
among Mexican Americans, 463.
The Mexican American family: tradition and
change, 1478.
A Mexican American woman encounters sociology:
an autobiographical perspective, 619.
Role making among married Mexican American
women: issues of class and ethnicity, 527.
Williams, Ronald L., et al.
Pregnancy outcomes among Spanish-surname women
in California, 2459.
Winkler, Karen J.
Scholars say issues of diversity have
"revolutionized" field of Chicano Studies,
1129.
Winter, Michael
The use of inpatient mental health services by
Hispanic women, 3992.
Winzelberg, Andrew
Ethnicity, locus of control for family
planning, and pregnancy counselor
credibility, 241.
Wolff, Cindy Brattan
Diet and pregnancy outcome in Mexican-American
women, 2460.
Woodward, Carolyn
Dare to write: Virginia Woolf, Tillie Olsen,
Gloria Anzaldua, 360.
Wooldredge, John
Ethnic and educational effects on marriage
choice, 1778.
Worth, Dooley
Latina women and AIDS, 1479.
Yanez, Rosa H.
The complimenting speech act among Chicano
women, 3188.
Yarbro-Bejarano, Yvonne
Cherrie Moraga's GIVING UP THE GHOST: the
representation of female desire, 2577.
Chicana literature from a Chicana feminist
perspective, 2361.
Chicana's experience in collective theatre:
ideology and form, 115.
De-constructing the lesbian body: Cherrie
Moraga's LOVING IN THE WAR YEARS, 2805.
The female subject in Chicano theater:
sexuality, race, and class, 2362.
The image of the Chicana in teatro, 2608.
Primer encuentro de lesbianas feministas
latinoamericanas y caribenas, 1035.
Teatropoesia by Chicanas in the Bay Area:
TONGUES OF FIRE, 4560.

TITLE INDEX

industrial sociology of women workers in
transnational labor processes, 849.
Beyond stereotypes: the critical analysis of
Chicana literature, 3453.
Beyond stereotypes: who becomes a single teenage
mother?, 2368.
A bibliography of criticism of contemporary
Chicano literature, 553.
[Bibliography of Special Issue: Chicana Creativity
and Criticism], 668.
Bibliography on Chicanas and public policy, 689.
Bibliography on maternal and child health across
class, race and ethnicity, 692.
The biocultural context of low-income
Mexican-American women with type II
non-insulin dependent diabetes and its
implications for health care delivery, 1594.
Birth control and low-income Mexican-American
women: the impact of three values, 85.
The birthing of the poetic "I" in Alma
Villanueva's MOTHER MAY I?: the search for a
feminine identity, 2919.
Birthweight of infants born to Hispanic women
employed in agriculture, 2170.
The bittersweet nostalgia of childhood in the
poetry of Margarita Cota-Cardenas, 1393.
Black and Latina womens' AIDS related knowledge,
attitudes, and practices, 175.
Black, Anglo, and Chicana women's construction of
mental illness, 305.
Body, spirit, and the text: Alma Villanueva's LIFE
SPAN, 1256.
Border crossings, 2192.
Borderlands/La frontera: the new mestiza, 624.
[Bornstein-Somoza, Miriam], 529.
Breaking boundaries: Latina writing and critical
readings, 3457.
Breast cancer prognosis in a mixed
Caucasian-Hispanic population, 260.
Breast feeding preference of Hispanic and Anglo
women, 267.
Breastfeeding among Hispanics [letter], 915.
Breast-feeding and social class mobility: the case
of Mexican migrant mothers in Houston,
Texas, 909.
Breast-feeding intentions and practice among
Hispanic mothers in Southern California,
916.
The broken web: the educational experience of
Hispanic American women, 39.
Brujeria: a sociological analysis of Mexican
American witches, 925.
By the day or week: Mexicana domestic workers in
El Paso, 1691, 1692.
Cactus flowers: in search of Tejana feminist
poetry, 542.
California's early pioneers: Spanish/Mexican
women, 958.
Un camino por transitar, 5549.
Campesinas: women farmworkers in the California
agricultural labor force, report of a study
project, 944.
Cannery women/cannery lives: Mexican women,
unionization, and the California food
processing industry, 1930-1950, 167.
Canning comes to New Mexico: women and the
agricultural extension service, 1914-1919,
985.
La caracterizacion de los personajes femeninos en
...Y NO SE LO TRAGO LA TIERRA, 3496.
Career Latinas: facing the challenges of a family
and a career, 1023.
Carmen Lomas Garza: traditional and
non-traditional, 412.
Challenge and counter challenge: Chicana literary
motifs, 317.
Changes in extended family relationships for
Mexican American and Anglo single mothers,
341.
Changes in funeral patterns and gender roles among
Mexican Americans, 463.
Changes in the friend network during the first
year of single parenthood for Mexican
American and Anglo women, 342.

Characteristics of college bound Mexican American
females, 2672.
Characteristics of professional and traditional
Mexican American women related to family of
origin, role models, and conflicts: a case
study, 1010.
"Chavalas de maquiladora": a study of the female
labor force in Ciudad Juarez' offshore
production plants, 835.
Cherrie Moraga's GIVING UP THE GHOST: the
representation of female desire, 2577.
Chicago's new Hispanic health alliance, 186.
La Chicana, 1178, 1183.
La Chicana: a bibliographic survey, 680.
Chicana adolescents and contraception issues, 741.
The Chicana and employment: needs analysis and
recommendations for legislation, 963.
Chicana and Mexican immigrant women at work: the
impact of class, race, and gender on
occupational mobility, 1897.
La Chicana and the Chicano family, 1489.
The Chicana and the women's rights movement, 2297.
La Chicana and "women's liberation", 2307.
The Chicana as a literary critic, 3538.
Chicana caucus, 1154.
La Chicana: changing roles in a changing society,
100.
Chicana creativity and criticism: charting new
frontiers in American literature, 386.
Chicana discourse: negations and mediations, 570.
Chicana employment--options for the future, 1836.
Chicana feminism, 2299.
Chicana feminism: in the tracks of 'the' native
woman, 1503.
The Chicana feminist, 2214.
The Chicana: her attitudes towards the woman's
liberation movement, 508.
La Chicana: her role in the past and her search
for a new role in the future, 2327, 2328.
Chicana historiography: a research note regarding
Mexican archival sources, 366.
Chicana history: a review of the literature, 2782.
Chicana history and historical significance: some
theoretical considerations, 1124.
Chicana identity, 6504.
Chicana identity: gender and ethnicity, 2931.
A Chicana in academe, 1620.
The Chicana in American literature, 1191, 1192.
The Chicana in American history: the Mexican women
of El Paso, 1880-1920 - a case study, 110.
The Chicana in Chicano literature, 3409.
The Chicana in literature, 1955.
La Chicana in literature, 1544.
La Chicana in politics, 1815.
Chicana journals, 3207.
The Chicana labor force, 1896.
Chicana labor history: a critique of male
consciousness in historical writing, 2712.
Chicana lesbians: fear and loathing in the Chicano
community, 1959.
Chicana lesbians: the girls our mothers warned us
about, 2803.
Chicana literary motifs: challenge and
counter-challenge, 318.
Chicana literature and related sources: a selected
and annotated bibliography, 685.
Chicana literature from a Chicana feminist
perspective, 2361.
La Chicana: Malinche or virgin?, 3781.
Chicana novelists in the process of creating
fictive voices, 562.
La Chicana organizes: the Comision Femenil
Mexicana in perspective, 815.
The Chicana perspective: a design for
self-awareness, 1142.
A Chicana perspective on Mexican culture and
sexuality, 956.
The Chicana: perspectives for education, 1281.
Chicana poets: re-visions from the margin, 552.
La Chicana: principle of life, survival and
endurance, 2883.
Chicana prose writers: the case of Gina Valdes and
Sylvia Lizarraga, 581.
Chicana reference sources, 672.

414

Chicana regional conference, 1117.
Chicana rights: a major MALDEF issue (reprinted
    from MALDEF Newsletter, Fall 1977), 1118.
Chicana Studies: a selected list of materials
    since 1980, 671.
Chicana: the forgotten woman, 10.
La Chicana: the Mexican-American woman, 2080.
La Chicana: transcending the old and carving out a
    new life and self-image, 1077.
Chicana use of abortion: the case of Alcala, 23.
Chicana voices: intersections of class, race, and
    gender, 1120.
Chicana Welfare Rights challenges Talmadge
    amendment, 1134.
Chicana Welfare Rights vs. the Talmadge amendment,
    1135.
The Chicana woman: a historical materialist
    perspective, 1001.
Chicana women writers and their audience, 560.
Chicana writer breaking out of the silence, 580.
Chicana writers and critics in a social context :
    towards a contemporary bibliography, 664.
Chicanas and alcoholism: a sociocultural
    perspective of women, 185.
Chicanas and Chicanos: barriers to progress in
    higher education, 1304.
Chicanas and el Movimiento, 1179.
Chicanas and Mexicanas within a transnational
    working class: theoretical perspectives,
    3318, 3322.
Chicanas and Mexican immigrant families 1920-1940:
    women's subordination and family
    exploitation, 2055.
Chicanas and Mexican immigrant women in the labor
    market: a study of occupational mobility and
    stratification, 2998.
Chicanas and political representation, 1817.
Chicanas and the issue of involuntary
    sterilization: reforms needed to protect
    informed consent, 749.
Chicanas and the law, 128.
Chicanas as healers, 2182.
Chicanas en la literatura y el arte (El Grito Book
    Series: Book 1, September 1973), 387.
Chicana's experience in collective theatre:
    ideology and form, 115.
Chicana's feminist literature: a re-vision through
    Malintzinl or Malintzin: putting flesh back
    on the object, 2185.
Chicanas holding doctoral degrees: social
    reproduction and cultural ecological
    approaches, 24.
Chicanas identify, 1173.
Chicanas in California post secondary education: a
    comparative study of barriers to the program
    progress, 26.
Chicanas in film: history of an image, 2471.
Chicanas in postsecondary education, 1274.
Chicanas in the 80s: unsettled issues, 1359.
Chicanas in the Great Depression, 1111.
Chicanas in the history of the Southwest, 37..
Chicanas in the labor force, 1653.
Chicanas in the struggle for unions, 2590.
Chicanas in the television media, 1022.
Chicanas in the workforce = Chicanas en la fuerza
    de trabajo: "Working 9 to 5", 1852.
Chicanas live in Aztlan also, 2280.
Chicanas modernize domestic service, 1688.
Chicanas: myths and roles, 2283.
Chicanas on the move, 2194.
Chicanas: power and control in the domestic
    sphere, 2022, 2023.
Chicanas speak out, 381.
Chicanas: their voices, their lives, 4117.
Las Chicanas/The Chicanas, 1152.
The Chicano family and sex roles: an overview and
    introduction, 2031.
Chicano family history---methodology and theory: a
    survey of contemporary research directions,
    146.
Chicano family research: conceptual distortions
    and alternative directions, 1431.
The Chicano index: a comprehensive subject,
    author, and title index to Chicano

materials, 3092.
Chicano intermarriage: a theoretical and empirical
    study, 458.
Chicano intermarriage in the United States: a
    sociocultural analysis, 52.
Chicano literature: beyond beginnings, 583.
Chicano men and masculinity, 1432.
Chicano Periodical Index: a cumulative index to
    selected Chicano periodicals between 1967
    and 1978, 4523, 4524.
Chicano sex role attitudes: a comparative study of
    sex differences in an urban barrio, 490.
Chicano-Anglo intermarriage in Arizona, 1960-1980:
    an exploratory study of eight counties, 375.
Chicano-produced celluloid mujeres, 639.
Chicanos and sociological research: 1970-1980,
    676.
Child behavior in Mexican American/Chicano
    families: maternal teaching and
    child-rearing practices, 75.
Childbearing among Hispanics in the United States:
    an annotated bibliography, 14.
Childbearing among young Latino women in the
    United States, 1973.
The childbearing beliefs and practices of pregnant
    Mexican-American adolescents living in
    Southwest border regions, 74.
Childbearing characteristics of U.S.- and
    foreign-born Hispanic mothers, 2457.
CHISMEARTE: La mujer special issue, 382.
Cholas: Latino girls and gangs, 646.
Cigarette smoking among San Francisco Hispanics:
    the role of acculturation and gender, 73.
Class, gender, and machismo: the
    "treacherous-woman" folklore of Mexican male
    workers, 2522.
The class politics of abstract labor:
    organizational forms and industrial
    relations in the Mexican maquiladoras, 850.
Cleofas M. Jaramillo on marriage in territorial
    Northern New Mexico, 3193.
Clinical observations of Mexican-American,
    Caucasian, and Black pregnant teenagers,
    271.
Clinical psychiatric case presentation; culturally
    responsive diagnostic formulation and
    treatment in an Hispanic female, 109.
A cohort analysis approach to the empty nest
    syndrome among three ethnic groups of women:
    a theoretical position, 1933.
College attendance and persistence among Hispanic
    women: an examination of some contributing
    factors, 25.
Comision Femenil Mexicana, 15, 16.
A comment on Schoen and Cohen, 1270.
Commentary, 3431.
Commentary [on "And Miles to Go": Mexican Women
    and Work, 1930-1985], 232, 233, 234.
Commentary on the Chicana and health services,
    3941.
Como Chicana mi madre, 2901.
Companeras: Latina lesbians (an anthology), 2799.
A comparative analysis of the wages of Hispanics,
    Blacks, and non-Hispanic whites, 320.
A comparative analysis of wife abuse among
    Anglo-American and Mexican-American battered
    women: attitudes, nature, severity,
    frequency and response to the abuse, 337.
Comparative frontiers: the migration of women to
    Alta California and New Zealand, 873.
A comparative study of female Mexican and American
    working nurses in the border corridor, 297.
A comparison of behavioral characteristics of
    Hispanic and Anglo female administrators in
    the resolution of critical incident
    situations, 282.
A comparison of fertility adaptation between
    Mexican immigrants to the U.S. and internal
    migrants in Mexico, 2424.
A comparison of occupational goal orientations of
    female Mexican-Americans and Anglo
    high-school seniors of the classes of 1972
    and 1980, 27.
Comparisons of the psychocultural characteristics

El discurso femenino en la literatura chicana, 2339.

Distress and the traditional female role: a comparison of Mexicans and Anglos, 322.

The distribution of Mexican American women in school organizations, 1793.

Diversity among Northwest Hispanics, 4372.

Division of household labor, strain, and depressive symptoms among Mexican Americans and non-Hispanic whites, 283.

Divorce likelihood among Anglos and Mexican Americans, 308.

Do you know me?: I wrote THE HOUSE ON MANGO STREET, 543.

Dolores Huerta talks about Republicans, Cesar, children and her home town, 165, 166.

Domestic service in the transition from rural to urban life: the case of la Chicana, 1690.

Dona Josefa: bloodpulse of transition and change, 1047.

The double bind, 1020.

A double edge sword: Hispanas and liberal feminism, 2195.

Dreams lost, dreams found: undocumented women in the land of opportunity, 551.

Drinking patterns and drinking-related problems of Mexican-American husbands and wives, 188.

Drug use by small town Mexican American youth: a pilot study, 252.

Early childbearing and employment among young Mexican origin, Black, and white women, 312.

Early grandmotherhood: an exploratory study, 154.

Economic and fertility differences between legal and undocumented migrant Mexican families: possible effects of immigration policy changes, 1738.

Economic restructuring in the United States: Hispanic women in the garment and electronics industries, 929.

Ecos de una convencion, 1344.

[Edicion feminista (Special Issue)], 3560.

Educacion y papel de la mujer en Mexico, 1782.

Education and discrimination against Mexican Americans in the Southwest, 1643.

Education and the Spanish-speaking woman: a sad reality, 1641.

Educational attainment of Chicana adolescents, 35.

The effect of maternal age on the well-being of children, 144.

The effect of unions on the employment of Blacks, Hispanics, and women, 791.

The effect of welfare eligibility on the labor force participation of women of Mexican origin in California, 170.

The effects of employment and marital relations on depression among Mexican American women, 1578.

The effects of nativity, legal status and welfare eligibility on the labor force participation of women of Mexican origin in California, 1857.

The effects of occupational type, educational level, marital status, and race/ethnicity on women's attitudes towards feminist issues, 18.

The effects of socialization on goal actualization of public school Chicana principals and superintendents, 1019.

Effects of stress, social support and coping style on adjustment to pregnancy among Hispanic women, 2437.

The effects of two parent training programs on parental attitudes and self-concepts of Mexican American mothers, 491.

The election day immigration raid at Lilli Diamond Originals and the response of the ILGWU, 2568.

The elliptic female presence as unifying force in the novels of Rolando Hinojosa, 1964.

Elucubraciones y antielucubraciones: critica feminista desde perspectivas poeticas, 1948.

El embarazo precoz: childbearing among Hispanic teenagers in the United States, 2404.

El embrion nacionalista visto a traves de la obra de Sor Juana Ines de la Cruz, 556.

Emergence of the modern Mexican woman: her participation in revolution and struggle for equality, 1910-1940, 2344.

The emerging Chicana: a review of the journals, 1601.

Emerging leadership among Hispanic women: the role of expressive behavior and nonverbal skill, 279.

Empirical and theoretical developments in the study of Chicano families, 2116.

Employment and education of Mexican-American women: the interplay of modernity and ethnicity in eight families, 55.

Employment and psychological well-being in Mexican American women, 488.

Employment counseling and the Chicana, 1869.

Employment of women by cities in the Southwest, 1862.

Employment status and women's protection against coronary heart disease, 289.

Entrevista con Lucha Corpi: poeta chicana, 568.

Entry into marriage and parenthood by young men and women: the influence of family background, 304.

Equality, 274.

ERA: the Latina challenge, 1941.

Las escritoras: romances and realities, 574.

Escritura chicana: la mujer, 3507.

Essays on la mujer, 5554.

Esta [sic] puente, mi espalda: voces de mujeres tercermundistas en los Estados Unidos, 1981.

Estela Portillo Trambley's fictive search for paradise, 1545.

Ethnic and educational effects on marriage choice, 1778.

Ethnic and sexual patterns of alcohol use: Anglo and Mexican American college students, 194.

Ethnic differences in hip fracture: a reduced incidence in Mexican-Americans, 244.

Ethnic differences in the substance use patterns of low-income pregnant women, 195.

Ethnic identity and cultural awareness among the offspring of Mexican interethnic marriages, 91.

Ethnic integration, socioeconomic status, and fertility among Mexican Americans, 451.

Ethnic women: a critique of the literature, 1971-1981, 673.

Ethnicity, division of household tasks and equity in marital roles: a comparison of Anglo and Mexican American couples, 3830.

Ethnicity, locus of control for family planning, and pregnancy counselor credibility, 241.

Evaluation of three treatment modalities with preorgasmic Hispanic women treated without partners, 4792.

Every woman's right: the right to quality education and economic independence, 1251.

Excerpts from los testamentos: Hispanic women folk artists of the San Luis Valley, Colorado, 368.

Expanding a feminist view: challenge and counter-challenge in the relationship between women, 2323.

Experience and meaning: an interpretive study of family and gender ideologies among a sample of Mexican-American women of two generations, 151.

The exploitation of Mexican women in the canning industry and the effects of capital accumulation on striking workers, 986.

An exploration of the finding and seeking of meaning in life and the Mexican-American nurse's mood state, 3933.

Exploring the applicability of the Dyadic Adjustment Scale for assessing level of marital adjustment with Mexican Americans, 1730.

Export processing, women's work, and the employment problem in developing countries: the case of the maquiladora program in Northern Mexico, 894.

Fables of the fallen guy, 1106.

Factorial invariance of the California achievement tests across race and sex, 316.

Factors affecting breastfeeding among women of Mexican origin or descent in Los Angeles, 98.

Factors associated with acculturative stress and depressive symptomatology among married Mexican immigrant women, 92.

Factors associated with low birth weight in Mexican-Americans and Mexicans, 311.

Factors discriminating pregnancy resolution decisions of unmarried adolescents, 12.

Factors predicting pregnancy resolution decision satisfaction of unmarried adolescents, 13.

Factors relating to the continuation of breast feeding by low income Hispanic women, 912.

Factors relating to frequency of breast self-examination among low-income Mexican American women: implications for nursing practice, 908.

Facts and figures on Hispanic Americans, women, and education, 1765.

La familia: Chicano families in the urban Southwest, 1848 to the present, 2057.

La familia [special issue of DE COLORES], 2044.

La familia: the Mexican immigrant family, 1900-1930, 452.

Familism and employment among Chicanas and Mexican immigrant women, 1898.

Family and gender in Chicano and border studies research, 204.

Family life, 871.

Family planning among the urban poor: sexual politics and social policy, 258.

Family planning needs and behavior of Mexican American women: a study of health care professionals and their clientele, 69.

Family planning practices of Mexican Americans, 742.

Family roles of Hispanic women: stereotypes, empirical findings, and implications for research, 2018.

Fear of success: Mexican-American women in two work environments, 45.

Fears of success and women employees, 1881.

La fecundidad entre los Mexicano-Norteamericanos en relacion a los cambiantes patrones reproductivos en Mexico y los Estados Unidos, 2370.

Female and male in Chicano theatre, 661.

Female archetypes in Mexican literature, 3459.

The female hero in Chicano literature, 3407.

Female Mexican Americans: minority within a minority, 455.

Female Mexican immigrants in San Diego County, 1902.

The female subject in Chicano theater: sexuality, race, and class, 2362.

Femenismo [sic] chicano, 2293.

El femenismo [sic] chicano: un panorama historico, 2246.

La femenista [sic], 309.

Femininity and womanhood: virginity, unwed motherhood, and violence, 750.

Feminism on the border: from gender politics to geopolitics, 324.

Feminism: the Chicana and Anglo versions: a historical analysis, 254.

Fertility among Mexican Americans and Anglos in Texas, 1900, 333.

Fertility and fertility-related behavior among Mexican-American and non-Hispanic white female adolescents, 238.

The fertility and language characteristics of Mexican-American and non-Hispanic husbands and wives, 330.

Fertility and mortality, 878.

Fertility expectations and behavior among Mexican Americans in Los Angeles, 1973-82, 2444.

Fertility, expectations and ethnic identity among Mexican-American adolescents: an expression of cultural ideals, 99.

The fertility related behavior of Mexican American adolescents, 2425.

Fighting to open the doors to opportunity, 927.

Film portrayals of La Mujer Hispana, 2473.

First conversations: verbal content of mother-newborn interaction, 1475.

Flesh pots, faith, or finances? Fertility rates among Mexican Americans, 1073.

La flor mas bella de la maquiladora: historias de vida de la mujer obrera en Tijuana, B.C.N., 821.

Folate status of Mexican American, Cuban, and Puerto Rican women, 1417.

For we are sold, I and my people: women and industry in Mexico's frontier, 836.

Forging paths in power and profit, 932.

Fostering the advancement of Latinas, 4015.

The fotonovela as a cultural bridge of Hispanic women in the United States, 2536.

Four representative Hispanic women poets of Central Texas: a portrait of plurality, 658.

Frequency and adequacy of breast cancer screening among elderly Hispanic women, 228.

From honor to love: transformations of the meaning of sexuality in colonial New Mexico, 1063.

From Luisa Espinel to Lalo Guerrero: Tucson's Mexican musicians before World War II, 737.

From the fields to the picket line: Huelga women and the boycott, 1965-1975, 904.

Fuentes para la historia de la mujer en los archivos de Guadalajara, 365.

Game theory in Chicana poetry, 3499.

Gender and aging: a case of Mexicana/Chicana elderly, 218.

Gender and ethnic differences in psychosocial stress and generalized distress among Hispanics, 325.

Gender and ethnic identity among Chicanos, 2857.

Gender and ethnicity in contemporary Chicana poetry, 3518.

Gender and mental health in the Mexican origin population of South Texas, 1562.

Gender gap in politics: no laughing matter, 473.

Gender identification and working-class solidarity among maquila workers in Ciudad Juarez: stereotypes and realities, 446.

Gender, race, and culture: Spanish-Mexican women in the historiography of frontier California, 640.

Gender roles, 5205.

Gender roles, illness, and illness behavior in a Mexican American population, 2065.

Generation, female education and Mexican American fertility, 138.

Generational differences in fertility among Mexican Americans: implications for assessing the effects of immigration, 140.

Getting started in Chicana Studies, 686.

Ghosts and voices: writing from obsession, 544.

"Go after the women": Americanization and the Mexican immigrant woman, 1915-1929, 95, 96.

Grappling with difference: gender, race, class, and ethnicity in contemporary Chicana/o literature, 209.

Grounded theory study: Chicana administrators in Colorado and New Mexico, 1013.

Group counseling Chicana troubled youth: an exploratory group counseling project, 1400.

Group psychotherapy for elderly female Hispanic outpatients, 220.

Group therapy with aged Latino women: a pilot project and study, 221.

Growing up Chicano: Tomas Rivera and Sandra Cisneros, 1234.

A guide to Hispanic women's resources: a perspective on networking among Hispanic women, 1599.

Hacia una bibliografia de poesia femenina chicana, 688.

Hacia una teoria para la liberacion de la mujer, 2265.

Having a job gives you some sort of power: reflections of a Chicana working woman, 1728.

Hay que inventarnos/we must invent ourselves, 380.

Headship and household composition among Blacks,

Recent changes in marital instability among
    Mexican Americans: convergence with Black
    and Anglo trends, 145.
Recent increases in intermarriage by Mexican
    American males: Bexar County, Texas from
    1971 to 1980, 663.
Reconceptualizing undocumented labor immigration:
    the causes, impact and consequences in
    Mexican women's lives, 1845.
Reflections on diversity among Chicanas, 1502.
Reflexiones de una estudiante chicana, 607.
Reflexiones sobre el feminismo y la Raza, 2286,
    2287.
EL REGIDOR and LA PRENSA: impediments to women's
    self-definition, 3570.
Reinforcing children's effort: a comparison of
    immigrant, native-born Mexican American and
    Euro-American mothers, 58.
Relating to privilege: seduction and rejection in
    the subordination of white women and women
    of color, 294.
The relationship between sociocultural variables
    and Chicano and Anglo high school student
    responses on the Potency Dimension of the
    Semantic Differential, 319.
The relationship between gender role incongruity
    on measures of coping and material resources
    and blood pressure among Mexican-American
    women, 2647.
The relationship between sex-role identity and
    ethnicity to styles of assertiveness and
    aggression in women, 310.
The relationship between state and trait anxiety
    and acculturation in Mexican-American women
    homemakers and Mexican-American community
    college female students, 53.
The relationship of independence to achievement: a
    comparative study of Hispanic women, 440.
The relationship of marital status, confidant
    support, and depression among Mexican
    immigrant women, 1585.
The relationship of nativity, social support and
    depression to the home environment among
    Mexican-American women, 105.
Relationship satisfaction of the Mexican American
    woman: effects of acculturation,
    socioeconomic status, and interaction
    structures, 88.
Religion and fertility in the United States: the
    importance of marriage patterns and Hispanic
    origin, 1069.
Religiosity and fertility: the case of Chicanas,
    1072.
Remarkable Latinas, 734.
The remembering voice in Chicana literature, 1516.
Report from the National Women's Political Caucus,
    1348.
Reproductive characteristics of Mexican-American,
    mainland Puerto Rican, and Cuban-American
    women: data from the Hispanic Health and
    Nutrition Examination Survey, 759.
Reproductive choice for Hispanas, 20.
Reproductive histories of low weight girls and
    women, 2409.
Research, action, and social betterment, 1112.
Research brief: sex and ethnic differences in
    mathematics achievement of Black and
    Mexican-American adolescents, 768.
Research guide to the literature on Northern
    Mexico's maquiladora assembly industry, 691.
The resourceful woman in THERE ARE NO MADMEN HERE,
    3465.
Resources for the Chicana feminist scholar, 1125.
Response to Cynthia Orozco, 4445.
La revolucion se trata de amor: Mercedes Soberon,
    389.
The rise and demise of women's liberation: a class
    analysis, 2228.
Risk factors for invasive cervical cancer among
    Latinas and non-Latinas in Los Angeles
    County, 980.
Risk of postmenopausal hip fracture in
    Mexican-American women, 213.
Role conflict in Mexican-American college women,

1279.
Role incompatibility and the relationship between
    fertility and labor supply among Hispanic
    women, 1416.
Role making among married Mexican American women:
    issues of class and ethnicity, 527.
The role of ethnic loyalty among Mexican immigrant
    women, 94.
The role of machismo and the Hispanic family in
    the etiology and treatment of alcoholism in
    the Hispanic American males, 192.
The role of the Chicana within the student
    movement, 1167.
The role of the Latina, 3363.
The role of women in Chicano literature, 3514.
Role perceptions of Hispanic young adults, 1476.
Role-model history and demographic factors in the
    social composition of the family of forty
    Hispanic women leaders in four occupational
    groups, 2036.
Rosita the riveter: Midwest Mexican American women
    during World War II, 1941-1945, 2778.
Rural female adolescent dissatisfaction, support
    and helpseeking, 191.
Sample representativeness in a three-generation
    study of Mexican Americans, 150.
Sandra Cisneros' THE HOUSE ON MANGO STREET and the
    poetics of space, 1238.
Sandra Cisneros' THE HOUSE ON MANGO STREET:
    community-oriented introspection and the
    demystification of patriarchal violence,
    1237.
Sangre joven: las maquiladoras por dentro, 829.
Sanitary product use by white, Black, and Mexican
    American women, 272.
Santos by twentieth-century santeras: continuation
    of a traditional art form, 394.
Sara Estela Ramirez: una rosa roja en el
    movimiento, 738.
Sara Estela Ramirez: the early twentieth century
    Texas-Mexican poet, 557.
Sara Estela Ramirez: sembradora, 558.
The sardonic powers of the erotic in the work of
    Ana Castillo, 1053.
Scholars say issues of diversity have
    "revolutionized" field of Chicano Studies,
    1129.
Se me acabo la cancion: an ethnography of
    non-consenting sterilizations among Mexican
    women in Los Angeles, 1995.
Secondary earner strategies and family poverty:
    immigrant-native differentials, 1960-1980,
    296.
Secondary victimization: confronting public
    attitudes about rape, 522.
El segundo sexo en Mexico: experiencia, estudio e
    introspeccion, 1983-1987, 369.
Select bibliography on Hispanic women and
    education, 681.
Selected bibliography, 682.
Selected cultural, organizational, and economic
    factors related to prenatal care utilization
    by middle-income Hispanic women, 2453.
Selected maternal-infant care practices of
    Spanish-speaking women, 3885.
Selective acculturation of female Mexican
    migrants, 79.
Self, family and community: the social process of
    aging among urban Mexican-American women,
    54.
Self-care agency and limitations with respect to
    contraceptive behavior of Mexican-American
    women, 753.
The self-concept of Mexican-American adolescent
    females, 2926.
Self-help support groups for Hispanic mothers,
    2067.
Self-reports of spousal violence in a
    Mexican-American and non-Hispanic white
    population, 332.
Senora Flores de Andrade, 605.
Separating a myth from reality: socio-economic and
    cultural influences on Chicanas and the
    world of work, 523.

Service delivery and mental health services for Chicano elders, 215.

Sex, age, and cultural differences in self-reported assertiveness, 439.

Sex and ethnic differences in the use of power, 242.

Sex education, abortion views of Mexican Americans typical of U.S. beliefs, 21.

Sex, ethnicity and Chicano status attainment, 47.

A sex role inventory with scales for "machismo" and "self-sacrificing woman", 3729.

Sex roles among Chicanos: stereotypes, challenges and changes, 2627.

Sex roles and perceptions of femininity and masculinity of Hispanic women: a review of the literature, 518.

Sex roles of the traditional Mexican family: a comparison of Chicano and Anglo students' attitudes, 285.

Sex stereotyping in Mexican reading primers, 1321.

Sexism in bilingual bicultural education, 700.

Sexism in Chicano Studies and the community, 118.

El sexo y su condicionamiento cultural en el mundo prehispanico, 4049.

Sex-related differences in the problem-solving abilities of rural Black Anglo, and Chicano adolescents, 180.

Sex-related speech accommodations among Mexican-American bilinguals: a pilot study of language choice in customer-server interactions, 706.

Sex-role attitudes and labor force participation among young Hispanic females and non-Hispanic white females, 313, 314.

Sexual knowledge, sexual interests, and sources of sexual information of rural and urban adolescents from three cultures, 746.

Sexual politics and the theme of sexuality in Chicana poetry, 1175.

The sexual stereotypes of the Chicana in literature, 5344.

Sexual stereotypes--psychological and cultural survival: a description of child-rearing practices attributed to the Chicana (the Mexican American woman) and its psychological and cultural implications, 1438.

La sexualidad en la narrativa femenina mexicana 1970-1987: una aproximacion, 3566.

Sexuality among Mexican Americans: a case of sexual stereotyping, 155.

Sexuality and discourse: notes from a Chicana survivor, 2315.

The sexuality of Latinas [special issue of THIRD WOMAN], 3554.

Sexuality, pregnancy, and motherhood among Mexican-American adolescents, 262.

Sharing bed and board: cohabitation and cultural difference in central Arizona mining towns, 376.

Sharing her tiny pieces of the past, 608.

Shattering the stereotype: Chicanas as labor union organizers, 2152.

Shipwrecked in the desert: a short history of the adventures and struggles for survival of the Mexican Sisters of the House of the Providence in Douglas, Arizona during their first twenty-two years of existence (1927-1949), 1062.

Silences: "Hispanics", AIDS, and sexual practices, 171.

Sisterhood, 495.

Sites of struggle: immigration, deportation, prison, and exile, 356.

Six reference works on Mexican-American women: a review essay, 1113.

Sobre la experiencia educativa chicana, 30.

Social, attitudinal and behavioral correlates of weight change among Mexican American women, 4387.

Social equity in film criticism, 2470.

Social influences on the participation of Mexican-American women in science: final report, 377.

Social networks and survival strategies: an exploratory study of Mexican American, Black, and Anglo female family heads in San Jose, California, 343.

Social science stereotypes of the Mexican American woman: policy implications for research, 5086.

The socialization of a Chicano family, 66.

Socioeconomic differences in rates of cesarean section, 286.

Socioeconomic influences on fertility in the Mexican borderlands region, 888.

The socio-historical implication of the valley as a metaphor in three Colorado Chicana poets, 563.

La soldadera en la narrativa de la Revolucion, 122.

Soldaderas in the Mexican military: myth and history, 125, 126.

Some different thoughts concerning "machismo", 3718.

Some thoughts of a macho on the Chicana Movement, 3748.

Something old, something new: auxiliary work in the 1983-1986 copper strike, 373.

Soothing restless serpents: the dreaded creation and other inspirations in Chicana poetry, 3504.

Soy Chicana primero, 1165, 1166.

Spiritual power and the mundane world: Hispanic female healers in urban U.S. communities, 1526.

The status of Chicanas in medicine, 3900.

The status of Hispanic women in nursing, 1008.

The status of women in Mexico: the impact of the "International Year of the Woman", 22.

Steps for developing an idea into a public policy, 4827.

Sterilization among American Indian and Chicano mothers, 4286.

Sterilization: an overview, 4839.

Sterilization is not an alternative in family planning, 1636.

Stress and coping among Mexican women, 1439.

Stress and coping as determinants of adaptation to pregnancy in Hispanic women, 2438.

The struggles of class and gender: current research in Chicano Studies [review essay], 998.

A study of Mexican American women's perceptions of factors that influence academic and professional goal attainment, 1009.

A study of successful completion and attrition among Chicana Title VII Bilingual Education Doctoral Fellows at selected Southwestern universities, 31.

A study of the attitudes of Texas Mexican American women toward higher education, 481.

A study of the influence of culture on the development of identity among a group of Chicana artists, 411.

A study of the interaction of Hispanic junior high school students and their teachers, 1700.

A study of the value orientation of Lane County, Oregon, Mexican American mothers with a special focus on family/school relationships, 1313.

Studying Chicanas: bringing women into the frame of Chicano Studies, 1123.

Studying maternal-infant attachment: a Mexican-American example, 1206.

Support networks for adolescent mothers, 948.

A survey of selected literature on La Chicana, 3604.

The sweatshop: the garment industry's reborn child, 2567.

Symbolic strategies for change: a discussion of the Chicana women's movement, 117.

Symposium. Civil rights, affirmative action, and the aged of the future: will life chances be different for Blacks, Hispanics, and women? An overview of the issues, 132.

Synopsis on Senate Concurrent Resolution 43: an example in public policy making, 3391.

La tarea de la mujer es la liberacion, 2276.
Teaching strategies used by Chicano mothers with
    their Head Start children, 702.
Teatropoesia by Chicanas in the Bay Area: TONGUES
    OF FIRE, 4560.
Teen women: disparity between cognitive values and
    anticipated life events, 5421.
Teenagers and contraception in Cameron and Willacy
    Counties, 752.
Teenagers willing to consider single parenthood:
    who is at greatest risk?, 762.
Tending the beets: campesinas and the Great
    Western Sugar Company, 2176.
The terminology of machismo, 1143.
The theatre of Denise Chavez: interior landscapes
    with SABOR NUEVOMEXICANO, 972.
Thematic issue: Chicana issues, 1753.
Theoretical perspectives on Chicanas, Mexicanas
    and the transnational working class, 834.
The theoretical subject(s) of THIS BRIDGE CALLED
    MY BACK and Anglo-American feminism, 235,
    236.
"There was a woman": La Llorona in Oregon, 2517.
"They didn't call them 'padre' for nothing":
    patriarchy in Hispanic California, 953.
Third World women in the United States--by and
    about us: a selected bibliography, 683.
This bridge called my back: writings by radical
    women of color, 1982.
Three Latina artists = Tres artistas latinas, 421.
Three Latinas in Hollywood = Tres latinas en
    Hollywood, 114.
The three Rs of Chicana leadership, 3379.
Three times a woman: Chicana poetry, 4551.
"Tienes que ser valiente": Mexicana migrants in a
    midwestern farm labor camp, 2165.
The ties that bind: women and community in
    Evangelina Vigil's THIRTY AN' SEEN A LOT,
    2929.
To be aged, Hispanic, and female: the triple risk,
    230.
To serve Hispanic American female students:
    challenges and responsibilities for
    educational institutions, 1704.
To split a human: mitos, machos y la mujer
    chicana, 1635.
The Tolteca Strike: Mexican women and the struggle
    for union representation, 1083.
Tortuosidad: shop floor struggles of female
    maquiladora workers, 852.
Toward a democratic women's movement in the United
    States, 2229.
Toward a feminist pedagogy for Chicana
    self-actualization, 1163.
Toward a reconceptualization of women's economic
    activities: the informal sector in urban
    Mexico, 1866.
Toward a science of women's liberation, 2262.
Toward an understanding of suicide risks in young
    Hispanic females, 107.
Toward understanding the educational trajectory
    and socialization of Latina women, 50.
Towards a Chicano poetics: the making of the
    Chicano subject, 1387.
Towards a definition of, and critical approaches
    to, Chicano(a) literature, 2231.
Trabajadoras mexicanas y chicanas en las artes
    visuales, 385.
Traddutora, traditora: a paradigmatic figure of
    Chicana feminism, 2188.
Tradition and mythology: signatures of landscape
    in Chicana literature, 577.
Traditional and nontraditional patterns of female
    activism in the United Farm Workers of
    America, 1962-1980, 905.
Traditional attitudes toward marriage, marital
    adjustment, acculturation, and self-esteem
    of Mexican-American and Mexican wives, 71.
Traditional sex-roles, ethnic integration, marital
    satisfaction, and psychological distress
    among Chicanas, 3849.
Translating ideas of public policy into public
    institutions, 4829.
The treacherous woman archetype: a structuring

agent in the corrido, 1386.
Trends in the employment of minority women as
    administrators in Texas public
    schools--1976-1981, 427.
Trends in the incidence of breastfeeding for
    Hispanics of Mexican origin and Anglos on
    the US-Mexican border, 329.
Tres modelos culturales: la Virgen de Guadalupe,
    la Malinche y la Llorona, 2607.
The triple bias: rural, minority and female, 1740.
Trivial lives: artists Yolanda Lopez and Patricia
    Rodriguez, 408.
Turnover and recruitment in the maquila industry:
    causes and solutions, 862.
Twice protected?: assessing the impact of
    affirmative action on Mexican-American
    women, 133.
UCAPAWA, Chicanas, and the California food
    processing industry, 1937-1950, 991.
Undocumented female labor in the United States
    Southwest: an essay on migration,
    consciousness, oppression and struggle, 378.
Undocumented Hispanas in America, 3022.
Undocumented immigrant women in the Houston labor
    force, 1841.
Unequal opportunity and the Chicana, 1626, 1627,
    1628.
Unequal sisters: a multicultural reader in U.S.
    women's history, 323.
The university setting reinforces inequality,
    1632.
The unspeakable crime, 4885.
Unsung heroine of La Causa, 135.
[Untitled interview with State Senators (Colorado)
    Polly Baca-Barragan and Lena Guerrero], 633.
Urban Chicano workers in historical perspective: a
    review of recent literature, 3219.
Urban kinship and Midwest Chicano families:
    evidence in support of revision, 1319.
U.S. Hispanics: changing the face of America,
    1749.
Use of clinic versus private family planning care
    by low-income women: access, cost and
    patient satisfaction, 2142.
Use of folk medicine by elderly Mexican-American
    women, 152.
The use of inpatient mental health services by
    Hispanic women, 3992.
El uso del cuerpo femenino en la epoca colonial
    mexicana a traves de los estudios de
    demografia historica, 3839.
The vaginal serpent and other themes from
    Mexican-American women's lore, 1428.
Valiant migrant women = Las mujeres valerosas,
    650.
Variation in patterns of marital instability among
    Hispanics, 1419.
Variations in Mexican American family life: a
    review synthesis of empirical research, 80.
La vela prendida: home altars, 200.
La vela prendida: Mexican-American women's home
    altars, 201.
Victorian attitudes affecting the Mexican woman
    writing in LA PRENSA during the early 1900s
    and the Chicana of the 1980s, 2274.
"La vieja Ines," a Mexican folkgame: a research
    note, 1208.
A view from within: midwife practices in South
    Texas, 2418.
[Villanueva, Alma], 566.
La violacion sexual: the reality of rape, 483.
Virgen de Guadalupe and the American dream: the
    melting pot bubbles on in Toledo, Ohio, 456.
La vision chicana, 264.
Una vista al pasado: la mujer en Nuevo Mexico,
    1744-1767, 2785.
Voces de Hispanas: Hispanic women and their
    concerns, 4017.
Walking the thin line: humor in Chicana
    literature, 1225.
Watsonville shows "it can be done", 992.
Well-being in the postparental stage in
    Mexican-American women, 156.
Western women: their land, their lives, 327.

What is the Talmadge Amendment?: justicia para las madres, 1140.
What kind of lover have you made me, Mother?: towards a theory of Chicanas' feminism and cultural identity through poetry, 923.
When Jesus came, the corn mothers went away: marriage, sexuality, and power in New Mexico, 1500-1846, 3829.
When wives work: the impact on the Chicano family, 2118.
White, Black, and Hispanic female youths in central city labor markets, 270.
Why migrant women feed their husbands tamales: foodways as a basis for a revisionist view of Tejano family life, 1494.
The widowed women of Santa Fe: assessments on the lives of an unmarried population, 1850-80, 2053, 2054.
Widowhood: its impact on morale and optimism among older persons of three ethnic groups, 212.
Woman of her word: Hispanic women write, 388.
The woman of La Raza, 123, 124.
Women and cancer, 982.
Women and education: sex role modifications of Mexican American women, 97.
Women and intercultural relations: the case of Hispanic New Mexico and Colorado, 1292.
Women artists of Texas: MAS = More + Artists + Women = MAS, 379.
Women as metaphor in the patriarchal structure of HEART OF AZTLAN, 207.
Women at Farah: an unfinished story, 2151.
Women at Frontera, CA, 1781.
Women, border industrialization program, and human rights, 827.
Women, development and human rights: issues in integrated transnational production, 828.
Women farmworkers: their workplace and capitalist patriarchy, 1002.
Women in early New Mexico: a preliminary view, 129.
Women in El Teatro Campesino: "A poco estaba molacha la Virgen de Guadalupe?", 112.
Women in prison--C.I.W.: an editorial, 1364.
Women in the Chicano Movement, 1182.
Women in the global factory, 839.
Women in the Mexican-American community: religion, culture, and reproductive attitudes and experiences, 7.
Women in the United Farm Workers: a study of Chicana Mexicana participation in a labor union, 1950-1980, 2765.
Women, labor, and the U.S.-Mexico border: Mexican maids in El Paso, Texas, 867.
Women, mental health, and the workplace in a transnational setting, 840.
Women migrant workers in the U.S., 4140.
Women: new voice of La Raza, 1369.
Women of color and southern women: a bibliography of social science research, 1975 to 1988, 690.
Women of the depression: caste and culture in San Antonio, 1929-1939, 1411.
Women of the Valley of the Sun: women and family work culture in Woodlake, California, 2030.
Women on the U.S.-Mexico border: responses to change, 854.
Women, power and the vote, 6134.
Women: prisoners of the word, 3493.
Women then and now: an analysis of the Adelita image versus the Chicana as political writer and philosopher, 121.
Women, work and family in the Chicano community: cannery workers of the Santa Clara Valley, 995.
The women's movement and the left in Mexico: the presidential candidacy of Dona Rosario Ibarra, 715.
The women's movement in Mexico: the first and second feminist congresses in Yucatan, 1916 1366.
Women's networks and the social needs of Mexican immigrants, 1872.
Women's rights: a Chicana's viewpoint, 2212.

Women's rights and the Mexican American woman, 1772.
Women's task is to gain liberation, 1082.
Women's work and Chicano families: cannery workers of the Santa Clara Valley, 996.
Women's work and unemployment in northern Mexico, 825.
Work and family: a comparative analysis of professional, clerical and blue-collar Chicana workers, 2093.
Work and sex-role attitudes in relation to education and other characteristics, 486.
The work experience of undocumented Mexican women migrants in Los Angeles, 3002.
Work force participation among Mexican immigrant women in Texas, 1900, 1904.
Work related networks and household organization among Chicana cannery workers, 997.
Working for wages: Mexican women in the Southwest, 1930-1980, 1893.
Working with women of color: an empowerment perspective, 437.
The working women's reactions to the traditional marriage role: a crosscultural study within the symbolic interactionism framework, 2989.
Working-class women in nineteenth century Mexico, 1858.
Workshop resolutions - First National Chicana Conference, May 1971, 1343.
THE WORLD WALL: A VISION OF THE FUTURE WITHOUT FEAR: an interview with Judith F. Baca, 398.
"Yo sola aprendi": contra-patriarchal containment in women's nineteenth-century California personal narratives, 612.
Young Chicana speaks up on problems faced by young girls, 11.
You've come a long way, baby. Or have you?, 931.
Zinc supplementation during pregnancy: zinc concentration of serum and hair from low-income women of Mexican descent, 3684.
Zinc supplementation during pregnancy in low-income teenagers of Mexican descent: effects on selected blood constituents and on progress and outcome of pregnancy, 2417.